A
HISTORY OF
ECONOMIC DOCTRINES

FROM THE TIME OF THE PHYSIOCRATS
TO THE PRESENT DAY

BY

CHARLES GIDE

LATE PROFESSOR OF SOCIAL ECONOMICS IN
THE FACULTY OF LAW UNIVERSITY OF PARIS

AND

CHARLES RIST

PROFESSOR OF POLITICAL ECONOMY IN THE
FACULTY OF LAW UNIVERSITY OF PARIS

AUTHORIZED TRANSLATION

BY

R. RICHARDS B.A.

SECOND ENGLISH EDITION

WITH ADDITIONAL MATTER FROM THE LATEST
FRENCH EDITIONS TRANSLATED BY
ERNEST F. ROW B.Sc. (Econ.) F.R. Econ. S.

GEORGE G. HARRAP & COMPANY LTD
LONDON   SYDNEY   TORONTO   BOMBAY

First published June 1915
by GEORGE G. HARRAP & CO. LTD
182 High Holborn, London, W.C.1
Reprinted : June 1917; *December* 1919;
February 1923; *February* 1925; *March* 1927;
October 1928; *July* 1930; *April* 1932;
October 1937; *October* 1943; *June* 1945
Second edition, reset 1948

*Composed in Baskerville type and printed by Western Printing Services, Ltd
Bristol. Made in Great Britain*

PUBLISHERS' NOTE

THIS work was first published in France in 1909. A translation of the second French edition (1913) appeared in England in 1915, and has been reprinted without alteration many times since. In France, however, seven successive editions have been published—although often with little substantial change in contents. The present English edition is based on the original translation of the second French edition, but also incorporates the amendments and additions made in the French sixth and seventh editions.

In carrying out the work of revision Professor Rist has freely altered and added to the chapters originally written by himself, but—for reasons stated in his Preface to the sixth edition—has been more conservative of alteration to the chapters written by his late co-author. These chapters may thus lose some of their significance unless the reader bears in mind the date at which they were originally written. This danger is, however, lessened by the statement of authorship of each chapter given in the table of contents. This arrangement, which is followed in both the sixth and seventh (French) editions, is confidently passed on to the English-speaking public in the belief that the late Charles Gide's analysis of economic theories is too valuable to be discarded after less than forty years' service.

PREFACE TO THE SEVENTH EDITION

This new edition differs very little from the sixth edition. The latter was prepared and printed during the enemy occupation, though it did not appear until after the Liberation, so it was difficult for me to write freely about both Bolshevism and National Socialism. I have not felt called upon, however, to restore in this edition the pages devoted to Bolshevism in the Fifth Edition, or to include a study of the economic aspect of National Socialism. It would in fact be a great mistake, in my opinion, to regard these two political doctrines as embodying anything economically new. The economic methods employed by revolutionary Russia in order to create large-scale industry were imposed on her by necessity; for, being unable to raise either an internal or an external loan for setting up the war industry that she wanted, the U.S.S.R. had to resort to compulsion and the issue of a paper currency to achieve her ends. As for the collectivization of industry and part of agriculture, what is interesting to study here is its realization in practice, for its theoretical basis is to be found in all previous socialist systems. The National Socialists organized their entire economy with a view to war, and it is of interest only as a system of war economy.

What determines to-day the differences between economists is, in my opinion, the opposition between a war economy and a peace economy. The *dirigisme*, or system of State control, which appeals to so many thinkers, is a consequence of the war economy. But it does not follow that the end of the war means also the disappearance of its economic consequences. In particular, the concentration of certain large-scale industries that was a wartime necessity is undoubtedly bound to extend yet further, and this will facilitate the intervention of the State to control it and share in it. But so long as production is determined primarily by the demand of consumers this concentration will in itself make little change in the economic machinery. So long as the economic world remains a world in which abundance is never anything but relative, economic calculation and, therefore, economic theories will retain their importance.

Is it possible now to foresee a day when abundance will be no longer relative but absolute? Can we imagine a world in which technical mastery over matter has reached such a point that man can draw from nature whatever product he pleases—a world like that pictured by

3

Sismondi, where one man, by turning a handle, can provide everything needed by a whole community? So boundless are the horizons opened up by the triumphs of physical science that some people believe this absolute abundance to be already within reach. If this dream were to come true the economic planning of human resources would become unnecessary and political economy would disappear, along with its economic laws, which means the psychological laws which it was its purpose to study. Work itself would become unnecessary for the vast majority of people, and what would need planning would be leisure, not toil. To my younger colleagues I suggest this as a subject for thought. They will perhaps discover that the 'curse' of labour pronounced in the Garden of Eden against Adam's descendants is after all the most salutary law of moral and physical health.

But we have not yet reached that point, and the history of economic doctrines still retains all its interest. Ours may be criticized, and with justice, for not bringing out clearly enough all the analogies that are apparent between ancient and modern doctrines. For instance, the reasoning methods of Lord Keynes were directly inspired by the Ricardian tradition, and on reading him one could well imagine that Walras and even Jevons had never written a line. So too there are many curious points of identity between his position and Sismondi's; and yet I believe I am right in thinking that Keynes had never read Sismondi.

Here is another very suggestive point. The whole of the Swedish School, for example, has based its teaching on the theory of Walras. The whole Italian School, so remarkable in many ways, is founded, by way of Pareto, on the same principles. And the best of the American economists have also adopted these principles. Yet part of the English School, with a curious continuity of tradition and ancestor-worship, persists in ignoring them.

But to lay stress on all these resemblances between the present and the past would have meant rewriting part of the book, besides abandoning the fundamental aim that we set before ourselves when we started our undertaking—namely, to concentrate in the case of each doctrine or each author on such developments as are indispensable to an understanding of his own thought. To the reader, therefore, we must leave the task of unearthing for himself those analogies between certain doctrines that we have merely noted in passing. We believe that they will come to light of their own accord from our analysis of each author.

PARIS   CHARLES RIST
1947

PREFACE TO THE SIXTH EDITION

THIS edition appears over thirty years after the first and fifteen years after the fifth. The eminent man who conceived the idea of this book, and whose name will henceforth be inscribed in the history of doctrines as one of the most original of French economists, has passed away, and I have therefore undertaken single-handed the necessary task of revision. I have felt it my duty to leave almost unaltered the chapters written by M. Gide, for the marks of his genius are too plainly visible for them to be susceptible to amendment or addition.

In the remaining chapters I have made few changes. My chief concern has been with the last two chapters, intended to bring the history down to date. I need not emphasize the difficulties and dangers of such a task. To try to set down in a hundred pages the essence of the economic ideas of the last twenty years will seem to many a rash undertaking. But I felt unable to resist the friendly entreaties of my publisher and my kindly colleagues.

Once again, and more emphatically than ever, I must express my regret at being unable to mention more names and more books. But the very character of this work, which should on no account resemble a catalogue or a bibliography, obliged me to select and to confine myself to what a historian of ideas is physically capable of reading and judging for himself, and this inevitably means leaving gaps. That is the risk in such a work as this. When one wishes to include not only the past—in which case the task of selection (though still subject to revision) has been done by time itself—but also the present, no one can pretend to indicate unerringly the names that will live in history. I have honestly chosen, according to my lights, those that seem to me the most important, without losing sight of the fact that the future may bring fame—as in the case of Cantillon or Gossen—to works neglected by, or even unknown to, their contemporaries.

I have had to modify slightly the original plan of the book. The title "Recent Doctrines" is no longer applicable to the doctrines collected together in Book V, most of which are now upward of fifty or sixty years old. The events of the past thirty years have also profoundly altered our attitude to pre-1914 doctrines. What chiefly marks the period 1870–1914 is, in my view, the discovery and development of the concepts of equilibrium and final utility on the one hand,

and on the other the social doctrines that arose during a prolonged period of peace: hence the new title given to Book V and the regrouping of certain chapters.

The post-war doctrines I have made into a sixth Book, in which I have attempted a general review of the theories of international trade and the conflict between the various theories of crises, both subjects evoked by the events which have upset world economy during the past twenty-five years. This shows the influence exerted on our views, not only of the present but also of the past, by a period entirely dominated by war, in contrast to the years in which this book was first conceived and written, when most minds were dominated by the habit of peace and the assumption that it would continue.

PARIS   CHARLES RIST
1944

PREFACE

IN the economic curricula of French universities much greater stress is laid upon the history of economic theory than is the case anywhere else. Attached to the Faculty of Law in each of these universities is a separate chair specially devoted to this subject; at the examination for the doctor's degree a special paper is set in the history of theory, and if necessary further proof of competence is demanded from the student before his final admission to the degree. At the Sorbonne, where there is only one chair in economics, that chair is exclusively devoted to the history of doctrines, and the same is true of the chair recently founded at the École des Hautes Études.

Such prominence given to the history of theory must seem excessive, especially when it is remembered that in economic history, as distinct from the history of economics, there is not a single chair in the whole of France. Those who believe that the French people are somewhat prone to ideology will not fail to see in this fact a somewhat unfortunate manifestation of that tendency. Elsewhere the positions are reversed, the premier place being given to the study of facts rather than ideas. Extreme partisans of the historical method, especially the advocates of historical materialism, regard doctrines and systems as nothing better than a pale reflection of facts. It is a part of their belief that facts are the only things that matter, and that the history of the evolution of property or the rise of the wage system may prove quite as instructive as the history of the controversies concerning the nature of the right of property or the wages-fund theory.

Such views as we have just expressed, however, are not altogether devoid of exaggeration, though of a kind directly opposite to that which we would naturally impute to them. The influence exerted by the economic environment, whence even the most abstract economist gets material for reflexion and the exercise of his logical acumen, is indisputable. The problems which the theorist has to solve are suggested by the rise of certain phenomena which at one moment cut a very prominent figure and at another disappear altogether. Such problems must vary in different places and at different times. The peculiar economic condition in which England found herself at the beginning of the nineteenth century had a great deal to do in directing Ricardo's thought to the study of the problems of rent and note

7

issue. But for the advent of machinery, with the subsequent increase in industrial activity and the parallel growth of a proletarian class, followed by the recurrence of economic crises, we may be certain that neither the doctrine of Sismondi nor that of Karl Marx would ever have seen the light of day. It is equally safe to assume that the attention which economists have recently bestowed upon the theory of monopoly is not altogether unconnected with the contemporary development of the trust movement.

But, while recognizing all this, it is important that we should remember that facts alone are not sufficient to explain the origin of any doctrines, even those of social politics, and still less those of a purely scientific character. If ideas are determined solely by time and environment how are we to explain the emergence at the same time and in the same environment of such different and even contradictory doctrines as J. B. Say's and Sismondi's, Bastiat's and Proudhon's, Schulze-Delitzsch's and Marx's, Francis Walker's and those of Henry George? With what combination of historical circumstances are we to connect Cournot's foundation of the Mathematical school in France, or how are we to account for the simultaneous discovery in three or four countries of the theory of final utility?

Although anxious not to seem to make any extravagant claims for the superiority of the history of theory, we are not ashamed of repeating our regrets for the comparative neglect of economic history, and we are equally confident in claiming for our subject the right to be regarded as a distinct branch of the science.[1] We shall accordingly omit all reference to the history of economic facts and institutions except in so far as such reference seems indispensable to an understanding of either the appearance or disappearance of such and such a doctrine or to the better appreciation of the special prominence which a theory may have held at one moment, although it is quite unintelligible to us to-day. Sometimes even the facts are connected with the doctrines, not as causes, but as results, for, notwithstanding the scepticism of Cournot, who was wont to declare that the influence exerted by economists upon the course of events was about equal to the influence exerted by grammarians upon the development of language, it is impossible not to see a connexion between the commercial treaties of 1860, say, and the teachings of the Manchester school, or between labour legislation and the doctrine of State Socialism.

To write a history of economic doctrines which should not exceed the limits of a single volume was to attempt an almost impossible task,

[1] See an article by M. Deschamps in the *Réforme sociale* of October 1, 1902, on the value of this kind of teaching.

and the authors cannot pretend that they have accomplished such a difficult feat. Even a very summary exposition of such doctrines as could not possibly be neglected involved the omission of others of hardly less importance.

But in the first place it was possible to pass over the pioneers by taking the latter part of the eighteenth century as the starting-point. There is no doubt that the beginnings of economic science lie in a remoter past, but the great currents of economic thought known as the "schools" only began with the appearance of those two typical doctrines, individualism and socialism, in the earlier half of the nineteenth century.[1] Moreover, the omission is easily made good, for it so happens that the earlier periods are those most fully dealt with in such works as have already appeared on the subject. For the period of antiquity we have the writings of Espinas[2] and Souchon; the medieval and post-medieval periods, right up to the eighteenth century, are treated of in the works of Dubois and Rambaud; while, in addition to these, we have the writings of Ashley, Ingram, Hector Denis, Brants, and Cossa, to mention only a few. Modern theories, as contrasted with those of the earlier periods, have received comparatively little attention.

Not only have we been obliged to confine our attention to certain periods, but we have also had to restrict ourselves to certain countries. We would claim the indulgence of those of our readers who feel that French doctrines have been considered at disproportionate length, reminding them that we had French students chiefly in view when writing. Each author is at liberty to do the same for his own particular country, and it is better so, for readers generally desire to learn more about those things of which they already know something. But, despite the prominence given to France, England and Germany were bound to receive considerable attention, although in the case of the latter country we had to make considerable omissions. With regard to the other countries, which we were too often obliged to pass by in silence or to mention only very casually in connexion with some theory or other, we are most anxious not to appear indifferent to the eminent services rendered by them, and especially Italy and the United States, to the cause of economic science, both in the past and in the present.

---

[1] In an article on the teaching of the history of economic doctrines (*Revue de l'Enseignement*, March 15, 1900) M. Deschamps declares that it is unpardonable that we should be unable to make better use of the marvellous economic teachings of which both ancient and medieval history are full, but he adds that "as far as the history of the science is concerned there is no need to go farther back than the Physiocrats."

[2] In the new edition of M. Espinas's work an entire volume is devoted to the study of economic doctrines in ancient and medieval times.

But, notwithstanding such restrictions, the field was still too wide, and we were obliged to focus attention on the minimum number of names and ideas, with a view to placing them in a better light. Our ambition has been, not to write as full or detailed a history as we possibly could, but merely to draw a series of pictures portraying the more prominent features of some of the more distinct epochs in the history of economic doctrines.

Such choice must necessarily be somewhat arbitrary, for it is not always an easy matter to fix upon the best representative of each doctrine. Especially is this the case in a science like economics, where the writers, unknown to one another, not infrequently repeat the same ideas, and it becomes a matter of some difficulty to decide the claim to priority. But although it may be difficult to hit upon the exact moment at which a certain idea first made its appearance, it is comparatively easy to determine when such an idea attracted general attention or took its place in the hierarchy of accepted or scarcely disputed truths. This has been our criterion. With regard to those whose names do not figure in our list, although quite worthy of a place in the front rank, we cannot believe that they will suffer much through this temporary eclipse, especially in view of the partiality of the age for the pioneers. That we are not unduly optimistic in this matter may be inferred from the numerous attempts recently made to discover the *poetæ minores* of the science, and to make amends for the scant justice done them by the more biased historians of the past.

Not only was selection necessary in the case of authors, but a similar procedure had to be applied to the doctrines. It must be realized, however, that a selection of this character does not warrant the conclusion that the doctrines dealt with are in any way superior to those which are not included, either from the standpoint of moral value, of social utility, or of abstract truth, for we are not of the number who think with J. B. Say that the history of error can serve no useful purpose.[1] We would rather associate ourselves with Condillac when he remarks: "It is essential that every one who wishes to make some progress in the search for truth should know something of the mistakes committed by people like himself who thought they were extending the boundaries of knowledge." The study of error would be thoroughly well

[1] "What useful purpose can be served by the study of absurd opinions and doctrines that have long ago been exploded, and deserved to be? It is mere useless pedantry to attempt to revive them. The more perfect a science becomes the shorter becomes its history. Alembert truly remarks that the more light we have on any subject the less need is there to occupy ourselves with the false or doubtful opinions to which it may have given rise. Our duty with regard to errors is not to revive them, but simply to forget them." (*Traité pratique*, Vol. II, p. 540.)

justified even though the result were simply a healthy determination to avoid it in future. It would be even more so if Herbert Spencer's version of the saying of Shakespeare, that there is no species of error without some germ of truth in it, should prove correct. One cannot, moreover, be said to possess a knowledge of any doctrine or to understand it until one knows something of its history, and of the pitfalls that lay in the path of those who first formulated it. A truth received as if it has fallen from the sky, without any knowledge of the efforts whereby it has been acquired, is like an ingot of gold got without toil—of little profit.

Moreover, it is to be remembered that this book is intended primarily for students, and that it may be useful to show them in what respects certain doctrines are open to criticism, either from the point of view of logic or of observation. We have attempted to confine such criticism within the strictest limits, partly because we did not wish the volume to become too bulky, and partly because we felt that what is important for our readers are not our own opinions, but the opinions of the masters of the science with which we deal. Wherever possible these have been given the opportunity of speaking for themselves, and for this reason we have not been afraid to multiply quotations.

A special effort has been made to bring into prominence such doctrines—whether true or false—as have contributed to the formation of ideas generally accepted at the present time, or such as are connected with these in the line of direct descent. In other words, the book is an attempt to give an answer to the following questions: Who is responsible for formulating those principles that constitute the framework—whether provisionary or definitive it is not for us to determine—of economics as at present taught? At what period were these principles first enunciated, and what were the circumstances which accounted for their enunciation just at that period? Thus we have thought it not altogether out of place to pay some attention to those ideas which, although only on the borderland of economics, have exercised considerable influence either upon theory itself, upon legislation, or upon economic thought in general. We refer to such movements as Christian Socialism, Solidarism, and Anarchism. Had we considered it advisable to retain the official title by which this kind of work is generally known, we should have had to describe it as *A History of the Origin and Evolution of Contemporary Economic Doctrines*.

The plan of a history of this kind was a matter that called for some amount of deliberation. It was felt that, being a history, fairly close correspondence with the chronological order was required, which meant either taking a note of every individual doctrine, or breaking up the work into as many distinct histories as there are separate schools.

The former procedure would necessitate giving a review of a great number of doctrines in a single chapter, which could only have the effect of leaving a very confused impression upon the reader's mind. The alternative proposal is open to the objection that, instead of giving us a general outline, it merely treats us to a series of monographs, which prevents our realizing the nature of that fundamental unity that in all periods of history binds every doctrine together, similar and dissimilar alike. We have attempted to avoid the inconveniences and to gain something of the advantages offered by these alternative methods by grouping the doctrines into families according to their descent, and presenting them in their chronological order. This does not mean that we have classified them according to the date of their earliest appearance; it simply means that we have taken account of such doctrines as have reached a certain degree of maturity. There is always some culminating-point in the history of every doctrine, and in deciding to devote a separate chapter to some special doctrine we have always had such a climacteric in mind. Nor have we scrupled to abandon the chronological order when the exigencies of the exposition seemed to demand it.

The first epoch comprises the end of the eighteenth and the beginning of the nineteenth centuries. It deals mainly with the founders of Classical political economy, with the Physiocrats, Smith and Say, and with Malthus and Ricardo, the two writers whose gloomy forebodings were to cloud the glory of the "natural order."

The second epoch covers the first half of the nineteenth century. The "adversaries" include all those writers who either challenged or in some way disputed the principles which had been laid down by their predecessors. To these writers five chapters are devoted, dealing respectively with Sismondi, Saint-Simon, the Associative Socialists, List, and Proudhon.

A third epoch deals with the middle of the nineteenth century and the triumph of the Liberal school, which had hitherto withstood every attack, though not without making some concessions. It so happened that the fundamental doctrines of this school were definitely formulated about the same time, though in a very different fashion, of course, in the *Principles* of Stuart Mill in England and the *Harmonies* of Bastiat in France.

The second half of the nineteenth century constitutes a fourth period. Those who dissented from the Liberalism of the previous epoch are responsible for the schisms that began to manifest themselves in four different directions at this time. The Historical school advocates the employment of the inductive method, and the State Socialists press the claims of a new social policy. Marxism is an attack upon the scientific basis of the science, and Christian Socialism a challenge to its ethical implications.

A fifth epoch comprises the end of the nineteenth century and the beginning of the twentieth. The heading "Recent Doctrines" includes several theories that are already well known to us, but which seem transfigured—or disfigured, as some would prefer to put it—in their new surroundings. The Hedonistic doctrine and the theory of rent represent a kind of revision of the Classical theories. Solidarism is an attempt to bridge the gap that exists between individualism and socialism, while Anarchism can only be described as a kind of impassioned Liberalism.

This order of succession must not be taken to imply that each antecedent doctrine has either been eliminated by some subsequent doctrine or else incorporated in it. The rise of the Historical school in the middle of the nineteenth century, for example, happened to be contemporaneous with the triumph of the Liberal school and the revival of Optimism. In a similar fashion the new Liberalism of the Austrian school was coincident with the advent of State intervention and the rise of Collectivism.

We cannot, however, help noticing a certain rhythmical sequence in this evolutionary process. Thus we find the Classical doctrine, as it is called, outlined in the earliest draft of the science, but disappearing under the stress of more or less socialistic doctrines, to reappear in a new guise later on. There is no necessity for regarding this as a mere ebb and flow such as distinguishes the fortunes of political parties under a parliamentary regime. Such alternation in the history of a doctrine has its explanation not so much in the character of the doctrine itself as in the favour of public opinion, which varies with the fickleness of the winds of heaven.

But doctrines and systems have a vitality of their own which is altogether independent of the vagaries of fashion. It were better to regard their history, like all histories of ideas, as a kind of struggle for existence. At one moment conflicting doctrines seem to dwell in harmony side by side, content to divide the empire of knowledge between them. Another moment witnesses them rushing at each other with tumultuous energy. It may happen that in the course of the struggle some of the doctrines are worsted and disappear altogether. But more often than not their conflicting interests are reconciled and the enmity is lost in the unity of a higher synthesis. And so it may happen that a doctrine which everybody thought was quite dead may rise with greater vigour than ever.

The bibliography of the subject is colossal. In addition to the general histories, which are already plentiful, the chapters devoted to the subject in every treatise on political economy, and the numerous articles which have appeared in various reviews, there is scarcely an author, however obscure, who is not the subject of a biography. To have attempted to enumerate all these works would merely have meant increasing the bulk of the book without being able to pretend that our list was exhaustive. It is scarcely necessary to add that this meant that we had to confine ourselves to the work done by the 'heroes' of this volume. Their commentators and critics only came in for our attention when we had to borrow either an expression or an idea directly from them or when we felt it necessary that the reader should fill up the gaps left by our exposition. This accounts for the number of names which had to be relegated to the footnotes. But such deliberate excision must not prevent our recognizing at the outset the debt that we owe to the many writers who have traversed the ground before us. They have facilitated our task and have a perfect right to regard themselves as our collaborators. We feel certain that they will find that their labours have not been ignored or forgotten.

Although this book, so far as the general task of preparation and revision is concerned, must be regarded as the result of a collective effort on the part of the two authors whose names are subjoined, the actual work of composition was undertaken by each writer separately. The Contents will sufficiently indicate the nature of this division of labour.

The authors refuse to believe that collaboration in the production of a scientific history of ideas need imply absolute agreement on every question that comes up for consideration. Especially is this the case with the doctrines of political and social economy outlined herein; each of the authors has retained the fullest right of independent judgment on all these matters. Consequently any undue reserve or any extravagant enthusiasm shown for some of these doctrines must be taken as an expression of the personal predilection of the signatory of the particular article.

PARIS   CHARLES GIDE
1909   CHARLES RIST

CONTENTS

BOOK I: THE FOUNDERS

BOOK II: THE ANTAGONISTS

BOOK III: LIBERALISM

BOOK IV: THE DISSENTERS

BOOK V: RECONSTRUCTION OF DOCTRINES AT THE END OF THE NINETEENTH CENTURY AND BIRTH OF SOCIAL DOCTRINES

BOOK VI: PREDOMINANCE OF PRODUCTION AND EXCHANGE PROBLEMS AFTER THE FIRST WORLD WAR

Book I: The Founders

CHAPTER I: THE PHYSIOCRATS

POLITICAL economy as the name of a special science is the invention of one Antoine de Montchrétien, who first employed the term about the beginning of the seventeenth century. Not until the middle of the eighteenth century, however, does the connotation of the word in any way approach to modern usage. A perusal of the article on Political Economy which appeared in the *Grande Encyclopédie* of 1755 will help us to appreciate the difference. That article was contributed by no less a person than Jean Jacques Rousseau, but its medley of politics and economics seems utterly strange to us. Nowadays it is customary to regard the adjective 'political' as unnecessary, and an attempt is made to dispense with it by employing the terms 'economic science' or 'social economics,' but this article clearly proves that it was not always devoid of significance. It also reveals the interesting fact that the science has always been chiefly concerned with the business side of the State, especially with the material welfare of the citizens—"with the fowl in the pot," as Henry IV put it. Even Smith never succeeded in getting quite beyond this point of view, for he declares that "the object of the political economy of every nation is to increase the riches and the power of that country."[1]

But the counsels given and the recipes offered for attaining the desired end were as diverse as they were uncertain. One school, known as the Mercantilist, believed that a State, like an individual, must secure the maximum of silver and gold before it could become wealthy. Happy indeed was a country like Spain that had discovered a Peru, or Holland, which, in default of mines, could procure gold from the foreigner in exchange for its spices. Foreign trade really seemed a quite inexhaustible mine. Other writers, who were socialists in fact though not in name—for that term is of later invention—thought that happiness could only be found in a more equal distribution of wealth, in the abolition or limitation of the rights of private property, or in the creation of a new society on the basis of a new social contract —in short, in the foundation of the Utopian commonwealth.

It was at this juncture that Quesnay appeared. Quesnay was a

---

[1] *Wealth of Nations* (Cannan's edition), Vol. I, p. 351.

doctor by profession, who now, when on the verge of old age, had turned his attention to the study of 'rural economy'—the problem of the land and the means of subsistence.[1] Boldly declaring that the solution of the problem had always lain ready to hand, needing neither inventing nor discovering, he further maintained that all social relations into which men enter, far from being haphazard, are, on the contrary, admirably regulated and controlled. To those who took the trouble to think, the laws governing human associations seemed almost self-evident, and the difficulties they involved no greater than the difficulties presented by the laws of geometry. So admirable were these laws in every respect that once they were thoroughly known they were certain to command allegiance. Dupont de Nemours cannot be said to have exaggerated when, in referring to this doctrine, he spoke of it as "very novel indeed."[2]

It is not too much to say that this marks the beginning of a new science—the science of Political Economy. The age of forerunners is past. Quesnay and his disciples must be considered the real founders of the science. It is true that their direct descendants, the French economists, very inconsiderately allowed the title to pass to Adam Smith, but foreign economists have again restored it to France, to remain in all probability definitely hers. But, as is the case with most sciences, there is not very much to mark the date of its birth or to determine the stock from which it sprang; all that we can confidently say is that the Physiocrats were certainly the first to grasp the conception of a unified science of society. In other words, they were the first to realize that all social facts are linked together in the bonds of inevitable laws, which individuals and Governments would obey if they were once made known to them. It may, of course, be pointed out that such a providential conception of economic laws has little in common with the ordinary naturalistic or deterministic standpoint of the science, and that several of the generalizations are simply the product of their own imaginations. It must also be admitted that Smith had far greater powers of observation, as well as a superior gift of lucid exposition, and altogether made a more notable contribution to the science. Still, it was the Physiocrats who constructed the way along which Smith and the writers of the hundred years which follow have all marched. Moreover, we know that but for the death of

---

[1] Quesnay's first economic articles, written for the *Grande Encyclopédie*, were on *Les Grains* and *Les Fermiers*.

[2] Professor Hector Denis, speaking of the Physiocratic doctrine, remarks that its imperfections are easily demonstrated, but that we seldom recognize its incomparable greatness.

Quesnay in 1774—two years before the publication of the *Wealth of Nations*—Smith would have dedicated his masterpiece to him.

The Physiocrats must also be credited with the foundation of the earliest 'school' of economists in the fullest sense of the term. The entrance of this small group of men into the arena of history is a most touching and significant spectacle. So complete was the unanimity of doctrine among them that their very names and even their personal characteristics are for ever enshrouded by the anonymity of a collective name.[1]

Their publications follow each other pretty closely for a period of twenty years, from 1756 to 1778.[2]

[1] "The genuine economists are easily depicted. In Dr Quesnay they have a common master; a common doctrine in the *Philosophie rurale* and the *Analyse économique*. Their classical literature is summed up in the generic term Physiocracy. In the *Tableau économique* they possess a formula with technical terms as precise as old Chinese characters." This definition of the Physiocrats, given by one of themselves, the Abbé Baudeau (*Ephémérides*, April 1776)—writing, we may be sure, in no malicious spirit —shows us that the school possessed not a little of the dogmatism of the Chinee.

[2] The first not only in chronological order but the chief recognized by all was Dr Quesnay (1694–1774), the physician of Louis XV and of Mme de Pompadour. He had already published numerous works on medicine, especially the *Essai physique sur l'Économie animale* (1736), before turning his attention to economic questions, and more especially to problems of 'rural economy.' His first contributions, the essays on *Les Grains* and *Les Fermiers*, which appeared in the *Grande Encyclopédie* in 1756 and 1757, were followed by his famous *Tableau économique* in 1758, when he was sixty-four years of age, and in 1760 by his *Maximes générales du Gouvernement économique d'un Royaume agricole*, which is merely a development of the preceding work.

His writings were not numerous, but his influence, like that of Socrates, disseminated as it was by his disciples, became very considerable.

The best edition of his works is that published by Professor Oncken of Berne, *Œuvres économiques et philosophiques de F. Quesnay* (Paris and Frankfort, 1888). Our quotations from the founders are taken from the *Collection des principaux économistes*, published by Daire.

The Marquis de Mirabeau, father of the great orator of the Revolution, a man of a fiery temperament like his son, published at about the same date as the production of the *Tableau* his *L'Ami des hommes*. This book, which created a great sensation, does not strictly belong to Physiocratic literature, for it ignores the fundamental doctrine of the school. *La Théorie de l'impôt* (1760) and *La Philosophie rurale* (1763), on the other hand, owe their inspiration to Physiocracy.

Mercier de la Rivière, a parliamentary advocate, published *L'Ordre naturel et essentiel des Sociétés politiques* in 1767. Dupont de Nemours refers to this as a "sublime work," and though it does not, perhaps, deserve that epithet it contains, nevertheless, the code of the Physiocratic doctrine.

Dupont de Nemours, as he is called after his native town, published about the same time, 1768, when he was only twenty-nine, a book entitled *Physiocratie, ou Constitution essentielle du Gouvernement le plus avantageux au Genre humain*. To him we owe the term from which the school took its name—Physiocracy, which signifies 'the rule of nature.' But the designation 'Physiocrats' was unfortunate and was almost immediately abandoned for 'Economists.' Quesnay and his disciples were the first 'Economists.' It was only much later, when the name 'Economist' became generic and useless as a distinctive mark for a special school, that writers made a practice of reverting to the older term 'Physiocrat.'

Turgot was the only literary person among them, but like his *confrères* he was devoid of wit, though the age was noted for its humorists. On the whole they were a sad and solemn sect, and their curious habit of insisting upon logical consistency—as if they were the sole depositaries of eternal truth—must often have been very tiresome. They soon fell an easy prey to the caustic sarcasm of Voltaire.[1] But despite all this they enjoyed a great reputation among their more eminent contemporaries. Statesmen, ambassadors, and a whole galaxy of royal personages, including the Margrave of Baden, who attempted to apply their doctrines in his own realm, the Grand Duke

---

An enthusiastic disciple of Quesnay, Dupont's rôle was chiefly that of a propagandist of Physiocratic doctrines, and he made little original contribution to the science. At an early date, moreover, the great political events in which he took an active part proved a distraction. He survived all his colleagues, and was the only one of them who lived long enough to witness the Revolution, in which he played a prominent part. He successively became a deputy in the Tiers État, a president of the Constituent Assembly, and later on, under the Directoire, Président du Conseil des Anciens. He even assisted in the restoration of the Empire, and political economy was first honoured at the hands of the Institut when he became a member of that body.

In 1777 Le Trosne, an advocate at the Court of Orleans, published a book entitled *De l'Intérêt social, par rapport à la Valeur, à la Circulation, à l'Industrie et au Commerce*, which is perhaps the best or at least the most strictly economic of all. Mention must also be made of the Abbé Baudeau, who has no less than eighty volumes to his credit, chiefly dealing with the corn trade, but whose principal work is *L'Introduction à la Philosophie économique* (1771); and of the Abbé Roubaud, afterwards Margrave of Baden, who had the advantage of being not merely a writer but a prince, and who carried out some Physiocratic experiments in some of the villages of his small principality.

We have not yet mentioned the most illustrious member of the school, both in respect of his talent and his position, namely, Turgot (1727–81). His name is generally coupled with that of the Physiocrats, and this classification is sufficiently justified by the similarity of their ideas. Still, as we shall see, in many respects he stands by himself, and bears a close resemblance to Adam Smith. Moreover, he commenced writing before the Physiocrats. His essay on paper money dates from 1748, when he was only twenty-one years of age, but his most important work, *Réflexions sur la formation et la distribution des richesses*, belongs to 1766. As the Intendant of Limoges and again as a minister of Louis XVI he possessed the necessary authority to enable him to realize his ideas of economic liberty, which he did by his famous edicts abolishing taxes upon corn passing from one province to another, and by the abolition of the rights of wardenship and privilege.

Unlike the other Physiocrats, who swore only by Dr Quesnay, Turgot owed a great deal to a prominent business man, Vincent de Gournay, who at a later date became the Intendant of Commerce. Gournay died in 1759, at the early age of forty-seven. Of Gournay we know next to nothing beyond what Turgot says of him in his eulogy (see Schelle, *Vincent de Gournay*, 1897).

Bibliography. Books dealing with the Physiocratic system, both in French and other languages, are fairly numerous. A very detailed account of these may be found in Weulersse's work *Le Mouvement physiocratique en France de 1756 à 1770*, published in 1910, which also contains a very complete exposition of the Physiocratic doctrine. In English there is a succinct account of the system in Higgs's *Physiocrats* (1897).

[1] Especially in the celebrated pamphlet *L'Homme aux quarante écus*.

Leopold of Tuscany, the Emperor Joseph II of Austria, Catherine, the famous Empress of Russia, Stanislaus, King of Poland, and Gustavus III of Sweden, were numbered among their auditors. Lastly, and most unexpectedly of all, they were well received by the Court ladies at Versailles. In a word, Physiocracy became the rage. All this may seem strange to us, but there are several considerations which may well be kept in view. The society of the period, *raffiné* and licentious as it was, took the same delight in the 'rural economy' of the Physiocrats as it did in the pastorals of Trianon or Watteau. Perhaps it gleaned some comfort from the thought of an unchangeable "natural order," just when the political and social edifice was giving way beneath its feet. It may be that its curiosity was roused by that terse saying which Quesnay wrote at the head of the *Tableau économique*: "Pauvres paysans, pauvre royaume! Pauvre royaume, pauvre roi!" or that it felt in those words the sough of a new breeze, not very threatening as yet, but a forerunner of the coming storm.

An examination of the doctrine, or the essential principles, as they called them, must precede a consideration of the system or the proposed application of those principles.

I

I: THE NATURAL ORDER

The essence of the Physiocratic system lay in their conception of the 'natural order.' *L'Ordre naturel et essentiel des Sociétés politiques* is the title of Mercier de la Rivière's book, and Dupont de Nemours defined Physiocracy as "the science of the natural order."

What are we to understand by these terms?

It is hardly necessary to say that the term 'natural order' is meant to emphasize the contrast between it and the artificial social order voluntarily created upon the basis of a social contract.[1] But a purely negative definition is open to many different interpretations.

[1] J. J. Rousseau, the author of the *Contrat Social* (1762), was a contemporary of the Physiocrats, but he never became a member of the school. Mirabeau's attempt to win his allegiance proved a failure. The 'natural order' and the 'social contract' seem incompatible, for the natural and spontaneous can never be the subject of contract. One might even be tempted to think that Rousseau's celebrated theory was formulated in opposition to Physiocracy, unless we remembered that the social-contract theory is much older than Rousseau's work. Traces of the same idea may be found in many writings, especially those inspired by Calvinism. To Rousseau the social question seemed to be a kind of mathematical problem, and any proposed solution must satisfy certain complicated conditions, which are formulated thus: "To find a form of association which protects with the whole common force the person

In the first place, this 'natural order' may be conceived as a state of nature in opposition to a civilized state regarded as an artificial creation. To discover what such a 'natural order' really was like man must have recourse to his origins.

Quotations from the Physiocrats in support of this view might easily be cited.[1] This interpretation has the further distinction of being in accord with the spirit of the age. The worship of the 'noble savage' was a feature of the end of the eighteenth century. It pervades the literature of the period, and the cult which began with the tales of Voltaire, Diderot, and Marmontel reappears in the anarchist writers of to-day. As an interpretation of the Physiocratic position, however, it must be unhesitatingly rejected, for no one bore less

---

and property of each associate, and in virtue of which every one, while uniting himself to all, obeys only himself and remains as free as before." Nothing could well be further from the Physiocratic view. Their belief was that there was nothing to find and nothing to create. The 'natural order' was self-evident.

It is true that Rousseau was an equally enthusiastic believer in a natural order, in the voice of nature, and in the native kindness of mankind. "The eternal laws of nature and order have a real existence. For the wise they serve as positive laws, and they are engraved on the innermost tablets of the heart by both conscience and reason." (*Émile*, Book V.) The language is identical with that of the Physiocrats. But there is this great difference. Rousseau thought that the state of nature had been denaturalized by social and especially by political institutions, including, of course, private property; and his chief desire was to give back to the people the equivalent of what they had lost. The 'social contract' is just an attempt to secure this. The Physiocrats, on the other hand, regarded the institution of private property as the perfect bloom of the 'natural order.' Its beauty has perhaps suffered at the hands of turbulent Governments, but let Governments be removed and the 'natural order' will at once resume its usual course.

There is also this other prime difference. The Physiocrats regarded interest and duty as one and the same thing, for by following his own interest the individual is also furthering the good of everybody else. To Rousseau they seemed antagonistic: the former must be overcome by the latter. "Personal interest is always in inverse ratio to duty, and becomes greater the narrower the association, and the less sacred." (*Contrat Social*, II, chapter iii.) In other words, family ties and co-operative associations are stronger than patriotism.

[1] "There is a natural society whose existence is prior to every other human association. . . . These self-evident principles, which might form the foundation of a perfect constitution, are also self-revealing. They are evident not only to the well-informed student, but also to the simple savage as he issues from the lap of nature." (Dupont, Vol. I, p. 341.) Some Physiocrats even seem inclined to the belief that this 'natural order' has actually existed in the past and that men lost it through their own remissness. Dupont de Nemours mournfully asks: "How have the people fallen from that state of felicity in which they lived in those far-off, happy days? How is it that they failed to appreciate the natural order?" But even when interpreted in this fashion it had no resemblance to a savage state. It must rather be identified with the Golden Age of the ancients or the Eden of Holy Scripture. It is a lost Paradise which we must seek to regain.

The view is not peculiar to the Physiocrats, but it is interesting to note how unfamiliar they were with the modern idea of evolutionary progress.

resemblance to a savage than a Physiocrat. They all of them lived highly respectable lives as magistrates, *intendants*, priests, and royal physicians, and were completely captivated by ideas of orderliness, authority, sovereignty, and property—none of them conceptions compatible with a savage state. "Property, security, and liberty constitute the whole of the social order."[1] They never acquiesced in the view that mankind suffered loss in passing from the state of nature into the social state; neither did they hold to Rousseau's belief that there was greater freedom in the natural state, although its dangers were such that men were willing to sacrifice something in order to be rid of them, but that nevertheless in entering upon the new state something had been lost which could never be recovered.[2] All this was a mere illusion in the opinion of the Physiocrats. Nothing was lost, everything was to be gained, by passing from a state of nature into the civilized state.

In the second place, the term 'natural order' might be taken to mean that human societies are subject to natural laws such as govern the physical world or exercise sway over animal or organic life. From this standpoint the Physiocrats must be regarded as the forerunners of the organic sociologists. Such interpretation seems highly probable because Dr Quesnay, through his study of "animal economy" (the title of one of his works) and the circulation of the blood, was already familiar with these ideas. Social and animal economy, both, might well have appeared to him in much the same light as branches of physiology. From physiology to Physiocracy was not a very great step. At any rate, the Physiocrats succeeded in giving prominence to the idea of the interdependence of all social classes and of their final dependence upon nature. And this we might almost say was a change tantamount to a transformation from a moral to a natural science.[3]

[1] Mercier de la Rivière, Vol. II, p. 615. "Natural right is indeterminate in a state of nature [note the paradox]. The right only appears when justice and labour have been established." (Quesnay, p. 43.)

[2] "By entering society and making conventions for their mutual advantage men increase the scope of natural right without incurring any restriction of their liberties, for this is just the state of things that enlightened reason would have chosen." (Quesnay, pp. 43, 44.)

[3] Pursuing this same idea, Dupont writes as follows: "It is thirteen years since a man of exceptional genius, well versed in profound disquisition, and already known for his success in an art where complete mastery only comes with careful observation and complete submission to the laws of nature, predicted that natural laws extended far beyond the bounds hitherto assigned to them. If nature gives to the bee, the ant, or the beaver the power of submitting by common consent and for their own interest to a good, stable, and equable form of government, it can hardly refuse man the power of raising himself to the enjoyment of the same advantages. Convinced of the importance of this view, and of the important consequences that might follow from it, he applied his whole intellectual strength to an investigation of the physical laws

Even this explanation seems to us insufficient. Dupont, in the words which we have quoted in the footnote at p. 27, seems to imply that the laws of the beehive and the ant-hill are imposed by common consent and for mutual benefit. Animal society, so it seemed to him, was founded upon social contract. But such a conception of 'law' is very far removed from the one usually adopted by the natural sciences, by physicians and biologists, say. And, as a matter of fact, the Physiocrats were anything but determinists. They neither believed that the 'natural order' imposed itself like gravitation nor imagined that it could ever be realized in human society as it is in the hive or the ant-hill. They saw that the latter were well-ordered communities, while human society at its present state is disordered, because man is free whereas the animal is not.

What are we to make of this 'natural order,' then? The 'natural order,' so the Physiocrats maintained, is the order which God has ordained for the happiness of mankind. It is the providential order.[1] To understand it is our first duty—to bring our lives into conformity with it is our next.

But can a knowledge of the 'order' ever be acquired by men? To this they reply that the distinctive mark of this 'order' is its obviousness. This word occurs on almost every page they wrote.[2] Still, the self-evident must in some way be apprehended. The most brilliant light can be seen only by the eye. By what organ can this be sensed? By instinct, by conscience, or by reason? Will a divine voice by means of a supernatural revelation show us the way of truth, or will it be Nature's hand that shall lead us in the blessed path? The Physiocrats seem to have ignored this question, for every one of them indifferently gives his own answer, regardless of the fact that it may contradict another's. Mercier de la Rivière recalls the saying of St John concern-

---

which govern society." Elsewhere he adds: "The natural order is merely the physical constitution which God Himself has given the universe." (Introduction to Quesnay's works, p. 21.)

Hector Denis in his *Histoire des Doctrines* expresses the belief that the most characteristic feature of the Physiocratic system is the emphasis laid upon a naturalistic conception of society. He illustrates this by means of diagrams showing the identity of the circulation of wealth and the circulation of the blood.

[1] "Its laws are irrevocable, pertaining as they do to the essence of matter and the soul of humanity. They are just the expression of the will of God. . . . All our interests, all our wishes, are focused at one point, making for harmony and universal happiness. We must regard this as the work of a kind Providence, which desires that the earth should be peopled by happy human beings." (Mercier de la Rivière, Vol. I, p. 390; Vol. II, p. 638.)

[2] "There is a natural judge of all ordinances, even of the sovereign's. This judge, which recognizes no exceptions, is just the evidence of their conformity with or opposition to natural laws." (Dupont, Vol. I, p. 746.)

ing the "Light which lighteth every man that cometh into the world." This may be taken to be an internal light set by God in the heart of every man to enable him to choose his path. Quesnay, so Dupont affirms, "must have seen that man had only to examine himself to find within him an inarticulate conception of these laws. In other words, introspection clearly shows that men are unwittingly guided by an 'inherent' knowledge of Physiocracy."[1] But, after all, it seems that this intuitive perception is insufficient to reveal the full glory of the order. For Quesnay declared that a knowledge of its laws must be enforced upon men, and this afforded a *raison d'être* for an educational system which was to be under the direct control of the Government.

To sum up, we may say that the 'natural order' was that order which seemed obviously the best, not to any individual whomsoever, but to rational, cultured, liberal-minded men like the Physiocrats. It was not the product of the observation of external facts; it was the revelation of a principle within. And this is one reason why the Physiocrats showed such respect for property and authority. It seemed to them that this formed the very basis of the 'natural order.'

It was just because the 'natural order' was 'supernatural,' and so raised above the contingencies of everyday life, that it seemed to them to be endowed with all the grandeur of the geometrical order, with its double attributes of universality and immutability. It remained the same for all times, and for all men. Its fiat was "unique, eternal, invariable, and universal." Divine in its origin, it was universal in its scope, and its praises were sung in litanies that might rival the *Ave Maria*.[2] Speaking of its universality, Turgot writes as follows: "Whoever is unable to overlook the accidental separation of political states one from another, or to forget their diverse institutions, will never treat a question of political economy satisfactorily."[3] Referring to its immutability, he adds: "It is not enough to know what is or what has been; we must also know what ought to be. The rights of man are not founded upon history: they are rooted in his nature."

It looked as if this dogmatic optimism would dominate the whole Classical school, especially the French writers, and that natural law would usurp the functions of Providence. To-day it is everywhere discredited, but when it first loomed above the horizon its splendour dazzled all eyes. Hence the many laudatory remarks, which to us seem hyperbolical, if not actually ridiculous.[4] But it was no small

[1] Dupont, introduction to Quesnay's works, Vol. I, pp. 19 and 26.
[2] Baudeau, Vol. I, p. 820. [3] Letter to Mlle Lespinasse (1770).
[4] See some remarks on the *Tableau économique* on p. 37.

B

thing to found a new science, to set up a new aim and a fresh ideal, to lay down the framework which others were to fill in.

It was the practical results, however, that revealed the full powers of the 'natural order.' It so happened that the mass of regulations which constituted the old regime fell to the ground before its onslaughts almost immediately, and it all came about in this fashion.

Knowledge of the 'natural order' was not sufficient. Daily life must also conform to the knowledge. Nothing could be easier than this, for "if the order really were the most advantageous"[1] every man could be trusted to find out for himself the best way of attaining it without coercion of any kind.[2]

This psychological balance which every individual was supposed to carry within himself, and which, as the basis of the Neo-Classical school, is known as the Hedonistic principle, is admirably described by Quesnay.[3] "To secure the greatest amount of pleasure with the least possible outlay should be the aim of all economic effort." And this was what the 'order' aimed at. "When every one does this the natural order, instead of being endangered, will be all the better assured." It is of the very essence of that order that the particular interest of the individual can never be separated from the common interest of all, but this happens only under a free system. "The movements of society are spontaneous and not artificial, and the desire for joy which manifests itself in all its activities unwittingly drives it towards the realization of the ideal type of State."[4] This is *laissez-faire* pure and simple.[5]

These famous formulæ have been so often repeated and criticized since that they appear somewhat trite to-day. But it is certain that

[1] Baudeau, *Éphémérides du citoyen.*

[2] "The laws of the natural order do not in any way restrain the liberty of mankind, for the great advantage which they possess is that they make for greater liberty." (Quesnay, *Droit naturel*, p. 55.) And Mercier de la Rivière says (Vol. II, p. 617): "The institution of private property and of liberty would secure perfect order without the help of any other law."

[3] *Dialogues sur les Artisans.*

[4] Mercier de la Rivière, Vol. II, p. 617.

[5] The origin of the famous formula is uncertain. Several of the Physiocrats, especially Mirabeau and Mercier de la Rivière, assign it to Vincent de Gournay, but Turgot, the friend and biographer of Vincent de Gournay, attributes it, under a slightly different form, *laissez-nous faire*, to Le Gendre, a merchant who was a contemporary of Colbert. Oncken thinks that the credit must go to the Marquis d'Argenson, who employed the term in his *Mémoires* as early as the year 1736. The formula itself is quite commonplace. It only became important when it was adopted as the motto of a famous school of thinkers, so that this kind of research has no great interest. For a discussion of this trivial question, see the work of M. Schelle, *Vincent de Gournay* (1897), and especially Oncken's *Die Maxime laissez-faire et laissez-passer* Berne, 1886).

they were not so at the time. It is easy to laugh at their social philosophy, to mock at its naïveté and simplicity, and to show that such supposed harmony of interests between men does not exist, that the interests of individuals do not always coincide with those of the community, and that the private citizen is not always the best judge even of his own interests. It was perhaps necessary that the science should be born of such extreme optimism. No science can be constructed without some amount of faith in a pre-established order.

Moreover, *laissez-faire* does not of necessity mean that nothing will be done. It is not a doctrine of passivity or fatalism. There will be ample scope for individual effort, for it simply means leaving an open field and securing fair play for every one, free from all fear lest his own interests should injure other people's or in any way prejudice those of the State. It is true that there will not be much work for the Government, but the task of that body will by no means be a light one, especially if it intends carrying out the Physiocratic programme. This included upholding the rights of private property and individual liberty by removing all artificial barriers, and punishing all those who threatened the existence of any of these rights; while, most important of all, there was the duty of giving instruction in the laws of the 'natural order.'

II: THE NET PRODUCT

Every social fact had a place within the 'natural order' of the Physiocrats. Such a wide generalization would have entitled them to be regarded as the founders of sociology rather than of economics. But there was included one purely economic phenomenon which attracted their attention at an early stage, and so completely captivated their imaginations as to lead them on a false quest. This was the predominant position which land occupied as an agent of production—the most erroneous and at the same time the most characteristic doctrine in the whole Physiocratic system.

Every productive undertaking of necessity involves certain outgoings—a certain loss. In other words, some amount of wealth is destroyed in the production of new wealth—an amount that ought to be subtracted from the amount of new wealth produced. This difference, measuring as it does the excess of the one over the other, constitutes the net increase of wealth, known since the time of the Physiocrats as the 'net product.'

The Physiocrats believed that this 'net product' was confined to

reap → harvest

one class of production only, namely, agriculture. Here alone, so it
seemed to them, the wealth produced was greater than the wealth
consumed. Barring accidents, the labourer reaped more than he consumed, even if we included in his consumption his maintenance
throughout a whole year, and not merely during the seasons of harvest
and tilth. It was because agricultural production had this unique and
marvellous power of yielding a 'net product' that economy was
possible and civilization a fact.[1] It was not true of any other class of
production, either of commerce or of transport, where it was very
evident that man's labour produced nothing, but merely replaced or
transferred the products already produced. Neither was it true of
manufacture, where the artisan simply combined or otherwise modified
the raw material.[2]

It is true that such transfer or accretion of matter may increase the
value of the product, but only in proportion to the amount of wealth
which had to be consumed in order to produce it; because the price
of manual labour is always equal to the cost of the necessaries consumed by the worker. All that we have in this case, however, is a
collection of superimposed values with some raw material thrown into
the bargain. But, as Mercier de la Rivière put it, "addition is not
multiplication."[3]

Consequently, industry was voted sterile. This implied no contempt
for industry and commerce. "Far from being useless, these are the
arts that supply the luxuries as well as the necessaries of life, and upon
these mankind is dependent both for its preservation and for its well-

---

[1] "The prosperity of mankind is bound up with a maximum net product." (Dupont
de Nemours, *Origine d'une Science nouvelle*, p. 346.)
"This physical truth that the earth is the source of all commodities is so very evident
that none of us can doubt it." (Le Trosne, *Intérêt social*.)
"The produce of the soil may be divided into two parts . . . what remains over is
free and disposable, a pure gift given to the cultivator in addition to the return for
his outlay and the wages of his labour." (Turgot, *Réflexions*.)
[2] "Labour applied anywhere except to land is absolutely sterile, for man is not a
creator." (Le Trosne, p. 942.)
"Raw material is transformed into beautiful and useful objects through the diligence of the artisan, but before his task begins it is necessary that others should supply
the raw material and provide the necessary sustenance. When their part is completed
others should recompense them and pay them for their trouble. The cultivators, on
the other hand, produce their own raw material, whether for use or for consumption,
as well as everything that is consumed by others. This is just where the difference
between a productive and a sterile class comes in." (Baudeau, *Correspondance avec
M. Graslin*.)
[3] "A weaver buys food and clothing, giving 150 francs for them, together with a
quantity of flax, for which he gives 50 francs. The cloth will be sold for 200 francs, a
sum that will cover all expenditure." (Mercier de la Rivière, Vol. II, p. 598.)
"Industry merely superimposes value, but does not create any which did not previously exist." (*Ibid.*)

being."[1] They are unproductive in the sense that they produce no 'extra' wealth.

It may be pointed out, on the other hand, that the 'gains,' both in industry and commerce, are far in excess of those of agriculture. All this was immaterial to the Physiocrats, for "they were gained, not produced."[2] Such gains simply represented wealth transferred from the agricultural to the industrial classes.[3] The agricultural classes furnished the artisans not only with raw material, but also with the necessaries of life. The artisans were simply the domestic servants, or, to use Turgot's phrase, the hirelings of the agriculturists.[4] Strictly speaking, the latter could keep the whole net product to themselves, but finding it more convenient they entrust the making of their clothes, the erection of their houses, and the production of their implements to the artisans, giving them a portion of the net product as remuneration.[5] It is possible, of course, that, like many servants in fine houses, the latter manage to make a very good living at their masters' expense.

The 'sterile classes' in Physiocratic parlance simply signifies those who draw their incomes second-hand. The Physiocrats had the good sense to try to give an explanation of this unfortunate term, which threatened to discredit their system altogether, and which it seemed unfair to apply to a whole class that had done more than any other towards enriching the nation.

It is a debatable point whether the Physiocrats attributed this virtue

[1] Baudeau, Éphém. IX (1770). One feels that the Physiocrats go too far when they say that "the merchant who sells goods may occasionally prove as useful as the philanthropist who gives them, because want puts a price upon the service of the one just as it does upon the charity of the other." (Du Marchand de grains, in the Journal de l'Agriculture, du Commerce, et des Finances, December 1773, quoted in a thesis on the corn trade by M. Curmond, 1900.) We must insist upon the fact that 'unproductive' or 'sterile' did not by any means signify 'useless.' They saw clearly enough that the labour of the weaver who makes linen out of flax or cloth out of wool is at any rate as useful as that of the cultivator who produced the wool and the flax, or rather that the latter's toil would be perfectly useless without the industry of the former. They also realized that although we may say that agricultural labour is more useful than that of the weaver or the mason, especially when the land is used for raising corn, one cannot say as much when that same land is employed in producing roses, or mulberry-trees for rearing silkworms.
[2] Le Trosne, p. 945.
[3] "It seems necessary as well as simple and natural to distinguish the men who pay others and draw their wealth directly from nature, from the paid men, who can only obtain it as a reward for useful and agreeable services which they have rendered to the former class." (Dupont, Vol. I, p. 142.)
[4] It is rather strange that Turgot should have added this qualification, because he was more favourable to industry and less devoted to agriculture than the rest of the Physiocrats.
[5] "I must have a man to make my clothes, just as I must have a doctor whose advice I may ask concerning my health, or a lawyer concerning my affairs, or a servant to work instead of me." (Le Trosne, p. 949.)

of furnishing a net product solely to agriculture or whether they intended it to apply to extractive industries, such as mining and fishing. They seem to apply it in a general way to mines, but the references are rare and not infrequently contradictory. We can understand their hesitating, for, on the one hand, mines undoubtedly give us new wealth in the form of raw materials, just as the land or sea does; on the other hand, the fruits of the earth and the treasures of the deep are not so easily exhausted as mines. Turgot put it excellently when he said, "The land produces fruit annually, but a mine produces no fruit. The mine itself is the garnered fruit," and he concludes that mines, like industrial undertakings, give no net product, that if anyone had any claim to that product it would be the owner of the soil, but that in any case the surplus would be almost insignificant.[1]

This essential difference which the Physiocrats sought to establish between agricultural and industrial production was at bottom theological. The fruits of the earth are given by God, while the products of the arts are wrought by man, who is powerless to create.[2] The reply is obvious. God would still be creator if He decreed to give us our clothes instead of our daily bread. And, although man cannot create matter, but simply transform it, it is important to remember that the cultivation of the soil, like the fashioning of iron or wood, is merely a process of transformation. They failed to grasp the truth which Lavoisier was to demonstrate so clearly, namely, that in nature nothing is ever created and nothing lost. A grain of corn sown in a field obtains the materials for the ear from the soil and atmosphere, transmuting them to suit its own purpose, just as the baker, out of that same corn, combined with water, salt, and yeast, will make bread.

But they were sufficiently clear-sighted to see that all natural products, including even corn, were influenced by the varying condition of the markets, and that if prices fell very low the net product disappeared altogether. In view of such facts can it still be said that the

---

[1] On this point see M. Pervinquière, *Contribution à l'Étude de la Productivité dans la Physiocratie.* The indifference of the Physiocrats to mines shows a want of scientific spirit, for even from their own point of view the question was one of prime importance. No commodity could be produced without raw material, and wealth is simply a collection of commodities. Raw material is furnished by the mine as well as by the soil. In the history of mankind iron has played as important a part as corn. Agriculture itself is an extractive industry, where the miner—the agriculturist—uses plants instead of drills, and in both cases the product is exhaustible.

[2] Le Trosne, p. 942.
"Land owes its fertility to the might of the Creator, and out of His blessing flow its inexhaustible riches. This power is already there, and man simply makes use of it." (*Ibid.*, chapter i, sec. ii.)

earth produces real value or that its produce differs in any essential respects from the products of industry?

The Physiocrats possibly thought that the *bon prix*—*i.e.*, the price which yielded a surplus over and above cost of production—was a normal effect of the 'natural order.' Whenever the price fell to the level of the cost of production it was a sure sign that the 'order' had been destroyed. Under these circumstances there was nothing remarkable in the disappearance of the net product. This is doubtless the significance of Quesnay's enigmatic saying: "Abundance and cheapness are not wealth, scarcity and dearness are misery, abundance and dearness are opulence."[1]

But if the *bon prix* simply measures the difference between the value of the product and its cost of production, then it is not more common in agriculture than in other modes of production. Nor does it extend over a longer period in the one case than in the other, provided competition be operative in both cases; on the contrary, it will become manifest in the one case as easily as in the other, especially if there be any scarcity. It remains to be seen then whether monopoly values are more prevalent in agricultural production than in industrial. In a very general way, seeing that there is only a limited quantity of land, we may answer in the affirmative, and admit a certain degree of validity in the Physiocratic theory. But the establishment of protective rights and the occurrence of agricultural crises clearly prove that competition also has some influence upon the amount of that revenue.

The net product was just an illusion. The essence of production is not the creation of matter, but simply the accretion of value. But it is not difficult to appreciate the nature of the illusion if we recall the circumstances, and try to visualize the kind of society with which the Physiocrats were acquainted. One section of the community, consisting solely of nobility and clergy, lived upon the rents which the land yielded. Their luxurious lives would have been impossible if the earth did not yield something over and above the amount consumed by the peasant. It is curious that the Physiocrats, while they regarded the artisans as nothing better than servants who depended for their very existence upon the agriculturists, failed to recognize the equally complete dependence of the worthless proprietor upon his tenants. If there had existed instead a class of business men living in ease and luxury, and drawing their dividends, it is quite possible that the Physiocrats would have concluded that there was a net product in industrial enterprise.

[1] Quesnay, p. 325.

So deeply rooted was this idea of nature, or God operating through nature, as the only source of value that we find traces of it even in Adam Smith. Not until we come to Ricardo do we have a definite contradiction of it. With Ricardo, rent, the income derived from land, instead of being regarded as a blessing of nature—the *Alma Parens*—which was bound to grow as the 'natural order' extended its sway, is simply looked upon as the inevitable result of the limited extent and growing sterility of the land. No longer is it a free gift of God to men, but a pre-imposed tax which the consumer has to pay the proprietor. No longer is it the net product; henceforth it is known as rent.

As to the epithet 'sterile,' which was applied to every kind of work other than agriculture, we shall find that it has been superseded, and that the attribute 'productive' has been successively applied to every class of work—first to industry, then to commerce, and finally to the liberal professions. Even if it were true that industrial undertakings only yield the equivalent of the value consumed, that is not enough to justify the epithet 'sterile,' unless, as Adam Smith wittily remarks, we are by analogy to consider every marriage sterile which does not result in the birth of more than two children. To invoke the distinction between addition and multiplication is useless, because arithmetic teaches us that multiplication is simply an abridged method of adding.

It seems very curious that that kind of wealth which appeared to the Physiocrats to be the most legitimate and the most superior kind should be just the one that owed nothing to labour, and which later on, under the name of rent, seems the most difficult to justify.

But we must not conclude that the Physiocratic theory of the net product possessed no scientific value.

It was a challenge to the economic doctrines of the time, especially Mercantilism. The Mercantilists thought that the only way to increase wealth was to exploit neighbours and colonists, but they failed to see that commerce and agriculture afforded equally satisfactory methods. Nor must we forget the Physiocrats' influence upon practical politics. Sully, the French minister, betrays evidence of their influence when he remarks that the only two sources of national wealth are land and labour. Let us also remember that, despite some glaring mistakes, agriculture has never lost the pre-eminence which they gave it, and that the recent revival of agricultural Protection is directly traceable to their influence. They were always staunch Free Traders themselves, but we can hardly blame them for not being sufficiently sanguine to expect such wholehearted acceptance of their views as to anticipate some of the more curious developments of their doctrines. It is almost certain that if they were living to-day they would not be found supporting the Protectionist movement. At least this is the opinion of M. Oncken, the economist, who has made the most thorough study of their ideas.[1]

Although the Physiocratic distinction between agriculture and industry was largely imaginary, it is nevertheless true that agriculture does possess certain special features, such as the power of engendering the forces of life, whether vegetable or animal. This mysterious force, which under the term 'nature' was only very dimly understood by the Physiocrats, and still is too often confused with the physico-chemical forces, does really possess some characteristics which help us to differentiate between agriculture and industry. At some moments agriculture seems inferior because its returns are limited by the exigencies of time and place; but more often superior because agriculture alone can produce the necessaries of life. This is no insignificant fact; but we are trenching on the difficult problems connected with the name of Malthus.

III: THE CIRCULATION OF WEALTH

The Physiocrats were the first to attempt a synthesis of distribution. They were anxious to know—and it was surely a praiseworthy ambition —how wealth passed from one class in society to another, why it always followed the same routes, whose meanderings they were successful in unravelling, and how this continual circulation, as Turgot said, "constituted the very life of the body politic, just as the circulation of the blood did of the physical."

A scholar like Quesnay, the author of the work on animal economy[2] and a diligent student of Harvey's new discovery, was precisely the man to carry the biological idea over into the realm of sociology. He made use of the idea in his *Tableau économique,* which is simply a graphic representation of the way in which the circulation of wealth takes place. The appearance of this table caused an enthusiasm among his contemporaries that is almost incredible,[3] although Professor Hector

[1] *Geschichte der National Oekonomie,* Part I, *Die Zeit vor Adam Smith.*

M. Méline's book *Le Retour à la Terre,* though Protectionist in tone, is wholly imbued with the Physiocratic spirit.

[2] *Essai physique sur l'Économie animale* (1747).

[3] "There have been since the world began three great inventions which have principally given stability to political societies, independent of many other inventions which have enriched and advanced them. The first is the invention of writing, which alone gives human nature the power of transmitting without alteration its laws, its contracts, its annals, and its discoveries. The second is the invention of money, which binds together all the relations between civilized societies. The third is the Economical Table, the result of the other two, which completes them both by perfecting their object; the great discovery of our age, but of which our posterity will reap the benefit." (Mirabeau, quoted in *Wealth of Nations,* Book IV, chapter ix.) Baudeau is no less

Denis declares that he is almost ready to share in Mirabeau's admiration.[1]

We know by this time that this circulation is much more complicated than the Physiocrats believed, but it is still worth while to give an outline of their conception.[2]

Quesnay distinguishes three social classes:

1. A productive class consisting entirely of agriculturists—perhaps also of fishermen and miners.

2. A proprietary class, including not only landed proprietors, but also any who have the slightest title to sovereignty of any kind—a survival of feudalism, where the two ideas of sovereignty and property are always linked together.

3. A sterile class, consisting of merchants and manufacturers, together with domestic servants and members of the liberal professions.

The first class, being the only productive class, must supply all that flow of wealth whose course we are now to follow. Let us suppose, then—the figures are Quesnay's and seem sufficiently near the facts —that the value of the total wealth produced equals 5 milliard francs.

---

enthusiastic. "These figures," he writes, "are borrowed with the consent and upon the advice of the great master whose genius first begat the sublime idea of this *Tableau*. The *Tableau* gives us such a clear idea of the premier position of the science that all Europe is bound to accept its teaching, to the eternal glory of the invention and the everlasting happiness of mankind." (P. 867.)

The first edition of the *Tableau*, of which only a few copies were printed, is missing altogether, but a proof of that edition, corrected by Quesnay himself, was recently discovered in the Bibliothèque Nationale in Paris by Professor Stephan Bauer, of the University of Bâle. A facsimile was published by the British Economic Association in 1894. [A facsimile is printed also in Alexander Gray's *Development of Economic Doctrine*, 1931.]

[1] "The discovery of the circulation of wealth in economic societies occupies in the history of the science the same position as is occupied by the discovery of the circulation of the blood in the history of biology."

[2] Quesnay's table consists of a number of columns placed in juxtaposition with a number of zigzag lines which cross from one column to another. If he had been living now he would almost certainly have used the graphic method, which would have simplified matters very considerably, and it is somewhat strange that no one has attempted this with his *Tableau*. Hector Denis has compared his tables with those of the anatomist and traced a parallel between the links of the economical world and the plexus of veins and arteries in the human body. Quesnay's explanation of the *Tableau* by means of mathematical tables gives him a claim to be considered a pioneer of the Mathematical school. Full justice has been done to him in this respect. An article by Bauer in the *Quarterly Journal of Economics*, 1890, recognizes his claim, and there is another by Oncken in the *Economic Journal* for June 1896, entitled *The Physiocrats as Founders of the Mathematical School*. His contemporary Le Trosne is even more emphatic on the point: "Economic science, being a study of measurable objects, is an exact science, and its conclusions may be mathematically tested. What the science lacked was a convenient formula which might be applied to test its general conclusions. Such a formula we now have in the *Tableau économique*" (*De l'ordre social*, VIII, p. 218.)

Of this 5 milliards 2 milliards are necessary for the upkeep of the members of this class and its oxen during harvest and sowing. This portion does not circulate. It simply remains where it was produced. The produce representing the remaining 3 milliards is sold. But agricultural products alone do not suffice for the upkeep of Class 1. Manufactured goods, clothes, and boots also are required, and these are got from the industrial classes, for which a milliard francs is given.

There remain just 2 milliards, which go to the landowners and the Government in rents and taxes. By and by we shall see how they attempted to justify this apparent parasitism.

Let us pass on to consider the propertied class. It manages to live upon the 2 milliards which it receives by way of rents, and it lives well. Its food it must obtain from the agricultural class (unless, of course, the rents are paid in kind), and for this it possibly pays a milliard francs. It also requires manufactured goods, which it must get from the sterile class, and for which it pays another milliard francs. This completes their account.

As to the sterile class, it produces nothing, and so, unlike the preceding class, it can only get its necessaries second-hand from the productive class. These may be got in two ways: a milliard from the agricultural class in payment for manufactured goods and another milliard from the landed proprietors. The latter milliard, being one of the two which the landed proprietors got from the agriculturists, has in this way described the complete circle.

The 2 milliards obtained as salaries by the sterile class are employed in buying the necessaries of life and the raw material of industry. And since it is only the productive class that can procure these necessaries and raw materials, this 2 milliards passes into the hands of the agriculturists. The 2 milliards, in short, return to their starting-point. Adding the milliard already paid by the landed proprietors to the 2 milliards' worth of products unsold, the total of 5 milliards is replaced in the hands of the productive class, and so the process goes on indefinitely.[1]

This résumé gives but a very imperfect idea of the vast complexities and difficulties involved in tracing the growth of revenues—an evolu-

---

[1] Turgot, although he is not speaking of the *Tableau* itself in this case, sums it up admirably in the following: "What the labourers get from the land in addition to what is sufficient to supply their own needs constitutes the only wages fund [note the phrase] which all the other members of society can draw upon in return for their labour. The other members of society, when they buy the commodities which the labourer has produced, simply give him the bare equivalent of what it has cost the labourer to produce them." (Vol. I, p. 10.) For a more detailed account see Baudeau, *Explication du Tableau économique*.

tion which the Physiocrats followed with the enthusiasm of children. They imagined that it was all very real.[1] The rediscovery of their millions intoxicated them, but, like many of the mathematical economists of to-day, they forgot that at the end of their calculations they only had what they had assumed at the beginning. It is very evident that the table proves nothing as to the essential point in their system, namely, whether there really exist a productive and a sterile class.[2]

The most interesting thing in the Physiocratic scheme of distribution is not the particular demonstration which they gave of it, but the emphasis which they laid upon the fact of the circulation of wealth taking place in accordance with certain laws, and the way in which the revenue of each class was determined by this circulation.

The singular position which the proprietors hold in this tripartite division of society is one of the most curious features of the system.

Anyone examining the table in a non-Physiocratic fashion, but simply viewing it in the modern spirit, must at once feel surprised and disappointed to find that the class which enjoys two-fifths of the national revenue does nothing in return for it. We should not have been surprised if such glaring parasitism had given to the work of the Physiocrats a distinctly socialistic tone. But they were quite impervious to all such ideas. They never appreciated the weakness of the landowners' position, and they always treated them with the greatest reverence. The epithet 'sterile' is applied, not to them, but to manufacturers and artisans! Property is the foundation-stone of the 'natural order.' The proprietors have been entrusted with the task of supplying the staff of life, and are endued with a kind of priestly sacredness. It is from their hands that all of us receive the elements of nutrition. It is a 'divine' institution—the word is there.[3] Such idolatry needs some explanation.

One might have expected—even from their own point of view— that the premier position would have been given to the class which they termed productive, i.e., to the cultivators of the soil, who were mostly farmers and métayers. The land was not of their making, it is

---

[1] "This movement of commerce from one class to another, and the conditions which give rise to it, are not mere hypotheses. A little reflexion will show that they are faithfully copied from nature." (Quesnay, p. 60.)

[2] They imagined that it was actually so. "On the one hand, we see the productive class living on a series of payments, which are given in return for its labour, and always bearing a close relation to the outlay upon its upkeep. On the other, there is nothing but consumption and annihilation of goods, but no production." (Ibid.)

[3] "It is impossible not to recognize the right of property as a divine institution, for it has been ordained that this should be the indirect means of perpetuating the work of creation." (La Rivière, p. 618.) "The order of society presupposes the existence of a third class in society, namely, the proprietors who make preparation for the work of cultivation and who dispense the net product." (Quesnay, p. 186.)

true. They had simply received it from the proprietors. This latter class takes precedence because God has willed that it should be the first dispenser of all wealth.[1]

There is no need to insist on this strange aberration which led them to look for the creator of the land and its products, not amid the cultivators of the soil, but among the idlers.[2] Such was the logical conclusion of their argument. We must also remember that the Physiocrats failed to realize the inherent dignity of all true labour simply because it was not the creator of wealth. This applied both to the agricultural labourer and the industrial worker, and though the former alone was considered productive it was because he was working in co-operation with nature. It was nature that produced the wealth, and not the worker.

Something must also be attributed to their environment. Knowing only feudal society, with its economic and political activities governed and directed by idle proprietors, they suffered from an illusion as to the necessity for landed property similar to that which led Aristotle to defend the institution of slavery.[3]

Although they failed to foresee the criticisms that would be levelled against the institution of private property, they were very assiduous—especially the Abbé Baudeau—in seeking an explanation of its origin and a justification of its existence. The reasons which they advanced are more worthy of quotation than almost any argument that has since been employed by conservative economists.

The most solid argument, in their opinion—at least the one that was most frequently used—is that these proprietors are either the men who cleared and drained the land or else their rightful descendants. They have incurred or they are incurring expenditure in clearing the land, enclosing it, and building upon it—what the Physiocrats call the *avances foncières*.[4] They never get their revenues through some one else as

---

[1] "Immediately below the landed proprietors come the productive classes, whose labour is the only source of their income, but who cannot exercise that labour unless the landlord has already incurred some outlay in the way of ground expenses." (Baudeau, *Philosophie économique*, p. 691.)

[2] The Physiocrats never mention the agricultural workers, and one might almost think that there were none. Their solicitude for the agriculturists does not extend beyond the farmers and *métayers*. M. Weulersse has referred to their system, not without some justification, as an essentially capitalistic one.

[3] "We may call them the nobility, as well as the propertied class. Nobility in this sense, far from being illusory, is a very useful institution in the history of civilized nations." (Baudeau, p. 670.)

[4] "In the third line—they generally occupy the first rank—we have the landed proprietors who prepare the soil, build houses, make plantations and enclosures at their own expense, or who pay for those outlays by buying property already developed. This revenue, they might argue, belongs to us because of the wisdom and forethought

the manufacturers do, and they are anything but parasites. Their portion is *optimo jure*, in virtue of a right prior and superior even to that of the cultivators, for although the cultivators help to make the product, the proprietors help to make the land. The three social classes of the Physiocratic scheme may be likened to three persons who get their water from the same well. It is drawn from the well by members of the productive class in bucketfuls, which are passed on to the proprietors, but the latter class gives nothing in return for it, for the well is of their making. At a respectable distance comes the sterile class, obliged to buy water in exchange for its labour.[1]

---

we have exercised in preparing the land, in undertaking to keep it in repair, and to improve it still further." (Baudeau, *Philosophie économique*, p. 757.) "The foremost and most essential agent of production must be that man who makes it possible. But who is this agent but the landed proprietor, whose claims to his prerogatives are based upon the need for his productive services?" (Mercier de la Rivière, pp. 466–467.)

"It is this expenditure that makes the claim of proprietors real and their existence just and necessary. Until such expenditure is incurred the right of property is merely an exclusive right to make the soil capable of bearing fruit." (Baudeau, p. 851.) In other words, so long as the proprietor has not incurred some expenditure the right of property is simply reduced to occupation.

The Physiocrats distinguished three kinds of *avances*:

1. The annual expenditure (*avances annuelles*) incurred in connexion with the actual work of cultivation, which recurs every year, such as the cost of seed and manure, cost of maintaining labourers, etc. The annual harvest ought to repay all this, which to-day would be called circulating capital.

2. The 'original' outlay (*avances primitives*) involved in buying cattle and implements which render service for a number of years, and for which the proprietor does not expect to be recompensed in a single year. The return is spread out over a number of years. Here we have the distinction between fixed and circulating capital, and the idea of the gradual redemption of the former as against the total repayment of the latter at one single use. It did not escape the Physiocrats' notice that an intelligent increase of the fixed might gradually reduce the annual expenditure. Such ideas were quite novel. But they immediately took their place as definite contributions to the science. They are no longer confined to agriculture, however, but apply equally to all branches of production.

3. The *avances foncières* are the expenses which are undertaken with a view to preparing the land for cultivation. (The adjective 'primitive' would have been better applied here.)

The first two kinds of expenditure are incumbent upon the agriculturist and entitle him to a remuneration sufficient to cover his expenses.

The third is incumbent upon the proprietor and constitutes his claim to a share of the funds. "Before you can set up a farm where agriculture may be steadily practised year in and year out, what must be done? A block of buildings and a farmhouse must be built, roads made and plantations set, the soil must be prepared, the stones cleared, trees cut down and roots removed; drains must also be cut and shelters prepared. These are the *avances foncières*, the work that is incumbent upon proprietors, and the true basis of their claim to the privileges of proprietorship." (Baudeau, *Éphémérides*, May 1776. A reply to Condillac.)

[1] "Without that sense of security which property gives, the land would still be uncultivated." (Quesnay, *Maximes*, IV.) "Everything would be lost if this fount of wealth were not as well assured as the person of the individual." (Dupont, Vol. I, p. 26.)

The Physiocrats failed to notice the contradiction involved in this. If the revenue which the proprietor draws represents the remuneration for his outlay and the return for his expenditure it is no longer a gift of nature, and the net product vanishes, for, by definition, it represented what was left of the gross product after paying all initial expenses—the excess over cost of production. If we accept this explanation of the facts there is no longer any surplus to dispose of. It is as capitalists pure and simple and not as the representatives of God that proprietors obtain their rents.

Must we really believe that although these outlays afford some explanation of the existence of private property they supply no means of measuring or of limiting its extent? Is there no connexion between these outlays and the revenues which landed proprietors draw?

Or must we distinguish between the two portions of the revenue—the one, indispensable, representing the reimbursement of the original outlay, and in every respect comparable to the revenue of the farmer, and the other, being a true surplus, constituting the net product? How can they justify the appropriation of the latter?

There is another argument held in reserve, namely, that based upon social utility. They point out that the cultivation of land would cease and the one source of all wealth would become barren if the pioneer were not allowed to reap the fruits of his labour.

The new argument is a contradiction of the old. In the former case land was appropriated because it had been cultivated. In the present case land must be appropriated before it can be cultivated. In the former labour is treated as the efficient cause, in the latter as the final cause of production.

Finally, the Physiocrats believed that landed proprietorship was simply the direct outcome of 'personal property,' or of the right of every man to provide for his own sustenance. This right includes the right of personal estate, which in turn involves the right of landed property. These three kinds of property are so closely connected that in reality they form one unit, and no one of the three can be detached without involving the destruction of the other two.[1] They were full of veneration for property of every description—not merely for landed property. "The safety of private property is the real basis of the economic order of society," says Quesnay.[2] Mercier de la Rivière writes: "Property may be regarded as a tree of which social institutions are branches growing out of the trunk."[3] We shall encounter this cult of property even during the terrible days of the French Revolution

---

[1] Mercier de la Rivière, Vol. I, p. 242.
[2] *Maximes*, IV.   [3] Pp. 615, 617.

and the Reign of Terror. When all respect for human life was quite lost there still remained this respect for property.

The defence of private property was already well-nigh complete.[1] But if they were strong in their defence of the institution they did not fail to impose upon it some onerous duties—which counterbalanced its eminent dignity. Of course, every proprietor should always be guided by reason and be mannerly in his behaviour, and he should never allow mere authority to become the rule of life.[2] Their duties are as follows:

1. They must continue without fail to bring lands into cultivation —*i.e.*, they must continue the *avances foncières*.[3]

2. They must dispose of the wealth which the nation has produced in such a way as to further the general interest; this is their task as the stewards of society.[4]

3. They must aim during their leisure at giving to society all those gratuitous services which they can render, and which society so sorely needs.

4. They must bear the whole burden of taxation.

5. Above all they must protect their tenants, the agriculturists, and be very careful not to demand more than the net product. The Physiocrats never go the length of advising them to give to their tenants a portion of the net product, but they impress upon them the importance of giving them the equivalent of their annual expenditure and of dealing liberally with them. It does not seem much, but it must have been something in those days. "I say it boldly," writes Baudeau,

> cursed be every proprietor, every sovereign and emperor that puts all the burden upon the peasant, and the land, which gives all of us our sustenance. Show them that the lot of the worthy individuals who employ their own funds or who depend upon those of others is to none of us a matter of complete indifference, that whoever hurts or degrades, attacks or robs them is the cruellest enemy

[1] It is necessary to make a note here of one of the many differences between Turgot and the Physiocrats. Turgot seems much less firmly convinced of the social utility of landed property and of the legitimacy of the right of property. He thinks that its origin is simply due to occupation. This weakens the Physiocratic case very considerably. "The earth is peopled and cultivation extends. The best lands will in time all be occupied. For the last comers there will only be the unfertile lands rejected by the first. In the end every piece of land will have its owner, and those who possess none will have no other resource than to exchange the labour of their arm for the superfluous corn of the proprietor." (Vol. I, p. 12.) We are here not very far from the Ricardian theory.

[2] Baudeau, *Philosophie économique*, p. 378.

[3] "A proprietor who keeps up the *avances foncières* without fail is performing the noblest service that anyone can perform on this earth." (Baudeau.)

[4] "The rich have the control of the fund from which the workers are paid, but they are doing a great injustice if they appropriate it." (Quesnay, Vol. I, p. 193.)

of society, and that he who ennobles them, furthers their well-being, comfort, or leisure increases their output of wealth, which after all is the one source of income for every class in society.[1]

Such generous words, which were none too common at the time, release the Physiocrats from the taunt of showing too great a favour to the proprietors. In return for such privileges as they gave them they demanded an amount of social service far beyond anything that was customary at the time.

II

So far we have considered only the Physiocratic theory. But the Physiocratic influence can be much more clearly traced if we turn to applied economics and examine their treatment of such questions as the regulation of industry, the functions of the State, and the problems of taxation.[2]

I: TRADE

All exchange, the Physiocrats thought, was unproductive, for by definition it implies a transfer of equal values. If each party only receives the exact equivalent of what it gives there is no wealth produced. It may happen, however, that the parties to the exchange are of unequal strength, and the one may grow rich at the expense of the other.[3] In giving a bottle of wine in exchange for a loaf of bread there

[1] Pp. 835, 839. And Mercier de la Rivière writes in terms not less severe: "He is responsible under pain of annihilation for the products of society, and no part of the produce which goes to support the cultivator should wittingly be employed otherwise." The history of Ireland is an interesting commentary on these words.

But let us always remember that when the Physiocrats speak of the rights of the cultivator they think only of the farmer and *métayer* and never of the paid agriculturist. They are content to demand merely a decent existence for the latter. Were they put too much at ease they would perhaps leave off working. See Weulersse, Vol. II, p. 729. He seems a little unjust, and quotes some words of Quesnay, who protests against the belief that "the poor must be kept poor if they are not to become indolent."

[2] One is perhaps surprised to find that freedom of work—in other words, the abolition of corporations—is not included in their list, especially since the credit for the downfall of those institutions is usually given to the Physiocrats. Their writings contain only very occasional reference to this topic, because industrial labour is regarded as sterile, and reform touching its organization concerned them but little. They did, however, protest against the rule that confined the right to engage in a trade to those who had received an express privilege from the Crown. They considered that "to an honest soul this was the most odious maxim which the spirit of domination and rapacity ever invented." (Baudeau, in *Éphémérides*, 1768, Vol. IV.) Turgot's famous *Edict* of January 1776, abolishing the rights of corporations and establishing liberty for all, is, with good reason, attributed to Physiocratic influence.

[3] "Exchange is a contract of equality, equal value being given in exchange for equal value. Consequently it is not a means of increasing wealth, for one gives as

is a double displacement of wealth, which evidently affords a fuller satisfaction of wants in both cases, but there is no wealth created, for the objects so exchanged are of equal value. To-day the reasoning would be quite different. The present-day economist would argue as follows: "If I exchange my wine for your bread, that is a proof that my hunger is greater than my thirst, but that you are more thirsty than hungry. Consequently the wine has increased in utility in passing from my hands into yours, and the bread, likewise, in passing from your hands into mine, and this double increase of utility constitutes a real increase of wealth." Such reasoning would have appeared absurd to the Physiocrats, who conceived of wealth as something material, and they could never have understood how the creation of a purely subjective attribute like utility could ever be considered productive.

We have already had occasion to remark that industry and commerce were considered unproductive. This was a most significant fact, so far as commerce was concerned, because all the theories that held the field under Mercantilism, notably the doctrine that foreign commerce afforded the only possible means of increasing a country's wealth, immediately assumed a dwindling importance. For the Mercantilists the prototype of the State was a rich merchant of Amsterdam. For the Physiocrats it was John Bull.

And foreign trade, like domestic, produced no real wealth: the only result was a possible gain, and one man's gain is another man's loss.

> Every commercial nation flatters itself upon its growing wealth as the outcome of foreign trade. This is a truly astonishing phenomenon, for they all believe that they are growing rich and gaining from one another. It must be admitted that this gain, as they call it, is a most remarkable thing, for they all gain and none loses.[1]

A country must, of course, obtain from foreigners the goods which it cannot itself produce in exchange for those it cannot itself consume. Foreign trade is quite indispensable, but Mercier de la Rivière thinks that it is a necessary evil[2] (he underlines the word). Quesnay contents himself with referring to it merely as a *pis aller*.[3] He thought that the

---

much as the other receives, but it is a means of satisfying wants and of varying enjoyment." (Le Trosne, *Intérêt social*, pp. 903, 904.) But what does this satisfying of wants and variation of enjoyment signify if it does not mean increased wealth?

[1] Mercier de la Rivière, p. 545.   [2] P. 548.

[3] "The settlement of international indebtedness by payment of money is a mere *pis aller* of foreign trade, adopted by those nations which are unable to give commodities in return for commodities according to custom. And foreign trade itself is a mere *pis aller* adopted by those nations whose home trade is insufficient to enable them to make the best use of their own productions. It is very strange that anyone should have laid such stress upon a mere *pis aller* of commerce." (*Dialogues*, p. 175.)

only really useful exchange is one in which agricultural products pass directly from producers to consumers, for without this the products would be useless and would simply perish in the producer's hands. But that kind of exchange which consists in buying products in order to resell them—trafficking, or a commercial transaction, as we call it —is sheer waste, for the wealth instead of growing larger becomes less, because a portion of it is absorbed by the traffickers themselves.[1] We meet with the same idea in Carey. Mercier de la Rivière ingeniously compares such traders to mirrors, arranged in such a way that they reflect a number of things at the same time, all in different positions. "Like mirrors, too, the traders seem to multiply commodities, but they only deceive the superficial."[2]

That may be; but, admitting a contempt for commerce, what conclusions do they draw from it? Shall they prohibit it, or regulate it, or shall they just let it take its own course? Any one of these conclusions would follow from their premises. If commerce be as useless as they tried to make out, the first solution would be the best. But it was the third that they were inclined to adopt, and we must see why.

It seems quite evident that the Physiocrats would have condemned both the Mercantile and the Colbertian systems. Both of these aimed at securing a favourable balance of trade—an aim which the Physiocrats considered illusory, if not actually immoral. But if they thought all trade was useless it is not easy to understand their enthusiasm for Free Trade. Those economists who nowadays favour Free Trade support it in the belief that it is of immense benefit to every country wherein it is practised, and that the more it is developed the richer will the exchanging countries become. But such was not the Physiocratic doctrine. It is a noteworthy fact that they are to be regarded as the founders of Free Trade, not because of any desire to favour trade as such, but because their attitude towards it was one of disdainful *laissez-faire*. They were not, perhaps, altogether free from the belief that *laissez-faire* would lead to the disappearance of commerce altogether. They were Free Traders primarily because they desired the freedom of domestic trade, and we must not lose sight of those extraordinary regulations which completely fettered its movements at this time.[3]

---

[1] "After all merchants are only traffickers, and the trafficker is just a person who employs his ability in appropriating a part of other people's wealth." (Mercier de la Rivière, p. 551.) "Merchants' gains are not a species of profit." (Quesnay, p. 151.)

[2] *Ordre Naturel*, p. 538.

[3] Enforcing sales in open market and in limited quantities only, keeping corn beyond two years, etc. Corn was to be supplied to consumers in the first place, then to bakers, and finally to merchants, etc.

The 'natural order' also implied that each one would be free to buy or sell wherever he chose, within or without the country. It recognized no frontiers,[1] for only through 'liberty' could the 'good price' be secured. The 'good price' meant the highest price and not the lowest, dearth and not cheapness. "Free competition with foreign merchants can alone secure the best possible price, and only the highest price will enable us to increase our stock of wealth and to maintain our population by agriculture."[2] This is the language of agriculturists rather than of Free Traders. It is the natural result of thinking about agricultural problems, and especially about the question of raising corn; and since Free Trade at this time gave rise to no fears on the score of importation, free exchange meant free exportation. Oncken points out that the commercial regime which the Physiocrats advocated was identical with that in operation in England about this time, where in case of over-abundance exportation was encouraged in order to keep up the price, and in case of dearth importation was permitted in order to ensure a steady supply and to prevent the price from rising too much.[3]

In a word, Free Trade meant for the Physiocrats the total abolition of all those measures which found so much favour with the Mercantilists, and which aimed at preventing exportation to places outside

[1] "Let entire freedom of commerce be maintained, for the surest, the exactest, the most profitable regulator both of home and of foreign trade for the nation as well as for the State is perfect freedom of competition." (Quesnay's *Maximes*, XXV.) "We must tell them that free trade is in accordance with the order and with the demands of justice, and everything that conforms to the order bears its own reward." (Le Trosne, p. 586.)

[2] *Dialogues*, p. 153. The dearth of plenty, as they paradoxically put it, stimulates production, and Boisguillebert, in an equal paradox, remarks that "Low price gives rise to want." In the *Maximes*, p. 98, Quesnay contents himself by saying that free trade in corn makes the price more equal. "It is clear," he adds, "that leaving aside the question of foreign debt, equal prices will increase the revenue yielded by the land, which will again result in extended cultivation, which will provide a guarantee against those dearths that decimate population."

Mercier de la Rivière writes in a similar vein. "A good constant average price ensures abundance, but without freedom we have neither a good price nor plenty." (P. 570.)

Turgot in his *Lettres sur le Commerce des Grains* develops the argument at great length and tries to give a mathematical demonstration of it. There was no need for this. It is a commonplace of psychology that a steady price of 20 is preferable to alternative prices of 35 and 5 francs respectively, although the average in both cases is the same.

[3] It is worth noting that the nature of American competition was clearly foreseen by Quesnay—one of the most remarkable instances of scientific prevision on record. In his article on corn in the *Encyclopédie* he says that he views the fertility of the American colonies with apprehension and dreads the growth of agriculture in the New World, but the fear is provisionally dismissed because the corn is inferior in quality to that of France and is damaged in transit. (See our remarks concerning the Physiocratic connexion with modern Protectionist theories.)

the country and checking the growth of free intercourse within it.[1] Narrow as their conception of Free Trade at first was, it was not long in growing out of the straitened circumstances which gave it birth, and it developed gradually into the Free Trade doctrine as we know it, which Walras expressed as follows: "Free competition secures for every one the maximum final utility, or, what comes to the same thing, gives the maximum satisfaction." We no longer admit that international trade is a mere *pis aller*. But all the arguments which have been used in its defence on the Free Trade side were first formulated by the Physiocrats. We shall refer to a few of them.

The fallacy lurking behind the 'balance of trade' theory is exposed with great neatness by Mercier de la Rivière. "I will drown the clamour of all your blind and stupid policies. Suppose that I gave you all the money which circulates among the nations with whom you trade. Imagine it all in your possession. What would you do with it?" He goes on to show how not a single foreign country will any longer be able to buy, and consequently all exportation will cease. The result of this excessive dearness will be that buying from foreign countries will be resorted to, and this will result in the exportation of metallic currency, which will soon readjust matters.[2]

The contention that import duties are paid by the foreigner is also refuted. Nothing will be sold by the foreigner at a lower price than that which other nations would be willing to give him. An import duty on such goods will increase the real price, which the foreigner will demand, and this import duty will be paid by those who buy the goods.[3]

There is also a refutation of the policy known as reciprocity.

[1] It must not be forgotten that the Protectionist system aided the development of industry and retarded that of agriculture by its policy of encouraging the exportation of manufactured products and its restrictions on the exportation of agricultural products and raw materials with a view to securing cheap labour and a plentiful supply of raw materials for the manufacturing industries. The Protectionists were not concerned to prevent the exportation of corn. Both Colbertism and Mercantilism sacrificed the cultivator by preventing the exportation of corn and by allowing of its importation, while doing the exact opposite for manufactured products.

[2] "Upon final analysis do you find that you have gained anything by your policy of always selling to foreigners without ever buying from them? Have you gained any money by the process? But you cannot retain it. It has passed through your hands without being of the least use. The more it increases the more does its value diminish, while the value of other things increases proportionally." (Mercier de la Rivière, pp. 580–583.)

[3] Turgot, *Œuvres*, Vol. I, p. 189. "If you succeed in keeping back foreign merchants by means of your protective tariffs they will not bring you those goods which you need, thus causing those impositions which were designed for others to retaliate upon your own head." (Quesnay, *Dialogues*.)

A nation levies an import duty upon the goods of another nation, but it forgets that in trying to injure the selling nation it is really checking the possible consumption of its own goods. This indirect effect, of course, is inevitable, but can nothing be done to remedy this by means of reprisals? England levies a heavy duty on French wines, thereby reducing its debit account with France very considerably, but more French wine will not be bought if a tax is also placed upon the goods which England exports to France. Do you think that the prejudice which England has taken against France can be remedied in this way?

We have multiplied instances, for during the whole of the hundred years which have since elapsed has anyone deduced better arguments?

These theories immediately received legal sanction in the edicts of 1763 and 1766 establishing free trade in corn, first within the country and then without, but some very serious restrictions were still retained. Unfortunately Nature proved very ungrateful to her friends. For four or five years she ran riot with a series of bad harvests, for which, as we may well imagine, the Physiocratic regime and its inspirers were held responsible. Despite the protests of the Physiocrats, this liberal Act was repealed in 1770. It was re-established by Turgot in 1774, and again repealed by Necker in 1777—a variety of fortune that betokens a fickleness of public opinion.

This new piece of legislation, and, indeed, the whole Physiocratic theory, was subjected to severe criticism by an abbot of the name of Galiani. Galiani was a Neapolitan monsignor residing at the French court. At the age of twenty-one he had written a remarkable work in Italian dealing with money, and in 1770, written in splendid French, appeared his *Dialogues sur le Commerce des Blés*. It was an immediate success, and it won the unqualified approval of Voltaire, who was possibly attracted more by the style than by the profundity of thought. Galiani was not exactly opposed to *laissez-faire*. "Liberty," he wrote, "stands in no need of defence so long as it is at all possible. Whenever we can we ought to be on the side of liberty."[1] But he is opposed to general systems and against complete self-surrender into the hands of Nature. "Nature," says he, "is too vast to be concerned about our petty trifles."[2] He shares the realistic or historical views of the writers of to-day, and thinks that before applying the principles of political economy some account should be taken of time, place, and circumstances. "The state of which the Physiocrats speak—what is it? Where is it to be found."[3]

[1] *Dialogues*, pp. 254, 274.   [2] *Ibid.*, p. 237.
[3] *Ibid.*, p. 22. He proposed a highly complicated system imposing moderate duties both upon the importation and exportation of corn—a 5 per cent. *ad valorem* duty in the one case and a 10 per cent. in the other.

Along with Galiani we must mention the great financier Necker, who in a bulky volume entitled *La Législation et le commerce des grains* (1775) advocates opportunistic views almost identical in character with those of Galiani, and who, as Minister of State (1776–81 and 1788–90), put an end to free trade in corn.

In monetary matters, especially on the question of interest, the Physiocrats were willing to recognize an exception to their principle of non-intervention. Mirabeau thought that whenever a real increase of wealth resulted from the use of capital, as in agriculture, the payment of interest was only just. It was simply a sign or symbol of the net product. But in trade matters he thought it best to limit if not to prohibit it altogether. It often proved very harmful, and frequently was nothing better than a tax levied by order of "the corrosive landowners." Quesnay could not justify it except in those cases where it yielded a net product, but he was content simply to suggest a limitation of it. The Physiocrats are at least logical. If capital sunk in industrial and commercial undertakings yields no income it is evident that the interest must be taken from the borrower's pocket, and they condemned it just as they condemned taxing the industrial and commercial classes.

Turgot[1] is the only one of them who frankly justifies taking interest. The reason that he gives is not the usual Physiocratic argument, but rather that the owner of capital may either invest it in the land or undertake some other productive work—capital being the indispensable basis of all enterprise[2]—and that, consequently, the capital will never be given to anyone who will offer less than what might have been made out of it did the owner himself employ it. This argument implies that every undertaking is essentially a productive one, and indeed one of the traits which distinguishes Turgot from the other Physiocrats is the fact that he did not think that industry and commerce were entirely unproductive.

II: THE FUNCTIONS OF THE STATE

Seeing that the Physiocrats believed that human society was pervaded by the principle of 'natural order,' which required no adventitious aid from any written law, and since Nature's voice, without any artificial restraint, was sufficient guide for mankind, it might have been expected that the trend of Physiocracy would have been towards the

---

[1] Turgot was the author of a work on this subject, entitled *Mémoire sur les Prêts d'Argent* (1769).

[2] *Réflexions sur la formation des richesses*, paras. 59, 61, 74.

negation of all legislation, of all authority—in a word, towards the subversion of the State.

It is certain that the Physiocrats wished to reduce legislative activity to a minimum, and they expressed the belief—which has often been repeated since by every advocate of *laissez-faire*—that the most useful work any legislative body can do is to abolish useless laws.[1] If any new laws are required they ought simply to be copies of the unwritten laws of Nature. Neither men nor Governments can make laws, for they have not the necessary ability. Every law should be an expression of that Divine wisdom which rules the universe. Hence the true title of lawgiver, not lawmaker.[2] It is in this connexion that we meet with those anecdotes—some of more than doubtful authenticity, it is true— that have gathered round their names. Of these the best-known is that which tells of Mercier de la Rivière's visit to St Petersburg, and his laconic reply to Catherine the Great. He had been invited there to advise the Empress about a new constitution for the country. After dilating upon the great difficulties of the undertaking and the responsibilities it involved he gave it as his opinion that the best way of achieving her object was just to let things take their course. Whereupon the Empress promptly wished him good-bye.

But it would be a great mistake to think of the Physiocrats as anarchists. What they wanted to see was the minimum of legislation with a maximum of authority. The two things are by no means incompatible. The liberal policy of limitation and control would have found scant favour with them. Their ideal was neither democratic self-government, as we have it in the Greek republics, nor a parliamentary regime such as we find in England. Both were detested.[3]

[1] "Remove all useless, unjust, contradictory, and absurd laws, and there will not be much legislative machinery left after that." (Baudeau, p. 817.) "It is not a question of procuring immense riches, but simply a question of letting people alone, a problem that hardly requires a moment's thought." So wrote Boisguillebert sixty years before.

[2] Quesnay, *Maximes*, Vol. I, p. 390. Mercier de la Rivière writes in much the same style: "The positive laws that are already in existence are merely expressions of such natural rights." (Vol. II, p. 61.) It sounds like a preamble to the Declaration of the Rights of Man.

[3] "The Physiocrats had the most absolute contempt for political liberty." (Esmein, *La Science politique des Physiocrates*, address at the opening session of the Congress of Learned Societies, Paris, 1906.)

"The Greek republics never became acquainted with the laws of the order. Those restless, usurping, tyrannical tribes never ceased to drench the plains with human blood, to cover with ruins and to reduce to waste the most fertile and the best situated soil in the then known world." (Baudeau, p. 800.)

"It is evident that a democratic sovereign—*i.e.*, the whole people—cannot itself exercise its authority, and must be content to name representatives. These representatives are merely agents, whose functions are naturally transitory, and such temporary

On the other hand, great respect was shown for the social hierarchy, and they were strong in their condemnation of every doctrine that aimed at attacking either the throne or the nobility. What they desired was to have sovereign authority in the guise of a hereditary monarchy. In short, what they really wanted—and they were not frightened by the name—was despotism.[1]

> The sovereign authority should be one, and supreme above all individual or private enterprise. The object of sovereignty is to secure obedience, to defend every just right, on the one hand, and to secure personal security on the other. A government that is based upon the idea of a balance of power is useless.[2]

This should help us to realize the distance separating the Physiocrats from the Montesquieuian idea of the distribution of the sovereign authority, and from the other idea of local or regional control. There is no mention of representation as a corollary of taxation. This form of guarantee, which marks the beginnings of parliamentary government, could have no real significance for the Physiocrats. Taxation was just a right inherent in the conception of proprietary sovereignty, a territorial revenue, which was in no way dependent upon the people's will.

It seems strange that such should be the opinion of a future President of the Constituent Assembly. How can we explain this apparent contradiction and such love of despotism among the apostles of *laissez-faire?*

Despotism, in the eyes of the Physiocrats, had a peculiar significance of its own. It was the work of freedom, not of bondage. It did not signify the rule of the benevolent despot, prepared to make men happy,

---

agents cannot always be in complete harmony with every interest within the nation. This is not the kind of administration contemplated by the Physiocrats. The sovereignty of the natural order is neither elective nor aristocratic. Only in the case of hereditary monarchy can all interests, both personal and individual, present and future, be clearly linked with those of the nation, by their copartnership in all the net products of the territory submitted to their care." (Dupont, Vol. I, pp. 359–360.)

This sounds very much like a eulogy of the House of Hohenzollern, delivered by William II.

Very curious also are Dupont's criticisms of the parliamentary regime. In his letter to J. B. Say (p. 414) he notes "its tendency to corruption and canker," which had not then manifested itself in the United States of America. These letters, though very interesting, hardly belong to a history of economic doctrines.

[1] "It is only when the people are ingenuous that we find real despots, because then the sovereign can do whatever he wills." (Dupont, p. 364.)

[2] Quesnay, *Maximes*, I. The Physiocrats were in favour of a national assembly, but would give it no legislative power. It was to be just a council of State concerned chiefly with public works and with the apportionment of the burden of taxation. See M. Esmein's *mémoire* on the proposed National Assembly of the Physiocrats (*Comptes rendus de l'Académie des Sciences Morales et Politiques*, 1904).

even against their own will. It was just the sovereignty of the 'natural order'[1]—nothing more. Every reasonable person felt himself bound to obey it, and realized that only through such obedience could the truth be possibly known.

It is quite different from the despotism of the ancient maxim, *Sicut principi placuit legis habet vigorem*.[2] They would never have subscribed to the doctrine that the king's word is law, but they were equally energetic in rejecting the claim of the popular will.[3] They are as far from modern democracy as they are from monarchical absolutism.

This despotism was incarnate in the person of the sovereign or king. But he is simply an organ for the transmission of those higher laws which are given to him. They would compare him with the leader of an orchestra, his sceptre being the baton that keeps time. The conductor's despotism is greater than the Tsar's, for every musician has to obey the movement of the hand, and that immediately. But this is not tyranny, and whoever strikes a false note in a spirit of revenge is not simply a revolter, but also an idiot.

Sovereignty appealed to the Physiocrats in the guise of hereditary monarchy, because of its associations with property under the feudal regime, and since hereditary rights were connected with landed property so must royalty be. The sovereign who best represents the Physiocratic ideal is perhaps the Emperor of China.[4] As the Son of Heaven he represents the 'natural order,' which is also the 'divine order.' As an agricultural monarch he solemnly puts his hand to the plough once a year. His people really govern themselves; that is, he rules them according to custom and the practice of sacred rites.[5]

[1] "The personal despotism will only be the legal despotism of an obvious and essential order. In legal despotism the obviousness of a law demands obedience before the monarch enjoins it. Euclid is a veritable despot, and the geometrical truths that he enunciates are really despotic laws. The legal and personal despotism of the legislator are one and the same. Together they are irresistible." (Mercier de la Rivière, pp. 460-471.) This despotism is really not unlike that of Comte, who remarks that there is no question of liberty of conscience in geometry.

[2] "On the contrary," says Quesnay in a letter to Mirabeau, "this despotism is a sufficient guarantee against the abuse of power."

[3] "That is an abominable absurdity," says Baudeau, "for on this reckoning a mere majority vote would be sufficient to justify parricide."

Is it necessary to point out that this is exactly the reverse of the view held by interventionists and socialists of these later times, who think that the mission of the State is to redress the grievances caused by natural laws?

[4] "This single supreme will which exercises supreme power is not, strictly speaking, a human will at all. It is just the voice of nature—the will of God. The Chinese are the only people whose philosophy seems to have got hold of this supreme truth, and they regard their emperor as the eldest son of God." (Baudeau, p. 798.)

[5] Some writers—for example, Pantaleoni in his introduction to Arthur Labriola's book *Le Dottrine economiche di Quesnay*—seem to think that the Physiocratic criticism proved fatal to feudal society, just as the socialistic criticism of the present time is

In practice there will be nothing of great importance for the despot to do. "As kings and governors you will find how easy it is to exercise your sacred functions, which simply consist in not interfering with the good that is already being done, and in punishing those few persons who occasionally attack private property."[1] In short, the preservation of the 'natural order' and the defending of its basis—private property —against the attacks of the ignorant and the sacrilegious is the first and most important duty of the sovereign. "No order of any kind is possible in society unless the right of possession is guaranteed to the members of that society by the force of a sovereign authority."[2]

Instruction is the second duty upon which the Physiocrats lay special stress. "Universal education," says Baudeau, "is the first and only social tie." Quesnay is specially anxious for instruction on the 'natural order,' and the means of becoming acquainted with it. Further, the only guarantee against personal despotism lies in well-diffused instruction and an educated public opinion. If public opinion, as Quesnay said, is to lead, it should be enlightened.

Public works are also mentioned. A wise landlord has good roads on his property, for good roads and canals improve it. These represent a species of *avances foncières*, similar to those undertaken by proprietors.

This is by no means all.[3] There are a number of duties recognized as belonging to the State, of which every economist of the Liberal school up to Bastiat and M. de Molinari approves.

We will add one other trait. Like the Liberal school, the Physiocrats were whole-hearted 'internationalists.' In this respect they differ from their prototypes, the Chinese. They believed that all class distinctions and all international barriers ought to be removed in the interest of political development, as well as in that of scientific study.[4] The peace advocates of to-day would do well to make the acquaintance of their illustrious predecessors.

---

undermining the bourgeois society. Politically this is true enough, for the Physiocrats advocated the establishment of a single supreme monarch with undivided authority. Economically it is incorrect, for their conception even of sovereignty and taxation is impregnated with feudal ideas.

[1] Dupont, *Discours en tête des Œuvres de Quesnay*, Vol. I, p. 35.

[2] *Ibid.*, p. 22.

[3] Turgot, who is less inclined to favour agriculture, thinks that certain royal privileges must be granted before manufacturers can compete with agriculture (*Œuvres*, Vol. I, p. 360).

[4] "One has come to regard the various nations as drawn up against one another in a perpetual state of war. This unfortunate prejudice is almost sacred, and is regarded as a patriotic virtue." (Baudeau, p. 808.)

The three errors usually committed by States, and the three that led to the downfall of Greece, Baudeau thought, were arbitrary use of legislative authority, oppressive taxation, and aggressive patriotism. (P. 801.)

III: TAXATION

The bulk of the Physiocratic system is taken up with the exposition of a theory of taxation, which really forms one of the most characteristic portions of their work. Though inextricably bound up with the theory of the net product and with the conception of landed proprietorship, curiously enough it has survived the rest of their doctrine, and quite recently has been given a new lease of life.

In the table showing the distribution of the national income three participators only are mentioned—the landed proprietor, the farmer, and the artisan. But there is also a fourth—the Physiocratic sovereign, who is none other than the State itself, and who thoroughly deserves a share. This benevolent despot, whose duties we have just mentioned, cannot be very exacting, for, having little to do, his demands must be moderate. In addition to his double mission of maintaining security and giving instruction, he must also contribute towards increasing the productivity of the land by establishing public works, making roads, etc.[1] Money is required for all this, and the Physiocrats argued that taxes ought to be paid liberally,[2] and not grudgingly, as is too often the case under a parliamentary regime. Where is this money to come from?

The reply is obvious if we have grasped their system. The only available fund is the net product, which is the only new wealth that is really dispensable the rest is necessarily absorbed in the repayment of the advances made for the upkeep of the agricultural and industrial classes. Were taxation to absorb a proportion of the revenues that are devoted to production it would gradually drain away the source of all wealth. So long as it only takes the surplus—the true net product, which is a mere tributary of the main stream—no harm will be done to future production.

All this is quite clear. But if taxation is to absorb the net product the question arises as to who is to pay it. It is equally evident that

[1] "Before a harvest can be reaped not only must the cultivators incur the usual outlay upon stock, etc., and the proprietors upon clearing the land, but the public authority must also incur some expense, which might be designated *avances souveraines*." (Baudeau, p. 758.)

[2] "The Government ought to be less concerned with the task of saving than with the duty of spending upon those operations that are necessary for the prosperity of the realm. This heavy expenditure will cease when the country has become wealthy." (Quesnay, *Maximes*, XXVI.)

"It is a narrow and churlish English idea which decrees that an annual sum should be annually voted to the Government, and that Parliament should reserve to itself the right of refusing this tax. Such a procedure is a travesty of democracy." (Dupont, in a letter to J. B. Say.)

it can only be taken from those who already possess it, namely, from the landed proprietors, who must bear the whole burden of taxation. Just now we were amazed at the privileges which the Physiocrats so light-heartedly granted them: this is the ransom, and it is no light one. The next problem is how to assess this tax.

The Physiocrats were extremely loth to rob the gentry of their incomes, and a number of pages in their writings are devoted to a justification of their claims upon them. Not only were they willing to leave them everything that was necessary to compensate them for the outlay of capital and labour, but also all that might be required to make the property thoroughly valuable and the position of the land-owner a most enviable one.[1] The preference shown for the landowner is just the result of the social importance attributed to him by the Physiocrats. "If some other class were preferable," says Dupont de Nemours, "people would turn their attention to that." They would no longer spend their capital in clearing or improving the land. But if the possession of land be so desirable, is there not some danger lest everybody should become a landlord and neglect the other walks of life? The Physiocrats thought not, for, since Nature has set a limit to the amount of land in existence, there must also be a limit to the number of landowners.

A third of the net product, or, if we accept Baudeau's figures, six-twentieths—i.e., 30 per cent.—was to be paid in taxes. Taking the net product at 2 milliard francs, which is the figure given in the *Explication du tableau économique*, this gives us exactly 600 million francs as the amount of the tax.[2]

The proprietors, who were then for the most part free from taxa-tion, felt that this was a very considerable contribution, and that the Physiocrats demanded a heavy price for the high honour which they had conferred upon them. Even to-day a tax of 30 per cent. on the gross revenue of landlords would cause some consternation. The

---

[1] "The amount of the tax as compared with the amount of the net product should be such that the position of the landed proprietor shall be the best possible and the state of being a landowner preferable to any other state in society." (Dupont, p. 356.)

[2] If we compare this figure with the total gross revenue of France, valued then at 5 milliard francs, it would represent a tax of 12 per cent., which is rather heavy for a State that was supposed to be governed by the laws of the 'natural order.' The pro-portion which the present French Budget bears to the total revenue of the country is 16 per cent.

The French Budget of 1781, introduced by Necker, corresponded almost exactly with the figure given by the Physiocrats, namely, 610 millions. Of course, we ought to add to this the ecclesiastical dues, the seigniorial rights, and the compulsory labour of every kind, which were to disappear under the Physiocratic regime.

Physiocrats anticipated this objection, and in reply brought forward an argument which shows that they possessed exceptionally keen economic insight. They argued that none would feel the burden, seeing that no one was really paying it. Land would now be bought at 70 per cent. of its former value, so that the 30 per cent. nominally paid by the proprietor was in reality not paid by him at all.[1] Land let at £10,000 would be valued at £200,000. But with a tax of £3000 it is really only yielding £7000, and its value will be £140,000. The buyer who pays this price, despite the fact that he has paid a tax of £3000, will enjoy all the revenue to which he has any claim, for he can only lay claim to what he has paid for, and he did not pay for that portion of the revenue which is affected by the tax. It is exactly as if he had only bought seven-tenths of the land, the remaining three-tenths being the State's. And if at some later time this tax should be abolished, it would merely mean making him a present of £3000 a year—the equivalent of a lump sum of £60,000.[2]

The reaso ing was excellent for those buying land after the tax had been levied. It had, however, a much wider import than the Physiocrats thought, for it might be applied not merely to taxes on land, but also to taxes on capital. But this gave little consolation to those who were to have the honour of inaugurating the new regime, and the first task evidently was to convert them.[3]

The sovereign's position in the main is like that of the landed proprietors, which is in agreement with the Physiocratic conception of sovereignty. The landed proprietors and the king in reality form one class of fellow landowners, with the same rights, the same duties, and

[1] "The tax is a kind of inalienable common property. When proprietors buy or sell land they do not buy and sell the tax. They can only dispose of that portion of the land which really belongs to them, after deducting the amount of the tax. This tax is no more a charge upon property than is the right of fellow proprietors a burden upon one's property. And so the public revenue is not burdensome to anyone, costs nothing, and is paid by no one. Hence, it in no way curtails the amount of property which a person has." (Dupont, Vol. I, pp. 357–358.)

[2] In order to give every security to proprietors the Physiocrats were anxious that the value of the property, when once it was fixed, should vary as little as possible. Baudeau, however, recognized the advisability of periodical revaluations "in order that the sovereign power should always share in both the profits and the losses of the producer." And he addresses this important caution to the proprietors: "Take no credit to yourselves for the increase in the revenue of land. The thanks are really due to the growing efficiency of the sovereign authority." (P. 708.)

[3] "Let us observe, in passing, that the terms 'taxation' and 'public revenue' have unfortunately become synonymous in the public mind. The term 'taxation' is always unpopular. It implies a charge that is hard to bear, and which everybody is anxious to shirk. The public revenue is the product of the sovereign's landed property, which is distinct from his subjects' property." (Mercier de la Rivière, p. 451.)

the same revenues. Hence the sovereign's interests are completely
bound up with those of his country.[1]

The Physiocrats attached the greatest practical importance to their
fiscal system, and were thoroughly convinced that the misery of the
people was due to the unequal distribution of the burden of taxation.
They thought that this was the true source of injustice—in short, that
this was the social problem. To-day we ascribe misery to unequal
distribution of wealth rather than to any particular fiscal system, and
consequently the Physiocratic view seems to us somewhat extreme.
Still, it was perhaps not so difficult to justify, in view of the frightful
conditions of fiscal organization under the old regime.

The objections which a single tax, levied only on the landed interest,
was bound to provoke were not unforeseen by the Physiocrats, nor did
they neglect to answer them.

To the objection that it was unjust to place the burden of taxation
upon the shoulders of a single class of the nation,[2] instead of distributing it equally among all classes, the Physiocrats replied that the
statesman's ideal was not equal taxation, but the complete abolition of
all taxation. This could only be achieved by taxing the 'net product.'

Suppose that we agree that the taxes should be paid by some other
class. The question then is to determine what class of the community
should be chosen.

Shall we say that the farmer must pay them? But after the 'net
product' has been deducted what remains for the farmer is just the bare
equivalent of his original outlay. Consequently, if we take 600 millions
from the farmers by way of taxation there will be so much less capital
for the land, resulting in a smaller gross product the following year,[3]
unless they agitate for a reduction of 600 millions in their rents. If
they succeed this will leave the proprietors in the position of having

[1] "The sovereign takes a fixed amount of the net product for his annual income.
This amount of necessity grows with every increase of the net product and diminishes
with every shrinking of the product. The people's interests and the sovereign's are,
consequently, necessarily one." (Baudeau, p. 769.)

[2] This was the basis of Voltaire's lively satire *L'Homme avec quarante écus*. It treats
of a wealthy financier who escapes taxation, and who makes sport of the poor agriculturist who pays taxes for both, although his income is only forty *écus*.

[3] "Such a reduction of the necessary expenditure must result in diminished production, because there can be no harvest without some amount of preliminary expense.
You may check your expenditure, but it will mean diminishing your harvest—a
decrease in the one means an equal decrease of the other. Such a fatal blow to the
growth of population would, in the long run, injure the landed proprietor and the
sovereign." (Dupont de Nemours, p. 353.)

"A fall in the expenditure means a smaller harvest, which means that less will be
expended upon making preparation for the next harvest. This cyclical movement
seems a terrible thing to those who have given it some thought." (Mercier de la
Rivière, p. 499.)

paid over the 600 millions to the State. But we must also reckon the losses and friction incurred in every deviation from the 'natural order.' Suppose we decide that the sterile classes should pay the taxes. This class is *ex hypothesi* sterile—that is, it produces the exact equivalent of what it consumes. To take 600 millions from this class is tantamount to a reduction of its consumption by 600 millions, or an equivalent limitation of its purchases of raw material. The result would be a diminished product in the future, unless the industrial classes succeeded in increasing prices by an equivalent amount. Even in that case the landed proprietors will have to bear the brunt of it: firstly, they will have to reduce their own consumption, and secondly, their tenants', whose efficiency will thereby be impaired.[1]

This process of reasoning seems to imply that the revenues of the agricultural and industrial classes are not squeezable because they represent the indispensable minimum necessary for the expenses of production. This seems to be an anticipation of the notorious 'iron law.' Turgot's formula incisively stating this law, but containing no attempt at a justification, is known to most people.[2] Long before his day, however, it had been stated by Quesnay in terms no less pronounced, though perhaps not so well known.

> It is useless to urge that wage-earners can pay the tax so levied upon them, by restricting consumption and depriving themselves of luxuries without thereby causing the burden to fall upon the classes who pay the wages. The rate of wages, and consequently the amount of comfort and luxury which wages can purchase, are fixed at the irreducible minimum by the action of the competition which prevails among them.[3]

This is quite a characteristic trait. The author of the 'natural order,'

---

[1] "There would be something to say for this if the rich repaid them by increased wages or additional almsgiving. But the poor give to the rich, and so add to their misery, already sufficiently great. The State demands from those who have nothing to give, and directs all its penalties and exercises all its severity upon the poor." (Turgot, *Œuvres*, Vol. I, p. 413.)

"It would be better for the landed proprietors to pay it direct to the Treasury and thus save the cost of collection." (Dupont, p. 352.)

[2] "It might happen—and, indeed, it often does happen—that the worker's wage is only equal to what is necessary for his subsistence." (*Réflexions*, VI.)

It is also possible that Jesus was not formulating a general law when He said that we have the poor always with us. Turgot likewise wished to state the simple fact, and not to draw a general conclusion.

[3] Quesnay, *Second Problème économique*, p. 134. The argument which follows is rather curious. He does not seem to think that a fall in wages even below the minimum would result in the death of many people, but simply that it would result in emigration to other countries, and that as a consequence of such emigration the diminished supply at home would soon lead to higher wages being paid—a fairly optimistic conclusion for the period.

without any hesitation, admits that the direct outcome of the establishment of that order would be to reduce the life of the wage-earners to a level of bare subsistence.

It is also remarkable that in their study of the industrial classes wages should have claimed the exclusive attention of the Physiocrats. Profits even then were by no means unsqueezable, but curiously enough they failed to realize this. Voltaire's rich banker would have proved embarrassing here. They would have had some difficulty in showing how a reduction of his extravagance could possibly have endangered production. But they might have replied that since he had so little difficulty in squeezing the 400,000 *livres* out of his fellow-citizens he would not experience much more trouble in getting another 400,000 out of them and paying them over to the State.

Another objection consists in the insufficiency of a single tax to meet all the needs of the State. "In some States it is said that a third, a half, or even three-fourths of the clear net revenue from all sources of production is insufficient to meet the demands of the Treasury, and consequently other forms of taxation are necessary."[1]

In reply to this the Physiocrats would point out that the mere application of their fiscal system would result in such an increase in the net product that the yield from the tax would progressively grow. We must also take account of the economies resulting from the simplicity of the tax, and the almost complete absence of expenses of collection. But the most interesting point of all is that they thought the State should adapt its needs to meet its revenue, and not *vice versa*. The great advantage of the Physiocratic *impôt*, however, was that it was regulated by a natural norm, which gave the amount of the net product. Without this, taxation becomes arbitrary.[2] At bottom the system affords a barrier against the autocracy of the sovereign—a barrier that is much more effective than a parliamentary vote.

One of the disciples of Quesnay put the theory to the test of practice. The Margrave of Baden had the advantage of being a prince, and he proceeded to experiment on his own subjects. The system was

[1] Baudeau (p. 770) points out the error of confusing the gross revenue with the net revenue. Allowance should be made for the cost of collecting the revenue, etc.

[2] "If unfortunately it be true that three-tenths of the annual product is not sufficient to cover the ordinary expenditure, there is only one natural and reasonable conclusion to be drawn from this, namely, curtail the expenditure." (Dupont de Nemours, p. 775.)

"The tax must never be assessed in accordance with individual caprice. The amount is determined by the natural order." (Dupont, *Sur l'Origine d'une Science nouvelle*.) Neither should the State, in their opinion, exceed the limit, because it would mean having recourse to borrowing, which would simply mean increased deferred taxation.

C

tried in three communes of his principality, but, like most social experiments, failed. In two of the communes it was abandoned at the end of four years. In a third, despite its evil effects, it was prolonged until 1802. The increase in the land tax caused a veritable slump in the value of property just when the remission of taxes upon consumption was resulting in the rapid multiplication of wineshops and beer-houses.[1] It is unnecessary to add that the failure of the experiment did nothing to weaken the faith of the Margrave or his fellow Physiocrats. An experiment on so small a scale could not possibly be accepted as decisive. This is the usual retort of innovators when social experiments prove failures, but we must recognize the element of truth contained in their reply.

But if we wish to see the real results of the Physiocratic system we must look beyond the private experiments of a prince. Elsewhere the effects were much more far-reaching.

The fiscal aspect of the French Revolution owed its guiding inspiration to their ideas. Out of a budget of 500 million francs the Constituent Assembly decreed that about half of it—that is, 240 millions—should be got out of a tax levied upon land, equal to a tax of 2400 million francs nowadays; and the greatest part of it was to be raised by direct taxation.

Distrust of indirect taxation, and of all taxes on commodities, is also a consequence of the Physiocratic system—a distrust that is bound to grow as society becomes more democratic. Most of the arguments in favour of direct taxation are to be found in the Physiocratic writings. But the chief one employed nowadays—namely, that indirect taxes often bear no proportion to the amount of the revenue, but weigh heaviest upon those who have least, is not among them. This concern about proportionality, which is merely another word for justice, was quite foreign to their thoughts.[2]

At a later stage of this work it will be our duty to call attention to the enthusiasm aroused by this old theory of an *impôt unique* as advocated in the works of an eminent American economist,[3] who renders homage to the Physiocrats for inspiring him with ideals altogether opposed to those of the landed proprietors. And a similar movement under the very same name—the single-tax system—is still vigorous in the United States.

---

[1] See Garçon's instructive brochure *Un Prince allemand physiocrat* for a résumé of the Margrave's correspondence.

[2] We find the word in one of Dupont's letters to Say, but that is much later.

[3] Henry George dedicated his volume entitled *Protection or Free Trade* to them because he considered that they were his masters. But his tribute loses its point somewhat when we remember that he admitted that he had never read them.

IV: RÉSUMÉ OF THE PHYSIOCRATIC DOCTRINE. CRITICS AND DISSENTERS

A brief résumé of the contributions made to economic science by the Physiocrats will help us to realize their great importance.

From the theoretical point of view we have:

1. The idea that every social phenomenon is subject to law, and that the object of scientific study is to discover such laws.

2. The idea that personal interest if left to itself will discover what is most advantageous for it, and that what is best for the individual is also best for everybody. But this liberal doctrine had many advocates before the Physiocrats.

3. The conception of free competition, resulting in the establishment of the *bon prix*, which is the most advantageous price for both parties, and implies the extinction of all usurious profit.

4. An imperfect but yet searching analysis of production, and of the various divisions of capital. An excellent classification of incomes and of the laws of their distribution.

5. A collection of arguments which have long since become classic in favour of landed property.

From a practical point of view we have:

1. The freedom of labour.

2. Free trade within a country, and an impassionate appeal for the freedom of foreign trade.

3. Limitation of the functions of the State.

4. A first-class demonstration of the superiority of direct taxation over indirect.

It is unjust to reproach the Physiocrats, as is sometimes done, with giving us nothing but social metaphysics. A little over-systemization may prove useful in the early stages of a science. Its very faults have some usefulness. We must admit, however, that although their conception of the 'natural order' supplied the foundation, or at least the scaffolding, for political economy, it became so intertwined with a kind of optimism that it nullified the work of the Liberal school, especially in France.[1]

---

[1] Listen to Mercier de la Rivière: "We must admire the way in which one man becomes an instrument for the happiness of others, and the manner in which this happiness seems to communicate itself to the whole. Speaking literally, of course I do not know whether there will not be a few unhappy people even in this State, but their numbers will be so few and the happy ones will be so numerous that we need not be much concerned about helping them. All our interests and wills will be linked to the interest and will of the sovereign, forming for our common good a harmony which can only be regarded as the work of a kind Providence that wills that the land

But the greatest gap in the Physiocratic doctrine is the total absence of any reference to value, and their grossly material, almost terrestrial, conception of production. They seldom mention value, and what little they do say is often confused and commonplace. Herein lies the source of their mistakes concerning the unproductive character of exchange and industry, which are all the more remarkable in view of the able discussions of this very question by a number of their contemporaries. Among these may be mentioned Cantillon,[1] who resembles them in some respects and whose essay on commerce was published in 1755; the Abbé Galiani, who dealt with the question in his *Della Moneta* (1750); and the Abbé Morellet, who discussed the same topic in his *Prospectus d'un nouveau dictionnaire du commerce* (1769). More important than any of them, perhaps, is Condillac, whose work *Du Commerce et du Gouvernement* was unfortunately not published until 1776; but by that time the Physiocratic system had been completed, and their pre-eminence well established.

Turgot, though one of their number, is an exception. He was never a thoroughgoing Physiocrat, and his ideas concerning value are much more scientific.[2] He defines it as "an expression of the varying esteem which man attaches to the different objects of his desire." This definition gives prominence to the subjective character of value, and the phrases "varying esteem" and "desire" give it greater precision.[3] It is true that he also added that besides this relative attribute value always implied "some real intrinsic quality of the object." He has frequently been reproached for this, but all that he

shall be full of happy men." (Vol. II, p. 638.) This enchanting picture only applies to future society when the 'natural order' will be established. The optimism of the Physiocrats is very much like the anarchists'.

[1] Very little seems to have been known about Cantillon for more than a century after his death. But, like all the rediscovered founders of the science, he has received considerable attention for some years past. His influence upon the Physiocrats has perhaps been exaggerated. Mirabeau's earliest book, *L'Ami des Hommes*, which appeared just twelve months after Cantillon's work, is undoubtedly inspired by Cantillon. No discussion of his work is included in the text because it was felt that it might interfere with the plan of the work as already mapped out. There are several articles in various reviews which deal with Cantillon's work, the earliest being that contributed by Stanley Jevons to the *Contemporary Review* in 1881.

[2] *Valeurs et Monnaies*, which dates from 1769, and again in his *Réflexions*. Quesnay's conception of value may be gleaned from his article entitled *Hommes*, which remained unpublished for a long time, and has only recently appeared in the *Revue d'histoire des doctrines économiques et sociales*, Vol. I, No. 1.

[3] He dilates at considerable length on the distinction between estimative value (what would now be called subjective value) and appreciative (or social) value. The first depends upon the amount of time and trouble we are willing to sacrifice in order to acquire it. In this connexion the notion of labour-value appears. As to appreciative value, it differs from the preceding only in being an "average estimative value."

meant to say was that our desire always implies a certain correctness of judgment, which is indisputable unless every judgment is entirely illusory—and Turgot would never have admitted that.

It is possible that Turgot inspired Condillac, and that he himself owed his inspiration to Galiani, whose book, which appeared twenty years earlier, he frequently quotes. This work contains a very acute psychological analysis of value, showing how it depends upon scarcity on the one hand and utility on the other.

Besides a difference in his general standpoint, there are other considerations which distinguish Turgot from the members of the Physiocratic school, and it would have been juster to him as well as more correct to have devoted a whole chapter to him.[1] Generally speaking, his views are much more modern and more closely akin to Smith's. In view of the exigencies of space we must be content to draw attention to the principal doctrines upon which he differs from the Physiocrats.

1. The fundamental opposition between the productivity of agriculture and the sterility of industry, if not altogether abandoned, is at least reduced in importance.

2. Landed property is no longer an institution of divine origin. Even the appeal to the "ground expenses" is dropped. As an institution it rests merely upon the fact of occupation and public utility.

3. Movable property, on the other hand, holds a prominent place. The function of capital is more carefully analysed and the legitimacy of interest definitely proved.

But we must turn to Condillac's book if we want to see how the Physiocratic doctrine should be completed and expurgated of its errors. Condillac was already well known as a philosopher when, in his sixtieth year, he published this new work in 1776. This admirable book, entitled *Le Commerce et le Gouvernement considérés relativement l'un à l'autre*, contains an outline of most modern problems. The title gives no adequate indication of the character of the work, and possibly accounts for the oblivion into which the book has fallen.

It is a genuine economic treatise, and not a medley of economic and political suggestions concerning social science, with an admixture of ethics and jurisprudence. Value is regarded as the foundation of the science, and the Physiocrats are thus out-classed from the very first.[2] Value itself is considered to be based upon utility, which is stripped of

[1] Turgot, though a disciple of Quesnay, remained outside the Physiocratic school. He always referred to them contemptuously as "the sect."

[2] "I am so struck with this notion that I think it must serve as the basis of this whole treatise." (Chapter i.)

its popular meaning, and given a scientific connotation which it has never lost. It no longer implies an intrinsic, physical property of matter, but connotes a degree of correspondence between a commodity and a given human want. "Value is not an attribute of matter, but represents our sense of its usefulness, and this utility is relative to our need. It grows or diminishes according as our need expands or contracts." This is the foundation of the psychological theory of value.[1]

But this is not all—though a great deal. He clearly realizes that utility is not the only determinant of value; that quantity, *i.e.*, scarcity or abundance, also exercises an important influence. With admirable judgment he seizes upon the connexion between them, and shows how the two statements are united in one, for quantity only influences value according as its action upon utility intensifies or weakens demand.

> But since the value of things is based upon need it is natural that a more keenly felt need should endow things with greater value, while a less urgent need endows them with less. Value increases with scarcity and diminishes with plenty. In case of plenty it may even disappear; a superabundant good will be valueless if one has no use for it.[2]

This could not be put more clearly to-day. Here we have the germ of the theories of Jevons and the Austrian school, though it took a long time to develop.

We might naturally expect a superior treatment of exchange following upon this new theory of value. If value is simply the satisfaction of want, exchange creates two values when it satisfies two needs at the same time. The characteristic of exchange is that each of the two parties yields what it has in superabundance in return for what it needs. But what is given up is superabundant, is useless, and consequently valueless; what is demanded has greater utility, and consequently greater value. Two men come to market each with a useless thing, and each returns with a useful one.[3] Consequently the Physiocratic saying that exchange means no gain to anyone, or at least that the gain of one only compensates for the loss of the others, is seen to be radically false. The Physiocrats—notably Le Trosne—attempted a reply, but, for reasons already given, they never succeeded in realizing the subjective character of value.

[1] *Le Commerce et le Gouvernement*, p. 15.   [2] *Ibid.*, Part I, chapter i.
[3] "It is not correct to say that the exchanged values are equal; on the contrary, each party seeks to give a smaller value in exchange for a larger one. The process proves advantageous to both; hence, doubtless, the origin of the idea that the values must be equal. But one ought to have come to the conclusion that if each gains both must have given less and obtained more." (*Ibid.*, pp. 5, 56.) Compare this with the quotation from Le Trosne, p. 45, and note its psychological superiority.

This same theory should have carried Condillac a stage further, and helped in the rectification of the Physiocratic error concerning production. If value is simply utility and utility itself is just the correspondence between things and our demand for them, what is the agency that produces this harmony between things and desires? It is very seldom that nature succeeds in establishing it. "Nature is frequently fertile in things we have no desire for and lavish of what is useless"—a profound remark that ought to have cooled the Physiocrats' love of the *Alma Parens*. "Matter is transformed and made useful by dint of human labour. Production means giving new form to matter."[1] If this be true, then there is no difference between agricultural and industrial production, for they both transform what already exists.[2]

Moreover, the theory proves very clearly that if artisans and proprietors are dependent upon the agriculturists—as, indeed, they are—the latter in their turn are nothing but artisans. "If some one asks whether agriculture ought to be preferred to manufacture or manufacture to agriculture, we must reply that we have no preferences, and that the best use should be made of both."[3]

Lastly, his definition of wages, short as it is, is of immense significance. "Wages represent the share of the product which is due to the workers as co-partners."[4] Wages only 'represent' the share that is due to the workers. In other words, the wage-earner, either through want of will or of power, cannot exercise his rightful claim to his own work, and simply surrenders the claim in return for a money price. This constitutes his salary, which is regulated, like every other price, by competition between buyers and sellers. Condillac makes no reference to an iron law of wages, but regards them as determined by the forces of demand and supply. He does, however, hint at the implicit alliance which exists between capital and labour.[5]

From a practical standpoint also, especially in his defence of free labour and his condemnation of corporations, Condillac is more categorical than the Physiocrats. "All these iniquitous privileges," he writes, "have no claim to a place in the order beyond the fact that they are already established." He is as persistent as Turgot in his

---

[1] *Le Commerce et le Gouvernement*, Part I, chapter ix.
[2] "Even where the land is covered with products there is no additional material beyond what there was formerly. They have just been given a new form, and wealth consists merely of such transformations."
[3] *Ibid.*, Part I, chapter xxix.
[4] In a study of the wage bargain we find Chatelain giving expression to similar ideas, though apparently knowing nothing of Condillac's work.
[5] *Ibid.*, chapter xv, para. 8.

justification of the taking of interest and in his demand for the determination of the rate by competition. This very elegant argument is employed to show its similarity to exchange: Exchange implies compensation for overcoming the drawbacks of distance, whether of place or of time.[1] Exchange generally refers to place, interest to time, and this is really the foundation of the modern theory.

CHAPTER II: ADAM SMITH

NOTWITHSTANDING the originality and vigour displayed by the Physiocrats, they can only be regarded as the heralds of the new science. Adam Smith,[2] it is now unanimously agreed, is its true founder. The

---

[1] See Turgot, *Mémoire sur les prêts d'argent*, p. 122: "In every bargain involving the taking of interest a certain sum of money is given now in exchange for a somewhat larger sum to be paid at some future date; difference of time as well as of place makes a real difference to the value of money." Further on he adds (p. 127): "The difference is familiar to every one, and the well-known proverb 'A bird in the hand is worth two in the bush' is simply a popular way of expressing it."

[2] The life of Adam Smith presents nothing remarkable. It is easily summed up in the story of his travels, his professional activities, and the records of his friendships, and among these his intimacy with Hume the philosopher has become classical. He was born at Kirkcaldy, in Scotland, on June 5, 1723. From 1737 to 1740 he studied at the University of Glasgow under Francis Hutcheson, the philosopher, to whom he became much attached. From 1740 to 1746 he continued his studies at Oxford, where he seems to have worked steadily, chiefly by himself. The intellectual state of the university was at that time extremely low, and a number of the professors never delivered any lectures at all. Returning to Scotland, he gave two free courses of lectures at Edinburgh, one on English literature and the other on political economy, in the course of which he defended the principles of commercial liberty. In 1751 he became Professor of Logic at Glasgow, at that time one of the best universities in Europe. Towards the end of the year he was appointed to the chair of Moral Philosophy, which included the four divisions of Natural Theology, Ethics, Jurisprudence, and Politics within its curriculum. In 1759 he published his *Theory of Moral Sentiments*, which speedily brought him a great reputation. In 1764, when forty years of age, he quitted the professorial chair at Glasgow University and accompanied the young Duke of Buccleuch, son-in-law of Charles Townshend, the celebrated statesman, on his travels abroad. With the young nobility of this period foreign travel frequently took the place of a university training, on account of the disrepute into which the latter had fallen. Smith was given a pension of £300 a year for the rest of his life, so that the mere material advantage was considerably in excess of his earnings as a professor. The years 1764–66 were spent in this way. A year and a half was passed at Toulouse, two months at Geneva, where he met Voltaire, and another ten months at Paris. While in Paris he became acquainted with the Physiocrats, particularly with Turgot and the Encyclopædists. It was at Toulouse that he began his *Wealth of Nations*. Returning to Scotland in 1767, he went to live with his mother, with the sole object of devoting himself to this work. By 1773 the book was nearly complete. But Smith moved to London, and the work did not appear till 1776. By this achievement Smith

appearance of his great work on the *Wealth of Nations* in 1776 instantly eclipsed the tentative efforts of his predecessors. To-day the Physiocratic doctrines scarcely do more than arouse historical curiosity, while Smith's work has been the guide for successive generations of economists and the starting-point of all their speculation. Even at the present day, despite many changes in the fundamental principles of the science, no economist can afford to neglect the old Scots author without unduly narrowing his scientific horizon.

Several reasons account for the commanding position held by this

---

crowned the great celebrity which he already enjoyed. In January 1778 Smith was appointed Commissioner of Customs at Edinburgh, a distinguished position which he held until his death in 1790.

All that we know of Smith's character shows him to have been a man of tender feelings and of great refinement of character. His absent-mindedness has become proverbial. In politics his sympathies were with the Whigs. In religion he associated himself with the deists, a school that was greatly in vogue towards the end of the eighteenth century, and of which Voltaire, who was much admired by Smith, was the most celebrated representative.

For a long time the only life of Smith which we possessed was the memoir written by Dugald Stewart, *Account of the Life and Writings of Adam Smith*, and read by him in 1793 before the Royal Society of Edinburgh. It appeared in the *Transactions* of the society for 1794, and was published in volume form in 1811 along with other biographies, under the title of *Biographical Memoirs of Adam Smith, Robertson, etc.*, by Dugald Stewart. To-day we are more fortunate. John Rae in his charming *Life of Adam Smith* (London, 1895) has succeeded in bringing to light all that we can know of Smith and his circle. To him we are indebted for most of the details we have given. In 1894 James Bonar published a catalogue of Smith's library, containing about 2300 volumes, and comprising about two-thirds of his whole library. A still more important contribution to the study of Smith's ideas has been made by Dr Edwin Cannan, who in 1896 published *Lectures on Justice, Police, Revenue, and Arms, delivered in Glasgow by Adam Smith, from Notes taken by a Student in 1763* (Oxford). This represents the course of lectures on political economy delivered by Smith while professor at Glasgow. A manuscript copy of the notes taken in this course by a student, probably in 1763, was accidentally discovered by a London solicitor in 1876. These notes were in 1895 forwarded to Dr Cannan for publication. They are especially precious in helping us to understand Smith's ideas before his stay in France and his meeting with the Physiocrats. Of the numerous editions of the *Wealth of Nations* which have hitherto been published, the more important are those of Buchanan, McCulloch, Thorold Rogers, and Nicholson. The best critical edition is that of Dr Cannan, published in 1904 by Methuen, containing very valuable notes. This is the edition we have used.

In 1937 a very valuable addition was made to our knowledge of the life and family of Adam Smith by W. R. Scott, who, on the 200th anniversary of Smith's matriculation at Glasgow University, published a large volume entitled *Adam Smith as Student and Professor* (Glasgow, 1937, 445 pp. 4to). Its contents include, besides unpublished letters, a document of very great value—a summary of Smith's economic ideas, compiled by himself and sent, about the year 1760, to Charles Townshend. This manuscript contains an admirable account of the division of labour, even more interesting than that given in *The Wealth of Nations*, and allows us a glimpse of the entire sociological and philosophical range ascribed by Smith to the division of labour as the foundation of the wealth of human societies. The manuscript was rediscovered by Scott among the papers preserved in one of the residences of the late Duke of Buccleuch.

book—a position which no subsequent treatise has ever successfully rivalled.

First is its supreme literary charm. It is above all an interesting book, bristling with facts and palpitating with life. The burning questions of the hour, such as the problems presented by the colonial regime, the trading companies, the mercantile system, the monetary question, and taxation, supply the author with congenial themes for his treatment. His discussion of these questions is marked by such mastery of detail and such balance of judgment that he convinces without effort. His facts are intermixed with reasoning, his illustrations with argument. He is instructive as well as persuasive. Withal there is no trace of pedantry, no monotonous reiteration in the work, and the reader is not burdened with the presence of a cumbersome logical apparatus. All is elegantly simple. Neither is there the slightest suggestion of the cynic. Rather a passion of genuinely human sympathy, occasionally bordering upon eloquence, breathes through the pages. Thanks to rare qualities such as these we can still feel something of the original freshness of this old book.

In addition to this, Smith has been successful in borrowing from his predecessors all their more important ideas and welding them into a more general system. He superseded them because he rendered their work useless. A true social and economic philosophy was substituted for their fragmentary studies, and an entirely new value given to their contributions. Taken out of their isolation, they help to illustrate his general theory, becoming themselves illuminated in the process.

Like most great writers, Smith knows how to borrow without impairing his originality. Over a hundred authors are quoted in his book, though their names are not always mentioned. Some, at least, of the writers who exercised such influence over him, and opened up the path which he afterwards followed, deserve more than a passing reference.

The first place among these belongs, perhaps, to Hutcheson, Smith's predecessor in the chair of Moral Philosophy at Glasgow. The divisions of the subject are almost identical with those given by Hutcheson, and many of Smith's best-known theories can be traced in the *System of Moral Philosophy* published by Hutcheson in 1755, but which we know was written long before. Hutcheson laid great stress upon the supreme importance of division of labour, and his views on such questions as the origin and variations in the value of money and the possibility of corn or labour affording a more stable standard of value closely resemble those of the *Wealth of Nations*.

David Hume is a near second. Smith refers to him as "by far the most illustrious philosopher and historian of the present age,"[1] and from 1752 onward they were the closest of friends. Hume was already the author of some essays on economic questions, the most important among them dealing with money, foreign trade, the rate of interest, etc. These, along with several other writings, were published in the *Political Discourses* in 1752. Hume's examination of these problems displays his original penetrative thought, and there is evident the profundity and lucidity of treatment characteristic of all his writings. The absurdity of the Mercantile policy and of interfering with the natural tendency of money to adapt itself to the needs of each community, the sophistry of the balance of trade theory, and the impious consequences resulting from commercial jealousy among nations are exposed with admirable force in these essays. No doubt the essays left a great impression upon Smith. He quoted them in his lectures at Glasgow, and Hume consulted him before bringing out a second edition. It is true that Smith eventually became the stauncher Liberal of the two. Hume, in his essay on the *Balance of Trade*, recognized the legitimacy of certain protective rights which Smith wished removed altogether. Still, it was to Hume that Smith owed his conversion to the Liberal faith.

On this matter of commercial liberty there was already, towards the end of the seventeenth and the beginning of the eighteenth centuries, a small but a growing band of Mercantilists who had begun to protest against the irksomeness of the Customs regulations. They were, of course, still largely imbued with mercantile prejudice, but they are rightly classed as "Liberals." Just as in France Boisguillebert had foreshadowed the Physiocrats, so in England Child, Petty, Tucker, Dudley North, and Gregory King had been preparing the way for a more liberal policy in foreign trade.[2]

In addition to Hutcheson and Hume one other writer must be mentioned in this connexion, namely, Bernard de Mandeville. He was not an economist at all, but a doctor with considerable philosophical interests. In 1704 he had published a poem, which, along with a number of additions, was republished in 1714 under the title of *The Fable of the Bees; or, Private Vices Public Benefits*. The fundamental idea of the book, which caused quite a sensation at the time, and which was seized by order of the Government, is that civilization—understanding by that term not only wealth, but also the arts and sciences—is the outcome, not of the virtues of mankind, but of what

---

[1] *Wealth of Nations* (Cannan's edition), Vol. II, p. 275.
[2] On this point, as on all that concerns Mercantilism, see Heckscher's book with that title, published in Swedish in 1931 and since translated into German and English.

Mandeville calls its vices; in other words, that the desire for well-being, comfort, luxury, and all the pleasures of life arises from our natural wants. The book was a sort of apology for the natural man and a criticism of the virtuous.

Smith criticized Mandeville in his *Theory of Moral Sentiments*,[1] and reproached him particularly for referring to tastes and desires as vices though in themselves they were nowise blameworthy. But despite his criticism Mandeville's idea bore fruit in Smith's mind. Smith in his turn was to reiterate the belief that it was personal interest (in his opinion no vice, but an inferior virtue) that unwittingly led society in the paths of well-being and prosperity. A nation's wealth for Smith as well as for Mandeville is the result, if not of a vice, at least of a natural instinct which is not itself virtuous, but which is bestowed upon us by Providence for the realization of ends that lie beyond our farthest ken.

Such are the principal writers in whose works we may find an outline of some of the more important ideas which Smith was to incorporate in a true system.

Mere systematization, however, would not have given the *Wealth of Nations* its unique position. Prior to Smith's time attempts had been made by Quesnay and the Physiocrats to outline the scope of the science and to link its various portions together by means of a few general principles. Although he was not the first to produce a connected scientific treatise out of this material, he had a much greater measure of success than any of his predecessors.

Smith owed much to the Physiocrats, but he had little personal acquaintance with them beyond that afforded by his brief stay in Paris in 1765. Slight as the intimacy was, however, there is no doubt about the influence they had upon him. It is also very improbable that he had read all their works: Turgot's *Réflexions*, for example, written in 1766, but only published in 1769–70, was probably not known to him. But frequent personal converse with both Turgot and Quesnay had helped him in acquiring precise first-hand knowledge of their views. We can easily guess which ideas would attract him most.

On one point at least he had no need to be enlightened, for in the matter of economic liberalism he had long been known as a doughty champion. But the ardent faith of the Physiocrats must have strengthened his own belief very considerably.

On the other hand, it appears that he borrowed from the Physiocrats the important idea concerning the distribution of the annual

---

[1] Chapter iv of sec. ii of the 7th part of the *Theory of Moral Sentiments* is entitled *Of Systems of License.*

revenue between the various classes in the nation. In his lectures at Glasgow he scarcely mentions anything except production, but in the *Wealth of Nations* an important place is given to distribution. The difference can hardly be explained except upon the hypothesis of Smith's growing acquaintance with the *Tableau économique* and the theory of the 'net product.'

But admitting that he borrowed what was most characteristic and most suggestive in their teaching, his treatment of its many complicated aspects is altogether superior to theirs. The Physiocrats were so impressed by the importance of agriculture that they utterly failed to see the problem in its true perspective. They scanned the field through a crevice, and their vision was consequently narrow and limited. Smith, on the other hand, took the whole field of economic activity as his province, and surveyed the ground from an eminence where the view was clearest and most extensive.

The economic world he regarded as a vast workshop created by division of labour, one universal psychological principle—the desire of every one to better his lot—supplying unity to its diverse phenomena. Political economy was at last to be based, not on the interests of a particular class, whether manufacturing or agricultural, but upon a consideration of the general interest of the whole community. Such are the directing principles that inspire the whole work, the guiding lines amidst what had hitherto seemed a mere chaos of economic facts. Contemporaries never counted upon the difficulties which the new science was bound to encounter, so great was their enthusiasm at having a fixed standpoint from which for the first time the complex interests of agriculture, industry, and commerce might be impartially surveyed. With Smith the study emerged from the 'system' stage and became a science.

Our examination of Smith's views will be grouped around three points:

(I) Division of labour.

(II) The 'natural' organization of the economic world under the influence of personal interest.

(III) Liberalism.

I: DIVISION OF LABOUR

It was Quesnay who had propounded the theory that agriculture was the source of all wealth, both the State's and the individual's.[1] Adam Smith seized upon the phrase and sought to disprove it in his

[1] Oncken's edition, p. 331.

opening sentence by giving to wealth its true origin in the general activity of society.

> The annual labour of every nation is the fund which originally supplies it with all the necessaries and conveniences of life which it annually consumes, and which consist always either in the immediate produce of that labour or in what is purchased with that produce from other nations.

Labour is the true source of wealth. When Smith propounded this celebrated theory, which has given rise to so many misunderstandings since, it was not intended that it should minimize the importance of natural forces or depreciate the part which capital plays in production.[1] No one, except perhaps J. B. Say, has been more persistent in emphasizing the importance of capital, and to the land, as we shall presently see, he attributed a special degree of productivity. But from the very outset Smith was anxious to emphasize the distinction between his doctrine and that of the Physiocrats. So he definitely affirms that it is human activity and not natural forces which produces the mass of commodities consumed every year. Without the former's directing energy the latter would for ever remain useless and fruitless.

He is not slow to draw inferences from this doctrine. Work, employed in the widest sense, and not nature, is the parent of wealth—not the work of a single class like the agriculturists, but the work of all classes. Hence all work has a claim to be regarded as productive. The nation's annual income owes something to every one who toils. It is the result of their collaboration, of their "co-operation," as he calls it. There is no longer any need for the distinction between the sterile and the productive classes, for only the idle are sterile.

A nation is just a vast workshop, where the labour of each, however diverse in character, adds to the wealth of all. The passage in which Adam Smith expresses this idea is well known, but no apology is needed for quoting it once again.[2]

> What a variety of labour too is necessary in order to produce the tools of the meanest of those workmen! To say nothing of such complicated machines as the ship of the sailor, the mill of the fuller, or even the loom of the weaver, let us consider only what a variety of labour is requisite in order to form that very simple machine, the

---

[1] The theory that there are three factors of production, which has since become a commonplace of economics, is not to be found in Smith. Indirectly, however, it was he who originated the idea by distinguishing in his treatment of distribution between the various sources of revenue. The distinction once made, it was quite natural to consider each source as a factor of production; and this is just what J. B. Say did in his *Treatise* (2nd ed., chapters iv and v). *Cf.* Cannan's *History of the Theories of Production and Distribution*, p. 40 (1894).

[2] *Wealth of Nations*, Book I, chapter i; Cannan's edition, Vol. I, pp. 13–14.

shears with which the shepherd clips the wool. The miner, the builder of the furnace for smelting the ore, the feller of the timber, the burner of the charcoal to be made use of in the smelting-house, the brick-maker, the brick-layer, the workmen who attend the furnace, the mill-wright, the forger, the smith, must all of them join their different arts in order to produce them. Were we to examine, in the same manner, all the different parts of his dress and household furniture, the coarse linen shirt which he wears next his skin, the shoes which cover his feet, the bed which he lies on, and all the different parts which compose it, the kitchen-grate at which he prepares his victuals, the coals which he makes use of for that purpose, dug from the bowels of the earth, and brought to him perhaps by a long sea and a long land carriage, all the other utensils of his kitchen, all the furniture of his table, the knives and forks, the earthen or pewter plates upon which he serves up and divides his victuals, the different hands employed in preparing his bread and his beer, the glass window which lets in the heat and the light, and keeps out the wind and the rain, with all the knowledge and art requisite for preparing that beautiful and happy invention, without which these northern parts of the world could scarce have afforded a very comfortable habitation, together with the tools of all the different workmen employed in producing those different conveniencies; if we examine, I say, all these things, and consider what a variety of labour is employed about each of them, we shall be sensible that without the assistance and co-operation of many thousands, the very meanest person in a civilized country could not be provided, even according to, what we very falsely imagine, the easy and simple manner in which he is commonly accommodated.

Division of labour is simply the spontaneous realization of a particular form of this social co-operation. Smith's peculiar merit lies in placing this fact in its true position as the basis of his whole work. The book opens upon this note, whose economic and social importance has been so frequently emphasized since that it sounds almost commonplace to-day.

This division of labour effects an easy and natural combination of economic efforts for the creation of the national dividend. Whereas animals confine themselves to the direct satisfaction of their individual needs,[1] men produce commodities to exchange them for others more immediately desired. Hence there results for the community an enormous increase of wealth; and division of labour, by establishing the co-operation of all for the satisfaction of the desires of each, becomes the true source of progress and of well-being.

[1] "In almost every other race of animals each individual, when it is grown up to maturity, is entirely independent, and in its natural state has occasion for the assistance of no other living creature." (*Wealth of Nations*, Book I, chapter ii; Cannan, Vol. I, p. 16.)

In order to illustrate the growth in total production as the outcome of division of labour, Smith gives an example of its effects in a particular industry. "The effects of the division of labour, in the general business of society, will be more easily understood by considering in what manner it operates in some particular manufactures." It is in this connexion that he introduces his celebrated description of the manufacture of pins.

> A workman not educated to this business (which the division of labour has rendered a distinct trade), nor acquainted with the use of the machinery employed in it (to the invention of which the same division of labour has probably given occasion), could scarce, perhaps, with his utmost industry, make one pin in a day, and certainly could not make twenty. But in the way in which this business is now carried on, not only the whole work is a peculiar trade, but it is divided into a number of branches, of which the greater part are likewise peculiar trades. One man draws out the wire, another straights it, a third cuts it, a fourth points it, a fifth grinds it at the top for receiving the head; to make the head requires two or three distinct operations; to put it on, is a peculiar business, to whiten the pins is another; it is even a trade by itself to put them into the paper; and the important business of making a pin is, in this manner, divided into about eighteen distinct operations, which, in some manufactories, are all performed by distinct hands, though in others the same man will sometimes perform two or three of them. I have seen a small manufactory of this kind where ten men only were employed, and where some of them consequently performed two or three distinct operations. But though they were very poor, and therefore but indifferently accommodated with the necessary machinery, they could, when they exerted themselves, make among them about twelve pounds of pins in a day.[1]

Such is the picture of man as we find him in society. Division of labour and exchange have resulted in augmenting production a hundredfold, and thus increasing his well-being, whereas left to himself he could scarcely supply his most urgent needs.

In a subsequent analysis Smith ascribes the gain resulting from division of labour to three principal causes: (1) the greater dexterity acquired by each workman when confined to one particular task; (2) the economy of time achieved in avoiding constant change of occupation; (3) the number of inventions and improvements which suggest themselves to men absorbed in one kind of work.

Criticism has been levelled at Smith for his omission to mention the disadvantages of division of labour which might possibly counterbalance its many advantages. The omission is the result of his method of treating the whole question, and it is not of much real importance.

[1] *Wealth of Nations*, Book I, chapter i; Cannan, Vol. I, pp. 6–7.

The disadvantages, moreover, were not altogether lost sight of, and it would be difficult to find a more eloquent plea for some counteracting influence than that which Smith puts forward in the fifth book of the *Wealth of Nations*. "In the progress of the division of labour," he remarks

> the employment of the far greater part of those who live by labour, that is, of the great body of the people, comes to be confined to a few very simple operations; frequently to one or two. But the man whose whole life is spent in performing a few simple operations, of which the effects too are, perhaps, always the same, or very nearly the same, has no occasion to exert his understanding, or to exercise his invention in finding out expedients for removing difficulties which never occur. He naturally loses, therefore, the habit of such exertion, and generally becomes as stupid and ignorant as it is possible for a human creature to become.[1]

This passage seems in contradiction with the ideas expressed above. At one moment constant application to one particular kind of work is regarded as the mother of invention, at another the unremitting task is branded as a fertile cause of stupefaction. The contradiction is, however, more apparent than real. An occupation at first stimulating to the imagination may, if constantly pursued, result in mental torpor. Smith's conclusions are at any rate interesting. In order to remove the inconveniences resulting from over-specialization he emphasizes the need for bringing within reach of the people, even of imposing upon them, a system of education consisting of the three R's[2]—such education to be supplied through institutions partly supported by the State. We can imagine the shock which such heterodoxy must have given to the prophets of *laissez-faire*. Fortunately it was not the only one they had to bear.

Smith next proceeds to indicate the limits of this division of labour. Of such limits he mentions two: (1) In the first place it must be limited by the extent of the market.

> When the market is very small, no person can have any encouragement to dedicate himself entirely to one employment, for want of the power to exchange all that surplus part of the produce of his own labour, which is over and above his own consumption, for such parts of the produce of other men's labour as he has occasion for.[3]

[1] *Wealth of Nations*, Book V, chapter i, Part III, art. 2; Cannan, Vol. II, p. 267.

[2] "For a very small expence the public can facilitate, can encourage, and can even impose upon almost the whole body of the people, the necessity of acquiring those most essential parts of education." (*Ibid.*, Book V, chapter i, Part III, art. 2; Vol. II, p. 270.)

[3] *Ibid.*, Book I, chapter iii; Vol. I, p. 19.

This is why foreign trade, including trade with the colonies, by extend-ing the market for some products is favourable to further division of labour and a further increase of wealth. (2) The other consideration which, according to Smith, limits division of labour is the quantity of capital available.[1] The significance of this observation is not quite so obvious as that of the former one. Here it seems to us that a con-clusion drawn from one particular trade has been applied to industry as a whole. It may be true of a private manufacturer that he will be able to push technical division of labour further than any of his rivals provided he has more capital than they; but taking society as a whole it is clear that the existence of division of labour enables the same product to be produced with less capital than is necessary for the single producer.[2]

Such is an outline of Adam Smith's theory of division of labour—a theory so familiar to every one to-day that we are often unable to realize its importance and to appreciate its originality, and this despite the fact that certain sociologists like Durkheim have hailed it as supplying the basis of a new ethic. Juxtaposed with the Physiocratic theory, it is not very difficult to realize its superiority.

To the Physiocrats the economic world was a hierarchy of classes. The agriculturist in some mysterious way bore the "whole weary weight of this unintelligible world" upon his own shoulders, giving to the other classes a modicum of that sustenance which he had wrested from the soil. Hence the fundamental importance of the agricultural classes and the necessity for making the whole economic system sub-ordinate to them. Adam Smith, on the other hand, attempted to get a view of production as a whole. He regarded it as the result of a series of joint undertakings engineered by the various sections of society and linked together by the tie of exchange. The progress of each section is bound up with that of every other. To none of these classes is entrusted the task of keeping all the others alive; all are equally indispensable. The artisan who spares the labourer the task of building his house or of making his shoes contributes to the accumu-lation of agricultural products just as much as the ploughman who

---

[1] "As the accumulation of stock must, in the nature of things, be previous to the division of labour, so labour can be more and more subdivided in proportion only as stock is previously more and more accumulated." (*Wealth of Nations*, Book II, Introd.; Cannan, Vol. I, p. 259.) It is true that in another passage he speaks of the quantity of stock which can be employed in any branch of business depending very much upon that of the labour which can be employed in it. (*Ibid.*, Book I, chapter x, Part II; Vol. I, p. 137.) But this observation remains isolated, while the former represents his true teaching.

[2] *Cf.* Cannan's penetrating criticism of this idea of Smith's in *Theories of Production and Distribution*, pp. 80–83.

frees the artisan from turning the furrow or sowing the seed. The progress of national wealth cannot be measured in terms of a single net product; it must be estimated by the increase in the whole mass of commodities placed at the disposal of consumers.

One very evident practical conclusion follows; namely, that taxation should fall, not upon one class, as the Physiocrats wished, but upon all classes alike. As against the *impôt unique*, Smith advocates multiple taxation which shall strike every source of revenue equally, labour and capital as well as land; and the fundamental rule which he lays down is as follows: "The subjects of every State ought to contribute towards the support of the Government, as nearly as possible, in proportion to their respective abilities; that is, in proportion to the revenue which they respectively enjoy under the protection of the State."[1] This is his famous maxim of equality so frequently quoted in every financial discussion.[2]

It is very curious that Smith should have failed to make the best possible use of this theory. Its full significance was lost upon him. The theory of division of labour alone was sufficient to dispose of the whole Physiocratic system. Nevertheless, in the last chapter of Book IV we find him still valiantly struggling to disprove the conclusions of the Physiocrats, by the aid of arguments not always very convincing. Forgetting his principle of division of labour, he even adopts a part of their thesis and finds himself entangled by the invalid distinctions which they had drawn between productive and unproductive workers. He simply gives another definition and describes as unproductive all works which "perish in the very instant of their performance, and seldom leave any trace or value behind them for which an equal quantity of service could afterwards be procured."[3] All these services,

---

[1] This is the first of the four celebrated maxims in Smith's theory of taxation. Here are the other three: "(ii) The tax which each individual is bound to pay ought to be certain and not arbitrary. The time of payment, the manner of payment, the quantity to be paid, ought all to be clear and plain to the contributor, and to every other person. (iii) Every tax ought to be levied at the time, or in the manner, in which it is most likely to be convenient for the contributor to pay it. (iv) Every tax ought to be so contrived as both to take out and to keep out of the pockets of the people as little as possible, over and above what it brings into the public treasury of the State." (*Wealth of Nations*, Book V, chapter ii, Part II; Cannan, Vol. II, pp. 310–311.)

[2] This rule of payment according to ability did not prevent his pronouncing in another paragraph in favour of progressive taxation. This is an instance of a want of logic frequently evidenced in his writings. Speaking of taxes upon rent, he remarks that they weigh more heavily upon rich than upon poor, because the former in proportion to their income spend more upon house rent than the latter. But "it is not very unreasonable that the rich should contribute to the public expence, not only in proportion to their revenue, but something more than in that proportion." (*Ibid.*, Book V, chapter ii, Part II, art. 1; Vol. II, p. 327.)

[3] *Ibid.*, Book II, chapter iii; Vol. I, p. 314.

which comprise the labours of domestic servants, of administrators and magistrates, of soldiers and priests, of counsellors, doctors, artists, authors, musicians, etc., Say classed together as 'immaterial products.' By restricting the term 'productive' to material objects only, Smith gave rise to a very useless controversy on the nature of productive and unproductive works—a controversy that was first taken up by Say and revived by Mill, but which to-day seems to be decided against Smith, thanks to a more exact interpretation of his own doctrines. It is, indeed, quite clear that all these services constitute a part of the annual revenue of the nation, and that 'production' in a general sense would be diminished if some persons did not exclusively devote themselves to the performance of such tasks.

After criticizing the Physiocratic distinction drawn between the wage-earning classes and the productive, Smith immediately admits that the labour of artisans and traders is not as productive as that of farmers and agricultural labourers, for the latter not only return the capital employed by them together with profits, but they also furnish the proprietor with rent.[1]

Whence this hesitation on the part of Smith? Where did he come by the idea of the special and superior productivity of agriculture? An attempt to account for it may prove interesting, and it will help us to give Smith his true place in a history of economic doctrines.

Notwithstanding his recantation, Smith was never quite rid of Physiocratic influence. Writing of the Physiocratic system, he described it as perhaps "the nearest approximation to the truth that has yet been published."[2] So indelible was the impression which the Physiocrats left upon him that both they and their doctrines, even when the latter are directly opposed to his own, are always spoken of with the greatest respect. The most important evidence of their power over him is the thesis just mentioned which he attempted to defend, namely, that between agriculture and other industries lies an essential distinction, because in industry and commerce the forces of nature are never brought into play, whereas in agriculture they always collaborate with man. "No equal quantity of productive labour employed in manufactures can ever occasion so great a reproduction. In them

---

[1] "Farmers and country labourers, indeed, over and above the stock which maintains and employs them, reproduce annually a neat produce, a free rent to the landlord. As a marriage which affords three children is certainly more productive than one which affords only two; so the labour of farmers and country labourers is certainly more productive than that of merchants, artificers, and manufacturers. The superior produce of the one class, however, does not render the other barren or unproductive." (*Wealth of Nations*, Book IV, chapter ix; Cannan, Vol. II, p. 173.)

[2] *Ibid.*, Book IV, chapter ix; Vol. II, p. 176.

nature does nothing; man does all; and the reproduction must always
be in proportion to the strength of the agents that occasion it."[1] We
almost think we are dreaming when we read such things in the work of
a great economist. Water, wind, electricity, and steam, are they not
natural forces, and do they not co-operate with man in his task of
production?

Considerations such as these were allowed to pass quite unheeded,
and Smith persisted in his error because he believed that this new
doctrine furnished him with an explanation of rent, that strange enigma
which had puzzled English economists for so long. How was it that
while other branches of production gave a return only sufficient to
remunerate the capital and labour employed, agriculture, in addition
to these two revenues, yielded a supplementary income known as rent?
It was because "in agriculture nature labours along with man: and
though her labour costs no expence, its produce has its value as well
as that of the most expensive workman." Thus "rent may be considered as the produce of those powers of nature, the use of which the
landlord lends to the farmer."[2] Had Smith arrived at a true theory
of rent this recourse to the natural powers of the soil to furnish an
explanation of the proprietor's revenue would have been quite unnecessary, and in all probability he would not have so easily accepted
the idea of the special productivity of the soil. But this false conception of nature has persisted in economic theory, and in it Smith

---

[1] *Wealth of Nations*, Book II, chapter v; Vol. I, p. 344.
[2] *Ibid.* Note that in this, as in other matters, Smith entertains more than one
opinion. In other passages in the same work he regards rent as a monopoly price
that "enters into the composition of the price of commodities in a different way from
wages and profit. High or low wages and profit, are the causes of high or low price;
high or low rent is the effect of it. It is because high or low wages and profit must
be paid, in order to bring a particular commodity to market, that its price is high
or low. But it is because its price is high or low; a great deal more, or very little
more, or no more, than what is sufficient to pay those wages and profit, that it
affords a high rent, or a low rent, or no rent at all." (*Ibid.*, Book I, chapter xi;
Vol. I, p. 147.)
It is impossible to reconcile these statements. In the one case rent is regarded as a
constituent element of price, in the other it is the effect of price.
In the first edition this contradiction was still more evident. In that edition rent,
along with profit and wages, was treated as a third determinant of value. (See
Cannan's edition, Vol. I, p. 51, note 7.) The paragraph was deleted from the second
edition, and rent was treated merely as a component part of the price. This modification was perhaps the outcome of a letter written by Hume to Smith on April 1, 1776,
after he had read the *Wealth of Nations* for the first time. "I cannot think," says
Hume, "that the rent of farms makes any part of the price of the produce, but that
the price is determined altogether by the quantity and the demand." (Quoted by
Rae in his *Life of Adam Smith*, p. 286.) The celebrated controversy as to whether
rent enters into prices is not a thing of yesterday. Its origin dates from the birth of
political economy itself, and it will probably only die with it.

thought he saw an additional reason for adhering to those errors which the Physiocrats had first induced him to commit.[1]

Apart from his personal attachment to the Physiocrats we must also remember that Smith more than shared their predilection for agriculture.

Nothing can be more incorrect, though it is frequently done, than to regard Smith as the prophet of industrialism and to contrast him with the Physiocrats, the champions of agriculture. When the *Wealth of Nations* appeared in 1776 the economic transformation known to history as the Industrial Revolution, which consisted in the rapid substitution of machine production for the old domestic regime, had as yet scarcely begun. Hargreaves and Arkwright had doubtless some inventions to their credit. The one had produced the spinning jenny in 1765, and the other had perfected the water frame in 1767, improvements that had given considerable impetus to the cotton trade. James Watt,[2] who was known to Smith, took out a patent for a steam-engine in 1769. But these inventions were as yet quite novel, and required time before they could modify the industrial system. The more important among them, Crompton's "mule"[3] and Cartwright's weaving machine, were as yet of the future. These dates are significant; they prove conclusively that the Industrial Revolution had scarcely begun when Smith's great work appeared. Moreover, several of the more important themes treated of in the *Wealth of Nations* may be discovered in the course of lectures which Smith delivered at Glasgow about 1759, so that it is quite impossible to establish anything like an exact connexion between the Industrial Revolution which was just beginning and the ideas embodied in the *Wealth of Nations*. One

[1] His error is partly due to the fact that he failed to distinguish between the profits of the *entrepreneur* and the interest of the capitalist. Both with Smith and with his successors the word 'profit' signified a twofold revenue, and this was perfectly correct so long as the *entrepreneur* was also a capitalist. The word 'interest' was reserved for the income of that person who lent capital but who did not himself produce anything. The revenue "derived from stock, by the person who manages or employs it, is called profit. That derived from it by the person who does not employ it himself, but lends it to another, is called the interest or the use of money." (*Wealth of Nations*, Book I, chapter vi; Cannan, Vol. I, p. 54.) J. B. Say was the first to give us a definite idea of the *entrepreneur*. Had Smith realized more clearly the functions of the *entrepreneur* he would probably have perceived: (1) that the *entrepreneur*, in addition to paying interest on his capital, frequently has to pay rent for the use of the soil; (2) that profit strictly so called includes an element analogous to rent. According to Smith, profit was simply payment for risks undergone or for work undertaken.

[2] James Watt in 1756 had set up his workshop within the precincts of the University of Glasgow, for which he manufactured mathematical instruments. The corporation had refused him permission to set it up in the town—a striking illustration of the narrowness and inflexibility of "the corporative regime."

[3] A combination of Hargreaves's spinning jenny and Arkwright's water frame.

cannot even say that Smith was particularly enamoured of the manufacturing regime—apart from the mechanical advance which it implied. For, as Marx says,[1] the characteristic trait of English economic
life, despite the undisputed advance that industry was making at that
time, was commercial rather than industrial.[2] Especially was this true
of Glasgow, where Smith made most of his observations. Glasgow
then was an essentially commercial town, principally engaged in the
importation of American tobacco.[3]

Far from constituting a prophetic manifesto of the new age, Smith's
work reveals even to the most superficial reader a thorough abhorrence
of traders and manufacturers. All his sarcasm is reserved for them,
all his criticism levelled at them. While the interest of landed proprietors and workers appears to him always to accord with a country's
general interest, that of traders and manufacturers "is never exactly
the same with that of the public," the manufacturers having "generally
an interest to deceive and even to oppress the public, and who accordingly have, upon many occasions, both deceived and oppressed it."[4]

Again, when it comes to choosing between capitalists and workmen
the issue is not long in doubt. It is quite clear from more than one
passage that Smith's sympathy was wholly with the workers. Several
paragraphs could be cited in proof of this. Suffice it to recall the very
sympathetic way in which he speaks of the high wages of workmen and
contrast it with his discussion of profits.

> Is this improvement in the circumstances of the lower ranks of the
> people to be regarded as an advantage or as an inconveniency to the
> society? The answer seems at first sight abundantly plain. Servants,
> labourers and workmen of different kinds, make up the far greater
> part of every great political society. But what improves the circum-
> stances of the greater part can never be regarded as an inconveniency
> to the whole. No society can surely be flourishing and happy, of which
> the far greater part of the members are poor and miserable. It is but
> equity, besides, that they who feed, cloath, and lodge the whole body
> of the people, should have such a share of the produce of their own
> labour as to be themselves tolerably well fed, cloathed, and lodged.[5]

[1] Marx speaks of Smith as the economist who is the very epitome of the manufacturing period. (*Das Kapital*, Vol. I, p. 313, note.)

[2] See Mantoux's work *La Révolution industrielle au XVIIIe Siècle*, p. 71 (Paris, 1905).
"We are mistaken," says he, "if we think that manufacture was the dominant feature
of the period preceding the factory system. Logically it may be the necessary antecedent, but historically its claim to priority is weak, although it left its indelible
marks upon industry. The appearance of industry at the time of the Renaissance is
an event of the greatest importance and significance, but it played a part of only
secondary importance for a century or two."

[3] Rae's *Life of Adam Smith*, p. 89.

[4] *Wealth of Nations*, Book I, chapter xi; Cannan, Vol. I, p. 250.

[5] *Ibid.*, Book I, chapter viii; Vol. I, p. 80.

High wages, moreover, are normally associated with a low cost of labour. This distinction between the cost of labour and the level of wages is not to be found in the *Wealth of Nations* but in the admirable summary of it that Adam Smith made in 1760, recently discovered by Professor Scott. "In an opulent and commercial society," he writes,

> labour becomes dear and work cheap, and those two events which vulgar prejudice and superficial reflection are apt to consider as altogether incompatible, are found by experience to be perfectly consistent. The high price of labour is to be considered not meerly [*sic*] as a proof of the general opulence of Society which can afford to pay well all those whom it employs; it is to be regarded as what constitutes the expence [*sic*] of public opulence, or as the very thing in which public opulence properly consists. That state is properly opulent in which opulence is easily come at, or in which a little labour properly and judiciously employed, is capable of procuring any man a great abundance of all the necessaries and conveniences of life.[1]

The tune changes when he comes to speak of profits. He is of opinion that high profits raise the price of commodities much more than high wages, and he dismisses the consideration of the problem with this ironical remark:

> Our merchants and master-manufacturers complain much of the bad effects of high wages in raising the price, and thereby lessening the sale of their goods both at home and abroad. They say nothing concerning the bad effects of high profits. They are silent with regard to the pernicious effects of their own gains. They complain only of those of other people.[2]

The contrast is significant. It is still more deeply marked in that phrase which one is surprised not to see more frequently quoted by the champions of labour legislation. "Whenever the legislature attempts to regulate the differences between masters and their workmen, its counsellors are always the masters. When the regulation, therefore, is in favour of the workmen, it is always just and equitable; but it is sometimes otherwise when in favour of the masters."[3]

This is not the tone of most of his contemporaries. Nor do we meet with this note in the writings of the appointed champions of the industrial system—the McCullochs, the Ures, and the Babbages of the next fifty years. His words ring with that generous pity which proved a source of inspiration to Lord Shaftesbury and Michael Sadler in their efforts to secure the passing of the Factory Act of 1833.

Smith cannot, accordingly, be regarded as the herald of dawning

[1] W. R. Scott, *Adam Smith as Student and Professor* (Jackson, Glasgow, 1937), p. 332.
[2] *Wealth of Nations*, Book I, chapter ix, *in fine*; Cannan, Vol. I, p. 100.
[3] *Ibid.*, Book I, chapter x, Part II; Vol. I, p. 143.

industrialism. He clung to agriculture with all the tenacity of his nature, and no opportunity of showing his preference was ever missed. The difficulties of agriculture are quite beyond those of any other craft. "After what are called the fine arts, and the liberal professions, however, there is perhaps no trade which requires so great a variety of knowledge and experience."[1] Not only is it more difficult, but it is also more useful. Between agriculture, manufacture, and commerce he draws a long comparison (to which we shall have to make reference again) purporting to show that of all employments agriculture is the most profitable field of investment, and the one most in accord with the general interest. For the more progressive nations "the natural course of things" would seem to suggest the investment of capital firstly in agriculture, in the second place in industry, and finally in foreign trade. The whole of Book III is an endeavour to show how the policy of European nations had for many centuries been hostile to agriculture and how the natural order had been inverted in the interests of merchants and artisans. Agriculture had always been the victim. In his theory of taxation he shows how a portion of the taxes on profits and wages ultimately falls upon property. In his discussion of duties on imported corn—those duties which aroused the indignation of Ricardo against the landlords—he reveals the same partiality. And he even goes the length of saying that it is not because of their personal interest, but owing solely to a badly conceived imitation of the doings of merchants and manufacturers, that "the country gentlemen and farmers of Great Britain so far forgot the generosity which is natural to their station, as to demand the exclusive privilege of supplying their countrymen with corn and butchers'-meat."[2]

Smith's preference for agriculture and agriculturists need not be further insisted upon. Despite his own theory of division of labour, he still cherished a secret regard for the Physiocratic prejudice. He never subjected agriculture to the indignity of equal treatment along with other forms of economic activity. In his work at least it still retains its ancient pre-eminence.

II: THE 'NATURALISM' AND 'OPTIMISM' OF SMITH

In addition to the conception of the economic world as a great natural community created by division of labour, we can distinguish in Smith's work two other fundamental ideas, around which his more

---

[1] *Wealth of Nations*, Book I, chapter x, Part II; Cannan, Vol. I, p. 128. The whole passage contains a curious eulogy of proprietors and farmers.

[2] *Ibid.*, Book IV, chapter ii; Vol. I, p. 427.

characteristic theories group themselves. First is the idea of the spontaneous origin of economic institutions, and secondly their beneficent
character—or, more briefly, Smith's naturalism and optimism.

The two ideas, though frequently intermingled and sometimes even
confused in Smith's work, must be carefully distinguished by the
historian of economic thought.

Spontaneity and beneficence were intimately connected for Smith.
In the eighteenth century anything natural or spontaneous was immediately voted good, and the terms 'natural,' 'just,' and 'advantageous' were often used as synonymous. Smith did not escape the
confusion of ideas. Having shown the natural origin of economic
institutions, he imagined that at the same time he had demonstrated
their useful and beneficent character.[1] The confusion is no longer
permissible. To give a scientific demonstration of the origin of social
institutions and to gauge their value from the point of view of the
general interest are two equally legitimate but very different intellectual pursuits. We may agree with Smith that our economic organizations, both in their origin and functions, participate of the spontaneity
of natural organisms, but we may at the same time reserve judgment
as to their real worth. Pessimism no less than optimism may be engendered by contemplation of the spontaneous character of economic
institutions. While this conception of the spontaneity of economic
institutions seems to us just and fruitful, the demonstration given of
their beneficent character appears insufficient and doubtful. The
former conception is a commonplace with all the greatest economists;
the latter is rejected by the majority of them.

These two ideas which have played such an important part in the
history of economic doctrines must be separately examined.

The conception of spontaneity is the one to which Smith refers most
frequently. *Il mondo va da se*. Here at any rate he and the Physiocrats
were entirely at one. There is no need for organization, no call for
the intervention of any general will, however far-seeing or reasonable,
and no necessity for any preliminary understanding between men.
Such are the reflexions that the study of the economic world suggests
ever anew to our author. The present aspect of the economic world
is the result of the spontaneous action of millions of individuals, each
of whom follows his own sweet will, taking no heed of others, but
never doubting the ultimate result. The noble outlines of the economic
world as we know it have been traced, not by following a plan issuing

[1] For the connexion between Smith's system and the philosophy of his time see
W. Hasbach, *Die allgemeinen philosophischen Grundlagen der von F. Quesnay und A. Smith
begründeten politischen Œkonomie* (Leipzig, 1890).

complete from the brain of an organizer and deliberately carried out by an intelligent society, but by the accumulation of numberless deeds designed by a crowd of individuals in obedience to an instinctive force wholly unconscious of the work which it was encompassing.

This idea of the spontaneous constitution of the economic world is in some aspects analogous to the conception of an 'economic law' of a later period. Both ideas suggest the presence of something superior to individual wills, and imposed upon them even despite their resistance. The differences are equally marked, however, the scope of the former being far greater than that of the latter. The words 'natural law,' in the first place, suggest regularity and repetition—the constant recurrence of the same phenomena under similar conditions. This is not the aspect that particularly struck Smith. He insists less upon the constancy of economic phenomena and more on their spontaneity, their instinctive and natural character. Say's delight was to compare the economic and the physical worlds. Smith loves to regard the economic world as a living organism which creates for itself its own indispensable organs. Nowhere is the term 'economic law' employed, but his delineation of the chief economic institutions and the account of their functions always results in the same conclusion.

First of all take division of labour, which we have just studied, and which more than any other institution contributes to the increase of wealth.

This marvellous institution is "not originally the effect of any human wisdom, which foresees and intends that general opulence to which it gives occasion." "It is the necessary, though very slow and gradual, consequence of a certain propensity in human nature which has in view no such extensive utility; the propensity to truck, barter, and exchange one thing for another."[1] This tendency itself is the outcome of personal interest.

Man has almost constant occasion for the help of his brethren, and it is in vain for him to expect it from their benevolence only. He will be more likely to prevail if he can interest their self-love in his favour, and show them that it is for their advantage to do for him what he requires of them. Whoever offers to another a bargain of any kind, proposes to do this: Give me that which I want, and you shall have this which you want, is the meaning of every such offer; and it is in this manner that we obtain from one another the far greater part of those good offices which we stand in need of. It is not from the benevolence of the butcher, the brewer, or the baker that we expect our dinner, but from their regard to their own interest. We address ourselves, not to their humanity,

[1] *Wealth of Nations*, Book I, chapter ii; Cannan, Vol. I, p. 15.

but to their self-love, and never talk to them of our own necessities, but of their advantages.[1]

This gives rise to exchange, and with exchange comes division of
labour.

> And thus the certainty of being able to exchange all that surplus
> part of the produce of his own labour, which is over and above his
> own consumption, for such parts of the produce of other men's
> labour as he may have occasion for, encourages every man to apply
> himself to a particular occupation, and to cultivate and bring to
> perfection whatever talent or genius he may possess for that particu-
> lar species of business.

Division of labour is the outcome of a tendency common to all men,
the tendency to barter; and this tendency itself is spontaneously
developed under the influence of personal interest, which acts simultaneously for the benefit of each and all.

Next comes money, and nothing has so facilitated exchange or so
greatly increased wealth. Every economic treatise since Smith's has
demonstrated its advantages in terms almost identical with his. But
how did money first come to be employed? It was not by the act of
a public body, nor was it the outcome of a nation's reflective judgment.
It is simply the result of the operation of a collective instinct. Some
men who were keener than others saw the inconveniences of the truck
system. And

> in order to avoid the inconveniency of such situations, every prudent
> man in every period of society, after the first establishment of the
> division of labour, must naturally have endeavoured to manage his
> affairs in such a manner, as to have at all times by him, besides the
> peculiar produce of his own industry, a certain quantity of some
> one commodity or other, such as he imagined few people would be
> likely to refuse in exchange for the produce of their industry.[2]

Money is thus the product of the simultaneous though not concerted
action of a great number of people, each obeying his personal inclination. The intervention of the public authority is much later, and its
object is merely to guarantee by means of a design the weight and
purity of such coins as are already in circulation.

Take another well-known phenomenon—capital.[3] With the excep-

[1] The whole passage, almost word for word, may be found in Smith's course of
lectures at Glasgow, and was itself taken from Mandeville's *Fable des Abeilles*.

[2] *Wealth of Nations*, Book I, chapter iv; Cannan, Vol. I, pp. 24–25.

[3] For a long time economists were quite content with Smith's theory of capital.
Like other portions of his work, it readily became classic, and subsequent writers
simply repeated it. To-day, however, this success hardly seems to have been war-
ranted. "It can scarcely be denied," writes Cannan, "that Smith left the whole
subject of capital in the most unsatisfactory state." (*Theories of Production and Distribu-*

tion of division of labour and the invention of money, Smith thought
there was no phenomenon of greater importance and no more essential
fount of national wealth than capital. The larger the store of capital,
the greater the number of productive workers, makers of tools and
machinery—the essentials of increased productivity—the further will
division of labour extend. To increase a nation's capital is to expand
its industry and to further its well-being.[1] In some passages the growth
of wealth appears not merely as the chief but as the only method of
augmenting a nation's wealth. "The industry of the society can
augment only in proportion as its capital augments, and its capital
can augment only in proportion to what can be gradually saved out
of its revenue."[2] In short, capital limits industry,[3] a phrase that was
destined to become classic, and one that was repeated by every economist down to Mill. Capital is the true source of economic life. Let
capital increase and industry will expand in every direction; diminish
it, and a bar is set to all improvement. Capital fertilizes the earth,
whereas the labour of man simply leaves it a weary waste.

Criticism has been freely levelled at this exaggerated importance
which capital is made to assume. It is certainly somewhat curious

tion, p. 89.) If this remark needs any justification we have it in the many discussions
which have taken place on this subject during the past, and which are not yet at an
end. Some of the most original works of the last century—Böhm-Bawerk's *Positive
Theory of Capital*, for example—are entirely taken up with this topic. In England,
America, and Italy the best-known economists, Cannan, Fisher, and Pareto, have
recently revived the ancient notions, and the discussions which have followed are
sufficient evidence that Smith had by no means exhausted the subject. If we carefully read Book II of the *Wealth of Nations*, which is entirely devoted to this topic,
what do we find? We have a distinction drawn between fixed and circulating capital
borrowed from practical affairs, but possessing no great scientific value; the very
doubtful identification of national capital with the sum of private capitals; a very
unsatisfactory attempt at differentiating between the notions of capital and revenue;
the affirmation that saving involves consumption, a paradox repeated *ad nauseam*
down to the days of Mill; the commonplace statement that capital increases as saving
grows; and, finally, the proposition that "capital limits industry."

[1] *Wealth of Nations*, Book II, chapter iii; Cannan, Vol. I, p. 325. "The annual
produce of the land and labour of any nation can be increased in its value by no
other means, but by increasing either the number of its productive labourers, or the
productive powers of those labourers who had before been employed. The number
of its productive labourers, it is evident, can never be much increased, but in consequence of an increase of capital, or of the funds destined for maintaining them. The
productive powers of the same number of labourers cannot be increased, but in
consequence either of some addition and improvement to those machines and instruments which facilitate and abridge labour; or of a more proper division and distribution of employment. In either case an additional capital is almost always required."

[2] *Ibid.*, Book IV, chapter ii; Vol. I, p. 423.

[3] "The general industry of the society never can exceed what the capital of the
society can employ." (*Ibid.*, Book IV, chapter ii; Vol. I, p. 419.) John Stuart Mill
was the first to employ the formula in its condensed form, "Industry is limited by
capital."

that labour should now be treated as altogether subordinate to capital, whereas earlier in the volume labour alone was regarded as the great wealth-producing agent. But we are not here concerned with the revival of these threadbare controversies.[1] We merely wish to note that Smith finds in this accumulation of capital a new illustration of spontaneity. The saving of capital is not the result of any foresight on the part of society, but is solely due to the simultaneous and concurrent actions of thousands of individuals. These individuals, urged on by a desire to better their situation, are spontaneously urged to save their earnings and to employ those savings productively.

> The principle which prompts to save, is the desire of bettering our condition, a desire which, though generally calm and dispassionate, comes with us from the womb, and never leaves us till we go into the grave. . . . An augmentation of fortune is the means by which the greater part of men propose and wish to better their condition. It is the means the most vulgar and the most obvious; and the most likely way of augmenting their fortune, is to save and accumulate some part of what they acquire.

This desire is so powerful that even the greatest follies perpetrated by governments have never succeeded in annulling its beneficial effects.

> The uniform, constant, and uninterrupted effort of every man to better his condition, the principle from which public and national as well as private opulence is originally derived, is frequently powerful enough to maintain the natural progress of things toward improvement, in spite both of the extravagance of government, and of the greatest errors of administration. Like the unknown principle of animal life, it frequently restores health and vigour to the constitution, in spite, not only of the disease, but of the absurd prescriptions of the doctor.[2]

But the idea of the spontaneity of economic institutions finds its most interesting illustration in the theory of demand and supply, upon which we must dwell a little.

In a society based upon division of labour, where every one produces for a market without previous arrangement with his fellow producers

---

[1] We have spoken of the controversies as threadbare, for every economist is by this time persuaded that, assuming the necessity for the co-operation of capital, land, and labour in production, it is quite clear that the amount of produce raised must depend upon the amount of each of these factors employed, and not upon the amount of any one of them.

Smith had anticipated the arguments advanced by such socialists as Rodbertus and Lassalle, who regard saving rather than labour as the source of capital. "Parsimony, and not industry, is the immediate cause of the increase of capital. Industry, indeed, provides the subject which parsimony accumulates. But whatever industry might acquire, if parsimony did not save and store up, the capital would never be the greater." (*Wealth of Nations*, Book II, chapter iii; Cannan, Vol. I, p. 320.)

[2] *Ibid.*, Book II, chapter iii; Vol. I, pp. 323, 324, 325.

and without any external direction, the great difficulty lies in the adapting of the amount of goods supplied to the amount demanded. How, as a matter of fact, are these producers to know at any particular moment what they ought to produce and in what quantities? Moreover, who is to direct and who can restrain them? It is true that Smith was careful to point out that they are not concerned with the satisfaction of all needs, of whatever kind they may be. Their duty lies towards what he calls the "effectual," not the "absolute," demand. By effectual demand we are to understand the demand of those who are capable of offering not merely something in exchange for the products which they desire, but of offering at least enough to cover the expenses of raising those products.[1] Society founded upon division of labour and exchange implies that nothing can be gratuitous and every loss involves a sacrifice on the part of some person or other.[2] But if production is carried on in this haphazard fashion how are we to avoid an occasional over-production or an accidental under-supply?

Before we can understand this we must acquaint ourselves with Adam Smith's theory of prices.

In the preceding chapter we had occasion to note how Condillac in 1776 put forward a theory of value which was altogether superior to the Physiocrats'. Smith's book, also published in 1776, betrays not the least sign of Condillac's influence, and the new theory never comes up for discussion. The very success of the *Wealth of Nations* had eclipsed the fame of the French philosopher, and Smith's theory, though quite inferior to Condillac's, held the field for so many years simply because

---

[1] *Wealth of Nations*, Book I, chapter vii; Cannan, Vol. I, p. 58. "The market price of every particular commodity is regulated by the proportion between the quantity which is actually brought to market, and the demand of those who are willing to pay the natural price of the commodity, or the whole value of the rent, labour, and profit, which must be paid in order to bring it thither. Such people may be called the effectual demanders, and their demand the effectual demand; since it may be sufficient to effectuate the bringing of the commodity to market. It is different from the absolute demand. A very poor man may be said in some sense to have a demand for a coach and six; he might like to have it; but his demand is not an effectual demand, as the commodity can never be brought to market in order to satisfy it."

[2] For Smith oppression meant the tyranny either of producers or consumers. When profits are above the normal rate "it is a proof that something is either bought cheaper or sold dearer than it ought to be, and that some particular class of citizens is more or less oppressed either by paying more or by getting less than what is suitable to that equality which ought to take place, and which naturally does take place among all the different classes of them." (*Ibid.*, Book IV, chapter vii, Part III; Vol. II, p. 128.)

The correspondence between selling price and the cost of production seemed to Smith to be of the very essence of justice. Complete correspondence would realize the ideal of the just price.

it won the allegiance of the English economists, whose influence was paramount throughout the first half of the nineteenth century. Its popularity only waned with the publication of the works of Walras, Jevons, and Menger. Its historic interest is further enhanced by the fact that it had the singular good fortune to win the approval both of the socialists and the Liberal economists. It is the fate of writers like Smith, remarkable for wealth of ideas rather than for logical presentation, to impel minds along different and sometimes even opposite paths. Unfortunately the theory of value is not the only one that presents a somewhat hazy outline. We cannot here enter into the details of the theory, but must content ourselves with a mere sketch of it. Even this, however, will immediately enable us to understand its insufficiency, and appreciate the twofold influence which it exercised upon subsequent doctrines.

Smith opens his treatment by emphasizing the fundamental distinction which exists between 'value in use' and 'value in exchange.'[1] By value in use he means almost[2] exactly what we understand by utility, or what other writers call subjective value, desirability, or ophelimity.

Present-day economists when treating of prices—the exchange value of things—chiefly rely upon this conception of 'value in use.' The explanation of the 'ratio of exchange' of commodities is based upon a previous analysis of their utility for those who exchange them. Smith proceeds in a different fashion. 'Value in use' is mentioned, but only for the purpose of contrasting it with value in exchange. It is then dismissed without further consideration. The two notions seem to have no point of contact. Value in exchange was the only one that

---

[1] *Wealth of Nations*, Book I, chapter iv; Cannan, Vol. I, p. 30. The passage is well known. "The word 'value,' it is to be observed, has two different meanings, and sometimes expresses the utility of some particular object, and sometimes the power of purchasing other goods which the possession of that object conveys. The one may be called 'value in use,' the other 'value in exchange.' The things which have the greatest value in use have frequently little or no value in exchange; and, on the contrary, those which have the greatest value in exchange have frequently little or no value in use. Nothing is more useful than water: but it will purchase scarce anything; scarce anything can be had in exchange for it. A diamond, on the contrary, has scarce any value in use; but a very great quantity of other goods may frequently be had in exchange for it."

[2] The statement has been qualified because in the passage referred to Smith seems to define utility in the vulgar sense (*i.e.*, utility as contrasted with mere agreeableness). This want of exactness was corrected by Ricardo, and is the subject of a searching criticism by Mill. The following passage from his *Lectures on Justice* may serve to throw some light upon the definition: "There is no demand for a thing of little use; it is not a rational object of desire." Smith could not conceive the possibility of a demand or even a desire for a commodity which was useless from a rational point of view. But this is evidently a great mistake.

was of any interest to Smith; hence there was all the more reason for denying its derivative character.[1]

Thus from the very first the only avenue that might have led to a satisfactory solution of this problem of prices was closed. One could easily have predicted that this was bound to land Smith in difficulty; as a matter of fact he is doubly involved.[2] Two different but equally erroneous solutions have been successively adopted by him, but he has never actually decided between them. The socialists and economists who are to follow will be engaged in the same task, and the cleavage between them will be marked by their adoption of one or other of these two theories.

Smith was led to the study of prices because he wished to know something of the constant oscillation which is such a feature of their history. The actual or market price is unstable because of the unstable connexion between demand and supply,[3] or, as he puts it, "It is adjusted, however, not by any accurate measure, but by the higgling and bargaining of the market, according to that sort of rough equality which, though not exact, is sufficient for carrying on the business of common life."[4] It seemed impossible that their perpetual fluctuation should represent the true value of the commodity. Its real value could not vary from this moment to the next or from one place to another. Underneath the constantly oscillating market price may be discerned another price, referred to by Smith as the real or sometimes as the natural price. The discovery of a more stable and a more constant element beneath the continual fluctuations of price movements still constitutes the great problem of pure economics.[5]

Smith's first theory makes the true value of any commodity depend upon the amount of labour or effort which it has taken to produce. "Labour, therefore, is the real measure of the exchangeable value of all

[1] The radical separation of the two ideas was perhaps more a matter of expression than of reasoning, for in his *Lectures on Justice*, p. 176, value in use, coupled with the purchasing power possessed by those who desired the commodity, was regarded as one of the elements which determined the demand for it and fixed its market price. The whole discussion of the theory of value by Smith is very unsatisfactory.

[2] We ought perhaps to have said that he had to choose between three possible definitions, for in the *Lectures on Justice* we find a third definition of 'natural price' (p. 176).

[3] *Wealth of Nations*, Book I, chapter vii; Cannan, Vol. I, p. 58.

[4] *Ibid.*, Book I, chapter v; Vol. I, p. 33.

[5] Pareto in his recent article *L'Économie et la Sociologie au point de vue scientifique* (*Rivista di Scienza*, 1907, No. 2) expresses himself as follows: "Underneath the actual prices quoted on the exchanges, prices varying according to the exigencies of time and place and dependent upon an infinite number of circumstances, is there nothing which has any constancy or is in any degree less variable? This is the problem that political economy must solve."

D

commodities." "The real price of every thing, what every thing really costs to the man who wants to acquire it, is the toil and trouble of acquiring it."[1] Labour—that is, the effort expended upon the production of a commodity—is both the origin and the measure of its exchange value. The theory that labour or effort is the cause of value (if value can be said to have a cause) was first formulated by the father of political economy himself. It is curious to think that it was this same theory that was used with such good effect by Karl Marx in his attack upon capitalism.

This first attempt to find a firmer foundation for exchange value than that afforded by the shifting sands of demand and supply was scarcely made before Smith became aware of some difficulties in the path. For example, how was this work and the value dependent upon it to be measured?

> There may be more labour in an hour's hard work than in two hours' easy business; or in an hour's application to a trade which it cost ten years' labour to learn, than in a month's industry at an ordinary and obvious employment. But it is not easy to find any accurate measure either of hardship or ingenuity.[2]

A second objection arises when the theory is applied to civilized society. Work by itself cannot produce anything; something must be contributed by both land and capital. But neither of these is a free good, and they must cost something to those who employ them. Accordingly primitive societies[3] are the only ones where "the quantity of labour commonly employed in acquiring or producing any commodity" is the only circumstance determining its value. We must nowadays take some account of land and capital. So that labour is not the only source of value, nor is it its sole measure.

Another hypothesis becomes necessary forthwith. This time cost of production is hit upon as the likely regulator of value. Hitherto the 'real' price has signified the price that is based upon labour. Now the 'natural' price is defined as the price of goods valued at their cost of production. The change of name is not of any great significance. What Smith was in search of on both occasions was that true value

[1] *Wealth of Nations*, Book I, chapter v; Cannan, Vol. I, p. 32. In this passage Smith seems to imply that the value of an object is determined, not by the amount of labour which it cost to produce it, but by the amount of labour which can be bought in exchange for it. Fundamentally the two ideas are one, for objects of equal value only can be exchanged, so that the amount of labour anyone can buy with any given object is equal to the amount of labour which that object cost to produce. "Goods," says Smith, "contain the value of a certain quantity of labour, which we exchange for what is supposed at the time to contain the value of an equal quantity."

[2] *Ibid.*, Book I, chapter v; Vol. I, p. 33.

[3] *Ibid.*, Book I, chapter vi; Vol. I, pp. 49–50.

which always kept in hiding behind the fluctuations of market prices. It is the same problem, but with a new solution. Just now we were informed that if a commodity sold at a price representing the labour which it cost to produce, that price would also represent its real cost. With no less assurance we are now told that a commodity sold at cost of production "is then sold precisely for what it is worth, or for what it really costs the person who brings it to market."[1] The true value of goods corresponds to their cost of production. By this we are to understand a sum sufficient to pay at normal rates the wages of labour, the interest of capital, and the rent of land, all of which have collaborated in the production of the particular commodity.

Smith, having discarded labour, finds a new determinant of value in cost of production, and if socialists rallied to his first hypothesis the great majority of economists right up to Jevons have clung to his second. As for Smith himself, he never had the courage to choose between them. They remain juxtaposed in the *Wealth of Nations* because he never made up his mind which to adopt. As a result his work is full of contradictions which it would be futile to try to reconcile. For example, land and capital in one place are regarded as sources of new values, adding to and increasing the value which labour creates, and producing normally an element of profit and rent, which, together with the wages of labour, makes up the cost of production. In another connexion they are treated as deductions made by capitalists and landlords from the value created by labour alone.[2] Some writers

---

[1] *Wealth of Nations*, Book I, chapter vii; Cannan, vol I, p. 57.

[2] *Ibid.*, Book I, chapter vi; Vol. I, p. 51. Here, for example, is a passage in which, as Böhm-Bawerk forcibly remarks (*Kapital und Kapitalzins*, 2nd ed., 1900, p. 84), the two conceptions are found in juxtaposition without any attempt at reconciliation: "In this state of things [where labour and capital have already been appropriated] the whole produce of labour does not always belong to the labourer. He must in most cases share it with the owner of the stock which employs him. Neither is the quantity of labour commonly employed in acquiring or producing any commodity, the only circumstance which can regulate the quantity which it ought commonly to purchase, command, or exchange for. An additional quantity, it is evident, must be due for the profits of the stock which advanced the wages and furnished the materials of that labour." At the beginning of the passage the workman shared the produce of his labour and profits constituted a deduction from the value created by labour alone; at the end of the paragraph profits issue from a supplementary value which is an addition to the value already given it by labour. Other passages where the two conceptions come into contact are also cited by Böhm-Bawerk. Interest and rent are also occasionally taken as evidence that the workman is being exploited, and this entitles Smith to be regarded as the father of socialism. More than one passage in his work seems to point to this conclusion. "In other countries, rent and profit eat up wages, and the two superior orders of people oppress the inferior one." (Book IV, chapter vii, Part II; Vol. II, p. 67.) Concerning property he writes: "Civil government, so far as it is instituted for the security of property, is in reality instituted for the defence of the rich against the poor, or of those who have some property against

accordingly argue that Smith must have been a socialist. On the whole the cost of production theory prevailed, and the natural price of commodities is taken to mean that price which coincides with their cost of production. As to market price, he makes the remark that it is higher or lower than the natural price according as the quantity offered diminishes or increases as compared with the quantity demanded.

Such is Smith's theory of prices. The element of truth which it contains, namely, that the prices of goods tend to coincide with their cost of production (the remark is not originally Smith's at all), must not blind us to its many faults. It is open to at least two very serious objections.

An attempt is made to explain the price of goods by referring to the price of the services (wages, interest, and rent) which make up the cost of production. When the cost of those services comes up for consideration it is assumed that their cost is dependent upon the price of the goods. Wages, for example, are determined by the selling price of the commodities which labour has produced. Escape from the vicious circle is only possible by availing ourselves of the modern theory of economic equilibrium. That theory shows us how prices generally, whether of goods or of services, are interdependent; all being determined simultaneously—like the unknown in an algebraical formula—just when the exchange is taking place. But this theory of economic equilibrium was, of course, unknown to Smith.

Cost of production being the regulator of price, it is very important that an analysis of cost of production and a study of the causes which determine the rates of wages, profit, and rent should be made. One might have expected that this study would have cleared away any obscurity that still clung to the theory of prices. But this analysis is one of the least satisfactory portions of Smith's work. We have already had occasion to note the unsatisfactory character of his theory of rent.

---

those who have none at all." (Book V, chapter i, Part II; Vol. II, p. 207.) And finally there is the famous passage from the sixth chapter: "As soon as the land of any country has all become private property, the landlords, like all other men, love to reap where they never sowed, and demand a rent even for its natural produce. . . . He [the workman] must then pay for the licence to gather them; and must give up to the landlord a portion of what his labour either collects or produces. This portion, or, what comes to the same thing, the price of this portion, constitutes the rent of land, and in the price of the greater part of commodities makes a third component part." (Book I, chapter vi; Vol. I, p. 51.) Dr Cannan in his *History of the Theories of Production and Distribution* goes the length of declaring that the theory of spoliation is the only one in Smith's work. It is to Smith that we owe that idea so frequently expressed by socialists, namely, that the workman in modern society never really obtains the produce of his toil.

That of profits—which Smith fails to distinguish from interest—is equally useless;[1] and his theory of wages is hopelessly inconsistent. He hesitates between the subsistence theory of wages and the other theory which makes them depend upon the relations between demand and supply, without ever making a final choice.

We cannot agree with Say in considering Smith's theory of distribution one of his best claims to fame. His treatment of this problem, which afterwards became the kernel of Ricardian economics, is altogether inferior to his handling of production. We also know that this is the least original part of his work. It was simply added as a kind of afterthought, the original intention being to deal only with production. This becomes evident if we compare the *Wealth of Nations* with the Glasgow course of 1763, the whole of which is devoted to production. The addition of a theory of distribution to the original skeleton was probably due to the Physiocrats, with whom in the meantime he had become acquainted; and the hesitations and uncertainties which mar this part of the work merely go to prove that Smith had not thought it out as clearly as the other sections.

The subject cannot be pursued here. We can only point to the inference which Smith draws from his theory of value, and how it is made to support the contention that demand adapts itself spontaneously to the conditions of supply. This is how Smith explains the continual oscillation of prices:

> When the quantity brought to market exceeds the effectual demand, it cannot be all sold to those who are willing to pay the whole value of the rent, wages and profit, which must be paid in order to bring it thither. Some part must be sold to those who are willing to pay less, and the low price which they give for it must reduce the price of the whole. The market price will sink more or less below the natural price according as the greatness of the excess increases more or less the competition of the sellers, or according as it happens to be more or less important to them to get immediately rid of the commodity.

The reverse will happen when demand exceeds supply.

> When the quantity brought to market is just sufficient to supply the effectual demand and no more, the market price naturally comes to be either exactly, or as nearly as can be judged of, the same with the natural price. The whole quantity upon hand can be disposed of for this price, and cannot be disposed of for more. The competition of the different dealers obliges them all to accept of this price, but does not oblige them to accept of less.

[1] *Cf. supra*, p. 82, note 1.

Thus "the quantity of every commodity brought to market naturally suits itself to the effectual demand."[1]

And this very remarkable result is simply the outcome of personal interest.

> If at any time it exceeds the effectual demand, some of the component parts of its price must be paid below their natural rate. If it is rent, the interest of the landlords will immediately prompt them to withdraw a part of their land; and if it is wages or profit, the interest of the labourers in the one case, and of their employers in the other, will prompt them to withdraw a part of their labour or stock from this employment. The quantity brought to market will soon be no more than sufficient to supply the effectual demand. All the different parts of its price will rise to their natural rate, and the whole price to the natural price.

And so, in the majority of cases at least, this natural and spontaneous mechanism secures a constant balancing of the quantities of goods produced and the quantities effectively demanded. The circumstances under which such a result does not follow are really quite exceptional—although Smith does not deny that sometimes they do exist. Whenever such conditions obtain—that is, when the market price remains for a considerable length of time above the natural price—we find that it is always due to the capitalists' action in concealing the high rate of profits which they draw, or in retaining possession of some patent or natural monopoly, such as wine of a special quality. It occasionally happens also as the result of an artificial monopoly.[2] But these are mere exceptions, their rare occurrence confirming the fundamental rule concerning the spontaneous adaptation of the quantity offered to the quantity demanded, thanks to this oscillation of the market price about the natural.

This theory of adaptation, we know, is one of the most important in the whole of political economy. Since Smith wrote it has been reproduced by almost every economist, and without any very substantial alteration. It remains even to this day the basis of our theory of production.

It is interesting to note the manner in which Smith makes use of his theory to illustrate his thesis. We shall refer to two cases which are intrinsically important as well as affording admirable illustrations of that spontaneity upon which Smith laid such stress.

[1] *Wealth of Nations*, Book I, chapter vii; Cannan, Vol. I, p. 59.
[2] Smith only gives at most seven or eight lines to monopoly price. He simply states that "the price of monopoly is upon every occasion the highest which can be got." (*Ibid.*, Book I, chapter vii; Vol. I, p. 63.) To-day the theory of monopoly prices is one of the most important in the whole of economics.

The first concerns population. Population, like commodities, may be superabundant or it may be insufficient. What regulates its numbers? "The number of people," Smith replies,

> depends upon the demand of society, and this is how it works. Among the proletariat, generally speaking, children are plentiful enough. It is only when wages are very low that poverty and misery cause the death of many of them; but when wages are fairly high several of them manage to reach maturity.

"It deserves to be remarked, too," he continues,

> that it necessarily does this as nearly as possible in the proportion which the demand for labour requires. If this demand is continually increasing, the reward of labour must necessarily encourage in such a manner the marriage and multiplication of labourers as may enable them to supply that continually increasing demand by a continually increasing population. If the reward should at any time be less than what was requisite for this purpose, the deficiency of hands would soon raise it; and if it should at any time be more, their excessive multiplication would soon lower it to this necessary rate. The market would be so much under-stocked with labour in the one case, and so much over-stocked in the other, as would soon force back its price to that proper rate which the circumstances of the society required. It is in this manner that the demand for men, like that for any other commodity, necessarily regulates the production of men; quickens it when it goes on too slowly, and stops it when it advances too fast.[1]

The second case relates to the demand for money and its supply. We have already seen how the problem of its origin is solved. Alongside of that problem is now placed another, namely, how is the quantity in circulation regulated to meet the requirements of exchange? Smith's first task was to expose the popular fallacy concerning this topic.[2] According to one school of thinkers, money was wealth *par excellence*, and it was all the more important that he should get rid of this view seeing that it constituted the very foundation of the Mercantile theory, the overthrow of which was the immediate object in publishing the *Wealth of Nations*. The Mercantilists contended that a country should export more than it imports, receiving the balance in money. If it can be proved that this balance is useless because money is a mere commodity possessing no greater and no less utility than any other, then the Mercantilist foundation is completely destroyed.

[1] *Wealth of Nations*, Book I, chapter viii; Cannan, Vol. I, pp. 81–82.
[2] "That wealth consists in money, or in gold and silver, is a popular notion which naturally arises from the double function of money, as the instrument of commerce, and as the measure of value." (*Wealth of Nations*, Book IV, chapter i; Cannan, Vol. I, p. 396.) The whole chapter is an attempt to get rid of this prejudice.

Smith thought that money was less indispensable than some other goods, seeing that we are anxious to pass it on as often as we can. The disdain with which Smith regarded money was the result of a reaction against Mercantilism, and it led some of his followers to over-emphasize his point of view and to misconceive the special character of monetary phenomena. A nation's true wealth "consists," Smith tells us, "not in its gold and silver only, but in its lands, houses, and consumable goods of all different kinds."[1] "It is the annual produce of the land and labour of the society."[2] Hence in evaluating a country's net revenue we must omit money, because it is not consumed. It only serves as an instrument for the circulation of wealth and for the measurement of value. It is the "great wheel of circulation."[3] In virtue of this title, although Smith himself classed money along with circulating capital, he remarks that it might be likened to the fixed capital of an industry, to machinery or workshops. The greater the economy in the use of fixed capital, provided there is no diminution in production, the better, for the larger will be the net product. This is equally true of money—a necessary but a very costly instrument of social production. "Every saving in the expence of collecting and supporting that part of the circulating capital which consists in money is an improvement of exactly the same kind"[4] as that which reduces the fixed capital of industry.[5]

This is why bank-notes—the circulation of which diminishes the quantity of money needed—have proved such a precious invention. What they do is to set free a certain quantity of gold and silver which may be sent abroad to pay for machinery and other instruments of

[1] *Wealth of Nations*, Book IV, chapter i; Cannan, Vol. I, p. 416; also Book II, chapter ii; Vol. I, p. 274. "Though the weekly or yearly revenue of all the different inhabitants of any country in the same manner, may be, and in reality frequently is, paid to them in money, their real riches, however, the real weekly or yearly revenue of all of them taken together, must always be great or small in proportion to the quantity of consumable goods which they can all of them purchase with this money. The whole revenue of all of them taken together is evidently not equal to both the money and the consumable goods; but only to one or other of those two values, to the latter more properly than to the former."

[2] We meet with this expression several times: in the Introduction (Vol. I, p. 4), in Book I, chapter xi, Part III (Vol. I, p. 240), and in Book II, chapter iii (Vol. I, pp. 315, 323).

[3] An expression that is met with three times—in chapter ii of Book II (Vol. I, pp. 272, 275, 279).

[4] *Ibid.*, Book II, chapter ii; Vol. I, p. 275.

[5] All these questions so obscurely treated in Smith's work are handled with admirable lucidity in Irving Fisher's *Nature of Capital and Income* (New York, 1907). Revenue is entirely stripped of that material suggestion which was always associated with it in Smith's work, and is looked upon as a continual flow of services, while capital as a whole is regarded as total wealth existing at one particular moment and from which these services flow out.

production, and which will in turn increase the true revenue of the country. Smith's parable in which he illustrates these advantages has long since become classic:

> The gold and silver money which circulates in any country may very properly be compared to a highway, which, while it circulates and carries to market all the grass and corn of the country, produces itself not a single pile of either. The judicious operations of banking, by providing, if I may be allowed so violent a metaphor, a sort of waggon-way through the air, enable the country to convert, as it were, a great part of its highways into good pastures and cornfields, and thereby to increase very considerably the annual produce of its land and labour.[1]

The conclusion is that every policy—the Mercantilist, for example—which aims at increasing the quantity of money within the country, whether by direct or indirect methods, is absurd, for money, far from being indispensable, is really an encumbrance.

It is not only absurd, but also useless. Have we not seen already that money is a mere commodity designed to facilitate circulation and that the demand for it is entirely determined by that object? But the supply of any commodity usually adapts itself spontaneously to the demand for it. No one concerns himself with supplying the nation with wine or with crockery. Why trouble about money?[2] If the quantity of goods diminishes, exchange slackens and a part of the money becomes useless. But the "interest of whoever possesses it requires that it should be employed."[3] Accordingly "it will, in spite of all laws and prohibitions, be sent abroad, and employed in purchasing consumable goods which may be of some use at home."

On the other hand, as the prosperity of a nation grows it necessarily attracts the precious metals because a multiplication of exchanges leads to a growing demand for money. These exportations and importations will depend, as Hume[4] had already shown, upon the relative cheapness or dearness of money. What is true of metallic money is also true of a special kind of money known as bank-notes. Smith has given us a vivid description of the functions of banks, and especially of the fortunes of the most famous bank of this period, the Bank of Amsterdam. This afforded him another opportunity of demonstrating how the quantity of notes offered spontaneously adapts itself to the quantity demanded. If banks issue more notes than the

[1] *Wealth of Nations*, Book II, chapter ii; Cannan, Vol. I, p. 304.
[2] *Ibid.*, Book IV, chapter i; Vol. I, pp. 402, 406.
[3] *Ibid.*, Book II, chapter iii; Vol. I, p. 322.
[4] Hume's treatment of the quantity theory of money in his essays on *Money* and *The Balance of Trade* is much clearer than Smith's.

circulation warrants prices will rise. Buying from foreign countries
will be resorted to and the notes will be returned to the banks to be
exchanged for gold and silver—the only international money. The
banks clearly have no interest in issuing too many notes, because it
involves a greater metallic reserve as the result of the more frequent
demands for payment which they will have to face. Of course, "every
particular banking company has not always understood or attended
to its own particular interest, and the circulation has frequently been
overstocked with paper money."[1] But this does not affect the main
principle, and we have one further proof of the spontaneous activity
of the economic mechanism.

We have now reviewed some of Smith's principal themes, and we
have seen how every phenomenon impresses him in the same fashion.
Had space permitted we might have cited other examples all pointing
to the same conclusion.[2] This conception of spontaneity and wise
beneficence is by no means the product of mere *a priori* thinking. It
was no abstract theory that needed the backing of a rigid demonstration. It was a belief gradually borne in upon him in the course of his
review of the economic field. This is characteristic of all his thought,
and with every new vista we are reminded of it. The conclusion is
hinted at again and again, and the impression left upon the reader's
mind is that no other conclusion could ever be possible. Smith thought
of the economic order as an organism—the creation of a thousand
human wills unconscious of the end whither they are tending, but all
of them obedient to the impulse of one instinctive, powerful force.
This force, the root of all economic activity, its constancy and uniformity triumphant over every artificial obstacle and giving unity to
the whole system, what is it?

We have already encountered it on more than one occasion. It is
personal interest, or, as Smith prefers to call it, "the natural effort of
every individual to better his own condition."[3] Hidden deep in the
heart of every individual lies this essential spring of human life and
social progress.

Doubtless it is not the only one. Smith is never exclusive. He knew

[1] *Wealth of Nations*, Book II, chapter ii; Cannan, Vol. I, p. 285.
[2] For instance, a high rate of exchange immediately readjusts the commercial
indebtedness of nations. (*Ibid.*, Book IV, chapter i; Vol. I, p. 400.) Elsewhere he
points out that the advantages enjoyed by Europe from the possession of colonies were
not exactly sought by her. The search for colonies, their discovery and exploitation,
all this was undertaken without any preconceived plan, and in spite of the disastrous
regulations imposed by European Governments. (*Ibid.*, Book IV, chapter vii, Part II;
Vol. II, pp. 90, 91.)
[3] *Ibid.*, Book II, chapter iii; Vol. I, p. 323: Book IV, chapter v; Vol. II, p. 43:
Book IV, chapter ix; Vol. II, p. 172.

that there were other passions[1] besides self-interest, and he is not afraid of naming them, as when he attributes an economic revolution which had such beneficial effects as the emancipation of the rural classes to "the most childish vanity of proprietors."[2] Neither did he omit to point out that personal interest is not equally strong in the breast of every one, and that there is the greatest diversity in human motives. All this he had forgotten, according to some of his critics, while others charge him with the creation of the *homo œconomicus*, a poor representation of reality and a mere automaton exclusively guided by material interests. Some one has remarked that if you add to this figure a tinge of patriotism you have a faithful picture of the English-man and Scotsman of his day. Had he been acquainted with Germans or Frenchmen, with their less sordid attachment to material gain, he might have judged differently. It may be that our reading of him is incorrect. He seems to have taken care to note that his remarks do not apply to *all*, but only to the generality of men. He continually recalls the fact that he is speaking of men of common understanding,[3] or of those gifted with common prudence.[4] He knew well enough that the principles of common prudence do not always govern the conduct of *every* individual, but he was of opinion that they always influenced that of the majority of every class and order.[5] His reasoning is applic-able to men *en masse*, and not to individuals in particular. Moreover, he does not deny that man may be unacquainted with or may even entirely ignore his own interest. We have just quoted a passage wherein he remarks that bankers who temporarily issue too many notes are at that moment ignorant of their own interests.

These reservations notwithstanding, and full account being taken of all the exceptions to the principles as laid down by Smith, it is still true to say that as a general thesis he considers "the natural effort of every individual to better his own condition"—that is, personal in-terest—as the fundamental psychological motive in political economy. Any reference to the case of business men who are really actuated by a desire to take general welfare as their guide in matters of conduct is treated with a measure of scepticism which it is difficult not to share. "I have never known much good done by those who affected to trade

[1] "It is thus that the private interests and passions of individuals naturally dispose them to turn their stock towards the employments which in ordinary cases are most advantageous to the society." The word 'passions' was not inserted by chance. It occurs no less than three times on the same page. (*Wealth of Nations*, Book IV, chapter vii, Part III; Cannan, Vol. II, p. 129.)
[2] *Ibid.*, Book III, chapter iv; Vol. I, pp. 389, 390.
[3] *Ibid.*, Book II, chapter i, *in fine*; Vol. I, p. 267.
[4] *Ibid.*, Book II, chapter iv, beginning of chapter; Vol. I, p. 332.
[5] *Ibid.*, Book II, chapter ii; Vol. I, p. 278.

for the public good. It is an affectation, indeed, not very common among merchants, and very few words need be employed in dissuading them from it."[1] Not that sentiment does not play a part, and a important part, in the philosophy of Smith; but sentiment, or sympathy, as he calls it, has the domain of morality for its own, while interest dominates that of economics. All his thinking led him to a firm belief in a spontaneous economic order founded and guided by self-interest.

Comparison with the Physiocratic doctrine concerning the natural and essential order of societies is illuminating. To the Physiocrats the 'natural order' implied a system—an ideal. It required a genius to discover it, and only an enlightened despotism could realize it. For Smith the 'spontaneous order' was a fact. It was not a thing to be brought into being. It already existed. It was doubtless held in check by a hundred imperfections, including, among others, the stupidity of human legislation.[2] But it was triumphant over them all. Beneath the artificial constitution of society lay the natural constitution which completely dominated it. This natural constitution, which for the Physiocrats was nothing more than an ideal, Smith discovered in actual operation, and he was able to describe its *modus operandi*. Political economy, which with Quesnay was nothing better than a system of rules and regulations, became in Smith's hands a natural science based upon the observation and analysis of existing facts. In a passage written in his usual lucid style Smith shows the superiority of his system over that of the Physiocrats.

Some speculative physicians seem to have imagined that the health of the human body could be preserved only by a certain precise regimen of diet and exercise, of which every, the smallest, violation necessarily occasioned some degree of disease or disorder proportioned to the degree of the violation. . . . Mr Quesnai, who was himself a physician, and a very speculative physician, seems to have entertained a notion of the same kind concerning the political body, and to have imagined that it would thrive and prosper only under a certain precise regimen, the exact regimen of perfect liberty and perfect justice. He seems not to have considered that in the political body, the natural effort which every man is continually making to better his own condition, is a principle of preservation capable of preventing and correcting, in many respects, the bad effects of a political economy in some degree both partial and oppressive. Such a political œconomy, though it no doubt retards more or less, is not always capable of stopping altogether the natural progress of a nation towards wealth and prosperity, and still

[1] *Wealth of Nations*, Book IV, chapter ii; Cannan, Vol. I, p. 421. After having just said: "By pursuing his own interest, he frequently promotes that of the society more effectually than when he really intends to promote it."
[2] *Ibid.*, Book IV, chapter v; Vol. II, p. 43.

less of making it go backwards. If a nation could not prosper
without the enjoyment of perfect liberty and perfect justice, there
is not in the world a nation which could ever have prospered. In
the political body, however, the wisdom of nature has fortunately
made ample provision for remedying many of the bad effects of the
folly and injustice of man; in the same manner as it has done in
the natural body, for remedying those of his sloth and intemperance.[1]

This passage leads us to his second thesis, namely, the excellence of
these economic institutions. As we have already remarked, these two
ideas of spontaneity and excellence, though confused by Smith, ought
to be treated apart. His naturalism and optimism are inseparable,
and both of them find expression in the same paragraph. The passage
just quoted affords a proof of this. Personal interest not only creates
and maintains the economic organism, but at the same time ensures
a nation's progress towards wealth and prosperity. The institutions
are not only natural, but are also beneficial. They interest him not
merely as objects of scientific curiosity, but also as the instruments of
public weal. Herein lies their chief attraction for him, for political
economy to him was more of a practical art than a science.[2]

But this is hardly emphatic enough. Natural economic institutions are not merely good: they are providential. Divine Providence
has endowed man with a desire to better his condition, whence arises
the 'natural' social organism: so that man, following where this desire
leads, is really accomplishing the beneficent designs of God Himself.
By pursuing his own interest, man "is in this as in many other cases"
(he is writing now of the employment of capital) "led by an invisible
hand to promote an end which was no part of his intention."[3] The
Physiocrats could hardly have improved upon that.

We can scarcely share in his optimism to-day. But it has played
too prominent a role in the history of ideas not to detain us for a
moment. We must examine the arguments upon which it is based
and endeavour to grasp their import.

Let us note, in the first place, that every example hitherto deduced
with a view to proving the spontaneity of economic institutions at
the same time furnishes a demonstration of the beneficial effects of
personal interest. Owing to a coincidence by no means fortuitous
every institution mentioned by Smith as owing its existence to the

[1] *Wealth of Nations*, Book IV, chapter ix; Cannan, Vol. II, p. 172.
[2] "The great object of the political œconomy of every country, is to increase the
riches and power of that country." (*Ibid.*, Book II, chapter v; Vol. I, p. 351.) The expression "the political economy of every country," which Smith frequently employed,
might be used in answer to writers such as Knies, who speak of the Universalism or
Internationalism of Smith.
[3] *Ibid.*, Book IV, chapter ii; Vol. I, p. 421.

prevalence of action of this kind is at the same time favourable to economic progress. Division of labour, the invention of money, and the accumulation of capital are so many natural social facts that also increase wealth. The adaptation of demand and supply, the distribution of money according to the need for a circulating medium, the growth of population according to the demand for it, are so many spontaneous phenomena which ensure the efficient working of economic society. A perusal of Smith's work leaves us with the impression that these spontaneous institutions must also be the best.

The general proof of this thesis is scattered throughout the whole book. But there was one point especially upon which Smith was very anxious to show complete accord between public and private interest. This was in connexion with the investment of capital. In his opinion capital spontaneously seeks, and as spontaneously finds, the most favourable field for investment—most favourable, that is to say, to the interest of society in general. This proof at first sight seems to apply only to one special fact, but it really has a more general import. We know the great stress which Smith laid upon capital. Division of labour depends upon it, and so does the abundance or scarcity of produce. It determines the quantity of work and fixes the limit of population. To show that the investment of capital conforms to the general interest is to show that all production is organized in the manner most favourable to national prosperity.

Smith distinguishes between four methods of investing capital: in agriculture, in industry, in the wholesale and in the retail trades. Wholesale industry is further divided into three classes: domestic trade; foreign trade, furnishing the nation with foreign products; and carrying trade, which transports those goods from one country to another. Smith maintained that the order in which these various forms of activity were mentioned was also the order of their utility, agriculture being the most advantageous, industry the second-best, etc.

He also proposes two criteria for testing this hierarchy: (1) the quantity of productive labour put into operation by means of the capital employed by each; (2) the amount of exchange value annually added to the revenue by each of these employments. As we pass from agriculture to the other branches, the quantity of productive labour brought into operation and the amount of exchange value obtained gradually decreases, and with this decrease goes a diminishing utility for the country. Smith thought that a nation ought to employ its capital in the way he had suggested. It ought to give the preference to agriculture, and engage in the other branches only as the accumulation of capital permitted.

But this is precisely what the capitalists would do were they entirely free. Every one of them, in fact, is interested in keeping his capital as near home as possible, with a view to better supervision. Only as a last resource does he venture to engage in foreign commerce. Again, even among the industries carried on in his own country every capitalist will preferably choose that which will result in the production of the greatest exchange value, seeing that his profit varies with the amount of this exchange value. His investments will accordingly be made in the order mentioned, an order which roughly corresponds to the greater or lesser quantity of exchange values produced by each industry. And finally, when contemplating investment in foreign trade he will for the same reason follow the order specified above—the order of greatest general utility. Thus the double desire of keeping one's capital within one's reach and of finding for it the most lucrative field of investment leads every capitalist to employ his capital in the fashion which is most advantageous for the nation. Such is the argument, whatever its value.

Even if we adopted his criteria it is obvious that his classification is altogether too arbitrary. How, for example, can we justify the statement that an industrial enterprise or the carrying trade employs less capital than agriculture? The exact contrary would be nearer the truth, and agriculture ought to be given a much more modest position. Moreover, the conception of such a hierarchy does not accord very well with the theory of division of labour, which seeks to put the various forms of human activity more nearly on an equality.

As a matter of fact we cannot even accept a criterion which takes the amount of exchange values furnished by an industry as the test of its social utility. This increase in the quantity of exchange values simply proves that the demand for the goods concerned is stronger than the demand for some others. When capital flows into certain industries it only points to the spontaneous satisfaction of social demand. But social demand and social utility are not necessarily the same. Demand is the outcome of human desires, and its intensity depends upon the revenue drawn by the individual. But we can neither regard these desires in themselves nor the system of distribution that makes such desires 'effective' as sufficient tests of social utility. And to say that production follows demand is to prove nothing at all. Smith himself seems to have realized this; hence his other criterion— the quantity of productive labour employed by capital. According to this test those industries that employ the least amount of machinery and the greatest amount of hand labour are the most useful—quite an untenable view.

A demonstration of a somewhat similar character has been attempted

by the Hedonistic school. They have shown how free competition
always tends to direct production into such channels as will result in
maximum utility, or, in other words, that it affords the best method
of satisfying the actual demands of the market. But they have been
very careful to note that social utility and ophelimity are two very
different expressions that must never be confused, and they admit
that they have failed to find any scientific test of social utility.

Smith's argument is unsatisfactory, and its foundation untrust-
worthy. We do not forget that his optimism is based not so much
upon this specious demonstration as upon the great number of
observations which he had occasion to make in the course of his work.
This idea of a harmony between private interest and the general well-
being of a society was not put forward as a rigidly demonstrable *a
priori* theory, open to no exceptions. It was rather a general view of
the whole position—the conclusion drawn from repeated observations,
the résumé of a detailed inquiry which had covered every corner of
the economic field. A particular process of reasoning may have helped
to confirm this conclusion, but the reasoning itself was largely based
upon experience, the universal experience of history. It was the study
of this experience that led to the discovery of a 'vital' principle of
health and progress in the 'body social.' Smith would have been the
first to oppose the incorporation of his belief in any dogma. He was
content to say that "most frequently" and in a "majority of cases"
general interest *was* satisfied by the spontaneous action of private
interest. He was also the first to point out instances—in the case of
merchants and manufacturers, for example—where the particular and
the general interest came into conflict. We might cite many characteristic passages in which he takes pains to qualify his optimism.

Absolute his optimism was not, neither was it universal. In fact,
it would not be difficult to prove that it was never intended to apply
to anything other than production. Nowhere does the great Scots
economist pretend that the present distribution of wealth is the justest
possible—a trait that distinguishes him from the optimists of Bastiat's
school. His optimism deserted him when he reached that portion of
his subject. On the contrary, he showed that landed proprietors as
well as capitalists "love to reap where they have not sown," that inequalities in social position give masters an advantage in bargaining
with their men.[1] In more than one passage he speaks of interest and

[1] *Wealth of Nations*, Book I, chapter viii; Cannan, Vol. I, p. 68. The masters possess
the advantage in discussion (1) because they can combine much more easily; (2)
because, thanks to their superior funds, they can afford to wait while "many workmen
could not subsist a week, few could subsist a month, and scarce any a year without
employment."

rent as deductions from the produce of labour.[1] Smith, indeed, might well be regarded as a forerunner of socialism. There is no difficulty in believing, so far as the experience of old countries goes, that "rent and profit eat up wages and the two superior orders of people oppress the inferior one."[2]

It is especially important that we should make a note of the opinions of those people who think that Smith intended his optimism to extend to distribution as well as to production. As a matter of fact he was too level-headed to entertain any such idea. Even Say himself in the last edition of his *Treatise* expresses some doubts as to the equity of the present system of distribution.[3] Smith was not really concerned with the question at all. It is only at a much later date, when the socialists had demonstrated the importance of the problem, that we hear of this belief in the beneficence of economic institutions. It really represents a reaction against the socialistic teaching and an attempt at a justification of the present methods of distribution.

We must beware of confusing Smith's optimism with that of modern Hedonism, or of identifying it with Bastiat's answer to the socialists. It lacks the scientific precision of the one and has none of the apologetic tone of the other. It is little more than a reflection prompted by the too naïve confidence of the eighteenth century in the bounty of 'nature,' and an expression of profound conviction rather than the conclusion of a logical argument.

III: ECONOMIC LIBERTY AND INTERNATIONAL TRADE

The practical conclusion to which naturalism leads and to which Smith's optimism points is economic liberty. So naturally does it proceed from what we have just said that the reader finds himself quite prepared for Smith's celebrated phrases:

> All systems either of preference or of restraint, therefore, being thus completely taken away, the obvious and simple system of natural liberty establishes itself of its own accord. Every man, as long as he does not violate the laws of justice, is left perfectly free to pursue his own interest his own way, and to bring both his industry and capital into competition with those of any other man, or order of men.

As to the Government, or "sovereign," as Smith calls him, "he is

[1] *Cf. supra*, p. 95.
[2] *Wealth of Nations*, Book IV, chapter vii, Part II, the beginning; Vol. II, p. 67.
[3] Say, speaking of the working classes, remarks: "Are we quite certain that the workman obtains that share of wealth which is exactly proportioned to the amount which he has contributed to production?" (*Treatise*, 6th ed., p. 116.)

completely discharged from a duty, in the attempting to perform which he must always be exposed to innumerable delusions, and for the proper performance of which no human wisdom or knowledge could ever be sufficient; the duty of superintending the industry of private people, and of directing it towards the employments most suitable to the interests of the society."

Smith, following the Physiocrats, but in a more comprehensive and scientific fashion, finds himself driven to the same conclusion, namely, the wisdom of non-intervention by the State in matters economic.[1]

But here, as elsewhere in his work, the sense of the positive and the concrete, so remarkable in Smith, prevents his being content with a general demonstration. He is not satisfied with proving the inefficiency of intervention as compared with the efficiency of those institutions which are spontaneously created by society itself, but he attempts to show that the State, by its very nature, is unfitted for economic functions. His arguments have been the arsenal from which the opponents of State intervention have been supplied with ammunition ever since.

Let us briefly recall them.

"No two characters seem more inconsistent than those of trader and sovereign."[2] Governments are "always, and without any exception, the greatest spendthrifts in the society."[3] The reasons for this are numerous. In the first place, they employ money which has been gained by others, and one is always more prodigal of the wealth of others than of one's own. Moreover, the Government is too far removed from the centres of particular industries to give them that minute attention which they deserve if they are going to prosper.

> The attention of the sovereign can be at best but a very general and vague consideration of what is likely to contribute to the better cultivation of the greater part of his dominions. The attention of the landlord is a particular and minute consideration of what is likely to be the most advantageous application of every inch of ground upon his estate.[4]

This necessity for a thorough cultivation of the soil and for the best employment of capital, for direct and careful superintendence, is an idea to which he continually reverts. He regrets, among other things, that the growth of public debts causes a portion of the land and the

[1] *Wealth of Nations*, Book IV, chapter ix, *in fine*; Cannan, Vol. II, p. 184.
[2] *Ibid.*, Book V, chapter ii, Part I; Vol. II, p. 304. He makes exception only of the post-office, "perhaps the only mercantile project which has been successfully managed by, I believe, every sort of government." (P. 303.)
[3] *Ibid.*, Book II, chapter iii; Vol. I, p. 328.
[4] *Ibid.*, Book V, chapter ii, Part II, art. 1; Vol. II, p. 318.

national capital to pass into the hands of fund-holders, who are doubt-less interested in the good administration of a country, but "are not interested in the good condition of any particular portion of land, or in the good management of any particular portion of capital stock."[1]

Lastly, the State is an inefficient administrator because its agents are negligent and thriftless, not being directly interested in adminis-tration, but paid out of public funds. Should the administration of the land pass into the hands of the State he exclaims that not a fourth of the present produce would ever be raised, because of "the negligent, expensive, and oppressive management of his factors and agents."[2] On the contrary, he proposes that the remainder of the common land should be distributed among individuals. On this point European Governments have followed his advice somewhat too closely.[3] For the same reason—the necessity for stimulating personal interest wherever possible—he commends, instead of a fixed salary for public officers, payment by those who benefit by their services, such payment in every case to be in strict proportion to the zeal and activity dis-played. This was to apply, for example, to judges and professors.[4]

State administration is accordingly a *pis aller*, and intervention ought to be strictly limited to those cases in which individual action is impossible. Smith recognizes three functions only which the State can perform—namely, the administration of justice, defence.

and, thirdly, the duty of erecting and maintaining certain public works and certain public institutions, which it can never be for the interest of any individual, or small number of individuals, to erect and maintain; because the profit could never repay the expence to any individual or small number of individuals, though it may fre-quently do much more than repay it to a great society.[5]

We must beware, however, lest we exaggerate this point. Although Smith, in the majority of cases, preferred individual action, we must not conclude from this that he had unlimited confidence in individuals. Smith's individualism was of a particular kind. It was not a mere blind preference for every private enterprise, for he knew that industry frequently falls a prey to the spirit of monopoly. "People of the same trade seldom meet together, even for merriment and diversion, but the conversation ends in a conspiracy against the public, or in some

[1] *Wealth of Nations*, Book V, chapter iii; Cannan, Vol. II, p. 413.
[2] *Ibid.*, Book V, chapter ii, Part I; Vol. II, p. 308.
[3] *Cf.* particularly Burgin, *Les Communaux et la Révolution française*, in *Nouvelle Revue historique de Droit*, Nov.–Dec. 1908.
[4] *Wealth of Nations*, Book V, chapter i, Part III, art. 2; Cannan, Vol. II, p. 250.
[5] *Ibid.*, Book IV, chapter ix, *in fine*; Vol. II, p. 185.

contrivance to raise prices."[1] In order that a private enterprise may be useful for the community two conditions are necessary. The *entrepreneur* must be: (1) actuated by personal interest; (2) his actions must by means of competition be kept within the limits of justice. Should either of these two conditions be wanting, the public would run the risk of losing as much by private as they would by State enterprise.

Thus Smith throughout remains very hostile to certain collective enterprises of a private nature, such as joint-stock companies,[2] because of the absence of personal interest. The only exceptions which he would tolerate are banks, insurance companies, and companies formed for the construction or maintenance of canals or for supplying great towns with water, for the management of such undertakings can easily be reduced to a kind of routine, "or to such a uniformity of method as admits of little or no variation."[3]

His opposition to every kind of monopoly granted either to an individual or to a company is even more pronounced. A whole chapter is devoted to an attack upon the great trading companies of the seventeenth and eighteenth centuries, which were created with a view to the development of colonial trade, and of which the East India Company was the most famous.

One other observation remains to be made. Non-intervention for Smith was a general principle, and not an absolute rule. He was no doctrinaire, and he never forgot that to every rule there are some exceptions. An interesting list could be made, giving all the cases in which, according to Smith, the legitimacy of State intervention was indisputable—legal limitation of interest,[4] State administration of the post-office, compulsory elementary education, State examinations as a condition of entry into the liberal professions or to any post of confidence whatever, bank-notes of a minimum value of £5, etc.[5] In a characteristic phrase he gave expression to his feeling on the question of restricting the liberty of banks.

Such regulations may, no doubt, be considered as in some respects a violation of natural liberty. But those exertions of the natural liberty of a few individuals, which might endanger the security of the

---

[1] *Wealth of Nations*, Book I, chapter x, Part II; Cannan, Vol. I, p. 130.

[2] *Ibid.*, Book V, chapter i, Part III, art. 1; Vol. II, p. 233.

[3] *Ibid.*, Book V, chapter i, Part III, art. 1; Vol. II, p. 246.

[4] *Ibid.*, Book II, chapter iv, *in fine*; Vol. I, p. 338. It is probable that his conversion to belief in absolute liberty took place later as the result of his perusal of Bentham's *Defence of Usury* (1787) advocating the right of taking interest. This seems to have been the case if we can credit the report of a conversation which Smith had with one of Bentham's friends, mentioned in a letter written to Bentham by another of his friends—George Wilson. *Cf.* John Rae, *Life of Adam Smith*, p. 423.

[5] *Wealth of Nations*, Book II, chapter ii; Cannan, Vol. I, p. 307.

whole of society, are, and ought to be, restrained by the laws of all governments; of the most free, as well as of the most despotical.[1]

Despite these reservations it is still very evident that the whole of Smith's work is a plea for the economic freedom of the individual. It is an eloquent appeal against the Mercantilist policy and a violent attack upon every economic system inspired by it.

On this point there is absolute agreement between the work done by Smith in England and that carried on at the same time by the Physiocrats in France. Both in foreign and domestic trade producers, merchants, and workmen were hemmed in by a network of restrictions either inherited from the traditions of the Middle Ages or imposed by powerful party interests and upheld by false economic theories. The corporations still existed in the towns; although their regulations could not be applied to industries born after the passing of Elizabeth's famous law concerning apprenticeship. The Colbertian system, with its mob of officials entrusted with the task of superintending the processes of production, of examining the weight, the length, and the quality of the material employed, was still a grievance with the woollen manufacturers.[2] The fixing of the duration of apprenticeship at seven years, the limitation of the number of apprentices in the principal industries, the obstacles put in the way of the mobility of labour by the Poor Law, and by the series of statutes passed since the reign of Elizabeth, fettered the movement of labour and the useful employment of capital. Smith opposed these measures with the whole of his energy. England, unlike France, had fortunately escaped internal restrictions upon trade, but the restraints placed upon foreign trade still kept England and Ireland commercially separated. These checks upon foreign trade proved as irksome in England as they did everywhere else. Manufactured goods from foreign countries were heavily taxed or were prohibited entrance altogether. Certain natural products—e.g., French wine—were similarly handicapped; the importation of a number of commodities necessary for national industry was banned; a narrow and oppressive policy regarded the colonies as the natural purveyors of raw materials for the mother-country and the

[1] *Wealth of Nations*, Book II, chapter ii; Cannan, Vol. I, p. 307. He continues: "The obligation of building party walls in order to prevent the communication of fire is a violation of natural liberty, exactly of the same kind with the regulations of the banking trade which are here proposed." This passage proves that Smith was in favour of public regulations which would further the material security of the citizens. Elsewhere he shows his partiality for adopting hygienic precautions against the spread of contagious diseases (Book V, chapter i, Part III, art. 2; Vol. II, p. 272).

[2] *Cf.* Mantoux, *op. cit.*, pp. 65–66. This work gives most interesting details bearing upon all the points mentioned here. Internal restrictions are criticized by Smith in the second part of chapter x of Book I.

willing buyers of its manufactured goods. Against all this mass of regulations, destined, it was thought, to secure the supremacy of England among other commercial nations, Smith directed his most spirited onslaughts. The fourth book of the *Wealth of Nations* is an eloquent and vigorous attack upon Mercantilism, admirable alike for the precision and the extent of its learning. It was this section of his work that interested his contemporaries most. For us it would have been the least interesting but for its theory of international trade and its criticism of Protection in general. On this account, however, it is of considerable importance in the study of economic doctrines.

In the struggle for Free Trade, as on other points, Smith was forestalled by the Physiocrats. But again has he shown himself superior in the breadth of his outlook. Physiocratic Liberalism was the result of their interest in agriculture, foreign trade being of quite secondary importance. Smith, on the other hand, considered foreign trade in itself advantageous, provided it began at the right moment and developed spontaneously.[1] Although his point of view is far superior to that of the Physiocrats, even Smith failed to give us a satisfactory theory. It was reserved for Ricardo and his successors, particularly John Stuart Mill, to find a solid scientific basis for the theory of international trade. The doctrine of the Scots economist is somewhat lame. But the hesitancy of a great writer is often interesting, and some of his arguments deserve to be recalled.

Already in our review of his theory of money we have become familiar with Smith's criticism of the balance of trade theory. But the balance of trade theory is not the whole of Protection, and we find in Smith something more than its mere refutation. In the first place, we have a criticism of Protectionism in general considered in its Mercantilistic aspect, followed by an attempt to demonstrate the positive advantages of international commerce.

The first criticism that he offers might be summed up in the well-known phrase: "Industry is limited by capital." "The general industry of the society can never exceed what the capital of the society can employ." But Protection, perhaps, increases the quantity of capital? No, "for it can only divert a part of it into a direction into which it might not otherwise have gone." But the direction spontaneously given to their capital by individuals is the most favourable to a country's industry. Has not Smith demonstrated this already?

[1] "Each of those different branches of trade, however, is not only advantageous, but necessary and unavoidable, when the course of things, without any constraint or violence, naturally introduces it," says he, after giving an exposition of the respective advantages of the various forms of economic activity. (*Wealth of Nations*, Book II, chapter v; Cannan, Vol. I, p. 352.)

Protection, consequently, is not merely useless; it may even prove injurious.[1]

The argument does not appear decisive, especially when we recall the criticism of Smith's optimism given above. To borrow an expression of M. Pareto, it is the maximum of ophelimity and not the maximum of utility that is realized by the capitalists under the action of personal interest.

A second and a more striking argument shows the absurdity of manufacturing a commodity in this country at a great expense when a similar commodity might be supplied by a foreign country at less cost. "It is the maxim of every prudent master of a family, never to attempt to make at home what it will cost him more to make than to buy. . . . What is prudence in the conduct of every private family, can scarce be folly in that of a great kingdom."[2] It is foolish to grow grapes in hothouses in Scotland when better and cheaper can be got from Portugal or France. Everybody is convinced of that. But a similar stupidity prevails when we are hindered by tariffs from profiting by the natural advantages which foreign nations possess as compared with ourselves. All "the mean rapacity and the monopolizing spirit of merchants and manufacturers"[3] was necessary to blind men to their true interests on this point. According to Smith, there exists a natural distribution of products among various countries, resulting in an advantage to all of them. It is Protection that hinders our sharing in the advantages. This is the principle known as the "territorial division of labour."

This is the best argument for Free Trade. Later on Ricardo and Mill were to think they had improved it by their theory of 'comparative cost,' but they only managed to complicate it, and the most recent theories have returned to this original view. It is a strange thing that Smith himself did not adopt it, and when he wanted to demonstrate directly the advantages of international trade he became to some extent disloyal to his own doctrine.

The real and decisive argument in favour of free exchange turns upon a consideration of the consumer's interests. Increased utilities placed at his disposal mark the superiority of free exchange, or, as John Stuart Mill puts it, "the only direct advantage of foreign commerce consists in the imports."[4] With Smith this is the point of view developed least of all. True, he wrote that "consumption is the sole

---

[1] *Wealth of Nations*, Book IV, chapter ii; Cannan, Vol. I, p. 419.
[2] *Ibid.*, Book IV, chapter ii; Vol. I, p. 422.
[3] *Ibid.*, Book IV, chapter iii, Part II; Vol. I, pp. 457-458.
[4] *Principles of Political Economy*, Book III, chapter xvii.

end and purpose of all production. But, in the mercantile system, the interest of the consumer is almost constantly sacrificed to that of the producer."[1] This criticism, however, was placed at the end of his examination of the Mercantilist system in chapter viii of Book IV. It is not found in the first edition of the work, and was only added in the third.[2]

It is the point of view of the producer that Smith invariably adopts when attempting to illustrate the advantages of international trade.[3]

Just now foreign trade seemed to afford a means of disposing of a country's surplus products, and this extension of the market, it was argued, would lead to further division of labour and increased productivity.[4] But one is led to ask why, instead of producing the superfluous goods which it must export, it does not produce those things which it is obliged to import.

Smith, being now desirous of showing that international trade necessarily benefits both countries, bases his argument upon the fact that the merchants in both countries must make a profit—*i.e.*, get an additional exchange value, which must be added to the others. To this Ricardo justly replied that the profits of a merchant do not necessarily increase the sum of utilities possessed by any country.

Here again, in striking contrast with the attitude of the Physiocrats, Smith, despite himself, has championed his own adversaries. As yet he is not sufficiently rid of Mercantilist prejudice not to be concerned with the welfare of the producer, and in his great work we find excellent argument and debatable points of view placed side by side. It does not appear that he himself realized this incompatibility. An irresistible tide was sweeping everybody before it in the direction of a more liberal policy. It proved too powerful for his contemporaries, who were not concerned to give a careful consideration to every part of his thesis. Enough that they found in him an ardent champion of an attractive cause.

We have already noticed more than once the hesitation which

[1] *Wealth of Nations*, Book IV, chapter viii; Cannan, Vol. II, p. 159.

[2] It is true that in Book IV, chapter iii, Part II, he declares: "In every country it always is and must be the interest of the great body of the people to buy whatever they want of those who sell it cheapest. The proposition is so very manifest, that it seems ridiculous to take any pains to prove it." (Cannan, Vol. I, p. 458.)

[3] Speaking of duties on corn, he writes: "To prohibit by a perpetual law the importation of foreign corn and cattle, is in reality to enact, that the population and industry of the country shall at no time exceed what the true produce of its own soil can maintain." (*Ibid.*, Book IV, chapter ii; Vol. I, p. 427.) He always views the question from the standpoint of increased population and labour, and not from that of the consumer.

[4] *Ibid.*, Book II, chapter v. *Cf.* Book IV, chapter i.

Smith displays when he comes to apply his principle, and we must again refer to it in this connexion.

Theoretically a champion of absolutely free exchange, he mitigates his belief in practice, and mentions an exception to his policy which seemed to him a mere matter of common sense.

> To expect, indeed, that the freedom of trade should ever be entirely restored in Great Britain, is as absurd as to expect that an Oceana or Utopia should ever be established in it. Not only the prejudices of the public, but what is more unconquerable, the private interests of many individuals, irresistibly oppose it.[1]

Facts have belied this prophecy, like many others. England of the nineteenth century succeeded in realizing this Utopia of free exchange —almost to perfection.

Without any illusion as to the future, his condemnation of the past was not altogether unqualified. He justified some of the acts that were inspired by Mercantilism. "The act of navigation[2] is not favourable to foreign commerce," said he; "as defence, however, is of much more importance than opulence, the act of navigation is, perhaps, the wisest of all the commercial regulations of England."[3] In another instance he justifies an import duty where a tax is levied upon goods similar to those imported. Here an import duty merely restores that normal state of competition which was upset by the imposition of the Excise. Retaliation as a means of securing the abolition of foreign duties is not altogether under his ban.[4] And he finally admits that liberty is best introduced gradually into those countries in which industry has long enjoyed Protection or where a great number of men are employed.[5]

His practical conclusion is somewhat as follows: Instead of innumerable taxes which hinder importation and hamper production, England ought to content herself with the establishment of a certain number of taxes of a purely fiscal character, placed upon commodities

---

[1] *Wealth of Nations*, Book IV, chapter ii, *in fine*; Cannan, Vol. I, p. 435.

[2] The 'Navigation Laws' is a generic term for a number of laws, the most famous of them dating from the time of Cromwell. Their immediate object was the destruction of the Dutch fleet, and English commerce was organized with a view to securing this. There is no doubt but that they contributed very considerably to the development of English maritime power.

[3] *Ibid.*, Book IV, chapter ii; Vol. I, p. 429.

[4] But "when there is no probability that any such repeal can be procured it seems a bad method of compensating the injury done to certain classes of our people, to do another injury ourselves, not only to those classes, but to almost all the other classes of them." (*Ibid.*, Book IV, chapter ii; Vol. I, p. 433.)

[5] The discussion of these various cases is to be found towards the end of chapter ii of Book IV.

such as wine, alcohol, sugar, tobacco, cocoa. Such a system, though perfectly consonant with a great deal of free exchange, would yield abundant revenue to the Treasury, and would afford ample compensation for the losses resulting from the introduction of Free Trade.[1]

England has followed his advice, and her financial system is to-day founded on these bases. Few economists can boast of such a complete realization of their projects.

IV: THE INFLUENCE OF SMITH'S THOUGHT AND ITS DIFFUSION. J. B. SAY

The eighteenth century was essentially a century of levelling down. In Smith's conception of the economic world we have an excellent example of this. Its chief charm lies in the simplicity of its outlines, and this doubtless accounted for his influence among his contemporaries. The system of natural liberty towards which both their political and philosophical aspirations seemed to point were here deduced from, and supported by, evidence taken direct from a study of human nature—evidence, moreover, that seemed to tally so well with known facts that doubt was out of the question. Smith's work still retains its irresistible charm. Even if his ideas are some day shown to be untenable—a contingency we cannot well imagine—his book will remain as a permanent monument of one of the most important epochs in economic thought. It must still be considered the most successful attempt made at embracing within a single purview the infinite diversity of the economic world.

But its simplicity also constituted its weakness. To attain this simplicity more than one important fact that refused to fit in with the system had to remain in the background. The evidence employed was also frequently incomplete. None of the special themes—price, wages, profits, and rent, the theory of international trade or of capital—which occupy the greater portion of the work, but has been in some way corrected, disputed, or replaced. But the structure loses stability if some of the corner-stones are removed. And new points of view have appeared of which Smith did not take sufficient account. Instead of the pleasant impression of simplicity and security which a perusal of Smith's work gave to the economists of the early nineteenth century, there has been gradually substituted by his successors a conviction of the growing complexity of economic phenomena.

To pass a criticism on the labours of Adam Smith would be to review the economic doctrines of the nineteenth century. That is the

[1] This system is expounded in Book V, chapter ii, Part II.

best eulogy one can bestow upon his work. The economic ideas of a whole century were, so to speak, in solution in his writings. Friends and foes have alike taken him as their starting-point. The former have developed, extended, and corrected his work. The latter have subjected his principal theories to harsh criticism at every point. All with tacit accord admit that political economy commenced with him. As Garnier, his French translator, put it, "he wrought a complete revolution in the science."[1] To-day, even although the *Wealth of Nations* may no longer appear to us as a truly scientific treatise on political economy, certain of its fundamental ideas remain incontestable. The theory of money, the importance of division of labour, the fundamental character of spontaneous economic institutions, the constant operation of personal interest in economic life, liberty as the basis of rational political economy—all these appear to us as definite acquisitions to the science.

The imperfections of the work will be naturally demonstrated in the chapters which follow. In order to complete our exposition of Smith's doctrines it only remains to show how they were diffused.

The rapid spread of his ideas throughout Europe and their incontestable supremacy remains one of the most curious phenomena in the history of ideas. Smith persuaded his own generation and governed the next.[2] History affords us some clue. To attribute it solely to the influence of his book is sheer exaggeration. A great deal must be set to the credit of circumstances more or less fortuitous.

M. Mantoux remarks with much justice that it was the American War rather than Smith's writings which demonstrated the decay of the ancient political economy and compassed its ruin. The War of Independence proved two things: (1) The danger lurking in a colonial system which could goad the most prosperous colonies to revolt; (2) the uselessness of a protective tariff, for on the very morrow of the war English trade with the American colonies was more flourishing than ever before. "The loss of the American colonies to England was really a gain to her." So wrote Say in 1803, and he adds: "This is a fact that I have nowhere seen disputed."[3] To the American War other causes must be added: (1) The urgent need for markets felt by English merchants at the close of the Napoleonic Wars; they were already abundantly supplied with excellent machinery. (2) Coupled with this was a growing belief that a high price of corn as the result of agricultural protection increased the cost of hand labour. These

---

[1] In the preface to his translation, 1821 ed., p. lxix.
[2] Rae, *Life of Smith*, p. 103. The author of this famous phrase is not known.
[3] J. B. Say, *Traité*, 1st ed., p. 240.

two reasons were enough to create a desire for a general lowering of the customs duties.

Subsequent events have justified Smith's attitude on the question of foreign trade. In the matter of domestic trade he has been less fortunate.

The French Revolution, which owed its economic measures to the Physiocrats, gave a powerful impulse to the principle of liberty. The influence of the movement was patent enough on the Continent. Even in England, where this influence was least felt, everybody was in favour of *laissez-faire*. Pitt became anxious to free Ireland from its antiquated system of prohibitions, and he succeeded in doing this by his Act of Union of 1800. The regulations laid down by the Elizabethan Statute of Apprentices, with its limitation of the hours of work and the fixing of wages by justices of the peace, became more and more irksome as industry developed. Every historian of the Industrial Revolution has described the struggle between workers and masters and shown how the former clung in despair to the old legislative measures as their only safeguard against a too rapid change, while the latter refused to be constrained either in the choice of workmen or the methods of their work.[1] They wished to pay only the wages that suited them and to use their machines as long as possible. These repeated attacks rendered the old Statute of Apprentices useless, and Parliament abolished its regulations one after another, so that by 1814 all traces of it were for ever effaced from the Statute Book.

But Smith did not foresee these things. He did not write with a view to pleasing either merchants or manufacturers. On the contrary, he was never weary of denouncing their monopolistic tendencies. But by the force of circumstances manufacturers and merchants became his best allies. His book supplied them with arguments, and it was his authority that they always invoked.

His authority never ceased growing. As soon as the *Wealth of Nations* appeared, men like Hume, and Gibbon, the historian, expressed to Smith or to his friends their admiration of the new work. In the following year the Prime Minister, Lord North, borrowed from him the idea of levying two new taxes—the tax on malt and the tax on inhabited houses. Smith was yet to make an even more illustrious convert in the person of Pitt. Pitt was a student when the *Wealth of Nations* appeared, but he always declared himself a disciple of Smith, and as soon as he became a Minister he strove to realize his ideas. It was he who signed the first Free Trade treaty with France—the

---

[1] Mantoux, *La Révolution industrielle*, p. 83. M. Halévy gives expression to a similar idea in his *La Jeunesse de Bentham*, p. 193 (Paris, 1901).

Treaty of Eden, 1786.[1] When Smith came to London in 1787 Pitt met him more than once and consulted him on financial matters. The story is told that after one of these conversations Smith exclaimed: "What an extraordinary person Pitt is! He understands my ideas better than myself."

While Smith made converts of the most prominent men of his time, his book gradually reached the public. Four editions in addition to the first appeared during the author's lifetime.[2] The third, in 1784, presents important differences in the way of additions and corrections as compared with the first. From the date of his death in 1790 to the end of the century three other editions were published.[3]

Similar success attended the appearance of the work on the Continent. In France he was already known through his *Theory of Moral Sentiments*. The first mention of the *Wealth of Nations* in France appears in the *Journal des Savants* in the month of February 1777. Here, after a brief description of the merits of the work, the critic gives expression to the following curious opinion:

> Some of our men of letters who have read it have come to the conclusion that it is not a book that can be translated into our language. They point out, among other reasons, that no one would be willing to bear the expense of publishing because of the uncertain return, and a bookseller least of all. They are bound to admit, however, that the work is full of suggestions and of advice that is useful as well as curious, and might prove of benefit to statesmen.

In reality, despite the opinion of those men of letters, several translations of the work did appear in France, as well as elsewhere in Europe. In little more than twenty years, between 1779 and 1802, four translations had appeared. This in itself affords sufficient proof of the interest which the book had aroused.[4]

Few works have enjoyed such complete and universal success. But despite admiration the ideas did not spread very rapidly. Faults of composition have been burdened with the responsibility for this, and it is a reproach that has clung to the *Wealth of Nations* from the first. Its organic unity is very pronounced, but Smith does not seem to

---

[1] So called in honour of the leading English representative, Lord Eden.

[2] In 1778, 1784, 1786, 1789.   [3] In 1791, 1793, 1796.

[4] Professor Kraus, writing in 1796, declared that no book published since the days of the New Testament would effect so many welcome changes when it became thoroughly known (J. Rae, p. 360). By the beginning of the nineteenth century its influence had become predominant. All the Prussian statesmen who aided Stein in the preparation and execution of those important reforms that gave birth to modern Prussia were thoroughly versed in Smith's doctrines, and the Prussian tariff of 1821 is the first European tariff in which they are deliberately applied. (*Cf.* Roscher, *Geschichte der Nationalökonomik in Deutschland.*)

have taken the trouble to give it even the semblance of outward unity. To discover its unity requires a real effort of thought. Smith whimsically regarded it as a mere discourse, and the reading occasionally gives the impression of conversation. The general formulæ which summarize or recapitulate his ideas are indifferently found either in the middle or at the end of a chapter, just as they arose. They represent the conclusions from what preceded as they flashed across his mind. On the other hand, a consideration of such a question as money is scattered throughout the whole work, being discussed on no less than ten different occasions. As early as April 1, 1776, Hume had expressed to Smith some doubts as to the popularity of the book, seeing that its reading demanded considerable attention. Sartorius in 1794 attributed to this difficulty the slow progress made by Smith's ideas in Germany. Germain Garnier, the French translator, gave an outline of the book in order to assist his readers. It was generally agreed that the work was a striking one, but badly composed and difficult to penetrate owing to the confused and equivocal character of some of the paragraphs. When Say referred to it as "a chaotic collection of just ideas thrown indiscriminately among a number of positive truths,"[1] he expressed the opinion of all who had read it.

But a complete triumph, so far as the Continent at least was concerned, had to be the work of an interpreter. Such an interpreter must fuse all these ideas into a coherent body of doctrines, leaving useless digressions aside.[2] This was the task that fell into the hands of J. B. Say. Among his merits (and it is not the only one) is that of popularizing the ideas of the great Scots economist on the Continent, and of giving to the ideas a somewhat classical appearance. The task of discrediting the first French school of economists and of facilitating the expansion of English political economy fell, curiously enough, to the hands of a Frenchman.

J. B. Say was twenty-three years of age in 1789.[3] At that time he

---

[1] In his introduction to the *Traité*, 1st ed. (The phrase was deleted in the 6th ed.)

[2] J. B. Say, *Traité*, 1st ed., introduction, p. xxxiii.

[3] He was born at Lyons on January 5, 1767. After a visit to England he entered the employment of an assurance company, and took part as a volunteer in the campaign of 1792. From 1794 to 1800 he edited a review entitled *Décade philosophique, littéraire et politique, par une société de républicains*. He was nominated a member of the Tribunate in 1799. After the publication of his *Traité* the First Consul, having failed to obtain a promise that the financial proposals outlined in the first edition would be eliminated in the second, dismissed him from the Tribunate, offering him the post of director of the *Droits réunis* as compensation. Say, who disapproved of the new regime, refused, and set up a cotton factory at Auchy-les-Hesdins, in the Pas-de-Calais. He realized his capital in 1813, returned to Paris, and in 1814 published a second edition of his treatise. In 1816 he delivered a course of lectures on political economy at the Athénée, probably the first course given in France. These lectures were pub-

was Clavières's secretary. Clavières became Minister of Finance in 1792, but at this period he was manager of an assurance company, and was already a disciple of Smith. Say came across some stray pages of the *Wealth of Nations*, and sent for a copy of the book.[1] The impression it made upon him was profound. "When we read this work," he writes, "we feel that previous to Smith there was no such thing as political economy." Fourteen years afterwards, in 1803, appeared *Le Traité d'économie politique*. The book met with immediate success, and a second edition would have appeared had not the First Consul interdicted it. Say had refused to support the Consul's financial recommendations, and the writer, in addition to having his book proscribed, found himself banished from the Tribunate. Say waited until 1814 before republishing it. New editions rapidly followed, in 1817, 1819, and 1826. The treatise was translated into several languages. Say's authority gradually extended itself; his reputation became European; and by these means the ideas of Adam Smith, clarified and logically arranged in the form of general principles from which conclusions could be easily deduced, gradually captivated the more enlightened section of public opinion.

It would, however, be unjust to regard Say as a mere popularizer of Smith's ideas. With praiseworthy modesty, he has never attempted to conceal all that he owed to the master. The master's name is mentioned in almost every line, but he never remains content with a mere repetition of his ideas. These are carefully reconsidered and reviewed with discrimination. He develops some of them and emphasizes others. Amid the devious paths pursued by Smith, the French economist chooses that which most directly leads to the desired end. This path is so clearly outlined for his successors that "wayfaring men, though fools, could not err therein." In a sense he may be said to have filtered the ideas of the master, or to have toned his doctrines with the proper tints. He thus imparted to French political economy its distinctive character as distinguished from English political economy, to which at about the same time Malthus and Ricardo were to give an entirely new orientation. What interests us more than his borrowing is the personal share which he has in the work, an estimate of which we must now attempt.

---

lished in 1817 in his *Catéchisme d'économie politique*. In 1819 the Restoration Government appointed him to give a course on 'Industrial Economy' (the term 'Political Economy' was too terrible). In 1831 he was made Professor of Political Economy in the Collège de France. He died in 1832. His *Cours complet d'économie politique* was published, in six volumes, in 1828–29.

[1] *Cf.* a letter to Louis Say in 1827 (*Œuvres diverses*, p. 545).

(1) In the first place, Say succeeded in overthrowing the work of the Physiocrats.

The work of demolition was not altogether useless. In France there were many who still clung to the 'sect.' Even Germain Garnier, Smith's translator, considered the arguments of the Physiocrats theoretically irrefutable. The superiority of the Scots economist was entirely in the realm of practice.[1] "We may," says he, "reject the *Economistes'* theory [meaning the Physiocrats'] because it is less useful, although it is not altogether erroneous." Smith himself, as we know, was never quite rid of this idea, for he recognized a special productiveness of land as a result of the co-operation of nature, and doctors, judges, advocates, and artists were regarded as unproductive. But Say's admission was the last straw. Not in agriculture alone, but everywhere, "nature is forced to work along with man,"[2] and by the funds of nature was to be understood in future all the help that a nation draws directly from nature, be it the force of wind or rush of water.[3] As to the doctors, lawyers, etc., how are we to prove that they take no part in production? Garnier had already protested against their exclusion. Such services must no doubt be classed as immaterial products, but products none the less, seeing that they possess exchange value and are the outcome[4] of the co-operation of capital and industry. In other respects also—*e.g.*, in the pleasure and utility which they yield—services are not very unlike commodities. Say's doctrine meets with some opposition on this point, for the English economists were unwilling to consider a simple service as wealth because of its unendurable character, and the consequent fact that it could not be considered as adding to the aggregate amount of capital. But he soon wins over the majority of writers.[5] Finally Say, like Condillac, discovered a decisive argument against Physiocracy in the fact that the production of material objects does not imply their creation. Man never can create, but must be content with mere transformation of matter. Production is merely a creation of utilities, a furthering of that capacity of responding to our needs and of satisfying our wants which is possessed by commodities; and all work is productive which

[1] Garnier's translation of Adam Smith, 1802, Vol. V, p. 283.

[2] *Traité*, 1st ed., p. 39.

[3] *Ibid.*, p. 21. Later on he employs the more comprehensive term 'natural agents.'

[4] *Ibid.*, Book I, chapters xlii and xliii. By 'industry' Say understands every kind of labour. *Cf.* 6th ed., pp. 70 *et seq.*

[5] Malthus still appeared hostile to the doctrine of immaterial products, but Lauderdale, Tooke, McCulloch, and Senior accepted it, and it seemed definitely fixed when Stuart Mill confined the word 'product' to material products only. For Tooke's view see his letter to J. B. Say in the *Œuvres diverses* of the latter.

achieves this result, whether it be industry, commerce, or agriculture.[1] The Physiocratic distinction falls to the ground, and Say refutes what Smith, owing to his intimacy with his adversaries, had failed to disprove.

(2) On another point Say carries forward Smith's ideas, although at the same time superseding them. He subjects the whole conception of political economy and the role of the economist to a most thorough examination.

We have already noticed that the conception of the 'natural order' underwent considerable modification during the period which intervened between the writings of the Physiocrats and the appearance of the *Wealth of Nations*. The Physiocrats regarded the 'order' as one that was to be realized, and the science of political economy as essentially normative. For Smith it was a self-realizing order. This spontaneity of the economic world is analogous to the vitality of the human body, and is capable of triumphing over the artificial barriers which Governments may erect against its progress. Practical political economy is based upon a knowledge of the economic constitution of society, and its sole aim is to give advice to statesmen. According to Say, this definition concedes too much to practice. Political economy, as he thinks, is just the science of this "spontaneous economic constitution," or, as he puts it in 1814, it is a study of the laws which govern wealth.[2] It is, as the title of his book suggests, simply an exposition of the production, distribution, and consumption of wealth. It must be distinguished from politics, with which it has been too frequently confused, and also from statistics, which is a simple description of particular facts and not a science of co-ordinate principles at all.

Political economy in the hands of J. B. Say became a purely theoretical and descriptive science. The role of the economist, like that of the savant, is not to give advice, but simply to observe, to analyse, and to describe. "He must be content to remain an impartial spectator," he writes to Malthus in 1820. "What we owe to the public is to tell them how and why such-and-such a fact is the consequence of another. Whether the conclusion be welcomed or rejected, it is enough that

---

[1] *Traité*, Book I, chapter ii. Is it not strange that Say should have failed to apply this idea to commerce? He regards the latter as productive because it creates exchangeable values. Nevertheless he criticizes Condillac for having said that mere exchange of goods increases wealth because it increases the utility of objects. This is because Say is perpetually mixing up utility and exchange value, a confusion that leads him into many serious mistakes.

[2] *Traité*, 6th ed., p. 6. The word 'laws' does not appear in the first edition. Say merely speaks of general principles. It is found for the first time in the edition of 1814: "General facts or, if one wishes to call principles by that name, general laws" (p. xxix).

E

the economist should have demonstrated its cause; but he must give no advice."[1]

In this way Say broke with the long tradition which, stretching from the days of the Canonists and the Cameralists to those of the Mercantilists and the Physiocrats, had treated political economy as a practical art and a guide for statesmen and administrators. Smith had already tried to approach economic phenomena as a scientist, but there was always something of the reformer in his attitude. Say's only desire was to be a mere student; the healing art had no attraction for him, and so he inaugurates the true scientific method. He, moreover, instituted a comparison between this science and physics rather than between it and natural history, and in this respect also he differed from Smith, for whom the social body was essentially a living thing. Without actually employing the term 'social physics,' he continually suggests it by his repeated comparison with Newtonian physics. The principles of the science, like the laws of physics, are not the work of men. They are derived from the very nature of things. They are not established; they are discovered. They govern even legislators and princes, and one never violates them with impunity.[2] Like the laws of gravity, they are not confined within the frontiers of any one country, and the limits of State administration, which are all-important for the student of politics, are mere accidents for the economist.[3] Political economy is accordingly based on the model of an exact science, with laws that are universal. Like physics, it is not so much concerned with the accumulation of particular facts as with the formulation of a few general principles from which a chain of consequences of greater or smaller length may be drawn according to circumstances.

A delight in uniformity,[4] love of universality, and contempt for isolated facts, these are the marks of the savant. But the same qualities in men of less breadth of view may easily become deformed and result in faults of indifference or of dogmatism, or even contempt for all facts. And are not these very faults produced by the stress which he lays upon these principles? Was not political economy placed in a vulnerable position for the attacks of Sismondi, of List, of the Historical school, and of the Christian Socialists by this very work of Say? In

[1] Correspondence with Malthus, in *Œuvres diverses*, p. 466.
[2] *Traité*, Introd., 1st ed., p. ix; 6th ed., p. 13.
[3] *Ibid.*, 1st ed., Book I, p. 404.
[4] There is no need for exaggeration, and no need to regard Say as indifferent to suffering and misery. He declares that "for many homes both in town and country life is one long privation," and that thrift in general "implies, not the curtailment of useless commodities, such as expediency and humanity would welcome, but a diminution of the real needs of life, which is a standing condemnation of the economic system of many Governments." (*Traité*, 1st ed., Vol. I, pp. 97–98; 6th ed., p. 116.)

his radical separation of politics and economics, in avoiding the 'practical' leanings of Adam Smith, he has succeeded in giving the science a greater degree of harmony. But it also acquired a certain frigidity which his less gifted successors have mistaken for banality or crudity. Rightly or wrongly, the responsibility is ascribed to Say.

(3) We have just seen the influence which the progress of the physical sciences had upon Say's conception of political economy; but he was also much influenced by the progress of industry. Between 1776, the date of the appearance of the *Wealth of Nations*, and the year 1803, when Say's treatise appeared, the Industrial Revolution had taken place. This is a fact of considerable importance for the history of economic ideas.

When Say visited England a little before 1789 he found machine production already in full swing there. In France at the same date manufactures were only just beginning. They increased rapidly under the Empire, and the progress after 1815 became enormous. Chaptal in his work, *De l'Industrie française* reckons that in 1819 there were 220 factories in existence, with 922,200 spindles consuming 13 million kilograms of raw cotton. This, however, only represented a fifth of the English production, which twenty years later was quadrupled. Other industries were developing in a similar way. Everybody was convinced that the future must be along those lines—an indefinite future, it is true, but it was to be one of wealth, work, and well-being. The rising generation was intoxicated at the prospect. The most eloquent exposition of this debauchery will be found in Saint-Simonism.

Say did not escape the infection. While Smith gives agriculture the premier place, Say accords the laurels to manufactures. For many years industrial problems had been predominant in political economy, and the first official course of lectures given by Say himself at the Conservatoire des Arts et Métiers was entitled "A Course of Lectures on Industrial Economy."

In that hierarchy of activities which Smith had drawn up according to the varying degree of utility each possessed for the nation Smith had placed agriculture first. Say preserved the order, but placed alongside of agriculture "all capital employed in utilizing any of the productive forces of nature. An ingenious machine may produce more than the equivalent of the interest on the capital it has cost to produce, and society enjoys the benefit in lower prices."[1] This sentence is not found in the edition of 1803, and appears only in the second edition. Say in the meantime had been managing his factory at Auchy-les-Hesdins, and he had profited by his experience. This

Traité, 6th ed., p. 403.

question of machinery, which was merely touched on by Smith in a
short passage, finds a larger place in every successive edition of Say's
work. The general adoption of machinery by manufacturers both in
England and France frequently incited the workers to riot. Say does
not fail to demonstrate its advantages. At first he admits that the
Government might mitigate the resulting evils by confining the employment of machinery at the outset to certain districts where labour
is scarce or is employed in other branches of production.[1] But by the
beginning of the fifth edition he changed his advice and declared that
such intervention involved interference with the inventor's property,[2]
admitting only that the Government might set up works of public
utility in order to employ those men who are thrown out of employment on account of the introduction of machinery.

The influence of these same circumstances must be accounted
responsible for the stress which is laid by Say upon the role of an
individual whom Smith had not even defined, though Cantillon had
already emphasized that role, and who is henceforth to remain an
important personage in the economic world, namely, the *entrepreneur*.[3]
At the beginning of the nineteenth century the principal agent of
economic progress was the industrious, active, well-informed individual,
either an ingenious inventor, a progressive agriculturist, or an experienced business man. This type became quite common in every
country where mechanical production and increasing markets became
the rule. It is he rather than the capitalist properly so called, the
landed proprietor, or the workman, who is "almost always passive,"
who directs production and superintends the distribution of wealth.
"The power of industrial *entrepreneurs* exercises a most notable influence upon the distribution of wealth," says Say. "In the same kind
of industry one *entrepreneur* who is judicious, active, methodical, and
willing makes his fortune, while another who is devoid of these qualities
or who meets with very different circumstances would be ruined."[4]
Is it not the master spinner of Auchy-les-Hesdins who is speaking here?
We are easily convinced of this if we compare the edition of 1803
with that of 1814, and we can trace the gradual growth and development of this conception with every successive edition of the work.

Say's classic exposition of the mechanism of distribution is based
upon this very admirable conception, which is altogether superior to
that of Smith or the Physiocrats. The *entrepreneur* serves as the pivot

[1] *Traité*, 1st ed., Vol. I, p. 48.   [2] *Ibid.*, 5th ed., Vol. I, p. 67.
[3] The *entrepreneur* in fact has an important place in Cantillon's admirable *Essai sur
la nature du commerce*, written in the middle of the eighteenth century.
[4] Criticial examination of McCulloch's treatise (1825), in *Œuvres diverses*, pp. 274-
275.

of the whole system. The following may be regarded as an outline of his treatment.

Men, capital, and labour furnish what Say refers to as productive services. These services, when brought to market, are given in exchange for wages, interest, or rent. It is the *entrepreneur*, whether merchant, manufacturer, or agriculturist, who requires them, and it is he who combines them with a view to satisfying the demand of consumers. "The *entrepreneurs*, accordingly, are mere intermediaries who set up a claim for those productive services which are necessary to satisfy the demand for certain products." Accordingly there arises a demand for productive services, and the demand is "one of the factors determining the value of those services."

> On the other hand, the agents of production, both men and things, whether land, capital, or industrial employees, offer their services in greater or less quantities according to various motives, and thus constitute another factor which determines the value of these same services.[1]

In this fashion the law of demand and supply determines the price of services, the average rate of interest, and rent. Thanks to the *entrepreneur*, the value produced is again distributed among these "various productive services," and the various services allotted according to need among the industries. This theory of distribution is in complete accordance with the theory of exchange and production.

Say's very simple scheme of distribution constitutes a real progress. In the first place, it is much more exact than the Physiocrats', who conceived of exchange as taking place between classes only, and not between individuals. It also enables us to distinguish the remuneration of the capitalist from the earnings of the *entrepreneur*, which were confounded by Adam Smith. The Scots economist assumed that the *entrepreneur* was very frequently a capitalist, and confused the two functions, designating his total remuneration by the single word 'profit,' without ever distinguishing between net interest of capital and profit properly so called. This regrettable confusion was followed by other English authors, and remained in English economic theory for a long time. Finally, Say's theory has another advantage. It gave to his French successors a clear scheme of distribution which was wanting in Smith's work, just at the time when Ricardo was attempting to overcome the omission by outlining a new theory of distribution. According to Ricardo, rent, by its very nature and the laws which give rise to it, is opposed to other revenues, and the rate of wages and of profits must be regarded as direct opposites, so that the one can

[1] *Traité*, 6th ed., p. 349.

only increase if the other diminishes—an attractive but erroneous
theory, and one which led to endless discussion among English economists, with the result that they abandoned it altogether. Say, by
showing this dependence, which becomes quite clear if we regard
wages and profits from the point of view of demand for commodities,
and by his demonstration that rent is determined by the same general
causes—*viz.*, demand and supply—as determine the exchange value
of other productive services, saved political economy in France from
a similar disaster. It was he, also, who furnished Walras with the first
outlines of his attractive conception of prices and economic equilibrium. This explains why he never attached to the theory of rent the
supreme importance given to it by English economists. In this respect
he has been followed by the majority of French economists. On the
other hand, and for a similar reason, he never went to the opposite
extreme of denying the existence of rent altogether by regarding it
merely as the revenue yielded by capital sunk in land. In this way he
avoided the error which Carey and Bastiat attempted to defend at a
later period.[1]

(4) So far it is Say's brilliant power of logical reasoning that we have
admired. But has he contributed anything which is entirely new to
the science?

His theory of markets was for a long time considered first-class
work. "Products are given in exchange for products." It is a happy
phrase, but it is not in truth very profound. It simply gives expression
to an idea that was quite familiar to the Physiocrats and to Smith,
namely, that money is but an intermediary which is acquired only to
be passed on and exchanged for another product. "Once the exchange
has been effected it is immediately discovered that products pay for
products."[2] Thus goods constitute a demand for other goods, and the
interest of a country that produces much is that other countries should
produce at least as much. Say thought that the outcome of this would
be the advent of the true brotherhood of man. "The theory of markets
will change the whole policy of the world," said he.[3] He thought

[1] "Rent," he says, "doubtless is partly interest on capital buried in the soil, for
there are few properties which do not owe something to improvements made in them.
But their total value is seldom due to this alone. It might be if the land were fertile
but lacked the necessary facilities for cultivation. But this is never the case in civilized countries." (Critical examination of McCulloch's treatise (1825), in *Œuvres
diverses*, p. 277.)

[2] *Traité*, 1st ed., p. 154.

[3] "The theory of heat and of weight and the study of the inclined plane have
placed the whole of nature at the disposal of mankind. In the same way the theory
of exchange and of markets will change the whole policy of the world." (*Ibid.*,
6th ed., p. 51.)

that the greater part of the doctrine of Free Trade could be based upon this principle. But to expect so much from such a vague, self-evident formula was to hope for the impossible.

Still more interesting is the way in which he applied this "theory of markets" to a study of over-production crises, and the light which that sheds upon the nature of Say's thought. Garnier had already pointed out that a general congestion of markets was possible. As crises multiplied this fear began to agitate the minds of a number of thinkers. "Nothing can be more illogical," writes Say. "The total supply of products and the total demand for them must of necessity be equal, for the total demand is nothing but the whole mass of commodities which have been produced: a general congestion would consequently be an absurdity."[1] It would simply mean a general increase of wealth, and "wealth is none too plentiful among nations, any more than it is among individuals."[2] We may have an inefficient application of the means of production, resulting in the over-production of some one commodity or other—*i.e.*, we may have partial over-production.[3] Say wishes to emphasize the fact that we need never fear general over-production, but that we may have too much of some one product or other. He frequently gave expression to this idea in the form of paradoxes. We might almost be led to believe that he denies the existence of crises altogether in the second edition of his work.[4] In reality he was very anxious to admit their existence, but he wished to avoid everything that might prove unfavourable to an extension of industry.[5]

He thought that crises were essentially transient, and declared that

---

[1] *Traité*, 1st ed., Vol. II, p. 175.   [2] *Ibid.*, p. 179.   [3] *Ibid.*, p. 178.

[4] "One kind of product would seldom be more plentiful than another and goods would seldom be too many if every one were given complete freedom." Too much stress has possibly been laid on the phrase "Certain products are superabundant just because others are wanting," and it has been taken as implying that even partial over-production is an impossibility. A note inserted on the next page helps to clear up the matter and to prevent misunderstanding. "The argument of the chapter," says he, "is not that partial over-production is impossible, but merely that the production of one thing creates the demand for another." He certainly seems unfaithful to his own position in the letters he wrote to Malthus, in which he tries to defend his own point of view by saying that "production implies producing goods that are demanded," and that consequently if there is any excessive production it is not the fault of production as such and cannot be regarded as *over-production*. In greater conformity with his own views and much nearer the truth is his reply to an article by Sismondi published in 1824 in the *Revue encyclopédique* under the title *Sur la Balance des Consommations avec les Productions* (*Œuvres diverses*, p. 250). His statements vary from one edition to another, and anything more unstable than Say's views on this question would be difficult to imagine. The formula "Products exchange for products" is so general that it includes everything, but means nothing at all; for what is money, after all, if it is not a product?

[5] Letters to Malthus (*Œuvres diverses*, p. 466).

individual liberty would be quite enough to prevent them. He was
extremely anxious to get rid of the vague terrors which had haunted
those people who feared that they would not be able to consume all
this wealth, of a Malthus who thought the existence of the idle rich
afforded a kind of safety-valve which prevented over-production,[1] of a
Sismondi who prayed for a slackening of the pace of industrial progress
and a checking of inventions. Such thoughts arouse his indignation,
especially, as he remarks, when it is remembered that even among
the most flourishing nations "seven-eighths of the population are
without a great number of products which would be regarded as
absolute necessities, not by a wealthy family, but even by one of
moderate means."[2] The inconvenience—and he is never tired of
repeating it—is not the result of over-production, but is the effect of
producing what is not exactly wanted.[3] Produce, produce all that
you can, and in the natural course of events a lowering of prices will
benefit even those who at first suffered from the extension of industry.

In this once-famous controversy between Say, Malthus, Sismondi,
and Ricardo (the last sided with Say) we must not expect to find a
clear exposition of the causes of crises. Indeed, that is nowhere to be
found. All we have here is the expression of a sentiment which is at
bottom perfectly just, but one which Say wrongly attempted to state
in a scientific formula.

J. B. Say plays a by no means negligible part in the history of doctrines. Foreign economists have not always recognized him. Dühring,
who is usually perspicacious, is very unjust to him when he speaks of
"the labour of dilution" to which Say devoted his energies.[4] His want
of insight frequently caused him to glide over problems instead of
attempting to fathom them, and his treatment of political economy
occasionally appears very superficial. Certain difficulties are veiled
with pure verbiage—a characteristic in which he is very frequently
imitated by Bastiat. Despite Say's greater lucidity, it is doubtful
whether Smith's obscurity of style is not, after all, more stimulating
for the mind. Notwithstanding all this, he was faithful in his transmission of the ideas of the great Scots economist into French. Happily
his knowledge of Turgot and Condillac enabled him to rectify some of
the more contestable opinions of his master, and in this way he avoided

[1] Malthus, *Principles of Political Economy*, Book II, chapter i, sec. ix.
[2] *Sur la Balance des Consommations avec les Productions*, p. 252.
[3] *Ibid.*, p. 251.
[4] Dühring, *Kritische Geschichte der Nationalökonomie und des Socialismus*, 2nd ed., 1875,
p. 165. For the other side of the question one may profitably peruse the interesting
study of Say contributed by M. Allix to the *Revue d'économie politique*, 1910 (pp. 303–
341), and the *Revue d'Histoire des Doctrines*, 1911 (p. 321).

many of the errors of his successors. He has left his mark upon French political economy, and had the English economists adopted his conception of the *entrepreneur* earlier, instead of waiting until the appearance of Jevons, they would have spared the science many useless discussions provoked by the work of a thinker who was certainly more profound but much less judicious than Say, namely, David Ricardo.[1]

CHAPTER III: THE PESSIMISTS

A NEW point of view is presented to us by the economists of whom we are now going to speak. Hitherto we have heard with admiration of the discovery of new facts and of their beneficent effects upon both nations and individuals. We are now to witness the enunciation of new doctrines which cast a deepening shadow across the radiant dawn of economics, giving it that strangely sinister aspect which led Carlyle to dub it "the dismal science."

Hence the term 'Pessimists,' although no reproach is implied in our use of that term. On the contrary, we shall have to show that the theories of the school are often truer than those of the Optimists, which we must study at a later stage of our survey. While nominally subscribing to their predecessors' doctrine concerning the identity of individual and general interests, the many cogent reasons which they have adduced against such belief warrants our classification. The antagonism existing between proprietors and capitalists, between capitalists and workmen, is a discovery of theirs. Instead of the 'natural' or 'providential' laws that were to secure the establishment of the 'order' provided they were once thoroughly understood and obeyed, they discovered the existence of other laws, such as that of rent, which guaranteed a revenue for a minority of idle proprietors—a revenue that was destined to grow as the direct result of the people's growing need; or the 'law of diminishing returns,' which sets a definite limit to the production of the necessaries of life. That limit, they

---

[1] Stanley Jevons (*Theory of Political Economy*, 1888) has recognized in words too rarely quoted, but clearly confirmed by the modern development of economics, the superiority of the French economists over Ricardo. "The true doctrine may be more or less clearly traced through the writings of a succession of great French economists, from Condillac, Baudeau, and Le Trosne, through J. B. Say, Destutt de Tracy, Storch, and others, down to Bastiat and Courcelle-Seneuil. The conclusion to which I am ever more clearly coming is that the only hope of attaining a true system of economics is to fling aside, once and for ever, the mazy and preposterous assumptions of the Ricardian School." (Preface, p. xlix.)

asserted, was already being approached, and mankind had no prospect of bettering its lot save by the voluntary limitation of its numbers. There was also the tendency of profits to fall to a minimum—until it seemed as if the whole of human industry would sooner or later be swallowed up by the stagnant waters of the stationary State.

Lastly, they deserve to be classed as pessimists because of their utter disbelief in the possibility of changing the course of these inevitable laws either by legislative reform or by organized voluntary effort. In short, they had no faith in what we call progress.

But we must never imagine that they considered themselves pessimists or were classed as such by their contemporaries. This verdict is posterity's, and would have caused them no little surprise. As for themselves, they seem to stand aloof from their systems with an insouciance that is most disconcerting. The 'present order of things' possessed no disquieting features for them, and they never doubted the wisdom of 'Nature's Lord.' They believed that property had been put upon an immovable basis when they demonstrated the extent of its denotation, and that the spirit of revolt had been disarmed by impressing upon the poor a sense of responsibility for their own miseries.[1]

The best-known representatives of the school are Malthus and Ricardo. They claimed to be philanthropists and friends of the people, and we have no reason to suspect their sincerity.[2] Their contemporaries, also, far from being alarmed, received the new political economy with the greatest enthusiasm. A warm welcome was extended to its apostles by the best of English society,[3] and ladies of distinction contended with one another for the privilege of popularizing the abstract thoughts of Ricardo in newspaper articles and popular tales.[4]

Neither should we omit to pay them full homage for the eminent services rendered to the science, and among these not the least impor-

[1] "The people must comprehend that they are themselves the cause of their own poverty." (Malthus, p. 458.) Doubtless this is the reason why M. Halévy, among others, in his book Le Radicalisme philosophique, remarks that Ricardo, Malthus, and their disciples were regarded as the exponents of optimism and quietism. But in what sense were they optimists? Of course they believed that the existing economic order is the best possible, and that it would be impossible to change it for a better. That may be. But we prefer to think of them as "contented pessimists."

[2] "Every reader of candour must acknowledge that the practical design uppermost in the mind of the writer, with whatever want of judgment it may have been executed, is to improve the condition and increase the happiness of the lower classes of society." It is with this declaration that Malthus brings his book on population to a close.

[3] Miss Edgeworth, a contemporary of Ricardo, states in her letters that political economy was so much the fashion that distinguished ladies before engaging a governess for their children inquired about her competence to teach political economy.

[4] Conversations on Political Economy, by Mrs Marcet (1816). Illustrations of Political Economy, by Miss Martineau (9 vols., containing thirty stories, 1832–34).

tant was the antagonism which their theories aroused in the minds of the working classes. Pessimists unwittingly often do more for progress than optimists. To these two writers fell the task of criticizing economic doctrines and institutions, a task that has been taken up by other writers in the course of the century, but which seems as far from completion as ever. Karl Marx, another critic, is intellectually a scion of the Ricardian family. It would be a mistake to imagine that all their theories savour of pessimism, but their reputation has always been more or less closely linked with the gloomier aspect of their teaching.

I: MALTHUS [1]

Malthus is best known for his "law of population." That he was a great economist, even apart from his study of that question, might easily be proved by reference to his treatise on political economy, or by a perusal of the many miscellaneous articles which he wrote on various economic questions. A consideration of many of these theories, notably the theory of rent, must be postponed until we come to study them in connexion with the name of Ricardo.

THE LAW OF POPULATION

Twenty years had elapsed since the publication of Smith's immortal work, without economics making any advance, when the appearance of a small anonymous volume, known to be the work of a country clergyman, caused a great sensation. Even after the lapse of a century the echo of the controversy which it aroused has not altogether passed

---

[1] Thomas Robert Malthus was born in 1766. His father, a country gentleman, was a man of learning and a friend of most of the philosophers of his time, especially Hume, and, it also seems, J. J. Rousseau. He was the youngest son of the family, and was intended for the Church and given an excellent education. After leaving Cambridge he took a living in the country, but in 1807 was appointed professor at a college founded by the East India Company at Haileybury, in Hertfordshire, where he remained until his death in 1834. He married when thirty-nine years of age, and had three sons and a daughter.

Malthus was a young unmarried clergyman living in a small country parish when, at the age of thirty-two, he in 1798 published anonymously his famous *Essay on the Principle of Population as it affects the Future Improvement of Society.* His critics were legion. In order to devote more study to the subject, he took a three years' tour (1799–1802) on the Continent—avoiding France, because France at this period was anything but inviting to an Englishman. In 1803 he published—under his own name this time—a second edition, much modified and amplified, and with a slightly different title: *An Essay on the Principle of Population, or a View of its Past and Present Effects on Human Happiness.* Four other editions were published during his lifetime.

We must not forget his other works, although they were all eclipsed by his earliest effort. These were: *The Principles of Political Economy considered with a View to their Practical Application* (1820); *A Series of Short Studies dealing with the Corn Laws* (1814–15); *On Rent* (1815); *The Poor Law* (1817); and finally his *Definitions in Political Economy* (1827).

away. At first sight one might be led to think that the book touches
only the fringe of economics, seeing that it is chiefly a statistical study
of population, or demography, as the science is called to-day. But
this new science, of which Malthus must be regarded as the founder,
was separated from the main trunk of economics at a much later date.
Furthermore, we shall find that the influence of his book upon all
economic theories, both of production and distribution, was enormous.
The essay might even be considered a reply to that of Adam Smith.
The same title with slight modification would have served well enough,
and James Bonar wittily remarks that Malthus might have headed it
An Essay on the Causes of the Poverty of Nations.

The attempt to explain the persistence of certain economic phenomena by connecting them with the presence of a new factor, biological
in its character and differing in its origin both from personal interest
and the mere desire for profit, considerably expanded the economic
horizon and announced the advent of sociology. We know that
Darwin himself acknowledged his indebtedness to the work of Malthus
for the first suggestion of what eventually became the most celebrated
scientific doctrine of the nineteenth century, namely, the conception
of the struggle for existence and the survival of the fittest as one of
the mainsprings of progress.

There is no necessity for thinking that the dangers which might
result from an indefinite growth of population had not engaged the
attention of previous writers. In France Buffon and Montesquieu had
already shown some concern in the matter. But a numerous population was usually regarded as advantageous, and fear of excess was
never entertained inasmuch as it was believed that the number of
people would always be limited by the available means of subsistence.[1]
This was the view of the Physiocrat Mirabeau, stated in his own
characteristic fashion in his book *L'Ami des hommes,* which has for its
sub-title *Traité de la population.* Such a natural fact as the growth of
population could possess no terrors for the advocates of the 'natural
order.' But in the writings of Godwin this "natural" optimism
assumed extravagant proportions. His book on *Political Justice* appeared in 1793 and greatly impressed the public. Godwin, it has been
well said, was the first anarchist who was also a doctrinaire. At any
rate he seems to have been the first to employ that famous phrase,
"Government even in its best state is an evil." His illimitable confidence in the future of society and the progress of science, which he
thought would result in such a multiplicity of products that half a day's
work would be sufficient to satisfy every need, and his belief in the

[1] See Stangeland, *Pre-Malthusian Doctrines* (New York, 1904).

efficacy of reason as a force which would restrain personal interest
and check the desire for profit, really entitles him to be considered a
pioneer. But life having become so pleasant, was there no possibility
that men might then multiply beyond the available means of subsistence? Godwin was ignorant of the terrible intricacies of the problem he had thus raised, and he experienced no difficulty in replying
that such a result, if it ever came to pass, must take several centuries,
for reason may prove as powerful in controlling the sexual instinct as
in restraining the desire for profit. Godwin even goes so far as to outline a social State in which reason shall so dominate sense that reproduction will cease altogether and man will become immortal.[1]

Almost at the same time there appeared in France a volume closely
resembling Godwin's, entitled *Esquisse d'un Tableau historique des progrès
de l'esprit humain*, written by Condorcet (1794). It displays the same
confidence in the possibility of achieving happiness through the all-
powerful instrumentality of science, which, if not destined actually to
overcome death, was at least going to postpone it indefinitely.[2] This
optimistic book, written by a man who was about to poison himself in
order to escape the guillotine, cannot leave us quite unmoved. But,
death abolished, Condorcet finds that he has to face the old question
propounded to Godwin: "Can the earth always be relied upon to
supply sufficient means of subsistence?" To this question he gives
the same answer: either science will be able to increase the means of
subsistence or reason will prevent an inordinate growth of population.

It was inevitable, in accordance with the law of rhythm which
characterizes the movements of thought no less than the forces of
nature, that such hasty optimism should provoke a reaction. It was
not long in coming, and in Malthus's essay we have it developed in
fullest detail.

To the statement that there are no limits to the progress of mankind either in wealth or happiness, and that the fear of over-population
is illusory, or at any rate so far removed that it need cause no apprehension, Malthus replied that, on the contrary, we have in population
an almost insurmountable obstacle, not merely looming in the distant
future, but pressing and insistent[3]—the stone of Sisyphus destined to be

[1] Godwin, *Political Justice*, Book VIII, chapter vii (reprinted, London, 1890).
[2] "Man doubtless will never become immortal, but it is possible that the span of
human life may be indefinitely prolonged."
[3] Chapter viii is entitled "The Error of Thinking that the Danger resulting from
Population is Remote." "There are few States in which there is not a constant effort
in the population to increase beyond the means of subsistence. This constant effort
as constantly tends to subject the lower classes of society to distress, and to prevent
any great permanent amelioration of their condition." (P. 10.)

the cause of humanity's ceaseless toil and final overthrow. Nature has planted an instinct in man which, left to itself, must result in starvation and death, or vice. This is the one fact that affords a clue to men's suffering and a key to the history of nations and their untold woes.

Every one, however little acquainted with sociological study, knows something of the memorable formula by which Malthus endeavoured to show the contrast between the frightful rapidity with which population grows when it is allowed to take its own course and the relative slowness in the growth of the means of subsistence. The first is represented by a geometrical series where each successive number is a multiple of the previous one. The second series increases in arithmetical progression, that is, by simple addition, the illustration being simply a series of whole numbers:

1	2	4	8	16	32	64	128	256
1	2	3	4	5	6	7	8	9

Every term corresponds to a period of twenty-five years, and a glance at the figures will show us that population is supposed to double every twenty-five years, while the means of subsistence merely increases by an equal amount during each of these periods. Thus the divergence between the two series grows with astonishing rapidity. In the table given above, containing only nine terms, the population figure has already grown to twenty-seven times the means of subsistence in a period of 225 years. Had the series been extended up to the hundredth term a numerical representation of the divergence would have required some ingenuity.

The first progression may be taken as correct, representing as it does the biological law of generation. The terms 'generation' and 'multiplication' are not used as synonyms without some purpose. It is true that doubling supposes four persons to arrive at the marriageable age, and this means five or six births if we are to allow for the inevitable wastage from infant mortality. This figure appears somewhat high to those who live in a society where limitation of the birthrate is fairly usual. But it is certain that among living beings in general, including humankind, who are least prolific, the number of births where no restraint of any kind exists is really much higher. Women have been known to give birth to twenty or even more children. And there are no signs of diminishing capacity among the sexes, for population is still growing. In taking two as his coefficient Malthus has certainly not overstepped the mark.[1]

[1] If two children were the normal issue of every marriage, population would evidently diminish, for all the children will not reach the marriageable age. Of those

The period of twenty-five years as the interval between the two terms is more open to criticism.[1] The practice of reckoning three generations to a century implies that an interval of about thirty-three years must elapse between one generation and another.

But these are unimportant details. It is immaterial whether we lengthen the interval between the two terms from twenty-five to thirty-three years, or reduce the ratio from 2 to $1\frac{1}{2}$, or even to something between $1\frac{1}{4}$ and $1\frac{1}{10}$. The movement will be a little slower, but it is enough that its geometrical character should be admitted, for however slow it moves at first it will grow by leaps and bounds until it surpasses all limits. These corrections fail to touch the real force of Malthus's reasoning concerning the law of reproduction.

The series representing the growth of the means of subsistence is also open to criticism. It is evidently of a more arbitrary character, and we cannot say whether it is simply supposed to represent a possible contingency like the first, or whether it pretends to represent reality. At least it does not correspond to any known and certain law, such as the law of reproduction. As a matter of fact it rather seems to give it the lie; for, in short, what is meant by means of subsistence unless we are to understand the animal and vegetable species that reproduce themselves according to the same laws as human beings, only at a much faster rate? The power of reproduction among plants, like corn or potatoes, or among animals, like fowls, herrings, cattle even, or sheep, far surpasses that of man. To this criticism Malthus might have replied as follows. This virtual power of reproduction possessed by these necessaries of life is in reality confined to very limited areas of the habitable globe. It is further restricted by the difficulty of obtaining the proper kind of nourishment, and by the struggle for existence. But if we admit exceptions in the one case why not also in the other? It certainly seems as if there were some incon-

---

that do all will not become parents. Experience seems to show that with a birth-rate of less than three per family population does not increase, or if it does grow at all it is almost imperceptibly. This is the case in France, where on an average there are 2·70 births to every marriage.

To justify multiplying by two, Malthus regards a family of six as being a normal one. Of the six, two will die before attaining marriageable age, or will remain celibates, so that we are left with four, who will in turn become parents, and so we have the series 2, 4, etc.

[1] The statement that population doubles every twenty-five years might appear to be confirmed by the growth of population in the United States. It is curious to find that the population there during the nineteenth century conforms exactly to Malthus's formula. In 1800 it was 5 millions. Doubling four times (4 periods of 25 years = 100) gives us a population of 80 millions, which is actually the figure for 1905, five years after the end of the century. But of course this is pure chance, the increase resulting from immigration rather than a rising birth-rate.

sistency here. As a matter of fact we have two different theses. The one attempts to show how multiplication or reproduction need not of necessity be less rapid among plants or animals than it is among men. The other expresses what actually happens by showing that the obstacles to the indefinite multiplication of men are not less numerous than the difficulties in the way of an indefinite multiplication of vegetables or animals, or, in other words, that the former is a function of the latter.

In order to grasp the true significance of the second formula it must be translated from the domain of biology into the region of economics. Malthus evidently thought of it as the amount of corn yielded by a given quantity of land. The English economists could think of nothing except in terms of corn! What he wished to point out was that the utmost we can expect in this matter is that the increase in the amount of the harvest should be in arithmetical progression— say, an increase of two hectolitres every twenty-five years. This hypothesis is really rather too liberal. Lavoisier in 1789 calculated that the French crop yielded on an average about $7\frac{3}{4}$ hectolitres per hectare. Before the First World War it averaged about 16, and if we admit that the increment was regular throughout the 120 years which had since elapsed there was an increase of 2 hectolitres per 25 years. This rate of increase proved sufficient to meet the small increase which has taken place in the population of France. But would it have sufficed for a population growing as rapidly as that of England or Germany? Assuredly not, for these countries, despite their superior yields, are forced to import from outside a great proportion of the grain which they consume. The question arises whether France can continue indefinitely on the same basis during the course of the coming centuries. This is, indeed, unlikely, for there must be a physical limit to the earth's capacity on account of the limited number of elements it contains. The economic limit will be reached still earlier because of the increasing cost of attempting to carry on production at these extreme limits. Thus it seems as if the law of diminishing returns, which we must study later, were the real basis of the Malthusian laws, although Malthus himself makes no express mention of it.

It is a truism that the number of people who can live in any place cannot exceed the number of people who can gain subsistence there. Any excessive population must, according to definition, die of hunger.[1]

[1] It was in this connexion that Malthus penned those famous words which have been so frequently brought up against him, although they were omitted from a later edition. "A man who is born into a world already possessed, if he cannot get

This is just what happens in the animal and vegetable kingdoms. Germs are extraordinarily prolific, but their undue multiplication is pitilessly retarded by a law which demands the death of a certain proportion, so that life, like a well-regulated reservoir, always remains at a mean level, the terrible gaps made by death being replenished by a new flow. Among savages, just as among animals, which they much resemble, a large proportion literally dies of hunger. Malthus devoted much attention to the study of primitive society, and he must be regarded as one of the pioneers of prehistoric sociology—a subject that has made much headway since then.

He proceeds to show how insufficient nourishment always brings a thousand evils in its train, not merely hunger and death, but also epidemics and such terrible practices as cannibalism, infanticide, and slaughter of the old, as well as war, which, even when not undertaken with a definite view to eating the conquered, always results in robbing them of their land and the food which it yielded. These are the 'positive' or 'repressive' checks.

But it may be replied that both among savages and animals the cause of this insufficiency of food is an incapacity for production rather than an excess of population.

Malthus has no difficulty in answering this objection by showing how savage customs prevailed among such civilized people as the Greeks. And even among the most modern nations the repressive checks, somewhat mitigated it is true, are never really absent. Famine in the sense of absolute starvation is seldom experienced nowadays, except perhaps in Russia, but it is by no means a stranger even to the most advanced communities. Tuberculosis, which involves such terrible bodily suffering, is nothing but a deadly kind of famine. Lack of food is also responsible for the abnormally high rate of infant mortality and for the premature death of the adult worker. As for war, it still demands its toll. Malthus was living during the wars of the Revolution and the First Empire—bloody catastrophes that caused the death of about ten million men, all in the prime of life.

In civilized communities equilibrium is possible through humaner methods, in the substitution of the preventive check with its reduced birth-rate for the repressive check with its abnormal death-rate. Here is an expedient of which only the rational and the provident can avail

---

subsistence from his parents on whom he has a just demand, and if the society do not want his labour, has no claim of *right* to the smallest portion of food, and, in fact, has no business to be where he is. At Nature's mighty feast there is no vacant cover for him. She tells him to be gone. . . ." On the other hand, let us remember his services in reorganizing public assistance in England in 1832.

themselves, an expedient open only to man. Knowing that his children are doomed to die—perhaps at an early age—he may abstain from having any. In reality this is the only efficacious way of checking the growth of population, for the positive check only excites new growth, just as the grass that is mown grows all the more rapidly afterwards. The history of war furnishes many a striking illustration of this. The year following the terrible war of 1870–71 remains unique in the demographic annals of France on account of the sudden upward trend of the declining curve of natality.

It was in the second edition of his book that Malthus expanded his treatment of the preventive checks, thus softening the somewhat harsher aspects of his first edition. It is very important that we should grasp his exact meaning. We therefore make no apology for frequently quoting his views on one point which is in itself very important, but upon which the ideas of the reverend pastor of Haileybury have been so often misrepresented.

The preventive check must be taken to imply moral restraint. But does this mean abstaining from sexual intercourse during the period of marriage after the birth, say, of three children, which may be taken as sufficient to keep the population stationary or moderately progressive? We cannot find that Malthus ever advocated such abstention. We have already seen that he considered six children a normal family, implying the doubling of the population every twenty-five years. Neither is it suggested that six should be the maximum, for he adds: "It may be said, perhaps, that even this degree of prudence might not always avail, as when a man marries he cannot tell what number of children he shall have, and many have more than six. This is certainly true." (P. 536.)

But where does moral restraint come in? This is how he defines it: "Restraint from marriage which is not followed by irregular gratifications may properly be termed moral restraint" (p. 9); and to avoid any possible misunderstanding he adds a note: "By moral restraint I would be understood to mean a restraint from marriage from prudential motives with a conduct strictly moral during the period of this restraint, and I have never intentionally deviated from this sense." All this is perfectly explicit. He means abstention from all sexual intercourse outside the bonds of marriage, and the postponement of marriage itself until such time as the man can take upon himself the responsibility of bringing up a family—and even the complete renunciation of marriage should the economic conditions never prove favourable.

Malthus unceremoniously rejected the methods advocated by those who to-day bear his name, and expressly condemned all who favoured the free exercise of sexual connexion, whether within or without the marriage bond, through the practice of voluntary sterilization. All these preventive methods are grouped together as vices and their evil effects contrasted with the practice of moral restraint. Malthus is equally explicit on this point.

> Indeed, I should always particularly reprobate any artificial and unnatural modes of checking population. The restraints which I have recommended are quite of a different character. They are not only pointed out by reason and sanctioned by religion, but tend in the most marked manner to stimulate industry. (P. 572.)

And he adds these significant words, so strangely prophetic so far as France is concerned: "It might be easy to fall into the opposite mistake and to check the growth of population altogether."

It is quite needless to add that if Malthus thus made short work of conjugal frauds he all the more strongly condemned that other preventive method, namely, the institution of a special class of professional prostitutes.[1] He would similarly have condemned the practice of abortion, of which scarcely anything was heard in his day, but which now appears like a scourge, taking the place of infanticide and the other barbarous practices of antiquity. Criminal law seems powerless to suppress it, and it has already received the sanction of a new morality.

But apart from the question of immoral practices, did Malthus really believe that moral restraint as he conceived of it would constitute an effective check upon population?

He doubtless was anxious that it should be so, and he tried to rouse men to a holy crusade against this worst of all social evils. "To the Christian I would say that the Scriptures most clearly and precisely point it out to us as our duty to restrain our passions within the bounds of reason. . . . The Christian cannot consider the difficulty of moral restraint as any argument against its being his duty." (P. 452.) And to those who wish to follow the dictates of reason rather than the observances of religion he remarks: "This virtue [chastity] appears to be absolutely necessary in order to avoid certain evils which would otherwise result from the general laws of nature." (P. 452.)[2]

[1] "The effect of anything like a promiscuous intercourse which prevents the birth of children is evidently to weaken the best affections of the heart and in a very marked manner to degrade the female character. And any other intercourse would, without improper arts, bring as many children into the society as marriage, with a much greater probability of their becoming a burden to it." (P. 450.)

[2] "These considerations show that the nature of chastity is not, as some have supposed, a forced produce of artificial society; but that it has the most real and solid foundation in nature and reason; being apparently the only virtuous means of avoiding the vice and misery which result so often from the principle of population." (P. 450.)
He also notes that this virtue has usually been especially commended to women,

At bottom he was never quite certain as to the efficacy of moral restraint. The threatening hydra always peered over the fragile shield of pure crystal with which he had hoped to do battle.[1] He also felt that celibacy might not merely be ineffective, but would actually prove dangerous by provoking the vices it was intended to check. Its prolongation, or worse still its perpetuation, could never be favourable to good morals.

Malthus was faced with a terrible dilemma, and the uncompromising ascetic is forced to declare himself a utilitarian philosopher of the Benthamite persuasion. He has now to condone those practices which satisfy the sexual instinct without involving maternity, although at an earlier stage he charactized them as vices. It seemed to him to be the lesser of two evils, for over-population[2] is itself the cause of much immorality, with its misery, its promiscuous living and licence. All of which is very true.[3] At the same time the rule of conduct now prescribed is no longer that of "perfect purity." It is, as he himself says, the grand rule of utility. "It is clearly our duty gradually to

---

but that "there is no reason for supposing that the violation of the laws of chastity are not equally dishonourable for both sexes." Malthus evidently believed in one moral law for both sexes.

Consequently whenever the reverend gentleman is reproached with encouraging blasphemy, a point upon which he is particularly sensitive—for example, when it is pointed out that God's injunction to man was to increase and multiply—he has no difficulty in showing that if procreation is the will of Providence, chastity is dictated by Christianity, and that the glorious work of chastity is to aid Providence in keeping the balance of life even.

[1] "Of the other branch of the preventive check, which comes under the head of vice, though its effect appears to have been very considerable, yet upon the whole its operation seems to have been inferior to the positive checks." (P. 140.)

"I have said what I conceive to be strictly true, that it is our duty to defer marriage till we can feed our children; and that it is also our duty not to indulge ourselves in vicious gratifications; but I have never said that I expected either, much less both, of these duties to be completely fulfilled. In this and a number of other cases, it may happen that the violation of one of two duties will enable a man to perform the other with greater facility. . . . The moralist is still bound to inculcate the practice of both duties, and each individual must be left to act as his conscience shall dictate." (P. 560.)

[2] "I should be extremely sorry to say anything which could either directly or remotely be construed unfavourably to the cause of virtue; but I certainly cannot think that the vices which relate to the sex are the only vices which are to be considered in a moral question." (P. 462.) Malthus omits to mention the particular vice which he has in mind. "I have not the slightest hesitation in saying that the prudential check [note the word—no longer "moral restraint"] to marriage is better than premature mortality." (P. 560.) We are far removed from the first edition, where there is no mention of a third alternative between chastity and vice.

[3] "Abject poverty is a state the most unfavourable to chastity that can well be conceived. . . . There is a degree of squalid poverty in which if a girl was brought up I should say that her being really modest at twenty was an absolute miracle." (P. 464.) And elsewhere he writes: "I maintain that the diminution of the vice which results from poverty would afford a sufficient compensation for any other evil that might follow."

acquire a habit of gratifying our passion, only in that way which is unattended with evil." (P. 500.) These concessions only served to prepare the way for the Neo-Malthusians.

Malthus gives us a picture of man at the cross-roads. Straight in front of him lies the road to misery, on the right the path of virtue, while on the left is the way of vice. Towards the first man is impelled by a blind instinct. Malthus warns him to rein in his desires and seek escape along either by-road, preferably by the path on his right. But he fears that the number of those who will accept his advice and choose "the strait road of salvation" will be very small. On the other hand, he is unwilling to admit, even in the secrecy of his own soul, that most men will probably follow the road that leads on to vice, and that masses will rush down the easy slope towards perdition. In any case the prospect is anything but inviting.

No doctrine ever was so much reviled. Imprecations have been showered upon it ever since Godwin's memorable description of it as "that black and terrible demon that is always ready to stifle the hopes of humanity."

Critics have declared that all Malthus's economic predictions have been falsified by the facts, that morally his doctrines have given rise to the most repugnant practices, and not a few French writers are prepared to hold him responsible for the decline in the French birth-rate. What are we to make of these criticisms?

History certainly has not confirmed his fears. No single country has shown that it is suffering from over-population. In some cases—that of France, for example—population has increased only very slightly. In others the increase has been very considerable, but nowhere has it outstripped the increase in wealth.

The following table, based upon the decennial censuses, gives the *per capita* wealth of the population of the United States, the country from which Malthus obtained many of his data:

Year			Dollars	Year			Dollars
1850	.	.	308	1890	.	.	1036
1860	.	.	514	1900	.	.	1227
1870	.	.	780	1905	.	.	1370
1880	.	.	870				

In fifty years the wealth of every inhabitant has more than quadrupled, although the population in the same interval also shows a fourfold increase (23 millions to 92 millions).[1]

[1] These figures only give the values expressed in money by capitalizing them at the market rate of interest, which gives a rather fictitious result. It does not warrant

Great Britain—*i.e.*, England and Scotland—at the time Malthus wrote (1800–5), had a population of 10½ millions. To-day it has a population of 45 millions. Such a figure, had he been able to foresee it, would have terrified Malthus. But the wealth and prosperity of Great Britain have in the meantime probably quadrupled also.

Does this prove the claim that is constantly being made, that Malthus's laws are not borne out by the facts? We think that it is correct to say that the laws still remain intact, but that the conclusions which he drew from them were unwarranted. No one can deny that living beings of every kind, including the human species, multiply in geometrical progression. Left to itself, with no check, such increase would exceed all limits. The increase of industrial products, on the other hand, must of necessity be limited by the numerous conditions which regulate all production—that is, by the amount of space available, the quantity of raw material, of capital and labour, etc. An American naturalist, Professor Edward East,[1] has given renewed support to the idea that the number of regions of the world available for agriculture will soon be inadequate to supply the needs of the human race if it continues to grow at its present rate. One of the masters of political economy in Sweden, Knut Wicksell,[2] has taken the fundamental principle of Malthus as one of the bases of his economic system, and predicted on the eve of the war the fall that would be necessitated in the world birth-rate. If the growth of population has not outstripped the increase in wealth, but, as appears from the figures we have given, has actually lagged behind it, it is because population has been voluntarily limited, not only in France, where the preventive check is in full swing, but also in almost every other country. This voluntary limitation which gave Malthus such trouble is one of the commonest phenomena of the present time.

Malthus's apprehensions appear to involve some biological confusion. The sexual and the reproductive instincts are by no means one and the same;[3] they are governed by entirely different motives. Only to the first can be attributed that character of irresistibility which he wrongly attributes to the second. The first is a mere animal

---

the belief that an American citizen of to-day, however much his consumption may have increased, is any better off than his ancestors.

[1] In a work published in 1923 entitled *Mankind at the Crossroads*. East was professor at Harvard University.

[2] Knut Wicksell, regarded by the modern Swedish School as its founder and master, even suffered imprisonment at one time for having defended the Malthusian thesis.

[3] These differ, again, from the desire for marriage, which is influenced by other considerations. French people marry in order to have a home, but a desire for a home and a desire for love or for children are very different things.

instinct which rouses the most impetuous of passions and is common to all men. The second is frequently social and religious in its origins, assuming different forms according to the exigencies of time and place.

To the religious peoples who adopted the laws of Moses, of Manu, or of Confucius to beget issue was to ensure salvation and to realize true immortality.[1] For the Brahmin, the Chinese, or the Jew not to have children meant not merely a misfortune, but a life branded with failure. Among the Greeks and Romans the rearing of children was a sacred duty laid upon every citizen and patriot. An aristocratic caste demanded that the glories of its ancestors and founders should never be allowed to perish for the want of heirs. Even among the working classes, whose lot is often miserable and always one of economic dependence, there are some who are buoyed up by the hope that the more children they have the larger will be their weekly earnings and the greater their power of enlisting public sympathy. And in every new country there is a demand for labourers to cultivate its virgin soil and to build up a new people.

The reproductive instinct, on the other hand, may be thwarted by antagonistic forces—by the selfishness of parents who shun their responsibilities, or of mothers who dread the pains and perils of child-bearing; by the greed of parents who would endow old age rather than foster youth; by the desire of women to enjoy independence rather than seek marriage; by the too early emancipation of children, which leaves to the parents no gains and no joys beyond the cost and trouble of up-bringing; by insufficient house-room or exorbitant taxation, or by any one of a thousand causes.

Thus the considerations that influence reproduction are infinitely varied, and being of a social character they are neither necessary nor permanent, nor yet universal. They may very well be defeated by motives that belong to the social order, and this is just what happens. And it is at least possible to conceive of a state of society where religious faith has vanished and patriotism is dead, where the family lasts only for one generation, and where all land has been appropriated so that the calling of the father is denied to the son; where existence has again

[1] "By a son a man obtains victory over all people; by a son's son he enjoys immortality; and afterwards by the son of that grandson he reaches the solar abode." "The son delivers his father from hell." "A son of a Brahmin if he performs virtuous acts redeems from sin his ten ancestors." (P. 105.)

This is Manu's law, which Malthus quotes in support of his contention. But he failed to see that as soon as one begins to doubt Manu's teaching the argument is the other way. One of the reasons why sterility was considered a dishonour by Jewish women was that each of them secretly hoped that she might become the mother of the promised Messiah. But when the Jews ceased to hope for the Deliverer that was to come, then the incentive to childbirth was gone.

become nomadic and suffering unbearable, and where marriage, easily annulled by divorce, has become more or less of a free union. In such a community, with all incentives to reproduction removed and all antagonistic forces in full operation, the birth-rate would fall to zero. And if all nations have not yet arrived at this stage they all seem to be tending towards it. It is true that a new social environment may give rise to new motives. We believe that it will, but as yet we are ignorant of the nature of these promptings.

Paradoxical as it may seem, the sexual instinct plays quite a secondary role in the procreation of the human species. Nature doubtless has united the two instincts by giving them the same organs, and those who believe in final causes can admire the ruse which Nature has adopted for securing the preservation of the species by coupling generation with sexual attraction. But man has displayed ingenuity even greater than Nature's by separating the two functions. He now finds that (since he has known how to get rid of reproduction) he can gratify his lust without being troubled by the consequences. The fears of Malthus have vanished; the other spectre, race suicide, is now casting a gloom over the land.

Malthus's condemnation of such practices was of little avail. Other moralists more indulgent than the master have given them their sanction by endeavouring to show that this is the only way in which men can perform a double function, on the one hand giving full scope to sexual instinct in accordance with the physiological and psychological laws of their being, and on the other taking care not to leave such a supreme duty as that of child-bearing to mere chance and not to impose upon womankind such an exhausting task as that of maternity save when freely and voluntarily undertaken. This is quite contrary to the pastor's teaching concerning moral restraint. The Neo-Malthusians, on the other hand, consider his teaching very immoral, as being contrary to the laws of physiology, infected with ideas of Christian asceticism, and altogether worse than the evil it seeks to remedy. His rule of enforced celibacy might, in their opinion, involve more suffering even than want of food, and late marriages simply constitute an outrage upon morality by encouraging prostitution and increasing the number of illegitimate births. The Neo-Malthusians[1]

---

[1] In recent years this movement has acquired unexpected strength almost everywhere, but especially in France, where it certainly seemed quite superfluous. The origins and history of the Neo-Malthusian movement were recounted by M. Chachuat in 1934 in a book entitled *Le mouvement de Birth Control dans les pays Anglo-Saxons* (*Bibliothèque de l'institut de droit comparé de Lyon*, Vol. XXXII.) The movement was started by Francis Place, the eccentric tailor who was connected with the beginnings of English trade unionism and whose papers have provided material for all the historians of that

persist in regarding themselves as his disciples because they think that he clearly demonstrated—despite himself, perhaps—that the exercise of the blind instinct of reproduction must result in the multiplication of human beings who are faced by want and disease and liable to sudden extinction or slow degradation, and that the only way of avoiding this is to check the instinct.

There is reason to believe, however, that were Malthus now alive he would not be a Neo-Malthusian. He would not have willingly pardoned his disciples the perpetration of sexual frauds which enable man to be freed from the responsibilities which Nature intended him to bear. Nevertheless we must recognize that the concessions which he made prepared the way for this further development.

Malthus did not seem to realize the full import of these delicate questions which contributed so powerfully to the overthrow of his doctrine. Especially is this true of the emphasis which he laid upon chastity, involving as he thought abstention from the joys of marriage. Such celibacy he would impose only upon the poor.[1] The rich are obviously so circumstanced that children cannot be a hindrance. We know well enough that it was in the interests of the poor themselves that Malthus imposed his cruel law "not to bring beings into the world for whom the means of support cannot be found." But that does not prevent its emphasizing in the most heartless fashion imaginable the inequality of their conditions, forcing the poor to choose between want of bread and celibacy. Malthus gave a quietus to the old song which eulogizes love in a cottage as the very acme of happiness. It is only just to remark, however, that he does not go so far as to put an interdict upon marriage altogether, which has been the case in some countries. The old liberal economist asserts himself here. He sees clearly enough that, leaving aside all humanitarian considerations, the remedy offered would be worse than the evil, for its only result would be a diminution in the number of legitimate

---

movement. His propaganda dates from the 1820's and is directly associated with the ideas of Malthus. The first book on the subject was that published anonymously in 1854 by Dr Drysdale, entitled *Elements of Social Science*, but it was not till 1877 that Drysdale founded the Malthusian League. It has since made rapid progress in America and England.

[1] He categorically declares that "we must suppose the general prevalence of such prudential habits among the poor as would prevent them from marrying when the actual price of labour joined to what they might have saved in their single state would not give them the prospect of being able to support a wife and five or six children without assistance." (P. 536.) Marriage seems prohibited to every worker whose wages are not enough to keep eight persons, which practically would mean that no workman could marry.

children and an increase in the number of those born out of wedlock.[1]

When telling the poor that they themselves were the authors of their misery,[2] because of their improvident habits, their early marriages, and their large families, and that no written law, no institution, and no effort of charity could in any way remedy it, he failed to realize that he was furnishing the propertied classes with a good pretext for dissociating themselves from the fate of the working classes.[3] And during the century which has passed since he wrote the way to every comprehensive scheme of socialistic or communistic organization has been barred and every projected reform which claimed to ameliorate the condition of the poor effectively thwarted by the argument that the only result would be to increase the number of participators as well as the amount to be distributed, and that consequently no one would be any the better off.

[1] "I have been accused of proposing a law to prohibit the poor from marrying. This is not true. . . . I am, indeed, most decidedly of opinion that any positive law to limit the age of marriage would be both unjust and immoral." (P. 357.)

[2] It is worth while recalling the passage to which we have already incidentally drawn attention: "The poor are themselves the cause of their own poverty." (P. 458.)

[3] His views concerning charity are exceedingly interesting, and are directly connected with his theory of population. This was the practical question about which he was most concerned, and his influence in this direction has been very considerable. He showed himself an uncompromising opponent of the English Poor Law as it then existed. Speaking of the famous 43rd of Elizabeth, he declares that one of its clauses is "as arrogant and as absurd as if it had enacted that two ears of wheat should in future grow where one only had grown before. Canute, when he commanded the waves not to wet his princely foot, did not in reality assume a greater power over the laws of nature." Since public assistance cannot create wealth, it cannot either keep alive a single pauper. "It may at first appear strange, but I believe it is true, that I cannot by means of money raise the condition of a poor man . . . without proportionally depressing others in the same class." But it may be pointed out that although charity cannot beget wealth it does transfer a certain portion of wealth from the pockets of the rich to fill the mouths of the hungry poor. The consumption of the one is increased just as much as the other is decreased.

Not only does he condemn charity in the way of almsgiving, but also the practice of giving work for charity's sake. He admits an exception in the case of education, of which everybody can partake without making anyone else the poorer. Such arguments would seem to imply the prohibition of all charity, whether public or private, and as a matter of fact he demands the gradual abolition of the Poor Laws and of every kind of systematic assistance which offers to the poor any kind of help upon which they can always reckon. But he recognizes the "good results of private charity, discriminately and occasionally exercised." Though he failed to remove the Poor Laws, the effect of his teaching is clearly seen in the Poor Law Amendment Act of 1834.

Malthus's doctrine is just the reverse of the social teaching on the question in France at the present time. There you have an attempt to substitute solidarity for Christian charity. That means that the poor should be able to demand assistance, not as a gift, but as a right, and that the place of individual or private charity should be taken by a public institution with a view to giving effect to this. His teaching concerning the preventive obstacle has been so thoroughly taken to heart that there is not much fear of legal assistance resulting in a growth of population.

Whatever opposition Malthus's doctrines may have aroused, his teaching has long since become a part and parcel of economic science. Occasionally it has thwarted legitimate claims, while at other times it has been used to buttress some well-known Classical doctrine, such as the law of rent or the wages fund theory. On more than one occasion it has done service in the defence of family life and private property, two institutions which are supposed to act as effective checks upon the growth of population, because of the responsibilities which they involve.[1]

The population question has lost none of its importance, although it has somewhat changed its aspect. What Malthus called the preventive check has got such a hold of almost every country that modern economists and sociologists are concerned not so much with the question of an unlimited growth of population as with the regular and universal decline of the birth-rate. It has already been predicted in some countries that in a short time the population will either become stationary or begin to fall. What is called the "net reproduction rate" has fallen in some countries of Northern, Central, and Western Europe below that which is necessary to keep the population at the existing level.[2]

It is generally agreed, however, that these causes are not natural or pathological laws, but simply the deliberate will of parents to have no children or to limit their number.[3] But this explains nothing at

[1] It is not proved, however, that such were Malthus's views. Private property, at least peasant proprietorship, acts as a stimulus to population. And it is very curious to think that he should have taken his illustration from France, where the multiplication of small farms is considered one of the causes of the falling birth-rate. "At all times the number of small farmers and proprietors in France was great, and though such a state of things is by no means favourable to the clear surplus produce or disposable wealth of a nation, yet sometimes it is not unfavourable to the absolute produce, and it has always a strong tendency to encourage population." And again: "Even in France, with all her advantages of situation and climate, the tendency of population is so great and the want of foresight among the lower classes so remarkable . . ." Godwin and Young express similar opinions. The latter is quoted by Malthus: "The predominant evil of the kingdom is the having so great a population that she can neither employ nor feed it." (P. 509.)

Marriage, Malthus thought, had a restraining influence upon population. He admits that the simplest and most natural obstacle is to oblige every father to rear his own children. He also admits that the shame which the mother of a bastard and her child have to endure is a matter of social necessity. He does not approve of forcing the man who has betrayed a woman to marry, but he declares that seduction ought to be seriously punished. This was a very novel view at the time, although later it came to be commonly adopted.

[2] See *La Population de la France*, by Huber, Bunle, and Boverat (Hachette, Paris), p. 186.

[3] There are some sociologists who, like Malthus, would seek an explanation both of depopulation and of over-population in biological causes. Fourier and Doubleday, for example, are among the number. Doubleday, who wrote forty years before

all, for the question is *why* people no longer wish to have children, and, in regard to France, why this deliberate abstinence—which in most countries began only in the latter half of the nineteenth century, though it is of longer standing in France—has increased so much. To explain it we must discover its causes, which are not peculiar to France or to our own generation, and which should therefore be observable elsewhere, though perhaps in different proportions. It may be, as Paul Leroy-Beaulieu believes, that a fall in the birth-rate results simply from the progress of civilization—rather too flattering an explanation in the case of France—creating needs and expenses incompatible with the duties and burdens of parenthood. Or we may agree with Dumont,[1] who ascribes it to the progress of democracy, which stimulates the desire to succeed, to rise more quickly and as high as possible—what he calls very ingeniously the *law of capillarity*. Or again we may attribute it to more specific causes, varying from one school of thought to another, such as the system of equal inheritance, as the Le Play school believes, or the weakening of moral and religious beliefs, which is the view of Paul Bureau, or intemperance in all its forms, such as debauchery, alcoholism, and so forth. One of the most interesting explanations is that suggested by Landry in his *La Révolution démographique*.[2] According to this view there are "populational systems" which are not the same in all periods or in all human groups. He distinguishes three of these, corresponding to three groups of doctrines, and defines them as follows: "In some communities marriages and births are unrestrained, the standard of life—at all events for the most numerous class—is fixed at what is called 'subsistence level,' and the *death-rate* may be said to determine population changes. In certain other communities the aim of parents is to secure for their children the same conditions as they themselves enjoy. In this case the standard of life is above subsistence level, but there is no voluntary limitation of procreation and it is by variations in the *marriage-rate* that the object aimed at is (more or less successfully)

Malthus, believed that fecundity varied inversely with subsistence, and that this acted as a kind of natural check upon the growth of population. There are others, again, who think that reproductive capacity varies inversely with intellectual activity. Both explanations seem to suggest a kind of opposition between the development of the individual and the progress of the race which is very suggestive. But their views have not gained many adherents. If they are ever proved, which is not very likely, the prospect is not an attractive one. It would mean that those nations and classes who have risen to a position of ease through their superior culture would disappear, while the poorer, uncultured masses would continue to increase.

[1] Arsène Dumont, *La Capillarité sociale* (Paris, 1890).

[2] Sirey, Paris, 1934. Landry's theory has been dealt with by the Belgian economist and statistician Armand Julin in the *Revue internationale de Statistique* for 1942 and 1943.

achieved. What we see nowadays in the most civilized countries is population changes determined principally by variations in the *birth-rate*: birth control is commonly practised, partly from the desire not to be burdened with the expense of a large family, and partly so that the children may live in greater comfort than their parents and rise higher in the social scale" (p. 202). The true cause of the decline in the birth-rate would therefore be that "rationalization" which since the eighteenth century has been introduced into all parts of life, whether public or private, in place of the former devotion to tradition, custom, and instinct (p. 40). Other writers, such as Sauvy,[1] instead of dwelling on the causes of the decline in the birth-rate, have tried to define what is nowadays called the "optimum" population—a difficult concept to define precisely—and have calculated the results and repercussions of the decline on production and financial conditions in the countries in which it occurs.

These researches, however useful they may be, still leave unsolved the mystery of the forces that determine at any given moment the rapid increase, the stagnation, and even the decline of a population. These forces have roots going down into the depths of man's instinctive feelings, where it is hardly permissible for the sociologist or the economist to reach them and analyse them. All we can say is, like the German demographer Mombert,[2] that a higher degree of comfort and well-being acts more often as a restraint than as a stimulus.

II: RICARDO

Next to Smith, Ricardo is the greatest name in economics, and fiercer controversy has centred round his name than ever raged around the master's. Smith founded no school, and his wisdom and moderation saved him from controversy. Hence every economist, whatever his views, is found sitting at his feet straining to catch the divine accents as they fall from his lips.

But Ricardo was no dweller in ethereal regions. He was in the thickest of the fight—the butt of every shaft. In discussions on the question of method the attack is always directed against Ricardo, who is charged with being the first to lead the science into the fruitless paths of abstraction. The Ricardian theory of rent affords a target for every Marxian in his general attack upon private property. The Ricardian theory of value is the starting-point of modern socialism—a kinship that he could never have disavowed, however little to his

[1] *Richesse et population* (1943).
[2] Mombert has devoted many works to the demonstration of this thesis.

taste. The same thing is true of controversies concerning banks of issue and international trade: Ricardo's place was ever with the vanguard.

His defects are as interesting as his merits, and have been equally influential. Of his theories, especially his more characteristic ones, there is now little left, unless we recall what is after all quite as important—the criticisms they aroused and the adverse theories which they begot. The city banker was a very indifferent writer, and his work is adorned with none of those beautiful passages so characteristic of Smith and Stuart Mill. No telling phrase or striking epithet ever meets the eye of the reader. His principal work is devoid of a plan, its chapters being mere fragments placed in juxtaposition. His use of the hypothetical method and the constant appeal to imaginary conditions makes its reading a task of some difficulty. This abstract method has long held dominion over the science, and it is still in full activity among the Mathematical economists. His thoughts are penetrating, but his exposition is frequently obscure, and a remark which he makes somewhere in speaking of other writers, namely, that they seldom know their own strength, may very appropriately be applied to him. But obscurity of style has not clouded his fame. Indeed, it has stood him in good stead, as it did Marx at a later date. We hardly like to say that a great writer is unintelligible—a feeling prompted partly by respect and partly arising out of fear lest the lack of intelligence should really be on our side. The result is an attempt to discover a profound meaning in the most abstruse passage—an attempt that is seldom fruitful, especially in the case of Ricardo.

It is clearly impossible to outline the whole of this monumental work. We shall content ourselves with an attempt to place the leading conceptions clearly before our readers.[1]

[1] David Ricardo was descended from a Jewish family originally domiciled in Holland. He was born in 1772 in London, where his father had settled as a stock-broker. He entered business at an early age, and soon became thoroughly conversant with the intricacies of banking and exchange. On the occasion of his marriage he changed his religion, and thus incurred the displeasure of his family. Setting up as a broker on his own account, he was not long in amassing a huge fortune, estimated at about £2,000,000—an enormous sum for those days.

Naturally enough, his earliest interest in economics centred round banking questions. The French wars had caused a depreciation in the value of the bank-note, and this aroused the interest not only of the specialists, but also of the public. His first essay, published in 1810, when he was thirty-eight years of age, was entitled *The High Price of Bullion a Proof of the Depreciation of Bank-notes*. It was soon followed by other studies dealing with banks and with the credit system. But these short polemical efforts gave scarcely any indication of the great attention which he was bestowing upon the principles of the science. His interest was primarily personal, for it appears that he had no intention of publishing anything on the subject. In 1817, however, the results were seen in a volume entitled *The Principles of Political Economy*. Ricardo

Speaking generally, Ricardo's chief concern is with the distribution of wealth. He was thus instrumental in opening up a new field of economic inquiry, for his predecessors had been largely engrossed with production. "To determine the laws which regulate this distribution is the principal problem in political economy." We have already some acquaintance with the tripartite division of revenues corresponding with the threefold division of the factors of production—the rent of land, the profits of capital, and the wages of labour. Ricardo wanted to determine the way in which this division took place and what laws regulated the proportion which each claimant got. Although unhampered by any preconceptions concerning the justice or injustice of distribution, we can easily understand how he ushered in the era of polemics and of socialistic discussion, seeing that the natural laws pale into insignificance when contrasted with the influence wielded by human institutions and written laws. The latter override the former, and individual interests which may co-operate in production frequently prove antagonistic in distribution.

We shall follow him in his exposition of the laws of rent, wages, and profits, but especially rent, for according to him the share given to land determines the proportions which the other factors are going to receive.

One would imagine that an indispensable preliminary to this study would be an examination of the Ricardian theory of value, especially when we recall the importance of his theory of labour-value in the history of economic doctrine and how it prepared the way for the Marxian theory of surplus value, which is the foundation-stone of contemporary socialism. Despite all this we shall only refer to his theory of value incidentally, and chiefly in connexion with the laws of distribution. We have Ricardo's own authority for doing this: "After all, the great problem of rent, of wages, or of profits might be elucidated by determining the proportions in which the total product

---

the business man could hardly have guessed that it would shake the capitalistic edifice to its very foundations.

In 1819 he was elected a member of the House of Commons, but he was as indifferent a speaker as he was a writer. He was always listened to, however, with the greatest respect. "I have twice attempted to speak," he writes, "but I proceeded in the most embarrassed manner: and I have no hope of conquering the alarm with which I am assailed the moment I hear the sound of my own voice." In 1821 he founded the Political Economy Club, the earliest of those numerous societies for the study of economic subjects which have since been established in every country. In 1822 he published a work on *Protection to Agriculture*. The following year he died at the comparatively early age of fifty-one.

Since his death all his writings have been carefully collected, and his correspondence with the chief economists of his day, with Malthus, McCulloch, and Say, published. The correspondence is extremely important for an understanding of his doctrines.

is distributed between the proprietors, the capitalists, and the workers, but this is not necessarily connected with the doctrine of value."[1]

It is, moreover, probable that Ricardo himself did not begin with an elaborate theory of value from which he deduced the laws of distribution, but after having discovered, or having convinced himself that he had discovered, the laws of distribution he attempted to deduce from them a theory of value. One idea had haunted him his whole life long—namely, that with the progress of time nature demanded an ever-increasing application of human toil. No doubt it was this that suggested to him that labour was the foundation, the cause, and the measure of value. But he never came to a final decision on the question, and his statements concerning it are frequently contradictory. We must also confess that his theory of value is far from being his most characteristic work. In the elucidation of that difficult question, vigorous thinker though he was, he has not been much more fortunate than his predecessors. He himself acknowledged this on more than one occasion, and shortly before his death, with a candour that does him honour, he recognized his failure to explain value.[2]

I. THE LAW OF RENT

Of all Ricardian theories that of rent is the most celebrated, and it is also the one most inseparably connected with Ricardo's name. So well known is it that Stuart Mill spoke of it as the economic *pons asinorum*, and it has always been one of the favourite subjects of examiners.

The question of rent—that is, of the return which land yields—had occupied the attention of others besides Ricardo. It was the burning question of the day. The problem of rent dominated English political economy during the first half of the nineteenth century, and a later period has witnessed a revival of it in the land nationalization policy of Henry George. In France there was but a feeble echo of the controversy, for France even long before the Revolution had been a country of small proprietors. Landlordism was far less common there, and where it existed its characteristics were very different. That threefold hierarchy which consisted of a worker toiling for a daily wage in the employ of a capitalist farmer who draws his profits towered

---

[1] Letter to McCulloch, July 13, 1820, quoted by H. Denis, Vol. II, p. 171.

[2] In his correspondence with McCulloch, under date December 18, 1819, he writes: " I am not satisfied with the explanation which I have given of the principles which regulate value. I wish a more able pen would undertake it."

In a letter to Malthus written on August 15, 1820, speaking of his own theory of value and of McCulloch's, he despairingly adds: "Both of us have failed." See Halévy, *Le Radicalisme philosophique,* and Hector Denis, *op. c t.*

over by a landlord in receipt of rents formed a kind of microcosmic picture of the universal process of distribution, but it was seldom as clearly seen in France as it was in England.

The first two incomes presented no difficulties. But how are we to explain that other income—that revenue which had created English aristocracy and made English history? The Physiocrats had named it the "net product," and they argued a liberality of nature and a gift of God. Adam Smith, although withholding the title of creator from nature and bestowing it upon labour, nevertheless admits that a notable portion—perhaps as much as a third of the revenue of land— is due to the collaboration of nature.[1]

Malthus had already produced a book on the subject,[2] and Ricardo hails him as the discoverer of the true doctrine of rent. Malthus takes as his starting-point the explanation offered by the Physiocrats and Adam Smith, namely, that rent is the natural outcome of some special feature possessed by the earth and given it by God—that is, the power of enabling more people to live on it than are required to till it. Rent is the result, not of a merely physical law, but also of an economic one, for nature seems to have a unique power of creating a demand for its products, and consequently of maintaining and even of increasing indefinitely both its own revenue and value. The reason for this is that the population always tends to equal and sometimes to surpass the means of subsistence. In other words, the number of people born is seldom less than the maximum number that the earth can feed. This new theory of rent is a simple deduction from Malthus's law concerning the constant pressure of population upon the means of subsistence.

Malthus emphasized another important feature of rent, and it was this characteristic that especially attracted Ricardo. Seeing that different parts of the earth are of unequal fertility, the capitals employed in cultivation must of necessity yield unequal profits. The difference between the normal rate of profit on mediocre lands and the superior rate yielded by the more fertile land constitutes a special kind of profit which is immediately seized by the owner of the more fertile land. This extra profit afterwards became known as differential rent.

To Malthus, as well as to the Physiocrats, this kind of rent seemed perfectly legitimate and conformed to the best interests of the public. It was only the just recompense for the "strength and talent" exercised

[1] Smith had likened industry to a household with two children—wages and profits; agriculture to a household with three—wages, profits, and rent.
[2] *An Inquiry into the Nature and Progress of Rent* (1815).

F

by the original proprietors. The same argument applies to those who have since bought the land, for it must have been bought with the "fruits of industry and talent." Its benefits are permanent and independent of the proprietor's labour, and in this way the possession of land becomes a much-coveted prize, the *otium cum dignitate* which is the just reward of meritorious effort.

Ricardo enters upon an entirely new track. He breaks the connexion with Smith and the Physiocrats—a connexion that Malthus had been most anxious to maintain. All suggestion of co-operation on the part of nature is brushed aside with contempt. Business-man and owner of property as he was, he had no superstitious views concerning nature, whose work he contemplated without much feeling of reverence. As against the celebrated phrase of Adam Smith he quotes that of Buchanan: "The notion of agriculture yielding a produce and a rent in consequence because nature concurs with human industry in the process of cultivation is a mere fancy."[1] He proceeds to defend the converse of Smith's view and to show how rent implies the avarice rather than the liberality of nature.

The proof that the earth's fertility, taken by itself, can never be the cause of rent is easily seen in the case of a new country. In a newly founded colony, for example, land yields no rent, however fertile, if the quantity of land is in excess of the people's demand. "For no one would pay for the use of land when there was an abundant quantity not yet appropriated, and therefore at the disposal of whosoever might choose to cultivate it."[2] Rent only appears "when the progress of population calls into cultivation land of an inferior quality or less advantageously situated." Here we have the very kernel of Ricardo's theory. Instead of being an indication of nature's generosity, rent is the result of the grievous necessity of having recourse to relatively poor land under the pressure of population and want.[3]

---

[1] It is necessary to remember, however, that the old theory survived and appears here under the very name of Ricardo, for he was unsuccessful in freeing himself altogether from its influence. He defines rent as "that portion of the produce of the earth which is paid to the landlord for the use of the original and indestructible powers of the soil." He continually refers to these powers of the soil, which are described as "natural," "primitive," "indestructible," *i.e.*, as independent of all labour.

[2] "Nothing is more common than to hear of the advantages which the land possesses over every other source of useful produce on account of the surplus which it yields in the form of rent. Yet when land is most abundant, when most productive and most fertile, it yields no rent, and it is only when its powers decay . . . that rent appears." (*Principles*, ed. Gonner, p. 52.)

[3] "The labour of Nature is paid, not because she does much, but because she does little. In proportion as she becomes niggardly in her gifts she exacts a greater price for her work." (*Ibid.*, p. 53, note.)

"Rent is a creation of value, not of wealth," says Ricardo—a profound saying, and one that has illuminated many a mystery attaching to the theory of rent. In that sentence he draws a distinction between wealth born of abundance and satisfaction and value begotten of difficulty and effort, and he declares that rent is of the second category and not of the first.

Still, this cannot be accepted as the final explanation. It is difficult to understand how a purely negative condition such as the absence of fertile land could ever create a revenue. It were better to say that the want of suitable land supplies the occasion for the appearance of rent, although it is not its cause. The cause is the high price of agricultural products—say corn—due to the increased difficulty of cultivating the less fertile lands.[1] In short, the cause and the measure of the rent of corn-land are determined by the quantity of labour necessary to produce corn under the most unfavourable circumstances, "meaning by the most unfavourable circumstances the most unfavourable under which the quantity of produce required renders it necessary to carry on production."[2]

Let us assume, as Ricardo did, that first-class land yields a bushel of corn as the result of ten hours' work, the corn selling for ten shillings a bushel.[3] In order to supply a population that is increasing in accordance with the Malthusian formula, land of the second class has to be cultivated, when the production of a bushel requires fifteen hours' work. The value of corn will rise proportionately to fifteen shillings, and landed proprietors of the first class will draw a surplus value or a bonus of five shillings per bushel. So rent emerges. Presently the time for cultivating lands of the third class will approach, when twenty hours' labour will be necessary for the production of a bushel. The price of corn goes up to twenty shillings, and proprietors of the first class see their gift increased or their rent raised from five to ten shillings per bushel, while the owners of the second-class land obtain a bonus of five shillings per bushel. This marks the advent of a new class of rent-receivers, who modestly take their place a little below the

---

"The comparative scarcity of the most fertile lands is the cause of rent." (*Principles*, ed. Gonner, p. 395.)

Adam Smith had already offered this as an explanation in the case of the products of the mine, but he failed to see that arable land is really nothing but a sort of mine.

[1] To-day we simply say that it is determined by increased demand. But this is quite contrary to Ricardo's views, for in his opinion it is labour and not demand that creates value.

[2] "The value of corn is regulated by the quantity of labour bestowed on its production on that quality of land [or with that portion of capital] which pays no rent." (*Ibid.*, p. 51.)

[3] The illustration as given by Ricardo is somewhat more complicated.

first class. The third class of landowner will receive a rent whenever the cultivation of fourth-class land becomes a necessity.[1]

It has been said in criticism of the theory that the hierarchy of lands has simply been invented for the purpose of illustrating the theory. But what Ricardo has really done is to put in scientific language what every peasant knows—what has been handed down to him from father to son in unbroken succession, namely, that all land is not equally fertile.

Ricardo, so often represented as a purely abstract thinker, was in reality a very practical man and a close observer of those facts that were then occupying the attention of both public and Parliament. High rents, following upon high prices, constituted the most important phenomenon in the economic history of England towards the end of the eighteenth and the beginning of the nineteenth centuries. Right through the eighteenth century—that is, up to 1794—the highest price paid for corn was only a few pence above 60s. per quarter. But in 1796 the price rose to 92s., and in 1801 it reached 177s.—nearly three times the old price. The exceptionally high price, due to extraordinary causes, chief among them being the Napoleonic Wars and the Continental blockade, could not last long, although the average during the years 1810–13 remained as high as 106s.[2]

This high price of corn was not entirely due to accidental causes. Something must be attributed to the fact that the available land was insufficient for the upkeep of the population, and that new land had to be cultivated irrespective of situation or degree of fertility. The pastures which had formerly covered England were daily disappearing before the plough. It was the period of the iniquitous Enclosure Acts, when landlords set their hearts upon enclosing the common lands. Professor Cannan has drawn up an interesting chart to show the close correspondence between the progress of the enclosure movement and the high price of corn.[3]

[1] "When land of an inferior quality is taken into cultivation the exchangeable value of raw produce will rise because more labour is required to produce it." (*Principles*, ed. Gonner, p. 49.)

[2] See Cannan's delightful volume *The Theories of Production and Distribution*, p. 150, where the average decennial price works out as follows:

	s.	d.
1770–1779	45	0
1780–1789	45	9
1790–1799	55	11
1800–1809	82	2
1810–1813	106	2

[3] The number of Enclosure Acts which Parliament, acting with the sanction of public opinion, passed during the latter part of the eighteenth and the beginning of the nineteenth centuries increased very rapidly. Between 1700 and 1845 no fewer

In 1813 a Commission appointed by the House of Commons to inquire into the price of corn—for the proprietors dreaded the day when the return of peace would allow of importation—came to the conclusion that new lands could not produce corn at a less cost than 80s. a quarter. What an argument for Ricardo's theory![1]

But is there no possible means of avoiding the cultivation of lands of the second and third order? Intensive cultivation might doubtless do something to swell the returns on the older lands, but only up to a certain point. It would be absurd to imagine that on a limited area of land an unlimited quantity of subsistence can be produced. There must be a limit somewhere—an elastic limit, perhaps, and one which the progress of science will push farther and farther away, even beyond our wildest hopes. But the cultivator stops long before this ideal limit is reached, for practice has taught him that the game is not worth the candle, because the outlay of capital and labour exceeds the profits on the return. This practical limit is determined for him by the law of diminishing returns.[2]

That law is indispensable to an understanding of the Ricardian theory, and is implied in Malthus's theory of population. Its discovery is still earlier, and we have an admirable statement of it in Turgot's writings: "It can never be imagined that a doubling of expenditure would result in doubling the product." Malthus, unconsciously no doubt, repeated Turgot's dictum.[3] It is evident, says he, that as

---

than 3835 such Acts were passed, involving the enclosure of 7,622,664 acres, most of it common land. Not until 1845 do we find a change either in the attitude of public opinion or in the action of Parliament.

[1] It is not quite clear whether the high price of corn is due to the cultivation of new lands or whether this high price is the cause of the cultivation of new lands. The second interpretation appears to us to be the most natural, but it involves the abandonment of the Ricardian theory.

[2] Some critics—e.g., Fontenay, Bastiat's disciple—suggested that land No. 4 might very well become No. 1, if, instead of being employed in the cultivation of corn, an intelligent husbandman were to put it to viticulture or rose-growing. But this is to beg the question. The law of rent implies products of the same kind, for it is this identity of quality that enables them to be sold at the same price. If bad corn-land could become good rose-growing ground, then of course it would take its place among rose-growing areas, yielding rent as soon as less fertile lands were employed for the same purpose.

[3] Turgot, Observations sur un Mémoire de M. de Saint-Péravy (Œuvres, Vol. I, p. 420). "It can never be imagined that a doubling of expenditure would result in doubling the product. . . . It is more than probable that by gradually increasing the expenditure up to the point where nothing would be gained on the return, such items would successively become less fruitful. The earth's fertility resembles a spring that is being pressed downwards by the addition of successive weights. If the weight is small and the spring not very flexible, the first attempts will leave no results. But when the weight is enough to overcome the first resistance then it will give to the pressure. After yielding a certain amount it will again begin to resist the extra force put upon

cultivation extends, the annual addition made to the average product must continually diminish.[1] Ricardo witnessed the operation of the law under his very eyes, and he frequently hinted at the decreasing returns yielded by capital successively applied to the same land. Even in cases of that kind, where recourse to new lands was impossible, rents were bound to increase.

Taking again land No. 1, which yields corn at 10s. a bushel, let us imagine that there is an increased demand for wheat. Instead of breaking up land No. 2 an attempt might be made to increase the yield on No. 1, but nothing will be gained by it because the new bushel produced on No. 1 will cost 15s., which is just what it would cost if raised on second-class land. Furthermore, the price will now rise to 15s., and the two bushels will be disposed of for 30s., thus giving the proprietor a rent of 5s., because they have only cost 25s. to produce.[2]

There is still another possibility, however. Resort might be had to emigration and colonists might be encouraged to cultivate the best soils of distant lands, soils equal in fertility to those in the first class. The products of such lands would be got in exchange for the manufactured goods of the home country, to which the law of diminishing

---

it, and weights that formerly would have caused a depression of an inch or more will now scarcely move it by a hair's breadth. And so the effect of additional weights will gradually diminish.

"The comparison is not very exact, but it is near enough to enable us to understand that when the earth is producing nearly all it can, a great deal of expense is necessary to obtain very little more produce."

Turgot, with his usual perspicacity, has noted a fact which the Classical writers generally failed to perceive, namely, that at the beginning of the process of cultivation there may be a period when the return shows no signs of diminishing.

[1] We must note the fact that the law of diminishing returns was already implied in the second of the famous progressions given by Malthus, for an arithmetical progression that shows an increase of one every twenty-five years implies an addition slower than the growth of the series itself—i.e., slower than the movement of time. Let us take land that yields one; in twenty-five years it will yield two, an increase of 100 per cent. But this is only the first step. At the end of another twenty-five years it will yield three, the increase being always one. But the increase from two to three means an increase of only 50 per cent., from three to four of only 33 per cent., and so on to 25 per cent. and 20 per cent. When the hundredth place has been reached, the increase will only be 1 per cent., and it will continue to fall further, only more slowly.

[2] Ricardo gives a slightly different explanation. "If with a capital of £1000 a tenant obtains 100 quarters of wheat from his land, and by the employment of a second capital of £1000 he obtains a further return of eighty-five, his landlord would have the power at the expiration of his lease of obliging him to pay fifteen quarters, or an equivalent value for additional rent, for there cannot be two rates of profit." (*Principles*, ed. Gonner, p. 48.) He means to say that if profits fall because new capital is less productive than old, rent must necessarily appear, because by definition rent is what remains of the produce after deducting profits and wages. This explanation closely resembles that one given by West in his *Application of Capital to Land*, published in 1815, and Ricardo was not above acknowledging his indebtedness to West.

returns does not apply. But some account of the cost of transport, which increases the cost of production, must be taken, and this leads to the same result, namely, a rent for those nearest the market, because of the advantages of a superior situation. Distance and sterility, as J. B. Say remarks, are the same thing. If land in America yields corn at 10s. a bushel and freightage equals 5s., it is clear that corn imported into England must sell for 15s.—exactly the same condition of things as if land of the second order had been cultivated, and English landlords of the first class will still draw a rent of 5s. This third possibility was scarcely mentioned by Ricardo, and he could hardly have foreseen the wonderful developments in transportation that took place during the next fifty years, which resulted in a reversal of the law of diminishing returns and the confuting of the prophets.[1]

The great Ricardian theory, *prima facie* self-evident, is in reality based upon a number of postulates to which we must pay more attention. Some of them must be regarded as economic axioms, but the validity of others is somewhat more doubtful.

In the first place there is the assumption that the produce of lands unequally fertile and representing unequal amounts of labour will always sell at the same price, or, in other words, will always possess the same exchange value. Is this proposition demonstrably sound? It is true when the product in question—for example, corn—is of uniform quality and kind. When the goods offered on the same market are so much alike that it is a matter of indifference to the buyer whether he takes the one or the other, then it is true that he will not pay a higher price for the one than he will for the other. This is what Jevons called the "law of indifference."[2]

[1] Shortly afterwards a German landowner published a book dealing with just that side of the problem of rent which had been neglected by Ricardo, namely, the influence of distance from a market upon cultivation and the price of products. We are referring to Thünen, who in his book *Der Isolerte Staat* (Vol. I, 1826) draws a picture of a town surrounded by a belt of land, and shows how cultivation will be distributed in concentric zones around that centre, and how the kind of cultivation adopted will be a function of the distance.

[2] But the honour of discovering this law, which is so important for an understanding of exchange value, does not belong entirely to Ricardo. Forty years before a humble Scots farmer named Anderson had observed the phenomenon and given a very satisfactory analysis of it in his book *Observations on the Means of Exciting a Spirit of National Industry* (1777). "Now as the expense of cultivating the least fertile soil is as great or greater than that of the most fertile field, it necessarily follows that if an equal quantity of corn, the produce of each field, can be sold at the same price, the profit on cultivating the most fertile soil must be much greater than that of cultivating the other, and as this continues to decrease as the sterility increases, it must at length happen that the expense of cultivating some of the inferior soils will equal the values of the whole produce." (Quoted by Jevons, *Theory of Political Economy*, p. 229.) Anderson's name was forgotten until quite recently, when it attracted a certain

In the second place it is implied that this exchange value, uniform for all identical products, is determined by the maximum amount of labour required for its production, or, in other words, by the amount of labour necessary for the production of the more costly portion.

This brings us to the Ricardian theory of value. We know that he considered that the value of everything was determined by the amount of labour necessary for its production.[1] Adam Smith had already declared that value was proportional to the amount of labour employed, but that this was the case only in primitive societies. "In civilized society, on the contrary, there is a still smaller number [of cases] in which it consists altogether in the wages of labour." Labour was regarded by Smith as one of the factors determining value—though by no means the only one, land and capital being obviously the others.

But Ricardo simplified matters, as abstract thinkers frequently do, by neglecting the last-named factors. This leaves us only labour. Land is dismissed because rent contributes nothing to the creation of value, but is itself entirely dependent upon value.[2] Corn is not dear because land yields rent, but land yields rent because corn is dear. "The clearly understanding this principle is, I am persuaded, of the utmost importance to the science of political economy." As for capital, why should we make a special factor of it, seeing that it is only labour? Its connotation might be extended so as to include "the labour bestowed not on their immediate production only, but on all those implements or machines required to give effect to the particular labour to which they were applied."[3] But Ricardo was not thoroughly satisfied with this identification of capital and labour, and, great capitalist that he was, it must have caused him much searching of heart. Furthermore, it was not very easy to apply the conception to such commodities as timber and wine, which increase in value as they advance in age. In a letter to McCulloch he admits the weakness of

---

amount of attention as a precursor of Ricardo. Ricardo himself does not seem to be aware of his existence; at least, he never quotes him. The only two writers mentioned by Ricardo are Malthus and West.

[1] "In speaking, however, of labour as being the foundation of all value, and the relative quantity of labour as almost exclusively determining the relative value of commodities, I must not be supposed to be inattentive to the different qualities of labour." (*Principles*, ed. Gonner, p. 15.)

[2] Hume had already pointed out the objection to this view. *Cf. supra*, p. 81, note 2.

[3] "If fixed capital be not of a durable nature it will require a great quantity of labour annually to keep it in its original state of efficiency, but the labour so bestowed may be considered as really expended on the commodity manufactured, which must bear a value in proportion to such labour." (*Principles*, ed. Gonner, p. 32.)

his theory. After all the study that he had given to the matter, he had to confess that the relative value of commodities appeared to be determined by two causes: (1) the relative quantity of labour necessary for its production; (2) the relative length of time required to bring the commodity to market. He seems to have had a presentiment of the operation of a new and distinct factor, to which Böhm-Bawerk was to ascribe such importance.

The usual method of stating the Ricardian theory of value is to say that value is determined by cost of production. It is also the correct way, inasmuch as he stated it thus himself. It is, however, quite a different thing to say on the one hand that value is determined by labour and on the other that it depends upon the sum of wages and profits (supposing we omit rent).[1] On this point, as on several others, obscurity of thought alone saves Ricardo from the reproach of self-contradiction.

Suppose we proceed a step farther. The statement that value is determined by labour is not enough to account for the phenomenon of rent. Let us imagine a market where three sacks of corn are available for sale. Let us further suppose that the production of each involved a different quantity of labour, one being produced on land that was very fertile, the other on soil that was less generous, etc. Every sack will sell at the same price, but the question is, which of those different quantities of labour is the one that determines the price? Ricardo replies that it is the maximum quantity, and the value of the corn is determined by the value of that sack which is produced under the greatest disadvantages. But why should it not be determined by the value of the sack grown under the most favourable circumstances, or by the value of that other sack raised under conditions of average difficulty?

That is impossible. Let us imagine that the three sacks of corn came from three different kinds of land, A, B, and C, where the necessary quantities of labour were respectively 10, 15, and 20. It is inconceivable that the price should fall below 20, the cost of production of corn grown on C, for if it did C would no longer be cultivated; but the produce of C is *ex hypothesi* indispensable. The market price cannot rise above 20, for in that case lands of the fourth class would be brought under cultivation, and their yield would be added to the quantity already on the market. The supposition is that the quantity of corn on the market is already sufficient to meet the demand, and

---

[1] In a note on section vi, chapter i, he adds: "Malthus appears to think that it is a part of my doctrine that the cost and value of a thing should be the same—it is, if he means by cost ,cost of production including profits." (*Principles*, ed. Gonner, p. 39.)

the increase in supply would soon cause the price to fall again to the irreducible minimum of 20.

We cannot but admire the ingenuity of a demonstration that seeks to explain a phenomenon like rent—which is a revenue obtained independently of all labour—by the aid of a generalization which regards labour as the one source of value. But the explanation is ingenious rather than convincing, for it is quite clear that only in the case of one of the sacks do value and amount of labour actually coincide. In the two other instances the quantity of labour and exchange value are absolutely and indefinitely divergent.

Most contemporary economists, while denying that value is solely the product of labour and preferring to regard it as a reflection of human preferences, would willingly recognize the element of truth contained in the Ricardian view. But it must be understood in the sense that competition, although tending to reduce price to the level of cost of production, cannot reduce it below the maximum cost of production, or the price necessary to repay the expenses of producing the most costly portion of the total amount demanded by the market.[1] In this sense it is true not only of agricultural but also of all other products, and it has a wider scope than was at first ascribed to it by its authors. Rent is nowadays recognized as an element which enters into all incomes. But with an extension of sway has gone attenuation, and the term has lost something of its original significance and precision. To-day rent is treated as the outcome of certain favourable conjunctures, which are to be found in all stations in life, and it is no uncommon thing to speak of consumer's rent, even.

The Ricardian theory, moreover, presupposed the existence of a class of land which yielded no rent, the returns which it gave being only just sufficient to cover cost of production. In other words, Ricardo only recognized the existence of differential rents, and dismissed the other cases mentioned by Malthus.

It really seems as if Malthus were in this instance more correct than Ricardo. It is quite possible that in the colonies, for example, there may be lands which yield no rent because of the superabundance of fertile land. Or the same thing may occur in an old country because of the extreme poverty of the land. But it is quite evident that in a society having a certain density of population the mere fact that there exists only a limited amount of land is enough to give to all lands and to their products a scarcity value independent of unequal returns.

[1] Still we must note that Ricardo and Karl Marx, like every one who has tried to base a theory of value upon labour, tacitly assume the operation of the law of demand and supply in order that their theories may fit in with the facts.

Nor would the case be materially different if all lands were supposed to be of equal fertility, for who would be willing to cultivate land which only yielded the bare equivalent of the expenses of production?

Ricardo's unwillingness to recognize this other class of rent, which depends solely upon the limited quantity of land, was due to the fact that it would have contradicted his other theory that there is no value except labour. It is true that he made an exception of some rare 'products,' such as valuable paintings, statuary, books, medals, first-class wines, etc., the quantity of which could not be increased by labour. Nobody would have taken any notice of such a slight omission as that, but had he left out such an important item of wealth as the earth itself there would be great danger of the whole theory crumbling to dust.[1]

Such is the theory of rent, celebrated above all economic doctrines, and concerning which it might be said that no doctrine, not even that of Malthus, has ever excited such impassioned criticism. For this there are several reasons.

In the first place, it led to an overthrow of the majesty of the 'natural order' by simply depicting some of its gloomier aspects. Men had been led to believe that the 'order' was for ever beyond challenge. Now, however, it seemed that if the new doctrine was true then the interests of the landed proprietors were opposed not only to those of every other class in the community—for sharing always begets antagonism—but also to the general interest of society as a whole.

For what are the real interests of proprietors? First, that population and its demands should increase as rapidly as possible in order that men may be forced to cultivate new lands, and that these new lands should be as sterile as possible, requiring much toil and thus causing an increase in rents. Exhaustive labour bestowed upon the cultivation of land that is gradually becoming poorer and poorer would soon make the fortune of every landlord.

As a class, proprietors have every interest in retarding the progress of agricultural science, a paradox which the slightest reflection will show to be true. Every advance in agricultural science must mean more products from the same amount of land and a check upon the law of diminishing returns, resulting in lower prices and reduced rents, since it would no longer be necessary to cultivate the poorer soils. In

---

[1] But how was it that he never realized that land at least in any given country, and indeed for that matter over the whole world, is simply a kind of wealth "of which no labour could increase the quantity"?

a word, since rent is measured by reference to the obstacles which thwart cultivation, just as the level of water in a pond is determined by the height of the sluice, everything that tends to lower this obstacle must reduce the rent. In mitigation of this charge it must, however, be noted that, taken individually, every proprietor is of necessity interested in agricultural improvement, because he may have an opportunity of benefiting by larger crops before the improvements have become general enough to lower prices and to push back the margin of cultivation. If every proprietor argued in this way, individual interest would finally cheat itself, to the advantage of the general public. But this is nothing to be very proud of.

Ricardo set out to demonstrate the antagonism,[1] and with what a vigorous pen does he not picture it! The study of this question of rent made of him a Free Trader stauncher than Adam Smith, more firmly convinced than the Physiocrats. Free Trade was for them founded upon the conception of a general harmony of interests, while Ricardo built his faith upon one clearly demonstrated fact—the high price of corn and its concomitant, high rents. Free Trade seemed to be the means of checking this disastrous movement. The free importation of corn implied the cultivation of distant lands as rich as or even richer than any in Britain. All this meant avoiding the cultivation of inferior lands and reducing the high price of corn.

He was also desirous of proving to the proprietors that the practice of free exchange, even though it might involve some loss of revenue to them, was really to their interest. Their opposition, he thought, was very short-sighted. "They fail to see," he writes,

that commerce everywhere tends to increase production, and that as a result of this increased production general well-being is also

---

[1] "The dealings between the landlord and the public are not like dealings in trade, whereby both the seller and the buyer may equally be said to gain, but the loss is wholly on one side and the gain wholly on the other." (*Principles*, ed. Gonner, p. 322.) And so when a proprietor sells corn to a consumer it is not of the nature of an ordinary bargain where both parties gain something. The consumer gets nothing in return for what he gives—*i.e.*, for what he gives over and above what it has cost to produce the corn. To get nothing in return for something given is the kind of transaction that generally goes by the name of theft.

Ricardo soon finds a reply to the comfortable doctrine of Smith, that the interests of the landlords are nowhere opposed to those of the rest of the community. "The interest of the landlord is always opposed to that of the consumer and manufacturer. Corn can be permanently at an advanced price only because additional labour is necessary to produce it, because its cost of production is increased. It is therefore for the interest of the landlord that the cost attending the production of corn should be increased. This, however, is not the interest of the consumer. . . . Neither is it the interest of the manufacturer that corn should be at a high price, for the high price of corn will occasion high wages, but will not raise the price of his commodity." (*Ibid.*, p. 322.)

improved, although there may be partial loss as the result of it. To be consistent with themselves they ought to try to arrest all improvement in agriculture and manufacture and all invention of machinery.[1]

The theory of rent, in the second place, endangered the reputation of landowners by showing that their income is not the product of labour, and is consequently anti-social. No wonder that it has been so severely criticized by conservative economists. Ricardo himself, however, seemed quite unconscious of the nature of the blow thus aimed at the institution of private property. His indifference, which appears to us so surprising, is partly explained by the fact that the theory absolved the proprietor from all responsibility in the matter. Unlike profits and wages, rent does not figure in cost of production because it makes no contribution to the price of corn, but is itself wholly determined by that price.[2] The landed proprietor thus appears as the most innocent of the co-partners, playing a purely passive role. He does not produce rent, but simply accepts it.

That may be; but the fact that the proprietor plays no part in the production of rent, whilst exonerating him from complicity in its invidious consequences, spells ruin to his title of proprietor—that is, if we consider labour to be the only title to proprietorship. It was just this aspect of the question that drew the attention of Ricardo's contemporary James Mill. Mill advocated the confiscation of rent or its socialization by means of taxation.[3] He thus became a pioneer in the

[1] "Wealth increases most rapidly in those countries where the disposable land is most fertile, where importation is least restricted, and where, through agricultural improvements, productions can be multiplied without any increase in the proportional quantity of labour, and where consequently the progress of rent is slow." (*Principles*, ed. Gonner, p. 54.) The contrast between fertile lands, free exchange, and the development of agricultural science on the one hand, and the growth of rent on the other, is very strikingly brought out in this paragraph.

[2] "Rent does not and cannot enter in the least degree as a component part of its price." (*Ibid.*, p. 55.) And he adds: "The clearly understanding of this principle is, I am persuaded, of the utmost importance to the science of political economy." It is true that Smith, writing long before this time, had declared that the "high rate of rent is the effect of price," but he does not seem to have attached any great importance to the remark.

[3] Ricardo wisely admits the possibility of confiscating this rent by means of taxation, the reason for this being that "a tax on rent would affect rent only; it would fall wholly on landlords and could not be shifted to any class of consumers." (*Ibid.*, p. 154.) And the argument which he advances in proof of this, namely, that the tax could not be shifted, seems to indicate that this particular kind of revenue is not quite as intangible as that of some other classes in society. But his advocacy is somewhat restrained, for, as he points out, it would be unjust to put all the burden of taxation upon the shoulders of one class of the community. Rent is often the property of people who, after years of toil, have invested their earnings in land. The original injustice, if any, would thus be got rid of in the process of selling the land. This might be a sufficient reason for indemnifying the expropriated, but it is not enough to condemn expropriation altogether.

movement for land nationalization, a cause that has since been championed by such writers as Colins, Gossen, Henry George, and Walras.

Finally, the theory of rent seems to give colour to certain theories which predict an extremely dark future for the race, corroborating the gloomy forebodings of Malthus. As society grows and advances it will be forced to employ lands that are less fertile and means of production that are more onerous. It seems as if the curse uttered in Genesis has been scientifically verified. "Thorns also and thistles shall it bring forth to thee; . . . in the sweat of thy face shalt thou eat bread."

True, he did not carry his pessimism so far as to say that as the result of this fatal exhaustion of this most precious instrument of production the progress of mankind would for ever be arrested by the ravages of famine. Other beneficent forces, the progress of agricultural science and a larger employment of capital, would surmount the difficulty.

Although the lands that are actually being cultivated may be inferior to those which were in cultivation some years ago, and consequently production is becoming more difficult, can anyone doubt that the quantity of products does not greatly exceed that formerly produced?

Ricardo's theory does not involve a denial of progress. But it shows how the struggle is becoming more and more difficult, and how scarcity and want, if not actual famine, must lie in the path along which we are advancing. Suppose Great Britain were now to attempt to feed her 45 million inhabitants from her own soil, would there be much doubt as to the correctness of Ricardo's prophecy?

It is an easy matter to reproach Ricardo[1] with his failure to foresee the remarkable development in the methods of transport and cheap importation which resulted in the arrest, if not the reversal, of the upward movement of the rent curve. The complaints of landlords both in England and Europe seem to belie the Ricardian theory.[2]

[1] "Malthus and Ricardo have both proved false prophets and mistaken apostles The much-vaunted Ricardian law is a pure myth." (Article by M. de Foville or Les Variations de la Valeur du Sol en Angleterre au XIXᵉ Siècle, in L'Économiste français March 21, 1908.

[2] Mr Robert Thompson, in a paper read before the Royal Statistical Society on December 17, 1907, has shown how the average rent per acre, valued at 11s. 2d. in 1801-5, reached the figure of 20s. in 1841-45, and despite the abolition of protection continued to rise up to 1872-77, when it reached a maximum of 29s. 4d. It then continued to fall until it reached the present amount of 20s. This figure is double what it was in Ricardo's time, but considerable deductions are necessary in view of the improvements made in the character of the soil. Thompson, after making these deductions, puts the amount at 15s. 5d., leaving just 4s. 7d. for rent pure and simple. The 11s. for rent at the beginning of the century covered something besides

But who can tell whether the peril is finally removed or not? The inevitable day will arrive when new countries will consume the corn which to-day they export. This may not come about in the history of England and Europe for some centuries yet, but when it does happen, rent, instead of being stationary and retrogressive, as it has been so long, will again resume its upward trend.

It is true that we may reckon upon the aid of agricultural science even if foreign importation should fail us. Ricardo was ever mindful of the great possibilities of human industry. Other economists, notably Carey and Fontenay, one of Bastiat's disciples, have propounded a theory which is the exact antithesis of the Ricardian, namely, that human industry in its utilization of natural forces always begins with the feeblest as being more easily tamed, the more powerful and recalcitrant forces only coming in for attention later on. The earth is no exception to the rule, and agricultural industry might well become not less but more productive.

This thesis, which implies a negation of the law of diminishing returns, is based upon a very debatable analogy.

When speaking of the future of industry it is well to remember that forces used for the first time in the Second World War, such as the energies liberated by chemical and intermolecular action, may hold infinite resources in reserve for mankind. But agriculture is different. Admitting that with nitrogen got from the atmosphere, or with phosphorus extracted from the subsoil, we may enrich the land indefinitely, still we are continually confronted with the limitations of time and space, which must determine the development of living things, and of agricultural products among them. When albumen can be scientifically produced then will the Ricardian theory become obsolete. Until then it holds the field.

2. OF WAGES AND PROFITS

Let us now approach these two laws of Malthus and Ricardo—the law of population and the law of rent—and ask what effect they are likely to have upon the condition of the worker and the amount of

economic rent. Considerable deductions are again necessary, but the amount of capital employed in agriculture was much less then.

One seems justified in saying that in England and even in France and other Protective countries the land has lost both in revenue and value during the last quarter of the nineteenth century almost all that it had gained from the time of Ricardo up till then. But is the recoil sufficient to justify Foville's description of Ricardo's vaunted law as a pure myth? We think not. It has the experience of seventy-five years behind it and of twenty-five years against it, that is all. Anyone who would predict a further fall in rent would probably be running the risk of becoming a false prophet.

his wages. The answer is not very reassuring. On the one hand there is an indefinite increase in the numbers of the proletariat—the result of unchecked procreation, for 'the moral restraint' can hardly be said to have influence at all. The inevitable result is the degradation of human labour. On the other hand, the law of diminishing returns causes a continuous rise in the price of necessaries. Between low wages on the one hand and high prices on the other, the worker feels himself crushed as between the hammer and the anvil.

Turgot had long since given utterance to the tragic thought that the wages of the worker are only just sufficient to keep him alive. His contemporary Necker gave expression to the view in terms still more melancholy. "Were it possible," writes Necker, "to discover a kind of food less agreeable than bread but having double its sustenance, people would then be reduced to eating only once in two days." These must be looked upon as mere isolated statements, sufficiently well attested by contemporary facts, perhaps, but laying no claim to be considered general, permanent, and inevitable laws such as Ricardo and Malthus would have regarded them.

And Ricardo still more emphatically declares that "the natural price of labour is that price which is necessary to enable the labourers one with another to subsist and to perpetuate their race without either increase or diminution." Note the last words, "without increase or diminution"; that is, if a working man has more children than are necessary for replacing their parents, then their wages will fall below the normal rate until increased mortality shall have again established equilibrium.

This is not tantamount to saying that nominal wages measured in terms of money cannot increase. Indeed, it is absolutely necessary that they should increase, seeing that the price of commodities is continually rising. If they were to remain the same the workman would soon be reduced to starvation. Wages accordingly will show a tendency to rise in sympathy with the rising price of corn, so that the workman will always be able to procure just the same quantity of bread, no more and no less. It is his real wages measured in corn that remain stationary, and upon this depends the well-being of the working class.

But do they really remain stationary? Ricardo does not seem to think so. "In the natural advance of society the wages of labour will have a tendency to fall, as far as they are regulated by supply and demand; for the supply of labourers will continue to increase at the same rate, whilst the demand for them will increase at a slower rate."[1]

It is even possible that an increase in nominal wages may hide a

[1] "The condition of the labourer will generally decline, and that of the landlord will always be improved." (*Principles*, ed. Gonner, p. 79.)

decrease in real wages. In that case, of course, wages will appear to rise, but "the fate of the labourer will be less happy; he will receive more money wages it is true, but his corn wages will be reduced." Only when the working classes are sufficiently thoughtful to limit the number of their children will it be possible to hope for a preservation of the *status quo*.

> It is a truth which admits not a doubt, that the comforts and well-being of the poor cannot be permanently secured without some regard on their part or some effort on the part of the legislature to regulate the increase of their numbers, and to render less frequent among them early and improvident marriages.

In other words, there will always be a demand for a certain number of individuals in order to supply the needs of industry. So long as this indispensable minimum is not exceeded the wages even of the very lowest order must be sufficient to maintain existence, for they must all be kept alive at any rate. But should the working population exceed this demand nothing can prevent wages from falling even below the minimum necessary for existence, for there will no longer be any necessity for keeping them all alive.

It must be remarked here that on this question, as on that of rent, Malthus is less pessimistic than Ricardo. Far from maintaining that every rise in wages of necessity involves an excess of population and a consequent lowering of wages, Malthus believed that a capacity for forethought, which constitutes the most efficacious check upon the operation of blind instinct, may be engendered even among the working classes, and that a high standard of life once secured may become permanent. All this may be very true, but the reasoning involves us in a vicious circle. In order that a high rate of wages may produce its beneficial effects it must first of all be established, but how can it possibly be established as long as the working classes remain steeped in the misery caused by not exercising this forethought?

An exit from the circle is only possible by recalling the fact that the market wage incessantly oscillates about the natural wage according to the exigencies of demand and supply. If this accidental rise could be prolonged a little it might become permanent and modify the workman's standard of life.[1]

Such is the law of wages, which has long since passed into an axiom, and whose authority is invoked in every discussion on social reform.

---

[1] "It generally happens, indeed, that when a stimulus has been given to population an effect is produced beyond what the case requires. . . . The increased wages are not always immediately expended on food, but are first made to contribute to the other enjoyments of the labourer. His improved condition, however, induces and enables him to marry." (*Principles*, ed. Gonner, p. 95.)

To every socialistic scheme, to every proposal for social reform, there is always one answer: "There is no means of improving the lot of the worker except by limiting the number of his children. His destiny is in his own hands."[1] Latter-day socialism, commencing with Lassalle, makes a careful study of the law, and returns to the charge against the existing economic order by affirming that in no respect is it a natural law, but merely a result of the capitalist regime, upon which it supplies an eloquent commentary.

We must not fail to note that in the Ricardian theory there is not what we can exactly call antagonism between the landed proprietor and the proletarian. To the latter it is a matter of indifference whether rents be high or low, for his money wages move in sympathy with the price of corn, but his real wages never change. The proprietor on his side is equally indifferent to rising or falling wages, for they never affect his receipts. His rent, as a matter of fact, is determined by the quantity of labour employed on the least fertile lands, but this quantity of labour has nothing to do with the rate of wages. The landlords are the grandees of a different order.[2]

The real struggle lies between capitalist and worker. Once the value of corn has been determined by the cost of producing it on the least-favoured land, the proprietor seizes whatever is over and above this, saying to both worker and capitalist, "You can divide the rest between you." This clearly is Ricardo's view.[3] "Whatever raises the

---

[1] "Every suggestion which does not tend to the reduction in number of the working people is useless, to say the least of it. All legislative interference must be pernicious." (Quoted by Graham Wallas, *Life of Francis Place*. Place was the author of a book on population which appeared in 1822.)

[2] This is a fundamental distinction upon which Ricardo is always insisting. The greater or smaller quantity of labour employed in the production of corn bears no necessary relation to the worker's wages. The one is merely a question of production, the other of distribution. The one is the task, the other the reward. But some might ask if the Ricardian theory of value does not state that the value of the product is determined by the quantity of labour necessary for its production, that this value will be subsequently divided between capitalist and worker, and that the greater this quantity the greater will be the share of each. Labour's share may increase, but not the labourer's, for we must not forget that when the price of corn goes up from 10s. to 20s. it is because the cultivation of poorer lands requires twice the number of labourers demanded by the better kind of land. Besides, it would be a strange thing to pay a man more as the work becomes less remunerative. All that one could hope for would be that the workers under the new conditions might be able to retain their old standard of life—that is, might be able to purchase the same quantity of bread despite the rise in price.

[3] "Thus, then, I have endeavoured to show that a rise of wages would invariably lower profits."

"Thus in every case . . . profits are lowered . . . by a rise of wages."

On the inexactness of the term "high rate of profits" as a synonym for a proportionally larger share of the produce see note, p. 177.

wages of labour lowers the profits of stock." Wages can only rise at
the expense of profits, and *vice versa*—a terrible prophecy that has been
abundantly illustrated by the fortunes of the labour movement, but
never more clearly than at the present moment.

But the mere statement of the fatal antagonism between capitalist
and workman must have caused both grief and surprise to those
economists who had endeavoured to demonstrate the solidarity of
interests between them as between brothers. Bastiat was one of these,
and he tried to show that in the course of economic evolution the share
of each factor tends to grow, but that labour's shows the greatest
increase.

There can be no objection to Ricardo's method of stating the law.
The whole thing is so evident that it is almost a truism. A cake is
being shared between two persons. If one gets more than his due
share is it not evident that the other must get less? It may be pointed
out, on the other hand, that the amount available for distribution is
continually on the increase, so that the share which each participant
gets may really be growing bigger. But that is hardly the problem to
be solved.[1] Increase the cake tenfold, even a hundredfold, but if one
person gets more than half of it the other must have less. Ricardo's
implication is just that. His law deals with proportions and not with
quantities.

Admitting that the proportion which one of the two factors receives
can be increased only if the other is lessened, the problem is to discover which of the two, capital or labour, has the bigger portion. It
really seems as if it were labour, for Ricardo speaks of another law of
profits, namely, "the tendency of profits to a minimum." Here is
another thesis which has had a long career in the history of economics,
but what are the reasons that can be adduced in support of it? The
natural tendency of profits, then, is to fall; "for in the progress of
society and wealth the additional quantity of food required is obtained
by the sacrifice of more labour." It is determined by the same cause
as determined rent—the system is a solid piece of work at any
rate.

But how does the cultivation of inferior land affect the rate of profits?
We have already seen how the worker's share, the minimum necessary
for keeping body and soul together, goes to swell the high price of

[1] Ricardo does not deny this. Indeed, he lays stress upon the fact that he is arguing
on the assumption that the value produced remains the same. "I have therefore made
no allowance for the increasing price of the other necessaries, besides food of the
labourer; an increase which would be the consequence of the increased value of the
raw materials from which they are made, and which would of course further increase
wages and lower profits."

corn.[1] But the manufacturer cannot transfer the cost of high wages
to the consumer, for the rate of wages has no effect on prices. (Labour
has, but wages have none.) As a consequence, the capitalist's share
must be correspondingly reduced. We must remember that the workman gains nothing by the high rate of wages, for his consumption of
food is limited by nature, but this does not hinder the capitalist from
losing a great deal by it.

And so there must come a time when the necessary wage will have
absorbed everything and nothing will remain for profit. There will
be a new era in history, for every incentive to accumulate capital will
disappear with the extinction of profit. Capital will cease growing,
no new lands will be cultivated, and population will be brought to a
sudden standstill.[2] The stationary state with its melancholy vistas will
be entered upon. Mill has described it in such eloquent terms that
we are almost reconciled to the prospect. But it could hardly have
been a pleasant matter for Ricardo, who was primarily a financier
and had but little concern with philosophy. He was very much
attached to his prophecies, and there is a delicate piece of irony in
the thought that the tendency of profits towards a minimum should
have been first noted by this great representative of capitalism. At
the same time he felt a little reassured when he thought of the opposing
forces which might check its downward trend and arrest the progress
of rent. In both instances the best corrective seemed to lie in the
freedom of foreign trade.

The general lines of distribution are presented to us in a strikingly
simple fashion. The demonstration is neater even than the famous
Tableau économique, and it has the further merit of being nearer the
actual facts as they appeared in Ricardo's day, for they are no longer
quite the same. It may be represented by means of a diagram consisting of three lines.

At the top is an ascending line representing rent—the share of
Mother Earth. The proprietor's rent reveals a double increase both
of money and kind, for as population and its needs grow it requires
an increasing quantity of corn at an increased price. Still, the high
price cannot be indefinitely prolonged, for beyond a certain point a

---

[1] But this only means a rise in the nominal or money wage. It does not mean that
the worker gets more corn; he only gets the same amount as before, because the price
of corn has gone up and it makes no difference whether the man is paid in money or
in kind.

[2] "For as soon as wages should be equal to the whole receipts of the farmer, there
must be an end of accumulation; for no capital can then yield any profit whatever,
and no additional labour can be demanded, and consequently population will have
reached its highest point." (*Principles*, ed. Gonner, p. 67.)

high price of corn would arrest the growth of population and at the same time the growth of rent; then it would no longer be necessary to cultivate new lands.

In the middle is a horizontal line representing wages—labour's share. The real wages of labour remain stationary, for it simply receives the quantity of corn necessary to keep it alive. It is true that as the corn is gradually becoming dearer the worker's nominal wages increase, but with no real benefit to him.

Below this is a descending line representing profits—capital's share.[1] It shows a downward trend for the simple reason that it finds itself squeezed between the proprietor's share, which tends to increase, and the labourer's, which is stationary. The capitalist is brought to our notice in the guise of an English farmer who is obliged to raise his servants' wages as the corn becomes dearer, but who gains nothing by this rise because the extra revenue is taken by the proprietor in the form of higher rent. But profits cannot fall indefinitely, for beyond a certain point it would involve an end to the employment of old capital and the formation of new capital. This would hinder the cultivation of new lands, and would arrest the high price of corn and lower rent.

3. THE BALANCE OF TRADE THEORY AND THE QUANTITY THEORY OF MONEY

Such are the more characteristic of Ricardo's doctrines—at any rate, those that left the deepest impression upon his successors and caused the greatest stir among his contemporaries. There are other doctrines besides which, regarded as contributions to the science, are much more important and more definite; but just because they figured almost directly in the category of universally accepted truths whose validity and authorship have never been questioned they have contributed less to his fame. Such are his theories of international trade and banking, where the theorist becomes linked to a first-rate practical genius. Here at any rate there is no note of pessimism and no suggestion of conflicting interests. On the contrary, he was able to point out that "under a system of perfectly free commerce the pursuit of

[1] When speaking of a reduction of capital's share Ricardo frequently employs the phrase "a lowering of the rate of profits," or "a fall in the rate of profits." A fall in the rate is not necessarily synonymous with a reduction of capital's share, however. The rate of profit simply implies a certain proportion between revenue and capital —5 per cent., for example; there is no suggestion of comparison between the quantities drawn by capitalist and workers respectively. Doubtless we must admit that when the rate of profit is diminished, *ceteris paribus*, the part drawn by capital relatively to labour's share also diminishes, but it is clear that if the quantity of capital employed in any industry were to be doubled, or the product halved, capital, even at the rate of 3 instead of 5 per cent., would be drawing a more considerable share and leaving labour with less. Bastiat, as we shall have to note, made the same mistake.

individual advantage is admirably connected with the universal good of the whole."

In the matter of international trade he showed himself a more resolute Free Trader than either Smith or the Physiocrats. It seemed to him that the only way of arresting the terrible progress of rent and of checking the rising price of corn and the downward tendency of profits was by the freest importation of foreign corn.[1]

In addition to this twofold argument in favour of Free Trade, Ricardo brings forward another which is of considerable importance even at the present time. This argument is based upon the advantages which accrue from the territorial division of labour. "By stimulating industry, by rewarding ingenuity, and by using most efficaciously the peculiar powers bestowed by Nature, it distributes labour most effectively and most economically."

It may be worth while remarking that his illustrious contemporary Malthus remained more or less of a Protectionist.[2] It might seem strange that Malthus, continually haunted as he was by the spectre of famine, should refuse to welcome importation. But his point of view was doubtless largely that of the modern agricultural Protectionist, who believes that the surest way of preserving a country from famine is not to abandon its agriculture to the throes of foreign competition, but, on the contrary, to strengthen and develop the home industry by securing it a sufficiently high price for its products. We must also remember that Malthus's theory of rent differed somewhat from Ricardo's, and that he was not so violently opposed to State intervention.[3]

But Ricardo's principal contribution to the science was his discovery of the laws governing the movements of commodities and the counter-movements of money from one place to another, and the admirable demonstration which he has given us of this remarkable ebb and flow.

As soon as the balance of commerce becomes unfavourable to

---

[1] In a letter to Malthus, December 18, 1814, he admits with a sigh of regret that even if a belt of fertile land were added to this island of ours profits would still keep up. Free Trade has added the illimitable zone of fertile land which Ricardo dreamed of, with the result that both profits and rents have fallen.

In his essay *On Protection to Agriculture* (1822) he shows how Protection, by forcing the cultivation of less fertile lands at home, raises the price of corn and increases rents; and his demand was not for free importation, but for a reduction of the duty to 10s. a quarter.

[2] See *An Inquiry into the Nature and Progress of Rent.*

[3] *Cf.* this unexpected remark to which H. Denis has recently drawn attention: "It is evidently impossible for any Government to let things just take their natural course." (Malthus, introduction to the *Principles.*)

France, let us say—that is, as soon as importation exceeds exportation say by £1,000,000—money is exported to pay for this excessive
importation. Money becomes scarce, its value rises, and prices fall.
But a fall in price will check foreign importation and will encourage
exportation, so that imports will show signs of falling off while exports
will grow. Money will no longer be sent abroad, and the current
will begin to run the other way, until the £1,000,000 sent abroad is
returned again. Moreover, the £1,000,000 sent abroad will cause a
movement in the opposite direction—superabundance and a depreciation in the value of money, high prices, a premium on importation
and a check upon exportation. Accordingly economic forces on both
sides will conspire to bring back the balance of commerce to a position
of equilibrium—that is, to that position where each country will
possess just the quantity of money that it needs.

It might be pointed out, on the other hand, that this somewhat
complicated mechanism can only operate very slowly, and that considerable time must elapse before the prices of goods begin to respond
to the change in the quantity of money. But as a matter of fact it is
not necessary to wait until this phenomenon becomes established, for
another striking feature precedes it and announces its approach so to
speak, and this is, as Smith had already noted, a change in the value
of bills drawn on foreign countries. The foreign exchanges are so
sensitive that the slightest rise is enough to stimulate exportation and
to check importation.

Accordingly money seldom leaves a country, or only leaves it for a
short time. In other words, contrary to the generally accepted opinion,
silver and gold in international trade do little more than oil the
wheels of commerce. The trade is carried on as if the metals were
non-existent. In short, it is essentially of the nature of barter.[1]

The explanation is very schematic. Every incidental phenomenon
is omitted, and the whole theory implies the validity of the quantity
theory of money, which is now open to considerable criticism as being
altogether inadequate for an explanation of the facts involved. But
this theory of the automatic regulation of the balance of trade by means
of variations in the value of money, although already hinted at by Hume
and Smith, is none the less a discovery of the first order, and one that
has done service as a working hypothesis for a whole century.[2]

[1] "Gold and silver having been chosen for the general medium of circulation, they
are by the competition of commerce distributed in such proportions among the
different countries of the world as to accommodate themselves to the natural traffic
which would take place if no such metals existed and the trade between countries
were purely a trade of barter."

[2] Ricardo also points out that "if, which is a much stronger case, we agreed to pay

Its explanation turns upon a particular theory of international trade which we can only mention in passing, but which we shall find more fully developed in Stuart Mill's theory of international values.

4. PAPER MONEY, ITS ISSUE AND REGULATION

The enunciation of the principles which should govern the conduct of bankers in issuing paper money is another debt that we owe to the genius of Ricardo. The Bank Act of 1822, and that of 1844 especially, which laid down the future policy of the Bank of England, represent an attempt on the part of the Government to put his principles into practice.

Ricardo was an eye-witness of the great panic of February 26, 1797, when the reserves of the Bank of England fell from ten millions to a million and a half, necessitating an Order in Council suspending cash payments. The suspension, which was supposed to be a temporary expedient, extended right up to 1821. The depreciation in the value of the bank-note averaged about 10 per cent., but at one period towards the end of the Napoleonic Wars it rose as high as 30 per cent. He also witnessed the suffering which such depreciation caused. Landlords demanded the payment of their rents in gold, or claimed an increase in the rent equal to the fall in the value of the note.

Ricardo tried to unravel the causes of this depreciation in his pamphlet entitled *The High Price of Bullion*, published in 1809, and came to the conclusion that there was only one cause, namely, an excessive supply of paper. At this distance of time it might not be thought such an extraordinary discovery after all. Still, he had the greatest difficulty in getting people to admit this, and in refuting the absurd explanations which had previously been suggested. He showed how a depreciation in the value of the note necessarily resulted in the exportation of gold, although most of his contemporaries, on the contrary, believed that the exportation of gold was the cause of all the mischief which they sought to check by an Act of Parliament.

The remedy which I propose for all the evils in our currency is that the Bank should gradually decrease the amount of their notes in circulation until they shall have rendered the remainder of equal value with the coins which they represent, or in other words till the prices of gold and silver bullion shall be brought down to their Mint price.[1]

---

a subsidy to a foreign Power, money would not be exported whilst there were any goods whch could more cheaply discharge the payment." (McCulloch's edition, p. 269.) As a matter of fact, the European Powers who were leagued against Napoleon were subsidized in this fashion, the exports exceeding the imports by many millions. The indemnity of 5 milliards of francs paid by France to Germany affords another illustration of the same truth.

[1] Ricardo's works, McCulloch's edition, p. 287.

But if that is the case why not cut the Gordian knot and suppress paper money altogether? The reply shows how well Ricardo had studied Smith: "A well-regulated paper currency is so great an improvement in commerce that I should greatly regret if prejudice should induce us to return to a system of less utility." "The introduction of the precious metals for the purposes of money may with truth be considered as one of the most important steps towards the improvement of commerce and the arts of civilized life; but it is no less true that with the advancement of knowledge and science we discover that it would be another improvement to banish them again from the employment to which, during a less enlightened period, they had been so advantageously applied."[1]

Proceeding, he points out that where you have only metallic money it might happen that the production of gold fails to keep pace with the growth of population, in which case you have a rise in the value of gold accompanied by a fall in prices. This danger might be obviated by a careful issue of notes in accordance with the demands of society. In short, Ricardo is so little disposed to abandon the system of paper money and to return to the previous system of metallic money that, on the contrary, he would prefer to abolish the metallic system altogether, taking good care that paper money did not become superabundant.

So convinced was he of the superiority of paper money that he had no desire to see the Bank resume cash payment. The result of the resumption would be a demand on the part of the public for a conversion of their paper money, "and thus, to indulge a mere caprice, a most expensive medium would be substituted for one of little value."

But if the notes are not convertible into cash, what is there to guarantee their value or to regulate their issue and prevent depreciation? This can be done merely by keeping a reserve of gold at the bank, not necessarily in the form of money, but in the form of ingots. The bank would not be allowed to issue any notes beyond the value of these ingots. This regulation would have the effect of keeping the value of the note at par, for bankers and money-dealers would immediately proceed to convert these notes into gold as soon as they showed any signs of depreciation. This would not mean, however, that the public at large would again return to the use of metallic money, for these ingots would be of little use for purposes of everyday life.

It is a curious system. One would hardly expect the great champion of Liberal political economy to outline a banking system which could only operate through a State bank. This was clearly his opinion, how-

[1] Ricardo's works, McCulloch's edition, p. 404.

ever. He declared himself utterly opposed to the free banking system, and doubted the ability of such a system to regulate the currency. "In that sense there can be no excess whilst the bank does not pay in specie, because the commerce of the country can easily employ and absorb any sum which the bank may send into circulation."[1] This shows what little confidence a Liberal individualist like Ricardo had in the liberty of individuals and their ability to judge of the kind of money that is most serviceable.

Ricardo's disciples are legion, and among them is every economist of standing of the earlier part of the nineteenth century. The best-known among these are the three writers who immediately follow him in chronological order: James Mill, the father of John Stuart Mill (*Elements of Political Economy*, 1821), his friend McCulloch (*Principles of Political Economy*, 1825), and Nassau Senior (*Political Economy*, 1836).

The two first-named writers contented themselves with a vigorous defence of the master's views without contributing anything very new. We have already referred to the very different conclusions which James Mill draws from the theory of rent, and how he became an advocate of land nationalization. McCulloch also was one of the earliest advocates of the right to strike.

Senior deserves a few pages to himself, for his work in systematizing the Classical doctrines. We shall deal with him in our chapter on John Stuart Mill.

---

[1] Ricardo's works, McCulloch's edition, p. 349.

Book II : The Antagonists

WITH the completion of the work of Say, Malthus, and Ricardo it really seemed as if the science of political economy was at last definitely constituted.

It would, of course, be extravagant to imagine that these three writers were unanimous on all questions. There were several points that still remained obscure, and more than one theory that was open to discussion. Despite its apparent rigidity, it would not have required much critical ability to detect flaws in the symmetrical doctrine so recently elaborated and to predict its ultimate discredit.

Hardly, indeed, was their task completed before the new doctrine found itself subjected to a most formidable attack, which was simultaneously directed against it from all points of the compass. The criticisms and objections advanced against the new science of political economy form the subject-matter of this second book.

First comes Sismondi, a purely critical mind, with a haunting catalogue of the sufferings and miseries resulting from free competition. Spirits still more daring will essay the discovery of new principles of social organization. The Saint-Simonians will demand the suppression of private property, the extinction of inheritance, and the centralized control of industry by the arm of an omniscient government. The voluntary socialists—Owen, Fourier, Louis Blanc—will claim the substitution of voluntary co-operation for personal interest. Proudhon will dream of the reconciliation of liberty and justice in a perfect system of exchange from which money shall be excluded. Finally, the broad cosmopolitanism of the Classical writers is to find a formidable antagonist in Friedrich List, and a new Protectionism, based on the sentiment of nationality, is to regild the old Mercantilism which seemed so hopelessly battered under the blows of Adam Smith and the Physiocrats.

These very diverse doctrines, along with much that is fanciful and erroneous, contain many just ideas, many original conceptions. They never succeeded in supplanting the doctrine of the founders; but they demonstrated, once for all, that the science, apparently complete, was in reality far from perfection. To the Orthodox school they flung the taunt which Hamlet cast at Horatio: "There are more things in heaven and earth than are dreamt of in your philosophy." In this way fruitful discussions were frequently raised, and the public proved sympathetic listeners. The economists who were still faithful to the Classical creed began to doubt the validity of their deductions and were forced to modify their methods and to overhaul their conclusions.

Let us now attempt to realize the importance of the part which these critics played.

CHAPTER I: SISMONDI AND THE ORIGINS OF THE CRITICAL SCHOOL

THE first thirty years of the nineteenth century witnessed profound transformations in the structure of the economic world.

Economic Liberalism had everywhere become triumphant. In France the corporation era was definitely at an end by 1791. Some manufacturers, it is true, demanded its re-establishment under the First Empire; but they were disappointed, and their demands were never re-echoed. In England the last trace of the Statute of Apprentices, that shattered monument of the Parliamentary regime, was removed from the Statute Book in 1814. Nothing remained which could possibly check the advent of *laissez-faire*. Free competition became universal. The State renounced all rights of interference either with the organization of production or with the relations between masters and men, save always the right of prohibiting combinations in restraint of trade, and this restriction was upheld with a view to giving free play to the law of demand and supply. In France the Penal Code of the Empire proved as tyrannous as the old regime or the Revolution; and although freedom of combination was granted in England by an Act of 1825, the defined limits were so narrow that the privilege proved quite illusory. The general opinion of the English legislator is well expressed in the report of a Commission appointed by the House of Commons in 1810, quoted by Mr and Mrs Webb.[1]

> No interference of the legislature with the freedom of trade, or with the perfect liberty of every individual to dispose of his time and of his labour in the way and on the terms which he may judge most conducive to his own interest, can take place without violating general principles of the first importance to the prosperity and happiness of the community.

In both countries—in England as well as in France—a regime of

[1] S. and B. Webb, *History of Trade Unionism*, p. 54.

ndividual contract was introduced into industry, and no legal intervention was allowed to limit this liberty—a liberty, however, which
eally existed only on the side of the employers.

Under this regime the new manufacturing industry, born of many
nventions, was wonderfully developed. In Great Britain Manchester,
Birmingham, and Glasgow, in France Lille, Sedan, Rouen, Elbeuf,
Mulhouse, became the chosen centres of large-scale production.

Alongside of these brilliant successes we have two new phenomena
which were bound to draw the attention of observers and to invite the
reflection of the thoughtful. First we have the concentration in the
great centres of wealth of a new and miserable class—the workers; and,
secondly, we have the phenomenon of over-production.

Factory life during the earlier half of the nineteenth century has
been the subject of countless treatises, and attention has frequently
been drawn to the practice of employing children of all ages under
circumstances that were almost always unhealthy and often cruel,[1] to
the habit of prolonging the working day indefinitely, to the inadequate
wages paid, to the general ignorance and coarseness of the workers, as
well as to the deformities and vices which resulted under such un-
natural conditions. In England, medical reports, House of Commons
inquiries, and the speeches and publications of Owen aroused the
indignation of the public, and in 1819 an Act of Parliament was
passed limiting the hours of work of children in cotton factories. This,
the first rudiment of factory legislation, was to be considerably extended
during the course of the century. J. B. Say, who in 1815 was travelling
in England, declared that a worker with a family, despite efforts often
of an heroic character, could not gain more than three-quarters and
sometimes only a half of what was needed for his upkeep.[2]

In France we must wait until 1840 to find in the great work of Dr
Villermé a complete description of the heartrending life of the workers
and the martyrdom of their children. Here, for example, we learn
that "in some establishments in Normandy the thong used for the
punishment of children in the spinner's trade appears as an instrument of production."[3] Even before this, in an inquiry into the state

[1] In 1835 Andrew Ure (*Philosophy of Manufactures*, p. 481) reckoned that in the manufacture of cotton, wool, linen, and silk in England there were employed 4800 boys
and 5308 girls below 11 years of age, 67,000 boys and 89,000 girls between 11 and 18
years of age, and 88,000 men and 102,000 women above 18 years; a total of 160,000
boys and men against 196,000 girls and women.
[2] J. B. Say, *De L'Angleterre et des Anglais*, in *Œuvres*, Vol. IV, p. 213.
[3] Villermé's report in *Mémoires de l'académie des sciences morales*, Vol. II, p. 414, note.
Villermé's observations were made in 1835 and 1836, although his celebrated work
Tableau de l'État physique et moral des ouvriers was not published till 1840. This book
is a reproduction of his report to the Academy.

of the cotton industry in 1828, the Mulhouse masters expressed thei belief that the growing generation was gradually becoming enervatec under the influence of the exhaustive toil of a day of thirteen or fifteer hours.[1] The *Bulletin* of the Industrial Society of Mulhouse of the same year states that in Alsace, among other places, the general working day averaged from fifteen to sixteen hours, and sometimes extendec even to seventeen hours.[2] And all evidence goes to show that thing were equally bad, if not worse, in other industrial towns.[3]

Crises supplied phenomena no less disquieting than the suffering of the proletariat. In 1815 a first crisis shook the English market throwing a number of workmen on to the street and resulting in riot and machine-breaking. It arose from an error of the English manu facturers, who during the war period had been forced to accumulate the stocks which they could not export, so that on the return of peace their supplies far exceeded the demands of the Continent. In 1818 a new commercial panic, followed by fresh riots, again paralysed the English market. In 1825 a third and more serious crisis, begot probably of the extensive credit given to the newly opened markets of South America, caused the failure of about seventy English provincial banks bringing much ruin in its train, as well as a shock to several neighbour ing countries. During the whole of the nineteenth century similar phenomena have recurred with striking regularity, involving ruin to ever-widening areas, as production on a large scale has extended it sway. No wonder some people were driven to inquire whether the economic system beneath all its superficial grandeur did not conceal some lurking flaw or whether these successive shocks were merely the ransom of industrial progress.

. Poverty and economic crises were the two new facts that attractec immediate attention in those countries where economic liberty hac secured its earliest triumphs; and no longer could attention be divertec from them. Henceforth they were incessantly employed by writers o the most various schools as weapons against the new regime. In many minds they gradually engendered a want of confidence in the doc trines of Adam Smith. With some philanthropic and Christian writer they provoked sentimental indignation and aroused the vehemen protest of humanity against an implacable industrialism which was the source of so much misery and ruin. With others, especially with the socialists, who pushed criticism to much greater lengths, even to an

---

[1] *Enquête sur l'Industrie du coton*, 1829, p. 87. Evidence of Messrs Witz and Son manufacturers.

[2] *Vide Bulletin de la Société*, etc., 1828, pp. 326–329.

[3] *Cf.* Rist, *Durée du Travail dans l'Industrie française de 1820 à 1870*, in the *Revu d'Économie politique*, 1897, pp. 371 *et seq.*

examination of the institution of private property itself, they resulted
in a demand for the complete overthrow of society. All critics whatsoever rejected the idea of a spontaneous harmony between private and
public interests as being incompatible with the circumstances which we
have just mentioned.

Among such writers no one has upheld the testimony of these facts
more strongly than Sismondi.[1] All his interest in political economy,
so far as theory was concerned, was summed up in the explanation of
crises; so far as practice, in the amelioration of the condition of the
workers. No one has sought the explanation or striven for the remedy
with greater sincerity. He is thus the chief of a line of economists
whose works never ceased to exercise influence throughout the whole
of the nineteenth century, and who, without being socialists on the
one hand or totally blind to the vices of *laissez-faire* on the other,
sought that happy mean which permits of the correction of the abuses
of liberty while retaining the principle. The first to give sentiment a
prominent place in his theory, his work aroused considerable enthusiasm at the time, but was subjected to much criticism at a later
period. For the reasons given above Sismondi's views became singularly applicable to the situation after the First World War, and in our
last chapter, dealing with crises, we shall see striking resemblances
between his theories and some of the modern ones, such as those of
Keynes.

I: THE AIM AND METHOD OF POLITICAL ECONOMY

Sismondi began his career as an ardent supporter of economic
Liberalism. In 1803, the year that witnessed the production of Say's
treatise, he published an exposition of the ideas of Adam Smith in a
book entitled *La Richesse commerciale*, a volume which achieved a certain
measure of success. During the following years he devoted himself to
work exclusively historical, literary, or political, and he only returned
to the study of political economy in 1818. "At this period," he writes,

I was keenly interested in the commercial crises which Europe had
experienced during the past years, and in the cruel sufferings of the
factory hands, which I myself had witnessed in Italy, Switzerland,

[1] Sismondi was a native of Geneva. His family was originally Italian, but took
refuge in France in the sixteenth century, and migrated to Geneva after the Revocation of the Edict of Nantes. Here Sismondi was born in 1773. He is even better known
for his two great works *L'Histoire des Républiques italiennes* and *L'Histoire des Français*
than for his economic studies. He was a frequent guest of Mme de Staël at the
Château Coppet, and among the other visitors whom he met there was Robert Owen.
He died in 1842.

and France; and which, according to public reports, were at least equally bad in England, Belgium, and Germany.[1]

It was at this moment that he was asked to write an article on political economy for the *Edinburgh Encyclopædia*. Upon a re-examination of his ideas in the light of these new facts he found to his surprise that his conclusions differed entirely from those of Adam Smith. In 1819 he travelled in England, "that wonderful country, which seems to have undergone a great experience in order to teach the rest of the world."[2] This seemed to confirm his first impressions. He took the article which he had contributed to the *Encyclopædia* and developed it. From this work sprang the treatise which appeared in 1819 under the significant title of *Nouveaux Principes d'économie politique* and made him celebrated as an economist. His path was already clear. His want of agreement with the predominant school in France and England was further emphasized by the appearance of his studies in economics,[3] in which he illustrates and confirms the ideas already expounded in the *Nouveaux Principes* by means of a great number of descriptive and historical studies bearing more especially upon the condition of the agriculturists in England, Scotland, Ireland, and Italy.

Sismondi's disagreement was not upon the theoretical principles of political economy. So far as these were concerned he declared himself a disciple of Adam Smith.[4] He merely disagreed with the method, the aim, and the practical conclusions of the Classical school. We will examine his arguments on each of these points.

First of all as regards method. He draws an important distinction between Smith and his followers, Ricardo and J. B. Say. "Smith," says he, "attempted to study every fact in the light of its own social environment," and "his immortal work is, indeed, the outcome of a philosophic study of the history of mankind."[5] Towards Ricardo, who is accused of having introduced the abstract method into the science, his attitude is quite different, and much as he admired Malthus, who, "possessed of a singularly forceful and penetrative mind, had cultivated

---

[1] *Nouveaux Principes*, Vol. II, p. xxii. Our quotations are taken from the second edition, published in 1827.

[2] *Ibid.*, p. iv.

[3] Two volumes, Paris, 1837 and 1838.

[4] *Nouveaux Principes*, Vol. II, pp. 50–51. "Adam Smith's doctrine is also ours, but the practical conclusion which we draw from the doctrine borrowed from him frequently appears to us to be diametrically opposed to his."

[5] *Ibid.*, p. 56. "Adam Smith recognized the fact that the science of government was largely experimental, that its real foundation lay in the history of various peoples, and that it is only by a judicious observation of facts that we can deduce the general principles. His immortal work is, indeed, the outcome of a philosophic study of the history of mankind." *Cf.* also Vol. I, pp. 47, 389.

the habit of a conscientious study of facts,"[1] still his spirit shrank from admitting those abstractions which Ricardo and his disciples demanded from him.[2] Political economy, he thought, was best treated as a "moral science where all facts are interwoven and where a false step is taken whenever one single fact is isolated and attention is concentrated upon it alone."[3] The science was to be based on experience, upon history and observation. Human conditions were to be studied in detail. Allowance was to be made for the period in which a man lived, the country he inhabited, and the profession he followed, if the individual was to be clearly visualized and the influence of economic institutions upon him successfully traced. "I am convinced," says he, "that serious mistakes have ensued from the too frequent generalizations which have been made in social science."[4]

This criticism was levelled not only at Ricardo and McCulloch, but it also included J. B. Say within its purview, for Say had treated political economy as an exposition of a few general principles. It also prepared the way for that conception of political economy upon the discovery of which the German Historical school so prided itself at a later date. Sismondi, himself an historian and a publicist interested in immediate reforms, could not fail to see quite clearly the effects that social institutions and political organization were bound to have upon economic prosperity. A good illustration of his method is furnished by his treatment of the probable effects of a complete abolition of the English Corn Laws. The question, he remarks, could not be decided by theoretical arguments alone without taking some account of the various methods of cultivating the soil. A country of tenant farmers such as England would find it difficult to meet the competition of feudal countries such as Poland or Russia, where corn only costs the proprietor "a few hundred lashes judiciously bestowed upon the peasants."[5]

Sismondi's conception of economic method is incontestably just so long as the economist confines himself to the discussion of practical problems or attempts to gauge the probable effects of a particular legislative reform or is unravelling the causes of a particular event.

---

[1] *Nouveaux Principes*, Vol. II, p. 268. *Cf.* also pp. 388, 389.

[2] *Ibid.*, p. 56. In several other passages he takes Ricardo to task (Vol. I, pp. 257, 300, 336, 366, 423; Vol. II, pp. 184, 190, 218, 329).

[3] *Ibid.*, p. 56.

[4] *Études sur l'Économie politique*, preface, p. v. Already in his first work, *La Richesse commerciale*, he had declared: "Political economy is based upon the study of man or of men. We must know human nature, the character and destiny of nations in different places and at different times. We must consult historians, question travellers, etc. . . . The philosophy of history . . . the study of travels, etc., are parallel studies."

[5] *Nouveaux Principes*, Vol. I, p. 257.

G

But should the economist wish to picture to himself the general aspect of the economic world, he cannot afford to neglect the abstract method, and Sismondi himself was forced to have recourse to it. It is true that he used it with considerable awkwardness, and his failure to construct or to discuss abstract theories perhaps explains his preference for the other method. At any rate it does partly explain the keen opposition which his book aroused among the partisans of what he was the first to call by the happy title of the "Orthodox" school.

But to imagine anything more confused than the reasonings by which he attempts to demonstrate the possibility of a general crisis of over-production is difficult.[1] For his point of departure he takes the distinction between the annual revenue and the annual production of a country. According to him the revenue of one year pays for the production of the following.[2] Accordingly, if the production of any one year exceeds the revenue of the previous year a portion of the produce will remain unsold and producers will be ruined. Sismondi reasons as if the nation were composed of agriculturists who buy the manufactured goods they need with the revenue received from the sale of the present year's crop. Consequently, if manufactured products are superabundant the agricultural revenue will not be enough to pay a sufficient price.

But within the argument there lurks a twofold confusion. At bottom a nation's annual revenue is its annual produce, and the one cannot be less than the other. Moreover, it is not the produce of two different years that is exchanged, but the various products of the same year, or rather (for this subdivision of the movements of the economic

[1] Sismondi's awkwardness in the manipulation of abstract reasoning is clearly visible in a host of other passages, especially in the vagueness of his definitions. Labour in one place is defined as the source of all revenues (*Nouveaux Principes*, Vol. I, p. 85); elsewhere, as the workers' revenue as contrasted with interest and rent (Vol. I, pp. 96, 101, 110, 113, 114; Vol. II, p. 257, etc.). He never distinguishes between national and private capital, and wages are sometimes treated as capital, sometimes as revenue (p. 379). He constantly uses such vague terms as "rich" and "poor" to designate capitalist and worker (Vol. II, chapter 5). In his explanation of how the rate of interest is fixed he says that the strength of the lenders of capital just balances the strength of the borrowers, and, as in all other markets, they hit upon a proportional mean (Vol. II, p. 36). In a similar fashion he is constantly confusing revenue in kind with money revenue.

[2] "Last year's revenue pays for the production of this." (*Ibid.*, Vol. I, p. 120.) Farther on he adds: "After all, what we do is to exchange the total product of this year against the total product of the preceding one" (p. 121). Sismondi attached great importance to the distinction between the national revenue and the annual product. "The confusion of the annual revenue with the annual product casts a thick veil over the whole science. On the other hand, all becomes clear and facts fall in with the theory as soon as one is separated from the other." (*Ibid.*, pp. 366–367.) It is he himself, on the contrary, who creates the confusion.

world into annual periods has no counterpart in actual life) it is the
different products created at every moment that are being continually
exchanged, thus constituting a reciprocal demand for one another.
At any one moment there may be too many or too few products of a
certain kind, resulting in a severe crisis in one or more industries. But
of every product, at one and the same time, there can never be too
much. McCulloch, Ricardo, and Say victoriously upheld this view
against Sismondi.[1] We shall see in Book VI how the whole problem
has been studied afresh by the most recent writers, starting from the
concept of *monetary incomes*, and how a crisis not general but *generalized*
then becomes easily explicable.

It is not only on the question of method, but still more on the question of aim, that Sismondi finds himself in opposition to the Classical
school. To them political economy was the science of wealth, or
chrematistics, as Aristotle called it. But the real object of the science
should be man, or at least the physical well-being of man. To consider wealth by itself and to forget man was a sure way of making a
false start.[2] This is why he gave such prominence to a theory of
distribution alongside of the theory of production, which had received
the exclusive attention of the Classical writers. The Classical school,
it is true, might have retorted that they gave first place to production
because the multiplication of products was a *sine qua non* of all progress
in distribution. But Sismondi regarded it otherwise. Wealth only
deserves the name when it is proportionately distributed. He could
not conceive of an abstract treatment of distribution, and consequently
could not appreciate it. In his own treatment of distribution he devoted
a special section to the "poor," who live by their labour and toil from
morn till eve in field or workshop. They form the bulk of our population, and the changes wrought in their way of life by the invention of

---

[1] McCulloch criticized Sismondi in an article in the *Edinburgh Review* of October
1819. For J. B. Say see pp. 130–132.
With regard to Ricardo, Sismondi relates that in the very year of his death he had
two or three conversations with him on this subject at Geneva. In the end he seems
to have accepted Ricardo's point of view, but not without several reservations. "We
arrive then at Ricardo's conclusion and find that when circulation is complete (and
having nowhere been arrested) production does give rise to consumption"; but he
adds: " This involves making an abstraction of time and place, and of all those obstacles
which might arrest this circulation."
Sismondi defended his point of view against his three critics in two articles reprinted
at the end of the second edition of the *Nouveaux Principes*.
[2] "The accumulation of wealth *in abstracto* is not the aim of government, but the
participation by all its citizens in the pleasures of life which the wealth represents.
Wealth and population in the abstract are no indication of a country's prosperity:
they must in some way be related to one another before being employed as the basis
of comparison." (*Nouveaux Principes*, Vol. I, p. 9.)

machinery, the freedom of competition, and the regime of private property was what interested him most. "Political economy at its widest," he says, "is a theory of charity, and any theory that upon last analysis has not the result of increasing the happiness of mankind does not belong to the science at all."[1]

What really interested Sismondi was not so much what is called political economy, but what has since become known as *économie sociale* in France and *Sozialpolitik* in Germany. His originality, so far as the history of doctrines is concerned, consisted in his having originated this study. J. B. Say scorned his definitions, so different were they from his own.

> M. de Sismondi refers to political economy as the science charged with guarding the happiness of mankind. What he wishes to say is that it is the science a knowledge of which ought to be possessed by all those who are concerned with human welfare. Rulers who wish to be worthy of their positions ought to be acquainted with the study, but the happiness of mankind would be much jeopardized if, instead of trusting to the intelligence and industry of the ordinary citizen, we trusted to governments.[2]

And he adds: "The greater number of German writers, by following the false notions spread by the Colbertian system, have come to regard political economy as being purely a science of administration."

II: SISMONDI'S CRITICISM OF OVER-PRODUCTION AND COMPETITION

Deceived as to the best method to follow, mistaken in its conception of the nature of the object to be kept in view, it is not surprising that the "Chrematistic school" should have gone astray in its practical conclusions. The teaching of the school gave an undoubted incentive to unlimited production, for it was loud in its praise of free competition. It preached the doctrine of harmony of interests, and considered that the best form of government was no government at all. These were the three essential points to which Sismondi took exception.

First as regards its immoderate enthusiasm for production. According to the Classical writers, the general growth of production presented no inconvenience, thanks to that spontaneous mechanism which immediately corrected the errors of the *entrepreneur* if he in any way underestimated the necessities of demand. Falling prices warned him

---

[1] *Nouveaux Principes*, Vol. II, p. 250. Elsewhere he adds: "Should the Government ever propose to further the interests of one class at the expense of another that class should certainly be the workers." (*Ibid.*, Vol. I, p. 372.)

[2] *Cours complet*, Vol. II, p. 551.

against a false step and influenced him in directing his efforts towards other ends. In a similar way rising prices proved to the producers that supplies were insufficient and that more must be manufactured. Hence the evils committed would always be momentary and transient.

To this Sismondi replied: If instead of reasoning in this abstract fashion economists had considered the facts in detail, if instead of paying attention to products they had shown some regard for man, they would not have so lightheartedly supported the producers in their errors. An increased supply, if supply were already insufficient to meet a growing demand, would injure no one, but would be profitable for all. That is true. But the restriction of an over-abundant supply when the needs grow at a less rapid rate is not so easily accomplished. Does anyone think that capital and labour could on the morrow, so to speak, leave a declining industry in order to engage in another? The worker cannot quickly leave the work he lives by, to which he has served a long and costly apprenticeship, and wherein he is distinguished for a professional skill that will be lost elsewhere. Rather than consent to leave it, he will let his wages fall, he will prolong the working day, remaining at work for fourteen hours, and will toil during those hours that would otherwise be spent in pleasure or debauchery; so that the produce raised by the same number of workmen will be very much increased.[1] As for the manufacturer, he will not be less loath than the worker to quit an industry into the management and construction of which he has put half or even three-quarters of his fortune. Fixed capital cannot be transferred from one use to another, for even the manufacturer is bound by custom—a moral force whose strength is not easily calculated.[2] Like the worker, he is tied to the industry which he has created and from which he draws a living. Consequently production, far from being spontaneously restrained, will remain the same or will even perhaps tend to increase. In the end, however, he must yield, and adaptation will take place, but only after much ruin. "Producers will not withdraw from that industry entirely, and their numbers will diminish only when some of the workshops have failed and a number of workmen have died of misery." "Let us beware," says he in conclusion, "of this dangerous theory of equilibrium which is supposed to be automatically established. A certain kind of equilibrium, it is true, is re-established in the long run, but it is only after a frightful amount of suffering."[3] The dictum which was to some extent true in Sismondi's day controls the policy of every trust and kartel of the present day.

Nowadays production chiefly grows as the result of the multiplica-

---

[1] *Nouveaux Principes*, Vol. I, p. 333.   [2] *Ibid.*, p. 336.   [3] *Ibid.*, pp. 220–221.

tion of machinery, and Sismondi's most telling attacks were directed
against machinery. Consequently he has been regarded as a reactionary and treated as an ignoramus, and for half a century was
refused a place among the economists.

On the question of machinery the Classical writers were unanimous.[1]
Machinery they considered to be very beneficial, furnishing commodities at reduced rates and setting free a portion of the consumer's
revenue, which accordingly meant an increased demand for other
products and employment for those dismissed as a result of this introduction. Sismondi does not deny that theoretically equilibrium is in
the long run re-established.

> Every new product must in the long run give rise to some fresh
> consumption. But let us examine things as they really are. Let us
> desist from our habit of making abstraction of time and place. Let
> us take some account of the obstacles and the friction of the social
> mechanism. And what do we see? The immediate effect of
> machinery is to throw some of the workers out of employment, to
> increase the competition of others, and so to lower the wages of all.
> This results in diminished consumption and a slackening of demand.
> Far from being always beneficial, machinery produces useful results
> only when its introduction is preceded by an increased revenue,
> and consequently by the possibility of giving new work to those
> displaced. No one will deny the advantage of substituting a machine
> for a man, provided that man can obtain employment elsewhere.[2]

[1] The unanimity is not quite absolute, however. Ricardo in the third edition of
his *Principles* added a chapter on machinery in which he admitted that he was mistaken
in the belief that machines after a short period always proved favourable to the
interests of the workers. He recognized that the worker might suffer, for though the
machine increases the net product of industry it frequently diminishes the total
product. He seemed to think that this might happen frequently, but in reality it is
quite exceptional.

[2] We may here recall the celebrated winch argument. Suppose, says Sismondi,
that England succeeded in tilling her fields and doing all the work of her towns by
means of steam power, so that her total products and revenue remain the same as
they are to-day, though her population is only equal to that of the republic of Geneva.
Is she to be regarded as being richer and more prosperous? Ricardo would reply in
the affirmative. Wealth is everything, men nothing. Really, then, a single king,
dwelling alone on the island, by merely turning a winch might conceivably automatically perform all the work done in England to-day. One can only reply to this
argument by saying that long before arriving at this state the community itself would
have devised some machinery for distributing the product between all its members.
To suppose that a portion of the population dies of hunger through want of employment while the other part continues to manufacture the same quantity of goods as
before is sufficiently contradictory. But at bottom, disregarding the paradoxical
form given it by Sismondi, the question set by him is insoluble. What is the best
equilibrium between production and population? Are we to prefer a population
rapidly increasing in numbers, but making no advance in wealth, to a population
which is stationary or even decreasing, but rapidly advancing in wealth? Every one
is free to choose for himself. Science gives us no criterion.

Neither Ricardo nor Say denies this; they affirmed that the effect of machinery is just to create some part of this demand for labour. But Sismondi's argument is vitiated by the same false idea that, as we have seen above, made him admit the possibility of general over-production—the idea that increased production, if it is going to be useful, must always be preceded by increased demand. He was unwilling to admit that the growth of production itself created this demand. On the other hand, what is true in Sismondi's attitude—and we cannot insist too much on this—is the protest he makes against the indifference of the Classical school in the face of the evils of these periods of transition.

The Classical school regarded the miseries created by large-scale production with that sang-froid which was to characterize the followers of Marx amid the throes of the 'inevitable Revolution.' Among many similarities which may be pointed out between the writings of Marx and the doctrines of the Classical school, this is one of the most characteristic. The grandeur of the new regime is worthy of some sacrifice. But Sismondi was an historian. His interest lay primarily in those periods of transition which formed the exit from one regime and the entrance into another, and which involved so much suffering for the innocent. He was anxious to mitigate the hardships in order that the process of transition might be eased. Nothing can be more legitimate than a claim of this kind. J. B. Say recognized its validity to a certain extent, and this is precisely the role of social economics.

Sismondi makes another remark which is no less just. What disgusted him was not merely that workmen should be driven out by machinery, but that the workers who were retained only had a limited share of the benefits which they procured.[1] For the Classical school it was enough that workers and consumers should have a share in the general cheapening of production. But Sismondi demanded more. So long as toil is as laborious as it is to-day, is it not just that the workman should benefit by the introduction of machinery in the way of

---

[1] "We have said elsewhere, but think it essential to repeat it, that it is not the perfection of machinery that is the real calamity, but the unjust distribution of the goods produced. The more we are able to increase the quantity of goods produced with a given quantity of labour, the more ought we to increase our comforts or our leisure. Were the worker his own master, after accomplishing in two hours with a machine a task which formerly took him twelve he would then desist from toil, unless he had some new need or were able to make use of a larger amount of products. It is our present organization and the workman's servitude that has forced him to work not less but more hours, at the same wage, and this despite the fact that machinery has increased his productive powers." (*Nouveaux Principes*, Vol. II, p. 318.) In this passage we have Sismondi's real opinion on the subject of machinery most clearly expressed.

increased leisure? In the social system as at present existing, owing to the competition among workers as the result of excessive population, machinery does not increase leisure, but it rather strengthens competition, diminishes wages, provokes a more intense effort on the part of the workman, and forces him to extend his working day. Here again Sismondi appears correct. We cannot see why the consumer alone should reap all the profit of improved machinery, which never benefits the workman unless it affects articles which enter into his consumption. There would be nothing very striking if the benefits of progress, at least during a short time, were to be shared between consumer and worker just as to-day they are shared between inventor, *entrepreneur*, and society. This idea is the inspiring motive of certain trade unions to-day, which only accept a new machine in exchange for less work and more pay.

Sismondi's method when applied to production and machinery leads to conclusions very different from those of the Classics. This is also true of his treatment of competition.

Adam Smith had written: "In general, if any branch of trade, or any division of labour, be advantageous to the public, the freer and more general the competition it will always be the more so."[1] Sismondi considered this doctrine false, and invoked two reasons of unequal value in support of his view.

The first is a product of the inexact idea already mentioned above, which regards any progress in production as useless unless preceded by more intensive demand. Competition is beneficial if it excites the *entrepreneur* to multiply products in response to an increased demand. In the opposite case it is bad, for if consumption be stationary, its only effect will be to enable the more adroit *entrepreneur* or the more powerful capitalist to ruin his rivals by means of cheap sales, thus attracting to himself their clientele, but giving no benefit to the public. This is the spectacle that in reality is too often presented to us. The movements of our captains of industry are directed, not by any concern for the presumed advantage of the public, but solely with a view to increased profits.

Sismondi's argument is open to the same objection as was made above. Cheapened production dispenses with a portion of the income formerly spent, and creates a demand for other products, thus repairing the evil it has created. Concentration of industry gives to society the same advantage as is afforded by machinery, and the same arguments may be used in its defence.

But against competition Sismondi directs a more serious argument.

---

[1] *Wealth of Nations*, Book II, chapter ii, *in fine*.

Pursuit of cheapness, he remarks, has forced the *entrepreneur* to econo-mize not only in the matter of stuff, but also of men. Competition has everywhere enticed women and children to bear the burden of production instead of adults. Certain *entrepreneurs*, in order to secure a maximum return from human energy, have enforced day and night toil with only a scanty wage in return. What is the use of cheapness achieved under such circumstances? The meagre advantage enjoyed by the public is more than counterbalanced by the loss of vigour and health experienced by the workers. Competition impairs this most precious capital—the life-energy of the race. He points to the work-men of Grenoble earning six or eight sous for a day of fourteen hours, children of six and eight years working for twelve or fourteen hours in factories "in an atmosphere loaded with down and dust" and perish-ing of consumption before attaining the age of twenty. He concludes that the creation of an unhappy and a suffering class is too great a price to pay for an extension of national commerce, and in an oft-quoted phrase he says,

> The earnings of an *entrepreneur* sometimes represent nothing but the spoliation of the workmen. A profit is made not because the in-dustry produces much more than it costs, but because it fails to give to the workman sufficient compensation for his toil. Such an industry is a social evil.[1]

It is futile to deny the justice of the argument. When cheapness is only obtained at the cost of permanent deterioration in the health of the workers, competition evidently is a producer of evil rather than of good. The public interest is no less concerned with the preservation of vital wealth than it is with facilitating the production of material wealth. Sismondi showed that competition was a double-edged sword, and in doing so he prepared the way for those who very justly demand that the State should place limits upon its use and prescribe rules for its employment.

We might be tempted to go farther and see in the passage just cited an unreserved condemnation of profits, even. That would involve placing Sismondi among the socialists, and this is sometimes done, although, as we think, wrongly.

In certain passages he doubtless expresses himself in a manner similar to Owen, the Saint-Simonians, and Marx. Thus in his studies on political economy we come across phrases such as the following: "We might almost say that modern society lives at the expense of the proletariat, seeing that it curtails the reward of his toil."[2] And else-where: "Spoliation indeed we have, for do we not find the rich robbing

[1] *Nouveaux Principes*, Vol. I, p. 92.   [2] *Études sur l' Économie politique*, Vol. I, p. 35.

the poor? They draw in their revenues from the fertile, easily cultivated fields and wallow in their wealth, while the cultivator who
created that revenue is dying of hunger, never allowed to enjoy any
of it."[1] We might even say that Sismondi enunciated the theory of
surplus value, which was worked out by Marx, when he makes use of
the term *mieux value*.[2] But the similarity is simply a matter of words.
Sismondi, speaking of surplus value, means to imply the value that is
constantly growing or being created every year in a progressive country,
not by the effort of labour alone, but by the joint operation of capital
and labour.[3] Marx's idea that labour alone created value, and that
consequently profit and interest constituted a theft, is entirely foreign
to Sismondi. Sismondi, indeed, recognized that the revenues of landed
proprietors and capitalists were due to efforts which they themselves
had never put forth. He rightly distinguished between the wages of
labour and the revenues of proprietors, but to him the latter were not
less legitimate than the former, for, says he, "the beneficiaries who
enjoy such revenues without making any corresponding effort have
acquired a permanent claim to them in virtue of toil undertaken at
some former period, which must have increased the productivity of
labour."[4] When Sismondi says that the worker is robbed he merely
means to say that *sometimes* the worker is insufficiently paid; in other
words, that he does not always receive enough remuneration to keep
him alive, and that, if only for the sake of humanity, he ought to
be better paid. But he does not consider that appropriation by proprietors or capitalists of a portion of the social product is in itself

[1] *Études sur l'Économie politique*, pp. 274–275.

[2] *Nouveaux Principes*, Vol. I, p. 103.

[3] On this point we must dissociate ourselves from the interpretation placed upon
the passage by M. Aftalion in his otherwise excellent monograph *L'Œuvre économique
de Simonde de Sismondi* (Paris, 1899), as well as from the view expressed by M. Denis
(*Histoire des Systèmes économiques*, Vol. II, p. 306). But Sismondi's text appears to us
to leave no room for doubt. "As against land we might combine the other two sources
of wealth, life which enables a man to work and capital which employs him. These
two powers when united possess an expansive characteristic, so that the labour which
a worker puts in his work one year will be greater than that put in the preceding year
—upon the product of which the worker will have supported himself. It is because
of this surplus value [*mieux value*], which increases as the arts and sciences are progressively applied to industry, that society obtains a constant increment of wealth."
(*Nouveaux Principes*, Vol. I, p. 103.)

[4] *Ibid.*, pp. 111–112. *Cf.* also p. 87: "Wealth, however, co-operates with
labour. And its possessor withholds from the worker the part which the worker
has produced beyond his cost of maintenance—as compensation for the help
which he has given him." It is true that this proportion is a considerable one.
"The *entrepreneur* is bound to leave to the worker just enough to keep him alive,
reserving for himself all that the worker has produced over and above this." (P. 103.)
But this is not a matter of necessity, a deduction from the laws of value, as it is with
Marx.

unjust.[1] His point of view is not unlike that adopted at a later period by the German socialists when they sought to justify their social policy.

But although Sismondi's criticism does not amount to socialism, he causes considerable consternation among Liberals by the telling manner in which he shows the falsity of the theory affirmed by the Physiocrats and demonstrated by Smith, namely, the natural identity of individual and general interests. It is true that Smith hesitated to apply it except to production. But Sismondi's peculiar merit lies in the fact that he examined its content in relation to distribution. Sismondi finds himself forced by mere examination of the facts to dispute the very basis of economic Liberalism. Curiously enough, he seems surprised at his own conclusions. A priori the theory of identity of interests appeared to him true, for does it not, in fact, rest upon the two ideas (1) that "each knows his own interest better than an ignorant or a careless Government ever can," and (2) that "the sum of the interests of each equals the interests of all"? "Both axioms are true."[2] Why, then, is the conclusion false?

Here we touch the central theme of Sismondi's system, the point where he leaves the purely economic ground to which the Classical writers had stuck and approaches new territory—the question of the distribution of property. Sismondi discovered the explanation of the contradiction which exists between private and general interests in the unequal distribution of property among men and the resulting unequal strength of the contracting parties.[3]

III: THE DIVORCE OF LAND FROM LABOUR AS THE CAUSE OF PAUPERISM AND OF CRISES

Sismondi was the first writer to give expression to the belief that industrial society tends to separate into two absolutely distinct classes —those who work and those who possess, or, as he often put it, the

---

[1] "The poor man, by his labour and his respect for the property of others, acquires a right to his home, to warm, proper clothing, to ample nourishment sufficiently varied to maintain health and strength. . . . Only when all these things have been secured to the poor as the fruit of their labour does the claim of the rich come in. What is superfluous, after supplying the needs of every one, that should constitute the revenue of opulence." (Études sur l'Économie politique, Vol. I, p. 273.) Here we see quite clearly the sense in which Sismondi uses the term "spoliation."

[2] Nouveaux Principes, Vol. I, p. 407. Cf. also pp. 200, 201.

[3] "Every one's interest if checked by everybody else's would in reality represent the common interest. But when every one is seeking his own interest at the expense of others as well as developing his own means, it does not always happen that he is opposed by equally powerful forces. The strong thus find it their interest to seize and the weak to acquiesce, for the least evil as well as the greatest good is a part of the aim of human policy." (Ibid., p. 407.) Cf. also infra, p. 201, note 2.

rich and the poor. Free competition hastens this separation, causing the disappearance of the intermediate ranks and leaving only the proletariat and the capitalist.[1] "The intermediate classes," says he at one point,

> have all disappeared: the small proprietor and the peasant farmer of the plain, the master craftsman, the small manufacturer, and the village tradesmen, all have failed to withstand the competition of those who control great industries. Society no longer has any room save for the great capitalist and his hireling, and we are witnessing the frightfully rapid growth of a hitherto unknown class—of men who have absolutely no property.[2]

"We are living under entirely new conditions of which as yet we have no experience. All property tends to be divorced from every kind of toil, and therein is the sign of danger."[3]

This law of the concentration of capital which plays such an important role in the Marxian system, though true of industry, seems hardly applicable to property, for a considerable concentration of labour is not incompatible with a fairly even distribution of property. It was a memorable exposition that Sismondi gave of this law, showing how it wrought its ravages in agriculture, in industry, and in commerce all at the same time.

> The tillage of the 34,250,000 acres under cultivation in England was, in 1831, accomplished by 1,046,982 cultivators, and now it is expected that the number may be still further reduced. Not only have all the small farmers been reduced to the position of labourers, but a great number of the day labourers have been forced to abandon field work altogether. The industry of the towns has adopted the principle of amalgamation of forces, and capital has been added to capital with a vigour greater than that which has joined field unto field. The manufacturer with a capital of £1000 was the first to disappear. Soon those who worked with £10,000 were considered small—too small. They were reduced to ruin and their places taken by larger employers. To-day those who trade with a capital of £100,000 are considered of an average size, and the day is not far distant when these will have to face the competition of manufacturers with a capital of £1,000,000. The refining mills of the Gironde dispensed with millers; the cask mills of the Loire ruined the coopers; the building of steamboats, of diligences, of omnibuses and railways with the aid of vast capitals have replaced

---

[1] "There is one fundamental change which is still possible in society, amid this universal struggle created by competition, and that is the introduction of the proletariat into the ranks of human beings—the proletariat, whose name, borrowed from the Romans, is so old, but who is himself so new." (*Études sur l'Économie politique*, Vol. I, p. 34.)

[2] *Revue mensuelle d'économie politique*, 1834, Vol. II, p. 124.

[3] *Nouveaux Principes*, Vol. II, p. 434.

the unpretentious industries of the independent boatman, carriage-
or wagon-maker. Wealthy merchants have entered the retail trade
and have opened their immense shops in the great capitals, where,
in virtue of the improved means of transit, they are able to offer
their provisions even to consumers who live at the very extremities
of the empire. They are well on the way towards suppressing the
wholesale trader as well as the retail dealer, and the petty shopkeeper of the provinces. The places of these independent tradesmen
will soon be taken over by clerks, hirelings, and proletarians.[1]

And now for the consequences of such a condition of things. In
this opposition existing between these two social classes which formerly
lived together harmoniously we shall find an explanation of the
workman's misery and of economic crises.

The sufferings of workmen, whence do they spring, if not from the
fact that their numbers are in excess of the demand for their labour,
thus forcing them to be content with the first wage that is offered them,
even though it be opposed to their own interests and the interest of
the whole class?[2] But "whence the necessity of submitting to these
onerous conditions and of tolerating a burden that is ever becoming
heavier under pain of hunger and death?" The explanation lies in
the separation of property and toil.[3] Formerly the workman, an independent artisan, could gauge his revenue and limit his family accordingly, for population is always determined by revenue.[4] Robbed of
his belongings, all his revenue is to-day got from the capitalist who
employs him. Ignorant of the future demand for his products, as

[1] *Études sur l' Économie politique*, introd., pp. 39 *et seq.*
[2] "That every one understands his own interest better than any Government ever
can is a maxim that has been considerably emphasized by economists. But they have
too lightly affirmed that the interest of each to avoid the greatest evil coincides with
the general interest. It is to the interest of the man who wishes to impoverish his
neighbour to rob him, and it may be the latter's interest to let him do it provided he
can escape with his life.

"But it is not in the interest of society that the one should exercise the force and
that the other should yield. The interest of the day labourer undoubtedly is that the
wages for a day of ten hours should be sufficient for his upkeep and the upbringing of
his children. It is also the interest of society. But the interest of the unemployed is
to find bread at any price. He will work fourteen hours a day, will send his children
to work in a factory at six years of age, will jeopardize his own health and life and
the very existence of his own class in order to escape the pressure of present need."
(*Nouveaux Principes*, Vol. I, pp. 200–201.)
[3] *Ibid.*, p. 201.
[4] "Population will then regulate itself simply in accordance with the revenue.
Where it exceeds this proportion it is always just because the fathers are deceived as
to what they believe to be their revenue, or rather because they are deceived by
society." (*Ibid.*, Vol. II, p. 254.) "The more the poor is deprived of all right of property
the greater is the danger of its mistaking its revenue and contributing to the growth of
a population which, because it does not correspond to the demand for labour, will
never find sufficient means of subsistence." (*Ibid.*, pp. 263–264.)

well as of the quantity of labour that may be necessary, he has no longer any excuse for exercising forethought, and accordingly he discards it. Population grows or diminishes in accordance with the will of the capitalist. "Let there be an increased demand for labour and a sufficient wage offered it and workmen will be born. If the demand fails, the workmen will perish."[1]

This theory of population and wages is really Smith's, who tried to prove that men, like commodities, extended or limited their numbers according to the needs of production. Sismondi, rather than accept it as a proof of the harmonious adaptation of demand to supply. emphasizes the lamentable effects of the separation of wealth from labour.[2] Smith and Sismondi both fell into the error of Malthus and Ricardo, who imagined that high wages of necessity increased population. To-day facts seem to show that a higher standard of well-being, on the contrary, tends to limit it, and the proletarians, who constitute the majority of the nation, can no longer be treated as mere tools in the hands of the capitalists, to be taken up or thrown aside according to fancy or interest.

What is true of industrial employees is no less true of the toilers of the field. In this connexion Sismondi introduces the celebrated distinction between net and gross production which has occupied the attention of many economists since then. If the peasants collectively owned all the land they would at least of a certainty find both the security and the support of their life in the soil. They would never let the gross produce fall below what was sufficient to support them.[3] But with great landed proprietors, and with the peasant transformed into the agricultural labourer, things have changed. The large proprietors have the net product only in view—that is, the difference between the cost of production and the sale price. It matters little to them if the

---

[1] *Nouveaux Principes*, Vol. II, p. 286.

[2] We note that Sismondi does not accept Malthus's theory of population. He never admits that population depends upon the means of subsistence; he holds that it varies according to the will of the proprietor, who stimulates or retards it according to his demand, but who is interested in its limitation in order to secure for himself the maximum net product. "Population has never reached the limits of possible subsistence, and probably it never will. But all those who desire the subsistence have neither the means nor the right to extract it from the soil. Those, on the contrary, to whom the laws give the monopoly of the land have no interest in obtaining from it all the subsistence it might produce. In all countries proprietors are opposed, and must be opposed, to any system of cultivation which would tend merely to multiply the means of subsistence while not increasing the revenue. Long before being arrested by the impossibility of finding a country which produced more subsistence population would be checked by the impossibility of finding the people to buy those means or to work and bring them into being." (*Ibid.*, pp. 269–270.)

[3] *Ibid.*, Vol. I, pp. 263, 264.

gross produce is sacrificed for the sake of increasing the net produce. Here you have land which, when well cultivated, brings gross produce of the value of 1000 shillings to the farmer and yields 100 shillings in rent to the proprietor. But the proprietor thinks that he would gain 110 shillings if he left it fallow or let it as unprofitable pasture.

> His gardener or vinedresser is dismissed, but he gains 10 shillings and the nation loses 890. By and by the capital employed in producing this plentiful supply will no longer be so employed, and there will be no profit. The workers whose former toil produced these products will no longer be employed and no wages will be paid.[1]

Examples are plentiful enough. A number of the great Scots proprietors, in order to replace the ancient system of cultivation by the open pasture system, sent the tenants from their dwellings and drove them into the towns or huddled them on board ships for America. In Italy a handful of speculators called the *Mercanti di tenute*, animated by similar motives, have hindered the repopulation and cultivation of the Roman Campagna,

> that territory formerly so very fertile that five acres were sufficient to provide sustenance for a whole family as well as sending a recruit to the army. To-day its scattered homesteads, its villages, the whole population, together with the farm enclosures, the vineyards, and the olive plantations—products that require the continual loving attention of mankind—have all disappeared, giving place to a few flocks of sheep tended by a few miserable shepherds.[2]

The criticism is just, but is directed rather against the abuse of private property than against the principle of the net product, for this principle is incident to peasant proprietorship as well. It is inevitable wherever production for a market takes place.[3]

It is just this opposition between proprietorship and labour that supplies an explanation of economic crises.

---

[1] *Nouveaux Principes*, Vol. I, p. 153.

[2] *Ibid.*, p. 235. This problem of the net and gross produce occupied Sismondi's attention for a long time. We find a suggestion of it in his first work, *Le Tableau de l'Agriculture toscane* (Geneva, 1801), and though he does not definitely take the side of the gross produce, he shows some leanings that way. "Why is the gain of a single rich farmer considered more profitable for a State than the miserable earnings of several thousand workers and peasants?" The book, however, is a treatise on practical agriculture, and includes only a few economic dicta. It is here that we have his beautiful description of his farm at Val Chiuso (p. 219).

[3] It is true that Sismondi wished to get rid of the practice of producing corn for a market, so as to free the nation's food from the fluctuations of that market. Neither is he over-enthusiastic in his praise of the gross produce. He recognizes that the gradual growth of the gross produce might, in its way, be the consequence of a state of suffering if population were to progress too rapidly (*Ibid.*, p. 153). This shows what a hesitating mind we are dealing with.

Sismondi holds the view that crises are due partly to the difficulty of acquiring exact knowledge of a market that has become very extensive, and partly to the fact that producers are guided in their actions by the amount of their capital rather than by the demand of the market.[1] But above all he thinks that they are due to the unequal distribution of revenues. The consequence of the separation of property from labour is that the revenues of those who possess lands increase while the incomes of the workers always remain strictly at the minimum. The natural result is a want of harmony in the demand for products. With property uniformly divided and with an almost general increase in the revenue there would result a certain degree of uniformity in the growth of demand. Those industries which supply our most essential and most general wants would experience a regular and not an erratic expansion. But as a matter of fact at the present time it is the revenue of the wealthy alone that increases. Hence there is a growing demand for the more refined objects in place of a regular demand for the ordinary things of life; a neglect of the more fundamental industries, and a demand for the production of luxuries. If the latter do not multiply quickly enough, then the foreigner will be called in to satisfy the demand. What is the result of these incessant changes? The old, neglected industries are obliged to dismiss their workmen, while the new industries can only develop slowly. During the interval the workmen who have suffered dismissal are forced to reduce their consumption of ordinary goods, and permanent under-consumption, attended by a crisis, immediately follows. "Owing to the concentration of wealth in the hands of a few proprietors, the home market is contracted and industry must seek other outlets for its products in foreign markets, where even more considerable revolutions are possible."[2] Thus "the consumption of a millionaire master who employs 1000 men all earning but the bare necessities of life is of less value to the nation than a hundred men each of whom is much less rich but who employ each ten men who are much less poor."[3]

Sismondi's explanation of crises, though adopted by many writers since then, is not one of the best. The difficulty of adaptation would

[1] *Nouveaux Principes*, Vol. I, p. 368.   [2] *Ibid.*, p. 361.

[3] Elsewhere he remarks: "The petty merchants, the small manufacturers, disappear, and a great *entrepreneur* replaces hundreds of them whose total wealth was never equal to his. Taken altogether, however, they consumed more than he does. His costly luxury gives much less encouragement to industry than the honest ease of the hundred homes which it has replaced." (*Ibid.*, Vol. II, p. 327.) The theory is more than doubtful. What we want to know is whether the demand will remain the same in amount, not whether there will be no change in its character—a contingency that need not result in a general crisis, but simply in a passing inconvenience.

in all probability not disappear even if wealth were to be more equally distributed. Moreover, what he attempts to explain is an evil that is chronic in certain industries and not the acute periodical crises. But the theory has the merit of attempting to explain what still remains obscure, and what J. B. Say and Ricardo preferred to pass over in silence or regarded as of secondary importance under pretext that in the long run equilibrium would always be re-established. We shall return to this subject in Book VI.

IV: SISMONDI'S REFORM PROJECTS. HIS INFLUENCE UPON THE HISTORY OF DOCTRINES

The principal interest of Sismondi's book does not lie in his attempt to give a scientific explanation of the facts that occupied his attention. Indeed, these attempts have little that is altogether satisfactory, for the analysis is frequently superficial, and even commonplace. His merit rather lies in having placed in strong relief certain facts that were consistently neglected by the dominant school of economists. Taken as a whole, his doctrine must be regarded as pessimistic. He deliberately shows us the reverse of the medal, of which others, even those whom we have classed as Pessimists—Ricardo and Malthus— wished only to see the brighter side. It is no longer possible to speak of the spontaneous harmony of interests, or to forget the misery and suffering which lie beneath an appearance of economic progress. Crises cannot be slipped over and treated as transient phenomena of no great moment. No longer is it possible to forget the important effects of an unequal division of property and revenues, which frequently results in putting the contracting parties in a position of fundamental inequality that annuls freedom of bargaining. In a word, it is no longer possible to forget the social consequences of economic transformations. And herein lies the sphere of social politics, of which we are now going to speak.

The new point of view occupied by Sismondi enables him to see that the free play of private interests often involves injury to the general interest, and that the *laissez-faire* doctrine preached by the school of Adam Smith has no longer any *raison d'être*. On the contrary, there is room for the intervention of society, which should set a limit to individual action and correct its abuses. Sismondi thus becomes the first of the interventionists.

State action, in the first place, ought to be employed in curbing production and in putting a drag upon the too rapid multiplication of inventions. Sismondi dreams of progress accomplished by easy stages, injuring no one, limiting no income, and not even lowering the rate of interest.[1] His sensitiveness made him timid, and critics smile at his philanthropy. Even the Saint-Simonians, too sympathetic to certain of his views, reproach him with having allowed himself to be misled by it.[2] This state of mind was reflected in his habits in private life. Sainte-Beuve[3] relates of him how he used to employ an old locksmith who had become so useless and awkward that everybody had left him. Sismondi remained faithful to the old man even to the very end, despite his inefficiency, lest he should lose his last customer. He wished society to treat the older industries in a similar fashion. He has been compared to Gandalin, the sorcerer's apprentice in the fable, who, having unlocked the water-gate with the magic of his words, sees wave succeed wave, and the house inundated, without ever being able to find the word which could arrest its flow.

Governments ought to temper their 'blind zeal' instead of urging on production.[4] Addressing himself to the savants, he begs them to desist from invention and recall the sayings of the economists, *laissez-faire, laissez-passer*, by giving to the generations which their inventions render superfluous at least time to pass away. For the old regime, with its corporations and wardens, he had the sincerest regard, while condemning them as being harmful to the best interests of production. Still he wondered whether some lesson could not be gleaned from them which might help us in fixing limits to the abuses of competition.[5]

Sismondi never seems to have realized that any restriction placed upon production with a view to alleviate suffering might hinder the progress and well-being of the very classes that interested him most. The conviction that the production of Europe was enough to satisfy all demands supported these erroneous views.[6] Sismondi never suspected the relative poverty of industrial society, a fact that struck J. B. Say very forcibly. Moreover, he felt that on this point the policy of Governments was not so easily modified, a feeling that undermined his previous confidence.

[1] Sismondi applies the same principles to a consideration of a fall in the rate of interest as he does to the growth of production or the increase of machinery. "An increase of capital is desirable only when its employment can be increased at the same time. But whenever the rate of interest is lowered it is a certain sign that the employment of capital has proportionally diminished as compared with the amount available; and this fall in the rate, which is always advantageous to some people, is disadvantageous to others—some will have to be content with smaller incomes and others with none at all." (*Nouveaux Principes*, Vol. I, p. 393.)

[2] Compare the Saint-Simonian review, *Le Producteur*, Vol. IV, pp. 557–558.

[3] *Nouveaux Lundis*, Vol. VI, p. 81.

[4] *Études sur l'Économie politique*, Vol. I, pp. 60, 61.

[5] *Nouveaux Principes*, Vol. I, p. 341; Vol. II, p. 459.

[6] *Ibid.*, Vol. II, pp. 415, 435. See also *Études*, Vol. I, p. 25.

Since the causes of the evils at present existing in society are (1) the absence of property, (2) the uncertainty of the earnings of the working classes, all Government action ought to be concentrated on these points.

The first object to be aimed at, wherever possible, was the union of labour and property, and Sismondi eulogizes the movement towards a new patriarchal state—that is, towards a revival of peasant proprietorship. The *Nouveaux Principes* contains a celebrated description of the idyllic happiness of such a state. In industry he wished for a return of the independent artisan.

> I am anxious that the industries of the town as well as country pursuits should be carried on by a great number of independent workers instead of being controlled by a single chief who rules over hundreds and even thousands of workers. I hope to see manufactures in the hands of a great number of capitalists of average means, and not under the thumb of one single individual who constitutes himself master over millions. I long to see the chance—nay, even the certainty—of being associated with the master extended to every industrious workman, so that when he gets married he may feel that he has a stake in the industry instead of dragging on through the declining years of life, as he too often does, without any prospect of advancement.[1]

This for an end.

But the means? On this point Sismondi shows extraordinary timidity. Appeal to the legislator is not followed up by a plan of campaign, and in moments of scepticism and despair he even doubts whether reform is ever possible. He declares himself an opponent of communism. He rejects the Utopias of Owen, of Thompson, and of Fourier, although he recognizes that their aim was his also. He failed to perceive that his 'breaking up' process was quite as illusory as the communistic Utopias which he shunned. He rejected Owen's system because he saw the folly of attempting to substitute the interest of a corporation for that of the individual. But he never realized that it had nothing to do with a corporation, and it is possible that were he alive at the present time he would be an ardent champion of co-operation.

But until the union of property and labour is realized Sismondi is content with a demand for a simpler reform, which might alleviate the more pressing sufferings of the working classes. First of all he appeals for the restoration, or rather the granting, of the right of combination.[2] Then follows a limitation of child labour, the abolition of Sunday toil, and a shortening of the hours of labour.[3] He also

[1] *Nouveaux Principes*, Vol. II, pp. 365–366. [2] *Ibid.*, p. 451. [3] *Ibid.*, p. 338.

demanded the establishment of what he called a "professional guarantee," whereby the employer, whether agriculturist or capitalist, would be obliged to maintain the workman at his own expense during a period of illness or of lock-out or old age. This principle once admitted, the employers would no longer have any interest in reducing the wages of the workman indefinitely, or in introducing machinery or in multiplying production unduly. Having become responsible for the fate of the workers, they would then take some account of the effect which invention might have on their well-being, whereas to-day they simply regard them from the point of view of their own profits.[1] One might be tempted to regard this as an anticipation of the great ideal which has to a certain extent been realized by the social insurance Acts passed during the last thirty years. But this is only partly so. Sismondi placed the charge of maintenance upon the master and not upon society, and his criticism of methods of relief, especially of the English Poor Law, was that they tended to decrease wages and to encourage the indifference of masters by teaching the workers to seek refuge at the hands of the State rather than at the hands of the masters.

In short, his reform projects, like his criticism of the economists, reveal a certain degree of hesitation, due, no doubt, to the perpetual conflict between reason and sentiment. Too keen not to see the benefits of the new industrial regime, and too sensitive not to be moved by some of its more painful consequences, too conservative and too wise to hope for a general overthrow of society, he is content to remain an astonished but grieved spectator of the helplessness of mankind in the face of this evil. He did not feel himself competent to suggest a remedy. He himself has confessed to this in touching terms:

> I grant that, having indicated what in my opinion is the principle of justice in this matter, I do not feel myself equal to the task of showing how it can be realized. The present method of distributing the fruits of industry among those who have co-operated in its production appears to me to be curious. But a state of society absolutely different from that with which we are now acquainted appears to be beyond the wit of man to devise.[2]

It is a striking fact that most of the important social ideas in the nineteenth century can be traced back to Sismondi's writings. They have been confirmed by the events that have followed the First World War. He was the first critic whom the Classical school encountered in its march, and he treats us to a full résumé of its many heresies. In the bitter struggle which ensued the heretics won the day, their nostrums taking the place of the Classical doctrines in the public

[1] *Nouveaux Principes*, Vol. II, p. 661.   [2] *Ibid.*, p. 364.

favour. But it seems hardly possible that Sismondi's work should have determined the course of these newer tendencies. His immediate influence was extremely limited. It scarcely told at all except upon the socialists. His book was soon forgotten, and not until our own day was its importance fully realized. It would be truer to say that in the course of the nineteenth century there was a spontaneous revival of interest in the ideas promulgated by Sismondi. None the less he was the first writer to raise his voice against certain principles which were rapidly crystallizing into dogmas. He was the earliest economist who dared resist the conclusions of the dominant school, and to point to the existence of facts which refused to tally with the large and simple generalizations of his predecessors. If not the founder of the new schools that were about to appear, he was their precursor. They are inspired by the same feelings and welcome the same ideas. His method is an anticipation of that of the Historical school. His definition of political economy as a philosophy of history[1] works wonders in the hands of Roscher, Knies, and Hildebrand. His plea for a closer observation of facts, his criticism of the deductive process and its hasty generalizations, will find an echo in the writings of Le Play in France, of Schmoller in Germany, and of Cliffe Leslie and Toynbee in England. The founders of the German Historical school, in their ignorance of foreign writers, regarded him as a socialist,[2] but the younger representatives of that school have done full justice to his memory, and recognize him as one of their earliest representatives.

By his appeal to sentiment and his sympathy for the working classes, by his criticism of the industrial regime of machines and competition, by his refusal to recognize personal interest as the only economic motive, he foreshadows the violent reaction of humanitarianism against the stern implacability of economic orthodoxy. We can almost hear the eloquence of Ruskin and Carlyle, and the pleading of the Christian Socialists, who in the name of Christian charity and human solidarity protest against the social consequences of production on a large scale. Like Sismondi, social Christianity will direct its attack, not against the science itself, but against the easy bourgeois complacency of its advocates. A charge of selfishness will be brought, not against economic science as such, but against its representatives and the particular form of society which it upholds.

Finally, by his plea for State intervention Sismondi inaugurated a reaction against Liberal absolutism, a reaction that deepened in intensity and covered a wider area as the century wore on, and which

---

[1] See section i of present chapter.
[2] Knies, strangely enough, classes him with the socialists.

found its final expression in State socialism, or "the socialism of the chair." He was the first to advocate the adoption of factory legislation in France and to seek to give the Government a place in directing economic affairs. The impossibility of complete abdication on the part of the State would, he thought, become clearer every day. But it was little more than an aspiration with him; it never reached the stage of a practical suggestion.

Thus in three different ways Sismondi's proposals were destined to give rise to three powerful currents of thought, and it is not surprising that interest in his work should have grown with the development of the new tendencies which he had anticipated.

His immediate influence upon contemporary economists was very slight. Some of them allowed themselves to be influenced by his warm-heartedness, his tenderness for the weak, and his pity for the workers, but they never found this a sufficient reason for breaking off their connexions with the Classical school. Blanqui[1] in particular was a convert to the extent that he admitted some exceptions to the principle of *laissez-faire*. Theodore Fix and Droz[2] seemed won over for a moment, and Sismondi might rightly have expected that the *Revue mensuelle d'économie politique*, started by Fix in 1833, would uphold his views. But the days of the *Revue* were exceedingly few, and before finally disappearing it had become fully orthodox. Only one author, Buret, in his work on the sufferings of the working classes in England and France,[3] has the courage to declare himself a wholehearted disciple of Sismondi. The name of Villeneuve-Bargemont, author of *Économie politique chrétienne*, must be added to these. His work, which was published in three volumes in 1834, bears frequent traces of Sismondi's influence.

Sismondi, though not himself a socialist, has been much read and carefully studied by socialists. It is among them that his influence is most marked. This is not very surprising, for all the critical portion of his work is really a vigorous appeal against competition and the inequalities of fortune. Louis Blanc read him and borrowed from him more than one argument against competition. The two German

---

[1] A. Blanqui, in his *Histoire de l'Économie politique en Europe* (1837), considers him a writer of the modern school, which he describes as follows: "Writers of this school are no longer willing to treat production as a pure abstraction apart from its influence upon the workers. To produce wealth is not enough; it must be equitably distributed." (Introd., 3rd ed., p. xxi.)

[2] Droz (1773–1850) published in 1829 his *Économie politique, ou Principes de la Science des Richesses*. It is in this work that we find the famous phrase, "Certain economists seem to think that products are not made for men, but that men are made for the products."

[3] Paris, 1841, two volumes. Buret died in 1842 when thirty-two years of age.

socialists Rodbertus and Marx are still more deeply indebted to him. Rodbertus borrowed from him his theory of crises, and owes him the suggestion that social progress benefits only the wealthier classes. Rodbertus quotes him without any mention of his name, but Marx in his *Manifesto* has rendered him full justice, pointing out all that he owed to his penetrative analysis. The most fertile idea borrowed by Marx was that which deals with the concentration of wealth in the hands of a few powerful capitalists, which results in the increasing dependence of the working classes. This conception is the pivot of the *Manifesto*, and forms a part of the very foundation of Marxian collectivism. The other idea of exploitation does not seem to have been borrowed from Sismondi, although he might have discovered a trace of the surplus value theory in his writings. Marx endeavours to explain profit by drawing a distinction between a worker selling his labour and parting with some of his labour force. Sismondi employs terms that are almost identical, and says that the worker when selling his labour force is giving his life. Elsewhere he speaks of a demand for 'labour force.' Sismondi never drew any precise conclusion from these ideas, but they may have suggested to Marx the thesis he took such pains to establish.

Many a present-day socialist, without acknowledging the fact, perhaps without knowing it, loves to repeat the arguments which Sismondi was the first to employ, to stir up his indifferent contemporaries.

CHAPTER II: SAINT-SIMON, THE SAINT-SIMONIANS, AND THE BEGINNINGS OF COLLECTIVISM

SISMONDI, by supplementing the study of political economy by a study of social economics, had already much enlarged the area traced for the science by its founders. But while giving distribution the position of honour in his discussion, he never dared carry his criticism as far as an examination of that fundamental institution of modern society —private property. Property, at least, he thought legitimate and necessary. Every English and French economist had always treated it as a thing apart—a fact so indisputable and inevitable that it formed the very basis of all their speculations.

Suddenly, however, we come upon a number of writers who, while definitely rejecting all complicity with the earlier communists and admitting neither equality of needs nor of faculties, but tending to an agreement with the economists in claiming the maximum of production as the one aim of economic organization, dare lay their hands upon the sacred ark and attack the institution of property with whole-hearted vigour. Venturing upon what had hitherto been holy ground, they displayed so much skill and courage that every idea and every formula which became a commonplace of the socialistic literature of the later nineteenth century already finds a place in their system. Having definite ideas as to the end which they had in view, they challenged the institution of private property because of its effects upon the distribution and production of wealth. They cast doubt upon the theories concerning its historical evolution, and concluded that its abolition would help the perfection of the scientific and industrial organization of modern society. The problem of private property was at last faced, and a recurrence of the discussion was henceforth to become a feature of economic science.[1]

---

[1] It was not intended that any reference should be made in this volume to the doctrine of socialism before the opening of the nineteenth century, but the question whether the French Revolution of 1789 was socialist in character or simply middle-class, as the socialists of to-day would put it, has been so frequently discussed that we cannot ignore it altogether.

There is no doubt that the leaders of the Revolution—including Marat, even, who is wrongly regarded as a supporter of that agrarian law which he condemned as fatal and erroneous—always showed unfailing respect for the institution of private property. The confiscation of the property of the Church and of the émigré nobles was a political and not an economic measure, and in that respect is fairly comparable with the historic confiscation of the property of Jews, Templars, Huguenots, and Irish, which in no case was inspired by merely socialist motives. The confiscation of endowments —of goods belonging to legal persons—was regarded as a means of defending individual or real property against the encroachments of merely fictitious persons and the tyranny of the dead hand. When it came to the abolition of feudal rights great care was taken to distinguish the tenant's rights of sovereignty, which were about to be abolished, from his proprietary rights, which deserved the respect of every one who recognized the legitimacy of compensation. In practice the distinction proved of little importance. Scores of people were ruined during those unfortunate months— some through mere misfortune, others because of the muddle over the issue of assignats, and others, again, because of the confiscation of rents; but the intention to respect the rights of property remains indisputable still. It would seem that in this matter the revolutionary leaders had come under the influence of the Physiocrats, whose cult of property has already engaged our attention. And how easy it would be to imagine a Physiocrat penning Article 17 of the Declaration of the Rights of Man when it speaks of property as an inviolable, sacred right! But, on the other hand, it is true that Rousseau in his article Économie politique speaks of the rights of property as the most sacred of the citizen's rights.

It was not only on the question of property that the revolutionists of 1789 showed themselves anti-socialist. They were also anti-socialist in the sense that they paid no attention to class war and ignored the antagonism that exists between capitalists and workers. All were to be treated as citizens and brothers, all were equal and alike. However, those who claim the most intimate connexion with the spirit of the Revo-

Not that it had hitherto been neglected. Utopian communists from Plato and More up to Mably, Morelly, Godwin, and Babeuf, the eighteenth-century equalitarians, all rest their case upon a criticism of property. But hitherto the question had been treated from the point of view of ethics rather than of economics.[1] The originality of

---

lution remain undismayed by such considerations. They endeavour to show that the Revolution was not quite so conservative nor so completely individualistic as is generally supposed, and after diligent search they claim to have discovered certain decrees bearing unmistakable traces of socialism. But a much more general practice is to plead extenuating circumstances. "Are we to demand that the social problems which appeared fifty years afterwards, when industry had revolutionized the relations of capital and labour, should have been solved at the end of the eighteenth century? It would have been worse than useless for the men of 1789 and 1793 to try to regulate such things in advance." (Aulard, Address to Students, April 21, 1893. Cf. his Histoire politique de la Révolution, chapter viii, paragraph entitled "Le Socialisme.")

We must not lose sight of the communist plot hatched by François Babeuf during the period of the Revolution. But in this case, at any rate, the exception proves the rule, for, despite the fact that Babeuf had assumed the suggestive name of Gaius Gracchus, he found little sympathy among the men of the Convention, even in La Montagne, and he was condemned and executed by order of the Directory. Babeuf's plot is interesting, if only as an anticipatory protest of revolutionary socialism against bourgeois revolution. Cf. Aulard, loc. cit., p. 627.

[1] Not to speak of celebrated Utopians like Plato, More, and Campanella, a number of writers who have been minutely studied by Lichtenberger undertook to supply such criticism in the eighteenth century. Morelly, Mably, Brissot, and Meslier the curé in France, and Godwin in England, attacked the institution of property with becoming vigour. Babeuf, who in 1797 suffered death for his attempt to establish a community of equals, has left us a summary of their theories. But the Saint-Simonians owe them nothing in the way of inspiration. Eighteenth-century socialism was essentially equalitarian. What aroused the anger of the eighteenth-century writers most of all was the inequality of pleasure and of well-being, for which they held the institution of private property responsible. "If men have the same needs and the same faculties they ought to be given the same material and the same intellectual opportunities," says the Manifeste des Égaux. But the Saint-Simonians recognize neither equality of needs nor of faculties, and they are particularly anxious not to be classed along with the Babeuvistes—the champions of the agrarian law. Their socialism, which is founded upon the right to the whole produce of labour and would apportion wages according to capacity, aims at neither equality nor uniformity.

The Saint-Simonians seem to have remained in ignorance of the socialist theories of their contemporaries, the French Fourier and the English Thompson and Owen. Fourier's work only became known to Enfantin after his own economic doctrine had been formulated. Saint-Simon and Bazard appear never to have read him. It is probable that Enfantin only became aware of Fourier's writings after 1829, and when he did he interested himself merely in those that dealt with free love and the theory of passions. As Bourgin put it: "If Fourier did anything at all, he has rather hastened the decomposition of Saint-Simonism." (Henry Bourgin, Fourier, p. 419; Paris, 1905.)

The English socialists are never as much as mentioned. The Ricardian doctrine of labour-value, which is the basis of Thompson's theory and of Owen's, and later still of that of Marx, seems never to have become known to them. "Questions of value, price, and production, which demand no fundamental knowledge either of the composition or the organization of society," are treated as so many details (Le Producteur, Vol. IV, p. 388). Their doctrine is primarily social, containing only occasional allusions to political economy. Enfantin is careful to distinguish between

the Saint-Simonian treatment is that it is the direct outcome of the economic and political revolution which shook France and the whole of Europe towards the end of the eighteenth and the beginning of the nineteenth centuries. The socialism of Saint-Simon is not a vague aspiration for some pristine equality which was largely a creation of the imagination. It is rather the naïve expression of juvenile enthusiasm in the presence of the new industrial regime begotten of mechanical invention and scientific discovery. The modern spirit at its best is what it would fain reveal. It sought to interpret the generous aspirations of the new bourgeois class, freed through the instrumentality of the Revolution from the tutelage of baron and priest, and to show how the reactionary policy of the Restoration threatened its triumph. Not content, however, with confining itself to the intellectual orbit of the bourgeoisie, it sought also to define the sphere of the workers in future society and to lay down regulations for their benefit. But its appeal was chiefly to the more cultured classes—engineers, bankers, artists, and savants. It was to these men—all of them members of the better classes—that the Saint-Simonians preached collectivism and the suppression of inheritance as the easiest way of founding a new society upon the basis of science and industry. Hence the great stir which the new ideas caused.

Consequently Saint-Simonism appears to be a somewhat unexpected extension of economic Liberalism rather than a tardy renewal of ancient socialistic conceptions.

We must, in fact, distinguish between two currents in Saint-Simonism. The one represents the doctrine preached by Saint-Simon himself, the other is that of his disciples, the Saint-Simonians. Saint-Simon's creed can best be described as "industrialism" plus a slight admixture of socialism, and it thus naturally links itself with economic Liberalism, of which it is simply an exaggerated development. The disciples' doctrine, on the other hand, can only be described as collectivism. But it is a collectivism logically deduced from two of the master's principles which have been extended and amplified. For a history of economic ideas it is the theories of the disciples that matter most, perhaps. But it would be impossible to understand these without knowing something of Saint-Simon's theory. We shall give an explanation of his doctrine, first attempting to show the links which surely,

Quesnay and his school and Smith or Say. The Physiocrats gave a social character to their doctrine, which the economists wrongfully neglected to develop. Aug. Comte, in the fourth volume of the *Cours de Philosophie*, has criticized political economy in almost identical terms, which affords an additional proof of his indebtedness to Saint-Simonism.

hough strangely enough, affiliate the socialism of Saint-Simon with
:conomic Liberalism.

I: SAINT-SIMON AND INDUSTRIALISM

Saint-Simon was a nobleman who led a somewhat dissolute, adven-
urous life. At the early age of sixteen he took part in the American
War of Independence. The Revolution witnessed the abandonment
of his claim to nobility, but by successful speculation in national
property he was enabled to retrieve his fortune to some extent. Imprisoned as a suspect at Sainte-Pélagie, set free on the 9th Thermidor,
he attained a certain notoriety as a man of affairs interested chiefly
n travels and amusements and as a dilettante student of the sciences.
From the moment of his release he began to regard himself as a kind
of Messiah.[1] He was profoundly impressed by what seemed to him
to be the birth of a new society at which he had himself assisted, in
which the moral and political and even physical conditions of life
were suddenly torn up by the roots, when ancient beliefs disappeared
and nothing seemed ready to take their place. He himself was to be
the evangelist of the new gospel, and with this object in view on the
4th Messidor, An. VI, he called together the capitalists who were
already associated with him and, pointing out the great necessity for
restoring public confidence, proposed the establishment of a gigantic
bank whose funds might be employed in setting up works of public
utility—proof of the curious way in which economic and philosophic
considerations were already linked together in his thoughts.[2] An ill-
considered marriage which was hastily broken off, however, was
followed by a period of much extravagance and great misery. By
the year 1805 so reduced were his circumstances that he was glad to
avail himself of the generosity of one of his old servants. After her
death he lived partly upon the modest pension provided him by his
family and partly upon the contributions of a few tradesmen, but he
was again so miserable that in 1823 he attempted suicide. A banker
of the name of Olinde Rodrigues came to the rescue this time and
supplied him with the necessary means of support. He died in 1825,
surrounded by a number of his disciples who had watched over the
last moments of his earthly life. During all these years, haunted as he
was by the need for giving to the new century the doctrine it so much
required, he was constantly engaged in publishing brochures, new

[1] *Cf.* especially Dumas, *Psychologie de deux Messies positivistes, Saint-Simon et A. Comte*
(Paris, 1905), and for biographical details Weill, *Saint-Simon et son Œuvre* (1894).
[2] Weill, *Saint-Simon et son Œuvre*, p. 15.

works, or selections from his earlier publications, sometimes alone and
sometimes in collaboration with others,[1] in which the same suggestion
are always revived and the same ideas keep recurring, but in slightly
different forms.

Saint-Simon's earlier work was an attempt to establish a scientific
synthesis which might furnish mankind with a system of positive
morality to take the place of religious dogmas. It was to be a kind of
'scientific breviary' where all phenomena could be deduced from one
single idea, that of 'universal gravitation.' He himself has treated us
to a full account of this system, which is as deceptive as it is simple,
and which shows us his serious limitations as a philosopher whose
ambition far outran his knowledge. Auguste Comte, one of his
disciples, attempted a similar task in his *Cours de Philosophie positive*
and in the *Politique positive*, so that Saint-Simon, who is usually considered the father of socialism, finds himself also the father of positivism

From 1814 up to his death in 1825 he partly relinquished his interest
in philosophy and devoted himself almost exclusively to the exposition
of his social and political ideas, which are the only ones that interest
us here.

His economics might be summed up as an apotheosis of industry,
using the latter word in the widest sense, much as Smith had employed
the term as synonymous with labour of all kinds.

His leading ideas, contained within the compass of a few striking
pages, have since become known as "Saint-Simon's Parable."

"Let us suppose," says he,

that France suddenly loses fifty of her first-class doctors, fifty first-
class chemists, fifty first-class physiologists, fifty first-class bankers,
two hundred of her best merchants, six hundred of her foremost
agriculturists, five hundred of her most capable ironmasters, etc.
[enumerating the principal industries]. Seeing that these men are
its most indispensable producers, makers of its most important
products, the minute that it loses these the nation will degenerate
into a mere soulless body and fall into a state of despicable weakness
in the eyes of rival nations, and will remain in this subordinate
position so long as the loss remains and their places are vacant.
Let us take another supposition. Imagine that France retains all

[1] In 1814 *De la Réorganisation de la société européenne*, by Saint-Simon and A. Thierry,
his pupil; 1817–18, *Industrie*, in 4 Vols. (the 3rd Vol. and the first book of the 4th Vol.
are the work of A. Comte); 1819, *La Politique*; 1821, *Le Système industriel*; 1823–24,
Le Catéchisme des Industriels (the third book, by A. Comte, bears the title *Système de
Politique positive*); 1825, *Le Nouveau Christianisme*. Our quotations from Saint-Simon
are taken from the *Œuvres de Saint-Simon et d'Enfantin*, published by members of the
committee instituted by Enfantin for carrying out the master's last wishes (Paris,
Dentu, 1865), and from the *Œuvres choisies de Saint-Simon*, published in 3 Vols. by
Lemonnier of Brussels (1859).

her men of genius, whether in the arts and sciences or in the crafts and industries, but has the misfortune to lose on the same day the king's brother, the Duke of Angoulême, and all the other members of the royal family; all the great officers of the Crown; all ministers of State, whether at the head of a department or not; all the Privy Councillors; all the masters of requests; all the marshals, cardinals, archbishops, bishops, grand vicars and canons; all prefects and sub-prefects; all Government employees; all the judges; and on top of that a hundred thousand proprietors—the cream of her nobility. Such an overwhelming catastrophe would certainly aggrieve the French, for they are a kindly-disposed nation. But the loss of a hundred and thirty thousand of the best-reputed individuals in the State would give rise to sorrow of a purely sentimental kind. It would not cause the community the least inconvenience.[1]

In other words, the official Government is a mere façade. Its action is wholly superficial. Society might exist without it and life would be none the less happy. But the disappearance of the savants, industrial leaders, bankers, and merchants would leave the community crippled. The very sources of wealth would dry up, for their activities are really fruitful and necessary. They are the true governors who wield real power. Such was the parable.

According to Saint-Simon, little observation is needed to realize that the world we live in is based upon industry, and that anything besides industry is scarcely worth the attention of thinking people. A long process of historical evolution, which according to Saint-Simon commenced in the twelfth century with the enfranchisement of the communes and culminated in the French Revolution, had prepared the way for it.[2] At least industry is the one cardinal feature of the present day.

The political concerns of his contemporaries were regarded with some measure of despair. The majority of them were engaged either in defending or attacking the Charter of 1814. The Liberals were simply deceiving themselves, examining old and meaningless formulæ

[1] *L'Organisateur*, Part I, 1819, pp. 10–20. This passage was republished by Olinde Rodrigues in 1832 under the title of *Une Parabole politique* in a volume of miscellaneous writings by Saint-Simon, with the result that Saint-Simon was prosecuted before the Cour d'Assises. He was acquitted, however.

[2] "With the enfranchisement of the communes we shall witness the middle classes at last in enjoyment of their liberty, setting up as a political power. The essence of that power will consist in freedom from being imposed upon by others without consent. Gradually it will become richer and stronger, at the same time growing in political importance and improving its social position in every respect, with the result that the other classes, which may be called the theological or feudal classes, will dwindle in estimation as well as in their real importance. Whence I conclude that the industrial classes must continue to gain ground, and finally to include the whole of society. Such seems to be the trend of things—the direction in which we are moving." (*Lettres à un Américain*, *Œuvres*, Vol. II, p. 166.)

such as 'the sovereignty of the people,' 'liberty,' and 'equality'—conceptions that never had any meaning,[1] but were simply meta physical creations of the jurists,[2] and they ought to have realized tha this kind of work was perfectly useless now that the feudal regime wa overthrown. Men in future will have something better to do than t defend the Charter against the 'ultras.' The parliamentary regim may be very necessary, but it is just a passing phase between th feudalism of yesterday and the new order of to-morrow.[3] That futur order is Industrialism—a social organization having only one end i view, the further development of industry, the source of all wealtl and prosperity.

The new regime implies first of all the abolition of all class distinc tion. There will be no need for either nobles, bourgeois, or clergy There will be only two categories, workers and idlers—or the bees anc the drones, as Saint-Simon puts it. Sometimes he refers to them a the national and anti-national party. In the new society the seconc class[4] is bound to disappear, for there is only room for the first. Thi class includes, besides manual workers,[5] agriculturists, artisans, manu facturers, bankers, savants, and artists.[6] Between these persons ther

[1] "Industry is the basis of liberty. Industry can only expand and grow strong with the growth of liberty. Were this doctrine, so old in fact but so new to many people, once fully grasped instead of those fictitious dreams of antiquity, we shoulc have heard the last of such sanguinary phrases as 'equality or death.'" (*Œuvres* Vol. II, pp. 210–211.)

[2] "Lawyers and metaphysicians are wont to take appearance for reality, the name for the thing." (*Syst. indust.*, *Œuvres*, Vol. V, p. 12.)

[3] "Parliamentary government must be regarded as an indispensable step in the direction of industrialism." (*Œuvres*, Vol. III, p. 22.) "It is absolutely necessary i the transition from the essentially arbitrary regime which has existed hitherto is tc be replaced by the ideal liberal regime which is bound to come into being by and by." (*Ibid.*, p. 21.)

[4] Writing in 1803 in his *Lettres d'un Habitant de Genève*, he uses the following words "Every one will be obliged to do some work. The duty of employing one's personal ability in furthering the interests of humanity is an obligation that rests upon the shoulders of every one." (*Œuvres*, Vol. I, p. 55.)

[5] "I find it essential to give to the term 'labour' the widest latitude possible. The civil servant, the scientist, the artist, the manufacturer, and the agriculturist are all working as certainly as the labourer who tills the ground or the porter who shoulders his burden." (Introduction to *Travaux scientifiques*, *Œuvres choisies*, Vol. I, p. 221.)

[6] The national or industrial party includes the following classes:

1. All who till the land, as well as any who direct their operations.

2. All artisans, manufacturers, and merchants, all carriers by land or by sea, as well as every one whose labour serves directly or indirectly for the production or the utilization of commodities; all savants who have consecrated their talents to the study of the positive sciences, all artists and liberal advocates; "the small number of priests who preach a healthy morality; and, finally, all citizens who willingly employ either their talents or their means in freeing producers from the unjust supremacy exercised over them by idle consumers."

"In the anti-national party figure the nobles who labour for the restoration of the

ought to be no difference except that which results from their different capacities, or what Saint-Simon calls their varying stakes in the national interest. "Industrial equality," he writes, "consists in each drawing from society benefits exactly proportionate to his share in the State—that is, in proportion to his potential capacity and the use which he makes of the means at his disposal—including, of course, his capital."[1] Saint-Simon evidently has no desire to rob the capitalists of their revenues; his hostility is reserved for the landed proprietors.

Not only must every social distinction other than that founded upon labour and ability disappear, but government in the ordinary sense of the term will largely become unnecessary. "National association" for Saint-Simon merely meant "industrial enterprise." "France was to be turned into a factory and the nation organized on the model of a vast workshop"; but "the task of preventing thefts and of checking other disorders in a factory is a matter of quite secondary importance and can be discharged by subordinates."[2] In a similar fashion, the function of government in industrial society must be limited to "defending workers from the unproductive sluggard and maintaining security and freedom for the producer."[3]

So far Saint-Simon's 'industrialism' is scarcely distinguishable from the 'Liberalism' of Smith and his followers, especially J. B. Say's. Charles Comte and Dunoyer, writing in their review, *Le Censeur*, were advancing exactly similar doctrines,[4] sometimes even using identical terms. "Plenty of scope for talent" and *laissez-faire* were some of the favourite maxims of the Liberal bourgeois. Such also were the aspirations of Saint-Simon.

But it is just here that the tone changes.[5]

---

old regime, all priests who make morality consist of blind obedience to the decrees of Pope or clergy, owners of real estates, noblemen who do nothing, judges who exercise arbitrary jurisdiction, as well as soldiers who support them—in a word, every one who is opposed to the establishment of the system that is most favourable to economy or liberty." (*Le Parti national*, in *Le Politique, Œuvres*, Vol. III, pp. 202–204.)

[1] *Syst. indust., Œuvres*, Vol. VI, p. 17, note.   [2] *Ibid.*, Vol. VI, pp. 91–92.
[3] *Ibid.*, Vol. III, pp. 35–36.
[4] On this point see Halévy's article in the *Revue du Mois* for December 1907, *Les Idées économiques de Saint-Simon*, and Allix, article mentioned *supra*, p. 132.
[5] In the following passage the opposition is very marked: "One must recognize that nearly all Government measures which have presumed to influence social prosperity have simply proved harmful. Hence people have come to the conclusion that the best way in which a Government can further the well-being of society is by letting it alone. But this method of looking at the question, however just it may seem when we consider it in relation to the present political system, is evidently false when it is adopted as a general principle. The impression will remain, however, until we succeed in establishing another political order." (*L'Organisateur, Œuvres*, Vol. IV, p. 201.)

Later on the Saint-Simonians abandoned this idea and demanded Governmental

Assuming that France has become a huge factory, the most important task that awaits the nation is to inaugurate the new manufacturing regime and to seek to combine the interests of the *entrepreneurs* with those of the workers on the one hand and of the consumers on the other. There is thus just enough room for government of a kind. What is required is the organizing of forces rather than the governing of men.[1] Politics need not disappear altogether, but "must be transformed into a positive science of productive organization."[2]

Under the old system the tendency was to increase the power of government by establishing the ascendancy of the higher classes over the lower. Under the new system the aim must be to combine all the forces of society in such a fashion as to secure the successful execution of all those works which tend to improve the lot of its members either morally or physically.[3]

Such will be the task of the new government, where capacity will replace power and direction will take the place of command.[4] Applying itself to the execution of those tasks upon which there is complete unanimity, most of them requiring some degree of deliberation and yet promptness of action, it will gradually transform the character of politics by concentrating attention upon matters affecting life or well-being—the only things it need ever concern itself with.[5]

In order to make his meaning clearer, Saint-Simon proposes to confine the executive power to a Chamber of Deputies recruited from the representatives of commerce, industry, manufacture, and agriculture. These would be charged with the final acceptance or refusal of the legislative proposals submitted to them by the other two Chambers, composed exclusively of savants, artists, and engineers. The sole con-

---

control of all social relations. "Far from admitting that the directive control of Government in social matters ought to be restricted, we believe that it ought to be extended until it includes every kind of social activity. Moreover, we believe that it should always be exercised, for society to us seems a veritable hierarchy." (*Doctrine de Saint-Simon, Exposition, Deuxième Année*, p. 108; Paris, 1830.)

[1] "Under the old regime men were considered inferior to things," according to a brochure entitled *Des Bourbons et des Stuarts* (1822; *Œuvres choisies*, Vol. II, p. 447). "The object of the new system will be to extend man's hold over things." (*Œuvres*, Vol. IV, p. 81.) "In the present state of education what the nation wants is not more government, but more cheap administration." (*Syst. indust., Œuvres*, Vol. V, p. 151.) Engels, in his book written in reply to Eugen Dühring, makes use of identical terms in speaking of the socialist regime. "When the administration of things and the direction of the processes of production take the place of the governing of persons the State will not merely be abolished: it will be dead." (*Philosophie, Économie politique, Socialisme*, French translation by Laskine, p. 316; Paris, 1911.)

[2] *Lettres à un Américain, Œuvres*, Vol. II, p. 189.
[3] *Des Bourbons et des Stuarts, Œuvres choisies*, Vol. II, pp. 437–438.
[4] *L'Organisateur, Œuvres choisies*, Vol. IV, pp. 86 and 150–151.
[5] *Lettres à un Américain, Œuvres*, Vol. II, p. 188.

cern of all legislation would, of course, be the development of the country's material wealth.[1]

An economic rather than a political form of government, administering things instead of governing men, with a society modelled on the workshop and a nation transformed into a productive association having as its one object "the increase of positive utility by means of peaceful industry"[2]—such are the ruling conceptions which distinguish Saint-Simon from the Liberals and serve to bring him into the ranks of the socialists. His central idea will be enthusiastically welcomed by the Marxian collectivists, and Engels speaks of it as the most important doctrine which its author ever propounded.[3] Proudhon accepts it, and as a practical ideal proposes the absorption of government and its total extinction in economic organization. The same idea occurs in Menger's *Neue Staatslehre*,[4] and in Sorel's writings, where he speaks of "reorganizing society on the model of a factory."[5]

It is this novel conception of government that most clearly distinguishes Saint-Simon's industrialism from economic Liberalism.[6]

But, despite the fact that he gave to socialism one of its most fruitful conceptions, we hardly know whether to class Saint-Simon as a socialist or not, especially if we consider that the essence of socialism consists in the abolition of private property. It is true that in one

---

[1] This is not the only plan of government proposed by Saint-Simon, although it is the one most characteristic of him. It is to be found in *L'Organisateur* immediately after the Parable. We have to remember that Saint-Simon was very hostile to a Government of savants. Power was to be placed in the hands of the industrial leaders —the savants were simply to advise. "Should we ever have the misfortune to establish a political order in which administration was entrusted to savants we should soon witness the corruption of the scientists, who would readily adopt the vices of the clergy and become astute, despotic quibblers." (*Syst. indust., Œuvres*, Vol. V, p. 161.)

[2] *Ibid.*, Vol. VI, p. 96.

[3] F. Engels, *Herrn Eugen Dührings Umwälzung der Wissenschaft*, 4th ed., p. 277. French translation, Paris, 1911, p. 334. The whole of this chapter in Engels's book is from the pen of Karl Marx.

[4] French translation under the title *L'État socialiste*, Paris, 1906.

[5] This is the full text: "The object of socialism is to set up a new system of society based upon the workshop as a model. The rights of the society will be the customary rights of the factory. Not only will socialism stand to benefit by the existence of the industrial system which has been built up by capital and science upon the basis of technical development, but it will gain even more from that spirit of co-operation which has long been a feature of factory life, drawing out the best energy and the best skill of the workman." Earlier in the same volume he writes: "Everything will proceed in an orderly, economical fashion, just like a factory." (G. Sorel, *Le Syndicalisme révolutionnaire*, in *Le Mouvement socialiste*, November 1 and 15, 1905.)

[6] Saint-Simon often quotes Say and Smith with distinct approval. But he charges Say with the separation of politics from economics instead of merging the former in the latter, and with inability to realize to the full extent what he "dimly saw, as it were, in spite of himself, namely, that political economy is the one true foundation of politics." (*Lettres à un Américain, Œuvres*, Vol. II, p. 185.)

H

celebrated passage he speaks of the transformation of private property.[1]
But it is quite an isolated exception. Capital as well as labour, he
thought, was entitled to remuneration. The one as well as the other
involved some social outlay. He would probably have been quite
content with a purely governmental reform.

[1] Saint-Simon is classed among the socialists for two reasons: (1) the interest he
takes in the condition of the poor; (2) his opinions concerning the necessity for reforming the institution of private property. But none of the texts that are generally quoted
seem to have the significance that is occasionally given them. With regard to the first
point, a celebrated passage from the *Nouveau Christianisme* is the one usually quoted:
"Society should be organized in such a fashion as to secure the greatest advantage
for the greatest number. The object of all its labours and activities should be the
promptest, completest amelioration possible of the moral and physical condition of
the most numerous class." (*Œuvres*, Vol. VII, pp. 108–109.) Already in his *Système
industriel* Saint-Simon had said that the direct object which he had in view was to
better the lot of that class that had no other means of existence than the labour of its
own right arm. (*Ibid.*, Vol. VI, p. 81.) But is this not just the old Benthamite formula
—the greatest good of the greatest number? Besides, how does Saint-Simon propose
to secure all this? By giving the workers more power? Not at all. "The problem of
social organization must be solved for the people. The people themselves are passive
and listless and must be discounted in any consideration of the question. The best
way is to entrust public administration to the care of the industrial chiefs, who will
always directly attempt to give the widest possible scope to their undertakings, with
the result that their efforts in this direction will lead to the maximum expansion of
the amount of work executed by the mass of the people." (*Ibid.*, Vol. VI, pp. 82–83.)
A Liberal economist would hardly have expressed it otherwise.

As to the question of private property, Saint-Simon certainly regarded its transformation as at least possible. This is seen in a number of passages. "Property should
be reconstituted and established upon a foundation that might prove more favourable for production," says he in *L'Organisateur*. (*Ibid.*, Vol. IV, p. 59.) Elsewhere, in
a letter written to the editor of the *Journal général de la France*, he mentions the fact
that he is occupied with the development of the following ideas: (1) That the law
establishing the right of private property is the most important of all, seeing that it is
the basis of our social edifice; (2) the institution of private property ought to be
constituted in such a fashion that the possessors may be stimulated to make the best
possible use of it. (*Ibid.*, Vol. III, pp. 43–44.) In his *Lettres à un Américain* he gives
the following résumé of the principles which underlie the work of J. B. Say (an incidental proof of his attachment to the Liberal economists): "The production of useful
objects is the only positive, reasonable aim which political societies can propose for
themselves, and consequently the principle of respect for production and producers
is a much more fruitful one than the other principle of respect for property and
proprietors." (*Ibid.*, Vol. II, pp. 186–187.) But all that this seems to us to imply
is that the utility of property constitutes its legality and that it should be organized
with a view to social utility. Admitting that he did conceive of the necessity of a
reform of property, it does not appear that he intended this to mean anything beyond
a reform of landed property. We have already seen how he regarded capital as a
kind of social outlay which demanded remuneration. The following passage bears
eloquent testimony to his respect for movable property: "Wealth, generally speaking,
affords a proof of the manufacturers' ability even where that wealth is derived from
inherited fortune, whereas in the other classes of society it is apparently true to say
that the richer are inferior in capacity to those who have received less education but
have a smaller fortune. This is a truth that must play an important part in positive
politics." (*Syst. indust., Œuvres*, Vol. V, p. 49, note.)

It would not be difficult, however, to take the ideal of industrialism as outlined by Saint-Simon as the basis of a demand for a much more radical reform and a much more violent attack upon society. Such was the task which the Saint-Simonians took upon themselves, and our task now is to show how collectivism was gradually evolved out of industrialism.

II: THE SAINT-SIMONIANS AND THEIR CRITICISM OF PRIVATE PROPERTY

Saint-Simon's works were scarcely ever read. His influence was essentially personal, and the task of spreading a knowledge of his ideas devolved upon a number of talented disciples whom he had succeeded in gathering round him. Augustin Thierry, who was his secretary from 1814 to 1817, became his adopted son. Auguste Comte, who occupied a similar post, was a collaborator in all his publications between 1817 and 1824. Olinde Rodrigues and his brother Eugène were both among his earliest disciples. Enfantin, an old student of the Polytechnic, and Bazard, an old Carbonaro who had grown weary of political experiments, were also of the number. Soon after the death of Saint-Simon his following founded a journal called *Le Producteur* with a view to popularizing his ideas. Most of the articles on economics were contributed by Enfantin. The paper lasted only for one year, although the number of converts to the new doctrine was rapidly increasing. All of them were persuaded that Saint-Simon's ideas furnished the basis of a really modern faith which would at once supplant both decadent Catholicism and political Liberalism, the latter of which, in their opinion, was a purely negative doctrine.

In order to strengthen the intellectual ties which already united them, this band of enthusiasts set up among themselves a sort of hierarchy having at its summit a kind of college or institution composed of the more representative members of the group, upon whom the title "fathers" was bestowed. The next lower grade was composed of "sons," who were to regard one another as "brothers." It was in 1828, under the influence of Eugène Rodrigues, that the Saint-Simonians assumed this character of an organized sect. About the same time Bazard, one of their number, was giving an exposition of the creed in a series of popular lectures. These lectures, delivered during the years 1828–30, and listened to by many men who were afterwards to play an important part in the history of France, such as Ferdinand de Lesseps, A. Carrel, H. Carnot, the brothers Péreire, and Michel Chevalier, were published in two volumes under the title *Exposition de la Doctrine de Saint-Simon.* The second volume is more particularly concerned with philosophy and ethics. The first includes the social doctrine of the school, and according to Menger forms one of the most important expositions of modern socialism.[1]

Unfortunately, under the influence of Enfantin the philosophical and mystical element gained the upper hand and led to the downfall of the school.

The Saint-Simonians considered that it was not enough to take modern humanity into its confidence and reveal to it its social destiny. It must be taught to love and desire that destiny with all the ardour of romantic youth. For the accomplishment of this end there must exist a unity of action and thought such as a common religious conviction alone can confer. And so Saint-Simonism became a religion, a cult with a moral code of its own, with meetings organized and churches founded in different parts of the country, and with apostles ready to carry the good tidings to distant lands. A striking phenomenon surely, and worthy the fullest study. It was a genuine burst of religious enthusiasm among men opposed to established religion but possessed of fine scientific culture—the majority of whom, however, as it turned out, were better equipped for business than for the propagation of a new gospel.

Enfantin and Bazard were to be the popes of this new Catholicism. But Bazard soon retired and Enfantin became "supreme Father." He withdrew, with forty of the disciples, into a house at Ménilmontant, where they lived a kind of conventual life from April to December 1831. Meanwhile the other propagandists were as active as ever, the work being now carried on in the columns of *Le Globe*, which became the property of the school in July 1831. This strange experiment was cut short by judicial proceedings, which resulted in a year's imprisonment for Enfantin, Duverger, and Michel Chevalier, all of whom were found guilty of forming an illegal association. This was the signal for dispersion.

The last phase was the most extravagant in the whole history of the school, and naturally it was the phase that attracted most attention. The simple social doctrine of Saint-Simon was overwhelmed by the new religion of the Saint-Simonians, much as the Positivist religion for

[1] The exact title is *Doctrine de Saint-Simon, Exposition, Première Année*, 1829. Our quotations are taken from the second edition (Paris, 1830). One ought to mention, in addition to these, the articles contributed by Enfantin to *Le Globe* and republished under the title of *Économie politique et Politique*, in one volume (2nd ed., 1832). But none of these articles is as interesting as the *Doctrine*, and they only reproduce the ideas already discussed by Enfantin in his articles in *Le Producteur*. A new edition of the *Doctrine* was published in 1924 by Rivière, edited by Bouglé and Elie Halévy.

a while succeeded in eclipsing the Positive philosophy. Our concern, of course, is chiefly with the social doctrine as expounded in the first volume of the *Exposition*. That doctrine is sufficiently new to be regarded as an original development and not merely as a résumé of Saint-Simon's ideas. Both Bazard and Enfantin had some hand in it. But it is almost certain that it was the latter who supplied the economic ideas,[1] and that to the formation of those ideas Sismondi's work contributed not a little. The work is quite as remarkable for the vigorous logical presentation of the doctrine as it is for the originality of its ideas. The oblivion into which it has fallen is not easily explicable, especially if we compare it with the many mediocre productions that have somehow managed to survive. There are not wanting signs of a revived interest in the doctrines, and for our own part we are inclined to give them a very high place among the economic writings of the century.

The *Doctrine de Saint-Simon* resolves itself into an elaborate criticism of private property.

The criticism is directed from two points of view—that of distribution and that of the production of wealth, that of justice and that of utility. The attack is carried on from both sides at once, and most of the arguments used during the course of the century are here hurled indiscriminately against the institution of private property. The doctrines of Saint-Simon contributed not a little to the success of the campaign.

(*a*) Saint-Simon had already emphasized the impossibility of workers and idlers coexisting in the new society. Industrialism could hold out no promise for the second class. Ability and labour only had any claim to remuneration. By some peculiar misconception, however, Saint-Simon had regarded capital as involving some degree of personal sacrifice which entitled it to special remuneration. It was here that the Saint-Simonians intervened. Was it not perfectly obvious that

[1] Despite the fact that the oral exposition of the doctrine was the work of Bazard and was prepared for the press by his disciples—Hippolyte Carnot among others—most of the economic ideas contained in it must be attributed to Enfantin. Enfantin also was responsible for the majority of the economic articles that appeared in *Le Producteur*. But the doctrine set forth in *Le Producteur* differs considerably from that expounded in the *Exposition*. Interest and rent are subjected to severe criticism as tributes paid to idleness by industry. Inheritance, on the other hand, though treated with scant sympathy, is not condemned. A lowering of the rate of interest would, Enfantin thinks, help to enfranchise the workers, and a sound credit system would solve the greatest of modern problems—that is, it would reconcile workers and idlers, "whose interests will never again be confused with the general interest, inasmuch as the possession of the fruits of past labour will no longer constitute a claim to the enjoyment of the benefits of labour in the present or future." (*Le Producteur*, Vol. II, p. 124.) These ideas are more fully developed in the *Exposition*.

private property in capital was the worst of all privileges? The Revolution had swept away caste distinctions and suppressed the right of primogeniture, which tended to perpetuate inequality among members of the same family, but had failed to touch individual property and its privilege of "laying a toll upon the industry of others." This right of levying a tax is the fundamental idea in all their definitions of private property.[1] Property, according to the generally accepted meaning of the term to-day, consists of wealth which is not destined to be immediately consumed, but which entitles its owner to a revenue. Within this category are included the two agents of production, land and capital. These are primarily instruments of production, whatever else they may be. Property-owners and capitalists—two classes that need not be distinguished for our present purpose—have the control of these instruments. Their function is to distribute them among the workers. The distribution takes place through a series of operations which give rise to the economic phenomena of interest and rent.[2] Consequently the worker, because of this concentration of property in the hands of a few individuals, is forced to share the fruits of his labour. Such an obligation is nothing short of the exploitation of one man by another,[3] an exploitation all the more odious because the privileges are carefully preserved for one section of the community. Thanks to the laws of inheritance, exploiter and exploited never seem to change places.

To the retort that proprietors and capitalists are not necessarily idle—that many of them, in fact, work hard in order to increase their incomes—the Saint-Simonians reply that all this is beside the point. A certain portion of the income may possibly result from personal effort, but whatever they receive either as capitalists or proprietors can obviously only come from the labour of others, and that clearly is exploitation.

It is not the first time we have encountered this word 'exploitation.' We are reminded of the fact that Sismondi made use of it,[4] and the same term will again meet us in the writings of Marx and others. None of them, however, uses it in quite the same sense, and it might be useful to distinguish here between the various meanings of a term which plays such an important role in socialist literature and which leads to so much confusion.

Sismondi, we know, regarded interest as the legitimate income of capital, but at the same time admitted that the worker may be exploited.

---

[1] *Doctrine de Saint-Simon*, p. 182.   [2] *Ibid.*, p. 190.   [3] *Ibid.*, p. 93.
[4] Sismondi's term was rather 'spoliation.' See *supra*, p. 198.

Such exploitation, he thought, took place whenever the wages were barely sufficient to keep the wage-earner alive, although at the same time the master might be living in luxurious ease. In other words, there is exploitation whenever the worker gets less than a 'just' wage. It is merely a temporary defect and not an ineradicable disease of the economic system. It certainly does occur occasionally, although there is no reason why it ever should, and it may be removed without bringing the whole system to ruin. Conceived of in this vague fashion, what is known as exploitation is as difficult to define as the 'just price' itself. It appears under several aspects, and is by no means peculiar to the master-servant relation. An individual is exploited whenever advantage is taken of his ignorance or timidity, his weakness or isolation, to force him to part with his goods or his services at less than the 'just price' or to pay more for the goods or services of others than they are really worth.

The Saint-Simonians, on the other hand, considered that exploitation was an organic defect of our social order. It is inherent in private property, of which it is an invariable concomitant. It is not simply an incidental abuse, but the most characteristic trait of the whole system, for the fundamental attribute of all property is just this right to enjoy the fruits of labour without having to undergo the irksome task of producing. Such exploitation is not confined to manual labourers; it applies to every one who has to pay a tribute to the proprietor. The *entrepreneur*, in his turn, becomes a victim because of the interest which he pays to the capitalist, who supplies him with the funds which he needs.[1]

The *entrepreneur*'s profit, on the other hand, is not the result of exploitation. It represents payment for the work of direction. The master may doubtless abuse his position and reduce the wages of the workers excessively. The Saint-Simonians would then agree with Sismondi in calling this exploitation. But this is not a necessity of the system. And the Saint-Simonians look forward to a future state of society in which exceptional capacity will always be able to enjoy exceptional reward.[2] This is one of the most interesting elements in their theory.

[1] "The mass of workers are to-day exploited by those people whose property they use. Captains of industry in their dealings with proprietors have to submit to a similar kind of treatment, only to a much less degree. But they occasionally share in the privilege of the exploiters, for the full burden of exploitation falls upon the working classes—that is, upon the vast majority of mankind." (*Doctrine de Saint-Simon*, p. 176.)

[2] "It is our belief that profits diminish while wages increase; but the term 'wages' as we use it includes the profits that accrue to the *entrepreneur*, whose earnings we regard as the price of his labour." (*Le Producteur*, Vol. I, p. 245. The article is by Enfantin.)

Marx conceives of exploitation as an organic vice inherent in capitalism. But with him the term has quite a different connotation from that given it by the Saint-Simonians. Following the lead of certain English socialists, Marx comes to the conclusion that the origin of exploitation must be sought in the present method of exchanging wealth. Labour, in his opinion, is the source of all value, and consequently interest and profit must be of the nature of theft. The *entrepreneur*'s revenue is quite as unjust as the capitalist's or landlord's.[1]

This last theory, with its wholesale condemnation of income of every kind save the worker's wage, seems much more logical than any of the others. But as a matter of fact it is much more open to criticism. If it can be demonstrated that the value of products is not the mere result of manual labour, then Marx's idea falls to the ground. The Saint-Simonians were never embarrassed by any theory of value. Their whole contention rests upon the distinction between the income which is got from labour and the revenue which is derived from capital, which every one can appreciate. It was a distinction which had already been emphasized by Sismondi, and no conclusion other than the illegitimacy of all revenue not derived from labour can be drawn from the premises thus stated. Some basis other than labour must be discovered if this revenue is ever to be justified, and a new defence of private property must somehow be attempted.

The exigencies of production itself may supply such justification. Private property and the special kind of revenue which is derived from its possession justifies itself, in the opinion of a growing number of economists, on account of the stimulus it affords to production and the accumulation of wealth. This seems the most advantageous method of defence, and it is one of the grounds chosen by the Physiocrats.[2]

But the Saint-Simonians from the very first set this argument aside and attacked the institution of private property in the interests of social utility no less than in the interest of justice. Production as well as distribution, in their opinion, demanded its extinction.

---

[1] We might sum up the different senses of the word "exploitation" as used by Sismondi, the Saint-Simonians, and Marx respectively as follows:

(1) Sismondi thinks that the worker is exploited whenever he is not paid a wage sufficient to enable him to lead a decent existence. Unearned income seems quite legitimate, however.

(2) Exploitation exists, in the opinion of the Saint-Simonians, whenever a part of the material produce raised by labour is devoted to the remuneration of proprietors through the operation of ordinary social factors.

(3) Marx speaks of exploitation whenever a portion of the produce of labour is devoted to the remuneration of capital either through the existence of social institutions or the operation of the laws of exchange.

[2] See p. 43.

(b) This brings us to the second point, which Saint-Simon did little more than suggest, namely, whether the institution of private property as at present existing is in the best interests of producers. The Saint-Simonians hold that it clearly is not, so long as the present method of distributing the instruments of production continues. At the present moment capital is transmitted in accordance with the laws of inheritance. Individuals chosen by the accident of birth are its depositors, and they are charged with the most difficult of all tasks, namely, the best utilization of the agents of production. Social interest demands that they should be placed in more capable hands and distributed in those places and among those industries in which the need for those particular instruments is most keenly felt, without any fear of a scarcity in one place or a glut in another.[1] To-day it is a blind chance that picks out the men destined to carry out this infinitely difficult task. And all the efforts of the Saint-Simonians are concentrated just on this one point—inheritance.

Their indignation is easily explained. There is certainly something paradoxical in the fact to which they draw attention. If we accept Smith's view, that government "is in reality instituted for the defence of those who have some property against those who have none at all" —a very narrow conception of the function of government[2]—inheritance is simply inevitable. On the other hand, if we put ourselves at the point of view of the Saint-Simonians, who lived in an industrial society where wealth was regarded, not as an end, but as a means, not merely as a source of individual income, but as the instrument of social production, it seems utterly wrong that it should be left at the disposal of the first comer. The practice of inheritance can only be justified on the ground that it provides a stimulus to the further accumulation of wealth, or that in default of a truly rational system the chances of birth are not much more open to criticism than any other.

Such scepticism was little to the taste of the Saint-Simonians. But they were firmly convinced that all the disorders of production, whether apparent or real, were due to the dispersion of property according to the chances of life and death.

Each individual devotes all his attention to his own immediate dependants. No general view of production is ever taken. There is no discernment and no exercise of foresight. Capital is wanting here and excessive there. This want of a broad view of the needs of consumers and of the resources of production is the cause of those industrial crises whose origin has given rise to so much fruitless

[1] *Doctrine*, p. 191.   [2] See p. 95, note.

speculation and so many errors which are still circulating in our midst. In this important branch of social activity, where so much disturbance and such frequent disorder manifests itself, we see the evil result of allowing the distribution of the instruments of production to be in the hands of isolated individuals who are at once ignorant of the demands of industry, of other men's needs, and of the means that would satisfy them. This and nothing else is the cause of the evil.[1]

Escape from such economic anarchy, which has been so frequently described, can only become possible through collectivism—at least, so the Saint-Simonians thought.[2] The State is to become the sole inheritor of all forms of wealth. Once in possession of the instruments of production, it can distribute them in the way it thinks best for the general interest. Government is conceived on the model of a great central bank where all the wealth of the country will be deposited and again distributed through its numerous branches. The uttermost ends of the kingdom will be made fertile, and the necessaries of life will be supplied to all who dwell therein. The best of the citizens will be put to work at tasks that will call forth their utmost efforts, and their pay will be as their toil. This social institution would be invested with all the powers which are so blindly wielded by individuals at the present moment.[3]

We need not insist too much on this project or press for further details, which the Saint-Simonians would have some difficulty in supplying.

Who, for example, is to undertake the formidable task of judging of the capacity of the workmen or of paying for their work? They are to be the "generals"—the superiors who are to be set free from the

---

[1] *Doctrine*, pp. 191–192.

[2] The Saint-Simonians never make use of the term, but they describe the doctrine admirably.

[3] "We may provisionally speak of this system as a general system of banking, ignoring for the time being the somewhat narrow interpretation usually placed upon that word. In the first place, the system would comprise a central bank, which would directly represent the Government. This bank would be the depository for every kind of wealth, of all funds for productive purposes and all instruments of labour— in a word, it would include everything that is to-day comprised within the term 'private property.' Depending upon this central bank would be other banks of a secondary character, which would be, as it were, a prolongation of the former and would supply it with the means of coming into touch with the principal localities, informing the central institution as to their particular needs and their productive ability. Within the area circumscribed for these banks would be other banks of a more specialized character still, covering a less extensive field and including within their ambit the tenderer branches of the industrial tree. All wants would be finally focused in the central bank and all effort would radiate from it." (*Doctrine*, pp. 206–207.) The idea is probably Enfantin's, for there is an exposition of the same idea in *Le Producteur*, Vol. III, p. 385.

trammels of specialization and whose instinctive feelings will naturally urge them to think only of the general interest. The chief will be he who shows the greatest concern about the social destiny of the community.[1] It is not very reassuring, especially when we remember that even with the greatest men there is occasionally a regrettable confusion of general and private interests.

But admitting the incomparable superiority of the "generals," what of obeying them? Will the inferiors take kindly to submission or will they have to be forced to it? The first alternative was the one which they seemed to favour, for the new religion, "Saint-Simonism," would always be at hand to inspire devotion and to deepen the respect of the inferiors for their betters.[2] One is tempted to ask what would become of the heretics if ever there happened to be any.

Further criticism of this kind can serve no useful purpose, and it applies to every collective system, differing only in matters of detail. Whenever it is proposed to set up an elaborate plan of economic activity, directed and controlled by some central authority, with a view to supplanting the present system of individual initiative and social spontaneity, we are met at the threshold with the difficulty of setting up a new code of morality. Instead of the human heart with its many mixed motives, its insubordination and weaknesses, in place of the human mind with all its failings, ignorance, and error, are to be substituted a heart and mind altogether ideal, which only serve to remind us how far removed they are from anything we have ever known. The Saint-Simonians recognized that a change so fundamental could only be accomplished through the instrumentality of religion. In doing this they have shown an amount of foresight which is rare among the critics who treat their ideas with such disdain.

It is more important that we should insist upon another fact, namely, that the Saint-Simonian system is the prototype of all the collectivist schemes that were proposed in the course of the century.

The whole scheme is very carefully thought out, and rests upon that penetrative criticism of private property which differentiates it from other social Utopias. The only equality which the Saint-Simonians demanded was what we call equality of opportunity—an equal

---

[1] *Doctrine*, p. 210, note. Elsewhere (p. 330): "We are weary of every political principle that does not aim directly at putting the destiny of the people in the hands of the most able and devoted among them."

[2] "We come back with real joy to this great virtue, so frequently misconceived, not to say misrepresented, at the present time—that virtue which is so easy and so delightful in persons who have a common aim which they want to attain, but which is so painful and revolting when combined with egoism. This virtue of obedience is one to which our thoughts return ever with love." (*Ibid.*, p. 330.)

chance and the same starting-point for every one. Beyond that there
is to be inequality in the interests of social production itself. To each
according to his capacity, and to every capacity according to the work
which it has accomplished—such is the rule of the new society.[1]

An interesting résumé of the Saint-Simonians' programme, given
in a series of striking formulæ which they addressed to the President
of the Chamber of Deputies,[2] is worth quoting:

> The Saint-Simonians do not advocate community of goods, for
> such community would be a manifest violation of the first moral law,
> which they have always been anxious to uphold, and which demands
> that in future every one shall occupy a situation becoming his
> capacity and be paid according to his labour.
> In view of this law they demand the abolition of all privileges of
> birth without a single exception, together with the complete extinc-
> tion of the right of inheritance, which is to-day the greatest of all
> privileges and includes every other. The sole effect of this system
> is to leave the distribution of social advantages to a chance few who
> are able to lay some pretence to it, and to condemn the numerically
> superior class to deprivation, ignorance, and misery.
> They ask that all the instruments of production, all lands and
> capital, the funds now divided among individual proprietors, should
> be pooled so as to form one central social fund, which shall be em-
> ployed by associations of persons hierarchically arranged so that
> each one's task shall be an expression of his capacity and his wealth
> a measure of his labour.
> The Saint-Simonians are opposed to the institution of private
> property simply because it inculcates habits of idleness and fosters
> a practice of living upon the labour of others.

(c) Critics of private property, generally speaking, are not content
with its condemnation merely from the point of view either of distribution or production. They almost invariably employ a third method
of attack, which might be called the historical argument. The argument generally takes the form of a demonstration of the path which
the gradual evolution of the institution of private property has hitherto
followed, coupled with an attempt to show that its further transformation along the lines which they advocate is simply the logical outcome
of that process. The argument has not been neglected by the Saint-
Simonians.

The history of this kind of demonstration is exceedingly interesting,

---

[1] The formula in the third edition of the *Doctrine* is a little different. "Each one,"
it runs there, "ought to be endowed according to his merits and rewarded according
to his work." We know that the first part of the formula refers to the distribution of
capital—*i.e.*, to the instruments of labour—while the second refers to individual incomes. The word 'classed' was substituted for 'endowed' in the second edition.

[2] Published as an appendix to the second edition of the *Doctrine de Saint-Simon,
Exposition, Première Année*, 1829.

and the role it has played in literature other than that of a socialist complexion is of considerable importance. Reformers of every type, whether the immediate objective be a transformation of private property or not, invariably base their appeals upon a philosophy of history.

Marx's system is really a philosophy of history in which communism is set forth as the necessary consummation of all industrial evolution. Many modern socialists, although rejecting the Marxian socialism, still appeal to history. M. Vandervelde builds his faith upon it.[1] So do Mr and Mrs Sidney Webb and all the Fabian Socialists. Dupont-White's State Socialism is inspired by similar ideas, and so is the socialism of M. Wagner. Friedrich List has a way of his own with history; and the earliest ambition of the Historical school was to transform political economy into a kind of philosophy of history. If we turn to the realm of philosophy itself we find somewhat similar conceptions—the best-known, perhaps, being Comte's theory of the three estates, which was borrowed directly from Saint-Simon.[2]

This is not the place to discuss historical parallels. The point will come up in a later chapter in connexion with the Historical school. What we would remark here is the good use which the Saint-Simonians made of the argument. All the past history of property was patiently ransacked, and the arguments of other writers who have extolled the merits of collectivism were thus effectually forestalled.

"The general opinion seems to be," says the *Doctrine de Saint-Simon*,[3]

> that whatever revolutions may take place in society, this institution of private property must for ever remain sacred and inviolable; it alone is from eternity unto eternity. In reality nothing could be less correct. Property is a social fact which, along with other social facts, must submit to the laws of progress. Accordingly it may be extended, curtailed, or regulated in various ways at different times.

This principle, once it was formulated, has never failed in winning the allegiance of every reformer. Forty years later the Belgian economist

---

[1] In his small volume *Le Collectivisme* (Paris, 1900).

[2] Littré has disputed Comte's indebtedness to Saint-Simon in his *Auguste Comte et le Positivisme*. Saint-Simon, however, in his preface to *Système industriel* remarks that in political matters the jurists form a connecting link between feudal government on the one hand and industrial government on the other, just as the metaphysicians are intermediate between the theological and the scientific regimes. In a note which he adds he states his position still more clearly (*Œuvres*, Vol. V, p. 9). It is true that the *Système industriel* dates from 1821, and is consequently subsequent to the beginning of the friendly relations between Comte and Saint-Simon. But textual evidence, however precise, cannot decide the question of the reciprocal influence which these two Messiahs exercised upon one another. A similar idea had already found expression in Turgot's work.

[3] P. 179.

Laveleye, who has probably made the most thoroughly scientific study of the question, used almost identical words in summing up his inquiry into the principal forms of property.[1]

The Saint-Simonians feel confident that a glance at the progress of this evolution is enough to convince anyone that it must have followed the lines which they have indicated. The conception of property was at first broad enough to include men within its connotation. But the right of a master over his slaves gradually underwent a transformation which restricted its exercise, and finally caused its disappearance altogether. Reduced to the right of owning things, this right of possession was at first transmissible simply according to the proprietor's will. But the legislature intervened long ago, and the eldest son is now the sole inheritor. The French Revolution enforced equal distribution of property between all children, and so spread out the benefits which the possession of the instruments of production confers. To-day the downward trend of the rate of interest is slowly reducing the advantages possessed by the owners of property, and goes a long way towards securing to each worker a growing share of his product.[2] There remains one last step which the Saint-Simonians advocate, which would secure to all workers an equal right to the employment of the instruments of production. This reform would consist in making everybody a proprietor, but the State the sole inheritor. "The law of progress as we have outlined it would tend to establish an order of things in which the State, and not the family, would inherit all accumulated wealth and every other form of what economists call the funds of production."[3]

These facts might be employed to support a conclusion of an entirely different character. That equality of inheritance which was preserved rather than created by the French Revolution might be taken as a proof that modern societies are tending to multiply the number of individual proprietors by dividing the land between an increasing number of its citizens. But such discussion does not belong to a work

---

[1] "Another mistake that is also very general is to speak of property as if it were an institution with a fixed, unchangeable form, while as a matter of fact it has assumed various aspects and is still capable of further modification as yet undreamt of." (Laveleye, *De la Propriété et de ses Formes primitives*, 1st ed., 1874, p. 381.) Stuart Mill, in a letter addressed to Laveleye on November 17, 1872, congratulated him on the demonstration he had given of this. (*Ibid.*, preface, p. xiii.)

[2] Note this argument, which has so frequently been employed by Liberal economists, and which we shall come across in Bastiat's work. The Saint-Simonians are constantly running with the hare as well as hunting with the hounds.

[3] *Doctrine*, p. 182. The historical argument of which we have just given a short summary is developed in the *Doctrine*, pp. 179–193. It is open to a still more fundamental criticism, inasmuch as it does not seem to be historically accurate.

of this kind. We are entitled to say, however, that the Saint-Simonian theory is a kind of prologue to all those doctrines that ransack the pages of history for arguments in favour of the transformation, or even the suppression, of private property.

Here again the Saint-Simonians have merely elaborated a view which their master had only casually outlined. Saint-Simon also believed that in history we have an instrument of scientific precision equal to the best that has yet been devised.

Saint-Simon, who owes something in this matter to Condorcet, regarded mankind as a living being having its periods of infancy and youth, of middle and old age, just like the individuals who compose it. Epochs of intellectual ferment in the history of the race are exactly paralleled by the dawning of intellectual interests in the individual, and the one may be foretold as well as the other. "The future," says Saint-Simon, "is just the last term of a series the first term of which lies somewhere in the past. When we have carefully studied the first terms of the series it ought not to be difficult to tell what follows. Careful observation of the past should supply the clue to the future."[1] It was while in pursuit of this object that Saint-Simon stumbled across the term 'industrialism' as one that seemed to him to express the end towards which the secular march of mankind appeared to lead. From family to city, from city to nation, from nation to international federation—such is the sequence which helps us to visualize the final term of the series, which will be some kind of "a universal association in which all men, whatever other relations they may possess, will be united."[2] In a similar fashion the Saint-Simonians interpret the history of individual property and predict its total abolition through a process of its gradual extension to all individuals combined with the extinction of private inheritance.

The doctrine of the Saint-Simonians may well be regarded as a kind of philosophy of history.[3] Contemplation of the system fills them with an extraordinary confidence in the realization of their dreams, to which they look forward not merely with confidence, but with feelings

[1] Saint-Simon, *Mémoire introductif sur sa Contestation avec M. de Redern* (1812) (*Œuvres*, Vol. I, p. 122).

[2] *Doctrine*, p. 144.

[3] The philosophy of history might be said to consist of attempts to show that history is made up of alternating periods of organic growth and destructive criticism. The former periods are marked by unity of thought and aim, of feeling and action in society; the latter by a conflict of ideas and sentiments, by political and social instability. The former periods are essentially religious, the latter selfish. Reform and revolution are the modern manifestations of the critical nature of the period in which we live. Saint-Simonism would lead us into a definitely organic epoch. Historical evolution seems to point to a religious and universal association.

of absolute certainty. "Our predictions have the same origins and are based upon the same kind of foundations as are common to all scientific discoveries."[1] They look upon themselves as the conscious, voluntary agents of that inevitable evolution which has been foretold and defined by Saint-Simon.[2] This is one trait which their system has in common with that of Marx. But there are two important differences. The Marxians relied upon revolution consummating what evolution had begun, while the Saint-Simonians relied upon moral persuasion.[3] The Saint-Simonians, true children of the eighteenth century that they were, believed that ideas and doctrines were sufficiently powerful agents of social transformation, while the Marxians preferred to put their hope in the material forces of production, ideas, in their opinion, being nothing better than a pale reflection of such forces.[4]

III: THE IMPORTANCE OF SAINT-SIMONISM IN THE HISTORY OF DOCTRINES

The doctrine of the Saint-Simonians consists of a curious mixture of realism and Utopianism. Their socialism, which makes its appeal to the cultured classes rather than to the masses, is inspired, not by a knowledge of working-class life, but by close observation and remarkable intuition concerning the great economic currents of their time.

The dispersion of the school gave the leaders an opportunity of

[1] *Doctrine*, p. 119.

[2] *Ibid.*, p. 121. "Man is not without some intuitive knowledge of his destiny, but when science has proved the correctness of his surmises and demonstrated the accuracy of his forecasts, when it has assured him of the legitimacy of his desires, he will move on with all the greater assurance and calmness towards a future that is no longer unknown to him. Thus will he become a free, intelligent agent working out his own destiny, which he himself cannot change, but which he may considerably expedite by his own efforts."

[3] This is developed at great length in the seventh lecture, *Doctrine*, pp. 211 *et seq.*

[4] "Politics," says Saint-Simon, "have their roots in morality, and a people's institutions are just the expression of their thoughts." (*Œuvres*, Vol. III, p. 31.) "Philosophy," he remarks elsewhere, "is responsible for the creation of all the more important political institutions. No other power would have the strength necessary to check the action of those that have already become antiquated or to set up others more in conformity with a new doctrine." (*Syst. indust.*, *Œuvres*, Vol. V, p. 167.) He further insists upon the part which philanthropists may play in the creation of a new society. "One truth," he writes, "that has been established in the course of human progress is this: a disinterested desire for the general well-being of the community is a more effective instrument of political improvement than the conscious self-regarding action of the classes for which these changes will prove most beneficial. In a word, experience seems to show that those who should naturally be most interested in the establishment of a new order of things are not those who show the greatest desire to bring it about." (*Œuvres*, Vol. VI, p. 120.) It would be difficult to imagine a neater refutation of Marxian ideas, especially the contention that the emancipation of the workers can only come from the workers themselves.

taking an active part in the economic administration of their own country, and we find them throwing themselves whole-heartedly into various schemes of a financial or industrial character. In 1863 the brothers Péreire founded a credit association which became the proto-type of the financial institutions of to-day. Enfantin took a part in the founding of the P.L.M. Railway, which involved an amalgamation of the Paris-Lyons, Lyons-Avignon, and Avignon-Marseilles lines. Enfantin was also the first to float a company for the purpose of making a canal across the isthmus of Suez. At the Collège de France Michel Chevalier defended the action of the State in undertaking certain works of a public character. It was he also who negotiated the treaty of 1860 with England, which was the means of inaugurating the era of commercial liberty for France. Other examples might be cited to show the important part which the Saint-Simonians played in nine-teenth-century economic history.[1]

More especially did they realize the enormous place which banks and institutions of a similar nature were bound to have in modern industrial organization. And whatever views we may hold as to the rights of property, we are bound to recognize how these deposit banks have already become great reservoirs of capital from which credit is distributed in a thousand ways throughout the whole realm of industry. Some writers, all of them by no means of the socialist way of thinking, would reproach the banks, especially in France, with their lack of courage in regulating and stimulating industry, which, as the Saint-Simonians foresaw, is a legitimate part of their duty.[2] The important part which they saw international financiers playing in the domestic affairs of almost every European nation during the Restoration period, coupled with their personal knowledge of bankers, helped the Saint-Simonians in anticipating the all-important role which credit was to play in modern industry.

Equally remarkable was the foresight they displayed in demanding a more rigorous control of production, and in emphasizing the need for some better method of adapting that production to meet the exigencies of demand than is possible under a competitive system. The State obviously has neither the ability nor the inclination to dis-charge such functions, but so great are the inconveniences of competition

---

[1] *Cf.* on these points Weill, *L'École Saint-Simonienne* (1896), and Charléty, *Histoire du Saint-Simonisme* (1896).

[2] "The object of credit," says Enfantin (*Économie politique et Politique*, p. 53), "in a society where one set of people possess the instruments of production but lack capacity or desire to employ them, and where another have the desire to work but are without the means, is to help the passage of these instruments from the former's possession into the hands of the latter." No better definition was ever given.

that manufacturers are forced to enter into agreements with one another in order to exercise some such control. This is nothing less than a partial application of the doctrine of Saint-Simon.

In addition to the considerable personal influence which they were able to exercise over economic development, we have to recognize that in their writings we have the beginnings both of the critical and of the constructive contribution made by socialists to nineteenth-century economics. Their doctrine is, as it were, little more than an index to later socialist literature.

In the first place one must be struck by the number of formulæ to be met with in their work which have since become the commonplaces of socialism. "The exploitation of man by man" was a phrase that was exceedingly popular up to 1848. The term 'class war,' which has taken its place since the time of Marx, expresses the same idea. They spoke of "the organization of labour" even before Louis Blanc, and employed the term 'instrument of labour' as a synonym for land and movable capital long before it was so used by Marx. Although we have not considered it necessary to group them with the Associationists, they have been as assiduous as any in proclaiming the superior merits of producers' associations. Moreover, they anticipated the use which the socialists would make of the theory of rent. In a curious passage written long before the time of Henry George they refer to the possibility of applying the doctrines of Ricardo and Malthus to justify the devotion of the surplus produce of good land to the general needs of society, thus anticipating the theory of another prominent socialist thinker.[1] Other ideas might be mentioned, though not of a specifically socialist character. Thus the theory of profit-sharing, as far as our knowledge goes, was first developed in an article in Le Producteur.[2]

The more one examines the doctrines of the Saint-Simonians the more conscious does one become of the remarkable character of these anticipations and of the injustice of the oblivion which has since befallen them. Marx's friend Engels called attention to the "genial perspicacity of Saint-Simon, which enabled him to anticipate all the doctrines of subsequent socialists other than those of a specifically economic character."[3] The specifically economic idea of which Engels speaks and which Saint-Simon, in his opinion, did wrong to neglect was the Marxian theory of surplus value. We are inclined to

[1] Doctrine, p. 226. Cf. p. 223 for an eloquent passage denouncing Ricardo and Malthus, who, as the result of their "profound researches into the question of rent," undertake to defend the institution of private property.

[2] The article is entitled De la Classe ouvrière, and may be found in Vol. IV of Le Producteur. See particularly pp. 308 et seq.

[3] Engels, Herrn Eugen Dührings Umwälzung der Wissenschaft, p. 277.

the opinion that it was more of a merit than a fault to place socialism on its real foundation, which must necessarily be a social one, rather than to found it upon an erroneous theory of value.

But new formulæ are not their only contribution. Due note was taken of that fundamental opposition which exists between economists and socialists and which has caused all the conflicts and misunderstandings that disfigure the history of the century and resulted in their speaking an entirely different language. We shall try to define the nature of the conflict, in order, if possible, to help the reader over the difficulties that arise just where the bifurcation of economic thought takes place.

No attempt was made either by Adam Smith, Ricardo, or J. B. Say to make clear the distinction between the science of political economy and the fact of social organization.[1] Property, as we have already had occasion to remark, was a social fact that was accepted by them without the slightest demur. The methods of dividing property and of inheriting it, the causes that determined its rise and the consequences that resulted from its existence, were questions that remained outside the scope of their discussions. By division or distribution of wealth they meant simply the distribution of the annual revenue between the various factors of production. Their interest centres round problems concerning the rate of interest or the rate of wages or the amount of rent. Their theory of distribution is simply a theory concerning the price of services. No attention was paid to individuals, the social product being supposed to be divided between impersonal factors— land, capital, and labour—according to certain necessary laws. For convenience of discussion the impersonal occasionally becomes personal, as when they speak of proprietors, capitalists, and workers, but that is not allowed to affect the general trend of the argument.

For the Saint-Simonians, on the other hand, and for socialists in general the problem of distribution consists especially in knowing how property is distributed. The question is to determine why some people have property while others have none; why the instruments of production, land, and capital should be so unevenly distributed, and why the revenues resulting from this distribution should be unequal. For a consideration of the abstract factors of production the socialists are anxious to substitute the study of actual living individuals or social classes and the legal ties which bind them together. These differing

[1] "The majority of economists, and especially Say, whose work we have just reviewed, regard property as a fixed factor whose origin and progress is no concern of theirs, but whose social utility alone concerns them. The conception of a distinctively social order is more foreign still to the English writers." (*Doctrine*, pp. 221 and 223.) No exception is made in favour of Sismondi or Turgot.

conceptions of distribution have given rise to two different problems, the one primarily economic, the other social, and sufficient care has not always been taken to distinguish between these two currents, which have managed to coexist, much to the confusion of social thinking in the nineteenth century.

Another essential difference between their respective points of view consists of the different manner in which economists and socialists conceive of the opposition that exists between the general interest and the interests of individuals.

Classical writers envisaged it as a conflict between the interests of consumers—*i.e.*, everybody—and the interests of producers, which are more or less the interests of a particular class.

The Saint-Simonians, on the other hand—and in this matter their distinction has met with the hearty approval of every socialist—think it better to regard it as between workers on the one hand and idlers on the other, or between workers and capitalists, to adopt the cramped formula of a later period. The worker's is the general interest; the particular interest is that of the idler who lives at the former's expense. "We have on several occasions," writes Enfantin,

> pointed out some of the errors in the classification adopted by most present-day economists. The antithesis between producer and consumer gives a very inadequate idea of the magnitude of the gap that lies between the various members of society, and a better differentiation would be that which would treat them as workers and idlers.[1]

The difference in the point of view naturally results in an entirely different conception of social organization. Economists think that society ought to be organized from the point of view of the consumer and that the general interest is fully realized when the consumer is satisfied. Socialists, on the contrary, believe that society should be organized from the standpoint of the worker, and that the general interest is only fully achieved when the workers draw their full share of the social product, which is as great as it possibly can be.[2]

There is one last element of difference which is very important.

---

[1] *Le Producteur*, Vol. III, p. 385.

[2] In the preface to *Économie politique et Politique* Enfantin again writes: "All questions of political economy should be linked together by a common principle, and in order to judge of the social utility of a measure or idea in economics it is absolutely necessary to consider whether this idea or measure is directly advantageous to the workers or whether it indirectly contributes to the amelioration of their lot by discrediting idleness." It is a pleasure to be able to concur in the opinion expressed by M. Halévy in his article on Saint-Simon (*Revue du Mois* for December 1907), in which he maintains that this idea is the distinctive trait of Saint-Simon's socialism. We have already called attention to another feature that seems to us equally important, namely, the suggested substitution of industrial administration for political government.

Classical writers made an attempt to reduce the apparent disorder of individual action within the compass of a few scientific laws. By the time the task was completed so struck were they with the profound harmony which they thought they had discovered that they renounced all attempts at amelioration. They were so satisfied with the demonstration which they had given of the way in which a spontaneous social force, such as competition, for example, tended to limit individual egoism and to complete the triumph of the general interest that they never thought of inquiring whether the action of these forces might not be rendered a little less harmful or whether the mechanism might not with advantage be lubricated and made to run somewhat more smoothly.

The Saint-Simonians, on the other hand—and in this matter it is necessary to couple with theirs the name of Sismondi—are convinced of the slowness, the awkwardness, and the cruelty with which spontaneous economic forces often go to work. Consequently they are concerned with the possibility of substituting a more conscious, carefully thought-out effort on the part of society. Instead of a spontaneous reconciliation of conflicting interests they suggest an artificial reconciliation, which they strive with all their might to realize. Hence the innumerable attempts to set up a new mechanism which might take the place of the spontaneous mechanism, and the childish efforts to co-ordinate or combine economic forces. These attempts, most of them of necessity unsuccessful, furnished the adversaries of socialism with their best weapons of attack. All of them, however, did not prove quite fruitless, and some of them were destined to exercise a notable influence upon social development.

It is in the Saint-Simonian doctrine that we find these contrasts between political economy and socialism definitely marked and in full detail. It matters little to us to-day that the school was ridiculed or that the eccentricities of Enfantin destroyed his propaganda work just when Fourier was pursuing his campaign with great success. Ideas are the things that stand out in a history of doctrines. To us, at any rate, Saint-Simonism appears as the first and most eloquent as well as the most penetrating expression of the sentiments and ideals that inspire nineteenth-century socialism.[1] This accounts for the influence

---

[1] It is impossible not to make a special mention of Anton Menger's excellent little book, *Das Recht auf den vollen Arbeitsertrag* (1886) (the English translation, with an excellent introduction by Professor Foxwell, is unfortunately out of print). It is indispensable in any history of socialism. We must also mention, with deep acknowledgments, Pareto's *Les Systèmes socialistes* (Paris, 1902, 2 vols.)—the most originally critical work yet published on this subject, though not always the most impartial—and Bourguin's *Les Systèmes socialistes et l'Évolution économique* (Paris, 1906), as containing the most scientific criticism of the economic theories of socialism.

it exerted on some of the most active minds of that period. We need name only Lamennais and Sainte-Beuve, for instance, to show its attraction for thinkers of the greatest diversity,[1] even when they were disinclined to adhere wholly to its 'doctrine.'

CHAPTER III: THE ASSOCIATIVE SOCIALISTS

THE name "Associative Socialists" is given to all those writers who believe that voluntary association on the basis of some preconceived plan is sufficient for the solution of all social questions. Unfortunately the plans vary very considerably, according to the particular system chosen.

They differ from the Saint-Simonians, who sought the solution in socialization rather than in association,[2] and thus became the founders of collectivism, which is quite another thing. The advocates of socialization always thought of 'Society' with a capital S, and of all the members of the nation as included in one collective organization. The term 'nationalization' much better describes what they sought. Associationism, on the other hand, more individualistic in character and fearing lest the individual should be merged in the mass, would have him safeguarded by means of small autonomous groups, where federation would be entirely voluntary, and any unity that might exist would be prompted from within rather than imposed from without.

On the other hand, the Associationists must be carefully distinguished from the economists of the Liberal school. Fortunately this is not very difficult, for by means of these very associations they claim to be able to create a new social *milieu*. They are as anxious as the Liberals for the free exercise of individual initiative, but they believe that under existing conditions, except in the case of a few privileged

---

[1] Sainte-Beuve wrote to Buchez: "I have felt some sympathy for the movement as a whole rather than with its details, though these perhaps are not yet clear in my mind." (*Correspondance générale de Sainte-Beuve*, Vol. III, p. 233, published by Jean Bonnerot, Paris, 1939.) For Sainte-Beuve's Saint-Simonian ideas see Maxime Leroy's interesting book *La politique de Sainte-Beuve* (Paris, 1941), pp. 29–115.

[2] "Association, which is destined to put an end to antagonism, has not yet found its true form. Hitherto it has consisted of separate groups which have been at war with one another. Accordingly antagonism has not yet become extinct, but it certainly will as soon as association has become universal." (*Doctrine de Saint-Simon, Exposition, Première Année*, p. 177.)

individuals, this very initiative is being smothered. They believe that liberty and individuality never can expand unless transplanted into a new environment. But this new environment will not come of itself. It must be created, just as the gardener must build a conservatory if he is to secure a requisite environment. Each one has his own particular recipe for this, and none of them is above thinking that his own is the best.[1] It is this conception of an artificial society set up in the midst of present social conditions, bound by strict limitations which to some extent isolate it from its surroundings, that has won for the system its name of Utopian Socialism.

Had the Associationists only declared that the social environment can and ought to be modified, despite the so-called permanent and immutable laws, just as man himself is capable of modification, they would have enunciated an important truth and would have forestalled all those who are to-day seeking a solution of the social question in syndicalism, in co-operation, and in the garden-city ideal.

On the other hand, had they succeeded in carrying out their plans on an extensive scale, if we may judge by the desire to evade them on the part of those experimented on, it seems probable that the new kind of liberty would have proved less welcome than the liberty which is enjoyed under the present constitution of society.

They would have been very indignant, however, if anyone had charged them with desiring to create an artificial society. On the contrary, their claim was that the present social environment is artificial, and that their business was not to create but merely to discover that other environment which is already so wonderfully adapted to the true needs of mankind in virtue of its providential, natural harmony. At bottom it is the same idea as the 'natural order' of the Physiocrats, much as their conception differs from that of the Physiocrats—an incidental proof that the order is anything but 'natural,' seeing that it varies with those who define it. Some of their sayings, however, might very well have been borrowed directly from Quesnay or Mercier de la Rivière—for example, that of Owen's in which he speaks of the commune as God's special agent for bringing society into harmony with nature. It is just the "good despot" of the Physiocrats over again. Or take Fourier's comparison in which he ranks himself with Newton

---

[1] In Owen's paper, the *Economist*, for August 11, 1821, we meet with the following words: "The secret is out! . . . The object sought to be obtained is not *equality* in rank or possessions, is not *community of goods*, but full, complete, unrestrained co-operation on the part of all the members for every purpose of social life." Fourier writes in a similar strain: "Association holds the secret of the union of interests." (*Assoc. domestique*, Vol. I, p. 133.) Elsewhere he writes: "To-day, Good Friday, I discovered the secret of association."

as the discoverer of the law of "attraction of passion," and believes that his "stroke of genius," as Zola calls it, lies in knowing how to utilize the passions which God has given us to the best advantage.

What is still more interesting is that this newer socialism marks a veritable reaction against the principles of 1789.[1] The Revolutionists hated every form of association, and suspected it of being a mere survival of the old regime, a chain to bind the individual. Not only was it omitted from the Declaration of the Rights of Man,[2] but it was formally prohibited in every province—prohibitions which have been withdrawn only quite recently. It is difficult to imagine a greater contrast to the spirit of the Revolution than the beliefs which inspired Owen, Fourier, and Cabet, the founders of the new order.

But the men of 1789 were not so far wrong, nor were they deceived by their recollections of corporations and guilds, when they expressed the belief that any form of association was really a menace to liberty. There is an old Italian proverb which states that every man who has an associate has also a master. The Liberal school has to a certain extent always shared these apprehensions, and ample justification might be found for them in the many despotic acts of associates, whether capitalists or workmen.

But the 'associative' socialists of the early part of the last century were impressed, even more than Sismondi and Saint-Simon were, by the new phenomenon of competition. The mortal struggle for profit among producers and the keen competition for wages among working men which immediately ensued upon the disappearance of the old framework of society seemed to them to wear all the hideousness of an apocalyptic beast. With wonderful perspicacity they predicted that such breakneck competition must inevitably result in combination and monopoly.[3] Voluntary association of a co-operative character (they paid hardly any attention to the possibilities of corporative association) appeared to supply the only means of suppressing this competition

[1] On the relations of socialism to the French Revolution see the preceding chapter on Saint-Simon (p. 212, note).

[2] The Declaration of the Rights of Man speaks of liberty, property, resistance to oppression, but there is not a word about the right of association. Trade association, one of the oldest and most democratic forms of association, was proscribed by the famous decree of Le Chapelier (1791), and severe penalties were imposed upon associations of more than twenty persons by the Penal Code of 1810. These prohibitions were gradually removed in the course of the nineteenth century. Friendly societies were the first to be set free, then followed trade unions, but these laws were not definitely repealed until July 1, 1901.

[3] "It is obvious that the present regime of free competition which is supposed to be necessary in the interests of our stupid political economy, and which is further intended to keep monopoly in check, must result in the growth of monopoly in almost every branch of industry." (Victor Considérant, *Principes de Socialisme.*)

without either endangering liberty or thwarting the legitimate ambitions of producers. And it is not very clear as yet that they were altogether mistaken in their point of view.

The two best known representatives of this school are Robert Owen and Charles Fourier. Although they were contemporaries—the one was born in 1771, the other in 1772[1]—it does not appear that they ever became known to one another. Owen never seems to have paid any attention to Fourier's system, and Fourier never refers to "Owen's communistic scheme" without showing some trace of bitterness. Indeed, it is doubtful whether he knew anything at all about it except from hearsay.[2]

Such reciprocal ignorance does little credit to their powers of observation. Still, it is easily explained. Despite a certain similarity in their plans for social regeneration—for example, they both proceed to create small autonomous associations, the microcosms which were to serve as models for the society of the future, or the yeast which was to leaven the lump—and notwithstanding that after their deaths they were both hailed as the parents of one common offspring, co-operation, they spent their whole lives in two very different worlds. Without any rhetorical exaggeration and without making any invidious distinctions we may truthfully say that Owen was a rich, successful manufacturer and one of the greatest and most influential men of his day and country, while Fourier was a mere employee in the realm of industry, or a "shop-sergeant," as he liked to call himself. Later on Fourier became the recipient of a small annuity; but his reputation only spread slowly and with much difficulty among a small circle of friends. Contrary to what might have been expected, the millionaire manufacturer was the more ardent socialist of the two. A militant communist and an anti-cleric, he loved polemics, and advanced his views both in the Press and on the platform. His humble rival was just a grown-up boy with the habits of an old woman. He scarcely ever left his house except to listen to a military band; he wrote sedulously, attempting to turn out the same number of pages each day, and spent most of his life on the look-out for a sleeping partner, who, unfortunately, never turned up.

[1] Fourier's first book, *Les Quatre Mouvements*, was published in 1808, and his last, *La Fausse Industrie*, in 1836. Owen's earliest work, *A New View of Society; or Essays on the Formation of Human Character*, was published in 1813, and his last work, *The Human Race governed without Punishment*, in 1858.
[2] "According to details supplied by journalists, Owen's establishments seem to have at least three serious drawbacks which must inevitably destroy the whole enterprise—the numbers are excessive, equality is one of his ideals, and there is no reference to agriculture." (*Unité universelle*, Vol. II, p. 35.)

Other writers of whom we shall have something to say in connexion with this school are Louis Blanc, Leroux, and Cabet.

I: ROBERT OWEN

Robert Owen of all socialists has the most strikingly original, not to say unique, personality. One of the greatest captains of industry of his time, where else have we such a commanding figure? Nor is his socialism simply the philanthropy of the kind-hearted employer. It is true that it is not revolutionary, and that he could not bring himself to support the Chartist movement, which seems harmless enough now.[1] He never suggested expropriation as an ideal for working men, but he exhorted them to create new capital, and it is just here that the co-operative programme differs from the collectivist even to this day. But for all practical purposes Owen was a socialist, even a communist. Indeed, he was probably the first to inscribe the word 'socialism' on his banner.[2]

[1] Despite the fact that Chartism was essentially a working-class movement, controlled by the Working Men's Association, its demands were exclusively political, the chief of them being universal suffrage.

[2] It is quite possible that Owen regarded the term as his own invention, but we now know that it had been previously employed by Pierre Leroux, the French socialist. The publication of Owen's *What is Socialism?* in 1841, however, is the earliest instance of the term being employed as the title of a book.

Owen lived an extremely active life, and died in 1857 at the advanced age of eighty-seven. Of Welsh artisan descent, he began life as an apprentice in a cotton factory, setting up as a master spinner on his own account with a capital of £100, which he had borrowed from his father. His rise was very rapid, and at the age of thirty he found himself co-proprietor and director of the New Lanark Mills. It was then that he first made a name for himself by his technical improvements and his model dwellings for his workmen. It was at this period that his ideas on education also took shape. By and by it became the fashion to make a pilgrimage to view the factory at New Lanark, and among the visitors were several very distinguished people. His correspondents also included more than one royal personage. Among these we may specially mention the King of Prussia, who sought his advice on the question of education, and the King of Holland, who consulted him on the question of charity.

The crisis of 1815 revealed to Owen the serious defects in the economic order, and this marks the beginning of the second period of his life, when he dabbled in communal experiments. In 1825 he founded the colony of New Harmony in Indiana, and the same year witnessed the establishment of another colony at Orbiston, in Scotland. But these lasted only for a few years. In 1832 we have the National Equitable Labour Exchange, which was not much more successful.

Owen, sixty-three years of age, and thoroughly disappointed with his experiments, but as convinced as ever of the truth of his doctrines, entered now upon the third period of his life, which, as it happened, was to be a fairly long one. This period was to be devoted wholly to propagating the gospel of the New Moral World—*The New Moral World* being the title of his chief work and of the newspaper which he first published towards the end of 1834. He took an active part in the Trade Union movement, but does not seem to have been much interested in the co-operative experiments

His passion for Utopias did not prevent him from initiating a number of reforms and establishing several institutions of a thoroughly practical character. Special mention ought to be made of his interest in the welfare of his workers, an inspiration that has been caught by several manufacturers since.

Nor must we imagine, simply because we have placed him along with the Associative socialists, that association was the only solution that met with his approval. As a matter of fact there is scarcely a solution of any description which was not to some extent tried by him.

Beginning with the establishment of model workshops in his factory at New Lanark, there is hardly a suggestion incorporated in his exposition of socialism which was not attempted and even successfully applied in the course of his experiments there. Among them are included such important developments as workmen's dwellings, refectories, the appointment of officials to look after the social and moral welfare of the workers, etc.

These experiments had the further distinction of serving as a model for the factory legislation of the next fifty years. We have only to glance at the following programme of reforms effected by him to realize this:

1. He reduced the hours of labour from seventeen to ten *per diem*.

2. No children under ten years of age were employed, but free education was supplied them in schools built for the purpose.

3. All fines—then a common feature of all workshops—were abolished.[1]

---

which were started by the Rochdale Pioneers in 1844, although curiously enough this is his chief claim to fame.

Owen was in no sense a *littérateur*, being essentially a man of affairs, and we are not surprised to find that the number of books which he has left behind him is small. But he was an indefatigable lecturer, and wrote a good deal for the press. We must confess, however, that it is not easy, as we read his addresses and articles to-day, to account for the wonderful contemporary success which they had.

There is an excellent French work by Dolléans dealing with his life and doctrines (1907). The best English life, that of Podmore, is unfortunately out of print.

[1] To his fellow employers who complained of his almost revolutionary proposals Owen made reply as follows—and his words are quite as true now as they were then: "Experience must have taught you the difference between an efficiently equipped factory with its machinery always clean and in good working order and one in which the machinery is filthy and out of repair and working only with the greatest amount of friction. Now if the care which you bestow upon machinery can give you such excellent results, may you not expect equally good results from care spent upon human beings, with their infinitely superior structure? Is it not quite natural to conclude that these infinitely more delicate and complex mechanisms will also increase in force and efficiency and will be really much more economical if they are kept in good working condition and treated with a certain measure of kindness? Such kindness

Seeing that neither his experiments nor his prestige as an employer were sufficient to influence his fellow employers, he now tried to gain the sympathetic attention of the legislature. He turned first of all to the British Government, and then to that of other countries, looking to legislation to provide what he believed should have been supplied by the goodwill of the ruling classes themselves.

Even before the days of Lord Shaftesbury he had inaugurated a campaign in favour of limiting the hours of children working in factories. In 1819 the first Factory Act was passed, fixing the minimum age at which children might be employed at nine years, although Owen himself would have put it at ten.

Discouraged by the little support which he obtained for his projects, and having satisfied himself as to the impotence of both patronage and legislation as forces of social progress, he turned his attention to a third possibility, namely, association. Association, he imagined, would create that new environment without which no solution of the social question was ever possible.

1. THE CREATION OF THE MILIEU

The creation of a social *milieu* was the one impelling force that inspired all Owen's various experiments. This was his one desire, whether he asked it of the masters, the State, or of the workers themselves.

He has thus some claim to be regarded as the father of etiology—etiology being the title given by sociologists to that part of their subject which treats of the subordination and adaptation of man to his environment. His theory concerning the possibility of transforming the organism by influencing its surroundings occupies the same position in economics as Lamarck's theory does in biology. By nature man is neither good nor bad. He is just what his environment has made him, and if at the present moment he is on the whole rather bad, it is simply because his environment is so detestable. Scarcely any stress is laid upon the natural environment which seemed of such supreme importance to writers like Le Play. Owen's interest was in the social environment, the product of education and legislation or of deliberate individual action.[1] Change the environment and the

---

would do much to remove the mental friction and irritation which always results whenever the nourishment is insufficient to keep the body in full productive efficiency, as well as to arrest deterioration and to prevent premature death."

[1] Education is given a very prominent place in Owen's system, and once we accept his philosophy we realize what an important place it was really bound to have. Education was to make men, just as boots and caps are made. Were it not altogether foreign to our purpose it would be interesting to compare his educational ideals with those of Rousseau as outlined in *Émile*.

individual would be changed. He failed to see that this meant begging the whole question. If man is simply the product of his environment, how can he possibly change that environment? It is like asking a man to raise himself by the hair of his head. But the futility of such criticism will be readily appreciated if we remind ourselves that it is to such insignificant beginnings as these that we owe the conception of the garden city. It was Owen's concern for the worker and his great desire to provide him with a home where some degree of comfort and some measure of beauty might be obtainable that gave the earliest impetus to that movement.

From a moral point of view this deterministic conception resulted in the absolute denial of all individual responsibility.[1] Every noble or ignoble deed, every act, whether deserving of praise or blame, of reward or punishment, reflects neither credit nor discredit upon its author, for the individual can never be other than he actually is.

There was all the more reason, then, why all religious influences, especially that of Christianity, should be excluded. This contempt for religion explains why Owen found so little support in English society, which revolted against what appeared like cynical atheism, although Owen himself was really a deist.[2]

Economically, the doctrine of payment according to work rather than capacity was to result in absolute equality. For why should higher intelligence, greater vigour, or capacity for taking pains entitle a man to a greater reward if it is all a question of environment? Hence Owen's associations were to be communal.

We need not here detail the history of his experiments in colonization. It is the usual story of failure and disappointed hopes. At last Owen himself was driven to the conclusion that his attempt to mould the environment which was to re-create society had proved unsuccessful. He renounced all his ambitions for building up a new social order, and contented himself with an attempt to rid society as at present constituted of some of the more potent evils that were sapping its strength. And this brings us to his second essential idea, the abolition of profit.

2. THE ABOLITION OF PROFIT

The first necessity, if the environment was ever to be changed, was

[1] "The idea of responsibility is one of the absurdest, and has done a great deal of harm." (*Catechism of the New Moral World*, 1838.)
[2] On the other hand, Owen had great influence with the working classes, and this he attributed to the fact that, "freed from all religious prejudice, he was able to look upon men and human nature in general with infinite charity, and in that light men no longer seemed responsible for their actions." (Quoted by Dolléans.)

to get rid of profit. There was *the* essential evil, the original sin. Profit was the forbidden fruit which had compassed the downfall of man and caused his expulsion from the Garden of Eden. Its very definition conveyed an implication of injustice, for it was always defined as whatever was over and above cost of production. Products ought to be sold for what they cost; the net price is the only just price. But profit is not merely an injustice, it is a perpetual menace. Economic crises resulting from over-production, or rather from under-consumption,[1] may always be traced back to an unhealthy desire for profit. The existence of profit makes it impossible for the worker to repurchase the product of his toil, and consequently to consume the equivalent of what he produced. Immediately it is completed the product is snatched up by a superior body which makes it inaccessible either to the maker or to the men who could furnish an equivalent amount of labour or who could offer as the price of acquiring it a value equal to that labour.

The problem is to abolish this parasitism, and the first question that suggests itself is whether the ordinary operation of competition, assuming it were altogether free and perfect, would be sufficient to get rid of it. The economists declare that it would, and the Hedonistic school makes bold to affirm that under a regime of perfect competition the rate of profit would fall to zero. But Owen believed nothing of the kind.[2] He regarded competition and profit as inseparable, and if one was war the other was simply the spoils of conflict.

Accordingly some form of combination must be devised which will suppress profit, together with "all that gives rise to that inordinate desire for buying in the cheapest market and selling in the dearest."

[1] Like most of the economists and socialists of that time, Owen was very much impressed with the crisis of 1815.

[2] On the other hand, there is this objection:

Whenever profit forms a part of cost of production it is impossible to distinguish it from interest. In that case it is true that even perfect competition would not do away with profit, since it will only reduce the price to the level of cost of production. In that case profit cannot be said to be either unjust or parasitic, for the product is sold exactly for what it cost.

When profit does not enter into cost of production there is no possibility of confusing it with interest. It is simply the difference between the sale price and the cost of replacing the article. In this it is certainly parasitic, and would disappear under a regime of perfect competition, which must to some extent destroy the monopoly upon which such profit rests.

But the distinction between profit and interest was not known in Owen's time, and Owen would have said that they are both one, and that if profit occasionally claims a share in the cost of production with a view to defying competition it has no right to any such refuge, for cost of production should consist of nothing but the value of labour and the wear and tear of capital. Accordingly it ought to be got rid of altogether.

But the instrument of profit is gold or money. Profits are always realized in the form of money.[1] Gold is an intermediary in every act of exchange, and its intervention goes a long way towards explaining the anomaly of selling a commodity for more than cost price. The objective, then, must be money, and it must be replaced by labour notes, which will supply us with a measure of value altogether superior to money. Seeing that labour is the cause and substance of value, it is only natural that it should afford us the best means of measuring value. It is quite obvious that ample homage is paid to the Ricardian theory of value, but conclusions both novel and unproved are drawn from it.

The producer who wishes to dispose of his produce will be given labour notes in proportion to the number of hours which he has worked. In the same way the consumer who wishes to buy that product will be called upon to pay an equivalent number of labour notes, and so profit will be eliminated.

The condemnation of money was not new, but what was original was the discovery that labour notes could supply the place of money, a discovery which Owen considered "more valuable than all the mines of Mexico and Peru." It has truly been a wonderful mine, and has been freely exploited by almost every socialist. But it hardly squares with Owen's communistic ideal, which aimed at giving to each according to his needs. The labour notes evidently imply payment according to the capacity of each. Besides, what is the use of any system of exchange that is not to be employed for purposes of distribution?[2]

It remained to be seen whether this elimination of money could actually be realized in practice. An experiment to that effect was tried in London with the establishment of the National Equitable Labour Exchange. This was the most interesting experiment in the whole movement, although Owen himself was not very proud of his connexion with it. It took the form of a co-operative society with a central depot where each member of the society could deposit the product of

[1] "Metallic money is the cause of a great deal of crime, injustice, and want, and it is one of the contributory causes which tend to destroy character and to make life into a pandemonium.

"The secret of profit is to buy cheap and to sell dear in the name of an artificial conception of wealth which neither expands as wealth grows nor contracts as it diminishes."

[2] This contradiction did not escape Owen. But we must not forget that he regarded this merely as a compromise, and that he looked forward to a time when the establishment of a communistic association with a new environment would lead to a complete solution of the problem. He began in the New Harmony colony by making *pro rata* payment for the work done, but the object was to arrive gradually at a state of complete equality where no distinction was to be made between the service rendered or the labour given—with the result that the colony was extinct in six months.

his labour and draw the price of it in labour notes, the price depending upon the number of hours of work the product had cost, which the member himself was allowed to state. These products, or goods as they were now called, marked with a figure which indicated the number of hours they had taken to produce, were at the disposal of any member of the Exchange who wished to buy them. All that a member had to do was to pay the ticketed price in labour notes. And so every worker who had taken, say, ten hours to make a pair of stockings was certain of being able to buy any other article which had also cost ten hours' labour. In this fashion every one got whatever his product had cost him, and every trace of profit automatically disappeared. The profit-maker, whether industrial or commerical or merely an intermediary, was effectively removed, because producers and consumers were brought into direct contact with one another, and so the problem was apparently solved.[1]

The experiment, which had about the same measure of success as the attempts to establish a communal colony in America, did not last very long. The slightest acquaintance with the laws of value would

[1] The Labour Exchange, which was opened in September 1832, at first enjoyed a slight measure of success. There were 840 members, and they even went the length of establishing a few branches. Among the chief causes of the failure of the scheme may be enumerated:

(a) The associates, being themselves allowed to state the value of their products, naturally exaggerated, and it became necessary to relieve them of a task which depended entirely upon their honour, and to place the valuation in the hands of experts. But these experts, who were not at all versed in Owen's philosophy, valued the goods in money in the ordinary way, and then expressed those values in labour notes at the rate of 6d. for every hour's work. It could hardly have been done on any other plan. But it was none the less true that Owen's system was in this way inverted, for instead of the labour standard determining the selling value of the product, the money value of the product determined the value of the labour.

(b) As soon as the society began to attract members who were not quite as conscientious as those who first joined it, the Exchange was flooded with goods that were really unsaleable. But for the notes received in exchange for these the authorities would be forced to give goods which possessed a real value, that is, goods which had been honestly marked, and which commanded a good price, with the result that in the long run there would be nothing left in the depot except worthless products. In short, the Exchange would be reduced to buying goods which cost more than they were worth, and selling goods that really cost less than they were worth.

Since the notes were not in any way registered, anyone, whether a member of the society or not, could buy and sell them in the ordinary way and make a handsome profit out of the transaction. Three hundred London tradesmen did this by offering to take labour notes in payment for merchandise. They soon emptied the Exchange, and when they saw that nothing valuable was left they stopped taking the notes, and the trick was done.

M. Denis very aptly points out that the Exchange was really of not much use to the wage-earner, who was not even allowed to own what he had produced. There is some doubt after all as to whether the system would prove quite successful in abolishing the wage-earners.

have convinced the reformer of the futility of his attempt. But it marks an important departure in the history of economic doctrines as being the first of a long line of experiments designed to solve the same problem, but with very different methods. It is the same idea that inspires Proudhon's Bank and Solvay's *Comptabilisme social*.

The particular mechanism wherewith the elimination of profit was essayed is really of quite secondary importance. But the essential idea which lay behind the whole attempt—namely, the abolition of profit—is at least partly realized in that solid and useful institution which is now found all over the world, and which was bequeathed to us by this experiment of Owen's—the co-operative stores. Their first appearance dates from 1832, the year of the Bank of Exchange experiment, but it was not until ten years later that they assumed their present form as the outcome of the efforts of the Rochdale Pioneers.

The co-operative retail societies have as their rule either to make no profits or to restore any profit that may accrue to their members in proportion to the amount of their purchases at the stores. In reality there is no profit, but simply a cancelling of insurance against risks which has been shared in by all the members. The process of elimination is strictly in accordance with Owen's method of putting producer and consumer in direct contact with one another with a view to getting rid of the middleman. But the elimination of profit is accomplished without eliminating money.[1] That close relation which Owen and a number of other socialists believed to exist between money and profit is purely imaginary. We know as a matter of fact that the highest profits are to be got under the truck system, in the African equatorial trade, for example, where guns are exchanged at five times their value for caoutchouc reckoned at a third of its value, representing a profit of 1500 per cent. The employment of money has brought such definiteness into the method of valuation that the rate of profit per unit on a yard of cloth, say, has become almost infinitesimal. Such exactness of calculation would have been impossible under either the truck or the labour note system.

The co-operative association, with its system of no profits, will for ever remain as Owen's most remarkable work, and his fame will for ever be linked with the growth of that movement. But he was hardly conscious of the important part which he was playing in the inaugura-

[1] This does not imply that consumers' associations, when they are better organized and federated, with large central depots at their command, will not take up this project once again—that is, will not try to dispense with money in their commercial transactions. They will certainly keep an eye on that problem.

I

tion of the new movement. It is seldom that we meet with the word
'co-operation' in his writings, although that is not a matter of any
great consequence, because the term at that time had not the significance which it has to-day, being then simply synonymous with communism. Not only was Owen unwilling to assume any parental
responsibility for the co-operative society, his latest offspring, but he
expressly refused to consider it as at all representative of his system.
Shops of that description seemed to him little better than philanthropic
institutions, quite unworthy of his great ideal.[1] Before passing judgment
upon him it is only fair to remember that since those early days the
character of the co-operative stores has been completely changed. He
lived to see the establishment of the Rochdale society, with its twenty-
eight pioneers, six of whom were ardent disciples of Owen himself,
and two of these, Charles Howarth and William Cooper, were the very
soul of that immortal association. But Owen was by this time seventy-
three years of age, and he scarcely realized that a child had been born
to him. This somewhat late arrival was to perpetuate his name, and
more than any of his other schemes was to save it from oblivion.

Owen had founded no school, unless of course we consider that the
co-operators are deserving of the title. There were, however, a few
disciples who attempted to apply his theories. One of these was William
Thompson, whose writings, forgotten for many years, have recently
come in for a good deal of extravagant praise. His principal work, *An
Inquiry into the Principles of the Distribution of Wealth*, was published in
1824. As compared with Owen he reveals a greater depth of thought
and shows a more thorough acquaintance with economic science, and
he ought perhaps to be given premier place as the founder of socialism.
But, as we have pointed out in the Preface, we cannot readjust the
judgment of history, and we are bound to accept the names which
tradition has made sacred. And if a person's rank in history is to be
measured by his influence rather than his talent, then Thompson's
influence was nil, for at the time his work seems to have passed almost
unnoticed.

We will only remark that Thompson's grasp of the idea that labour
does not enjoy all it produces is much firmer than Owen's. This
meant opening the way for a discussion of surplus value and unproductive labour, of which more anon. He agrees with Owen in thinking that expropriation would not remedy the evil, and he also would
rather build up a new form of enterprise in which the worker would

---

[1] That was Holyoake's view (*History of Co-operation*, Vol. I, p. 215). But, according
to a passage quoted by Dolléans, Owen contemplated making an appeal to the
co-operative societies to come to the rescue of his National Labour Exchange.

be able to retain for himself all the produce of his labour. This was precisely the co-operative ideal.[1]

II: CHARLES FOURIER

Owen's practical influence has been much greater than Fourier's, for most of the important socialistic movements of the last century can easily be traced back to Owen. But Fourier's intellectual work, when taken as a whole, though more Utopian and less restrained in character than Owen's, has a considerably wider outlook, and combines the keenest appreciation of the evils of civilization with an almost uncanny power of divining the future.[2]

To some writers Fourier is simply a madman, and it is difficult not to acquiesce in the description when we recall the many extravagances that disfigure his work, which even his most faithful disciples can only explain by giving them some symbolic meaning of which we may be certain Fourier would never have thought.[3] The term 'bourgeois socialist' seems to us to describe him fairly accurately, but its employment lays us open to the charge of using a term that he himself would never have recognized. But what are we to make of one who speaks of Owen's communistic scheme as being so pitiable as to be hardly worth refuting; who "shudders to think of the Saint-Simonians and of all their monstrosities, especially their declamations against property and hereditary rights[4]—and all this in the nineteenth century"; who in his scheme of distribution scarcely drew any distinction between labour, capital, and business ability, five-twelfths of the product being given to labour, four-twelfths to capital (which is probably more than

[1] To the workers he wrote: "Would you like to enjoy yourselves the whole products of your labour? You have nothing more to do than simply to *alter the direction of your labour.* Instead of working for you know not whom, *work for each other.*" (Quoted by Foxwell in his introduction to Anton Menger's *The Right to the Whole Produce of Labour.*)

[2] See the lecture on *Les Prophéties de Fourier* in Gide's *Co-opération.*

[3] It is hardly necessary, however, to credit him with a greater amount of eccentricity than he actually possessed, and I seize this opportunity of refuting once more a story told by more than one eminent economist, attributing to him the statement that the members of the Phalanstère would all be endowed with a tail with an eye at the end of it. The caricaturists of the period—"Cham," for example—represent them in that fashion. The legend doubtless grew out of the following passage from his works, which is fantastic enough, as everybody will admit. After pointing out that the inhabitants of other planets have several limbs which we do not possess, he proceeds: "There is one limb especially which we have not, and which possesses the following very useful characteristics. It acts as a support against falling, it is a powerful means of defence, a superb ornament of gigantic force and wonderful dexterity, and gives a finish as well as lending support to every bodily movement." (*Fausse Industrie*, Vol. II, p. 5.)

[4] *Nouveau Monde industriel*, p. 473.

it gets to-day) and three-twelfths to management; who outbid the most brazen-faced company promoter by offering a dividend of 30 to 36 per cent., or for those who preferred it a fixed interest of 8 per cent.;[1] who held up the right of inheritance as one of the chief attractions that would be secured by the Phalanstère; and who finally declared that inequality of wealth and "even poverty are of divine ordination, and consequently must for ever remain, since everything that God has ordained is just as it ought to be"?[2]

To the men of his time, and to every one who has not read him, which means practically everybody, Fourier appears as an ultra-socialist or communist. That opinion is founded not so much upon the extravagance of his view or the hyperbolical character of his writing as upon the popular conception of the Phalanstère, which was the name bestowed upon the new association he was going to create. Visions of a strange, bewildering city where the honour of women as well as the ownership of goods would be held as common property are conjured up at the mention of that word. Our exposition of his system must obviously begin with an examination of the Phalanstère, upon the understanding of which everything turns.

I. THE PHALANSTÈRE

As a matter of fact nothing could be more peaceful than the prospect which the Phalanstère presents to our view. Anything more closely resembling Owen's New Harmony or Cabet's Icaria or Campanella's Civitas Solis or More's Utopia would be difficult to imagine. Externally it looks for all the world like a grand hotel—a Palace Hotel on a gigantic scale with 1500 persons *en pension*. One is instinctively reminded of those familiar structures which have lately become such a feature of all summer and winter resorts, containing all manner of rooms and apartments, concert halls and lecture rooms, etc. All of this is described by Fourier with the minutest detail. No restrictions would be placed upon individual liberty. Anyone so choosing could have a suite of rooms for himself, and enjoy his meals in the privacy of his own room—that is, if he preferred it to the *table d'hôte*. Hotel life is generally open only to the few. The Phalanstère would have rooms and tables at all prices to suit all five classes of society, with a free table in addition.

A number of people living under the same roof and eating at the same table, and adopting this as their normal everyday method of

---

[1] Letter dated January 23, 1831, quoted by Pellarin, *Vie de Fourier* (Paris, 1850).

[2] *Nouveau Monde industriel*, p. 26. For further details see *Œuvres choisies de Fourier*, with introduction by Charles Gide, and Hubert Bourgin's big volume on Fourier.

living, sums up the element of communism which the scheme contained. And the question is naturally asked, Why should Fourier attach such supreme importance to this mode of existence as to make it the *sine qua non* of his whole system and the key to any solution of the problem? The answer lies in the conviction, which he fully shared with Owen, that no solution is possible until the environment is changed, and so changed that an entirely new type of man will result from it.

Economically, of course, life under the same roof can offer to the consumer the maximum of comfort at a minimum of cost. Cooking, heating, lighting, etc., would under such conditions be cheaper and more efficient, and all the worries and anxieties of individual housekeeping would be swept aside.

Socially a common life of this kind would gradually teach different persons to appreciate one another. Sympathy would take the place of mutual antipathy, which under the present regime, as Fourier eloquently remarks, shows an "ascending scale of hatred and a descending scale of contempt." Besides, the multiplicity of relations and interests, and even of intrigues, which would occasionally enliven this little world would at any rate make life more interesting.

On this double series of advantages Fourier is quite inexhaustible. He reckons up the economies with the painstaking care of an old clerk, and boasts the superiority of the *table d'hôte* over the family meal with the enthusiasm of an old bachelor. The social and moral advantages seem somewhat more doubtful. It is not very obvious that contact with the rich would make the poor more polished or amicable, nor is it very clear that either would be much happier for it. Fourier's Utopia is already in operation in the United States, where, owing to the increase in the cost of living, the economic advantages of a communal life are more fully taken advantage of. Not only are there a great number of bachelors living at the clubs, but young couples have recently made a practice of taking up their abode at the hotels. They are already on the way to the Phalanstère.

This shows that Fourier was considerably in advance of his time, and those who hold that doctrines, after all, are always suggested by facts would find it difficult to discover anything pointing towards such communal experiments in the earlier part of the nineteenth century.

His solution of the servant problem, which is becoming more difficult every day, has since been largely adopted. His suggestion was the substitution of collective for individual services as being more compatible with human dignity and independence, and the development of industrial rather than domestic production. This has taken place in the case of bread-making and laundry work, and has been extended to house-sweeping (by means of the vacuum cleaner), carpet-cleaning, etc. A further extension to the art of cooking has also taken place.[1]

2. INTEGRAL CO-OPERATION

Careful scrutiny of the internal arrangements of the Phalanstère shows it to be something other than an ordinary hotel, after all. It may perhaps be regarded as a kind of co-operative hotel, belonging to an association and accommodating members of that association only. It is much more thoroughgoing than the ordinary co-operative society, which is just content to buy commodities as an association without making any real attempt to practise communism, except in those rare cases where a co-operative restaurant is set up alongside of a co-operative warehouse.

The "Phalange," not content to remain a mere consumers' association, was to attempt production as well. Around the hotel was to be an area of 400 acres, with farm buildings and industrial establishments that were to supply the needs of the inmates. The Phalange was to be a small self-sufficing world, a microcosm producing everything it consumed, and consuming—as far as it could—all it produced. Occasionally, no doubt, there would be occasional surpluses or some needs would remain unsatisfied, and then recourse would be had to exchange with other Phalanges. Every Phalange was to be established as a kind of joint-stock company. Private property was not to be extinguished altogether, but to be transformed into the holding of stock—a transformation of a capitalistic rather than of a socialistic nature. M. de Molinari states that the future will witness the almost universal application of the joint-stock principle, and he for one would welcome its extension. Fourier has forestalled his prophecy by three-quarters of a century, with an insight that is truly remarkable for the time in which he wrote, for joint-stock undertakings were then exceedingly rare. He enumerates the many advantages which would result from such a transformation in the nature of property, and he roundly declares that "a share in such concerns is really more valuable than any amount of land or money."

[1] It is necessary to point out that Fourier's suggestions for a solution of the domestic servant problem are really not quite so definite as we have given the reader to understand in the text. They are mixed up with a number of other ideas of a more or less fantastic description, but very suggestive nevertheless. This is especially true of the suggestion to transform domestic service by making it mutually gratuitous—an idea that is worth thinking about.

How were the extravagant dividends which he promised when propounding his scheme to be paid out? The usual method in financial and commercial transactions is to distribute them according to the holding of each individual. But such was not to be his plan. Capital was to have a third of the profits, labour five-twelfths, and ability three-twelfths. 'Ability,' which signifies the work of management, was to devolve upon those individuals who were chosen by the society and were considered best fitted for the work. Fourier never realized that there was a possibility of the wrong man being chosen. He had no experience of universal suffrage, and he believed that within such a tiny group the election would be perfectly *bona-fide*.

Associations known as Phalanges have actually been established in Paris, and to some extent at any rate they have realized the ideal as outlined by Fourier. The profits are divided in almost strict accordance with Fourier's formula,[1] and in order to emphasize their descent from him the members have caused a statue to be raised to his memory in their quarter of the town—the Boulevard de Clichy.

Not content with giving us an outline of a co-operative productive society, Fourier has also left us an admirably concise statement of the problem that faces modern society. "The first problem for the economist to solve," says he, "is to discover some way of transforming the wage-earner into a co-operative owner."[2]

The necessity for such transformation consists in the fact that this is the only way of making labour at once attractive and productive, for "the sense of property is still the strongest lever in civilized society."[3] "The poor individual in Harmony who only possesses a portion of a share, say a twentieth, is a part proprietor of the whole concern. He can speak of *our* land, *our* palaces and castles, *our* forests and factories, for all of them belong partly to him."[4] "Hence the role of capitalist and proprietor are synonymous in Harmony."[5]

The worker will draw his share of the profits not merely as a worker, but also as a capitalist who is a shareholder in the concern, and as a member of the directorate, in which every shareholder has a voice. The administration of the business will form a part of his responsibilities. It is just what we are accustomed to call co-partnership. He will,

[1] We were thinking especially of associations like that of the painters under the leadership of M. Buisson, where distribution is as follows: labour 50 per cent., capital 27 per cent., administration 12 per cent.

[2] *Association domestique*, Vol. I, p. 466.

[3] *Ibid.*, p. 466. Note that Fourier says that this only applies to civilized societies. For those who live in the future Harmony city there will be other and more powerful motives.

[4] *Unité universelle*, Vol. III, p. 517.

[5] *Ibid.*, p. 451.

moreover, participate in the privileges and management of the Phalange as a member of a consumers' association.

All this seems very complicated, but it was a part of Fourier's policy to transmute the divergent interests of capitalists, workers, and consumers by giving to each individual a share in these conflicting interests.[1] Under existing conditions they are in conflict with one another simply because they are focused in different individuals. Were they to be united in the same person the conflict would cease, or at any rate the battle-ground would be shifted to the conscience of each individual, where reconciliation would not be quite such a difficult matter.

A programme which aims, not at the abolition of property, but at the extinction of the wage-earner by giving him the right of holding property on the joint-stock principle, which looks to succeed, not by advocating class war, but by fostering co-operation of capital with labour and managing ability, and attempts to reconcile the conflicting interests of capitalist and worker, of producer and consumer, debtor and creditor, by welding those interests together in one and the same person, is by no means commonplace. Such was the ideal of the French working classes until Marxian collectivism took its place, and it is quite possible that its deposition may be only temporary after all. The programme which the Radical Socialists swear allegiance to, and which they set against the purely socialistic programme, is the maintenance and extension of private property and the abolition of the wage-earner. By taking this attitude they are unconsciously following in the wake of Fourier.[2]

[1] The system of integral association proposed by Fourier, including both co-operative production and co-operative distribution, will be better understood if we look at the facts of the present situation.

On the one hand we have co-operative associations of producers who are not particularly anxious that their products should be distributed among themselves; they simply produce the goods with a view to selling them and making a profit out of the transaction. On the other hand, the distributing societies simply aim at giving their members certain advantages, such as cheaper goods, but they make no attempt to produce the goods which they need.

In countries where co-operative societies are properly organized, as they are in England, for example, many of these societies have undertaken to produce at least a part of what they consume, and some of them have even acquired small estates for the purpose; but only a small proportion of the employees are members of the societies, with the result that their position is not very different from that of other working men. One understands the difficulty of grouping people in this way. But if the associations are to live it is absolutely necessary that they should produce what they require under conditions that are more favourable than those of ordinary producers; in a word, that they should be able to create a kind of new economic environment.

Even in the colonies one does not find many instances of vigorous associations of this kind.

[2] Co-partnership as outlined by M. Briand is to-day an item in the programme of the Radical Democratic party. See *Les Actions du Travail*, by M. Antonelli.

3. BACK TO THE LAND

The title at the head of this section is to-day adopted as a motto by several social schools. It also figured in Fourier's programme long ago. Fourier, however, employed the phrase in a double sense.

In the first place, he thought that there must be a dispersion of the big cities and a spreading out of their inhabitants in Phalanstères, which would simply mean moderate-sized villages with a population of 1600 people, or 400 families. Great care was to be exercised in choosing a suitable site. Wherever possible the village was to be placed on the bank of a beautiful river, with hills surrounding it, the slopes of which would yield to cultivation, the whole area being flanked by a deep forest. It was not, as some one has remarked, intended as an Arcadia for better-class clerks.[1] It was simply an anticipation of the garden cities which disciples of Ruskin and Morris are building all over England. These are designed, as we know, not merely with a view to promoting health and an appreciation of beauty, but also to encouraging the amenities of life and to solving the question of housing by counteracting the high rental of urban land.

In the second place, industrial work of every description, factory and machine production of every kind, were to be reduced to the indispensable minimum—a condition that was absolutely necessary if the first reform was ever to become practicable. Contrary to what might have been expected, Fourier felt no antipathy towards capitalism, but entertained the greatest contempt for industrialism, which is hardly the same thing.[2] A return to the land, if it was to mean anything at all, was to mean more agriculture. But care must be taken not to interpret it in the old sense of tillage or the cultivation of cereals. It was in no measured terms that he spoke of the cultivation of corn and the production of bread, which has caused mankind to bend under the cruellest yoke and for the coarsest nourishment that history knows. The only attractive forms of cultivation, in his opinion, were horticulture and arboriculture, apple-growing, etc., joined, perhaps, with poultry-keeping and such occupations as generally fall to the lot of the small-holder.[3] The inhabitant of the Phalanstère would be employed

[1] M. Faguet, *Revue des Deux Mondes*, August 1, 1896.
[2] "Industrialism is the latest scientific illusion." (*Quatre Mouvements*, p. 28.) We must also draw attention to his suggestion for co-operative banks, where agriculturists could bring their harvest and obtain money in exchange for it—a rough model of the agricultural credit banks. But he only regarded this as a step towards the Phalanstère.
[3] The kinds of labour which Fourier selects as examples are always connected with fruit-growing—cherry orchards, pear orchards, etc. Fruit and flowers have a very important place in his writings. He seems to have anticipated the fruit-growing rancher of California.

Without stopping to examine some of the more solid reasons—which unfortunately

almost exclusively in looking after his garden, just as Adam was before
the Fall and Candide after his misfortunes.

4. ATTRACTIVE LABOUR

The attractiveness of labour was made the pivot of Fourier's system.
Wherever we like to look, whether in the direction of so-called civilized
societies or towards barbarian or servile communities, labour is everywhere regarded as a curse. There is no reason why it should be, and
in the society of the future it certainly will not be, for men will then
labour not because they are constrained to either by force or by the
pressure of need or the allurement of self-interest. Fourier's ideal was
a social State in which men would no longer be forced to work, whether
from the necessity of earning their daily bread or from a desire for gain
or from a sense of social or religious duty. His ambition was to see
men work for the mere love of work, hastening to their task as they do
to a gala. Why should not labour become play, and why should not
the same degree of enthusiasm be shown for work as is shown by youth
in the pursuit of sport?[1]

Fourier thinks this would be possible if every one were certain that
he would get a minimum of subsistence by his work. Labour would
lose all its coercive features, and would be regarded simply as an
opportunity for exercising certain faculties, provided sufficient liberty
were given every one to choose that kind of work which suited him
best, and provided also the labour were sufficiently diversified in
character to stimulate imagination and were carried on in an atmosphere of joy and beauty. The sole object of the Phalanstère, as we
have already seen, was to make labour more attractive by creating a
new kind of social life in which production as well as distribution would
be on a co-operative basis and horticulture would take the place of
agriculture. But Fourier was not content to stop at that, and he proceeds to show the importance of combining different kinds of employment. Some of his suggestions are very ingenious; others, on the other
hand, are equally puerile. The most notable of these is his proposal
to bring individuals together into what he calls groups and series. A

---

are buried beneath a great deal of rubbish—why fruit-growing should take the place
of agriculture, we must just recall the curious fact that he was always emphasizing
the superiority of sugar and preserves over bread, and pointed to the 'divine instinct'
by which children are enabled to discover this. The suggestion was ridiculed at the
time, but is to-day confirmed by some of the most eminent doctors and teachers of
hygiene.

[1] It is interesting to contrast this view with Bücher's, who thinks that the evolution
of industry simply increases its irksomeness. A conception of regressive or spiral
evolution might reconcile the two views.

person would be allowed to join these groups according to his own individual preferences, and as it would not involve his spending his whole life in any one of them, he would be free to 'flit' from one to the other.

But it is about time we took leave of our guide. We cannot pretend to follow the twists and turns of his labyrinthine psychology, with its dozen passions, of which the three fundamental ones are the desire for change, for order, and for secrecy; nor can we bring ourselves to accept his theodicy, nor his views on climatic and cosmogenic evolution, which was some day to result in sweetening the waters of the ocean, in melting the polar glaciers, in giving birth to new animals, and in putting us in communication with other planets. Yet even this muddy torrent is not without some grain of gold in it.

Take the question of education, for example, which holds a very prominent place in his writings. Old bachelor that he was, he never cared very much for children, but he nevertheless foreshadowed the development of modern education on several important points. Froebel, who conceived the idea of the kindergarten (1837), was among his disciples.[1]

His teaching on the sex question bears all the marks of lax morality, and indicates the fallacy of thinking that untrained passions and instincts can be morally justified.[2] His extreme views on this question, which even go beyond the advocacy of free union, have contributed a great deal to the downfall of Fourierism. Paul Janet remarks somewhere that the socialists have not been very happy in their treatment of the woman question, and we have already shown how this weakness led to the downfall of Saint-Simonism. But even on this subject Fourier has penned a few pithy sentences. "As a general rule," he says,

> it may be said that true social progress is always accompanied by the fuller emancipation of woman, and there is no more certain evidence of decadence than the gradual servility of women. Other events undoubtedly influence political movements, but there is no other cause that begets social progress or social decline with the same rapidity as a change in the status of women.[3]

[1] Let us not forget his *Petites Hordes*, which consisted of groups of boys who undertook the sweeping of public paths, the surveillance of public gardens, and the protection of animals. The idea was very much ridiculed at the time, but a number of similar organizations, each with its badge and banner, were instituted by Colonel Waring in the city of New York.

[2] "My theory is that every passion given by nature should be allowed the fullest scope. That is the key to my whole system. Society requires the full exercise of all the faculties given us by God."

[3] *Quatre Mouvements*, p. 194.

Unfortunately his feminism was not so much inspired by respect for the dignity of woman as by his hatred of family life, and the liberty which he thought to be the true test of progress was generally nothing better than free love.

The anti-militarists have good claim to regard him as a forerunner. Speaking of present-day society, he said that "it consists of a minority of armed slaves who hold dominion over a majority of disarmed."

It was not Fourier's intention to introduce men into the world of Harmony at one stroke. He thought that as an indispensable preliminary they should go through a stage of transition which he calls *Garantisme*, where each one would be given a minimum of subsistence, security, and comfort—in short, everything that is considered necessary by the advocates of working-class reform.

Fourierism never enjoyed the prestige and never exercised the influence which Saint-Simonism did, but its action, though less startling, and confined as it was to a narrower sphere, has not been less durable. Nothing has been heard of Saint-Simonism these last fifty years, but there is still a Phalanstère school. It is not very numerous, perhaps, if we are only to reckon those who formally adhere to the doctrine, but if we take into consideration the co-operative movement, as we ought at least to some extent, it is seen to be very powerful still. For a long time Fourier's ideas were scouted by everybody, but later much more sympathetic attention was given them.[1]

Among his disciples there are at any rate two who deserve special mention. Victor Considérant, one of the strongest advocates of Fourierism, has left us the best exposition of the doctrine that we have, in his book *Doctrine sociale* (1834–44). Like Owen, he experimented in American colonization,[2] and gained a measure of notoriety in the Revolution of 1848 by insisting upon the right to work as a necessary compensation for the loss of property.

André Godin left a monument more permanent than books, in the famous Familistère which was founded by him. It consists of an

[1] See, for example, such works as Zola's *Travail*, and Barrès's *L'Ennemi des Lois*; and as an example of the general change in the tone of the economists we may refer to Paul Leroy-Beaulieu's latest writings, in which he speaks of Fourier as a "genial thinker."

[2] It is no part of our task to relate the story of the several colonies founded either by disciples of Fourier or of Owen. Experiments of this kind were fairly general in the United States between 1841 and 1844, when no less than forty colonies were founded. Brook Farm, which is the best known of these, included among its members some of the most eminent Americans—Channing and Hawthorne, for example—but none of the settlements lasted very long

Similar attempts have been made in France at a still more recent period, notably in the colony at Condé-sur-Vesgres, near Rambouillet, where a few faithful disciples of Fourier came together.

establishment for the manufacture of heating apparatus at Guise, run entirely on co-partnership lines, the profits being distributed in accordance with the rules of the master.[1] It is not a new co-operative society of the humdrum kind, however. Close to the works, right in the middle of a beautiful park, are one or two huge blocks which contain the 'flats' where the co-partners live, as well as schools, crèches, a theatre, and a co-operative stores. But despite its fame, and notwithstanding the fact that it has become a kind of rendezvous for co-operators all the world over, there is nothing very attractive about it, and if one wants to get a good idea of what a real Phalanstère is like it is better to visit either Bournville or Port Sunlight, or Agneta Park in Holland.

III: LOUIS BLANC

It is not the most original work that always attracts most attention. Stuart Mill, writing of Saint-Simonism and Fourierism, claims that "they may justly be counted among the most remarkable productions of the past and present age." To apply such terms to the writings of Louis Blanc would be entirely out of place. His predecessors' works, despite a certain mediocrity, are redeemed by occasional remarks of great penetration; but there is none of that in Louis Blanc's. Moreover, his treatment is very slight, the whole exposition occupying about as much space as an ordinary review article.[2] And there is no evidence of exceptional originality, for the sources of its inspiration must be sought elsewhere—in the writings of Saint-Simon, of Fourier, of Sismondi, and of Buonarotti, one of the survivors of the Babeuf conspiracy,[3] and in the democratic doctrines of 1793. In short, Blanc was content to give a convenient exposition of such socialistic ideas as the public had become accustomed to since the Restoration.

Nevertheless, no sooner was the *Organisation du Travail* published in 1841 than it was read and discussed by almost everybody. Several editions followed one another in rapid succession. The title, which is borrowed from the Saint-Simonians, supplied one of those popular formulæ which conveniently summed up the grievances of the working classes in 1848, and during the February Revolution Louis Blanc came to be regarded as the best-qualified exponent of the views

---

[1] Founded in 1859, it only became a co-partnership in 1888, the year of Godin's death.

[2] As a matter of fact it first appeared as an article in the *Revue du Progrès* in 1839.

[3] Buonarotti was the author of *La Conspiration pour l' Égalité, dite de Babeuf*, published in 1828. Little notice was taken of the volume by the public, but it was much discussed in democratic circles.

of the proletariat. Even for a long time after 1848 the work was considered to be the most characteristic specimen of French socialistic
writing.

Its success was in a measure due to the circumstances of the period.
The brevity of the book and the directness of the exposition made the
discussion of the theme a comparatively easy matter. The personal
notoriety of the author also had a great deal to do with the interest
which his work aroused. During the short career of the July monarchy
Blanc, both in the Press and on the platform, had found himself one
of the most valiant supporters of the advanced democratic wing. His
Histoire de Dix ans gave him some standing as a historian. Later on
the role which he played as a member of the Provisional Government
of 1848, and afterwards at the inauguration of the Third Republic,
contributed to his fame as a public man. And, last of all, his unfortunate experience in connexion with the failure of the national workshops, for which he was unjustly blamed, added to the interest which
the public took in him.

All this, however, would not justify his inclusion in our history were
it not for other reasons which give to the *Organisation du Travail* something more than a mere passing interest.

In no other work is the opposition between competition and association so trenchantly stated. Every economic evil, if we are to believe
Blanc, is the outcome of competition. Competition affords an explanation of poverty and of moral degradation, of the growth of crime and
the prevalence of prostitution, of industrial crises and international
feuds. "In the first place," writes Blanc, "we shall show how competition means extermination for the proletariat, and in the second place
how it spells poverty and ruin for the bourgeoisie."[1] The proof spreads
itself out over the whole work, and is based upon varied examples
gleaned from newspapers and official inquiries, from economic treatises
and Government statistics, as well as from personal observations
carried on by Blanc himself. No effort is spared to make the most
disagreeable facts contribute of their testimony. Everything is arranged
with a view to one aim—the condemnation of competition. Only one
conclusion seems possible: "If you want to get rid of the terrible effects
of competition you must remove it root and branch and begin to build
anew, with association as the foundation of your social life."

Louis Blanc thus belonged to that group of socialists who thought
that voluntary associations would satisfy all the needs of society. But
he thinks of association in a somewhat different fashion from his predecessors. He dreams neither of New Harmony nor of a Phalanstère.

[1] *Organisation du Travail*, 5th ed. (1848), p. 77.

Neither does he conceive of the economic world of the future as a series of groups, each of which forms a complete society in itself. Fourier's integral co-operation, where the Phalanstère was to supply all the needs of its members, is ignored altogether. His proposal is a social workshop, which simply means a co-operative producers' society. The social workshop was intended simply to combine members of the same trade, and is distinguished from the ordinary workshop by being more democratic and equalitarian. Unlike Fourierism, it does not contain within itself all aspects of economic life. By no means self-contained, it merely undertakes the production of some economic good, which other folk are expected to buy in the ordinary way. Louis Blanc's is simply the commonest type of co-operative society.[1] The schemes of both Owen and Fourier were much more ambitious, and attempted to apply the principle of co-operation to consumption as well as to production.

Nor was the idea altogether a new one. A Saint-Simonian of the name of Buchez had already in 1831[2] made a similar proposal, but it met with little success. Workers in the same trade—carpenters, masons, shoemakers, or what not—were advised to combine together, to throw their tools into the common lot, and to distribute among themselves the profits which had hitherto gone to the *entrepreneur*. A fifth of the annual profits was to be laid aside to build up a "perpetual inalienable reserve," which would thus grow regularly every year. "Without some such fund," says Buchez, with an unerring instinct for the future,

> association will become little better than other commercial under-takings. It will prove beneficial to the founders only, and will ban every one who is not an original shareholder, for those who had a share in the concern at the beginning will employ their privileges in exploiting others.[3]

Such is the destiny that awaits more than one co-operative society, where the founders become mere shareholders and employ others who are simply hirelings to do the work for them.

[1] We refer to it as the commonest type because in the previous section we have shown that other co-operative societies exist, such as Le Travail, for example, which claims to be modelled upon Fourier's scheme, especially in the matter of borrowed capital. But the usual type is affiliated to the Chambre consultative des Associations de Production. Article 2 of its regulations reads as follows: "No one will be allowed to become a subscriber who is not a worker in some branch of production or other." See the volume published by the Office du Travail in 1898, *Les Associations Ouvrières de Production.*

[2] In the *Journal des Sciences morales et politiques*, December 17, 1831. Only one association—the goldsmiths', in 1834—was founded as the result of this article.

[3] Quoted by Festy, *Le Mouvement ouvrier au Début de la Monarchie de Juillet*, p. 88 (Paris, 1908).

Whereas Buchez was greatly interested in *petite* industry,[1] Blanc was in favour of the great industry, and that seems to be the only difference between his social workshop and an ordinary co-operative society. But in Blanc's opinion the social workshop was just a cell out of which a complete collectivistic society would some day issue forth. Its ultimate destiny did not really interest him very much. The ideal was much too vague and too distant to be profitably discussed. The important thing was to make a beginning and to prepare for the future in a thoroughly practical fashion, but "without breaking altogether with the past." That seemed clearly to be the line of procedure. To give an outline of what that future would be like seemed a vain desire, and would simply mean outlining another Utopia.

It is just because his plan was precise and simple that Louis Blanc succeeded in claiming attention where so many beautiful but quite impossible dreams had failed. Here at last was a project which every one could understand, and which, further, would not be very difficult to adopt. This passion for the concrete rather than the ideal, for some practical formula that might possibly point the way out of the morass of *laissez-faire*, may be discovered in more than one of his contemporaries. It is very pronounced in Vidal's work, for example. Vidal was the author of an interesting book on distribution which unfortunately seems to be now quite forgotten.[2] Much of the success of the project, like that of the State Socialism of a later period, was undoubtedly due to this feeling.

The projected reform seemed exceptionally simple. A national workshop was to be set up forthwith in which all branches of production would be represented. The necessary capital was to be obtained from the Government, which was expected to borrow it. Every worker who could give the necessary moral guarantee was allowed to compete for this capital. Wages would be equal for everybody, a thing which is quite impossible under present conditions, largely because of the false anti-social character of a good deal of our education. In the future, when a new system of education will have improved morality and begotten new ideas, the proposal will seem a perfectly natural one. Here we come across a suggestion that seems common to all the associationists, namely, the idea of a new environment effecting a revolution in the ordinary motives of mankind. As to the hierarchy of the workshop, that will be established by election, except during the first year, when the Government will undertake to conduct the or-

[1] Buchez's proposals for the reform of the "great industry" were of an entirely different character.

[2] François Vidal, *De la Répartition des Richesses* (1846).

ganization, because as yet the members will hardly be sufficiently
trained to choose the best representatives. The net revenue will be
divided into three portions, of which the first will be distributed
between the various members of the association, thus contributing to
a rise in their wages; the second portion will go towards the upkeep
of the old, the sick, and the infirm, and towards easing the burdens of
some other industries; while the third portion will be spent in supplying
tools to those who wish to join the association, which will gradually
extend its sway over the whole of society. The last suggestion inevitably
reminds us of Buchez's "inalienable and perpetual capital."

Interest will be paid on the capital employed in founding the industry, such interest being guaranteed against taxation. But we must
not conclude that Blanc favoured this condition because he believed
in the legitimacy of interest, as Fourier did. He was too pronounced
a disciple of the Saint-Simonians ever to admit that it was legitimate.
The time will come, he thinks, when it will no longer be necessary,
but he gives no hint as to how to get rid of it. For the present at any
rate it must be paid, were it only to enable the transition to be made.
"We need not with savage impatience destroy everything that has
been founded upon the abuses which as a whole we are so anxious to
remove." The interest paid, along with the wages, will form a part
of the cost of production. The capitalists, however, will have no share
in the net profit unless they have directly contributed to it.

It seems that the only difference between the social workshop and
the present factory is its somewhat more democratic organization, and
the fact that the workers themselves seize all the profit (*i.e.*, over and
above the net interest), instead of leaving it, as was hitherto the case,
to the *entrepreneur*.

But this social workshop, as we have said, is a mere cell out of which
a new society is expected to form. The amusing feature is this, that
the new society can only come into being through the activity of
competition—competition purged of all its more abominable features,
that is to say. "The arm of competition must be strengthened in order
to get rid of competition." That ought not to be a very difficult task,
for the "social workshop as compared with the ordinary private factory
will effect greater economies and have a better system of organization,
for every worker without exception will be interested in honestly performing his duty as quickly as possible." On every side will private
enterprise find itself threatened by the new system. Capital and workers
will gravitate towards the social workshop with its greater advantages.
Nor will the movement cease until one vast association has been formed
representing all the social shops in the same industry. Every important

industry will be grouped round some central factory, and "the different shops will be of the nature of supplementary establishments." To crown the edifice, the different industries will be grouped together, and, instead of competing with one another, will materially help and support each other, especially during a time of crisis, so that the understanding existing between them will achieve a still more remarkable success in preventing crises altogether.

Thus, merely by being given greater freedom the competitive regime will gradually disappear, to make way for the associative regime, and as the social workshops realize these wonderful ideals the evils of competition will disappear, and moral and social life will be cleansed of its present evils.

The remarkable feature of the whole scheme is that hardly anything new is needed to effect this vast change. Just a little additional pressure on the part of Government, some capital to set up the workshops, and a few additional regulations to guide it in its operations, that is all.

This is really a very important point in Louis Blanc's doctrine, which clearly differentiates it from both Owen's and Fourier's. They appeared to think that the State was not necessary at all: private initiative seemed quite sufficient. It was hoped that society would renew itself spontaneously without any extraneous aid, and this is still the working creed of the co-operative movement. Wherever the co-operative movement has flourished the result has been entirely due to the efforts of its members. But Louis Blanc's attention was centred on the highly trained artisan, and the problem was to find capital to employ him. Were they to rely upon their own savings, they would never make a beginning.[1] Moreover, somebody must start the thing, and power is wanted for this. That power will be organized force, which will be employed, however, not so much as an ally, but rather as a 'starter.' Intervention will necessarily be only temporary. Once the scheme is started its own momentum will keep it going. The State, so to speak, "will just give it a push: gravity and the laws of mechanics will suffice for the rest." That is just where the ingenuity of the whole system comes in, and as a matter of fact the majority of the producing

[1] "The emancipation of the working classes is a very complicated business. It is bound up with so many other questions and involves such profound changes of habit. So numerous are the various interests upon which an apparent though perhaps not a real attack is contemplated, that it would be sheer folly to imagine that it could ever be accomplished by a series of efforts tentatively undertaken and partially isolated. The whole power of the State will be required if it is to succeed. What the proletarian lacks is capital, and the duty of the State is to see that he gets it. Were I to define the State I should prefer to think of it as the poor man's bank." (*Organisation du Travail*, p. 14.)

co-operative societies now at work owe their existence to the financial aid and administrative ability of public bodies, without which they could hardly keep going.

Louis Blanc, accordingly, is one of the first socialists to take care to place the burden of reform upon the shoulders of the State. Rodbertus and Lassalle make an exactly analogous appeal to the State, and for this reason the French writer deserves a place among the pioneers of State Socialism.

This appeal of the socialists is beautifully naïve. On the one hand they invite the adherence of Government to a proposal that is frankly revolutionary, in which case it is asked to compass its own destruction —naturally not a very attractive prospect. On the other hand the project seems harmless enough, and the support which the Government is asked to extend further emphasizes the modest nature of the undertaking. State socialism cannot escape the horns of this dilemma by proclaiming itself frankly conservative, as it has done in Germany.

Louis Blanc, like Lassalle after him, was much concerned with immediate results, and he failed to notice this objection. He paid considerable attention to another line of criticism, however, and one that he considered much more dangerous. He sought a way of escape by using an argument which was afterwards frequently employed by the State Socialists, as we shall see by and by.

The question was whether State intervention is contrary to liberty or not. "It clearly is," says Louis Blanc,

if you conceive of liberty as an abstract right which is conferred upon man by the terms of some constitution or other. But that is no real liberty at all. Full liberty consists of the power which man has of developing and exercising his faculties with the sanction of justice, and the approval of law.[1]

The right to liberty without the opportunity of exercising it is simply oppression, and wherever man is ignorant or without tools he inevitably has to submit to those who are either richer or better taught than him-

[1] "The illusive conception of an abstract right has had a great hold upon the public ever since 1789. But it is nothing better than a metaphysical abstraction, which can afford but little consolation to a people who have been robbed of a definite security that was really theirs. The 'rights of man,' proclaimed with pomp and defined with minuteness in many a charter, has simply served as a cloak to hide the injustice of individualism and the barbarous treatment meted out to the poor under its ægis. Because of this practice of defining liberty as a right, men have got into the habit of calling people free even though they are the slaves of hunger and of ignorance and the sport of every chance. Let us say once for all that liberty consists, not in the abstract right given to a man, but in the power given him to exercise and develop his faculties." (*Organisation du Travail*, p. 19.)

self, and his liberty is gone. In such cases State intervention is really
necessary, just as it is in the case of inferior classes or minors. Lacor-
daire's saying is more pithy still: "As between the weak and the
strong, liberty oppresses and law sets free." Sismondi had already
employed this argument, and much capital has been made of it by
every opponent of *laissez-faire*.[1]

In the writings of Louis Blanc may be found the earliest faint outline of a movement that had assumed considerable proportions before
the end of the century. State socialism, which was as yet a temporary
expedient, by and by becomes an important economic doctrine with
numerous practical applications.

The events of 1848 gave Louis Blanc an opportunity of partly
realizing his ideas. We shall speak of these experiments when we
come to discuss the misdirected efforts of the 1848 socialists. But the
ideas outlined in the *Organisation du Travail* were destined to a more
permanent success in the numerous co-operative productive societies
which were founded as a result of its teaching. They are still quite
popular with a certain class of French working men.

Though inferior to both Fourier and Owen, Blanc gave considerable impetus to the Associative movement, and quite deserves his
place among the Associative socialists.

Beside Louis Blanc it may be convenient to refer to two other
writers, Leroux and Cabet, who took part in the same movement right
up to the Revolution of 1848.

Pierre Leroux exercised considerable influence over his contemporaries. George Sand's works are full of social dissertations, and she
herself declares that most of these she owed to Leroux. However, one
can hardly get anything of the nature of a definite contribution to the
science from his own writings, which are vaguely humanitarian in
character. We must make an exception, perhaps, of his advocacy of
association,[2] and especially of the idea of solidarity, a word that has
been exceedingly fortunate in its career. Indeed, it seems that he was
the first to employ this famous term in the sense in which it is used
to-day—as a substitute for charity.[3]

Apparently, also, he was the first to contrast the word 'socialism'

---

[1] *Cf.* pp. 199 *et seq.*

[2] "Your want of faith in association," he wrote to the National Assembly of 1848,
"will force you to expose civilization to a terribly agonizing death."

[3] *L'Humanité* (1840). It would be wrong to conclude, however, that this desire
for secularizing charity meant that Leroux was anti-religious. On the contrary, he
admits his indebtedness for the conception of solidarity to the dictum of St Paul,
"We are all members of one body."

with its antithesis 'individualism.'[1] The invention of these two terms is enough to save his name from oblivion in the opinion of every true sociologist.

Cabet had one experience which is rare for a socialist: he had filled the office of Attorney-General, though only for a short time, it is true. Far greater celebrity came to him from the publication of his novel, *Le Voyage en Icarie*. There is nothing very original in the system outlined there. He gives the usual easy retort to those who question him concerning the fate of idlers in Icaria: "Of idlers in Icaria there will be none." In his enthusiasm for his ideal he went farther than either Owen or Considérant by personally superintending the founding of a colony in the United States (1848). Despite many a grievous trial the settlement managed to exist for fifty years, finally coming to grief in 1898.[2]

Cabet is frankly communistic, and in that respect resembles Owen rather than Fourier, although he always considered himself a disciple of the latter. But this was perhaps due to his admiration for Fourier, with whom he was personally very well acquainted. Although he was a communist he was no revolutionist. He was a good-natured fellow who believed in making his appeal to the altruistic feelings of men, and was sufficiently optimistic to believe that moral conversion was not a difficult process.[3]

CHAPTER IV: FRIEDRICH LIST AND THE NATIONAL SYSTEM OF POLITICAL ECONOMY

By the middle of the nineteenth century the doctrine of Adam Smith had conquered the whole of Europe. Former theories were forgotten and no rival had appeared to challenge its supremacy. But during the course of its triumphant march it had undergone many changes and

[1] "I was the first to employ the term 'socialism.' It was a neologism then, but a very necessary term. I invented the word as an antithesis to 'individualism.'" (*Grève de Samarez*, p. 288.) As a matter of fact, as far back as 1834 he had contributed an article entitled *De l'Individualisme et du Socialisme* to the *Revue encyclopédique*. The same word occurs in the same review in an article entitled *Discours sur la Situation actuelle de l'Esprit humain*, written two years before. See his complete works, Vol. I, pp. 121, 161, 378. For a further account of Leroux see M. F. Thomas's *Pierre Leroux* (1905), a somewhat dull but highly imaginative production.

[2] For Cabet's life and the story of Icaria see Prudhommeaux's two volumes *Étienne Cabet* and *Histoire de la Communauté icarienne*.

[3] "The communists will never gain much success until they have learned to reform themselves. Let them preach by example and by the exercise of social virtues, and they will soon convert their adversaries."

had been subjected to much criticism. Even disciples like Say and Malthus, and Ricardo especially, had contributed many important additions and effected much improvement. Through the influence of Sismondi and the socialists new points of view had been gained, involving a departure from the narrow outlook of the master in the direction of newer and broader horizons.

Of the principles of the Classical school the Free Trade theory was the only one which still remained intact. This, however, was the most important of all. Here the triumph had been complete. Freedom of international trade was accepted as a sacred doctrine by the economists of every country. In Germany as in England, in France as in Russia, there was complete unanimity among scientific authorities. The socialists at first neglected this topic, and when they did mention it it was to express their complete approval of the orthodox view.[1] A few isolated authors might have hinted at reservations or objections, but they never caught the public ear.[2] It is true that Parliaments and Governments in many countries hesitated to put these new ideas into practice. But even here, despite the strength of the opposing forces, one can see the growing influence of Smith's doctrine. The liberal tariff of Prussia in 1818, the reforms of Huskisson in England (1824–27), were expressly conceived by their authors as partial applications of those principles.

However, there arose in Germany a new doctrine for which the

---

[1] Protection was attacked by Sismondi in *Nouv. Princ.*, Book IV, chapter xi. He considered it a fruitful source of over-production, and uttered his condemnation of the absurd desire of nations for self-sufficiency. Saint-Simon considered Protection to be the outcome of international hatred (*Œuvres*, Vol. III, p. 36), and commended the economists who had shown that "mankind had but one aim and that its interests were common, and consequently that each individual in his social connexion must be viewed as one of a company of workers" (*Lettres à un Américain, Œuvres*, Vol. II, pp. 186–187). The Saint-Simonians never touched upon the question directly, but it is quite clear that Protective rights were to have no place in the universal association of which they dreamt. According to Fourier, there was to be the completest liberty in the circulation of goods among the Phalanstères all the world over. (*Cf.* Bourgin, *Fourier*, pp. 326–329; Paris, 1905.)

[2] We refer to two of them only: Augustin Cournot and Louis Say of Nantes. The former, in his *Recherches sur les Principes mathématiques de la Théorie des Richesses* (1838), a work that is celebrated to-day but which passed unnoticed at the time of its publication, has criticized the theory of Free Trade. But the reputation which he subsequently achieved was not based upon this part of the book. Louis Say (1774–1840) was a brother of J. B. Say. He published a number of works, now quite forgotten, in which he criticized several doctrines upheld by his brother, whose displeasure he thus incurred. We refer to his last work, *Études sur la Richesse des Nations et Réfutation des principales Erreurs en Économie politique* (1836), for this is the work to which List alludes. It is probable that Louis Say's name would have remained in oblivion but for List. Richelot, in his translation of List (second edition, p. 477), quotes some of the more important passages of Say's book.

peculiar economic and political conditions of that country at the beginning of the nineteenth century afforded a favourable environment. Although the development was slow it was none the less startling. Friedrich List, in his work entitled *Das Nationale System der Politischen Oekonomie*, promulgated the theory of the new Protection. "The history of my book," he remarks in his preface, "is the history of half my life." He might have added that it was also the history of Germany from 1800 to 1840. It was no mere coincidence that led to the creation of an economic system based exclusively upon the conception of nationality in that country, where the dominant political note throughout the nineteenth century was the realization of national unity. List's work was a product of circumstances, and these circumstances we must understand if we are to judge of the author and his work.

I: LIST'S IDEAS IN RELATION TO THE ECONOMIC CONDITIONS IN GERMANY

The Germany of the nineteenth century presents a unique spectacle. Her population was at first essentially agricultural, and the various states politically and economically isolated. Her industry was fettered by the corporative regime, and her agriculture was still in feudal thraldom. Freed from these encumbrances, and having established first her economic and then her political unity, she took her place during the last three decades of the century among the foremost of industrial Powers.

The Act of Union of 1800 had ensured the economic unity of the British Isles. The union of England and Scotland was already a century old, and Smith regarded it as "one of the chief causes of the prosperity of Great Britain."[1] France had accomplished the same end by the suppression of domestic tariffs in 1791. But Germany even in 1815 was still a congeries of provinces, varying in importance and separated from one another by tariff walls. List, in the petition which he addressed in 1819 to the Federal Assembly in the name of the General Federation of German Trade and Commerce, could reckon no less than thirty-eight kinds of tariffs within the German Confederacy, without mentioning other barriers to commerce. In Prussia alone there were no fewer than sixty-seven different tariffs.[2] "In short,"

[1] The union of England and Scotland dates from 1707. Compare the passage in Adam Smith, Book V, chapter ii, Part II, art. 4; Cannan's edition, Vol. II, p. 384.
[2] List, *Werke*, ed. Häusser, Vol. II, p. 17. The seventh edition of the *National System*, which was published in 1883 by M. Eheberg, contains an excellent historical and critical introduction. Our quotations are from the English translation by Lloyd, published in 1885, republished, with introduction by Professor Shield Nicholson, in 1909.

says List in another petition, "while other nations cultivate the sciences and the arts whereby commerce and industry are extended, German merchants and manufacturers must devote a great part of their time to the study of domestic tariffs and taxes."[1]

These inconveniences were still further aggravated by the complete absence of import duties. The German states were closed to one another, but, owing to the absence of effective central control, were open to other nations—a peculiarly galling situation on the morrow of the Continental Blockade. The peace treaty was scarcely signed when England—so long cut off from her markets and forced to overstock her warehouses with her manufactured goods—began to flood the Continent with her products. Driven from France by the protective tariff established by the Restoration Government, these goods, offered at ridiculously low prices, found a ready market in Germany.

The German merchants and manufacturers became thoroughly alarmed, and there arose a general demand for economic unity and a uniform tariff. Public opinion urged a reform which appeared to be the first step in the movement towards national unity. In 1818 Prussia secured her own commercial unity by abolishing all internal taxation, retaining only those duties which were levied at the frontier. Her new tariff of 10 per cent. on manufactured goods, with free entrance for raw material, was not regarded as prohibitive, and was actually approved of by Huskisson as a model which the British Parliament might well imitate. But this reform, confined as it was to Prussia alone, did nothing to improve the lot of the German merchants elsewhere, for the Prussian tariff applied just as much to them as to foreigners.

This particular reform, far from staying the movement towards uniform import duties, only accelerated it. A General Association of German Manufacturers and Merchants was founded at Frankfort in 1819 to urge confederation upon the Government. The agitation was inspired by Friedrich List. He had been for a short time professor at Tübingen and was already well known as a journalist. He was nominated general secretary of the association, and became the soul of the movement. He wrote endless petitions and articles, and made personal application to the various Governments at Munich, Stuttgart, Berlin, and Vienna. He was anxious that Austria should take the lead. But all in vain. The Federal Assembly, hostile as it was to every manifestation of public opinion, refused to reply to the petition of the

[1] Petition presented to a meeting of the German princes at Vienna in 1820 (*Werke*, Vol. II, p. 27).

merchants and manufacturers. List himself was soon taken up with other interests. He was named as the deputy for Reutlingen, his native town, in the state of Würtemberg, in 1820, but was banished from the Assembly and condemned to ten months' imprisonment for criticizing the bureaucracy of his own country. After seeking refuge in France he spent a few years travelling in England and Switzerland, and then returned to Würtemberg, where he again suffered imprisonment. Upon his release from prison he resolved to emigrate to America, where Lafayette, whom he had met in Paris, promised him a warm welcome.

Returning to Germany in 1832, after having made numerous friends and accumulated a fortune, he found the tariff movement for which he had struggled thirteen years before just coming to a head. It was to be established, however, in a fashion quite different from what he had expected. It was not to be a general reform, and Austria was not to be leader. Prussia was to be the pivot of the movement, which was to be accomplished by means of a series of general agreements. In 1828 there were formed almost simultaneously two Tariff Unions, the one between Bavaria and Würtemberg, the other between Prussia and Hesse-Darmstadt. Within the areas of both of these unions goods were to circulate freely, and a common rate of duty was to be established at the frontiers. From the very first there was a *rapprochement* between the unions, but a definite fusion in one Zollverein was only decided upon on March 22, 1833. The new regime actually came into being on January 1, 1834. Even before that date Saxony and some of the other states had already joined the new union.

Thus by 1834 the commercial union of modern Germany was virtually accomplished. The Zollverein united the principal German states,[1] Austria excepted, and under this regime industry, assured of a large domestic market, increased by leaps and bounds. But a new problem presented itself, namely, what system of taxation was to be adopted by the union as a whole. In 1834 the liberal Prussian tariff of 1818 was adopted without much opposition, but nothing more was attempted just then. Many of the manufacturers, however, especially the iron-smelters and the cotton and flax spinners, demanded a more substantial means of protection against foreign competition. This clamour became more intense as the need for iron and manufactured goods increased the demand for raw material. Hence from 1841—the date of the completed Zollverein—a new discussion arose between the

[1] Baden, Nassau, and Frankfort joined in 1835 and 1836. But there still remained outside Mecklenburg and the Free Towns of the Hanse, Hanover, Brunswick, and Oldenburg.

partisans of the *status quo*, inclining towards free exchange, and the advocates of a more vigorous protection.

List's *National System*, advocating Protection, appeared at the psychological moment. This delightfully eloquent work is full of examples borrowed from history and experience. The peculiar condition of contemporary Germany was the one source of List's inspiration, and since the work was written for the public at large it is remarkably free from all traces of the 'schools.' Germany's industry, the sole hope of her future greatness, had found scope for development only during the peace which followed 1815. It was still in its infancy, and found itself hard hit by the competition of England, with her long experience, her perfected machinery, and her gigantic output. This was the all-important fact for List. England, whose rivalry appeared so dangerous, had closed her markets to German agriculturists by her Corn Laws, while industrial competition was out of the question. Two other nations, France and the United States, destined, like Germany, to become great industrial Powers, indicated the path of emancipation. France, warned by the results of the Treaty of Eden (1786) as to the evils of English competition, hastened to defend her fortunes by means of prohibitive tariffs. Still more significant was the example of the United States, whose situation was in all respects comparable with that of Germany. In both cases economic independence was hardly yet fully established, the natural resources were abundant, the territory was vast, the population intelligent and industrious, with the hope of a great political future. Though scarcely free as yet, the Americans made the establishment of industry and the shutting out of English goods by means of protective tariffs their first care. Thus there was everywhere the same danger, the tyrannical supremacy of England, and the same method of defence, Protection. Would Germany alone stand aloof from adopting similar measures?

That is the essential point of List's thesis. But these very practical views tended to damage the well-known arguments of those economists whom List refers to collectively as "the school." The 'school' maintained that nations as well as individuals should buy in the cheapest markets and devote all their energies to producing just those commodities which yield them the greatest gain. Industry can only grow in proportion to the amount of capital saved, but a protective regime hinders accumulation and so defeats its own end. To overcome these objections it is not necessary to combat them one by one, for the discussion may be carried to an entirely different field. The 'school' adopts a certain ideal of commercial policy as the basis of its thesis, namely, the increase of consumable wealth, or, as List

puts it, in an awkward enough fashion, "the increase of its exchangeable values."[1] This fundamental point of view must be changed if we
would avoid the consequences which naturally follow from it. List
realized this, and in his attempt to accomplish the task he gave expression to new truths which make his book one of lasting theoretical
value and ensure for it an important place in the history of economic
doctrines.

In fact, he introduces two ideas that were new to current theory,
namely, the idea of nationality as contrasted with that of cosmopolitanism, and the idea of productive power as contrasted with that of
exchange values. List's whole system rests upon these two ideas.

(a) List accuses Adam Smith and his school of cosmopolitanism.
Their hypothesis rested on the belief that men were henceforth to be
united in one great community from which war would be banished.
On such a hypothesis humanity was merely the sum of its individuals.
Individual interests alone counted, and any interference with economic
liberty could never be justified. But between man and humanity must
be interpolated the history of nations, and the 'school' had forgotten
this. Every man forms part of some nation, and his prosperity to a
large extent depends upon the political power of that nation.[2]

Universal *entente* is doubtless a noble end to pursue, and we ought
to hasten its accomplishment. But nations to-day are of unequal
strength and have different interests, so that a definite union could
only benefit them if they met on a footing of equality. The union
might even only benefit one of them while the others became dependent. Viewed in this new light, political economy becomes the science
which, by taking account of the actual interests and of the particular
condition of each nation, shows along what path each may rise to that
degree of economic culture at which union with other civilized nations,
accompanied by free exchange, might be both possible and useful.[3]

---

[1] List's expression "exchangeable value" merely signifies the mass of present advantages—the material profit existing at the moment. It is not a very happy phrase,
and it would be a great mistake to take it literally or to attach great importance to it.
In his *Letters to Ingersoll*, p. 186, he gives expression to the same idea by saying that
Smith's school had in view "the exchange of one material good for another," and
that its concern was chiefly with "such exchanged goods rather than with productive
forces." We note that List never speaks of Ricardo, but only of Smith and Say,
whose works alone he seems to have read.

[2] "In the Italian and the Hanseatic cities, in Holland and England, in France and
America, we find the powers of production and consequently the wealth of individuals
growing in proportion to the liberties enjoyed, to the degree of perfection of political
and social institutions, while these, on the other hand, derive material and stimulus
for their further improvement from the increase of the material wealth and the
productive power of individuals." (*National System*, p. 87.)

[3] He defines "political or national economy" as "that which, emanating from the

List distinguishes several 'degrees of culture,' or what we would
to-day call 'economic stages,' and he even claims actual historical
sequence for his classification into the savage, the pastoral, the agricultural, the agricultural-manufacturing, and the agricultural-manufacturing-commercial stage.[1] A nation becomes 'normal'[2] only when
it has attained the last stage. List understands by this that such is the
ideal that a nation ought to follow. As a matter of fact, he would allow
it to possess a navy and to found colonies only on condition that it
kept up its foreign trade and extended its sphere of influence. It is
only at this stage that a nation can nourish a vast population, ensure
a complete development of the arts and sciences, and retain its independence and power. The last two ideas constitute the *sine qua non*
of nationality.[3] Not all nations, it is true, can pretend to this complete development. It requires a vast territory, with abundant natural
resources, and a temperate climate, which itself aids the development

idea and nature of the nation, teaches how a given *nation*, in the present state of the
world and its own special national relations, can maintain and improve its economical
conditions." (*National System*, p. 99.)

[1] It was the example of England that gave List the idea, but the whole conception
is based upon a historical error. England possessed a navy, had founded colonies, and
developed her international trade long before she became a manufacturing nation.
Since the time of List various categories of national development have been proposed.
Hildebrand speaks of periods of natural economy, of money economy, and of credit
economy (*Jahrbücher für National Oekonomie*, Vol. II, pp. 1–24). Bücher proposed the
periods of domestic economy, of town economy, and of national economy as a substitute (*Die Entstehung der Volkswirtschaft*, 3rd ed., p. 108). Sombart, in his turn, has very
justly criticized this classification in his book *Der moderne Kapitalismus* (Vol. I, p. 51;
Leipzig, 1902). But would that which he proposes himself be much better?
No one, we believe, has as yet remarked that List borrowed this enumeration of
the different economic states, almost word for word, from Adam Smith. In chapter v
of Book II, speaking of the various employments of capital, Smith clearly distinguished
between three stages of evolution—the agricultural state, the agricultural-manufacturing, and the agricultural-manufacturing-commercial. Smith considered that this
last stage was the most desirable, but in his opinion its realization must depend upon
the natural course of things.
[2] The term 'normal' is one of the vaguest and most equivocal we have in political
economy. It would be well if we were rid of it altogether. What controversies have
not raged around the ideas of a normal wage or a normal price! One of the chief
merits of the Mathematical school lies in the success with which it has effected the
substitution of the idea of an equilibrium price. The idea of a normal nation is about
as vague as that of a normal wage, and it is curious that our author describes as
normal a whole collection of characteristics which, according to his own account,
were at the moment when he wrote only realized by one nation, namely, England.
[3] P. 292. The idea of national power is, moreover, not completely lost sight of by
Smith, as is proved by the following passages: "The riches and, so far as power
depends upon riches, the power of every country must always be in proportion to the
value of its annual produce. . . . But the great object of the political economy of every
country is to increase the riches and power of that country." (*Wealth of Nations*,
Book II, chapter v; Cannan's edition, Vol. I, p. 351.)

of manufactures.[1] But where these conditions are given then it becomes a nation's first duty to exert all its forces in order to attain this stage. Germany possessed these desiderata to a remarkable degree. All that was needed was an extension of territory, and List lays claim to Holland and Denmark as a portion of Germany, declaring that their incorporation would be regarded even by themselves as being both desirable and necessary. Accordingly, he wished them to enter the Confederacy of their own free will.[2]

Hence the aim of a commercial policy is no longer what it was for Smith, *viz.*, the enriching of a nation. It is a much more complex ideal that List proposes, both historically and politically, but an ideal which implies as a primary necessity the establishment of manufactures.

(*b*) This necessity becomes apparent from still another point of view. The estimate of a nation's wealth should not be confined to one particular moment. It is not enough that the labour and economy of its citizens should at the present moment assure for it a great mass of exchange values. It is also necessary that these resources of labour and of economy should be safeguarded and that their future development should be assured, for "the power of creating wealth is infinitely more important than the wealth itself." A nation should concern itself with the growth of what List in a vague fashion calls its productive forces even more than with the exchange values which depend upon them.[3] Even a temporary sacrifice of the second may be demanded for the sake of the first. In these expressions List merely wishes to emphasize the distinction between a policy which takes account of a nation's future as compared with one which takes account only of the present. "A nation must sacrifice and give up a measure of material property in order to gain culture, skill, and powers of united

[1] On the question of the industrial vocation of the temperate zone and the agricultural vocation of the torrid compare *National System*, Book II, chapter iv.

[2] "The German nation will at once obtain what it is now in need of, namely, fisheries and naval power, maritime commerce and colonies." (*National System*, p. 143.) List has no difficulty in allying his patriotic idealism with the practical side of his nature.

[3] List deliberately distinguishes between exchange values and productive forces; but the distinction is by no means a happy one. For a policy which aims at encouraging productive forces has no other way of demonstrating its superiority than by showing an increase of exchange value. The two notions are not opposed to one another, and in reckoning a nation's wealth we must take some account of its present state as well as of its future resources. In his *Letters to Ingersoll* (*cf.* Letter IV, referred to above) he distinguishes between "natural and intellectual capital" on the one hand and "material productive capital" on the other (Adam Smith's idea of capital). "The productive powers of the nation depend not only upon the latter, but also and chiefly upon the former."

production; it must sacrifice some present advantages in order to ensure to itself future ones."[1]

But what are these productive forces which constitute the permanent source of a nation's prosperity and the condition of its progress?

With particular insistence List first of all mentions the moral and political institutions, freedom of thought, freedom of conscience, liberty of the Press, trial by jury, publicity of justice, control of administration, and parliamentary government. All these have a stimulating and salutary effect upon labour. He is never weary of recalling to mind the loss of wealth caused by the Revocation of the Edict of Nantes, or by the Spanish Inquisition, which, says he, "had passed sentence of death upon the Spanish navy long ere the English and the Dutch fleets had executed the decree" (p. 88). He unjustly[2] accuses Smith and his school of materialism, and condemns them for neglecting to reckon those infinitely powerful but perhaps less calculable forces.

But of all the productive forces of a nation none, according to List, can equal manufactures, for manufactures develop the moral forces of a nation to a superlative degree.

> The spirit of striving for a steady increase in mental and bodily acquirements, of emulation and of liberty, characterize a State devoted to manufactures and commerce. . . . In a country devoted to mere raw agriculture, dullness of mind, awkwardness of body, obstinate adherence to old notions, customs, methods, and processes, want of culture, of prosperity, and of liberty prevail.[3]

[1] *National System*, p. 117.

[2] Unjustly as we think, for on more than one occasion Smith did take account of moral forces. He dated the prosperity of English agriculture from the time when farmers were freed from their long servitude and became henceforth independent of the proprietors. He remarks that towns attain prosperity quicker than the country, because a regular government is earlier established there. "The best effect which commerce and manufactures have is the gradual introduction and establishment of order and good government, and with them the liberty and security of individuals among the inhabitants of the country. This, though it has been the least observed, is by far the most important of their effects. Mr Hume is the only writer who so far as I know has hitherto taken notice of it." (Book III, chapter iv; Cannan, Vol. I, p. 383.) Speaking of the American colonies, Smith (Cannan, Vol. II, p. 73) makes the remark that although their fertility is inferior to the Spanish, Portuguese, and the French colonies, "the political institutions of the English colonies have been more favourable to the improvement and cultivation of this land than those of any of the other three nations." How could List have forgotten the celebrated passage in which Smith attributes the prosperity of Great Britain largely to its legal system, which guarantees to each individual the fruits of his toil and which must be reckoned among the definitive achievements of the Revolution of 1688? "That security which the laws in Great Britain give to every man that he shall enjoy the fruits of his own labour is alone sufficient to make any country flourish, notwithstanding these and twenty other absurd regulations of commerce; and this security was perfected much about the same time that the bounty was established." (Book IV, chapter v; Cannan, Vol. II, pp. 42–43.)   [3] *National System*, chapter xvii, beginning.

Manufactures permit of a better utilization of a country's products than is the case even with agriculture. Its water-power, its winds, its minerals, and its fuel supplies are better husbanded. The presence of manufactures gives a powerful impetus to agriculture, for the agriculturist profits even more than the manufacturer, owing to the high rent, increased profits, and better wages that follow upon an increased demand for agricultural products. The very proximity of manufactures constitutes a kind of permanent market for those agricultural products, a market which neither war nor hostile tariffs can ever affect. It gives rise to varied demands and allows of a variation of cultivation, which results in a regional division of labour. This enables each district to develop along the most advantageous line, whereas in a purely agricultural country each one has to produce for his personal consumption, which means the absence of division of labour and a consequent limitation of production.[1]

Industry for List is not what it was for Smith. For him it is a social force, the creator of capital and of labour, and not the natural result of labour and saving. It deserves introduction even at the expense of a temporary loss, and its justification is that of all liberal institutions, namely, the impetus given to future production. In a beautiful comparison which would deserve a niche in a book of classical economic quotations he writes as follows:

It is true that experience teaches that the wind bears the seed from one region to another, and that thus waste moorlands have been transformed into dense forests; but would it on that account be wise policy for the forester to wait until the wind in the course of ages effects this transformation?[2]

The tariff, apparently, is the only method of raising the wind.

By placing himself at this point of view List is able to defeat the most powerful arguments used by his opponents. All we can say in reply is that manufactures will not produce these effects if they have not already a *raison d'être* in the natural evolution of a nation—that is, if they do not demand too costly a sacrifice. The land on which the settler sows his corn can scarcely be regarded as ready to receive it if it lacks the power to make it grow.

List's Protectionism, as we may guess from what precedes, possesses original features. It is not a universal remedy which may be indifferently applied to every country at any period or to all its products. It is a particular process which can only be used in certain cases and

[1] Compare chapters vii and xv, where he treats of the manufacturing industry in its relation to each of the great economic forces of the country.

[2] *National System*, p. 87.

under certain conditions. Subjoined are some of the characteristic traits of this Protectionism which List himself has neatly described.

(1) The Protectionist system can only be justified when it aims at the industrial education of a nation.[1] It is thus inapplicable to a nation like the English, whose industrial education is already complete. Nor should it be attempted by countries that have neither the aptitude nor the resources necessary for an industrial career. The nations of the tropical zone seem destined to the pursuit of agriculture, while those of the temperate zone are accustomed to engage in many and varied forms of production.[2]

(2) But a further justification is also necessary. It must be shown that the nation's progress is retarded by the competition of a powerful manufacturing rival which has already advanced farther on the industrial path.[3] "The reason for this is the same as that why a child or a boy in wrestling with a strong man can scarcely be victorious or even offer steady resistance."[4] This was precisely the case with Germany in her struggle with England. (It is interesting to come across a full account of the process of 'dumping' in List's letters to Ingersoll. 'Dumping,' which has received much attention in connection with the trust movement, consists in selling at a low price in foreign markets in order to keep up prices in the home market.[5])

[1] *National System*, p. 150.

[2] "It may in general be assumed that where any technical industry cannot be established by means of an original protection of 40 to 60 per cent., and cannot continue to maintain itself under a continued protection of 20 to 30 per cent., the fundamental conditions of manufacturing power are lacking." (*Ibid.*, p. 251.)

[3] "Solely in nations of the latter kind, namely, those which possess all the necessary mental and material conditions and means for establishing a manufacturing power of their own and of thereby attaining the highest degree of civilization and development of material prosperity and political power, but which are retarded in their progress by the competition of a foreign manufacturing Power which is already farther advanced than their own—only in such nations are commercial restrictions justified for the purpose of establishing and protecting their own manufacturing power." (*Ibid.*, p. 144.)

[4] *Ibid.*, p. 240.

[5] "Everyone knows," says he (quoted by Hirst, pp. 231 *et seq.*), "that the cost of production of a manufactured good depends very largely upon the quantity produced—that is, upon the operation of the law of increasing returns. This law exercises considerable influence upon the rise and fall of manufacturing power. . . . An English manufacturer producing for the home market has a regular sale of 10,000 yards at 6 dollars a yard. . . . His expenses being thus guaranteed by his sales in the home market, the cost of producing a further quantity of 10,000 yards for the foreign market will be considerably reduced and would yield him a profit even were he to sell for 3 or 4 dollars a yard. And even though he should not be making any profit just then, he can feel pretty confident about the future when he has ruined the foreign producer and driven him out of the field altogether." List thinks that this shows how impossible it is for manufacturers in a new country without any measure of protection to compete with other countries whose industry is better established. But this is one

(3) Even in that case Protection can be justified "only until that manufacturing Power is strong enough no longer to have any reason to fear foreign competition, and thenceforth only so far as may be necessary for protecting the inland manufacturing power in its very roots."[1]

(4) Lastly, Protection ought never to be extended to agriculture. The reasons for this exception are that on the one hand agricultural prosperity depends to a great extent upon the progress of manufactures—the protection of the latter indirectly benefits the former—and on the other hand an increase in the price of raw materials or of food would injure industry. Moreover, there exists a natural division which is particularly advantageous to the system of cultivation pursued by each country, a division dependent upon the natural qualities of their soils, which Protection would tend to destroy. This territorial division does not exist for manufactures, "for the pursuit of which every nation in the temperate zone seems to have an equal vocation."[2]

One might experience some difficulty in understanding the sudden *volte-face* of List in favour of free exchange in agriculture did we forget the particular situation in Germany, to which his thoughts always returned. This is equally true of many other points in his system. Germany was an exporter of corn and suffered from the operation of the English Corn Laws. German agriculture needed no protection, but suffered from want of markets, and List would have been very happy to persuade England to abandon her Corn Laws. Agricultural protection was only revived in Germany towards the end of 1879, when the agriculturists thought they were being threatened by foreign competition.

II: SOURCES OF LIST'S INSPIRATION. HIS INFLUENCE UPON SUBSEQUENT PROTECTIONIST DOCTRINES

The question of the origin of List's Protectionist ideas has frequently

---

of the arguments that has been most frequently used by British manufacturers in the past in demanding protection against American competition. We would like to know what List would have thought of this.

[1] *National System*, p. 144, and the whole of chapter xvi of Book II. He considered that "it would be a further error if France, after her manufacturing power has become sufficiently strong and established, were not willing to revert gradually to a more moderate system of Protection and by permitting a limited amount of competition incite her manufacturers to emulation." (*Ibid.*, p. 249.)

[2] *Ibid.*, p. 253, and especially p. 162, etc., where with a sudden change of front he declares himself in favour of Free Trade in agriculture, and employs the arguments which Free Traders had applied to all products. Compare again p. 230, where he declares that agriculture "by the very nature of things is sufficiently well protected against foreign competition."

K

been raised. The works of the Frenchmen Dupin and Chaptal undoubtedly gave him some material for reflection, but he was really
confirmed in his opposition to *laissez-faire* by the men whom he met
in America. While there he came into intimate contact with the
members of a society which had been founded at Philadelphia for the
encouragement of national industry. The founder of this society was
an American statesman named Hamilton, the author of a celebrated
report upon manufactures, who as far back as 1791 had advocated
the establishment of Protection for the encouragement of struggling
American industries.[1] Hamilton's argument, as List fully recognized,
bears a striking similarity to the thesis of the *National System*.[2] The

[1] Hamilton's Report on the Encouragement and Protection of Manufactures, as
well as the very important Report on the creation of a National Bank and the two
on Public Credit, was fortunately republished in 1934 by the Columbia University
Press in an easily accessible volume, through the good offices of Mr Samuel McKee.

[2] It is very probable that List had read the work of another American Protectionist,
Daniel Raymond, whose *Thoughts on Political Economy* appeared in 1820 and ran into
four editions (*cf. Daniel Raymond*, by Charles Patrick Neill, Baltimore, 1897). This
seems to be the opinion of the majority of writers who during the last few years have
especially concerned themselves with the study of List's opinions (Miss Hirst, in her
Life of Friedrich List, and M. Curt Kohler in his book *Problematisches zu Friedrich List*,
Leipzig, 1909). But to regard Raymond as his only inspirer, as is done by Rambaud
in his *Histoire des Doctrines*, seems to us mere exaggeration. Apart from the facts that
Raymond's ideas are not particularly original and that List had lived some years in
America in a Protectionist environment, List never quotes him at all. On the other
hand, he frequently and enthusiastically refers to both Dupin and Chaptal in his
Letters to Ingersoll. The expression 'productive forces' was probably borrowed from
Baron Dupin's *Situation progressive des Forces de la France* (Paris, 1827), which opens
with the following words: "This forms an introduction to a work entitled *The Productive and Commercial Forces of France*. By *productive forces* I mean the combined forces of
men, animals, and nature applied to the work of agriculture, of industry, or of commerce." Again, the idea of protecting infant industries is very neatly put by Chaptal.
On p. xlvi of the introduction to his *De l'Industrie française* (published in 1819) we meet
with the following words: "It does not require much reflection to be convinced of the
fact that something more than mere desire is needed to overcome the natural obstacles
in the way of the development of industry. Everywhere we feel that 'infant industries'
cannot struggle against older establishments cemented by time, supported by much
capital, freed from worry and carried on by a number of trained, skilled workmen,
without having recourse to prohibition in order to overcome the competition of
foreign industries."

It is certain that List, during his first stay in France, had read these two authors,
and had there found a confirmation of his own Protectionist ideas. It is not less
certain, from a letter written by him in April 1825 (quoted by Miss Hirst, p. 33),
that he was converted before going to America, but that he expected to find some new
arguments there which would strengthen him in his opposition to Smith. Marx's
assertion made in his *Theorien über den Mehrwerth*, Vol. I, p. 339 (published by Kautsky,
Stuttgart, 1905), that List's principal source of inspiration was Ferrier (*Du Gouvernement considéré dans ses Rapports avec le Commerce*, Paris, 1805) has not the slightest foundation. Neither has the attempt to credit Adam Müller with being the real author of
the conception of a national system of political economy. List, we know, was
acquainted with Müller, a Catholic writer who wished for the restoration of the feudal
system. But to be a German writer in the Germany of the nineteenth century was

Philadelphian society, which was then presided over by Matthew Carey (the father of the economist of whom we shall have to speak by and by), immediately after List's arrival in America inaugurated an active campaign on behalf of a revision of the tariffs. Ingersoll, the vice-president, persuaded List to join in the campaign, which he did by publishing in 1827 a number of letters which caused quite a sensation.[1] They are really just a résumé of the *National System*. The policy which in the course of a few years he was to advocate in Germany he now recommended to the consideration of the Americans.

But facts were even more eloquent than books, and what chiefly struck the practical mind and the observant eye of List was the material success of American Protection, just as in Germany he had been impressed by the beneficial effects which temporary Protection enforced by the Continental Blockade had produced there.[2]

Far from being injurious to the economic development of the United States, it seemed as if Protection had really helped it. What it actually did was to quicken by the space of a few years an evolution which Nature herself was one day bound to accomplish. So vast was the territory, so abundant the natural resources, and so advantageously were they placed for the application of human energy that no system, however defective, could long have delayed the accumulation of wealth. The similar condition of Germany lent colour to the belief that the same experiment carried on in similar circumstances would also succeed there.

Accordingly, List's work, though not directly connected with any known American system, is the first treatise which gives a clear indication of the influence upon European thought of the economic experiences of the New World.

In a beautiful paragraph in the *National System* List has himself confessed to this.

> When afterwards I visited the United States, I cast all books aside—they would only have tended to mislead me. The best work

---

quite enough to imbue one with the idea of nationality. Moreover, Protectionists' arguments are extremely limited in number, so that they do not differ very much from one epoch to another, and it is a comparatively easy task to find some precursors of Friedrich List.

[1] Published in a volume entitled *Outlines of a New System of Political Economy, in a Series of Letters addressed by F. List to Charles Ingersoll* (Philadelphia, 1827). This publication did not find a place in the collected edition published by Häusser, but the whole of it has been incorporated in the interesting *Life of Friedrich List* by Margaret E. Hirst (London, 1909).

[2] This was the consideration that influenced him in adopting a Protectionist attitude, although hitherto he had regarded himself as a disciple of Smith and Say. (*Letters to Ingersoll*, p. 173.)

on political economy which one can read in that modern land is
actual life.   There one may see wildernesses grow into rich and
mighty states; and progress which requires centuries in Europe goes
on there before one's eyes, *viz.*, that from the condition of the mere
hunter to the rearing of cattle, from that to agriculture, and from
the latter to manufactures and commerce.   There one may see how
rents increase by degrees from nothing to important revenues.
There the simple peasant knows practically far better than the most
acute savants of the Old World how agriculture and rents can be
improved; he endeavours to attract manufacturers and artificers to
his vicinity.   Nowhere so well as there can one learn the importance
of means of transport, and their effect on the mental and material
life of the people.   That book of actual life I have earnestly and
diligently studied, and compared with the results of my previous
studies, experience, and reflections.[1]

Though from this point of view List's Protectionism seems closely
connected with the most modern of economic units, a still closer tie
links him to the Mercantilism of old.   Nor did he ever dissemble his
love for the Mercantilists, especially for Colbert.   He accused Smith
and Say of having misunderstood them, and he declared that they
themselves more justly deserved the title of Mercantilists because of
their attempt to apply to whole nations a very simple conception
which they had merely copied from a merchant's note-book, namely,
the advice to buy in the cheapest and sell in the dearest market.   He
distinguishes between two classes of Mercantilists according as they
are influenced by one or other of two dominating ideas.   On the one
hand we have those who emphasize the importance of industrial
education, which is the dominant note in List's philosophy.   This idea
has quite taken the place of the older idea of a favourable balance of
trade, and has been adopted by such a Liberal thinker as John Stuart
Mill, whereas the other has been definitely rejected by the science.
Furthermore, the Mercantilism of the seventeenth century was a special
instrument employed in the interests of a permanent policy, which
was exclusively national; while List's Protection, according to his own
opinion, was merely a means of leading nations towards the possibility
of union on a footing of equality.   It was a mere transitory system, a
policy dictated by circumstances.

List's system cannot be regarded as the inspirer of modern Protection, any more than he himself can be regarded as a direct descendant
of the old Mercantilists.   Even in Germany, despite the great literary
success of his work, its influence was practically nil, unless we credit it
with the slight increase of taxation upon which the Zollverein decided
in 1844, and couple with it the Protectionist campaign afterwards

---

[1] *National System*, preface, p. 54.

carried on by List in the columns of his newspaper.[1] But the Liberal reforms carried out by the English Parliament under the Premiership of Peel were during that very same year crowned by the abolition of the Corn Laws. This measure caused much consternation throughout Europe, and the confirmation which Cobden's ideas thus received influenced public opinion a good deal and gave a Liberal trend to the commercial policy of Europe during the next few years. The regime of commercial treaties inaugurated by Napoleon III was an outcome of this change of feeling.

Towards the end of 1879 a vague kind of Protectionism made its appearance in Europe. Tariff walls were raised, but they never seemed to be high enough. One would like to know whether these new tariffs, established successfully by Germany and France, were in any way inspired by List's ideas.

It does not seem that they were. Neither of the two countries which have remained faithful to a thoroughgoing Protection any longer needs industrial education. Both of them have long since arrived at that complex state which, according to List, is necessary for the full development of their civilization and the expansion of their power. Were he to return to this world to-day, List, who so energetically emphasized the relative value of the various commercial systems, and the necessity of adapting one's method to the changing conditions of the times and the character of the nation, but always laid such stress upon the essentially temporary character of the tariffs raised, would perhaps find himself ranged on the side of those who demand a lowering of those barriers in the interest of a more liberal expansion of productive forces. Has he himself not declared that "in a few years the civilized nations of the world, through the perfection of the means of transport, through the influence of material and intellectual ties, will be as united, nay, even more closely knit together, than were the counties of England, a hundred years ago"?[2]

Even the profound changes in the international economic situation during the nineteenth and twentieth centuries fail to supply a serious justification for the Protectionist policy of the great commercial nations, and the essential traits of this new regime differ *toto cælo* from the out-

---

[1] The *Zollvereinsblatt*, which was published by him towards the end of 1843.

[2] *National System*, p. 230. We do not by any means imply that the Germany of List's day was in greater need of Protection than the Germany of to-day. Indeed, if we accept Chaptal's view, we may well deny this, for, writing in 1819, he said that Saxony occupied a place in the front rank of European nations in the matter of industry. Speaking of Prussia, he declared that the industry of Aix-la-Chapelle alone was enough to establish the fame of any nation (*De l'Industrie française*, Vol. I, p. 75). It is to be remembered that the great industrial prosperity enjoyed by Germany between 1871 and 1914 was based on a very liberal economic system.

lines supplied by List. Far from allowing agriculture to develop naturally, there has arisen the cry for some protection for the farmer, which has served as a pretext for a general reinforcement of tariffs in many cases, notably in France and Germany. The competition of American corn has hindered European agriculture from benefiting by the advancement of industry as List had predicted. Modern tariffs, involving as they do the taxation of both agricultural and industrial products, imply a conception of Protection entirely different from List's. He would have confined Protection to the most important branches of national production—to those industries from which the other and secondary branches receive their supplies. Only on this ground would he have justified exceptional treatment.[1] It is an essentially vigorous conception, and what he sought of Protection was an energetic stimulant and an agent of progress. But a tariff which indifferently protects every enterprise, which no longer distinguishes between the fertilizing and the fertilized industries, and increases all prices at the same time, can have only one effect—a loss for one producer and a gain for another. Their relative positions remain intact. It is no longer a means of stimulating productive energy; it is merely a general instrument of defence against foreign competition, and is essentially conservative and timorous.

To speak the truth, tariff duties are never of the nature of an application of economic doctrines. They are the results of a compromise between powerful interests which often enough have nothing in common with the general interest, but are determined by purely political, financial, or electoral considerations. Hence it is futile to hope for a trace of List's doctrines in the Protective tariffs actually in operation. His influence, if indeed it is perceptible anywhere, must be sought amid the subsidiary doctrines which uphold them.

The only complete exposition of Protectionism that has been given us since List's is that of Carey,[2] the American economist. Carey was at first a Free Trader, but in 1858 became a Protectionist, and his ideas, which were expounded in his great work *The Principles of Social Science*,

---

[1] "Neither is it at all necessary that all branches of industry should be protected in the same degree. Only the most important branches require special protection, for the working of which much outlay of capital in building and management, much machinery and therefore much technical knowledge, skill, and experience, and many workmen are required, and whose products belong to the category of the first necessaries of life and consequently are of the greatest importance as regards their total value as well as regards national independence (as, for example, cotton, woollen, and linen manufactures, etc.). If these main branches are suitably protected and developed, all other less important branches of manufacture will rise up around them under a less degree of protection." (*National System*, p. 145.)

[2] On Carey, see *infra*, Book III.

published in 1858–59, bear a striking resemblance to those of his German predecessor.

Carey, like List, directs his attack against the industrial pre-eminence of England, and substitutes for the ideal of international division of labour the ideal of independent nationality, each nation devoting itself to all branches of economic activity, and thus evolving its own individuality. According to him, Free Trade tends to "estab-lish one single factory for the whole world, whither all the raw produce has to be sent whatever be the cost of transport."[1] The effect of this system is to hinder or retard the progress of all nations for the sake of this one. But a society waxes wealthy and strong only in proportion as it helps in the development of a number of productive associations wherein various kinds of employments are being pursued, which in-crease the demand for mutual services and aid one another by their very proximity. Such associations alone are capable of developing the latent faculties of man[2] and of increasing his hold upon nature. These two traits help to define economic progress. Under a slightly different form we have a picture of the normal nation or the complex State so dear to the heart of Friedrich List—an ideal of continuous progress as the object of commercial policy being substituted for one of immediate enrichment.

Following List, but in a still more detailed fashion, Carey sought to show the beneficial effects that the proximity of protected industry would have upon agriculture. But unfortunately there are other arguments upon which Carey lays equal stress that are really of a much more debatable character.

Protection, according to Carey, by furnishing a ready market for agricultural products, would free agriculture from the burden of an exorbitant cost of carriage to a distant place. This argument, which List[3] merely threw out as a passing suggestion, continually recurs with the American author. But, as Stuart Mill justly remarked,[4] if America consents to such expenditure it affords a proof that she procures by means of international exchange more manufactured goods than if she manufactured them herself.

Another no less debatable point: The exportation of agricultural products, says Carey, exhausts the soil, for the products being con-sumed away from the spot where they are grown, the fertilizing agents which they contain are not restored to the earth; a manufacturing population in the immediate neighbourhood[1] would remedy this. But,

---

[1] Carey, *Principles of Social Science.*   [2] *Ibid.*
[3] *National System*, Book II, chapter iii.
[4] *Principles of Political Economy*, Book V, chapter x, para. 1.

as John Stuart Mill again remarks,[2] and justly enough, it is not Free
Trade that forces America to export cereals. If she does so, it is
because exhaustion of soil appears to her an insignificant inconvenience
compared with the advantage gained by exportation.

Carey, finally, was one of the first to discover in Protection a means
of increasing wages. Once the complex economic State is established
there arises a keen competition between the *entrepreneurs* who require
the service of labour—a competition which naturally benefits the workman. But this advantage, granting that it does exist, is more than
counterbalanced by the increased price of goods.

We see that Carey, although sharing the fundamental conceptions
of List, employs arguments that are much less valid. Both in power
of exposition and in the scientific value of his work, the German author
shows himself vastly superior to his American successor. He is also
much more moderate. Carey is not content with industrial Protection;
he demands agricultural Protection as well, and the duties, though they
are a little higher than those proposed by List, seem hardly sufficient
for him.

Despite all this similarity of views, Carey does not owe his inspiration to List. He was acquainted with the *National System* and he quoted
it. But American economic literature had already supplied him with
analogous suggestions. Even more than books, the economic life of
America itself as it evolved before his very eyes had contributed to the
formation of his ideas. It was the progress of America under a Protective regime, it was the spectacle of a country as yet entirely new and
sparsely populated, increasing the produce of her soil as colonization
extended, and multiplying her wealth as population became more
dense, that inspired him with the idea of a policy of isolation with a
view to hastening the utilization of those enormous resources. More
fortunate than List, Carey lived to see his ideas accepted, if not by
the scientific experts of his country (who on the whole remained aloof),
at least by the American politician, who has applied his principles
rather freely.[3]

Carey's doctrine, accordingly, cannot be attributed directly to the

[1] "Of all the things required for the purposes of man, the one that least bears transportation, and is, yet, of all the most important, is manure. The soil can continue
to produce on the condition, only, of restoring to it the elements of which its crop
had been composed. That being complied with, the supply of food increases, and
men are enabled to come nearer together and combine their efforts—developing
their individual faculties, and thus increasing their wealth; and yet this condition
of improvement, essential as it is, has been overlooked by all economists." (*Principles
of Social Science*, Vol. I, pp. 273–274.)
[2] *Principles of Political Economy*, Book V, chapter x, para. 1.
[3] On this point see Jenks, *Henry C. Carey als Nationalökonom*, chapter i (Jena, 1885).

influence of List. It remains to be seen whether List had any influence upon European doctrines.

He undoubtedly succeeded in forcing the acceptance of the idea of a temporary Protection for infant industries even upon Free Traders. The most notable convert to this view was John Stuart Mill.[1] But it was a somewhat Platonic concession that he made. He thought it inapplicable to old countries, for their education was no longer incomplete, and at best useful only for new countries.

Can modern Protectionists claim descent from List? In the absence of any systematic treatise dealing with their ideas, it is not always easy to glean the significance of their doctrines from the various articles, discourses, and brochures amid which they are scattered.[2] Neglecting those writers who are merely content to reproduce the old fallacies of the Mercantile arguments concerning the balance of trade,[3] the majority of them appear to base their case more or less explicitly upon two principal arguments: (1) the necessity for economic autonomy; (2) the patriotic necessity of securing a national market for national products.[4] These two points of view, which are more or less clearly

---

[1] Compare the long passage in the *Principles*, Book V, chapter x, para. 1, which begins: "The only case in which on mere principles of political economy protecting duties can be defensible is when they are imposed temporarily (especially in a young and rising nation) in hopes of naturalizing a foreign industry, in itself perfectly suitable to the circumstances of the country. The superiority of one country over another in a branch of production often varies only from having begun it sooner." Stuart Mill, however, does not refer to List, and one wonders whether the paragraph owes anything to his influence.

[2] We must make an exception of M. Cauwès, whose Protectionism, on the contrary, is a quite logical adaptation of List's idea, *viz.*, the superiority of nations possessing a complex economy. This is the only scientific system of Protection that we are to-day acquainted with. But it must be confessed that the majority of writers are very far removed from Cauwès's point of view. Compare his *Cours d'Économie politique*, 3rd ed., Vol. III.

[3] Such, *e.g.*, are the economists who are always speaking of a "commercial deficit," *i.e.*, of an unfavourable balance of commerce. Despite the frequent refutations which have been given of it, it is still frequently quoted as an axiomatic truth. List criticized the school for its complete indifference to the balance of imports and exports. But he did not favour the Mercantilist theory of the balance of trade; on the contrary, he regarded that as definitely condemned (p. 218). He regarded the question from a special point of view, that of monetary equilibrium. When a nation, says he, imports much, but does not export a corresponding amount of goods, it may be forced to furnish payment in gold, and a drainage of gold might give rise to a financial crisis. The indifference of the school with regard to this question of the quantity of money is very much exaggerated (Book II, chapter xiii). The policy of the great central banks of to-day aims at easing those tensions in the money market which appear as the result of over-importation, and in this matter they have proved themselves much superior to any system of Protection.

[4] Some writers go even farther. Patten (*Economic Foundations of Protection*) longs to see a national type established peculiar to each country, as the result of forcing the inhabitants to be nourished and clothed according to the natural resources of the

avowed and accepted as political maxims, would, if applied with logical strictness, result in making all external commerce useless. Each nation would thus be reduced to using just those resources with which Nature had happened to endow it, but it could get little if any of the goods produced by the rest of mankind. These two ideas were not absolutely foreign to List's thought, although they never assumed anything more than a secondary or subordinate character. He never considered them as the permanent supports of a commercial policy.

List frequently spoke of making a nation independent of foreign markets by means of industry. He considered that nation highest which "has cultivated manufacturing industry in all its branches within its territory to the highest perfection, and whose territory and agricultural production is large enough to supply its manufacturing population with the largest part of the necessaries of life and raw materials which they require." But he also recognized that such advantages were exceptional, and that it would be folly for a nation to attempt to supply itself by means of national division of labour— that is, by home production—with articles for the production of which it is not favoured by nature, and which it can procure better and cheaper by means of international division of labour, or, in other words, through foreign commerce. Complete autonomy is accordingly an illusion. But we cannot deny that some of his expressions seem to give credit to the false idea that a country which obtains a considerable portion of its consumption goods from foreigners must be dependent upon those foreigners.[1] In fact, it is no more dependent upon the foreigner than the foreigner is upon it. In the case of a buyer and seller who is the dependent person? There is but one instance in which the expression is justified, and that is when a foreign country has become the only source of supply for certain commodities. Then the buyer does become dependent, and List rightly enough had in view the manufacturing monopoly enjoyed by England—a monopoly that no longer exists.

He also spoke of retaining the home market for home-made goods;

---

country in which they live. We should, as a consequence of this, have an American type quite superior to any European type. "Then," says he, "we should be able to exercise a preponderant influence upon the fate of other nations and could force them to renounce their present economic methods and adopt a more highly developed social State." Until then no foreign goods are to enter the country. Here, as is very frequently the case, Protectionism is confounded with nationalism or imperialism.

[1] "A merely agricultural State is an infinitely less perfect institution than an agricultural-manufacturing State. The former is always more or less economically and politically dependent on those foreign nations which take from it agricultural products in exchange for manufactured goods. It cannot determine for itself how much it will produce: it must wait and see how much others will buy from it." (*National System*, p. 145.)

but he thought that this guarantee would of necessity have to be limited to the period when a nation is seeking to create an industry for itself: at a later period foreign competition becomes desirable in order to keep manufacturers and workmen from indolence and indifference.[1]

At no period was List anxious to make economic autonomy or the preservation of the home market the pivot of his commercial policy. The creation of native industry is the only justification of protective rights, but this is the one point which modern Protectionists cannot insist upon without anachronism.

List left no marked traces of his influence either upon practical politics or upon Protectionist doctrines. It is in his general views that we must seek the source of his influence and the reason for the position which he holds in the history of economic doctrines.

III: LIST'S REAL ORIGINALITY

List's method is essentially that of the pioneer. He was the first to make systematic use of historical comparison as a means of demonstration in political economy. Although he can lay no claim to be the founder of the method, still the brilliant use which he made of it justifies us in classifying him as the equal, if not the superior, of those who at the same moment were attempting the creation of the Historical school and the transformation of history into the essential organon of economic research.

List also introduced new and useful points of view into economics. The principle of free exchange as formulated by Smith, and especially by Ricardo and Say, was evidently too absolute and rested upon a demonstration that was too abstract for the ordinary politician. If, as List justly remarks, the practice of commercial nations has so long remained contrary to a doctrine that all economists regard as admirable, it is not without some just cause. As a matter of fact, can the statesman ever place himself outside of the point of view of national interest of which he is the custodian? It is not enough for him to know that the interchange of products will in some degree increase wealth.[2] He must be certain that this increased wealth will benefit his

---

[1] "A nation which has already attained manufacturing supremacy can only protect its own manufactures and merchants against retrogression and indolence by the free importation of means of subsistence and raw materials, and by the competition of foreign manufactured goods." (*National System*, p. 153.) Hence the appeal to England in the name of this theory to abolish her tariffs, but gracefully to allow France, Germany, and the United States to continue theirs.

[2] See M. Pareto's *Economia Politica* (Milan, 1906) for a demonstration that international exchange is not necessarily advantageous for both parties (chapter ix, para. 45).

own nation. He must be equally well assured that Free Trade will not result in too sudden a displacement of population or industry, the social and political results of which might be very harmful. In other words, political economy must be subordinated to politics in general, and to-day there is no single economist who does not recognize the impossibility of separating them in practice.[1] There is none that does not perceive the influence of political power on economic prosperity, and that consequently does not recognize the necessity for the different complexion which the peculiar circumstances of each country imposes upon the practical application of the principle of commercial liberty.

This is not all. List, by abandoning the favourite habit of eighteenth-century writers who contrasted man and society, and by giving us a picture of man as he really is, as a member of a nation, has introduced a fruitful conception into economics of which we have not yet seen the full results. He rightly treats of nations not merely as moral and political associations created by history, but also as economic associations. Just as a nation is politically strengthened by the moral cohesion of its citizens, so its economic cohesion increases the productive energy of each individual and enhances the prosperity of the whole nation.

And Governments, while charged with maintaining the political unity of a country, ought also to retain its economic unity by subordinating all local interests to the general interest, by preserving intact the liberty of internal trade, by organizing railways and canals on a national basis, by keeping watch over the central bank, and by aiming at a uniform code of commercial legislation. This was the programme outlined by List in his paper the *Zollvereinsblatt*.

This belief in the power which a unified economic organization can bring to a nation is by no means too common among individualists, who at bottom are often particularists. But List possessed it in the highest degree. He devoted many years of his life to advocating the establishment of a German railway system, and it was he who traced the principal highways which have since been established in Germany. Protection, in his opinion, was one means of increasing the economic cohesion of Germany, because of the solidarity of interests which would result from the presence of a powerful industry.

---

[1] But the line is sometimes difficult to follow. In our days statesmen are concerned not only with the exportation of goods but also with the migration of capital. Ought the Minister for Foreign Affairs to veto the raising of a loan in the home market on behalf of a foreign Power or an alien company? To what extent ought bankers and capitalists to accept his advice? Such are some of the questions that for some years past have been repeatedly asked in France, England, and Germany. And it seems in almost every case that political economy has had to bow before political necessity, and not *vice versa*.

With similar enthusiasm he devoted himself to two apparently contradictory tasks—the suppression of inter-State duties and the establishment of protective rights. To him there was no element of contradiction in this, any more than there would be for us in a national system of political economy with no protective rights.[1]

He also extended the political horizon of the Classical school and substituted a dynamic for their purely static conception of national development. His thorough examination of the conditions of economic progress is a contribution to the study of international trade exactly analogous to the contribution made by Sismondi to the study of national welfare. But, unlike Sismondi, who wished to retard this progress, he is anxious to stimulate it, and so he charges the State with the duty of safeguarding the future prosperity of the country and with furthering its production. The actual procedure, involving as it did the establishment of protective rights, may appear to us to be unfortunate.[2] But the idea which inspires it—the recognition that in the interests of the future national power has a definitely economic role— is essentially sound. To-day it is a mere commonplace. But when List enunciated it it was quite a novel idea.

In attempting to define List's real significance one feels that he failed in the achievement of his chief aim. He has not succeeded in breaking down the abstract theory of international trade. But if his work has retained any lasting value—apart from the literary talent that characterizes it—it is because he tries, by adopting for the first time since the great eighteenth-century economists a purely national standpoint, to define, for a given country at a given moment, a positive objective for its economic policy. It is not a general theory of foreign trade that List endeavours to formulate, but a precise view, after the

[1] It is very remarkable that List's greatest admirer, Dühring, in his *Kritische Geschichte der Nationalökonomie und des Sozialismus* (2nd ed., p. 362), insists on the fact that Protection is not an essential element, but a mere temporary form of the principle of national economic solidarity, which is List's fundamental conception, and which must survive all forms of Protection. Dühring is the only real successor of List and Carey. He has developed their ideas with a great deal of ability and has shown himself a really scientific thinker. But what he chiefly admires in both writers is not their Protection, but their effort to lay hold of the material and moral forces which lie below the mere fact of exchange, and upon which a nation's prosperity really depends. His *Kursus der National- und Social-oekonomie* (Berlin, 1873) is very interesting reading.

[2] Except the Saint-Simonians nobody seems to have conceived of the State's responsibility for a nation's productive forces. List refers to them sympathetically, especially to those who, like Michel Chevalier, "sought to discover the connexion of these doctrines with those of the premier schools, and to make their ideas compatible with existing circumstances" (*National System*, p. 287). But List differs from them in his love of individual liberty and in the importance which he attaches to moral, political, and intellectual liberty as elements of productive efficiency.

manner of a statesman, of what is practically desirable for his country at a definite period. Thereby he also sets the limits within which his ideas can be applied, since the end to be sought will naturally vary from State to State and from period to period. None the less he is the forerunner of all who in other times and in other lands seek to determine and improve the future—a task that science alone cannot accomplish but which politics cannot neglect. Nor must it be forgotten that by drawing up for Germany a programme of economic development that was to make her a great manufacturing and maritime State and that needed for its full development the adhesion of neighbouring countries like Holland and Denmark, List may be considered one of the precursors of that economic imperialism which led William II's Empire into the First World War and, later, transformed into the doctrine of 'living space,' inspired National Socialism. The part played by List in this respect has been noted in an interesting book by F. A. Hayek.[1]

CHAPTER V: PROUDHON AND THE SOCIALISM OF 1848

PROUDHON comes next, though his place in the history of economic doctrines is not easily defined. Like all socialists, he begins with a criticism of the rights of property. The economists had carefully avoided discussing them, and political economy had become a mere résumé of the results of private property. Proudhon regarded these rights as the very basis of the present social system and the real cause of every injustice. Accordingly he starts with a criticism of property in opposition to the economists who defended it.

But how can we reform the present system or replace it by a better? Herein lies the difficulty. Born twenty years earlier, Proudhon, like many others, would perhaps have invented a Utopia. But what was possible in 1820 was no longer so twenty years later. Public opinion was already satiated with schemes of reform. Owen, Saint-Simon, Fourier, Cabet, and Louis Blanc had each in his turn proposed a remedy. The fancy of reformers had roamed at will over the whole wide expanse of possible reforms. Proudhon was well acquainted with all these efforts, and had come to the conclusion that they were all

---

[1] *The Road to Serfdom* (Routledge, London, 1944), p. 23. Mr Hayek, an Austrian economist, is now a professor in London.

equally useless. Hence he turns out to be a critic of the socialists as well as of the economists.

Proudhon attempts the correction of the vices of private property without becoming a party to what he calls the "crass stupidity of socialism." Every Utopian scheme is instinctively rejected. He cares nothing for those who view society as they do machinery and think that an ingenious trick is all that is needed to correct all anomalies and to reset the machine in motion. To him social life means perpetual progress.[1] He knows that time is required for the conciliation of those social forces that are warring against one another. He was engrossed with his attempt to find a solution for this difficult problem when the Revolution of 1848 broke out, and Proudhon, suddenly thrown into action, finds himself forced to express his ideas in a concrete form, such that all could understand. The critic has to try his hand at construction, and almost despite himself he outlines another Utopia in his Exchange Bank.

Other writers had sought a solution in the complete overthrow of the present methods of production and distribution. But Proudhon thought it lay in improved circulation. It was an ingenious idea, and it deserves mention in a history of economic doctrines because of the truth, mingled with error, which it contains, and because it has become the type of a series of similar projects. It is upon this conception that we wish to dilate here. Leaving aside his other ideas, which are no whit less interesting, we shall treat of Proudhon the philosopher, moralist, and political theorist only in so far as these have influenced Proudhon the economist.[2]

I: CRITICISM OF PRIVATE PROPERTY AND SOCIALISM

The work that first brought Proudhon to the notice of the public was a book published in 1840 entitled *Qu'est-ce que la Propriété?* Proudhon

[1] *Philosophie du Progrès, Œuvres*, Vol. XX, p. 19: "Growth is essential to thought, and truth or reality whether in nature or in human affairs is essentially historical, at one time advancing, at another receding, evolving slowly, but always undergoing some change." In his *Contradictions économiques* he defines social science as "the systematized study of society, not merely as it was in the past or will be in the future, but as it is in the present in all its manifold appearances, for only by looking at the whole of its activities can we hope to discover intelligence and order." (Vol. I, p. 43.) "If we apply this conception to the organization of labour we cannot agree with the economists when they say that it is already completely organized, or with the socialists when they declare that it must be organized, but simply that it is gradually organizing itself; that is, that the process of organization has gone on since time immemorial and is still going on, and that it will continue to go on. Science should always be on the look-out for the results that have already been achieved or are on the point of realization." (Vol. I, p. 45.)

[2] A vigorous exposition of his other ideas is given in Bouglé's *La Sociologie de Proudhon* (Paris, 1911).

was then thirty-one years of age.[1] Born at Besançon, he was the son of a brewer,[2] and was forced to earn his living at an early age. He first became a proof-corrector, and then set up as a printer on his own account. Despite hard work he became a diligent reader, his only guide being his insatiable thirst for knowledge. The sight of social injustice had sent the iron into his soul. Economic questions were faced with all the ardour of youth, with all the enthusiasm of a man of the people speaking on behalf of his brothers, and with all the confidence of one who believes in the convincing force of logic and common sense. All this is very evident in his brilliantly imaginative work. Mingled with it is a good deal of that provoking swagger which was noted by Sainte-Beuve as one of his characteristics, and which appears in all his writings.

Throughout this treatise from first page to last there periodically flashes one telling phrase which sums up his whole argument, " Property is theft."[3]

[1] The following are Proudhon's principal works: 1840, *Qu'est-ce que la Propriété?* (studies in ethics and politics); 1846, *Système des Contradictions économiques* (the "philosophy of destitution"); 1848, *Organisation du Crédit et de la circulation et solution du problème social*; 1848, *Résumé de la Question sociale, Banque d'Échange*; 1849, *Les Confessions d'un Révolutionnaire*; 1850, *Intérêt et Principal* (a discussion between M. Bastiat and M. Proudhon); 1858, *De la Justice dans la Révolution et dans l'Église* (three volumes); 1861, *La Guerre et la Paix*; 1865, *De la Capacité politique des Classes ouvrières*. Our quotations are taken from the *Œuvres complètes*, published in twenty-six volumes by Lacroix (1867-70).

[2] " Do you happen to know, madam, what my father was? Well, he was just an honest brewer whom you could never persuade to make money by selling above cost price. Such gains, he thought were immoral. 'My beer,' he would always remark, 'costs me so much, including my salary. I cannot sell it for more.' What was the result? My dear father always lived in poverty and died a poor man, leaving poor children behind him." (Letter to Madame d'Agoult, *Correspondance*, Vol. II, p. 239.)

[3] It has been said that Proudhon borrowed this formula from Brissot de Warville, the author of a work entitled *Recherches philosophiques sur le Droit de Propriété et sur le Vol, considérés dans la Nature et dans la Société*. It was first published in 1780, and reappeared with some modifications in Vol. VI, pp. 261 *et seq.*, of his *Bibliothèque philosophique du Législateur* (1782). But this is a mistake. Proudhon declares that the work was unknown to him (*Justice*, Vol. I, p. 301); and, moreover, the formula is not there at all. Brissot's point of view is entirely different from Proudhon's. The former believes that in a state of nature the right of property is simply the outcome of want, and disappears when that want is satisfied; that man, and even animals and plants, has a right to everything that can satisfy his wants, but that the right disappears with the satisfaction of the want. Consequently theft perpetrated under the pressure of want simply means a return to nature. The rich are really the thieves, because they refuse to the culprit the lawful satisfaction of his needs. The result is a plea for a more lenient treatment of thieves. But Brissot is very careful not to attack civil property, which is indispensable for the growth of wealth and the expansion of commerce, although it has no foundation in a natural right (p. 333). There is no mention of unearned income. Proudhon, on the other hand, never even discusses the question as to whether property is based upon want or not. He would certainly have referred to this if he had read Brissot.

The question then arises as to whether Proudhon regards all property as theft. Does he condemn appropriation, or is it the mere fact of possession that he is inveighing against? This is how the public at large have viewed it, and it would be useless to deny that Proudhon owes a great deal to this interpretation, and the consequent consternation of the bourgeoisie. But his meaning is quite different. Private property in the sense of the free disposal of the fruits of labour and saving is in his opinion of the very essence of liberty. At bottom this is nothing more than man's control over himself.[1] But why attack property, then? Property is attacked because it gives to the proprietor a right to an income for which he has not worked. It is not property as such, but the right of escheat, that forms the butt of Proudhon's attack; and following the lead of Owen and other English socialists, as well as the Saint-Simonians, he directs his charges against that right of escheat which, according to circumstances and the character of the revenue, is variously known as rent, discount, money interest, agricultural privilege, sinecure, etc.[2]

Like every socialist, Proudhon considered that labour alone was productive.[3] Land and capital without labour were useless. Hence the demand of the proprietor for a share of the produce as a return for the service which his capital has yielded is radically false. It is based upon the supposition that capital by itself is productive, whereas the capitalist in taking payment for it literally receives something for nothing.[4]

[1] *Contradictions*, Vol. I, pp. 219, 221.

[2] *Résumé de la Question sociale*, p. 29. We meet with the same idea in other passages. "Property under the influence of division of labour has become a mere link in the chain of circulation, and the proprietor himself a kind of toll-gatherer who demands a toll from every commodity that passes his way. Property is the real thief." (*Banque d'Échange*, p. 166.) We must also remember that Proudhon did not consider that taking interest was always illegal. In the controversy with Bastiat he admits that it was necessary in the past, but that he has found a way of getting rid of it altogether.

[3] We must distinguish between this and Marx's doctrine. Marx believed that all value is the product of labour. Proudhon refuses to admit this. He thinks that value should in some way correspond to the quantity of labour, but that this is not the case in present-day society. Marx was quite aware of the fact that Proudhon did not share his views (see *Misère de la Philosophie*). Proudhon follows Rodbertus, who taught that the products only and not their values are provided by labour.

[4] *Propriété*, 1er *Mémoire*, pp. 131–132. It is true that Proudhon adds that without land and capital labour would be unproductive. But he soon forgets his qualifications when he proceeds to draw conclusions, especially when he comes to give an exposition of the Exchange Bank, where we meet with the following sentence: "Society is built up as follows: All the raw material required is gratuitously supplied by nature, so that in the economic world every product is really begot of labour, and capital must be considered unproductive." Elsewhere he writes: "To work is not necessarily to produce anything." (*Solution du Problème social, Œuvres*, Vol. VI, pp. 261 *et seq.*, and p. 187.)

All this is simply theft. His own definition of property is, "The right to enjoy the fruits of industry, or of the labour of others, or to dispose of those fruits to others by will."[1]

The theme is not new, and the line of thought will be resumed—by Rodbertus among others. The originality of the work consists not so much in the idea as in the brilliance of the exposition, the vehemence of the style, and the verve of the polemics hurled against the old arguments which based property only upon labour, upon natural right, or upon occupation. A German writer[2] has said that, published in Germany or in England, the book would have passed unnoticed, because in both those countries the defence of property had been much more 'scientific' than in France.

The whole force of the work lies, not in itself, but in the weakness of the opposing arguments, and this fact is quite sufficient to give it a certain permanent value. Moreover, Proudhon has himself shown in a later work, *Théorie de la propriété*, that property does in fact perform a 'social function' which nothing could replace, and which is the "spontaneous product of the collective being."[3] The first treatise sent an echo through the whole world, and its author may be said to have done for French socialism what Lassalle did for German. The ideas set forth are not new, but they are expressed in phrases of wonderful penetration.

There is also a wealth of ingenious remarks which, if not, perhaps, true, deserve retention because of their originality. How such spoliation on the part of capitalists and proprietors can continue without a revolt of the working men is a question which has been asked by every writer on theoretical socialism, without its full import ever being realized. Is there not something very improbable in this? The problem is a curious one, indeed, and requires much ingenuity for its solution. Marx disposed of it by his theory of surplus value. Rodbertus in a simpler fashion showed the opposition between economic distribution as realized in exchange and the social distribution which lurks

---

[1] *Propriété*, 1er *Mémoire*, p. 133.

[2] L. von Stein, *Geschichte der sozialen Bewegung in Frankreich*, Vol. III, p. 362 (Leipzig, 1850). A remarkable piece of work altogether.

[3] In this new book, published in 1860, he recognizes the necessity of private property as the sole means of combating the omnipotence of the State. "Modern property," he writes (p. 144), "created apparently against all legal right and all common sense, may be regarded as the triumph of liberty." And, again, at p. 166: "Property founded on egoism is the fire in which egoism is refined." It is to the wide extension of property that he looks for the equalitarian reform of society. "The aim of the theory that I propose to you," he says, "is to show you how, if you wish, there will be no revolution. All that is needed is for the 'have-nots' to make it easy for themselves to acquire property, and for the 'haves' to fulfil their duty to the Government better."

behind it. Proudhon has his own solution. There is, says he, between
master and men continual miscalculation.[1] The master pays each
workman in proportion to the value of his own individual labour, but
reserves for himself the product which results from the collective force
of all—a product which is altogether superior to that yielded by the
sum of their individual efforts. This excessive product represents
profits.

It is said that the capitalist pays his workmen by the day. But to
be more exact we ought to say that he pays a *per diem* wage multiplied by the number of workmen employed each day—which is not
the same thing. For that immense force which results from union
and from the harmonious combination of simultaneous efforts he
has paid nothing. Two hundred grenadiers can deck the base of
the Louqsor statue in a few hours, a task which would be quite impossible for one man though he worked two hundred days. According to the capitalist reckoning the wages paid in both cases would
be the same.[2] And so the worker is led to believe that he is paid for
his work, whereas in reality he is only partly paid for it. Even after
receiving his wage he still retains a right of property in the things
which he has produced.[3]

His explanation, though very subtle, is none the less erroneous, because
it is precisely the function of the *entrepreneur*—and therefore the justification for his remuneration—to collect and organize the forces of
labour so as to achieve a result that could not be achieved separately.

The appearance of the pamphlet made Proudhon famous, not
merely in the eyes of the public, who knew little of him beyond his
famous formula, but also in the opinion of the economists. Blanqui
and Garnier, among others, interested themselves in his work. "It is
impossible to have a higher opinion of anyone than I have of you,"
writes the former.[4] Blanqui by his favourable report to the Academy
of Moral Sciences was instrumental in thwarting the legal proceedings
which the Minister of the Interior was anxious to take against
Proudhon. And it was upon Garnier's advice that the publisher
Guillaumin, although a strong adherent of orthodox economics, con-
sented to issue a new work by Proudhon in 1846. The book was
entitled *Les Contradictions économiques*, and Guillaumin was not a little
startled by it.[5]

[1] "This is the fundamental idea of my first *Mémoire*." (Quoted by Sainte-Beuve,
P. J. Proudhon, p. 90.) Later on he complains that the suggestion was never even
discussed.
[2] *Propriété*, 1er *Mémoire*, p. 94.   [3] *Ibid.*, p. 91.
[4] Blanqui's letter dated May 1, 1841, in reply to a communication from Proudhon
concerning the second *Mémoire* on property.
[5] *Cf.* Sainte-Beuve, *P. J. Proudhon*, pp. 202, 203; and see on this point Proudhon's
amusing letters to Guillaumin (*Correspondance*, Vol. II).

The sympathy of the economists is easily explained. They realized from the first that Proudhon was a vigorous opponent of their views, but it was not long before they discovered that he was an equally resolute critic of socialism. Let us briefly examine his attitude with regard to the latter.

No one has ever referred to socialists in harsher terms. "The Saint-Simonians have vanished like a masquerade."[1] "Fourier's system is the greatest mystification of our time."[2] To the communists he writes as follows: "Hence, communists! Your presence is a stench in my nostrils and the sight of you disgusts me." Elsewhere he says: "Socialism is a mere nothing. It never has been and never will be anything."[3] The violence of his attitude towards his predecessors springs from a fear of being confused with them. The procedure is intended to put the reader on his guard against all equivocation, and to afford him valuable preparation for appreciating Proudhon's solutions by showing how utterly impossible the other solutions are.

His attack upon the socialists roughly amounts to a charge of failure to realize that the destruction of the present regime would involve taking a course in the opposite direction. The difficult problem which he set out to solve was not merely the suppression of existing economic forces, but also their equilibration.[4] He never contemplated "the extinction of such economic forces as division of labour, collective effort, competition, credit, property, or even economic liberty."[5] His

---

[1] *Propriété*, 1er *Mémoire*, p. 203.

[2] An article in *Le Peuple*, in 1848. Proudhon's attacks are more especially directed against Fourier. Fourier's was at this time the only socialist school that had any influence, and this was largely due to the active propaganda of Victor Considérant. See *Contradictions*, Vol. II, p. 297, and *Propriété*, 1er *Mémoire*, pp. 153 *et seq.*

[3] *Contradictions*, Vol. II, p. 285. For the attack on Cabet, Louis Blanc, and the communists see the whole of chapter xii of the *Contradictions*. Louis Blanc "has poisoned the working classes with his ridiculous formulæ" (*Idée générale de la Révolution*, p. 108). Louis Blanc himself is summed up as follows: "He seriously thought that he was the bee of the Revolution, but he turned out to be only a grasshopper." (*Ibid.*)

[4] "I believe that I am the first person possessed of a full knowledge of the phenomena in question who has dared to uphold the doctrine that instead of restraining economic forces whose strength has been so much exaggerated we ought to try to balance them against one another in accordance with the little-known and less perfectly understood principle that contraries, far from being mutually destructive, support one another just because of their contrary nature." (*Justice*, Vol. I, pp. 265–266.) The same idea also finds expression on pp. 302–303. Elsewhere he remarks that what society is in search of is a way of balancing the natural forces that are contained within itself. (*Révolution démonstrée par le Coup d'État*, p. 43.)

[5] "Division of labour, collective force, competition, exchange, credit, property, and even liberty—these are the true economic forces, the raw materials of all wealth, which, without actually making men the slaves of one another, give entire freedom to the producer, ease his toil, arouse his enthusiasm, and double his produce by creating a real solidarity which is not based upon personal considerations, but which

chief concern was to preserve them, but at the same time to suppress the conflict that exists between them. The socialists aim merely at destruction. For competition they would substitute an associative organization of labour; instead of private property they would set up community of goods[1] or collectivism; instead of the free play of personal interest they would, according to Fourier, substitute love, or love and devotion, as the Saint-Simonians put it, or the fraternity of Cabet. But none of these satisfies Proudhon.

He dismisses association and organization as being detrimental to the liberty of the worker.[2] Labour's power is just the result of "collective force and division of labour." Liberty is the economic force *par excellence*. "Economic perfection lies in the absolute independence of the workers, just as political perfection consists in the absolute independence of the citizens."[3] "Liberty," he remarks in an address delivered to the electors of the department of the Seine in 1848, "is the sum total of my system—liberty of conscience, freedom of the Press, freedom of labour, of commerce, and of teaching, the free disposal of the products of labour and industry—liberty, infinite, absolute, everywhere and for ever." He adds that his is "the system of '89," and that he is preaching the doctrines of Quesnay, of Turgot, and of Say. Indeed, it would not be difficult to imagine ourselves reading the Classical rhapsodies concerning the advantages of Free Trade over again.[4]

---

binds men together with ties stronger than any which sympathetic combination or voluntary contract can supply." (*Idée générale de la Révolution au XIXᵉ Siècle*, p. 95.) The economic forces are somewhat differently enumerated in chapter xiii of *La Capacité des Classes ouvrières*. Association and mutuality are mentioned; but while recognizing the prestige of the word "association," especially among working men, Proudhon concludes that the only real association is mutuality—not in the sense of a mutual aid society, which he thinks is altogether too narrow.

[1] It is true that Fourier was not a communist. Proudhon shows that on the one hand his Phalanstère would abolish interest, while it would give a special remuneration to talent on the other, simply because "talent is a product of society rather than a gift of nature." (*Propriété, 1er Mémoire*, p. 156.)

[2] Proudhon's opposition to the principle of association is very remarkable. He refers to it more than once, but especially in the *Idée générale de la Révolution*. "Can association be regarded as an economic force? For my own part I distinctly say, No. By itself it is sterile, even if it does not check production, because of the limits it puts upon the liberty of the worker." (P. 89.) "Association means that everyone is responsible for some one else, and the least counts as much as the greatest, the youngest as the oldest. It gets rid of inequality, with the result that there is general awkwardness and incapacity." (*Ibid.*)

[3] *La Révolution démontrée par le Coup d'État*, pp. 53, 54. Elsewhere: "When you speak of organizing labour it seems as if you would put out the eyes of liberty." (*Organisation du Crédit et de l'Échange, Œuvres*, Vol. VI, p. 91.)

[4] *Programme révolutionnaire*. To the electors of the Seine, in the *Représentant du Peuple*. (*Œuvres*, Vol. XVII, pp. 45, 46.)

Communism as a juridical system is rejected no less energetically. There is no suggestion of suppressing private property, which is the necessary stimulant of labour, the basis of family life, and indispensable to all true progress. His chief concern is to make it harmless and to place it at the disposal of every one.[1] "Communism is merely an inverted form of private property. Communism gives rise to inequalities, but of a different character from those of property. Property is the exploitation of the weak by the strong, communism of the strong by the weak."[2] It is still robbery. "Communism," he exclaims, "is the religion of misery."[3] "Between the institution of private property and communism there is a world of difference."[4]

Racial devotion or fraternity as possible motives for action are not recognized. They imply the sacrifice and the subordination of one man to another. All men have equal rights, and the freer exercise of those rights is a matter of justice, not of fraternity. Proudhon thinks the axiom so very evident that he takes no trouble to explain it, but merely gives us a definition of justice. In his first *Mémoire* it is defined as "a kind of respect spontaneously felt and reciprocally guaranteed to human dignity in any person and under all circumstances, even though the discharge of that feeling exposes us to some risk."[5]

His justice is tantamount to equality. If we apply the definition to the economic links which bind men together, we find that the principle of mutual respect is transformed into the principle of reciprocal service.[6] Men must be made to realize this need for reciprocal service. It is the only way in which equality can be respected. "Do unto others as you would that others do unto you"—this principle of justice is the

[1] "I should like everybody to have some property. We are anxious that they should have property in order to avoid paying interest, because exorbitant interest is the one obstacle to the universal use of property." (*Le Peuple*, September 2, 1849.)

[2] *Propriété*, 1er *Mémoire*, p. 204.   [3] *Contradictions*, Vol. II, p. 203.

[4] *Organisation du Credit et de la circulation*, p. 131. Elsewhere: "To adopt Hegelian phraseology, the community is the first term in social development—the thesis; property the contradictory term—the antithesis. The third term—the synthesis—must be found before the solution can be considered complete." (*Propriété*, 1er *Mémoire*, p. 202.) That term will be possession pure and simple—the right of property with no claim to unearned income. "Get rid of property, but retain the right of possession, and this very simple change of principle will result in an alteration of the laws, the method of government, and the character of a nation's economic institutions. Evil of every kind will be entirely swept away." Proudhon employed Hegelian terminology as early as 1840, four years before Karl Grün's visit to Paris. For Proudhon's relation to Grün see Sainte-Beuve's *P. J. Proudhon*.

[5] *Justice dans la Révolution*, Vol. I, pp. 182–183.

[6] *Ibid.*, p. 269. "It is easy to show how the principle of mutual respect is logically convertible with the principle of reciprocal service. If men are equal in the eyes of justice they must also have a common necessity, and whoever would place his brothers in a position of inferiority, against which it is the chief duty of society to fight, is not acting justly."

ethical counterpart of the economic precept of mutual service.[1] Reciprocal service must be the new principle which must guide us in rearranging the economic links of society.

And so a criticism of socialism helps Proudhon to define the positive basis of his own system. The terms of the social problem as it presents itself to him can now be clearly followed. On the one hand there is the suppression of the unearned income derived from property—a revenue which is in direct opposition to the principle of reciprocal service. On the other hand, property itself must be preserved, liberty of work and right of exchange must be secured. In other words, the fundamental attribute of property must be removed without damaging the institution of property itself or endangering the principle of liberty.[2]

It is the old problem of how to square the circle. The extinction of unearned incomes must involve the communal ownership of the instruments of production, although Proudhon did not seem to think so. Hitherto the reform of property had been attempted by attacking the production and distribution of wealth. No attention was ever paid to exchange. But Proudhon thought that in the act of exchange inequality creeps in and a new method of exchange is needed. Towards the end of the *Contradictions économiques* he gives us an obscure hint of the kind of reform to be aimed at. After declaring that nothing now remains to be done except "to sum up all contradictions in one general equation," he proceeds to ask what particular form that equation is to take. We have already, he remarks, been permitted a glimpse of it. "It must be a law of exchange based upon a theory of mutual help. This theory of mutualism—that is, of natural exchange—is from the collective point of view a synthesis of two ideas—that of property and that of communism."[3] No further definition is attempted. In a letter written after the publication of the *Contradictions* he still refers to himself as a simple seeker, and states that he has a new book in preparation, in which these propositions are to be further developed.

About the same time he had laid out his plans for active propaganda in the Press. But the Revolution of 1848 threw him into the *mêlée* of party politics and hastened the publication of his theories.

In order to give a better idea of the place occupied by Proudhon's ideas, and to show how they were connected with the socialist experiments of the time, we must say a few words about the Revolution itself.

---

[1] This idea of mutual service is further developed, especially in *Organisation du Crédit et de la circulation* (*Œuvres*, Vol. VI, pp. 92–93), and in *Idée générale*, p. 97.

[2] That is how the problem is put in the preface to the first *Mémoire*.

[3] *Contradictions*, Vol. II, p. 414.

II: THE REVOLUTION OF 1848 AND THE DISCREDIT OF SOCIALISM

Socialists of all shades of opinion, who from 1830 to 1840 had been advocating radical reforms, were given a unique opportunity of putting their theories to the test during the Revolution of 1848. During the four months (February to June) which preceded the terrible ruin of the socialist Republic by the bourgeoisie, projects of all kinds which for many years had been discussed in books and newspapers appeared to be on the point of bearing fruit. For a number of weeks nothing seemed impossible. 'The right to work,' 'organization of labour,' and 'association,' instead of being so many formulæ, were by a mere stroke of the magic wand to be translated into realities.

Enthusiasts were not wanting to attempt this task of transformation, but, alas! only to find every scheme tumble into ruins. Every formula, when put to the test, was found to be void. The malevolence of some people, the impatience of others, the awkwardness and haste of the promoters even, made the experiments odious and ridiculous. Public opinion was at last thoroughly wearied and all the reformers were indiscriminately condemned.

The year 1848 is accordingly a memorable one in the history of social ideas. The idealistic socialism of Louis Blanc, of Fourier, and of Saint-Simon was definitely discredited. Bourgeois writers thought that it was utterly destroyed. Reybaud, who contributed the article on Socialism to the *Dictionnaire d'Économie politique* (edited by Coquelin and Guillaumin) in 1852, writes as follows: "To speak of socialism nowadays is to deliver a funeral oration. It has exhausted itself. The vein is worked out. Should the human mind in its vertigo ever take it up again it will be in a different form and under the influence of other illusions."

It fared scarcely better at the hands of subsequent socialists. Marx referred to all his predecessors under the rather misleading title of Utopians, and against their fantastic dreams he set up the 'scientific socialism' of *Das Kapital*. Between the two epochs lies a distinct cleavage, marked by the Revolution of 1848. We must briefly see how this was brought about, and rapidly review the more important experiments that were made.

First of all there is 'the right to work.' Fourier's formula, which was developed by Considérant and adopted by Louis Blanc and other democrats, became extremely popular during the reign of Louis Phillipe. Proudhon speaks of it as the only true formula of the February Revolution. "Give me the right to work," he declares, "and I will give you the right of property."[1] The same idea has been revived in our own day, after the long period of post-war unemployment, but with a new formula: 'full employment' is now proposed as the fundamental objective of economic policy.

Workmen thought that the first duty of the Provisional Government was to give effect to this formula. On February 25 a small group of Parisian workmen came to the Hôtel de Ville to urge their claims, and the Government hastened to recognize them. The decree drawn up by Louis Blanc was as follows: "The Provisional Government of the French Republic undertakes to guarantee the existence of every worker by means of his labour. It further undertakes to give work to all its citizens." The following day another decree announced the immediate establishment of national workshops with a view to putting the new principle into practice. All that was necessary to gain admission was to have one's name inscribed in one of the Parisian municipal offices.

Louis Blanc in his book of 1841 had demanded the establishment of 'social' workshops. Public opinion, misled by the similarity of names, and encouraged to persist in its error by the enemies of socialism, thought that the national workshops were the creation of Louis Blanc. Nothing could be more incorrect. The 'social' workshops, as we know, were to engage in co-operative production, whereas the national workshops were to provide employment for idlers. Similar institutions had been established during every crisis between 1790 and 1830, generally under the name of "charity works." Moreover, it was Marie, the Minister of Public Works, and not Louis Blanc, who organized them. Far from providing work as the socialists had hoped, the Government soon realized that the workshops afforded an admirable opportunity for binding the workmen together into brigades which might act as a check upon the socialistic tendencies of the Luxembourg Commission, then presided over by Louis Blanc. The workshops were placed under the management of Émile Thomas, the engineer, who was an avowed opponent of the scheme. In his *Histoire des Ateliers nationaux*, written in 1849, he tells us how they were controlled by him in accordance with the wishes of the anti-socialist majority of the Provisional Government.[2]

[1] *Le Droit du Travail et le Droit de Propriété*, pp. 4, 5, 58 (1848).

[2] Every historian is agreed on this point, which Louis Blanc has dealt with at great length in his *Histoire de la Révolution de 1848* (chapter xi). The testimony of contemporaries, especially Lamartine in his *Histoire de la Révolution de 1848* (Vol. II, p. 120), is also very significant. "These national workshops were placed under the direction of men who belonged to the anti-socialist party, whose one aim was to spoil the experiment, but who managed to keep the sectaries of the Luxembourg and the rebels of

But they were mistaken in their calculations. Those who thought that the national workshops could be used for their own political ends were soon undeceived. The Revolution greatly increased the number of idlers, already fairly considerable as the result of the economic crisis of 1847. Moreover, the opening of the workshops brought the workmen from the provinces into Paris. Instead of the estimated 10,000, 21,000 had been enrolled by the end of March, and by the end of April there were 99,400. They were paid two francs a day while at work, and a franc when there was no work for them. In a very short time it became impossible to find employment for so many. The majority of them, whatever their trade, were employed upon useless earthworks, and even these soon proved inadequate. Discontent soon became rife among this army of unfortunate workers, humiliated by the nature of the ridiculous labour upon which they were employed, and scarcely satisfied with the moderate salary which they received. The wages paid, however, were more than enough for the kind of work that was being done. The workshops became centres of political agitation, and the Government, thoroughly alarmed, and acting under pressure from the National Assembly, was constrained to abandon them.

Suddenly, on June 21, a summons was executed upon all men between seventeen and twenty-five enrolled in the shops, ordering them to join the army or to leave for the country, where more digging awaited them. The exasperated workmen rose in revolt. Rioting broke out on June 23, but it was crushed in three days. Hundreds of the workers died in the struggle, and the country was terrorized into reaction.

That simple logic which is always so characteristic of political parties held the principle of 'the right to work' responsible for this disastrous experience, and it was definitely condemned. This is quite clear from the constitutional debates in the National Assembly. The constitutional plan laid down by Armand Marrast on June 19, a few days

---

the clubs apart until the meeting of the National Assembly. Paris was disgusted with the quantity and the character of the work accomplished, but it little thought that these men had on more than one occasion defended and protected the city. Far from being in the pay of Louis Blanc, as some people seem to think, they were entirely at the beck and call of his opponents." É. Thomas in his *Histoire des Ateliers nationaux* (pp. 146–147) relates how Marie sent for him on May 23 and secretly asked him whether the men in the workshops could be relied upon. "Try to get them strongly attached to you. Spare no expense. If there is any need we shall give you plenty of money." Upon Thomas asking what was the purpose of all this, Marie replied: "It is all in the interest of public safety. Make sure of the men. The day is not far distant when we shall need them in the streets."

before the riots, recognized 'the right to work.' "The Constitution," says Article 2, "guarantees to every citizen liberty, equality, security, instruction, work, property, and public assistance." But in the new plan of August 29—after the experience of June—the article disappeared. The right to relief only was recognized. In the discussion on the article an amendment re-establishing 'the right to work' was proposed by Mathieu de la Drôme. A memorable debate followed, in which Thiers, Lamartine, and Tocqueville opposed the amendment, while the Radical Republicans Ledru-Rollin, Crémieux, and Mathieu de la Drôme defended it.[1] The socialists had become extinct. Louis Blanc was in exile, Considérant ill, while Proudhon was afraid of startling his opponents and of compromising his friends. Besides, the Assembly had already made up its mind. The amendment was defeated, and Article 8 of the preamble to the Constitution of 1848 runs as follows: "The Republic by means of friendly assistance should provide for its necessitous citizens, either by giving them work as far as it can, or by directly assisting those who are unable to work and have no one to help them."

During the reign of the July Monarchy 'the organization of labour' was another phrase which divided the honours with 'the right to work.' With the spread of the Revolution came a similar menacing demand for its realization. By a strange coincidence the author of this formula was also a member of the Provisional Government. And so when on February 28, three days after the recognition of 'the right to work,' the workers came in a body and claimed the creation of a Minister of Progress, the organization of labour, and the abolition of all exploitation, Louis Blanc immediately seized the opportunity to urge his unwilling colleagues to accede to their demands. He himself had pressed the Government to take the initiative in social reform, and now that the Revolution had made him a member of the Government how could he escape his responsibility? After some difficulty his colleagues succeeded in persuading him to accept the alternative of a Government commission on labour, of which he was to be president. The commission was entrusted with the task of drawing up the proposed reforms, which were afterwards to be submitted to the National Assembly. To mark the contrast between the old and the new regime the commission carried on its deliberations in the Palais du Luxembourg, where the Chambre des Pairs formerly sat.

The Luxembourg commission was composed of representatives elected by workmen and masters, three for each industry. The representatives met in a general assembly to discuss the reports prepared

[1] These addresses were afterwards published in a volume entitled *Le Droit au Travail.*

by a permanent committee of ten workers and an equal number of masters, to which Louis Blanc had added a few Liberal economists and socialists, such as Le Play, Dupont-White, Wolowski, Considérant, Pecqueur, and Vidal. Proudhon was also invited, but refused to join. As a matter of fact, only the workers took part in the sittings.

The commission, although it possessed no executive power, might have been of some service. But Louis Blanc, as he himself confessed, regarded it as "a golden opportunity where socialism had at its disposal a tribunal from which it could address the whole of Europe."[1] He still kept up his role of orator and writer, and devoted most of the sittings to an eloquent appeal for the theories already outlined in his 'organization of labour.'[2] Vidal and Pecqueur undertook the task of elaborating the more definite proposals. In a lengthy report which appeared in the *Moniteur*[3] they outlined a plan of State Socialism, with workshops and agricultural colonies, with State depots and bazaars as places of sale. Money in the form of warrants was to be borrowed on the security of goods, and a State system of insurance—excepting life policies—was to be established. Finally, the Bank of France was to be transformed into a State bank. This was to extend the operation of credit, and to reduce the rate of discount simply to insurance against risk. Vidal and not Pecqueur is obviously the author of the report, for it contains some of the projects that had already appeared in his book *De la Répartition des Richesses*. And it is easy to see here the origin of those demands for nationalization that are common to all socialist parties since the First World War and that they have succeeded in putting into practice throughout Europe after the Second World War.

None of the projects was even discussed by the National Assembly. The only positive piece of work accomplished by Louis Blanc's commission was done under pressure from the workmen. This was the famous decree of March 2, abolishing piece-work and reducing the working day to ten hours in Paris and eleven hours in the provinces. This decree, though it was never put into operation, marks the first rudiments of French labour legislation. Louis Blanc was forced to grant it because the working-class element on the commission refused to take part in its proceedings until they were satisfied on this point.

[1] Louis Blanc, *Histoire de la Révolution de 1848*, Vol. II, p. 135.

[2] See the addresses in his *La Révolution de Février au Luxembourg* (Paris, 1849).

[3] *Moniteur*, April 27, May 2, 3, and 6, 1848. The dismissal of the commission meant an interruption of the *Exposé général*, but Vidal in his work *Vivre en travaillant! Projets, Voies, et Moyens de Réformes sociales* (1848) continued the exposition. It contains a plan for agricultural credit, a State land-purchase scheme in order to get rid of rent, a proposal for buying up railways and mines and for erecting cheap dwellings. It affords an interesting example of State Socialism in 1848 which seems to have struck many people then as being very amusing.

The commission must also be credited with several successful attempts at conciliation.

Not only did the commission fail to do anything permanent, but its degeneracy into a mere political club thoroughly alarmed the public. It became involved in elections, and even intervened in street riots. It finally took a part in the demonstration of May 15, which, under pretext of demanding intervention in favour of Poland, resulted in an invasion of the National Assembly by the mob. Louis Blanc had already retired. Since the reunion of the National Assembly the Government had been replaced by an executive commission, and Blanc, no longer a supporter of the Government, sent in his resignation on May 13. After that the commission was at an end, and, like the national workshops, it all resulted in nothing save a general discredit of socialist opinion.

There still remained the 'working men's associations.' Every socialist writer of the early nineteenth century was agreed on this principle of association. Every reformer, with the exception of Proudhon,[1] who always pursued a path of his own, regarded it as the one method of emancipation. It was quite natural that it should be put to the test.

In its declaration of February 26 the Provisional Government stated that besides securing the right to work, the workers must combine together before they could secure the full benefit of their labour. The moment Louis Blanc attained to power he sought to guide the energies of the commission in this direction. The 'Association' was to be of the nature of a co-operative productive society, supported by the State. Under the influence of Buchez, an old Saint-Simonian, a Republican Catholic and the founder of the newspaper called *L'Atelier*, there had been formed in 1834 an association of jewellers and goldsmiths.[2] But it was a solitary exception.

Louis Blanc was more fortunate. He successively founded associations of tailors, of saddlers, of spinners and lace-makers, and he secured Government orders for tunics, saddles, and epaulettes for them. Other associations followed, and by July 5 the National Assembly was sufficiently interested in these experiments to vote the sum of three millions to their credit. A good portion of this sum passed into the hands of mixed associations of masters and men formed with the sole purpose of benefiting by the Government's liberality. The workmen's associations pure and simple, however, received more than a million, and there was not a sou of it left by 1849.

The first co-operative movement inspired by the ideas of Louis Blanc

---

[1] *Cf. supra*, p. 305, note 2.   [2] *Cf. supra*, "The Associative Socialists."

was of short duration. The National Assembly took good care to place the new societies under Ministerial control by appointing a *Conseil d'Encouragement*, nominated by the Ministry to fix the conditions under which loans should be granted. The *Conseil* hastened to publish model regulations which left the associations little scope for internal organization. So stringent were the rules that several of them were immediately jeopardized, and every society which failed to conform to one of the three models outlined in Article 19 of the Commercial Code was obliged to dissolve. This meant every society which was not nominally a collective society or a joint stock or a limited liability company. By 1855, according to the testimony of Reybaud, there remained only nine out of those subsidized in 1848. Consumers' co-operative societies, that is, the societies which aimed at securing cheap commodities, established at Paris, Lille, Nantes, and Grenoble, were also dissolved.

And so all these experiments—the only ones that had not already brought reformers into discredit—were destined to fail in their turn. Their extinction was due partly to political causes, partly to their founders, who had not yet been trained in the difficult task of building up such associations.

The social experiments of 1848 one after another foundered, bringing a distrust of theories in their train. There still remained one other experiment connected with Proudhon's name—that of free credit. But it also was destined to fail like the rest.

III: THE EXCHANGE BANK THEORY

The Revolution of 1848 did not take Proudhon quite unawares, although he considered the outbreak was rather sudden. He was soon convinced that the real problem to be determined was economic rather than political, but he also realized that the education of the masses was too backward to permit of a peaceful solution. Proudhon, in this matter at one with his French *confrères*, had hoped for such a solution.[1] He thought the February Revolution was a child prematurely born.[2] In a striking article in the columns of *Le Peuple* he gave wistful expression to his fears as he foresaw the Revolution impending. Its solution had been delivered to none and its interpretation baffled the ingenuity of all.

[1] "I need hardly say that this measure of fiscal reform [namely, the abolition of private property] must be carried out without any violence or robbery. There must be no spoliation, but ample compensation must be given." (*Résumé de la Question sociale*, p. 27.)

[2] *Solution du Problème social* (*Œuvres*, Vol. VI, p. 32).

I have wept over the poor workman, whose daily bread is already sufficiently uncertain and who has now suffered misery for many years. I have undertaken his defence, but I find that I am powerless to succour him. I have mourned over the bourgeois, whose ruin I have witnessed and who has been driven to bankruptcy and goaded to opposition of the proletariat. My personal inclination is to sympathize with the bourgeois, but a natural antagonism to his ideas and the play of circumstance have made me his opponent. I have gone in mourning and paid penance for the spirit of the old Republic long before there were any signs of its offspring. This Revolution which was to restore the public order merely marks the beginning of a new departure in social revolution which no one understands.[1]

But the Revolution having once begun, Proudhon did not feel himself justified in being behindhand. He had been a most severe critic of the existing regime, and he felt that he was bound to attempt a solution of the practical problems which suddenly came to the front. He became a journalist and threw himself wholeheartedly into the struggle. Hitherto he had been content with vague suggestions as to where the evil lay. But now he was anxious to make reform practicable and to fill in the details of the scheme; and so he invented the Exchange Bank.

Proudhon's exposition of the scheme is contained in a number of pamphlets, in newspapers, and in his books.[2] The explanations do not always tally, and he is not always happy in stating exactly what he thinks. This explains why he has been so often misunderstood. We shall try to give a résumé of his ideas before proceeding to criticize them and to compare them with analogous projects formulated both before and after his time. This will help us to understand where the originality of the scheme lay.

The fundamental principle on which the whole scheme rests is

---

[1] *Œuvres*, Vol. XVIII, pp. 6–7. See also the letter dated February 25, 1848 (*Correspondance*, Vol. II, p. 280): "France will certainly accomplish it, whether it remains a republic or not. It might even be carried out by the present decadent Government, at a trifling cost." This thought did not prevent his taking a hand in the Revolution.

[2] In a pamphlet entitled *Organisation du Crédit et de la circulation*, and dated March 31, 1848, he expounds the principle of the scheme and indicates some of its general features. The scheme is dealt with in a number of articles contributed to *Le Représentant du peuple* for April, afterwards published in book form by Darimon, under the title of *Résumé de la Question sociale*. The plan differs slightly from the statutes of the People's Bank as they appear in Vol. VI of the *Œuvres*, but the guiding principle is much the same. A further exposition was given in *Le Peuple* in February and March 1849, just when the Bank was being founded. There is still another account contained in the volume entitled *Intérêt et Principal: Discussion entre M. Proudhon and M. Bastiat sur l'intérêt du capitaux* (Paris, 1880). This controversy was carried on in the columns of *La Voix du peuple* from October 1849 to October 1850. Proudhon frequently refers to the same idea in his other works, notably in *Justice dans la Révolution*, Vol. I, pp. 289 *et seq.*, and in *Idée générale*, pp. 197 *et seq.*

somewhat as follows: Of all the forms of capital which allow of a right of escheat to the product of the worker, whether in the form of rent, of interest, or of discount, the most important is money, for it is only in the form of money that these dues are actually paid.[1] If we could suppress the right of escheat in the case of this universal form of capital—in other words, if interest were abolished—the right of escheat in every other case would soon disappear.

Let us suppose that by means of some organization or other money required for the purchase of land, machinery, and buildings for industrial purposes could be procured without interest. Were this the case the required capital would then be obtained in that way instead of by payment of interest or rent as is the case to-day. The suppression of money interest would enable the worker to borrow capital gratuitously, and would give him immediate control over all useful capital instead of renting it. All attempts to hold up capital for the sake of receiving interest without labour would thus be frustrated. The right of property would be reduced to mere possession. Exchange would be reciprocal, and the worker would secure all the produce of his labour without having to share it with others. In short, economic justice would be secured.

This is all very well, but how can the necessary money be obtained without paying interest? Everything depends upon that.

Proudhon invites us to consider what money really is. It is a mere medium of exchange which is designed to facilitate the circulation of goods. Proudhon, who had hitherto regarded money as capital *par excellence*, now treats it as a mere instrument of exchange. "Money by itself is of no use to me. I merely take it in order to part with it. I can neither consume it nor cultivate it."[2] It is a mere medium of exchange, and the interest paid merely covers this cost of circulation.[3] But paper money will fulfil this function quite as well and much more cheaply. Banks advance money in exchange for commodities or supply bills which are immediately transferable into cash. In exchange for this service the banker receives a discount which goes to remunerate the shareholders who have supplied the capital. Why not establish a bank without any capital which, like the Bank of France, will discount goods with bills—either circulation or exchange notes? The bills would be inconvertible, and consequently would cost scarcely anything, and there would be no capital to remunerate.

[1] See *Solution du Problème social*, pp. 178, 179.

[2] *Intérêt et Principal*, p. 112.

[3] "Money is simply a supplementary kind of capital, a medium of exchange or a credit instrument. If this is the case what claim has it to payment? To think of remunerating money for the service which it gives!" (*Ibid.*, p. 113.)

The service given would be equal to that given by the banks, but would cost a great deal less. All that would be required to ensure the circulation of the bills would be an understanding on the part of the clientele of the new bank that they would accept them as payment for goods. The bearer would thus be certain that they were always immediately exchangeable, just as if they were cash. The clients would lose nothing by accepting them, for the statutes would decree that the bank should never trade in anything except goods actually delivered or under promise of delivery. The notes in circulation would never exceed the demands of commerce. They would always represent goods already produced and actually sold, but not yet paid for.[1] Following the example of other banks, the bank would advance to the seller of the goods a sum of money which it would subsequently recover from the buyer. The merchants and manufacturers would obtain not only their circulating capital without payment of interest, but also the fixed capital necessary for the founding of new industries. These advances obtained without interest would enable them to buy and not merely to rent the instruments of production which they needed.[2]

The consequences of a reform of this kind cannot be easily enumerated. Not only would capital be freely placed at the disposal of every one, but every class distinction would disappear[3] as soon as the worker ceased selling his products at cost price[4] and government itself would become useless. The aim of all government is to check the oppression of the weak by the strong.[5] But the moment fair exchange

---

[1] Cf. Résumé de la Question sociale, p. 39.

[2] Moreover, the advances will take the form of discount. The entrepreneur who has some scheme which he wishes to carry out "will in the first place collect orders, and on the strength of those orders get hold of some producer or dealer who has such raw material or services at his disposal. Having obtained the goods, he pays for them by means of promissory notes, which the bank, after taking due precaution, will convert into circulation notes." The consumer is really a sleeping partner in the business, and between him and the entrepreneur there is no need for the intervention of money at all. (Organisation du Crédit, Œuvres, Vol. VI, p. 123.) Discount was the fundamental characteristic of the bank, and no criticism is directed against this feature of its operations.

[3] "How to resolve the bourgeoisie and the proletariat into the middle class, the class which lives upon its income and that which draws a salary into a class which has neither revenue nor wages, but lives by inventing and producing valuable commodities to exchange them for others. The middle class is the most active class in society, and is truly representative of a country's activity. This was the problem in February 1848." (Révolution démontrée par le Coup d'État, p. 135.)

[4] "Reciprocity means a guarantee on the part of those who exchange commodities to sell at cost price." (Idée générale de la Révolution, pp. 97–98.)

[5] "The very existence of the State implies antagonism or war as the essential or inevitable condition of humanity, a condition that calls for the intervention of a coercive force which shall put an end to the struggle continually waging between the weak and the strong." (Voix du Peuple, December 3, 1849; Œuvres, Vol. XIX, p. 23.)

L

318 PROUDHON AND THE SOCIALISM OF 1848

becomes possible, free contract is sufficient to secure this; there is no
longer anyone who is oppressed. All are equally favoured, for the
cause of contention has been removed. "Once capital and labour are
identified, society will subsist of its own accord, and there will no
longer be any need for government." Government has "its origin and
its whole being immersed in the economic system." Proudhon's
system means anarchy—the absence of government.[1]

Such is Proudhon's plan, and such its consequences. To understand
its full significance we must inquire whether (1) the substitution of
exchange notes for bank-notes payable at sight is practicable, and,
(2) supposing it to be practicable, if it is likely to have the effects
anticipated by its author.

Proudhon states that his system merely involves the universal adoption of exchange notes.[2] The Exchange Bank would merely append
the manager's signature against the particular commodity discounted.
But the issue of bank-notes at the present time involves nothing more
than this. Instead of the bill of exchange which it now buys, and which
enjoys only a limited circulation because the signatories have only a
very limited credit, it is proposed that the Bank of France should
substitute a note bearing its own signature, which is universally known
and testifies to an illimitable amount of credit. In what respects, then,
does Proudhon's circulating medium differ from a bank-note? It
differs simply in the fact that the signature of the Bank of France
involves a promise of reimbursement in metallic money, a commo-

---

"When economic development has resulted in the transformation of society even
despite itself, then the weak and the strong will alike disappear. There will only be
workers; and industrial solidarity, and a guarantee that their products will be sold
will tend to make them equal both in capacity and wealth." (*Œuvres*, Vol. XIX, p. 18.

[1] "Consequently we consider ourselves anarchists and we have proclaimed the
fact more than once. Anarchy is suitable for an adult society just as hierarchy is for
a primitive one. Human society has progressed gradually from hierarchy to anarchy."
(*Ibid.*, p. 9.) A little later, in *Idée générale de la Révolution* (p. 196), he states that
the aim of the Revolution was "to build up a property constitution and to dissolve
or otherwise cause the disappearance of the political or government system by reducing
or simplifying, by decentralizing and suppressing the whole machinery of the State."
This idea was borrowed from Saint-Simon, and Proudhon has acknowledged the
debt in his *Idée générale*. This conception of industrial society rendering government
useless or reducing it to harmless proportions is a development, though perhaps somewhat extravagant, of the economic Liberalism of J. B. Say. The first edition of the
Mémoire sur la Propriété contains an admission of anarchical tendencies. "What are
you, then? I am an anarchist.—I understand your doubts on this question. You
think that I am against the Government.—That is not so. You asked for my confession of faith. Having duly pondered over it, and although a lover of order, I
have come to the conclusion that I am in the fullest sense of the word an anarchist."

[2] "The whole problem of circulation is how to make the exchange note universally
acceptable, how to secure that it shall always be exchangeable for goods and service
and convertible at sight." (*Organisation du Crédit, Œuvres*, Vol. VI, pp. 113, 114.)

dity universally accepted and demanded, while Proudhon's Exchange
Bank enters into no such definite agreement, but merely undertakes
to accept it in lieu of payment.

Theoretically, perhaps, the difference may appear insignificant,
since the signatures are the only guarantee of the solvency of the notes
of the Bank of France and the Exchange Bank alike. But in practice it
is enormous. The certainty that the note can be exchanged for money
gives it a wide currency and makes it acceptable to many people who
rely implicitly upon their confidence in the bank. They need give no
thought to the question of its solvency. A mere circulating medium,
on the other hand, in addition to transferring a claim to certain goods
belonging to clients of the bank, involves a certain amount of confidence in the solvency of those clients—a confidence not always easily
justified. A note of this kind will only circulate among the bank's
clientele. It will never reach the general public as the bank-note
actually does. The clients themselves will keep their engagements
just so long as the bank continues to discount goods that have actually
been delivered and never refuses payment when it falls due. Failing
this, the exchange notes, instead of regularly returning to the bank, will
remain in circulation. A slight crisis or a little tension, and many of
the clients will become insolvent. The total nominal value of the
exchange notes will quickly surpass the actual value of the goods which
they represent. There will be a rapid depreciation, and clients even
will refuse to take them.

It is just possible to conceive of the circulation of such exchange
notes, but the area of circulation will be a very limited one, and it will
be utterly impossible if all the clients are not perfectly solvent.

Let us, however, suppose that the practical difficulties have been
overcome, and that the exchange notes are already in circulation.
Interest will not disappear even then, and herein lies the essential
weakness of the system.

Why does the Bank of France charge a discount? Is it, as Proudhon
suggests, because it supplies cash in return for a bill of exchange, so
that "the seigneurial right of discount"[1] would disappear with the
adoption of a non-metallic currency? The bank charges discount
simply because it gives a certain quantity of money immediately
exchangeable in return for a bill of exchange payable some months
hence. It gives a tangible commodity in exchange for a promise—a
present sum for a future. What the bank takes is the difference between
the present value of the bill of exchange and its value when it falls
due. It is not the mere whim of the banker or the employment of a

[1] *Organisation du Crédit.*

particular kind of money that gives rise to discount. It belongs to the
very nature of things. Proudhon notwithstanding, a sale for cash and
a sale with future payment must remain two different operations,[1] at
least as long as the immediate possession of a sum of money is judged
to be more advantageous than its future possession. Experience of
forced circulation has shown this clearly. The Bank of France still
charged discount after its notes ceased to be convertible. The disappearance of metallic money made no difference to the phenomenon
of discount.

To this Proudhon would reply that the clients of the bank, under
the terms of their agreement, are debarred from taking any such
premiums. Of course, if they remained faithful to their promise,
interest or discount would be suppressed; but this would result, not
from the organization of the Exchange Bank, but because of mutual
agreement. This would be a purely moral reform requiring no banking contrivance to aid it, but one in which progress must inevitably
be very slow.

The Bank of Exchange failing to suppress discount, or to check the
right of escheat in general, Proudhon's other conclusions fall to the
ground.

There is something else that Proudhon forgets: that even if it is
possible to multiply at will the instruments of circulation it is not
possible to do the same with the capital that results from saving—
i.e., the division of income between consumption and production.
The multiplication of exchange notes without any increase in social
wealth would have no other effect than to raise all prices—of land,
houses, and machinery, as well as of consumption goods.[2] Capital
would be lent as before, and being less plentiful the high rate of in-

---

[1] Proudhon always maintained that his reform merely consisted in transforming a
credit sale into a cash one. But he might as well have said that black was white. Far
from giving mutual benefit, the borrower will be the one who will gain most advantage.
Elsewhere he says that to give credit is merely to exchange. This is true enough, but
discount is employed just to equalize different credit transactions.

[2] The war of 1914–18 gave us the remarkable experience of a system under which
all commercial operations were on a cash basis, and when the savings of the public
did not come along fast enough the State made its purchases with paper money which,
though inconvertible, was accepted by every one. The result on prices in general was
not long in showing itself, though almost everywhere there were some economists
to demonstrate (!) that the rise in prices was a cause and not an effect of the issue of
paper money. Moreover, in countries where bank-notes were not used and where
the State borrowed from the banks by means of credit entries to be drawn on by
cheque, the results of this creation of supplementary purchasing power, added to the
normal results of saving, were precisely the same. The rise of prices in England, where
cheques take the place of bank-notes, was caused by the multiplication of these
cheques, just as in France the increase in the number of notes was the principal
cause of the rise.

:erest or rent would tend to maintain the high level of prices, and these would in turn be still further increased—a strange outcome of a reform intended to lower them! Proudhon, having exaggerated the evil effects of gold, now accepts Say's formula too literally. J. B. Say allowed himself to be led into error by his own formula that "Goods exchange for goods," and it is interesting to note that the Exchange Bank is the logical, though somewhat paradoxical, outcome of the reaction against the Mercantilist ideas concerning money which can be traced to Adam Smith and the Physiocrats.

This does not imply that Proudhon's idea is devoid of truth. The false ideal of free credit contains the germ of a true ideal, namely, mutual credit. The Bank of France is a society of capitalists whose credit is established by the public who accept their notes. They really deal in public credit. Proudhon saw clearly enough that their notes are ultimately guaranteed by the public. The public are the true signatories of these commercial goods. Were the public insolvent the bank would never recover its advances, which really constitute the security for the bills. The shareholders' capital is only a supplementary guarantee. The Comte Mollien, the Financial Minister of Napoleon I, declared that in theory a bank of issue should be able to operate without any capital. The public lends money to itself through the intermediary, the bank. Why not operate without the intermediary? Why not eliminate the *entrepreneur* of credit just as the industrial or commercial *entrepreneur* is eliminated in the case of the co-operative society? Discount would not disappear altogether, perhaps, but the rate of discount for borrowers would be diminished in proportion to the extent to which they stood to gain as lenders. This is the principle of the mutual credit society, where the initial capital is almost entirely superseded, its place being taken by the joint liability of the co-operators. Proudhon's initial conception seems to be reducible to this very simple idea.[1]

It seems that Proudhon was merely following the idea of a co-operative credit bank, just as in other parts of the work he copies other forms of co-operation without ever showing much sympathy for the principle itself.[2]

[1] In the *Idée générale de la Révolution au XIXᵉ Siècle*, p. 198: "The citizens of France have a right to demand and if need be to join together for the establishment of bake-houses, butchers' shops, etc., which will sell them bread and meat and other articles of consumption of good quality at a reasonable price, taking the place of the present chaotic method, where short weight, poor quality, and an exorbitant price seem to be the order. For a similar reason they have the right to establish a bank, with the amount of capital which they think fit, in order to get the cash which they need for their transactions as cheaply as possible."

[2] "Association avoids the waste of the retail system. M. Rossi recommends it to

In addition to a correct conception of the value of mutual credit, there runs throughout his whole system a more fundamental idea which helps to distinguish it from other forms of official socialism which arose either before or after his time. This is his profound belief in individual liberty as the indispensable motive of economic activity in industrial societies. He realized better than any of his predecessors that economic liberty is a definite acquisition of modern societies, and that every true reform must be based on liberty. He has estimated the strength of spontaneous economic forces more clearly than anyone else. He has demonstrated their pernicious effects, but at the same time he has recognized, as Adam Smith had done, that this was the most powerful lever of progress. His passionate love of justice explains his hatred of private property, and his jealous belief in liberty aroused his hostility to socialism. Despite his famous formula, *Destruam et ædificabo*, he destroyed more than he built. His liberalism rested on his profound hold of economic realities, and the social problem of to-day, as Proudhon clearly saw, is how to combine justice with liberty.

Proudhon's project for an Exchange Bank must not be confused with analogous schemes that have appeared either before or after his day. All these schemes have a common basis in a reform of exchange as a remedy for social inequalities. Apart from this one idea the resemblance is frequently superficial, and the economic bases differ considerably:

(1) Proudhon's idea has often been contrasted with Robert Owen's labour notes, and with the scheme prepared by Mr Bray in 1839, in a work entitled *Labour's Wrongs and Labour's Remedy*,[1] as well as with the later system outlined by Rodbertus. Proudhon's circulating notes have nothing in common with the labour notes described by these writers. The circulating notes represent commercial goods produced for the purpose of private exchange. Prices are freely fixed by buyer and seller, and they bear no relation to the labour time, as is the case with the labour notes. The final result, doubtless, was expected to be the same. Proudhon hoped that in this way the price of goods, now that it was no longer burdened with interest on capital, would equal

those small householders who cannot afford to buy wholesale. But this kind of association is wrong in principle. Give the producer, by helping him to exchange his products, an opportunity of supplying them with provisions at wholesale prices, or, what comes to the same thing, organize the retail trade so as to leave only just the same advantage as in the case of the wholesale transaction, and 'association' will be unnecessary." (*Idée générale de la Révolution*, p. 92.)

[1] This system was criticized by Marx in his *Misère de la Philosophie*, published in 1847 (Giard and Brière's edition, 1896, pp. 92 *et seq.*). A more recent and more complete exposition is given in Foxwell's introduction to Anton Menger's *The Right to the Whole Produce of Labour*, pp. lxv, etc.

cost of production. This result was to be obtained indirectly. The economic errors in the two cases are also different. Proudhon's error lay in his failure to realize that metallic money is a merchandise as well as an instrument of circulation. The error of Owen, of Bray, and of Rodbertus consisted of a failure to see that the price of goods includes something more than the mere amount of labour which they have cost to produce—an error which Proudhon at any rate did not commit.

(2) Proudhon's bank has also been confused with other banks of exchange which are really quite different. The ideas underlying such schemes had become prominent before Proudhon's days, and numerous practical experiments had been attempted along the lines indicated. These banks aimed, not at the suppression of interest, but at a gradual *rapprochement* between producer and consumer, the goods offered for sale being bought by the bank, and paid for in exchange notes upon an agreed basis of calculation. Buyers in their turn would come to the bank to obtain the necessaries of life, paying for them in exchange notes. An experiment of this kind was made by a certain Fulcrand Mazel in 1829.[1] In this case the bank was merely an *entrepôt* which facilitated the marketing of the goods produced. Such a system is open to the objection that the value of the notes issued in payment for goods would necessarily vary with the fluctuations in the value of these goods during the interval which would elapse between the time they are taken in by the bank and their eventual purchase by consumers.

---

[1] Mazel gave an exposition of his scheme in a series of pamphlets written in very bombastic language, but only of very slight interest to the economist. Another bank, known as Bonnard's Bank, was established at Marseilles in 1838, and afterwards at Paris. The ideas are somewhat similar, but much more practical. Both branches are still in active operation. Proudhon refers to this bank in his *Capacité politique des Classes ouvrières*. Courcelle-Seneuil gives a very eulogistic account of it in his *Traité des Banques*, and in an article in the *Journal des Économistes* for April 1853. The *modus operandi* is explained in three brochures, which may be seen in the Bibliothèque Nationale. One of these is entitled *Liste des Articles disponibles à la Banque*; the other two describe the mechanism of the bank. Darimon, one of Proudhon's disciples, in his work *De la Réforme des Banques* (Paris, Guillaumin, 1856), gives an account of a large number of similar institutions which were founded during this period. Several systems of the kind have also been discussed by M. Aucuy in his *Systèmes socialistes d'Échange* (Paris, 1907). But we cannot accept his interpretation of various points.

Bonnard's Bank differs from the others in this way. The client of the bank, instead of bringing it some commodity or other which may or may not be sold by the bank, gets from the bank some commodity which he himself requires, promising to supply the bank with a commodity of his own production whenever the bank requires it. The bank charges a commission on every transaction. Its one aim is to bring buyer and seller together, and the notes are simply bills, payable according to the conditions written on them. But they cannot be regarded as substitutes for bank bills. *Cf. Banque d'Échange de Marseille*, C. Bonnard et Cie, *fondée par Acte du* 10 *Janvier*, 1849 (Marseilles, 1849).

Proudhon's plan was to discount the goods already bought or actually delivered. The bank would only advance what was actually promised, but would make no charge for accommodation. Depreciation could only arise if the buyer were insolvent. It could never result from a fall in price as a result of a diminished demand for the product. Proudhon renounced all dealings with solidarity when he dismissed Mazel's project.[1]

(3) M. Solvay, a Belgian *entrepreneur*, has recently elaborated a scheme of 'social accounting.' He also proposes the suppression of metallic money and the introduction of a perfect system of payment. Here, however, the analogy ends.

What Solvay proposed was the replacement of metallic money, not by bank-notes, but by a system of cheques and clearing-houses. His plan owes its inspiration to the modern development of the clearing-house system. Solvay thought that the system might be so extended as to make the employment of money entirely unnecessary. To every such clearing-house the State would hand over a cheque-book, covering a sum varying with the amount of real or personal property which the house possessed. This cheque-book was to have two columns, one for receipts, the other for expenditure. Whenever any commodity was sold, the liquidation of debt would be effected by the buyer's stamping the book on the receipt side and the seller's stamping it on the expenditure side. As soon as the total value of these transactions equalled the initial sum which the cheque-book was supposed to represent the book would be returned to the State bureau, where each

---

[1] "I repudiate Mazel's system root and branch," he declares in an article contributed to *Le Peuple* of December 1848 (*Œuvres*, Vol. XVII, p. 221). He also adds that when he wrote first he had no acquaintance of any kind with Mazel. "It was M. Mazel who on his own initiative introduced himself to me and told me of his idea." In one of his projects, published on May 10, 1848, Proudhon seems inclined to adopt this idea, just for a moment at any rate. Article 17 seems to hint at this. "The notes will always be exchangeable at the bank and at the offices of members, but only against goods and services, and in the same way commodities and services can always be exchanged for notes." (*Résumé de la Question sociale*, p. 41.) This article justifies the interpretation which Courcelle-Seneuil puts on it, in his *Traité des Opérations de Banque* (9th ed., 1899, p. 470), and which Ott accepts in his *Traité d'Économie sociale* (1851), which, moreover, contains a profound analysis and some subtle criticism of Proudhon's idea. But we think that this article was simply an oversight on Proudhon's part; for beyond a formal refutation of Mazel's idea there is no reference to it in any of his other works, not even in the scheme of the People's Bank. Moreover, it seems to contradict the statement that the notes would be issued against commodities which had been actually sold and delivered, as well as other articles of the scheme—*e.g.*, Article 30, dealing with buying and selling. It also conflicts with the idea that the discounting of goods is the prime and essential operation of the bank. In our opinion, Dehl in his book on Proudhon (*P. J. Proudhon, Seine Lehre u. sein Leben*, Vol. II, p. 183) is wrong in thinking that the Exchange Bank would issue notes against all kinds of goods without taking the trouble to discover whether they had been sold or not.

individual account would be made up. "In this way everybody's receipts and expenditure will always be known with absolute clearness."[1]

The advantage of such a system would in the first place consist in the economy of metallic money. In the second place it would furnish the State with information as to the extent of everybody's fortune. The State would then be in possession of the information necessary for setting up an equable scheme of succession duties which would gradually suppress the hereditary transmission of acquired fortune. Such gradual suppression would result in the total extinction of the fundamental injustice of modern society, namely, the inequality of opportunity.[2] It would also help the application of that other principle of distributive justice, namely, 'to each according as he produces.' The idea is Saint-Simon's rather than Proudhon's.

The scope of the proposed reform is quite clear. Social accounting, according to Solvay, is a mere element in a more general conception, that of 'productivism,' which in various ways is to result in increasing productivity to its maximum.[3]

In all this it is impossible to see anything of Proudhon's ideas. With the exception of the suggestion of suppressing metallic money the fundamental conceptions are utterly different. M. Solvay makes no pretence to ability to suppress interest, and he never imagines that money is the cause of interest. The cheque and clearing system is a mere device for facilitating cash payment. It has nothing in common with the Proudhonian system, whereby circulating notes are supposed to place credit sales and cash payments on an equal footing.[4]

The most serious objection to Solvay's system lies in the fact that the suppression of money as a circulating medium must also involve its suppression as a measure of value. It seems difficult to imagine that the universal cheque bank with no monetary support would not result in a rapid inflation of prices because of the superabundance of paper. But although the particular process advocated by Solvay is open to criticism there can be no objection to his desire to diminish the quantity

---

[1] *Annales de l'Institut Solvay*, Vol. I, p. 19.   [2] *Ibid.*, p. 25.

[3] *Cf. Principes d'Orientation sociale*, a résumé of Solvay's studies in productivism and accounting (Brussels, 1904).

[4] Although Solvay's scheme seems very different from Proudhon's, it possesses features that received the highest commendation from the Luxembourg Commission. In *L'Exposé général de la Commission de Gouvernement pour les Travailleurs*, which appeared in *Le Moniteur* of May 6, 1848, we read: "When in the future association has become complete, there will be no need for notes even. Every transaction will be carried on by balancing the accounts. Book-keepers will take the place of collecting clerks. Money, both paper and metallic, is largely superfluous even in present-day society." The author then proceeds to outline a scheme of clearing-houses.

of metallic money or to further the ideal of equal opportunity for all.

The project was never successfully put into practice. Like the cognate ideas of 'the right to work,' 'the organization of labour,' and 'working men's associations,' the idea of 'free credit' has left behind it a mere memory of a sudden check.

On January 31, 1849, Proudhon, in the presence of a notary, set up a society known as the People's Bank, with a view to showing the practicability of free credit. The actual organization differs considerably from the theoretical outline of the Exchange Bank. The Exchange Bank was to have no capital: the People's Bank had a capital of 5,000,000 francs, divided into shares of the value of 5 francs each. The Exchange Bank was to suppress metallic money: the People's Bank had to be content with issuing notes against certain kinds of commercial goods only. The Exchange Bank was to suppress interest: the People's Bank fixed it at 2 per cent., expecting that it could be reduced to a minimum of $\frac{1}{4}$ per cent.

Despite these important changes the bank would not work. At the end of three months the subscribed capital was only 18,000 francs, although the number of subscribers was almost 12,000. Just at that moment—March 25, 1849—Proudhon was brought before the Seine Assize Court to answer for two articles published on January 16 and 27, 1849, containing an attack on Louis Bonaparte. He was sentenced to three years' imprisonment and fined 3000 francs. On April 11 he announced that the experiment would be discontinued, and that "events had already proved too strong for it," which seemed to suggest that he had lost faith in the scheme.

From that moment free credit falls into the background, and political and social considerations obtain first place in his later works.

IV: PROUDHON'S INFLUENCE AFTER 1848

It is extremely difficult to follow the influence of Proudhon's thought after 1848.

Karl Marx, who was almost unknown in 1848, became by the publication of his *Kapital* in 1867 practically the sole representative of theoretical socialism. Marx's *Misère de la Philosophie*,[1] published in 1847, is a bitter criticism of the *Contradictions économiques*, and shows how violently he was opposed to Proudhon's ideas. To the champion of collectivism the advocate of peasant proprietorship is scarcely

[1] A hit at Proudhon's *Philosophie de la Misère*, which was the sub-title of his *Contradictions économiques*.

comprehensible; the theorist of class war can hardly be expected to sympathize with the advocate of class fusion, the revolutionary with the pacificist.[1] The success of Marx's ideas after 1867 cast all previous social systems into the shade. Proudhon, he thought, was a mere *petit bourgeois.* When the celebrated International Working Men's Association was being founded in London in 1864 the Parisian workmen who took part in it seemed to be entirely under the influence of Proudhon. At the first International Congress, held at Geneva in 1866, a memorial was presented which bore clear indications of Proudhon's influence, and its recommendations were adopted. At the following Congress, in 1867, Proudhon's ideas met with a more determined resistance, and by the time of the Congress of Brussels (1868), and that of Basle (1869), Marx's influence had become predominant.

One might even doubt whether the Proudhonian ideas defended by the Parisian workmen in 1866 were really those of the Proudhon of 1848. They seemed much more akin to the thesis of his last work, *La Capacité politique des Classes ouvrières,* published in 1865. This book was itself written under the inspiration of a working men's movement which had arisen in Paris after 1862 as the result of a manifesto signed by sixty Parisian workmen. This manifesto had been submitted to Proudhon as the best-known representative of French socialism. The attitude of the French workmen at the opening of the "International," then, was the effect of a revival of Proudhonism as the outcome of the publication of this new volume rather than a persistence of the ideas of 1848.[2]

The revival was of short duration. Since then, however, the Marxian

---

[1] In a letter written to Karl Marx on May 17, 1846 (*Correspondance*, Vol. II, p. 199), *à propos* the expression "at the moment of striking," which Marx had employed, Proudhon takes the opportunity of declaring that he is opposed to all kinds of revolution. "You are perhaps still of opinion that no reform is possible without some kind of struggle or revolution, as it used to be called, but which is nothing more or less than a shock to society. That opinion I shared for a long time. I was always willing to discuss it, to explain it, and to defend it. But in my later studies I have completely changed my opinion. I think that it is not in the least necessary, and that consequently we ought not to consider revolution as a means of social reform. Revolution means an appeal to force, which is clearly in contradiction to every project of reform. I prefer to put the question in a different fashion, namely, How can we arrange the economic activities of society in such a fashion that the wealth which is at present lost to society may be retained for its use?" And in the *Confessions d'un Révolutionnaire,* p. 61: "A revolution is an explosion of organic forces, an evolution spreading from the heart of society through all its members. It can only be justified if it be spontaneous, peaceful, and gradual. It would be as tyrannous to try to suppress it as to bring it about through violence." See M. Bourguin's article on Proudhon and Karl Marx in the *Revue d'Économie politique,* 1893.

[2] On this point see Puech, *Proudhon et l'Internationale* (Paris, 1907); preface by M. Andler; and Maxime Leroy's introduction to the book *De la Capacité des Classes ouvrières* in the edition of his complete works published by Marcel Rivière (Paris, 1924).

ideas have been submitted to very thorough criticism, and many
twentieth-century French writers have displayed an entirely new interest in Proudhon's ideas. These writers, chief among whom is Georges
Sorel, combine a great admiration for Marx with a no less real respect
for Proudhon. The fact is that Proudhon, though commonly considered
a socialist, is above all else an individualist. We shall meet him again
in our chapter on the Anarchists. The fault he finds with liberalism
is that it could never bring liberty and equality *to every one*. The all-
powerful State remains for him the supreme danger in modern communities. In his *Théorie nouvelle de la propriété* he returns at the end of
his life to his earlier ideas, and regards property as "the greatest
revolutionary effort in existence that can put up an opposition to
power." "The State," he writes,

> though constituted in the most rational and the most liberal fashion
> and animated by the purest intentions, is none the less a mighty
> power, capable of wiping out everything around it if it is not given
> some counterweight. What is this counterweight to be? Where
> shall we find a power capable of counterbalancing this formidable
> might of the State? There is no other except property. Take the
> sum total of all the forces of property and you have a might equal
> to that of the State. (P. 137.)

Thus it is that "property, in its origin and nature a vicious and anti-
social principle, is yet destined to become by its very universality and
the co-operation of other institutions the pivot and mainspring of the
entire social system."

This social system is really nothing but generalized liberalism in
which the exchange of services will no longer be vitiated by the
monopolies and privileges that existing liberalism has neither prevented
nor opposed. This new liberalism, freed from the defects of the older
liberalism, is the system of 'mutualism,' in which each will receive a
value exactly equal to what he gives in exchange. Proudhon thus
remains the most impassioned and the most eloquent exponent of the
ideas of the French Revolution, whose principles he extends to the
whole of social life and not merely to the realm of politics. It is for
this reason that his prestige as a writer has continued to grow during
the last twenty years, so that writers belonging to parties to which he
was always hostile claim kinship with him. In this respect he remains
the most marked opponent of that State socialism which, as we shall
see in a later chapter, has at length won over almost every country
during the last half-century, and that finds its completest embodiment
in German National Socialism and Russian socialism.

Book III: Liberalism

It is time we returned to the Classical writers. Now that the combat had grown fierce among its critics, we are anxious to know what the Classical school itself was doing to repel the onslaughts of the enemy. Its apparent quiescence must not mislead us into the belief that it was already extinct. Although the great works of Ricardo, Malthus, and Say were produced early in the century, it cannot be said that economic literature even after that period, especially in England, had remained at a standstill. But no work worthy of comparison with the writings of the first masters or their eloquent critics had as yet appeared. Now, however, the science was to captivate the public ear a second time, and for a short period at least to unite its many votaries.

But the union was no true one. The Classical school itself was about to break up into two camps, the English and the French. In no sense can they be regarded as rivals, for they are defenders of the same cause. They are both champions of the twin principles of Liberalism and Individualism. But while the first, with John Stuart Mill as its leader, lent a sympathetic ear to the vigorous criticism now rampant everywhere, which claimed that the older theories ought to yield place to the new, the French school, on the other hand, with Bastiat as its chief, struggled against all innovation, and reaffirmed its faith in the 'natural order' and *laissez-faire*.

This divergence really belongs to the origin of the science. Traces of it may be discovered if we compare the Physiocrats with Adam Smith, or J. B. Say with Ricardo; but it was now accentuated, for reasons that we shall presently indicate.

Our third Book naturally divides itself into two parts, the one devoted to the French Liberal school, the other to the English.

CHAPTER I: THE OPTIMISTS

The previous Book has shown us the unsettled state of economic science. It has also indicated how the science was turned from its original course by reverses suffered at the hands of criticism, socialism, and interventionism, which were now vigorous everywhere. The time had come for an attempt to bring economic science back into its true path and to its old allegiance to the 'natural order,' a position which it had renounced since the days of the Physiocrats and Adam Smith. This was the task more specially undertaken by the French economists.

The attitude of the French school is not difficult to explain, for the French economists found themselves faced by both socialism and Protection. We must never forget that France is the classic land of socialism.[1] The influence exercised in England by Owen and in Germany by Weitling or Schuster is unworthy of comparison with the exalted role played by Saint-Simon, Fourier, or Proudhon in France. The latter writers wielded a veritable charm, not merely over working men, but also over the intellectuals, and on that account were all the more dangerous, in the opinion of economists.

French Protection was never represented by such a prominent champion as Germany had in List, but it was none the less active. Protection in England succumbed after a feeble resistance to the repeal movement led by Cobden, but in France it was powerful enough to resist the campaign inaugurated by Bastiat. It is true that Napoleon III suppressed it, but it soon reappeared, as vigorous as ever.

The French school had thus to meet two adversaries, disguised as one; for Protection was but a counterfeit of socialism, and all the more hateful because it claimed to increase the happiness of proprietors and manufacturers—of the wealthy; while socialists did at least aim at increasing the happiness of the workers—of the poor. Protection was also more injurious, for being in operation its ravages were already felt, whereas the other, happily, was still at the Utopian stage. But in hitting at both adversaries at once the French school discovered that it possessed this advantage: it was free from the reproach that it was serving the interests of a particular class, and could confidently reply that it was fighting for the common good.

A war of a hundred years can scarcely fail to leave a mark upon the nation which bears the brunt of it, and we think that this affords some explanation of the apologetic tendencies and of the normative and finalistic hypotheses for which the French school has so often been reproached.

It is necessary that we should try to understand the line of argument adopted by the French writers in defending the optimistic doctrines

[1] This fact is recognized even by German socialists themselves. "The people who gave socialism to the world even in its earlier forms have immortalized themselves," says Karl Grün, when speaking of France just about the time that our chapter refers to. (Quoted by Puech, *loc. cit.*, p. 57.)

which they so easily mistook for the science itself. They argued somewhat as follows:

"Pessimism is the great source of evil. The sombre prophecies of
the pessimists have destroyed all belief in 'natural' laws and in the
spontaneous organization of society, and men have been driven to seek
for better fortune in artificial organization. What is especially needed
to refute the attacks of the critics, both socialists and Protectionists, is
to free the science from the compromising attitude adopted by Malthus
and Ricardo, and to show that their so-called 'laws' have no real
foundation. We must strive to show that natural laws lead, not to
evil, but to good, although the path thither be sometimes by way of
evil; that individual interests are at bottom one, and only superficially
antagonistic; that, as Bastiat put it, if every one would only follow his
own interest he would unwittingly find that he was advancing the
interests of all." In a word, if pessimism is to be refuted it can only be
by the establishment of optimism.

It is true that the French school protests against the adjective
'optimistic,' and refuses to be called 'orthodox.' Its protests would be
justified if optimism implied quietism—that selfish contentment of the
well-to-do bourgeois who feels that everything is for the best in this
best of all worlds—or the attenuated humanitarianism of those who
think that they can allay suffering by kind words or good deeds. It
is nothing of the kind. We have already protested against interpreting
laissez-faire as a mere negation of all activity. It ought to be accepted
in the English sense of fair play and of keeping a clear field for the
combatants. The economists both of the past and of the present have
always been indefatigable wranglers and controversialists of the first
order, and they have never hesitated to denounce abuses. But their
optimism is based upon the belief that the prevalence of evil in the
economic structure is due to the imperfect realization of liberty. The
best remedy for these defects is greater and more perfect liberty;[1]
hence the title "Liberal," to which the school lays claim. The liberty
of the worker is the best guarantee against the exploitation of his
labour and the reduction of wages. M. Émile Ollivier, the author of
the law which suppressed combination fines, declared that freedom of
combination would put an end to strikes. Free loans would cause the
disappearance of usury. Freedom of trade would put an end to the
adulteration of goods and the reign of trusts. Competition would
everywhere secure cheap production and just distribution.[2]

---

[1] "So many things have we attempted! How is it that liberty, the easiest of all,
has never been given a trial?" (Bastiat, *Harmonies*, chapter ix, p. 125.)

[2] One of the sections of Dunoyer's *La Liberté du Travail* is entitled: "Of the True

This optimism, strengthened and intensified, deepened their distrust of every kind of social reform undertaken with a view to protecting the weak, whether by the masters themselves or through the intervention of the State. Liberty, so they thought, would finally remedy the evils which it seemed to create, while State intervention merely aggravated the evils it sought to correct.[1]

What seems still more singular is their scant respect for 'associationism' as outlined in our previous chapter. It found just as little favour as State control. They did not display quite the same contempt for it as was shown by the Revolutionists. It was no longer actually condemned, and they put forward a formal plea for the right of combination, in politics, in religion, industry, commerce, and labour. But they always interpreted it as a mere right of coalition or association with a view to protecting or strengthening individual activity. Association as an instrument of social transformation that would set up co-operation in place of competition, and which in the name of solidarity demanded certain sacrifices from the individual for the sake of the community, was not to the liking of the Liberal Individualist school. Even the less ambitious and less complete forms, such as the co-operative and the mutual aid society, seemed to them to be full of illusions and deceptions, if not actually vicious.[2]

The most striking characteristic of the French school is its unbounded faith in individual liberty. This distinctive trait has never been lacking throughout the century and a half that separates us from the time of the Physiocrats. Its most eminent representatives, while spurning the title Orthodox or Classical, have repeatedly declared that they wish for no other name than Liberal.[3]

Means of remedying the Evils from which the Workers suffer, by extending the Sphere of Competition." (Book IV, chapter x, para. 18.)

"As a matter of fact," says Dunoyer elsewhere, "this competition which seems such an element of discord is really the one solid bond which links together all the various sections of the social body."

[1] "Whenever the State undertakes to supply the wants of the individual, the individual himself loses his right of free choice and becomes less progressive and less human; and by and by all his fellow citizens are infected with a similar moral indifference." (Bastiat, *Harmonies*, chapter xvii, p. 545.)

[2] Dunoyer says: "You may search the literature of association as much as you like, but you will never come across a single intelligent discussion of an equitable means of distribution." (*Liberté du Travail*, Vol. II, p. 397.) Further, he asserts that association has damaged social even more than individual morality, because nothing will be considered lawful unless done by society as a whole. It is true that in this case he was speaking chiefly of corporative association, but the condemnation has a wider import.

[3] On the occasion of the international gathering of economists at the Paris Exposition in July 1900, Levasseur, one of the most moderate members of the Liberal school, said: "There is no need to draw any distinction between us. Liberal economists

It is also marked by a certain want of sympathy with the masses in their sufferings. Science, doubtless, does not make for sympathy. But what we merely wish to note is the presence of a certain tendency— already very pronounced in Malthus—to believe that people's misfortunes result from their vices or their improvident habits.[1] The Liberal school was quite prepared to extend an enthusiastic welcome to the teaching of Darwin. He pointed out that a necessary condition of progress was the natural selection of the best by the elimination of the incapable, and that the price paid is not a bit too high. Belief in the virtue of competition led to the glorification of the struggle for life.

But the Liberal school failed to demonstrate the goodness of all natural laws; neither did it succeed in arresting the progress of either socialism or Protection. The end of the nineteenth century found it submerged beneath the waters of both currents. Yet it never once lost confidence. Its fidelity to principle, its continuity of doctrine, its resolute, noble disdain of unpopularity, have won for it a unique position; and it deserves better than the summary judgment of foreign economists, who describe it as devoid of all originality, or at best as only a pale reflection of the doctrine of Adam Smith.

In this chapter we are to study the period when Liberalism and Optimism were at the height of their fame. It runs from 1830 to 1850. It was during this epoch that the union of political and economic liberty took place. Henceforth they are combined in a single cult known as Liberalism. Economic liberty—that is, the free choice of vocation and the free exchange of the fruits of one's toil—no longer figured in the category of necessary liberties, alongside of liberty of conscience or freedom of the Press. Like the others it was one of the successes already achieved by democracy or civilization, and to attempt to suppress it was as vain as to try to make a river flow backward. It was just a part of the wider movement towards freedom from all servitude.

The appearance of political economy at the time when the old regime was showing signs of disintegration is not without significance. The Physiocrats, who were the first Liberal Optimists, were unjustly

---

ought not to be divided in this way. There may be different opinions on the question of applying our principles, but we are all united on this question of liberty. A man becomes wealthy, successful, or powerful all the sooner if he is free. The more liberty we have, the greater the stimulus to labour and thought and to the production of wealth." (*Journal des Économistes*, August 15, 1900.)

[1] "It is a good thing to have a number of inferior places in society to which families that conduct themselves badly are liable to fall, and from which they can rise only by dint of good behaviour. Want is just such a hell." (Dunoyer, *La Liberté du Travail*, p. 409.)

ignored and neglected by their own descendants, not because of their economic errors so much as because of their political doctrines, especially their acceptance of legal despotism, which seemed to the Liberals of 1830, if not an actual monstrosity, at least a sufficiently typical survival of the old regime to discredit the whole Physiocratic system.[1]

Charles Dunoyer's book, which appeared in 1845,[2] and which bears the significant title of *De la Liberté du Travail, ou simple Exposé des Conditions dans lesquelles les Forces humaines s'exercent avec le plus de Puissance*, exactly marks this era of politico-economic Liberalism. But although Dunoyer's book is a eulogy of liberty in all its forms, especially its competitive aspects, the optimistic note is not so marked as it is in another much more celebrated work which appeared about the same date—*Les Harmonies économiques* of Bastiat (1850). The *Harmonies* and the other works of Bastiat contain all the essential traits of the Liberal doctrine. His extreme optimism and his belief in final causes have been disavowed by a great many of the Liberal economists, but he remains the best-known figure of the Optimistic Liberal group, and possibly of the whole French school.

Another economist whose name is inseparably linked with the Optimistic doctrine, and of whom we have already made some mention, is the American Carey.[3] In many respects Carey ought to be given first place, were it only because of his priority as a writer, and especially, perhaps, since he accuses Bastiat of plagiarism. In his treatment of certain aspects of the subject, such as the question of method, in the logical consistency of his argument, and in the scope

[1] See the discussion of the political doctrine of the Physiocrats, pp. 51 *et seq.*

[2] Editions of the same work appeared between 1825 and 1830; but the volume was much smaller and had a different title. Dunoyer will again engage our attention towards the end of this chapter. *Cf.* Villey, *L'Œuvre économique de Dunoyer* (Paris, 1899).

[3] Henry Charles Carey was born at Philadelphia in 1793, and died in 1879. Up to the age of forty-two he followed the profession of a publisher, retiring in 1835 to devote himself to economic studies. The three volumes of his *Principles of Political Economy* were issued in 1837, 1838, and 1840 respectively. In 1848 appeared *The Past, the Present, and the Future*, which contains his theory of rent. In 1850 his *Harmony of Interests, Agricultural, Manufacturing, and Commercial*, was published, and in 1858–59 his *Principles of Social Science*.

These dates possess some importance. At the time of the publication of the *Harmonies* in 1850 Carey wrote a letter to the *Journal des Économistes* accusing Bastiat of plagiarism. Bastiat, who was already on the point of death, wrote to the same paper to defend himself. He admitted that he had read Carey's first book, and excuses himself for not making any reference to it on the ground that Carey had said so many uncomplimentary things about the French that he hesitated to recommend his work. Several foreign economists have since made the assertion that Bastiat merely copied Carey, but this is a gross exaggeration. Coincidence is a common feature in literary and scientific history. We have quite a recent instance in the simultaneous appearance of the utility theory in England and France.

of his discussion of such a problem as that of rent, he displays a marked
superiority. In our exposition of Bastiat's doctrine we shall give to
Carey's the attention which it deserves. Our decision to give Bastiat
and not Carey the central position in this chapter is due in the first
place to the consideration that we are writing primarily for French
students, who will be more frequently called upon to read Bastiat than
Carey; and, in the second place, to the fact that the works of the
American economist appeared at a time when economic instruction
scarcely existed in the United States, and consequently his writings
never exercised the same influence as those of the French economist,
which appeared just when the war of ideas was at its fiercest. Finally,
Carey's doctrine is lacking in the beautiful unity of conception of the
Harmonies, so that alongside of the advocacy of free competition among
individuals is presented an outline of national Protection. Thus we
have been forced to divide our treatment of Carey into two sections.
The heterogeneous, not to say contradictory, character of his doctrines
accounts for his appearing in two different chapters.

Bastiat,[1] both at home and abroad, has always been regarded as
the very incarnation of bourgeois political economy. Proudhon,

[1] Frédéric Bastiat, born in 1801 near Bayonne, belonged to a family of fairly wealthy
merchants, and he himself became in turn a merchant, a farmer in the Landes district, a justice of the peace, a councillor, and finally a deputy in the Constituent
Assembly of 1848. He made little impression in the Assembly; but he scarcely had
time to become known there before his health gave way. He died at Rome in 1850,
at the age of forty-nine.

Brief as was Bastiat's life, his literary career was shorter still. It lasted just six
years. His first article appeared in the *Journal des Économistes* in 1844. His one book,
appropriately called *Les Harmonies économiques*, written in 1849, remains a fragment.
In the meantime he published his *Petits Pamphlets* and his *Sophismes*, which were aimed
at Protection and socialism. He was very anxious to organize a French Free Trade
League on the lines of that which won such triumphs in England under the guidance
of Cobden, but he did not succeed.

His life was that of the publicist rather than the scholar. He was not a bookworm,
although he had read Say before he was nineteen, and Franklin's *Poor Richard's
Almanac* soon afterwards. He was very enthusiastic about the merits of Franklin's
works, and Franklin's influence upon his writings, even upon his personal appearance
and behaviour, is very marked. "With his long hair, his small cap, his long frock-
coat, and his large umbrella, he seemed for all the world like a rustic on a visit to
town." (Molinari in the *Journal des Économistes*, February 1851.)

These biographical details should not be lost sight of, especially by those who
accuse him of lacking scientific culture and of being more of a journalist than an
economist.

Despite the fact that he has been severely judged by foreign economists, he is still
very popular in France. His wit is a little coarse, his irony somewhat blunt, and his
discourses are perhaps too superficial, but his moderation, his good sense, and his
lucidity leave an indelible impression on the mind. And we are by no means certain
that the *Harmonies* and the *Pamphlets* are not still the best books that a young student
of political economy can possibly read. Moreover, we shall find by and by that the
purely scientific part of his work is by no means negligible.

Lassalle, in his famous pamphlet *Bastiat Schulze-Delitzsch*, Cairnes, Sidgwick, Marshall, and Böhm-Bawerk all think of him as the advocate of the existing order. None of them considers him a scientific writer. They treat his writings as a kind of amplification of Franklin's *Poor Richard's Almanac*, where apologues take the place of demonstration and a much-vaunted transparency of style is simply due to absence of thought.

Bastiat deserves a juster estimate. The man who wrote that "if capital merely exists for the advantage of the capitalist I am prepared to become a socialist," or who declared that "one important service that still requires to be done for political economy is to write the history of spoliation," was not a mere well-to-do bourgeois. It is true that he carried the 'isms' of the French school to absurd lengths. An unkind fate decreed that his contribution should mark the culminating-point of the doctrine, to be followed by the inevitable reaction. To the force of that reaction he had to bow, and his whole work was demolished.

Bastiat's arguments against socialism are somewhat antiquated, but so are the peculiar forms of socialist organization which he had in view when writing. This is not true of the arguments dealing with Protection. These have not been entirely useless. Though they failed to check the policy of Protection, they definitely invalidated some of its arguments. If modern Protectionists no longer speak of the "inundation of a country" or of an "invasion of foreign goods," and if the old and celebrated argument concerning national labour is less frequently invoked as a kind of final appeal, we too often forget that all this is due to the small but admirable pamphlets written by Bastiat. Such were *The Petition of the Candle-makers* and *The Complaint of the Left Hand against the Right*. No one could more scornfully show the laughable inconsistency of tunnelling the mountains which divide countries, with a view to facilitating exchange, while at the same time setting up a customs barrier at each end; or expose the patent contradiction involved in guaranteeing a minimum revenue to the landed proprietors and capitalists by the establishment of protective rights, while refusing a minimum wage to the worker. No one has better emphasized the difficulty of justifying an import duty as compared with an ordinary tax, for a tax is levied upon the individual for the benefit of all, while a duty is levied upon all for the benefit of the few.

He has not been quite so happy in his exposition of individualism. The problem has been over-simplified: individual and international exchange have been treated as if they were on all fours. Analogies, more amusing than solid, are employed to show that the advantages of international trade are greater if a country has an unfavourable balance against it, and that international exchange benefits poor countries most.[1]

The thesis of the constructive portion of his work is as follows: "The general laws of the social world are in harmony with one another, and in every way tend to the perfection of humanity." *A priori*, however, are we not confronted with rank disorder everywhere? To that he replies in his well-known apologue, "Things are not what they seem," pointing out that we cannot always trust what we see, and that what is not seen is very often true. Apparent antagonisms on closer view often reveal harmonious elements. But man's freedom sometimes breaks the harmony and destroys the liberty of others. Especially is this the case with spoliation, which Bastiat never attempts to justify, but denounces whenever he has the chance. But around man and within him are diverse forces which must lead him the way of the good, deviate he never so often, and which will finally and automatically re-establish the harmony. "My belief is that evil, far from being antagonistic to the good, in some mysterious way promotes it, while the good can never end in evil. In the final reckoning the good must surely triumph."[2]

It is quite evident that this doctrine goes far beyond the conception of 'natural laws,' and implies a belief in a Providential order. Bastiat never shrinks from this position. He never misses an opportunity of declaring his faith in language much clearer than that of the Physiocrats. "God," he writes, "has placed within each individual an irresistible impulse towards the good, and a never-failing light which enables him to discern it."[3]

Auguste Comte has delivered an eloquent protest against the vain and irrational disposition to think that only the spontaneous can be regarded as conforming to the 'order' of nature. Were this the case any practical difficulty "that presented itself in the course of industrial development could only be met with a kind of solemn resignation under the express sanction of political economy."[4]

Even as an exposition of the Providential order Bastiat's faith is not

---

[1] On this question of who benefits by international trade see our discussion of Mill's treatment of the problem (pp. 369–370).

[2] *Harmonies*, p. 21. Our quotations are taken from the tenth edition of the *Œuvres complètes*.

[3] "Economic phenomena are not without their efficient cause and their Providential aim." (*Harmonies*, last page.)

"Looking at this harmony, the economist can join with the astronomer and the physiologist and say: *Digitus Dei est hic*." (*Ibid.*, chapter x, p. 39.)

"If every one would only look after his own affairs, God would look after everybody's." (*Ibid.*, chapter viii, p. 290.)

[4] Auguste Comte, *Cours de Philosophie positive*, Vol. IV, p. 202.

easy to justify. It by no means agrees with the Christian teaching on
the point. For we cannot forget that although Scripture teaches us
that both man and nature were declared good when first created by
God, it also teaches that both have been entirely perverted by man's
iniquity, and that never will they become good of their own accord,
since there is no natural means of salvation.[1] Christian people are
exhorted to kill the natural man within them and to foster the growth
of the new man. Christianity promises a new heaven and a new earth
—an infinitely more revolutionary doctrine than that of the economic
Optimists. Bastiat's God is, after all, just "*Le Dieu des bonnes gens*"
whose praises are sung by Béranger.

What are the facts of this pre-established harmony? What are its
laws, and where are they operative? They are in evidence everywhere,
Bastiat thinks—in value and exchange, in the institution of private
property, in competition, production and consumption, etc. We shall
content ourselves with a consideration of the circumstances under
which Bastiat thought it was most clearly seen.

I: THE THEORY OF SERVICE-VALUE

First of all we have the law of value, "which is to political economy
what numbers are to arithmetic."[2]

Ricardo taught that value was determined by the quantity of labour
necessary for production. This theory is entirely at one with Bastiat's,
and he would have felt no compunction about inserting it in the
Harmonies, for a theory of value which showed that every form of
property is really based upon labour seemed to accord with the requirements of justice. But although Bastiat's method was almost exclusively deductive, and as little realistic as possible, he could never
content himself with an explanation which was all too clearly in conflict with the facts. Such a theory could never explain why the value
of a pearl accidentally discovered should equal the value of another
laboriously brought from the depths of the sea. Accordingly he sought
another explanation, juster, and more in accordance with facts, than
Ricardo's.

Carey effected just the needed correction of the Ricardian theory,
by propounding another ingenious explanation, namely, that value is
determined, not by the quantity of labour actually employed in produc-

[1] The liturgy of the Reformed Church reads as follows: "We acknowledge and
confess our manifold sins." See our chapter on "Doctrines that owe their Inspiration
to Christianity" (pp. 514–544).
[2] *Harmonies*, chapter v, p. 140.

tion, but by the quantity of labour saved. This would account for
those facts that refused to fit in with the Ricardian theory, and the
chance pearl was no longer a stumbling-block. Bastiat was evidently
attracted by this theory.[1] But his satisfaction was by no means complete, for it is not quite clear how a value which is proportional to the
amount of lavour saved—that is, to labour which never has been and
never will be undertaken—can be considered as an economic harmony. But a ray of light illumines the darkness. The labour saved is
a kind of service rendered to the person who acquires the commodity.
The long-sought explanation is found at last! "Value is the ratio
between two exchanged services."[2] And, seeing that individual
property and private fortunes represent sums of values, we might say
that a person's property is merely the sum of the services rendered by
him. Herein lies the harmony. Nothing better could be wished for,
and Bastiat exults in his discovery. Everything becomes quite clear,
every contradiction is removed, every difficulty solved, if we take for
our starting-point the crux of economic theory—namely, why diamonds
are considered more valuable than water. The diamond is more
valuable simply because the person who gives it to me is rendering
me a greater service than he who merely gives me a glass of water.
This was not the case on the Medusan raft, but even in that instance,
seeing that the service rendered was incalculable, the value must have
been immense.

Every solution propounded by economists—utility, scarcity, difficulty of acquisition, cost of production, labour—is included within this
conception of service, and "economists of all shades of opinion ought
to feel satisfied." "My decision is favourable to every one of them,
for they have all seen some aspect of the truth; error being on the
other side of the shield."[3] Moreover, the word 'service' has the

[1] "I have attempted to show that value is based not so much upon the amount of
labour which a thing has cost the person who made it, as upon the amount of labour
it saves the persons who obtain it. [He ought to have acknowledged his indebtedness
to Carey in this matter.] Hence I have adopted the term 'service,' which implies
both ideas." (*Harmonies*, chapter ix, p. 341.)

[2] *Ibid.*, chapter v, p. 145.   [3] *Ibid.*, chapter v, p. 193.

"Socialists and economists, champions of equality and fraternity, I challenge you,
however numerous you may be, to raise even a shadow of objection to the legitimacy
of mutual service voluntarily rendered, and consequently against the institution of
private property as I have defined it. With regard to both these considerations, men
can only possess values, and values merely represent equal services freely secured
and freely given." (*Ibid.*, chapter viii, pp. 265, 268.)

Had the limits of this work permitted us to speak of the Italian economists we
should have had to refer to Ferrara, professor at Turin from 1849 to 1858, whose
theory of value and economic harmony link him to his contemporaries Carey and
Bastiat. The whole economic edifice, according to Ferrara, was built upon cost of
production. The value of a commodity is not measured by the amount of labour

advantage of including, besides value properly so called (that is, the price of goods), the price of all productive services such as appear under the heads of loans, rent, discount, and interest—in short, "everything that can be said to render a service."[1]

One cannot help smiling at Bastiat's naïve exultation, for he never realizes that his formula is so comprehensive and includes everything within itself simply because it is an empty form—a mere *passe-partout*. It really amounts to saying that value depends upon desirability, and we are not so much farther on after all.[2] On closer view, it even lacks that apologetic tone which evidently attracted Bastiat to it. It legitimizes neither value nor property, and even if it did it would simply be by the help of a hypocritical formula, for the word 'service' gives rise to the belief that all value implies a benefit for those who receive it and a virtue in those who give it. But very frequently it is nothing of the kind. The owner of a house or of a piece of land in the city of London which is let or sold at a fabulous price, the capitalist who lends money to a needy borrower at a usurious rate, or the politician even who in return for an enormous bribe secures some financial concession, cannot be said to be rendering any real service, for all these

which it really has cost to produce, but by the amount of labour that would be required to produce another similar commodity, or, if the commodity in question be absolutely limited in quantity, such as is the case with an old work of art, by the labour necessary to produce a new one that would satisfy the same need equally well —an application of the principle of substitution which had not been formulated when Ferrara wrote. The progress of industry gradually reduces the cost of labour and dispenses with human effort; hence harmony.

Everything, including the earth and its products, even capital, are subject to this same law, and a gradual diminution of rent and a lowering of the rate of interest are thus assured.

Ferrara's principal writings consist of prefaces to Italian translations of the works of the chief economists. They were published in a collection known as *Biblioteca dell' Economista* (Turin, 1850–70, 26 vols.).

[1] *Harmonies*, chapter vii, p. 236. The controversy between Bastiat and Proudhon in 1849 concerning the legitimacy of interest was published under the title of *Gratuité du Crédit*, but the argument is scarcely worth examining here. Bastiat's argument is based upon the supposition that the person who lends money performs some service or other, and that the service, whenever given, should be paid for; in other words, he maintains that capital is productive. A plane means more planks produced, and it is only just that the owner of the plane should get some of them. Proudhon replies that he does not deny the legitimacy of interest under present conditions, but that interest itself is just a historical category—to use a phrase that only became current after Proudhon's time—and that it will be quite unnecessary under the new regime. The Exchange Bank was to be the parent of the new order. The two combatants never really come to blows. They keep on arguing about nothing. The result is that this discussion is very trying and brings little honour to either.

[2] "The relative importance of any service must vary with the circumstances. This will depend upon its utility, and the number of people who are willing to give the amount of labour, of ability or training necessary to produce it, as well as the amount of labour which it will save us." (*Harmonies*, chapter v, p. 146.)

have either been solicited or demanded, or perhaps even extorted under pressure. Such abnormal rates of discount, interest, or rent can find no place in Bastiat's formula. From a moral and ethical point of view it is equally futile. It is a mere mask which affords protection as well to the worst exploiter as to the honest tradesman: all are thrown promiscuously into the 'universal harmony.'[1]

Despite the justness of these criticisms, and although Bastiat's attempt to explain value by employing the term 'service' must be regarded as futile, the word has not remained a mere ingenious epithet. On the contrary, it has won for itself a permanent place in economic terminology. We shall again meet with it in the vocabulary of that school which prides itself upon the exactness of its method, namely, the Hedonistic and Mathematical school. These later writers constantly make use of the term 'productive services,' and would find it hard to discover another word having a sufficiently wide connotation.[2] It is true that the word 'service,' with all the noble associations of unselfish interest and professional honour which cling to it (compare the phrase 'his Majesty's service'), may lead us astray as to the economic arrangements of society, and that a recollection of the less distinguished uses of the term may cause us to doubt the wisdom of Bastiat's choice. Still, it is the best that we can imagine when speaking of the society of the future. It is employed in the same sense as Auguste Comte used the term 'social function,' or as the equivalent of Marshall's 'economic chivalry.'[3] In attempting to present to ourselves the society of the future, or at least the society of our dreams, we must hope that the present incentive to economic activity, which is merely the desire for profit, will gradually give place to the idea of social service. When that day dawns a statue ought to be erected to the memory of Bastiat.

II: THE LAW OF FREE UTILITY AND RENT

Ricardo's law of rent was the optimist's nightmare. Should it by

---

[1] Bastiat himself was obliged to recognize this. "I have not taken the trouble to ask whether all these services are real and proper or whether men are not sometimes paid for services which they never give. The world is full of such injustices." (*Harmonies*, chapter v, p. 157.)

But if the world is full of people who are paid for services which they have never given or for merely imaginary and improper work, what is the use of speaking of value and property as if they were founded upon service rendered?

See Gide's article on *La Notion de la valeur dans Bastiat*, in the *Revue d'Économie politique*, 1887.

[2] J. B. Say had already employed the term 'service' without giving it any normative significance, simply using it to distinguish between wealth which consists of acts and wealth which consists of material products.

[3] *Social Possibilities of Economic Chivalry*, in *Economic Journal*, March 1907.

any chance prove true, then the institution of property must be abandoned altogether, and victory must lie with the socialists, whom the economists regarded as somewhat of a social nuisance. It was necessary, then, at all costs, to show that this law had in reality no foundation, and with this end in view Bastiat attempts to defend the paradox that nature or land gratuitously gives its products to all men. But must we really say that corn and coal, the products of soil and mine, literally do not pay for the trouble of getting them? In other words, have they no value? Bastiat replies that they doubtless possess some value, but that the price paid for them does not cover the natural utility of those products. It merely covers cost of production, and is only just sufficient to reimburse the proprietor for the expense incurred.

Every product contains two layers of superimposed utilities. The one is begot of onerous toil and must be paid for. It constitutes what we call value. The other, which is thrown into the bargain, is a gift of nature, and as such is never paid for. This lower stratum, though it is of considerable importance, is ignored simply because it is not revealed in price. It is invisible because it is free.

But when a commodity is free, like air, light, or running water, it is the common possession of everybody. The same idea may be expressed by saying that below the apparent layer of value which constitutes individual property there lies an invisible layer of common property which benefits everybody alike. "What Providence decreed should be common has remained so throughout the whole history of human transactions."

"This," says Bastiat, "is the essential law of social harmony." The proprietor, who in the Ricardian theory figures as a kind of dragon, jealously guarding the treasures of national wealth, which can only be enjoyed on payment of a fine, or who in Proudhon's passionate invectives is denounced as an interceptor of the gifts of God, appears to Bastiat as a mere intermediary between nature and consumer. He is like a good servant who draws water from a common fount, and receives payment, not for the water drawn, but solely for the trouble of drawing it.[1]

---

[1] "And I also declare that you have not intercepted any of the gifts of God. It is true that you received them free out of nature's hand. But it is equally true that you have handed them on freely, reserving nothing for yourself. Fear not, but live in peace and freedom from every qualm." (*Harmonies*, chapter viii, p. 257.)

"Coal is free for every one. There is neither paradox nor exaggeration in that. It is as free as the water of the brook, if we only take the trouble to get it, or pay others for getting it for us." (*Ibid.*, chapter x.) Bastiat would not regard the shareholders' dividends as payments for the trouble which the shareholders have taken in getting the coal. The dividends simply pay for the trouble taken to save the money which made the exploitation possible.

Say spoke of free natural agents. What he meant to refer to was such natural commodities as air and water, which are at the disposal of every one.

But there is a still greater degree of harmony. Of the two elements —the onerous and the gratuitous—which enter into the composition of all forms of wealth, the former gradually tends to lose its importance relatively to the latter. It is a general law of industry that as invention progresses the human effort necessary to obtain the same satisfaction diminishes. New labour is almost always more productive than old, and this is true with regard to all products, whether corn or coal, steel or cotton. It is true not only of the products of the land, but also of the land itself. The cost of clearing new land is diminishing, just as the expense of making new machinery is decreasing. The natural utility, on the contrary, is never diminished. Corn has to-day exactly the same utility as it had on the morrow of the Deluge.

Property being nothing more than a sum of values, every diminution of value must be interpreted as a constant restriction of the rights of property.

Hence this result, "which reveals a most important fact for the science, a fact, if I mistake not, as yet unperceived,"[1] namely, that in every progressive society common or gratuitous utility never stops growing, while the more arduous portion, which is usually appropriated, gradually contracts. Present society is already communistic, and is becoming more so every day.

The idea is indeed an attractive one. Individual property is like a number of islands surrounded by a vast communal sea which is continually rising, fretting their coasts and reducing their areas. When labour has become all-powerful and when science had dispensed with effort the last islet of property will sink beneath the wave of free utility. And so Bastiat triumphantly exclaims: "You communists dream of a future communism. Here you have the actual thing. All utilities are freely given by the present social order provided we facilitate exchange."[2]

Bastiat, usually so logical, seems inclined to be sophistical here. If we seek beneath this brilliant demonstration we shall merely find the statement that rent is non-existent because the value of commodities —including all natural products—can never exceed cost of production. This cost of production is being continually lowered, and so the value of goods must be falling.

But the statement requires proof. There is nothing to show how the price of natural goods under the influence of competition would tend to fall to the level of cost of production—still less to the minimum level. There is no refutation either of the differential or monopolistic theory of rent. There is doubtless this much truth in it: nature does

[1] *Harmonies*, chapter viii, p. 256. [2] *Ibid.*, chapter v, p. 142.

not create value, nor does it demand payment for it. No one would to-day say that a single cent of the price of corn or coal was meant as payment for the alimentary properties of the one or the calorific capacity of the other. But although it is true that nature asks nothing in return, it is not correct to say that the landowner demands nothing except payment for trouble and expenditure incurred. And this extra gain he never relinquishes unless under pressure of competition. But this very seldom happens, and economic theorists have to be content merely with showing how the sale price usually exceeds the cost of production, and how this excess is variously known as rent, profits, or surplus value.

Bastiat was fully conscious of the weakness of his argument. He saw quite clearly that possession of a suitable piece of land in the Champs-Élysées would earn something more than mere payment for labour and outgoings. It is then that he takes refuge in his theory of value, and attempts to show that the proprietor will never draw more than the price of the service rendered. This may be true. But the mere fact of possessing a natural source of wealth permits of the raising of the price of these goods a great deal, and then what becomes of community of interests, and of the theory that the goods are handed on by the proprietor free of any charge?

How superior is Carey's theory, both in its scientific value and in its social import! Carey follows Ricardo step by step, whereas it seems that Bastiat had only a very imperfect acquaintance with the Ricardian theory.[1] In reply to the statement that the value of corn rises progressively because the more fertile lands are occupied first, and the less fertile have to be utilized afterwards, Carey points out that, on the contrary, cultivation begins with the poorer land first, and that the richest is the last to be cultivated. The consequence is just the reverse of what Ricardo predicted. As production increases, the price of corn will be lowered. The process of reasoning by which this reversal of the order of cultivation is demonstrated is very interesting. The domestication of land, if the phrase be permissible, like the

---

[1] Bastiat does not seem to have studied rent. The chapter of the *Harmonies* on this subject was never completed. Fontenay, one of his disciples, wrote a brilliant book called *Du Revenu foncier* (1854), which is almost forgotten to-day. He attempted to show:

(1) That Ricardian or differential rent would not exist were all the land equally fertile and suitably cultivated.

(2) That it is incorrect to speak of the rent of natural fertility, as Adam Smith and the Physiocrats did, if all utility (and not merely value) is the product of human labour. A fish, a grape, a grain of wheat, a fat ox, all of them have been created by human industry. Nature is for ever incapable of doing this. This is quite true if we say nature alone, but it is equally true of labour taken by itself.

utilization of all natural forces, takes place according to the inverted order of their strength. Animals are domesticated before man harnesses wind or water, and water and wind are employed before there is any thought of vapour or electricity. The same is true of land. Fertile land in its natural state is either overrun with vegetation, which must be grubbed up, or is covered with water, which must be drained off. "Rich land is the terror of the emigrant."[1] Its virgin forests must be felled, its wild animals destroyed, its marshes drained, and its pestilential miasmas rendered innocuous if it is not to become a mere graveyard. And not until several generations have given of their toil will it be of much use. Rather than undertake the task the earliest emigrant seeks the lighter soils of the hill-side, which are better adapted to his feeble means, as well as safer and more easily defended.

That this theory is well founded may be very clearly seen if we watch the progress of cultivation or the colonization of new lands, or glance at the general history of civilization. Men group themselves in villages on the higher levels or build their castles on the slopes of the hills, and only descend slowly and carefully into the lower plains. How many are the localities in France where the new town may be seen overspreading the plain close to the old city which still crests the hill! The various national gods—Hercules, for example, who stifled the hydra of Lerna in his arms and shot the birds of Stymphalus's pool with his arrows—are in all probability just the men who first dared to break up the alluvial soils.

This theory, again, is open to the same objection as Ricardo's. It applies to some cases only, and under certain conditions. Ricardo's theory explained the facts relative to England, where population presses heavily upon the limited area of a small island already well occupied. Carey's theory is equally well adapted to an immense continent, with a thinly scattered population, occupying only a few cultivated islets amid the vast ocean of virgin forest and prairie. The two theories are not contradictory. They apply to two different sets of conditions, or to successive phases of economic evolution. And seeing that Ricardo's applies to the more advanced stage of civilization, it certainly ought to have the last word. If Carey were writing now he would probably express himself somewhat differently, for it is no longer true even of the United States that the more fertile lands are still awaiting cultivation. Only the poorer and the more arid plains remain uncultivated, and here dry farming has to be resorted to. So that even in the 'Far West' Ricardo's theory is closer to the facts than Carey's. Rents are

---

[1] Carey, *Principles of Social Science.*

rising everywhere, and not a few American millionaires owe their fortunes to this fact.[1]

It is just possible that Bastiat had some knowledge of Carey's theory, for the theory is outlined in *The Past, the Present, and the Future,* published by Carey a little before Bastiat's death, as well as in his *Social Science,* which appeared ten years later. At any rate, let us render thanks to both of them for the suggestive thought that as human power over nature increases, effort, difficulty, and value, which is the outcome of difficulty, will disappear, and that, consequently, the sum total of real wealth at the disposal of every one will increase, but that the poor will be those who will benefit most.[2]

III: THE RELATION OF PROFITS TO WAGES

The law of rent was not the only discordant note. That other law which stated that profits vary inversely with wages was also dissonant and needed refuting. Bastiat emphasizes the contrast between it and his new law of harmony, according to which the interests of capital and labour are one, their respective shares increase together, and the proportion given to labour grows more rapidly even than capital's.[3]

That is the conclusion which Bastiat wishes to illustrate by means of the following table:

	Total Product	Capital's Share	Labour's Share
First period	1000	500 (50 per cent.)	500 (50 per cent.)
Second period	2000	800 (40 „)	1200 (60 „)
Third period	3000	1050 (35 „)	1950 (65 „)
Fourth period	4000	1200 (30 „)	2800 (70 „)

This law he speaks of as "the great, admirable, comforting, necessary, and inflexible law of capital."

The proof is very simple—too simple, perhaps. It rests entirely upon the law concerning the lowering of the rate of interest, noted by Turgot and other economists long before Bastiat's time. If capital, instead of asking 5 per cent., only demands 3 per cent., then its share

[1] Even in Algeria, for example, where Carey's theory was at first true, now that the fertile plain of the Mitidja has been cultivated by two generations of colonists it is certain that there is only second-class land available.

[2] "Wealth consists of the right to command the services of nature, which are always free." (Carey, *Principles of Social Science,* Vol. I, chapter xiii.)

"As man's power over nature grows, his power over his fellow-men seems to dwindle and equality becomes possible." (*Ibid.,* Vol. III, p. 122.)

Compare, for example, the relative equality of comfort enjoyed by those who travel by rail irrespective of class distinctions (which are only to be found in some countries) with the former method of travelling by post-chaise.

[3] "Capitalists and workers, don't look at one another with an air of defiance and vengeance!" (*Harmonies,* p. 252.)

is diminished, and any further diminution of its share must mean an increase of the proportion available for labour.

But a *relative* diminution of this kind will not prevent capital drawing an *absolutely* greater share, provided the total produce goes on increasing, as is the case in every progressive community. Its total share, though on the increase, may be decreasing relatively to the share which goes to labour. For example, the total product may be tripled, capital's share having doubled in the meantime, while labour's portion is quadrupled. Unfortunately this is a purely sophistical argument. The figures given in the table are simply invented to meet the needs of the case. Even the universality of the law concerning the lowering of the rate of interest is open to dispute. Economic history seems to point to a series of periodic oscillations of the rate, and quite recently it has risen very considerably.

The so-called 'law' becomes more than doubtful if, following Bastiat, we include under the term interest, not merely net interest, but also profits and dividends and all kinds of returns from capital.

But, even admitting that such a law is thoroughly established, does that prove that capital's share is decreasing? A lowering of the rate of interest cannot affect the capital already invested in factories, mines, railways, State funds, etc. The latter will not draw a penny less, and a fall in the rate of interest will increase the value of all old capital. Every capitalist knows this and speculates on the chance of its happening.[1]

Only in the case of new capital, then, will a lower rate of interest reduce the capitalist's share. If by any chance this new capital should prove less productive than the old it may then happen that the reduced rate of interest will mean an equal or even a greater rise in the remuneration of labour. This is quite a probable contingency, and the proof advanced by economists who believe in a gradual lowering of the rate of interest is just this very fact that new capital is generally less productive than old.

In short, the problem presented by the rate of interest, implying as it does a certain connexion between the value of the capital and the value of the revenue, is entirely different from the question as to what share of the produce will eventually fall to the lot of the capitalist and what to the workers.[2]

[1] A lowering of the rate of interest from 5 to 3 per cent. means that what formerly cost £60 and yielded 3 per cent. will now cost £100. There is no decrease of the revenue and there is an increase in the capital. It is quite a good bargain. A lowering of the rate of interest will simply reduce the amount of capital in those instances where the borrower can effect a conversion to his own advantage.

[2] This truth is so obvious that Rodbertus, as we shall see by and by, took the opposite point of view and attempted to argue on the strength of the "iron law" that

Not only is the demonstration which Bastiat thought he had given false, but the thesis itself is very doubtful when tested by the facts. Statistics seem to show quite clearly—Bastiat's law notwithstanding, and not depreciating the influence of other powerful factors, such as trade unions, strikes, and State intervention—that during the course of the nineteenth century the share of the social revenue which falls to the lot of capital has increased more rapidly than labour's.[1]

IV: THE SUBORDINATION OF PRODUCER TO CONSUMER

Bastiat laid considerable stress upon this principle, but it is not easy to realize its harmonic significance.

The subordination of producer to consumer is nothing less than the subordination of private to general interest. Producers always consult their own interests, and are continually in search of profits. Still, everything invented with a view to increasing profits results in lowering prices, so that the consumer is the person who finally benefits by it.[2] And so economic laws, the law of competition and of value, constrain the producer who really wishes to be selfish to be altruistic, even despite himself. The laws outwit him, but his undoing benefits every one else. While working for a maximum profit he is really toiling to satisfy the needs of others in the most economical fashion, and therein lies the harmony.

In all difficult economic problems the criterion should be this: What solution will prove most advantageous to consumers? Never ought we ask what will be most profitable for producers, although, unfortunately, this is the more usual question. In matters of international trade, when the interest of the producer is uppermost, Protection is established. If we only consulted the interest of consumers, Free Trade would become an immediate necessity. Or take the case of public or private expenditure. The producer can bring himself to

---

capital's share is always increasing, while labour's is decreasing. This thesis seems to have no better foundation than the other. See an article by Rist entitled *Deux Sophismes économiques*, in the *Revue d'Économie politique* for March 1905.

Bastiat's thesis may also be seen in Carey. The Liberal school has clearly adopted it. See Paul Leroy-Beaulieu's *Répartition des Richesses*.

[1] See Gide's *Political Economy*, p. 599 (English translation), and Colson's *Political Economy*, Vol. III, p. 366. According to Colson, capital's share has quadrupled since 1820, while labour's has only increased in the proportion of 1 : 3½.

[2] "Just as the earth is the great reservoir of electricity, so the public or the consumer is the one source of any gain or loss which the producer makes or suffers. Everything comes back to the consumer. Consequently every important question must be studied from the consumer's point of view if we want to get hold of its general and permanent results." (*Harmonies*, chapter xi, p. 414.)

excuse or even to approve of breaking windows or wasting powder,[1] but the consumer unceremoniously condemns all such destruction of wealth as useless consumption.

But Bastiat is not content with giving the consumer mere economic pre-eminence. He is equally anxious to demonstrate his moral superiority. "If humanity is to be perfected, it must be by the conversion of consumers, and not by the moralizing of producers,"[2] and so, he holds consumers responsible for the production of unnecessary or worthless commodities, such as alcohol.[3] Bastiat's contribution to this subject is quite first-class, and may possibly be his best claim to a place among the great economists. He was not far wrong when on his deathbed he delivered to his disciples as his last instructions—his *novissima verba*, "Political economy should be studied from the consumer's standpoint." This distinguishes him from his famous antagonist, Proudhon, who always had the producer's interest at heart.

The only things with which we can reproach Bastiat are a too persistent faith in natural harmonies and a belief in the efficacy of ordinary economic laws to bring about the supremacy of the consumer. In fact, the consumer's reign has not yet come, and the economic mechanism is becoming more and more the tool of the profit-maker. The consumer has had to seek in organization a method of defending his own interests and those of the public, with whose interests his own are often confused. This is why we have institutions like the co-operative society and the consumers' league. His moralization, moreover, is not entirely his own affair. Before the consumer realizes the full measure of his responsibility and the extent of his duties a great deal of work will be necessary on the part of buyers' social leagues, temperance leagues, etc.

Strangely enough, economists of the Liberal Individualist school view such institutions with a somewhat critical eye.[4]

V: THE LAW OF SOLIDARITY

We must not forget, as most writers on the subject seem to have done, that Bastiat was the first to give the law of solidarity—so popular in the economics of to-day—a position of honour within the science of political economy.[5] One of the unfinished chapters of the *Harmonies*,

[1] See one of Bastiat's best-known pamphlets, *La Vitre cassée*.
[2] *Harmonies*, chapter vi, p. 419.
[3] Quoted by his friend Paillottet in his preface to the *Œuvres complètes*.
[4] *E.g.*, Yves Guyot in the *Journal des Économistes* for 1904 *et passim*. See p. 326.
[5] The word is not his invention. That honour is claimed by Pierre Leroux. See p. 246.

M

entitled "Solidarity," was meant to expound the thesis that "society is just a collection of solidarities woven together."[1]

The name is deceptive, however, and his conception of solidarity is quite different from the one current to-day, while the conclusions drawn are by no means similar.

The fundamental doctrine upon which the Solidarists of to-day would base a new morality is briefly this: Every individual owes all the good with which he is endowed, and all the evil with which he is encumbered, to others. So whether he is wealthy or poor, virtuous or vicious, it is his duty to share with those who are worse off, and he has a right to demand a share from those who are better off. Only in this way can we justify legal assistance, insurance, Factory Acts, education, and taxation. The doctrine is a negation, or at the very least a modification, of the strict principle of individual responsibility.

But Bastiat views it differently. He has no desire to weaken individual responsibility, for responsibility must be the indispensable corrective of liberty. And solidarity, because of the feeling of interdependence to which it gives rise, is so bewildering that Bastiat anxiously asks whether solidarity is actually necessary "in order to hasten or to secure the just retribution of deeds done." A closer survey reconciles him to the prospect, for he sees in it a means of extending and deepening individual responsibility. Seeing that the results of good and bad deeds react upon every one, everybody must be interested in furthering every good deed and in repressing the bad, especially since every deed reacts upon its author with its original force multiplied a thousand, and perhaps a million times.[2] The harmony just consists in that. Bastiat's solidarity aims, not at the development of fraternity, but at the strengthening of justice. It does not urge upon society the duty of permitting no differences among its members, but it does emphasize the importance of handling the scourge or bestowing the palm with greater impartiality. And Bastiat, despite his law of solidarity—nay, possibly *because* of that very law— definitely rejects all legal assistance, even in the case of deserted children! National insurance, old age pensions, profit-sharing, free

[1] *Harmonies*, chapter xxi, p. 624.
"There is not a man living whose character has not been determined by a thousand factors entirely beyond his control." (*Ibid.*, p. 623.)
"All profit by the progress of the one, and the one by the progress of the many." (*Ibid.*, chapter xi, p. 411.)
[2] "Solidarity implies a kind of collective responsibility. And so solidarity as well as responsibility is a force that makes for progress. It is a system that is admirably calculated to check evil and to advance the good." (*Ibid.*, chapter xxi, pp 622–626.)

education, everything that is comprised under the term 'social solidarity' is cast aside.[1]

It is a terribly individualistic conception of solidarity. Comparison
with Carey's ideas is again interesting. Carey may seem to ignore it
altogether, inasmuch as he never mentions the name. But if the name
was unknown to him he gave a good description of the principle itself
when he referred to it as "the power of association." And he was also
probably the first to put the double character of solidarity, as we
know it to-day, in a clear light:

(1) As the differences among mankind increase in number and
intensity the more perfect will solidarity become.

(2) Individuality, instead of being weakened by it, is strengthened
and intensified.[2]

Some one may perhaps point out that in our treatment of the
Optimists' attack upon the great Classical laws no mention has been
made of that terribly discordant theme, Malthus's law of population,
which ascribes all vice and misery to the operation of a natural instinct.
On this particular point Bastiat's treatment is lacking in both vigour
and originality. His reply merely amounts to showing that the preventive obstacles, such as shame and continence, religious feeling and the
desire for equality, all of which limit the number of children, are equally
natural, so that nature has placed a remedy alongside of the evil.

A more solid argument, borrowed from Carey, attempts to show
how a growing density of population allows of a growth of production,
so that the production of commodities may develop *pari passu* with the
growth of population, or may even exceed it. Carey relied upon his
own observations. All over the vast American continent, especially on
the immense plains of the Mississippi, he noticed that the few encamp-
ments of the poor tribes that dwelt there were being rapidly replaced

[1] "Workers must understand that these collective funds [pension funds] must be
voluntarily contributed by those who are to have a share in them. It would be quite
unjust, as well as anti-social, to raise them by means of taxation—that is, by force—
from the classes who have no share in the benefits." (*Harmonies*, chapter xiv, p. 471.)

"A peasant marries late in the hope of having a small family, and we force him to
rear other people's children. He has to contribute towards the rearing of bastards."
(*Ibid.*, chapter xx, pp. 617, 618.)

Speaking of sharing in the benefits, he remarks: "That is really not worth talking
about." (*Ibid.*, chapter xiv, p. 457.)

[2] "Organisms in nature have their rank and degree of perfection determined by
the number of organs which they possess and the amount of difference which exists
between each of them." (*Social Science*, Vol. III, p. 461.)

"Life has been defined as an exchange of mutual obligations, but if there were no
difference between the various objects how could the exchange take place?" (*Ibid.*,
Vol. I, pp. 54–55.)

"The more perfectly co-ordinated the whole is, the better developed will be each of
its parts." (*Ibid.*, Vol. III, p. 462.)

by large industrial centres. Such an increase of population in immediate contiguity naturally resulted in a great amassing of wealth.

We have already noted the fact that the growth of wealth in the
United States has outstripped the increase in its population. The
simultaneous development of Germany, both in numbers and wealth,
is still more striking.

But Carey's population theory is open to the same criticism as was
urged against his theory of rent. Up to a certain degree of density it
is undoubtedly true, but there is no ground for believing that it holds
good beyond this.

Bastiat's name is frequently linked with Dunoyer's, to whom we
have already had occasion to refer.[1] Dunoyer was one of the most
militant of the politico-economic Liberals, and fully shared their
belief that free competition was a sufficient solution for every social
problem.[2] The obvious drawbacks of free competition, he thought,
were due to its imperfect character. No one was more opposed to
State Socialism and to intervention of every kind. He was opposed
to labour legislation, to Protection, to the regulation of the rights of
property, and even to the State management of forests. As we have
already remarked, he was against every kind of combination, because
it stood as an obstacle in the path of free competition.

Logically enough he was in favour of the free disposal of land, and
would not even make any reservations in favour of heirs. He refuses
to recognize the right of entail because the exercise of the testator's
liberty necessarily involves the curtailment of the liberty of his
successors.[3]

Some of the arguments which he employs in support of free exchange are quite novel. The following is one of the most interesting.
Admitting that it is not to the advantage of a poor country to trade
with another which is wealthier or industrially superior, the same thing
must apply to the poorer districts of a country in their dealings with

---

[1] Charles Dunoyer was Bastiat's senior. The first edition of *De la Liberté du travail*,
to which we have already referred, dates from 1825, and the last edition from 1845.
He took an active part in opposing the Restoration Government, but he became
prefect and subsequently Conseiller d'État under Louis Philippe.

[2] Molinari, a modern French economist, holds similar views.

[3] If a person died intestate Bastiat was in favour of equal division of wealth. The
arguments which he employed are very interesting, especially those directed against
the upholders of primogeniture. They thought that by depriving the younger sons of
their inheritance they became more industrious and thoughtful. Dunoyer replies by
asking whether it would not be an advantage to deny the right of succession to the
eldest son as well, "for it is obviously unfair that he should be deprived of that kind
of training which is so profitable to his younger brothers." Dunoyer forgot that it
would have gone ill with his arguments if the socialists had taken him at his word.

other provinces that have suddenly become rich, or with rich
provinces recently acquired by conquest. But "as soon as they
are annexed their superiority presumably disappears." The argument is amusing, but not very solid. It is not impossible that free
exchange, even within the bounds of the same country, may have the
effect of drawing capital and labour from the poorer districts towards
the richer, from Creuse or Corsica to Paris. This is just what does
happen. It is not, perhaps, a very serious evil, because what France
loses on the one hand she gains on the other; but if Creuse or Corsica
were independent states, anxious to preserve their individuality, we
could understand their taking measures to prevent this drainage. It is
true that it is not easy to see how protective rights could accomplish
this—a point which Dunoyer might well have emphasized.

We cannot speak of Dunoyer without saying a word about his
theory of production. Labour with him is everything. Nature and
raw material are nothing. He stands at the opposite pole to the
Physiocrats,[1] and supplied a handle to those socialists who before
Marx's day had thought that labour was the only source of wealth,
and that consequently all wealth should belong to the worker. But he
pays no very great attention to this idea. His chief concern is with
production, and not with distribution.

From this view of production he draws several interesting conclusions.

In the first place, it matters little to him whether labour is applied
to material objects or not. That makes no difference, so far as its
character or productivity is concerned, for in both cases what is produced is an immaterial thing called utility. What the baker produces
is not bread, but the wherewithal to satisfy a certain desire. This is
exactly what the *prima donna* produces. The so-called liberal professions are placed in the same category as manual work, and in this
respect again Dunoyer takes up a position opposed to that of the
Physiocrats.[2]

[1] "Labour is the only source of productive power. Capital is a human creation,
and land is simply a form of capital." (*De la Liberté du Travail*, Book VI.)

[2] Say had already recognized the claims of immaterial wealth alongside of material,
and he had employed the term 'services' in describing them. In this way he considered that the professor, the doctor and the actor had claims to be regarded as
producers. Dunoyer, while accepting his conclusion, criticizes his way of putting it.
He recognizes no distinction between material and immaterial wealth. There is
nothing but utility. "It is true that taste, education, etc., are immaterial, but so is
everything that man produces." But he is entirely wrong when he says that a good
teacher is a producer of enlightened men and a doctor a producer of healthy persons.
We are at a loss to explain why at one moment he refuses to recognize the material
element in production, while at another he grossly exaggerates the material results of
purely intellectual labour.

Contrary to what might have been expected, this large extension of the concept production fails to include commerce. Dunoyer applies the title productive to the singer, but refuses it to the merchant, and by this strange reversal he arrives once again at the Physiocratic position. Exchange is not productive[1] because buying and selling does not involve any work, and where there is no work there is no production. Exchange creates utilities, and it is not easy to understand what more Dunoyer expects from it, seeing he admits that labour can do nothing more. Exchange, he thought, was a purely legal transaction, and he was loath to admit that any act of a 'corporate will' without labour or physical effort could create wealth, just as the Physiocrats found it impossible to think of wealth other than as a product of the soil.

CHAPTER II: THE APOGEE AND DECLINE OF THE CLASSICAL SCHOOL. JOHN STUART MILL

WHILE the French economists, alarmed at the consequences involved in the theories of Malthus and Ricardo, strove to transmute the Brazen laws into Golden ones, the English economists pursued their wonted tasks, never once troubled by the thought that they were possibly forging a weapon for their own destruction at the hands of socialists.

The thirty years which separate the publication of Ricardo's *Principles of Political Economy* (1817) from Mill's book bearing the same title are occupied by economists of the second rank, who apply themselves, not to the discovery of new principles, but to the development and co-ordination of those already formulated. Of course we must not lose sight of the mass of critical work bearing upon certain aspects of current doctrines, which was produced by English economists just about this time. But their ideas attracted as little attention as did Cournot's in France or Gossen's in Germany.[2]

These were the days when Miss Martineau and Mrs Marcet gave expositions of political economy in the form of tales, or conversations

---

[1] "Labour and exchange belong to two categories of facts which are absolutely distinct in their nature. Labour implies production. Commerce and exchange imply nothing of the kind." (*De la Liberté du Travail*, p. 599.)

[2] Seligman in the *Economic Journal* for 1903, pp. 335 and 511, devotes two very interesting articles to such writers under the title of *Some Neglected British Economists*. One is astonished to find how many there are and the originality which they show, and to learn that several of the more important modern theories are simply rediscoveries.

with "young Caroline,"[1] when MacWickar, writing his *First Lessons in Political Economy for the use of Elementary Schools*, expressed the belief that the science was already complete. "The first principles of political economy," he wrote, "are mere truisms which children might well understand, and which they ought to be taught. A hundred years ago only savants could fathom them. To-day they are the commonplaces of the nursery, and the only real difficulty is their too great simplicity."[2]

We cannot attempt the individual study of all the economists of this period.[3] However, one of them, Nassau Senior,[4] certainly deserves more space than we can give him in this history, and is perhaps the best representative of the Classical school, showing its good and bad points better than any other writer. He removed from political economy every trace of system, every suggestion of social reform, every connexion with a moral or conscious order, reducing it to a small number of essential, unchangeable principles. Four propositions seemed sufficient for this new Euclid,[5] all necessary corollaries being easily deducible from one or other of these. Senior's ambition was to make an exact science of it, and he deserves to be remembered as one of the founders of pure economics.

He is responsible for the introduction into political economy of a new and hitherto neglected element, namely, an analysis of abstinence, or saving. (The former word, which is Senior's choice, is the more striking and precise term.) It is true enough, as Senior remarks, that abstinence does not create wealth, but it constitutes a title to wealth, because it involves sacrifice and pain just as labour does. Hitherto the income of capital had been the least defensible of all revenues, for Ricardo had only discussed it incidentally, and had represented it as a surplus left over after paying wages. The claim of capital was believed to be as evident as that of land or labour, and there was no need for

---

[1] Mrs Marcet's *Conversations* belong to 1817, Miss Martineau's *Illustrations* to 1832. The latter had a wonderful vogue.

[2] Quoted by Seager in a lecture on economics at Columbia University in 1908.

[3] We have already referred to McCulloch and James Mill, two of Ricardo's immediate disciples. We must just add the names of Torrens and Gibbon Wakefield. Wakefield was the author of a book which had a great reputation at one time, but which was simply an attempt to apply the Ricardian principles to the practice of colonization.

[4] Nassau Senior during a part of his life was Professor of Political Economy at Oxford. The Oxford chair, created in 1825, was the first chair of economics to be established in England. His writings, which treat of various subjects, belong to the period 1827–52. The bulk of his doctrine is contained in his *Political Economy*, contributed to the *Encyclopædia Britannica* in 1836 and afterwards published separately. This small volume may be regarded as the earliest manual of political economy.

[5] The four principles were (i) the Hedonistic Principle; (ii) the Principle of Population; (iii) the Law of Increasing Returns in Industry; (iv) the Law of Diminishing Returns in Agriculture.

any further inquiry. But has it any real right to separate remuneration, seeing that, unlike the other two agents, it is itself a product of those two and not an original factor of production? Here at last is its title, not in labour, but in abstinence.

But if on the one hand Senior succeeds in establishing the claim of interest, he invalidates the claim of most other capital revenues on the other. Let us follow his argument. Cost of production is made up of two elements, labour and abstinence, and wherever free competition obtains, the value of the products is reduced to this minimum. Where competition is imperfect, where there is a greater or less degree of monopoly, then between cost of production and value lies a margin which constitutes extra income for those who profit by it. This revenue by definition of labour and abstinence is independent of every sacrifice or personal effort. This revenue Senior calls rent, and his theory is thus a mere extension of the Ricardian. Rent is not the result of appropriating the better situated or the more fertile lands only. It may be due to the appropriation of some natural agent or to the possession of some personal quality such as the artiste's voice or the surgeon's skill,[1] or it may simply be the result of social causes or fortuitous circumstances. Senior shows that rent, far from being an exceptional phenomenon, is really quite normal. This kind of revenue which is wanting in title—drawn, but not earned—is extremely important, and absorbs a great share of the total wealth. Indeed, Senior goes much further, and states that whenever, as in the case of death, capital passes from the hands of those who have earned it into the possession of others, it immediately becomes rent. The inheritor cannot plead abstinence—the virtue is not transmissible, and he has no title to his fortune except just good luck.[2]

---

[1] "But a considerable part of the produce of every country is the recompense of no sacrifice whatever; is received by those who neither labour nor put by, but merely hold out their hands to accept the offerings of the rest of the community." (*Political Economy*, p. 89.) He takes the income of a successful doctor as an illustration, and divides it up as follows (*ibid.*, p. 189):

Wages or payment for labour	. . .	£40
Profit or payment for abstinence	. .	£960
Rent	. . . .	£3000

See *Senior's Theory of Monopoly*, by Richard Ely (American Economic Association 1899).

[2] This confusion between rent and the income of inherited wealth does little honour to Senior, for the two facts belong to entirely different categories. Rent is a purely economic phenomenon, resulting from the necessary conditions of exchange. It owes nothing to social organization, not even to the institution of private property. Inheritance, on the other hand, is a purely juridical phenomenon, the product of civil law. Even if inheritance were abolished it would make no difference to the existence and growth of rent, whether obtained from the soil or from some other source; whereas under the hypothetical regime of perfectly free competition, although rent would no

No revolutionary socialist could ever have invented a better argument for the abolition of the existing order. And how different from the 'natural order'! But Senior is quite unmoved, and the superb indifference with which economists of the Ricardian school affirm their belief in their doctrines without taking any account of the consequences which might uphold or might destroy those very beliefs has a peculiar scientific fascination for us.

Also, it was Senior who laid stress upon scarcity as the basis of economic value. But a thing to possess value must be not merely rare, it must also satisfy some want. It must be a rare utility. It is the same term, 'scarcity,' that was employed by Walras.

The Classical doctrines were taught during the first half of the nineteenth century, not in England alone, but in every country of the world. In Germany they were expounded by von Thünen, of whom we have already spoken, and by his contemporary Rau.[1] In France, despite the growing influence of the optimistic politico-liberal creed considered in our last chapter, English Classical economics was still taught by a large number of economists, among whom Rossi deserves special mention. His *Cours d'Économie politique*, published in 1840, enjoyed a fair success, due, not to any originality in the contribution itself, but to the somewhat oratorical style of the work.[2]

But to proceed to the central figure of this chapter—John Stuart Mill.[3] With him Classical economics may be said in some way to

---

longer be known, inheritance, together with all its privileges, might still continue to exist. Senior evidently understands by the term 'rent' any kind of income that is not obtained by personal effort. But this is clearly a perversion of the original meaning.

[1] Rau's treatise on political economy belongs to the years 1826–37, and von Thünen's *Der Isolirte Staat* appeared in 1826.

[2] Pellegrino Rossi, who became a naturalized Frenchman in 1833, was an Italian by birth. He succeeded Say as professor at the Collège de France. He afterwards became Lecturer on Constitutional Law, and his name is commemorated in one of the annual prizes. He eventually entered the diplomatic service, and was attached to the Papal See during the pontificate of Pius IX. He was assassinated at Rome in 1848.

[3] John Stuart Mill, born in 1806, was the son of James Mill the economist of whom we have already spoken. The system of education which his father planned for him can only be described as extraordinary. Practised on anyone else it would have been fatal. At the age of ten he was already well versed in universal history and in the literatures of Greece and Rome. At thirteen he had a fair grasp of science and philosophy, and had written a history of Rome. By the time he was fourteen he knew all the political economy that there was to know then. In 1829, then a young man of twenty-three, he published his first essays on political economy. In 1843 appeared his well-known *System of Logic*, which immediately established his fame. In 1848 he issued the admirable *Principles of Political Economy*. Mill was in the service of the East India Company up to the time when it lost its charter in 1858. From 1865 to 1868 he was a member of the House of Commons. After the death of his wife, who collaborated with him in the production of several of his works, especially *Liberty* (1859),

have attained its perfection, and with him begins its decay. The middle of the nineteenth century marks the crest of the wave. What makes his personality so attractive is his almost dramatic appearance, and the consciousness that he was placed between two schools, even between two worlds. To the one he was linked by the paternal ties which bound him to the Utilitarian school, wherein he was nurtured; the other beckoned him towards the new horizons that were already outlined by Saint-Simon and Auguste Comte. During the first half of his life he was a stern individualist; but the second found him inclined to socialism, though he still retained his faith in liberty. His writings are full of contradictions; of sudden, complete changes, such as the well-known *volte-face* on the wages question. Mill's book exhibits the Classical doctrines in their final crystalline form, but already they were showing signs of dissolving in the new current.

Like other theorists of the 'Pure' school, he declared that there was no room in political economy for the comparative judgment of the moralist, but it was he also who wrote:

> If, therefore, the choice were to be made between communism with all its chances and the present state of society with all its sufferings and injustices; if the institution of private property necessarily carried with it as a consequence that the produce of labour should be apportioned as we now see it, almost in an inverse ratio to the labour—the largest portions to those who have never worked at all, the next largest to those whose work is almost nominal, and so in a descending scale, the remuneration dwindling as the work grows harder and more disagreeable, until the most fatiguing and exhausting bodily labour cannot count with certainty on being able to earn even the necessaries of life; if this or communism were the alternative, all the difficulties, great or small, of communism, would be but as dust in the balance.[1]

It was Mill the utilitarian philosopher who declared that a person of strong conviction "is a social power equal to ninety-nine who have only interests." It was he also who wrote that "competition may not be the best conceivable stimulus, but it is at present a necessary one, and no one can foresee the time when it will not be indispensable to progress." But he also admits that "co-operation is the noblest ideal," and that it "transforms human life from a conflict of classes struggling for opposite interests to a friendly rivalry in the pursuit of a good common to all."[2]

---

being unwilling to quit the spot where she lay buried, he spent the last years of his life, except those taken up by his Parliamentary work, at Avignon. His autobiography contains a precious account of his life and of his gradual conversion to socialistic views.

[1] *Principles*, Book II, chapter i, para 3.   [2] *Ibid.*, Book IV, chapter vii, para. 7.

Mill, it has been said, was simply a gifted popular writer. But this is to under-estimate his ability. It is true that, unlike Ricardo, Malthus, or Say, his name is not associated with any economic law, but he opened up a wider prospect for the science which will secure him a reputation long after the demise of these so-called laws. His fame is doubly assured, for in no other work on political economy, not excepting even the *Wealth of Nations*, are there so many pages of fine writing, so many unforgettable formulæ which will always be repeated by every one who has to teach the science. It is not for naught that the *Principles* has served as a text-book for so long in many of the English universities.

Before examining the changes in the Classical doctrines which Mill himself effected, we must give a brief outline of those theories as they appeared in all their inflexible majesty towards the middle of the nineteenth century, during the period between the publication of the *Principles* and the death of John Stuart Mill, between 1848 and 1873. This was the period when the Classical Liberal school believed that its two old rivals, Protectionism and socialism, were definitely crushed. Reybaud, in his article on socialism in the *Dictionnaire d'Économie politique* of 1852, wrote as follows: "To speak of socialism to-day is to deliver a funeral oration." Protection had just been vanquished in the struggle that led to the repeal of the English Corn Laws, and was to suffer a further check, alike in France and in the other countries of Europe, as a result of the treaties of 1860. The future lay with the Classics. It was little thought that 1867 would witness the publication of *Kapital*, that in 1872 the Congress of Eisenach would reassemble, when the treaties of 1860 would be publicly denounced.

Let us profit by its hour of glorious existence to give an exposition of the doctrines which it taught. The treatment must necessarily be very summary, seeing that we are not writing a treatise on political economy, and that our attention must be confined to writers who are definitively members of the Liberal school.

I: THE FUNDAMENTAL LAWS

A belief in natural laws was always an article of faith with the Classical school. Without some such postulate it seemed to them that no collection of truths, however well attested, could ever lay claim to the title of science. But these natural laws had none of that 'providential,' 'finalistic,' and 'normative' character so frequently dwelt upon by the Physiocrats[1] and the Optimists. They are simply natural

[1] Dupont de Nemours, writing very much in the spirit of the Classical school, had

laws like those of the physical order, and are clearly non-moral. They may prove useful or they may be harmful, and men must adapt themselves to them as best they can. To say that political economy is a "dismal science" because it shows that certain laws may have unfortunate results is as absurd as it would be to call physics a "dismal science" because lightning kills.

Far from being irreconcilable with individual liberty, these laws are among its direct results. They are the spontaneous links which bind together all free men. Freedom is always subject to conditions. Men are not free in the matter of eating or not eating, and if they would eat they *must* cultivate the soil. Freedom is limited not only by the actions of other human beings, but also by the laws of the physical world which surrounds us.

These laws are universal and permanent, for the elementary needs of mankind are always and everywhere the same. Economics is in quest of such permanent laws, and has no concern with the merely temporary. It is only by seeking the more general and consequently the more nearly universal laws that economics can apprehend truth or hope to become a science. It must study man, not men—the type, not the individual—the *homo œconomicus* stripped of every attribute except self-interest. It does not deny the existence of other qualities, but merely relegates them to the consideration of other sciences.

It now remains to see what those natural laws were.

(1) *The Law of Self-interest.* This law has since been named the Hedonistic principle—a term that was never employed by the Classical school. Every individual desires well-being, and so would be possessed of wealth. Similarly he would, if possible, avoid evil and escape effort. This is a simple psychological law. Could anything be more universal or permanent than this law, which is simply the most natural and the most rational (using the term in its Physiocratic sense) statement of the law of self-preservation? In virtue of this fundamental principle the Classical school is frequently known as the Individualist school.

But individualism need imply neither egoism nor egotism. This confusion, which is repeatedly made with a view to discrediting the Classical writers, is simply futile. No one has displayed greater vigour in protesting against this method of treating individualism than Stuart Mill. To say that a person is seeking his own good is not to

---

already given an excellent definition of natural law. "By natural law we are to understand those essential conditions that regulate all things in accordance with the design laid down by the Author of Nature. They are the 'essential conditions' to which men must submit if they would obtain all the benefits which the natural order offers them." (Introduction to Quesnay's works, p. 21.)

imply that he desires the failure of others. Individualism does not
exclude sympathy,[1] and a normal individual feels it a source of
gratification whenever he can give pleasure to others.

But this did not prevent Ricardo and Malthus from showing the
numerous instances in which individual interests conflict, where it is
necessary that one interest should be sacrificed to another. And Mill,
far from denying the existence of these conflicts, has taken special pains
to emphasize them. The Classical writers, together with the Optimists,
reply that such contradictions are apparent only, and that beneath
these appearances there is harmony; or they point out that these
antinomies are due to the fact that both individualism and liberty
are only imperfectly realized, and as yet not even completely understood, but that as soon as they are securely established the evils which
they have momentarily created will be finally healed.[2] Liberty is like
Achilles's lance, healing the wounds it inflicts. Other individualists,
such as Herbert Spencer, declare that the conflict of individual interests
is not merely advantageous to the general interests of society, but is
the very condition of progress, weeding out the incapable to make
room for the fittest.

(2) *The Law of Free Competition.* Admitting that each individual is
the best judge of his own interests, then it is clearly the wisest plan to
let every one choose his own path. Individualism presupposes liberty,
and the Individualist school is also known as the Liberal school. This
second title is more exact than the first, and is the only one which
the French school will accept. It emphatically repudiates every other,
whether Individualist, Orthodox, or Classical.[3]

[1] Adam Smith, let us remember, also wrote a book on the *Theory of Moral Sentiments*
(see Book I, chapter ii), and Stuart Mill writes as follows: "In the golden rule of
Jesus of Nazareth we read the complete spirit of the ethics of utility. To do as you
would be done by and to love your neighbour as yourself constitute the ideal perfection of utilitarian morality." (*Utilitarianism*, chapter ii.)

[2] This is how Mill views it: "It is only in a very imperfect state of the world's
arrangements that anyone can best serve the happiness of others by the absolute
sacrifice of his own. (*Utilitarianism*, chapter ii.) But it is scarcely necessary to add,
seeing that the two propositions are necessarily complementary, that one of the best
ways of securing happiness is to sacrifice one's self in the cause of others. All that is
required is a little patience. "Education and opinion will so use that power as to
establish in the mind of every individual an indissoluble association between his
happiness and the good of the whole." Interpreted in this way, individualism is closely
akin even to the most transcendent form of solidarity.

[3] One is sometimes asked to state the differences between the Classical, the Individualist, the Liberal, and the Optimist schools. The question does not seem to us
to be a very important one, but we may answer it in this way:

(a) The Individualist school, according to the worst interpretation put upon it,
thinks that egoism is the only possible system of ethics and that each for himself is
the sole principle of action. But, naturally enough, every one is anxious to avoid the
taunt of selfishness, and the existence of such economic ties as exchange and division

The English school is equally decisive in its preference for 'Liberalism.' The terms 'Manchesterism' and 'Manchesterthum' have also been employed, especially by German critics, in describing this feature of their teaching.

But the Classical school itself thought of *laissez-faire* neither as a dogma nor a scientific axiom. It was treated merely as a practical rule which it was wise to follow, not in every case, but wherever a better had not been discovered. Those who act upon it, in Stuart Mill's opinion, are nearer the truth nineteen times out of twenty than those who deny it.[1] This practical Liberalism is intended to apply to every aspect of economic life, and their programme includes liberty to choose one's employment, free competition, free trade beyond as well as within the frontiers of a single country, free banks, and a competitive

---

of labour make egoism impossible as an ethical system. According to the broadest interpretation of the term, individualism implies the recognition of individual welfare as the sole aim of every activity, whether individual or social, economic or political. But this does not take us very far, for every socialist and individualist would accept this interpretation. We seldom speak of the welfare of society *per se* as an entity possessed of conscious feeling. This definition is much too wide. It includes solidarity and association, State intervention and labour legislation, provided the aim be to protect the individual against certain dangers. Self-sacrifice is not excluded, for what can strengthen individualism like self-sacrifice? This is the interpretation which Schatz puts upon it in his *L'Individualisme économique et social*. But the term 'individualist' is too indefinite and we must avoid it whenever we can.

(*b*) The so-called Liberal school uses the term in a much more definite fashion. The individual is to be not merely the sole end of economic action, but he is also to be the sole agent of the economic movement, because no one else can understand his true interests or realize them in a better way. Interpreted in this fashion, it means letting the individual alone and removing every external intervention, whether by the State or the master.

According to the one definition, individualism is a creed which every one can adopt; according to the other it is open to very serious objections. Experience shows that the individual, whether as consumer buying injurious, costly, or useless commodities, or as worker working for wages that ruin his health and lower his children's vitality, is a poor judge of his own interest, and is helpless to defend himself, even where science and hygiene are on his side.

(*c*) If we push this interpretation a stage farther and admit not only that each individual is best qualified to speak for himself, but also that the social interest is simply the sum of the individual interests, all of which converge in a harmonious whole, then the Liberal school becomes the Optimistic. In France it has the tradition of a generation behind it, and an attempt has been made to revive it in certain recent works; still it may now be regarded as somewhat antiquated.

(*d*) When we speak of the Classical school we mean those who have remained faithful to the principles enunciated by the earlier masters of economic science. An effort has been made to improve, to develop, and even to correct the older theories, but no attempt has been made to change their essential aspects. Individualistic and liberal by tradition, this school has never been optimistic. It lays no claim to finality of doctrine or to the universality of its aim, but simply confines itself to pure science.

[1] *Auguste Comte and Positivism.*

rate of interest; and on the negative side it implies resistance to all
State intervention wherever the necessity for it cannot be clearly
demonstrated, as in the case of protective or parental legislation.

In the opinion of Classical writers, free competition was the sovereign
natural law. It was sufficient for all things. It secured cheapness for
the consumer, and stimulated progress generally because of the rivalry
which it aroused among producers. Justice was assured for all, and
equality attained, for the constant pursuit of profits merely resulted in
reducing them to the level of cost of production. The *Dictionnaire
d'économie politique* of 1852, which may perhaps be considered as the
code of Classic political economy, expressed the opinion that competition is to the industrial world what the sun is to the physical. And
Stuart Mill himself, the author of *Liberty*, no longer distinguishing
between economic and political liberty, in less poetic but equally con-
clusive terms states that "every restriction of competition is an evil,"
but that "every extension of it is always an ultimate good."[1] On this
point he was a stern opponent of socialism, although in other respects
it possessed many attractions for him. "I utterly dissent," says he,
"from the most conspicuous and vehement part of their teaching, their
declamations against competition."

But the Classical school, despite its glorification of free competition,
never had any intention of justifying the present regime. The complaints urged against it on this score, like the similar charge of egoism,
are based upon a misconception. On the contrary, the Classics, both
new and old, complain of the imperfect character of competition.
Senior had already pointed out what an enormous place monopoly
still holds in the present regime. A regime of absolutely free competition is as much a dream as socialism, and it is as unjust to judge
competition by the vices of the existing order as it would be to judge
of collectivism by what occurred in the State arsenals.

(3) *The Law of Population* also held an honourable place among
Classical doctrines, so honourable, indeed, that even the Optimists
never dared contradict it. And of all economists Mill seems most
obsessed by it.[2] In his dread of its dire consequences he surpasses
Malthus himself. And he reveals a far greater regard for moral considerations than was ever shown by the latter. Mill was already a
Neo-Malthusian in the respect which he felt for the rights and liberty
of women, which are too seldom consulted when maternity is forced

[1] *Principles*, Book IV, chapter vii, para. 7 (Ashley's ed., p. 793). See the work of
Molinari, or *La Morale de la Concurrence*, by Yves Guyot.
[2] "It is in vain to say that all mouths which the increase of mankind calls into
existence bring with them hands. The new mouths require as much food as the old
ones and the hands do not produce as much." (*Principles*, Book I, chapter xi, para. 2.)

upon them.[1] A numerous family appeared to him as vicious and
almost as disgusting as drunkenness.[2] Time and again he declares
that the working classes can hope for no amelioration of their lot
unless they check the growth of population. One reason for his
favourable view of peasant proprietorship is the restraint which it
exercises upon the birth-rate. "The rate of increase of the French
population is the slowest in Europe," he writes, and this result he
thought very encouraging.

To exorcize this terrible demon he would even sacrifice the principle
of liberty which everywhere else he is at so much pains to defend. He
was prepared to support a law to prohibit the marriage of indigents,[3]
a proposal to which Malthus was absolutely opposed. His plea for
this measure of restraint is expounded, not in the *Principles*, but in
another of his works entitled *Liberty*. It is, of course, possible that
Liberty may owe something to the collaboration of Mrs Stuart Mill.

(4) *The Law of Demand and Supply*—the law that determines the
value of products and of productive services, such as labour, land, and
capital—is usually stated in the following terms: Price varies directly
with demand, inversely with supply. One of the most important
contributions which Mill made to the science was to show that this
apparently mathematically precise formula was merely a vicious circle.
If it be true that demand and supply cause a variation of price, it is
equally true that price causes a variation of demand and supply.
Mill corrects the dictum by saying that price is fixed at a margin
where the quantity offered is equal to the quantity demanded. All
price variations move about this point, just as the beam of a balance

---

[1] "It is seldom by the choice of the wife that families are too numerous; on her
devolves (along with all the physical suffering and at least a full share of the priva-
tions) the whole of the intolerable domestic drudgery resulting from the excess."
(*Principles*, Book II, chapter xiii, para. 2.)

[2] "While a man who is intemperate in drink is discountenanced and despised by
all who profess to be moral people, it is one of the chief grounds made use of in appeals
to the benevolent that the applicant has a large family and is unable to maintain
them." (*Ibid.*, Book II, chapter xiii, para. 1.) "Little improvement can be expected
in morality, until the producing large families is regarded with the same feelings as
drunkenness or any other physical excess. But while the aristocracy and clergy are
foremost to set the example of this kind of incontinence what can be expected of the
poor?" (*Ibid.*, Ashley's ed., p. 375, note.)

He complains that the Christian religion inculcates the belief that God in His
wisdom and care blesses a numerous family.

[3] "The laws which in many countries on the Continent forbid marriage unless
the parties can show that they have the means of supporting a family, do not exceed
the legitimate powers of the State. They are not objectionable as violations of
liberty." (*Liberty*, chapter v.)

On the other hand he thought that a law which limited the number of public-
houses involved a violation of liberty because it meant treating the workers as children.
(*Ibid.*, chapter v.)

oscillates about a point of equilibrium.[1] He thus gave to the law of demand and supply a scientific precision which it formerly lacked, and by substituting the conception of equilibrium for the causal relation he introduced a new principle into economics which was destined to lead to some important modifications.

The law of demand and supply explains the variations of value, but fails to illuminate the conception of value itself. A more fundamental cause must be sought, which can be found in cost of production. Under a regime of free competition the fluctuations in value tend towards this fixed point, just as "the sea tends to a level; but it never is at one exact level."[2]

A temporary, unstable value dependent upon the variations of demand and supply, a permanent, natural, or normal value regulated by cost of production, such was the Classical law of value. Mill was entirely satisfied with it, as will be seen from the following phrase, which seems rather strange, coming from such a cautious philosopher. "Happily," says he, "there is nothing in the laws of value which remains for the present or any future writer to clear up; the theory of the subject is complete."[3]

The law which regulates the value of goods applies also to the value of money. Money also has a temporary value, determined by the quantity in circulation and the demand for it for exchange purposes —the celebrated quantity theory. But it also has a natural value, determined by the cost of production of the precious metals.

(5) *The Law of Wages.* A similar law determined wages—the price of hand-labour. Here again is a double law. Temporary wages depend upon demand and supply—understanding by supply the quantity of capital available for the upkeep of the workers, the wages fund, and by demand the number of workers in search of employment.[4] This law was more familiarly expressed by Cobden when he said that wages rose whenever two masters ran after the same man, and fell whenever two men ran after the same master.

---

[1] "The rise or the fall continues until the demand and supply are again equal to one another: and the value which a commodity will bring in any market is no other than the value which in that market gives a demand just sufficient to carry off the existing or expected supply." (*Principles*, Book III, chapter 2, para. 4.)

Cournot in his criticisms of the law of demand and supply had anticipated Mill. But it is very probable that Mill was not acquainted with the *Recherches*.

[2] *Principles*, Book III, chapter iii, para 1.

[3] *Ibid.*, Book III, chapter i, para. 1.

[4] "Wages depend, then, on the proportion between the number of the labouring population and the capital or other funds devoted to the purchase of labour, and cannot under the rule of competition be affected by anything else." (*Ibid.*, Book II, chapter xi, Parts I and III.)

Natural or subsistence wages in the long run are determined by the cost of production of labour—by the cost of rearing the worker. The oscillations of temporary wages always tend to a position of equilibrium about this point.

This "brazen law," as Lassalle calls it, well deserves its title. According to it wages depend entirely upon causes extraneous to the worker, and bear no relation either to his need or to the character of his work or his willingness to perform it. He is at the mercy of a fatalistic law, and is as helpless to influence his market as a bale of cotton. And not only is the law independent of him, but no intervention, legal or otherwise, no institution, no system, can alter this state of things without influencing one or other of the two terms of the equation, the quantity of capital employed as wages—the wage fund—or the numbers of the working population in search of work. "Every plan of amelioration which is not founded upon this principle is quite illusory." Only by encouraging the growth of capital by means of saving, or by discouraging the growth of population and restraining the sexual instinct, can the terms of the equation be favourably modified. Upon final analysis there are only two chances of safety for the workers, and of these the first is beyond their power,[1] while the second means the condemnation to celibacy or onanism of all proletarians, as they are ironically called.

And thus Mill, who formulated the law with greater rigour than any of his predecessors, found himself alarmed at its consequences. He was specially impressed by the courageous but impotent efforts of trade unionism, then at the beginning of its career. Mill and the economists of the Liberal school were as strongly in favour of the removal of the Combination Laws as they were persistent in their demands for the repeal of the Corn Laws; but of what use was the right of association and combination when a higher law frustrated every attempt to raise wages? Just at this time Longe, writing in 1866, and Thornton, in his volume on *Labour*, began to question the validity of the wage fund theory. They experienced no difficulty in converting John Stuart Mill, who followed with his famous recantation in the pages of the *Fortnightly*. His defection caused a remarkable stir, and was thought almost an offence against the sacred traditions of the Classical school. The conversion was not quite complete, however, for the last edition of the *Principles* still contains the passages we have already quoted, as well

[1] Saving with a view to augmenting the wage fund is only possible for the rich, and Mill is as insistent upon their doing it as he is upon the workers refraining from marriage. He also tries to impress upon the workers the importance of saving, but his way of showing its advantages is often laborious and obscure.

as others equally discouraging to the working classes, and equally fatal to the hopes which they had reasonably placed in their own efforts.[1]

The wage fund theory, though badly shaken as a result of Mill's defection, was not abandoned by all the Classical writers, and some American publications later attempted a revival of it.[2]

(6) *The Law of Rent.* The law of competition tends to reduce the selling price until it is equal to the cost of production. But suppose, as is often the case, that there are two costs of production, which of the two will determine the price? The higher will be the determinant, and so there exists a margin for all similar products whose cost of production is less. Ricardo showed that this was the case with agricultural products as well as with certain manufactured goods.[3] Mill included personal ability, and though the conception of rent was thus very considerably extended, it had not the scope which it had with Senior.

(7) *The Law of International Exchange.* According to the Liberal economists Ricardo and Dunoyer (see p. 352), international trade is subject to the laws regulating individual exchange, and the results in the two cases are almost identical, namely, a saving of labour to both parties. One party exchanges a product which has cost fifteen hours' labour for another which, had an attempt been made to produce it directly, would have involved a labour of twenty hours. The gain is

[1] Stuart Mill admitted that trade unions might modify the relations between demand and supply, forgetting for the moment that this meant a contradiction of the Classical theory.

The unions might limit the number of available men. He feared that this would result in high wages for the small number of organized labourers and in low wages for the others. They might check the birth-rate, their members becoming accustomed to such a degree of comfort and well-being as would raise their standard of life. He was always a strict Malthusian.

[2] See the quarterlies of Harvard and Columbia. It was an American, however, Francis Walker, in his *Wages Question* (1876), who did more than anyone to destroy the old wage fund theory.

[3] "The cost value of a thing means the cost value of the most costly portion of it." (*Principles*, Book II, chapter vi, para 1, prop. 7.)

"The extra gains which any producer or dealer obtains through superior talents for business or superior business arrangements are very much of a similar kind. If all his competitors had the same advantages, and used them, the benefit would be transferred to their customers through the diminished value of the article: he only retains it for himself because he is able to bring his commodity to market at a lower cost while its value is determined by a higher." (*Ibid.*, Book III, chapter v, para. 4.)

Senior had already emphasized one important difference between agricultural and industrial production, namely, that while the law of diminishing returns operates in the former case, the law of increasing returns is operative in the second. In other words, the cost of production diminishes as the quantity produced increases. The result is, as Mill points out elsewhere, that the industrial employer is anxious to reduce the sale price in order to produce more and to recoup himself for a reduction in price by a reduced cost of production.

credited to the importing side, for exportation is merely the means whereby it is obtained. Its measure is the excess of the imported value over the value exported.

It is clear that each party gains by the transaction. It is not quite clear, nor is it altogether probable, that the advantages are equally distributed. But it is generally believed that if any inequality does exist the greater gain goes to the poorer country—to the one that is less gifted by nature or less fitted for industrial life. The latter country by very definition would experience great difficulty in attempting the direct production of the imported goods, and would even, perhaps, find it quite impossible. On this point the English Classical or the Manchester school is in complete agreement with the French school.[1]

It might possibly be pointed out that under a regime of free competition all values would be reduced to the level of cost of production, and products would be exchanged in such a fashion that a given quantity of labour embodied in one commodity would always exchange for an equal quantity embodied in any other. But in such a case where would be the advantage of exchanging? Ricardo had already anticipated this objection, and had shown that if the rule of equal quantity in exchange for equal quantity were true of exchange between individuals, it did not hold of exchange between different countries, for the equalizing action of competition no longer operated, because of the difficulty of moving capital and labour from one to the other. A comparison should be made, not of the respective costs of the same product in the two countries, but of the respective costs of the imported and the exported products in the same country. Another buttress to strengthen the theory which measures the advantages of international commerce by the amount of labour economized![2]

[1] Ricardo, moreover, gives an exposition of the advantages of international trade in terms that Bastiat might have adopted. "Under a system of perfectly free commerce each country naturally devotes its capital and labour to such employments as are most beneficial to each. This pursuit of individual advantage is admirably connected with the universal good of the whole. By stimulating industry, by rewarding ingenuity, and by using most efficaciously the peculiar powers bestowed by nature, it distributes labour most effectively and most economically: while by increasing the general mass of productions it diffuses general benefit and binds together, by one common tie of interest and intercourse, the universal society of nations throughout the civilized world. It is this principle which determines that wine shall be made in France and Portugal, that corn shall be grown in America and Poland, and that hardware and other goods shall be manufactured in England." (Ricardo, *Works*, p. 75.)

[2] The following apparent paradox may be deduced from Ricardo's theory. A country is wise in importing not only those commodities which it can only produce at a disadvantage as compared with its rivals, but also those goods in which it has a distinct advantage in the matter of production, though not so great as the advantage enjoyed in some other case. Under those circumstances it is better that it should

But the value of the exchanged product is still undetermined. It lies somewhere between the real cost of production of the goods exported and the virtual cost of production of the goods imported, in such a way that each country gains something. That is all we are able to say. Mill has gone a step farther. He has abandoned the comparison of costs of production, which is purely abstract, and can afford no practical measure of the advantages, preferring to measure the value of the imported product by the value of the product which must be given in exchange for it.[1] We require to find the causes that enable a country like England to obtain a greater or a lesser quantity of wine in exchange for her coal. In other words, the law of international values no longer involves a comparison of costs of production, but is simply the law of demand and supply. The prices of the two goods arrange themselves in such a fashion that the quantities demanded by the respective countries exactly balance. If there is a greater demand for coal in France than there is for wine in England, England will obtain a great quantity of wine in exchange for her coal, and will consequently find herself in a very advantageous position.

Mill's theory[2] constitutes a real advance as compared with Ricardo's, for it affords a means of gauging the strength of the foreign demand, and of judging of the circumstances favourable to a good bargain. Mill was of the opinion that a poor country stood to benefit most by the transaction—thus confirming Bastiat's belief. A rich country will always have to pay more for its goods than a poor one.[3]

---

produce that product in the making of which it has the greater advantage and exchange it for some other product in which it has less.

"Two men can both make shoes and hats, and one is superior to the other in both employments; but in making hats, he can only exceed his competitor by one-fifth, or 20 per cent., and in making shoes he can excel him by one-third, or 33 per cent. Will it not be for the interest of both that the superior man should employ himself exclusively in making shoes, and the inferior man in making hats?" (Ricardo, *Political Economy*, chapter vii, para. 47, note.)

And so England might find it advantageous to exchange her coal for French cloths, although she may be able to produce those cloths cheaper herself. In Book VI we shall see how this theory was developed and transformed.

[1] "The value of a thing in any place depends on the cost of its acquisition in that place; which in the case of an imported article means the cost of production of the thing which is exported to pay for it." (*Principles*, Book III, chapter xviii, para. 1.)

[2] Mill first treated of the theory in his *Unsettled Questions of Political Economy*. A more complicated but more precise exposition is given in the *Principles*, Book III, chapter xviii, para 7. The whole process of reasoning, based as it is upon the hypothetical conduct of two persons, is purely abstract, and is of very little practical use. What is really important is to know the relation between the advantages gained by either side. It is true that on the whole imports and exports balance one another, thanks to the operation of money, but that is another question. (We shall examine it in Book VI.)

[3] "It still appears, that the countries which carry on their foreign trade on the most

Protectionists affect the opposite belief, holding that it is the poor country that is duped. The English trade with Portugal is one of their favourite illustrations. But it is simply an illustration, and it can never take the place of actual proof.

Notwithstanding these divergent views, Mill is more sympathetic to the Protectionists than any other economist of the Liberal school. His theory provides them with at least one excellent argument. Seeing that the advantages of international commerce depend upon demand and supply, a country may make it operate to its own advantage by merely pursuing a different policy. New industries might be developed whenever there is a considerable demand for new products, and that demand might easily be so considerable that the price would be lowered.

Besides this, Mill makes an important concession to the Protectionists when he shows that import duties are not always paid by the consumer in the form of higher prices, but may in certain cases be paid by the foreigner, notably when the imported product, such as rare and high-priced wines, enjoys a monopoly price.[1]

Finally, though Mill remained faithful to Free Trade, he resembled List (whom he did not know) in accepting Protection for infant industries, imposed "in hopes of naturalizing a foreign industry, in itself perfectly suitable to the circumstances of the country." But he makes one reservation, that "the protection should be confined to cases in which there is good ground of assurance that the industry which it fosters will after a time be able to dispense with it." That, he says, is "the only case in which, on mere principles of political economy, protecting duties can be defensible." In truth, however, this "only case" opens the door very wide to a very large measure of Protection.[2]

The Free Trade doctrine has not remained where it was any more than the other special doctrines of the Classical school. It gave birth to one of the most powerful movements in economic history, which

---

advantageous terms are those whose commodities are most in demand by foreign countries, and which have themselves the least demand for foreign commodities, from which, among other consequences, it follows that the richest countries, *ceteris paribus*, gain the least by a given amount of foreign commerce, since, having a greater demand for commodities generally they are likely to have a greater demand for foreign commodities and thus modify the terms of interchange to their own disadvantage." (*Principles*, Book III, chapter xviii, para. 8.) Note the phrase 'a given amount of foreign commerce.' That is, although the rate of interchange is less advantageous for the rich country than it is for the poor, still, since the former exchanges much more than the latter it gains more on the whole transaction. Mill states this expressly elsewhere. The rich and the poor country are like the wholesale house and the little shop. The former gains very little on each article sold, but gains much on the whole turnover.

[1] *Ibid.*, Book V, chapter iv, para. 6.   [2] *Ibid.*, Book V, chapter x, para. 1.

led to the famous law of June 25, 1846, abolishing import duty on corn. This law was followed by others, and ended in the complete removal of all tariff barriers. But the eloquence of Cobden, of Bright, and of others was necessary before it was accomplished. A national Anti-Corn League had to be organized, no less than ten Parliamentary defeats had to be endured, the allegiance of Peel and the approval of the Duke of Wellington had to be secured before they were removed. All this even might have proved futile but for the poor harvest of 1845. This glorious campaign did more for the triumph of the Liberal economic school and for the dissemination of its ideas than all the learned demonstrations of the masters. Fourteen years were still to elapse before Cobden and Michel Chevalier were able to sign the treaty of 1860. Even this was due to a personal act of Napoleon III, and Cobden was not far wrong when he declared that nine-tenths of the French nation was opposed to it.

II: MILL'S INDIVIDUALIST-SOCIALIST PROGRAMME

Such were the doctrines taught by the Classical school about the middle of the nineteenth century. The writers in question, however, strongly objected to the term 'school,' believing that they themselves were the sole guardians of the sacred truth. And we must admit that their doctrines are admirably interwoven, and present an attractive appearance. On the other hand, it must be confessed that the prospects which they hold out for anyone not a member of the landowning class are far from attractive. For the labourer there is promise of daily toil and bare existence, and at best a wage determined by the quantity of capital or the numbers of the population—causes which are clearly beyond the workers' influence, and even beyond the assuaging influence of association and combination. And although the latter rights are generously claimed for the workers, the occasional antagonism between masters and men presages the eternal conflict between profits and wages. The possession of land is a passport to the enjoyment of mono-polistic privileges, which the right of free exchange can only modify very slightly. Rent—the resultant of all life's favourable chances—reserved for those who need it least, monopolizes a growing proportion of the national revenue. Intervention for the benefit of the worker, whether undertaken by the State or by some other body, is pushed aside as unworthy of the dignity of labour and harmful to its true interests. 'Each for himself' is set up as a principle of social action, in the vain hope that it would be spontaneously transformed into the principle of 'Each for all.' The search for truth was the dominant interest of the school, and these doctrines were preached, not for the pleasure they yielded, but as the dicta of exact science. Little wonder that men were prepared to fight before they would recognize these as demonstrable truths. And just as it was Mill who so powerfully helped to consolidate and complete the science of economics that Cossa refers to his *Principles* as the best résumé, the fullest, most complete and most exact exposition of the doctrines of the Classical school that we have,[1] it was Mill also who, in successive editions of his book, and in his other and later writings, pointed out the new vistas opening before the science, freed the doctrine from many errors to which it was attached, and set its feet on the paths of Liberal Socialism.

We might say without any suggestion of bias that Mill's evolution was largely influenced by French ideas.[2] A singularly interesting volume might be written in illustration of this statement. Without referring to the influence of Comte, which Mill was never tired of recognizing, and confining our attention only to economics, he has himself acknowledged his debt to the Saint-Simonians for the greater part of his doctrines of heredity and unearned increment, to Sismondi for his sympathy with peasant proprietorship, and to the socialists of 1848 for his faith in co-operative association as a substitute for the wage nexus.

It would hardly be true to say that Mill became a convert to socialism, although he showed himself anxious to defend it against every undeserved attack. To those who credit socialism with a desire to destroy personal initiative or to undermine individual liberty he disdainfully points out that "a factory operative has less personal interest in his work than a member of a communist association, since he is not, like him, working for a partnership of which he is himself a member," and that "the restraints of communism would be freedom in comparison with the present condition of the majority of the human race."[3] And although he expresses the belief that "communism would even now be practicable among the elite of mankind, and may become so among the rest," and hopes that one day education, habit, and culture will so alter the character of mankind that digging and weaving for one's country will be considered as patriotic as to fight for it,[4] still he was far from being a socialist. Free competition, he thought, was an absolute necessity, and there could be no interference with the essential rights of the individual.

[1] *Histoire des Doctrines économiques*, p. 338.
[2] Mill was for many years resident in France, and died at Avignon. An article written by him in defence of the Revolution of 1848 has been translated into French and published in book form by M. Sadi Carnot.
[3] *Principles*, p. 210.   [4] *Representative Government*, chapter iii.

The first blow which he dealt at the Classical school was to challenge its belief in the universality and permanence of natural law. He never took up the extreme position of the Marxian and Historical schools, which held that the so-called natural laws were merely attempts at describing the social relations which may exist at certain periods in economic history, but which change their character as time goes on. He draws a distinction between the laws which obtain in the realm of production and those that regulate distribution. Only in the one case can we speak of 'natural' laws; in the other they are artificial—created by men—and capable of being changed, should men desire it.[1] Contrary to the opinion of the Classical school, he tries to show that wages, profits, and rent are not determined by immutable laws against which the will of man can never prevail.

The door was thus open for social reform, which was no small triumph. Of course it cannot be said of the Classical school, or even of the Optimists, that they were prepared to deny the possibility or the efficacy of every measure of social reform, but it must be admitted that they were loath to encourage anything beyond private effort, or to advocate the abolition of any but the older laws. Braun, speaking at a conference of Liberal economists at Mayence in 1869, expressed the opinion that "that conference had given rise to much opposition because it upheld the principle that human legislation can never change the eternal laws of nature, which alone regulate every economic action." Similar declarations abound in the French works of the period. But, thanks to the distinction drawn by Mill, all this was changed. Though the legislator be helpless to modify the laws of production, he is all-powerful in the realm of distribution, which is the real battle-ground of economics.

But, as a matter of fact, Mill's distinction is open to criticism, especially his method of stating it; and we feel that he is unjust to himself when he regards this as his most important and most original contribution to economic science. Production and distribution cannot be treated as two separate spheres, for the one invariably involves the other. And Mill himself is forced to abandon his own thesis when he advocates the establishment of co-operative associations or peasant proprietorship, for each of these belongs as much to the domain of production as to that of distribution. Rodbertus, at almost the same

---

[1] "The laws and conditions of the production of wealth partake of the character of physical truths. There is nothing optional or arbitrary in them. . . . It is not so with the distribution of wealth. This is a matter of human institution solely. The things once there, mankind, individually or collectively, can do with them as they like." (*Principles*, Book II, chapter i, para. 1.) Karl Marx, a little later than this, claimed that distribution is wholly determined by production.

period, gave a much truer expression to Mill's thought by emphasizing the distinction which exists between economic and legal ties.[1] Even these may mutually involve one another; still we know that the economic laws which regulate exchange value or determine the magnitude of industrial enterprise are not of the same kind as the rules of law which regulate the transfer of property or lay down the lines of procedure for persons bound by agreement concerning wages, interest, or rent. The first may well be designated natural laws, but the latter are the work of a legislative authority.

Stuart Mill, not content with merely opening the door to reform, deliberately enters in, and, in striking contrast to the economists of the older school, outlines a comprehensive programme of social policy, which he formulates thus:[2] "How to unite the greatest individual liberty of action, with a common ownership in the raw material of the globe, and an equal participation of all in the benefits of combined labour."

We may summarize his proposals as follows:

(1) Abolition of the wage system and the substitution of a co-operative association of producers.

(2) The socialization of rent by means of a tax on land.

(3) Lessening of the inequalities of wealth by restrictions on the rights of inheritance.

This threefold measure of reform possesses all the desiderata laid down by Mill. Moreover, it does not conflict with the individualistic principle, but would somewhat strengthen it. It involves no personal constraint, but tends to extend the bounds of individual freedom.

Let us briefly review these projects seriatim.

(1) Mill thought that the wages regime was detrimental to individuality because it deprived man of all interest in the product of his labour, with the result that a vast majority of mankind is living under conditions which socialism could not possibly make much worse.

It is necessary to replace this condition of things by

a form of association which, if mankind continue to improve, must be expected in the end to predominate, and is not that which can exist between a capitalist as chief and workpeople without a voice in the management, but the association of the labourers themselves on terms of equality, collectively owning the capital with which they carry on their operations, and working under managers elected and removable by themselves.[3]

[1] See Chatelain's introduction to Rodbertus's *Kapital*.
[2] See *Autobiography*, p. 133 ("Popular" edition).
[3] "If the improvement which even triumphant military despotism has only retarded, not stopped, shall continue its course there can be little doubt that the status of hired

This noble ideal of a co-operative community was borrowed, not from Owen, but from the French socialists. Mill had already eulogized the French movement, even before its brilliant but ephemeral triumph in 1848. He was not the only one to be attracted by the idea of a co-operative community, for the English Christian Socialists drew their inspiration from the same source.

Mill lived long enough to witness the decline of co-operative production in England, and of the Co-operative Consumers' Union in France, but neither failure seems to have had any influence upon his projects.[1] Whatever the method might be, the object in his ideal was always the same, the self-emancipation of the workers.

(2) The rent of land, which Ricardo and his disciples accepted as a natural if not as a necessary phenomenon, appeared to Mill as an abnormal fact which was as detrimental to individuality as the wage system itself. Its peculiar danger was, of course, not quite the same. What rent did was to secure to certain individuals something which was not the result of their own efforts, whereas individualism always aimed at securing for every one the fruits of his own labour—*suum cuique*. On the principle of giving to each what each produced, everything not directly produced by man himself was to be restored to the community. It is immaterial whether this extra product is due to the collaboration of nature, as Smith and the Physiocrats believed, or whether it is the result of the pressure of population, as Ricardo and Malthus thought, or the mere result of chance and favourable circumstance, as Senior put it. Nothing could be easier than to levy a land tax which would gradually absorb rent, and which could be periodically increased as rents advanced. The idea was a brilliant one, and Mill had learned it from his father. It soon became the rallying-cry of a new school of economists closely akin to the socialists.

---

labourers will gradually tend to confine itself to the description of workpeople whose low moral qualities render them unfit for anything more independent, and that the relation of masters and workpeople will be gradually superseded by partnership in one of two forms: in some cases, association of the labourers with the capitalist; in others, and perhaps finally in all, association of labourers among themselves." (*Principles*, Book IV, chapter vii, para. 4.)

"In this or some such mode, the existing accumulations of capital might honestly and by a kind of spontaneous process become in the end the joint property of all who participate in their productive employment—a transformation which, thus effected, would be the nearest approach to social justice and the most beneficial ordering of industrial affairs for the universal good which it is possible at present to foresee." (*Ibid.*, Book IV, chapter vii, para. 6.)

[1] The co-operative movement probably suggested this idea to him. He several times expresses the opinion that middlemen's profits exceed those of the capitalists, and that the working class would gain more by the removal of the former than they would by the extinction of the latter.

The movement begot of this idea of confiscation deserves the fuller treatment which will be found in another chapter of this work.

Meanwhile, and until the larger and more revolutionary reform becomes practicable, Mill would welcome a modest instalment of emancipation in the shape of peasant proprietorship. Like the co-operative ideal, this also was of French extraction. Admiration of the French peasant had been a fashionable cult in England ever since the days of Arthur Young.[1] Mill thought that among the principal advantages of peasant proprietorship would be a lessening of the injustice of rent, because its benefits would be more widely distributed. The feeling of independence would check the deterioration of the wage-earner, individual initiative would be encouraged, the intelligence of the cultivator developed, and the growth of population checked.

Mill inspired a regard for the frugal French peasantry in the English Radical party. To his influence are due the various Small Holdings Acts which have resulted in the establishment of small islets of peasant tillers amid the vast territories of the English aristocracy.

(3) Mill was equally shocked at our antiquated inheritance law, which permits people to possess wealth which they have never helped to produce. To Senior inheritance ranked with the inequality of rent, and he placed both in the same category. To Mill it appeared to be not merely antagonistic to individual liberty, but a source of danger to free competition, because it placed competitors in positions of unequal advantage. In this matter Mill was under the influence of the Saint-Simonians, and he made no attempt to hide his contempt for the 'accident of birth.'

---

[1] But Young remained a champion of *grande culture*, while Mill was a complete convert to peasant proprietorship. But peasant proprietorship is proposed simply as a step towards association.

"The opinion expressed in a former part of this treatise respecting small landed properties and peasant proprietors may have made the reader anticipate that a wide diffusion of property in land is the resource on which I rely for exempting at least the agricultural labourers from exclusive dependence on labour for hire. Such, however, is not my opinion. I indeed deem that form of agricultural economy to be most groundlessly cried down, and to be greatly preferable in its aggregate effects on human happiness to hired labour in any form in which it exists at present. But the aim of improvement should be not solely to place human beings in a condition in which they will be able to do without one another, but to enable them to work with or for one another in relations not involving dependence." (*Principles*, Book IV, chapter vii, para. 4.)

Mill was not the only one who looked to peasant proprietorship partly to solve the social problem. Not to mention Sismondi, who was very much taken up with the idea, we have Thornton in England in his *Plea for Peasant Proprietors* (1848) and Hippolyte Passy in France in his excellent little volume *Des Systèmes de Culture* (1852) strongly advocating it. The Classical economists for the most part took the opposite point of view, especially Lavergne in his *Essai sur l'Économie rurale de l'Angleterre*.

This right of bequest, he felt, was a very difficult problem, for the right of free disposal of one's property even after death constituted one of the most glorious attributes of individuality. It implied a kind of survival or persistence of the human will. Mill showed considerable ingenuity in extricating himself from this difficult position. He would respect the right of the proprietor to dispose of his goods, but would limit the right of inheritance by making it illegal to inherit more than a certain sum. The testator would still enjoy the right of bequeathing his property as he wished, but no one who already possessed a certain amount of wealth could inherit it. Of all the solutions of this problem that have been proposed, Mill's is the most socialistic. He puts it forward, however, not as a definite project, but as a mere suggestion.[1]

Mill might well have been given a place among the Pessimists, especially as he inherits their tendency to see the darker side of things. Not only did the law of population fill him with terror, but the law of diminishing returns seemed to him the most important proposition in the whole of economic science; and all his works abound with melancholy reflections upon the futility of progress. There is, for instance, the frequently quoted "It is questionable if all the mechanical inventions yet made have lightened the day's toil of any human being."[2] In his vision of the future of society he prophesies that the river of human life will eventually be lost in the sea of stagnation.

It is worth while dwelling for a moment on this idea of a stationary state. Though the conception is an old one, it is very characteristic of Mill's work, and he feels himself forced to the belief that only by reverting to the stationary state can we hope for a solution of the social question.

Economists, especially Ricardo, had insisted upon the tendency of profits to a minimum as a correlative of the law of diminishing returns. This tendency, it was believed, would continue until profits had wholly disappeared and the formation of new capital was arrested.[3] Mill took

---

[1] "Were I framing a code of laws according to what seems to me best in itself, without regard to existing opinions and sentiments, I should prefer to restrict, not what anyone might bequeath, but what anyone should be permitted to acquire by bequest or inheritance. Each person should have power to dispose by will of his or her whole property; but not to lavish it in enriching some one individual beyond a certain maximum." (*Principles*, Book II, chapter ii, para. 4.)

It is hardly necessary to say that this limitation of the right of inheritance is a purely personal opinion of Mill, and that it is rejected along with his other solutions by most individualists. It is not quite correct to say then, as Schatz has said in his *Individualism*, that Stuart Mill is "the very incarnation of the individualistic spirit." He was really a somewhat sceptical disciple of the school, and his frequent change of opinion was very embarrassing!

[2] *Principles*, Book II, chapter vi, para. 2.

[3] "There is at every time and place some particular rate of profit, which is the lowest that will induce the people of that country and time to accumulate savings ...

up the theory where Ricardo had left it, and arrived at the conclusion that industry would thus be brought to a standstill, seeing that the magnitude of industry is dependent upon the amount of available capital. Population must then become stationary, and all economic movement must cease. Though alarmed at the economic significance of this prospect, Mill acquiesced in its ethical import. On the whole he thinks that such a state would be a very considerable improvement on our present condition. With economic activity brought to a standstill the current of human life would simply change its course and turn to other fields.[1] The decay of Mammon-worship and the thirst for wealth would simply mean an opportunity for pursuing worthier objects. He hoped that the arrest of economic progress would result in a real moral advance, and in the appeasement of human desires he looked for a solution and for the final disappearance of the social problem. And as far as we can see the reformers of to-day have nothing better to offer us.

III: MILL'S SUCCESSORS

Mill's influence was universal, though, properly speaking, he had no disciples. This was, no doubt, partly because writers like Toynbee, who would naturally have become disciples, were already enrolled in the service of the Historical school.

The Classical school failed to follow his socialistic lead. It still

---

But though the minimum rate of profit is thus liable to vary, and though to specify exactly what it is would at any given time be impossible, such a minimum always exists; and whether it be high or low, when once it is reached no further increase of capital can for the present take place. The country has then attained what is known to political economists under the name of the Stationary State." (*Ibid.*, Book IV, chapter iv, para. 3.)

Mill indicates the causes that contribute to a fall in the rate of profits as well as the causes that arrest that fall, such as the progress of production and the destruction of wealth by wars and crises.

It may be worth while pointing out that the word profit as employed by the English economists, and especially by Mill, has not the same meaning as it has with the French writers. French economists since the time of Say have employed the term profit to denote the earnings of the *entrepreneur*, the capitalist's income being designated interest. The English economists do not distinguish between the work of the *entrepreneur* and that of the capitalist, and the term profit covers them both. The result is that the French Hedonistic economists can say that under a regime of absolutely free competition profit would fall to zero, while the English economists cannot accept their thesis because profits include interest, which will always remain as the reward of waiting.

The French point of view is more generally adopted to-day.

[1] In a letter to Gustave d'Eichthal, recently published, speaking of Auguste Comte, he writes as follows: "How ridiculous to think that this law of civilization requires as its correlative constant progress! Why not admit that as humanity advances in certain respects it degenerates in others?"

preached the old doctrines, but with waning authority, and no new work was produced which is at all comparable with the works which we have already studied. We will mention a few of the later writings, however, for, though belonging to the second class, they are in some respects excellent.

In the first place we have several books written by Cairnes,[1] notably *Some Leading Principles of Political Economy* (1874). Cairnes is generally regarded as a disciple of Mill, though as a matter of fact he was nothing of the kind. Cairnes was purely Classic, and shared the Classical preference for the deductive method, which he thought the only method for political economy. His preference for that method sometimes resulted in his abusing it, and he was curiously indifferent to all social iniquities. He accepted *laissez-faire*, not as the basis of a scientific doctrine, but simply as a safe and practical rule of conduct.[2] The old wage fund theory has in him a champion who attempted to defend it against Stuart Mill. It cannot be said that he made any new contribution to the science, unless we except his teaching concerning competition. He pointed out that competition has not the general scope that is usually attributed to it. It only obtains between individuals placed in exactly similar circumstances. In other words, it operates within small areas, and is inoperative as between one area and another. This theory of non-competing groups helps to throw some light upon the persistent inequality shown by wages and profits.

In France the most prominent representative of political economy during the Second Empire was Michel Chevalier, a disciple of Saint-Simon. He nevertheless remained faithful to the Classical tradition of Say and Rossi,[3] his predecessors at the Collège de France. He waged battle with the socialists of 1848, made war upon Protection, and had the good fortune to be victorious in both cases, sharing with Cobden the honour of being a signatory to the famous commercial treaty of 1860. He realized the important place that railways would some day occupy in national economy, and the great possibilities of an engineering feat like the Suez Canal. He was also alive to the importance of credit institutions, which were only at the commencement of their useful career just then.[4] Although connected with the Liberal school,

---

[1] On the question of co-operation as a method of social reform, Cairnes, who simply refers to it as a possible alternative, may have owed something to Mill.

[2] *Essays*, p. 281.

[3] Since 1830 there have only been four professors—J. B. Say, Rossi, Michel Chevalier, and Chevalier's son-in-law, M. Paul Leroy-Beaulieu. The history of the chair is a fair summary of the history of French economics.

[4] His most curious book, perhaps, was *De la Baisse probable de l'or*, a title that caused a good deal of amusement during the latter half of the nineteenth century, but which proved somewhat of a prophecy after all.

he was not indifferent to the teaching of the Saint-Simonians on the importance of the authority and functions of the State, and he impressed upon the Government the necessity of paying attention to labour questions—a matter to which Napoleon III was naturally somewhat averse. Every subject which he handles is given scholarly and eloquent treatment.

About the same time Courcelle-Seneuil published a treatise on political economy which was for a long time regarded as a standard work. Seneuil was a champion of pure science—or "plutology," as he called it, in order to distinguish it from applied science, to which he gave the name "ergonomy." For a long time he was regarded as a kind of pontiff, and the pages of the *Journal des Économistes* bear evidence of the chastisement which he bestowed upon any of the younger writers who tried to shake off his authority. This was the time when Maurice Block was meting out the same treatment to the new German school in those bitterly critical articles which appeared in the same journal.

It is to be regretted that we cannot credit France with the *Précis de la Science économique et de ses Principales Applications*, which appeared in 1862. Cherbuliez, the author, was a Swiss, and was professor first at Geneva and then at Zurich. Cossa, in his *Histoire*, speaks of it as "undoubtedly the best treatise on the subject published in France," and as being "possibly superior even to Stuart Mill's." Cherbuliez belonged to the Classical school. He was opposed to socialism, and wrote pamphlets *à la* Bastiat in support of Liberal doctrines and the deductive method. But, like the Mills before him, and Walras, Spencer, Laveleye, Henry George, and many others who came after, he found it hard to reconcile private property with the individualistic doctrine, 'To each the product of his labour.' He reconciles himself to this position merely because he thinks that it is possibly a lesser evil than collective property.

The Liberal school had still a few adherents in Germany, although a serious rival was soon to make its appearance. Prince Smith (of English extraction) undertook the defence of Free Trade, pointing out "the absurdity of regarding it as a social question," and "how much more absurd it is to think that it can ever be solved other than by the logic of facts." Less a doctrinaire than a reformer, Schulze-Delitzsch, about 1850, inaugurated that movement which, notwithstanding the gibes of Lassalle, has made magnificent progress, and to-day includes thousands of credit societies; though up to the present it has not benefited anyone beyond the lower middle classes—the small shopkeeper, the well-to-do artisan, and the peasant proprietor.

Book IV : The Dissenters

WITH Bastiat economic Liberalism, threatened by socialism, sought precarious refuge in Optimism. With Mill the older doctrines found new expression in language scientific in its precision and classical in its beauty.

It really seemed as if political economy had reached its final stage and that there could be no further excuse for prolonging our survey.

But just when Liberalism seemed most triumphant and the principles of the science appeared definitely settled there sprang up a feeling of general dissatisfaction. Criticism, which had suffered a temporary check after 1848, now reasserted its claims, and with a determination not to tolerate any further interruption of its task.

The reaction showed itself most prominently in Germany, where the new Historical school refused to recognize the boundaries of the science as laid down by the English and French economists. The atmosphere of abstractions and generalizations to which they had confined it was altogether too stifling. It demanded new contact with life —with the life of the past no less than that of the present. It was weary of the empty framework of general terms. It was athirst for facts and the exercise of the powers of observation. With all the ardour of youth it was prepared to challenge all the traditional conclusions and to reformulate the science from its very base.

So much for the doctrine. But there was one thing which was thought more objectionable than even the Classical doctrine itself, and that was the Liberal policy with which the science had foolishly become implicated, and which must certainly be removed.

In addition to such critics as the above there are also the writers who drew their inspiration from Christianity, and in the name of charity, or morality, or of religion itself, uttered their protest against optimism and *laissez-faire*. Intervention again, so tentatively proposed by Sismondi, makes a bold demand for wider scope in view of the pressure of social problems, and under the name of State Socialism becomes a definitely formulated doctrine.

Socialism, which Reybaud believed dead after 1848, revived in its turn. Marx's *Kapital*, published in 1867, is the completest and most powerful exposition of socialism that we have. It is no longer a pious aspiration, but a new and a scientific doctrine ready to do battle with the champions of the Classical school, and to confute them out of their own mouths.

None of these currents is entirely new. Book II has shown us where they originated, and their beginnings can be traced to the earlier critical writers.

But we must not forget the striking difference between the ill-fated doctrines of the pre-1848 period and the striking success achieved by the present school. Despite the sympathy shown for the earlier critics, they remained on the whole somewhat isolated figures. Their protests were always individualistic—Sismondi's no less than Saint-Simon's, Fourier's no less than Owen's. Proudhon and List never seriously shook the public confidence in Liberalism. Now, on the contrary, Liberalism finds itself deserted, and sees the attention of public opinion turning more and more in the direction of the new school.

The triumph, of course, was not immediate. Many of the doctrines were formulated between 1850 and 1875, but victory was deferred until the last quarter of the century. But when it did come it was decisive. In Germany history monopolized the functions of economics, at least for a time. Intervention has only become universal since 1880. Since then, also, collectivism has won over the majority of the workers in all industrial countries, and has exercised very considerable influence upon politics, while Christian Socialism has discovered a way of combining all its most fervent adherents, of whatever persuasion, in one common faith.

The advance of this new school meant the decline of the Classical doctrine and the waning of Liberalism. Public interest gravitated away from the teaching of the founders. But in the absence of a new and a definite creed, what we find is a kind of general dispersion of economic thought, accompanied by a feeling of doubt as to the validity of theory in general and of theoretical political economy in particular. The old feeling of security gave place to uncertainty. Instead of the comparative unanimity of the early days we have a complete diversity of opinions, amid which the science sets out on a new career.

In Book V we shall find that certain eminent writers have succeeded in renewing the scientific tradition of the founders. But every connexion with practical politics had to be removed and a new body of closely knit doctrines had to be created before social thinkers could have this new point of view from which to co-operate.

CHAPTER I: THE HISTORICAL SCHOOL AND THE CONFLICT OF METHODS

THE second half of the nineteenth century is dominated by Historical ideas, though their final triumph was not fully established until the last quarter of the century. The rise of these ideas, however, belongs to a still earlier period, and dates from 1843, when there appeared a small volume by Roscher entitled *Grundriss*. We shall have to return to that date if we wish to understand the ideas of the school and to appreciate their criticisms.

The successors of J. B. Say and Ricardo gave a new fillip to the abstract tendency of the science by reducing its tenets to a small number of theoretical propositions. The problems of international exchange, of the rate of profits, wages, and rent, were treated simply as a number of such propositions, expressed with almost mathematical precision. Admitting their exactness, we must also recognize that they are far from being adequate, and could not possibly afford an explanation of the different varieties of economic phenomena or help the solution of the many practical problems which the development of industry presents to the statesman. But McCulloch, Senior, Storch, Rau, Garnier,[1] and Rossi, the immediate successors of Ricardo and Say in England and France, repeated the old formulæ without making any important additions to them. The new system of political economy thus consisted of a small number of quite obvious truths, having only the remotest connexion with economic life. It is true that Mill is an exception. But the *Principles* dates from 1848, which is subsequent to the foundation of the Historical school. With this exception we may say, in the words of Schmoller, that after the days of Adam Smith political economy seems to have suffered from an attack of anæmia.[2]

Toynbee gives admirable expression to this belief in his article on *Ricardo and the Old Political Economy*:[3] "A logical artifice became the accepted picture of the real world. Not that Ricardo himself, a benevolent and kind-hearted man, could have wished or supposed, had he asked himself the question, that the world of his treatise actually was the world he lived in; but he unconsciously fell into the habit of

[1] Joseph Garnier, who must not be confused with Germain Garnier, the translator of Smith's works, published the first edition of his *Éléments d'Économie politique* in 1845. From 1848 up to his death in 1881 he was chief editor of the *Journal des Économistes*.

[2] G. Schmoller, *Zur Litteraturgeschichte der Staats- und Sozialwissenschaften* (Leipzig, 1888). The expression will be found in his study of Roscher.

[3] A. Toynbee, *The Industrial Revolution*.

regarding laws which were those only of that society which he had created in his study for purposes of analysis as applicable to the complex society really existing around him. And the confusion was aggravated by some of his followers and intensified in ignorant popular versions of his doctrines." In other words, there was a striking divergence between economic theory and concrete economic reality, a divergence that was becoming wider every day, as new problems arose and new classes were being formed. But the extent of the gap was best realized when an attempt was made to apply the principles of the science to countries where the economic conditions were entirely different from those existing either in England or in France.

This divergence between theory and reality might conceivably be narrowed in one of two ways. A more harmonious and a more comprehensive theory might be formulated, a task which Menger, Jevons, and Walras attempted about 1870. A still more radical suggestion was to get rid of all abstract theory altogether and to confine the science to a simple description of economic phenomena. This was the method of procedure that was attempted first, and it is the one followed by the Historical school.

Long before this time certain writers had pointed out the dangers of a too rigid adherence to abstraction. Sismondi—an essentially historical writer—treated political economy as a branch of moral science whose separation from the main trunk is only partial, and insisted upon studying economic phenomena in connexion with their proper environment. He criticized the general conclusions of Ricardo and pleaded for a closer observation of facts.[1] List showed himself a still more violent critic, and, not content with the condemnation of Ricardian economics, he ventured to extend his strictures even to Smith. Taking nationality for the basis of his system, he applied the comparative method, upon which the Historical school has so often insisted,[2] to the commercial policy of the Classical school; but history was still employed merely for the purpose of illustration. Finally, socialists, especially the Saint-Simonians, whose entire system is simply

---

[1] It is curious that the Historians never refer to Sismondi as one of the pioneers of historical study. Roscher and Hildebrand never mention him at all, and Knies only thinks of him as a socialist (cf. Die Nationalökonomie vom historischen Standpunkt, 2nd ed., p. 322).

[2] Even List did not escape criticism at their hands. Hildebrand thinks that he was infected with the atomic views of Adam Smith and never showed himself sufficiently conscious of the ethical nature of society. "List seems to think that the entire subordination of private interest to public utility is dictated by custom, and even by private interest when properly understood, but he never regards it as a public duty rising out of the very nature of society itself." (Hildebrand, Die Nationalökonomie der Gegenwart und Zukunft, p. 73.) Note the ethical standpoint of the school.

one vast philosophy of history, had shown the impossibility of isolating economic from political and juridical phenomena, with which they are always intermingled.

But no author as yet had deliberately sought either in history or in the observation of contemporary facts a means of reconstructing the science as a whole. It is just here that the originality of the German school lies.

Its work is at once critical and constructive. On the critical side we have a profound and suggestive, though not always a just, analysis of the principles and methods of the older economists, while its constructive efforts gave new scope to the science, extended the range of its observations, and added to the complexity of its problems.

Generally speaking, it is not a difficult task to give an exposition of the critical ideas of the school, as we find them set forth in several books and articles, but it is by no means easy to delineate the conceptions underlying the positive work. Though implicit in all their writings, these conceptions are nowhere explicitly stated; whenever they have tried to define them it has always been, as their disciples willingly admit, in a vague and contradictory fashion.[1] To add further to the difficulty, each author defines them after his own fashion, but claims that his definition represents the ideas of the whole school.

In order to avoid useless repetitions and discussions without number we shall begin with a rapid survey of the outward development of the school, following with a résumé of its critical work, attempting, finally, to seize hold of its conception of the nature and object of political economy. From our point of view the last-named object is by far the most interesting.

I: THE ORIGIN AND DEVELOPMENT OF THE HISTORICAL SCHOOL

The honour of founding the school undoubtedly belongs to Wilhelm Roscher, a Göttingen professor, who published a book entitled *Grundriss zu Vorlesungen über die Staatswirtschaft nach geschichtlicher Methode* in 1843. In the preface to that small volume he mentions some of the leading ideas which inspired him to undertake the work, which reached fruition in the celebrated *System der Volkswirtschaft* (1st ed., 1854). He makes no pretence to anything beyond a study of economic history.

[1] See, among others, Max Weber's articles in Schmoller's *Jahrbuch* for 1903, p. 1181, and 1905, p. 1323. The methodological errors of Roscher, Knies, and Hildebrand get their due meed of criticism.

"Our aim," says he,

> is simply to describe what people have wished for and felt in matters
> economic, to describe the aims they have followed and the successes
> they achieved—as well as to give the reasons why such aims were
> chosen and such triumphs won. Such research can only be accom-
> plished if we keep in close touch with the other sciences of national
> life, with legal and political history, as well as with the history of
> civilization.[1]

Almost in the same breath he justifies an attack upon the Ricardian
school. He recognizes that he is far from thinking that his is the only
or even the quickest way of attaining the truth, but thinks that it will
lead into pleasant and fruitful quests, which once undertaken will
never be abandoned.

What Roscher proposed to do was to try to complete the current
theory by adding a study of contemporary facts and opinions, and, as
a matter of fact, in the series of volumes which constitute the *System*,
every instalment of which was received with growing appreciation by
the German world of letters, Roscher was merely content to punctuate
his exposition of the Classical doctrines with many an erudite excursus
in the domain of economic facts and ideas.[2]

Roscher referred to his experiment as an attempt to apply the
historical method which Savigny had been instrumental in introducing with such fruitful results into the study of jurisprudence.[3]
But, as Karl Menger[4] has well pointed out, the similarity is only superficial. Savigny employed history in the hope of obtaining some light
upon the organic nature and the spontaneous origin of existing institutions. His avowed object was to prove their legitimacy despite the
radical pretensions of the Rationalist reformers of the eighteenth
century. Roscher had no such aim in view. He was himself a Liberal,
and fully shared in their reforming zeal. History with him served
merely to illustrate theory, to supply rules for the guidance of the
statesman or to foster the growth of what he called the political sense.

Schmoller thinks that Roscher's work might justly be regarded as
an attempt to connect the teaching of political economy with the
'Cameralist' tradition of seventeenth- and eighteenth-century Germany.[5] These Cameralists were engaged in teaching the principles

---

[1] *Grundriss*, preface.
[2] Knies is of the same opinion. He remarks that Roscher's work simply means "a
completion of historiography rather than a correction of political economy." (*Die
Nationalökonomie vom geschichtlichen Standpunkte*, p. 35.) [3] *Grundriss*, preface, pp. iv–v.
[4] *Untersuchungen über die Methode der Sozialwissenschaften und der Politischen Oekonomie
insbesondere.* (Leipzig, 1883.)
[5] Schmoller, *loc. cit.* For further information concerning the Cameralists see
Geschichte der Nationalökonomie, by M. Oncken. Menger and Schmoller also connect

of administration and finance to students who were to spend their lives in administrative work of one kind or another, and they naturally took good care to keep as near actual facts as possible. Even in England and France political economy soon got involved in certain practical problems concerning taxation and commercial legislation. But in a country like Germany, which was industrially much more backward than either England or France, these problems wore a very different aspect, and some correction of the Classical doctrines was absolutely necessary if they were to bear any relation to the realities of economic life. Roscher's innovation was the outcome of a pedagogic rather than of a purely scientific demand, and he was instrumental in reviving a university tradition rather than in creating a new scientific movement.

In 1848 another German professor, Bruno Hildebrand, put forward a much more ambitious programme, and his *Die Nationalökonomie der Gegenwart und Zukunft* shows a much more fundamental opposition to the Classical school. History, he thought, would not merely vitalize and perfect the science, but might even help to recreate it altogether. Hildebrand points to the success of the method when applied to the science of language. Henceforth economics was to become the science of national development.[1]

In the prospectus of the *Jahrbücher für Nationalökonomie und Statistik*, founded by him in 1863, Hildebrand goes a step farther. He challenges the teaching of the Classical economists, especially on the question of national economic laws, and he even blames Roscher because he had ventured to recognize their existence.[2] He did not seem to realize that a denial of that kind involved the undoing of all economic science and the complete overthrow of those "laws of development" which he believed were henceforth to be the basis of the science.

Roscher with Heeren, Gervinus, and the other historians of Göttingen who during the first quarter of the nineteenth century tried to found a science of politics upon a general study of history. Roscher had studied history under them, and his aim is in every respect similar to theirs.

[1] In the introduction, p. v, he declares that the object of his work is "to open a way for an essentially historical standpoint in political economy and to transform the science of political economy into a body of doctrines dealing with the economic development of nations."

[2] Even Roscher had ventured to say that they partook of a mathematical nature. This is how he expresses his views as against those of Hildebrand on the real aim of political economy in the *Jahrbücher für Nationalökonomie und Statistik*, Vol. I, p. 145: "Economic science need not attempt to find the unchangeable, identical laws amid the multiplicity of economic phenomena. Its task is to show how humanity has progressed despite all the transformations of economic life, and how this economic life has contributed to the perfection of mankind. Its task is to follow the economic evolution of nations as well as of humanity as a whole, and to discover the bases of the present economic civilization as well as of the problems that now await solution."

But Hildebrand's absolutism had no more influence than Roscher's eclecticism, unless we make an exception of his generalization concerning the three phases of economic development, which he differentiates as follows: the period of natural economy, that of money economy, and finally that of credit. Beyond that he merely contented himself with publishing a number of fragmentary studies on special questions of statistics or history, without, for the most part, making any attempt to modify the Classical theory of production and distribution.

The critical study of 1848 hinted at a sequel which was to embody the principles of the new method. But the sequel never appeared, and the difficult task of carrying the subject farther was entrusted to Karl Knies, another professor, who in 1853 published a bulky treatise bearing the title of *Political Economy from the Historical Point of View*.[1] But there is as much divergence between his views and those of his predecessors as there is between Roscher's and Hildebrand's. He not only questions the existence of natural laws, but even doubts whether there are any laws of development at all—a point Hildebrand never had any doubts about—and thinks that all we can say is that there are certain analogies presented by the development of different countries. Knies cannot share in the belief of either Hildebrand or Roscher, nor does he hold with the Classical school. He thinks that political economy is simply a history of ideas concerning the economic development of a nation at different periods of its growth.

Knies's work passed almost unnoticed, ignored by historians and economists alike, until the younger Historical school called attention to his book, of which a new edition appeared in 1883. Knies makes frequent complaints of Roscher's neglect to consider his ideas.

Such heroic professions naturally lead us to expect that Knies would spare no effort to show the superiority of the new method. But his subsequent works dealing with money and credit, upon which his real reputation rests, bear scarcely a trace of the Historical spirit.

The three founders of the science devoted a great deal of time to a criticism of the Classical method, but failed to agree as to the aim and scope of the science and left to others the task of applying their principles.

This task was attempted by the newer Historical school, which sprang up around Schmoller towards the end of 1870. This new school possesses two distinctive characteristics.

(1) The useless controversy concerning economic laws which

---

[1] The exact title of the first edition was *Die Politische Oekonomie vom Standpunkte der geschichtlichen Methode*. A second edition appeared in 1883 with a slightly different title. Our quotations are taken from the second edition.

Hildebrand and Knies had raised is abandoned. The members of the school are careful not to deny the existence of natural social laws or uniformities, and they considered that the search for these was the chief object of the science. In reality they are economic determinists. "We know now," says Schmoller,[1] "that physical causation is something other than mechanical, but it bears the same stamp of necessity." What they do deny is that these laws are discoverable by Classical methods, and on this point they agree with every criticism made by their predecessors.

As to the possibility of formulating 'the laws of development' upon which Hildebrand laid such stress, they professed themselves very sceptical. "We have no knowledge of the laws of history, although we sometimes speak of economic and statistical laws,"[2] writes Schmoller. "We cannot," he regretfully says later, "even say whether the economic life of humanity possesses any element of unity or shows any traces of uniform development, or whether it is making for progress at all."[3] This very characteristic passage from Schmoller was written in 1904,[4] and forms the conclusion of the great synthetic treatise. All attempts at a philosophy of history are treated with the same disdain.[5]

(2) The newer Historical school, not content merely with advocating the use of the Historical method, hastened to put theory into practice. Since about 1860 German economists have shown a disposition to turn away from economic theory and to devote their entire energy to practical problems, sociological studies, and historical or realistic research. The number of economic monographs has increased enormously. The institutions of the Middle Ages and of antiquity,

[1] Schmoller, *Grundriss der Volkswirtschaftslehre*, Vol. I, p. 107 (1904).
[2] *Ibid.*, Vol. I, p. 108.   [3] *Ibid.*, Vol. II, p. 653.
[4] All historians, however, are not equally sceptical. Ashley in his preface to *English Economic History and Theory* writes as follows: "Just as the history of society, in spite of apparent retrogressions, reveals an orderly development, so there has been an orderly development in the history of what men have thought, and therefore in what they have thought concerning the economic side of life." And Ingram, in his *History of Political Economy*, points out that "As we have more than once indicated, an essential part of the idea of life is that of development—in other words, of ordered change. And that such a development takes place in the constitution and working of society in all its elements is a fact which cannot be doubted. . . . That there exist between the several social elements such relations as make the change of one element involve or determine the change of another is equally plain; and why the name of natural laws should be denied to such constant relations of co-existence and succession it is not easy to see. These laws being universal admit of the construction of an abstract theory of economic development." (P. 205.)
[5] Schmoller thinks that the science in the present stage of development, while it cannot be prevented from attempting a philosophy of history, is much better employed in building up simple scientific hypotheses with a view to gauging the future course of development than in getting hold of 'absolute truths.'

the economic doctrines of the ancients, statistics, the economic organization of the present day, these are some of the topics discussed. Political economy is lost in the maze of realistic studies, whether of the present day or of the past.

Although the Historical school has done an enormous amount of work we must not forget that historical monographs were printed before their time, and that certain socialistic treatises, such as Marx's *Kapital*, are really attempts at historical synthesis. The special merit of the school consists in the impulse it gave to systematic study of this description. The result has been a renewed interest in history and in the development of economic institutions. We cannot attempt an account of all these works and their varied contents. We must remain satisfied if we can catch the spirit of the movement. The names of Schmoller, Brentano, Held, Bücher, and Sombart are known to every student of economic history. Marshall, the greatest of modern theorists, has on more than one occasion paid them a glowing tribute.[1]

The movement soon left Germany, and it was speedily realized that conditions abroad were equally favourable for its work.

By the end of 1870 practical Liberalism had spent its force. But new problems were coming to the front, especially the labour question, which demanded immediate attention.[2] Classical economists had no solution to offer, and the new study of economic institutions, of social organization, and of the life of the masses seemed to be the only hopeful method of gaining light upon the question. Comparison with the past was expected to lead to a better understanding of the present. The Historical method seemed to social reformers to be the one instrument of progress, and a strong desire for some practical result fostered belief in it. When we remember the prestige which German science has enjoyed since 1871, and the success of the Germans in combining historical research with the advocacy of State Socialism, we can understand the enthusiasm with which the method was greeted abroad.

Even in England, the stronghold of Ricardian economics, the influence of the school becomes quite plain after 1870.

Here, as elsewhere, a controversy as to the method employed manifests itself. Cairnes in his work, *The Character and Logical Method of*

[1] Marshall, *Principles*, Appendix A.

[2] Its influence has been noted by Toynbee in his article on *Ricardo and the Old Political Economy*. "It was the labour question, unsolved by that removal of restrictions which was all deductive political economy had to offer, that revived the method of observation. Political economy was transformed by the working classes." Elsewhere he adds: "The Historical method is often deemed conservative, because it traces the gradual and stately growth of our venerable institutions; but it may exercise a precisely opposite influence by showing the gross injustice which was blindly perpetrated during this growth." (*Industrial Revolution*, p. 58.)

Political Economy (1875[1]), writing quite in the spirit of the old Classical authors, strongly advocates the employment of the deductive method. In 1879 Cliffe Leslie, in his *Essays on Political and Moral Philosophy*, enters the lists against Cairnes and makes use of the new weapons to drive home his arguments. The use of induction rather than deduction, the constant necessity for keeping economics in living touch with other social sciences, the relative character of economic laws, and the employment of history as a means of interpreting economic phenomena, are among the arguments adopted and developed by Leslie. Toynbee, in his *Lectures on the Industrial Revolution*, gave utterance to similar views, but showed much greater moderation. While recognizing the claims of deduction, he thought that history and observation would give new life and lend a practical interest to economics. The remoteness and unreality of the Ricardian school constituted its greatest weakness, and social reform would in his opinion greatly benefit by the introduction of new methods. Toynbee would undoubtedly have exercised tremendous influence; but his life, full of the brightest hopes, was cut short at thirty.

The lead had been given; the study of economic institutions and classes was henceforth to occupy a permanent position in English economic writings, and the remarkable works which have since been published, such as Cunningham's *Growth of English Industry and Commerce*, Ashley's *Economic History*, the Webbs' *Trade Unionism* and *Industrial Democracy*, Booth's *Life and Labour of the People*, bear witness to the profound influence exerted by the new ideas.

In France the success of the movement has not been quite so pronounced, although the need for it was as keenly felt there. Although it did not result in the founding of a French school of economic historians, the new current of ideas has influenced French economic thought in a thousand ways. In 1878 political economy became a recognized subject in the various curricula of the Facultés de Droit. The intimate connexion between economic study and the study of law has given an entirely new significance to political economy, and the science has been entirely transformed by the infusion of the historical spirit. At the same time professional historians have become more and more interested in problems of economic history, thus bringing a spirit of healthy rivalry into the study of economic institutions. Several Liberal economists also, without breaking with the Classical tradition, have devoted their energies to the close observation of contemporary facts or to historical research.[2]

---

[1] The first edition appeared in 1857.

[2] We would specially mention Levasseur's excellent work *Histoire des Classes ouvrières en France* (first edition, 1867).

Finally, we have a new group of workers in the sociologists. Sociology is interested in the origin and growth of social institutions of all kinds and in the influence which they have exerted upon one another. After studying institutions of a religious, legal, political, or social character it is only natural that they should ask that the study of economic institutions should be carried on in the same spirit and with the help of the same method. This object has been enthusiastically pursued for some time. The mechanism and the organization of the economic system at different periods have been closely examined by the aid of observation and history. Abstraction has been laid aside and a preference shown for minute observation, and for induction rather than deduction.[1]

II: THE CRITICAL IDEAS OF THE HISTORICAL SCHOOL

Among so many writers whose works cover such a long period of time we can hardly expect to find absolute unanimity, and we have already had occasion to note some of the more important divergencies between them, especially those separating the newer from the older writers of the Historical school. We cannot here enter into a full discussion of all these various shades of opinion, and we must be content to mention the more important features upon which they are almost entirely at one, noticing some of the prinicipal individual doctrines by the way.

The German Historical school made its debut with a criticism of Classical economics, and we cannot better begin than with a study of its critical ideas.[2]

Although these ideas had already found expression in the writings of Knies, Hildebrand, and Roscher, there was nothing like the

[1] More especially we must mention the group of workers associated with M. Durkheim and the *Année sociologique*. But it would be a great mistake to confuse the two methods, the Historical and the Sociological. See Simiand, *Méthode historique et Science sociale*, in the *Revue de Synthèse historique*, 1903. See also *La Méthode positive en Science économique* (Paris, 1912), which contains a study of the methodological problems presented by political economy.

[2] There is one aspect of the critical work of the German school with which we have not dealt in this book—namely, the criticism of *laissez-faire*. Some of the members—*e.g.*, Hildebrand—have insisted on the ethical criterion, but none of them share in the optimism of either Smith or Bastiat. The emphasis laid upon relativity made this quite impossible. But all the more eminent writers have remained faithful to the Liberal teaching of the founders. See Hildebrand's confession of faith at the beginning of Vol. I of the *Jahrbücher für Nationalökonomie*, 1863, Vol. I, p. 3. And although some of them—*e.g.*, Brentano and Schmoller—seem to be connected with the new current of ideas that gave rise to State Socialism, the association was quite accidental. They never considered it an organic part of their teaching, and they made no very original contribution to that part of the study. Their connexion with economics must always depend upon the light which they have thrown upon the question of method.

discussion which was provoked by them when the newer Historical school, at a much later period, again brought them to public notice. The publication of Karl Menger's work *Untersuchungen über die Methode der Socialwissenschaften*, in 1883—a classic both in style and matter—ushered in a new era of active polemics. This remarkable work, in which the author undertakes the defence of pure political economy against the attacks of the German Historical school, was received with some amount of ill-feeling by the members of that school,[1] and it caused a general searching of hearts during the next few years. We must try to bring out the essential elements in the discussion, and contrast the arguments advanced by the Historians with the replies offered by their critics.

Broadly speaking, three charges are levelled at the Classical writers. (i) It is pointed out that their belief in the universality of their doctrines is not easily justified. (ii) Their psychology is said to be too crude, based as it is simply upon egoism. (iii) Their use, or rather abuse, of the deductive method is said to be wholly unjustifiable. We will review these charges seriatim.

The Historians held that the greatest sin committed by Smith and his followers was the inordinate stress which they laid upon the universality of their doctrines. Hildebrand applies the term 'universalism' to this feature of their teaching, while Knies refers to it as 'absolutism' or 'perpetualism.' The belief of the Anglo-French school, according to their version of it, was that the economic laws which they had formulated were operative everywhere and at all times, and that the system of political economy founded upon them was universal in its application. The Historians, on the other hand, maintained that these laws, so far from being categorically imperative, should be regarded always as being subject to change in both theory and practice.

First with regard to practice. A uniform code of economic legislation cannot be indifferently applied to all countries at all epochs of their history. An attempt must be made to adapt it to the varied conditions of time and place. The statesman's art consists in adapting principles to meet new demands and in inventing solutions for new problems. But, as Menger points out, this obvious principle, which was by no means a new one, would have met with the approval of Smith and Say, and even of Ricardo himself;[2] although they

---

[1] *Cf.* Schmoller's account of Menger's work published in the *Jahrbuch* in 1884. The article appears also in the volume entitled *Zur Litteraturgeschichte der Staats- und Sozialwissenschaften* (1888).

[2] *Cf.* Menger, *loc. cit.*, pp. 130 *et seq.* Marshall's ironical remark is very apposite here: "German economists have done good service by insisting on this class of consideration, but they seem to be mistaken in supposing that it was overlooked by the older English economists." (*Principles*, Book I, chapter vi, note.)

occasionally forgot it, perhaps, especially when judging the institutions of the past or when advocating the universal adoption of *laissez-faire*.

The second idea, namely, that economic theory and economic laws have only a relative value, is treated with even greater emphasis, and this was another point on which the older economists had gone wrong. Economic laws, unlike the laws of physics and chemistry, with which the Classical writers were never tired of comparing them, have neither the universality nor the inevitability of the latter. Knies has laid special stress on this point.

> The conditions of economic life determine the form and character of economic theory. Both the process of argument employed and the results arrived at are products of historical development. The arguments are based upon the facts of concrete economic life and the results bear all the marks of historical solutions. The generalizations of economics are simply historical explanations and progressive manifestations of truth. Each step is a generalization of the truth as it is known at that particular stage of development. No single formula and no collection of such formulæ can ever claim to be final.[1]

This paragraph, though somewhat obscure and diffuse, as is often the case with Knies, expresses a sound idea which other economists have stated somewhat differently, by saying that economic laws are at once provisional and conditional. They are provisional in the sense that the progress of history continually gives rise to new facts of which existing theories do not take sufficient account. Hence the economist finds himself obliged to modify the formulæ with which he has hitherto been quite content. They are conditional in the sense that economic laws are only true so long as other circumstances do not hinder their action. The slightest change in the conditions as ordinarily given might cancel the usual result. Those economists who thought of their theory as a kind of final revelation, or considered that their predictions were absolutely certain, needed reminding of this.

But Knies is hopelessly wrong in thinking that this relativity is enough to separate the laws of economics from the laws of other sciences. Professor Marshall justly remarks that chemical and physical laws likewise undergo transformation whenever new facts render the old formulæ inadequate. All these laws are provisional. They are also hypothetical in the sense that they are true only in the absence of

---

[1] Knies, *loc. cit.*, pp. 24–25. Ashley gives an unmistakable expression to the same opinion in his *History*. "Political economy is not a body of absolutely true doctrines, revealed to the world at the end of the last and the beginning of the present century, but a number of more or less valuable theories and generalizations. . . . Modern economic theories, therefore, are not universally true; they are true neither for the past, when the conditions they postulate did not exist, nor for the future, when, unless society becomes stationary, the conditions will have changed." (Preface.)

any disturbing cause. Scientists no longer consider these laws as inherent in matter. They are the product of man's thought and they advance with the development of his intelligence.[1] They are nothing more or less than formulæ which conveniently express the relation of dependence that exists between different phenomena; and between these various laws as they are framed by the human mind there is no difference except a greater or lesser degree of proof which supports them.

What gives to the laws of physics or chemistry that larger amount of fixity and that greater degree of certainty which renders them altogether superior to economic law as at present formulated is a greater uniformity in the conditions that give rise to them, and the fact that their action is often measurable in accordance with mathematical principles.[2]

Not only has Knies exaggerated the importance of his doctrine of relativity,[3] but the imputation that his predecessors had failed to realize the need for it was hardly deserved. We shall have to refer to this matter again. Mill's *Principles* was already published, and even in the *Logic*, which appeared for the first time in 1843, and several editions of which had been issued before 1853, the year when Knies writes, we meet with the following sentence:[4]

> The motive that suggests the separation of this portion of the social phenomenon from the rest . . . is that they do mainly depend at least in the first resort on one class of circumstances only; and that even when other circumstances interfere, the ascertainment of the effect due to the one class of circumstances alone is a sufficiently intricate and difficult business to make it expedient to perform it once for all and then allow for the effect of the modifying circumstances.

Consequently sociology, of which political economy is simply a branch, is a science of tendencies and not of positive conclusions. No better expression of the principle of relativity could ever be given.

Notwithstanding all this, modern economists have come to the conclusion that the criticisms of the Historical school are sufficiently well founded to justify them in demanding greater precision so as to avoid

[1] See Karl Pearson, *The Grammar of Science*.
[2] Marshall, *Principles*, 4th ed., Book I, chapter vi, para. 6.
What we say about the mathematical method does not imply any criticism of the Mathematical method in political economy. To establish mathematical relations between economic phenomena, as Walras and his school did, and to deduce economic conclusions from general mathematical theories are two different things.
[3] Knies employs the differences there set up in order to deny that economic laws have even the character of national laws. The new Historical school does not go quite so far, as we shall see presently.
[4] Chapter iv, "Of the Logic of the Moral Sciences."

those mistakes in the future. Dr Marshall, for one, adopts Mill's expression, and defines an economic law as "a statement of economic tendencies."[1]

Even the founders of pure political economy, although their method is obviously very different from that of the Historians, have taken similar precautions. They expressly declare that the conclusions of the science are based upon a certain number of preliminary hypotheses deliberately chosen, and that the said conclusions are only provisionally true. "Pure economics," says Walras, "has to borrow its notion of exchange, of demand and supply, of capital and revenue, from actual life, and out of those conceptions it has to build the ideal or abstract type upon which the economist exercises his reasoning powers."[2] Pure economics studies the effects of competition, not under the imperfect conditions of an actual market, but as it would operate in a hypothetical market where each individual, knowing his own interests, would be able to pursue them quite freely, and in full publicity. The conception of a limited area within which competition is fully operative enables us to study as through a magnifying-glass the results of a hypothesis that really very seldom operates in the economic life of to-day.

We may dispute the advantages of such a method, but we cannot say that the economists ever wished to deny the relativity of a conclusion arrived at in this fashion.

While willing to admit that the Historians have managed to put this characteristic in a clear light just when some economists were in danger of forgetting it, and that it is a universally accepted doctrine to-day, we cannot accept Knies's contention that it affords a sufficient basis for the distinction between natural and economic laws. And such is the opinion of a large number, if not of the majority, of economists.[3]

The second charge is levelled against the narrowness and insufficiency of the psychology. Adam Smith treated man as a being solely dominated by considerations of self-interest and completely absorbed in the pursuit of gain. But, as the Historians justly point out, personal interest is far from being the sole motive, even in the economic world. The motives here, as elsewhere, are extremely varied: vanity, the desire for glory, pleasure afforded by the work itself, the sense of duty, pity, benevolence, love of kin, or simply custom.[4] To say that man is always and irremediably actuated by purely selfish motives, says Knies, is to deny the existence of any better motive or to regard man

---

[1] *Principles*, Book I, chapter vi, para. 6.   [2] Walras, *Économie politique pure.*
[3] Some authors would not admit complete assimilation—*e.g.*, Wagner. (*Grundlegung*, French translation, Vol. I, p. 335.   [4] Schmoller especially insists on this point.

as a being having a number of centres of psychical activity, each operating independently of the other.[1]

We cannot deny that the Classical writers believed that 'personal interest'—not in the sense of egoism, which is the name given it by Knies, and which somewhat distorts their view—held the key to the significance and origin of economic life. But the claims of the Historians are again immoderate. Being themselves chiefly concerned with concrete reality in all its complexity of being, and with all its distinctive and special features rather than its general import, they forgot that the primary aim of political economy is to study economic phenomena *en masse*. The Classical economists studied the crowd, not the individual. If we neglect the differences that occasionally arise in special cases, and allow for the personal equation, do we not find that the most constant motive to action is just this personal desire for well-being and profit? This is the opinion of Wagner, who on this question of method is not quite in agreement with other members of the school. In his suggestive study of the different motives that influence economic conduct he definitely states that the only motive that is really constant and permanent in its action is this self-interest. "This consideration," he says, "does something to explain and to justify the conduct of those writers who took this as the starting-point of their study of economics."[2]

But having admitted this, we must also recognize, not that they denied the changes occasionally undergone by self-interest under the pressure of other motives, as Knies suggests, but that they have neglected to take sufficient account of such modifications. Sometimes it really seems as if they would "transform political economy into a mere natural history of egoism," as Hildebrand says.

We can only repeat the remark which we have already made, namely, that when this criticism was offered it was scarcely justified. Stuart Mill had drawn attention to this point in his *Logic* ten years previously.[3] "An English political economist, like his countrymen in general, has seldom learned that it is possible that men in conducting the business of selling their goods over the counter should care more about their ease or their vanity than about their pecuniary gain." For his own part he ventures to say that "there is perhaps no action of a man's life in which he is neither under the immediate nor under the remote influence of any impulse but the mere desire of wealth."[4]

It is evident that Mill did not think that self-interest was the one

[1] Knies, *op. cit.*, p. 23.
[2] A. Wagner, *Grundlegung*, para. 67; French translation, Vol. I, p. 249.
[3] Vol. II, p. 502. [4] *Logic*, Vol. II, p. 497.

unchangeable and universal human motive. Much less 'egoism,' for, as we have seen in the previous chapter, his 'egoism' includes a considerable admixture of altruism.

But here again the strictures of the Historians, though somewhat exaggerated, have forced economists of other schools to be more precise in their statements. The economists of to-day, as Marshall remarks, are concerned "with man as he is; not with an abstract or 'economic' man, but a man of flesh and blood."[1] And if the economist, as Marshall points out, pays special attention to the desire for gain among the other motives which influence human beings, this is not because he is anxious to reduce the science to a mere 'natural history of egoism,' but because in this world of ours money is the one convenient means of measuring human motive on a large scale.[2] Even the Hedonists, whose economics rest upon a calculus of pleasure and pain, are careful to note that their hypothesis is just a useful simplification of concrete reality, and that such simplification is absolutely necessary in order to carry the analysis of economic phenomena as far as possible. It is an abstraction—imposed by necessity, which is its sole justification, but an abstraction nevertheless.

It is just here that the final reproach comes in, namely, the charge of abusing the employment of abstraction and deduction, and greater stress is laid upon this count than upon either of the other two.

Instead of deduction the new school would substitute induction based upon observation.

Their criticism of the deductive method is closely connected with their attack upon the psychology of the older school. The Classical economists thought, so the Historians tell us, that all economic laws could be deduced by a simple process of reasoning from one fundamental principle. If we consider the multiplicity of motives actually operative in the economic world, the insufficiency of this doctrine becomes immediately apparent. The result is not a faithful picture, but a caricature of reality. Only by patient observation and careful induction can we hope to build up an economic theory that shall take full account of the complexity of economic phenomena. "There is a new future before political economy," writes Schmoller in 1883, in reply to a letter of Menger,

> thanks to the use that will be made of the historical matter, both descriptive and statistical, that is slowly accumulating. It will not come by further distillation of the abstract propositions of the old dogmatism that have already been distilled a hundred times.[3]

[1] *Principles*, Book I, chapter v, para. 9.
[2] *Ibid.*, Book I, chapter v, para. 7.   [3] *Zur Litteraturgeschichte*, p. 279.

The younger school especially has insisted on this; and Menger has ventured to say that in the opinion of the newer Historical school

the art of abstract thinking, even when distinguished by profundity and originality of the highest order, and when based upon a foundation of wide experience—in a word, the exercise of that gift which has in other sciences resulted in winning the highest honour for the thinkers—seems to be of quite secondary importance, if not absolutely worthless, as compared with some elaborate compilation or other.[1]

But the criticism of the Historical school confuses two things, namely, the particular use which the Classical writers have made of the abstract deductive method, and the method itself.

No one will deny that the Classical writers often started with insufficient premises. Even when the premises were correct, they were too ready to think and not careful enough to prove that their conclusions were always borne out by the facts. No one can defend their incomplete analyses, their hasty generalizations, or their ambiguous formulæ.[2]

But this is very different from denying the legitimacy of abstraction and deduction. To isolate a whole class of motives with a view to a separate examination of their effects is not to deny either the presence or the action of other motives, any more than a study of the effect of gravitation upon a solid involves the denial of the action of other forces upon it. In a science like political economy, where experiment is practically impossible, abstraction and analysis afford the only means of escape from those other influences which complicate the problems so much. Even if the motives chosen were of secondary importance, the procedure would be quite legitimate, although the result would not be of any great moment. But it is of the greatest service and value when the motive chosen is one, like the search for gain or the desire for personal satisfaction, which exercises a preponderant influence upon economic action.[3]

[1] *Untersuchungen über die Methode*, p. 48.

[2] The English economists, even the most eminent, are often mistaken, says Wagner (*Grundlegung*, chapter iv, para. 4), but their errors are not to be imputed to their method as much as to the use they make of it. And Menger, who so energetically undertook the defence of deduction, further undertakes to renew the Classical theories. Economic theory, says he, as constituted by the English Classical school, has not succeeded in giving us a satisfactory science of economic laws (Menger, *loc. cit.*, p. 15).

[3] *Cf.* Menger, *loc. cit.*, p. 79: "The student of pure mechanics does not deny the existence of air or friction, any more than the student of pure mathematics denies the existence of real bodies, of surfaces, and lines, or the student of pure chemistry denies the influence of physical forces or the physicist the presence of chemical factors in actual phenomena, although each of these sciences only considers one side of the real world, making an abstraction of every other aspect of it. Nor does the economist pretend that men are only moved by egoism or that they are infallible and omniscient

So natural, we may even say so indispensable, is abstraction, if we are to help the mind steer its way amid the complexity of economic phenomena, that the criticism of the Historical school has done nothing to hinder the remarkable development which has resulted from the use of the abstract method during the last thirty years. But, although the Neo-Classical school has succeeded in replacing the old methods in their position of honour once more, it no longer employs those methods in the way the older writers did. A more solid foundation has been given them in a more exact analysis of the needs which personal interest ought to satisfy.[1] And the mechanism of deduction itself has been perfected by a more rigid use of the ordinary logical forms, and by the adoption of mathematical phraseology.

Happily the controversy as to the merits of the rival methods, which was first raised by the Historical school, has no very great interest at the present moment. Most eminent economists consider that both are equally necessary. There seems to be a general agreement among writers of different schools to consider the question of method of secondary importance, and to forget the futile controversies from which the science has gained so little. Before concluding this section it may be worth while to quote the opinion of men who represent very different tendencies, but are entirely agreed with regard to this one subject. "Discussion of method," says Pareto, "is a pure waste of time. The aim of the science is to discover economic uniformities, and it is always right to follow any path or to pursue any method that is likely to lead to that end."[2] "For this and other reasons," says Marshall,

> there always has been, and there probably always will be, a need for the existence side by side of workers with different aptitudes and different aims. . . . All the devices for the discovery of the relations between cause and effect which are described in treatises on scientific method have to be used in their turn by the economist.[3]

These writers generally employ the abstract method. Let us now hear some of the Historians. Schmoller is the author of that oft-

---

because they envisage social life from the point of view of the free play of individual interest uninfluenced by other considerations, by sin or ignorance." Wagner and Marshall take the same view.

[1] So great is the respect for psychology among the deductive writers of to-day that it has been suggested that the Austrian school should be known as the Psychological school. We can say that they have done much more in this direction than the Historical school.

[2] *Manuale di Economia politica*, p. 24 (Milan, 1906).

[3] *Principles*, 4th ed., Book I, chapter iii.

quoted phrase, "Induction and deduction are both necessary for the science, just as the right and left foot are needed for walking."[1]

More remarkable still, perhaps, is the opinion of Bücher, an author to whom the Historical school is indebted for some of its most valuable contributions.

> It is therefore a matter of great satisfaction that, after a period of diligent collection of material, the economic problems of modern commerce have in recent times been zealously taken up again and that an attempt is being made to correct and develop the old system in the same way in which it arose, with the aid, however, of a much larger store of facts. For the only method of investigation which will enable us to approach the complex causes of commercial phenomena is that of abstract isolation and logical deduction. The sole inductive process that can likewise be considered—namely, the statistical—is not sufficiently exact and penetrating for most of the problems that have to be handled here, and can be employed only to supplement or control.[2]

III: THE POSITIVE IDEAS OF THE HISTORICAL SCHOOL

What made the criticism of the Historians so penetrating was the fact that they held an entirely different view concerning the scope and aim of economics. Behind the criticism lurked the counter-theory. Nothing less than a complete transformation of the science would have satisfied the founders, but the younger school soon discovered that so ambitious a scheme could never be carried out. It is important that we should know something of the view of those older writers on this question, and the way they had intended to give effect to their plans. The positive contribution made by the Historical school to economic study is even more important than its criticisms, for it gives a clue to an entirely different point of view with which we are continually coming into contact in our study of economic doctrines.

The study of economic phenomena may be approached from two opposite standpoints, which we may designate the mechanical and the organic. The one is the vantage-ground of those thinkers who love generalizations, and who seek to reduce the complexity of the economic world to the compass of a few formulæ; the other of those writers who are attracted by the constant change which concrete reality presents.

---

[1] *Handwörterbuch der Staatswissenschaften.* In his *Grundriss* we read: "The writers who figure as representatives of inductive research in recent German economics are not opposed to the practice of deduction as such, but they do believe that it is too often based upon superficial and insufficient principles and that other principles derived from a more exact observation of facts might very well be substituted for these." Every one would subscribe to this view.

[2] *Die Entstehung der Volkswirtschaft*, Dr Wickett's translation.

The earlier economists for the most part belonged to the former class. Amid all the wealth and variety of economic phenomena they confined their attention almost entirely to those aspects that could be explained on simple mechanical principles. Such were the problems of price fluctuations, the rate of interest, wages, and rent. Production adapting itself to meet variation in demand, with no guide save personal interest, looked for all the world like the intermolecular action of free human beings in competition with one another. The simplicity of the idea was not without a certain grandeur of its own.

But such a conception of economic life is an extremely limited one. A whole mass of economic phenomena of the highest importance and of the greatest interest is left entirely outside. The phenomena of the economic world, as a matter of fact, are extremely varied and changeable. There are institutions and organizations without number, banks and exchanges, associations of masters and unions of men, commercial leagues and co-operative societies. Eternal struggle between the small tradesman and the big manufacturer, between the merchant and the combine, between the peasant proprietor and the great landowner, between classes and individuals, between public and private interests, between town and country, is the common feature of economic life. A state rises to prosperity again to fall to ruin. Competition at one moment makes it superior, at another reduces its lead. A country changes its commercial policy at one period to reintroduce the old regime at another. Economic life fulfils its purposes by employing different organs that are continually modified to meet changing conditions, and are gradually transformed as science progresses and manners and beliefs are revolutionized.

Of all this the mechanical conception tells us nothing. It makes no attempt to explain the economic differences which separate nations and differentiate epochs. Its theory of wages tells us nothing about the different classes of work-people, or of their well-being during successive periods of history, or about the legal and political conditions upon which that well-being depends. Its theory of interest tells us nothing of the various forms under which interest has appeared at different times, or of the gradual evolution of money, whether metallic or paper. Its theory of profits ignores the changes which industry has undergone, its concentration and expansion, its individualistic nature at one moment, its collective trend at another. No attempt is made to distinguish between profits in industry or commerce and profits in agriculture. The Classical economists were simply in search of those universal and permanent phenomena amid which the *homo œconomicus* most readily betrayed his character.

The mechanical view is evidently inadequate if we wish to delineate concrete economic life in all its manifold activity. We are simply given certain general results, which afford no clue to the concrete and special character of economic phenomena.

The weakness of the mechanical conception arises out of the fact that it isolates man's economic activity, but neglects his environment. The economic action of man must influence his surroundings. The character of such action and the effects which follow from it differ according to the physical and social, the political and religious surroundings wherein they are operative. A country's geographical situation, its natural resources, the scientific and artistic training of its inhabitants, their moral and intellectual character, and even their system of government, must determine the nature of its economic institutions, and the degree of well-being or prosperity enjoyed by its inhabitants. Wealth is produced, distributed, and exchanged in some fashion or other in every stage of social development, but each human society forms a separate organic unit, in which these functions are carried out in a particular way, giving, accordingly, to that society a distinctive character entirely its own. If we want to understand all the different aspects of this life we must make a study of its economic activity, not as it were *in vacuo*, but in connexion with the medium through which it finds expression, and which alone can help us to understand its true nature.[1]

This was the first doctrine on which they laid stress: the other follows immediately. This social environment cannot be regarded as fixed. It is constantly undergoing some change. It is in process of transformation and of evolution. At no two successive moments of its existence is it quite the same. Each successive stage calls for explanation, which history alone can give. Goethe has given utterance to this thought in a memorable phrase which serves as a kind of epigraph to Schmoller's great work, the *Grundriss*. "A person who has no knowledge of the three thousand years of history which have gone by must remain content to dwell in obscurity, living a hand-to-mouth existence." We must have some knowledge of the previous stages of economic development if we are to understand the economic life of the present. Just

[1] "National life, like every other form of existence, forms a whole of which the different parts are very intimately connected. Complete understanding even of a single aspect of it requires a careful study of the whole. Language, religion, arts and sciences, law, politics and economics must all be laid under tribute." (Roscher, *Principles.*) *Cf.* also Hildebrand, *Die Nationalökonomie der Gegenwart und Zukunft*, p. 29. This is also Knies's thought.

as naturalists and geologists in their anxiety to understand the present
have invented hypotheses to explain the evolution of the globe and of
living matter upon it, so must the student of economics return to the
distant past if he wants to get hold of the industrial life of to-day.
"Man as a social being," says Hildebrand,

> is the child of civilization and a product of history. His wants, his
> intellectual outlook, his relation to material objects, and his con-
> nexion with other human beings have not always been the same.
> Geography influences them, history modifies them, while the
> progress of education may entirely transform them.[1]

The Historians maintained that the earlier economists, by paying
exclusive attention to those broader conclusions which had something
of the generality of physical laws about them, had kept the science
within too narrow limits. Alongside of theory as they had conceived
of it—some Historians would say instead of it—there is room for
another study more closely akin to biology, namely, a detailed description and a historical explanation of the constitution of the economic
life of each nation. Such is the positive contribution of the school to
the study of political economy, and it fairly represents the attitude of
most modern economists towards history.

Their aim was a perfectly natural and legitimate one, and at first
sight, at least, seemed very attractive. But beneath its apparent
simplicity there is some amount of obscurity, and its adversaries have
thought that upon close analysis it is really open to serious objections.

In the first place, is it the aim of the science to present us with an
exact, realistic picture of society, as the Historians loved to think?
On the contrary, do we not find that a study can only aspire to the
name of a science in proportion as its propositions become more
general in their nature? There is no science without generalization,
according to Aristotle, and concrete description, however indispensable,
is only a first step in the constitution of a science. A science must be
explanatory rather than descriptive.

Of course Historians are not always content with mere description.
Some Historians have attempted explanation and have employed
history as their organon. Is the choice a suitable one?

"History," says Marshall, "tells of sequences and coincidences; but
reason alone can interpret and draw lessons from them."[2]

Moreover, is there a single important historical event whose cause

---

[1] *Die Nationalökonomie der Gegenwart und Zukunft*, p. 29.
[2] *Principles*, Book I, chapter vii. "History," says Wagner (*Grundlegung*, para. 83),
"may well affirm the existence of causal or conditional relations, but it can never
prove it."

has ceased to be a matter of discussion? It will be a long time before people cease to dispute about the causes of the Reformation or the Revolution, and the relative importance of economic, political, and moral influences in determining the course of those movements has yet to be assigned. The causes that led to the substitution of credit for money or money for barter are equally obscure. Before narrative can become science there must be the preliminary discovery by a number of other sciences of the many diverse laws whose combination gives rise to concrete phenomena.[1] Not history but the sciences give the true explanation. The evolutionary theory has proved fruitful in natural history simply because it took the succession of animal species as an established fact and then discovered that heredity and selection afforded a means of explaining that succession. But history cannot give us any hypothesis that can rival the theory of evolution either in its scientific value or in its simplicity. In other words, history itself is in need of explanation. It gives no clue to reality and it can never take the place of economics.[2]

The earlier Historians claimed a higher mission still for the historical study of political economy. It must not only afford an explanation of concrete economic reality, but it must also formulate the laws of economic development. This idea is only held by a few of them, and even the few are not agreed as to how it should be done. Knies, for example, thinks that it ought to be sufficiently general to include the economic development of all nations. Saint-Simon held somewhat similar views. Others, and among them Roscher, hold that there exist parallelisms in the history of various nations; in other words, that every nation in the course of its economic development passes through certain similar phases or stages. These similarities constitute the laws of economics. If we were to study their movements in the

[1] History may, as a matter of fact, become explanatory, but only in a particular sense. In other words, although it cannot discover the general laws regulating phenomena, it may show what special circumstances (whose general laws are already supposed to be known) have given rise to some event equally specialized in character. But every honest historian has to admit that such explanations are definitely personal and subjective in character. For a recent examination of these ideas from the pen of a historian see the profound yet charming introduction contributed by Meyer to the second edition of his *Geschichte des Alterthums*. *Cf.* also Simiand, pp. 14–16.

[2] *Cf.* Marshall, *Principles*, Book I, chapter vi, para. 4, and especially Menger, *Untersuchungen*, pp. 15–17: "We may be said to have historical knowledge of a particular phenomenon when we have traced its individual genesis, *i.e.*, when we have succeeded in representing to ourselves the concrete circumstances among which it came into being, with their proper qualifications, etc. We may be said to have a theoretical knowledge of some concrete phenomenon when we are enabled to envisage it as a particular instance of a certain law or regularity of sequence or coexistence, *i.e.*, when we are able to give an account of the *raison d'être* and the nature of its existence as an exemplification of some general law."

civilizations of the past we might be able to estimate their place in existing societies.[1]

Neither point seems very clear. Even if we admit that there is only one general law of human development we cannot forecast the line of progress, because scientific prediction is only applicable to recurrent phenomena. They fail just when the conditions are new. Of course one can always guess at the nature of the future, but divination is not knowledge. And predictions of this kind are almost always false.[2] Historical parallelism rests on equally shaky foundations. A nation, like any other living organism, passes through the successive stages of youth, maturity, and old age, but we are not justified in thinking that the successive phases through which one nation has passed must be a kind of prototype to which all others must conform. All that we can say is that in two neighbouring countries the same effects are likely to follow from the same causes. Production on a large scale, for example, has been accompanied by similar phenomena in most countries in Western Europe. But this is by no means an inevitable law. It is simply a case of similar effects resulting from similar causes. Such analogies are hardly worthy of the name of laws. The discovery of the law, as Wagner says,[3] may be a task beyond human power; and Schmoller, as we have already seen, is of the same opinion.

One remark before concluding. There is a striking similarity between the ideas just outlined and those of a distinguished philosopher whose name deserves mention here, although his influence upon political economy was practically nil. We refer to Auguste Comte.

[1] A full exposition of this idea is given in his *Grundriss*, but Knies, in the name of the conception of a unique evolution, contests the view.

[2] This is what M. Renouvier thinks of this conception: "If we proceed to ask another question in addition to the difficult one already asked and inquire as to the circumstances under which different nations have advanced or declined in the path of goodness and of truth and transmitted their triumphs or their defeats to the next generations, and if we support ourselves in the quest by the belief that we already have some knowledge of a scientific law and consequently of the aim of human society (this kind of knowledge generally begins with formulating such aims), we shall find ourselves in the position of a religious prophet who, not merely content with an inspired version of the truth, and of the destiny of mankind, proceeds to expound to his auditors the necessity under which both preacher and auditors are compelled to believe and to act in accordance with what will undoubtedly come to pass. Philosophical and religious imagination seeks in external observation the elements of a confidence which it can no longer place in itself. History becomes a kind of inspiring divinity. But although the object of the illusion is different its nature is still the same, for the new deity is as little effective as were the ancient ones in the opinion of those who have no faith in it, and it only inspires those who already believe." (*Introduction à la Philosophie analytique de l'Histoire*, 2nd ed., Vol. I, p. 121.) Bergson's philosophy also contests the possibility of guessing what the future may be like from the character of the present. See especially *Creative Evolution*.

[3] *Grundlegung*, para. 90; French translation, p. 342.

It is curious that the earliest representatives of the school should have ignored him altogether, but just as Mill remained unknown to them, so the *Cours de Philosophie positive*, though published in 1842, remained a sealed book so far as they were concerned. Comte's ideas are so very much like those of Knies and Hildebrand that some Positivist economists, such as Ingram and Hector Denis, have attempted to connect the Historical tendency in political economy with the Positive philosophy of Comte.[1]

The three fundamental conceptions which formed the basis of the teaching of the Historical school are clearly formulated by Comte. The first is the importance of studying economic phenomena in connexion with other social facts. The analysis of the industrial or economic life of society can never be carried on in the 'positive' spirit by simply making an abstraction of its intellectual, political, or moral life, whether of the past or of the present.[2] The second is the employment of history as the organon of social science. "Social research," says he, "must be based upon a sane analysis of the all-round development of the best of mankind up to the present moment, and the growing predilection for historical study in our time augurs well for the regeneration of political economy." He was fully persuaded that the method would foster scientific prediction—a feature which is bound to fuse all those diverse conditions which will form the basis of Positive politics.

Comte wished to found sociology, of which political economy was to be simply a branch. The Historical school, and especially Knies, regarded economics in the same spirit. Hence the analogies with which Knies had to content himself, but which the younger school refused to recognize. But there was a fundamental difference between their respective points of view, and this will help us to distinguish between them.

Comte was a believer in inevitable natural laws, which, according to the earlier Historians, had wrought such havoc. The Historical method also, as he conceived of it, was something very different from what the older or the newer Historical school took it to be.

Adopting a dictum of Saint-Simon, Comte speaks of the Historical method as an attempt to establish in ascending or descending series the curve of each social institution, and to deduce from its general outlines conclusions as to its probable growth or decline in the future. This is how he himself defines the process:

The essence of this so-called historical spirit, it seems to us, consists in the rational use of what may be called the social series method, or,

[1] *Cf.* Ingram, *History of Political Economy*, and Denis, *Histoire des Systèmes*.
[2] A. Comte, *Cours*, Vol. IV, p. 198.

in other words, in the due appreciation of the successive stages of human development as reflected in a succession of historical facts. Careful study of such facts, whether physical, intellectual, moral, or political, reveals a continuous growth on the one hand and an equally continuous decline on the other. Hence there results the possibility of scientific prophecy concerning the final ascendancy of the former and the complete overthrow of the latter, provided always such conclusion is in conformity with the general laws of human development, the sociological preponderance of which must never be lost sight of.[1]

It was in virtue of this method that Saint-Simon predicted the coming of industrialism and that Comte prophesied the triumph of the positive spirit over the metaphysical and religious.

There is considerable difference between this attitude and the Historical method as we know it,[2] and the attempt at affiliation seems to us altogether unwarranted. But the coincidence between Comte's views and those of Knies and Hildebrand is none the less remarkable, and it affords a further proof of the existence of that general feeling which prompted certain writers towards the middle of the century to attempt a regeneration of political economy by setting it free from the tyranny of those general laws which had nearly stifled its life.

It seems to us, however, that the Historical school is mistaken if it imagines that history alone can afford an explanation of the present or will ever enable us to discover those special laws which determine the evolution of nations.

On the other hand, it has a perfect right to demand a place beside economic science, and it is undoubtedly destined to occupy a position still more prominent in the study of economic institutions, in statistical investigation, and above all in economic history. Not only is a detailed description of the concrete life of the present of absorbing interest in itself, but it is the condition precedent to all speculations concerning

---

[1] *Cours*, Vol. IV, p. 328.

[2] It is interesting to learn the views of historians on this point. Meyer thinks that the object of history is not to discover the general laws of development, but to describe and explain particular concrete events as they succeed one another. Such descriptions can only be made in accordance with the rules of historical criticism, but explanation is only possible with the aid of analogy. "It is only by the use of analogy that the historian can explain past events, especially where there are psychological motives that require analysis. The explanation thus given will necessarily be of a subjective character, and from its very nature somewhat problematic." *Cf.* Ed. Meyer, *Geschichte des Alterthums*, Introduction, 2nd ed., paras. 112 *et seq.* There does not seem to be any connexion between this method and that o f Aug. Comte. One becomes still more convinced of this after reading Langlois and Seignobos's *Introduction aux Études historiques* or G. Monod's study in historical method in *De la Méthode dans les Sciences* (Paris, 1909), or, finally, the numerous articles dealing with this question of method which have appeared in the *Revue de Synthèse historique*.

the future. The theorist can never afford to neglect the minute observation of facts unless he wills that his structure shall hang in the void. Most abstract economists feel no hesitation in recognizing this. For example, Jevons, writing in 1879,[1] gave it as his opinion that "in any case there must arise a science of the development of economic forces and relations."

This newer historical conception came to the rescue just when the science was about to give up the ghost, and though they may have failed to give us that synthetic reconstruction which is, after all, within the ability of very few writers, its advocates have succeeded in infusing new life into the study and in stimulating new interest in political economy by bringing it again into touch with contemporary life. They have done this by throwing new light upon the past and by giving us a detailed account of the more interesting and more complex phenomena of the present time.[2] Such work must necessarily be of a fragmentary character. The school has collected a wonderful amount of first-class material, but it has not yet erected that palace of harmonious proportions to which we in our fond imagination had likened the science of the future. Nor has it discovered the clue which can help it to find its way through the chaos of economic life. This is not much to be wondered at when we remember the shortcomings of the method to which we have already had occasion to refer. Indeed, some of the writers of the school seem fully convinced of this. Professor Ashley, in an article contributed to the *Economic Journal*, employs the following words:[3]

> As I have already observed, the criticisms of the Historical school have not led so far to the creation of a new political economy on historical lines: even in Germany it is only within very recent years that some of the larger outlines of such an economics have begun to loom up before us in the great treatise of Gustav Schmoller.

In view of considerations like these one might have expected that the Historical school would have shown greater indulgence to the attempts made both by the Classical and by the Hedonistic schools to give by a different method expression to the same instinctive desire to simplify matters in order to understand them better.[4]

[1] *Theory of Political Economy*, preface to the second edition, 1879.
[2] Schmoller's *Jahrbuch* contains descriptive studies of present-day commercial and industrial undertakings which are veritable models.
[3] *The Present Position of Political Economy*, in the *Economic Journal*, 1907, p. 487.
[4] We have not the necessary space in this volume to refer to the history of statistics. This science, though independent of political economy, is, however, such a powerful auxiliary that its progress has to some extent been parallel with the growth of economics. During the last twenty years the methods of interpreting statistics (we are speaking merely of observation) have been very considerably improved. The logical

CHAPTER II: STATE SOCIALISM

THE nineteenth century opened with a feeling of contempt for government of every kind, and with unbounded confidence on the part of at least every publicist in the virtue of economic liberty and individual initiative. It closed amid the clamour for State intervention in all matters affecting economic or social organization. In every country the number of public men and of economists who favour an extension of the economic function of government has been continually growing, and after two world wars such men are certainly in the majority. To some writers this change of opinion has seemed sufficiently important to warrant special treatment as a new doctrine, variously known as State Socialism or "the Socialism of the Chair" in Germany and Interventionism in France.

Really it is not an economic question at all, but a question of practical politics upon which writers of various shades of economic opinion may agree despite extreme differences in their theoretical preconceptions. The problem of defining the limits of governmental action in the matter of producing and distributing wealth is one of the most important in the whole realm of political economy, but it can hardly be considered a fundamental scientific question upon which economic opinion is hopelessly divided. It is clear that the solution of the problem must depend not merely upon purely economic factors, but also on social and political considerations, upon the peculiar conception of general interest which the individual has formed for himself and the amount of confidence which he can place in the character and ability of Governments.[1] The problem is always changing, and whenever a new kind of society is created or a new

---

problems involved have been studied with much care, and the application of mathematics to these problems has proved very fruitful. No student of the social sciences can afford to neglect such mathematical theories as those of combination, correlation, degree of error, etc. The history of statistics, which contains many eminent names, from Quetelet to Karl Pearson, would certainly deserve a chapter in a book dealing with method, although there would be some risk of giving it too statistical a bias. We must rest content with referring the reader to Udny Yule's *Introduction to the Theory of Statistics*, which constitutes what is perhaps the best recent introduction to the discussion concerning the method to be employed in this social science, and forms an indispensable complement to the study of the problems examined in this chapter.

[1] Dupont-White makes the remark somewhere that the State, strictly speaking, has only existed since 1789. It appears, then, that a State which is not constitutional, democratic, and liberal has none of the virtues of the true State. Such exclusion, although permissible in the publicist, is indefensible in the theorist or historian.

Government is established a fresh solution is required to meet the changed conditions.

How is it, then, that this question has assumed such extravagant proportions at certain periods of our history?

Had the issue been confined to the limits laid down by Smith it is probable that such passionate controversies would have been avoided. Smith's arguments in favour of *laissez-faire* were largely economic. Gradually, however, under the growing influence of individual and political liberty, a kind of contempt for all State action took the place of the more careful reasoning of the earlier theory, and the superiority of individual action in matters non-economic became an accepted axiom with every publicist.

This method of looking at the problem is very characteristic of Bastiat. The one feature of government that interested him was not the fact that it represented the general interest of the citizens, but that whenever it took any action it had to employ force,[1] whereas individual action is always free. Every substitution of State for individual action meant victory for force and the defeat of liberty. Such substitution must consequently be condemned. Smith's point of view is totally different. To appreciate this difference we need only compare their treatment of State action. In addition to protecting the citizens from invasion and from interference with their individual rights, Smith adds that the sovereign should undertake

the duty of erecting and maintaining certain public works and certain public institutions, which it can never be for the interest of any individual, or small number of individuals, to erect and maintain; because the profit could never repay the expense to any individual or small number of individuals, though it may frequently do much more than repay it to a great society.[2]

The scope is sufficiently wide, at any rate. If we turn to Bastiat, on the other hand, we find that the Government has only two functions to perform, namely, "to guard public security and to administer the common land."[3] Viewed in this light, the problem of governmental intervention, instead of remaining purely economic, becomes a question of determining the nature, aims, and functions of the State, and individual temperament and social traditions play a much more

[1] "The distinctive character of the State merely consists in this necessity to have recourse to force, which also helps to indicate the extent and the proper limits of its action. Government is only possible through the intervention of force, and its action is only legitimate when the intervention of force can be shown to be justifiable." (*Harmonies*, 10th ed., pp. 552–553.)

[2] *Wealth of Nations*, Book IV, chapter ix; Cannan's ed., Vol. II, p. 185.

[3] *Harmonies*, 10th ed., p. 556.

important part than either the operation of economic phenomena or
any amount of economic reasoning. It is not surprising that some
writers thought that the one aim of economics was to defend the
liberty and the rights of the individual!

Such exaggerated views were bound to beget a reaction, and the
defence of State action assumes equally absurd proportions with some
of the writers of the opposite school. Even as far back as 1856 Dupont-
White, a French writer, had uttered a protest against this persistent
depreciation of the State, in a short work entitled *L'Individu et l'état*.
His ideas are so closely akin to those of the German State Socialists
that they have often been confused with them, and it is simpler to
give an exposition of both at the same time. But he was a voice crying
in the wilderness. Public opinion under the Second Empire was very
little disposed to listen to an individual who, though a Liberal in
politics, was yet anxious to strengthen the power and to add to the
economic prerogative of the Crown. More favourable circumstances
were necessary if there was to be a change of public opinion on the
matter. The times had ripened by the last quarter of the century, and
the elements proved propitious, especially in Germany, where the
reaction first showed itself.

The reaction took the form not so much of the creation of a new
doctrine as of a fusion of two older currents, which must first be
examined.

During the course of the nineteenth century we find a number of
economists who, while accepting Smith's fundamental conception,
gradually limit the application of his principle of *laissez-faire*. They
thought that the superiority of *laissez-faire* could not be scientifically
demonstrated and that in the great majority of cases some form of
State intervention was necessary.

On the other hand, we meet with a number of socialists who prove
themselves to be more opportunistic than their comrades, and though
equally hostile to private property and freedom of production, yet
never hesitate to address their appeals on behalf of the workers to
existing Governments.

State Socialism represents the fusion of these two currents. It surpasses the one in its faith in the wisdom of Governments, and is distinguished from the other by its greater attachment to the rights of
private property; but both of them contribute some items to its
programme. In the first place we must try to discover the source of
these separate tendencies, and in the second place watch their
amalgamation.

I: THE ECONOMISTS' CRITICISM OF *LAISSEZ-FAIRE*

The doctrine of absolute *laissez-faire* was not long allowed to go unchallenged. From the time of Smith onward there is an uninterrupted sequence of writers—all of them by no means socialists—who ventured to attack the fundamental propositions of the great Scotsman and who attempted to show that his practical conclusions were not always borne out by the facts.

Smith based his advocacy of *laissez-faire* upon the supposed identification of public and private interests. He showed how competition reduced prices to the level of cost of production, how supply adapted itself to meet demand in a perfectly automatic fashion, and how capital in an equally natural way flowed into the most remunerative occupations.

This principle of identity of interests was, however, rudely shaken by the teachings of Malthus and Ricardo, although both of them remained strong adherents of the doctrine of individual liberty.

Sismondi, who was the next to intervene, laid stress upon the evils of competition, and showed how social inequality necessitated the submission of the weak to the will of the strong. His whole book was simply a refutation of Smith's providential optimism.

In Germany even, as early as 1832, that brilliant economist Hermann was already proceeding with his critical analysis of the Classical theories; and after demonstrating how frequently individual interest comes into conflict with public welfare, and how inadequate is the contribution which it can possibly make to the general well-being, he declares his inability to subscribe to the doctrine laid down by most of Smith's followers, namely, that individual activity moved by personal interest is sufficient to meet all the demands of national economy. Within the bounds of this national economy[1] he thinks there ought to be room for what he calls the civic spirit (*Gemeinsinn*) as well.

The next critic, List, bases his whole case upon the opposition between immediate interests, which guide the individual, and the permanent interests of the nation, of which the Government alone can take account.

Stuart Mill, in the famous fifth book of the *Principles*, refuses even to discuss the doctrine of identity of interests, believing it to be quite untenable. On the question of non-intervention he admits the validity of one economic argument only, namely, the superiority of self-interest as an economic motive. But he is quick to recognize its shortcomings and the exceptions to its universal operation—in the natural incapacity

[1] Hermann, *Staatswirtschaftliche Untersuchungen*, 1st ed., pp. 12–18.

o

of children and of the weak-minded, the ignorance of consumers, the difficulty of achieving it, even when clearly perceived, without the help of society as a whole, as in the case of the Factory Acts. Mill also points out how this motive is frequently wanting in modern industrial organization, where, for example, we have joint stock companies acting through the medium of a paid agency, or charitable work undertaken by an individual who has to consider, not his own interests, but those of other people. Private interest is also frequently antagonistic to public interest, as in the case of the public supply of gas or water, where the individual *entrepreneur* is influenced by the thought of a maximum profit rather than by considerations of general interest. In matters of that kind Stuart Mill was inclined to favour State intervention.[1]

M. Chevalier, from his professorial chair in the Collège de France, extended his congratulations to Mill upon his successful restoration of the legitimate duties of Governments.[2] Chevalier thought that those who believed that the economic order could be set up simply by the aid of competition acting through personal interest were either illogical in their arguments or irrational in their aims. Government was simply the manager of the national organization, and its duty was to intervene whenever the general interest was endangered. But the duties and privileges of government are not exactly those of the village policeman.[3] Applying this principle to public works, he points out that they are more or less State matters, and the guarantee for good work is quite as great when the State itself undertakes to perform it as when it is entrusted to a private individual.

In 1863 Cournot, whose reputation was unequal to either Mill's or Chevalier's, but whose penetrating thought, despite its small immediate influence, is quite important in the history of economic doctrines, treats of the same problem in his *Principes de la théorie des richesses*. Going straight to the heart of the problem, he asks whether it is possible to give a clear definition of this general interest—the economic *optimum* which we are anxious to realize—and whether the system of free

---

[1] A similar idea is contained in *Liberty*, where it is stated that "trade is a social act," that the conduct of every merchant "comes within the jurisdiction of society," and that "as the principle of individual liberty is not involved in the doctrine of Free Trade, so neither is it in most of the questions which arise respecting the limits of that doctrine; as, for example, what amount of public control is admissible for the prevention of fraud by adulteration; how far sanitary precautions, or arrangements to protect workpeople employed in dangerous occupations, should be enforced on employers. . . . But that they [people] may be legitimately controlled for these ends is in principle undeniable." (Chapter v.)

[2] Michel Chevalier, Introductory Lectures, No. 10, in *Cours*, Vol. I, p. 221.

[3] *Cours*, Vol. I, pp. 211, 214; Vol. II, pp. 38, 115.

competition is clearly superior to every other. He justly remarks that
the problem is insoluble. Production is determined by demand,
which depends both upon the preliminary distribution of wealth and
also upon the tastes of consumers. But if this be the case, it is impossible to outline an ideal system of distribution or to fix upon the
kind of tastes that will prove most favourable for the development of
society. A step farther and Cournot must have hit upon the distinction so neatly made by Pareto between maximum utility, which is a
variable, undefined notion, and maximum ophelimity, "the investigation of which constitutes a clearly defined problem wholly within the
realm of economics."[1]

But Cournot does not therefore conclude that we ought to abstain
from passing any judgment in the realm of political economy and
abandon all thought of social amelioration. Though the absolutely
best cannot be defined, it does not follow that we cannot determine
the relatively good. "Improvement or amelioration is possible," says
he, "by introducing a change which operates upon one part of the
economic system, provided there are no indirect effects which damage
the other parts of the system."[2] Such progress is not necessarily the
result of private effort. Following Sismondi, he quotes several instances
in which the interests of the individual collide with those of the public
and in which State intervention might prove useful.

Every one of these authors—in varying degrees, of course—admits
the legitimacy of State intervention in matters economic. Liberty
doubtless is still the fundamental principle. Sismondi was content
with mere aspiration, so great did the difficulties of intervention appear
to him. Stuart Mill thought that the *onus probandi* should rest with the
innovator. Cournot considered liberty as being still the most natural
and simple method, and should the State find it necessary to intervene
it could only be in those instances in which science has clearly defined
the aim in view and demonstrated the efficacy of the methods proposed. Every one of them has abandoned liberty as a scientific
principle. To Cournot it was an axiom of practical wisdom;[3] Stuart
Mill upheld it for political reasons as providing the best method of
developing initiative and responsibility among the citizens. They all
agree that the State, far from being a *pis aller*, has a legitimate sphere
of action. The difficulty is just to define this.[4] This was the task to

[1] Pareto, *Cours d'Économie politique*, Vol. II, para. 656 (1897).
[2] *Principes*, p. 422.
[3] *Ibid.*, pp. 444, 462, 521.
[4] Stuart Mill has tried to do so in a formula that is not very illuminating: "To
individuality should belong the part of life in which it is chiefly the individual that
is interested; to society, the part which chiefly interests society." (*Liberty*, chapter iv.)

which Walras addressed himself with remarkable success in his lectures on the theory of the State, delivered in Paris in 1867-68.[1]

And so we find that the progress of thought since the days of Adam Smith had led to important modifications of the old doctrines concerning the economic functions of the State. The publicists, however, were not immediately converted. Even when the century was waning they still remained faithful to the optimistic individualism of the earlier period. The organon of State Socialism merely consists of these analyses incorporated into a system. The authors just mentioned must consequently be regarded, if not as the precursors of State Socialism, at any rate as unconsciously contributing to the theory.

II: THE SOCIALISTIC ORIGIN OF STATE SOCIALISM. RODBERTUS AND LASSALLE

State Socialism is not an economic doctrine merely. It has a social and moral basis, and is built upon a certain ideal of justice and a particular conception of the function of society and of the State. This ideal and this conception it received, not from the economists, but from the Socialists, especially Rodbertus and Lassalle. The aim of these two writers was to effect a kind of compromise between the society of the present and that of the future, using the powers of the modern State simply as a lever.

The idea of a compromise of this kind was not altogether new. A faint suggestion of it may be detected more than once in the course of the century, and an experiment of the kind was mooted in France towards the end of the July Monarchy. At that time we find men like Louis Blanc and Vidal—who were at least socialists in their general outlook—writing to demand State intervention not merely with a view to repairing the injustice of the present society, but also with a view to preparation for the society of the future with as little break with the past as possible. Louis Blanc was in this sense the first to anticipate the programme of the State Socialists. But its more immediate inspirers were Rodbertus and Lassalle, both of whom belonged to that country in which its effects were most clearly seen.

Their influence upon German State Socialism cannot be exactly measured by the amount of direct borrowing that took place. They were linked by ties of closest friendship to the men who were responsible for creating and popularizing the new ideas, and it is important that we should appreciate the personal influence which they wielded.

[1] Republished in his *Études d'Économie sociale*, 1896. See a brief résumé in our chapter on Rent.

Rodbertus formed the centre of the group, and during the two years 1862–64 he carried on an active correspondence with Lassalle. They were brought together by the good offices of a common friend, Lothar Bucher, an old democrat of 1848 who had succeeded in becoming the confidant of Bismarck. Strangely enough, Bismarck kept up his friendship with Lassalle even when the latter was most busily engaged with his propaganda work.[1] Wagner, also, the most eminent representative of State Socialism, was in frequent communication with Rodbertus, and he never failed to recognize his great indebtedness to him. Wagner himself was on more than one occasion consulted by Bismarck.

But apart altogether from their connexion with State Socialism, Rodbertus and Lassalle would deserve a place in our history. Rodbertus is a theoretical writer of considerable vigour and eloquence, and his thoughts are extraordinarily suggestive. Lassalle was an agitator and propagandist rather than an original thinker, but he has left a lasting impression upon the German labour movement. Hence our determination to give a somewhat detailed exposition of their work, especially of that of Rodbertus, and to spare no effort in trying to realize the importance of the contribution made by both of them.

I. RODBERTUS

In a history of doctrines Rodbertus has a place peculiarly his own. He forms, as it were, a channel through which the ideas first preached by Sismondi and the Saint-Simonians were transmitted to the writers who belong to the last quarter of the century. His intellectual horizon —largely determined for him by his knowledge of these French sources[2] —was fixed as early as 1837, when he produced his *Forderungen*, which

---

[1] For a general account of Lassalle's life, and especially his relations with Bismarck, see Hermann Oncken, *Lassalle* (Stuttgart, 1904).

[2] There has been no dispute concerning the French origin of Rodbertus's ideas since the evidence was sifted by Menger in his *Das Recht auf den vollen Arbeitsertrag* (1st ed., 1886). But Menger only mentions two sources of inspiration, Proudhon and the Saint-Simonians. The text will sufficiently indicate his indebtedness to the Saint-Simonians, but we think that Sismondi might well have been substituted for Proudhon. The only Proudhonian doctrine that is discoverable in Rodbertus is the theory concerning the constitution of value. But in the second of the *Soziale Briefe* (*Schriften*, Vol. II, p. 46, note) he states definitely that the idea was not a borrowed one, and that he himself was the first to formulate it, although he omits to state in what connexion. He may be referring to a passage in his *Forderungen*, where the idea is quite clearly expressed. Speaking of Ricardo's theory of value, he says: "That theory comes to grief on a single issue, namely, in regarding a thing as existing when it only exists in the mind, and treating a thing as a reality when it only becomes real in the future." (*Schriften*, Vol. III, p. 120.) It is clearly pointed out that the task of the future is to determine what value is. The *Forderungen*, where all the master ideas of Rodbertus may be studied, was published in 1837, nine years before the *Contradictions économiques* was published by Proudhon, who made his first reference to the question in that work.

the *Gazette universelle d'Augsburg* refused to publish. His first work appeared in 1842,[1] and the earliest of the *Soziale Briefe*[2] belong to 1850 and 1851. At the time these passed almost unnoticed. It was only when Lassalle in his treatise in 1862 referred to him as the greatest of German economists, and when conservative writers like Rudolf Meyer and Wagner drew attention to his work, that his books received the notice which they deserved. The German economists of the end of the last century were greatly influenced by him. His ideas, it is true, are largely those of the earliest French socialists, who wrote before the movement had lost its purely intellectual tone and become involved in the struggle of the July Monarchy, but his clear logic and his systematic method, coupled with his knowledge of economics, which is in every way superior to that of his predecessors, gives to these ideas a degree of permanence which they had never enjoyed before. This "Ricardo of socialism," as Wagner[3] calls him, did for his predecessors' doctrines what Ricardo had succeeded in doing for those of Malthus and Smith. He magnified the good results of their work and emphasized their fundamental postulates.

Rodbertus's upbringing decreed that he should not become involved in that democratic and radical socialism which was begotten of popular agitation, and whose best-known representative is Marx. Marx considered socialism and revolution, economic theory and political action, as being indissolubly one.[4] Rodbertus, on the other hand, was a great liberal landowner who sat on the Left Centre in the Prussian National Assembly of 1848, and his political faith is summed up in the two phrases 'constitutional government' and 'national unity.'[5] The success won

---

[1] *Zur Erkenntniss unserer staatswirtschaftlichen Zustände* (New Brandenburg, 1842). The work was to consist of three parts, only the first of which was published, and that has not been reissued since.

[2] The first three *Soziale Briefe*, as well as the *Forderungen*, have been republished in *Schriften von Dr Karl Rodbertus-Jagetsow* (Berlin, 1899, 3 Vols.). This is the edition we quote. The fourth *Brief*, entitled *Das Kapital*, was written in 1852, but was not published until after Rodbertus's death. It was translated into French in 1904 by M. Chatelain, and published by Messrs Giard and Brière. Our references in the succeeding pages are to this edition. Two other articles written by Rodbertus have been published, one by R. Meyer under the title *Briefe u. Sozialpolitische Aufsätze* (Berlin, 1882), the other by Moritz Wirth under the title of *Kleine Schriften* (Berlin, 1890). For a complete bibliography of Rodbertus's work see Andler's *Le Socialisme d'État en Allemagne* (Paris, 1897). Professor Gonner has written an illuminating study of his political philosophy.

[3] In his introduction to the *Briefe von Lassalle an Rodbertus*, p. 8 (Berlin, 1878).

[4] On the other hand, as Menger shows, the sources of Marx's theory are English rather than French—another point of difference between the two socialists.

[5] He was for a short time Minister of Public Worship. Appointed on July 4, he resigned at the end of a fortnight because his colleagues refused to recognize quite as fully as he wished the rights of the Parliament of Frankfort.

by the Bismarckian policy gradually drew him nearer the monarchy, especially towards the end of his life.[1] His ideal was a socialist party renouncing all political action and confining its attention solely to social questions. Although personally favourably inclined towards universal suffrage, he refused to join Lassalle's *Arbeiterverein* because Lassalle had insisted upon placing this article of political reform on his programme.[2] The party of the future, he thought, would be at once monarchical, national, and socialistic, or at any rate conservative and socialistic.[3] At the same time we must remember that "in so far as the Social Democratic party was aiming at economic reforms he was with it heart and soul."[4]

Despite his belief in the possibility of reconciling the monarchical policy with his socialistic programme, he carefully avoided the economic teachings of the socialists. His too logical mind could never appreciate their position, and he had the greatest contempt for the Socialists of the Chair. He would be the first to admit that in practice socialism must content itself with temporary expedients, although he cannot bring himself to believe that such compromise constitutes the whole of the socialistic doctrine. He refers to the Socialists of the Chair as the "sweetened water thinkers,"[5] and he refused to join them at the Eisenach Congress of 1872—the "bog of Eisenach," as he calls it somewhere. He regarded the whole thing as a first-class comedy. Even labour legislation, he thought, was merely a caprice of the humanitarians and socialists.[6] So that whenever we find him summing up his programme in some such sonorous phrase as *Staat gegen Staatslosigkeit*[7] ("the State as against the No-State") we must be careful to distinguish it from the hazy doctrines of the State Socialists.[8]

[1] A characteristic sign of this evolution is the substitution throughout the second edition of the *Soziale Briefe* of the word *Staatswille* ("the will of the State") for the word *Volkswille* ("the people's will"). This second edition, comprising the second and third letters, was published by him in 1875 under the title *Zur Beleuchtung der sozialen Frage*.
[2] Letter to R. Meyer, November 29, 1871. This point of view is developed at length in his "Open Letter to the Committee of the Association of German Workmen at Leipzig," April 10, 1863, published by Moritz Wirth in the *Kleine Schriften*.
[3] Letter to R. Meyer, March 12, 1872. *Cf.* the letters of January 23 and February 3, 1871.
[4] *Ibid.*, November 30, 1871. In 1874 he proposes to offer himself as a socialist candidate for the Reichstag, but recognizes that the State must first of all be strengthened on the military side as well as on the religious.
[5] *Ibid.*, October 17, 1872.   [6] *Ibid.*, January 6, 1873.
[7] *Ibid.*, March 10, 1872, and *Physiokratie u. Anthropokratie*, in *Briefe u. Sozialpolitische Aufsätze*, pp. 521, 522.
[8] He protests vigorously against the title of *Katheder Sozialist* in a letter of August 26, 1872. A vigorous criticism of the Socialism of the Chair, written in a private letter of Rodbertus, is quoted at length by Rudolf Meyer in his *Emancipationskampf des 4ten Standes*, pp. 60–63 (Berlin, 1874).

Despite himself, however, he proved one of the most influential pre-cursors of the school, and therein lies his real significance.

Rodbertus's whole theory rests upon the conception of society as an organism created by division of labour. Adam Smith, as he points out, had caught a faint glimmer of the significant fact that all men are linked together by an inevitable law of solidarity which takes them out of their isolation and transforms an aggregate of individuals into a real community having no frontiers and no limits save such as division of labour imposes, and sufficiently wide in scope to include the whole universe.[1] As soon as an individual becomes a part of economic society his well-being no longer depends upon himself and the use which he makes of the natural medium to which he applies himself, but upon the activity of his fellow-producers. The execution of certain social functions, which Rodbertus enumerates as follows, and which he borrows partly from Saint-Simon, henceforth become the deter-mining factors: (1) The adaptation of production to meet demand; (2) the maintenance of production at least up to the standard of the existing resources; (3) the just distribution of the common produce among the producers.

Should society be allowed to work out these projects spontaneously, or should it endeavour to carry out a preconceived plan? To Rodbertus this was the great problem which society had to consider. The econo-mists of Smith's school treated the social organism as a living thing. The free play of natural laws must have the same beneficial effects upon it as the free circulation of the blood has upon the human body. Every social function would be regularly discharged provided "liberty" only was secured. Rodbertus thought this was a mistake. "No State," says he,

is sufficiently lucky or perhaps unfortunate enough to have the natural needs of the community satisfied by natural law without any conscious effort on the part of anyone. The State is an historical organism, and the particular kind of organization which it possesses must be determined for it by the members of the State itself. Each State must pass its own laws and develop its own organization. The organs of the State do not grow up spontaneously. They must be fostered, strengthened, and controlled by the State.[2]

[1] "Communion or community of labour would be a better term than division of labour" (*Kapital*, p. 74); and in another connexion: "The only real division of labour is territorial division of labour" (*ibid.*). Elsewhere (p. 87) he warns his readers against confusing the terms 'social' and 'national.' Adopting the Saint-Simonian philosophy of history, he declares history to be a process of unification which brings gradually widening circles into closer unity with one another (*Zur Geschichte der römischen Tributsteuer*, in the *Jahrbücher für Nationalökonomie u. Statistik*, 1865, Vol. V, p. 2). "The course of history is just the expansion of communism." (*Kapital*, p. 85, note.)

[2] *Physiokratie u. Anthropokratie*, in *Briefe u. Sozialpolitische Aufsätze*, p. 519.

Hence, after 1837 we find Rodbertus proposing the substitution of a system of State direction[1] for the system of natural liberty, and his whole work is an attempt to justify the introduction of such a system. Let us examine his thesis and review the various economic functions which we defined above. Let us also watch their operation at the present day and see how differently these functions would be discharged in a better-organized community.

1. It is hardly correct to speak of production adapting itself to social need under existing conditions, because production only adapts itself to the effective demand—i.e., to the demand when expressed in terms of money. This fact had been hinted at by Smith, and Sismondi had laid considerable stress upon it; but Rodbertus was the earliest to point out that this really meant that only those people who already possess something can have their wants satisfied.[2] Those who have nothing to offer except their labour, and find that there is no demand for that labour, have no share in the social product. On the other hand, the individual who draws an income, even though he never did any work for it, is able to make effective his demand for the objects of his desire. The result is that many of the more necessitous persons must needs go unsatisfied, while others wallow in luxury.

Truer word was never spoken. Rodbertus had a perfect right to insist on the fundamental fallacy lurking within a system which could treat unemployment—that modern form of famine—as simply an over-production of goods, and which found itself unable to modify it except through public or private charity. His remedy consisted of a proposal to set up production for social need as a substitute for production for demand. The first thing to be done was to find out the time which each individual would be willing to give to productive work, making a note of the character and quantity of goods required at the same time.[3] He thought that "the wants of men in general form an even series, and that the kind and number of objects required can easily be calculated."[4] Knowing the time which society could afford to give to production, there would be no great difficulty in distributing the products among the various producers.

This is to go to work a little too precipitately and to shun the greatest

---

[1] *Schriften*, Vol. III, p. 216.

[2] "In a social State of this description people produce, not with a view to satisfying the needs of labour, but the needs of possession; in other words, they produce for those who possess." (*Kapital*, p. 161. *Cf.* also p. 51.)

[3] "Provided we knew the time that a person could afford to devote to the work of production, we could easily determine the quantity that would be sufficient to satisfy the needs of everybody." (*Ibid.*, p. 109.)

[4] *Ibid.*, p. 103.

difficulty of all. The uniform series of wants of which Rodbertus speaks exist only in the imagination. What we really find is a small number of collective needs combined with a great variety of individual needs. Social need is merely a vague term used to designate both kinds of wants at once. The slightest reflection shows that every individual possesses quite a unique series of needs and tastes. To base production upon social need is to suppress liberty of demand and consumption. It implies the establishment of an arbitrary scale of needs which must be satisfied and which is to be imposed upon every individual. The remedy would be worse than the evil.

But the opposition between social need and effective demand by no means disposes of his argument. The opposition needs some proving, and some explanation of the producers' preference for demand rather than need ought to be offered. The explanation must be sought in the fact that the capitalistic producer of to-day manages his business in accordance with the dictates of personal interest, and personal interest compels him to apply his instruments to produce whatever will yield him the largest net product. He is more concerned about the amount of profit made than about the amount of produce raised. He produces, not with a view to satisfying any social need, but simply because it yields him rent or profit.[1]

This contrast between profit-making and productivity deserves some attention. Sismondi had already called attention to it by distinguishing between the net and the gross product. A number of writers have treated of it since, and it holds a by no means insignificant place in the history of economic doctrines.[2]

The opposition is dwelt upon in no equivocal fashion by Rodbertus. This pursuit of the maximum net product is clearly the producer's only guide, but the conclusions which he proceeds to draw from it are somewhat more questionable. If we accept his opinion that the satisfaction of social need and not of individual demand is the determining factor in production, we are driven to the conclusion that modern

[1] *Kapital*, p. 143.

[2] The question of the net and gross product was one of the outstanding problems of this period. Vidal (*Répartition des Richesses*, p. 219, Paris, 1846) and Ott (*Traité d'Économie sociale*, p. 95, 1851) lay stress upon it. Since then Cournot, Dühring, and more recently Effertz and Landry, have handled the problem anew. But each of them when he comes to define the word 'productivity' defines it in his own fashion, so that they do not really discuss the same question. Rodbertus, as we shall have occasion to point out in the text, uses the word in a very vague fashion indeed, but still it is the basis of his whole discussion. It seems to us that under a regime of division of labour rentability should be the one criterion. But it would be a mistake to imagine that when dwindling profits make a change in the methods of production imperative, that change will be welcomed with equal enthusiasm by everybody, by both master and worker alike.

society, actuated as it is by this one motive, cannot possibly satisfy every individual demand. But we have already shown that the phrase 'social need' has no precise connotation; neither has the term 'productivity,' which is so intimately connected with it. Further, if society has no desire to impose upon its members an arbitrary scale of wants that must be satisfied—in other words, if demand and consumption are to remain free—it can only be by adopting that system which recognizes a difference between the present and the future 'rentability' of the product. This difference between the sale price and the real cost of production of any commodity must, it seems to us, be recognized even by a collectivist society as the only method of knowing whether the satisfaction which a commodity gives is in any way commensurate with the labour involved in its production.[1] Pareto has given an excellent demonstration of this by showing how collectivist society will have to take account of price indications if social demand is to be at all adequately supplied.

2. Turning to the other desideratum, namely, a fuller utilization of the means of production, Rodbertus contents himself with quoting the criticisms of the Saint-Simonians concerning the absence of conscious direction which characterizes the present regime and the hereditary element which is such a common feature of economic administration. He is in full agreement with Sismondi when the latter declares that production is entirely at the option of the capitalist proprietor.[2] In this matter he is content merely to follow his leaders, without making any contribution of his own to the subject.

3. There still remains a third economic function which society ought to perform, and which Rodbertus considered the most important of all, namely, the distribution of the social product. An analysis of the present system of distribution was one of the tasks he had set himself to accomplish, believing with Sismondi and other socialists that a solution of the problem of distribution and the explanation of such phenomena as economic crises and pauperism constitute the most vital problems which face the science at the present moment.

A just distribution, in Rodbertus's opinion, should secure to every one the product of his labour.[3] But does not the present regime of free competition and private property accomplish this?

---

[1] He is dealing merely with individual wants. Rentability is not the only guide. Many collective wants must be satisfied, but the process is not always a profitable one. The problem is to determine which are those wants. Rodbertus is speaking of private wants; he has taken good care to leave the public needs aside, so that his argument applies only to the former.　　　[2] *Kapital*, pp. 164–166.

[3] Rodbertus further adds that a portion of everybody's income should be expended in supplying such public needs. (*Kapital*, pp. 132–133.)

Let us watch the mechanism of distribution as we find it operating at the present time. Rodbertus's description of it is not very different from J. B. Say's, and it tallies pretty closely with the Classical scheme. On the one hand we have the *entrepreneur* who purchases the services of labour, land, and capital, and sells the product which results from this collaboration. The prices which he pays for these services and the price he himself receives from the consumer are determined by the interaction of demand and supply. What remains after paying wages, interest, and rent constitutes his profits.[1]

The distribution of the product is effected through the mechanism of exchange, and the result of its operation is to secure to the owner of every productive service the approximate market value of that service. Could anything be juster? Apparently not. But if we examine the social and economic hinterland behind this mechanism what we do find is the callous exploitation of the worker by every capitalist and landlord. The various commodities which are distributed among the different beneficiaries are really the products of labour. They are begotten of effort and toil—largely mechanical. Rodbertus did not under-value intellectual work or under-estimate the importance of directive energy. But intelligent effort seemed to him an almost inexhaustible force, and its employment should cost nothing, just as the forces of nature may be got for nothing. Only manual labour implies loss of time and energy—the sacrifice of something that cannot be replaced.[2] Consequently he does not recognize the intellectual or moral effort (the name is immaterial) involved in the postponement of consumption, whereby a present good is withheld with a view to contributing to the sum total of future good.[3] And he proceeds to define and to develop the opening paragraph of Smith's *Wealth of Nations*: "The annual labour of every nation is the fund which originally supplies it with all the necessaries and conveniences of life which it annually consumes, and which consist always either in the

---

[1] *Kapital*, pp. 150–160.

[2] Cf. *Zur Erkenntniss*, pp. 7–10: "Every economic good costs labour and only labour." In the third of the *Soziale Briefe* he expresses this idea in a slightly different form: "All economic goods are the product of labour" (*Schriften*, Vol. II, pp. 105–106). Developing the same thought, he declares that this formula means: (1) that "only those goods which have involved labour should figure in the category of economic goods"; (2) that, "economically speaking, goods are regarded, not as the product of nature or of any other force, but simply as the product of labour"; (3) that "goods economically considered are just the product of labour, carried out by means of the material operations which are necessary for production." The work of industrial direction and its remuneration are regarded in the same light. Cf. *Schriften*, Vol. II, p. 219.

[3] On this point see Rist's *Le Capital provient-il uniquement du Travail?* in the *Revue d'Économie politique*, February 1906.

immediate produce of that labour or in what is purchased with that produce from other nations."

The difference between his attitude and Marx's is also interesting. Marx was thoroughly well versed in political economy, and had made a special study of the English socialists. His one object was to set up a new theory of exchange, with labour as the source of all value. Rodbertus, who drew his inspiration from the Saint-Simonians, focused attention upon production, and treated labour as the real source of every product—a simpler, a truer, but a still incomplete proposition. Rodbertus never definitely commits himself to saying that labour by itself creates value, but, on the other hand, he never denies it.[1] Social progress, he always maintained, must consist in the greater degree of coincidence[2] between the value of a product and the quantity of labour contained in it. But this is a task which the future must take in hand.[3] Again, if it be true that the worker creates the product, but that the proprietors of the soil and the capitalists who have had no share in its production are able to manipulate exchange in such a way as to retain a portion of it for themselves, it is clear that our judgment concerning the equity of the present system needs some revision. This secret embezzlement for the profit of the non-worker and to the injury of the diligent proceeds without any outward display of violence through the free play of exchange operating within a system of private property.

[1] Rodbertus expressly declares that to say that goods are the product of labour is not to imply that the value of the product is always equal to what it cost in the way of labour, or, in other words, that the labour spent on it does not always measure its value (*Schriften*, Vol. II, pp. 104, 105). A similar statement is made in the *Forderungen* (1837). In the *Zur Erkenntniss* (1842) (pp. 129-131) he gives some of the reasons why he thinks that the value of a product is not equal to the labour it has cost: (1) There is the necessity for equalizing the gains of capital; (2) the price of a unit of any commodity is fixed by the price of the unit which costs most to reproduce. In the second of the *Soziale Briefe* he repeats the statement that the labour value theory is nothing better than an ideal (*Kapital*, Appendix, p. 279). In a letter written to R. Meyer on January 7, 1872, he affirms the demonstration which he had already given, "that goods do not and cannot exchange merely in proportion to the quantity of labour which has been absorbed by them simply because of the existence of capital"; and he adds the significant words: "a demonstration that might in case of need be employed against Marx."

[2] "The coincidence between the value of the products and the quantity of labour involved in their production is simply the most ambitious ideal that economics has ever formulated." (Second *Sozial Brief*.)

[3] Occasionally Rodbertus admits for the sake of hypothesis or demonstration that prices do coincide with the labour cost; but his essential theory has no need of any such hypothesis, and it really plays quite an auxiliary or subordinate rôle. It is in the course of his exposition of the theory concerning the distribution of unearned income between landed proprietors and capitalists (quite an erroneous theory, by the way) that he is driven to admit that "the exchange value of each completed product, as well as of each portion of the product, is equal to its labour value." (Third *Sozial Brief*, *Schriften*, Vol. II, p. 101.)

Its sole cause lies in the present social system, "which recognizes the claim of private landowners and capitalists to a share of the wealth distributed, although they have contributed nothing towards its production."[1]

Hence his exposition of the twofold aspect of distribution. Economically exchange attributes to each of the factors land, capital, and labour a portion of the produce corresponding to the value of their respective services as estimated in the market. Socially it often means taking away from the real producers—from the workers—a part of the goods which their toil has created. This portion Rodbertus refers to under the simple name "rent," which includes both the revenue of capitalists and the income of landlords.

No economist ever put the twofold aspect of the problem in a clearer light. Laying hold of the eternal opposition between the respective standpoints, he emphasizes the difficulties which they present to so many minds. Justice would relate distribution to merit, but society is indifferent provided its own needs are satisfied. Society simply takes account of the market value of these products and services without ever showing the least concern for their origin or the efforts which they may originally have involved—the weary day of the industrious labourer and the effortless lounge of the lazy capitalist being similarly rewarded. Rodbertus's great merit was to separate this truth from the other issues so frequently confused with it in the writings of the earlier economists and to bring it clearly before the notice of his fellow economists.

Rodbertus's criticism did not end there, although the demonstration which we have just given of the distinction between the social and the purely economic point of approach to distribution constitutes its essential merit. We must not omit the practical conclusions which he draws from it.

What concerned Rodbertus most—at least, so we imagine from the standpoint which he adopted—was not the particular way in which the rate of wages or interest, high or low rents, are determined, but the proportion of the revenue that goes to the workers and non-workers respectively. The former question is a purely economic one of quite secondary importance compared with this other social problem. Believing that he had already shown the possibility of the workers being robbed, the problem now was to determine whether this spoliation was likely to continue. Does economic progress give any ground for hoping that rent or unearned income will gradually disappear? Bastiat and Carey had replied in the affirmative. The proportion that goes to

[1] *Kapital*, p. 105.

capital, so they affirmed, is gradually becoming less, to the great advantage of the labourer. Ricardo, faced with the same dilemma, had come to the conclusion that with the inevitable increase in the cost of producing food the landowner's share must be constantly growing. Say had asked himself the same question in the earliest edition of his treatise, but had found no reply. Rodbertus adopts none of their solutions, but independently arrives at the conclusion that the worker's share gradually dwindles, to the advantage of the other participants.[1]

Theorist as he was, a simple deduction was all that was needed to convince him of the truth of this view. The rate of wages, we have already seen, is determined by the interaction of demand and supply in the labour market. The market price of labour, however, like that of any other product, is always gravitating towards a normal value— this normal value being none other than Ricardo's necessary wage. "The share of the product that falls to the lot of the producer both in an individual instance and as a general rule is not measured by the amount which he himself has produced, but by that quantity which is sufficient for the upkeep of his strength and the upbringing of his children."[2] This celebrated 'brazen law' became the pivot of Lassalle's propaganda, although it was never definitely recognized by Marx.

Granting the existence of such a law, and admitting also that the amount produced by labour is always increasing, so that the mass of commodities produced always keeps growing, a very simple arithmetical calculation suffices to show that the total quantity obtained by the workers always remains the same, representing a diminished fraction of the growing totality.

A similar demonstration affords a clue to the prevalence of crises. The *entrepreneur* keeps adding to the mass of commodities produced until he touches the full capacity of social demand.[3] But while production grows and expands the worker's share dwindles, and thus his

[1] "Whenever exchange is allowed to take its own course in the matter of distributing the national dividend, certain circumstances connected with the development of society and with the growing productivity of social labour cause the wages of the working classes to diminish so as to constitute a decreasing fraction of the national product." (Second *Sozial Brief*, *Schriften*, Vol. II, p. 37.)

[2] *Kapital*, p. 153.

[3] The idea that *entrepreneurs* base their production upon the demand of the higher classes is a somewhat novel one, but it is quite definitely stated by Rodbertus. "The classes can only influence the market in proportion to the quantity of the social product which is given them. But the *entrepreneurs* must determine the quantities which they will produce, according to the size of their demands." (*Kapital*, pp. 51–52. *Cf.* also pp. 170–171.) It is quite obvious, on the contrary, that the *entrepreneurs* base their production solely upon the demand for the particular goods which they manufacture, and that they are quite indifferent to the share which goes to the higher classes.

demand for some products remains permanently below production level. The structure is giving way under the very feet of the unsuspecting producer.[1] This theory of crises is simply a re-echo of Sismondi,[2] and gives an explanation of a chronic evil rather than of a crisis pure and simple. Its scientific value is just about equal to Sismondi's other theory concerning proportional distribution.

This theory upon which Rodbertus laid such emphasis had already been outlined in his *Forderungen*, and a fuller development is given in his *Soziale Briefe*, where he expressly states it to be the fundamental point of his whole system, all else being mere scaffolding. His one ambition all his life long was to be able to give a statistical proof of it, but its importance is not nearly as great as he imagined it to be.

In the first place, doubt as to the validity of the 'brazen' or 'iron law of wages'—upon which the theory is based—is entertained not merely by economists, but also by socialists. And even if it were true, Rodbertus's proof would still be inconclusive, for the workers' share of the total product depends not upon one fact alone, but upon two —the rate of wages *and* the number of workers. Rodbertus's error and Bastiat's are very similar. Bastiat had tried to determine the capitalists' share of the total product by taking account of one fact only, namely, the rate of interest, whereas he ought to have taken the amount of existing capital into consideration as well.

But we must admit that although the arguments used by Rodbertus are scarcely more reliable than Bastiat's, his theory itself is nearer the facts as judged by statistics. No amount of *a priori* reasoning without some recourse to statistics can ever solve the problem. Statistics themselves seem to prove that labour's portion, in the Western countries, showed signs of diminishing between the beginning of the present century and the First World War; and the same is true—in France at least—after the Second World War.

This does not necessarily mean that the worker must be worse off, for it may well happen that a diminution in the general share obtained by labour is accompanied by a growth of individual wages. All that we can conclude is that wages have not increased as rapidly as has

[1] *Kapital*, p. 53.

[2] We shall soon be convinced of the similarity that exists between the two theories if we read the passage in the article on *Balance des Consommations avec les Productions*, published by Sismondi as an appendix to the second edition of the *Nouveaux Principes*, Vol. II, p. 430. Rodbertus agrees with Sismondi that equilibrium will be re-established in the long run, but that in the meantime a crisis may have to intervene. (*Kapital*, p. 171, note; *cf.* p. 190, *supra*.)

[3] Such, as we have already seen, is Colson's conclusion (*Cours*, Vol. III, p. 366), and such is the verdict of M. Chatelain after studying the United States census returns. According to Chatelain (*Questions pratiques de Législation ouvrière*, June and July 1908),

capital's share,[3] but this has not prevented the workers from sharing in the general growth of prosperity. Nor is there any reason why at another time the workers' *share* should not increase, even without any improvement in their *absolute* remuneration.

Logically enough, Rodbertus proceeds to draw certain practical conclusions, including the necessity for the suppression of private property and of individual production. The community should be the sole owner of the means of production. Unearned income must go. Every one should contribute something to the national dividend, and each should share in the total produce in proportion to his labour. The value of all commodities will depend upon the amount of time spent on them and effort put into them; and since the supply will always adapt itself to the needs of society the measure will be constant and exact, and equal distribution will be assured.

But Rodbertus recoils from his own solution, and the ardent socialist becomes a simple State Socialist. What frightens him is not the terrible tyranny of a system under which production and even consumption would be strictly regulated. "There would be as much personal freedom under a system of this kind as in any other form of society," he remarks,[1] 'society' evidently always implying some measure of restraint. His apprehension was of a different kind. He had a perfect horror of any revolutionary change, and stood aghast at the lack of education displayed by the masses. He realized how unwilling they were to sacrifice even a part of their wages in order to enable other men to have the necessary leisure to pursue the study of the arts and sciences—the noblest fruits of civilization. Finally, it seemed to him that illegal appropriation and the rightful ownership which results from vigorous toil are too often confused by being indiscriminately spoken of as private property. "There is," says he, "so much that is right mixed up with what is wrong that one goads the lawful owner into revolt in trying to lay hold of the unlawful possessor."[2]

the American metal-workers' share in the product fell from 71 to 68 per cent. between the years 1890 and 1905, while capital's share increased from 28 to 32 per cent. The men's wages during the same period rose from 551 dollars to 626, while the rate of interest fell from 9 to 8 per cent. Despite this diminution in labour's share of the total product it is impossible to say whether the remuneration of labour in general is moving upward or downward, for the working classes do not depend solely upon the wages of their labour. Some of them have a little capital—a very small amount, perhaps, but there is no reason for thinking that it will not grow in future.

It is quite clear that this complicated question must be carefully defined. Three different factors must be distinguished: (1) The individual's wage; (2) labour's share in the product; (3) the income of the working class. On this problem see Edwin Cannan's article in the *Quarterly Journal of Economics*, 1905, and his statements in his *Theory of Production and Distribution, 1776–1848*.

[1] *Kapital*, p. 176. [2] *Ibid.*, p. 187.

Some kind of compromise should at all costs be effected. If private property—one of the great evils of the present day—cannot be got rid of without some inconvenience, cannot we possibly dispense with freedom of contract, the other source of inequality? Let us assume, then, that we have got rid of free contract while retaining the institution of private property. By doing this, although we are not immediately able to clear away unearned income, we shall have removed some of the greatest inconveniences that result from it. We shall arrest the downward trend of labour's remuneration, and poverty and crises will disappear together.[1]

Such an attempt might be made even now. Let the State estimate the total value of the social product in terms of labour and determine the fraction that should go to the workers. Let it give to each *entrepreneur* in accordance with the number of workers he employs a number of wage coupons, in return for which the *entrepreneur* shall be obliged to put on the market a quantity of commodities equal in value. Lastly, let the said workers, paid in wage coupons, supply themselves with whatever they want from the public stores in return for these coupons. The national estimate would from time to time be subject to revision; and in order that the proportions should always be the same, the number of coupons given to labour would have to be increased if the number of commodities produced ever happened to increase. Rodbertus's aim was to give the workers a share in the general progress made, and such was the plan which he laid down.[2]

There is no need to emphasize its theoretical, let alone its practical, difficulties. We were led to mention it for a double reason. In the first place, it is interesting as an attempt to effect a compromise between the society of the present and the collectivism of the future. Marx regards the growing servility of the worker with a certain

[1] "And so I believe that just as history is nothing but a series of compromises, the first problem that awaits economic science at the present moment is that of effecting some kind of a working compromise between labour, capital, and property." (*Kapital*, p. 187.) In a letter written on September 18, 1873, to R. Meyer, he declares that the great problem "is to help us to pass by a peaceful evolution from our present system, which is based upon private property in land and capital, to that superior social order which must succeed it in the natural course of history, which will be based upon desert and the mere ownership of income, and which is already showing itself in various aspects of social life, as if it were already on the point of coming into operation."

[2] *Cf. Kapital*, pp. 109 *et seq.*, and especially his article *Der Normalarbeitstag*, which appeared in 1871 and was republished in *Briefe u. Sozialpolitische Aufsätze*, pp. 552 *et seq.* The idea of determining value in the way Rodbertus intended was criticized by Marx in his *Misère de la Philosophie*, *à propos* of Proudhon's attempt in 1847. The socialization of production involves the socialization of exchange as well. This is another point upon which Marx and Rodbertus differ.

measure of equanimity as a necessary preliminary to his final emancipation. Rodbertus would speed the process of amelioration and would better his lot here and now.[1] It also throws an interesting light upon his extraordinary confidence in the all-powerful sovereignty of the State, and the ability of government to bend every individual will, even the most recalcitrant, to the general will. At the same time it reveals his utter indifference to individual liberty as an economic motive.

This indifference gradually merges into extreme hostility, while his confidence in the centralized executive becomes all the more thoroughly established. His later historical works contain an exposition of an organic theory of the State which is meant to justify such confidence. Just as in the animal world the higher animals are found to possess the most highly differentiated organs as well as the most closely coordinated, so in history as we pass from the lower social strata to the higher ones

> the State advances both in magnitude and efficiency; and its action, while increasing in scope, grows in intensity as well. The State in its passage from one evolutionary stage to another presents us not merely with a greater degree of complexity, each function being to a greater and greater extent discharged by some special organ, but also with an increasing degree of harmony. The social organisms, despite their ever-increasing variation, are placed in growing dependence upon one another by being linked to some central organ. In other words, the particular grade that a social organism occupies in the organic hierarchy depends upon the degree to which division of labour and centralization have been carried.[2]

We are thus driven back upon the fundamental question set by Rodbertus at the outset of his inquiry: Can the various social functions, acting spontaneously, efficiently further the good of the social body, or should these functions be discharged by the mediation of a special organ, the State or Government? There is also the further question as to whether the reply which he gives is entirely satisfactory.

We are immediately struck by a preliminary contradiction: the economic boundaries of the community do not coincide with its political boundaries. The one is the result of division of labour and is coextensive with the limits set by division of labour, while the second is the product of the changing conditions of history. It is only logical that the economic functions of the State should be performed by other organs than those of the political Government, since its sphere of action is necessarily different. But it is to the State, as evolved in the

[1] *Cf. Kapital,* p. 188, note.
[2] *Zur Geschichte der römischen Tributsteuer,* in *Jahrbücher für Nationalökonomie u. Statistik,* Vol. VIII, pp. 446–447, note.

course of a long historical process, that Rodbertus would entrust this directing power. Between Rodbertus's description of the State's economic activity and his final recourse to a national monarchical State is an element of contradiction which strikes us rather forcibly, especially when he comes to speak of "national" socialism.

In order to demonstrate how inadequately the present social organization performs its duties, Rodbertus appeals to an ideal method of discharging them which he himself has created, and he has not the slightest difficulty in showing that hardly any of his ideal functions are being performed at the present time. Production is not based upon social need, nor is the wealth produced distributed in accordance with the labour spent. But we must never forget that Rodbertus's conception of the social need was extremely arbitrary. His distribution formula, "to every one according as he produces," if applied logically is impossible, and satisfies neither the demands of humanity nor the needs of production. Had his definition of social function been less ambitious, his argument, perhaps, would have been more convincing.

Let us admit, however, that the existence of an economic society implies the successful accomplishment of certain functions which we need not trouble to define just now. The question then arises—a question that implies the severest criticism of the present organization: Can the control and oversight which men ought to exercise over these functions be performed otherwise than through the instrumentality of the State? There was only one alternative for Rodbertus—extreme individualism or State control. But nature and history both escape the dilemma. The biological analogy has been carried too far, and most writers would be content to abandon it altogether. Like most of his contemporaries, Rodbertus imagined that economic individualism and personal liberty were indissolubly bound together, and that it was impossible to check individualism without endangering liberty. It is now realized, however, that this association of ideas, like many another, is temporary and not eternal, and the growth of voluntary associations intermediate between the State and the individual is every day showing it to be false.

We are now in a better position to appreciate the kind of appeal which this doctrine would make to State Socialists—people who are essentially conservative, but nevertheless genuinely desirous of seeing a larger element of justice introduced into our industrial regime. The distinction drawn between politics and economic socialism makes a first claim upon their respect. Then would follow the organic conception of society, which is a feature of all Rodbertus's writings. It was his belief that production and distribution could only be regarded as

social functions, and that the breakdown of individualism implied a
need for greater centralization or a greater degree of State control.
On the other hand, the State Socialists refuse to associate themselves
with the radical condemnation of private property and unearned
income, both of which are features of Rodbertus's teaching. The
State Socialists set out to transform the Rodbertian compromise into
a self-sufficing system, and instead of regarding their doctrine as a
diluted form of socialism they are rather inclined to treat socialism as
an exaggerated development of their theory.[1]

2. LASSALLE

Rodbertus's efforts to establish a doctrine of State Socialism upon
the firm foundation of a new social theory had already met with a
certain measure of success, but it was reserved for Lassalle to infuse
vitality into these new ideas.

Lassalle's brief but brilliant political career, ever memorable for
the natural vigour of his eloquence, at once popular and refined, and
its indelible impression of a strikingly original nature aflame with a
passion both for thought and action, together with the romantic,
dramatic character of his checkered existence, lent wonderful force to
his utterances. In 1848, at the early age of twenty-three, he was a
Marxian revolutionist. The revolutionary period was followed by a
time of enforced inactivity, when he devoted himself almost exclusively
to philosophical, legal, and literary pursuits. In 1862 the silence was
at last broken by his re-entry into the political arena. The whole
political life of Germany was at that moment convulsed by the half-
hearted opposition which the Prussian Liberal party was offering to
Bismarck's constitutional changes. Lassalle declared war both upon
the Government and upon the bourgeois Opposition—upon the latter
more than the former, perhaps. Turning to the working classes, he
urged them to form a new party which would avoid all purely political
questions and to concentrate upon their own economic emancipation.
For two eventful years the whole of Germany resounded with his
speeches and his declamations before various tribunals, while the
country was flooded with his pamphlets advocating the complete
establishment of the *Allgemeiner deutscher Arbeiterverein* (General Association of German Workers) which he had already founded at Leipzig in
1863. The workers of the Rhineland received with open arms the
agitator who thus took up in their midst the tangled skein of a broken

[1] "Extreme socialism," says Wagner, "is simply an exaggeration of that partial
socialism which has long been a feature of the economic and social evolution of all
nations, especially the most civilized." (*Grundlegung*, 3rd ed., p. 756.)

career, and welcomed him with songs and decked him with garlands. The Liberal Press, on the other hand, thoroughly taken aback by his unexpected onslaughts, mercilessly attacked him, even accusing him of having secret dealings with the Government. Suddenly the clamour ceased: Lassalle died on August 31, 1864, as the result of a wound which he had received in a duel,[1] and only the *Deutscher Arbeiterverein*, the earliest embryo of the great German Social Democratic party, remained as a memento of those violent attacks upon individualist Liberalism.

As far as theory goes, Lassalle's socialism is hardly distinguishable from Marx's. Social evolution is summed up in a stricter limitation of the rights of private property,[2] which in the course of a century or two must result in its total disappearance.[3] But Lassalle was pre-eminently a man of action, bent upon practical results. At that particular moment the German working class was only just waking up to the possibility of political existence. The path that it should follow was still undecided. In the year 1863 a number of workmen had tried to persuade their comrades to meet together in a kind of general congress. They further appealed to Lassalle and to other well-known democrats for their advice concerning the labour question. This gave Lassalle the opportunity he required for forming a political party of his own, with himself as chief. The next question was to fix upon a programme. "Working men," says Lassalle, "must have something definite,"[4] and, on the other hand, "it is almost impossible to get the public to understand the final object which we must keep in view."[5] So, without burdening his propaganda with too remote an ideal, he concentrates all his efforts upon two demands, the one political, the other economic—universal suffrage on the one hand and the establishment of producers' associations supported by the State on the other. In order to win over the masses, he invoked, not the doctrine of the exploitation of the workers by the proprietors—which would have alienated the middle classes from him[6]—but the 'brazen

[1] George Meredith in his *Tragic Comedians* weaves his story round this tragic adventure, giving us an admirable study of Lassalle's psychology. *Cf.* also *Lassalle*, by Georges Brandès, and Oncken's *Lassalle* (Stuttgart, 1904).

[2] *Théorie systématique des Droits acquis*, Vol. I, p. 274, note (Paris, 1904).

[3] *Briefe von Lassalle an Rodbertus*, p. 46 (Berlin, 1878).   [4] *Ibid.*, p. 44.

[5] "*Freilich darf man das dem Mob heut noch nicht sagen.*" (*Ibid.*, p. 46.)

[6] "No workman will ever forget that property whenever legally acquired is absolutely inviolable and just," says he in an address delivered to the workers of Berlin on April 12, 1862, and published under the title of *Arbeiterprogramm* (*Schriften*, Vol. I, p. 197). Elsewhere he defends himself against the charge of inciting the proletariat by claiming that his agitation was of a purely democratic character, and intended to facilitate the fusion of classes (*ibid.*, Vol. II, pp. 126–127). (Our quotations are taken from Pfau's edition. We were unable to obtain the best edition of Lassalle's works, published by Bernstein.)

law of wages,' which is the happy title by which he chose to designate
the Ricardian law of wages.

Rodbertus realized the necessity for distinguishing between an
esoteric and an exoteric Lassalle[1]—between the logical theorist of the
study and the opportunist politician of the public platform. Only to
his contemporaries was the latter Lassalle really known. But his
letters, which have been published since his death, go to show that
there is at least no need to attach any greater importance to his proposed reforms than he was prepared to give them himself. It is not
necessary to emphasize the fact that his plan was really borrowed
from Louis Blanc or to call attention to the letter written to Rodbertus
in which he declares himself quite prepared to change his plan provided
a better one can be found. This idea of association was one that was
by no means unknown to the German Liberal party; nor was it the
first time that it had been preached to the working classes. Lassalle's
rival, Schulze-Delitzsch, had begun an active campaign even as far
back as 1849, and had succeeded in establishing a great number of
co-operative credit societies, composed largely of artisans, and aiming
at supplying them with cheap raw materials. But such associations
were to receive no support from the Government.

What was new in Lassalle's scheme was just this appeal for State
intervention. It was his energetic protest against eternal *laissez-faire*
that impressed public opinion, and he himself was anxious that it
should be presented in this light. Speaking to the workers of Frankfort
on May 19, 1863, he declared that "State intervention is the one
question of principle involved in this campaign. That is the consideration that has weighed with me, and there lies the whole issue of the
battle which I am about to wage."[2]

---

[1] Wagner's introduction to *Briefe von Lassalle an Rodbertus*, p. 5. Lassalle has himself
defined this somewhat Machiavellian attitude in a letter written to Marx in 1859,
in which he speaks of a drama which he had just written dealing with Franz von
Sickingen. "It looks like the triumph of superior realistic ability when the leader of a
rebellion takes account of the limited means at his disposal and attempts to hide
from other men the real object which he has in view. But the success achieved by
deceiving the ruling classes in this way puts him in possession of new forces which
enable him to employ this partial triumph for carrying out his real object." (*Aus
dem litterarischen Nachlass von K. Marx, F. Engels, und Lassalle*, Vol. IV, p. 133; published
by F. Mehring, Stuttgart, 1902.)

[2] *Schriften*, Vol. II, p. 99. This address has been published under the title of
Arbeiterlesebuch. This is just the attitude of which Marx disapproved. In a letter
written to Schweitzer on October 13, 1868, quoted by Mehring (*Aus dem litterarischen
Nachlass*, etc., Vol. IV, p. 362), he expresses himself as follows: "He is too liable to
be influenced by the immediate circumstances of the moment. He exaggerates the
trivial difference between himself and a nonentity like Schulze-Delitzsch, until the
issue between them, governmental intervention as against private initiative, becomes
the central point of his agitation."

He harks back to this fundamental idea in all his principal writings. It was the theme of his first address delivered to the workers in Berlin in 1862. It is there presented with all his customary force. The bourgeois conception of the State is contrasted with the true conception, which is identical with the workers'. The bourgeoisie seem to think that the State has nothing to do except to protect the property and defend the liberties of the individual—a conception of State action that would be quite sufficient were everybody equally strong and intelligent, equally cultured and equally rich.[1] But where such equality does not exist the State is reduced to the position of a 'night watchman,' and the weak is left at the mercy of the strong. In reality the State exists for quite òther purposes. The history of mankind is the story of one long struggle to establish liberty in the face of natural forces, to overcome oppression of every kind, and to triumph over the misery, ignorance, want, and weakness with which human nature has always had to reckon. In that struggle the individual, in his isolation, is hopeless and union becomes indispensable. This union is a creation of the State, and its object is to realize the destiny of mankind, namely, the attainment of the highest degree of culture of which humanity is capable. It is a means of educating and of furthering the development of humanity along the path of liberty.

The formula savours of metaphysics rather than of economics. There is a striking similarity between it and the formula employed by Hegel, the philosopher.[2] Lassalle was really a disciple of Hegel and Fichte.[3] Through the influence of Lassalle the theories of the German

[1] *Schriften*, Vol. I, p. 213.

[2] See, among others, the chapter entitled *Hegel et la Théorie de l'État* in Lévy-Brühl's *L'Allemagne depuis Leibnitz*, especially p. 398 (Paris, 1890). The State, according to Hegel, is an expression of the spirit realizing itself in the conscience of the world, while nature is an expression of the same spirit without the conscience, an *alter ego* —a spirit in bondage. God moving in the world has made the State possible. Its foundation is in the might of reason realizing itself in will. It is necessary to think of it not merely as a given State or a particular institution, but of its essence or idea as a real manifestation of the mind of God. Every State, of whatever kind it may be, partakes of this divine essence. For full information concerning the philosophical origin of State Socialism see Andler's *Le Socialisme d'État en Allemagne* (1897).

[3] Fichte issued a very curious work in 1800 entitled *Der geschlossene Handelsstaat*, published in Vol. III of his complete works (Berlin, 1845), and containing ideas with many points of resemblance to those of State Socialism. Fichte thought that the State should not merely guarantee to every citizen his property, but should first of all rear its citizens, let them build their property, and then defend it. In order to do this every one should be given the necessary means of livelihood, for the one aim of all human activity is to live, and every one here has an equal right to live (p. 402)— a declaration of the right of existence. Until all are so provided for no luxuries should be allowed. No one should decorate his house until he feels certain that every one has a house, and every one should be comfortably and warmly clad before anyone is elegantly dressed (p. 400). "Nor is it enough to say that I can afford to pay for it,

idealists came into conflict with the economists', and his incomparable
eloquence contributed not a little to the rising tide of indignation with
which the Manchester ideas came to be regarded.

III: STATE SOCIALISM—PROPERLY SO CALLED

The years that elapsed between the death of Lassalle and the
Congress of Eisenach (1872) proved to be the decisive period in the
formation of German State Socialism.

Bismarck's remarkable *coups d'état* in 1866 and 1870 had done much
to discredit the political reputation of the leaders of the Liberal party,
who had shown themselves less than a match for the Chancellor's
political insight. This reacted somewhat upon economic Liberalism,
because it so happened that the leaders of both parties were the same.[1]
On the other hand, the idea of a rejuvenated empire incarnate in the
Iron Chancellor seemed to add fresh lustre to the whole conception of
the State. The *Jahrbücher für Nationalökonomie*, first issued by the
Historical school in 1863, had by this time become the recognized
organ of the University Economists, and had done a great deal to
accustom men's minds to the relative character of the principles of
political economy and to prepare their thoughts for an entirely new
point of view.

Labour questions had also suddenly assumed an importance quite

---

for it is unjust that one individual should be able to buy luxuries while his fellow
citizens have not enough to procure the necessaries of life. The money with which
the former purchases his luxuries would in a rational State not be his at all." Adopting this as his guiding principle, Fichte proposes to organize a State in which the
members of every profession, agriculturists, artisans, merchants, etc., would make a
collective contract with one another, in which they would promise not to encroach
upon one another's labour, but would guarantee to every one a sufficient number of
the goods which each has made for his own use. The State would also undertake to
see that the number of persons in every profession was neither too few nor too many.
It would also fix the price of goods. Lastly, in view of the fact that foreign trade
would naturally upset the equilibrium established by the contract which guaranteed
security of existence to each individual, the commercial State would have to be
entirely hemmed in by tariff walls. The whole work is original and interesting.
A. Menger, who gives a brief résumé of it in his second chapter of *The Right to the
Whole Produce of Labour*, thinks that Fichte was influenced by what he saw of the Convention during the Reign of Terror, by the issue of assignats, and perhaps by Babeuf.
Fichte, on the other hand, takes care to point out that his commercial State is not
realizable as such, but that a book like his is not less useful in view of the general hints
which it affords a statesman.
[1] It is remarkable that the majority of the commercial and financial measures introduced in Germany between 1866 and 1875, such as a uniform system of weights and
measures, the reform of the monetary system, banks, the tariffs, etc., were directly
inspired by the principles of economic Liberalism.

undreamt of before this. The German revolution of 1848 was presumably political in character: the great capitalistic industry had not reached that stage of development which characterized it both in England and in France; and it is a significant fact that the two great German socialists, Rodbertus and Marx, had to go abroad to either of those two countries to get their illustrations. But since 1848 German industry had made great strides. A new working-class community had come into being, and Lassalle had further emphasized this transformation by seeking to found a party exclusively upon this new social stratum. The association which was thus founded still survives. Another agitation, largely inspired by Marxian ideas, was begun about the same time by Liebknecht and Bebel. In 1867 both of them were elected to the Reichstag, and two years later they founded the *Social-demokratische Arbeiterpartei* (Social Democratic party), which was destined to play such an important part in the history of the next thirty years.

In this way labour questions suddenly attracted attention, just as they had previously done in France during the July Monarchy; and just as in France a new current of opinion—unceremoniously set aside by the *coup d'état*, it is true—had urged upon the educated classes the importance of abandoning the doctrine of absolute *laissez-faire* and of claiming the support of Government in the struggle with poverty, so in Germany an increasing number of authors had persuaded themselves that a purely passive attitude in face of the serious nature of the social problem which confronted them was impossible, and that the establishment of some sort of compact between the warring forces of capital and labour should not prove too much of an undertaking for the rejuvenated vitality of a new empire.

The new tendencies revealed themselves in unmistakable fashion at Eisenach in 1872. A conference, which was largely composed of professors and economists, of administrators and jurists, decided upon the publication of a striking manifesto in which they declared war upon the Manchester school. The manifesto spoke of the State as "a great moral institution for the education of humanity," and claimed that it should be "animated by a high moral ideal," which would "enable an increasing number of people to participate in the highest benefits of civilization."[1] At the same time the members of the congress determined upon the establishment of the *Verein für Sozialpolitik*, an association charged with the task of procuring the necessary scientific material for this new political development. This was the beginning

[1] A copy of the text translated into French by Saint-Marc appeared in the *Revue d'Économie politique*, 1892.

of the "Socialism of the Chair," as it was derisively named by the
Liberals on account of the great number of professors who took part
in this conference. The same doctrine, with a somewhat more radical
bias, became known as State Socialism. The imparting of such a bias
was the task undertaken by Wagner,[1] in his *Grundlegung*, which appeared
in 1876.[2]

Difficult though the task may prove, we must try to distinguish
between the work of the earlier economists and the special contributions made by the State Socialists. Like all doctrines that purport to
sum up the aspirations of a group or an epoch and to supply a working agreement between principles in themselves irreconcilable, it lacks
the definiteness of a purely individualistic or theoretical system. Its
ideas are borrowed from various sources, but it is not always scrupulous
in recognizing this.

It is first and foremost a reaction, not against the fundamental ideas
of the English Classical school, as is generally believed, but against the
exaggerations of their second-grade disciples, the admirers of Bastiat
and Cobden—known to us as the "Optimists" and styled the "Manchestrians" in Germany. The manifesto, drawn up by Professor
Schmoller at the Eisenach Congress, speaks of the "Manchester
school," but makes no mention of the Classical writers.[3] It is true
that a great many German writers regard the expressions "Smithianismus" and "Manchesterthum" as synonymous, but these are perhaps
polemical exaggerations upon which we ought not to lay too much
stress. On the other hand, Liberalism had nowhere assumed such
extravagant proportions as it had in Germany. Prince Smith, who is
the best-known representative of Liberalism after Dunoyer, was convinced that the State had nothing to do beyond guaranteeing security,

[1] In addition to Wagner we might mention Albert Schaeffle, who has shown considerable literary activity, but who is more of a sociologist than an economist. His
great work, *Bau und Leben des sozialen Körpers* (1875–78), contains an organic and
biological theory of society, but his best-known book is the *Quintessenz des Sozialismus*.

[2] Wagner's principal works, which contain an exposition both of the ideas and
programme of State Socialism, are *Grundlegung* (1st ed. 1876), translated into French
in 1900 under the title *Fondements de l'Économie politique*; *Finanzwissenschaft*; his article
Staat in the *Handwörterbuch der Staatswissenschaften*; and especially two articles entitled
Finanzwissenschaft and *Staatssozialismus*, published in the *Zeitschrift für die gesammte
Staatswissenschaft*, 1887, pp. 37–122, 675–746. One might profitably consult two
addresses, the one of March 29, 1895, *Sozialismus, Sozialdemokratie, Katheder u. Staatssozialismus*, the other of April 21, 1892, *Das neue sozialdemokratische Programm*.

[3] It is a curious fact that Wagner's definition of the province and functions of the
State is not very different from Smith's, though differing considerably from Bastiat's.
"As a general rule," says he, "the State should take charge of those operations which
are intended to satisfy the wants of the citizens, but which private enterprise or
voluntary associations acting for the community either cannot undertake or cannot
perform as well or as cheaply." (*Grundlegung*, 3rd ed., 1893, 1st part, p. 916.)

and denied that there was any element of solidarity between economic agents save such as results from the existence of a common market. "The economic community, as such, is a community built upon the existence of a market, and it has no facility to offer other than free access to a market."[1]

The State Socialists, on the contrary, are of opinion that there exists a moral solidarity which is much more fundamental than any economic tie between the various individuals and classes of the same nation—such solidarity as results from the possession of a common language, similar manners, and a uniform political constitution. The State is the organ of this moral solidarity, and because of this title it has no right to remain indifferent to the material poverty of a part of the nation. It has something to do besides protecting people against internal or external violence. It has a real work of "civilization and well-being"[2] which it ought to perform. In this way State Socialism becomes reconciled to the philosophic standpoint which Lassalle had chosen for it. Lassalle's insistence upon the mission of Governments and the importance of their historic role has been incorporated into its system, and the attention that is paid to national considerations reminds one of the teaching of Friedrich List.

It is impossible not to ask whether the State is capable of carrying out the duties that have been entrusted to it. There is little use in emphasizing duty where there is no capacity for discharging it. The State's incapacity as an economic agent has long been a notorious fact. Wagner and his friends were particularly anxious to correct this false impression, and as far as their doctrine contains anything original it may most conveniently be described as an attempt to rehabilitate the State. Optimists of Bastiat's genre looked upon the State as the very incarnation of incapacity. The State Socialists, on the other hand, regard government as an economic agent very similar to other agents which the community employs, only a little more sympathetic, perhaps. Much of their argument consists of an attempt to create a presumption in favour of government as against the ordinarily accepted opinion which individualism had begotten. Such was the nature of the task which they undertook.

Their first action was to insist upon the weaknesses of individuals. Following in the wake of Sismondi and other socialists, they empha-

[1] "Liberalism only recognizes one task which the State can perform, namely, the production of security." (Quoted by Schönberg, *Handbuch der politischen Oekonomie*, 3rd ed., Vol. I, p. 61. The quotation is taken from Rentzsch's dictionary, articles on *Freihandel* and *Handelsfreiheit*.)

[2] "Kultur und Wohlfahrtzweck" (Wagner, *Grundlegung*, p. 885.)

sized the social inconveniences of competition, which is, however, generally confused with individual liberty.[1] They also insisted upon the social inequality of masters and workers when it comes to a question of wage-bargaining—a fact that had already been noted by Adam Smith—as well as upon the universal opposition that exists between the weak and the strong. The inadequacy of merely individual effort to satisfy certain collective wants is another fact that was considerably emphasized.

As far back as the year 1856 Dupont-White, a Frenchman, had complained bitterly that all the paths of civilization remained closed merely because of the existence of one obstacle—the infirmity and malignity of the individual.[2] He also attempted to show how the collective interests of modern society are becoming increasingly complex in character and of such magnitude as to be utterly beyond the compass of individual thought.[3] "There are," says he in that excellent formula in which he summarizes the instances in which State intervention may be necessary,

> certain vital things which the individual can never do, either because he has not the necessary strength to perform them or because they would not pay him; or, again, because they require the co-operation of everybody, which can never be got merely by common consent. The State is the one person—the *entrepreneur*—who can undertake such tasks.[4]

But his words went unheeded.

Writing in a similar vein, Wagner invokes the testimony of history in support of his State doctrine, showing us how the State's functions vary from one period to another, so that one never feels certain about prescribing limits to its action. Individual interest, private charity, and the State have always had to divide the field of activity between them. Never has the first of these, taken by itself, proved sufficient, and in all the great modern states its place is taken by State action. To conclude that this solution was useful and necessary and in accordance with the true law of historical development only involved one further step.[5] One almost unconsciously proceeds from the mere statement of a fact to the definite formulation of a law. "Anyone," says Wagner,

[1] Wagner, *Grundlegung*, 3rd ed., pp. 811 *et seq*; 839 *et seq*. The State Socialists have a habit of wrongfully using the two expressions 'free competition' and 'economic liberty' as if they were synonymous terms. See *Grundlegung*, p. 97.

[2] Dupont-White, *L'Individu et l'État*, 5th ed., p. 9.

[3] *Ibid.*, p. 267.

[4] Preface to the French translation of Stuart Mill's *Liberty*.

[5] Wagner, *Grundlegung*, 3rd ed., pp. 892 *et seq*.

who has appreciated the immanent tendencies of evolution (*i.e.*, the essential features of economic, social, or political evolution) may very properly proceed from such a historical conception of social evolution to the formulation of postulates relative to what ought to be.[1]

In virtue of this conception there is a demand for the extension of the State's functions, which may easily be justified on the ground of its capacity for furthering the well-being and civilization of the community. The influence of Rodbertus's thought, especially his theory concerning the development of governmental organs to meet the needs of a higher social development,[2] is quite unmistakable in this connexion.

The similarity between his views and those of Dupont-White, though entirely fortuitous, perhaps, is sufficiently remarkable to justify our calling attention to it. White is equally emphatic in his demand that the State should exercise charity and act beneficently.[3] He shows how the modern State has extended its dominion, substituting local government for class dominion and parental despotism, taking women, children, and slaves successively under its care, and adding to its duties and responsibilities in proportion as civilization grows and liberty broadens downward. Fresh life requires more organs, new forces demand new regulations. But the ruler and the organ of society is the State.[4] In a moment of enthusiasm he even goes so far as to declare that "the State is simply man minus his passions; man at such a stage of development that he can commune even with truth itself, fearing neither God nor his own conscience. However imperfect it may be, the State is still vastly superior to the individual."[5] Such writing is not without a touch of mysticism.

Without going to the extent of admitting, as M. Wagner would have us do, that the simple demonstration of the truth of historical evolution is enough to justify his policy, we must commend State Socialism for the service it has performed in combating the Liberal contempt for government. If we admit the right of a central power to regulate social relations, it is difficult to understand why certain economic relations only should be subjected to such supervision.

But the real difficulty, even when the principle is fully recognized, is to define the spheres that should respectively belong to the State and to the individual. How far, within what limits, and according to what rules should the State intervene? We must at any rate, as Wagner says, begin with a rough distribution of attributes. It is impossible to proceed by any other method unless we are to assume, as

---

[1] *Finanzwissenschaft und Staatssozialismus*, p. 106.   [2] See *supra*, p. 431.
[3] Dupont-White, *Capital et Travail*, p. 353 (1847); *L'Individu et L'État*, p. 81.
[4] *L'Individu et l'État*, p. 65.   [5] *Ibid.*, pp. 163, 164.

the collectivists seem to do, a radical change in human psychology resulting in the complete substitution of a solicitude for the public welfare for private interest.

Dupont-White thought the problem insoluble,[1] and Wagner is equally emphatic about the impossibility of formulating an absolute rule. The statesman must decide each case on its merits. He does, however, lay down a few general rules. As a first general principle it is clear that the State can never completely usurp the place of the individual.[2] It can only concern itself with the general conditions of his development. The personal activity of the individual must for ever remain the essential spring of economic progress. The principle is apparently the same as Stuart Mill's, but there is quite a marked difference between them. Mill wished to curtail individual effort as little as possible, Wagner to extend Government action as much as he could. Mill insists throughout upon the negative role of Government; Wagner emphasizes the positive side, and claims that it should help an ever-increasing proportion of the population to share in the benefits of civilization. No inconvenience, Wagner thinks, would result from a little more communism in our social life. "National economy should be transferred from the control of the individual to the control of the community in general," he writes, in a sentence that might have been borrowed directly from Rodbertus.[3] Both he and Mill are agreed that the limit of Government action must be placed just at that point where it threatens to cramp individual development.[4]

The practical application of these ideas would affect both the production and the distribution of wealth. But on this question State

[1] "No means has as yet been suggested which will help to delimit the functions of the State from those of the individual. But that is not a consideration of any great moment, for we can always arrange matters so as to make them balance roughly when it comes to a particular case." (*L'Individu et l'État*, pp. 298 and 301.) Elsewhere (in his preface to the French translation of Mill's *Liberty*) he gives the opinion that such a delimitation is impossible and that when we speak of the State and the individual we speak of two distinct powers, such as life and law (p. vii). Law has to follow in the footsteps of life, reproving its excesses and correcting its faults (p. xiii).

[2] Wagner, *Grundlegung*, p. 887.

[3] State enterprise is to be recommended wherever possible, "not only for specific reasons which make the State ownership of certain industries highly desirable, but also for reasons of social policy, such as the advisability of helping industry to pass from a regime of individual ownership to that of communal control." (*Finanzwissenschaft und Staatssozialismus*, p. 115.)

[4] Dupont-White's individualism is as unimpeachable as Wagner's, which proves that an individualist need not always be a Liberal. "The author of *Liberty*," says he in his preface to Mill's *Liberty*, p. lxxxix, "has a keen sympathy for individualism, which I share to the full, though without any misgivings as to the future destiny of this unalterable element. Individualism is life. In that sense individualism is imperishable."

Socialism has done little more than seize hold of ideas that were current long before its day.

In the matter of distribution it takes exactly the same standpoint as Sismondi. There is no condemnation either of profits or interest as a matter of principle, such as is the case with the Socialists, nor is there any suggestion of doing away with private property as the fundamental institution of society; but there is the expression of a desire for a more exact correspondence between income and effort[1] and for such a limitation of profits as the economic conjuncture will allow of, and, on the other hand, for such an increase of wages as will permit of a more humane existence. It is impossible to disguise the fact that all this sounds very vague.[2]

The State would thus undertake to see that distribution conformed to the moral sentiment of each period. Taxation was to be employed as the instrument of such reforms. Dupont-White, in his *Capital et Travail*,[3] which was written as early as the year 1847, had hit upon the precise formula in which to describe these projects: "To levy a tax such as will strike the higher classes and to apply the yield to help and reward labour."

Wagner says just the same thing.

Logically State Socialism must undertake two tasks which are closely connected with one another. In the first place it must raise the lower strata of the working classes at the expense of the higher classes, and in the second place it must put a check upon the excessive accumulation of wealth among certain strata of society or by certain members of the propertied classes.[4]

In the matter of production State Socialism has simply been content to reproduce the list given by Mill, Chevalier, and Cournot of the cases in which there is no economic principle against the direct control or management of an industrial enterprise by the State. Speaking generally, Wagner is of the opinion that the State should take upon

[1] *Cf.*, for example, Schmoller's open letter to von Treitschke (1874–75), translated in his *Politique sociale et Économie politique* (Paris, 1902). To the objection that the civil list of European monarchs is condemned by this principle Schmoller replies that he is "speaking of the average man," but that "the Hohenzollerns, when considered in this light, have no more than they deserve" (p. 92).

[2] Wagner recognizes the arbitrary nature of his suggestions. Theoretically, he says, this method of procedure is quite legitimate, but practically it is not so simple, "for the object, in short, is to employ the principles of equity and of social utility, which are by no means difficult to formulate, and to transmute those principles into legislative enactments, so as to put a check upon the arbitrary and excessive accumulation of wealth in the hands of a few individuals, such as is the case under a regime of free competition." (*Finanzwissenschaft und Staatssozialismus*, p. 719.)

[3] P. 398.

[4] *Finanzwissenschaft und Staatssozialismus*, p. 718.

itself the control of such industries as are of a particularly permanent
or universal character, or such as require either uniform or specialized
methods of control or are likely to become monopolies in the hands of
private individuals. The same argument would apply to industries
satisfying some general want, but in which it is almost impossible to
determine the exact advantage which the consumer derives from them.
The State administration of rivers, forests, roads, and canals, the
nationalization of railways and banks, and the municipalization of
water and gas, are justified on the same grounds.

Such are the essential features of State Socialism, which bases its
appeal, not on any precise criticism of property or of unearned income,
such as we are accustomed to get from the socialists, but entirely upon
moral and national considerations. A juster distribution of wealth
and a higher well-being for the working classes appear to be the only
methods of maintaining that national unity of which the State is the
representative. But it neither specifies the rules of justice nor indicates
the limits of the ameliorative process. The fostering of collective effort
affords another means of developing moral solidarity and of limiting
purely selfish action; but the maintenance of private property and
individual initiative seemed indispensable to the growth of production
—a consideration which renders it inimical to collectivism. Its moral
character explains the contrast between the precise nature of some of
its positive demands and the somewhat vague character of its general
principles, which may be applied to a greater or lesser extent according to individual preferences. It is impossible to deny the essentially
subjective character of its criteria, and this affords some indication of
the vigorous criticism offered by the economists, who are above all
anxious for scientific exactitude, and the measure of enthusiasm with
which it has been welcomed by all practical reformers. It forms a
kind of crossroads where social Christianity, enlightened conservatism,
progressive democracy, and opportunistic socialism all come together.

But its success was due much less to the value of its principles than
to the peculiar nature of the political and economic evolution towards
the end of the century. Its most conspicuous representative in Germany was Prince Bismarck, who was totally indifferent to any theory
of State Socialism, and who preferred to justify his policy by an appeal
to the principles of Christianity or the Prussian Landrecht.[1] One of

[1] The imperial message of November 17, 1881, announcing the celebrated series of
Insurance Acts admits the necessity for a more marked policy of State intervention:
"To lay hold of the ways and means whereby the working classes may best be helped
is by no means an easy task, but it is one of the highest which a moral and Christian
community can set its heart upon." Bismarck, in his speech of May 9, 1884, said: "I
unhesitatingly recognize the rights of labour, and so long as I occupy this place I

P

his great ambitions was to consolidate and cement the national unity which he had succeeded in creating. A system of national insurance financed and controlled by the State appealed to him as the best way of weaning the working classes from revolutionary socialism by giving them some positive proof of the sympathy of the Government in the shape of pecuniary interest in the welfare of the empire. In a somewhat similar fashion the French peasant became attached to the Revolution through the sale of national property. "I consider," says Bismarck, speaking of invalidity insurance,

> that it is a tremendous gain for us to have 700,000 annuitants among the very people who think they have nothing to lose, but who sometimes wrongly imagine that they might gain something by a change. These individuals would lose anything from 115 to 200 marks, which just keeps them above water. It is not much, perhaps, but it answers the purpose admirably.[1]

Such was the origin of those important laws dealing with sickness, accidents, invalidity, and old age which received the imperial seal between 1881 and 1889. But just because the Chancellor did not consider that there was the same pecuniary advantage to be derived from labour laws in the narrow sense of the term—that is, in laws regulating the duration of labour, Sunday rest, the inspection of factories, etc.—he was less favourably inclined towards their extension. The personal predilection of the Emperor William II, as expressed in the famous decrees of February 4, 1890, was needed to give the Empire a new impetus in this direction.

Accordingly it was the intelligent conservatism of a Government almost absolute in its power, but possessed of no definitely social creed, that set about realizing a part of the programme of the State Socialists. In England and France and the other countries where political liberty is an established fact similar measures have been carried out at the express wish of an awakening democracy. The working classes are beginning to find out how to utilize for their own profit the larger share of government which they have recently secured. Progressive taxation, insurance, protective measures for workmen, more frequent intervention of Government with a view to determining the conditions

---

shall uphold them. In so doing I base my plea, not upon socialism, but upon the Prussian Landrecht." Sec. ii of art. 19 of the second part of the Prussian Landrecht (February 5, 1794) reads as follows: "To such as have neither the means nor the opportunity of earning their own livelihood or that of their family, work shall be given, adapted to their strength and capacity." Despite its general tone, it did not contemplate giving relief.

[1] Speech delivered on March 18, 1889, quoted by Brodnitz, *Bismarcks Nationalökonomische Ansichten*, p. 141 (Jena, 1902).

of labour, are just the expressions of a tendency that operates independently of any preconceived plan.

The regulation of the relationship between masters and workmen gave to State Socialism a legislative bias. Governments and municipalities, not content with that, have long since extended their intervention to the domain of production, the new character of social life rather than any social theory being again the determining motive. Public works, such as canals, roads, railways, sea transport, and electric power have multiplied enormously in the course of the nineteenth century, thanks to the existence of new productive forces. The demand for public services such as lighting and heating has increased because of the increasing concentration of population. Communal life keeps encroaching upon what was formerly an isolated, dispersive existence, and community of interest is extending its sway in village and borough as well as in the great city and the nation at large. Industry also is being gradually linked together, and the area of free competition is perforce becoming narrower. In the labour market, as well as in the produce and the money markets, concentration has taken the place of dispersion. Monopoly is everywhere. Collective enterprise, instead of being the exception, tends to be the rule, and public opinion is gradually being reconciled to the idea of seeing the State—the "collective being' *par excellence*—becoming in its turn industrial.

Under conditions such as these it was impossible that the doctrine of State Socialism should not influence public opinion.

State Socialism has the peculiar merit of being able to translate the confused aspirations of a new epoch in the history of politics and economics into practical maxims without arousing the suspicions of the public to the extent that socialism generally does. Legislators and public men generally have been supplied with the necessary arguments with which to defend the inauguration of that new policy upon which they had secretly set their hearts. A common ground of action is found for parties that are generally opposed to one another and for temperaments that are usually incompatible. That is the outstanding merit of a doctrine that seems eminently suitable for the attainment of tangible results.

And so, by a curious inversion of functions by no means exceptional in the history of thought, State Socialism in our century finds itself playing the part of its great adversary, the Liberal Optimism of the early century. "Thou hast conquered, O State Divine," as the Emperor Julian said of Christianity, might well be the words of Proudhon if he came back to this world. One of the outstanding merits of that earlier Liberalism was the preparation it afforded for a policy of enfranchisement or liberty, which was absolutely necessary for the development of the industrial regime. And so it became the interpreter of the great economic currents of the time. In pursuance of this exclusive task all traces of its scientific origin disappeared, the elaboration of economic theory was neglected, and the habit of close reasoning so essential to systematic thinking was abandoned. In a somewhat similar manner State Socialism has become the creed of all those who desire to put an end to the abuses of economic liberty in its extremer aspects, or such as are generally concerned about the miserable condition of an increasing number of the working classes. It has continued to spread thence until it has gradually invaded the whole economic system without meeting any serious resistance from a public opinion growing less and less sympathetic towards economic liberalism. Yet there was a time when it could be asked whether this very multiplicity of government interventions would not arouse in consumers—as in the *entrepreneurs*, and even the workers—a growing mistrust of the economic competence of the State. The illusion was short-lived and only served to show up more clearly the universal triumph of State Socialism over all forms of liberalism, including syndicalist liberalism.

In conclusion, we must note another characteristic reaction. Whereas during the greater part of the nineteenth century the attacks of Socialism were directed against Liberalism and economic orthodoxy, Neo-Marxian syndicalism is concentrating its attention almost exclusively upon State Socialism. Sorel emphasizes the similarity that exists between Marxism and Manchesterism, and on more than one point he finds himself in agreement with a 'Liberal' like Pareto. On the other hand, no words are sufficiently vigorous to express his condemnation of the partisans of social peace and interventionism, which appear to him to corrupt the working classes. Syndicalist working men have on more than one occasion shown their contempt for the State by refusing to avail themselves of measures passed on their behalf—old-age pensions, for example. This attitude is perhaps due to the influence of the anarchists upon the leaders of French syndicalism. (See Book V, chapter v.)

The combined effect of this twofold current of ideas—the Neo-Marxian and the Anarchist—in turning the French working classes away from State Socialism in the years immediately preceding the First World War is an interesting and very generally recognized fact. In England at the same time a current of ideas called Guild Socialism, akin to this movement in many ways, was tending to replace the earlier State Socialism, represented especially by Mr and Mrs Sidney Webb, and to supersede trade unionism. It put in the forefront of its programme not the defence of the specific interests of labour but (after the abolition of the wage system) the general organization of production. This was to be directed in each branch of industry by the whole body of workers and technicians in the industry, who were to constitute a 'guild,' so that the State, though taking over the ownership of the national capital, would be as far as possible relieved of the task of administering it. The State, however, in the opinion of some at least of these writers, should retain the function of control and arbitration in respect of the guilds, as the representative of the consumers.[1]

But when an attempt was made after the First World War to translate these ideas into reality, and there arose a 'corporative' doctrine which combined in a somewhat confused manner not only trade unionist aspirations but also the paternalist tendencies of Social Catholicism (see Book V, chapter ii) and the desire of employers for the federation of industries, the influence of State Socialism on men's minds was once more apparent. For it was to the State that the direction of the new corporations was entrusted, when in various countries, especially Italy, they obtained the sanction of the law. It has been clearly shown by Gaëtan Pirou,[2] in a small but substantial volume, how corporatism, born of a reaction against the excesses alike of individualism and of étatisme, turned after all into a new ascendancy of the State over industry. In the same way the term 'controlled economy,' which has become increasingly popular during the last twenty years, is only a modern label for State Socialism, which is itself applied, through the interventionism of 1848, to the old étatisme of the eighteenth and preceding centuries.

[1] The principal writers in this movement were G. D. H. Cole and S. G. Hobson. A good summary of their ideas is to be found in an article (in French) by Laskine in the Revue d'Économie politique, 1920, p. 405. The Economic Journal has also published reviews of several of their works. G. D. H. Cole, one of the founders of the movement, summarizing its fundamental ideas in the American Encyclopedia of the Social Sciences in 1932, said that it had profoundly transformed socialist ideas on nationalization, and that English socialists now thought that socialized industries and services should to a great extent administer themselves, with the workers obtaining an increasing share of control. See the article on Guild Socialism in Vol. VII of the Encyclopedia.

[2] Essais sur le corporatisme (Sirey, Paris, 1936). M. Salleron, an ardent supporter of corporatism and especially of agricultural corporatism, writes in his Naissance de l'État corporatif (Grasset, Paris, 1942): "Truth compels us to say that the first year's experience of the peasant corporation is a success for étatisme. . . . This is a serious fact, to which it is our duty to call the attention of peasants everywhere" (p. 14). The same tendency of the State to absorb and dominate the corporation is noted in the very important little book by Jacques Valdour, Organisation corporative de la Société et de la profession (Rousseau, Paris, 1935).

IV: STATE CONTROL AND WAR

The fact is that war has provided State Socialism with its most decisive arguments. The term 'controlled economy' that has triumphed everywhere during the last quarter of a century is merely another name for a war economy. The nineteenth century had known a long spell of peace, but the twentieth, from 1914 to 1945, has been a continuous period of war or preparation for war. Now war, and especially 'total' war which affects all the principal nations in the world as well as every social class in each nation, and in which the distinction between soldiers and civilians virtually disappears, means the seizure of everything by the State. All productive activity is mobilized for the single purpose of defence. Every industry abandons production for peace and concentrates on armaments. Agriculture, deprived of its manpower, sees its products growing scarce. Foreign trade is limited to essential commodities. Exportation is reduced almost to nothing by the limitation of tonnage and the closing of frontiers. Every effort is directed to the maintenance of imports. The economy of abundance gives way to the economy of scarcity.

In these circumstances the State undertakes tasks that are normally left to individual initiative. Not only is production completely subject to its orders, but the distribution of existing products becomes one of its essential functions. The normal functions of commerce are entrusted to the Government. Prices are fixed, and every one's rations are determined by authority, so that the poorest shall not be deprived of essentials by the demand of the richest. In a word, the economic system that was formerly free becomes entirely the business of the State.

This situation, created by necessity, still continues when the war is over. The State finds it hard to relinquish the control it has become accustomed to, and there are many theorists to advise it not to. War-time economy is a foreshadowing of a communism regarded by many theorists as the ideal social organization, an end in itself and not a temporary exception. Thus Babeuf in 1795 saw in the war-time communism of the Revolutionary War the realization of a moral and social ideal of which he made himself the prophet. And thus too on the morrow of the 1914 war, and still more after the Second World War, longer and even more devastating, we have a great many voices clamouring for the continuance of what is called 'control' (*dirigisme*). In every country in the world a doctrine has developed that preaches the retention of price control, the rationing of consumption, and the planning of imports and exports. Along with the growth of economic nationalism in foreign trade has come the control of production at home.

The old and never-ending discussion of the parts to be played by the State and the individual in economic life has taken on a new vigour, and the national characteristics of the different countries has once more been revealed in the way in which each has solved the problem: between the Russian solution and the American the differences are immense. In these developments the historian of economic doctrines sees not the birth of any new ones, but the reinstatement of very old ones, adapted to the new forms of economic life and the use of technical power infinitely superior to that of past ages. He cannot regard them as original intellectual creations capable of giving us new conceptions of economic and social life, and for this reason we do not feel it incumbent on us to quote or analyse the views of any writer in particular.

The success of the system of 'control' will depend far more, in our opinion, on the *political* development of the great States than on their *social and economic* development. The more doubtful the chance of peace, the more numerous and disquieting the risks of war, and the greater the delay in achieving the pacification of the nations, the more will this *dirigisme* grow. And just so far as peace seems more assured, on the other hand, we shall find the peoples of the world drawing nearer in their relations with one another to a free economic federation, and in their domestic affairs to a free understanding between the associations of producers.[1]

[1] The German economist Professor Lexis has unfortunately not been mentioned in this chapter, for the Göttingen professor had the misfortune of being neither a State Socialist nor a member of the Historical school. His works, dealing with various topics—money, the population theory, and general economic theory—are scattered through a number of reviews and other publications, especially the *Jahrbücher für Nationalökonomie und Statistik*, Schönberg's *Handbuch*, and the great *Handwörterbuch der Staatswissenschaften*. His writings are distinguished not only by a definitely scientific method of treatment, but also by a remarkable clearness of thought. While appearing to continue the tradition of the Classical school, he takes care to reject the optimistic conclusions which are too often regarded as an inseparable element of that tradition. In 1900 Lexis gave us a general résumé of his teaching in the *Allgemeine Volkswirtschaftslehre*, where he treats of the economic world as concerned merely with the circulation of goods. In addition to an interesting theory of crises, upon which we cannot dwell just now, the most original part of the work consists of a theory concerning the method of distributing the social product between workers and capitalists. Lexis thought that all material goods were produced by labour and measurable in terms of labour. The problem then is to determine where the capitalist gets his income. The capitalist's profit is not the result of exploitation, as Marx thought, but is simply what is added to the sale price—a sum corresponding to the capitalist's interest is added to the sum representing the workmen's wages. Profit originates in the sphere of circulation. But how will this increased sale price benefit the capitalists, seeing that under existing conditions the workers can only buy the equivalent of the products which they have already helped to produce? We need

CHAPTER III: MARXISM

I: KARL MARX[1]

EVERY one knows of the spell cast over the socialism of the twentieth century by the doctrines of Karl Marx and the contempt with which this newer so-called scientific socialism refers to the earlier or Utopian kind. But what is even more striking than the success of Marxian socialism is its wants of sympathy with the heretical doctrines of its predecessors

---

to remember, however, that they produce for the capitalist as well as for themselves, and with the money thus obtained the working classes are enabled to buy whatever they need at market prices—*i.e.*, at a price that includes interest, which constitutes the capitalist's profit. Whenever the capitalists themselves purchase goods made by themselves they are reciprocally benefiting one another. Their class position is not modified by such procedure, for each *entrepreneur* simply draws profits in proportion to his capital. And so we avoid the most serious objection which can be raised to Marx's theory. This explanation of the surplus value received by the capitalists is at least very ingenious. Lexis was mostly influenced by Marx and Rodbertus, and he attempted a fusion of their more vigorous conceptions. Despite the objections that might be raised to it, the work is certainly one of the most original of the German School.

[1] Karl Marx, generally spoken of as a Jew, was born on May 5, 1818, of Jewish parents who had been converted to Protestantism. Born of a respectable bourgeois family and wedded to the daughter of a German baron, few would have predicted for him the career of a militant socialist. Such was to be his lot, however. In 1843, at the age of twenty-five, the authorities having suppressed a newspaper which he was conducting, he fled to Paris, and thence to Brussels. Returning to Germany during the Revolution of 1848, in which he took an active part, he was again expelled, and this time took refuge in London (1849). Here he spent the rest of his life (about thirty years), leaving for France a short time before his death in 1883. He died at London on March 14 in that year.

Although Marx was one of the founders and directors of the famous association known as the "International," which was the terror of every European Government between 1863 and 1872, he was not a mere revolutionary like his rival Bakunin, nor was he a famous tribune of the people like Lassalle. He was essentially a student, an affectionate father, like Proudhon, an indefatigable traveller, and a man of great intellectual culture.

The best-known of his works, which is frequently quoted but seldom read, is *Das Kapital*, of which the first volume—the only one published during his lifetime—appeared in 1867. The other two volumes were issued after his death, in 1885 and 1894, through the efforts of his collaborator Engels.

This book exercised a great influence upon nineteenth-century thought, and probably no work, with the exception of the Bible and the Pandects, has given rise to such a host of commentators and apologists. Marx's other writings, though much less frequently quoted, are also exceedingly important, especially *La Misère de la Philosophie*, published in 1847 in answer to Proudhon's *Les Contradictions Économiques*; *Zur Kritik der politischen Oekonomie* (1859); and particularly the *Communist Manifesto*, published in January 1848. The *Manifesto* is merely a pamphlet, and at first it attracted scarcely any attention, but Labriola goes so far as to say—not without some exaggeration, perhaps—that "the date of its publication marks the beginning of a

the Communists and Fourierists, and the pride it takes in regarding itself as a mere development or rehabilitation of the great Classical tradition.

To give within the limits of a single chapter a résumé of a doctrine that claims to review and to reconstruct the whole of economic theory is clearly impossible, and we shall merely attempt an examination of two of Marx's more essential doctrines, namely, his theory of surplus labour and value and his law of automatic appropriation, more familiarly but less accurately known as the law of concentration of capital. The first is based upon a particular conception of exchange value and the second upon a special theory of economic evolution. To employ Comtean phraseology, the one belongs to the realm of economic statics, the other to the domain of economic dynamics.

1. SURPLUS LABOUR AND SURPLUS VALUE

The laborious demonstration which follows will become clearer if we remind ourselves of the objects Marx had in view. Marx's aim was to show how the propertied class had always lived upon the labour of the non-propertied classes—the possessors upon the non-possessing. This was by no means a new idea, as we have already made its acquaintance in the writings of Sismondi, Saint-Simon, Proudhon, and Rodbertus. But the essence of the criticism of these writers was always social rather than economic, the institution of private property and its injustice being the chief object of attack. Karl Marx, on the other hand, deliberately directed the gravamen of the charge against economic science itself, especially against the conception of exchange.

---

new era" (*Essai sur la Conception matérialiste de l'Histoire*, p. 21). At any rate, it is the breviary of modern socialism. There is scarcely a single one of its phrases, each of which stings like a dart, that has not been invoked a thousand times. The *Programme of the Communist Manifesto* is included in Ensor's *Modern Socialism*.

It is a much-debated question as to whether Karl Marx was influenced by French socialists, and if so to what extent. On the question of his indebtedness to Pecqueur and Proudhon see Bourguin's article in *La Revue d'Économie politique*, 1892, on *Des Rapports entre Proudhon et K. Marx*. Proudhon's work, at any rate, was known to him, for one of his books was a refutation of the doctrines of the *petit bourgeois*, as he called him. Certain analogies between the works of these two writers to which we shall have to call attention will help us to appreciate the extent to which Marx is indebted to Proudhon. But, as Anton Menger has pointed out, we must seek Marx's antecedents among English socialists, in the works of writers like Thompson especially. Nor must we forget his friend and collaborator Friedrich Engels, who for the sake of his master has been content to remain in the background. Engels collaborated in the publication of the famous *Manifesto* in 1848, and it was he who piously collected and edited Karl Marx's posthumous work. It is difficult to know exactly what part he played in the development of Marx's ideas, but it is highly probable that it was considerable.

He endeavours to prove that what we call exploitation must always exist, that it is an inevitable outcome of exchange—an economic necessity to which both master and man must submit.

It is convenient to begin with an examination of economic value. Marx lays down the doctrine that labour is not merely the measure and cause of value, but that it is also its substance. We have already had occasion to note how Ricardo was somewhat favourably inclined to the same view, though hardly willing to adopt it. There is no such hesitation on the part of Marx: it is all accepted in a characteristically thorough fashion. Of course, he does not deny that utility is a necessary condition of value and that it is really the only consideration in the case of 'value in use.' But utility alone is not enough to explain value in exchange, since every act of exchange implies some common element, some degree of identity between the exchanged commodities. This identity is certainly not the result of utility, because the degree of utility is different in every commodity, and it is this difference that constitutes the *raison d'être* of exchange. The common or homogeneous element which is contained in commodities themselves heterogeneous in character is the quantity of labour, great or small, which is contained in them. The value of every commodity is simply the amount of crystallized human labour which it contains, and commodities differ in value according to the different quantities of labour which are "socially necessary to produce them."[1]

Let us take the case of a working man, an employee in any kind of industry, working ten hours a day.

What will be the exchange value of the produce of his labour? It will be the equivalent of ten hours' labour, whether the commodity produced be cloth or coal or what not. And since the master, or the capitalist, as Marx always calls him, in accordance with the terms of

---

[1] Marx calls attention to the fact that even Aristotle was puzzled by this common element which exchanged objects seemed to possess, and by the fact that exchange appeared to make them of equal value. We say that 5 beds = 1 house. "What is that equal something, that common substance, which admits of the value of the beds being expressed by a house? Such a thing, in truth, cannot exist, says Aristotle. And why not? Compared with the beds the house does represent something equal to them, in so far as it represents what is really equal, both in the beds and the house. And that is—human labour." (*Kapital*, p. 29; Moore and Aveling's translation—to which the Translator is indebted for the succeeding quotations also).

"If we make abstraction from its use-value we make abstraction at the same time from the material elements and shapes that make the product a use-value. . . . Its existence as a material thing is put out of sight. Neither can it any longer be regarded as the product of the labour of the joiner, the mason, the spinner, or of any other definite kind of productive labour . . . there is nothing left but what is common to them all; all are reduced to one and the same sort of labour—human labour in the abstract." (*Ibid.*, p. 5.)

ways, and an analysis of some of these processes is one of the most characteristic features of the Marxian doctrine. This analysis may be summed up under two main divisions.

1. The first method is to prolong the working day as much as possible in order to increase the number of hours of surplus labour. If the number of working hours can be increased from ten to twelve the surplus will automatically grow from five to seven. This is exactly what manufacturers have always tried to do. Factory legislation, however, has forced some of them to limit the number of hours, and this has resulted in checking the growth of surplus value somewhat. But this check applies only to a limited number of industries.

2. A second method is to diminish the number of hours necessary to produce the worker's sustenance. Were this to fall from five to three it is clear that the surplus would again rise from five to seven. Such reduction is possible through the perfection of industrial organization or through a reduction in the cost of living, a result which is usually effected by means of co-operation.[1] The capitalist also often manages to bring this about by setting up philanthropic institutions or by employing women and children, who require less for their upkeep than adults. Women and children have been taken from the house, and the task of housekeeping and cookery has been left in the hands of the men. But laws regulating the employment of women and children have again defeated these tactics.[2]

Such is a very brief summary of Marx's demonstration. Its real originality lies in the fact that it does not consist of commonplace recriminations concerning the exploitation of workers and the greed of exploiters, but shows how the worker is robbed even when he gets all that he is entitled to.[3] It cannot be said that the capitalist has

---

[1] The development of machinery, according to the Marxian theory, tends to reduce the cost of living, and consequently the price of labour, by producing cheaper clothes, furniture, etc., and to a lesser extent cheaper food.

By parity of reasoning ought it not to reduce the price of goods produced by the wage-earner and so lower the surplus value? We must be careful, however, not to confuse a reduction in the price of each unit with a reduction in the total value of the articles produced by machinery. A yard of cloth produced by a modern loom has not the same value as a yard produced by an old hand-loom. But the value of the total quantity produced each day must be equal to the value produced by hand, provided the same number of hours have been spent upon its production.

[2] Marx points out that there are other ways of increasing the amount of work done and of adding to the surplus value, such as the speeding up of labour. Speeding up does not increase the value of the goods, because the value depends upon the time spent upon them, and not upon the intensity of the effort put forth, but it does lower the cost of production.

[3] "Our friend Money-bags . . . must buy his commodities at their value, must sell them at their value, and yet at the end of the process must withdraw more value from circulation than he threw into it at starting. . . . These are the conditions of

robbed him. He has paid him a fair price for his labour; that is, he has given it its full exchange value. The conditions of the wage bargain have been observed in every particular: equal value has been given in exchange for equal value. Given the capitalistic regime and the free competition of labour, the result could not be otherwise. The worker, perhaps, may be surprised at this unexpected result, which only secures him half the value of his labour, but he can only look on like a bewildered spectator. Everything has passed off quite correctly. The capitalist, no doubt, is a shrewd person, and knows that when he buys labour power he has got hold of a good thing, because it is the only merchandise which possesses the mysterious capacity of producing more value than it itself contains.[1] He knows this beforehand, and, as Marx says, it is "the source of considerable pleasure to him." "It is a particularly happy condition of things when the buyer is also allowed to sell it wherever and whenever he likes without having to part with any of his privileges as a vendor." The result is that the worker has no means of defence either legal or economic, and is as helpless as a peasant who has sold a cow in calf without knowing it.

Hitherto we have spoken only of labour. But the outstanding personage in the book—the hero of the volume—is capital, whose name appears on the title-page. Our exposition of the Marxian doctrine of production would accordingly be very incomplete if we omitted to make reference to his treatment of capital.

Taken by itself capital is, of course, sterile, for it is understood that labour is the sole source of value. But labour cannot produce unless it consumes a certain proportion of capital, and it is important that we should understand something of the combination of capital and labour.

Marx distinguishes between two kinds of capital. The first serves for the upkeep of the working-class population, either in the way of wages or direct subsistence. The older economists referred to it as

---

the problem. *Hic Rhodus! hic salta!*" (*Kapital*, p. 145.) *Cf.* p. 215, where something is said about the different phases through which the idea of exploitation has passed.

Although Marx never says that the worker is actually robbed by the capitalist, but simply that the capitalist profits by circumstances which he is powerless to change, that has not prevented him from treating the capitalist somewhat harshly and unjustly even, judging from his own point of view. He speaks of the capitalist as "a vampire which thrives upon the blood of others and becomes stouter and broader the more blood it gets." He might have added that no blame could be attached to the vampire, seeing that it only obeyed the tendencies of its nature.

[1] "By turning his money into commodities that serve as the material elements of a new product, and as factors in the labour process by incorporating living labour with their dead substance, the capitalist at the same time converts value—*i.e.*, past, materialized, and dead labour—into capital, into value big with value, a live monster that is fruitful and multiplies." (*Ibid.*, p. 176.)

the Wages Fund, and Marx calls it "variable capital." If this kind of capital does not directly take part in production, it is this fund, after all, when consumed by labour that begets value and the surplus which is attached to it.

That other kind of capital which directly assists the productive activity of labour by supplying it with machinery, tools, etc., Marx calls "constant capital." This latter kind of capital, which is not absorbed or vitalized by labour, does not result in the production of surplus value. It simply produces the equivalent of its value, which is the sum total of all the values absorbed during the time when it was being produced. This constant capital is evidently the crystallized product of labour, and its value, like that of any other product, is determined solely by the number of hours of labour it has taken to produce. This value, whether it include the cost of producing the raw material or merely the cost of labour employed in elaborating it, should be rediscoverable in the finished product. But there is nothing more—no surplus. The economists refer to this as depreciation, and every one knows that depreciation implies no profits at any rate.[1]

It seems quite obvious that it is to the interest of the capitalist to employ only variable capital, or at least that it will pay him to reduce the amount of constant capital used to the irreducible minimum.[2] But we are here met with an anomaly which is the despair of all Marxian commentators, and which must have caused Marx himself some amount of embarrassment, if we may judge by the laborious demonstration which he gives.[3]

[1] A potter working with his hands makes a vase in ten hours; each vase, then, costs ten hours' labour. The same potter decides to make a wheel—a species of fixed capital. Setting up the wheel was a hundred hours' task. If he still continues to produce only one vase *per diem*, which is a perfectly absurd proposition, for he would never have gone to the trouble of making the wheel if it did not mean some advantage to him, the value of each vase will now be 10 hours + 100 hours divided by x, which is the number of vases he would have produced had he not wasted his time making a wheel.

[2] Take two industries, A and B, each employing a capital of £1000. In A the amount of fixed capital is £100 and circulating £900. In B the fixed = £900 and the circulating £100. Admitting that surplus value is at the rate of 100 per cent., as in the example chosen just now, the total surplus value in A will be £900, equal to a profit of 90 per cent. on a capital of £1000. B, on the other hand, will only make £100 profit, which is equal to 10 per cent.

[3] This explanation only appears in the later volumes, which were published after his death.

It is true that Marx had drawn attention to the contradiction in the first volume, but no explanation was forthcoming until the later volumes appeared. Having stated that the greater quantity of surplus value is the direct result of the greater proportion of circulating capital employed, he proceeds: "This law clearly contradicts all experience based on appearance. Every one knows that a cotton-spinner who, reckoning the percentage on the whole of his applied capital, employs much

If fixed capital is really unproductive, how is it that modern production is always increasing the quantity of fixed capital which it employs, until this has now become one of its most familiar features? Is it because it yields less profit than that yielded by the smaller handicrafts or agriculture? Again, how are we to account for the variation in the rates of profit in different industries according to the different quantities of capital employed, seeing that it is an axiom of political economy that under a regime of free competition with equal security for everybody the returns on different capitals should everywhere be the same?

Marx replies by saying that the rate of profit is the same for all capitalists within the country, but that this rate is the average of the different rates in all the different industries. In other words, it is the rate that would obtain if every industry in the country employing varying amounts of fixed and circulating capital formed a part of one whole. It must not be thought of as a kind of statistical average, but simply as a kind of average which competition brings about. The result is other than might have been expected.[1] Those industries which have a large amount of variable capital—agriculture, for example—find themselves with just the average rate of return, but draw much less in the way of surplus value than they had expected, and so Marx refers to them as undertakings of an inferior character. On the contrary, those industries which possess a large amount of constant capital draw more than their capital had led them to hope for, and Marx refers to them as industries of a superior character.[2] Hence those industries which employ a considerable amount of machinery expand at the expense of the others. It is because the former kind find themselves in a more favourable position, or, in other words, realize greater

---

constant and little variable capital, does not, on account of this, pocket less profit or surplus value than a baker who relatively sets in motion much variable and little constant capital. For the solution of this apparent contradiction many intermediate terms are as yet wanted, as from the standpoint of elementary algebra many intermediate terms are wanted to demonstrate that $\frac{0}{0}$ may represent an actual magnitude. . . . Vulgar economy, which, indeed, has really learnt nothing, here, as everywhere, sticks to appearances in opposition to the law which regulates and explains them." (*Kapital*, p. 274.)

It is probable that Marx was not very well satisfied with his explanation, which may account for his reluctance to publish it during his lifetime.

[1] In the example just given suppose A and B represent the total industry of the country: the whole national industry will be made up of £900 + £100 circulating capital and £100 + £900 fixed—£2000 altogether. If the surplus value be at the rate of 100 per cent. of the circulating capital, the total capital value will be £900 + £100 = £1000 on a capital of £2000, or a percentage of 50.

[2] Taking the example given on p. 459, the mean of £900 + £100 = £500, and industry A, instead of 90 per cent., will draw only 50 per cent. profit, while industry B, instead of drawing only 10 per cent., will draw 50 per cent.

profits, that they do employ surplus labour, from which surplus value is naturally derived.[1]

While admiring the ingenuity of the dialectics, we must not blind ourselves to the simple fact which Marx was so anxious to hide, but which is nevertheless implicit in all this, namely, that the rate of profit, which means also the value of the goods, is regulated by competition —that is, by demand and supply—but bears no relation to the quantity of labour employed. We must also remember that the *entrepreneur*, far from seeing his profits diminish as he employs less human labour, finds them increasing. This contradiction is just one of those flaws that finally cause the downfall of the majestic edifice so laboriously raised by Marx.

2. THE LAW OF CONCENTRATION OR EXPROPRIATION

The law of concentration of capital,[2] which can only be interpreted in the light of economic history, is an attempt to show that the regime of private property and personal gain under which we live is about to give place to an era of social enterprise and collective property.[3] Let us try to follow the argument as given by Marx.

[1] We have indifferently employed the terms 'profit' and 'surplus value' simply because the former is a much more familiar word. But we must warn the reader against thinking that the two terms are synonymous. The surplus value is all that part of the value of the produce which is over and above the expenses of labour involved in its production—that enormous slice which becomes the property of every class in society except the workers, not merely the employers, but merchants, land-lords, etc.; while profit is that part of the surplus value which the employers of labour keep for their own use. The rate of profit also is something quite different from the percentage of surplus value, as we shall see later.

We must call attention once more to the different interpretations which have been given of the term 'profit.' Marx and the English economists take the word to comprise the whole revenue of capital under a regime of free competition, no distinction being drawn between profit properly so called and interest. To-day we understand by profit the income drawn by the *entrepreneur*—as distinct from the capitalist—as the result of certain favourable circumstances, notably imperfect competition.

It would be absurd to speak of a law of equality of profit, seeing that profit, as we have defined it, is, like rent, a differential revenue.

[2] We are fully aware of the fact that our method of approach must appear absurd from the Marxian standpoint, because it lays Marx open to the charge of starting with a preconceived idea, much after the style of economists like Bastiat, for example. Such a method, it is contended, is utterly unscientific and unworthy of a great mind like Marx's.

However great he may have been, we cannot help thinking that, in common with most scientists, he discovered just what he was looking for, and it would be difficult to prove that Marx was not a socialist long before he began the writing of *Kapital*, even long before he had constructed a system at all.

Our object in stating the conclusion first of all is to help the reader to an understanding of the argument, but it is quite open to anyone who thinks differently to say that Marx had not the least idea where the analysis would lead him.

[3] The general use of the term 'collectivism' is largely due to Marx. While 'col-

Again must we cast back our thoughts to a period before the earliest beginnings of capital in the sixteenth century—a period when, according to the socialists, there existed neither capital nor capitalist. Capital in the economic sense of a mere instrument of production must have existed even before this time, but the socialists are of opinion that it had quite a different significance then, and it is important that we should appreciate their point of view. Their employment of the term is closely akin to the vulgar use of the word as anything that yields a rent, and yields the said rent as the result, not of the capitalist's labour, but of the toil of others. But under the guild system which preceded this condition of things the majority of the workers possessed most of the instruments of production themselves.

Then follows a description of a series of changes which we cannot attempt to study in detail, but which forms a singularly dramatic chapter in the writings of Marx. New means of communication are established and new markets opened as the result of important maritime discoveries coupled with the consolidation of the great modern States, the rise of banks and of trading companies, and the formation of public debts. All these resulted in the concentration of capital in the hands of a few and the expropriation of the small proprietor.

But this was only a beginning. If capital in this newer sense of an instrument for making profit out of the labour of others was ever to come into its own and develop, if the surplus labour and surplus value of which we have given an analysis were really to contribute to the growth and upkeep of this capital, it was necessary that the capitalist should be able to buy that unique merchandise which possesses such wonderful qualities in the open market. But labour-force can never be bought unless it has been previously detached from the instruments of production and removed from its surroundings. Every connexion with property must be severed, every trace of feudalism

lectivism' occurs almost on every page of the *Manifesto*, the term 'communism,' on the other hand, is never once employed.

James Guillaume, in the preface to Vol. II of the French edition of Bakunin's works, p. xxxvi, gives the following account of the origin of the word 'collectivism': "At the fourth General Congress of the International, held at Bâle in 1869, almost every delegate voted in favour of collective property. But there were two distinct opinions cherished by the delegates present. The German-Swiss, the English, and the German delegates were really State communists. The Spanish, Belgian, French-Swiss, and most of the French delegates were federal or anarchist communists who took the name of collectivists. Bakunin belonged to the second group, and to this group also belonged the Belgian Paepe and the French Varlin." Bakunin always spoke of himself as a collectivist and not a communist, and in this respect he differs from Marx. The habit of thinking that all anarchists are communists is largely due to Kropotkin.

and of the guild system must be removed. Labour must be free—that is, saleable; or, in other words, it "must be forced to sell itself because the labourer has nothing else to sell." For a long time the artisan was in the habit of selling his goods to the public without the intervention of any intermediary, but a day dawned when, no longer able to sell his products, he was reduced to selling himself.[1]

The creation of this new kind of property based upon the labour of others meant the extinction of that earlier form of property founded upon personal labour and the substitution for it of the modern proletariat. This was the task to which the bourgeoisie resolutely set itself for about three centuries, and its proclamation of the liberty of the labourer and the rights of man is just its pæan of victory. Its task was accomplished. The expropriated artisan who was already swelling the ranks of the proletariat seemed an established fact.

In reality this end was only partially accomplished even in the more capitalistic countries, but that there is a general movement in that direction seems clear in view of the following considerations.

(a) The most suggestive fact in this connexion is the growth of production on a large scale, resulting in the employment of machinery and in the rise of new forms of organization such as trusts and cartels, new systems that were unknown in Marx's day, but which have helped to confirm his suspicions. These trusts and cartels are especially important from a social point of view because they not only absorb the capital of the small independent proprietor, but swallow the medium-sized industry as well. This wonderful expansion of production on a large scale means a corresponding growth in the numbers of the proletariat, and capitalism, by increasing the number of wage-earners, helps to swell the ranks of its own enemies. "What the bourgeoisie produces, above all, therefore, are its own gravediggers."[2]

(b) Over-production is another fruitful method. A contraction of the market results in a superabundance of workmen whose services are always available. They form a kind of industrial reserve army upon which the capitalist may draw at his pleasure—at one moment indiscriminately taking on a number of them, and throwing them back on to the streets again as soon as the demand shows signs of slackening.[3]

[1] "We think we can perceive a change in the physiognomy of our *dramatis personæ*. He who before was the money-owner now strides in front as capitalist; the possessor of labour-power follows as his labourer. The one with an air of importance, smirking, intent on business; the other timid and holding back, like one who is bringing his own hide to market and has nothing to expect but—a hiding." (*Kapital*, p. 155.)

[2] *Manifesto*, para. 1.

[3] One of the chief objects of the trusts is the avoidance of over-production, but that does not mean less unemployment; on the contrary, a part of their policy consists in closing down certain establishments which appear to be unnecessary.

(c) The concentration of the rural population in towns is another contributing factor. This movement itself is the result of the disappearance of the small holder and the substitution of pastoral for arable farming, the outcome of it all being an addition to the ranks of the expropriated proletariat of an increasing number of hitherto independent proprietors and producers.

Such is the advent and growth of capitalism. It comes into the world "with bloody putrescence oozing out of every pore." How different is the real history of capital from the idyllic presentation to which we are treated by the economists! They love to picture it as the slowly accumulated fruit of labour and abstinence, and the co-existence of the two classes, the capitalists and the workers, is supposed to date from an adventure that befell them both a few days after creation, when the good and the wise decided to follow the high road of capitalism and the idle and vicious the stony path of toil.

In reality capitalism is the outcome of class struggle—a struggle that will some day spell the ruin of the whole regime, when the expropriators will themselves be the expropriated. We are given no details as to how this is to be accomplished, and this abstention from prophecy distinguishes Marx from the Utopian socialists of the last two thousand years. His one object was to show how those very laws that led to the establishment of the regime would some day encompass its ruin.[1] The force of circumstance seemed to make self-destruction inevitable. "The capital regime," writes one Marxian socialist, "begets its own negation, and the process is marked by that inevitability which is such a feature of all natural laws."[2] The following facts are deduced as proofs that this process of self-destruction is already in course of being accomplished.

(a) Industrial crises, whether of over-production or under-consumption, have already become a chronic evil. The fact that to some extent they are to be regarded as the direct outcome of the capitalist system of production cannot prevent their damaging that system. The continual growth of fixed at the expense of circulating capital, involving as it does the substitution of machinery for hand labour, must also involve a continual reduction of the surplus value. In order to counteract this tendency the capitalists find themselves forced to keep ahead with production; they are driven to rely upon quantity, as they put it. The workers, on the other hand, find that it is gradually becoming impossible for them to buy the products of their labour with the wages which they get, because they never get a wage which is equal to the value of the product of their labour. Moreover, they periodically find

[1] See the *Manifesto* for an eloquent statement of this.   [2] Labriola.

themselves out of employment altogether and almost on the verge of starvation. Proudhon, as we have already seen, laid considerable stress upon this, and it is one of the instances in which Marx is obviously influenced by Proudhon.

The idea which underlies the Marxian theory is that every crisis involves a readjustment of the equilibrium between fixed and circulating capital. The growth of the former, though continuous, is not always uniform, and whole sections of it may occasionally be found to be without solid foundation which would warrant such expansion. But the crises which result in the destruction of these speculative accretions give a new spirit to the creation of further surplus value, which results in the creation of further fixed capital and more crises, and so the process goes on.[1]

(b) The growth of pauperism, which is the direct outcome of crises and want, is another factor.

> The bourgeoisie is unfit any longer to be the ruling class in society, and to impose its conditions of existence upon society as an overriding law. It is unfit to rule because it is incompetent to assure an existence to its slave within his slavery, because it cannot help letting him sink into such a state that it has to feed him instead of being fed by him.[2]

(c) The rapid multiplication of joint-stock companies is the final buttress with which the Marxians have strengthened their contention. Under the joint stock principle the right of property is simply reduced to the possession of a few strips of paper giving the anonymous owner the right to draw dividends in some commercial concern or other. Profit is seen in all its nakedness as a dividend which is wholly independent of all personal effort and produced entirely as the result of the workers' drudgery. The duty of personally supervising the methods of production and of opening up new and better ways of manufacturing, which served to disguise the real character of the individual employer and to justify his existence, is no longer performed by the owner, but falls to the lot of two new functionaries, the parasitic company director on the one hand and the salaried official on the other.

Once the whole industry of a country becomes organized on a joint-stock basis—or, better still, once it passes over into the hands of a trust, which is simply a manifestation of the joint-stock principle at its highest—expropriation will be a comparatively simple matter. By a mere stroke of the pen property hitherto held by private shareholders will be transferred into the custody of the State with hardly a change in the economic mechanism itself.

[1] *Kapital*, p. 647.   [2] *Manifesto*, para. 1.

Thus the expropriation of the bourgeoisie will be a much easier task than was the expropriation of the artisan by the bourgeois a few centuries ago. In the past it was a case of the few subjugating the many, but in the future the many will overwhelm the few—thanks to the law of concentration.

But what is to be the outcome of the Marxian programme (we cannot speak of its aim or ideals, for Marx scorned such terms)? The general opinion seems to be that it involves the abolition of private property, and that the opinion is not altogether without foundation may be seen from a perusal of the Manifesto, where we read that "the theory of the Communists may be summed up in the single sentence: Abolition of private property."[1]

The Manifesto also explains in what sense we are to understand this. The private property which so much needs suppressing is not the right of the worker to the produce of his own toil, but the right of others to appropriate for themselves the produce of that labour. This is private property as they understand it. They think, however, it would be better to call it bourgeois property, and they feel quite confident that it is destined to disappear under a collectivistic regime. As to a man's right to the product of his own labour, that surely existed formerly, before the peasant and the craftsman were overwhelmed by capitalism and replaced by the proletariat. Collectivism, far from destroying this kind of property, will rather revive it, not in the antiquated individualistic form of letting each man retain his own, which is obviously impossible under division of labour and production on a large scale, but of giving to every man a claim upon the equivalent of what he has produced.[2]

This twofold task can only be accomplished by undoing all that capitalism has done; by taking from the capitalists the instruments of production which they now possess and restoring them to the workmen, not individually—that would be impossible under modern condi-

---

[1] Engels in his preface to the Manifesto admits that one of its objects was "to announce the inevitable and imminent downfall of bourgeois property."

Nowadays, however, it is more usual to characterize the aim of collectivism as an attempt to abolish the wage-earning class—abolition of property being simply a step towards that. This is how Labriola writes in his Essai sur la Conception matérialiste (2nd ed., p. 62): "The proletariat must learn to concentrate upon one thing, namely, the abolition of the wage-earner."

It is well to remember that such is also the aim of the Associationists, the co-operators, and the Radical Socialists. They proceed, however, from the opposite point of view, and would multiply property rather than abolish it, thinking that the latter process would merely universalize the wage-earner.

[2] "Communism deprives no man of the power to appropriate the products of society. All that it does is to deprive him of the power to subjugate the labour of others by means of such appropriation." (Manifesto, para. 2.)

tions—but collectively. To adopt the formula which figures at the head of the party's programme, this means the socialization of the means of production—land, including surface and subsoil, factories, and capital. The produce of every one's labour, after allowing for certain expenses which must be borne by the community as a whole, will be distributed according to each one's labour. Surplus labour and surplus value will thus disappear simultaneously.

This expropriation of the capitalists will be the final stage, for, unlike the preceding movements, it will not be undertaken for the benefit of a single class—not even for the benefit of the workers. It will be for the interest of everybody alike, for the benefit of the nation as a whole. It will also be adequate to cope with the change which industry has recently undergone; in other words, both production and distribution will be on a collective basis.

II: THE MARXIAN SCHOOL

After this summary exposition of the principal theories of Karl Marx, we must now try to fix the general character of the school that bears his name[1] and to distinguish it from the other socialist schools that we have already studied.

(a) In the first place, it proudly claims for its teaching the title of *scientific* socialism, but much care must be exercised in interpreting the formula. No economist has ever shown such contempt or betrayed such passion in denouncing Phalanstères, Utopias, and communistic schemes of every kind. To think that the Marxians should add to the number of such fantastic dreams! What they claim to do, as Labriola points out (may the shades of Fourier forgive their presumption!), is to give a thoroughly scientific demonstration of the line of

---

[1] To say that Karl Marx was the leader of a great socialist school is hardly the way to describe him, for it is necessary that we should remember that the vast majority of those who consider themselves socialists are more or less his disciples. The other socialist schools, the anarchists, the Fabians, the Collinsists, and the followers of Henry George, cut a very poor figure beside his.

The bulk of his adherents were at first drawn either from Germany or Russia, England being the country which did least to swell the ranks of his followers. In France the pure doctrine was vigorously preached since 1878 by Jules Guesde and Lefargue—the latter of whom was Marx's son-in-law. But a great many French socialists, though collectivists in name, refused their adhesion to the Marxian doctrine in all its rigidity. They accepted three of his main principles—the socialization of the means of production, class war, and internationalism—but rejected his theory of value and his materialistic conception of history. Moreover, they showed no desire to break with the French socialist tradition, which was pre-eminently idealistic. Benoît Malon, the founder of the *Revue socialiste* (1885), was one of the earliest representatives of French collectivism, and among his successors may be reckoned George Renard and Fournière.

progress which has actually been followed by civilized societies.[1] Their one ambition is to gauge the significance of the unconscious evolution through which society has progressed and to point the goal towards which this cosmic process seems to be tending.

The result is that the Marxian school has a conception of natural laws which is much nearer the Classical standpoint than that of its predecessors. Of this there can be no doubt. The Marxian theories are derived directly from the theories of the leading economists of the early nineteenth century, especially from Ricardo's. Marx is in the line of direct succession. Not only is this true of the labour-value theory and of his treatment of the conflict between profits and wages, but it also applies to his theory of rent and to a whole host of Ricardian doctrines that have been absorbed wholesale into the Marxian philosophy. And, paradoxical as it may sound, his abstract dogmatic method, his obscure style, which encourages disciples to retort that the critics have misunderstood his meaning and to give to many a passage quite an esoteric significance, is of the very essence of Ricardo.[2] Marx's theories are, of course, supported by a wealth of illuminating facts, which unfortunately have been unduly simplified and drawn upon for purely imaginary conclusions. We have already had occasion to remark that Ricardo also owes a good deal more to the observation of facts than is generally believed, and his practice of postulating imaginary conditions is of course notorious. The impenitent Marxian who still wishes to defend some of the more untenable theories of Marx, such as his doctrine of labour-value, generally finds himself forced to admit that Marx had supposed (the use of suppositions is an unfailing proof of Ricardian influence) the existence of society wherein labour would be always uniform in quality.[3]

---

[1] Labriola, *Essai sur la Conception matérialiste de l'histoire*, p. 24. The Saint-Simonians had already made a similar claim. It is hardly fair to class them among the Utopians, and some Marxians are quite ready to admit their claim to priority in this matter.

[2] Georges Sorel, one of Marx's disciples, writing in no derogatory spirit, we may be certain, expresses himself as follows: "Our experience of the Marxian theory of value convinces us of the importance which obscurity of style may lend to a doctrine" —a remark that is applicable to other writers besides Marx.

[3] See Sorrel's article, *Les Polémiques pour l'Interprétation du Marxisme*, in the *Revue internationale de Sociologie*, 1900, p. 248. There is no such thing as a theory of value— in the accepted sense of the term in Marx. What we have is a theory of economic equilibrium which would only be true of a very rudimentary kind of society. It is assumed, for example, that all industries are equally easy or difficult, that all the workers are of one type, that ten men working for one hour will produce the same amount of wealth no matter what task they are engaged upon. It is this equality that enables comparison to be made between one commodity and another, and this constitutes their value. We are simply treated to an abstraction which shows that with the exercise of a little ingenuity it is at least possible to reconcile the theory of time-value and the theory of market price.

Marxism is simply a branch grafted on the Classical trunk. Astonished and indignant as the latter may well seem at the sight of the strange fruit which its teaching has borne, it cannot deny the fact that it has nourished it with its own life-blood. "*Das Kapital*," as Labriola notes, "instead of being the prologue to the communal critique, is simply the epilogue of bourgeois economics."[1]

Not only has Marxism always shown unfailing respect for political economy even when attacking individual economists, who are generally accused of inability to grasp the full significance of their own teaching, but, strangely enough, it betrays an equal affection for capitalism.[2] It has the greatest respect for the task which it has already accomplished, and feels infinitely grateful for the revolutionary part (such are the words used) which it has played in preparing the way for collectivism, which is almost imperceptibly usurping its place.[3]

But the Marxians have one serious quarrel with the older economists. It seemed to them that the earliest writers on political economy never realized the relatively transient nature of the social organism which they were studying. This was possibly because they were conservative by instinct and had the interest of the bourgeois at heart. They always taught, and they fully believed it, that private property and proletarianism were permanent features of the modern world, and that social organization was for ever destined to remain upon a middle-class foundation. They were at least unwilling to recognize that this also, like the rest, was simply a historical category, and, like them, also was destined to vanish.[4]

(*b*) The Marxian school also differs from every previous socialist

---

[1] *Conception matérialiste*, p. 91. Sorel says: "Marxism is really much more akin to the Manchester doctrine than to the Utopian. We must never forget this." (*La Décomposition du Marxisme*, p. 44.)

[2] "The bourgeoisie, historically, has played a most revolutionary part. . . . The bourgeoisie cannot exist without constantly revolutionizing the instruments of production, and thereby the relations of production, and with them the whole relations of society. . . . All fixed, fast-frozen relations, with their train of ancient and venerable prejudices and opinions, are swept away, all new-formed ones become antiquated before they can ossify, all that is solid melts into air, all that is holy is profaned." (*Manifesto*, para. 1.)
Besides, the Marxians themselves have tried to prove that capital is actively undermining its own existence, which is surely the *ne plus ultra* of the revolutionary temperament.

[3] "The result is that capital has managed to solve problems which the Utopians tackled in vain. It has also given rise to conditions which permit of an entrance into a new form of society. Thus socialism will not need to invent new machinery or to get people accustomed to them," etc. (Sorel, *loc. cit.*, p. 41.)

[4] "The economists regard the feudal institutions as artificial, the bourgeois as natural. The existing economic ties, in their opinion, are elemental laws that must always bind society. . . . They have had some history, that is all we can really say." (Marx, *Misère de la Philosophie*, pp. 167–168.)

school in the comparative ease with which it has eschewed every
consideration of justice and fraternity, which always played such an
important role in French socialism. It is interested, not in the ideal,
but in the actual, not in what ought to be, but in what is likely to be.

> The theoretical conclusions of the communists are in no way based
> on ideas or principles that have been invented, or discovered by
> this or that would-be universal reformer. They merely express, in
> general terms, actual relations springing from an existing class
> struggle, from a historical movement going on under our very eyes.[1]

To economic facts they attributed an importance altogether
transcending their influence in the economic sphere. Their belief was
that the several links which unify the many-sided activities of society,
whether in politics, literature, art, morality, or religion, are ultimately
referable to some economic fact or other. None of them but is based
upon a purely economic consideration. Most important of all are the
facts relating to production, especially to the mechanical instruments
of production and their operation. If we take, for example, the production of bread and the successive stages through which the mechanical operation of grinding has passed from the hand-mill of antiquity
to the water-mill of the Middle Ages and the steam-mill of to-day, we
have a clue to the parallel development of society from the family to
the capitalistic system and from the capitalistic to the trust, with their
concomitants slavery, serfdom, and proletarianism. This affords a far
better explanation of the facts than any bourgeois cant about "the
growth of freedom" or humbug of that nature. These are the real
foundations upon which every theory has to be reared. This materialistic conception of history,[2] implying as it does a complete philosophy
of history, is no longer confined to the purely economic domain.

[1] *Manifesto*, para. 2.

[2] Whenever they change their method of production men also change their whole
social outlook. "The hand-mill gave us the servile State; the steam-mill is the parent
of the industrial, capitalist State." (*Misère de la Philosophie*, 2nd ed., p. 156.) This
oft-repeated phrase contains a picturesque antithesis rather than a scientific formula
of historical materialism. In his preface to his *Kritik der politischen Oekonomie* Marx
expresses himself with much more moderation. The following is the most important
passage of that celebrated page:

"In the course of their efforts at production men enter into certain definite and
necessary relations which may be wholly independent of their own individual
preferences—such industrial ties being, of course, correlative to the state of their productive forces. Taken together, all these links constitute the economic structure of
society. In other words, it supplies a basis upon which the legal and political superstructure is raised, and corresponding to it are certain social forms which depend
upon the public conscience. The method of producing commodities, speaking
generally, fixes the social, political, and intellectual *processus* of life. A man's conscience has less to do with determining his manner of life than has his manner of life
with determining the state of his conscience."

Taken in the vulgar sense, it seems to involve the exclusion of every moral and every humanitarian consideration. As Schäffle put it in that oft-quoted phrase of his, it means reducing the social question to a "mere question of the belly." The French socialists find the doctrine somewhat difficult to swallow, and they hardly display the same reverence for Marx as is shown in some other countries.[1]

The orthodox Marxians immediately proceed to point out that such criticism is useless and shows a complete misunderstanding of Marx's position. Materialism in the Marxian sense (and all his terms have a Marxian as well as the ordinary significance) does not exclude idealism, but it does exclude ideology, which is a different thing. No Marxian has ever advocated leaving mankind at the mercy of its economic environment; on the contrary, the Marxian builds his faith upon evolution, which implies man's conscious, but not very successful, effort to improve his economic surroundings.[2] The materialistic

---

The word 'fixes,' even when qualified by 'speaking generally,' seems a little pronounced, and Marxism has substituted the term 'explained,' which is somewhat nearer the mark. Labriola says that "it merely represents an attempt to explain historical facts in the light of the economic substructure." (*Conception matérialiste*, p. 120.)

This materialistic conception is developed in a very paradoxical fashion in Loria's *La Constitution sociale*. He shows how all history and every war, whether of Guelph or of Ghibelline, the Reformation and the French Revolution, and even the death of Christ upon Calvary, rest upon an economic basis. In Loria's opinion, however, this basal fact is not industrialism, but the various types of land systems. See our chapter on Rent.

It would not be correct to regard Marxism as a mere expression of fatalism or out-and-out determinism. The Marxian pretends to be, and as a matter of fact he really is, a great believer in will-power. Once the workers see where their interests really lie he would have them move towards that goal with irresistible strength. It is not always even necessary to define the end quite clearly before beginning to move. "Everything that has happened in history has, of course, been the work of man, but only very rarely has it been the result of deliberate choice and well-considered planning on his part." (Labriola, *Conception matérialiste*, p. 133.) Elsewhere: "The successive creation of different social environments means the development of man himself." (*Ibid.*, pp. 131-132.)

It would be beyond the scope of this work to enter into a metaphysical discussion of these theories, however much one would like to.

[1] See the works of Jaurès, *Études socialistes*; George Renard, *Le Régime socialiste*; Fournière, *L'Indivdiu, l'Association, et l'État*.

[2] Labriola, *op. cit.* Vandervelde (*L'Idéalisme Marxiste*, in *La Revue socialiste*, February 1904) says that "upon final analysis it will be found that Marx's whole argument rests upon a moral basis, which is that justice requires that every man should get all that he produces."

Landry, in a book of lectures delivered by different authors entitled *Études sur la Philosophie morale au XIXe Siècle* (p. 164), is of an entirely different opinion. He thinks that Marx's moral basis is simply potentiality. In other words, everything that has been created in the ordinary course of economic development is moral, everything that has been destroyed is immoral.

conception of history apparently is simply an attempt at a philosophy
of human effort.[1] Criticism of such elusive doctrines is not a very
easy task.

(c) The socialism of Karl Marx is exclusively a working-class gospel.
This is its distinctive trait and the source of the power it wields. To
some extent it also explains its persistence. Other socialist systems
have been discredited and are gone, but the Marxian gospel—no
longer, of course, the sublime masterpiece it was when its author first
expounded it—has lost none of its ancient vigour, despite the many
transformations which it has undergone.

The socialists of the first half of the nineteenth century embraced all
men without distinction, worker and bourgeois alike, within their
broad humanitarian schemes. Owen, Fourier, and Saint-Simon
reckoned upon the co-operation of the wealthy governing classes to
found the society of the future. Marxism implies a totally different
standpoint. There is to be no attempt at an understanding with the
bourgeoisie, there must be no dallying with the unclean thing, and
the prohibition is to apply not only to the capitalists, but also to the
intellectuals[2] and to the whole hierarchical superstructure that usually
goes by the name of officialdom. Real socialism aims at nothing but
the welfare of the working classes, which will only become possible
when they attain to power.

It may, of course, be pointed out that socialism has always involved
some such struggle between rich and poor, but it is equally correct
to say that the battle has hitherto been waged over the question of
just distribution. Beyond that there was no issue. But in the Marxian
doctrine the antagonism is dignified with the name of a new scientific
law, the 'class war'—the worker against the capitalist, the poor versus
the rich. The individuals are the same, but the *casus belli* is quite
different. 'Class war' is a phrase that has contributed not a little to
the success of Marxism, and those who understand not a single word
of the theory—and this applies to the vast majority of working men—
will never forget the formula. It will always serve to keep the powder
dry, at any rate.

'Class war' was not a new fact. "The history of all hitherto exist-

[1] Hence the alliance of the Marxians with what appears to be a directly opposite
philosophy—that of William James and Bergson (see Guy Grand, *La Philosophie
syndicaliste*).

[2] *Manifesto*. It is impossible to do away with the intellectuals altogether, but they
may be reduced to the rank of mere wage-earners. "The Marxians always regarded
revolution as the special privilege of the producers, by whom, of course, they understood the manual workers, who, accustomed as they are to nothing but the factory
regime, would force the intellectuals also to supply some of the more ordinary wants
of life." (Sorel, *Décomposition du Marxisme*, p. 51.)

ing society is the history of class struggles."[1] But although it has always existed, it cannot continue for ever. And the great struggle that is now drawing nigh and which gives us such a tragic interest in the whole campaign will be the last. The collectivist regime will destroy the conditions that breed antagonism, and so will get rid of the classes themselves. Let us note in passing that this prophecy is not without a strong tinge of that Utopian optimism which the Marxians considered such a weakness in the earlier French socialism.

(d) A final distinction of Marxism is its purely revolutionary or catastrophic character, which is again unmistakably indicated by its adoption of 'class war' as its watchword. But we have only to remind ourselves that the adjective 'revolutionary' is applied by the Marxians to ordinary middle-class action to realize that the term is employed in a somewhat unusual fashion.

The revolution will result in the subjection of the wealthier classes by the working men, but all this will be accomplished, not by having recourse to the guillotine or by resorting to street rioting, but in a perfectly peaceful fashion. The means may be political and the method even within the four corners of the law, for the working classes may easily acquire a majority in Parliament, seeing that they already form the majority of the electors, especially in those countries that have adopted universal suffrage. The method may be simply that of economic associations of working men taking all economic services into their own hands.[2]

The final catastrophe may come in yet another guise, and most Marxians seem to centre their hopes upon this last possibility. This would take the form of an economic crisis resulting in the complete overthrow of the whole capitalist regime—a kind of economic *felo de se*. We have already noted the important place which crises hold in the Marxian doctrines.

But if Marxism does not necessarily involve resort to violence, violent methods are not excluded. Indeed, it considers that some measure of struggle is inevitable before the old social forms can be

---

[1] *Manifesto*, para. 2. It is necessary that we should be reminded of the fact that the Saint-Simonians had already emphasized the antagonism by speaking, not of rich and poor, but of idlers and workers. The differentiation, that is to say, was economic. The Marxian distinction is quite different, for within the category workers the Saint-Simonians included bankers and employers, for example, who are excluded by the Marxians. In some cases the Saint-Simonians thought they had even better claims to inclusion than the ordinary worker.

[2] The first of these means, namely, the acquiring of public works by the State, is spoken of as unified socialism in France, whereas the second, which relies upon direct action without the assistance of any political organization, is known as syndicalism and is represented by the Confédération générale du Travail (see p. 481).

delivered of the new—before the butterfly can issue from the chrysalis. "Force is the birth-pangs of society."[1]

This is not the place for false sentimentalism. Evil and suffering seem to be the indispensable agents of evolution. Had anyone been able to suppress slavery or serfdom or to prevent the expropriation of the worker by the capitalist, it would have merely meant drying up the springs of progress, and more evil than good would probably have resulted.[2] Every step forward involves certain unpleasant conditions, which must be faced if the higher forms of existence are ever to become a reality. And for this reason the reform of the bourgeois philanthropist and the preaching of social peace would be found to be harmful if they ever proved at all successful. There is no progress where there is no struggle. This disdainful indifference to the unavoidable suffering involved in transition is inherited from the Classical economists, and provides one more point of resemblance between the two doctrines. Almost identical terms were employed by the Classical economists when speaking of competition, of machinery, or of the absorption of the small industry by a greater one. In the opinion of the Marxians no attempt at improving matters is worth the name of reform unless it also speeds the coming revolution. "But it can shorten and lessen the birth-pangs."[3]

III: THE MARXIAN CRISIS AND THE NEO-MARXIANS

To speak of Neo-Marxism, which is of quite recent growth, is to anticipate the chronological order somewhat, but some such procedure seems imperative in the interests of logical sequence. It has the further merit of dispensing with any attempt at criticism, a task which the Neo-Marxians[4] have exclusively taken upon their own shoulders.

The two phases of the crisis must needs be kept distinct. The one, which is predominantly critical—or reformative, if that phrase be preferred—is best represented by M. Bernstein and his school. The other, which is more or less of an attempt to revive Marxism, has become current under the name of Syndicalism.

[1] Marx, *Misère de la Philosophie*. "What does the word 'revolt' imply? Simply disobedience to law. But what are these laws that govern our lives? They are just the products of bourgeois society and of the institutions which they are supposed to defend. Revolution will simply mean replacing these laws by others which will have an entirely different kind of justification."

[2] "It is the worst side of things that begets movement and makes history by begetting strife." (*Ibid.*, 2nd. ed., p. 173.)

[3] Preface to *Kapital*, p. xix.

[4] For the evolution of Marxism see Sombart's lively volume *Sozialismus und soziale Bewegung im 19ten Jahrhundert* (6th ed., 1908), and also Georges Sorel, *La Décomposition du Marxisme* (1908).

I. THE NEO-MARXIAN REFORMISTS

If we take Marx's economic theories one by one as we have done, we shall find that there is nothing very striking in any of them, and that even the most important of them will not stand critical scrutiny. We might even go farther and say that this work of demolition is partly due to the posthumous labours of Marx himself. It was the publication of his later volumes that served to call attention to the serious contradiction between the later and the earlier sections of his work. Marxism itself, it seems, fell a prey to that law of self-destruction which threatened the overthrow of the whole capitalistic regime. Some of Marx's disciples have, of course, tried to justify him by claiming that the work is not self-contradictory, but that the mere enumeration of the many conflicting aspects of capitalistic production strikes the mind as being contradictory.[1] If this be so, then *Kapital* is just a new edition of Proudhon's *Contradictions économiques*, which Marx had treated with such biting ridicule. And if the capitalist regime is really so full of contradictions that are inherent in its very nature, how difficult it must be to tell whether it will eventuate in collectivism or not and how very rash is scientific prophecy about annihilation and a final catastrophe![2]

With the beginning of the twentieth century the fundamental theory of Marxism, that of labour-value, was abandoned by a great number of modern Marxians, who were gradually veering round and adopting either the 'final utility' or the 'economic equilibrium' theory.[3] Even Marx himself, despite his formal acceptance of the labour-value theory, is constantly obliged to admit—not explicitly, of course—that value depends upon demand and supply.[4] Especially is this the case with

---

[1] Labriola, *Socialisme et Philosophie*, p. 29. Others declare more unmistakably still that "these obscure formulæ [the writer is thinking of surplus labour] lead to equivocation and must be banished from the science altogether." (Sorel, *Revue internationale de Sociologie*, 1900, p. 270.)

[2] M. Sorel says of the revolutionary movement that everything connected with it s very improbable. (*Décomposition du Marxisme*.)

[3] The Italian syndicalist Arthur Labriola (*Revue socialiste*, 1889, Vol. I, p. 674) writes as follows: "While we Marxians are trying to repatch the master's cloak political economy is making some headway every day. If we compare Marx's *Kapital* with Marshall's *Principles*—chapter by chapter, that is to say—we shall find that problems which required a few hundred pages in the *Kapital* are solved in a few lines by Marshall." B. Croce (*Materialismo storico ed Economia marxistica*, 1900, p. 105) writes thus: "I am strongly in favour of economic construction along Hedonistic lines. But that does not satisfy the natural desire for a sociological treatment of profits, and such treatment is impossible unless we make use of the comparative considerations suggested by Marx." Lastly, Sorel, in *Saggi di Critica del Marxismo* (1903, p. 13) says: "It is necessary to give up the attempt to transform socialism into a science."

[4] Especially in that passage to which Bernstein calls attention: "According to the law of value not merely must one devote the socially necessary amount of time to the

profits, as we have already had occasion to remark. What appears as an indisputable axiom in the first volume is treated as a mere working hypothesis in the later ones.

But seeing that the other Marxian doctrines—the theories of surplus value and surplus labour, for example—are mere deductions from the principle of labour-value, it follows that the overthrow of the first principle must involve the ruin of the other two. If labour does not necessarily create value, or if value can be created without labour, then there is no proof that labour *always* begets a surplus value and that the capitalist's profit must largely consist of unremunerated labour. The Neo-Marxians in reply point to the fact that surplus labour and surplus value do exist, else how could some individuals live without working? They must obviously be dependent upon the labour of others.[1] All this is very true, but the fact had been announced by Sismondi long before, and the evil had been denounced both by him and the English critics. It is the old problem of unearned increment which formed the basis of Saint-Simon's doctrine and Rodbertus's theory, and which was taken up by the English Fabians.

It is difficult to see what definite contribution Marx has made to the question, and the old problem as to whether workers are really exploited or not and whether the revenues obtained by the so-called idle classes correspond to any real additional value contributed by themselves still remains unsettled. We can only say that his historical exposition contains several very striking instances which seem to prove this exploitation, and that this is really the most solid part of his work.

Passing on to the law of concentration—the vertebral column of the Marxian doctrine—we shall find upon examination that it is in an equally piteous condition. The most unsparing critic in this case has been a socialist of the name of Bernstein, who has adduced a great number of facts[2]—many of them already advanced by the older

---

production of each commodity, but each group of commodities must have such extra effort spent upon it as the nature of the commodity or the character of the demand requires. The first condition of value is utility or the satisfaction of some social need —that is, value in use raised to such a degree of potentiality as shall determine the proportion of total social labour to each of the various kinds of production." (*Kapital*, Vol. III.)

Bernstein adds: "This admission makes it impossible to treat the themes of Gossen, of Jevons, and of Böhm-Bawerk as so many insignificant irrelevances." (*Die Voraussetzungen des Sozialismus.*)

[1] "The surplus-value theory may be true or it may be false, but that will make no difference to the existence of surplus labour. Surplus labour is a fact of experience, demonstrable by observation, and requires no deductive proof." (Bernstein, *loc. cit.*) That Marx did not treat it with quite the same indifference is evident from the fact that the whole theory is developed, not incidentally in the course of the work, but at the very opening of the book.

[2] In the book already quoted, which was published in 1899

economists—which go to disprove the Marxian theory, and which may be summarized as follows. It may be impossible to deny that the number of great industries is increasing rapidly and that their power is growing even more rapidly than their numbers, but it certainly does not seem as if the small proprietors and manufacturers were being ousted. Statistics, on the contrary, show that the number of small independent manufacturers (the artisans who, according to Marxian theory, had begun to disappear as far back as the fourteenth century) is actually increasing. Some new invention, such as photography, cycling, or the application of electricity to domestic work, or the revival of an industry such as horticulture, gives rise to a crowd of small industries and new manufacturers.

But concentration as yet has scarcely made an appearance even in agriculture, and all the efforts of the Marxians to make this industry fit in with their theory have proved utterly useless. America as well as Europe has been laid under tribute with a view to supplying figures that would prove their contention. The statistics, however, are so confusing that directly opposite conclusions may be drawn from the same set of figures. The amount of support which they lend to the Marxian contention seems very slight indeed. On the whole they may be said to lend colour to the opposite view that the number of businesses is at least keeping pace with the growth of population. Were this to be definitely verified it would set a twofold check upon the Marxian theory. Not only would it be proved that *petite culture* is on the increase, but it would also be found that it is on the increase simply because it is more productive than 'the great industry.'

But suppose for the sake of hypothesis that we accept the law of concentration as proved. That in itself is not enough to justify the Marxian doctrine. To do this statistics proving an increasing concentration of property in the hands of fewer individuals are also necessary; but in this case the testimony of the figures is all in the opposite direction. We must not be deceived by the appearance of that remarkable species the American millionaire. There are men who are richer than the richest who ever lived before, but there are also more men who are fairly rich than ever was the case before. The number of men who make a fortune—not a very great one, perhaps, but a moderate-sized or even a small one—is constantly growing. Joint-stock companies, which according to the Marxian view afforded striking evidence of the correctness of his thesis, have, on the contrary, resulted in the distribution of property between a greater number of people, which proves that the concentration of industry and the centralization of property are two different things. Or take the wonderful development of the co-operative movement, and reflect upon the number of proletarians who have been transformed into small capitalists entirely through its instrumentality. To think that expropriation in the future will be easier because the number of expropriated will be few seems quite contrary to facts. It looks as if it were the masses, whose numbers are daily increasing, who will have to be expropriated, after all. More than half the French people at the present day possess property of one kind or another—movable property, land, or houses. And yet the collectivists never speak except with the greatest contempt of these rag-ends and tatters of property, fondly imagining that when the day of expropriation comes the expropriated will joyfully throw their rags aside in return for the blessings of social co-proprietorship. Apparently, however, the Marxians themselves no longer believe all this. Their language has changed completely, and just now they are very anxious to keep these rags and tatters in the hands of their rightful owners.

The changes introduced into the programme as a result of this have transformed its character almost completely. When it was first drawn up and issued as a part of the *Communist Manifesto* nearly a hundred years ago everybody expected that the final disappearance of the small proprietor was a matter of only a few years, and that at the end of that time property of every description would be concentrated in the hands of a powerful few. This continuous expropriation would, of course, swell the ranks of the proletariat, so that compared with their numbers the proprietors would be a mere handful. This would make the final expropriation all the easier. With such disparity in numbers the issue was a foregone conclusion, no matter what method was employed, were it a revolution or merely a parliamentary vote.

Unfortunately for the execution of this programme, not only do we find the great capitalist still waxing strong, which is quite in accordance with the orthodox Marxian view, but there is no evidence that the small proprietor or manufacturer is on the wane. The Marxian can scarcely console himself with the thought that the revolution is gradually being accomplished without opposition when he sees hundreds of peasant proprietors, master craftsmen, and small shopkeepers on every side of him. Nor is there much chance of forcing this growing mass of people, which possibly includes the majority of the community even now, to change its views. We can hardly expect them to be very enthusiastic about a programme that involves their own extinction.

A distinction has obviously been drawn between two classes of proprietors. The socialization of the means of production is only to apply to the case of wealthy landowners and manufacturers on a large scale—to those who employ salaried persons. But the property of the man who is supporting himself with the labour of his own hands will always be respected. The Marxians defend themselves from the reproach of self-contradiction and opportunism by stating that their action is strictly in accordance with the process of evolution. You begin by expropriating those industries that have arrived at the capitalistic and wage-earning stage. The criterion must be the presence or otherwise of a surplus value.

The conclusion is logical enough, but one would like to know what is going to become of the small independent proprietor. Will he be allowed to grow and develop alongside of the one great proprietor— the State? We can hardly imagine the two systems coexisting and hopelessly intermingled, as they would have to be, but still with freedom for the individual to choose between them. The collectivists have at any rate made no attempt to disguise the fact. They look upon it merely as a temporary concession to the cowardice of the small proprietor, who will presently willingly abandon his own miserable bit of property in order to share in the benefits of the new regime, or who will at any rate be put out of the running by its economic superiority. But since the prospects do not seem very attractive to those immediately concerned, it may be as well to dispense with any further consideration of the subject.

But there is another question. What has become of the class struggle in Neo-Marxism? The doctrine, though not altogether denied, is no longer presented as a deadly duel between two classes and only two, but as a kind of confused *mêlée* involving a great number of classes, which makes the issue of the conflict very uncertain. The picture of society as consisting merely of two superimposed layers is dismissed as being altogether too elementary. On the contrary, what we find is increasing differentiation even within the capitalist class itself. There is a perpetual conflict going on between borrower and lender, between manufacturer and merchant, between trader and landlord, the last of which struggles is especially prominent in the annals of politics. It has a long history, but in modern times it has taken the form of a political battle between the Conservative and Liberal parties.

These undercurrents complicate matters a great deal, and on occasion they have a way of dramatically merging with the main current, when both parties seek the help of the proletariat. In England, for example, the manufacturers succeeded in repealing the Corn Laws, which dealt a hard blow at the landed proprietors, who in turn passed laws regulating the conditions of labour in mines and factories. In both cases the working classes gained something—*tertius gaudens!* Then there are the struggles among the working classes themselves. Not to speak of the bitter animosity between the *syndicats rouges* and the *syndicats jaunes*, there is the rivalry between syndicalists and non-syndicalists, between skilled workmen and the unskilled. As Leroy-Beaulieu remarks, not only have we a fourth estate, but there are many signs of a fifth.

And what of the great catastrophe? The Neo-Marxians no longer believe in it. The economic crises which furnished the principal argument in support of the catastrophic theory are by no means as terrible as they were when Marx wrote. They are no longer regarded as of the nature of financial earthquakes, but much more nearly resemble the movements of the sea, whose ebb and flow may to some extent be calculated.

And the materialistic conception of history? "Every unbiased person must subscribe to that formula of Bernstein: The influence of technico-economic evolution upon the evolution of other social institutions is becoming less and less."[1] What a number of proofs of this we have! Marxism itself furnishes us with some. The principle of class war and the appeal to class prejudice owe much of the hold which they have to a feeling of antagonism against economic fatalism. In other words, they draw much of their strength from an appeal to a certain ideal. It is, of course, true that facts of very different character, economic, political, and moral, react upon one another, but can anyone say that some one of them determines all the others? Economists have been forced to recognize this, and the futile attempt to discover cause or effect has recently given place to a much more promising search for purely reciprocal relations.

It is by no means easy to determine how much Marxism there is in Neo-Marxism. "Is there anything beyond the formulæ which we have quoted, and which are becoming more disputable every day? Is it anything more than a philosophical theory which purports to explain the conflicts of society?"[2] Bernstein tells us somewhere that socialism is just a movement, and that "the movement is everything, the end is nothing."[3]

2. THE NEO-MARXIAN SYNDICALISTS

Doctrinaire Marxism seemed languishing when a number of pro-

[1] Sorel, *Les Polémiques pour l'Interprétation du Marxisme*, in the *Revue internationale de Sociologie*, 1900.

[2] Sorel, *Décomposition du Marxisme*, p. 33.

[3] *Socialisme et Social-démocratie*, p. 234. We have been told by Sorel that syndicalism is just a literal application of Bergson's philosophy.

fessed disciples found a fresh opportunity of reviving its ideals and of justifying its aims in a new movement of a pre-eminently working-class character known as Syndicalism.

Our concern is not with the reformist movement, occasionally spoken of as Trade Unionism, which constitutes the special province of M. Bernstein and the Neo-Marxians of his school,[1] but rather with militant syndicalism, which as yet scarcely exists anywhere except in France and Italy, and which in France is represented by the Confédération générale du Travail.

What connexion is there between Marxism and syndicalism? Of conscious, deliberate relationship there is scarcely any. The men who direct the Confédération have never read Marx, possibly, and would hardly concern themselves with the application of his doctrines. On the other hand, we have been told by Sorel that the programme of the Confédération générale du Travail (C.G.T.) is in strict conformity with the Marxian doctrine; that since the reforming passion has so seized hold of the Neo-Marxians as to drive them to undermine the older doctrine altogether, it is necessary to turn to the new school to find the pure doctrine. They make the further claim of having aroused new enthusiasm for the Marxian doctrines.

(a) Firstly, Georges Sorel and his followers have re-emphasized the essentially proletarian character of socialism. Not only is there to be no dealing with capitalist or *entrepreneur*, but no quarter is to be given to intellectuals or politicians. The professional labour syndicate is to exclude every one who is not a workman, and it has no interest at heart other than that of the working class.[2] Contempt for intellectualism is a feature of Marxism, and so is the emphasis laid upon the beauty and worth of labour, not of every kind of labour, but merely of that labour which moulds or transforms matter—that is, of purely manual labour.

No institution seems better fitted to develop class feeling—that is,

[1] This point of view is very neatly expressed in an article of M. Berth's (*Mouvement socialiste*, May 1908, p. 393): "From a purely negative or critical point of view we agree with Bernstein rather than the orthodox Kautsky. But what does Bernstein propose to substitute for the revolutionary ideal—impracticable as it was—of the German Social Democratic party? The alternative offered is a simple democratic, reformist evolution, a political or economic development which would just be a pale imitation of the bourgeois Liberal regime, which it is hoped would result in the emancipation of the workers by getting rid of bourgeois Liberalism altogether. The complete democratization of politics and economics would, it is hoped, effect the necessary improvement. On this point we syndicalists must definitely part company with Bernstein and his *confrères*, for what we want is not a mere evolution, but a revolutionary creation of new social forms."

[2] "An organization of producers who will be able to manage their own affairs without having recourse to the superior knowledge which the typical bourgeois is supposed to possess." (Sorel, *Décomposition du Marxisme*, pp. 60–61.)

the sense of community of interests binding all the proletarians together against the owners—than the *syndicat*. Organization is necessary if social consciousness is to develop. This is as true in the economic as it is in the biological sphere, and this is why the *syndicat* is just what was needed to transform the old socialistic conception into real socialism. Marx could not possibly have foreseen the vast potentialities of the *syndicat*. If he had only known it how his heart would have rejoiced! The Neo-Marxians can never speak of syndicalism without going into raptures. No other new source of energy seems left in this tottering middle-class system. But syndicalism has within it the promise of a new society, of a new philosophy, even of a new code of morality which we may call producers' ethics, which will have its roots in professional honour, in the joy that comes from the accomplishment of some piece of work, and in their faith in progress.[1]

(b) New stress has been laid upon the philosophy of class war, and a fresh appeal has been made for putting it into practice. The only real, sensible kind of revolution is that which must sooner or later take place between capitalists on the one hand and wage-earners on the other, and this kind of revolution can only be effected by appealing to class feeling and by resorting to every instrument of conflict, strikes, open violence, etc. All attempts at establishing an understanding with the bourgeois class, every appeal for State intervention or for concessions, must be abandoned. Explicit trust must be placed in the method of direct action.[2]

Strife is to be the keynote of the future, and in the pending struggle every trace of bourgeois legalism will be ruthlessly swept aside. The

[1] "Revolutionary syndicalism is the great educative force which contemporary society has at its disposal to prepare it for the tasks which await it." (Sorel, *Réflexions sur la Violence*, p. 244; 1909.)

"In the general ruin of institutions something new and powerful will remain intact. This will be what is generally known as the proletarian soul, which it is hoped will survive the general reassessment of moral values, but that will depend on the energy displayed by the workers in resisting the corruption of the bourgeoisie and in meeting their advances with the most unmistakable hostility." (*Ibid.*, p. 253.)

It is altogether a different point of view from that of the consumer, the shareholder, or the 'literary idler,' who are only interested in the success of buyers' social leagues, or in consumers' societies. *Cf.* p. 348.

[2] This incessant struggle is what Sorel has named violence, which he thinks is peculiarly healthy. "I have shown," says he, "that proletarian violence has an entirely different significance from that usually attributed to it by politicians and amateur students of society." It is incorrect, however, to say that he is in favour of sabotage. "Sabotage," says Sorel, "belongs to the old regime, but does nothing to set the worker in the way of emancipation." (*Mouvement socialiste*, 1905, November 1 and 15.)

One cannot fail to see the antagonism which exists in France between the Socialistes Unifiés (which is largely recruited from the old Marxian party) and the syndicalists, who condemn both universal suffrage and parliamentary action.

fighting spirit must be kept up, not with a view to the intensification of class hatred, but simply in order to hand on the torch.

The struggle has hitherto been the one concern of the revolutionary syndicalists. Unlike the socialists, they have never paid any attention either to labour or to social organization. All this has, fortunately, been done by the capitalist, and all that is required now is simply to remove him.[1]

(c) Nor has the catastrophic thesis been forgotten. This time it has been revived, not in the form of a financial crisis, but in the guise of a general strike. What will all the bourgeois generalship, all the artillery of the middle class, avail in a struggle of that kind? What is to be done when the worker just folds his arms and instantly brings all social life to a standstill, thus proving that labour is really the creator of all wealth? And although one may be very sceptical as to the possibility of a general strike—the scepticism is one that is fully shared in by the syndicalists themselves—still this "myth," as Sorel calls it, must give a very powerful stimulus to action, just as the Christians of the early centuries displayed wonderful activity in view of their expectation of the second coming of Christ.

The word 'myth' has been a great success, not so much among working men, to whom it means nothing at all, but among the intellectuals. It is very amusing to think that this exclusively working-class socialism, which is not merely anti-capitalist, but also violently anti-intellectual, and which is to "treat the advances of the bourgeoisie with undisguised brutality," is the work of a small group of 'intellectuals' possessed of remarkable subtlety, and even claiming kinship with Bergsonian philosophy.[2] A myth, perhaps! But what difference is there between being under the dominion of a myth and following in the wake of a star such as guided the wise men of the East, or being led by a pillar of flame or a cloud such as went before the Israelites on their pilgrimage towards the Promised Land?[3] Such faith and hope

[1] "One no longer thinks of drawing up a scheme which shall determine the way in which people in the future are to seek their own well-being. The problem now is how to complete the revolutionary education of the proletarian." (Sorel, *Décomposition du Marxisme*, introduction, p. 37.)

[2] This group was represented by the review called *Le Mouvement socialiste*, which was controlled by M. Lagardelle. Sorel withdrew from the group and at the end of his life was leading a campaign in favour of Catholic nationalism.

The literature of syndicalism is very extensive. We have already mentioned M. Guy Grand's *La Philosophie syndicaliste*.

[3] *Réflexions sur la Violence*, p. xxxv. We must note, however, that Sorel protests against any confusion being made between the myth as he understands it and Utopian socialism. The myth is obviously superior in the fact that it cannot be refuted, seeing that it is merely the expression of a conviction. See pp. xxv and 218 of the same work.

borrowed from the armoury of the triumphant Church of the first century, such a conception of progress which swells its followers with a generous, almost heroic passion, puts us out of touch with the historic materialism so dear to the heart of Marx and brings us into line with the earlier Utopian socialists whom he so genuinely despised. Sorel recognizes this. "You rarely meet with a pure myth," says he, "without some admixture of Utopianism."

Book V: Reconstruction of Doctrines at the End of the Nineteenth Century and Birth of Social Doctrines

THE forty years of almost uninterrupted peace in Europe following the Franco-German War were marked in the history of doctrines by a great reconstruction both of economic theory and of social doctrines.

In the realm of theory there was a veritable revolution in methods and conceptions. At the very moment when historians and State Socialists were proclaiming their contempt for all abstract speculation a brilliant attempt was being made in France, in England, and in Austria to establish economic theory on new foundations. Three great names stand out pre-eminently: Walras in France, Menger in Austria, and Jevons in England. By concentrating on the concept of utility, too much neglected since the days of Condillac, and following Cournot in their use of mathematics, these writers replaced the too elementary simplifications of the classical school by the concepts of economic equilibrium and mutual dependence of prices. These ideas, developed later in Italy, Austria, the United States, and England by economists like Pareto, Marshall, Edgeworth, Böhm-Bawerk, and Fisher, gradually won their way to recognition, though not without somewhat prolonged resistance in Germany and France. They led to original research in all directions, and ended by dominating economic thought and teaching in the principal countries of the world. Those who initiated them became the real 'classics' for later generations of economists, and their prestige definitely eclipsed that of Ricardo and Mill.

At the same time there was taking place a reconstruction of social doctrines. Throughout this period, of course, the number of adherents of State Socialism and Marxism continued to increase, but a reaction showed itself in several directions against the two fundamental ideas that inspired both these doctrines: the class war in the one case and *étatisme* in the other. While they both sought a solution of the problems raised by the claims of the working classes, some doctrines proclaimed, in opposition to the Marxian class conflict, the principle of class union, while others demanded a measure of freedom from all

State restrictions even more radical than that demanded by the liberals.

In the first place Christianity, long absent from the arena of social discussion, made a brilliant return to it through the champions of the two great Christian faiths, the Catholic and the Protestant. Nothing is more opposed to the idea of the class conflict than the teaching of Christianity, based entirely on the idea of charity. Is not this basis strong enough to form the foundation of a social doctrine bringing hope to the poorest classes of an improvement in their lot, and reminding the more fortunate of the too often forgotten duties that charity enjoins? That is what many generous-hearted men were thinking in various countries, almost at the same time. A Christian social doctrine would obviously be a doctrine of union, supported by aspirations common to workers and employers alike. It would find the solution of social problems in the fervour of a revived Christian sentiment and the *rapprochement* that results from it. For the most conservative can no longer ignore the gravity of these problems. Even in the preceding period various mighty voices had been raised in support of these ideas, but they met with little response in an age of bloody social strife. The belated flowering of such doctrines in all their glory did not come till the end of the nineteenth century, when Pope Leo XIII bestowed on them his authoritative consecration. All the Christian churches were more or less inspired by them, and their place should therefore be in this part of our work.

The idea of a union of classes instead of their deep-rooted antagonism was to find an echo in other quarters besides the consciences of Christian men. Among the great body of the indifferent, or of thinkers aloof from the traditional religious faiths but permeated by the individualist ideas of the French Revolution, there were some who felt the need of a principle that would reconcile these ideas with the admitted necessity of social reform. The question was how to incorporate in formulæ declaring above all the *rights* of the individual, new formulæ applying on the contrary to his *duties*, and justifying the sacrifices that the State might require him to make. From these considerations emerged the doctrine of 'Solidarism,' which has led increasingly in democratic countries to legislation similar to that which State Socialism has put into effect in authoritarian States.

Another effort to reconcile liberalism with socialism is seen in the attempts made to draw from Ricardo's theory of rent conclusions favourable to a more equitable distribution of the social product. The theory of rent covers all incomes produced by economic progress of its own motion: they cannot be attributed to the labour or saving of any one particular agent. They result from the dynamic tendency inherent in all societies, whereas the theory of equilibrium implies a static society. By being continually created anew they introduce variety and change into an economic system that pure theory regards as tending to stability and uniformity.

Could not part at least of these incomes be restored to society, so that society, which is their real author, should also benefit by them? The reply to this question is given in systems of land nationalization and those still wider plans which aim at confiscating all incomes analogous to rent. This was a strange attempt at reconciling liberalism with socialism and establishing a more equitable distribution of incomes without restricting freedom and competition among *entrepreneurs*.

The doctrine that opposed these attempts at reconciliation was entirely different. In opposition to the authoritarian trend of socialism it carried to their extreme limits the liberal tendencies that emerged from the French Revolution, and gave expression to the old revolutionary and individualist spirit that was always active, especially in the Latin countries. A strange rebirth of liberalism was apparent at this time among the working classes, but it was undoubtedly quite a different liberalism from that of its founders. It was harsher in its mode of expression, and Smith and Bastiat would certainly have repudiated it. So to avoid confusion with the older liberal doctrine it was called "libertarian." But for all that it is none the less genuine: it is *anarchism*. This libertarian, or anarchist, tendency, already perceptible in the International, eventually obtained an ever clearer ascendancy over the working classes and left its mark on the syndicalist movement in France and Italy. At the same time a kind of philosophical and moral anarchism appeared among middle-class writers and seemed to presage a rebirth of individualism.

Such, then, are the principal doctrinal currents which, under the favourable influence of the prolonged peace that followed the Franco-German War, showed the trend of thought among writers who were interested particularly in social reform. Almost all of them had their roots in writers of earlier periods, but their full brilliance and penetrating power belong to the period we have now to examine. It was not till a yet later period—after the First World War—that men returned with new ardour to the great problems of production and exchange that had engrossed the attention of the 'founders.' And it was to the impoverishment caused by so prolonged a conflict, as in the earlier period after the Napoleonic Wars, that these problems owed all their importance.

CHAPTER I: THE HEDONISTS

I: THE PSEUDO-RENAISSANCE OF THE CLASSICAL SCHOOL

IF we are to give this new doctrine its true setting we must return for a moment to our study of the Historical school. The criticism of that school, as we have already seen, was directed chiefly against the method of the Classical writers. The faith which their predecessors had placed in the permanence and universality of natural law was scornfully rejected, and the possibility of ever founding a science upon a chain of general propositions emphatically denied. Political economy, so it was decreed, was henceforth to be concerned merely with the classification of observed facts.

It would not have been difficult to foretell that the swing of the pendulum—in accordance with that strange rhythm which is such a feature of the history of thought—would at the opportune moment cause a reversion to the abstract method. That is exactly what happened. Just at the moment when Historical study seemed to be triumphantly forging ahead—that is, about the years 1872–74—several eminent economists in Austria, England, Switzerland, and America suddenly and simultaneously made their appearance with an emphatic demand that political economy should be regarded as an independent science. They brought forward the claims of what they called pure economics. Naturally enough there ensued the keenest controversy between the champions of the two schools, notably between Professors Schmoller and Karl Menger.

The new school had one distinctive characteristic. In its search for a basis upon which to build the new theory it hit upon the general principle that man always seeks pleasure and avoids pain, getting as much of the former with as slight a dilution of the latter as he possibly can.[1] A fact of such great importance and one that was not confined to the field of economic activities, but seemed present everywhere throughout nature in the guise of the principle of least resistance, could scarcely have escaped the notice of the Classical theorists. They had referred to it simply as "personal interest," but to-day we speak of it as Hedonism, from the Greek ἡδονή (pleasure or agreeableness).

---

[1] "Pleasure and pain are undoubtedly the ultimate objects of the calculus of economics. To satisfy our wants to the utmost with the least effort, to procure the greatest amount of what is desirable at the expense of the least that is undesirable, in other words, *to maximise pleasure*, is the problem of economics." (Stanley Jevons, *Theory of Political Economy*, p. 40.)

Hence the name Hedonists, by which we have chosen to designate these two schools.

The elimination of all motives affecting human action except one does not imply any desire on the part of these writers to deny the existence of others. They simply lay claim to the right of abstraction, without which no exact science could ever be constituted. In other words, they demand the right of eliminating from the field of research every element other than the one which they wish to examine. The study of the other motives belongs to the province of other social sciences. The *homo œconomicus* of the Classicals which has been the object of so much derision has been replaced on its pedestal. But it has in the meantime undergone such a process of simplification that it is scarcely better than a mere abstraction. Men are again to be treated as forces and represented by curves or figures as in treatises on mechanics. The object of the study is to determine the interaction of men among themselves, and their reaction upon the external world.

We shall also find that the new schools arrive at an almost identical conclusion with the old, namely, that absolutely free competition alone gives the maximum of satisfaction to everybody. Allowing for the differences in their respective points of view, to which we shall refer later on, what is this but simply a revival of the great Classical tradition?

Little wonder, then, that we find a good deal of sympathy shown for the old Classical school. Indeed, it is throughout regarded with almost filial piety.[1]

This does not mean that the Classical doctrine is treated as being wholly beyond reproach, although it does mean that the new school could scarcely accuse it of being in error, seeing that it comes to similar conclusions itself. But what it does lay to the charge of the older writers is a failure to prove what they assumed to be true and a tendency to be satisfied with a process of reasoning which too often meant wandering round in a hopeless circle. Especially was this the case with their study of causal relations, forgetting that as often as not cause was effect and effect cause. The attempt to determine which is cause and which effect is clearly futile, and the science must rest content with the discovery of uniformities either of sequence or of coexistence.

This applies especially to the three great laws which form the framework of economic science, namely, the law of demand and supply, the

[1] "The errors of the Classical school are, so to speak, the ordinary diseases of the childhood of every science." (Böhm-Bawerk, *The Austrian Economists*, in *Annals of the American Academy of Political and Social Science*, January 1891.)

law of cost of production, and the law of distribution, none of which is independent of the others. Let us review them briefly.

The law stating that "price varies directly with demand and inversely with supply" possessed just that degree of mathematical precision necessary to attract the attention of the new writers. In fact, it just served for the passage from the old to the new economics. But no sooner was the crossing effected than the bridge was destroyed. Little difficulty was experienced in pointing out that this so-called law which had been considered to be one of the axioms of political economy, the *quid inconcussum* upon which had been raised all the superstructure of economic theory, was an excellent example of that circular reasoning of which we have just spoken. There was a considerable flutter among the economists of the mid-nineteenth century when they found themselves forced to recognize this. However true it may be that price is determined by demand and supply, it is equally true that demand and supply are each in their turn determined by the price, so that it is impossible to tell which is cause or which is effect. Stuart Mill had already noted this contradiction, and had attempted correction in the way already described (p. 364). But he was ignorant of the fact that Cournot had completely demolished the formula by setting up another in its place, namely, that 'demand is a function of price.'[1] The substitution of that formula marks the inauguration of the Hedonistic calculus. Demand is now shown to be connected with price by a kind of see-saw movement, falling when prices rise and rising when prices fall. Supply is equally a function of price, but it operates in the opposite fashion, moving *pari passu* with it—rising as it rises and falling as it falls. Thus price, demand, and supply are like three sections of one mechanism, none of which can move in isolation, and the problem is to determine the law of their interdependence.

This does not by any means imply that there is no longer any place in economics for the law of demand and supply. It has merely been given a new significance, and the usual way of expressing it nowadays is by means of a supply and demand curve, which simply involves translating Cournot's dictum into figures.

The same is true of the law stating that cost of production determines value. There is the same *petitio principii* here. It is easy enough to see, on the contrary, that the *entrepreneur* regulates his cost of production according to price. The Classical school had realized this as far as one of the elements in the cost of production was concerned, for it was quite emphatic in its teaching that price determined rent, but that rent did not determine price. It is just as true of the other ele-

[1] *Recherches sur les Principes mathématiques de la théorie des richesses.*

ments. In other words, the second law is just as fallible as the first.
It is obviously imperative that the vain quest for causal relations
should be abandoned and that economists should be content with the
statement that between cost of production and price there exists a
kind of equilibrating action in virtue not of any mysterious solidarity
which subsists between them, but because the mere absence of equilibrium due either to a diminution or an increase in the quantity of
products immediately sets up forces which tend to bring it back to a
position of equilibrium. This interdependent relation, which is
extremely important in itself and upon which the Hedonists lay great
store, is simply one example taken from among many where the value
of one thing is just a function of another.

Similar criticism applies to the law of distribution, to the Classical
doctrine of wages, interest, and rent. The way the Classical writers
treated of these questions was extraordinarily naïve. Take the
question of rent. You just subtract from the total value of the product
wages, interest, and profit, and you are left with rent. Or take the
question of profit. In this case you will have to subtract rent, if there
is any, then wages and interest, the other component elements, and
what remains is profit. Böhm-Bawerk wittily remarks that the saying
that wages are determined by the product of labour apparently only
amounts to this—that what remains (if any) after the other co-operators
have had their share is wages. Each co-partner in turn becomes a
residual claimant, and the amount of the residuum is determined by
assuming that we already know the share of the other claimants![1]

The new school refuses any longer to pay honour to this ancient
trinity. It is impossible to treat each factor separately because of the
intimate connexion between them, and their productive work, as the
Hedonists point out, must necessarily be complementary. In any case,
before we can determine the relative shares of each we must be certain
that our unknown x is not reckoned among the known. This naturally
leads them on to the realm of mathematical formulæ and equations.

All the Hedonists, however, do not employ mathematics. The
Psychological school, especially the Austrian section of it, seems to
think that little can be gained by the employment of mathematical
formulæ. Some of the Mathematical economists, on the other hand,
are equally convinced of the futility of psychology, especially of the

---

[1] Let P = value of product and x, y, z represent wages, interest, and rent respectively
then $x + y + z = P$, which is insoluble.
Nor does it seem much more hopeful when written out thus:
$$x = P - (y + z)$$
$$y = P - (x + z)$$
$$z = P - (x + y)$$

famous principle of final utility, which is the corner-stone of the Austrian theory.[1]

For the sake of clearness it may be better to take the two branches —the Psychological and the Mathematical—separately.

II: THE PSYCHOLOGICAL SCHOOL

The feature of the Psychological school is its fidelity to the doctrine of final utility, whatever that may mean.[2] The older economists had got hold of a similar notion when they spoke of value in use, but instead of preserving the idea they dismissed it with a name, and it was left to the Psychological school to revive it in its present glorified form.

It must not be imagined that the term is employed in the usual

[1] "The theory of economic equilibrium is quite distinct from the theory of final utility, although the public are apt to confuse them and to think that they are both the same." (Vilfredo Pareto, *L'Économie pure*, 1902.)

[2] The name varies a little with different authors and in different countries. 'The final degree of utility' is the term used by Jevons, 'marginal utility' by the Americans, 'the intensity of the last satisfied want' by Walras. Walras also speaks of it as 'scarcity,' using the term in a purely subjective fashion to denote insufficiency for present need. This very plethora of terms suggests a certain haziness of conception. The term 'marginal' seems clearer than the term 'final,' although in some cases it may be impossible to oust the latter.

It appears that the first suggestion of final utility in the sense in which it is employed by the Psychological school is due to a French engineer of the name of Dupuit. He threw out the suggestion in two memoirs entitled *La Mesure de l'utilité des travaux publics* (1844) and *L'Utilité des voies de communication* (1849), both of which were published in the *Annales des Ponts et chaussées*, although their real importance was not realized until a long time afterwards. Gossen also, whose book is referred to on p. 499, was one of the earliest to discover it. These two memoirs were republished in Italy in 1933, in the collection of "unpublished or scarce economic works" edited by the eminent economist Luigi Einaudi at Turin.

In its present form it was first expounded by Stanley Jevons in his *Theory of Political Economy*, and by Karl Menger in his *Grundsätze der Volkswirtschaftslehre* (1871). Walras's conception of scarcity, which is just a parallel idea, was made public about the same time (1874). Finally Clark, the American economist, in his *Philosophy of Value*, which is of a somewhat later date (1881), seems to have arrived at a similar conclusion by an entirely different method—a remarkable example of simultaneous discoveries, which are by no means rare in the history of thought.

Despite its cosmopolitan origin, the school is generally spoken of as the Austrian school, because its most eminent representatives have for the most part been Austrians. Among these we may mention Karl Menger, already referred to, Professor Sax (*Das Wesen und die Aufgabe der Nationalökonomie*, 1884), Wieser (*Der natürliche Werth*, 1889), and of course Böhm-Bawerk (author of *Grundzüge der Theorie des wirthschaftlichen Güterwerths*, in *Jahrbücher für Nationalökonomie*, 1886, and the well-known book on capital and interest).

Since 1900 the theory of marginal utility has found its most brilliant exponents in the United States. The American professors J. B. Clark, Patten, Irving Fisher, Carver, Fetter, etc., were assiduous students of marginal utility, applying the conception not only to problems of capital and interest, but also to the question of distribution.

popular sense of something beneficial. All that it connotes is ability
to satisfy some human want, be that want reasonable, ridiculous, or
reprobatory. Bread, diamonds, and opium are all equally useful in
this sense.[1]

Nor must we fall into the opposite error of thinking of it as the
utility of things in general. Rather is it the utility of a particular unit
of some specific commodity relative to the demand of some individual
for that commodity, whether the individual in question be producer
or consumer. It is not a question of bread in general, but of the
number of loaves. To speak of the utility of bread in general is absurd,
and, moreoever, there is no means of measuring it. What is interesting
to me is the amount of bread which I want. This simple change in
the general point of view has effectively got rid of all the ambiguities
under which the Classical school laboured.[2]

1. The first problem that suggests itself in this connexion is this:
Why is the idea of value inseparable from that of scarcity? Simply
because the utility of each unit depends upon the intensity of the
immediate need that requires satisfaction, and this intensity itself
depends upon the quantity already possessed, for it is a law of physiology
as well as of psychology that every need is limited by nature and grows
less as the amount possessed increases, until a point zero is reached.
This point is called the point of satiety, and beyond it the degree of
utility becomes negative and desire is transformed into repulsion.[3]
Hence the first condition of utility is limitation of supply.

So long as people held to the idea of utility in general it was impossible to discover any necessary connexion between utility and
scarcity. It was easy enough to see that an explanation that was not

[1] To escape the confusion which would result from employing the same term in two
such very different senses—a confusion that is inevitable however one may try to
avoid it—Pareto has substituted the word 'ophelimity,' and Gide in his *Principles*
(1883) 'desirability.'

[2] "The idea of final utility is the 'open sesame,' the key to the most complicated
phenomena of economic life, affording a solution of its most difficult problems."
(Böhm-Bawerk, *The Austrian Economists*, in *Annals of the American Academy of Political
and Social Science*, 1891.)

[3] Condillac had already drawn attention to this fact (see p. 65), and Buffon had
noted it even before that. "The poor man's coin which goes to pay for the necessaries
of life and the last coin that goes to fill the financier's purse are in the opinion of the
mathematician two units of the same order, but to the moralist the one is worth a
louis, the other not a cent." (*Essai d'Arithmétique morale.*)

The connexion between quantity and demand is best expressed by means of a
curve either of utility or of demand (see p. 502). Along the horizontal line let the
figures 1, 2, 3, 4 denote the quantities consumed, and from each of these points draw
a vertical line to denote the intensity of demand for each of these quantities. The
height of the ordinate decreases more or less rapidly as the quantity increases, until
at last it falls to zero.

based upon one or other of these two ideas was bound to be unsatisfactory, but nobody knew why. As soon as the connexion between the
two was realized, however, it became evident that utility must be
regarded as a function of the quantity possessed, and that this degree
of utility constitutes what we call value.

2. Just as the notion of final utility solved one of the most difficult
problems in economics, namely, why water, for example, has less
value than diamonds, it also helped to clear up another mystery that
had perplexed many economists from the Physiocrats downward,
namely, how exchange, which by definition implies the equivalence
of the objects exchanged, can result in a gain for both parties. Here
at last is the enigma solved. In an act of exchange attention must be
focused not upon the total but upon the final utility. The equality
in the case of both parties lies in the balance between the last portion
that is acquired and the last portion that is given up.

Imagine two Congoese merchants, the one, A, having a heap of
salt, and the other, B, a heap of rice, which they are anxious to exchange. As yet the rate of exchange is undetermined, but let them
begin. A takes a handful of salt and passes it on to B, who does the
same with the rice, and so the process goes on. A casts his eye upon
the two heaps as they begin mounting up, and as the heap of rice
keeps growing the utility of each new handful that is added keeps
diminishing, because he will soon have enough to supply all his wants.
It is otherwise with the salt, each successive handful assuming an
increasing utility. Now, seeing that the utility of the one keeps increasing, while that of the other decreases, there must come a time
when they will both be equal. At that point A will stop. The rate of
exchange will be determined, and the prices fixed by the relative
measures of the two heaps. At that moment the heap of rice acquired
will not have for A a much greater utility than has the heap of salt
with which he has parted.

But A is not the only individual concerned, and it is not at all
probable that B will feel inclined to stop at the same moment as A;
and if he had made up his mind to stop before A had been satisfied
with the quantity of rice given him no exchange would have been
possible. We must suppose, then, that each party to the exchange
must be ready to go to some point beyond the limit which the other
has fixed *in petto*. This point can only be arrived at by bargaining.[1]

[1] It is in cases of this kind that figures become handy. If we take two curves, an
ascending one to represent the utility of each handful of salt parted with, and a
descending one to represent the utility of each handful of rice acquired, the two
curves must necessarily intersect, seeing that one is just the inverse of the other. The

3. Another question that requires answering is this: How is it that
there is only one price for goods of the same quality in the same market?
Once it is clearly grasped that the utility spoken of is the utility of
each separate unit for each separate individual it will be realized that
there must be as many different utilities as there are units, for each of
them satisfies a different need. But if this is the case, why does a
person who is famishing not pay a much higher price for a loaf than
a wealthy person who has very little need for it? or, why do I not pay
more when I am hungry than when I am not? The reason is that it
would be absurd to imagine that goods which are nearly identical and
even interchangeable should have different exchange values on the
same market and especially for the same person. This law of indifference,[1] as it is called, is derived from another law to which the
Psychological school rightly attaches great importance, and which
constitutes one of its most precious contributions to the study of

point of intersection marks the place where the utilities of the two exchanged handfuls
are exactly equal.

We must be careful not to confuse matters, however. It is not suggested that the
final utilities in the case of the two co-exchangers are equal. There is no common
measure by which the desires of different persons can be compared, and no bridge
from one to the other. What is implied is that the final utility of both commodities
for the *same person* are the same. The balance lies between two preferences of the same
individual. The actual market exchange is just the resultant of all these virtual
exchanges.

The Austrian school in its explanation makes use of a hypothesis known as the
double limit, which does not seem to be absolutely indispensable, seeing that other
economists of the same school—Walras, for example—appear to get on well enough
without it. They seem to think of buyers and sellers drawn up in two rows facing
one another. Every one of the sellers attributes to the object which he possesses and
which he wants to sell a certain utility different from his neighbour's. Each buyer
in the same way attributes to that object which he desires to buy a degree of utility
which is different from that which his neighbour puts upon it. The first exchange,
which will probably have the effect of fixing the price for all the other buyers and
sellers, will take place between the buyer who attributes the greatest utility to the
commodity he has to sell, and who is therefore least compelled to sell, and the buyer
who attributes the least utility to the commodity he wishes to buy and who is therefore least tempted to buy. At first sight it seems impossible that the party as a whole
should be bound by the action of the two individuals who show the least inclination
to come to terms. It would be more natural to expect the first move to take place
between the seller who is forced to sell and because of his urgency is content with a
price of 10s. per bushel, say, and the buyer who feels the strongest desire to buy and
who, rather than go without, would be willing to give 30s. for it. But upon consideration it will be found that the price is indeterminate just because these two are ready to
treat at any price. The most impatient individual will surely wait to see what terms
the least pressed will be able to make, and it is only natural that those who are nearest
one another should be the first to come together. These two co-exchangists who
control the market are known as the "limiting couple."

[1] It was Stanley Jevons who gave it this expressive name. It is meant to imply that
if two objects which fulfil very different needs, perhaps, can be interchanged they
cannot have very different values.

economics, namely, the law of substitution. This law implies that whenever one commodity can be exchanged for another for the purpose of satisfying the same need, the commodity replaced cannot be much more valuable than the commodity replacing it.[1]

For what is substitution but mutual exchange? And exchange implies equality, so that if there is a series of interchangeable goods none of them can be of greater value than any of the rest.

Consequently, if an individual has at his disposal 100 glasses of water, which is easily available everywhere except in the Sahara, perhaps, no one of these glasses, not even that one for which he would be willing to give its weight in gold were he very thirsty and that the only glassful available, will have a greater value than has the hundredth, which is worth exactly nothing. The hundredth is always there ready to be substituted for any of the others.

But the best way of getting a clear idea of final utility is not to consider the value of the object A, but of the object B, which can replace it. It becomes evident, then, that if I am about to lose some object, A, which I value a good deal but which can be perfectly replaced by another object, B, that object A cannot be much more valuable than B; and if I had the further choice of replacing it by C, C being less valuable than B, then A itself cannot be much more valuable than C.[2]

We arrive, then, at this conclusion: The value of wealth of every kind is determined by the value of its least useful portion—that is, by the least satisfaction which any one portion of it can give.

Hitherto we have been concerned with the notion of final utility as applied to the problems of value and exchange, but has it the same effect when applied to problems of production, distribution, or consumption? The Hedonists have no doubt as to the answer, for what are production, distribution, and consumption but modifications of exchange?

Take production, for example. How is it that under a system of free competition the value of the product is regulated by its cost of production? It is because a competitive regime is by every definition a regime where at any moment one product may be exchanged for

---

[1] The law of substitution applies not merely to different objects which satisfy the same need, but also to objects which supply different needs, provided those needs are to any extent interchangeable—to tea as a substitute for wines, to coffee as a substitue for both, to travel as a substitute for the life of a country gentleman.

[2] "The enjoyment derived from the least enjoyable unit is what we understand by final utility." (Böhm-Bawerk, *The Austrian Economists*, in the *Annals of the American Academy of Political and Social Science*, 1891.)

another of a similar character, the similarity in this case being simply the result of a certain transformation of the raw material. The law of substitution is operative here, and the reason why cost of production regulates value is that the cost of production at any moment represents the last interchangeable value.

The same is true of consumption, as we can see if we only watch the way in which each of us distributes his purchases and arranges his expenditure. There is evident everywhere an attempt to get the best out of life—to get all the enjoyment which our different incomes may be made to yield; here spending more on house-room and less on food, there curtailing on amusement and extending on charity, until a rough kind of equilibrium is reached where the final utility of the last exchanged objects—or, if another phrase be preferred, the intensities of the last satisfied needs—are equal. If the coin spent in purchasing the last cigar does not yield the same pleasure as the same coin yields when spent on a newspaper, the newspaper will in future probably take the place of the cigar. Consumption seems really to be a kind of exchange, with conscience for mart and desires as buyers and sellers.[1]

Nor is the realm of distribution even beyond the reach of the utility theory. Its application to the problems of interest, wages, and rent is largely the work of American economists, especially of J. B. Clark. It is quite impossible for us to give an exposition of the subtle analyses in which the quarterly reviews of the American universities take such a delight, and which undoubtedly afford a very welcome relaxation in an atmosphere so charged with pragmatism and realism. But we must just glance at the theory of wages. Wages, like other values, must be determined by final utility. But the final utility of what, and for whom? The final utility of the services which the worker renders to

---

[1] The new school deduces a very curious conclusion from this law of indifference. Although there is only one price for all corn buyers, say, the final utility of the corn for each individual is by no means the same. Let us assume that the price is 20s., but one of the buyers, rather than go without, would possibly have given 25s. for it, and others might have been willing to give 24s., 23s., 22s., etc. Every one of those who ex hypothesi only pay 20s. gains a surplus which Professor Marshall has called consumer's rent (Principles, Book III, chapter vi). He has given it that name in order to facilitate comparison with producer's rent, which had gained notoriety long before the Hedonistic school arose. Both are due to similar causes, namely, the existence of differential advantages which give rise to a substantial margin between the selling price and the cost of production.

Really, however, the similarity is simply a matter of words, because consumer's rent is purely subjective, whereas producer's rent is a marketable commodity. It would be better to say simply that in many cases of exchange it is not correct to argue that because the prices are equal the satisfaction given to different persons is necessarily equal.

the *entrepreneur*. Following other factors of production, the final productivity of the workers will determine their wages. That is, their final utility is fixed by the value produced by the marginal worker—no matter how worthless he may be—who only just pays the *entrepreneur*. The value produced by this almost supernumerary worker not only fixes the maximum which the employer can afford to give him, but also the wages given to all the other workers who can take his place— *i.e.*, who are employed upon the same kind of work as his—although they may produce much more than he does; just as in the case of the 100 glasses of water the least valuable glassful determines the value of all the rest.[1]

Thus is the productivity theory of wages at once confirmed and corrected. But this time it is the productivity of the least productive worker, of the individual who barely keeps himself. No wonder the theory has lost its optimistic note. Somehow or other it does not seem very different from the old 'brazen law.'

The rate of interest follows a similar line—the marginal item of capital fixing the rate. Iti s even more true of capital, which is more completely standardized, with the result that the principle of substitution works much more easily.[2]

Rent is treated at greater length in the next chapter.

Gradually we begin to realize how the observation of certain facts apparently of a worthless or insignificant character, such as the substitution of chicory for coffee or the complete uselessness of a single glove, enabled the Psychological school to propound a number of general theories such as the law of substitution and the doctrine of complementary goods which shed new light upon a great number of economic questions. There is something very impressive about this deductive process that irresistibly reminds one of the genie of the *Thousand and One Nights*, who grew gradually bigger and bigger until he finally reached the heavens. But then the genie was nothing but flame.

---

[1] It is scarcely necessary to point out that if workers are not really interchangeable on account of their different capacities the law can no longer be said to hold good, since it always presupposes free competition, whereas in this case we have a personal monopoly.

[2] It is not quite the same when the capital is fixed, for the law of substitution is no longer applicable in that case, and the incomes are very different.

III: THE MATHEMATICAL SCHOOL[1]

The Mathematical school is distinguished for its attachment to the study of exchange, from which it proposes to deduce the whole of political economy. Its method is based upon the fact that every exchange may be represented as an equation, $A = B$, which expresses the relation between the quantities exchanged. Thus the first step plunges us into mathematics.

However true this may be, the application of the method must necessarily be very limited if it is always to be confined to exchange.

[1] It must not be supposed that in applying the term 'school' to these writers we wish to suggest that they have a common programme. All we mean is that they make use of the same method.

It is generally recognized that the school dates from the appearance of Cournot's *Recherches sur les Principes mathématiques de la théorie des richesses* (1838). Cournot, who was a school inspector, died in 1877, leaving behind him several philosophical works which are now considered to be of some importance. The story of his economic work affords an illustration of the kind of misfortune which awaits a person who is in advance of his age. For several years not a single copy of the book was sold. In 1863 the author tried to overcome the indifference of the public by recasting the work and omitting the algebraical formulæ. This time the book was called *Principes de la Théorie des richesses*. In 1876 he published it again in a still more elementary form, and under the title of *Revue sommaire des Doctrines économiques*, but with the same result. It was only shortly before his death that attention was drawn to the merits of the work in a glowing tribute which was paid to him by Stanley Jevons.

Gossen's book, *Entwickelung der Gesetze des menschlichen Verkehrs*, which appeared much later (1853), was equally unfortunate. The author remained an obscure civil servant all his life. His book, of which there is still a copy in the British Museum—the only one in existence possibly—was accidentally discovered by Professor Adamson, and Stanley Jevons was again the first to recognize its merits. A brief résumé of the work will be found in our chapter on Rent.

Stanley Jevons (died 1882) belongs both to the Mathematical and to the Final Utility school. His charming book *The Theory of Political Economy* dates from 1871.

Léon Walras, who is persistently spoken of as a Swiss economist just because he happened to spend the greater part of his life at the University of Lausanne, also known as the School of Lausanne, was in reality a Frenchman. His *Éléments d'Économie politique pure*, of which the first part appeared in 1874, contains a full exposition of Mathematical economics. He says himself that he owes his ideas to the teaching of his father, Auguste Walras, a school inspector of an independent attitude of mind who retired in 1849. He had published in 1831 a thesis *De la nature de la richesse et de l'origine de la valeur* in which he criticized the vagueness of the ideas of the principal economists and attributed value to *scarce utility*. This work was republished in 1938 by Gaston Leduc in a new collection of the works of the leading economists (Alcan, Paris, 340 pp.). Léon Walras always considered that it was his father who initiated him into political economy and even mathematical economics. The Mathematical school to-day has exponents in every land, and even economists not specifically connected with it are in the habit of using algebraical symbols to clarify particularly complicated explanations or arguments. France, though rather late in entering this field, now has many Mathematical economists: Aupetit led the way with his *Théorie de la monnaie*, followed by Moret, the translator of Irving Fisher and author of many works, and notable contributions have been made by Colson and his successors, Divisia, Rueff, Allais, Lutfalla, and Roy.

It is, however, a mistake to suppose that this is really the case, and one of the most ingenious and fruitful contributions made by the new school was to show how this circle could be gradually enlarged so as to include the whole of economic science.

Distribution, production, and even consumption are included within its ambit. Let us take distribution first and inquire what wages and rent are. In a word, what are revenues? A revenue is the price of certain services rendered by labour, capital, and land, the agents of production, and paid for by the *entrepreneur* as the result of an act of exchange.

And what is production? It is but the exchanging of one utility for another—a certain quantity of raw materials and of labour for a certain quantity of consumable goods. Even nature might be compared to a merchant exchanging products for labour, and Xenophon must have had a glimpse of this ingenious theory when he declared that "the gods sell us goods in return for our toil." The analogy might be pushed still further, and every act of exchange may be considered an act of production. Pantaleoni puts it elegantly when he says that "a partner to an exchange is very much like a field that needs tilling or a mine that requires exploiting."[1]

And what are capitalization, investment, and loan but the exchange of present goods and immediate joys for the goods and enjoyments of the future?

It was a comparison instituted between the lending of money and an ordinary act of exchange that led Böhm-Bawerk to formulate his celebrated theory of interest. Böhm-Bawerk, however, is a representative of the Austrian rather than the Mathematical school.

Even consumption—that is, the employment of wealth—implies incessant exchanging, for if our resources are necessarily limited that must involve a choice between the object which we buy and that which with a sigh we are obliged to renounce. To give up an evening at the theatre in order to buy a book is to exchange one pleasure for another, and the law of exchange covers this case just as well as any other.[2] It is the same everywhere. To pay taxes is to give up a portion

---

[1] *Des Différences d'opinion entre économistes* (Geneva, 1897), inserted in *Scritti varii di Economia*, pp. 1–48 (1904).

[2] Value itself, the pivot of Classical economics, is simply a link in exchange with the new school, and thus it loses all its subjectivity; and since it is not a thing at all, but merely an expression, it would be ridiculous to struggle to find its cause, foundation, or nature, as the older writers did. This is why Jevons proposed to banish the word altogether and to employ the term 'ratio of exchange' instead. And Aupetit insists that "the expression 'value' is to-day devoid of content . . . and seems doomed to disappear from the scientific vocabulary altogether. There is no great harm in omitting this parasitical element as we have done, and in treating economic equilibrium as an entity without ever employing the term 'value.'" (*Théorie de la Monnaie*, p. 85.)

of our goods in order to obtain security for all the rest. The rearing of children involves the sacrifice of one's own well-being and comfort in exchange for the joys of family life and the good opinion of our fellow men.

It is not impossible, then, to discover among economic facts certain relations which are expressible in algebraical formulæ or even reducible to figures. The art of the Mathematical economist consists in the discovery of such relations and in putting them forth in the form of equations.

For example, we know that when the price of a commodity goes up the demand for it falls off. Here are two quantities, one of which is a function of the other.[1] Let us see how the law of demand in its amended form would express this.

If along a horizontal line A B we take a number of fixed points equidistant from one another to represent prices—e.g., 1, 2, 3, 4, 5 . . 10—and from each of these points we draw a vertical line to represent the quantity demanded at that price, and then join the summits of these vertical lines, which are known as the ordinates, we have a curve starting at a fairly high point—representing the lowest prices—and gradually descending as the prices rise until it becomes merged with the horizontal, at which point the demand becomes nil.[2]

What is very interesting is that the curve is different for different products. In some cases the curve is gentle, in others abrupt, according as the demand, as Marshall puts it, has a greater or lesser degree of elasticity. Every commodity has, so to speak, its own characteristic

---

[1] If demand be represented by d and price by p, then $d = f(p)$—i.e., demand is a function of price.

Geometrical figures can always take the place of equations, for every equation can be expressed in the form of a curve. Geometrical representation makes a quicker appeal to the eye, and it is extremely useful where people are not conversant with the calculus which is frequently employed by Cournot and other Mathematical writers. But it is hardly as fruitful, for a geometrical figure can only trace the relation between two quantities, one of which is fixed and the other is variable, or between three at most, when two would be variable. Even in this case recourse would be necessary to projections, and the figures in that case would not be very clear. In the case of algebraical formulæ, on the other hand, we can have as much variation as we like provided we have as many equations as there are variables.

[2] Dupuit, the engineer, was the first to make use of a demand curve. Cournot, who refers to it as the law of sale, gives an admirable illustration of its operation in the case of bottles of medicinal waters of wonderful curative power. At a very low price the demand and consequently the sale would be very great, though not infinite because of the limit which exists for each want. At a very high price it would be nil. Between the two extremes would be several intermediate curves. We cannot deal with all the ingenious deductions which Cournot makes concerning monopoly and the greater or lesser discord between monopoly and the general interest.

curve, enabling us, at least theoretically, to recognize that product among a hundred.[1]

We would naturally expect the supply curve to be just the inverse of the demand curve, rising with a rising price and descending with a falling one, so that by the time the price is zero supply is nil, whereas the demand is infinite.[2]

[1] The demand curve is generally concave, and this characteristic form is just the geometrical expression of the well-known fact that when prices are low enough to be accessible to everybody the sales increase rapidly, because, lean purses being much more numerous than fat ones, a slight lowering of the level of prices will bring the commodity within the reach of a fresh stratum of people. It may take different forms, however. For some products, such as common salt, a considerable fall in the price will not result in a large increase in the sales. In the case of diamonds a great fall in price may cause a falling off in demand because they have become too cheap. The supply curve, on the other hand, is generally convex, because the supply, which only enters upon the scene at a certain point, is very sensible to price movements, going up rapidly with a slight increase in price. Its upward trend is soon arrested, however, because production cannot keep up the pace. It is even possible that the supply may fall off at the next point, simply because there is no more of the commodity available.

[2] Below on the same diagram are traced a demand and a supply curve.

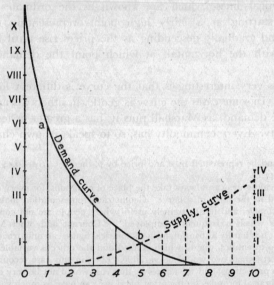

The figures along the horizontal line denote price, along the vertical the quantity demanded. In the given figure when price is 1, quantity demanded is VI, and with the price at 7 the quantity demanded falls to zero.

The dotted curve represents the supply. When price is 1, supply is nil. When price is 10, supply mounts up to IV. Exchange obviously must take place just where demand and supply are equal—i.e., at b—which marks the point of intersection of the two lines, when the amount demanded is equal to the quantity offered and the price is 5.

The vertical lines are called ordinates, and o X the axis of the ordinates. Distances along o X are called abscissæ. Each point on the curve simply marks the intersection

But it is not quite correct to regard it as merely the inverse of the demand curve. A supply curve is really a much more complicated affair, because supply itself depends upon cost of production, and there are some kinds of production—agriculture, for example—where the cost of production increases much more rapidly than the quantity produced. In industry, on the other hand, the cost of production decreases as the quantity produced increases.

Mathematical political economy, not content with seeking relations of mutual dependence between isolated facts, claims to be able to embrace the whole field within its comprehensive formulæ. Everything seems to be in a state of equilibrium, and any attempt to upset it is immediately corrected by a tendency to re-establish it.[1] To determine the conditions of equilibrium is the one object of pure economics.

The most remarkable attempt at systematization of this kind was made by Professor Walras, who endeavoured to bring every aspect of the economic world within his formula, a task almost as formidable as that attempted by Laplace in his *Mécanique céleste*.[2]

Let us imagine the whole of society included within one single room, say the London Stock Exchange, which is full of the tumult of those who have come to buy and sell, and who keep shouting their prices. In the centre, occupying the place usually taken up by the market, sits the *entrepreneur*, a merchant or manufacturer or an agriculturist, as the case may be, who performs a double function.

On the one hand he buys from producers, whether rural or urban, landlords, capitalists, or workers, what Walras calls their "productive services," that is, the fertility of their lands, the productivity of their capital or their labour force, and by paying them the price fixed by the laws of exchange he determines the revenue of each; to the proprietor he pays a rent, to the capitalist interest, to the workman wages. But

---

of these, of the ordinates and the abscissæ. This is true of the point *a*, for example, where the perpendicular denotes the price (1) and the other line the number of units sold, in this case VI.

Though in the diagram we have considered the ordinates to represent price and the abscissæ quantities, the reverse notation would work equally well.

[1] Mathematical economics also studies other forms of equilibrium which are much more complicated and not quite so important, perhaps, relating as they do to conditions of unstable equilibrium.

[2] Note Pareto's terms of appreciation (*Économie pure*, 1902, p. 11): "Walras was the first to show the importance of these equations, especially in the case of free competition. This capital discovery entitles him to all the praise that we can give him. The science has developed a good deal since then, and will undoubtedly develop still more in the future, but that will not take away from the importance of Walras's discovery. Astronomy has progressed very considerably since Newton published his *Principia*, but far from detracting from the merits of the earlier work it has rather enhanced its reputation."

how is that price determined? Just as at the Exchange all values whatsoever are determined by the law of demand and supply, so the *entrepreneur* demands so many services at such and such a price and the capitalist or workman offers him so many at that price, and the price will rise or fall until the quantity of services offered is equal to the quantity demanded.

The *entrepreneur* on his side disposes of the manufactured goods fashioned in his factory or the agricultural products grown on his farm to those very same persons, who have merely changed their clothes and become consumers. As a matter of fact the proprietors, capitalists, and workers who formerly figured as the vendors of services now reappear as the buyers of goods. And who else did we expect the buyers to be? Who else could they be?

And in this market the prices of products are determined in just the same fashion as we have outlined above.

All at once, however, a newer and a grander aspect of the equilibrium comes to view. Is it not quite evident that the total value of the productive services on the one hand and the total value of the products on the other must be mathematically equal? The *entrepreneur* cannot possibly receive in payment for the goods which he has sold to the consumers more than he gave to the same persons, who were just now producers, in return for their services. For where could they possibly get more money? It is a closed circuit, the quantity that comes out through one outlet re-enters through another.

With the important difference that it keeps much closer to facts, the explanation bears a striking resemblance to Quesnay's *Tableau économique*.[1]

---

[1] If this is to be taken as literally true, we have this curious result: the *entrepreneur*, receiving for the products which he sells just exactly what he paid for producing them, makes no profit at all.

Both Walras and Pareto fully admit the paradoxical nature of the statement. Of course it is understood that it can only happen under a regime of perfectly free competition, care being also taken to distinguish between profits and interest, a thing that is never done, apparently, by English economists, who treat both interest and profit as constituent elements of cost of production.

But this is not so wonderful as it seems at first sight. It simply means a return to the well-known formula that under a regime of free competition selling price must necessarily coincide with cost of production.

This does not prevent our recognizing the existence of actual profits. Profits are to be regarded as the result of incessant oscillations of a system round some fixed point with which it never has the good fortune actually to coincide. According to this conception they are but the waves of the sea. But the existence of waves is no reason for denying a mean level of the ocean or for not taking that mean level as a basis for measuring other heights. Some day, perhaps, equilibrium will become a fact, and profits will vanish. But if that day ever does dawn either upon the physical or the economic world, all activity will suddenly cease, and the world itself will come to a standstill.

We have two markets in juxtaposition,[1] the one for services and the other for products, and in each of them prices are determined by the same laws, which are three in number:

(a) On the same market there can be only one price for the same class of goods.

(b) This price must be such that the quantity offered and the quantity demanded shall exactly coincide.

(c) The price must be such as will give maximum satisfaction to the maximum number of buyers and sellers.

All these laws are mathematical in character and involve problems of equilibrium.

In some such way would the new school reduce the science of economics to a sort of mechanism of exchange, basing its justification upon the contention that the Hedonistic principle of obtaining the maximum of satisfaction at the minimum of discomfort is a purely mechanical principle, which in other connexions is known as the principle of least resistance or the law of conservation of energy. Every individual is regarded simply as the slave of self-interest, just as the billiard-ball is of the cue. It is the delight of every economist as of every good billiard-player to study the complicated figures which result from the collision of the balls with one another or with the cushion.[2]

[1] A full exposition of Walras's system involves the supposition not only of two but of three markets interwoven together. On the actual market where goods are exchanged the quantity of these commodities depends upon the quantity of productive services, land, capital, and labour, and the quantity of these productive services, at least the quantity of capital, depends to a certain extent upon the creation of new capital, which in turn depends upon the amount of saving. The third market, then, is that of capitalization. Since the new capital can only be paid for out of savings—i.e., out of that part of the revenue which has been employed in other ways than in buying consumable commodities—the price of capital must be such as to equal the quantity saved and the quantity of new capital demanded. If saving exceeds the demand the price will fall, etc.

To say that the price of capital has gone up is to say that the rate of interest or the reward of saving has fallen. But a fall in the rate of interest will check saving. The result will be a change of equilibrium, the price of new capital will fall, he rate of interest will go up, etc.

Briefly, then, the total maximum utilities on the one hand and the price on the other, these are the two conditions determining equilibrium in the economic world, no matter whether it be products or services or capital. "The same thing is true of gravity in the physical world, which varies directly with the mass and inversely with the square of the distance. Such is the twofold condition which determines the movement of the celestial bodies. . . . In both cases the whole science may be represented by a formula consisting of only two lines. Such a formula will include a great number of facts." (Walras, Économie politique pure, p. 306.)

[2] Professor Edgeworth employs a similar comparison, speaking of the economic man as a charioteer and of social science as consisting of a chariot and some such charioteer (Mathematical Psychics, p. 15). "'Mécanique Sociale' may one day take

Another problem of equilibrium is to discover the exact proportion in which the different elements combine in production. Jevons compares production to the infernal mixture which was boiled in their cauldron by the witches in *Macbeth*. But the ingredients are not mixed haphazard, and Pareto thinks that they conform to a law analogous to the law known in chemistry as the law of definite proportions, which determines that molecules shall combine in certain proportions only. The combination of the productive factors is perhaps not quite so rigidly fixed as is the proportion of hydrogen and oxygen which goes to form water. Similar results, for example, may be obtained by employing more hand labour and less capital, or more capital and less hand labour. But there must be some certain proportion which will yield a maximum utility, and this maximum is obtainable in precisely the same way as in other cases of equilibrium—that is, by varying the 'doses' of capital and labour until the final utility in the case both of capital and labour becomes equal. Generally speaking, this is the law that puts a limit to the indefinite expansion of industry, for whenever one element runs short, be it land or capital, labour or managing ability or markets, all the others are directly affected adversely and the undertaking as a whole becomes more difficult and less effective. Pareto rightly enough attaches the greatest importance to this law, and we have only to remember that it is the direct antithesis of the famous law of accumulation of capital to realize its full significance.

There are several other cases of interdependence to which the new school has drawn attention, as, for example, that of certain complementary goods whose values cannot vary independently. What is the use of one glove or one stocking without another, of a motor-car without petrol, of a table service without glasses? Not only is this true of consumption goods; it also applies to production goods. The value of coke is necessarily connected with the value of gas, for you cannot produce the one without the other, and this applies to all by-products. The possibility of utilizing a by-product always lowers the price of the main commodity.

IV: CRITICISM OF THE HEDONISTIC DOCTRINES

The triumph of the new doctrines has been by no means universal. England, Italy, and Germany, and even the United States, where one

---

her place along with 'Mécanique Céleste,' throned each upon the double-sided height of one maximum principle, the supreme pinnacle of moral as of physical science." (*Ibid.*, p. 12.)

Pareto regards political economy as a study of the balance between desires and the obstacles which stand in the way of their satisfaction.

would least expect enthusiasm for abstract speculation, have supplied many disciples, and several professorial chairs and learned reviews have been placed at their disposal. During many years France seemed altogether closed to them. Not only was Walras, the doyen of the new school, forced to leave France to find in foreign lands a more congenial environment for the promulgation of his ideas, but at one time it would have been quite impossible to mention a single book or a single course of lectures given either in a university or anywhere else in which these doctrines were taught or even criticized.[1]

We might have understood this antipathy more easily if France, like Germany, had already been annexed by the Historical school. There would have been some truth in a theory of incompatibility of tempers under circumstances of that kind. But the great majority of French economists were still faithful to the Liberal tradition, and one might naturally have expected a hearty welcome for a school that is essentially Neo-Classical and pretends nothing more than to give a fuller demonstration of the theories already taught by the old masters.[2]

The mere fact, however, that they presumed to draw fresh lessons or to deduce new principles from those already formulated by the older writers appeared an unwarranted interference with doctrines

---

[1] We have had, of course, Colson's great book on political economy, which contains a mathematical treatment of demand and supply and Landry's exposition of the Austrian theory in his *Manuel Économique*. We have already referred to Aupetit's book on money. We must also mention the translations of the *Manual of Political Economy* of Vilfredo Pareto and of Jevons's *Theory of Political Economy*. Since then the exponents of mathematical economics have become very numerous in France (*cf.* p. 499 *n.*).

[2] Paul Leroy-Beaulieu was particularly severe upon the Mathematical method. "It is a pure delusion and a hollow mockery. It has no scientific foundation and is of no practical use. It is as much a gamble as the scramble for prizes at the table at Monte Carlo. . . . The so-called curve of utility or demand is of no earthly use, for if the price of wine goes up the consumption of beer or cider will increase, that is all." (*Traité d'Économie politique*, Vol. I, p. 85; Vol. III, p. 62.)

This last criticism is somewhat unexpected, for we have already seen that the Hedonists are very far indeed from ignoring the law of substitution. If they did not actually discover it they immensely amplified it. And it is very probable that if there had been a contradiction between their doctrines and this law it would not have escaped them. Moreover, we note that beer and cider have their demand curves: cannot wine have one as well? Having to pass from one to the other does undoubtedly complicate matters, and the Mathematical economist frequently finds himself obliged to juggle not with one but with two or three balls. But this is just the kind of difficulty which is amenable to mathematical treatment—nay, even, perhaps, demands it. The connexion between the values of complementary or supplementary goods is one of the problems that has been most thoroughly investigated by the Hedonists. See Pantaleoni, *Economia pura*.

A criticism of Mathematical economics may be found in an article by Simiand entitled *La Méthode positive en science économique* (*Revue de Métaphysique et de morale*, November 1908), and a good reply in *La Méthode mathématique en économie politique*, by Bouvier.

that had hitherto seemed good enough for every one. Criticism of that kind, of course, is not worth serious attention.

An easier line of criticism, and one very frequently adopted, is to maintain that the wants and desires of mankind are incapable of measurement and that mathematical causations can never be reconciled with the doctrine of free will. But such claims as these were never put forward by the Mathematical school. On the contrary, it has always recognized that every man is free to follow his own bent— *trahit sua quemque voluptas*—merely inquiring how man is to act if he is to obtain the maximum satisfaction out of the means at his disposal and to overcome the obstacles that stand in his way. Neither has it ever ventured to say that such and such a man is forced to sell corn or to buy it, but simply that if he does buy or sell it will be with a determination to make the best of the bargain, and that such being the case the buying or selling will take place in such and such a fashion. It further claims that the action of a number of individuals under similar circumstances is equally calculable. So is the movement of the balls on the billiard-table, but that does not interfere with the liberty of the players.[1]

Nor do they pretend to be able to measure our desires. What they do—and it is not so absurd after all, because we are all doing it—is to express in pounds, shillings, and pence the value we put upon the acquisition or loss of an object that satisfies our desire. Moreover, the Mathematical school does not make much use of numbers, but confines itself to algebraical notation and geometrical figures—that is, to the consideration of abstract quantities. To write down a problem in the form of a mathematical equation is to show that the problem can be solved and to give the conditions under which solution is alone possible. Beyond this the economist never goes. He never tries to fix the price of corn, whatever it may be; he leaves that to the speculators.[2]

From the other side—that is, from the historians, interventionists, solidarists, socialists—comes criticism which is quite as bitter and not a whit easier to justify. The Hedonistic doctrine appears to them simply as a fresh attempt to restore the optimistic teaching of the Manchester school, with its individualism and egoism, its free competi-

<hr />

[1] Walras put it well when he wrote as follows: "We have never tried to analyse the motives of free human beings. We have simply tried to give a mathematical expression of the result." (*Éléments d'Économie politique pure*, p. 232.)

[2] "We do not know exactly what it is that binds the function and the variable together, or the intensity of the satisfied need to the quantity already consumed. But for every item on the one side we feel certain that there must be a corresponding item on the other." (Aupetit, *Théorie de la Monnaie*, p. 42.)

tion and general harmony, its insidious justification of interest, rent, and starvation wages—in the name of some imaginary entity which they call marginal utility. In short, it looks just like another proof of the thesis that the present economic order is the best possible—a proof that is all the less welcome seeing that it claims to be scientific and mathematically infallible.

This sort of criticism is nothing less than caricature. It would be futile to deny that the new school has undertaken the task of carrying on the work of the Classical writers, but what possible harm can there be in that? The royal road of science often turns out to be nothing better than a very narrow path—but it does lead somewhere. There would be no progress in economic science or in any other if every generation were to throw overboard all the work done by its predecessors. What the Hedonistic school has tried to do is to distinguish between the good and the bad work of the Classical writers and to retain the one while rejecting the other.

The main object of the equilibrium and final utility theories is not to justify the present economic regime, but merely to explain it,[1] which is quite a different matter. But it does happen in this case that the explanation justifies the conclusion that under the conditions of a free market the greatest good of the greatest number would naturally be secured. The term 'good,' however, is used in a purely Hedonistic and not in the ethical sense. No attention is paid to the pre-existing conditions of the exchange, and none is bestowed upon its possible consequences. The old-time bargain between Esau and Jacob, when the former sold his birthright for a mere mess of pottage, gave the maximum of satisfaction to both, even to Esau, of whom it is related that he was at the point of death, and to whom accordingly the pottage must have been of infinite value. Even if Jacob had offered him a bottle of absinthe instead the result would have been equally satisfactory from a Hedonistic standpoint. The theory takes as little account of hygiene as it does of morals.

The Hedonist, by way of amendment, might suggest that Esau would have made a better bargain if there had been, not one, but several Jacobs offering the pottage, which helps to explain why they are so partial to competition and so strongly opposed to monopoly.[2] No Hedonist would deny that Esau was exploited by Jacob; but, on

[1] For a vigorous refutation of this criticism see two articles by Rist entitled *Économie optimiste* and *Économie scientifique* in the *Revue de Métaphysique et de morale* for July 1904 and September 1907.

[2] Or he will argue, perhaps, that the market would have been much more favourable to Esau if Jacob had had more pottage than he could easily have disposed of—a case where even monopoly might offer some advantage to the buyer.

R

the other hand, they would point out that there is no necessity to imagine that society is made up only of Esaus and Jacobs.[1]

The same thing applies to Böhm-Bawerk's celebrated theory of interest. Indeed, Böhm-Bawerk quite definitely states that he merely wants to discover some explanation of interest, but does not anticipate that he will be able to justify it, and in that spirit he condemns the ethical justifications that were attempted some centuries back. His object is to show that interest is due neither to the productivity of capital nor to the differential advantages enjoyed by its possessor. Neither is it a tax levied upon the exploited borrower: it is simply a *time*-payment. In other words, it represents the difference between the value of a present good and the same good on some future occasion. It is just the result of exchanging a present good for a future one. A hundred francs a year hence are not equal in value to a hundred francs here and now. To make them equal we must either add something by way of interest to the future item or take away something by way of discount from the present one.[2]

Turning to the theory of wages, according to which the wages of each class of producers is supposed to be determined by the productivity of the marginal worker in that class, we are struck by the fact that it is only a little less pessimistic than the old 'brazen law.' What it really implies is that the marginal worker—the worker whom the *entrepreneur* is only just induced to employ—consumes all that he produces.

The Hedonistic school, in short, has no theory of distribution, neither does it seem very anxious to have one. It speaks, not of co-sharers, but of productive services, whose relative contributions it is interested to discover. But it is one thing to know exactly what fraction of the work is due to a certain unit of capital or a given individual workman, and quite another to know whether workers or capitalists are being unfairly treated.

The best proof that the Hedonists are not mere advocates of *laissez-faire* is the general attitude of the leaders. It is true that the Austrian school has always shown itself quite indifferent to the social or working-

[1] "For purposes of demonstration," says Pareto, "we have assumed the existence of private property. But to assume on the strength of the conclusion which we have established that a regime of private property gives the maximum of well-being would clearly be to beg the question."

[2] This doctrine is not accepted even by all the Hedonists. Walras especially is very critical in the fourth edition of his *Économie pure*. M. A. Landry in his *Intérêt du Capital* (1904) and Irving Fisher in *The Rate of Interest* (1907) have tried if not to demolish it at least to correct it by giving a more subtle analysis of the motives determining a preference for a future income as compared with a present one. This time-preference, of course, varies according to the fortune of each and other circumstances.

class question,[1] as it is sometimes called, but it certainly has a perfect right to confine itself to pure economics if it wishes. The other leaders of the school, however, have clearly shown that the method followed need involve no such approval or acquiescence. Not to mention Stanley Jevons, who in his book *Social Reform* makes a very strong case for intervention, we have also Professor Walras, who stands in the front rank of agrarian socialists. Leaving aside merely utilitarian considerations, he points out that in the interest of justice, which, as he has been careful to emphasize, involves quite a different point of view, he wants to establish a regime of absolutely free competition. But how is this to be accomplished? Merely by means of *laissez-faire*, as the old Liberal school had thought? Not at all. It can only be done through the abolition of monopoly of every kind, and land monopoly, which is the foundation of every other, must go first. The reform advocated in his *Économie sociale* consists of two items, land nationalization and the abolition of all taxation. The two items are intimately connected because the rents now become the possession of the State will take the place of the taxes, and the object of both is the same, namely, the extension of free competition by securing to every citizen the full produce of his work. Under existing conditions the producer is doubly taxed—in the first place by the landowner and then by the State.[2] Moreover, when we remember that the point of equilibrium in Walras's system occurs just where the selling price exactly coincides with the cost of production—in other words, where profit is reduced to zero—we begin to realize how far it is from anything in the nature of an apology for the present condition of things.

Vilfredo Pareto, another representative of this school, although ultra-individualistic in his opinions and extremely hostile to interventionism or solidarity, takes good care not to connect his personal opinion with the Hedonistic doctrines. As a matter of fact he thinks that, theoretically at least, the maximum of well-being might be

[1] We have already remarked on this in the case of M. Böhm-Bawerk. This is another respect in which the Hedonists have shown themselves faithful to the Classical tradition. The necessity for separating the art from the science of political economy, pure economics from applied, was especially emphasized by Courcelle-Seneuil and Cherbuliez. Pareto put it well when he said that the maximum of ophelimity can be put in the shape of an equation, but the maximum of justice can not.

[2] This system, according to Walras, would possess another advantage in that it would facilitate the establishment of free trade, which is an ideal of the science. The chief difficulties would thus be avoided, such as unequal import duties and unequal degree of fertility. "Free trade has always involved the absence of duties, and the nationalization of land would further result in the free movement of capital and labour to whatever place might prove most advantageous to them." (*La Paix par la justice sociale et par le libre-échange*, in *Questions pratiques de Législation ouvrière*, September–October 1907.)

equally attainable under a collectivist regime, although he does not think that collectivism is yet possible. But this opinion is founded upon "ethical and other considerations which are quite outside the scope of economics."[1]

M. Pantaleoni, who soars higher still into the realm of pure, transcendental science, ventures to declare that the substitution of purely altruistic motives for merely selfish ones would involve about as much change in the calculation as would the substitution throughout of a plus for a minus sign in an algebraical equation. All extremes meet. Complete disinterestedness and absolute egoism would necessarily work out very much the same. Devotion to duty would replace the clamour for rights; sacrifices would be exchanged instead of utilities. But the laws determining their exchange would still be the same. The Hedonists are not so much concerned with the morality of such laws as with the productive capacity of a given economic state, just as in the case of a piece of machinery the engineer's sole concern is to gauge the output of that machine.

But the most serious criticism passed upon the work of the school is that at the end of the reckoning nothing has been discovered that was not already known, to which the Hedonists reply that they have at least succeeded in making certain what was only tentative before. The discovery of truth appears to be an intermittent process, and the first vague presentiment is often as useful as the so-called scientific discovery. Astronomy, which is the most nearly perfect of the sciences, has progressed just in this way. The older economists felt fully convinced that the regime of free competition was best, but they gave no reason for the faith that was in them and no demonstration of the conditions under which the doctrine was true. Such a demonstration the Mathematical economists claim to have given by showing that a regime of free competition is the only one where a maximum of satisfaction is available at a minimum of sacrifice for both parties. The same consideration applies to the law of demand and supply, the law of indifference, cost of production, wages, interest, rent, etc. To have given an irrefutable demonstration of theories that were formerly little better than vague intuitions[2] or amorphous hypotheses is certainly something.

[1] The same is true of American economists, where the use of the Hedonistic method is by no means confined to one school. Professor Clark employs it, and he is rather inclined to set up an apology for the present economic order and to trust to the efficacy of free competition. But Professor Patten also makes use of it, and he is an interventionist of the extreme type.

[2] Economics will become a science when it can say that "what was just now nothing better than an intuition can now be fully proved." (Walras, Économie politique pure, p. 427.)

We may laugh as much as we like at the *homo œconomicus*, who is by this time little better than a skeleton, but it is the skeleton that has helped the science to stand upright and make progress. It has helped forward the process from the invertebrate to the vertebrate.

But admitting that all these doctrines have been definitely proved, as the Hedonists claim they have, is the science going to profit as much as they thought by it? Somebody has remarked that mathematics is a mere mill that grinds whatever is brought to it. The important question is, What is the corn like? In this case it consists of a mass of abstractions—a number of individuals actuated by the same selfish motives, alike in what they desire to get and are willing to give,[1] the assumed ubiquity of capital and labour, facility for substitution, etc. It is possible enough that the flour coming from the mill may not prove very nutritious. When ground out the result would at any rate be as unlike reality as the new society outlined by Fourier, the Saint-Simonians, or the anarchists, and its realization quite as improbable, unless we presuppose an equally miraculous revolution. The Hedonists frankly recognize this, and in this respect they show themselves superior to the Classical economists, who when they talk of free competition believe that it actually exists.[2]

But however sceptical they are about the possibility of ever realizing all this, they are somewhat emphatic about the virtues of the new method, and they are not exempt, perhaps, from a certain measure of dogmatic pride which irresistibly reminds one of the Utopian socialists. Could we not, for example, imagine Fourier writing in this strain: "What has already been accomplished is as nothing compared with what may be discovered" (by the application of the mathematical method);[3] or "The new theories concerning cost of production have the same fundamental importance in political economy that the substitution of the Copernican for the Ptolemaic system has in astronomy"?[4] We have already called attention to the comparison

---

[1] "It is necessary to apply the law of the variation of intensity of need to each separate individual in relation to each one of his needs." (Aupetit, *La Monnaie*, p. 93.)

[2] It is only those Hedonists who claim to be able to establish an exact science that make use of the mathematical and abstract method to the total exclusion of the historical and biological method. Professor Marshall expressly declares himself in favour of the biological method, and would advocate employing diagrams and curves as little as possible (*Economic Journal*, March 1898, p. 50).

[3] Pareto, *Giornali degli Economisti*, September 1901.

[4] Böhm-Bawerk, *The Austrian Economists, loc. cit.* On the other hand, one of the disciples of this school, M. Landry, writes: "To-day the Austrian school is somewhat played out" (*L'École économique*, in *Rivista di Scienza*, 1907). At the end of thirty years! —not a very long life.

of Walras's system with Newton's *Principia*—all of which rather savours of enthusiasm outrunning judgment.

While recognizing the very real services which the Mathematical and Austrian schools have rendered to the science, and admitting that they mark an era in the history of economics which can never be forgotten, we cannot do better than conclude with the advice of an economist who is himself an authority both in the Mathematical and Classical schools, and who is therefore well qualified to judge:

> The most useful applications of mathematics to economics are those which are short and simple and which employ few symbols; and which aim at throwing a bright light on some small part of the great economic movement rather than at representing its endless complexities.[1]

CHAPTER II: DOCTRINES THAT OWE THEIR INSPIRATION TO CHRISTIANITY

EVERY one who knows the Bible at all or has the slightest acquaintance with the writings of the early Fathers must have been struck by the number of texts which they contain bearing upon social and economic questions. And one has only to recall the imprecations of the prophets as they contemplate the misdeeds of merchants and the greed of land-grabbers, or strive to catch the spirit of the parables of Jesus or the epistles of the Fathers concerning the duty of the rich towards the poor —a point emphasized by Bossuet in his sermon on *The Eminent Dignity of the Poor*—or dip into the folios of the Canonists or the *Summa* of Aquinas, to realize how imperative were the demands of religion and with what revolutionary vehemence its claims were upheld.[2]

But not until the middle of the nineteenth century do we meet with social doctrines of a definitely Christian type, and not till then do we witness the formation of schools of social thinkers who place the teaching of the Gospel in the forefront of their programme, hoping that it may supply them with a solution of current economic problems and with a plan of social reconstruction.[3] It is not difficult to account

---

[1] Marshall, *Distribution and Exchange*, in *Economic Journal*, March 1898.

[2] We need only recall the doctrine of usury and the legislation on the question— all of it the outcome of Canonist teaching.

[3] A Catholic professor—long since forgotten—of the name of de Coux wrote as follows in a book entitled *Essai d'Économie politique*, published in 1832: "The practical application of Catholicism would result in the finest system of social economy that the world has ever seen."

for their appearance at this juncture. Their primary object was to bear witness to the heresy of socialism, and the nature of the object became more and more evident as socialism tended to become more materialistic and anti-Christian. It became the Church's one desire to win back souls from the pursuit of this new cult. It was the fear of seeing the people—her own people—enrol themselves under the red flag of the Anti-Christ that roused her ardour.[1] But to regard it as a mere question of worldly rivalry would be childish and misleading. Rather must we see in it a reawakening of Christian conscience and a searching of heart as to whether the Church herself had not betrayed her Christ, and in contemplation of her heavenly had not forgotten her earthly mission, which was equally a part of her message; whether in repeating the Lord's Prayer for the coming of the Kingdom and the giving of daily bread she had forgotten that the Kingdom was to be established on earth and that the daily bread meant, not charity, but the wages of labour.

Both doctrines and schools are of a most heterogeneous character, ranging from authoritative conservatism to almost revolutionary anarchism, and it will not be without some effort that we shall include them all within the limits of a single chapter. But it is not impossible to point to certain common characteristics, both positive and negative, which entitle us to regard them all as members of one family.

As a negative trait we have their unanimous repudiation of Classical Liberalism. This does not necessarily imply a disposition to invoke State aid, for some of them, as we shall see, are opposed even to the idea of a State. Neither does it imply a denial of a 'natural order,' for under the name of Providence and as a manifestation of the will of God the 'order' was a source of perennial delight to them. But man was to them an outcast without lot or portion in the 'order.' Fallen and sinful, bereft of his freedom, it was impossible that of himself he should return to his former state of bliss. To leave the natural man alone, to deliver him over to the pursuit of personal interest in the hope that it might lead him to the good or result in the rediscovery of the lost way of Paradise, was clearly absurd. It was as futile in the economic as it was in the religious sphere. On the contrary, the Christian schools maintained that the 'natural' man, the old man, the

---

[1] "Catholicism alone has the necessary cohesion and power to withstand socialism, which has been erected upon the ruins of the Liberal system." (Comte de Mun, *La Question sociale au XIXe siècle*, 1900.)

"There is no need to think of the Church as a kind of gendarme in cassock flinging itself against the people in the interest of capital. Rather it should be understood that it is working in the interests and solely for the defence of the weak." (Comte de Mun, *Discours*, April 1893.)

first Adam of the New Testament, must somehow be got rid of before room could be found for the new man within us. Every available force, whether religious, moral, or merely social, must be utilized to keep people from the dangerous slope down which egoism would inevitably lead them.[1]

The new doctrines are also distinct from socialism, despite the fact that their followers frequently outbid the socialists in the bitterness of their attacks upon capital and the present organization of society. They refuse to believe that the creation of a new society in the sense of a change in economic conditions or environment is enough. The individual must also be changed. To those who questioned Christ as to when the Kingdom of God should come, He replied, "The kingdom of God cometh not with observation . . . for, behold, the kingdom of God is within you," and His answer is witness to the fact that social justice will only reign when it has achieved victory over human hearts. Social Christianity must never be compared with the socialism of the Liberals or the Associationists, for the latter believed man to be naturally good apart from the deteriorating effects of civilization. Nor must it ever be classed with the collectivism of Marx, which has its basis in a materialistic conception of history and class war. Some of these Christian authors, it is true, regard State Socialism with a certain degree of favour and would possibly welcome co-operation, but to most of them legal coercion does not seem very attractive and they prefer to put their faith in associations such as the family, the corporation, or the co-operative society. We could hardly expect otherwise, seeing that every church is an organization of some kind or other. The Catholic Church especially, whatever opinion we may have of it, is at once the greatest and the noblest association that ever existed. Its bonds are even stronger than death. The Church militant below joins hands with the Church triumphant above, the living praying for the dead and the dead interceding for the living.

From a constructive standpoint they defy classification. They have

---

[1] The Social Christians somewhere make the remark that even if the orthodox account of creation is destined to disappear before the onslaughts of the evolutionary theory and Adam makes way for the gorilla, the problem would merely be intensified, for it would still be necessary to get rid of the "old man." "We live," says Brunetière, "in the strength of the victories won over the more primitive instincts of our nature" (*Revue des Deux Mondes*, May 1, 1895).

Kidd in his *Social Evolution*, a work which attracted great attention when it was first published in 1894, attempts to apply the Darwinian theory to Christianity. He accepts the Darwinian hypothesis that the struggle for existence and natural selection constitute the mainsprings of progress. But the struggle may demand, or the selection involve, the sacrifice of individual to collective interest, and the only force which can inspire such sacrifice is religion.

a common aspiration in their hope of a society where all men will be brothers, children of the one Heavenly Father,[1] but many are the ways of attaining this fraternal ideal. In the same spirit they speak of a just price and a fair wage much as the Canonists of the Middle Ages did. In other words, they refuse to regard human labour as a mere commodity whose value varies according to the laws of supply and demand. The labour of men is sacred, and Roman law even refused to recognize bartering in *res sacræ*. But when it becomes a question of formulating means of doing this, the ways divide. Numerous as are the Biblical texts which bear upon social and economic questions, they are extraordinarily vague. At least they seem capable of affording support to the most divergent doctrines.

Some might consider it a mistake to devote a whole chapter to these doctrines, seeing that they are moral rather than economic, and that, with perhaps the exception of Le Play, who is only indirectly connected with this school, we have no names that can be compared with those already mentioned. But not a few intellectual movements are of an anonymous character. The importance of a doctrine ought not to be measured by the illustrious character of its sponsor so much as by the effect which it has had upon the minds of men. No one will be prepared to deny the influence which these doctrines have exercised upon religious people, an influence greater than either Fourier's, Saint-Simon's, or Proudhon's. Moreover, they are connected with the development of important economic institutions, such as the attempt to revive the system of corporations in Austria, the establishment of rural banks in Germany and France, the development of co-operative societies in England, the growth of temperance societies, the agitation for Sunday rest, etc. Nor must we forget that the pioneers of factory legislation, the founders of workmen's institutes, men like Lord Shaftesbury in England, Pastor Oberlin, and Daniel Legrand the manufacturer, were really Christian Socialists.

I: LE PLAY'S SCHOOL

Le Play's[2] school is very closely related to the Classical Liberal,

[1] It was no Christian Socialist, but Auguste Comte, the founder of Positivism, who wrote: "The original equality of men is not a doctrine founded simply upon the observation of social facts. It was only clearly affirmed for the first time by Christianity." (*Traité de Politique*, Vol. I, p. 407.)

[2] Frédéric Le Play (1806–82) was a mining engineer, and was educated at the École polytechnique. He subsequently became a professor at the École des Mines and a Conseiller d'État. In 1855 he published a collection of monographs dealing with working-class families under the title of *Les Ouvriers européens*, in one volume (the second edition, which appeared in 1877, consisted of six volumes). In 1864 he

DOCTRINES INSPIRED BY CHRISTIANITY

some of its best-known representatives actually belonging to both. There is the same antipathy to socialism and the same dread of State intervention.

But it is not difficult to differentiate from the more extreme Liberal school which finds its most optimistic expression in the works of certain French writers. The cardinal doctrine of that school, namely, that individual effort is alone sufficient for all things, finds no place in Le Play's philosophy. Man, it seemed to him, was ignorant of what his own well-being involved. In the realm of social science no fact seemed more persistent or more patent than error. Every individual appeared to be born with a natural tendency to evil, and he picturesquely remarks that "every new generation is just an invasion of young barbarians that must be educated and trained. Whenever such training is by any chance neglected, decadence becomes imminent."[1]

Among the errors more particularly denounced by Le Play were the special idols of the French bourgeois—the "false dogmas of '89" as he calls them.[2] It seemed to him that no society could ever hope to exist for any length of time and still be content with the rule of natural laws, which merely meant being ruled by the untamed instincts of the brute. It must set to and reform itself. Hence his book is entitled *Social Reform*, and the school which he founded adopted the same title.

Some kind of authority is clearly indispensable; the question is what it should be. The old paterfamilias relation immediately suggests itself as being more efficacious than any other, seeing that it is founded in nature and not on contract or decree, and springs from love rather than coercion. The family group under the authority of its chief, which was the sole social unit under the patriarchal system, must again

---

published an exposition of his social creed in *La Réforme sociale*, a book that Montalembert declared to be "the most original, the most courageous, the most useful, and altogether the most powerful book of the century." It hardly deserves such extravagant praise, perhaps, but it is true that many of its more pessimistic prophecies concerning the future of France have been very curiously verified.

In 1856 Le Play founded La Société d'Économie sociale, which since 1881 has been responsible for the publication of *La Réforme sociale*. He organized the Universal Exhibition in 1867, and was one of the first to arrange exhibitions of social work. For a résumé of his life and work see *Frédéric Le Play d'après lui-même*, by Auburtin (Paris, 1906).

[1] *Programme des Unions de la Paix sociale*, chapter i.

[2] "The gravest and most dangerous error of all, and one that has been the parent of all our revolutions, is the false principle which the innovators of 1789 would put into practice and which affirms the original perfection of mankind. It also encourages the belief that a society composed of 'natural' men would enjoy peace and happiness without any effort at all, and that these desiderata are just the spontaneous outcome of every free society."

be revived in the midst of our complex social relations. But parental control cannot always be relied upon, for the parent is frequently engrossed with the other demands of life, and there is positive need for some social authority. This new social authority will not be the State—that is, if Le Play can possibly avoid it. The first chance will be given to 'natural' authorities—those authorities which rise up spontaneously. The nobility is well fitted for the task where it exists. In the absence of nobility, or where, as was unfortunately the case in France, they were impervious to a sense of duty, society must fall back upon the landed proprietors, the employers, and persons of ripe judgment—men who hardly deserve the title of savants, but nevertheless with considerable experience of life. Failing these it could still appeal to the local authorities, to those living nearest the persons concerned, to the parish rather than the county, the county rather than the State. State intervention is indispensable only when all other authorities have failed—in the enforcement of Sunday observance, for example, where the ruling classes have shown a disposition to despise it. The necessity for State intervention is evidence of disease within the State, and the degree of intervention affords some index of the extent of the malady.[1]

Seeing that he attaches such importance to the constitution of the family, Le Play is also bound to give equal prominence to the question of entail, which determines the permanence of the family. Herein lies the kernel of Le Play's system. He distinguishes three types of families:

1. The patriarchal family. The father is the sole proprietor, or, more correctly, he is the chief administrator of all family affairs. At his death all goods pass by full title to the eldest son. Such is the most ancient form of government of which we have any record. It is the political counterpart of the pastoral regime, and both may still be seen in full operation on the Russian steppes.

2. The family group. Children and grandchildren no longer remain under paternal authority throughout life. With a single exception they leave the family hearth and proceed to found new homes. Whoever remains at home becomes the heir, after first becoming his father's associate during the latter's lifetime. He becomes the new head of the family by paternal wish, and not of legal right or necessity. The property thus passes to the worthiest, to him who is thought best able to preserve it. It is this regime, Le Play thinks, that explains the extraordinary stability of China; and the

---

[1] "It is the great misfortune of France that the family should be immersed in the commune, the commune in the department, the department in the State." (*La Réforme sociale*, Vol. III, Book VII.)

same system, though somewhat shaken, is the source of England's strength and vitality. There were some parts of France where, in spite of the Civil Code, a similar system was still in vogue. There was one such family in particular, that of the Pyrenean peasant Melouga, whose history showed a wonderful continuity, and the story of that family recurs as a kind of *leitmotiv* through the whole of the writings of Le Play and his immediate disciples. The Melouga family has since become extinct.

3. The unstable family, where all the children, as soon as they arrive at maturity, quit the home and set up for themselves. At the father's death the family, already scattered, is completely dissolved. The patrimony is divided equally between all its members, and any business which the father may have possessed, whether agricultural or industrial, goes into immediate liquidation. This is the regime born of individualism which is characteristic of all modern societies, especially France.

Le Play's sympathy is entirely with the second, for the family group seems to hold the balance evenly between the two antagonistic forces which are both indispensable for the welfare of society, namely, the spirit of conservatism and the spirit of innovation. Under the patriarchal system the former preponderates,[1] while under the regime of the unstable family it is utterly wanting. The latter reminds us of Penelope's web—each generation making a fresh beginning. But this periodical division of wealth fails to give the desired degree of equality, for the removal of every trace of solidarity between the members means that the one may become rich and the other sink into poverty. Every one fights for his own hand. Moreover, when children only remain with their parents for just a short period of tutelage there is a powerful incentive given to race-suicide, as is clearly shown in the case of France. As soon as the offspring find themselves in a position of self-sufficiency they leave the old home, just as the young animal does. Under such circumstances it is clearly to the interest of parents to have as few children as possible.[2]

The family group, on the other hand, entrusts its traditions and their preservation to the keeping of the child who remains at home. Those who leave have their way to make, and become heirs of that

---

[1] "It [the patriarchal regime] in all matters relating to economic action or to social life shows greater attachment to the past than concern for the future. Obedience is the keynote rather than initiation. The family group tends to arrest the enterprise which would characterize the action of the more independent members of the family in a somewhat freer atmosphere." (*La Réforme sociale*, Book III.)

[2] "In short, I have never met with a social organization which to the same extent vitiates the laws both of nature and morality."

industrial spirit which has made England the mistress of the world. True fraternal equality is also preserved, for the old home always remains open—a harbour of refuge to those who fail in the industrial struggle. To mention but one instance, the 'old maid,' whose lot is often exceedingly hard, need never be without a home.

Apart from moral reform, there seemed only one way of establishing the family group in France, namely, by greater freedom of bequest, or at the very least by increasing the amount of goods that may be given to any one child, so that a father might be able to transmit the whole of his land or his business to any one of his children on condition that the heir fairly indemnified each of his brothers should their respective shares be insufficient.[1]

A father's authority over his children is an indispensable element in the stability of society, and a master's authority over his men, though derivative in character, is scarcely less so. The continuance of social peace largely depends upon the latter, and the preservation of social peace should be the essential aim of social science.[2] We are continually meeting with the expression 'social peace' in the writings of Le Play and his school, and the associations which they founded became known as "Unions of Social Peace."

Play's first essay, an admirably planned *Exposition of Social Economics*, was published in 1867. The sole object of its author was to further the establishment of such institutions as were likely to promote understanding among all persons employed in the production of the same goods. We might even be tempted to say that the whole co-partnership movement started by Dollfus at Mulhouse in 1850 with the utterance of the famous phrase, "The master owes something to the worker beyond his mere wages," was inspired by Le Play.[3] Le Play pinned his faith to the benevolent master. It was quite natural that the apostle of the family group should regard the factory as possessing a great deal of the stability and many of the other characteristics of the

---

[1] Le Play, who had some influence over Napoleon III, tried to get him to consent to some such modification of the Civil Code. But the Emperor, though favourably inclined, and despot as he was, dared not alienate public sympathy in the matter. And really fathers seldom exercised the full authority which the law gave them at one time. The evil, then, if it is an evil, is deeper than Le Play imagined, and seems to be moral rather than legal.

[2] "Human societies should aim not so much at the creation of wealth as such, but rather at increasing the well-being of mankind. Well-being includes daily bread, but it does not exclude social peace." (Claudio Jannet in a lecture on *Les Quatre Écoles d'Économie sociale*.)

[3] We must remember that these were the orthodox views then. Villermé, writing in 1840 in his celebrated *Tableau de l'État moral et physique des ouvriers*, thought it was the employers really who could best improve the circumstances and character of the workers.

family, such as its quasi-permanent engagements[1] and its various grades of working men all grouped together under the authority of a well-respected chief.

Le Play's thesis that the salvation of the working classes can only come from above seems to have even less foundation than the opposite doctrine of syndicalism, which claims that their deliverance is in their own hands, and it was once for all refuted in a brilliant passage of Stuart Mill's:[2]

> No times can be pointed out in which the higher classes of this or any other country performed a part even distantly resembling the one assigned them in this theory. All privileged and powerful classes as such have used their power in the interest of their own selfishness. . . . I do not affirm that what has always been must always be. This at least seems to be undeniable, that long before the superior classes could be sufficiently inspired to govern in the tutelary manner supposed, the inferior classes would be too much improved to be so governed.

Besides the master and the State there was still another factor of social progress which is of prime importance at the present time, namely, working men's unions. One might reasonably have expected a more sympathetic treatment for them at Le Play's hands, especially when we remember that they were proscribed by the "false dogmas of '89." But he had little faith in union, whether a corporation or a co-operative society.[3] Trade unionism especially seemed rather useless, because it tended to destroy the more natural and more efficient organization which appeared to him to be merely an extension of the family group. It is true that Le Play never saw unionism in operation, but it is hardly probable that he would have modified his opinion. At any rate, the attitude of his disciples is not much more favourable.

One feels tempted to say that there is nothing very new in all this. The remark would have been particularly gratifying to Le Play, who considered that invention was impossible in social science and that what he himself had done was merely to make a discovery.

The discovery of "the essential constitution of humanity," as he called it, was, he thought, the outcome of his methods of observation. His method was really always more important than his doctrine. It

---

[1] We get some idea of the importance which he attributed to the permanence of engagements when we realize that he contemplated the abolition of slavery with a measure of regret. (*La Réforme sociale.*)

[2] *Principles*, Book IV, chapter vii.

[3] "Among the panaceas advocated in our time none has been more criticized than 'association.' From a practical point of view these societies seem to present none of the advantages ordinarily associated either with complete independence or with a well-managed business concern."

has always enjoyed a considerable measure of success, and it seems as if it will survive the doctrine. Le Play was brought up as a mining engineer and had travelled extensively.[1] Twenty years of his life had been spent in this way, and during that period he had travelled over almost the whole of Europe, even as far as the Urals. It was while staying in the neighbourhood of those mountains that he conceived the idea of writing monographs dealing with individual families belonging to the working classes, a method of investigation which he is never weary of contrasting with that other "disdainful method of invention."[2]

To write a family monograph[3] *à la* Le Play is not merely to relate its history, to describe its mode of life, and to analyse its means of subsistence, but also to sum up its daily life in a kind of double-entry book-keeping where every item of expenditure is carefully compared and balanced with the receipts. But there is much that is artificial and a great deal that is childish in this seemingly mathematical precision, where not merely economic wants but such needs as those of education, of recreation, and of intemperance, virtues as well as vices, are catalogued and reckoned in terms of £ *s. d.* Its advantage lies in its holding the attention of the observer, even when he is a mere novice at the work, by obliging him to put something in every column and allowing nothing to escape his notice.[4]

But when Le Play proceeds to declare that this method has revealed the truth to him and helped him to formulate the doctrines of which we have just given a résumé it really seems as if he were making a great mistake. Actually it has only revealed what Le Play expected to find; in other hands it might have yielded quite different results. He declares that it has proved to him that only those families which

[1] "I have frequently posted as much as 1000 kilometres in order to consult some eminent landowner living on the confines of Europe." (Letter to M. de Ribbes, October 3, 1867.)

[2] "This method is based upon a careful observation of each fact and its past history. Nothing is left to the imagination, the presupposition, or the prejudices of the observer. It is essentially scientific and exact." (*La Réforme en Europe.*)

[3] These monographs appeared first of all, as we have seen, in his great work on the European workmen in 1855. The work has been carried on by his disciples and the results incorporated in the *Ouvriers des deux mondes*, which numbers about a hundred volumes. They have also employed the method in writing monographs on industries and communes, etc.

The method requires supplementing by reference to statistics of population and wages, which can only be supplied, of course, by Governments.

[4] "The comparison of receipts and expenditure should help to discover any oversight, just as the weight of a chemical substance both before and after an experiment helps to determine the nature of the chemical reaction." (Bureau, *L'Œuvre d'Henri de Tourville.*)

are grouped under paternal authority and which obey the Ten Commandments are really happy.[1] That may be, but how would he define a happy family? "A happy family is one that dwells in unity and abides in the love of God." He has thus armed himself with a definite *a priori* criterion of happiness;[2] but there is nothing to prove that the unstable disorganized family of the Parisian factory hand may not be infinitely more happy than the family group of Melouga or the patriarchal family of the Bashkirs of Turkestan.

A comparison has often been drawn between Le Play's school and the German Historical school. It is pointed out that both schools lay great emphasis upon the method of observation and focus attention upon the institutions of the past, and that to some extent they both represent a reaction against Liberalism and Classical optimism. But the resemblance is wholly superficial. At bottom the two schools are not merely different, but even divergent. The German school seeks the explanation of the present in the past, while Le Play's school is merely out to learn a few lessons. The one studies the germ which is to develop and to bear fruit, while the other admires the type and the model to which it thinks it necessary to conform. The one is evolutionary, the other traditional, and the conclusions of the former are radical in the extreme, and even socialistic, while those of the latter are usually conservative.

And so Le Play's true position is in the chapter dealing with Social Christianity, and not among the writers of the Historical school.

His unshaken belief in the natural propensity of man to evil and error is sufficient to give him his place. But we must beware of confusing his doctrine with that of the Social Catholics, for, unlike them, he is rather prone to invoke the authority of the Mosaic law, especially the Decalogue, and to take his illustrations from England, which is a Protestant country, or from China or Mohammedan lands. His importance among authorities on social questions is not very great, but his attitude towards Church and clergy was on the whole defiant,[3]

---

[1] With a good deal of candour he admits offering a reward to anyone who could show him a single happy family except under conditions of this kind. "But," he adds, "all my efforts proved fruitless." (*Les Ouvriers européens*, Vol. IV, introduction.)

[2] When Le Play teaches us that the essential condition of society implies

A double foundation—the Decalogue and paternal authority,

A twofold link—religion and sovereignty, and

Three kinds of material—the community, private property, and employers,

we cannot help thinking that the so-called method of observation has a very pronounced trait of dogmatism in its constitution.

[3] "The principal object to aim at here is the limitation of the ecclesiastical personnel with a view to keeping them all fully employed," as he adds later on. He had the same antipathy to religious congregations as he had to other forms of association.

and the plan of reform of which we have just given an outline is very different from that of the Social Catholics.

There was a schism in the school in 1885. The "Unions of Social Peace," with their organ *La Réforme sociale*, on the whole remained faithful to the programme as outlined in this chapter. The dissenting branch, on the other hand, with Demolins and the Abbé de Tourville as leaders, developed the doctrine on its ultra-individualistic or Spencerian side, so that only in origin could it be regarded as at all connected with the school of Le Play.

The "School of Social Science," as it was called—at least, that was the name it gave to its review—claimed that it was still faithful to the method of the master. It even went so far as to say that Le Play was ignorant of the full possibilities of this method, and condemned his failure to establish a positive science by means of it. In reality, however, the master's method had quite a subordinate role in the activities of this school, for the simple reason that it was practically useless except for the production of monographs. The school arranged its facts according to their natural relations, and attempted to link the study of social science to the study of geographical environment.[1] The study of environment received some attention in the works of Le Play himself, but it assumed much greater importance after then. To give but a single instance, the school attempted to show how the configuration of the Norwegian fiord, the almost complete absence of arable land, and the consequent recourse to fishing as a means of livelihood, even the very dimensions of their sea-craft, helped to fix the type of family and even the political and economic constitutions prevalent among the Anglo-Saxon race. In a similar fashion, the vast steppes of central and southern Asia had begotten a civilization of their own. It was the Historical materialism of the Marxian school reappearing in the more picturesque and more suggestive guise of geographical determinism.[2]

The new school, however, was not very favourably inclined to Le Play's programme of social reform, especially its teaching concerning the family. Their aim was not the preservation of the family, but the placing of each child in a position to found a family of his own as soon as possible. Their object was neither family nor communal solidarity, but self-help, not the family group, but the single individual

---

[1] "No social phenomenon can ever be explained if it is taken out of its own setting. All social science is based upon this law." (Demolins, *La Classification sociale*.)

[2] The similarity noted here has given rise to emphatic protests on the part of certain members of this school. There is no need to take offence at the epithet, however, provided we are careful to distinguish it from philosophic materialism and recognize that it does not necessarily exclude idealism.

family, not the English, but the American home. Demolins was an ardent believer in the struggle for existence, and no one ever professed greater contempt for the solidarist doctrine. "Social salvation, like eternal life," says he, "is essentially a personal affair"—a singularly heterodox declaration, by the way, for if salvation is a purely personal matter of what use is the Church?[1]

II: SOCIAL CATHOLICISM[2]

The term 'Catholic Socialism,' which is occasionally employed as an alternative to the above title, is objected to by the majority of Catholics as being excessively restrictive. The generic term 'Christian Socialism' was first employed by a Frenchman, Francis Huet, in a book entitled *Le Règne social du Christianisme*, published in 1853.[3]

But at least two other authors, namely, Buchez in his *Essai d'un Traité complet de philosophie au point de vue du catholicisme et du progrès* (1838–40), and the fiery Abbé de Lamennais in *La Question du travail* (1848), can lay considerable claims to priority in the matter. Buchez was the founder of the Co-operative Association of Producers (1832), and Lamennais outlined a scheme of co-operative banks almost exactly like those afterwards established in Germany by Raiffeisen.[4]

Present-day Catholicism, however, shows no great desire to honour any of them. The one ambition of these three republicans was to effect a union between the Church and the Revolution.[5] The most

[1] This branch of the school, of which Tourville and Demolins were the earliest leaders, has given us several excellent books. Demolins's own work on the superiority of the Anglo-Saxons caused quite a stir. Then there is M. de Rousiers's book on producers' industrial unions, and P. du Maroussem's. We would also specially mention Paul Bureau's *Le Contrat de Travail* (1902), *La Participation aux Bénéfices*, and *La Crise morale des Temps nouveaux*. Bureau's work is characterized by precise impartial analysis of facts combined with great moral fervour.

[2] For its doctrines and the movements connected with it see the important and interesting work by Georges Hoog, *Histoire du catholicisme social en France* (Domat-Montchrestien, Paris, 1942).

[3] Huet was a professor at Ghent, which accounts for his being considered a Belgian, just as Walras is generally considered a Swiss.

[4] He was the first to emphasize the importance of borrowers combining. Only in this way can the poor hope to offer some real security. "How is it that the worker cannot borrow? Simply because he has no security to offer except just his work in the future. That future guarantee can only become real and certain by means of combination. Union eliminates the uncertainty which hitherto made the security worthless and the loan impossible." (*La Question du travail*, p. 25.)

"The problem is to outline a state of society where working men will work only for themselves and not for others; where none will reap but has already sown, and where each will enjoy the fruits of his own labour." (*Ibid.*)

[5] "Christianity and revolution as far as humanity is concerned have identical aims, and the one is the natural outcome of the other." (Buchez, *Traité de la Politique*, Vol. II, p. 504.)

advanced of the Social Catholics of to-day, on the other hand, would
be well satisfied could they establish some kind of understanding
between the Church and democracy. Such at least was the programme
laid down by Marc Sangnier, the founder of the Sillon.

About the same time we find Monseigneur von Ketteler, Bishop of
Mayence, preaching a doctrine which drew its inspiration, not from
"the false dogmas of '89," but from the institutional life of the Middle
Ages, from the guilds and the other corporative associations, which
are minutely described by him and his disciples, especially Canon
Moufang and the Abbé Hitze. Some such institutional activity was
again to form the corner-stone of Social Catholicism.[1]

During the period of the Second Empire most of the Social Catholics
seem to have fallen asleep, but they were aroused from their slumbers
by the disaster of 1870. The Marquis de La Tour du Pin[2] and Count
Albert de Mun proved the inspirers this time, and the noble eloquence
of the latter, which led to the formation of unions of Catholic working
men, was instrumental in giving the movement a vigorous start. The
same period witnessed the appearance of *L'Association catholique*, a
review which took as its programme the study of economic facts in a
Catholic spirit—an object that has always been kept steadily in
view.

Organization in the form of corporations was given first place in
the Social Catholic programme.[3] Le Play's corner-stone—the family

[1] Ketteler's principal writings were published in France in 1864 under the title of
La Question ouvrière et le Christianisme. He could never make up his mind as between the
corporative and the co-operative ideal, however. The latter was very much to the
front just then, not only in France, but also with the English Christian Socialists and
with the German socialist Lassalle. This was before the co-operative movement was
eclipsed by trade unionism.

Hitze, however, shows none of his master's hesitation, but emphatically declares
that "the solution of the social question is essentially and exclusively bound up with
a reorganization of trades and professions. We must have the medieval regime of
corporations re-established—a regime which offers a better solution of the social
problem than any which existed either before or after. Of course times have changed,
and certain features of the medieval regime would need modification. But some
such corporative regime conceived in a more democratic spirit must form the economic
basis. (*Capital and Labour*.)

[2] His articles have been collected in two volumes: *Vers un ordre Social chrétien* (1907),
and *Aphorismes de politique sociale* (1909).

[3] "We must direct all our private initiative and concentrate public attention upon
this one reform—the corporative reorganization of society." (*Programme de l'Œuvre des
cercles ouvriers*, April 1894.)

Co-operative association is dismissed altogether. The Social Catholics have
especially little sympathy with the small retail co-operative stores, because they
threaten the existence of the small merchant and the small artisan—types of individuals that are dear to the heart of the Catholics. On the other hand, it shows itself
very favourably inclined towards co-operative credit, because of the possibility of
assisting the classes already referred to—the shopkeeper and the small merchant.

organization—was not rejected, but they considered that though the family was to remain the basis for moral reform a wider association of an economic character must serve as a basis for economic reform.

At first sight this may seem somewhat surprising. The connexion between these professional associations and the teaching of the Gospel is not very evident, nor is it very clear how such organizations could ever hope to Christianize society. But although the Gospels know nothing of a corporative or any other regime we must not forget their prominence during the Middle Ages—when the authority of the Church was in the ascendant. As long as this regime lasted what we understand as the social question—the vexed problem as to whether we possess sufficient moral strength to keep the peace between capital and labour—never presented itself. The problem is, of course, somewhat different to-day, but its solution may possibly require the exercise of similar virtues, namely, obedience to a detailed system of organization coupled with a feeling of brotherhood—the chastening of the whole complexity of social relations by the spirit of Christianity.

Some of their opponents have not hesitated to charge these Catholics with a desire to return to the feudalism of the Middle Ages, which is of course utterly false. What the Social Catholics wished to do was to build up the new social structure upon the basis of the modern trade union, or upon syndicalism; and the proof that the foundation is not at any rate too narrow lies in the fact that the new schools of socialists can conceive of none better. With this as the foundation they looked forward not merely to the development of a new society, but also to the rise of a new ethic. The fact that they forestalled the socialists in this respect shows that the Social Catholics were at least not hopelessly antiquated.

Early in the history of the movement they tried to organize a kind of mixed *syndicat* consisting both of masters and men, because this seemed to them to offer the best guarantee for social peace. But the results proved disappointing, and they were soon forced to relinquish that idea and to content themselves with a separate organization of masters and men co-operating only in matters relating to the regulation of work or the settling of differences.[1] Such collateral unions, it

[1] In 1894 the Congress of Catholic Circles which met at Rheims declared that, "without minimizing the difficulties which stand in the way of extending the mixed *syndicats*, the formation of such *syndicats* must be our chief aim." In 1904 Father Rutten, one of the leaders of the Belgian Catholic Syndical movement, in a report on the syndicalist movement writes as follows: "We do not despair of the mixed *syndicat*, which in theory we certainly think is nearest perfection. But we must not blind ourselves to facts, and whether we will or no we have to admit that at the present moment the mixed *syndicat* in ninety industries out of every hundred seems quite Utopian." (Quoted by Dechesne, *Syndicats Ouvriers belges*, p. 76; 1906.)

was at first thought, would gradually become the organs of labour legislation, and the State would entrust them with the discharge of that function because of their greater freedom in the making of experiments. All questions affecting the interests of a trade, the hours of labour, Sunday observance, apprenticeship, the sanitary condition of the workshops, the labour of women and children, and even the rate of wages paid, instead of being regulated as they are at present by brutal, inflexible laws which are seldom suited to meet every individual case, would henceforth be settled by the union, and the rules of the union would be incumbent upon all the members of the trade or profession, both masters and men. Every one would be free to enter the union or to decline membership just as he chose, but no member would be allowed to violate the rules of the union or to lower the conditions of labour in any way. "Free association within an organized profession," such is the formula.[1]

To those Liberals who feign indignation at seeing purely private institutions thus invested with legislative authority it may be answered that the 'labour union' so constituted forms an association which is as natural and as necessary—understanding by this that it is independent of the voluntary conventions of the parties interested—as one based upon community of residence. Everybody admits that the inhabitants of the commune ought to submit to the rule of the organized majority. What difference would it make if the majority thus organized constituted a corporation rather than a commune?[2]

Some go as far as to regard these professional associations as possessed of an important political role, and would even go the length of making

[1] Such is the programme as outlined especially in Austria, which is one of the countries where Social Catholicism seems fairly powerful. As a matter of fact, the corporative regime has never quite disappeared there, and for some years now attempts have been made to revive it in the smaller crafts. The new corporation would take the form of a centralized organization, whose regulations would be obligatory upon all the members of the craft.

[2] "The commune has always been organized. Is there any reason why the trade should not be? In both cases special relations are established, special needs arise, there are frequent conflicts and occasional harmony between the different interests. But all of them are nevertheless intimately bound together, and the links connecting them must be co-ordinated on some regular plan if every one is to be safe, and free to follow his own bent." (Henri Lorin, *Principes de l'Organisation professionnelle*, in *L'Association catholique*, July 15, 1892.)

To this it might be replied that the majority generally makes the law for the commune, but that in the case of a free corporation it is often the minority that rules. To which it might be retorted that the so-called majority is often not better than a minority of the electors, and a very small minority indeed of the whole inhabitants —who of course include women, who generally have no votes. Moreover, as soon as the rules of the *syndicat* became really obligatory the majority if not the whole of the workers in the trade would be found within the union.

this new corporative unit the basis of a new franchise for the election of at least one of the two Chambers.

It is not very easy, perhaps, to get a clear idea of what a society built upon a plan of this kind would really be like, but the difficulty is no greater in this case than in some others.

In the first place it would have to be a society professing the Catholic faith.[1] Should the enemies of religion or even the indifferent by any chance ever gain the upper hand in the social unit the whole structure would immediately fall to the ground. Its realization, accordingly, is quite hypothetical.

It would also be a society founded upon brotherhood in the full sense of the term. The only real brotherhood is that founded upon the fatherhood of God, and not upon any socialistic conception of equality. But even brotherhood and a common parentage may not be sufficient to prevent irregularities, and the family relation in addition to this almost inevitably implies the rights of the youngest and the duties of the oldest. Within the corporative unit already outlined true equality would always reign, for the humblest, meanest task would be of equal dignity with the most exalted office in the State, and every one would be content and even proud to live where God had placed him.[2]

Such a society would be a pure hierarchy. All the authority and responsibility, all the duties involved, would be on the master's side. On the worker's side would be rights respected, life assured on the minimum level, and a re-establishment of family life.[3]

Social Catholicism further undertook to disprove the first article in the socialist creed, namely, that "the emancipation of the workers

---

[1] Father Antoine writes as follows in his *Cours d'Économie sociale*, p. 154: "The social question can never be completely solved until we have a complete revival of Christian morals." Still more categorical is the declaration of M. Léon Harmel in *L'Association catholique* for December 1889: "We can see only one remedy, and that is that the authority of the Pope should be recognized all the world over, and his ruling accepted by all people."
The annual study reunions which go by the name of *les Semaines sociales*, and which afford one of the best manifestations of the kind of activities which Social Christianity gives rise to everywhere, are not so exclusive. Economic questions of all kinds are discussed, but the programme is not strictly Catholic at all, and the basis is wide enough to include every one who is a professed Christian.

[2] "The corporations which would be set up under the ægis of religion would aim at making all their members contented with their lot, patient in toil and disposed to lead a tranquil, happy life" (*sua sorte contentos, operumque patientes et ad quietam ac tranquillam vitam agendam inducant*). (Encyclical of Leo XII, December 28, 1878, called the *Quod Apostolici*. See *History of Corporations*, by M. Martin Saint-Leon.)

[3] "The corporation is simply the model of the Church. Just as for the Church all the faithful are equal in the sight of God, so here. But equality ends there. For the rest it is a hierarchy." (Ségur-Lamoignon, *L'Association catholique*, July 13, 1894.)

can only be accomplished by the workers themselves." It maintained that, on the contrary, this object could only be accomplished by the help of the masters and of all the other classes in society, not excluding even the non-professional classes, landed proprietors, rent-receivers, and consumers generally,[1] all of whom ought to be informed of the responsibilities which their different positions impose upon them and of the special duty which is incumbent upon all men of making the most of the talents with which the Master has entrusted them.

The German Christliche Gewerkvereine, which got most of its recruits among the Catholics, took an important part in German political life and did something to counterbalance the 'Reds,' or the revolutionary socialists. They advocated the union of masters and men, but were extremely anxious not to be confused with the 'Yellows,' or those who advocated mixed unions. In other words, they were independent of both the masters and the socialists.

State intervention might be necessary at first in order to establish the corporative regime, but once founded it would naturally monopolize all the legislative and police power which affects labour in any way, especially in the matter of fixing wages,[2] arranging pensions, etc. The legislature would still find ample material to exercise its powers upon outside these merely professional interests, especially in regulating the rights of property, prohibiting usury, protecting agriculture, etc.[3]

"The State," says the *Immortale Dei*, an Encyclical of Pope Leo XIII —repeating a text of St Paul—"is the minister of God for good." Elsewhere St Paul declares that the Law is the schoolmaster to bring us unto Christ, and if we paraphrase this to mean that the function of law is to lead men to a higher conception of brotherhood we have a fairly exact idea of what Social Catholicism considered to be the function of the State.

Between the corporatism preached by La Tour du Pin and Mgr

[1] The Ligue sociale d'Acheteurs, founded in Paris in 1900, is of Social Catholic inspiration.

[2] "More important even than free will, whether of masters or of men, is that higher and more ancient law of natural justice which demands that wages should always be sufficient to enable the worker to lead a sober and honest life. But lest the public authority in this case, as in some other analogous cases, such as the question of the length of the working day, should unwisely intervene, and in view of the great variety of circumstances, it is better that the solution should be left in the hands of the corporations or the unions." (Encyclical, *Rerum Novarum*, 1891.)

[3] The Social Catholics wherever found are usually Protectionists, the reason being that they think their "corporative regime could never be kept going without some protection against foreign competition," and also because most of their adherents are drawn from the ranks of the agricultural unions. (*Programme de l'Œuvre des cercles ouvriers*, art. 7.)

Ketteler on the one hand, and that which has been advocated by many writers since the end of the First World War on the other, there are striking resemblances. There is no doubt that the first was largely the ancestor of the second, though generally speaking the religious aspect is absent from the later forms. Corporatism, like Neo-Syndicalism in France and Guild Socialism in England, seems to provide the long-sought middle way between the pure individualism of the liberals and the complete *étatisme* of the socialists. The meeting of these three tendencies, arising in very different surroundings and of almost completely opposite political and social sympathies, is significant, and we have emphasized this in dealing with State Socialism. As a matter of fact it is not easy to give a precise idea of this 'corporatism,[1] because very varying formulæ are adopted by its adherents. Gaëtan Pirou, endeavouring to pick out its original features, defines its specific character thus: "The function of corporatism is to formulate rules to which every one in the profession must conform. . . . Corporatism means, therefore, something more than freely formed groups with voluntary membership. It exists only if the corporation is formed as a kind of statutory group, which within its own sphere makes the law and imposes it on defaulters." If this is a true definition of corporatism, as we believe it to be, it is in the right line of descent from social catholicism. It includes the notion of 'community of labour' mentioned earlier as peculiar to the founders of the latter movement. Existing corporatism may not be a religious system, but none the less it owes its most characteristic formula to the Kettelers and La Tour du Pins. The success of their ideas after more than fifty years is one example among many of that unexpected shining-forth of doctrines long hidden under a bushel, when new circumstances suddenly provide the opportunity. What has given new life to the corporative idea is the need to find, at any cost, some organization capable, it is hoped, of ending the class conflict. It is thought that a new incentive to action has been found in the interest of the 'profession,' to take the place of class solidarity. It remains to be seen whether this interest, detached

---

[1] The pamphlets, articles, and books on Corporatism, in Italy and France, would fill a library. This literature is very skilfully analysed in Gaëtan Pirou's *Essais sur le Corporatisme* (Sirey, Paris, 1938). In a matter of this kind actual events are more interesting than future prospects or plans in which corporatists differ from each other remarkably. These variations on an original theme are not very instructive, so we have merely noted the origin of the theme, leaving to others the task of describing the forms under which it will be incorporated in the existing economic system. Actually, the exponents of corporatism are generally not very satisfied with these forms. Jacques Valdour, for instance, considers that none of the known corporative codes embodies the ideal in his mind, except in Spain: they are either too *étatiste* or too syndicalist. No doubt the happy mean is not easy to achieve.

from any religious inspiration, will form a strong enough bond between the members of the corporation to put an end to their antagonisms, and, above all, whether corporatism, discredited since the last war by its alliance with the political systems that the war has destroyed, will not be born again under a new name.

Social Catholicism has sometimes shown very advanced tendencies, bringing it very near to socialism in the strict sense. But these tendencies have been confined to individual cases and have been formally condemned by Rome; those responsible for them have generally deferred to her authority.

It was Loesewitz in 1888 who made the first violent attack upon the so-called productivity theory of capital in *L'Association catholique*.[1] It caused quite a sensation at the time, and provoked a disapproving reply from the Comte de Mun. Afterwards, however, the article became the programme of a party known as "Les jeunes Abbés." Nor must we omit to mention the growth of the Sillon, founded in 1890, the political ambition of whose members is the reconciliation of the Church and democracy and even republicanism, and whose economic aim is the abolition of the wage-earner and his master.[2] This is also the aim of the syndicalists, and Article 2 of the Confédération générale du Travail (C.G.T.) declares that one of the avowed objects of the federation is the disappearance of the wage-earner and the removal of his master. Instead of seeking a solution of the problem in the parallel action of *syndicats* of men on the one hand and of masters on the other, it would suppress the latter altogether, leaving the men the right of possessing their own instruments of production and of keeping intact the produce of their labour. It is true that the Sillon has been put under the ban of the Pope, but this essentially syndicalist movement is still in existence, and its leaders have assumed great political influence since the end of the Second World War.

[1] "The so-called productivity of capital, which constitutes the greatest iniquity of profit-making society, and which is from an economical point of view the final cause of social suffering, is nothing better than a word invented to hide the real fact, namely, the appropriation of the fruits of labour by those who possess the instruments of labour." (Loesewitz, *Legislation du Travail*, in *L'Association catholique*, 1886.)

[2] Extract from a report of a meeting of the Sillon, November 1907:
"MARC SANGNIER. The social transformation which we desire to see, comrades, will aim, not at absorbing the individual, but rather at developing him. We want the factories, the mines, and the industries in the possession, not of the State, but of groups of workers.
"AN INTERRUPTER. That is socialism.
"MARC SANGNIER. You can call it socialism if you like. It makes no difference to me. But it is not the socialism of the socialists, of the centralizing socialists. We don't want to set the proletarians free from the control of the masters to put them under the immediate control of one great master, the State; we want the proletarians themselves, acting collectively, to become their own masters."

If the Catholic school has experienced some difficulty in throwing out a left wing it has never been without a right wing which has always shown a predilection for the masters. "The problem is not how to save the worker through his own efforts, but how to save him with the master's co-operation"—the benevolent master of Le Play's school over again.[1] The right wing, moreover, thinks that the existing institutions would prove quite equal to a solution of the so-called social question if they were once thoroughly permeated with the Christian spirit or if the leaders really knew how to deal with the people.

III: SOCIAL PROTESTANTISM

Belief in the essentially individualistic nature of Protestantism is fairly widespread.[2] For confirmation there is the emphasis it has always laid upon the personal nature of salvation and its denial of the necessity for any mediator between God and man, save only the Man Christ Jesus, whereas Roman Catholicism teaches that only through the Church—that great community of the faithful—is salvation ever possible. Protestantism is the religion of self-help, and naturally enough its social teaching is somewhat coloured by its theological preconceptions. Nor must we lose sight of its connexion with middle-class Liberalism; and thus while in politics it is generally regarded as belonging to the left, in matters economic it is generally on the extreme right.[3]

Whatever truth there may be in this attempt to sum up its doctrine and history, we shall find as a matter of actual fact that on economic grounds it is much more advanced than the Social Catholic school; and its extreme left, far from being content with the extinction of the proletariat, also demands the abolition of private property and the establishment of complete communal life.

[1] Milcent, in *L'Association catholique*, 1897, Vol. II, p. 58. There is a Catholic Social school which is Liberal and individualist in its tendencies, and which is represented by such writers as the late Charles Périn, professor at Louvain, author of *La Richesse et Le Socialisme chrétien*, and by M. Rambaud, author of *Cours d'Histoire des doctrines*. Nor ought we to forget their connexion with the development of agricultural credit banks of the Raiffeisen type which have been established in Germany, France, and Italy—although their inception in Italy is largely the work of a Jew named Wollemborg.

[2] Such, for example, is the opinion of Nitti in his book on Catholic Socialism, and because of that rather unsatisfactory reason he only devotes a few pages to it.

[3] There are several historical considerations that may with advantage be kept in mind in dealing with this subject, such as, for example, the notable fact that while the Catholic Church has always been opposed to usury, it was Calvin and Calvinists like Saumaise and the ancient jurist Dumoulin who first justified the practice of taking interest.

Social Protestantism, or Christian Socialism as it is known in England, has a birthday which may be determined with some degree of accuracy. It was in the year 1850 that there was founded in England a society for promoting working men's associations, having for its organ a paper entitled *The Christian Socialist*.[1] Its best-known representatives were Kingsley and Maurice, who subsequently became respectively professors of history and philosophy at Cambridge. A small number of lawyers also joined the society, among whom Ludlow, Hughes, and Vansittart Neale are the most familiar names. Kingsley was much in the public eye just then, not only because of his impassioned eloquence, but also on account of the success of his novel *Alton Locke*, which is perhaps the earliest piece of socialistic fiction that we possess. It is the story of a journeyman tailor and his sufferings under the sweating system—the horrors of which were thus revealed to the public for the first time.[2]

The object which the Christian Socialists[3] had in view, as we have already seen, was the establishment of working men's associations. What type they should adopt as their model was not very easily determined. The trade unions, little known as yet, were just then struggling through the convulsions of their early infancy. Moreover, they were exclusively concerned with professional matters, with the struggle for employment and the question of wages, and altogether did not seem very well fitted to develop the spirit of sacrifice and love which was indispensable for the realization of their ideal. Neither did the co-operative associations of consumers seem very attractive. True, they had attained to some degree of success at Rochdale, but they were

[1] *The Christian Socialist* was preceded by another paper called *Politics for the People*, founded in 1848, which may be taken as the birthday of the movement. In any case the date is significant in view of the contemporary revolution in France.

It is only just to note that Channing, the American pastor, who died in 1842, was one of the pioneers. His writings on social questions are still read.

Those who wish for more information either on the history or on the other aspects of Social Christianity should consult the *New Encyclopædia of Social Reform*, published in America.

[2] The following year Charles Kingsley preached a sermon in London which caused such a sensation that the vicar of the parish felt bound to protest against its tone even during the service. In the course of the sermon Kingsley remarked that any social system which enabled capital to become the possession of a few, which robbed the masses of the land which they and their ancestors had cultivated from time immemorial, and reduced them to the condition of serfs working for daily wage or for charity, was contrary to the spirit of the Kingdom of God, as revealed in Christ. The sermon was afterwards published under the title of *The Church's Message to the Workers*.

[3] Maurice declared that every one who is a Christian must also be a socialist. But the significance of the word 'socialist' has changed somewhat since then. According to Maurice, "The motto of the socialist is co-operation; of the anti-socialist, competition."

536 DOCTRINES INSPIRED BY CHRISTIANITY

inspired by the teaching of Owen, which was definitely anti-Christian. The fact also that they merely proposed to make life somewhat less costly and a little more comfortable implied a certain measure of stoicism which hardly fitted them to be the chosen vessels of the new dispensation. And so the Christian Socialists naturally turned their attention to producers' associations, just as the earliest Social Catholics had done before them. But it would be a mistake to imagine that they owed anything to Buchez, whom they appear to have ignored altogether. The reawakened interest in the possibilities of association which exercised such a fascination over John Stuart Mill in 1848 had touched their imagination, and Ludlow, one of their number, had the good fortune to be resident in Paris, and so witnessed this glorious revival. Such associations seemed to be just the economic instruments needed if a transformation was ever to be effected, and the very process of establishing them, it was hoped, would supply a useful means of discipline in the subordination of individual to collective interests. But the process of disillusion proved as rapid as it was complete. Contrary to what was the case in France, it cannot be said that they were ever really attempted in England.

But the work of the 'Association' had not been altogether in vain. Defeated in its attempts to arouse the worker from his lethargy, and thwarted in its efforts by legal restrictions of various kinds, it began a campaign in favour of a more liberal legislation in matters affecting the welfare of the working classes. The result was the passing of the Industrial and Provident Societies Acts of 1852–62, which conferred legal personality for the first time upon co-operative associations, with consequent benefit to themselves and to other working men's associations.

The Christian Socialists thought that the methods by which their ideals might be attained were of quite secondary importance. Experience had taught them that voluntary association or legislation even by itself could never be of much avail until the whole mental calibre of the worker was changed.[1] What they strove for above all else was moral reform, and whenever they use the word 'co-operation' they conceive of it not merely as a particular system of industry, but rather as the antithesis of the competitive regime or as the negation of the

[1] "There is no doubt about association being the form which industrial government will take in future, and I have no doubt as to its success, but a preliminary training extending possibly over a couple of generations is necessary before the worker has the requisite ability or moral strength to make use of it." (Kingsley in 1856.)

And this is how State intervention appealed to him: "The devil is always ready to urge us to change law and government, heaven and earth even, but takes good care never to suggest that we might change ourselves."

struggle for existence. Their thoughts are admirably summed up in a letter of Ludlow's to Maurice written from Paris in March 1848, in which he speaks of the necessity for "Christianizing socialism."

Christian Socialism in England, though it has survived its founders, has been obliged to change its programme. It has abandoned the idea of a producers' association, but still advocates other forms of co-operation. Its chief demand has been for a reorganization of private property, which is a particularly serious question in England, where the land is in the hands of a comparatively few people. In the words of the Psalmist, the Christian Socialists often cry out, "The earth is the Lord's," and they are never weary of pointing out how under the Mosaic law the land was redistributed every forty-nine years with a view to bringing it back to its original owners. And so it finds itself supporting the doctrines of Henry George, who may himself be classed as one of the Christian Socialists.[1] There is also the Institutional Church, with its network of organizations for the satisfaction of the material, intellectual, and moral needs of the worker, which is a prominent feature of most modern protestant Churches. Moreover, several of the early Labour leaders—Keir Hardie, for example—were earnest Christians. The Federation of Brotherhoods, which at one time included over 2000 societies, with a membership of over a million working men, combined an ardent evangelical faith with a strong advocacy of socialism.[2]

In the United States of America Christian Socialism is still more aggressive and outspoken in its attacks upon capitalism. The earliest society of Christian Socialists was founded at Boston in 1889. Since then these associations have multiplied rapidly. One of them defines its objects in the following terms: "To help the message of Jesus to permeate the Christian Churches and to show that socialism is necessarily the economic expression of the Christian life." A little farther on it declares itself persuaded "that the ideal of socialism is identical with that of the Church, and that the gospel of the co-operative commonwealth is the Gospel of the Kingdom of God translated into economic terms."[3]

For the other extreme—the extreme right—we must look to

[1] The official organ of the Christian Social Union, which is definitely connected with the Church of England, is the *Economic Review*, published at Oxford—not to be confused with the *Economic Journal*, which is published in London by the Royal Economic Society.

[2] E. Gounelle, *Le Mouvement des fraternités*.

[3] Josiah Strong, director of the Institute of Social Service at New York, was the publisher of a review called *The Gospel of the Kingdom*, which has for its programme "the study of economic facts in the light of the Gospel," and in which he maintains that "if the world is ever to be Christianized industry must be Christianized first of

Germany. In 1878 Pastors Stöcker and Todt founded the Christian Social Working Men's Party, which, despite its title, drew most of its recruits from the middle classes. Later on Stöcker became Court preacher, and during his occupation of that post this kind of socialism found such favour in official quarters that he was able to say that it was his personal conviction that a social revolution was within the bounds of practical politics.[1] But in 1890 the Emperor William II dismissed his pastor, and as a result Christian Socialism immediately lost its official status.[2]

At the Congress of Erfurt in 1896 two young pastors of Frankfort named Naumann and Goehre[3] tried to win the adherence of the working classes by endeavouring to give the Protestant churches a more distinctively socialist bias. But the suggestion was condemned by the official Lutheran Church, the masters opposed it, and it received but very slight support from the Social Democrats. Altogether the movement proved abortive, and the pastors soon turned aside to other interests.

In Switzerland also the movement made considerable headway, and in Professor Ragaz and Pastors Kutter[4] and Pflüger it found advocates whose views were at any rate sufficiently advanced.

In France there is at least one—there may possibly be more—Social Protestant school. But as it only includes a small fraction of Protestantism, which is itself in a hopeless minority, its influence is not very great. There are several important social movements, however, such

---

all. On the question of unemployment, for example, he refers us to Matthew xx, 6, and on the still more vexed question of the closed or open shop we are referred to 1 Corinthians xii, 16, 26. We must also mention Rauschenbusch's eloquent book *Christianity and the Social Crisis*.

The well-known economist Professor Richard T. Ely is another of the leaders of this movement. Nor must we omit Herron, who caused some sensation by declaring that it is necessary to go well beyond collectivism, which he thinks altogether too conservative and reactionary. He adds that Karl Marx is a crusted Tory compared with Jesus, "for anyone who accepts private property in any form whatsoever, even in matters of consumption, must reject Christ."

[1] At a conference held at Geneva in 1891. At this conference M. Stöcker defined his programme as follows: "We do not believe that we can do anything without the State, but we also believe in the spirit of association. We have told the masters that their duty is to make some sacrifice for the sake of solving the question in a way that will be agreeable to their men. We have also told the workers that they must work hard, economically, and conscientiously, even if they never obtain a better situation."

[2] He was formally repudiated by the Emperor in 1896 in a telegram addressed to a powerful employer, Baron Stumm.

[3] Goehre is the author of a work entitled *Three Months in a Workshop*. The book has been a great success and has produced a crop of imitations.

[4] Kutter's book *Sie Müssen* caused quite a flutter. The author attempts to show that the socialists are the real disciples of Christ, but have been disowned by the Church.

as the crusades against alcoholism and pornography, the revival of co-operation and the demand for the erection of 'People's Palaces'—known as *Solidarités*—which are entirely due to the activities of this school. An association for the inductive study of social questions was founded in 1887 by Pastor Gouth, another pastor named Tomy Fallot being its president and inspirer.[1] At first the demands of this group were extremely moderate, co-operation being their only mode of action and solidarity their social doctrine.[2] This new doctrine of solidarity, although rather belonging to the Radical wing, being the very antithesis of Christian charity, as we shall see by and by, was enthusiastically welcomed by the Social Protestants. The Protestants even claimed that it was originally their own peculiar doctrine, and that other schools merely borrowed it; for where can be found a fuller expression of the law of solidarity than the two Christian doctrines of the fall and redemption of man? "For as in Adam all die, even so in Christ shall all be made alive."

Curiously enough there is another group of young pastors who closely resemble what is known in Catholic circles as the Abbots' Party. They are dissatisfied with the moderate claims of the Catholics as a whole, and like their American colleagues they demand the establishment of a form of collectivism.[3] They think, at any rate, that the question of property ought to come up for consideration almost immediately.

In short, it seems true to say that in almost every country Social Christianity has taken over most of the elements of the socialist programme, and the change of title is an index to the difference of attitude.

[1] For over twenty years M. de Boyve, the leader of the co-operative movement in France, was the president, which confirms us in the suspicion that the two schools had a common parentage, both really springing from the École de Nîmes. Periodical congresses are held in connexion with it, and it also has a review called *Le Christianisme social*.

[2] Pastor Tomy Fallot, the initiator of this movement, indicates the path that should be followed thus: "The essential thing is to get a rough outline of that perfect type which is known as co-operation. Just now it seems the only thing that contains a prophecy of better times." (*L'Action Bonne.*) Compare this with Maurice's formula. "We are Social Christians because we are solidarists. In our search for solidarity we have found the Messiah and His Kingdom. Solidarity is the layman's term, the Kingdom of God the theologian's, but the two are the same." (Gounelle, *L'Avant-Garde*, 1907.)

[3] This group found its earliest recruits among the young pastors who ministered in the great industrial towns (M. Wilfred Monod at Rouen and M. Gounelle at Roubaix, for example), and thus found itself in close touch with poverty, suffering, and discontent. But several laymen also joined it, among them being a son of the economist who was regarded as the doyen of the Liberal school—Frédéric Passy. The Christian Socialist group had a journal of its own, entitled *L'Espoir du Monde*.

In other words, Social Protestantism accepts the essential principles of international socialism, such as the socialization of the means of production, class war, and internationalism, and endeavours to show that they are in complete accordance with the teaching of the Gospels.

But the stress which it lays upon the necessity for moral reform saves Social Protestantism from being hopelessly confused with collectivism, and the fact that it believes that individual salvation is impossible without social transformation helps to distinguish it from individual Protestantism.[1] Conversion implies a change of environment. What is the use of preaching chastity when people have to sleep together in the same room without distinction of age or of sex? "Society," says Fallot, "ought to be organized in such a fashion that salvation is at least possible for every one." "The regime of the great industry," says M. Gounelle, "is the greatest obstacle to the salvation of sinners that the religion of Christ has yet met." Protestant Socialism remains individualistic in the sense that while seeking to suppress individualism in the form of egoism as a centripetal force, it wishes to uphold it and to strengthen it as a principle of disinterested activity —as a centrifugal force. It takes for its motto those words of Vinet which may be found carved on the pedestal of his statue at Lausanne: "I want man to be his own master in order that he may give better service to everybody else."[2]

IV: THE MYSTICS

No review of Christian Social doctrines, however summary, can afford to omit the names of certain eminent writers who, though belonging to none of the above-mentioned schools, and having no definite standing either as socialists or economists, being for the most part *littérateurs*, historians, and novelists, have nevertheless lent the powerful support of their eloquence to the upholding of somewhat similar doctrines.[3]

[1] "'For I could wish that myself were accursed from Christ for my brethren,' writes St Paul; in other words, 'I do not want to be saved alone, and I shall be completely saved only when humanity as a whole has been saved.' And so the evangelical doctrine would subordinate the full realization of my personal salvation to the salvation of others." (W. Monod, *La Notion apostolique du salut*.)

[2] Or, as he epitomizes it elsewhere, "It is useless to speak of giving ourselves until we are certain that we own ourselves."

[3] Ruskin himself did not think that his doctrines were only of slight importance. The introduction to *Munera Pulveris* (1862) contains the following words: "The following pages contain, I believe, the first accurate analysis of the laws of Political Economy which has been published in England."

See also the preface to *Unto This Last*, which has for its sub-title "Four Essays on the First Principles of Political Economy."

Tolstoy and Ruskin are the best-known representatives of this movement on the borderland of Social Christianity, although they are by no means the only ones.[1] These two grand old men, who both died at an advanced age, appeared to their contemporaries in much the same light as the prophets of old did to Israel. True descendants of Isaiah and Jeremiah, they exultantly prophesied the downfall of capitalism—the modern Tyre and Sidon—and announced the coming of the New Jerusalem—the habitation of justice. Their language even is modelled on Holy Writ, and Ruskin, we know, was from his youth upward a diligent reader of the Bible.[2] Both of them condemn the Hedonistic principle and denounce money as an instrument of tyranny which has resulted in setting up something like a new system of slavery,[3] and they both advocate a return to manual labour as the only power that can free the individual and regenerate social life. They differ, however, in their conception of future society, which to Ruskin must be aristocratic, chivalrous, and heroic, while Tolstoy lays stress upon its being equalitarian, communal, and above all ethical. The one looks at society from the standpoint of an æsthete, the other from that of a *muzhik*: the one would breed heroes, the other saints.

Thomas Carlyle also deserves mention. Among the numerous books which he wrote we may mention, among others, his *French Revolution* (1837) and his *Heroes and Hero-worship*. Chronologically he precedes both Tolstoy and Ruskin, and his influence upon economic thought was greater than either of theirs. But we could hardly put him among the Christian Socialists because of his extreme individualism, and if he were to be given a place at all it would be with such writers as Ibsen and Nietzsche. In his influence, however, he resembles Ruskin; and nowhere but in the choruses of the old Greek tragedies do we get anything approaching the declamations of these two writers against the economic order of their time.[4]

[1] There are a great number of novels dealing with social questions. For the English novels bearing on this topic see M. Cazamian, *Le Roman social*.

[2] So much was this the case with Ruskin that Mme Brunhes has published a book called *La Bible et Ruskin*, and Tolstoy on his side has an edition of the Gospels to his credit which is said to be much nearer the original than the ordinary version of the canon.

[3] See *Fors Clavigera, passim*. Tolstoy writes in a similar strain. Money is just a conventional sign giving the right or the possibility of claiming the service of others. But although money is all-powerful in the matter of exploiting the worker it is quite useless when it comes to a question of furthering his well-being. There is a curious development of this thesis in Tolstoy's *What is to be Done?*

[4] "All this has come of the spreading of that thrice accursed, thrice impious doctrine of the modern economist, that 'To do the best for yourself, is finally to do the best for others.' Friends, our great Master said not so." (Ruskin, *Crown of Wild Olive*, Lecture II.)

S

Carlyle is possibly the strongest adversary that the old Classical school ever encountered. It was he who spoke of political economy as "the dismal science." That abstract creation of the Classicists the economic man afforded him endless amusement, and he very aptly described their ideal State as "anarchy plus the policeman." He is no less fierce in his denunciation of *laissez-faire* as a social philosophy.[1] But he left us no plan of social reconstruction, being himself content to wait upon individual reform—a trait which brings him into intimate connexion with the Christian Socialists.[2]

Ruskin, on the other hand, has given us a programme of social regeneration which might be summarized as follows:[3]

1. Manual labour should be compulsory for everybody. His readers were reminded of those words of St Paul, "If any would not work, neither should he eat." He thought it both absurd and immoral that a man should live in idleness merely by using money inherited from his ancestors to pay for the services of his fellow-men. Life is the only real form of payment; in other words, labour ought to be given in return for labour. To *live* upon the fruits of *dead* labour is surely absurd and contradictory. And it must be real human labour. Machinery of all kinds must be renounced except that which may be driven by wind or water—natural forces which, unlike coal, do not defile, but rather purify.

Ruskin wanted labour to be artistic, and he longed to see the artisan again become an artist as he was in the Middle Ages (which is a somewhat hasty generalization, perhaps). In practice this is not very easy. Some of his immediate disciples have set up as artistic bookbinders, but the number of people who can find employment at such trades must be exceedingly few.

Tolstoy, on the other hand, does not strive for artistic effect. His heart is set upon rural work, which he magnificently describes as "bread work," and which seemed to him sufficiently noble without embellishment of any kind.

---

[1] Especially in that celebrated passage: "It [Political Economy] sounds with Philosophico-Politico-Economic plummet the deep dark sea of troubles, and having taught us rightly what an infinite sea of troubles it is sums up with the practical inference and use of consolation that nothing whatever can be done in it by man, who has simply to sit still and look wistfully to 'time and general laws,' and thereupon without so much as recommending suicide coldly takes its leave of us." (*Chartism.*)

[2] "If thou ask again . . . What is to be done? allow me to reply: By thee, for the present, almost nothing. . . . Thou shalt descend into thy inner man, and see if there be any traces of a *soul* there; till then there can be nothing done! . . . Then shall we discern, not one thing, but, in clearer or dimmer sequence, a whole endless host of things that can be done. *Do* the first of these." (*Past and Present*, Book I, chapter iv.)

[3] See particularly *Fors Clavigera*.

2. Work for every one is the natural complement and the necessary corrective of the preceding rule of no idleness and no unemployment. In society as at present organized everybody is not obliged to work, while some individuals are obliged to be idle.[1] This monstrous inequality must be remedied. There would be no difficulty about finding plenty of work for every one if every one did something. Under such a system there would be no unemployment, although there would be more leisure for some.

3. Labour would no longer be paid for according to the exigencies of demand and supply, which tend to reduce manual work to the level of a mere commodity. It would be remunerated according to the eternal principles of justice, which would not of necessity imply an appeal to any written law, but solely to custom, which even now fixes the salaries of doctors, lawyers, and professors. In these professions there are no doubt some individual inequalities, but there is also the norm, and it is a breach of professional etiquette to take less than this. The norm does occasionally find expression in the rules of the association, and in some such way Ruskin would fix not merely a minimum but also a maximum wage. Whatever profession a person follows, whether he be workman, soldier, or merchant, he should always work not merely for profit but for the social good. He must, of course, be suitably rewarded if his position as a worker is to be maintained and the work itself efficiently performed, but it can never be done if gain becomes the end and labour merely the means.

4. The natural sources of wealth—land, mines, and waterfalls— and the means of communication should be nationalized.

5. A social hierarchy graded according to the character of the services rendered should be established. The gradation must be accepted in no intolerant spirit, and must be respected by everybody. Chivalry is as necessary in an industrial as in a military society, and a new crusade against Mammonism[2] should be preached both far and wide.

6. Above all else must come education—not mere instruction. What needs developing above everything is a sense of greatness, a love of beauty, respect for authority, and a passion for self-sacrifice. What

[1] "Why, the four-footed worker has already got all that this two-handed one is clamouring for, and you say it is impossible." (Carlyle, *Past and Present*, chapter iii; and see also *Chartism*, chapter iv.)

[2] This was the ideal which he had in mind in founding the Guild of St George. See an article by Professor Marshall, *The Social Possibilities of Economic Chivalry*, in the *Economic Journal*, March 1907. There is no reference to Ruskin in it, however.

especially need acquiring are the faculties of admiration, of hope, and of love.[1]

Only the last item on the programme seems anywhere near realization, but that by itself would justify our reference to Ruskin's scheme. Not only has the suggestion resulted in the creation of working men's colleges at Oxford and of Ruskin Colleges elsewhere, but it has also given rise to the garden city movement. These new cities are built with the express purpose of relieving the worst features of industrial life, and are so planned as not to interfere in any way either with the beauties of nature or with the health of the citizens.[2]

Ruskin speaks of himself somewhere as an out-and-out communist, but his communism had also a touch of the aristocrat and the æsthete about it which possibly proved a recommendation in English society. Tolstoy is a much more thoroughgoing communist, and is violently opposed to "that low, bestial instinct which men call the right of private property."[3] His cry was "Back to the land," and the practice of coaration; his ideal the mir. He was not anxious to know that every one was working at some trade or other, but he thought every one ought to produce his own food, which is the one inevitable law of human existence. Division of labour, which has been so extravagantly praised by economists, he thought of as a mere machination of the devil enabling men to evade the Divine commandment. At any rate it should only be adopted when the need for it arises, and after consultation with all the parties interested, and not indiscriminately, as is at present the case, with competition, over-production, and crises as the result.[4]

If we are to take Tolstoy's words literally, as he suggested we should take Christ's words, then the society that he dreamt of is very far beyond even the communist ideal. More towns, more commerce, more subdivision of trades, more money, more art for art's sake—such was to be the economic Nirvana of the communists.

[1] When the Christian Socialists in 1854 organized a course of lectures for working men in London Ruskin volunteered to give a few addresses, not on social economics or on history, but on drawing.

[2] One naturally thinks first of such industrial villages as Bournville and Port Sunlight. But in 1903 an entirely new city of this kind was begun at Letchworth, Herts. The idea has undergone a considerable development by a society that owes its inspiration to Ruskin.

[3] *Story of a Horse*, in his *First Stories* (1861).

[4] See a book entitled *Labour*, which consists of the meditations of a *muzhik* called Bondareff upon those words of Genesis, "In the sweat of thy face shalt thou eat bread," followed by a long commentary by Tolstoy.

CHAPTER III   THE SOLIDARISTS

I: THE CAUSES OF THE DEVELOPMENT OF SOLIDARISM

THE word 'solidarity,' formerly a term of exclusively legal import,[1] has during the twentieth century been employed to designate a doctrine which has aroused the greatest enthusiasm—at least in France. Every official speech pays homage to the ideal, every social conference ends with an expression of approval. Those who wish to narrow the scope of industrial warfare as well as those who wish to extend the bounds of commercial freedom base their demands upon 'a sense of social solidarity,' and it has become quite a common experience to find writers on ethics and education who have fallen under its spell. The result is that no history of French economic doctrines can pass it by.[2]

The fundamental idea underlying the doctrine of solidarity, namely, that the human race, taken collectively, forms one single body, of which individuals are the members, is not by any means new. St Paul and Marcus Aurelius among the writers of antiquity, not to mention Menenius Agrippa's well-known apologue, gave expression to this very idea in terms almost identical with those used by the Solidarist school.[3]

Nor was the importance of heredity wholly lost upon the ancients. The hereditary transmission of moral qualities was a doctrine taught with the express sanction of a revealed religion. This doctrine of

---

[1] Etymologically 'solidarity' is a corruption of *solidum*, which was employed by the Roman jurists to signify the obligation incurred by debtors who were each held responsible for the whole amount of a debt. One would naturally expect the French derivative to be *solidité*, which was the term used by the jurists under the old regime, especially by Pothier. *Solidarité* was substituted for it by the editors of the Civil Code.

[2] We should never come to an end if we began to quote passages in which the merits of solidarity are set forth. We must content ourselves with the following, chosen at random:

M. Millerand, at the time Minister of Commerce, in a speech delivered at the opening of the Exposition Universelle in 1900, said: "Science teaches men the true secret of material greatness and of social morality; and all its teaching, in a word, points to solidarity"

M. Deherme, the founder of the People's University movement, says: "The folly of solidarity should be the source of our inspiration, just as the martyrs of old were inspired by the folly of the Cross. The thing that wants doing is to organize democracy." (*La Cooperation des Idées*, June 16, 1900.)

[3] "For as we have many members in one body, and all members have not the same office; so we, being many, are one body in Christ, and every one members one of another." (Romans xii, 4 and 5.)

"As in physical organisms the unity is made up of separate limbs, so among reasoning things the reason is distributed among individuals constituted for unity of co-operation." (Marcus Aurelius, vii, 13; Rendall's translation.)

original sin is perhaps the most terrible example of solidarism that history has to reveal. Turning to profane history, we are reminded of the line of Horace:

Delicta majorum immeritus lues!

We must also remember that it was always something more than a mere theory or dogma. It was a practical rule of conduct, and as such was enjoined by law, exhorted by religion, and enforced by custom, with the result that what was preached was also practised with a thoroughness that is quite unknown at the present day. We have an illustration of this in the collective responsibility of all the members of a family or tribe whenever one of their number was found guilty of some criminal offence. A survival of this pristine custom is the Corsican vendetta of to-day.

Finally, there is that other aspect of solidarity which is based upon division of labour and the consequent necessity of relying upon the co-operation of others for the satisfaction of our wants. The Greek writers had caught a glimpse of this interdependence many centuries before the brilliant exposition of Adam Smith was given to the world.

All the manifold aspects of the doctrine, whether biological, socio-logical, moral, religious, legal or economic, were obviously matters of common knowledge to the writers of antiquity. But each phase of the subject seemed isolated from the rest, and it was not until the middle of the nineteenth century that it dawned upon thinkers that there was possibly something like unity underlying this apparent diversity. It has already been impressed upon us that Pierre Leroux and a few of the disciples of Fourier, as well as Bastiat, had realized something of the value of the doctrine of solidarity and of the appropriateness of the term. But it was reserved for Auguste Comte to appreciate its full possibilities.

> The new philosophy, viewed as a whole, emphasizes the intimacy that exists between the individual and the group in their different relations, so that the conception of social solidarity extending throughout time and embracing the whole of humanity has become a fairly familiar idea.[1]

It is necessary, however, to inquire somewhat more closely into the success of the new doctrine in holding the attention both of the public and of economists. It is possible that the seed would have borne little fruit but for the presence of extraneous circumstances which helped to impress the public with a sense of the importance of these new theories.

[1] *Discours sur L'Esprit positif.* In the *Cours de Philosophie* he frankly pays it this well-deserved compliment: "It is a truly capital idea, and thoroughly modern too."

Nothing has left a deeper impression upon the public or afforded a better illustration of the infinite possibilities of the new doctrine than the study of bacteriology. The prevalence of certain contagious maladies or epidemics had been too terribly prominent in the history of the human race to require any confirmation; but it was something to learn that the most serious diseases and maladies of all kinds were communicated from man to man by means of invisible bacilli. It was now realized that men who were supposed to be dying a natural death were in reality being slowly murdered. It was with something like horror that men learned that the consumptive, the hero of a hundred sentimental tales, every day expectorated sufficient germs to depopulate a whole town. Such 'pathological' solidarity is being more closely interwoven every day by the ever-increasing multiplicity and rapidity of the means of communication. The slow caravan journey across the desert was much more likely to destroy the vitality of the bacilli picked up at Mecca than the much more rapid railway journey of the future, which will speed the pilgrim across the sandy wastes in a few hours. The traveller of former days, who went either afoot or on horseback, ran less risk of infection than his descendant of to-day, who perhaps only spends a few hours in the metropolis.

Sociology has also brought its contingent of facts and theories.[1] The sociologist stakes his reputation upon being able to prove that the fable of the body and its members is no fable at all, but a literal transcription of actual facts, and that the union existing between various members of the social body is as intimate as that which exists between the different parts of the same organism. Such is the fullness and minuteness with which the analogy has been pushed even into obscure points of anatomical detail that it is difficult not to smile at the naïveté of its authors. It is pointed out that so close is the resemblance between the respective functions in the two cases that the term 'circulation' does duty in both spheres, and a comparison is instituted between nutrition and production, reproduction and colonization, and accumulation of fat and capitalism. In Florence during the Middle Ages the bourgeois were spoken of as the fat people, the workers as the small people. The organs also are very similar. Arteries and veins have their counterpart in the railway system, with its network of 'up' and 'down' lines. The nervous system of the one becomes the telegraphic system of the other, with its rapid communication of news and

[1] Social biology dates from the publication of Professor Schäffle's great work *Bau und Leben des sozialen Körpers* (1875–78); possibly from the publication of Rodbertus's work—at any rate, Rodbertus accuses Schäffle of plagiarism. See also Spencer's *Principles of Sociology.* Aristotle had already ventured to say that "an animal is just like a well-ordered city," a proposition that might well be inverted.

sensations. The brain becomes the seat of government, the heart is the bank; and between the two, both in nature and in society, there is a most intimate connexion. Even the white corpuscles have a prototype in the police force, whose duty is to rush to the seat of disorder and to attempt to crush it immediately.

The sociological analogy, ingenious rather than scientific, did not have a very long vogue.[1] But it has at least supplied a few conclusions which are thoroughly well established, and which serve as the basis of the solidarist doctrine. Among these we may mention the following:

(a) That solidarity in the sense of the mutual dependence of members of the same body is a characteristic of all life. Inorganic bodies are incomplete simply because they are mere aggregates. Death is nothing but the dissolution of the mysterious links which bind together the various parts of the living organism, with the result that it relapses into the state of a corpse, in which the various elements become indifferent to the presence of one another and are dissipated through space, to enter into new combinations at the further call of nature.

(b) That solidarity becomes more perfect and intimate with every rise in the biological scale. Completely homogeneous organisms scarcely differ from simple aggregates. They may be cut into sections or have a member removed without suffering much damage. The section cut off will become the centre of independent existence, and the amputated limb will grow again. In the case of some organisms of this kind reproduction takes the form of voluntary or spontaneous segmentation. But in the case of the higher animals the removal of a single organ sometimes involves the death of the whole organism, and almost always imperils the existence of some others.

(c) That a growing differentiation of the parts makes for the greater solidarity of the whole. Where every organ is exactly alike each is generally complete in itself. But where they are different each is just the complement of the other, and none can move or exist independently of the rest.

One has only to think of the treatment meted out to the innovator by primitive tribes to realize the tremendous solidarity of savage society. The 'boycotting' familiar in civilized countries provides a similar example.

Political economy, in addition to an unrivalled exposition of division of labour (which, as we have seen, was not unknown in classical times),

<hr>

[1] In spite of Worms's book, *Organisme et Société*, and Lilienfeld's *Pathologie sociale*.
Herbert Spencer, who was the pioneer of the analogy, had abandoned it; and Auguste Comte, the godfather of sociology, took good care to put sociologists on their guard against the method which he considered irrational.

has adduced several other incidental proofs of solidarity, such as bank failures in London or Paris and short time in the diamond or automobile industry as the result of a crisis in New York or an indifferent rice harvest in India. To take a simpler case, consider how easy it would be for the secretary of an electrical engineers' union to plunge whole cities into darkness. The general strike, the latest bugbear of the bourgeoisie, owes its very existence to the growing sense of solidarity among working men. A sufficient number of workmen have only to make up their minds to remain idle and society has either to give way to their demands or perish.

Add to this the remarkable development which has taken place in the spreading of news and the perfecting of telegraphic communication, by which daily and even hourly men of all nations are swayed with feelings of sorrow or joy at the mere recital of some startling incident which formerly would have influenced but a very small number of people.[1] Such agencies are not unworthy of comparison with those subtle human sympathies which are known by the name of spiritualism or telepathy. Thus from every side, from the limbo of occultism as well as from the full daylight of everyday life, the presence of numberless facts goes to show that each for all and all for each is not a mere maxim or counsel of perfection, but a stern, practical fact. The good or bad fortune of others involves our own well-being or misfortune. The ego, as some one has said, is a social product. These are some of the founts from which the stream of solidarism takes its rise.

But that is not all. The doctrine of solidarity had the good fortune to appear just when people were becoming suspicious of individualist Liberalism, though unwilling to commit themselves either to collectivism or to State Socialism.

In France especially a new political party in process of formation was on the look-out for a cry. The new creed which it desired must needs be of the nature of a *via media* between economic Liberalism on the one hand and socialism on the other. It must repudiate *laissez-faire* equally with the socialization of individual property; it must hold fast to the doctrine of the rights of man and the claims of the individual while recognizing the wisdom of imposing restrictions upon the exercise of those rights in the interests of the whole community. This was the party which called itself Radical then, but later preferred to be known as the Radical-Socialist party. German State Socialism as

---

[1] "The enormous development of steam communication and the spread of the telegraph over the whole globe have caused modern industry to develop from a gigantic starfish, any of whose members might be destroyed without affecting the rest, into a μέγα ζῷον which is convulsed in agony by a slight injury in one part." (Nicholson, *Effects of Machinery on Wages*, p. 117.)

expounded about the same time was closely akin to it. But the German conception of the State as something entirely above party was an idea that was not so easily grasped in France as in Prussia. History in the two countries had not emphasized the same truths. Solidarism, so to speak, is State Socialism in a French garb, but possessed of somewhat better grace in that it does not necessarily imply the coercive intervention of the State, but shows considerable respect for individual liberties.[1]

The new word performed one final service by usurping the functions of the term 'charity,' which no one was anxious to retain because of its religious connexion. The other term, 'fraternity,' which had done duty since the Revolution of 1848, was somewhat antiquated by this time, and charged with a false kind of sentimentalism. The word 'solidarity,' on the contrary, has an imposing, scientific appearance without a trace of ideology. Henceforth every sacrifice which is demanded in the interests of others, whether grants to friendly societies or workmen's associations, cheap dwellings, workmen's pensions, or even parish allowances, is claimed, not in the interests of charity, but of solidarity. And whenever such demand is made the approved formula is always used—it is not a work of charity, but of solidarity, for charity degradeth whereas solidarity lifteth up.

II: THE SOLIDARIST THESIS

The current is seldom very clear when the tributaries are numerous, and the stream must deposit its sediment before it becomes limpid. So here much greater precision was needed if the doctrine was ever to become general in its scope or even popular in its appeal.

[1] It was in 1889, if we mistake not, that the term 'solidarity' was proposed as the title of a new economic school in a lecture entitled *L'École nouvelle*. This lecture was published, along with others, in a small volume entitled *Quatre Écoles d'économie sociale* (1890, Geneva) (*L'École libérale*, by Frédéric Passy; *L'École catholique*, by Claudio Jannet; *L'École socialiste*, by M. Stiegler; and *L'École nouvelle*, by M. Gide). The characteristics of the various schools are summed up as follows: The one is the school of liberty, the other of authority, while the third is the school of equality. Gide then proceeds: "Were I asked to define what I understand by the New School in a single word, I should call it the Solidarity School. Unlike liberty, equality, and fraternity, solidarity is not a very high-sounding word, nor is it a mere ideal. It is just a fact, one of the best-established facts of history and experience, and the most important discovery of our time, and this fact of solidarity is becoming better established every day."

It would have been better, perhaps, to have spoken of a new movement rather than of a new school, seeing the variety of schools, some of them actually opposed to one another, such as the school of Biological Naturalism and the Christian school, the Anarchist school and the State Socialist school, that have adopted solidarity as a part of their creed.

M. Léon Bourgeois, one of the leaders of the Radical-Socialist party, to his eternal credit attempted some such clarification by employing the term 'solidarity,' hitherto so vaguely metaphysical, in a strictly legal fashion to designate a kind of quasi-contract. Quite a sensation was caused by M. Bourgeois's work—a result due alike to the prominent position of the author and the opportune moment at which the book appeared. The greatest enthusiasm was shown for the new doctrine, especially in the universities and among the teachers in 100,000 elementary schools. An equally warm welcome was extended to it in democratic circles, where the desire for some kind of lay morality had by this time become very strong. It becomes necessary, accordingly, to give a more detailed analysis of the theory than was possible within the compass of the small volume in which it was first expounded.[1]

In the first place it must be noted that the doctrine connotes something more than the mere application or extension of the idea of natural solidarity to the social or moral order. On the contrary, it is an attempt to remove some of the anomalies of natural solidarity. A firm belief in the injustice of natural solidarity, or at least a conviction that things are so adjusted that some individuals obtain advantages which they by no means desire while others are burdened with disadvantages which are none of their seeking, lies at the root of the doctrine. There is a demand for intervention in order that those who have benefited by the accidents of natural solidarity should divide the spoils with those who have been less fortunate in drawing prizes in the lottery of life. It is for Justice to restore the balance and correct the abnormalities which a fickle sister has created. Just as it has been seen that man may utilize the forces of nature, against which he formerly was wont to struggle, to further his own ends, so solidarity puts forth a claim for the co-operation of Justice to correct the anomalies begotten

---

[1] M. Léon Bourgeois's *La Solidarité* appeared originally as a series of articles contributed to the *Nouvelle Revue* in 1896. These were published in book form in the following year. The different aspects of the question have been dealt with in a series of lectures delivered by various authors at the École des Hautes Études sociales under the presidency of M. Bourgeois himself, and published in a volume entitled *Essai d'une Philosophie de la solidarité* (1902). An association for the propagation of the new ideas was founded in 1895 under the name of La Société d'Éducation sociale. An International Congress was called together on the occasion of the 1900 Exposition, but since then the signs of activity have been few.

French books and articles dealing with the subject are plentiful enough. We can only mention *La Solidarité sociale et ses Nouvelles formules*, by M. d'Eichthal (1903); the annual report of L'Académie des Sciences morales et politiques for 1903; M. Bouglé's book *Le Solidarisme* (1907); and Fleurant's *La Solidarité* (1907). There is hardly a manual for teachers published which does not contain a chapter devoted to this question.

of brute strength, believing that only in this way is real advance possible or any kind of improvement even remotely attainable.

Natural solidarity[1] tells us that as a result of the division of labour, of the influence of heredity, and of a thousand other causes which have just been described, every man owes either to his forebears or his contemporaries the best part of what he has, and even of what he himself is. As Auguste Comte has put it, "We are born burdened with all manner of social obligations." Nor is it an uncommon thing to meet with the word 'debt' or 'obligation' in the articles of the French Constitution. In the Constitution of 1793, for example, the duty of public assistance is spoken of as a sacred debt. But the term was loosely employed in the sense of *noblesse oblige* or *richesse oblige*, every individual being left free to carry out the obligation as best he could in accordance with the dictates of his own conscience. It is necessary, however, to transform the duty into a real debt, to give it a legal status, and when not voluntarily performed a legal sanction as well. If we are anxious to know exactly how this is to be done we have only to turn to Articles 1371-81 of the Civil Code, where in the chapter dealing with quasi-contracts we shall come across a section headed "Of Non-conventional Contracts."

The title would seem to imply the validity of debts not explicitly contracted—that is to say, the existence of obligations which have not involved any volitional undertaking on the part of either party concerned. The first case, that of injury inflicted upon others, whether wilfully or not, is referred to as quasi-misdemeanour, and other instances mentioned in the section are spoken of as quasi-contracts. Illustrations, which are plentiful enough, include payments made when not really due, attention to the business of another without any definite mandate authorizing such interference, the obligation of the inheritor of property to pay off debts incurred by the previous owner, the recognition of the common interest which people living in the same neighbourhood possess, and which also exists between those who own property and those who lease it, between those who use it and those who inherit it.

Wherever anything of the nature of a quasi-contract exists we may be tolerably certain that it is the product of *de facto* or natural solidarity.

---

[1] "The fact that such a thing as natural solidarity exists should not be taken to imply that it must necessarily be just. Justice can never be realized unless the laws of solidarity are first observed; but once these have been established, their effects must be modified to make them conform to the requirements of justice. The actual and the ideal should never be confused; they are the direct contraries of one another. But it is absolutely necessary that the first should be established before we can realize the moral necessity for the other." (Bourgeois, *Philosophie de la Solidarité*, pp. 13, 17.)

Such solidarity may take its rise in the mere fact of propinquity or the mere feeling of neighbourliness; but more often than not it involves a measure of control over the lives of others, which is one of the outstanding features of a regime of division of labour. Then follow the familiar phenomena of fortunes amassed to the detriment of others through the acquisition of unearned increment and the operation of the laws of inheritance—the source of so many inequalities. Nor must we forget the prejudicial effect of quasi-misdemeanour upon the fortunes of others. The result is that the whole of society seems built, if not upon an original explicit contract, as Rousseau imagined, at least upon a quasi-contract; and seeing that this quasi-contract receives the tacit submission of the parties concerned, there is no reason why it should not be legally binding as well.

Now the existence of a debt implies that some one must pay it, and the next question is to determine who that some one ought to be.

Obviously it can only be those who have benefited by the existence of natural solidarity—all those who have amassed a fortune, but whose fortune would be still to make but for the co-operation of a thousand collaborators, both past and present. Such individuals have already drawn more than their share and have a balance to make up on the debit account. This debt should certainly be paid. It is all the better if it is done voluntarily, as an act of liberality arising out of goodness of heart—*quia bonus*, as the Gospel narrative puts it, of the rich good man. But this is hardly probable. Most people will pay just when they are obliged to; but such people have no right to consider themselves free, and no claim to the free disposal of their goods until they have acquitted themselves honourably.[1] Individual property will be respected and free when every social debt which it involves has been adequately discharged, and not before then.[2] Until this is done it is useless to speak of the existence of competition.

The next question is to dermine who is to receive payment. Payment ought to be made to those who, instead of benefiting by the existence of natural solidarity, have suffered loss through its operation —the disinherited, as they are rightly called.[3] All those who have

---

[1] "There are some debts which are hardly noticed at all, but which ought to be paid all the same." (Bourgeois, *Philosophie de la Solidarité*, p. 60.) "There is a real claim where we thought there was only a moral obligation, and a debt where we thought there was only a sacrifice." As the Gospel says: "Unto whomsoever much is given, of him shall be much required." (Luke xii, 48.) "So that ye come behind in no gift." (1 Corinthians i, 7.)

[2] "No man is free as long as he is in debt. He becomes free the moment he pays off that debt. The doctrine of solidarity is just the corrective of the theories of private property and individual liberty." (Bourgeois, *op. cit.*, p. 45.)

[3] M. Bourgeois also points out that just as our ancestors were indebted to us, so

THE SOLIDARISTS

not received a fair share of the total wealth produced by the co-
operation of all naturally find themselves in the position of creditors.
It is not easy to name them, perhaps, but the State can reach them a
helping hand in a thousand different ways. State action of this kind
was formerly spoken of as public assistance; nowadays it is termed
solidarity or mutual insurance.

The payment may take the form either of a voluntary contribution
to help some solidarist effort or other, or of an obligatory contribution
levied by the State. Some advocate progressive taxation, for if it be true
that profits tend to grow progressively in proportion as an increase in
the variety and strength of the means of production takes place, why
not a progressive tax as well?[1] Besides, the tax would be of a semi-
sacred character, because it would mean the discharging of an important social debt. Nor is there anything very extravagant in the demand
that the State should see that every one makes a contribution in proportion to his ability, seeing that the natural function of the State is
to be the guardian of contracts.[2]

It is still more difficult to assess the rate of payment. The conditions
under which payment would be made, says M. Bourgeois, would be
such as the associates themselves would have adopted had they been
free to discuss the terms of their engagement. In other words, everything must be regulated as if society were the result of an express
convention, or rather of a retroactive contract mutually agreed upon.
The difficulty is to determine the conditions which individual associates would demand as the price of their adhesion to the terms of the
contract. We shall have to imagine what they would demand were
they able to make fresh terms.

But we are not much farther ahead after all, for the individual himself knows nothing at all about it. Renouncing the attempt to solve
the insoluble, one has to fix some kind of minimum claim which the
disinherited may reasonably expect to see fulfilled. Such a minimum
claim would be a guarantee against the ordinary risks of life. Society
would become a kind of association for mutual insurance, with the
good and bad fortune spread out equally over everybody.[3]

---

are we indebted to those that shall come after us. But that is a different thing, and
the theory does not seem very sound on this point. It is strange to think that creditors
long since dead should transfer the debt which was owing to them to the credit of
generations yet unborn!

[1] Bourgeois, op. cit., p. 94.

[2] Even the texts of the Civil Code seem to point to some such theory. Article 1370,
in addition to the cases of quasi-contract and quasi-misdemeanour of which it speaks,
also mentions 'law' as a general cause of obligation.

[3] "Wherever it is impossible to fix definitely the value of the personal effort put

THE SOLIDARIST THESIS 555

But a quasi-contract is something very different from this. Contracts and quasi-contracts are based upon the giving and receiving of equivalent values, *do ut des*, whereas mutual insurance is a kind of substitute for direct liability. A contract is essentially individualistic—mutualism is primarily socialistic.

This idea of a quasi-contract contributed not a little to the success of M. Bourgeois's theory, but it makes no vital contribution to the doctrine itself, and he might very easily have omitted it altogether.[1] It is nothing better than an artifice, almost a logomachy, invented for the express purpose of affording some kind of justification for demanding a legal contribution by treating it as an implicit or retroactive contract. It is more of a concession to individual liberty than anything else. A taxpayer grumbles at a tax which goes to provide pensions for the old, but it is pointed out to him that the contribution is owing from him in virtue not of an explicit agreement, perhaps, but at least of a quasi-agreement.

But what useful purpose can be served by such ironical subterfuge? If it can be shown that owing to inferior moral education the law must have the making of a conscience for those who have none, and must enforce a certain minimum of social duties which appear necessary for the preservation of life and the perpetuation of social amenities, what is that but a form of State Socialism? If it is pointed out, on the other hand, that moral progress consists in transforming debts into duties[2] rather than *vice versa*, one readily realizes that it is best to multiply the number of free institutions of a solidarist complexion, such as mutual aid and co-operative societies, trade unions, etc.

---

forth by a single individual, as in the case of a quasi-contract—that is, whenever it is impossible to determine the value of the debt on the one ha d or the credit on the other—*the best plan is to pool those risks and advantages*. This would mean that none would know who is really bearing the risk or who is reaping the advantages, the risks being shared by everybody and the advantages being thrown open to every one." (Bourgeois, *op. cit.*, p. 81.)

The end of the quotation apparently contradicts the statement we have italicized, in which he speaks of pooling risks and advantages. With regard to the latter, it is enough, apparently, to secure equal opportunity. It is not very obvious why the principle should be so rigidly enforced in the one case and so reluctantly in the other. If the principle of solidarity holds me responsible for the degradation of the drunkard in the one case, is there any reason why I should not be allowed to share in the good fortune of the lucky speculator in another? Is it because the logical application of this principle would directly lead to communism?

[1] One should add that the word "quasi-contract" is not so frequently used by M. Bourgeois as it is by his disciples. As in many another instance, the disciples have outdone the master. In his *Philosophie de la Solidarité* he scarcely uses the term at all, but seems to prefer to speak of mutualization.

[2] Such seems to be the ideal of Guyau, the philosopher, in his charming volume, *Esquisse d'une Morale sans Obligation ni Sanction*.

Another objective which the quasi-contract theory had in view was to supply the debtor with a kind of guarantee that nothing would be required of him beyond the exact equivalent of his debt.[1] But, as we have already noted, it would be a somewhat illusory guarantee, because it is almost impossible to determine the amount of the debt in the first place. Since the amount of this debt is in some way to be fixed by law it may be well to begin with it.

Should the legislator find himself driven to accept M. Bourgeois's valuation, the demands made upon the taxpayer will not be so exorbitant after all. The whole mass of obligations is summed up under three heads:

1. Free education for all classes of the community. Intellectual capital more than any other kind of capital is a collective good, and should never be other than common property, upon which every one may draw whenever he wishes. A necessary corollary would be a shorter working day.

2. A minimum of the means of existence for everybody. It is difficult to imagine a retroactive contract which refuses to grant men the right to live. Regarded in this light, the 'guarantism' of Sismondi and Fourier, the 'right to work' of Louis Blanc and Considérant, gain new significance and throb with fresh vitality.

3. Insurance against the risks of life, which, being fortuitous, are escaped by none. We know the promptness with which the feeling of kinship is aroused whenever one of these accidents happens on a scale somewhat larger than usual and assumes the proportions of a catastrophe. Why should it be otherwise when a single individual falls a victim to the fickleness of fate?

If M. Bourgeois has given his theory a distinctly politico-legal bias, M. Durkheim has taken good care to approach the question from the standpoint of moralist and sociologist.

M. Durkheim draws a distinction between two kinds of solidarities. The first of these, which he regards as a quite inferior type, depends upon external resemblances, and is of a purely mechanical character, like the cohesion of atoms in a physical body. The other, which consists of a union of dissimilars, is the result of division of labour, and of such is the union between the various members of the human body. Durkheim regards this kind of unity as of immense significance, not so much because of its economic consequence as of its important moral results,

---

[1] "The only thing that justice demands is the payment of debt; beyond that we have no right to impose any obligation whatsoever." (Bourgeois, *op. cit.*, pp. 45 and 56.)

"which might even supply the basis of a new moral order." Seeing that individuals really follow divergent paths, the struggle for existence cannot be quite so keen as it is generally supposed to be,[1] and this differentiation between the individual and the mass enables the former to dissociate himself from the collective conscience. Durkheim's desire was to see the new ethic developed by the professional associations; hence the important role which trade unionism holds in his philosophy.

Without disputing the validity of the distinction thus made, we may be allowed to question the advisability of treating one kind of solidarity with such contempt and of showing such enthusiasm for the other. Our hope is that the future lies with the former kind. For what is the object of evolution if it is not to make what seems similar really alike? The world is not merely marching in the direction of greater differentiation; it is also moving towards a deeper unity. This seems a well-established fact, at least so far as the physical world is concerned. Mountains are brought low and the hollow places filled. Heat is dissipated throughout space, causing minute gradations of temperature, and the establishment of a kind of final equilibrium.[2] The same law applies to human beings. Differences of caste, of rank, of manners and customs, of language and measurements, are everywhere being obliterated. And it seems by this time a tolerably well-established fact that the wars of the past were wars between strangers—strangers in race or religion, in culture or education—and consequently it was between people who were dissimilar that they appeared most violent. Therefore the march towards unity also represents a movement in the direction of peace.[3]

Such a conception of solidarity seems more akin to the ideal which we have formed respecting it, and has by far the greatest moral value; for if I am to be responsible for the evil that has befallen another, or

[1] "Thanks to this fact, rivals need not seek to eliminate one another, but may well be content to exist side by side. Specialization is undertaken, our author thinks, not with the idea of producing more, as the economists seem to teach, but merely with a view to enabling us to exist under the new conditions of life which await us." (*Division du Travail.*)

[2] "Every brook that flows, every lamp that burns, every word spoken, every gesture made, betokens a movement in the direction of the greater uniformity of the universe." (Lalande, *La Dissolution.*)

[3] This is the sense in which solidarity has been understood by the Lausanne philosopher Charles Secrétan, in his book *La Civilisation et la Croyance*, and the same point of view has been adopted by M. Alfred Fouillée. "Solidarity," writes Fouillée, "has all the practical value of an ideal force. The recognition of the profound identity which pervades humanity and the adoption of an ideal of perfect unity as the supreme object of rational desire must assume the form of a duty in the eyes of every human being. We should anticipate the unity of the human race, which is as yet far from being realized, and which will never be perfect perhaps, by acting as if we were already one." (*Revue des Deux Mondes*, July 15, 1901.)

to be considered an accomplice in the evil which he has done, that can only be just in proportion to the extent to which that other is also myself.[1] The practical result will be a preference for such modes of association as will group men together according to some general characteristic—a co-operative association rather than a trade union; for while the interest of the latter is in opposition both to that of the producer and to that of the public, the method of association in the former case is the most general imaginable, for every one at some time or other must be regarded as a consumer.

III: THE PRACTICAL APPLICATION OF SOLIDARIST DOCTRINES[2]

There is no such thing as a Solidarist school in the sense in which we speak of a Historical, a Liberal, or a Marxian school. Solidarity is a banner borne aloft by more than one school, and a philosophy that serves to justify aims that are occasionally divergent. As we have already had occasion to point out, the solidarists are more of a political party than a doctrinal school, and their best work has been done in association with the Radical-Socialist party. Behind them is the State Socialist or 'interventionist' school. It has been suggested that the social legislation of the twentieth century, such as the regulations governing the conditions of labour, factory and general hygiene, insurance against accidents and old age, State aid for the aged and the disabled,[3] the establishment of societies for mutual credit, rural banks

[1] Auguste Comte, in his usual authoritative manner, declared that solidarity rests upon the fact that men can represent one another, and consequently may be held responsible for one another.

[2] See a collection of addresses by various authors published under the title of *Les Applications sociales de la Solidarité* (1904).

[3] These laws of public assistance are among the most remarkable practical manifestations of the solidarist movement. They marked a new departure in French public life, and until their appearance relief, whether given by the State, the department, or the commune, was purely optional (except in a few isolated cases, such as in that of waifs and strays). To mention only the principal ones in France, the law of July 15, 1893, made relief in the form of medical attendance of all destitute invalids obligatory upon the communes. The law of July 14, 1905, extended a similar benefit to all invalids and to all persons over seventy years of age in the form of pensions varying in amount from 60 to 240 francs per annum (360 in Paris). Finally, the law of April 5, 1910, secures a pension to all workmen at the age of sixty, the charge being divided between the State, the employers, and the workmen themselves. It is a kind of payment made by the members of the present generation to the survivors of a past one. This relief is clearly of the nature of a social debt, and justifies us in treating it as the outcome of a quasi-contract, for on the one hand it constitutes an obligation fixed by law on the part of the commune, the department, or the State, as the case may be— an obligation which they cannot escape—and on the other hand a right on the part of the beneficiary, as in the case of a creditor in an action for the recovery of debt.

and cheap cottages, and school clinics, all of which are the direct outcome of preaching solidarity, as well as the grants in aid of these
objects which are paid out of the progressive taxation levied upon
inherited wealth or extraordinary incomes of such as have plucked
the fruit from the tree of civilization to the deprivation of those who
caused that fruit to grow, should be known as "the laws of social
solidarity."

Nor are workmen the only class who are likely to benefit by the
adoption of this principle. The Protectionist or Nationalist party
claims to be the party of solidarity, as well as the mutualists, who
employ the term oftener than anyone else. When the taxpayer complains about the taxes which he has to pay in order to grant a bounty
to certain proprietors or manufacturers, and the consumer grumbles
because the levying of import duties results in increasing his cost of
living, the reply is that the spirit of solidarity demands that preference
should be given to their own kith and kin.[1]

Fiscal reform, with its twofold attribute of a progressive tax at one
end of the scale and total exemption at the other, also claims to be
solidarist. Progressive taxation is justified on the ground that those
who have made their fortunes are the debtors of society, while exemption at the other end is only fair, seeing that the disinherited have
nothing to give, but have already a strong claim upon society.

However closely akin to State Socialism practical solidarism may
appear, the fact that the latter may achieve its results merely by means
of associationism is sufficient to distinguish it from the former. The
result is that it gave quite a fresh impetus to the associative movement. Syndicalists, mutualists, and co-operators vie with one another
in their anxiety to swear allegiance to the principle of free solidarism
as distinct from the forced solidarism of the State Socialists.[2] It is not
that they fail to recognize the necessity for the latter and its superiority
over free competition, but on moral grounds they think that such
forced solidarism is even inferior to competition. It is imperative,
however, that we should make some distinction between such

[1] A very curious application of this national solidarity has come to light since the
beginning of this century. Formerly the French Government would only sanction
foreign loans if the borrowing country promised to apply some part of its funds to
French industry. That meant linking the *rentier* and the French manufacturers by a
forced kind of solidarity, the first being unwilling to lend money unless that money
in some way returned to the second person for goods purchased. This is where the
claim of the workers, who justly demand a minimum wage, comes in.

[2] The doctrine of quasi-contract might lead to the one conclusion as well as to the
other. M. Bourgeois himself seems to incline rather in the direction of associationism.
"The Radical party has a social doctrine, a doctrine that might be summed up in
one word—association." (Preface to M. Buisson's *La Politique radicale*.)

heterogeneous elements as enter into the composition of the solidarist party.

The syndicalists, who come first, will hear of nothing except trade unionism, which is to become the basis of a new economic organization and a new kind of ethics. The sense of solidarity is in this case very strong, because the *syndicat* poses as the sworn foe of the bourgeoisie. Nothing develops this sense like a struggle, and the struggle becomes a means of discipline. The attempts made by the trade unionists to enforce this solidarity, not only upon their own members, but also upon workmen who are unwilling to enrol themselves as members of the union, the antagonism shown for the *jaunes*, and the advent of the solidarist or sympathetic strike, constitute one of the most interesting aspects of the syndicalist movement.

Next came the mutualists, who are loudest and most persistent in their appeal to solidarity.[1] It is not difficult to understand this when we realize the battle which they wage against the ills of life—invalidity, old age, poverty, and death. It is just here that men most feel the need of sticking together. But if we are to judge by the sacrifices which they make, the sense of solidarity among the mutualists themselves is not very great. They are loud in their demands that the State or the commune, or even voluntary subscribers, should complete what they have begun,[2] and that the State should delegate to them the task of establishing workmen's pensions and of dispensing State aid. Containing as they do some members of the middle classes as well as employees, they show no pronounced revolutionary leanings, nor have they even a plan of social reorganization.

Co-operation, on account of its scope and the variety of its aims, has some claim to be regarded as in a measure a realization of the ideals of solidarism. But co-operation presents a twofold aspect with different programmes and aims that are not always easily reconcilable. The oldest movements in which the fraternal tradition of 1848 may

[1] "The Apotheosis of Solidarity," printed in large type, appeared at one time as a headline in one of the French morning papers. The reference was to a banquet of 30,000 mutualists.

[2] Mutualists are so taken up with the idea of solidarity that they indignantly protest if any of their number happens to make use of the term 'beneficence' or 'charity.' "Every one has a right to demand his own," they say: that is clearly Bourgeois's thesis. On the other hand, their journal, *L'Avenir de la Mutualité*, for February 1909 claims that societies for mutual help have a right to organize tombolas and lotteries, and they base their case upon the law of May 21, 1836, which reserves the right of lottery to "efforts of an entirely charitable character." In order to defend its claim, *L'Avenir de la Mutualité* does not hesitate to affirm that the societies for mutual help "recognize the existence of an element of benevolence which is not exactly mutual and which is rightly connected with the superior modern principle of social solidarity, but which none the less justifies the application of the law of 1836."

still be viewed in all its pristine vigour are the producers' associations, of which we have already spoken. Their ideal is to emancipate the worker by setting up a kind of industrial republic, and they make a practical beginning with 'guarantism,' which Sismondi expected the masters to give and which Fourier thought would naturally follow the establishment of the Phalanstère.[1] But however rosy the prospects may be they can never affect more than a very small proportion of the working classes.

Distributive societies have met with a greater measure of success. Their membership is reckoned by the million, and in some towns in England, Germany, and Switzerland the members actually comprise the majority of the population. Such is the colossal magnitude of the 'wholesale' that it might even alter the whole character of commercial organization—that is, if we are to judge not merely by the record of its transactions, but also by the feeling of awe which it inspires in the minds of merchants in all countries, who are already claiming the protection of their respective Governments. Although the number of such societies increased in France, they never had quite the same practical influence there, simply because they have been lacking in the true spirit of solidarity. Curiously enough, these French co-operators have formulated a most ambitious programme of social reform which is wholly inspired by the experience of the Rochdale Pioneers.[2]

[1] "Solidarity is just an empty word if it is not supported by special organisms which can render it effective. This is why workmen's associations have deemed it necessary to establish what they call 'guarantism.' . . .

"The most unmistakable manifestation of solidarity consists in the employment of a part of the wealth produced by labour in order to repair the poverty caused by the deficient organization of labour, which leaves the worker and his family liable to the acutest suffering whenever illness, old age, or misfortune crosses their paths." (Programme on the cover of a journal known as *L'Association ouvrière*, the organ of the producers' associations.)

[2] This co-operatist programme is generally known in France as that of the École de Nîmes. Really it is a development of the suggestions thrown out by the Rochdale Pioneers in 1844. Renard, who gives it a place in his *Systèmes socialistes*, considers that it is a little indefinite. It seems to us, on the other hand, to be about as precise as any of the other socialist systems that attempt to envisage the future; and it has this advantage, that its prophecies were realized in a fashion that is most unmistakable. See a brief résumé of the programme in a lecture by Gide on the occasion of the centenary of the French Revolution, published in the volume entitled *Co-opération* (*Des Transformations que la Co-opération est appelée à réaliser dans l'Ordre économique*).

The task of reorganizing society belongs, not to the producers, but to the consumers, for while the former are inspired by the co-operative spirit, the latter are imbued with enthusiasm for the general well-being. Consumers have only to unite and all their wants are satisfied just in the way they desire, for they can either buy directly from the producers all that they need, or they can, when they have become sufficiently rich and powerful, produce for themselves in their own factories and on their own lands. This would mean the abolition of all profits, those of middlemen and manufacturers alike. The societies would retain only as much as would be

The gospel of solidarity has even penetrated into the rural districts, and although the temperament of the peasant is strongly individualistic it is already beginning to bear fruit in the shape of numerous associations of various kinds. The most interesting of these is the mutual credit society, which implies collective responsibility for social debts.[1]

This by no means exhausts the practical consequences of the solidarist ideal. One notable result which has already shown itself is a serious modification of the whole conception of the rights and attributes of private property. The old formula in which property was spoken of as a social trust rather than as a strictly individualistic right as the *dominium ex jure Quiritium*, but which until quite recently was

---

necessary for the further extension of the movement, returning all the rest to the consumers in proportion to the amount of their purchases. We have already had occasion to note how this idea of the abolition of profits had haunted John Stuart Mill, and how it seemed linked with an entirely new phase of social evolution, to which he gave the name of the "stationary State." We have also witnessed the Hedonists' arrival at exactly the same conclusion, though along a directly opposite path, namely, that of absolutely free competition.

We must not lose sight of the fact that this revolution is accomplished without affecting the foundations of the social order—property, inheritance, interest, etc.— and without having recourse to any measure of expropriation save such as naturally results from the free play of present economic laws. Co-operators have no desire to interfere with accumulated capital, their aim being merely to form new capital which shall render the old useless. If existing capital is merely accumulated profits made out of labour, why should not labour itself make a profit, and this time keep it for its own use?

Complaints have been made that a system of this kind, even if it were realized, would not result in the abolition of the wage-earner, seeing that the workers would still be employed, the only difference being that their employer would be a society instead of an individual. The reply is that a person who works for a society of which he himself is a member is very near to being his own master.

Moreover, has anyone a right to raise this objection? The upholder of the present economic order certainly has not when we remember that he considers the wage contract to be the definite type of pure contract. Neither are the collectivists entitled to make it, for under their system everybody would be a civil servant. Hence the only persons who are really justified in making this criticism are those who believe that the future will see an increase in the number of independent proprietors. The reply that we would make to them is this: The only hope of seeing this realized— which is also the ideal of some co-operators—is to set up producers' associations under the control and protection of consumers' societies. In fact, a regime of federated co-operative societies is not incompatible with the maintenance of a certain amount of autonomous production, thanks to various considerations which need not be detailed here.

[1] In France this rule of solidarity has only been adopted by a Catholic group of credit societies known as the Union Durand. It may be practised by a few other societies there, but it is quite obviously the exception, whereas in some German societies and in Italian and Swiss associations the rule is always followed—another proof that although the idea is French in origin we must look elsewhere for practical applications

nothing more than a mere metaphor, becomes a reality under the inspiration of this new doctrine of solidarity. Once it is realized that property is simply the result of the unconscious co-operation of a large number of causes, most of which are impersonal, the tendency will be to eliminate it altogether or to adapt it more and more to collective ends. Alfred Fouillée,[1] a French philosopher, aptly put this aspect of the question when he spoke of social co-proprietorship being grafted on to individual property.

The modifications introduced into the study of jurisprudence by emphasizing its solidarist aspect are occasionally spoken of as "juridical socialism," a term that is not very clear, to say the least. The jurists who have undertaken the task of applying this new principle to the study of jurisprudence have not merely adopted the quasi-contract theory as the basis of their work of reconstruction, but have also refused to recognize any absolute rights of property; in other words, they claim that the proprietor has other responsibilities besides the mere exercise of those rights (*qui suo jure utitur neminem lædere videtur*).

Instead of emphasizing the new principle known as the "abuse of rights," they prefer to claim the complete subjection of all private rights to the public weal. They point to a thousand instances in which a proprietor ought to be held responsible, though through no fault of his own, for the results following from the discharge of his economic duties.[2] The existence of such a thing as an acquired right is also denied, chiefly on the ground that fictitious rights of this kind bar the way to progress by setting up a claim for indemnity.[3]

---

[1] *La Propriété sociale et la Démocratie.*

[2] The result is that masters are nowadays held responsible whenever a workman meets with an accident, or falls ill even. They are also liable to damages whenever they pay off their men. Owners of urban property are no longer allowed to build according to their fancy, and any property set up in contravention of the sanitary regulations is immediately demolished. Further progress along these lines would lead to juridical socialism. See *Les Transformations du droit civil*, by Charmont, and *Le droit social et le droit individuel*, by Duguit.

[3] Anton Menger, of Vienna, is the protagonist of this view. See his book *Das bürgerliche Recht und die besitzlosen Volksklassen* (1890). Another of his works, *Das auf den vollen Arbeitsertrag*, has been translated into English and contains a valuable preface by Professor Foxwell. Menger maintains that at the basis of the economic order are three fundamental rights which may be compared with the political demands put forward in the Declaration of the Rights of Man. These rights are: (1) the right to the whole produce of labour, (2) the right to work , (3) the right to exist—all of which claims were put forward by Considérant, Louis Blanc, and Proudhon, the French socialists of 1848. See also Lassalle's book *Das System der erworbenen Rechte*. Mention should also be made of Emmanuel Lévy, who has published several articles of this kind, especially the pamphlet entitled *Capital et Travail.*

IV: CRITICISM

Notwithstanding the popularity of the term 'solidarity' and the numerous attempts made to give effect to the doctrine of which we have just given a summary account, it would be a mistake to imagine that the theory met with sympathy everywhere. On the contrary, it was subjected to the liveliest criticism, especially by the Liberal economists.

It is not that the Liberals deny the existence of solidarity or disapprove of the results which follow from its operation. The discovery of the law of solidarity under the familiar aspect of division of labour and exchange constitutes a part of their own title to fame, and extravagant were the eulogiums which they bestowed upon its working.

They still, however, hold firmly to the belief that economic solidarity is quite sufficient, and that it is also the best imaginable, despite the fact that it may be our duty to organize it afresh. Is it possible to improve upon a system of division of functions which gives every one, every day of his life, the equivalent of the service which he has rendered to society? Bastiat in his fable *The Blind and the Paralytic* compares this distribution of social effort to an understanding between two such persons, whereby the blind does the walking and the maimed indicates the direction.

Members of this school were strongly of the opinion that it was quite enough to let this principle of each for all work itself out under the pressure of competition. And as a matter of fact is it not to the interest of the producer to consult the wants and tastes and even the fancies of the public? Altruism pursued in this spirit, as it well might be, manifests itself as an incessant desire to satisfy the wants of others, and even to live for others. It loses none of its force by becoming, instead of a mere ideal, a professional necessity which no producer can afford to neglect without running the risk of failure.[1] And it is not only between producers and consumers, but also between capital and labour, that such solidarity exists. Neither can produce without the other, and the interest of both is to have as large a produce as possible. A similar kind of solidarity exists among nations. The richer our neighbours are the better chance of our finding an outlet for our products.

[1] "The producer is concerned about the well-being of his clients at every moment. His sympathies are wide enough to include the whole of humanity. The merchant and the transport agent are always on the look-out for what will prove most advantageous to those for whom they are working, as well as for new clients—that is, for more persons to whom they can be of service." These words, which might have been written by Bastiat, are taken from a small yet curious volume published by Yves Guyot, and entitled *La Morale de la Concurrence*.

Moreover, none of these *solidarités* but is essentially just, since every one receives the exact equivalent of what he gives. What can the new doctrine of solidarity add to this, unless it be, perhaps, an element of pure parasitism?[1]

For what is the essence of the new doctrine if it is not that those members of society who are possessed of a certain superiority of position, either material or intellectual (which is very often the result of the greater contribution which they have made to the material or intellectual capital of society), by a bold inversion of their material positions should find themselves treated as the debtors of such as have not succeeded? The natural result is that there are springing up everywhere in society whole classes who are living upon the claims of solidarity, just as their predecessors lived upon the claims of Christian charity. More daring than their forebears, they have none of the humility of the ordinary beggar, but boldly demand their due; not for the love of God, as was wont with the true mendicant, but in the name of some quasi-contract, with a policeman within hailing distance lest the debtor should not acquit himself in a sufficiently graceful fashion. Hence the swarm of pensioners and semi-invalids, of unemployed who patronize the relief works, and of victims of accidents more or less real, of parents who have their children reared for nothing, of manufacturers and proprietors who make a profit directly or indirectly out of the existence of public rights, and of public servants who in the name of professional solidarity trample national solidarity underfoot and sacrifice the interests of both taxpayer and consumer.

The economists have never held the doctrine that commutative justice by itself—mere *do ut des*—is enough. Adjacent to the realm of justice lies the domain of charity. But to annex this zone to the dominion of justice and to claim solidarity as a justification seems utter futility.

There is no avoiding this dilemma. Either they get the equivalent of what they give, which is the case under a system of free exchange, or they do not—in which case they must be getting either more or less. In other words, they are either parasites or destitutes—a case of exploitation or of charity.

It is further pointed out that the whole trend of evolution appears to

[1] "Solidarity serves as a pretext for those people who want to enjoy the fruits of the labour of others without taking a part in such labours themselves, and for politicians who want to win adherents to their cause; it is just a new name for an unhealthy kind of egoism." (Vilfredo Pareto, *Le Péril socialiste*, in the *Journal des Économistes*, May 15, 1900.)

"The solidarist theories would simply greatly increase the number and incapacity of the unemployable." (Demolins, *La Supériorité des Anglo-Saxons*.)

give no countenance to this doctrine of solidarity, and that consequently it is of the nature of a retrograde movement. Even in the biological realm we come across what looks like a persistent effort to attain independence or autonomy, a struggle on the part of the individual to free himself from the trammels of his descent.[1] Such must be the explanation of man's heroic efforts to leave the earth and rise towards the skies, and the consequent exultation which the aviator feels when he finds that he has overcome the force of gravity and broken the last link which bound man to his mother earth. Turning to criminal law, we are met with similar considerations there. The collective responsibility of the whole family or tribe seemed quite just to the primitive mind, and the sons of the Atridæ and the descendants of Adam suffered with hardly a murmur for the sins committed by their parents.[2] But to us the doctrine is simply revolting. Whenever such penalties are demanded by nature we can only submit with the best grace that we can command. We are reluctantly bound to admit that the innocent does suffer for the faults of others—that the child perishes because the parent was a drunkard. But we, at any rate, regard such things as evil, and valiantly struggle against them. We are not much given to raising altars to Eumenides. When solidarity breeds contamination we seek to counteract it by a strict individualism that immunes. The innumerable fetters that had been riveted together by the old co-operative regime were ruthlessly torn off by the French Revolution. Why attempt to forge new chains by giving to each individual a hypothetical claim upon his fellows?

The moralists in their turn have also raised objections. They want to know what new principle of morality solidarity professes to teach. When it has been shown that my neighbour's illness may easily compass my own death, what new feeling will the mere proving of this beget in me? Will it be love? Is it not much more likely to reveal itself as a desire to keep him as far from me as possible—to get rid of him altogether like a plague-stricken rat, or at least to see that he is locked up in some sanatorium or other? I may perhaps be found more

[1] "The distinctive feature of evolution seems to be the growing tendency among organisms to attain to a position of independence by acquiring a certain degree of specialized skill." (De Launay, *L'Histoire de la Terre.*) The crystal's action, says de Launay, in grouping itself in the form of a polyhedron is an expression of independence as well as a means of defence. The crystal is simply the earliest individual to break away from its environment. The animal form in the ocean depths that carries in its own body the essentials of a new environment marks a second step.

[2] "The primitive era was an age of solidarity. Crime was no individual thing then, and that the innocent should suffer for the sake of the guilty seemed a part of the order of things. It is only in an age of reflection that such dogmas appear absurd." (Renan, *Avenir de la Science,* p. 307.)

willing to contribute towards the upkeep of the sanatorium, but the dominant motive will be fear, or self-interest, if that word seems preferable.[1]

Thus solidarity, while it does not seem to contain any new doctrine of love, tends to weaken and to suppress the sense of responsibility by treating society as a whole, or at least the social environment, as the source of our errors, our vices and crimes. Individual responsibility, however, is the very basis of morality.

Such are the criticisms preferred by individualist economists. It would be a mistake to imagine, however, that the socialists, the anarchists, or the syndicalists have treated the doctrine with any greater degree of indulgence. The proposal to reconcile masters and workmen, rich and poor, in a kind of silly, sentimental embrace is a menace to socialism and a denial of the principle of class war.[2]

All such criticism, however, utterly fails to convince us. It may be well, perhaps, to get rid of the coercive element in the discharge of social debt, but that does not do away with the valuable contribution made by solidarity both to social economics and to ethics.

Solidarity by itself does not furnish a principle of moral conduct, since it is just a natural fact, and as such it is non-moral. Whenever we imagine that solidarity is something evil, that judgment in itself is a proof that we have had recourse to some criterion outside solidarity itself by which to judge of its good or evil features. It is quite possible also that the idea may be exploited for the profit of the egoist. If solidarity is nothing but a mere cord binding us together it may quite possibly happen that it will be used to exalt some people and to pull others down, and the number brought low may even exceed the number raised up. We need not be surprised if occasionally we find that instead of increasing the power of good we have extended the opportunity for evil. But we must speed the coming of these new powers in the hope that in the end good will triumph over evil. Solidarity by itself cannot furnish a rule of moral conduct to such as have none already; but, granting the existence of a moral principle, it

[1] Anti-kissing leagues, inspired not by any puritan motives, but arising solely out of fear of bacilli, were formed in the United States. One must not be surprised if a league against hand-shaking is established next; although this would be rather a curious result of a doctrine of solidarity that is always represented by the device of two hands clasped in one another!
In Paul Bureau's book *La Crise morale des Temps nouveaux* there is a lengthy, lively criticism of solidarism from the moral standpoint.
[2] This is how we find it appraised in *Le Mouvement socialiste*: "The development of solidarism is one of the most disquieting features of the present time. It affords a proof as well as being a cause of a considerable slackening of energy." (Issue for July 1907; Paul Olivier in a review of Bouglé's book on solidarism.)

matters not whether it be egoism or altruism, solidarity supplies us with a leverage of incomparable strength.

In short, it teaches us three important lessons:

1. It shows us that all the good which has happened to others has added to our own well-being, and that all the evil that has befallen them has done us harm, and that consequently we ought to encourage the one and discourage the other, so that a policy of indifferent abstention is no longer possible for any of us.

The mode of action prescribed may be frankly utilitarian, but there is an element of triumph in getting the egoist to forget himself and to remember others, even though it be but for a time. A heart that beats for others, though the reason perhaps be selfish, is a somewhat nobler heart. It is doubtful whether we can ever get pure altruism without some admixture of self-interest. The Gospel only asks that we should love our neighbour as ourselves. Solidarity makes a similar demand, neither more nor less, but undertakes to prove that the neighbour is really myself.

2. It shows us how the results of our actions return upon ourselves with their harvest of suffering or joy a thousand times increased. This gives it its character for solemnity and majesty which has made it such an exceedingly favourable instrument for moral education. To our care is entrusted the welfare of souls, and just as we are led to see that we never really had a right to say that this or that matter was no concern of ours, so we also find ourselves relieved of that other equally heinous maxim, namely, that certain matters concern ourselves alone. Far from weakening the sense of responsibility, as some writers maintain, it is obvious that it increases it indefinitely.

3. It is true that in a contrary fashion it renders us more indulgent of the faults of others, by showing how often we have been unconscious accomplices in their crime. Morally this is a gain, for it helps us to be more indulgent towards others, but more severe upon ourselves.

From the standpoint of sociological evolution we are confronted with the dissolution of many of the older forms of solidarity and with the emergence of new ones. What really takes place is an extension of the circle of solidarity through the family, the city, and the nation until it reaches humanity—such expansion being accompanied by a doubly fortunate result. On the one hand corporate egoism becomes so ennobled and extended that it includes the whole of humanity, with the result that the strife between antagonistic interests becomes less acute. The old argument from independence had already grown blunt in the struggle with division of labour. Degree of independence is not the sole measure of personality. The savage beneath his ancestral tree is independent, and so perhaps is Ibsen's hero in revolt against society. The king on his throne, on the other hand, who never speaks except in the plural number, is always conscious of his dependence. But the savage because of his independence is powerless, whereas the king because of his dependence is very powerful. Solidarity, whether it be like the rope that binds the Alpine climber to his guide which may lead them both to the abyss, or like the patriotism that rivets the soldier's gaze upon his country's flag, cannot detract from individuality. If it be true, as was said just now, that the crystal is the earliest effort of the individual to render itself independent of its environment, we must never forget that it is also the earliest realization of true solidarity in the form of association.

As to the argument of the economists that mere exchange is the only form of solidarity that is at all compatible with the demands of justice, all the schools whose fortunes we have followed in the course of this volume have declared against this view, not excepting even the Mathematical school, the latest offspring of the Classical tradition. Esau's bargain with Jacob, the contracts between the Congo Company and the blacks, or between the *entrepreneur* and the home-worker, are irreproachable from a Hedonistic standpoint (see p. 509). But no one would consider such primitive exchanges, which, as Proudhon eloquently remarks, savour of retaliation—an eye for an eye and a tooth for a tooth—as evidence of the existence of solidarity.

Even if we conceived of exchange as a balance the two sides of which are in equilibrium, it is impossible to escape the conclusion that the contracting parties fare rather differently when they do not start on a footing of complete equality. There is always a Brennus ready to throw his sword into the scales.

It is only natural that we should ask ourselves what is to be done under such circumstances. Must we be content simply to resign ourselves to our fate? This seems inevitable if it be true, as the economists seem to suggest, that human relations depend entirely upon exchange and its derivatives—selling, lending, wage-earning, etc. But it is quite otherwise when these human relations are regarded as the outcome of association, whether professional, mutualist, or co-operative.[1]

[1] Association, even when the object in view is purely mercenary, has a moral value superior to exchange:
(1) Inasmuch as it always implies, in addition to money payment, a certain sacrifice of time and trouble, perhaps even of independence. It involves something more than the obligation to attend meetings and to conform to rules.
(2) It implies something more than a mere act of exchange which is completed in an instant and at one stroke. It implies the indefinite collaboration of the parties concerned.

In this spirit the worker subscribes to his union with a view to increasing its strength. Undoubtedly he reckons upon getting a higher wage, but there is no necessary relation between his membership of the union and the eventual rise in wages which he expects. The mutualist supports his society in the hope that he may add to the general feeling of security. Undoubtedly in his case again he reckons upon the society paying his doctor should he fall ill, but scores of members pass through life without making any demand upon their society at all, contributing much more than they withdraw. In this way the good lives pay for the bad ones. The member of the co-operative society, in a similar fashion, is more concerned about a fuller satisfaction of his need than he is about the amount of profit that he can get out of it. In short, whereas under a competitive system each one tries to get rid of his neighbour, under a regime of association every one would try to make some use of him. The object of solidarity is to substitute 'each for all' as a principle of action instead of 'each for himself.'[1] Every step taken in this direction, whether we wish it or no, implies a movement away from the regime of exchange in the direction of solidarity.

CHAPTER IV: THE THEORY OF RENT AND ITS APPLICATIONS

THE revival of interest in Classical theories, of which mention was made in the last chapter, cannot be passed over without a special reference to the theory of rent. The theory of rent has always held a prominent place in economic science, especially during the earlier years of the nineteenth century, and the developments it has undergone since are significant equally from a theoretical as from a practical standpoint.

Theoretically it has been shown that the concept rent, which for a

[1] The solidarist regime must be distinguished from the exchange regime on the one hand and from charity on the other. Exchange implies giving something with a view to obtaining the exact equivalent. Charity, on the other hand, implies giving without expecting any return; hence it involves a sacrifice. Solidarity also implies a sacrifice: every appeal on behalf of solidarity is based upon the consciousness of a certain amount of sacrifice, but a sacrifice that is not entirely disinterested—it is the sacrifice of a part of the individual self in order to gain an equal share in the collective being.

long time was supposed to be indissolubly bound up with a particular economic phenomenon, namely, the revenue of landed proprietors, is capable of several applications and extensions, some of which might throw considerable light into more than one obscure corner of the economic world. Particularly does it seem applicable to a kind of revenue which the classics hardly mentioned—that is, the profits of the *entrepreneur* as distinct from the interest of the capitalist.

Practically also it is very important. Rent is 'unearned increment' *par excellence*. In other words, it is a revenue for which the receiver has ostensibly done nothing. One can well imagine what fruitful ground for socialistic theories this must be! And, as a matter of fact, all systems of land nationalization or of socialization of rent—and they are by no means few in number—trace descent from the old Ricardian theory.

What we propose to do in this chapter is to examine the doctrine of rent in its twofold aspect, inquiring in the first place into what developments it has undergone as a scientific theory, and, secondly, how it is proposed to apply this theory with a view to reforming society. The chief aim in view is, of course, to glean some knowledge of present-day theories, but to do this we shall often find ourselves obliged to follow the stream backward towards its source in Mill or Ricardo, for in many cases it is the only way of appreciating the development of ideas.

I: THE THEORETICAL EXTENSION OF THE CONCEPT RENT

In a former chapter we were led to investigate the utterly futile attempts made both by Carey and Bastiat to undermine the Ricardian theory of rent. Open to criticism the theory certainly is, but in their anxiety to do away with it altogether these critics were led to deny that the land had any value at all.

But this denial has been refuted in no equivocal fashion by the emergence of what was perhaps the most striking phenomenon in nineteenth-century history, namely, the fabulous prices paid for land in the neighbourhood of large cities. The last century was pre-eminently the century of big towns. No other epoch in history can point to such growth of urban centres. England, America, Germany, and to a lesser degree France, have all had a share in this development. One result of this rapid agglomeration of population in restricted areas has been a wonderful growth of rents, or unearned increment. A quarter of an acre of land in the city of Chicago which was bought in 1830 for $20, at a time when the population was only fifty, and which in 1836 was sold for $25,000, was valued at $1,250,000 at the time of the International Exhibition in 1894. It has been calculated that the increase in ground rents in London between 1870 and 1895 is represented by no less a sum than £7,000,000. Hyde Park, bought by the City of London in 1652 for £17,000, was valued in 1900 at about £8,000,000. M. d'Avenel states that in Paris a piece of land belonging to the Hotel Dieu which was valued at 6 fr. 40 c. a square metre in 1775 was worth 1000 fr. in 1900,[1] and M. Leroy-Beaulieu mentions a piece of land in the neighbourhood of the Arc de Triomphe which between 1881 and 1904—i.e., in twenty-three years—had doubled its value and was at that time selling at 800 fr. a metre as compared with 400 fr. formerly.[2] We have merely quoted a few isolated examples, but they may be regarded as typical.

Carey and Bastiat have not made many converts, evidently. The majority of economists have either accepted Ricardo's theory or, having been induced to examine his position thoroughly, have been led to develop it, but none of them has denied the reality of the income derived from land. Hence the very curious twofold evolution which the theory presents.

On the one hand there has been discovered a whole series of differential revenues analogous to the rent of land, which, according to the expression of a great contemporary economist, "is not a thing by itself, but the leading species of a large genus."[3] On the other hand (and this second line of development is perhaps more curious than the first), while Ricardo considered that the rent of land was an economic anomaly resulting from special circumstances, such as the unequal fertility of the land or the law of diminishing returns, modern theorists regard it simply as the normal result of the regular operation of the laws of value. The rent of land and similar phenomena seem to fit in with the general theory of prices, and the theory of rent so laboriously constructed by the Classical school falls into the background as being comparatively useless. Despite its prestige throughout the nineteenth century it is now regarded by many writers as a mere historical curiosity.

This double evolution is the result of simultaneous efforts on the part of a great number of economists. It is almost impossible to trace

[1] Our figures are taken from the well-informed pamphlet of M. Einaudi, *La Municipalisation du sol dans les grandes villes* (Giard et Brière, 1898), reprinted from *Devenir social*.

[2] P. Leroy-Beaulieu, *L'Art de placer et gérer sa fortune*, p. 34.

[3] Marshall, *Principles*, preface to the first edition.

a regular sequence of advances from one to the other, and we shall content ourselves with a mere mention of the names of those who have contributed most to it, their actual words being quoted whenever possible.[1]

(a) In the first place, we have a number of differential revenues which are exactly analogous to the rent of land. Equal quantities, or, as the English economists prefer to put it, equal doses of capital and labour applied to different lands yield different revenues: such was the classic statement of the law of rent. Ricardo attributed the existence of rent to the presence of particular phenomena appertaining only to land, such as diminishing returns, unequal fertility, greater or lesser distance from a market. But it has long been realized that agriculture is by no means the only domain in which capital and labour yield unequal returns.

All natural sources of wealth—mines, salt-works, and fisheries—give rise to exactly similar phenomena. Their productivity is not identical, their fertility (if the term is permissible) presents the same differences and their position relative to a market the same variety as in the case of cultivated lands. Consequently every mine, every salt-work and fishery that is not on the margin of cultivation yields a differential revenue or rent because of its greater productivity or more convenient situation. Ricardo had recognized this in the case of mines, and Stuart Mill insisted upon its further extension.[2]

Further, land is not employed for tilth only; it is also frequently used for building purposes. The services which it renders in this connexion are not less important than the others, and between different sites there are as many distinctions as there are between the various grades of cultivated lands. Their commercial productivity, if we may so put it, is by no means uniform.

> The ground-rent of a house in a small village is but a little higher than the rent of a similar patch of ground in the open fields, but that of a shop in Cheapside will exceed this by the whole amount at which people estimate the superior facilities of money-making in the more crowded place. In this way the value of these sites is governed by the ordinary principles of rent.[3]

[1] There is a good account of the evolution of which we have given a brief résumé in a work published as far back as 1868, entitled *Versuch einer Kritischen Dogmengeschichte der Grundrente*, by Edward Berens (Leipzig), but especially in *La Théorie de la rente et son extension récente*, by Paul Frézouls (Montpellier, 1908), and in the very interesting articles of Herr Schumpeter, *Das Rentenprinzip in der Vertheilungslehre*, which appeared in Schmoller's *Jahrbuch* in 1907, pp. 31 and 591.

[2] Ricardo's *Principles*, chapter iii, "On the Rent of Mines." *Cf.* Stuart Mill, *Principles*, Book III, chapter v, para. 3.

[3] Stuart Mill, *loc. cit.*

T

But why even confine attention to land and its uses? Degrees of productivity and differences of returns are equally evident in the case of capital. The machinery in one shop may be better, the organization more efficient, division of labour more fully developed than in another because of the relatively greater abundance of capital, with the result that the production in the one case will exceed the production in the other, resulting in a supplementary gain in the case of the first shop.[1] Similarly, the production of one worker as compared with another is frequently unequal. One man without any greater effort may get through more work than another, and the earnings of that man will exceed those of the other, so that even a workman may enjoy a supplementary gain of the nature of a differential rent. And not among workmen only do aptitudes differ, but also among *entrepreneurs*. Rent of ability plays an important role in determining the different degrees of success experienced by different undertakings and the unequal revenues which they yield. "The extra gains which any producer or dealer obtains through superior talents for business or superior business arrangements are very much of a similar kind." That is how Mill[2] expressed it, content merely to repeat an idea which Senior had expressed in his *Political Economy* as early as the year 1836,

---

[1] This fact was noted by Hermann even as far back as 1832 in his very remarkable *Staatswirtschaftliche Untersuchungen* (Munich, 1832), p. 166: "A phenomenon that is exactly analogous to rent becomes manifest whenever a country employs imported machinery the multiplication of which is difficult, possibly because the producing country discourages such exportation. [Such was the case with English machinery at the time Hermann wrote.] ... Suppose now that the price of the commodity manufactured with the aid of such machinery goes up. If the country under consideration can only manufacture with machinery that is more expensive but less efficient because of its defective character, the cost of production will still be higher than if the best [foreign] machinery were employed. The result is that the proprietors of the latter retain such advantages as the rise in price had secured them." Mangoldt (in *Die Lehre vom Unternehmergewinn*, Leipzig, 1855) expresses his view in a somewhat similar fashion: "Rent shows itself clearest and on the largest scale in the case of agricultural land, but it is equally evident wherever the difficulty of multiplying capital prevails or where it can only be replaced by other capital of a more expensive character or a less productive yield." Ricardo himself possibly had the rent of capital in mind when he said: "The exchangeable value of all commodities, whether they be manufactured or the produce of the mines or the produce of land, is always regulated, not by the less quantity of labour that will suffice for their production under circumstances highly favourable, and exclusively enjoyed by those who have peculiar facilities of production, but by the greater quantity of labour necessarily bestowed on their production by those who have no such facilities; by those who contrive to produce them under the most unfavourable circumstances—meaning by the most unfavourable circumstances the most unfavourable under which the quantity of produce required renders it necessary to carry on the production." (*Principles*, p. 37.) English writers, however, seldom speak of the rent of capital. Rent with them always signifies income due, not to the intervention of man, but to the natural resources of production.

[2] *Principles*, Book III, chapter v, para. 4.

where he applies the term 'rent' to "all peculiar advantages of extra-ordinary qualities of body and mind."[1]

The simple suggestion thrown out by Mill and Senior has long since been developed into a full-blown theory by Francis Walker, the American economist. The conception of profits as the remuneration of the *entrepreneur's* exceptional skill is examined in his *Treatise on Political Economy*, and is further treated in considerable detail in the *Quarterly Journal of Economics* for April 1887.[2]

We have already commented upon the optimistic tendencies of certain American economists. Carey was a case in point; so is Walker. In a work entitled *The Wages Question*, published in 1876, Walker made a successful attack upon that most pessimistic of theories the wages fund, and forced economists to recognize that to some extent at any rate the wages depended upon the productivity of the under-taking. But to show the possibility of wages growing with the increased productivity of industry was hardly enough to satisfy sensitive con-sciences. Walker was particularly anxious to foil the socialists by showing that profit is not the outcome of exploitation, and it was with a view to such demonstration that the doctrine of rent was so greedily seized upon.

By the term 'profit' Walker understands the special remuneration of the *entrepreneur*,[3] omitting any interest which he may draw as the possessor of capital. This distinguishes him from the majority of English economists, who, contrary to Continental practice, have always persisted in confusing the functions of the *entrepreneur* and the capitalist. Neither is he content to regard his work as confined to simple business arrangement and superintendence, which would result in his being paid a salary equal to that of a managing director. His work is

---

[1] "But as it is clearly a surplus, the labour having been previously paid for by average wages, and that surplus the spontaneous gift of nature, we have thought it most convenient to term it rent." (Quoted by Cannan, *Production and Distribution*, p. 198.)

[2] In an article entitled *The Source of Business Profit*.

[3] Walker is one of the first of the English-speaking economists to make this distinc-tion and to employ the term 'profit' in a narrow sense, distinguishing it from interest on the one hand and wages on the other. He even went so far as to subtract the wages of superintendence and direction because this work of supervision could be delegated to others (*Wages Question*, 2nd ed., 1891, pp. 230 *et seq.*), while the special function performed by the *entrepreneur*, namely, the adaptation of supply to demand, requires special remuneration, which he proposes to call profit. It is a little odd that a writer who seemed completely isolated should be shown, after all, to share the views of other economists. Walker declares that save his own father, Amasa Walker, he knew of no economist who had distinguished between capitalist and *entrepreneur*. But J. B. Say had already made the same distinction, which had been adopted by almost all Continental economists even at the beginning of the nineteenth century.

altogether of a more dignified character, and consists largely in anticipating the fluctuations of the market and in organizing production to meet them—in a word, in adapting supply to demand. The *entrepreneur* is the true leader of economic progress—a real "captain of industry."[1]

All this implies, says Walker, differences in industrial revenues exactly analogous to the differences in agricultural incomes. Some industries yield no profit at all beyond remunerating capital and labour at the normal rate and leaving enough for the *entrepreneur* to prevent his abandoning the undertaking altogether. Other industries yield a little more, and by imperceptible gradations we pass from such mediocre undertakings to more prosperous ones, and finally reach those that yield immense profits. The question then arises as to whether such abnormal profits in any way represent wages that have been withheld from the workers. This is not at all likely, because wages are often highest where profits are greatest. *Cæteris paribus*, the probability is that the greater profit in the one industry as compared with another implies the greater capacity of the *entrepreneur* in the one case than in the other. The superior income is a pure surplus like the rent of land. "Under free and full competition," says Walker,

> the successful employers of labour would earn a remuneration which would be exactly measured, in the case of each man, by the amount of wealth which he could produce, with a given application of labour and capital, over and above what would be produced by employers of the lowest industrial, or no-profits, grade, making use of the same amounts of labour and capital, just as rent measures the surplus of the produce of the better lands over and above what would be produced by the same application of labour and capital to the least productive lands which contribute to the supply of the market, lands which themselves bear no rent.[2]

Walker's theory contains a good deal of truth, although it is not, perhaps, quite as new as he thought it was. The opinions of Mill and Senior have already been referred to, and more than one Continental economist, from J. B. Say to Mangoldt, and including Hermann,[3] have propounded similar views. Nor has the doctrine ever been completely triumphant in economic circles. Most contemporary writers, no doubt, regard profit as a kind of rent, due partly, but only partly,

---

[1] This is how Walker summarizes his duties: "To furnish also technical skill, commercial knowledge, and powers of administration; to assume responsibilities and provide against contingencies; to shape and direct production, and to organize and control the industrial machinery." (*The Wages Question*, p. 245.)

[2] Walker, *Quarterly Journal of Economics*, April 1887, p. 278.

[3] Hermann, *Untersuchungen*, p. 206; for J. B. Say *cf. supra*, p. 128.

to the personal ability of the *entrepreneur*.[1] Other economists—such as Marshall,[2] for example—think that they can trace some other elements as well, such as insurance against risk and payment for the necessary expenses of training the *entrepreneur*.[3] Walras, on the other hand, omits these last two items and points out that under static conditions the *entrepreneur* would neither gain nor lose. The sole source of profit, then, are those 'dynamic' rents which are the result, so to speak, of the perpetual displacements of equilibrium in a progressive society. But these dynamic rents are extremely varied in character and bear no relation to the personal qualities of the *entrepreneur*.

Clark[4] and others, although subscribing to Walras's dictum that profits are really composed of rents, think that there may be static as well as dynamic rents and that Walras's hypothesis of a uniform net cost for all undertakings is altogether too abstract. Only in the case of the marginal producer, whose expenses are highest, is there any-thing like equilibrium between costs and price. The other producers, even when there is no such thing as a temporary displacement of equilibrium, are able to make substantial incomes out of the various species of differential rents already mentioned—proximity to market, better machinery, greater capital, etc. Marshall speaks of such incomes as composite rent.[5]

Walker's theory has evidently not been accepted without consider-able reservations. And we need only remind ourselves of the way in which dividends are usually distributed among shareholders to realize the inadequacy of his conception of rent and the exaggerated nature

---

[1] Pantaleoni (*Economia pura*, Part III, chapter iv) seems to be the only economist who accepts Walker's theory without any reservation.

[2] For his criticism of Walker see the *Quarterly Journal of Economics*, 1887, p. 479, and the *Principles*, 4th edition, p. 705, note. In conformity with English tradition, Marshall includes within profits any interest upon such capital as the *entrepreneur* possesses.

[3] Pantaleoni makes the same distinction: "Profits," says he, "may be the result of superior ability acquired either by assiduous study or prolonged preparation. In that case we are dealing, not with a kind of rent, but with a species of profit which may be very remunerative but which is nevertheless amenable to a very different law from that which generally regulates the investment of capital." (*Economia pura*, Part III, chapter iv.) On the other hand, Pantaleoni refuses to recognize the existence of an element of insurance against risk as an item in profits, because, as he points out, if the premium has been carefully reckoned up and compared with the risk, "it ought on an average to be equal to it at the end of a certain number of years, so that the net rent would become equal to zero." (*Ibid.*)

[4] Cf. *Distribution of Wealth* (1899) and *Essentials of Economic Theory* (1908).

[5] Moreover, the *entrepreneur* may find himself forced to yield a part of this composite rent either to the landlord or to the capitalist from whom he has borrowed his capital or to the workers by whose superior ability he has benefited. The difficult question of determining what proportion ought to be given in this way is discussed by Marshall in his *Principles*, Book V, chapter x, para. 4: Book VI, chapter viii, para. 9.

of his attempted justification. Would anyone suggest, for example, that such dividends are merely the result of exceptional ability?[1]

This attempted explanation of profit affords, perhaps, the most interesting illustration of the extension of the concept rent, although it is by no means the only one. The Ricardian theory, worked out to its logical conclusion, reveals the interesting fact that there are as many kinds of rents as there are different situations in the economic world. Whenever it becomes necessary to unravel the mystery surrounding individual inequalities of income recourse is had to a generalized theory of rent. "All advantages, in fact, which one competitor has over another, whether natural or acquired,[2] whether personal or the result of social arrangements . . . assimilate the possessor of the advantage to a receiver of rent."[3] Something of the variety of concrete life is thus reintroduced into the Classical theory of distribution, although all this was at first rigidly excluded by the doctrine of equality of interest and uniformity of wages.[4] The theory of rent is an indispensable complement of the Classical theory of distribution, giving the whole thing a much more realistic aspect. It is, as it were, the keystone of the whole structure.

(b) But the theory has also undergone another species of transformation. Ricardo conceived of rent as essentially a differential revenue arising out of the differences in the fertility of soils.[5] Were all lands equally fertile there would be no rent. The same remark applies to the various species of rent discovered since then. There is always some inherent difference which explains the emergence of rent, such as the greater suitability of a building site, the greater vigour of the worker, or the superior intelligence of the *entrepreneur*. They are all of a type. *Entrepreneurs* who produce the same article, workmen toiling at the same trade, capitals employed in the same kind of undertaking, may be grouped in an order of diminishing productivity, much as

[1] Walker might answer by saying that the dividend is simply the interest upon the capital. But we can hardly bring ourselves to believe this.

[2] This word 'acquired' is not quite in conformity with the pure theory of rent, for if these advantages are acquired the remuneration thus received should be considered merely as interest upon capital spent.

[3] Stuart Mill, *Principles*, Book III, chapter v, para. 4.

[4] "Wages and profits represent the universal elements in production, while rent may be taken to represent the differential and peculiar: any difference in favour of certain producers, or in favour of production in certain circumstances, being the source of a gain, which, though not called rent unless paid periodically by one person to another, is governed by laws entirely the same with it." (*Ibid.*, Book III, chapter v, para. 4.)

[5] "Rent, it should be remembered, is the difference between the produce obtained by equal portions of labour and capital employed on land of the same or different qualities." (Ricardo, *Principles*, chapter ix.)

Ricardo grouped the various species of lands. The last *entrepreneur* of the series, the last worker, or the last item of capital each earns just enough to keep them at that kind of employment. All the others produce more, and, seeing that they all sell their goods or services at the same price, they draw a rent which is greater than the income enjoyed by the others by the difference between their productivity and that of the last of the series. The whole economic world seems to be under the dominion of a kind of law of unequal fertility, not of lands merely, but of capital and individual capacity as well—a law which is sufficiently general in its application to explain all inequalities in the revenues of the different factors of production.

We cannot help feeling the artificiality of this conception and wondering whether the differences in revenues are not capable of explanation upon the basis of a simpler and more general principle. Is it impossible to take account of them directly and to treat them as something other than an exception or an anomaly? One cannot avoid asking such questions, and the reply is not far to seek.

Doubts arise as soon as we realize that land may yield rent apart from any inequality in its fertility. "If the whole land of a country were required for cultivation, all of it might yield a rent," says Stuart Mill.[1] Apparently all that is needed is an intense demand and a supply that is never equal to that demand, so that the price is permanently above the cost of production.[2] In such a case even the worst land—assuming that all is not of equal fertility—would yield a rent. Mill was of opinion that this rarely happened in the case of land, but was by no means uncommon in the case of mines.[3] Obviously, then, rent is not merely the outcome of unequal fertility, and the cause must be sought elsewhere. Stuart Mill had obviously foreseen this when he

---

[1] *Principles*, Book II, chapter xvi, para. 2.

[2] Ricardo had already made use of the following argument: "Suppose that the demand is for a million of quarters of corn, and that they are the produce of the land actually in cultivation. Now, suppose the fertility of all the land to be so diminished that the very same lands will yield only 900,000 quarters. The demand being for a million of quarters, the price of corn would rise, and recourse must necessarily be had to land of an inferior quality sooner than if the superior land had continued to produce a million of quarters." (*Principles*, chapter xxxii, p. 246.) Towards the end of his life Ricardo seems to have been more favourably inclined to a conception of rent somewhat closer akin to J. B. Say's. Compare the curious quotations given in Frézouls, *op. cit.*, p. 21.

[3] "A commodity may no doubt, in some contingencies, yield a rent even under the most disadvantageous circumstances of its production; but only when it is, for the time, in the condition of those commodities which are absolutely limited in supply, and is therefore selling at a scarcity value—which never is, nor has been, nor can be a permanent condition of any of the great rent-yielding commodities." (*Principles*, Book III, chapter v, para 4.) For the position with regard to mines see the same chapter, para. 3.

said that "a thing which is limited in quantity is still a monopolized article."[1]

But if such be the explanation of rent on land which is the last to be put under cultivation, what is the explanation in the case of better lands? We are not sure that Stuart Mill foresaw this problem.

This is how he explains the emergence of rent on land No. 1. Production having become insufficient to meet demand, prices go up; but it is only when they have reached a certain level—a level, that is to say, sufficiently high to secure a normal return on the capital and labour employed—that these lands will be brought under cultivation.[2]

The cause of rent in this case is obviously the growth of demand and not the cultivation of land No. 2, because the cultivation only took place when the prices had risen.[3] Moreover, the effect of this cultivation will be rather to check than to encourage the growth of rent by arresting this upward trend of prices through increasing the quantity of corn on the market. The rent of land No. 1 is consequently a scarcity rent which results directly from an increased demand and is independent of the quality of the land. The real cause of rent on all lands, whether good or bad, is really the same, namely, the insufficiency of supply to meet demand.

A similar process of reasoning might be applied to the other differential rents already mentioned, and the conclusion arrived at is that rent, whatever form it takes, is not an anomaly, but a perfectly normal consequence of the general laws of value. Whenever any commodity, from whatever cause, acquires scarcity value and its price exceeds its cost of production, there results a rent for the seller of that product.

---

[1] In this case Stuart Mill seems to compare rent to a monopoly revenue: "A thing which is limited in quantity, even though its possessors do not act in concert, is still a monopolized article." (*Principles*, Book II, chapter xvi, para. 2.) The expression, though adopted by several other writers, is not quite accurate. In the case of a monopoly the owners fix the quantity which they will produce beforehand with a view to getting a maximum of profit. But this cannot apply to landowners. At any rate, if there is any monopoly it must be an incomplete one.

[2] *Ibid.*, Book III, chapter v, para. 1.

[3] Such was the argument employed by J. B. Say in the course of a controversy with Ricardo. "It is perfectly obvious that if the needs of society raise the price of corn to such a level as to permit of the cultivation of inferior lands which yield nothing beyond wages for the workmen and profits on the capital, then that demand on the part of society, coupled with the price which it can afford to pay for the corn, allows of a profit on the most fertile or best situated lands." (*Traité*, 6th edition, p. 410.) Continuing, he remarks: "David Ricardo in the same chapter clearly shows that the profit from land is not the cause but the effect of the demand for corn, and the reasons which he adduces in support of this view may be turned against him to prove that other items in cost of production, notably the wages of labour, are not the cause but the effect of the current price of goods." Ricardo himself seemed on the point of being converted to this view. See p. 579, *supra*.

Such is the general formula, and therein we have a law that is quite independent of the law of diminishing returns and of the unequal fertility of land.[1]

But the issue was not decided at a single stroke. English political economy was so thoroughly impregnated with Ricardian ideas that it long adhered to the conception of a differential rent. Continental economists, on the other hand, have always regarded it as a more or less natural result of the laws of demand and supply. J. B. Say had long since made the suggestion that the existence of rent is due to the needs of society and the prices which it can afford to pay for its corn.[2] A German economist of the name of Hermann, a professor at Munich, in his original and suggestive work, *Staatswirtschaftliche Untersuchungen*, published in 1832, claims that the rent of land is simply a species of the income of fixed capital. Whereas circulating capital, because of its superior mobility, has almost always a uniform rate of interest, fixed capital, which has not that mobility and which cannot be increased with the same facility, has a revenue which is generally greater than that of circulating capital. This surplus revenue or rent, instead of being a mere transitory phenomenon, might easily become permanent provided the new fixed capital which enters into competition with it has a lesser degree of productivity. Such precisely is the case with land.[3] A little later another German, of the name of Mangoldt, defined rent as a scarcity price which does not benefit all the factors of production equally, but only those which cannot be readily increased in amount. And rent appears in the guise of a differential revenue simply because scarcity is always relative and is frequently kept in check by substitutes which generally give a smaller margin of profit.[4] Schäffle, in a work partly devoted to the subject of rent,[5] published in

---

[1] The theory of economic equilibrium enables us to give a still better demonstration of the general nature of this theory of rent. On this point we may refer to Pareto's *Cours* and Sensi's *La Teoria della Rendita* (Rome, 1912).

[2] *Cf. supra*, p. 580, note 3.

[3] Hermann, *Staatswirtschaftliche Untersuchungen*, Part V: *Vom Gewinn*. Even in the preface he declares that the doctrine of the rent of land must be regarded as a particular instance in the exposition of the law governing the returns from fixed capital in general.

[4] Mangoldt, *Die Lehre vom Unternehmergewinn* (Leipzig, 1855), pp. 109 *et seq.*

[5] *Die nationalökonomische Theorie der ausschliessenden Absatzverhältnisse* (Tübingen)—a work in which he attempts a justification of rents in general and of the rent of land in particular. Rent he regards as the reward offered to anyone who knows how to utilize either his personal capacity or his capital or land in a way that is particularly advantageous to society. It supplies an allurement that acts as the source of all progress and of all economic activity, a sort of natural right of ownership which society spontaneously confers upon those individuals who know how to serve society, and which competition causes to disappear at the opportune moment. The rent of land can be justified on this ground wherever legislation has not made an abuse of it.

1867, insists on the idea that the soil furnishes rent not because it is a gift of nature, but simply because of its immobility and the impossibility either of removing it or of increasing its quantity. Finally, Karl Menger, in his *Grundsätze der Volkswirtschaftslehre*, published in 1872, in outlining the foundations of the modern doctrine of value, assimilated the theory of rent to the general theory of prices by categorically declaring that "the products of land as far as the nature of their value is concerned afford no exception to the general rule, which applies to the value of the services of a machine or a tool, of a house or a factory, or any other economic good."[1]

The only difference, apparently, which present economists recognize between rents conceived of in this fashion is their greater or lesser duration. The rent furnished by a first-class machine will disappear very readily because new machines can be turned out to compete with it. But when the rent is due to superior natural qualities, whether of land or of men, the element of rent will not be so easily got rid of. To borrow a phrase of Pareto's, we may say that the rent will be of a more or less permanent character, according to the ease with which savings can be transformed into capital of a more or less durable kind.[2] Dr Marshall sums up his subtle analysis of the problem under consideration as follows: "In passing from the free gifts of nature through the more permanent improvements in the soil, to less permanent improvements, to farm and factory buildings, to steam-engines, etc., and finally to the less durable and less slowly made implements we find a continuous series [of rents]."[3]

This new claim on behalf of rent is very interesting, and those who regard rent as exclusively unearned increment may ponder over this new characteristic of unearned incomes.

[1] P. 148.

[2] "The sum paid for the use of land differs in no material respect from the sum paid for the use of other kinds of capital—a machine, for example. Although the land or the machine has to be returned to its rightful owner in the same condition as it was received, one ought to pay something just because such capitals are economically scarce; in other words, the amount existing at any one time or place is not greater than the demand. What differentiates land from machinery is that savings might easily be employed in turning out new machinery, but cannot very well increase the quantity of land in existence, or at any rate cannot transform existing soils in a manner that is profitable." (Pareto, *Cours d'Économie politique*, Vol. II, para. 759.) Marshall makes use of analogous terms: "If the supply of any factor of production is limited, and incapable of much increase by man's effort in any given period of time, then the income to be derived from it is to be regarded as of the nature of rent rather than profits in inquiries as to the action of economic causes during that period; although for longer periods it may rightly be regarded as profits which are required to cover part of the expenses of production and which therefore directly enter into those expenses." (*Principles*, 1st ed., Book VI, chapter iii, para. 1.)

[3] *Ibid.*, Book VI, chapter iii, para. 7.

The series, we might add, may be extended to a point at which rent becomes negative, *i.e.*, until the conditions of demand and supply become such that the factor of production which previously yielded a supplementary revenue no longer gives even the normal rate of remuneration. Thünen had suggested the possibility of a negative rent, and the idea has been further developed by Pareto.

These writers seem to regard rent simply as a result of the ordinary operation of the laws of supply and demand. The concept rent has been generalized so that it can no longer be regarded as a curiosity or an anomaly. The law of diminishing returns loses much of its economic importance, and even the Ricardian theory which is based upon it seems imperilled. After the numerous polemics to which it has given rise this theory, along with the Classical theory of value, has been practically relegated to the class of doctrines in which the historian is still interested but which are apparently of little practical value.[1]

II: UNEARNED INCREMENT AND THE PROPOSAL TO CONFISCATE RENT BY MEANS OF TAXATION

It does not appear that Ricardo fully realized the damaging consequences which would ensue if the doctrine of rent ever happened to be made the basis of an attack upon the institution of private property. He was quite satisfied with the inference which he had drawn from it in support of the free importation of corn, and did not feel called upon to defend the rent of land any more than the interest of capital, both of which seemed inseparable from a conception of private property.

[1] Did space permit, this would be the place to refer to the brilliant exposition of the doctrine of rent which is to be found in Clark's *Distribution of Wealth*, published in 1899. In that work, upon the strength of which the author enjoys a well-deserved reputation, revenues of various kinds are successively treated as rents. Imagine a fixed amount of capital applied along with successive doses of labour: each new dose of labour will produce less than the preceding one, while the production of the last dose regulates the remuneration of all the rest. But the product of the preceding doses is greater than that of the last, and a surplus value will be produced which will represent the product of capital and which will be exactly analogous to rent. Or suppose, on the other hand, that the quantity of labour is fixed and applied along with successive doses of capital; the productivity of the latter will in this case go on decreasing, and since the revenue of each dose will be proportionate to its productivity, any surplus left over will be of the nature of rent due to labour. There are other ingenious discussions which cannot be referred to in a note of this kind. But in our opinion the theory of economic equilibrium affords a simpler explanation of distribution, and the kind of optimism to which Clark's theory gives rise seems hardly justified. His attempt to combine the idea of marginal productivity with the law of diminishing returns is a further proof of the persistent influence exerted by Ricardian ideas upon English-speaking economists.

Other writers proved more exacting. Despite the numerous exceptions met with in actual life, the feeling that all forms of revenue ought to be justified by some kind of personal effort on the part of the beneficiary is fairly deeply rooted in our moral nature. But according to the Ricardian theory the rent of land is a kind of income got without corresponding toil—a reward without merit, and as such it is unjust. Such seems to be the logical conclusion of the Ricardian thesis.

The conclusion thus established is further confirmed by the natural feeling that not only is rent unjust, but the whole institution of private property as well. This feeling is one which all of us share (except those fortunate individuals who happen to be landlords, perhaps!), and is, of course, much older than any doctrine of rent. Movable property is generally the personal creation of man, the result of the toil or the product of the savings, if not of the present possessor, at least of a former one. But land is a gift of nature, a bountiful creation of Providence placed at the disposal of every one without distinction of wealth or of station. Proudhon's celebrated dictum is known to most people: "Who made the land? God. Get thee hence, then, proprietor."[1] That line of argument is really very old, and Ricardo unwittingly gave it new strength.

The idea of a natural right to the land and of a common interest in it is the instinctive possession of every nation. But in England the feeling seems more general than elsewhere, because, possibly, of the number of large proprietors and of the serious abuses to which the system has given rise. It seems rooted in the legal traditions of the nations. "No absolute ownership of land," writes Sir Frederick Pollock, "is recognized by our law-books except in the Crown. All lands are supposed to be held, immediately or mediately, of the Crown, though no rent or services may be payable, and no grant from the Crown on record."[2] Even as far back as the seventeenth century, Locke, in his work On Civil Government, had ventured to declare that God had given the land as common property to the children of men.

As one approaches the end of the eighteenth century the demands that all lands unlawfully taken from the public should be again restored to it become much more frequent. Sometimes the demand is put forward by otherwise obscure writers, but occasionally it finds support in distinguished and influential quarters. In 1775 a Newcastle schoolmaster of the name of Thomas Spence, in the course of a lecture given before the Philosophical Society of that town, proposed that the parishes should again seize hold of the land within their own area.

[1] Proudhon, Qu'est-ce que la Propriété?, p. 74.
[2] Pollock, The Land Laws, p. 12.

Thereupon he was obliged to flee to London, where he carried on an active propaganda in support of these ideas, achieving a certain measure of success. In 1781 a distinguished professor of the University of Aberdeen of the name of Ogilvie published an anonymous essay on the rights of landed proprietorship, wherein confiscation was proposed by taxing the whole of the value of the soil which was not due to improvements effected by proprietors. But little notice was taken of his suggestions, despite the fact that they had won the approval of Reid the philosopher. Tom Paine, in a pamphlet published in 1797, gave expression to similar ideas,[1] and the same views were put forward in a book published in 1850 by a certain Patrick Edward Dove.[2] The following year Herbert Spencer, in his book *Social Statics*, claimed that the State in taking back the land would be "acting in the interests of the highest type of civilization" and in perfect conformity with the moral law. It is true that in a subsequent work he took pains to point out that all that can be claimed for the community is the surface of the country in its original unsubdued state. "To all that value given to it by clearing, making up, prolonged culture, fencing, draining, making roads, farm buildings, etc., constituting nearly all its value, the community has no claim."[3] But despite this reservation the justice of the general principle is clearly recognized by him.

Other communities besides England have put forward a similar demand. Not to mention the claims made by socialists like Proudhon and the Belgian Baron Colins, and Christian Socialists like François Huet, we find that a similar method of procedure is advocated by philosophers like Renouvier, Fouillée, and Secrétan. Some of them even go the length of claiming compensation for the loss which this usurpation has involved to the present generation.

Thus, a conception that was already ancient even when the law of rent was first formulated proclaimed the inalienable right of man to the soil and demanded the re-establishment of that right. We shall hear an echo of that ancient belief in all the advocates of land nationalization, in Stuart Mill, Wallace, Henry George, and Walras;[4] and

[1] *Agrarian Justice opposed to Agrarian Law and Agrarian Monopoly.*
[2] *The Theory of Human Progression and Natural Probability of a Reign of Justice.* For further information concerning Spencer, Ogilvie, Dove, Paine, etc., see Escarra's *Nationalisation du Sol et socialisme* (Paris, 1904). We have drawn upon his book for the views here put forward, the works of these writers not being easily accessible.
[3] *Justice*, p. 92.
[4] "The land is the original heritage of the whole human race," says Mill in his *Dissertations and Discussions*. In the *Principles*, Book II, chapter ii, para. 5, he expresses his views thus: "The essential principle of property being to assure to all persons what they have produced by their labour and accumulated by their abstinence, this principle cannot apply to what is not the produce of labour, the raw material of the

this is one of the many links that bind them to those earlier writers. Gossen is a solitary exception.

But a simple pronouncement on the illegality of property does not take us very far. Appropriation of public property for private purposes is undoubtedly a great injustice, but the transaction is so old that retribution would serve little useful purpose, and the authors, were they still alive, would be safely ensconced behind their prescriptive rights. Moreover, most of the present proprietors, possibly all of them, cannot be accused of violent theft. They have acquired their land in a perfectly regular fashion, giving of their toil or their savings in exchange for it. To them it is merely an instrument of production, and their possession of it as legally justifiable as the ownership of a machine or any other form of capital. To take it away from them without some indemnity would not be to repair the old injustice, but to create a new one. Hence it is that the doctrine of the right of the community to the land had little more than philosophic interest until such time as it begot a new theory—the theory of rent.

What the Ricardian theory really proves is the accumulative nature of the benefits accruing from the possession of land. This spontaneous, automatic character of rent makes it unique : to no other form of revenue does it belong. The extension of cultivation, the increase of population, the growing demand for commodities, means an indefinite progression in the value of land. The interest, initiative, and intelligence of the proprietor are of no account. Everything depends upon the development of the social environment. This value which is created by the community should also belong to it. Just as the landed proprietors in times past filched the land, so they to-day absorb this income. But why allow this injustice to continue?

"Suppose," says Stuart Mill,

> that there is a kind of income which constantly tends to increase without any exertion or sacrifice on the part of the owners, these owners constituting a class in the community whom the natural course of things progressively enriches consistently with complete passiveness on their own part. In such a case it would be no violation of the principles on which private property is founded if the State should appropriate this increase of wealth, or part of it, as it arises. This would not properly be taking anything from anybody; it would merely be applying an accession of wealth created by circumstances

---

earth." Walras, in his *Théorie de la Propriété*, in the *Études d'Économie sociale*, p. 218, says that the land by a kind of natural right is the property of the State. Henry George, in *Progress and Poverty*, Book VII, chapter i, maintains that "the equal right of all men to the use of the land is as clear as their equal right to breathe the air—it is a right proclaimed by the fact of their existence."

to the benefit of society, instead of allowing it to become an unearned appendage to the riches of a particular class. Now this is actually the case with rent.[1]

The argument seems quite decisive. At any rate, Ricardo's book was hardly out of the press before the demand for confiscation was renewed.

His friend James Mill, writing in 1821, claimed that the State could legitimately appropriate to itself not only the present rent of land, but also all future increments of the same, with a view to compensating for public expenditure.[2] The Saint-Simonians, a little later, expressed a similar view.[3] But it was James Mill's son, John Stuart Mill, who showed the warmest attachment to this idea. The *Principles* contains a general outline of his reform plan, which took a still more definite shape in the programme of the Land Tenure Reform Association, founded in 1870, and in the discussions and explanations which accompanied it.[4]

The following are the essential points: (1) The State will only appropriate for its own use the future rents of land; that is, the rents paid after the proposed reform has been accomplished. (2) A practical beginning will be made by valuing the whole of the land, and a periodical revaluation will be made with a view to determining the increase in its value, and whether such increase is or is not the result of communal activity. A general tax would transfer this benefit to the State.[5] (3) Should any proprietor consider himself unfairly treated the State would give him the option of paying the new tax or of buying back the property at the price obtainable for it had he determined to sell just when the reform was being brought in.

Mill was opposed to immediate nationalization. Not that he thought it unjust; on the contrary, he was fully convinced of its equity. But our experience of State administration and of the work of municipal bodies did not seem to him to warrant any great faith in the utility of any such measure. He was afraid that "many years would elapse before the revenue realized for the State would be sufficient to pay

---

[1] *Principles*, Book V, chapter ii, para. 5.

[2] "This continual increase arising from the circumstances of the community and from nothing in which the landholders themselves have any peculiar share, does seem a fund no less peculiarly fitted for appropriation to the purposes of the State than the whole of the rent in a country where land has never been appropriated." (*Elements of Political Economy*, chapter iv, para. 5.)

[3] *Cf. supra*, chapter on Saint-Simon.

[4] *Principles*, Book V, chapter ii, para. 5. *Cf.* also chapter iii, paras. 2 and 6. For the programme of the League see *Dissertations and Discussions*, Vol. IV.

[5] Mill thought it impossible to distinguish in individual cases between the surplus value which is due to general circumstances and the surplus that results from the expenditure undertaken by the proprietor. Hence his conclusion that a general tax was the most equitable method of procedure with a view to effecting confiscation.

the indemnity which would be justly claimed by the dispossessed proprietors."[1]

Nor did he attempt to disguise the fact that the financial results would in his opinion be somewhat insignificant and the scope of the reform naturally somewhat limited. A few years only were to elapse before another writer proposed a much more radical measure which was to effect a veritable social revolution. It was a project to abolish poverty and to secure distributive justice that Henry George now launched on the strength of his belief in the doctrine of rent.

Henry George (1839–97) was not a professional economist. He was a self-made, self-taught man who followed a variety of occupations before he finally blossomed forth as a publicist. At the age of sixteen he went to sea, and led a roving life until 1861, when he settled down at San Francisco as a compositor, finally becoming editor of a daily paper in that city. He witnessed the rapid expansion of San Francisco and the development of the surrounding districts as the result of the great influx of gold-diggers. He also saw something of the agricultural exploitation of the western States. The enormous increase in the value of land and the fever of speculation which resulted from this naturally left a lasting impression upon him. *Progress and Poverty* (1879), the book which established his fame, is wholly inspired by these ideas.[2]

The book aroused the greatest enthusiasm. It has all the liveliness of journalism and the eloquence of oratory, but has neither the precision nor the finality of a work of science. Its economic heresies, though obvious enough, detracted nothing from its powerful appeal, and the wonderful setting in which the whole problem of poverty was placed has not been without its effect even upon economists;[3] nor is the powerful agitation to which the book gave rise by any means extinct.

It seemed to Henry George that landed proprietors, in virtue of the monopoly which they possess, absorb not merely a part but almost the whole of the benefits which accrue from the increase of population and the perfection of machinery. The progress of civilization seems helpless to narrow the breach separating the rich from the poor. While rents go up interest goes down and wages fall to a minimum.

---

[1] *Dissertations and Discussions*, Vol. IV, p. 256.

[2] *Progress and Poverty* was not his first effort, however. In 1871 *Our Land and Land Policy* had appeared, and in 1874 *The Land Question*. Later still he published *Protection or Free Trade* (1886), in which he puts forward a strong case for Free Trade, and in 1891 *An Open Letter to Pope Leo XIII* on the condition of the workers.

[3] Clark in his *Distribution of Wealth* states that the method by which he tries to determine the exact productivity of each factor of production is one that he borrowed from Henry George.

Every country presents the same phenomena—extreme poverty at one end of the scale accompanied by extravagant luxury at the other.

Is this unhappy result a kind of hybrid begotten of the Malthusian law and the law of diminishing returns? Must we, after all, agree with Malthus, Ricardo, and Mill when they say that the cause is to be sought in the increase of population outrunning the means of subsistence? Henry George thinks not, for experience everywhere seems to show that the rich are growing in numbers much more rapidly than the growth of population warrants, and that organization is really performing wonderful feats under very difficult conditions.[1]

Is it caused by the exploitation of labour by capital, as the socialists seem to think? George apparently thinks not, for the two factors, capital and labour, seem to him so intimately connected that both of them are easily exploited by the landowners. Every man, he thinks, could devote his energies either to the production of capital or to supplying labour—capital and labour being merely different manifestations of the same force, human effort. The benefits resulting from the formation of capital on the one hand and from the exercise of labour on the other tend to be equal, and any inequality is immediately counteracted by a larger production of one or other of these two factors, with the result that equilibrium is soon re-established. The rate of interest and the rate of wages can never vary inversely.[2]

But if we can neither accuse over-population nor lay the blame at the door of exploitation, how are we to account for the fact that the labourer is still so miserably paid? It is entirely, he thinks, the result of rent. Hitherto exceedingly severe in his handling of some Ricardian theories, George has no hesitation in pushing the doctrine of rent to its extreme limits.

He points out that owing to the existence of competition between capital and labour the rates of interest and wages are determined by

[1] "Twenty men working together will, where nature is niggardly, produce more than twenty times the wealth that one man can produce where nature is most bountiful." *Cf.* also the whole of Book II, which is a disproof of the Malthusian theory.

[2] "Labour and capital are but different forms of the same thing—human exertion. Capital is produced by labour; it is, in fact, but labour impressed upon matter. . . . The use of capital in production is, therefore, but a mode of labour. . . . Hence the principle that, under circumstances which permit free competition, operates to bring wages to a common standard and profits to a substantial equality—the principle that men will seek to gratify their desires with the least exertion—operates to establish and maintain this equilibrium between wages and interest. . . . And this relation fixed, it is evident that interest and wages must rise and fall together, and that interest cannot be increased without increasing wages, nor wages be lowered without depressing interest." (*Progress and Poverty*, Book III, chapter v.) It is hardly necessary to point out how very much simplified this doctrine concerning the relation between wages and interest really is.

the yield of that capital and labour when applied to land on the margin of cultivation—that is, to land that yields no surplus or rent. And in virtue of the natural monopoly which landowners possess they can exact for the use of other lands any amount they like beyond this minimum. The result is that rent goes on gradually increasing as the limits of cultivation extend. As population grows and needs become more extensive and varied, as technical processes become more perfect and labour becomes less and less necessary, new lands are brought under cultivation, such lands being generally of an inferior character. The result is that the lands which were previously cultivated will always yield a rent to the proprietor. Thus the progress of civilization, whatever form it take, always tends to the same result—a higher rent for the benefit of the landed proprietor.[1]

> Here is a little village; in ten years it will be a great city—in ten years the railroad will have taken the place of the stage-coach, the electric light of the candle; it will abound with all the machinery and improvements that so enormously multiply the effective power of labour. Will, in ten years, interest be any higher?

He will tell you "No!" "Will the wages of common labour be any higher?" He will tell you "No!" "What, then, will be higher?"

> Rent: the value of land. Go, get yourself a piece of ground, and hold possession. . . . You may sit down and smoke your pipe; you

[1] A résumé of this theory of distribution, whose very simplicity must make it suspect, may be found in Book V, chapter ii: "In every direction, the direct tendency of advancing civilization is to increase the power of human labour to satisfy human desires—to extirpate poverty and to banish want and the fear of want. . . . But labour cannot reap the benefits which advancing civilization thus brings, because they are intercepted. Land being necessary to labour, and being reduced to private ownership, every increase in the productive power of labour increases rent—the price that labour must pay for the opportunity to utilize its power; and thus all the advantages gained by the march of progress go to the owners of land, and wages do not increase." George, however, does not claim that real wages have fallen because technical improvements enable production to be carried on where it was formerly impossible. At most this will only enable capital and labour to preserve their old scale of remuneration; it will not give them any share in the progress that has been made, so that, relatively speaking, it is true to say that wages and interest have both fallen in comparison with rent. "When I say that wages fall as rent rises, I do not mean that the quantity of wealth obtained by labourers as wages is necessarily less, but that the proportion which it bears to the whole produce is necessarily less. The proportion may diminish while the quantity remains the same, or even increases." (Book VI, chapter vi. Cf. also Book IV, chapter iii.) George, like Ricardo and a good many socialists, confuses two different problems, namely, the price of productive services and the proportional distribution of the product between the different agents of production (Book V). He adds, however, that scientific discovery, by pushing the margin of cultivation back to that point where the law of diminishing returns is more than counterbalanced by increased productive efficiency, may even sometimes reduce the worker's real wages, and so impair his position not only relatively, but also absolutely. (Book IV, chapter iv.)

may lie around like the *lazzaroni* of Naples or the lepers of Mexico; you may go up in a balloon or down a hole in the ground; and without doing one stroke of work, without adding one iota to the wealth of the community, in ten years you will be rich! In the new city you may have a luxurious mansion; but among its public buildings will be an almshouse.[1]

Accordingly Henry George regards rent not so much as a species of revenue which, as Stuart Mill saw, is particularly easy to absorb by means of taxation, but as the very source of all evil. Once get rid of rent, poverty will be banished, inequality of wealth will be removed, and economic crises—which George thought were the result of speculation in land—will no longer disturb the serenity of commercial life. But it is hardly enough to aim at the future increments of rent, for the damning consequences of privilege would still remain if landowners were allowed to retain even their present rents. The whole abomination must be taxed out of existence.[2] Such a tax would yield sufficient to defray all State expenditure, and other forms of taxation could then be dispensed with. In the single tax advocated by Henry George we have a curious revival of the Physiocrats' *impôt unique*.

George's system is open to serious criticism both from the economic and from the ethical standpoint. From the economic point of view it is obvious that the right of private property does confer upon the proprietor the right to such benefit as may accrue from a possible surplus value, but it is not at all clear—nor has George succeeded in proving it—that such a right absorbs the *whole* benefit which accrues from social progress. Besides, it seems rather childish to think that rent is the sole cause of poverty and that its confiscation would result in the removal of the evils of poverty.

From the point of view of equity it seems clear that George in removing one injustice is at the same time creating another. To rob the present proprietors of the rents which they draw is simply to deprive them of advantages which many of them have acquired either by means of labour or economy. Land is no longer acquired merely by occupation: the usual way of getting hold of it to-day is to buy it. And if we consider that such a transaction is just, we are bound to recognize the legitimacy of rent just as much as the interest of capital. Confiscation might be justified in the case of those who first unlawfully occupied the land. But how many of them are left now?

Further, if we are going to relieve the landowner of the rent which results from the progress of civilization, we ought to indemnify him for

---

[1] *Progress and Poverty*, Book V, chapter ii.

[2] That portion of their revenue which represented the capital sunk in the land would still be the property of the landowners.

any 'decrement' which may have resulted through no error of his.
Stuart Mill anticipated this objection[1] and gave the dissatisfied proprietor the option of selling his land at a price equal to its market
value at the time when the reform was inaugurated.[2] Henry George
apparently never faced this aspect of the question. He thought that
'decrement' would be very exceptional indeed, and that the persistence
of increment values is as thoroughly established as any law in the
physical world ever was.

Mill's system, though much more moderate than George's, is by
no means beyond reproach. The common element in both systems—
i.e., the emphasis laid upon unearned increments—has been criticized
by both socialists and economists.

The socialists point out that if the object is to get rid of unearned
incomes the interest of capital as well as the rent of land ought to be
confiscated. While agreeing with the object, they claim that they are
more logical in demanding the extinction of both kinds. But this
criticism is not quite a complete answer to Mill and his supporters,
for the latter regarded interest as the legitimate remuneration, if not
of the labour, at least of the abstinence of the capitalist. Interest is
the remuneration of sacrifice.[3] But the socialists are not convinced.
They cannot see how the negative effort of the capitalist is to be compared with the positive effort of the labourer, and they have not been
sparing in their denunciation of Mill and his followers.

The economists adopt a different line of criticism. The argument
is that the rent of land is illegal because the progress of society has
contributed more to it than the work of the proprietor. But is there

---

[1] Mill points out that the answer to this objection is that the right of selling the
land at a price which depends upon two contrary conditions (gain or loss) establishes
a kind of equilibrium. The State would not lose anything by this, for a fall in value
in one place, unless it be accompanied by a general want of prosperity, implies a
corresponding increase somewhere else, of which the State will get the benefit.
(*Dissertations and Discussions*, Vol. IV.)

[2] M. Einaudi, however, in his excellent *Studi sugli effetti delle imposte*, p. 125 (Turin,
1902), remarks that this principle of indemnifying losses leads directly to a State
guarantee of values—the expediency of which is at least problematic. He makes the
further observation that the compensation would often be paid to a person other
than the one who paid the tax when it was levied—the property in the meantime
having changed hands.

[3] For the distinction between the legality of movable and immovable property see
Mill, *Principles*, Book II, chapter ii, para. 1, and Henry George, *Progress and Poverty*,
Book VII, chapter i. "The institution of private property," says Mill in the above
passage, "when limited to its essential elements, consists in the recognition, in each
person, of a right to the exclusive disposal of what he or she have produced by their
own efforts, or received either by gift or by fair agreement without force or fraud
from those who produced it." Such a definition at least implies that landed property
is illegal. A house is distinguished from the land upon which it is built; whereas the
former is legally held the latter is not.

any kind of revenue which is altogether free from such criticism? Every kind of revenue contains some elements that are essentially social in character; that is, elements that depend entirely upon the demands of society. The growth of social demand often brings to capital as well as to land, to labour as well as to capital, quite unexpected and occasionally extravagant incomes. Has not political economy in the course of its development been forced to recognize the existence of a whole series of rents differing from the rent of land merely in respect of their shorter duration? Was the fortune of the celebrated hunchback of Quincampoix Street, who lived in the glorious days of Law's system, in any way different from the fortune of the Duke of Westminster, who owns large areas of the City of London? Or is the surplus value conferred upon old capital by a mere fall in the rate of interest in any respect different from the surplus value acquired by land under the pressure of growing population? The most striking thing, apparently, about unearned increment is its ubiquity. Society, presumably, does not distribute its revenues in the way a schoolmaster rewards the most painstaking or the most meritorious pupil. It puts a premium upon the services that are rarest, but never inquires whether they involved any greater amount of sacrifice. Such premiums simply denote the intensity of its own demands. What right have we to isolate one of these and demand that it and it alone shall be confiscated?

Stuart Mill has given the only reply that is possible by showing that none of the other rents has either the persistence or the generality of the rent of land.[1] That reply seems clear enough to justify at least a partial application of the systems of Henry George and Stuart Mill.

About the year 1880 several leagues were founded in England, America, and Australia with a view to propagating what George's followers call his "sublime truths." On the other hand, several attempts have since been made, especially by municipalities, to tax surplus values.[2] As far back as 1807 a law was passed in France requiring riparian owners to pay compensation in cases where their estates bordered upon public works which in any way contributed to the greater value of the property. But the law is very seldom enforced.[3] In London the principle was recognized as far back as the seventeenth century,

[1] Mill, *Dissertations and Discussions*, Vol. IV, p. 298.
[2] Especially in England, where various schemes have been propounded and investigated by Royal Commissions since the beginning of this century. Such schemes are discussed in a very thorough fashion in Einaudi's book already mentioned, and in an article entitled *Recent Schemes for Rating Urban Land Values* contributed by Edgeworth to the *Economic Journal* in 1906.
[3] Article 30 of the Act of September 16, 1807, runs as follows: "If as the result of

but has long since fallen into desuetude.[1] The idea gained ground very rapidly in the beginning of the century, in England and Germany especially. Numerous projects were launched with a view to taxing the surplus value of urban lands not used for building purposes, and some of the schemes were fairly successful. The adoption of this principle was one of the more prominent features of the famous English Budget of 1909, which roused so much opposition and brought the long constitutional struggle between the Liberal Government and the House of Lords to a head. The economists are still divided on the question. The imposition of a *Werthzuwachssteuer* by certain German municipalities led to a fresh discussion of the topic in a number of reviews and polemical works, and the principle was adopted in the German Imperial Act of 1911, creating a special tax for increasing the war-tax.

These ideas have never obtained the same hold in France, where property is subdivided to a much greater extent than it is in England, and where rent is accordingly distributed among a greater number of cultivators and naturally raises less opposition. In addition to this, the slow growth of the population in France makes the problem less acute than it is in Germany, where the workers find that an increasing proportion of wages is absorbed in the payment of rent.

III: SYSTEMS OF LAND NATIONALIZATION

The 'land-nationalizers,' whose schemes now come under consideration, not content with the taxation of a part of the revenue of the land, demand that the whole of it should again become the property of the State.

Apparently a much more thorough-going suggestion than any of the preceding ones, especially Mill's, in reality it is a much simpler

---

the improvements already mentioned in this Act—through the making of new roads or the laying out of new squares, through the construction of quays or other public works—any private property acquires a notable increase in value, such property shall be made to pay an indemnity which may be equal to half the value of the advantage which has thus accrued to it." The principle was rarely applied, however. M. Berthélemy (*Traité élémentaire de Droit administratif*, 1908, p. 624) states that he can only find twenty occasions on which the law was brought into operation in the whole course of the nineteenth century.

[1] Professor Seligman (*Essays in Taxation*, 5th ed., p. 341) quotes an English law of 1662 relating to the widening of certain streets in Westminster in which the principle is neatly stated. But when it was proposed to apply it to certain public works undertaken in London in 1890 it was energetically opposed. It was admitted afresh in the Tower Bridge Act of 1895. A similar system is frequently adopted in America under the name of 'special assessment' or 'betterment.'

system that is proposed. The advocates of land nationalization think, with Mill, that the surplus value of the land should be reserved for the State, and, like him, they have great faith in the persistence and continuity of this surplus value. They also agree with him when he puts forward the claim of society to the possession of the soil, but they never suggest that it should be taken from its present owners. They reject the distinction between earned and unearned income and consider that they are both equally legitimate. But, unlike Mill, they never feel that they can say to the landed proprietor, "Thus far and no farther." Appropriation is advocated simply on the ground of its public utility, and care is taken to hedge it round with all kinds of guarantees. Proprietors are to be indemnified not merely for the loss of income it would immediately involve, but also for the loss of any future revenue upon which they had reckoned. Could anything be simpler or more reasonable?

The practical interest of a system of this kind cannot be very great. Such a fundamental change in the institution of private property, especially in old countries, could only be accomplished by means of a revolution. Revolutions are to be undertaken in no light-hearted fashion and never without the sanction of absolute necessity. Curiously enough, all the great changes in landed property during the last hundred years have been in the opposite direction. After the First World War in the Balkan countries (Hungary and Rumania, for example) the land was divided among the peasants, as it had been formerly in Russia after the emancipation of the serfs. Even in the Russia of to-day the first move of the Bolshevik revolution has been to create peasant property. Since 1930 the Russian agricultural reform has consisted not in nationalization of the soil but in the creation of Kolkhozy, which are co-operative farming enterprises. The prospects of nationalization are certainly not very rosy.

The extremely hypothetical character of the schemes now under consideration relieves us of the necessity of examining their organization in any detail, although this question of the minutiæ is apparently one that strongly appeals to the creative instinct of these Utopians.

Of greater interest are the grounds on which they base their demand and the economic processes by means of which they hope to accomplish their aims. From this point of view the most interesting systems are those of Gossen and Walras. Gossen's scheme is expounded in a curious volume entitled *Entwickelung der Gesetze des menschlichen Verkehrs*, and Walras's is developed in a memorandum addressed by the author to the Vaudoise Society of Natural Sciences in 1880. Both works contain ideas from which the economist may learn a good deal, and both writers claim that the successful adoption of their schemes would enable the State to make an offer of free land to all citizens.

(a) Gossen's book appeared in 1853.[1] It is a curious coincidence that the French Bastiat, the American Carey, and the German Gossen should all be engaged in developing an optimistic thesis just about the same time. Of the three, Gossen's was the most optimistic and by far the most scientific. He concurred in the judgment of the Physiocrats, who believed that the world was providentially subjected to the action of beneficent laws which men must know and obey if they are ever to become happy. Such, he thought, are the laws of enjoyment, or of utility or ophelimity, as we call them to-day. A person who merely follows his own interests finds that unconsciously, perhaps, he has been contributing to the happiness of the whole of society. Gossen gives a remarkably clear proof of the theory of maximum ophelimity, based upon a very ingenious analysis of wants. According to this theory, every individual who pursues the satisfaction of his own desires under a regime of free competition helps in the realization of the maximum satisfaction by everybody concerned.

If it be true that each individual in pursuit of personal enjoyment unwittingly contributes to the well-being of the whole community, it is clear that every one ought to be given the utmost possible freedom in the pursuit of his interests. But there are two great obstacles in the way of this. The first of these is want of capital, which Gossen thought could be obviated by creating a huge Government bank which would lend capital whenever required. The mechanism of the bank is described in considerable detail. The second obstacle is the existence of private property in land. If man is to develop all his faculties and to use them to their utmost extent in the production of wealth, he must be allowed to choose his work freely and to carry it on under the most advantageous circumstances possible. But private property hinders free choice. "Thanks to this one fact," says Gossen,

the obstinacy of a single proprietor often hinders the best development of the land which belongs to him and prevents its utilization in the fashion that would best meet the needs of production. The necessity for the compulsory purchase of land for industrial purposes, for the making of roads, railways, or for developing mines,

[1] No notice whatever was taken of it then, and even in the second edition of the great *Handwörterbuch der Staatswissenschaften*, published in 1900, no mention is made of Gossen's name, although the third edition of that work has made ample reparation. The book was reprinted in 1889. On the relation between the ideas of Gossen and those of Jevons and Walras see Walras's interesting article *Un Économiste inconnu, Hermann Henri Gossen*, published in the *Journal des Économistes* in 1885 and reproduced in his *Études d'Économie sociale*, pp. 351 *et seq.*

affords an indication of the unsatisfactory condition of landholding as it exists at present.[1]

It is obviously necessary that the community's right to the soil should again be restored to it, so that every one might be free to demand and to obtain the use of as much of it as he required. Every industry could then choose that locality which seemed best fitted for it. The right of using the land might be disposed of by public auction and given to the bidder who offered the highest rent. There would thus be a kind of guarantee that the organization of production at any one moment was being carried on in the most favourable fashion —relatively, that is to say, to the knowledge possessed by the community at that period.[2]

(b) Walras's position is not quite so frankly utilitarian as Gossen's. It was the analysis of the respective roles of the individual and the State, of which he gave an exposition in his lectures on *La Théorie générale de la société* (1867), that inspired his reform. Following Henry George, he sought a reconciliation of individualism and socialism[3]—a reconciliation which he variously speaks of under the terms 'liberal socialism,' 'synthetic socialism,' or simply 'syntheticism.'[4]

It was his opinion that no real opposition existed between the State and the individual, that the one is just the complement of the other. Taken separately, it has been well said that they are nothing better than abstractions; the only real man is the social man—man living in society. This man, as we know, has two kinds of interests—the one personal or individual, and as such opposed to the interests of other beings; the other social or collective, common both to himself and his fellows—and unless these are secured the existence of the race is immediately jeopardized. The two groups of interests are equally important, for they are both equally necessary for the life of the social being. The State and the individual are mere phases in the life of the

---

[1] *Entwickelung der Gesetze*, p. 250.

[2] Gossen sees other advantages that would follow such reform. He enumerates them thus: (1) The confiscation of rent would reduce the possibility of living without working, and this would increase the industrial activity of the class under consideration. (2) The legal transference of property would be greatly simplified. (3) Producers would be exempted from buying land and from keeping capital for this purpose. (4) Rent would take the place of taxation to a very considerable extent, and would free the collection of it from every trace of vexation or injustice. (*Ibid.*, p. 273.)

[3] *Cf.* the fragment entitled *Méthode de Conciliation ou de synthèse*, in the *Études d'Économie sociale*. Henry George in his preface to *Progress and Poverty* writes thus: "What I have done in this book ... is to unite the truth perceived by the school of Smith and Ricardo to the truth perceived by the school of Proudhon and Lassalle; to show that *laissez-faire* (in its full, true meaning) opens the way to a realization of the noble dream of socialism."

[4] *Études d'Économie sociale*, p. 239.

same being, according as we think of him pursuing the collective interests which he has in common with his fellow-men or his more personal and individual interests. Each has its own sphere of activity definitely marked off from the other by the diverse nature of the respective tasks which they have to perform.

The duty of the State is to secure those general conditions of existence which are necessary for everybody alike. Upon the individual devolves the duty of determining his own personal position in society through perseverance in the exercise of his own capacity in any line of activity which he may himself choose. But if both of them, individual and State alike, are to perform their respective tasks efficiently, they must be supplied with all necessary resources. To the individual should accrue the wealth which results from labour and saving, to the State the revenue which results from general social progress—*i.e.*, the rent of land. Provided for in the manner indicated, there would be no necessity for taking away from the individual a portion of the fruit of his labour by means of taxation. Collective ownership of land and rent, private ownership of capital and labour, together with their incomes—such is the social organization which Walras thought would solve the problem of distribution: equal conditions, coupled with unequal situations.[1]

The reforms of Gossen and Walras, starting from a different angle as they do, depend for their realization upon conditions that are exactly identical. Both of them evince the most scrupulous respect for the prescriptive rights of the present owners; and both agree that the State has no more right to appropriate future rents[2] upon which these owners rely, in the manner suggested by John Stuart Mill, than it has to confiscate present rents, as Henry George proposed. The only way in which reform can be fairly carried out is to buy back the land, including in the purchase price any surplus values upon which the present proprietors have set their hopes. The most expedient way, perhaps, would be to issue bonds and to offer these to the proprietors

[1] See the charming sixth lesson of the *Théorie générale de la Société* in the *Études d'Économie sociale*.

[2] "In order to justify a measure involving a slight diminution in the rent of landed proprietors, it is hardly necessary to invoke the fact that rents have a faculty of growing continuously without the co-operation of the proprietor. We need scarcely point out that this increase in rent over a certain period cannot enter into the price of land simply because it cannot be calculated. Consequently, when a buyer buys under the system of guarantee afforded by the State he has at the same time undoubtedly bought a claim to all the variations of rent which may ensue. . . . Even if the landed proprietor is indemnified by being paid a perpetual rent equal to the rent of his land at the time of confiscation, as is done to-day in the case of compulsory purchase, the injustice will not be as great as it otherwise would be, but it will not be removed altogether." (Gossen, *Entwickelung der Gesetze*, pp. 257–258.)

in exchange for the land. The rents, which would still be received by the State—for there is no prospect of cessation of growth—would be employed partly in paying interest on the debt and partly in redeeming it; so that at the end of a certain period, say fifty years, the State would have paid back all the capital and it alone would henceforth draw the rents.[1]

It would have been unnecessary to add anything to the exposition as given by Walras but for the objection which he himself raised to it, and which led him to give a very interesting account of his belief in the permanence of rent.

"If," says Walras, "the State pays to the proprietors the exact value of their lands, reckoning in that price a sum equal to the estimated value of the future rent, what is it going to gain by the bargain?" If the value of the soil is carefully computed in the manner indicated above, then the interest on the capital borrowed to effect the purchase and the rents received must exactly balance one another, for one is just the price of the other, and the State will find that the rent of land is insufficient to repay the outlay involved. The results will cancel one another. Some inconveniences will doubtless be avoided, but there will be no outstanding advantage. How are we to get rid of this objection?

The difficulty is soon removed, for once the system outlined above is adopted there will be an end to all speculation in land. When individual buyers find that they must pay the owners a price that covers all surplus values which the land may possibly yield in the future, which would mean that *they* would not get any of that surplus value themselves, they will not be quite so keen. This is not the case, however, at the present time. Speculation of this kind is rife everywhere, for the good reason that a surplus value is always a possible contingency. The more perspicacious or better informed a buyer is, the more firmly does he believe in this advance and the more careful is he to safeguard his future interests. The State, so soon as it has bought back the land, will be in the position of the speculator in question. Walras is of the opinion that the surplus value is certain to grow in future even more rapidly than the actual possessors of the land imagine. Thanks to economic evolution, what the private proprietor can only speculate on the State can rely upon with absolute certainty.[2]

---

[1] Gossen gives reasons for thinking that the State, owing to its superior position as compared with individuals, might offer better terms to the proprietors than ordinary buyers could—among others, that the State can borrow cheaply and could consequently offer a better price.

[2] A similar idea underlies Gide's proposal in an article contributed to the *Journal des Économistes* for July 1883. "The State would offer to buy the land and pay for it

I believe, along with several competent economists, that when humanity left the purely agricultural system under which it had lived for thousands of years and entered upon a regime of industry and commerce, under which agriculture is still necessary to feed a growing population, but only possible with the expenditure of a vast amount of capital, it achieved a notable triumph, and the step it then took marks a veritable advance in economic evolution. I also believe that as the result of this evolution rent will continue to grow, but without involving any scarcity or increase in the value of agricultural produce—a fact that has escaped every one except the wideawake and the well-informed, and by which proprietors alone have profited. I further believe that if the State had bought the land before this evolution had taken place and had then given of its resources to further such development, even the normal growth of this surplus value would have been ample to clear the debt.[1]

Walras agrees with Ricardo, and a kind of rehabilitation of the Ricardian thesis drives him to the conclusion that the future must witness a further growth of this surplus value of land—merely because of the limited quantity of land in existence. There is this difference, however. Whereas Ricardo bases his whole contention upon the validity of the law of diminishing returns, Walras will not even entertain the thought of a possible diminution in the amount of agricultural produce. The inevitable progress of society which leads it on from a purely agricultural stage right up to the industrial-commercial stage, from extensive to intensive cultivation, must result in increasing the value of land. The State would ease this transitional process by a measure of appropriation, and could make a solid contribution to the success of this gigantic undertaking, which is to apply not merely to land, but also to railways and mines, etc.[2]

(c) Numerous and various are the reasons invoked by the advocates of land nationalization. Gossen's ideal is the maximum product, while Walras's first care is to supply the State with all necessary resources. A final class of writers regards it as an excellent opportunity

on the basis of ninety-nine years' purchase. There is reason to think that hardly a buyer would be found who would refuse such an offer coupled with a slight compensation, for ninety-nine years is the equivalent of perpetuity as far as the individual is concerned. There would be nothing mean about such a price; really it would be more of a gift to the proprietor."

[1] Walras, *Études d'Économie sociale*, p. 368. A mathematical discussion of the theory is contained in the *Théorie mathématique du Prix des terres*. The same argument expressed in ordinary language may be found in the article entitled *Un Économiste inconnu* (*Études d'Économie sociale*, pp. 365 *et seq.*), and it is still more simply summed up in the *Problème fiscal*, pp. 446–449.

[2] "The same considerations would apply in the case of mines, railways, monopolies of every kind, natural and otherwise, where the principle of free competition is in operation or where any surplus value exists." (*Études d'Économie sociale*, p. 347, note. *Cf.* also pp. 237 *et seq.*)

of giving everybody access to the soil. It was this ideal of free land that inspired the late Alfred Russel Wallace to write his book *Land Nationalization: its Necessity and its Aims*, and to inaugurate his campaign in favour of nationalization in 1882.

Wallace imagined that the mere right of free land would put an end for ever to the worker's dependence upon the goodwill of the capitalist. Nobody would be found willing to work for starvation wages were every one certain that on a free piece of land he would always obtain his daily bread. None would suffer hunger any longer, for the soil, at any rate, would always be there awaiting cultivation. Free access to the land would by itself solve the problem of poverty and want, and this would be by no means one of the least of the benefits of land nationalization.[1]

The essential thing, in his opinion, is to give to every worker the right to possess and to cultivate a portion of the soil.[2] His proposal is that once nationalization is an accomplished fact every individual at least once in his lifetime should be given the opportunity of choosing a plot of land of from one to five acres in extent wherever he likes on condition that he personally occupies and cultivates it.[3]

The extremely simple character of the proposal makes it all the more notorious. Unlike the other schemes, it is not based upon any subtle complex economic analysis. But it supplies a most convincing platform theme. Closer scrutiny, however, reveals its almost childish nature.

The cultivation even of the smallest piece of land requires some capital, which the advocates of free land appear to forget altogether. The amount of capital so required may not infrequently be in excess of the modest sum possessed by the working man. They also seem oblivious of the fact that the land does not produce all the year round: there must of necessity be a period of quiescence when the seeds are germinating. And if we are to suppose that the worker has sufficient reserve to wait for the harvest, why not admit at once that he has also enough to tide over a period of unemployment? A few pounds in the bank to which he can have access whenever he likes would certainly be much more serviceable in mid-winter, say, than a plot of land

---

[1] *Cf.* Escarra, *op. cit.*, p. 224. See also Laveleye, *Le Socialisme contemporain*, 8th ed., Appendix I.

[2] Métin, *Le Socialisme en Angleterre*, p. 179 (1897).

[3] "The possession of a piece of land frees the workman from dependence upon the masters, which is one cause of poverty. The worker who possesses land is free. He has always something he can turn his hand to when out of work." Elsewhere: "If a certain quantity of land is given to the workers their wages will surely rise, for no one will work for another unless he can get more than he gets when working for himself." (Quoted by Escarra, p. 224, note.) The same idea occurs in Henry George, but not as a part of the general argument.

situated some distance away. Cultivation also requires capacity as well as capital. You cannot improvise the peasant, and a first-class artisan may be a very indifferent cultivator. The experience of distress committees seems to prove this point. The advocates of free land have a mistaken belief in the efficacy of the proposed remedy, and experience would quickly show them how difficult it would be to apply it.[1]

IV: SOCIALIST EXTENSIONS OF THE DOCTRINE OF RENT

The writers who have hitherto engaged our attention were all of them individualists. They had no quarrel with the institution of private property as such, nor were they hostile to the existence of capital or to the personal advantage which may accrue from the possession of exceptional talent or ability. The orthodox socialist, on the other hand, is distinguished by an aversion to both interest and rent, and some of them even go the length of denying the individual's claim to any special benefit accruing from personal ability if it has the effect of increasing his income beyond the mere remuneration of labour.

Between the two conceptions is a veritable abyss, and the question arises as to whether it can ever be bridged. Some writers confidently reply in the affirmative. "It is the easiest thing in the world. Just treat your interest on capital and the revenue derived from exceptional

---

[1] If we had not decided against the inclusion of the Italian economists, this would have been the place to devote a few words to the writings of Achille Loria. No one excels him as a writer on political economy. An elaborate superstructure of great economic, political, social, and even religious significance has been built upon the foundation of free land, which at least denotes a powerful imagination. A résumé of this thesis is contained in *La Terra ed il Sistema sociale*, translated for the *Revue d'Économie politique* in 1892. We cannot examine Loria's system here. Suffice it to say that in his *Costituzione economica odierna* (1900) he demands that the law should recognize each man's right to the land: either to a unit of land (*i.e.*, a quantity of land such as would enable a man to live and set up as an independent producer) or, failing that, to a fraction of such a unit.

Such is the theoretical solution, but the practical suggestion is somewhat milder, a kind of territorial wage being suggested. Every master would be obliged to give to his workmen, in addition to a minimum wage, a certain amount of land at the end of a given number of years. If during that period the workman has been employed by several masters, each master should contribute in proportion to the length of time he has been in his service.

At the end of a certain period every worker would thus become a proprietor. These would thus be in the same position as their primitive ancestors were as far as natural economy is concerned, and would be able to join with the older proprietors in a kind of association of capital and labour on a footing of absolute equality, which Signor Loria thought would be a most fruitful type of organization. During the intervening years a certain amount of pressure would have to be put upon the proprietors.

capacity as rent, and the theory of rent will supply a justification not only for the appropriation of land, but also for universal collectivism." It was in England that this idea was first mooted.

England, the true home of socialism, the England of Godwin and Hall, of Thompson and Owen, after the first outburst of socialist activity over seventy years before, had not given birth to a single socialist scheme. With the exception of John Stuart Mill, who was impressed by the French socialists, English writers had remained quite indifferent to the ideas that were agitating Europe. Karl Marx toiled at the production of his masterpiece, *Das Kapital*, in the very heart of London without arousing the curiosity of a single English economist. The formation of socialist parties in Germany and France after 1870 had to intervene before the ideas of the great collectivist aroused any real enthusiasm in Great Britain, and it was not until 1880 that a small Marxian party was formed in England.[1] Just about the same time another group of writers known as the Fabian Socialists began to preach an original and characteristically English kind of socialism.[2]

The Fabian Society at first consisted of a small group of young men, for the most part belonging to the middle classes, and holding themselves aloof from the older political parties. The object was "the prompt reconstruction of society in accordance with the highest moral possibilities." Success appearing somewhat remote, and being anxious for more immediate results, they allowed themselves to be led astray by ideas borrowed from the Marxian and anarchist doctrines of the Continent. But they very soon renounced the revolutionary spirit, which has so little in common with the English temperament; and in order to emphasize the difference between themselves and the advocates of brute force and the believers in a sensational historical crisis[3] they adopted the name Fabian, which is derived from Fabius Cunctator, the famous adversary of Hannibal. The school has always been very critical both of itself and of others, somewhat afraid of public ridicule, but possessing none of the enthusiasm of apostles. Always ready to banter one another,[4] to destroy their ancient idols, and to dispense with every social or definitely political creed, the Fabians rapidly became transformed into a society of students and propagandists whose

---

[1] The Social Democratic Federation was founded by Hyndman in 1881. See Métin, *Le Socialisme en Angleterre*, chapter vi (1897).

[2] Bernard Shaw, *The Fabian Society, what it has done and how it has done it* (1892; Fabian Tract, No. 41).

[3] *Report on Fabian Policy* (Fabian Tract, No. 70).

[4] "For it was at this period that we contracted the invaluable habit of freely laughing at ourselves which has always distinguished us, and which has saved us from becoming hampered by the gushing enthusiasts who mistake their own emotions for public movements." (Bernard Shaw, *loc. cit.*)

interests are exclusively intellectual, and who believe that "in the natural philosophy of socialism light is a more important factor than heat."[1]

Such an attitude is hardly conducive to success in a socialist crusade, but the Fabians have left a deep impression—not so much upon working men, perhaps, as upon members of the bourgeois or middle class. Several of their members were persons of great literary distinction, such as Bernard Shaw, Sidney and Beatrice Webb (later Lord and Lady Passfield), and H. G. Wells. By throwing themselves into the study of social conditions of different kinds, by collaborating in the publication of reviews and newspapers without distinction of party, by publishing pamphlets and calling conferences, they have managed to stimulate interest in their ideas. A résumé of these ideas is given in a curious collection of articles entitled the *Fabian Essays*, published in 1889. These essays represent the opinions of the more prominent Fabians rather than of the Fabian Society, for the society as such has only a practical policy, but no theoretical doctrine which it holds in common. It calls itself socialist,[2] and would welcome the transformation of individual into collective property. On the other hand, it declares that it has "no distinctive opinions on the marriage question, religion, art, abstract economics, historic evolution, currency, or any other subject than its own special business of practical democracy and socialism."[3] The economic theories which immediately interest us here are peculiar to certain members of the society. The society as a whole was doubtless inspired by these ideas, but they have not all received official recognition at its hands, and they are not even accepted by some adherents of the school.[4]

It is Sidney Webb more especially who has essayed the task of finding a new theoretical basis for Fabian collectivism. Having rejected

---

[1] *Report on Fabian Policy.*

[2] Socialism, as understood by the Fabian Society, means the organization and conduct of the necessary industries of the country, and the appropriation of all forms of economic rent of land and capital by the nation as a whole, through the most suitable public authorities, municipal, provincial, or central. The socialism advocated by the Fabian Society is State socialism exclusively (the term is used to distinguish it from anarchist socialism). On the other hand, it "steadfastly discountenances all schemes for securing to any person, or any group of persons, the entire product of their labour. It recognizes that wealth is social in its origin and must be social in its distribution, since the evolution of industry has made it impossible to distinguish the particular contribution that each person makes to the common product, or to ascertain its value." (*Report on Fabian Policy.*)   [3] *Ibid.*

[4] In addition to the *Fabian Essays*, the principal publications containing an exposition of Fabian ideas are the Fabian Tracts, a collection containing a great number of pamphlets on various subjects; *The History of Trade Unionism*, by Mr and Mrs Webb; *Industrial Democracy*, particularly chaps. i and iii of the third part, by the same authors; and, finally, *Problems of Modern Industry* (1898), a collection of lectures and articles, also by Mr and Mrs Webb.

the Marxian theory of labour-value, and conscious of the charm possessed by the modern theories of Jevons, of Marshall, and the Austrians, he felt the need of some new justification for the collective ownership of the means of production. Unable to free himself from the fascination which Ricardo has always exercised over his fellow-countrymen, he turns to the theory of rent of that great economist, and that theory, in his opinion, is "the very corner-stone of collectivist economy."[1]

It is perfectly obvious that this theory of rent affords ample justification for the appropriation of the revenue of land by proving that this revenue is purely supplementary, produced as it is only on the best lands and not on the worst, where the worker only produces the exact equivalent of his wages. There is nothing very new in this, however.

Equally valid is its justification of confiscated interest. Different kinds of capital, different machines, implements, and buildings, all of which are employed for purposes of production, show the same variety of quality, and consequently produce different quantities of material goods, just as different lands do. The employee who works with 'marginal capital,' if we may so put it, or, in other words, has to make shift with the minimum of tools and machinery, without which no work at all would be possible, barely produces the equivalent of his wages. Everything that exceeds this minimum may be claimed by the capitalist as payment for the superior yield of the capital which he has supplied. Interest, accordingly, is a differential revenue—a rent which ought to be expressed as a definite quantity of produce, for such it really is, and not as so much per cent.[2]

Finally, any who possess superior ability as compared with those who work not merely with a minimum of capital and labour, but with a minimum of intelligence and ability, produce a surplus, which they generally retain for themselves. This surplus is of the nature of a differential rent—the rent of ability. Generally it is the result of the better education received by the children of proprietors and capitalists, and it is thus the indirect outcome of private property.[3]

---

[1] Mr and Mrs Webb in their *History of Trade Unionism* reject "that confident sciolism and prejudice which has led generations of socialists to borrow from Adam Smith and the 'classic' economists the erroneous theory that labour is by itself the creator of value without going on to master that impregnable and more difficult law of economic rent which is the very corner-stone of collectivist economy."

[2] "The interest with which we are concerned must clearly be a definable quantity of produce." (*The National Dividend and its Distribution*, in *Problems of Modern Industry*, p. 227. We are indebted to this article for the exposition which we have given of the Fabian doctrine.)

[3] An exposition of the same theory is given in Tract No. 15, *English Progress towards Social Democracy*: "The individuals or classes who possess social power have at all

U

This ingenious argument is not very convincing. Even though we admit that interest and possibly the greater portion of wages may only be differential revenues, their confiscation would require special justification. The attributes of capital, unlike those of land as defined in the Ricardian theory, are not natural, but have been conferred upon it by the efforts of human beings. And as to the rent of ability, it still remains to be seen whether society would benefit by the confiscation of this rent. As a scientific explanation of distribution it does not seem to us a particularly attractive one. The distribution of incomes is effected by means of exchange and depends upon prices, but Webb makes an abstraction of prices in order to concentrate upon the material product. We do not deny the existence of rent derived from fixed capital, such rent being approximately measured by comparison with the current rate of interest. But after the labours of Böhm-Bawerk and Fisher it would seem impossible to explain this rate itself by reference to the material productivity of capital, which seems to be the essence of Webb's theory.

The latest attempt to deduce revolutionary conclusions from the older economics and to found a theory of collectivism upon the Ricardian doctrine of rent has proved a failure. Even Webb's friends have not shown the enthusiasm for it that they might[1]—and this despite the constant allusion to the "three monopolies" which one meets with in their writings.

The interest of the experiment lies not so much in itself as in the indication which it affords of the more recent trend of thought in this matter. We have already drawn attention to the fact that the more immediate disciples of Marx both in France and Germany have refuted his theory of value, showing a disposition to rally to the counter-theory of final utility. We have here a group of English socialists undergoing a somewhat similar process of evolution. On every hand it seems that socialism has given up all pretension to creating a working men's political economy alongside of the bourgeois, and it is now generally recognized that there can only be one political economy, independent

---

times, consciously or unconsciously, made use of that power in such a way as to leave to the great majority of their fellows practically nothing beyond the means of subsistence according to the current local standard. The additional product, determined by the relative differences in productive efficiency of the different sites, soils, capitals, and forms of skill above the margin of cultivation, has gone to those exercising control over these valuable but scarce productive factors. This struggle to secure the surplus or 'economic rent' is the key to the confused history of European progress, and an underlying, unconscious motive of all revolutions." Cf. also The Difficulties of Individualism, in Problems of Modern Industry, pp. 237-239.

[1] Bernard Shaw in his Economic Basis of Socialism, published in the Fabian Essays, makes a very neat distinction between interest properly so called and economic rent.

altogether of all parties and social ideals, whose sole function is to give a scientific explanation of economic phenomena.

The Fabians even outdo the syndicalists in their reaction against the Marxian theories. Not only is the theory of value thrown overboard, but Marx's whole social doctrine is rejected as well. There are two points on which the opposition is particularly marked, and although these may be outside the scope of the present chapter it is necessary to mention them in order to complete our exposition of Fabian ideas.

Marx's social doctrine was built upon the theory of class war. Socialism was simply the creed of the proletarian. Its triumph would mean the victory of the proletariat over the bourgeoisie. Its principles are the direct antithesis of those which govern society at the present time, just as the two classes are directly opposed to one another. The Fabians entertain no such views. They think of socialism as a mere extension of the ideals of bourgeois democracy, and they would be quite content with a logical development and application of the principles which at present govern society. "The economic side of the democratic ideal is, in fact, socialism itself," writes Sidney Webb.[1] Our object should not be to replace the bourgeois supremacy by the proletarian ascendancy, nor even to emancipate the worker from the tyranny of the wage system (for under the socialist regime, as the Fabians point out, everybody will be a wage-earner), but merely to organize industry in the interest of the community as a whole. "'We do not desire to see the mines and the profits from the mines transferred to the miners, but to the community as a whole."[2] Socialism is not a class doctrine, but a philosophy of general interest. "Socialism is a plan for securing equal rights and opportunities for all."[3] Webb questions the existence of an English class struggle in the Marxian sense of the word.[4] On the contrary: "In view of the fact that the socialist movement has been hitherto inspired, instructed, and led by members of the middle class or bourgeoisie, the Fabian Society . . . protests against the absurdity of socialists denouncing the very class from which socialism has sprung as specially hostile to it." One cannot see much similarity between this point of view and that of the French syndicalists.[5]

[1] *Fabian Essays*, p. 35.   [2] *Socialism True and False* (Tract No. 51).
[3] *What Socialism is* (Tract No. 13).
[4] In his preface to Kurella's German book *Sozialismus in England* (1898) he mentions the fact that the English working class is divided into a number of corporations who are either jealous of or misunderstand one another, but have not what we may properly call a class consciousness (p. 10).
[5] *Report on Fabian Policy*, p. 7.

The Fabian philosophy of history is equally distinct. For Marx the capital fact in nineteenth-century history is the concentration of property in the hands of a privileged few, and the consequent pauperization of the masses. The necessary consequence of this twofold development will be the revolutionary dispossession of the former by the latter.

Optimistic as they are, the Fabians are not prepared to deny the concentration of capital. According to their view, the prime fact in nineteenth-century history is not the servility of the masses, but the waning authority of the capitalists, the growing importance of collective government in national economy, and the gradual dispossession of the idlers for the sake of the workers, a process that is already well on the way towards consummation. Webb is of the opinion that socialism is being realized without any conflict, and even with the tacit approval of its victims.

> Slice after slice has gradually been cut from the profits of capital, and therefore from its selling value, by socially beneficial restrictions on its user's liberty to do as he liked with it. Slice after slice has been cut off the incomes from rent and interest by the gradual shifting of taxation from consumers to persons enjoying incomes above the average of the kingdom. . . . To-day almost every conceivable trade is, somewhere or other, carried on by parish, municipality, or the national Government itself without the intervention of any middleman or capitalist. . . . The community furnishes and maintains its own museums, parks, art galleries, libraries, concert halls, roads, streets, bridges, markets, slaughter-houses, fire-engines, lighthouses, pilots, ferries, surf-boats, steam-tugs, lifeboats, cemeteries, public baths, washhouses, pounds, harbours, piers, wharves, hospitals, dispensaries, gasworks, waterworks, tramways, telegraph cables, allotments, cow meadows, artisans' dwellings, schools, churches, and reading-rooms.

And even where private industry is allowed to survive it is rigorously supervised and inspected.

> The State in most of the larger industrial operations prescribes the age of the worker, the hours of work, the amount of air, light, cubic space, heat, lavatory accommodation, holidays, and mealtimes; where, when, and how wages shall be paid; how machinery, staircases, lift-holes, mines, and quarries are to be fenced and guarded; how and when the plant shall be cleaned, repaired, and worked. . . . On every side the individual capitalist is being registered, inspected, controlled, and eventually superseded by the community.[1]

We are already in the full current of socialism, declares Mr Webb.

[1] *Fabian Essays*, pp. 47–49.

Our legislators are socialists without knowing it. "The economic history of the century is an almost continuous record of the progress of socialism."[1] The Fabians, adopting a saying of the Saint-Simonians, point out to the socialists that they ought to be content with a clear exposition of the evolution of which every one knows something, although perhaps in a hazy fashion. "Instead of unconscious factors we become deliberate agents either to aid or resist the developments coming to our notice."[2]

We are some distance away from Marx here, and farther still from his syndicalist disciples. We have really been led back to the philosophy of history as it was interpreted by the German State Socialists. Must we, then, conclude that the Fabians are State Socialists who feign ignorance of the fact?

Fabian socialism, strictly speaking, is not a new scientific doctrine. It is rather a plea for economic centralization, an idea begotten of the modern conditions of existence in Europe, as against orthodox Liberalism, which is somewhat threadbare but still holds an honourable place in the opinion of many English writers. This tendency towards centralization has tended to become stronger. The industrial nationalizations carried out in many countries after the Second World War are proof of this. They are the outcome of a long evolution.

English politics even long before this had begun to shake off its individualism and to rid itself of the philosophic and political doctrines of the utilitarian Radicals, which Bentham and his friends had formulated early in the nineteenth century, and which still exercise a considerable influence over some people. The Fabians regard themselves as the special protagonists of the new standpoint. They would be proud to consider themselves the intellectual successors of the utilitarian Radicals, who simply claim to express the new desires of a great industrial democracy. Labour legislation and its many ramifications, municipal socialism spontaneously developing in all the big towns, the great co-operative 'wholesales' in Glasgow and Manchester, furnish persuasive illustration of the practical socialism which they advocate. "It is not," writes Mrs Sidney Webb,

> the socialism of foreign manufacture which cries for a Utopia of anarchy to be brought about by a murderous revolution, but the distinctively *English* socialism, the socialism which discovers itself

[1] *Fabian Essays*, p. 31.
[2] Sidney Webb, *The Difficulties of Individualism*, in *Problems of Modern Industry*. Also in the *Fabian Essays*, p. 35, he declares: "Socialists as well as individualists realize that important organic changes can only be (1) democratic . . . ; (2) gradual . . . ; (3) not regarded as immoral by the mass of the people; and (4) in this country, at any rate, constitutional and peaceful."

in works and not in words, the socialism that has silently embodied itself in the Factory Acts, the Truck Acts, Employers' Liability Acts, Public Health Acts, Artisans' Dwellings Acts, Education Acts—in all that mass of beneficent legislation forcing the individual into the service and under the protection of the State.[1]

The Fabian doctrine is the latest avatar of the Ricardian theory. It would really seem impossible to draw any further conclusions from it. Everything that could possibly be attempted in that direction has already been done, although other weapons of war forged against the institution of private property may yet come out of that old armoury. But that is hardly probable, especially when we remember that economic science no longer regards rent as a kind of anomaly amid the other economic phenomena. There is no doubt as to its reality, but it has been deprived of much of the social importance that was attributed to it by Ricardo and his followers, and it has consequently lost much of its revolutionary fecundity.

CHAPTER V: THE ANARCHISTS

THE social creed of the anarchist is a curious fusion of Liberal and socialist doctrines. Its economic criticism of the State, its enthusiasm for individual initiative, as well as its conception of a spontaneous economic order, are features which it owes to Liberalism; while its hatred of private property and its theory of exploitation represent its borrowings from socialism.

Doctrinal fusions of this kind which seek to combine two extreme standpoints not infrequently outdo them both. Dunoyer, for example, was the extremest of Liberals, but he took great care to remind his readers of at least one function which none but the State could perform: no other authority, he thought, could ever undertake to provide security. True bourgeois of 1830 that he was, Dunoyer always considered that 'order' was a prime social necessity.[2] But, armed with the criticism of the socialists, the anarchists soon get rid of this last vestige of the State's prerogative. In their opinion the security of which Dunoyer spoke merely meant the security of proprietors; 'order' is only necessary for the defence of the possessors against the attack of

---

[1] B. Potter (Mrs Sidney Webb), *The Co-operative Movement*, p. 16.

[2] See his article on Government in the *Dictionnaire* of Coquelin and Guillaumin.

the non-possessors. The socialists themselves (with the exception of Fourier, perhaps, whom the anarchists claim as one of themselves), however opposed to private property, were exceedingly anxious to retain considerable powers in the hands of the State, such as the superintendence of social production, for example. Armed this time with the criticism of the Liberal school, the anarchists experience no difficulty in demonstrating the economic and administrative incapacity of the State. "Liberty without socialism means privilege, and socialism without liberty means slavery and brutality"—so writes Bakunin.[1]

It is only fitting that a few pages at this stage of the book should be devoted to a doctrine that attempts to fuse the two great social currents that strove so valiantly for the upper hand in nineteenth-century history.

It is not our first acquaintance with anarchy, however. It has already been given a "local habitation and a name" by Proudhon, who is the real father of modern anarchism. This does not imply that similar doctrines may not be discovered in writings of a still earlier date, as in Godwin's, for example. But such writers remained solitary exceptions,[2] while the links connecting the anarchical teaching of Proudhon with the political and social anarchy of the last thirty years are easily traced. Not only is the similarity of ideas very striking, but their transmission from Proudhon to Bakunin, and thence to Kropotkin, Reclus, and Jean Grave, is by no means difficult to follow.

Alongside of the political and social anarchism which form the principal subject of this chapter there is also the philosophical and literary anarchism, whose predominant characteristic is an almost insane exaltation of the individual. The best-known representative of this school, which hails from Germany, is Max Stirner, whose book entitled *Der Einzige und sein Eigenthum* appeared in 1844.[3] The work was forgotten for a long time, although it enjoyed a striking success when it first appeared, and was bitterly criticized by Marx. Later when Nietzsche was beginning to win that literary renown which is so

---

[1] *Œuvres*, Vol. I, p. 59 (*Fédéralisme, Socialisme, et Antithéologisme*).

[2] Adler in his article *Anarchismus* in the *Handwörterbuch der Staatswissenschaften*, and in his *Geschichte des Sozialismus und Kommunismus* (1899), shows the indebtedness of the anarchist ideal to Greek philosophy.

[3] The work was republished in 1882 and again in 1893, and translated into French in 1902. There are also a few translations from the writings of Smith and Say from his pen. A very interesting account of his life, to which we must acknowledge our indebtedness for some of the information given here, is to be found in J. H. Mackay's *Max Stirner, sein Leben und sein Werk* (Berlin, 1898). Stirner's real name was Kaspar Schmidt. Born in 1806 at Bayreuth, in Bavaria, he died at Berlin in extreme poverty and wretchedness in 1856. For an account of the "left Hegelian school" and of Stirner himself see the very interesting articles of Saint-René Taillandier published in the *Revue des Deux Mondes*, 1842–50.

unmistakably his to-day, it was seen that in Stirner he had a precursor, although Stirner's works probably remained quite unknown to Nietzsche himself, with the result that Stirner has since enjoyed posthumous fame as the earliest *immoraliste*. A few words only are necessary to show the difference between his doctrines and those of Proudhon, Bakunin, and Kropotkin.[1]

I: STIRNER'S PHILOSOPHICAL ANARCHISM AND THE CULT OF THE INDIVIDUAL

Stirner's book was written as the result of a wager. The nature of the circumstances and the character of the epoch that gave birth to it were chiefly these. Stirner was a member of a group of young German Radicals and democrats whom Bruno Bauer had gathered round him in 1840. They drew their inspiration from Feuerbach, and accepted the more extreme views of the Hegelian philosophy. Their ideal was the absolute freedom of the human spirit, and in the sacred name of liberty they criticized everything that seemed in any way opposed to this ideal, whether nascent communism, dogmatic Christianity, or absolute government. The intellectual leaders of the German Revolution of 1848 were drawn from this group, but they were soon swept aside in the reaction of 1850. A few of them who were in the habit of meeting regularly in one of the Berlin restaurants assumed the name *die Freien*. Marx and Engels occasionally joined them, but soon left in disgust. A joint pamphlet by them, which bears the ironical title of *The Holy Family*, is supposed to refer to Bauer and his friends. A few of the German Liberal economists, including Julius Faucher among others, paid occasional visits to the Hippel Restaurant. Max Stirner, who was one of the most faithful members and a most attentive listener, although it does not seem that he contributed much to the discussion, conceived the idea of preparing a surprise for his friends in the form of a book in which he attempted to prove that the criticism of the supercritics was itself in need of criticism.

The extreme Radicals who formed the majority of the group were still very strongly attached to a number of abstract ideas which to Stirner seemed little better than phantoms. Humanity, Society, the

[1] Some may perhaps wonder why Nietzsche is not included, especially as he was a successor of Stirner's. But Nietzsche's interests were always exclusively philosophical and ethical. Stirner's work, on the other hand, is mainly social and political. We have already pointed out that even Stirner's book has only a rather remote connexion with economics, and a detailed study of it would be more in keeping with a history of political ideas. Nietzsche's work would lead us still farther afield, and would force us to examine every individualistic doctrine as it cropped up.

STIRNER'S PHILOSOPHICAL ANARCHISM

Pure, and the Good seemed so many extravagant abstractions; so many fetishes made with hands before whom men bow the knee and show as much reverence as ever the faithful have shown towards their God. Such abstractions, it seemed to him, possess about as much reality as the gods of Olympus or the ghosts that people the imagination of childhood. The only reality we know is the individual; there is no other. Every individual constitutes an independent original force, its only law its own personal interest, and the only limit to his development consists in whatever threatens that interest or weakens its force. Every man has a right to say, "I want to become all that it is within my power to become, and to have everything I am entitled to."[1] Bastiat had already expressed it as his opinion that there could be no conflict of legitimate rights, and Stirner declares that "every interest is legitimate provided only it is possible." "The crouching tiger is within his rights when he springs at me; but so am I when I resist his attacks." "Might is right, and there is no right without might."[2]

Granting that the individual is the only reality, all those collective unities that go by the name of the family, the State, society, or the nation, and all of which tend to limit his individuality by making the individual subservient to themselves, at once become meaningless. They are devoid of substance and reality.[3] Whatever authority they possess has been ascribed to them by the individual. Mere creatures of the imagination, they lose every right as soon as I cease to recognize them, and it is only then that I become a really free man.

> I have a right to overthrow every authority, whether of Jesus, Jehovah, or God, if I can. I have a right to commit a murder if I wish it—that is to say, unless I shun a crime as I would a disease. I decide the limits of my rights, for outside the ego there is nothing. . . . It may be that that nothing belongs to no one else; but that is somebody else's affair, not mine. Self-defence is their own look-out.[4]

The workers who complain of exploitation, the poor who are deprived of all property, have just one thing which they must do. They must recognize the right to property as inherent in themselves and take as much of it as they want.

---

[1] *Der Einzige und sein Eigenthum* (ed. Reklam), p. 164.   [2] *Ibid.*, p. 225.

[3] "This man has a body, and so has this man, and that man, right through society, so that you have a *collection of bodies* and not one *collective body*. Society has several bodies at its disposal, but has no body of its own. Just like the parallel notion of a nation, this corporate body is a mere phantom—an idea with no corporeal existence." (*Ibid.*, p. 138.) To make the possession of a body the test of reality is surely gross materialism. At this rate, law, custom, and language would have to be considered unreal. A historical fact such as a battle or a revolution has no body, but its *real* consequences are often palpable enough.

[4] *Ibid.*, p. 222.

The egoist's method of solving the problem of poverty is not to say to the poor, "Just wait patiently until a board of guardians shall give you something in the name of the community," but "Lay your hands upon anything you want and take that." The earth belongs to him who knows how to get hold of it, and having got hold of it knows how to keep it. If he seizes it, not only has he the land, but he has the right to it as well.[1]

But what kind of a society would we have under such conditions? It would simply be a 'Union of Egos,' each seeking his own and joining the association merely with a view to greater personal satisfaction. Present-day society dominates over the individual, making him its tool. The 'Union of Egos'—for we cannot call it a society—would be simply a tool in the hand of the individual. No scruples would be felt by anyone leaving the union if he thought something was to be gained by such withdrawal. Every individual would just say to his neighbour, "I am not anxious to recognize you or to show you any respect. I simply want you to be of some service to me."[2] It would be a case of *bellum omnium contra omnes*, with occasional precarious alliances. But it would at least mean liberty for all.

Such strange, paradoxical doctrines are irrefutable if we accept Stirner's postulates. But we must reject his whole point of view and dispute the stress laid upon the individual as the only reality, as well as his denial of the reality of society. Granting that the individual is the only reality, then society and the nation are mere abstractions created by man and removable at his pleasure. But that is just the mistake. The individual has no existence apart from society, nor has he any greater degree of reality. He is simply an element, not a separate entity. His existence or non-existence does not depend upon himself. Nor is society merely an idea. It is a natural fact. The individual may be quite as appropriately described as an abstraction or a mere phantom.

The fundamental difference between Stirner and the other anarchists who will engage our attention is just this recognition of the reality of the social fact which Stirner denies *in toto*. It also marks the cleavage between literary and political anarchism.[3]

---

[1] *Der Einzige und sein Eigenthum*, p. 223.   [2] *Ibid.*, p. 164

[3] In a pamphlet called *Les Nouveaux Aspects du Socialisme* (Paris, 1908), written by a syndicalist of the name of Berth, syndicalism and anarchism are contrasted, Proudhon's emphasis upon the reality of society being adopted as the crucial test. Unfortunately, however, Berth confines his examination to Stirner's system. Had he applied the test to Bakunin or Kropotkin he would have discovered that the emphasis laid by them upon the reality of society constitutes the most original feature in their theory. We are thus driven to the exactly opposite conclusion, and feel bound to admit—M. Berth notwithstanding—that anarchism and syndicalism in many respects closely resemble one another. Jean Grave, however, as we shall see later, seems more favourably inclined towards the naive individualism of Stirner.

II: SOCIAL AND POLITICAL ANARCHISM AND THE CRITICISM OF AUTHORITY

Stirner spent his life between his study and the Hippel Restaurant, the rendezvous of his friends. Bakunin and Kropotkin were men of a different stamp, who risked their freedom, and even their lives, for the sake of the cause which they had at heart. It is true that the seed sown in the mind of the ignorant as the result of their teaching often had most deplorable results, but no one can deny the quality of courage to either Kropotkin or Reclus, or withhold from them the title of greatness of both mind and character.

Bakunin was reared in much the same intellectual atmosphere as Stirner.[1] By birth he belonged to the Russian nobility, and spent the earliest years of his life in the Russian army. In 1834, at the age of twenty, he resigned his commission in order to devote himself to the study of philosophy, and, like Proudhon, Stirner, and Marx, he came under the universal spell of Hegel. In 1840 he proceeded to Berlin, where he became acquainted with the school of young Radicals of whom we have already spoken. From 1844 to 1847 we find him in Paris, where he used to spend whole nights in discussion with Proudhon. Proudhon's influence upon him is very marked, and one constantly meets with passages in the writings of the Russian anarchist which are nothing but paraphrases of ideas already put forward by Proudhon in the *Idée générale de la Révolution au XIXᵉ siècle*. The year 1848 revealed to the dilettante nobleman his true vocation, which he conceived to be that of a revolutionary. He successively took part in the risings at Prague and in the Saxon Revolution at Dresden. He was arrested and twice condemned to death, in Saxony and again in Austria, but was finally handed over to the Russian authorities, who imprisoned him in the fortress of St Peter and St Paul, where an attack of scurvy caused him to lose all his teeth. He was exiled to Siberia in 1857, but managed to escape in 1861. Making his way to London, he undertook the direction of a vigorous revolutionary campaign, which was carried on in Switzerland, Italy, and France. During the years 1870 and 1871

[1] See Bakunin's *Life*, written by his friend James Guillaume, included in the two-volume edition of his works; or the notice of him prefaced by Dragomanov to his volume *Michail Bakunins sozial-politischer Briefwechsel mit Herzen und Ogareff* (Stuttgart, 1895). A fairly full biography was written by Nettlau, but not published; a copy of the MS. may be seen in the Bibliothèque Nationale at Paris. See also M. Lagardelle's article on Bakunin in the *Revue politique et parlementaire* (1909). Bakunin's works have been published in French in four volumes, the first of which was issued in 1895, and the other three in 1907, 1908, and 1909 respectively (Paris, Stock). Some of his writings, however, are not included among these—*e.g.*, the *Statutes of the International Alliance for Social Democracy*.

he successfully planned a popular rising at Lyons. Bernard Lazare has graphically described him as

> a hirsute giant with an enormous head which seems larger than it really is because of the mass of bushy hair and untrimmed beard which surrounds it. He always sleeps rough, has no roof above him, and no homeland which he can call his own, and like an apostle is always prepared to set out on his sacred mission at any hour of the night or day.

The most striking fact in his history was his rupture with Karl Marx at the last International Congress, held at The Hague in 1872. Bakunin joined the International in 1869. Disgusted with the pontifical tendencies of the General Council, which was entirely under the heel of Marx, he proposed a scheme of federal organization under which each section would be left with considerable autonomy. The Jura Federation supported his proposals, and so did several of the French, Belgian, and Spanish delegates, as well as all the Italian. But he was expelled from the International by Marx's own friends. The official rupture between Marxian socialism and anarchy, grown to considerable proportions since, dates from that very moment. That Hague congress marks also the end of the International. Marx soon afterwards transferred the centre of the administration to the United States, and no conference was held afterwards. Bakunin also retired from the struggle about the same time, but not before he had set up a new association at Geneva, composed of a few faithful friends. In 1876 Bakunin died at Berne.

It was in the region of the Jura, in the neighbourhood of Neuchâtel, where Bakunin had still a few followers among the extremely individualistic but somewhat mystical population of those parts, that Kropotkin in the course of a short stay in the district in 1872 imbibed those anarchist ideas to the propagation of which he so strenuously devoted his life.[1] Although personally unacquainted with Bakunin, Kropotkin must be regarded as his direct descendant.

---

[1] "I returned from that journey with very definite sociological theories in my mind which I have ever since cherished, and I have done everything I can to give them a more clear and a more concrete expression." Kropotkin's principal works are: *Paroles d'un Révolté* (1884); *In Russian and French Prisons* (1887); *La Conquête du pain* (1888; Engl. trans. 1906); *The State, its Part in History* (1898); *Fields, Factories, and Workshops* (1899); *Memoirs of a Revolutionist* (1900); *Mutual Aid* (1902). He has also published a large number of pamphlets, among them *L'Anarchie: sa philosophie, son idéal* (1896). Our quotations are taken from Eltzbacher's *Der Anarchismus*, a work that consists almost entirely of quotations from the various anarchist authors, grouped under a few headings. [The references are to the French translation, 1902.—Tr.] These writers, and Kropotkin among them, have readily recognized the impartiality of the work.

Prince Kropotkin also was a Russian aristocrat, and he, like his master, joined the army after a short period of study. He attracted public notice first of all as the author of several remarkable works dealing with natural history and geography, which showed him to be a confirmed disciple of Darwin. But science was by no means his only interest. By 1871 Hegelian influence was on the wane in Russia, and the more thoughtful of the younger generation turned their attention to democracy. The new watchword was, "Go, seek the people, live among them, educate them and win their confidence if you want to get rid of the yoke of autocracy." Kropotkin caught the inspiration. He himself has told us how one evening after dinner at the Winter Palace he drove off in a cab, took off his fine clothes, and, putting on a cotton shirt instead of his silk one, and boots such as the peasants wore, hurried away to another quarter of the city and joined a number of working men whom he was trying to educate. But his propaganda proved short-lived, for one evening when he was leaving the headquarters of the Geographical Society, where he had just been reading a paper and had been offered the presidency of one of the sections, he was arrested on a charge of political conspiracy and imprisoned in the fortress of St Peter and St Paul. He managed to escape in 1876, and found refuge in England. Afterwards he was wrongfully condemned to three years' imprisonment at Clairvaux on account of his supposed complicity in an anarchist outbreak which took place at Lyons in 1884. But there was something extraordinary about a prisoner who could get the libraries of Ernest Renan and the Paris Academy of Sciences placed at his disposal during his term of imprisonment to enable him to pursue his scientific investigations. During his previous imprisonment in Russia the Geographical Society of St Petersburg had extended him a similar privilege. Afterwards Kropotkin lived in England, which he left after the Bolshevik Revolution to return to his country.

The best-known French anarchists, Élisée Reclus, the geographer, and Jean Grave, simply reproduce Kropotkin's ideas, with an occasional admixture of Bakunin's or Proudhon's.[1]

Our concern is with the expression of anarchist ideas as we find them in the best-known writers of the school. Consequently we must pass over the very striking but immature formulæ which are not infrequently to be met with in the works of more obscure writers.[2]

---

[1] Cf. L'Évolution, la révolution, et l'idéal anarchique, by Élisée Reclus (Paris, 1898), and La Société future, by Jean Grave (1895).

[2] On the position of anarchist ideas in France at that time see R. de Marmande, Les Forces révolutionnaires en France, in the Grande Revue, August 10, 1911.

Here again the distinguishing features are the emphasis laid upon individual rights and a passion for the free and full development of personality, which, as we have seen, was the keynote of Stirner's system. "Obedience means abdication," declares Élisée Reclus.[1] "Mankind's subjection will continue just so long as it is tolerated. I am ashamed of my fellow-men," writes Proudhon in 1850 from his prison at Doullens.[2] "My liberty," says Bakunin, "or what comes to the same thing, my honour as a man, consists in obeying no other individual and in performing only just those acts that carry conviction to me."[3] Jean Grave declares that society can impose "no limitations upon the individual save such as are derived from the natural conditions under which he lives."[4]

But this cult of the individual which is present everywhere in anarchist literature rests upon a conception which is the direct antithesis of Stirner's. To Stirner every man was a unique being whose will was his only law. The anarchists who follow Proudhon, on the other hand, regard man as a specimen of humanity, i.e., of something superior to the individual. "What I respect in my neighbour is his manhood,"[5] wrote Proudhon. It is this humanity or manhood that the anarchist would have us respect by respecting his liberty, for, as Bakunin declares, "liberty is the supreme aim of all human development."[6] It is not the triumph of the egoist but the triumph of humanity in the individual that the anarchists would seek, and so they claim liberty not merely for themselves but for all men. Far from wishing to be served by their fellow-men, as Stirner desired, they want equal respect shown for human dignity wherever found. "Treat others as you would that others should treat you under similar circumstances,"[7] writes Kropotkin, employing Kantian and even Christian phraseology. Bakunin, a faithful disciple of Proudhon's, considered that "all morality is founded on human respect, that is to say, upon the recognition of the humanity, of the human rights and worth in all men, of

---

[1] *L'Évolution, la révolution, et l'idéal anarchique*, p. 88; and he adds: "Our ideal implies the fullest and most absolute liberty of expression of opinion on all matters whatsoever. It further involves complete freedom to follow one's own inclinations or to do as one likes" (p. 143), with this single proviso: "that the individual is thereby developing a healthy moral life" (p. 141).

[2] Extract from *Carnets*, published in *Le Figaro*, January 16, 1909.

[3] *Œuvres*, Vol. I, p. 281.

[4] Jean Grave, *La Société future*, p. 157. *Cf.* also p. 199: "No individual must accept any restriction that will check his development, nor must he submit to the yoke of authority under any pretence whatsoever."

[5] *Justice dans la Révolution*, Vol. I, p. 185.

[6] Bakunin, *Œuvres*, Vol. I, p. 105.

[7] Quoted by Eltzbacher, *op. cit.*, p. 199.

whatever race or colour, degree of intellectual or moral development ";[1] and he adds that

> the individual can only become free when every other individual is free. Liberty is not an isolated fact. It is the outcome of mutual goodwill; a principle not of exclusion, but of inclusion, the liberty of each individual being simply the reflection of his humanity or of his rights as a human being in the conscience of every free man, his brother and equal.[2]

This idea of humanity, which the latest anarchists owe to Proudhon, is not simply foreign to Stirner, but is just one of those phantoms which Stirner was particularly anxious to waylay.[3]

Along with this extravagant worship of individual liberty goes a hatred of all authority. Here the political anarchists join hands with Stirner. For the exercise of authority of one man over another means the exploitation of one man by another and a denial of his humanity. The State is the summation of all authority, and the full force of anarchist hatred is focused upon the State. No human relation is too sacred for State intervention, no citizen but is liable to have his conduct minutely prescribed by law. There are officers to apply the law, armies to enforce it, lecturers to interpret it, priests to inculcate respect for it, and jurists to expound it and to justify everybody. Thus has the State become the agent *par excellence* of all exploitation and oppression.[4] It is the *one* adversary, in the opinion of every anarchist—"the sum total of all that negates the liberty of its members." "It is the grave where every trace of individuality is sacrificed and buried." Elsewhere, "it is a flagrant negation of humanity."[5] Bakunin, who in

---

[1] Bakunin, *Œuvres*, Vol. I, p. 281. "I can be really free when those around me, both men and women, are also free. The liberty of others, far from limiting or negating my own, is, on the contrary, its necessary condition and guarantee."

[2] *Ibid.*, Vol. I, p. 277.

[3] The idea of respecting man's humanity is vigorously criticized by Stirner. Proudhon is expressly mentioned as the chief representative of that view. The principle was also regarded with some favour by Feuerbach, who wanted to substitute emphasis upon the human in man for the stress generally laid upon the divine in his nature.

[4] Proudhon is the model here. "To be governed," says he (*Idée générale de la Révolution*) "is to have every deed of ours, every action and movement, noted, registered, reviewed, docketed, measured, filed, assessed, guaranteed, licensed, authorized, recommended, prohibited, checked, reformed, redressed, corrected; under pretence of public policy, to be taxed, dragooned, imprisoned, exploited, cajoled, forced, cheated, robbed; at the least sign of resistance or complaint to be repressed, convicted, vilified, vexed, hunted, mauled, murdered, stripped, garrotted imprisoned, shot, slaughtered, judged, condemned, deported, sacrificed, sold, betrayed, and finally mocked, flouted, outraged and dishonoured. That is government, such its justification and morality."

[5] Bakunin, *Œuvres*, Vol. I, pp. 143, 227, 151.

this matter as well as in many others is a follower of Bastiat, speaks of it as "the visible incarnation of infuriated force." That is enough to label it for ever with the evil things of life, for the aim of humanity is liberty, but force is "a permanent negation of liberty."[1].

A necessary agent of oppression, government always and inevitably becomes the agent of corruption. It contaminates everything that comes into contact with it, and the first to show signs of such contamination are its own representatives.

> The best man, whoever that may be, whatever degree of intelligence, magnanimity, and purity of heart he may have, is unavoidably corrupted by his trade. The person who enjoys any privilege, whether political or economic, is intellectually and morally a depraved character.

So Bakunin thought,[2] and Élisée Reclus writes in a similar strain. "Every tree in nature bears its own peculiar fruit, and government, whatever be the form it take, always results in caprice or tyranny, in misery, villainy, murder, and evil."[3] The governing classes are inevitably demoralized, but so are the governed, and for just the same reasons. Government is a worker of evil even when it would do good, for "the good whenever it is enjoined becomes evil. Liberty, morality, real human dignity consists in this, that man should do what is good not because he is told to do it, but simply because he thinks that it really is the best that he can ever wish or desire."[4]

It matters little what form government takes. Absolute or constitutional monarchy, democratic or aristocratic republicanism, government on the basis of a universal or a restricted suffrage, are all much the same, for they all presuppose a State of some sort. Authority, whether of a despot or of the majority of the community, is none the less authority, and implies the exercise of a will other than the individual's own. The great error committed by all the revolutions of the past has been this: one government has been turned out, but only to have its place usurped by another. The only true revolution will be that which will get rid of government itself—the fount and origin of all authority.

Still closer scrutiny reveals the interesting fact that the State, which is naturally oppressive, gradually becomes employed as the instrument for the subjugation of the weak by the strong, the poor by the rich. It was Adam Smith who ventured to declare that "civil government . . . is in reality instituted for the defence of the rich against the poor, or of those who have some property against those who have none at

---

[1] Bakunin, Œuvres, Vol. I, p. 228.   [2] Ibid., Vol. I, p. 176; Vol. III, p. 53.
[3] L'Évolution, la révolution, et l'idéal anarchiste, p. 164.   [4] Bakunin, Vol. I, p. 280.

all."[1] Pages of anarchist literature simply consist of elaborate paraphrases of this remark of Smith's.

Kropotkin thinks that every law must belong to one or other of three
categories. To the first category belong all laws concerned with the
security of the individual; to the second all laws concerned with the
protection of government; and to the third all those enactments where
the chief object in view is the inviolability of private property.[2] In
the opinion of the anarchist, all laws might more correctly be placed
under the last category only, for whenever the safety of the individual
is in any way threatened it is generally the result of some inequality of
fortune.[3] Indirectly, that is to say, the attack is directed against
property. The real function of government is to defend property, and
every law which is instrumental in protecting property is also effective
in shielding the institution of government from attack.

Property itself is an organization which enables a small minority of
proprietors to exploit and to hold in perpetual slavery the masses of
the people. In this instance the anarchists have not made any weighty
contribution of their own, but have merely adopted the criticisms of
the socialists.[4] Proceeding in the usual fashion, they point to the

[1] *Wealth of Nations*, Vol. II, p. 207. *Cf. supra*, p. 95, footnote. Adam Smith, it is
true, did write that "civil government, so far as it is instituted for the security of
property," etc.; but that does not imply that the great economist regarded this as the
only object of government, although it certainly is one of its chief aims.

[2] "The million and one laws that govern humanity naturally fall into one or other
of three categories: laws for the protection of property, of government, or of individuals. If we take these three divisions and analyse them we are inevitably forced
to realize how futile and even injurious all legislation is." (*Memoirs of a Revolutionist*,
p. 236.)

[3] "Society itself is every day creating beings imbued with anti-social feelings and
incapable of leading honest, industrious lives." (Kropotkin, quoted by Eltzbacher,
op. cit., p. 221.) "Seeing that the organization of society is always and everywhere
the one cause of all the crimes committed by men, its conduct in punishing criminals
is clearly absurd or obviously insincere. Every punishment implies guilt, but the
criminals in this case are never guilty. We deny the so-called right of society to
bestow punishment in this arbitrary fashion. A human being is simply the unwilling
product of the natural or social environment in which he was born and reared and
under whose influence he still remains. The three great causes of human immorality
are inequality, whether political, economic, or social; ignorance, which is its natural
result; and slavery, its inevitable consequence." (Bakunin, *Programme de l'Alliance
internationale de la Démocratie socialiste*, in *Sozial-politischer Briefwechsel*, pp. 332–333.)
"Property and want are the great incentives to crime. But if defective society
organization is the cause of crime, an improvement in organization should cause a
disappearance of crime." (Jean Grave, *La Société future*, pp. 137–138.)

[4] "Is it necessary," asks Bakunin, "to repeat the arguments of socialism, which
are still unanswerable and which no bourgeois economist has ever attempted to disprove? What are we to make of property and capital as they exist at the present
moment? In both cases it practically means a right or a power guaranteed and
protected by society to live without working; and since property and capital produce
absolutely nothing unless fertilized by labour, it means power and the right to live

miserable wages which are usually paid to the workers, and show how the masters always manage to reserve all the leisure, all the joys of existence, all the culture and other benefits of civilization for themselves. Private property is of the essence of privilege—the parent of every other kind of privilege. And the State becomes simply the bulwark of privilege. "Exploitation and government," says Bakunin, "are correlative terms indispensable to political life of every kind. Exploitation supplies the means as well as the foundation upon which government is raised, and the aim which it follows, which is merely to legalize and defend further exploitation."[1] "Experience teaches us," says Proudhon,[2] "that government everywhere, however popular at first, has always been on the side of the rich and the educated as against the poor and ignorant masses."[3]

Whether the extinction of private property, which would free the worker from the danger of being exploited by the rich, would also render the State unnecessary is a question upon which the anarchists are not agreed. Proudhon, we remember, hoped by means of the Exchange Bank to reduce the right of property to mere possession. Bakunin, on the contrary, was under the spell of the Marxians, and, like a true collectivist, he thought that all the instruments of production, including land, should be possessed by the community. Such instruments should always be at the disposal of groups of working men expert in the details of agriculture or industrial production, and such workers should be paid according to their labour.[4] Kropotkin, on the other hand, regarded communism as the ideal and looked upon the distinction drawn by the collectivist between instruments of production and objects of consumption as utterly futile. Food, clothing, and fuel were quite as necessary for production as machinery or tools, and nothing was gained by emphasizing the distinction between them. Social resources of every kind should be freely placed at the disposal of the workers.[5]

upon the labour of others and to exploit the labour of those who have neither property nor capital and are compelled to sell their productive force to the fortunate owner of the one or other of these." *Cf.* Kropotkin's *Conquest of Bread*, p. 56: "Multiply examples, choose them where you will, consider the origin of all fortunes, large or small, whether arising out of commerce, finance, manufactures, or the land. Everywhere you will find that the wealth of the wealthy springs from the poverty of the poor." In this sentence he sums up a long demonstration which he gives in proof of this contention.

[1] Bakunin, *Œuvres*, Vol. I, p. 324.

[2] *Idée générale de la Révolution*, p. 119.

[3] "Law is simply an instrument invented for the maintenance of exploitation and the domination of the idle rich over the toiling masses. Its sole mission is the perpetuation of exploitation." (Kropotkin, *Memoirs of a Revolutionist*, p. 235.)

[4] Bakunin, *Programme de l'Alliance*, in *Sozial-politischer Briefwechsel*, p. 339.

[5] Kropotkin, *Conquest of Bread*, pp. 61–62.

But the State and the institution of private property by no means exhaust the list of tyrannies. Individual liberty is as little compatible with irrevocable vows—that is, with a present promise which binds for ever the will of man—as it is with submission to external authority. The present marriage law, for example, violates both these conditions. Marriage ought to be a free union. A contract freely entered upon and deliberately fulfilled is the only form of marriage that is compatible with the true dignity and equality of both man and woman.[1] A free and not a legal contract is the only form of engagement which the anarchists recognize. Free contract between man and wife, between an individual and an association, between different associations pursuing the same task, between one commune and another, or between a commune and a whole country. But such engagements must always be revocable, otherwise they would merely constitute another link in the chain that has shackled humanity. Every contract that is not voluntarily and frequently renewed becomes tyrannical and oppressive and constitutes a standing menace to human liberty. "Because I was a fool yesterday, must I remain one all my life?"[2] asks Stirner; and on this point Bakunin, Kropotkin, Reclus, Jean Grave, and even Proudhon are agreed.

To regard their social philosophy as nothing but pure caprice because of the wonderful faith which they had in their fellow-men would, however, be a great mistake.

Notwithstanding the merciless criticism of authority of every kind, there was still left one autocrat, of a purely abstract character, perhaps, but none the less imperious in its demands. This was the authority of reason or of science. The sovereignty of reason was one of the essential features of Proudhon's anarchist society.[3] What Proudhon calls reason Bakunin refers to as science, but his obeisance is not a whit less devotional. "We recognize," says he,

the absolute authority of science and the futility of contending with natural law. No liberty is possible for man unless he recognize this

[1] "The anarchists want to see free unions established, resting upon mutual affection and based upon respect for one's self and for the dignity of others. And in that sense, in their desire to show respect and affection for all the members of the association, they are inimical to the family." (Élisée Reclus, op. cit., pp. 145–146.)

[2] Der Einzige, p. 229.

[3] Cf. Idée générale de la Révolution, p. 281, and p. 342: "Revolution follows revelation. Reason aided by experience reveals to us the nature of the laws which govern society as well as nature, and which in both cases are simply the laws of necessity. They are neither made by man nor imposed by his authority. They have only been discovered step by step, which is a proof of their independent existence. By obeying them a man becomes just and noble. Violation of them constitutes injustice and sin. I can suggest no other motive for human actions."

and seek to turn this law to his own advantage. No one except a
fool or a theologian, or perhaps a metaphysician, a jurist, or a
bourgeois economist, would revolt against the mathematical law
which declares that $2 + 2 = 4$.

The utmost that a man can claim in this matter is that "he obeys the
laws of nature because he himself has come to regard them as necessary, and not because they have been imposed upon him by some
external authority."[1]

Not only does Bakunin bow the knee to science, but he also swears
allegiance to technical or scientific skill.

> In the matter of boots I am willing to accept the authority of the
> shoemaker; of clothes, the opinion of the tailor; if it is a house, a
> canal, or a railway, I consult the architect and the engineer. What
> I respect is not their office but their science, not the man but his
> knowledge. I cannot, however, allow any one of them to impose
> upon me, be he shoemaker, tailor, architect, or savant. I listen to
> them willingly and with all the respect which their intelligence,
> character, or knowledge deserves, but always reserving my undis-
> puted right of criticism and control.[2]

Bakunin has no doubt that most men willingly and spontaneously
acknowledge the natural authority of science. He agrees with Descartes
and employs almost identical terms[3] when he declares that "common
sense is one of the commonest things in the world." But common
sense simply means "the totality of the generally recognized laws of
nature." He shares with the Physiocrats a belief in their obviousness,
and invokes their authority whenever he makes a vow. He is also
anxious to make them known and acceptable of all men through the
instrumentality of a general system of popular education. The moment
they are accepted by "the universal conscience of mankind the question
of liberty will be completely solved."[4] Let us again note how redolent
all this is of the rationalistic optimism of the eighteenth century, and
how closely Liberals and anarchists resemble one another in their
absolute faith in the "sweet reasonableness" of mankind. Bakunin
only differs from the Physiocrats in his hatred of the despot whom they
had enthroned.

A society of free men, perfectly autonomous, each obeying only himself, but subservient to the authority of reason and science—such is
the ideal which the anarchists propose, a preliminary consideration
of its realization being the overthrow of every established authority.

---

[1] Bakunin, *Œuvres*, Vol. III, p. 51.   [2] *Ibid.*, Vol. III, p. 55.

[3] "In general we may say that man's general life is almost entirely governed by
what we call good sense." (*Ibid.*, Vol. III, p. 50.)

[4] *Ibid.*, Vol. III, p. 51.

"No God and no master," says Jean Grave; "every one obeying his own will."[1]

III: MUTUAL AID AND THE ANARCHIST CONCEPTION OF SOCIETY

At first sight it might seem that a conception of social existence which would raise every individual on a pedestal and proclaim the complete autonomy of each would speedily reduce society to a number of independent personalities. Every social tie removed, there would remain just a few individuals in juxtaposition, and society as a 'collective being' would disappear.

But it would be a grievous mistake to conceive of the anarchist ideal in this light. There is no social doctrine where the words 'solidarity' and 'fraternity' more frequently recur. Individual happiness and social well-being are to them inseparable. Hobbes's society, or Stirner's, where the hand of every one is against his brother, fill the anarchists with horror. To their mind that is a faithful picture of society as it exists to-day. In reality, however, man is a social being. The individual and society are correlative: it is impossible to imagine the one without thinking of the other.

No one has given more forcible expression to this truth than Bakunin; and this is possibly because no one ever had a keener sense of social solidarity. "Let us do justice once for all," he remarks,

> to the isolated or absolute individual of the idealists. But that individual is as much a fiction as that other Absolute—God. . . . Society, however, is prior to the individual, and will doubtless survive him, just as Nature will. Society, like Nature, is eternal; born of the womb of Nature, it will last as long as Nature herself. . . . Man becomes human and develops a conscience only when he realizes his humanity in society; and even then he can only express himself through the collective action of society. Man can only be freed from the yoke of external nature through the collective or social effort of his fellowmen, who during their sojourn here have transformed the surface of the earth and made the further development of mankind possible. But freedom from the yoke of his own nature, from the tyranny of his own instincts, is only possible when the bodily senses are controlled by a well-trained, well-educated mind. Education and training are essentially social functions. Outside the bounds of society, man would for ever remain a savage beast.[2]

Whether we read Proudhon or Kropotkin, we always meet with the same emphasis on the reality of the social being, on the pre-existence of the State, or at least of its necessary coexistence, if the individual

[1] *La Société future*, p. 303.   [2] Bakunin, *Œuvres*, Vol. I, pp. 298, 286, 277.

is ever to reach full development. It is true that there are a few anarchists, such as Jean Grave, who still seem to uphold the old futile distinction between the individual and society, and who conceive of society as made up of individuals just as a house is built of bricks.

But is there no element of contradiction between this idea and the previous declaration of individual autonomy? How is it possible to exalt social life and at the same time demand the abolition of all traditional social links?[1]

The apparent antinomy is resolved by emphasizing a distinction which Liberalism had drawn between government and society. Society is the natural, spontaneous expression of social life. Government is an artificial organ, or, to change the metaphor, a parasite preying upon society.[2] Liberals from the days of Smith onward had applied the distinction to economic institutions; the anarchists were to apply it

---

[1] Bakunin on his death-bed confessed to his friend Reichel that "all his philosophy had been built upon a false foundation. All was vitiated because he had begun by taking man as an individual, whereas he is really a member of a collective whole" (quoted by Guillaume, *Œuvres*, preface to Vol. II, p. 60). In his *Philosophie du Progrès* (*Œuvres*, Vol. XX, pp. 36–38) Proudhon writes as follows: "All that reason knows and maintains is that the individual, like an idea, is really a group. All existence is in groups, and whatever forms a group also forms a unit, and consequently becomes perceptible and is then said to exist. In accordance with this general conception of being, I think it possible to prove the existence of positive reality and up to a certain point to demonstrate the laws of the social being or of the humanitarian group, and to establish a proof of the existence of an individuality superior to collective man and still quite other and different from his individual self." The same idea frequently comes up in different connexions, *e.g.*, in the *Petit Catéchisme politique* at the end of Vol. I of *La Justice dans la Révolution*, and in *Idée générale de la Révolution*.

Kropotkin thinks that man has always lived in society of one kind or another. "As far back as we can go in the palæo-ethnology of mankind, we find men living in societies, in tribes similar to those of the highest mammals." (*Mutual Aid*, p. 85.) "Man did not create society; society is older than man." (*The State, its Historic Role*, p. 6; London, 1898.) Jean Grave, on the other hand, thinks that "the individual was prior to society. Destroy the individual, and there will be nothing left of society. Let the association be dissolved and the individuals scattered, they will fare badly and will possibly return to savagery, their faculties will decay and not progress, but still they will continue to exist." (*La Société future*, pp. 160–162.) Grave's view is essentially his own and does not square with those of either Kropotkin, Bakunin, or Proudhon, the real founders of anarchy. It is, moreover, quite obvious that their theories are really much nearer the truth, for it is as impossible to conceive of society without the individual as it is to conceive of the individual without society. The individual, as Bakunin emphatically declares, is a fiction, or an abstraction, as Walras would say. Many people find it difficult to accept this doctrine. But it seems the only one that tallies with the facts, whether of nature or of history. We can no more imagine the individual without society than we can a fish without water. Deprived of water, it is not only less of a fish, but it is no longer a fish at all—except a dead one.

[2] Bastiat speaks of this error of confusing government and society as being the worst that has ever befallen the science. The State problem he defines as follows: "How to inscribe within the great circle which we call society that other circle called government." Dunoyer in so many words expresses the same idea.

to every social institution. Not only the economic but every form of social life is the outcome of the social instinct which lies deep in the nature of humanity. This instinct of solidarity urges men to seek the help of their fellow-men and to act in concert with them. It is what Kropotkin calls mutual aid, and seems as natural to man and as necessary for the preservation of the species as the struggle for existence itself. What really binds society together, what makes for real cohesion, is not constraint (which, contrary to the time-honoured belief of the privileged classes, is really only necessary to uphold their privileges), but this profound instinct of mutual help and reciprocal friendship, whose strength and force have never yet been adequately realized. "There is in human nature," says Kropotkin, "a nucleus of social habits inherited from the past, which have not been as fully appreciated as they might. They are not the result of any restraint and transcend all compulsion."[1]

Law, instead of creating the social instinct, simply presupposes it. Laws can only be applied so long as the instinct exists, and fall into desuetude as soon as the instinct refuses to sanction them. Government, far from developing this instinct, opposes it with rigid, stereotyped institutions which thwart its full and complete development. To free the individual from external restraint is also to liberate society by giving it greater plasticity and permitting it to assume new forms which are obviously better adapted to the happiness and prosperity of the race.[2] Kropotkin in his delightful book *Mutual Aid* gives numerous examples of this spontaneous social instinct. He shows how it assumes different forms in the economic, scientific, educational, sporting, hygienic, and charitable associations of modern Europe; in the municipalities and corporations of the Middle Ages; and how even among animals this same instinct, which forms the real basis of all human

---

[1] *Memoirs of a Revolutionist. Cf.* also *Paroles d'un Révolté*, p. 221.

[2] This idea finds frequent expression with both Reclus and Kropotkin. "The fact that we have instituted, regulated, codified, and encompassed with constraints and penalties, with gendarmes and jailers, the larger part of our more or less incoherent collection of political, religious, moral and social conceptions of to-day in order to enforce them upon the citizens of to-morrow is in itself sufficiently absurd, and it is bound to have contradictory results. Life, which is always improving and renewing itself, can never submit to regulations which have been drawn up in some period now past." (Reclus, *op. cit.*, pp. 108–109.) "Anarchist society," writes Kropotkin, "is one to which any pre-established, crystallized form of law will always be repugnant. It is also one which looks for harmony, which can only be temporary and fugitive perhaps, in the equilibrium between the mass of different forces and influences of every kind which pursue their course without the slightest deflection, and which because they are quite untrammelled beget reaction and arouse those activities which are favourable to them when they move in the direction of progress." (*L'Anarchie,* pp. 17, 18.)

societies, has enabled them to overcome the natural dangers that threaten their existence.

Anarchist society must not be conceived as a *bellum omnium contra omnes*, but as a federation of free associations which every one would be at liberty to enter and to leave just as he liked. This society, Kropotkin tells us, would be composed of a multitude of associations bound together for all purposes that demand united action. A federation of producers would have control of agricultural and industrial, and even of intellectual and artistic production; an association of consumers would see to questions of housing, lighting, health, food, and sanitation. In some cases the federation of producers would join hands with the consumers' league. Still wider groups would embrace a whole country, or possibly several countries, and would include people employed in the same kind of work, whether industrial, intellectual, or artistic, for none of these pursuits would be confined to some one territory. Mutual understanding would result in combined efforts, and complete liberty would give plenty of scope for invention and new methods of organization. Individual initiative would be encouraged; every tendency to uniformity and centralization would be effectively checked.[1]

In such a society as this complete concord between the general and the individual interests, hitherto so vainly sought after by the bourgeoisie, would be realized once for all in the absolute freedom now the possession of both the individual and the group, and in the total disappearance of all traces of antagonism between possessors and non-possessing, between governors and governed. Again we note a revival of the belief in the spontaneous harmony of interests which was so prominent a feature of eighteenth-century philosophy.[2]

Such an attractive picture of society was bound to invite criticism. The anarchists foresaw this, and have tried to meet most of the arguments.

In the first place, would such extravagant freedom not beget abuse,

[1] *Memoirs of a Revolutionist.*

[2] Proudhon had already set the problem as follows: "Can we find a method of transacting business that will unite divergent interests and identify individuals with the general well-being, replace the inequality of nature by equality of education, and remove all political and economic contradictions; when each individual will be at once both producer and consumer, citizen and sovereign, ruler and ruled; when liberty will always expand without involving any counter-loss; when the well-being of each will grow indefinitely without involving any damage to the property, the labour, or the revenue of any of his fellow-citizens, or of the State itself, without weakening the interests he has in common with his fellow-men, without alienating their good opinion or destroying their affection for him?" (*Idée générale*, p. 45.) Says Jean Grave: "Were society established on natural bases, individual and general interests would never conflict." (*Société future*, p. 156.)

unjustifiable repudiation of contracts, crimes and misdemeanours? Would it not give rise to chronic instability? and would the conscientious never find themselves the victims of the fickle and the fraudulent?

The anarchists agree that there may be a few pranks played, or, as Grave euphemistically calls them, "certain acts apparently altogether devoid of logic."[1] But can we not reckon upon criticism and disapproval checking such anti-social instincts? Public opinion, if it were once freed from the warping influence of present-day institutions, would possess far greater coercive force.[2] Our present system of building prisons, "those criminal universities," as Kropotkin calls them, will never check these anti-social instincts. "Liberty is still the best remedy for the temporary excesses of liberty."[3] Moreover, such a system would enjoy a superior sanction in the possible refusal of other people to work with those who could not keep their word.[4] "You are a man and you have a right to live. But as you wish to live under special conditions and leave the ranks, it is more than probable that you will suffer for it in your daily relations with other citizens "[5]

But there is still a more serious objection. Were there no compulsion, would anyone be found willing to work? The host of idlers is at the present time vast, and without the sting of necessity it would become still greater. Kropotkin remarks that "it is only about the sugar plantations of the West Indies and the sugar refineries of Europe that robbery, laziness, and very often drunkenness become quite usual with the bees."[6] Is it not possible that men are just imitating the bee?

The anarchists point out that many a so-called idler to-day is simply a madcap who will soon discover his true vocation in the free

[1] La Société future, p. 16. "We cannot disguise the fact," says Kropotkin, "that if complete liberty of thought and action were once given to the individual we should see some exaggerations, possibly extravagant exaggerations, of our principles." (Memoirs of a Revolutionist, p. 413.)

[2] "The only great and all-powerful authority at once rational and natural that we can respect is the public spirit of a collective society founded upon equality and solidarity, upon liberty and respect for the human qualities of all its members. It will be a thousand times more powerful than all your authorities, whether divine, theological, metaphysical, political, or juridical, whether instituted by Church or by State; more powerful than all your criminal codes, all your jailers and hangmen." (Bakunin, Œuvres, Vol. III, p. 79.)

[3] Memoirs of a Revolutionist, p. 414. This is also one of the favourite doctrines of the Liberals.

[4] Kropotkin, Conquest of Bread, p. 206.

[5] Grave, op. cit., p. 297. Proudhon is even more severe. "By making a contract you become a member of the fraternity of free men. In case of infringement, either on their side or on yours, you are responsible to one another, and the responsibility might even involve excommunication and death." (Idée générale, p. 343.)

[6] Kropotkin, Mutual Aid, p. 17.

society of the future, and will thus be gradually transformed into a useful member of society.[1] Moreover, does not the fact that so many people shun work altogether prove that the present method of organizing society must be at once cruel and repugnant? The certainty of being confined in an unhealthy workshop for ten or twelve hours every day, with mind and body "to some unmeaning task-work given," in return for a wage that is seldom sufficient to keep a family in decent comfort, is hardly a prospect that is likely to attract the worker. One of the principal aims of the anarchist regime—and in this respect it resembles the Phalanstère of Fourier— ill be to make labour both attractive and productive.[2] Science will render the factory healthy, well lighted, and thoroughly ventilated. Machinery will even come to the rescue of the housewife and will relieve her of many a disagreeable task. Inventors, who are generally ignorant of the unpleasant nature of many of these tasks, have been inclined to ignore them altogether. "If a Huxley spent only five hours in the sewers of London, rest assured that he would have found the means of making them as sanitary as his physiological laboratory."[3] Finally, and most important of all, the working day could then be reduced to a matter of four or five hours, for there would no longer be any idlers, and the systematic application of science would increase production tenfold.

The wonderful expansion of production under the influence of applied science is a favourite theme of the anarchists. Kropotkin has treated us to some delightful illustrations of this in his *Conquest of Bread*. He begins by pointing out the wonders already accomplished by market gardeners living in the neighbourhood of Paris. One of these, employing only three men working twelve to fifteen hours a day, was able, thanks to intensive cultivation, to raise 110 tons of vegetables on one acre of ground. Taking this as his basis, he calculates that the 3,600,000 inhabitants in the departments of the Seine and the Seine-et-Oise could produce all the corn, milk, vegetables, and fruit which they could possibly need in the year with fifty-eight half-days' labour per man. By parity of reasoning he arrives at the conclusion that twenty-eight to thirty-six days' work per annum would

[1] "In our opinion, and speaking strictly, there is no such thing as a really idle person. There are a few individuals, perhaps, who have not developed as they might have done and whose activity has never found a proper outlet under existing conditions. In a society where every one would be allowed to choose his own sphere of work the idlest people would be found doing something." (J. Grave, *La Société future*, pp. 277–278.) Kropotkin writes in the same strain (*Conquest of Bread*, chapter on *Objections*).

[2] Kropotkin, *Memoirs of a Revolutionist*, p. 414; *Conquest of Bread*, p. 156. The anarchists show no desire to expand the Phalanstère, but prefer the family life.

[3] *Conquest of Bread*, p. 204.

secure for each family a healthy, comfortable home such as is occupied
by English working men at the present time. The same thing applies
to clothing. American factories produce on an average forty yards of
cotton in ten hours.

> Admitting that a family needs two hundred yards a year at most,
> this would be equivalent to fifty hours' labour, or ten half-days of
> five hours each,[1] and that all adults save women bind themselves to
> work five hours a day from the age of twenty or twenty-two to forty-
> five or fifty. . . . Such a society could in return guarantee well-being
> to all its members.[2]

Élisée Reclus shares these hopes. It seems to him that "in the great
human family hunger is simply the result of a collective crime, and it
becomes an absurdity when we remember that the products are more
than double enough for all the needs of consumers."[3]

Amid such superabundant wealth, in a world thus transformed into
a land of milk and honey, distribution would not be a very difficult
problem. Nothing really could be easier. "No stint or limit to what
the community possesses in abundance, but equal sharing and dividing
of those commodities which are scarce or apt to run short."[4] Such
was to be the guiding principle. In practice the women and children,
the aged and the infirm, were to come first and the robust men last,
for such even is the etiquette of the soup kitchen, which has become a
feature of some recent strikes. As to the laws of value which are
supposed to determine the present distribution of wealth, and which
the economists fondly believe to be necessary and immutable, the
anarchists regard them as being no concern of theirs. The futility of
such doctrines is a source of some amusement to them.[5]

IV: REVOLUTION

But how is the beautiful dream to be realized? The way thither,
from the miserable wilderness wherein we now dwell to the Promised
Land of which they have given us a glimpse, lies through Revolution
—so the anarchist tells us.

A theory of revolution forms a necessary part of the anarchist doctrine. In the mind of the public it is too often thought to be the only
message which the anarchists have to give. We must content ourselves

---

[1] *Conquest of Bread*, p. 130.   [2] *Ibid.*, p. 133.
[3] Élisée Reclus, *L'Évolution*, etc., pp. 136–137.   [4] *Conquest of Bread*, p. 83.
[5] *Cf.* Grave, *La Société future*, chapter xiv, *La Valeur*. The anarchists frequently complain that their ideas are generally mutilated by the economists. To read this chapter
is to realize the amount of intelligence which they display when interpreting their
adversaries' doctrines!

with a very brief reference to it, for the non-economic ideas of anarchism have already detained us sufficiently long.

Proudhon is soon out of the running. We have already had occasion to refer to his disapproval of violence and revolution. It seemed to him that the anarchic ideal was for ever impossible apart from a change of heart and a reawakening of conscience. But his successors were somewhat less patient. To their minds revolution seemed an unavoidable necessity from which escape was impossible. Even if we could imagine all the privileged individuals of to-day agreeing among themselves on the night of some fourth of August to yield up every privilege which they possess and to enter the ranks of the proletariat of their own free will, such a deed would hardly be desirable. The people, says Reclus, with their usual generosity, would simply let them do as they liked, but would say to their former masters, "Keep your privileges."

> It is not because justice should not be done, but things ought to find a natural equilibrium. The oppressed should rise in their own strength, the despoiled seize their own again, and the slaves regain their own liberty. Such things can only really be attained as the result of a bitter struggle.[1]

It is not that Bakunin, Kropotkin, or their disciples revel in bloodshed or welcome outbreaks of violence. Bloodshed, although inevitably and inseparably connected with revolution, is none the less regrettable, and should always be confined within the narrowest limits.

> Bloody revolutions are occasionally necessary because of the crass stupidity of mankind; but they are always an evil, an immense evil, and a great misfortune; not only because of their victims, but also because of the pure and perfect character of the aims in view of which they are carried out.[2]

"The question," says Kropotkin,[3] "is not how to avoid revolutions, but how to secure the best results by checking civil war as far as possible, by reducing the number of victims, and by restraining the more dangerous passions." To do this we must rely upon people's instincts, who, far from being sanguinary, "are really too kind at heart not to be very soon disgusted with cruelty."[4] The attack must be directed

[1] *L'Évolution*, p. 154. Kropotkin says: "Those who wish the triumph of justice, who really want to put the new ideas into practice, understand the necessity for a terrible revolution which would sweep away this canker and revive the degenerate hearts with its invigorating rush, bringing back habits of devotion, of self-negation, and of heroism, without which society becomes vile, degraded, and rotten." (*Paroles d'un Révolté*, p. 280.)

[2] Bakunin, in *Sozial-politischer*, p. 297.   [3] *Memoirs of a Revolutionist*, p. 297.

[4] Kropotkin, quoted by Eltzbacher, p. 236. "Revolution, once it becomes socialistic, will cease to be sanguinary and cruel. The people are not cruel. It is the privileged

not against men but against their position, and the aim must be not individuals but their status. Hence Bakunin lays great stress upon setting fire to the national archives, and to papers of all kinds relating to title in property, upon the immediate suppression of all law courts and police, upon the disbanding of the army, and the instant confiscation of all instruments of production—factories, mines, etc. Kropotkin in the *Conquest of Bread* gives us a picture of an insurgent commune laying hold of houses and occupying them, seizing drapers' establishments and taking whatever they need, confiscating the land, cultivating it, and distributing its products. If revolutionists only proceeded in this fashion, never respecting the rights of property at all (which was the great mistake made by the Commune in its dealing with the Bank of France during the rising of 1871), the revolution would soon be over and society would speedily reorganize itself on a new and indestructible basis and with a minimum of bloodshed.

But the tone is not always equally pacific. Bakunin during at least one period of his life preached a savage and merciless revolution against privilege of every kind. At that time, indeed, he might justly have passed as the inventor of the active propaganda which, strenuously pursued for many years by a few exasperated fanatics, had the effect of rousing public opinion everywhere against anarchism. "We understand revolution," some one has remarked, "in the sense of an upheaval of what we call the worst passions, and we can imagine its resulting in the destruction of what we to-day term public order." "Brigandage," it is remarked elsewhere, "is an honourable method of political propaganda in Russia, where the brigand is a hero, a defender and saviour of the people."[1] In a kind of proclamation entitled *The Principles of Revolution*, which, as some writers point out, ought not to be attributed to Bakunin, but which at any rate appears to give a fair representation of his ideas at this period of his life, we meet with the following words: "The present generation should blindly and indiscriminately destroy all that at present exists, with this single thought in mind—to destroy as much and as quickly as possible."[2] The means advocated are of a

classes that are cruel. People are ordinarily kind and humane, and will suffer long rather than cause others any suffering." (Bakunin, *Œuvres*, Vol. III, pp. 184–185.) The same idea runs through Sorel's *Réflexions sur la Violence*.

[1] Bakunin, *Sozial-politischer*, pp. 225 and 353.

[2] *Sozial-politischer*, p. 361. The proclamation was addressed to Young Russia just after the Tsar Alexander II had accepted the challenge of Liberalism by emancipating the serfs. But he immediately proceeded to revive the cruel system of espionage and repression carried out by his father Nicholas I, and so roused the indignation of the more advanced leaders, who thought that they had in him a hero who would open the golden gates of liberty. Bakunin at the time was under the influence of an unscrupulous fanatic of the name of Netchaieff, whose savage and revolting passion

most varied description: "Poison, the dagger, and the sword . . . revolution makes them all equally sacred. The whole field is free for action."[1] Bakunin had always shown a good deal of sympathy for the role of the conspirator. In the *Statutes of the International Brotherhood*, which prescribed the rules of conduct for a kind of revolutionary association created by Bakunin in 1864, are some passages advocating violence which are as bloodcurdling as anything contained in Netchaieff's famous *Revolutionary Catechism*. It is difficult to find lines more full of violent revolutionary exasperation than that passage of the *Statutes of the International Socialist Alliance* which forms the real programme of the anarchists. Since it also seems to us to give a fairly faithful expression of Bakunin's thoughts on the matter, it will afford a fitting close to our exposition.

> We want a universal revolution that will shake the social and political, the economic and philosophical basis of society, so that of the present order, which is founded upon property, exploitation, dominion, and authority, and supported either by religion or philosophy, by bourgeois economics or by revolutionary Jacobinism, there may not be left, either in Europe or anywhere else, a single stone standing. The workers' prayer for peace we would answer by demanding the freedom of all the oppressed and the death of every one who lords it over them, exploiters and guardians of every kind. Every State and every Church would be destroyed, together with all their various institutions, their religious, political, judicial, and financial regulations; the police system, all university regulations, all social and economic rules whatsoever, so that the millions of poor human beings who are now being cheated and gagged, tormented and exploited, delivered from the cruellest of official directors and officious curates, from all collective and individual tyranny, would for once be able to breathe freely.[2]

A discussion of anarchist doctrine lies beyond our province. Moreover, such sweeping generalizations disarm all criticism. Their theories are too often the outbursts of passionate feeling and scarcely need refuting. Let us, then, try to discover the kind of influence they have had.

We are not going to speak of the criminal outrages which unfortunately have resulted from their teaching. Untutored minds already exasperated by want found themselves incapable of resisting the temptations to violence in face of such doctrines. Such deeds, or active propaganda as they call it, can have no manner of justification, but find an explanation in the extreme fanaticism of the authors. It is not very

for the execution of criminal deeds in the name of revolution had completely captivated him. Later on he vigorously reproved such acts, and declared that he had been mistaken.
[1] Bakunin, *Sozial-politischer Briefwechsel*, p. 361.   [2] *Ibid.*, p. 332.

easy to attribute such violence to a social doctrine which, according to the circumstances, may on the one hand be considered as the philosophy of outrage and violence, and on the other as an ideal expression of human fraternity and individual progress.

The influence of which we would speak is the influence which anarchy has had upon the working classes in general. Undoubtedly it has led to a revival of individualism and has begotten a reaction against the centralizing socialism of Marx. Its success has been especially great among the Latin nations and in Austria, where it seemed for a time as if it would supplant socialism altogether. Very marked progress has also been made in France, Italy, and Spain. Is it because individuality is stronger in those countries than elsewhere? We think not. The fact is that wherever liberty has only recently been achieved, order and discipline, even when freely accepted, seem little better than intolerable signs of slavery.

An anarchist party came into being between 1880 and 1895. But since 1895 it seems to have declined. This does not mean that the influence of anarchism has been on the wane, but simply that it has changed its character. In France especially many of the older anarchists joined the Trade Union movement, and occasionally managed to get the control of affairs into their own hands, and under their influence the trade unions tried to get rid of the socialist yoke. The Confédération générale du Travail took as its motto two words that are always coupled together in anarchist literature, namely, 'Welfare and liberty.' It also advocated 'direct action'—that is, action which is of a definitely revolutionary character and in defiance of public order. Finally, it betrayed the same impatience with merely political action, and would have the workers concentrate upon the economic struggle. Since the First World War the anarchist movement has practically disappeared.

The prophets of revolutionary syndicalism deny any alliance with anarchy. But, despite their protests, it would be a comparatively easy matter to point to numerous analogies in the writings of Bakunin and Kropotkin. Moreover, they admit that Proudhon, as well as Marx, has contributed something to the syndicalist doctrine; and we have already noted the intimate connexion which exists between Proudhon and the anarchists.

The first resemblance consists in their advocacy of violence as a method of regenerating and purifying social life. "It is to violence," writes M. Sorel, "that socialism owes those great moral victories that have brought salvation to the modern world."[1] The anarchists in a similar fashion liken revolution to the storm that clears the threatening

[1] *Réflexions sur la Violence*, p. 253.

sky of summer, making the air once more pure and calm. Kropotkin longs for a revolution because it would not merely renew the economic order, but would also "stir up society both morally and intellectually, shake it out of its lethargy, and revive its morals. The vile and narrow passion of the moment would be swept aside by the strong breath of a nobler passion, a greater enthusiasm, and a more generous devotion."[1]

In the second place, moral considerations, which find no place in the social philosophy of Marx, are duly recognized by Sorel and by the anarchist authors. Bakunin, Kropotkin, and Proudhon especially demand a due respect for human worth as the condition of every man's liberty. They also proclaim the sovereignty of reason as the only power that can make men really free. M. Sorel, after showing how the new school may be easily distinguished from official socialism by the greater stress which it lays upon the perfection of morals, proceeds to add that on this point he is entirely at one with the anarchists.[2]

Finally, their social and political ideals are the same. In both cases the demand is for the abolition of personal property and the extinction of the State. "The syndicalist hates the State just as much as the anarchist. He sees in the State nothing but an unproductive parasite borne upon the shoulder of the producer and living upon his substance."[3] And Sorel regards socialism as a tool in the hands of the workers which will some day enable them to get rid of the State and abolish the rights of private property.[4] "Free producers working in a factory where there will be no masters"[5]—such is the ideal of syndicalism, according to Sorel. There is also the same hostility shown towards democracy as at present constituted and its alliance with the State.

But despite many resemblances the two conceptions are really quite distinct. The hope of anarchy is that spontaneous action and universal liberty will somehow regenerate society. Syndicalism builds its faith upon a particular institution, the trade union, which it regards as the most effective instrument of class war. On this basis there would be set up an ideal society of producers founded upon labour, from which intellectualism would be banished. Anarchy, on the other hand, contents itself with a vision of a kind of natural society, which the syndicalist thinks both illusory and dangerous.

It has not been altogether useless, perhaps, to note the striking analogy that exists between these two currents of thought which have had such a profound influence upon the working-class movement during this century, and which have resulted in a remarkable revival of individualism.

---

[1] *Paroles d'un Révolté*, pp. 17–18. [2] *Réflexions sur la Violence*, p. 218.
[3] Berth, *Les Nouveaux Aspects du Socialisme*, p. 3.
[4] *Réflexions sur la Violence*, introduction. [5] *Ibid.*, p. 237.

Book VI: Predominance of Production and Exchange Problems after the First World War

In the preceding Book we have described the progress of economic theory and the emergence of social doctrines during a long period of peace that favoured both these things. Since 1914 the theories and doctrines that have been developed have borne the marks of war. Just as the founders of economics, from Adam Smith to Ricardo and J. B. Say, were strongly influenced by the Seven Years' War and the War of American Independence, and still more by the Revolutionary and Napoleonic Wars, so too was economic thought between 1914 and 1939 affected by the great world conflict whose shadow stretched far beyond the end of hostilities. Problems just like those that disturbed the founders of economics suddenly resumed all their former urgency and reality, but on an infinitely larger scale. They arose, too, in a world that had been transformed in a hundred years by a revolution in methods of transport and industrial technique, by an unprecedented increase in the population of the world, and by the economic influences that were henceforth to be exerted by such powerful new nations as the United States, Japan, and the British Dominions.

During the nineteenth century each country in turn had to review every ten years its financial, commercial, or monetary policy, but the scope of the discussions involved in this review hardly ever extended beyond the range of the nation itself, except in certain rare circumstances. After 1918, however, the same questions arose all at once, and all governments were faced by them at the same time. The result was a striking resemblance between the problems that exercised the economists of all lands, even in the realm of theory. In the vast literature to which these problems gave rise we find no longer the clearly defined schools of thought that we have distinguished in earlier pages. No economist is willing to be enrolled under any of the former standards.

On the other hand, however, there was also an accentuation of national characteristics, so that it would be very tempting to classify economists according to their nationality and to show how each of them has been constantly influenced by the circumstances peculiar to his country and by its scientific traditions. We should have to try to describe an 'English' school, still permeated, almost against its will, by

memories of Ricardo; an 'American' school, much closer in its methods
and conclusions to the 'continental' schools (Italian, French, or
Viennese) than to the English school; and a 'German' school, mainly
concerned with immediate problems. To these would have to be
added the brilliant school of 'Stockholm,' whose representatives
to-day enjoy well-merited prestige for the progress they have made in
some of the most difficult theoretical problems of our science.[1] But
this method seems out of keeping with the very spirit of a work in
which the history of political economy has been deliberately treated as
the history of a science in which national differences give way to the
common search for truth.

What is the historian of ideas concerned with? What will the
economist of to-morrow, to whom this book is addressed, be interested
in? Above all else it is the *permanent* changes that the flood of new facts
has brought about in the great theories and fundamental concepts of
political economy. The contribution made by certain original thinkers
to a better understanding of economic life, and their wider grasp of
existing theories in the light of the new combinations of forces revealed
by the war and the post-war period—these are of more importance
than the variety of attitudes adopted by economists in regard to
practical problems that are always the same, though differently
presented in different countries. From these problems, of course, we
cannot entirely withdraw our attention, but we shall attend particularly to the progress that science has made through them.

Looking at the matter from this point of view, we are struck by a
twofold trend of thought that has been apparent since the First World
War in almost all branches of our science. First there is the desire
to show in precise detail the mechanism by which some elements of
the economic system adapt themselves to changes in other elements—
the adaptation of commerce to exchange variations, of prices to monetary fluctuations, of production to crises, and so forth. The description
of these mechanisms and their representation in the form of simplified
schemes—what a Swiss economist has called "little models"—are one
of the main concerns of economists to-day, and especially of those who
in increasing numbers start from Walras's theory of equilibrium and
come to regard the different factors of economic life as closely interdependent.

The same writers are also concerned to describe the play of these
mechanisms *in an economy that is constantly changing*. It is the *dynamic*

[1] I will name here only Wicksell, Cassel, Lindhal, Myrdal, Ohlin, and Heckscher
among those whose works are partially available in translations and deserve to be
carefully studied.

aspect of economic phenomena, in contrast to their *static* aspect, that attracts them most. There is nothing surprising in this at a time when the mobility of economic life forces itself on the attention of the most careless observer. Nor is it surprising to see certain problems raised afresh[1] in the very terms in which they were dealt with by, say, Sismondi or Malthus in opposition to the classical economists.

These theoretical tendencies are particularly marked in the study of two problems to which for this reason we give the central place in our exposition: the problem of international trade and the problem of crises. Both of them have called forth some of the best books of the period just ended, and it is around them that the views of the most prominent economists of to-day and to-morrow can most conveniently be grouped. All these economists, near and far, and whatever their nationality, have taken part in the heated discussions aroused by these problems. The reader will see that, from the way they have been dealt with, we can observe marked and continuous progress. To this progress the most varied types of mind have contributed, and it is such as to encourage those who put their faith in the gradual transformation of political economy from a *normative* science, as it tended to be at the beginning to far too great an extent, to the *explicative* science that it has always wished to become.

It may perhaps be thought that along with theories relating to crises and foreign exchanges we should have kept a special chapter for monetary theories. But for various reasons we have not done so. Though practical monetary problems have been warmly debated for twenty years, the progress made in the theory of money does not seem to us proportionate to the volume of these discussions. Moreover, the complexity and the technical character of these problems would have meant giving them more space than we could afford in a work of this kind. And lastly, there was too great a risk of merely repeating what has recently been said in another work on this subject, to which the reader is referred.[2] He will see also that monetary questions have been dealt with more than once in the chapters that follow. They are inseparable from the problems of international trade and of crises, with which in their most modern aspects they are closely connected.[3]

[1] By Keynes, for instance.

[2] *Histoire des doctrines relatives au crédit et à la monnaie*, by Charles Rist (Sirey, Paris, 1936).

[3] Since the publication of the last edition of our *History of Economic Doctrines* many general histories of economic theories have appeared in France. We should mention particularly M. Gonnard's *Histoire des doctrines économiques*, and M. Gaëtan Pirou's *Les Doctrines économiques en France depuis 1870*, which makes a very useful complement to many chapters of our book. But special mention should be made of this author's series of volumes (Domat-Montchrestien) in which he makes a profound study of

CHAPTER I: GENERAL REVIEW OF THEORIES OF INTERNATIONAL TRADE

PROBLEMS of international trade assumed unprecedented importance after the First World War. The belligerents were left at the end of hostilities in a situation closely resembling that assumed by Ricardo as the starting-point for his theory of international commerce. He described countries, hitherto separate, entering suddenly into trading relations, and investigated the results on their economy. The end of the World War made real what had been looked on as only an abstract hypothesis. What would be the effects of this sudden resumption of contacts between countries isolated by the blockade and the long closing of frontiers? How would commodity prices behave when communications were once more established? What would be the fate of industrial and agricultural undertakings that had been abnormally developed by the war? And lastly, what economic policy ought States to adopt in the peace period? Should they strengthen the tendency towards more rigorous protection, already in evidence before the war, or encourage a return to greater freedom of trade?

A further serious difficulty was caused by the demand of the Allies for reparations from Germany and the American claim to repayment of the enormous advances made to the 'associated nations.' How were such gigantic sums of money to be found, and then transferred from one country to another? What would be the effect of such transfers on the international trade in commodities? Would not the process be likely to produce profound disturbances in the monetary equilibrium and the foreign exchanges, and upset national economies by creating imports and exports out of all proportion to the normal course of trade?

These problems seemed to have been solved at last, after a fashion, at the end of ten years of conferences, negotiations, and agreements (as well as disagreements) between States and central note-issuing banks, when suddenly the world crisis broke out in the autumn of 1929 and brought into question once more all the results so laboriously obtained. The profound fall in prices, creating grave difficulties for industrialists and farmers in all lands, evoked everywhere a violent reaction against the foreign competition that was held responsible for

---

all the great currents of thought relating to economic theory. This series, consisting of a large number of volumes, enables the reader to understand the very varied directions taken by doctrines and methods in foreign countries, particularly the United States.

this fall. National economies sought safety in methods hitherto unknown or long abandoned, such as import quotas and monetary devaluation. These methods in their turn raised new difficulties, so that discussion sprang up once more and original methods like the clearing system were employed to regulate trade between one country and another by means of systematically organized barter.

The lively economic discussion caused by this situation followed two different lines. It was pursued first on the lines of practical every-day policy. Statesmen, publicists, and representatives of the great agricultural, industrial, and commercial interests made known their views on parliamentary platforms or at meetings of the League of Nations, as well as at professional conferences and in the papers. These discussions revealed not only the main trends of thought but also the feelings, the passions, and the interests that disturbed men's minds. They reflected the struggle between the strictly national views of some and the more international conceptions of others, which aimed at restoring a universal economy after a war which had upset the normal course of trade. How was the increasingly close network of economic interdependence, to which the nineteenth century with its long spell of peace owed much of its prosperity, and which Keynes described so eloquently in 1919 in *The Economic Consequences of the Peace*, to be restored amid national passions aggravated by a bloody conflict? That was the fundamental problem that set the politicians by the ears. The very same problems had arisen after the Napoleonic Wars and even after the Seven Years War, but those far-off experiences had been forgotten.

However, the following passage from Ricardo might well have been studied, for he was announcing in advance all the difficulties by which men were later to be faced:

> The commencement of war after a long peace, or of peace after a long war, generally produces considerable distress in trade. It changes in a great degree the nature of the employments to which the respective capitals of countries were before devoted; and during the interval while they are settling in the situations which new circumstances have made the most beneficial, much fixed capital is unemployed, perhaps wholly lost, and labourers are without full employment. The duration of this distress will be longer or shorter according to the strength of that disinclination, which most men feel to abandon that employment of their capital to which they have long been accustomed. It is often protracted too by the restrictions and prohibitions, to which the absurd jealousies which prevail between the different states of the commercial commonwealth give rise.[1]

[1] Ricardo, *Principles of Political Economy*, chapter xix, para. 92 (chapter xvii of the first edition, 1817).

Before the time of Ricardo Adam Smith had written as follows:

> In the midst of the most destructive foreign war, therefore, the greater part of manufactures may frequently flourish greatly; and, on the contrary, they may decline on the return of peace. They may flourish amidst the ruin of their country, and begin to decay upon the return of its prosperity. The different state of many different branches of the British manufactures during the late war [the Seven Years War], and for some time after the peace, may serve as an illustration of what has been just now said. (*Wealth of Nations*, Book IV, chapter i.)

This passage is a perfect description of what happened after the First World War. To make it more complete we could add to it an equally forgotten passage from John Stuart Mill, though he was an optimist, pointing out by way of compensation the rapidity with which the public wealth is spontaneously created anew on the morrow of a war, if labour is left free to put forth its efforts. Mill gave the reason for this phenomenon, always neglected during the war and always marvelled at afterwards, in terms that might usefully be recalled even to-day.[1]

Public controversy is of more interest to the political historian than to the historian of economic doctrines, who is particularly concerned with the influence of these events on the considered opinions of economists. So great a mass of new experiences could not fail to fill out, correct, and widen the theory of international trade. The old formulæ, born of more limited experience and a state of affairs made obsolete by later events, had to be revised in the light of the recent past and to take account at the same time of both new and old facts. This work did not consist simply of throwing into relief and giving new force to certain views formulated long before the war by clear-sighted writers. It resulted also in really new doctrines. One of the most interesting aspects of this revision is the application to international trade of the very fertile concept of economic equilibrium formulated

---

[1] See Mill, *Principles of Political Economy*, Book I, chapter v, para. 7. The passage is too long to be quoted here in full, but it deserves to be carefully read. Mill pointed out that a country's capital is constantly destroyed and restored, that war only hastens this process, and that the restoration is accomplished by the aid of manual labour. "If there is as much of food left to them, or of valuables to buy food, as enables them by any amount of privation to remain alive and in working condition, they will in a short time have raised as great a produce, and acquired collectively as great wealth and as great capital as before; by the mere continuance of that ordinary amount of exertion which they are accustomed to employ in their occupations." Mill's words are profoundly true, and it need only be added that after a long period of rising prices there is always a rapid fall, as the result of the increase in production. This fall seems a far worse catastrophe to certain producers than the scarcity of commodities during the war.

between 1870 and 1880 by Walras and Jevons, whose wide scope enables us to understand much better than the artificial Ricardian simplifications the various combinations of circumstances that are continually taking us by surprise.

This revision has affected particularly the following points, which we shall examine in turn: (1) It has restored the theory of international trade to the general theory of trade, from which it had been arbitrarily separated by the classical economists. (2) It has resulted in a more satisfactory description of the mechanism by which the purchases and sales of each country with foreign countries are balanced, and has considerably diminished the part played (according to the classical economists) by gold in this mechanism. (3) It makes important additions to the explanation given by the classical economists of the differences in price levels between different countries. (4) It has clarified and completed Ricardo's theory of the distribution of gold between the countries of the world by showing the influence—too often forgotten—of monetary legislation on this distribution. (5) Finally, it puts the controversy between protection and free trade on to new ground, though without losing sight of some of the great truths set forth by the classical economists.

I: GRADUAL ABANDONMENT OF THE DOCTRINE OF COMPARATIVE COST

The only 'theory' of international trade known to the history of economic doctrines is the famous 'theory of comparative cost,' already mentioned, without being fully dealt with, in the chapter on the Fundamental Laws. It was formulated first by Ricardo (and still earlier by Torrens), developed in greater detail by John Stuart Mill, taken up again with some modifications by Cairnes and Bastable, and has had the somewhat peculiar fate of never being adopted without reserve by continental economists, even when they did not reject it altogether.[1] M. Sauvaire-Jourdan, in his preface to the translation of Bastable's book,[2] drew attention to this disregard, which he considered was not justified, and M. Reboud, in his excellent *Précis d'économie politique*, has given the best exposition of the doctrine that exists in France. But these belated efforts at rehabilitation have exactly

---

[1] For detailed quotations from various writers see James W. Angell's *Theory of International Prices*. In France Courcelle-Seneuil, like Cournot, expressly rejects any difference between home and foreign trade. A list of the opinions of the principal economists on the Ricardian doctrine will be found in an appendix to Sauvaire-Jourdan's translation of Bastable.

[2] Paris, Giard, 1903. Bastable's *Theory of International Trade* dates from 1897.

coincided with an increasingly marked tendency on the part of the best economists in Italy, America, and even England to reject the theory.

In Italy Pareto, in 1894,[1] and a little later Barone in his remarkable *Principi* (1908) paid courteous homage to Ricardo but formulated a theory of the equilibrium of international prices that rested in reality on new foundations. Edgeworth was not far from accepting Pareto's doctrine in the noteworthy article he contributed to the *Economic Journal* in 1894 on the pure theory of international values, a masterly summing-up of the doctrines worked out from the time of Ricardo to that date.[2]

The ground was therefore already prepared when after the First World War economists in ever increasing numbers, impressed by the inability of the Ricardian theory to account for the multitude of observed facts, decided simply to scrap it. To the Swedish author Ohlin belongs the honour of having deliberately set aside the old doctrine as inadequate, in a work full of facts and ideas entitled *Interregional and International Trade*, and constructing instead a theory of international trade on new foundations closely resembling those adopted by Pareto, though he was not then acquainted with Pareto's views. A little earlier (1926) the American James W. Angell, after tracing the entire history of doctrines relating to this great subject, reached the very same conclusion in a book that is remarkable alike for its critical spirit and its erudition.[3] The appearance at the same time of Taussig's *International Trade* (1927), far from retarding this development, actually encouraged it; for if on the one hand the American economist gave the most highly developed and detailed exposition that is to be found of the doctrine of comparative cost, which he still accepted, yet on the other hand, relying on his vast experience of American commercial policy, he showed the difficulties of the doctrine with such admirable honesty that he contributed as much as his declared opponents towards facilitating the necessary rejuvenation of that doctrine that was prepared by the remarkable work of his own pupils, of whom we must mention Viner, Williams, and Angell himself.

For a proper understanding of this development a brief reminder of the Ricardian theory is necessary. It actually comprises three distinct elements, not bound together by any organic link, which can most advantageously be considered separately. These are (*a*) an

[1] In an article entitled *Cambi Forestieri* in the *Giornale degli Economisti* (1894), and then in his *Cours d'économie politique* in 1896.
[2] The article is reprinted in the second volume of Edgeworth's *Papers relating to Political Economy* (London, 1925).
[3] Angell, *The Theory of International Prices* (Harvard, 1926).

explanation of the reasons why countries exchange their products; (*b*) a definition of the criterion that distinguishes domestic trade from international trade; and (*c*) a statement that international trade resolves itself into mere barter.

(*a*) Why, asks Ricardo first, do two countries exchange products— *e.g.*, corn and cloth—*when each of them is equally able to produce them in its own territory?* For it must be said at once that it is this case, and this case alone, to which the Ricardian theory relates. Cases in which the subject of exchange is not produced in both countries, though at least as numerous as the others, if not indeed more numerous, are set aside.[1]

The question was apparently one of pure theory. But actually it had a bearing on the most immediate interests, for it presented itself in an urgent form to England after the Napoleonic Wars, because of the special position of her agricultural industry.[2] English wheat-growing had increased greatly during the war, being stimulated both by high prices resulting from inflation and by the partial interruption of overseas commerce. The peace brought back the competition of foreign grain, and at the same time a rise in the purchasing power of gold. The landowners, anxious to preserve their monopoly, demanded an increase in protective duties against foreign competition and falling prices. Ricardo, in whose eyes the future of England was bound up with the development of her manufactures, advocated a decreasing duty which should give agriculture time to adapt itself without preventing a gradual fall in the price of corn, and therefore in the cost of living and wages. The same opposition of interests between agriculture and industry gave rise in France after the war of 1914–18 to a similar problem.[3] The theory of comparative cost was born of the

---

[1] The Classical school, by entirely ignoring the exchange between two countries of goods produced by one of them alone, leave out of their theory what is probably the most important part of all imports and exports. They evidently thought that these exchanges need no explanation. They might, strictly speaking, be regarded as only a special case of the general theory. That is how Barone, for example, did treat them, and the same idea is to be found in Ohlin, at the end of paragraph 7 of the first chapter of his great work. But one might equally well reverse the terms of the demonstration and take for our basis the hypothesis of entirely different commodities.

[2] Viner, in an article in the great *Encyclopedia of the Social Sciences* (published in New York in 1932), said in reference to the theory of international trade that the classical theory had been developed largely as an accidental by-product of current controversies about practical questions, and that in its choice of problems as well as in the relative importance assigned to them it reflected clearly the special circumstances in which it had been elaborated. (*Encyclopedia*, Vol. VIII, p. 201.)

[3] Similar, but not identical, and to some extent 'inverse.' French agriculture, in fact, had diminished instead of increasing during the First World War. On the return of the prisoners production increased, and falling prices should have enabled her to *sell* at a profit in an impoverished Europe. But this *exportation* might have resulted in an internal rise in the prices of agricultural products which would have

effort made by Ricardo to justify his own thesis in opposition to that of the agriculturists.

The argument of the English agrarian protectionists was a simple one. Why import wheat from Russia and Poland, they said, *when England can produce it just as well as those two countries?* It is the traditional argument put forward by protectionists in favour of the industries in which they are interested, and is met with in all discussions of this kind. Why, it is repeated on each occasion, import such and such a product when the importing country *could technically* make it as well as the foreigner, and even more cheaply? To this Ricardo replied— and his reply covers all similar cases—that it is because England has a *greater advantage* in producing and exporting textiles or other manufactured products than agricultural commodities. In fact the sale of these textiles to the foreigner enables her to obtain, and therefore to consume, *a greater quantity* of corn than she could herself produce *if she devoted to its cultivation the same amount of labour that she devotes now to the production of the textiles that she exports.* It is, he added, a simple application of the principle of the division of labour. He illustrated his idea by the following example, since taken up and developed with an abundance of complicated arguments by Mill and his successors:

> Two men can both make shoes and hats, and one is superior to the other in both employments; but in making hats he can only exceed his competitor by one-fifth, or 20 per cent., and in making shoes he can excel him by one-third, or $33\frac{1}{3}$ per cent. Will it not be for the interest of both that the superior man should employ himself exclusively in making shoes, and the inferior man in making hats?[1]

The whole of the doctrine of comparative cost is nothing but an academic dilution of this short and obscure footnote by Ricardo.

To know whether exchange between two countries is advantageous it is not necessary to know that the product imported would cost less labour to produce at home than abroad. What does matter is to discover whether, given the *relative labour costs* (within each country) of the two products to be exchanged, each of the two countries does not gain by devoting itself to the exclusive manufacture of one and acquiring the other by exchange.

hampered industry. At that juncture the Minister of Commerce felt it his duty to *prohibit exportation*, so as to prevent agricultural prices from rising and ensure low wages in industry. It was therefore the same opposition of interests as in England, between agriculture and industry, that led to intervention with the object of preventing agricultural prices following their natural course, though in France the aim was to make them fall and in England to make them rise. The results of this policy were, however, very unfortunate, for it retarded the restoration of agriculture after the war and granted a needless subsidy to industry.

[1] Ricardo, *Political Economy*, chapter vii, para. 47, note.

We need not stress the unfortunate lack of precision of the terms used by Ricardo, which has given much scope for the ingenuity of commentators. Nor has this lack of precision disappeared in the later elaborations of the theory, and Pareto in particular has emphasized it.[1] Here we will merely enumerate the reasons that have led an increasing number of economists to abandon the Ricardian theory as formulated in the above passage.

To begin with, why should the origin of exchange be explained by reference to the cost *in labour* instead of starting from the different *prices* of the products, as is the case in actual fact? Countries export and import because certain foreign products are dearer or cheaper than the home-produced ones. This common-sense statement, however, is not enough. It has in fact been observed that if all prices in each country, while differing in actual amounts, differed from each other *in the same proportion*, there would be no exchange. That is the form that the theory of comparative cost assumes when applied to prices. It has been rightly emphasized by Ohlin (p. 13), and before him, though in a slightly different form, by the great Dutch economist Pierson.[2] Suppose that the prices of commodities *a, b, c, d, e,* in France are in the ratio of 1, 2, 4, 8, 16, etc., while in England the scale of prices of the same commodities is 3, 6, 12, 24, etc. Then all the English prices are higher than the French ones, but the ratios of the prices in each country to each other are the same. In that case France will export to England but will not import from her: there will be no exchange. Owing to this unilateral trade, exchange on Paris will rise in London (assuming, like Ohlin, for the sake of simplicity, that both countries have a paper currency), so that the prices of all French

[1] Pareto, *Manuale di economia politica*, chapter ix, para. 42: "It is hard to say what is the meaning of one thing being produced *more easily* than another. Professor Bastable warns us that the comparison between the costs of the commodities A and B should relate not to their prices but to *sacrifices*, but he does not—and he cannot—tell us exactly what these sacrifices are. This theory can really be expounded strictly only by the help of mathematics." See also the important note by Ohlin on p. 425 of his work.

[2] See Vol. II of *Principles of Economics*, the English edition of his *Manual of Political Economy* published in Dutch between 1896 and 1902. Nikolaas Gerard Pierson played an important part as Minister of Finance, President of the Council, and President of the Netherlands Bank. In his remarkable Manual (not well enough known in France) he gave an extremely interesting and modernized exposition of the doctrine of comparative cost, which he sums up thus: "If all articles without exception involve in their production amounts of effort exactly proportional in one country to that which they involve in another, then trade between different countries would be impossible." (Part III, chapter iv, para. 2.) The Ricardian theory was presented in a similar form by the German Mangoldt, whose theory will be found explained in Edgeworth's important article on the pure theory of international commerce. We have been unable to procure Mangoldt's *Grundriss*, first published in 1863.

goods rise for the English. Suppose now that this rise in prices continues until the prices of all French goods in English currency are
trebled. Actual prices will then have become the same in both countries,
sales will stop, and there will no longer be any reason for exchange.
In other words, if lasting trade is to be established between two
countries not only must their prices be different but *the scale of 'relative
prices' must be different in each country*. There is no need, therefore, to
resort to so vague a notion as 'cost in labour' to explain exchange: all
that is needed is to speak of differences between relative prices. But
when that is done Ricardo's truth becomes so obvious a proposition
as to be almost a truism, for who ever imagined that the prices of all
products were in the same ratio to each other in two different countries?

But that is not all. In basing its explanation on the 'labour cost'
of products the classical theory entirely neglects the part played by
demand in the fixing of prices within each country and therefore in the
international trade that results from them. Ricardo admits, it is true,
that prices are proportional to 'cost in labour' and that exchange
takes place on this basis inside each country. But this proportionality
is actually only a tendency. Moreover, we must take account not only
of labour but of saving and interest also. In fact the market demand
operates at every moment to modify these theoretical prices. As
Angell says, however great may be the comparative advantages
expressed in terms of labour, current prices may be such that exchange
which ought to take place on the basis of comparative cost is in fact
impossible (p. 373). Ease or technical cheapness of production are
not enough to make an *entrepreneur* decide to produce: he must take
into account also the tastes and incomes of prospective buyers.

Ohlin has rightly shown that in production at home as well as in
foreign trade it is this consideration that determines the choice of crops
to be cultivated, and not merely the technical advantages and physical
output of labour. "In Southern Europe," he says, "corn is grown in
many places on land that gives a smaller yield than could be obtained
from land that grows vines, if it was turned over to corn-growing."
Why is this? It is because "the demand for wine is so great that these
vineyards yield more (in money) than if they were used for corn-
growing." (P. 46.) So also "in central Europe maize is hardly ever
grown on the land that would give the best actual yield of maize,"
this land being devoted to wheat because the price of wheat enables it
to pay a higher rent.

Taussig in his turn has taken typical examples from American
agriculture of crops, such as beet and hemp, being replaced on soils
that are technically more suitable for them by different crops, simply

because the latter are more profitable (p. 133)—*i.e.*, they bring in more money in view of the market demand and the prices of the other factors of production employed.[1] From these examples Ohlin draws the conclusion that the so-called law of comparative cost is only a particular instance of the tendency to find the cheapest combination of the factors of production (p. 47).

In reality this principle of comparative cost, which Ricardo looked upon as the basis of international commerce alone, is at the bottom of *all* trade between regions and between individuals. That is the most decisive criticism that can be levelled against his doctrine. The source of exchange and of the division of labour is always the same: namely, the *relative* preference of the exchanging parties for one commodity compared with another, or the *relative* advantage enjoyed by the producers in the production of one commodity compared with another. Why does Lyons specialize in the manufacture of silk and Roubaix in that of wool? Is it not because Roubaix has an even greater advantage in making woollens and exchanging them for Lyons silk (or other products) than in making both silk and woollen goods (or other products) at the same time for Northern France? Why does one industrialist specialize in weaving and another in spinning if it is not because he has an even greater advantage in producing only cloth and exchanging it for yarn? Is it not Ricardo himself who suggested this by his example of the hatter and the shoemaker? This is what a growing number of economists have seen more and more clearly as the prestige of the Ricardian economics wanes.

The consideration of relative costs "is not peculiar to international trade," says Pareto in his *Cours d'économie politique* (p. 859 *n.*); "it can be applied also to the individuals who form an economic unit." And at the same time Edgeworth said in his article on the Pure Theory of International Values that the fundamental principle of international trade is to be found in the general theory that Jevons called the theory of exchange and that Marshall defined as a study of the equilibrium

---

[1] Taussig, however, regards these examples as confirming the theory of comparative cost, in which he is an acknowledged believer. But we can equally well draw from them a conclusion in favour of the theory that takes prices directly as the point of departure. In a significant passage Taussig was himself led to introduce demand or utility as a criterion of the advantage of exchange: in his chapter iv he develops the doctrine of comparative cost and is led (pp. 29, 30) to notice the case in which one of the two countries, after the exchange, has *less* than before of one of the two commodities exchanged. How then are we to be sure that he has gained by the exchange? Taussig declares that the very fact that he consents to the exchange shows that *psychologically* there is an advantage. But is not this to take up entirely different ground from that taken up in his previous argument, according to which the criterion was the increase in *quantities* obtained, and not the satisfaction that they yielded?

between the forces of demand and supply, a theory which is at the centre of most of the problems of political economy. It follows from this theory that all the parties to an exchange gain by it. That, he concluded, is the general formula of the principle of comparative cost so far as its positive aspect is concerned. To make his view more precise he pointed out that *national* trade is, strictly speaking, a simple special case of *international* trade, and that even historically the latter preceded the former.

This truth obtained acceptance as the theory of equilibrium made its way into economic doctrine. In the United States and in England it gained important adherents. In a typical passage in his *Principles of Economics* the well-known American economist Seligman described the development of his ideas on this point. It had long been supposed, he said, that the principles of international trade differed from those of domestic trade in that the former was subject to the law of comparative cost, but we knew now that this law or the law of reciprocal demand explains *all* exchanges. Trade takes place between countries as between individuals because of its relative, not absolute, advantages.

In England Edwin Cannan, in his presidential address at the annual meeting of the Royal Economic Society in 1933, declared that the principal error of economists, from Ricardo's time until the present day, had been to try to construct a special theory of international trade, separate and distinct from the theory of trade within a single country.[1]

To sum up, Ricardo, seeking to explain briefly the reasons for international trade, thought to simplify the problem by assimilating nations to communities of workers exchanging their products between them. But this simplification, meant primarily to show the advantages of this trade, became so sketchy a picture that it left out some of the most important phenomena presented by it,[2] and these can be explained

---

[1] This does not mean that there are not some economists who remain faithful even to-day to the doctrine of comparative cost. I have already mentioned Reboud in France, and there are also Cabiati in Italy (in his important work on the Physiology of International Relations), de Leener in Belgium, in his book on International Commerce, and, as already stated, Taussig in the United States.

[2] Ohlin devoted Appendix 3 of his work to a penetrating criticism of the classical theory of foreign trade. He points out in para. 2 that in his simplified plan Ricardo assumed (1) that it is the marginal cost of production that is the basis of these calculations, and that rent is thus eliminated; (2) that the different kinds of labour are reduced to a common denominator, which is just "labour"; (3) that capital and labour are employed in the same proportions in the making of all commodities. These three assumptions are singularly far removed from reality.

Wilhelm Lexis had already observed in his remarkable and insufficiently known study of commerce in Schoenberg's *Grundriss* (Vol. II, p. 902) that Ricardo's theory implicitly and wrongly assumes that in each country, in different branches of production, equal quantities of capital correspond to equal quantities of labour.

only by taking *prices* for the basis. In answer to the objection that these prices themselves and their differences need explanation—an objection already raised by Mill and recently again by Taussig—Ohlin, like Angell, replied that the differing economic constitutions of different countries suffice to explain them. Each country is endowed with 'factors of production' differing in quality and quantity: one is rich in man-power and another in raw materials; one has workers of remarkable technical skill and another mainly unskilled labourers; one has abundant savings at its disposal while another has been unable to accumulate any capital; in one the demand for certain products is very keen and in another the demand for the same products is negligible, and so forth. The result of these natural and historical differences is that in different countries there are different prices for the same or similar products, and from these price differences exchange arises. The treatment accorded by Ohlin to the influence of these factors on international trade is among the most suggestive features of his book, as well as one of the most original.

But to replace the doctrine of comparative cost by a theory of price equilibrium is not enough: we must also construct for international as for national trade a group of equations to show that these mutually dependent prices are all determined and that the number of unknowns is equal to the number of equations. As Ohlin says, the theory of equilibrium *on a single market* must be supplemented by a theory of equilibrium *on several markets*. The first attempt at this was made by Pareto in the first edition of his *Course* in 1896,[1] and again in his *Manual* in 1906. To the old equations of equilibrium of production in an isolated country he added two new ones, taking into account on the one hand goods made in one country and sold in another, and on the other their price. The first equation expresses the equilibrium of purchases and sales between one country and the others; the second shows the price of one country's money in terms of that of another— that is to say, the exchange rate. Ohlin, on his part, constructed independently of Pareto a system of equations of international equilibrium, including two which took the same two circumstances into account, but he started with Cassel's equations of prices, leaving out the notion of 'ophelimity' contained in Pareto's equations.

In a historical work like this we can only refer to these algebraical demonstrations that are impossible to summarize. We will merely say that apart from their greater generality and their agreement with

---

[1] And even earlier in an article in the *Giornale degli Economisti* in 1894, whose bearing on the matter was realized by Edgeworth in the important study previously mentioned.

the now classical theory of price equilibrium, they have the advantage of taking into account two extremely important elements completely absent from the Ricardian doctrine. First there is the part played by *demand* in the determination of price. This we have already mentioned, and it was entirely neglected by Ricardo. And secondly there is the part played by the *rate of exchange* in the determination of commodities exchanged between different countries. This latter point is very important. Two countries such as France and England would, in fact, see a sudden change in their imports and exports if the price of the pound in francs should happen to fall suddenly (as the result, for instance, of a depreciation of the note issue or a legal devaluation). Suppose its price fell on the exchange market from 25 to 15 francs, either spontaneously or from legislative action taken by one of the two countries. A great mass of English goods would then immediately come within the range of French incomes while French goods would become dearer for the English. And the position would be reversed if the price of the pound rose. In such cases it would therefore be necessary to find a fresh equilibrium between purchases and sales. Meanwhile the country that had become suddenly cheaper would reap an advantage. These devaluations played an important part during the post-war years, and became an instrument of international commercial policy. Their effects in the seventeenth century had been noticed by Cantillon, but they had no place in the theory of Ricardo and his successors.[1] Mill expressly declares that a depreciation of the currency "does not affect the foreign trade of the country,"[2] because prices in the country whose currency is depreciated are immediately adjusted to the depreciation. The position taken up by Marshall in his famous depositions before the Gold and Silver Commission in 1887 and the

---

[1] On this point see Ohlin, chapter i, para. 6.

[2] Here is Mill's argument: "Let us suppose that England is the country which has the depreciated paper. Suppose that some English production could be bought, while the currency was still metallic, for £5, and sold in France for £5 10s., the difference covering the expense and risk, and affording a profit to the merchant. On account of the depreciation, this commodity will now cost in England £6, and cannot be sold in France for more than £5 10s., and yet it will be exported as before. Why? Because the £5 10s. which the exporter can get for it in France is not depreciated paper, but gold or silver: and since in England bullion has risen—in the same proportion with other things—if the merchant brings the gold or silver to England, he can sell his £5 10s. for £6 12s., and obtain as before 10 per cent. for profit and expenses" (*Principles of Political Economy*, Book III, chapter xxii, para. 3). It will be seen that Mill starts from the notion that the depreciation of paper money on the exchange market and the rise in the prices of goods, including gold, on the home market are two simultaneous phenomena and exactly balance each other. He forgets too that paper-money countries are in the habit of prohibiting the sale of gold or silver money, so that the transaction he imagines would be unlikely to take place.

Indian Currency Commission in 1899 already show very appreciable progress, and constitute a document of exceptional interest. Marshall recognizes that there may be a premium on exportation for a fairly long time in favour of the countries whose silver or paper money is depreciated in relation to gold, so long as prices in those countries have not changed, or have changed only slightly. This will happen especially when the fall in the exchange rate has *begun abroad*—a hypothesis that Mill did not even consider.[1] And he pointed out also that the excess of exports often lasts for a considerable time because it is accompanied by an export of capital, the foreign currency arising from the exports not being sent back in the form of imports into the country whose money is in process of depreciating. This penetrating observation has since been verified in a striking manner at the time of the depreciation of the franc during the years 1925–27, which explains the excess of French exports at that date.[2] But in spite of this observation he returned in other passages to the idea that an excess of exports must of necessity induce corresponding imports, so that the premium on exportation from countries with a depreciated currency does not involve the countries that receive the goods in any lasting inconvenience because these latter countries in turn see their goods demanded by the others. That is the situation that Marshall thought to exist in England in relation to India before the rupee was stabilized.

The controversies on this point, provoked at first by the fall in silver and later by the behaviour of paper money, continued at the end of the nineteenth century and the beginning of the twentieth "without providing economists with any opportunity of agreement," as Fontana

[1] According to the earliest members of the Classical school, since *depreciation always arises from a previous issue of paper money*, the rise in prices and the depreciation take place at the same time. The idea of depreciation preceding the price rise is foreign to them. Marshall already took up a different position. He admitted that the fall in the value of a currency may begin abroad (he admitted it in the special case of silver at p. 195 of his *Official Papers*), and that in consequence there may be a premium on the exportation of goods from a country with a depreciated currency. It is natural to conclude from this that the same position may arise in a country with a paper currency, though Marshall does not speak of this. In other words, the fall in the value of the paper money may *begin abroad*, that is to say on the exchange market, before making itself felt on the commodity market. We know now—and Nogaro has written many pages to demonstrate it—that this case is even the most frequent one, and this explains why the premium on exportation arising from paper currency appears so often. It is the very case that Taussig gave special prominence to (see below).

[2] See pp. 300–303 of Marshall's *Official Papers*, where the exposition is particularly clear and complete. The question of the premium (or bounty) on exportation is dealt with in the volume on several occasions and in a masterly fashion. Pierson, too, in a remarkable passage in his *Principles* (Book II, chapter iii, para. 4 of the English translation) stresses the differing effects produced by a change in the value of a currency on international trade according as the change takes place abroad or in the country itself.

Russo ironically puts it.[1] Yet post-war events have made all writers admit the influence exerted on international commerce, at least temporarily, by a fall in the exchange rate. Without accepting the Ricardian dogma, governments have not hesitated to base their commercial policy on this principle and to favour what has been called "exchange dumping." The whole problem has been clarified by the suggestive work of M. Subercaseau, Chilean Finance Minister and Professor at the University of Santiago, on paper money.[2] He has described for the first time, for the instruction of Europe, the innumerable experiments made by South America, where the absence of any proportional relation between monetary depreciation on the exchange market and on the commodity market has so frequently been shown. Taussig observes with his customary honesty that the problem has been neglected by the early economists and scarcely less so in the modern period—a remark that applies particularly to the Anglo-Saxon economists, who have remained more faithful than others to the Ricardian tradition—for in eighteenth-century France it gave rise to many controversies.[3] Taussig himself, departing from this tradition, did not hesitate to recognize the influence of exchange fluctuations on international commerce and the possibility of a premium on exportation being maintained for a considerable time, in the event of a sudden fall in the value of a currency.

Space does not permit us to go into detail on the discussions arising from this problem, which has created an immense quantity of literature. Such details belongs to special treatises on money and exchange. What matters here is to emphasize the imperative necessity of including exchange movements among the explanations of the international movements of goods. Otherwise they must either be denied —which is not possible in the long run—or they must be constrained by complicated arguments to enter the strait waistcoat of a doctrine constructed in view of different circumstances. The great merit of the recent writers of whom we are speaking here is that they have not

[1] Fontana Russo, *Traité de politique commerciale*, French translation (Giard, Paris, 1908).

[2] Subercaseau, *Le Papier-monnaie* (Giard, Paris, 1926).

[3] The frequency of monetary appreciations and depreciations had for a long time drawn attention to the effect of these manipulations on foreign commerce. Melon, Dutot, Law, Daguesseau, Paris-Duverney, and Forbonnais all dealt with the matter, but without reaching any agreement. A good study of these discussions, comparing them with present-day controversies, will be found in a thesis by Jean-Marie Pascal entitled *Manipulations monétaires et Commerce international* (Sirey, Paris, 1936). It is a pity that the obscure language of the so-called "financial economists" has made it so hard to read those writers who discussed in advance so many problems to which the two World Wars gave new importance.

hesitated to make the effort needed to build up a new construction, by including these so-called anomalies. But it is not correct to say that the opponents of the doctrine of comparative cost have not formulated any doctrine to replace it. Viner, who expresses this opinion,[1] yet makes an exception in favour of Pareto. But Ohlin and Angell must be added also, and still more Viner himself and the group of writers inspired by Taussig, who with him have carefully observed the actual facts and transformed the old conception in their noteworthy studies.

(b) The examination of the second element in the Ricardian theory will not detain us long. It is the question of the criterion chosen by Ricardo and his successors to distinguish between national and international trade. Assuming the perfect mobility of labour and capital within a country, then, they say, each industry is localized wherever conditions of production are most favourable.[2] Division of labour is carried to its highest point, and wages and profits are equalized throughout the whole of the country. In contrast to this, the circulation of capital and labour between one country and another is very difficult, and so the localization of industries and the division of labour cannot be completely carried out, and there is not the same equalization of wages and profits between different countries as there is within a single country. Nevertheless exchange of goods does take place, though not through equality of cost of production (or, as Ricardo prefers to say, equality of labour cost): it is determined entirely by the law of supply and demand.

Of the three propositions that make up the Ricardian doctrine none has been more keenly and more justly criticized than this one. Apart from the old objection to the theory that exchange is based on quantity of labour, or even on cost of production,[3] it evidently cannot be a question here merely of simple differences of *degree* rather than of *kind* between domestic and foreign trade. No one denies that division of labour is more easily practised within one country than between different countries,[4] but perfect mobility of labour and capital in one country is a myth. There are 'non-competing groups,' as Cairnes had already pointed out. Farm labourers do not become factory workers,

[1] In the American *Encyclopedia of the Social Sciences*, article on "Foreign Trade."

[2] This localization is limited, however, even in one country, by considerations of distance and means of transport, which Mill seems to have forgotten when he assumed, for instance, that the whole of the shoemaking industry would be concentrated in a single part of London (*Principles*, Book III, chapter xvii).

[3] See the admirable comments of Lexis on this subject in his article *Handel* in Schoenberg's *Grundriss*, especially para. 41.

[4] Cannan, in the address already mentioned, speaks angrily of Ricardo's "monstrous assertion," according to which the labour of 100 Englishmen cannot be exchanged for the labour of 80 (*Economic Journal*, 1933, p. 377).

and *vice versa*, according to whether industry or agriculture offers the highest wages. The French agricultural workers of the south do not willingly enter the mines of the north, nor do the northern miners go into the salt-works of the south according as the profit to be made is greater or less. In a single country there are the greatest differences between wages in different trades, just as there are between the profits of different undertakings (even in the same industry), and these differences are the greater as the size of the country is greater, as for example in the United States. On the other hand the immobility of capital and labour between different countries is purely relative: need we recall the sudden rush of labour from all lands to the gold-mines at the time of the successive discoveries of gold in Australia, California, South Africa, and Alaska? Is not emigration to new countries one of the most characteristic economic facts of the nineteenth century? Are there not periodic migrations across the frontiers from Belgium and Spain into France? And is not the transfer of capital from Europe to the South American countries, to Canada, to India, and to China a phenomenon of vast importance?

It has been very well said by the American economist Williams— one of Taussig's best disciples—in an article criticizing judicially the whole of the Ricardian theory of international trade, that it is not the Ricardian hypothesis of *immobility* that needs to be ruled out, but rather his hypothesis of *mobility*—of the free movement of the factors of production *within* each country.[1] This fact is even more evident over the vast area of the United States than elsewhere. Williams's article is important as marking the semi-official rejection of the classical doctrine by the best American economists of to-day. One example of this rejection had already been seen in Seligman, and Cannan in England was another. The same position had been taken up in Europe at an earlier date by the most varied kinds of writers, such as Lexis[2] in Germany, Ansiaux in Belgium, Nogaro in France, and so forth. The only real difference between the two kinds of trade—national and international—is that the currencies of different States are themselves different, and that therefore there intervenes in this trade a currency market in which exchange rates are fixed—rates that must of necessity modify the prices of the goods of one country for buyers in another. That is the conclusion reached by Angell in the work already often quoted.[3] Ohlin adopts a slightly different and more general criterion:

[1] Williams, *The Theory of International Trade Reconsidered* (*Economic Journal*, June 1929).

[2] Article *Handel* in Schoenberg's *Grundriss*, pp. 868 *ff.* and 902.

[3] Angell, p. 371: "The essential differences between international trade and internal, with respect to the process of price determination, are rather these. First,

"The most important distinction to be made," he writes, "is not between the theory of international commerce and that of national commerce, but between a theory of prices for a single market and a theory of prices that is valid for several markets." (P. 141.) This statement relates not so much to international commerce, in the strict sense, as to what the author calls 'interregional' commerce, including exchange between regions in a single country.

(c) The last proposition implied in the Ricardian doctrine is that which assimilates all international trade to mere barter. Here the doctrine joins the old law of markets of J. B. Say. The proposition, though incontestable, throws very little light on the workings of international trade (for domestic trade is equally a matter of barter if we mentally eliminate the intervention of money), and is a conclusion rather than a starting-point.

Now the English economists, regarding it as a starting-point, have for a long time made great efforts to include the whole theory of international trade in a theory of barter. Marshall in particular, by using ingenious curves that were reproduced by Pantaleoni and modified by Edgeworth, sought to represent the whole of the mechanism of trade between two countries by the mere process of barter of two kinds of goods between two individuals. Ohlin was right in considering that these simplifications did little to elucidate the complex state of affairs with which we are concerned in real life.[1] Here too, by setting aside the consideration of prices, we are making the question more obscure instead of clearer. Now, on this point a characteristic development appeared before the last war. In opposition to the kind of curve employed by Marshall some quite different curves were constructed by Cunynghame and Barone,[2] who replaced the curves representing direct barter between two countries by curves of supply and demand

---

the greater costs of transportation in international trade, which is a purely quantitative difference; second, the presence of tariffs and other legal obstacles; and third, the fact that currencies are dissimilar, and that a foreign exchange mechanism is therefore necessary. The principal objective distinctions between the establishment of internal and of international prices can be explained very largely in terms of these three elements alone."

It is obvious that transport costs and customs tariffs, which may be regarded as adding to transport costs, constitute a difference of degree only, and not of kind. In frontier regions transport costs between one country and another may be much lower than between two parts of the same country. So all that remains of any real importance is the monetary difference.

[1] "These studies have served as a recreation for some of the keenest intellects among nineteenth-century economists, but in my opinion they have added little to our real knowledge of international trade." (Ohlin, p. 419.)

[2] See especially Cunynghame, A Geometrical Political Economy (Oxford, 1904), chapter x, and Barone, Principi di Economie politica (Rome, 1908), Part III.

in the exchanging countries, superimposed one on the other, from which are deduced on the one hand the fixing of the price on the international market of the goods exchanged, and on the other hand the gains or losses for the consumers and producers. Here again the idea of the *cost in labour* of the goods is tacitly abandoned and a return made to the consideration of *prices* alone as the incentive to importation and exportation. This development, little noticed but significant, actually marks the tacit abandonment of the Ricardian system by the mathematical economists. Cannan protested vehemently in his address in 1933 (already quoted) against the idea that the conception of barter is appropriate to international trade.

> We want an entire abandonment of the stupid insistence on international trade being 'virtually barter'; of course, all trade is 'virtually barter' when you drop the intervening money out of the picture and think only of persons producing one set of goods and services for other people and receiving another set from them in exchange. It is the intervention of money which turns barter into selling and buying, and far from eliminating money, international trade usually involves the intervention of not only one money, but two different moneys.[1]

The graphic presentation of international trade in the form of barter made possible to the classical economists and their successors the simplified examination of a problem to which they attached considerable importance and to which they tried to find a general solution, though in reality its solution varies with time and circumstances. It is a question of what Anglo-Saxon economists call the "terms of trade." What does this mean? The barter of two commodities can take place only between maximum and minimum limits, above and below which one of the two countries would no longer reap any benefit from exchange. Between this maximum and minimum the advantages are shared between the exchanging parties, but in different proportions,[2] as the "terms of trade" are more or less favourable to one of the parties.

Mill, followed by his successors, elaborates at some length the division of these advantages between an industrial and an agricultural country, and between a large one and a smaller one. Starting from considerations of price alone, we find at once that *according to price variations within each country* the same quantity of exports from country A will enable it to procure sometimes more and sometimes

---

[1] Cannan, *The Need for Simpler Economics*, in the *Economic Journal*, 1933, p. 377.

[2] Reboud has explained this conception in detail and with the greatest clearness in sec. ii of chapter ii (on the theory of international trade) of his excellent *Précis d'économie politique* (Vol. II, pp. 136 ff.).

less goods in country B. But it is impossible to say *a priori* which kind of country—such as an industrial country—will obtain greater advantage than another from international trade.

Taussig re-examined the whole problem, which takes a very different form according to whether the balance of the account is made up of varied elements, as is the case nowadays for most countries, or consists solely of goods, as was always assumed by the classical economists in their expositions. Taussig distinguishes between what he calls "net" terms of trade and "gross" terms.[1] From the evidence of the index of prices he shows how these terms of trade have varied at different periods for England and the United States, becoming sometimes more and sometimes less advantageous. Such an investigation is by no means devoid of interest, although its importance may be a good deal less than the classical economists imagined.[2] All that can be said is that Taussig's method is in any case far superior, as an index to the advantages of international trade, to the method—long condemned but still too often employed in modern controversies, and even in some official reports—which consists in taking the size of the trade 'deficit' or 'excess' as a criterion of the more or less favourable situation of a country in its foreign trade.

What it comes to is this, that the Ricardian economists believed they could simplify the theory of international trade by leaving money out of their calculations, whereas in reality they made it more complicated. In the theories of economists like Ohlin and Aftalion money again takes its normal place, with the result that the necessary link between the foreign purchases and the sales of any country, which the classical economists tried to elucidate by assimilating trade to barter, becomes much clearer by the intervention of money. They observe quite truly, for instance, that every additional sale made by France to another country gives her possession of foreign currency— *i.e.*, of increased purchasing power *abroad*. This purchasing power must operate, in one way or another, exactly as the additional purchasing power acquired by an industry through an increase in sales

---

[1] This is how he defines them at p. 113: "There are thus two ways of looking at the barter terms of trade. One may be indicated by the phrase 'gross barter terms of trade'; the other by 'net barter terms of trade.' The first regards the whole volume of goods, both imports and exports. The second regards those goods only which pay for goods; it demarcates any movement of goods which serves for other payments."

[2] We are of the same opinion as Ohlin, who writes (p. 132): "The old question of the way in which the benefit arising from the establishment of international trade is divided between the trading countries is artificial and of little scientific or practical importance—even if it has any importance at all. . . . *Obviously what we need to find out is not how much total benefit results from international trade, but how much results from any given extension of this trade, or how much loss results from any given restriction on it.*"

in its own country operates *of necessity* in relation to other industries by purchasing additional products from them. The only difference between the two cases is that in the first case (selling abroad) the increased purchasing power (consisting of foreign currency) *can only be spent abroad*. The creditor country will thereby find itself in a position to obtain from abroad either goods or services or gold or capital, and the debtor country will not be compelled to 'offer' these things first at a higher price, as was claimed by those economists who followed Mill in describing the mechanism of international barter.[1] For the abundance of foreign exchange at the disposal of the creditor country causes its price in its own currency to fall *automatically*, and, moreover, on the great international market there is almost certain to be found a buyer prepared to acquire some goods or services or credit in the country in question. As for the importing country, it is deprived, for the benefit of the foreign country and at a price proportionate to its additional imports, of part of its own purchasing power with respect to home-produced goods, and this must lower their price and facilitate their export to foreign countries.

The consideration of purchasing power has very successfully replaced in the present theory (as we shall show presently) the complicated (and purely imaginary) mechanism by which two countries were supposed to act in the aggregate like two individuals bartering their products. All that can be said is that the barter theory has been much refined in these researches. It has all been worked out to explain the mechanism of trade by barter, which our own age, to its great astonishment, has seen reintroduced between individuals as well as between nations, under the influence of war and the monetary disasters that preceded it. But our understanding of international trade has not gained much thereby.

We have just shown how the doctrine of comparative cost has gradually lost ground since 1900, and especially since the First World War. It has, however, kept many adherents, and has found in F. W. Taussig in particular an advocate of high quality. In his *International Trade* (1927), which sums up the results of his long study of this problem, he gives it the place of honour. Nowhere has the doctrine been expounded with such care, precision, and clarity. Yet no one has pointed out its shortcomings better than Taussig. He himself shows where it is out of touch with reality, and he looks upon it as a 'heroic' simplification. He declares that it must be corrected

---

[1] This is one of the points very rightly emphasized by Ohlin in his controversy with Keynes, to be dealt with later.

by taking account of differences of wages in different industries and of differences in rates of interest. He thus manages, after making these additions, actually to explain international trade by means of prices even more than costs. In one particular case he is even obliged (as we said above, p. 649 n.) to introduce the *tastes* of consumers to justify an exchange in which its utility cannot be satisfactorily explained by an increase in the quantities obtained by the exchanging parties. He declares also that the notion of *cost* as used by the Classical school is very difficult to define.[1] Why, then, does Taussig remain faithful to the theory, despite the penetrating criticisms that he levels against it? The reason seems to lie in two circumstances regarded as particularly important by this great observer of reality, who was in regular contact, by reason of his profession, with industrial development and the effects of the customs tariff. It will be as well to dwell for a moment on these circumstances.

The first is that in the existing economic system international trade deals with an increasing number of products that originate not from *natural* differences, such as climate, latitude, and soil fertility, but from differences in *industrial* development. The great volume not only of manufactured products but of *instruments of production* (machines, agricultural implements, boilers, cables, etc.) that are included in the imports and exports of the great countries of the world, are constituting an ever-increasing part of this trade. This is the case, for instance, with the United States, as well as with the industrial countries of Europe, which are each other's best markets for this kind of product. How are we to explain this important fact, to which it is very expedient that attention should be drawn? The explanation, according to Taussig, is the greater *efficiency* of labour in the countries that export these products. By this is meant that the cost in labour of products of this kind that enter into trade is *less* in the exporting than in the importing countries—that with the same expenditure of time and the same number of workers the former produce more than the latter, so that the prices of the products are lower. So international trade is determined by the greater efficiency of labour, which is another way of expressing 'relative cost.' Taussig furnishes many interesting examples of this, and concludes from them that the 'cost' theory provides the best explanation of this important fact that was certainly worth emphasizing.

[1] See his chapter xv. "Cost in labour," he explains, does not mean what it means to accountants and employers—*i.e.*, the price paid for the labour embodied in a unit of product. It is the *quantity of labour* (measured in hours) that is devoted to the making of a product. And this quantity, he adds, is very difficult to discover, and still more difficult to compare with others.

To this it may be replied, however, that it is really still the *price* that is the determining factor here, and not the cost, which is almost impossible to measure. If America, for example, makes certain great standard products such as agricultural implements, calculating machines, etc., more cheaply, it is because of the widespread use of machinery for making them, the organizing ability of their managers, or the skill of their workmen—all circumstances leading to the cheapness of the American products. How are we to evaluate in labour cost the part played by machinery or by technical skill? We can try to, of course, but only by the aid of analogies and hypotheses far removed from reality.

There is a second consideration that causes Taussig to uphold the cost theory, and that is that the scale of wages may be very high in one country without raising the price of products exported above the price of similar products made in other countries by less well paid workmen. And every one knows what a large part is played in American protectionism by the desire to protect high wages. To meet this argument, which he considers inaccurate, and which, indeed, is for the most part inaccurate,[1] Taussig tries to show that it is cost in labour and not the scale of wages that counts in international competition. The latter may be high when the former is low, because the hours devoted to the production of a given commodity are fewer than elsewhere. To this again the reply is easy: it is not only in foreign trade but in domestic trade also that high wages are perfectly compatible with a low price of goods, provided that the equipment and organization of the factories are superior to those where low wages are paid. So the determining factor is really the superiority of equipment and organization. They constitute a 'relative advantage' which is translated into a lower level of prices, leading to greater power of expansion. The theory of comparative cost is singularly defective when it comes to synthesizing a complex aggregate of circumstances such as abundance of capital, rate of interest, inventive genius, ingenuity of the workers, and so forth, each having its effect on the price of the commodities produced. It is certainly good to investigate the factors that explain the lowness of certain prices and not to regard these prices as ultimate data: Taussig protests against this too simplified method, but none the less it is the price differences that determine the exchange.

Now, the source of these differences—as Ohlin has so well shown,

---

[1] We say "for the most part" because no one will deny (on this point see Edgeworth's article already mentioned) that a rise or fall of wages in a foreign industry may alter its ability to compete with the foreigner.

and as common sense had already discovered—is to be found in the unequal distribution among different countries of the 'factors of production,' whatever they may be: natural forces, capital, and man-power. Not only are these factors themselves divided into subdivisions (man-power is of different kinds in the same country as well as in different countries), but their relative abundance varies. The United States, where man-power is scarce and natural resources are abundant, has triumphed on the international market first by the cheapness of its agricultural products and then, when industry had developed, by the perfection of the mechanization employed to replace this scarce and dear man-power. All these elements could not be summed up in the single conception of 'cost in labour' or 'efficiency' of labour.

What gives Taussig's book its great value—apart from the expository gift that recalls the seductive clarity of the best pages of John Stuart Mill—is the analysis and description of a multitude of facts drawn from the writer's practical experience, which have a savour all their own, and are rich in lessons of all kinds, even if one does not accept his general theory.

II: THE PROBLEM OF REPARATIONS AND THE MECHANISM OF INTERNATIONAL TRANSFERS OF CAPITAL

Apart from exchanges of goods, transfers of capital are one of the essential elements of international commerce. But the classical econo-mists gave them hardly any attention. Economists of the twentieth century—the period of great international migrations of capital—cannot neglect them. The payment of the war indemnity in 1918 provided the occasion for a reconsideration of the whole problem.

The payment of a war indemnity, involving the transfer of a con-siderable sum by one country to another, is no novelty. France experienced it twice in the nineteenth century, first in 1815[1] and again after the Franco-German War, the sums involved being 900 million francs in the first case and five milliards in the second. We are very inadequately informed as to the method of payment on the first occasion, but for the second we learn from the famous report of Léon Say to the National Assembly in 1875 that it was mainly effected by bills of exchange, 'and especially bills on London.[2] But how could

[1] See Charléty, *Histoire de la Restauration*, pp. 114 ff.
[2] The method of payment of the Franco-German indemnity and reparations has been explained with perfect clarity by Reboud in his *Précis* (published by Dalloz). But the interesting chapter on war indemnities in Taussig's *International Trade* should

such a quantity of bills be collected in such a short time? Léon Say admits that he does not know: "If we knew," he says, "we should have an explanation of what would have been improbable, so to speak, if it had not actually occurred, but the theory of it may be said to have partly escaped us."[1] Now, however, we know the origin of those bills. They came either from subscriptions by foreigners in foreign currency to the two liberation loans, or from French subscriptions made sometimes directly in foreign currency by Frenchmen who owned it, and sometimes from the proceeds of the sale abroad of foreign securities belonging to Frenchmen.[2] This accounts for the relatively slight rise in the price of foreign stocks in Paris, which Say's report notes with satisfaction though with a little surprise. In other words, the pounds sterling, or money easily convertible into pounds, that the French Government needed, was obtained, directly or indirectly, from the subscribers to its loans. All that was necessary then was to remit these moneys to its German creditor, the eventual transfer being shifted on to the country whose money was thus handed over to Germany—i.e., England. But another part of the money came from a different source: it was provided by the excess of exports that the French balance of trade showed quite exceptionally in the years 1872–76. Léon Say regards this as merely a fortunate coincidence,[3] but there is no doubt that this temporary excess of exports was a consequence of the payment of the indemnity, for a transfer of capital results normally in a transfer of goods, in a way to be dealt with presently. This fact has been emphasized by C. Colson in his great treatise. The same exceptional excess of exports was seen later on at the time of the great fall in the value of the franc between 1922 and 1926, when the prolonged depreciation of the French currency led to an export of capital abroad, and the result of this phenomenon on the balance of trade was a temporary

---

also be consulted, as well as Moulton's *Reparation Payments*. I might also refer the reader to the chapter on reparations in my own *Finances de guerre de l'Allemagne* (Paris, 1921), which contains an outline of the history of ideas about war indemnities.

[1] See *Rapport sur l'indemnité de guerre*, printed at the end of the French edition of Goschen's *Theory of the Foreign Exchanges* (Paris, 1892), p. 313.

[2] The French owners of foreign securities sold them for foreign money which they offered on the exchange market to the French Government, and the Government bought it with francs obtained from subscriptions to its loans.

[3] "Immediately after the war," he writes, "French exports developed considerably. They surpassed in importance all that had been produced before and showed what had not previously been seen, *viz.*, an excess over imports of 518 million francs in 1872 and 1873. If the excess had been the other way there is no doubt that the settlement of the war indemnity would have met with enormous difficulties, and it is *a most fortunate circumstance* that this excess of exports occurred during these two critical years. But it is far from explaining the abundance of bills of exchange that have been offered to the Treasury." (*Report*, p. 317.)

excess of exports of goods (though this is still often looked upon by ill-informed publicists as a stroke of good fortune in French commercial history!).

In short, the transfer of the Franco-German indemnity (apart from a few hundred millions paid directly in gold and silver coin or in German notes and the cession of the railways of Alsace-Lorraine) was accomplished for the most part by bills of exchange directly provided by foreigners or Frenchmen who had sold their foreign capital, and for the other part by an increase in French exports to Germany, whose yield in marks served to effect the payment required.[1]

As for the *theory* of the transfer of a war indemnity, this, in spite of Léon Say's opinion, had been already formulated before the events of 1871. It is to be found in a noteworthy passage in Mill. It is true that he describes the mechanism in a different form from that in which the Franco-German operation was so efficiently performed, and that is perhaps why Say did not mention it. Yet Mill's description covers part, at least, of this operation. "Commerce being supposed to be in a state of equilibrium when the obligatory remittances begin," he says,

> the first remittance is necessarily made in money. This lowers prices in the remitting country, and raises them in the receiving. The natural effect is that more commodities are exported than before, and fewer imported, and that, on the score of commerce alone, a balance of money will be constantly due from the receiving to the paying country. When the debt thus annually due to the tributary country becomes equal to the annual tribute or other regular payment due from it, no further transmission of money takes place; the equilibrium of exports and imports will no longer exist, but that of payments will; the exchange will be at par, the two debts will be set off against one another, and the tribute or remittance will be virtually paid in goods.[2]

There are two points to be noted in this remarkable passage:

---

[1] We may note here a couple of historical points that are important for an understanding of the mechanism of the indemnity. (1) When France had supplied Germany mainly with bills on London the cost of transfer of these bills to Germany fell mainly on London, and this expense caused some anxiety in the City on more than one occasion. On this point see an interesting article by Newbold on the beginnings of the crisis of 1873 in the Historical Supplement to the *Economic Journal* for January 1932. (2) Germany herself did not escape the inconveniences caused by the sudden influx of money that the payment of the indemnity involved, *viz.*, a sudden increase in imports, an increase in her monetary circulation, a rise in prices, excessive investments of capital in business undertakings, and so forth. Such circumstances contributed to the violence of the crisis that occurred in Vienna in 1873 and spread thence to the rest of the Continent. This was the starting-point, though not the cause, of the prolonged fall in prices from which Europe suffered until 1895.

[2] *Principles of Political Economy*, Book III, chapter xxi, para. 4.

(1) the statement that a transfer of capital between two countries is accomplished essentially by a transfer of goods or services; (2) the statement that this transfer is dependent on a *previous alteration in price levels in both countries due to an initial export of gold* which, by increasing circulation in one country and diminishing it in the other, is actually the motive power that starts the whole mechanism. The first of these points is not open to dispute, but it needs to be completed. We have just seen that in the case of the Franco-German indemnity the direct handing-over to the creditor country of foreign assets possessed by the debtor country may partly relieve the latter of having to pay for goods by providing gold or services equal to its debt. It then shifts this burden, at least temporarily, and only in respect of the part that its creditor means to return, on to *the countries that supplied the property that is handed over*. In this way the transfer of the tribute money is broken down, as it were, into movements of goods or gold divided between several countries and several periods of time.

Mill's intention was to set forth only the essential part of the phenomenon—the fact that a transfer of capital takes place *as a rule* in the form of goods. He did not consider those other methods that modern credit facilities and the possession of capital abroad have put at the disposal of debtors for paying their debts—methods which are actually of great importance.

On the other hand the mechanism described by Mill, through which the flow of goods is set going, has met with increasingly numerous objections. The role unanimously assigned by economists (from the days of Hume, Ricardo, and Mill down to the First World War) to movements of gold in causing differences of price level between two or several countries was no longer in accordance with observed facts, not only in cases of 'tribute' but in the far more frequent cases of foreign loans, interest coupons, or temporary excesses of imports to be paid for by one country to another. In all these cases gold has actually played an insignificant part, and so economists have been led to examine more closely the mechanism of capital transfers. A new doctrine has been gradually evolved that is nearer to economic reality to-day. The authors who have contributed most to its formation belong to different doctrinal schools and to very different countries. Thus we find among them the names of Ohlin in Sweden, Aftalion in France, Taussig and his pupils (Angell, Viner, and Williams) in the United States. Rueff, although more akin to the Classical school, has made his contribution to the revision of the classical conception. We will try to summarize the conclusions reached by these economists.

The occasion of this general revision of the classical doctrine was the payment of the reparations imposed on Germany by the Treaty of Versailles and the simultaneous repayment to the United States of the advances made by her to her 'associates' during the war. How could payment be made of these enormous sums, whose actual figure was for a very long time not even determined, so that the whole problem assumed a tiresome air of indefiniteness, and what would be the consequences of payment? These two questions gave rise to prolonged controversy and an abundant output of literature of very varied quality, most of which deserves the oblivion into which it has already fallen. One book emerged, however, which had a resounding success and much of which is still instructive. This was *The Economic Consequences of the Peace*, by J. M. Keynes (afterwards Lord Keynes), an official of the British Treasury, a delegate to the Peace Conference, and already the author of a notable book on *Indian Currency and Finance* and a *Treatise on Probability*. But it was his book on the Peace that made him famous. In it he recalled certain fundamental truths that appeared paradoxical to the ill-informed public, that were new to many statesmen, and that many economists affected to forget, though they were merely applications of the classical doctrine formulated by Mill. Since Germany had lost by the war nearly all her foreign properties and even her gold reserve, and was unable to call on foreign credits so long as her currency remained unstable, the methods adopted by France in 1871 were not open to her. There could be no question for her of any other payment than in *goods*. She found herself in the simplified situation imagined by Mill. It was certain, said Keynes, that Germany could not make her annual payments except by diminishing her imports and increasing her exports—*i.e.*, by setting up a favourable balance of trade, which is the best way of making payments abroad. Germany could in the long run pay in goods, and in goods alone, whether they were delivered direct to the Allies or sold to neutrals, the credits thus obtained being handed over to the Allies. After recalling this thesis, which is completely in conformity with the classical doctrine, Keynes showed that most of the products that Germany could export competed with those of the creditor countries. Reparations, therefore, could not exceed a moderate figure without upsetting the entire world economy. The success of Keynes's book was considerable, and it contributed largely towards converting the governments to a thesis whose correctness could not but be recognized by economists and financiers in every land. It triumphed eventually in a famous document, extremely instructive to economists, that has become part of the classical literature of the subject, like Léon Say's Report. This is the Dawes Plan, named after the American general who presided over the commission of international experts in Paris who were responsible for drawing up the Plan in 1924.

Yet once again practice showed itself more elastic than theory, and the putting into effect of the Dawes Plan virtually contradicted Keynes's forecasts. Instead of the exports that were expected from a 'tributary' country, there was witnessed an enormous increase of *imports* into Germany. For the restoration of Germany's monetary stability by the Dawes Plan itself recreated Germany's credit and attracted foreign capital to that country. This influx of capital enabled her both to pay her debt by the help of the foreign money thus obtained and also to import goods in great quantity. Owing to the Dawes Plan Germany found herself in a position to use similar methods to those of France in 1873, which had enabled that country, through the system of international credit, to pay off her debt in due course. The simplified mechanism described by Mill and Keynes, though logically true, gave place in real life to a more complicated mechanism. Once again monetary stability was shown to be the necessary and sufficient condition of credit, and this credit the sole means of accomplishing a payment on such a vast scale.

Many writers, as we have said, had long been sceptical as to the part played by movements of gold in the process of transfer of capital. It was said first that in the case of great international loans the amounts of gold exported were very small, and it seemed unlikely that they could by themselves cause such an alteration in the price level that the export of goods was appreciably stimulated or checked. On the other hand it was remarkable how easily and quickly movements of goods began, corresponding to movements of capital, without any apparent disturbance of the money market, whereas an influx of gold can only slowly influence prices. Even authors who were most devotedly attached to the classical theory, such as Taussig, expressed doubts. "What is puzzling," wrote Taussig, "is the rapidity, almost simultaneity, of the commodity movements. The presumable intermediate stage of gold flow and price changes is hard to discern, and certainly is extremely short."[1] And again: "All in all, we have here a field quite insufficiently explored. The plain outstanding fact is that the exports and imports of goods adjust themselves, if not at once, certainly with quickness and ordinarily with ease, to the sum total of a country's transactions with other countries. The balance of payments is satisfied only to a slight extent by any shipment of specie, chiefly thru [*sic*] changes in the commodity sales and purchases."[2]

But the question then arises, If it is not through the movements of

[1] Taussig, *International Trade*, p. 261.   [2] *Ibid.*, p. 263.

gold that the disturbed equilibrium of international trade is restored, what is the actual mechanism? Two writers in particular, Ohlin in Sweden and Aftalion in France, have undertaken to describe it. The work of the former is constructive, that of the latter more critical, so the two supplement each other and both start from the same fundamental idea, already indicated above, which may be summarized as follows. Every selling or borrowing operation that puts the beneficiary in possession of what Aftalion would call "income" and Ohlin "purchasing power" leads *directly* to movements of goods, except in cases where the beneficiary is paying debts or investing the money as capital. These results occur in domestic transactions as well as foreign ones, the only difference being that in the latter case the money to be spent by the beneficiary is foreign, not national, currency, and cannot therefore be employed except abroad. But the mere existence of this purchasing power determines the international movements of goods and also price movements, *without the intervention of gold*.

To make this clearer Ohlin starts by considering what happens between two countries with the same currency when one lends to the other.[1] For instance, when England lends to Scotland there is a simple transfer of English purchasing power to Scotland. If the products bought by the Scottish borrowers arc exactly the same as those required by the English, there will be no change in the production of the two countries: products to the value of the loan will simply be dispatched to Scotland instead of England. The Scottish trade balance will become a debit balance and the deficit will be paid by Scotland to the English suppliers with the funds that have been borrowed and have remained on deposit in England. This assumption, however, is an improbable one: there is not likely to be this identity between the products demanded by the Scots and those demanded by the English with the same purchasing power. Scotland will undoubtedly increase her demand for her own products. If, for example, the loan is intended to create new undertakings in Scotland itself, part of the money will be spent on new buildings in that country. Hence there will be a tendency for some prices *in Scotland* to rise, whereas England, deprived by the loan of part of its purchasing power, will find the price of some of its own products falling. This fall in English prices will in turn stimulate Scottish purchases in England, creating a Scottish trade deficit which will be paid as before, without any monetary disturbance, by the English funds lent to the Scots. The price changes result from the mere changes in purchasing power,

[1] In what follows we are merely summarizing Ohlin's arguments in chapters xix and xx of his principal work.

Y

without being preceded by any transfer. But there is more in it than that: part of the activity of the Scottish industries which previously exported to England will be directed towards Scotland itself, because of the increased demand within that country, leading to a restriction of Scottish sales in England and an increase in the Scottish trade deficit. On the other hand certain short-term operations will result from this situation, for the Scottish banks now possess abundant resources, while the English ones find theirs depleted by the amount of the loan. So the former will be disposed to grant credit more readily and to lower their discount rate and the latter will do the reverse. Hence a stream of short-term loans begins to flow from the Scottish to the English banks—*in the opposite direction to the long-term stream*—which will prevent the sending of gold by the lender to the borrower. On the other hand, the credit facilities will produce in Scotland an additional activity whose influence will be added to all the preceding ones to increase Scottish imports and cause a new trade deficit that Scotland will pay with the borrowed funds deposited in England.

So there we have a series of effects due not to any transfer of money but simply to a change in the ownership of purchasing power handed over by way of loan: trade deficit in Scotland, price changes, with a general tendency to a rise in Scotland and a fall in England; short-term loans by Scotland to England; more or less strong inflation of credit in Scotland and relative deflation in England. Is it not natural to think that this same mechanism might operate between two countries with different currencies, without the need of any previous transfer of gold from one to the other to explain the price changes and set in motion the series of repercussions of the loan? That, indeed, is just what Ohlin thought, and this is how he sums up the different stages by which the foreign loan is paid in the form of goods and services by the lender to the borrower, without the intervention of any movements of gold: (1) If the borrowing country uses abroad the total amount of the loan there will be no need of any previous transfer of gold. The borrowing country has at its disposal in the lending country a sum in foreign currency which he merely has to spend directly in that country, so gold is not moved. (2) But the borrowing country will without doubt want to use part of the loan at home, which is equivalent to withdrawing from the lending country part of its purchasing power to be spent in the borrowing country. This withdrawal will be accomplished in the simplest manner by remitting to the banks of the borrowing country bills on the lending country, in exchange for which the banks will remit to the holders of the bills either by cheque or by national bank notes. This increased purchasing power in the borrowing country will cause a rise in the prices of certain commodities, while the corresponding decrease of purchasing power in the lending country will cause a fall in the prices of certain commodities. This double movement will have the effect of stimulating the export of goods or services from the lending country to the borrowing country. These exports will be paid for with the surplus of the loan deposited in the banks of the lending country, and thus the transfer of the loan will be accomplished entirely in the form of goods or services. (3) Finally, the abundance of bills on the foreign country in the borrowing country will compel the banks receiving these bills, which are equivalent to a surplus of cash, to expand their credit. This causes a new tendency towards a change in the price level between the borrowing and the lending countries. This is the moment when the banks of the borrowing country may be tempted to draw money from the lending country to increase their reserves. These imports of gold are then the *consequence* and not the cause of an increase of credit. They will take place automatically by the lowering of the price of the bills below the gold point in the country where they have become superabundant.

Such, then, are the stages by which a foreign loan will be eventually transferred almost entirely in the form of goods or services from one country to another. These transfers may be accompanied by a movement in the opposite direction of short-term loans; the banks in the borrowing country lending to those in the lending country so as to profit by the rise in the discount rate, which will help to prevent or reduce the sending of gold.

The manner in which a loan is transferred from one country to another is explained by Aftalion in a very similar way. Starting from the fundamental principle that there is necessarily equality between the income of a country and the value of its products—expressed by the equation $I = PQ$, where I is income, P is price, and Q is quantity of goods and services—he concludes that every additional purchase of foreign products by one country, or every loan granted by that country to another, causes a change of income, which in turn causes price changes between the two countries which lead to movements of goods from one to the other.[1]

---

[1] "By purchasing great quantities of foreign goods imported into the country, those individuals whose incomes are to that extent diminished reduce their purchases of home-produced goods. The capacity of the home market to absorb goods is decreased. Importers and holders of home-produced goods find some difficulty in disposing of them. Imports diminish, while on the other hand attempts are made to export more, and these are particularly successful in the case of 'marginal exporters'— *i.e.*, those who are doubtful whether to sell at home or abroad and are therefore on

The same reasoning may be applied to the transfer of capital, the working of which has been examined in detail by Aftalion. "The stimulus to re-equilibrium of the balance of accounts," he concludes, "may come into action even before there have been any payments and consequent changes in the total monetary circulation of the two countries" (p. 159).

Angell's conclusions agree closely with Ohlin's.[1]

Rueff begins by expounding the theory of the re-establishment of equilibrium according to the classical formula which, as a first approximation, considers effective transfers of gold giving rise in their turn to price changes. But even he is led, in passing from theory to practice, to recognize that things do not happen as simply as that. In cases of exchange disequilibrium it is not usually the stock of money in circulation that diminishes, but the gold held in reserve by credit institutions. These changes in the gold reserve in turn cause a rise in the discount rate in the exporting country and a fall in the importing country, a restriction of credit in the former and expansion in the latter, and in consequence a fall of prices on the one hand and a rise on the other, leading in their turn to movements of goods or securities.[2] But in Rueff's view it is the movement of gold that starts the restoration of equilibrium, whereas according to Angell and Ohlin these movements are the result, and not the cause, of previous movements of purchasing power. In the opinion of these writers the changes in purchasing power and their influence on prices take place independently of any movements of gold. On this point there is marked disagreement between the old conception and the new one which seems to us much nearer the truth.

A similar evolution of ideas has taken place in regard to the equilibrium

---

the margin between the two markets. Foreign purchases and sales will thus tend towards a new position of equilibrium, reaching together three or four milliards or even more. The inequality appearing between income and disposable production will speedily put an end to the risk of a deficit in the balance of accounts." (Aftalion, *L'Équilibre dans les Relations économiques internationales*, p. 151.)

[1] "The essential feature of the older analysis of mechanisms," says Angell (p. 418), "lies in the role assigned to specie flows. These flows were regarded as both certain to occur, and as being fairly rapid in their effects. Here, on the contrary, they have been relegated to a minor place. . . . The ultimate key to the maintenance of equilibrium in the balance of payments in the face of enduring disturbances, and the key to the problem of international equilibrium at large, must be sought in another direction. It lies in the effects that a persisting change in the relation between the demand and supply of bills of foreign exchange produces upon the volume of purchasing power in circulation, and through it upon the general level of prices.

"The analysis to this point has rested on the assumption that the countries concerned maintained common metallic standards of money."

[2] Rueff, pp. 212-319.

of payments *within one country*. Here also the first step was to explain certain price changes by gold investments and then to revert to a simple explanation by income changes. Although it means going back to the eighteenth century it will not be out of place here to recall this little-marked episode in the history of economic ideas.

Cantillon, in a noteworthy chapter marked by all his customary depth of vision, seeks to explain how equilibrium is brought about between two regions of the same country, and especially between the capital and the provinces. For this purpose he has recourse to the mechanism of the circulation of gold. Observing that the capital always has to receive very considerable sums of money, as payment of taxes or rents of landowners living in London or Paris, so that the capital is thus a creditor of the provinces, he writes, "This debt paid in specie will diminish the quantity of money in the provinces and increase it in the capital, so that commodities and merchandise will be dearer in the capital than in the provinces by reason of the greater abundance of money in the capital."[1] This inequality of prices between the capital and the provinces, he says, will create a flow of goods from the latter to the former which will enable the deficit in the provinces to be paid for. In this way Cantillon applies the quantity theory pure and simple to a debit balance between two different parts of the same country. According to him it is by movements of specie and their influence on prices that the mechanism is started, exactly as in the classical theory in the case of international trade.

No one to-day would dream of explaining this phenomenon by such an over-simplified application of the quantity theory of money. All we should say is that since the *income* to be received by the capital is much larger than that due to the provinces, and since the capital cannot make all that its large population needs, the *expenditure of this income* causes the sending of commodities from the provinces to the capital, which makes it a debtor to the provinces, and in this way the equivalence of credits and debits is established. The circulation of specie and its effect on prices have nothing to do with the matter. In other words the explanation of internal exchange equilibrium by the conception of income has been quietly substituted (for so far as we know there has never been any controversy on the point) for a quantitative explanation by the influx of gold and the resulting changes in the price-level.

A little reflection will show that Cantillon himself mixes up two notions: the expenditure of income and the transfer of specie. In his

---

[1] Cantillon, *Essai sur la nature du commerce*, p. 150 (ed. Higgs; London, Macmillan, 1931).

time income, especially in the country (France) that he used as an example, where the development of credit instruments was still in a rudimentary state, was received and spent to a large extent in money. Abundance of income and abundance of money were the same thing to him, as a careful reading of the chapter in which he deals with this problem will show. He admits that the incomes of the Parisians are received by them in specie and then redistributed to the provinces through the traders of the capital, who are thus enabled to draw from the provinces the products demanded by the Parisians. But even in the eighteenth century this procedure had already been much simplified by the bankers. And in the monetary system of the twentieth century, when new methods of payment have taken the place of movements of metallic money for internal trade, and transfers of income are accomplished almost without any movements of specie (this being confined to a single national reserve), the explanation by the greater or smaller abundance of specie and its effect on prices is even further removed from reality. A separation has imperceptibly been made between the idea of income and that of payment in metallic money.

A similar though less complete development has taken place also in international payments. A creditor country can either spend directly abroad the income that the loan provides it with, or create at once at home and in its own currency the means of payment which are to be transferred to it by another country, through the mechanism of credit that dispenses with the movement of gold. The reduction of income in a country is also accomplished in the same way by a movement of bank deposits or notes. No longer are the transfer of income and the transfer of gold identical operations, and theory has come more and more to separate the two notions of income and metallic money in the international as well as in the national sphere. It ascribes to movements of income (or purchasing power) the effects which used to be attributed exclusively to movements of metallic money.[1]

Differing views about the mechanism for restoring the exchanges broke out into a suggestive controversy, started by an article by Keynes in 1929 on the subject of the Young Plan[2] that was to replace the Dawes Plan. Keynes again took the view that in the long run (and despite the loans granted her in the foreign markets up to that time) Germany could pay only in goods, and he was frightened by the

[1] We have explained this development elsewhere by showing that the creation of bank deposits and notes by credit is simply one way of making metallic money circulate without displacing it.

[2] The articles by Keynes, Ohlin, and Rueff appeared in the *Economic Journal* in 1929.

thought that she would have to offer them at lower and lower prices in order to get other countries to accept them. Now this lowering of prices, he said, could be achieved only by a reduction in the nominal and real wages of her workers to an almost intolerably low level. Keynes's reasoning was based on the classical barter theory, according to which a country having to meet a new foreign debt is condemned to 'offer' its goods at ever lower prices to induce its creditors to accept them in payment.

To this argument Ohlin replied to this effect: let us set aside the old notion of barter and see what movements of *purchasing power* a war indemnity produces. We see at once that the creditor countries find their purchasing power increased by the amount of the indemnity while that of the debtor country is diminished by the same amount. This change by itself—without any obligation upon Germany to lower her prices and without any disturbance of the exchanges—ensures an additional market for the goods of the debtor country, and nothing can prevent German sales from increasing thirty, forty, or fifty per cent. The question is rather whether the creditor countries can regard such an influx of foreign goods without anxiety.

When Rueff intervened he started from a rather different point of view in which the rate of exchange played an essential part. If, said he, the German Government took in taxation the sum needed to pay the indemnity the problem of transfer would be solved at once without any need to assume an additional fall in wages. The German Government by seeking foreign bills for the amount of the indemnity would make the price of these bills rise to the point at which the price of German goods in foreign currency would be lowered sufficiently to attract foreign purchases. These purchases would exactly correspond to the total of the goods withdrawn by the tax from German consumption. "The result of the tax will be to reduce the resources of the people of the debtor country, and this reduction of purchasing power will be exactly equal to the increase in the resources of the people of the creditor country" (p. 389), in virtue of what Rueff calls the principle of the conservation of purchasing power. All German prices will be lowered for the foreigner in proportion to the depreciation of German exchange, and wages will not fall more than other forms of income. It is the sum total of these forms of income, and therefore the *general* standard of living, that will be reduced.

Another important question was raised in the course of this controversy. In one of his articles Keynes had put forth the idea that exchanges of goods are determined by the economic structure of the various countries, and cannot be adapted without difficulty to movements of capital. Rueff, on the contrary, asserted that the elasticity of commercial movements had been proved many a time by experience. It had been proved particularly by the extraordinarily rapid restoration of the French balance of payments when France was suddenly deprived of the support of American loans in 1919. The ease with which imports and exports of goods were readjusted at that time emphasized the elasticity of commercial movements and their dependence on movements of capital.

A little later Aftalion devoted a chapter of his fine book on *L'Équilibre dans les échanges internationaux* to the same question. "Do goods follow capital?" he asked himself, and he came to the conclusion that as a general rule, and apart from certain exceptional cases, the trade balance adapts itself to the needs of the balance of payments. Experience shows, indeed, that countries owing either interest or capital are distinguished in general by an excess of exports, whereas creditor countries are characterized by a trade deficit.

By the discussions that they aroused, then, the payment of German reparations and the repayment of the inter-Allied debts to the United States resulted in a general revision of ideas hitherto held as to the means by which the balance of payments is brought into equilibrium. The means are similar to those employed in internal payments, and the resemblance between internal and external trade is once more established. The reintroduction of purchasing power instead of the comparison with barter in explaining the equilibrium of international trade has been equally fruitful of results in other spheres. By starting from the idea of a transfer of purchasing power it is possible, in particular, to consider the influence exerted by the development of one particular industry on other industries in the same country. Thus the progress of the motor-car industry, or the wireless or the cinema, by increasing the incomes and purchasing power of these new industries, alters the demand for the products of the older industries and causes reactions on their part to get back the markets they have partly lost. These reactions tend in general to lower the prices of their products so as to get back their former incomes by wider sales. This is a simple application of Rueff's principle of the conservation of purchasing power. The progress of one industry leads immediately to a new distribution of the demand for the products of other industries and a readjustment of production in general. In these reactions is to be found the clue to that general lowering of prices that accompanies the progress of production when it is not compensated by a simultaneous creation of new monetary instruments. Thus the theory of equilibrium between international purchases and sales can be applied just as well to the establishment of equilibrium between different industries in one country, or between different regions of the same country when one develops more rapidly than the others. It is a general method of interpretation, rather delicate to handle, but much closer to reality.

Finally, it should not be necessary to stress the fact that the sudden introduction of a new element into the system of international trade, such as the payment of a war indemnity or credit operations on an unaccustomed scale, is bound to have repercussions on the entire economy of the country in question. During the ten years following the First World War these great transfers of funds caused much disturbance to money markets and even to commodity markets. Along with the monetary instability and the inevitable fall in prices that always follows the rise caused by a prolonged war, they contributed also to the economic uneasiness that persisted so long after the war.

In this respect, also, the classical theory of international commerce, by which the equilibrium of debits and credits seemed to be established or restored with incomparable simplicity, has been shown to be at fault. Taussig called attention to this forcibly in the following passage:

> The Ricardians imagined that changes in prices would follow quickly and smoothly from the inflow and outflow of specie; goods would also move in and out of the country with ease and promptness. The whole machinery would work without giving any trouble, without disconcerting either the business world or the public Treasury or the observing economist. The intellectually courageous simplification of the problem is quite out of accord with the experiences of their own times [the Napoleonic Wars] or of any later time when there was the sudden impact of a huge remittance.[1]

It is to be hoped that this lesson will not be forgotten in the future.

III: THE INFLUENCE OF INTERNATIONAL TRADE ON NATIONAL PRICES

Here is another long-neglected problem that has suddenly become of great practical importance through the war and the compulsory nationalization of all economic systems. What is the effect of international trade on national price-levels? It ought *a priori* to assimilate the prices of similar goods produced in different countries, but is this actually the case? Do there not remain great differences not only

[1] Taussig, *International Trade*, p. 276.

between the prices of products, but also between the prices of services in different countries? And are we not justified in speaking of different price-levels in different countries? In this case is not currency devaluation the simplest method of restoring the equilibrium that has been destroyed? This is a strictly practical problem that statesmen call upon economists to solve.

The answers given by economic science to these questions were, it must be admitted, both fragmentary and inadequate, and some theories which had formulated solutions—like that of Senior—were well-nigh forgotten. So the whole question was brought forward anew, with results that are certainly not very satisfactory, though they deserve mention, if only because of the fame of the economists associated with them and the very difficulty of the questions raised.

Two main facts were obvious to observers: (1) Between price-levels in countries with the same monetary standard there is a very striking agreement in the rate of movement. This was shown throughout the nineteenth century between gold-standard countries, and was confirmed by the worldwide fall in prices after 1925, and still more after 1930. (2) On the other hand, between the price-levels of different countries, as revealed by index numbers, there are at any given moment *divergences* that persist despite the general similarity of their movements. How are we to explain these two apparently contradictory facts? How can we reconcile the parallelism of the general movements and the relative independence of the price-levels?

On the first point recent writers, especially Angell and Ohlin, have done little more than confirm and give precision to the older ideas. Ohlin distinguishes two kinds of prices: those of commodities consumed on an international scale (metals, coal, essential agricultural products like corn, sugar, and so forth), and those of commodities whose consumption is for the most part confined to one country (bricks and stone, building slates, timber and woodwork, furniture, etc.). The former are sold simultaneously on the great international markets, and their prices scarcely differ from one region to another except by the amount of customs duties and transport costs (p. 152). The prices of the latter—what might be called internal or domestic goods—seem at first glance to show greater independence from country to country. Why, for example, should not houses of the same kind, built largely of materials obtained from the country itself, be much dearer in England than in France, or *vice versa*? Actually, however, says Ohlin (pp. 153 *ff.*), the prices of 'domestic' products bear even more similarity to each other in different countries than those of 'international' commodities. This is because they necessitate the

employment of numerous imported products and are naturally subject
to the influence of the prices of these. The price of wooden houses,
for instance, will be affected of necessity by variations in the price of
timber on the great markets. It is the same with food products.
The price of foreign butter will affect the price of 'national' milk,
because the more foreign butter is imported the smaller the demand
for 'national' milk to make into butter, and this will tend to lower
its price. The price of 'national' fats will vary according to the
amount of oil products imported. Again, the price of 'national'
apples will be influenced by that of bananas or oranges, which are
substitutes for them in everyday consumption, and so forth. Advocates
of agricultural protection make good use of these repercussions as
arguments for demanding the prohibition not only of a single commodity but of a whole group of commodities capable of meeting the
same need. These influences operate the more strongly the more
transport facilities are perfected, so that access to markets is made
easier. In short, the bonds that connect prices in one country to
those in other countries have become so numerous and so close that
we cannot imagine a rise or fall at one point without expecting repercussions at all other points. Hence arises the striking similarity
between the trend of price-index numbers in countries on the same
monetary standard.

But, on the other hand, it is none the less certain that in the case of
many commodities there are often considerable divergences in price
between two countries, and these divergences are sometimes remarkably
permanent. How is this to be explained? They are particularly
marked in the prices of services, and above all in the prices of labour.
It was in regard to these that a theory of price variations between
different countries was given its first rough outline. Ricardo was the
first to formulate it, and then, a little later, Senior gave it much more
precision in his book entitled *Three Lectures on the Cost of Obtaining
Money*.[1] Senior's thesis is summed up in the following two propositions:

[1] London, Murray, 1830. The most important passage is at p. 14: "In fact the
portableness of the precious metals and the universality of the demand for them
render the whole commercial world one country, in which bullion is the money, and
the inhabitants of each nation form a distinct class of labourers. We know that in
the small market of every district the remuneration paid to the producer is in proportion to the value produced. And consequently that if one man can by superior
diligence, or superior skill, or by the assistance of a larger capital, or by deferring for
a longer time his remuneration, or by any advantage natural or acquired, occasion
a more valuable product, he will receive a higher reward. It is thus that a lawyer
is better paid than a watchmaker, a watchmaker than a weaver, a first-rate than an
ordinary workman. And for the same reason in the general market of the world an
Englishman is better paid than a Frenchman, a Frenchman than a Pole, and a Pole
than a Hindoo." And just as in a land of gold-mines it is the output of gold that

THEORIES OF INTERNATIONAL TRADE

(1) wages in any country are determined by the wages paid in the export industries; (2) wages in these latter industries are fixed from country to country by the quality of the labour furnished. The purchasing countries will give higher pay to the worker who produces the greatest quantity or the best quality of a product in the same time as his competitor, or who makes things that these countries consider the most desirable. This explains the high wages paid in England in comparison with French, German, or Russian wages, English goods being more sought after on all markets. This doctrine, which served to explain in particular the high wages paid in England at that time, aroused little interest outside England. Taussig studied the same problem in 1906 in connexion with American wages, which in their turn astonished people by their high level—higher than those of other countries, including England. He said, quite truly, that nothing could be found in the writings of French or German economists to show that their attention had been turned to these subjects.[1]

But Taussig might have mentioned the Dutch economist and statesman Pierson, who took up the same problem at the same time as Taussig was studying it, and started, like Taussig, from the differences in wages in order to solve the wider problem of the differences in price-levels between different countries. It was, no doubt, the reputation of Holland as a 'dear' country that led him to pay attention to this question. In a very interesting chapter on the value of money in different countries Pierson asserted that the only way to compare the purchasing power of money in one country with that in another (*i.e.*, their price-levels) is to compare its purchasing power in regard to services, not goods. The problem of the conditions that determine the local value of money, he said, can be posed only in these terms: how is the price of labour, expressed in money, determined in a

---

determines the wages of all other workers, so too "the mine worked by England is the general market of the world: the miners are those who produce those commodities by the exportation of which the precious metals are obtained, and the amount of the precious metals, which by a given exertion of labour, and advance of capital, they can obtain, must afford the scale by which the remuneration of all other producers is calculated" (p. 241). If we try to give precision to these statements, which, despite their apparent clarity, are still rather vague, we reach the following conception. For all products that have an international market, the remuneration of the workers in each country will naturally be greater if they produce more goods by a day's work. Remuneration will be determined by productivity. On the other hand, for products that have cost the same amount of labour, those most in demand or most sought after on the international market will also be the best paid, and the rate of remuneration thus obtained will force itself by degrees upon the total wages paid in each country.

A cricitism of Ricardo, Senior, and Taussig will be found in Ohlin, pp. 280–283.

[1] *Free Trade, the Tariff, and Reciprocity*, p. 85, note (New York, Macmillan, 1920).

country or district? It should be noted to begin with that by 'price of labour' the author does not mean only the nominal wages of the worker, but includes also the profit of the *entrepreneur* and the interest of capital—*i.e.*, the price of *all* the services used in making a product. And his answer, which is the same as Senior's, is that the price of labour, or, more precisely, the scale of prices of labour in a given country, depends on the quantity of the standard metal that this country can obtain in exchange for the products it exports.[1] In other words, the price of labour—in the special sense that Pierson gives to the phrase—that is acquired by the exported products fixes the entire range of remuneration in the country. That is the very conclusion reached by Senior. But what can be deduced from it in regard to comparative price-levels for *goods*? The answer is hardly anything, for Pierson hastens to add that a high price for *services* is quite compatible with a low price for *products*. In his view, a low purchasing power of money in a country (*i.e.*, a high price of labour) is not synonymous with a high level of *prices*, for the productivity of labour, measured by the number of days taken to produce the same thing in two countries, may be greater than it is elsewhere, and that means low prices. In brief, the two phrases 'high level of prices of things in a country' and 'low purchasing power of money' are not identical, for the second relates to services alone and the first to *all* products. Pierson drew the conclusion that price-levels in two countries could not be compared in any satisfactory way. In any such comparison, he said, individual experiences play a preponderant part, and these depend on individual needs. A country that one person considers 'dear' may with equally good reason be regarded by another as 'cheap.' (P. 369.) He added that a high price of labour is always an indication of economic prosperity.

Taussig, dealing with the same problem in 1906,[2] reached very similar conclusions, which he reaffirmed in his book in 1927. But this is not to be wondered at, since his doctrine, like Pierson's, is in a direct line of descent from that of Senior. In his view each country exports those of its products in which its labour is relatively most "efficient"—*i.e.*, in which its productivity for the same time worked is relatively greatest. Its products are cheaper than their foreign counterparts because, by hypothesis, in the time taken to make, say, ten units, the other countries make five. Hence the advantage

[1] Pierson, *Principles*, Vol. I, p. 369, of the English translation.
[2] In an article in *The Quarterly Journal of Economics* (August 1906) on *Wages and Prices in their Relation to International Trade*, reprinted in 1920 in his *Free Trade, the Tariff, and Reciprocity*, pp. 70 ff.: see especially the note at p. 84.

possessed by a country like the United States, which manages to produce much more than its competitors in the same time by the use of machinery both in agriculture and industry, and by the skill shown by its workers in using this machinery. The remuneration of labour is therefore greater in the American export industries, and this remuneration determines what must be paid in all other industries. High wages are found in countries where labour is efficient in the production of *export* commodities, and whose exports fetch a good price in the markets of the world. But Taussig, like Pierson, is careful to add that high wages must not be identified with high prices. If, he says, in the 'domestic' industries (*i.e.*, those working for the home market) the efficiency of labour is also greater than it is elsewhere, then the prices of 'domestic' products will be relatively low, despite the high wages. He observes that in the United States a great number of 'domestic' products are cheaper than in Europe, while, on the other hand, all personal services are much dearer. To sum up, it may be said that the United States, though a country of high wages, is not a country of high prices for the great majority of the population, though it is very much so for the wealthy and well-to-do classes (p. 81).

In short, Taussig's theory, like Pierson's, though it considers wage differences between countries, fails to explain differences in price-levels. Taussig even leans to the belief that we cannot speak of a general level of prices, but must distinguish carefully according to kinds of products. All that can be said—and it is the conclusion already reached by Senior—is that high wages in a country are generally a sign of prosperity and well-being, because they are a sign of highly developed productivity, and consequently of the widespread use of machinery and improved methods of cultivation and manufacture.[1]

The solution of the problem discussed by Taussig and Pierson became a matter of peculiar urgency when, after the First World War, several States decided to devaluate their currency so as to lower the general level of their prices, because, they said, high prices hindered the exportation of their goods. The long-neglected problem of the relation between the price-levels of different countries again became one of immediate interest, for on this relation depended in part the rate at which each country meant to fix the level of its currency in relation to others. After the collapse of the pound in 1931 and the dollar in 1933 all French prices, expressed in sterling or dollars, were

---

[1] The notion that a manufacturing and exporting country draws much money from abroad, and therefore shows a high price-level, had already been categorically expounded by Cantillon, *Essai sur la nature de commerce*, ed. Higgs, chapter v, pp. 156–157.

suddenly raised in relation to English and American prices. When France decided in 1936 to devaluate the franc once again Switzerland hastened to follow suit, in order to avoid a price difference between the two countries that would threaten her exports. So too in 1931 the Scandinavian countries had followed England, so as not to lose the market that their products had hitherto found there. In this way the various governments showed their conviction that the general price-level of one country can for a fairly long time be higher than that of others, and that the effects of this are felt by foreign trade, at least temporarily. Many economists remained sceptical, being convinced that after a certain time-lag the temporary excess of exports from the favoured country must either diminish or evoke a contrary stream of imports, owing to the necessary equilibrium between a country's purchases and sales. But how long can this time-lag last? It may be months or even years before the former volume of exports is restored, as England found by experience after 1925 and France after 1931.

These circumstances again drew attention to the problem discussed by Taussig as early as 1906, and to the causes of the difference of price-levels in different countries. The solution proposed by Taussig met with numerous objections from Ohlin and Angell. The former, basing his argument on the idea of mutual dependence, was unwilling to give to a single factor—such as the efficiency of labour—a decisive role in the fixing of relative price-levels. It is the sum total of the factors that act on prices that must be considered. The comparatively high rate of wages in the United States results, according to Ohlin, from the relative scarcity of man-power in that country, and not only from the great advantages enjoyed by the export industries. Angell adopts a very similar view.

But it is the legitimacy of the problem itself that is open to question. Can we really speak of the price-level of one country compared to that of others, when the very nature of the goods of one country varies greatly from those of another, despite their identity of name? When we seek to compare the absolute prices of goods in various countries, the principal difficulty we are up against is that of finding lists of products that are really capable of being compared. Too little attention is generally paid to the differences between manufactured products in common consumption in different countries, such as clothing, furniture, and utensils. Each nation has its own habits and traditions adapted to its climate and its own particular needs. Food, clothing, and housing are very different, even to a superficial observer, in Norway and England, or in France and Italy. Commodities common to them all are confined to a certain number of staple international goods, such as metallic raw materials and a few major agricultural products like milk, butter, and oil. In these circumstances the very idea of comparing price-levels is faced by an objection at the outset, and the practical conclusions that can be drawn from it are of little importance.

It is for statistical observation to settle the problem. Attempts at a more precise comparison of price-levels have so far met with the greatest difficulty, the theoretical reasons for which were admirably explained by René Roy in a remarkable study published in the Paris *Journal de la Société de Statistique* for September–October 1941, as well as by Ohlin (p. 159). Some good writers, however, such as Knut Wicksell, who dealt with the question a few years before the Second World War, are content with the statement that "broadly speaking the price of the same commodity cannot vary in two different countries by much more than the import duty and the freight."[1] But this formula is too much simplified, as Ohlin has shown: it is true only of countries that are all importers of a commodity supplied by the *same* exporting country; for instance, all countries that buy their wood pulp from Sweden. It ceases to be true when we compare the price of this commodity in one of the importing countries with its price in another: the difference is often less than the cost of transport between the two countries.[2] In short, the problem of price differences between different countries is far from having been satisfactorily solved.

One notion that should be mentioned here—a very old one—is that a prosperous country is generally a country of high prices. From Cantillon to Ricardo and down to Pierson and Taussig we find it constantly reappearing. But Wicksell considers it an illusion,[3] though he does not say how it arose. We will try to explain, as a modest contribution to a problem whose solution is beset by so many pitfalls.

A prosperous country is one in which the quantity of products and services to be consumed per head of population is greater than elsewhere, or of better quality, or both. In such a country, therefore, the inhabitants enjoy on an average a higher standard of life than those in less prosperous countries. If we admit that prices of the same products are the same in this as in other countries, we are bound to

[1] Wicksell, *Lectures on Political Economy*, English translation, 1935, Vol. II, p. 158. The passage continues as follows: "A factor which certainly tends to raise the cost of living in prosperous countries is the high level of wages and the ensuing higher prices for all personal services and all work done by hand. But this does not appreciably affect commodity prices, or at any rate the prices of those commodities entering into commercial statistics."

[2] See Ohlin, *International and Interregional Trade*, p. 157.

[3] Wicksell, *op. cit.*, Vol. II, p. 157.

attribute the prosperity of this one to the fact that the nominal income of each person—*i.e.*, the amount he receives and spends per day or per month—is represented by a higher figure than elsewhere. A prosperous country, then, will be a country not necessarily of high prices but of high incomes. Now, in a country of high incomes it will be possible to obtain not only more things at the same price as elsewhere, but also things of better quality which, *if they were consumed in poor countries as well*, would have the same price, *but which are not consumed there*, because incomes are too low and these things are dear in relation to those incomes and not in relation to the same things made elsewhere. So in prosperous countries we find products that are too dear to be obtained in poor countries, but not dearer than they *would be* in the latter countries *if they were found there*. The entire range of consumption is different in those countries, so that superficial observers get the impression that the cost of living in general is higher. But that comes of comparing cost of living with *incomes* in the less wealthy countries, instead of with the prices of products, which are the same, or *would be* the same if they were met with there. In England, for instance, or in Holland, articles of toilet and clothing, etc., seem dear to an Italian or a Frenchman, but actually they are things *of better quality* than in France or Italy—more solid or more durable things, which in the latter countries are confined to the richer section of the community, whereas they are in common use in England and Holland. So we get back to a very similar idea of the problem to that of Pierson.

IV: THE INTERNATIONAL DISTRIBUTION OF GOLD

Closely connected with the problem of price-levels is another problem that greatly concerned the Classical school of political economy: that of the distribution of gold among the different countries.

The doctrine formulated for the first time by Hume (following Cantillon), and again in almost identical terms by Ricardo, Senior, Mill, and Bastable, remained for a long time without any important change. Its essential points are the two following ideas: (1) that gold is a commodity whose circulation from one country to another is determined by the same circumstances as other commodities; (2) that just as commodities are exported from a country where they are cheap to one where they are dearer, so is gold exported when it is cheaper in one country than in others (or, in other words, when the price-level is higher than elsewhere), and this export of gold tends after a short time to equalize the price-levels in the different countries.

From the beginning this doctrine has received many modifications. Ricardo's opponents observed that gold was exported whenever the balance of accounts was out of equilibrium, so that the rate of exchange rose. Now, the reasons for the disequilibrium of this balance are very numerous, so differences between the general price-levels of different countries are far from being the sole cause of gold movements.

To meet this objection a distinction has been made, as by Mill, between two kinds of disequilibrium in the balance of accounts, namely, those of short duration arising from temporary inequality between a country's credits and foreign debts, leading to very slight remittances of gold, and those of longer duration, where the outflow of gold may go on for a fairly long time, and which result from a marked inequality between the price-levels of exporting countries and the rest. These latter disequilibria are less frequent than the former kind and appear particularly at times when large quantities of the monetary metals are being produced.

This is the point at which the theory of the world distribution of gold was left by Mill and his successors. The second case, however, was more and more neglected as it was very rarely met with in practice: it is not even mentioned by Goschen in his famous *Theory of the Foreign Exchanges*.[1]

It is obvious that the origin of the classical doctrine is to be found in the great discoveries of gold and silver in the sixteenth century, the rise in prices that resulted from them, and the consequent distribution of the precious metals among the trading countries through the import and export of goods. The mechanism of this distribution continued to obsess the classical writers, and their notions were to be largely confirmed by the two great influxes of gold during the nineteenth century. After the discovery of the Australian and Californian gold-fields, as well as those of the Transvaal, a flood of gold poured on two occasions over the world, leading gradually to a general rise of prices, accompanied by an expansion of international commerce, by a method very similar to that described by Ricardo and his successors (and even earlier still by Cantillon). As to this mechanism there is fundamental agreement to-day between advocates and opponents alike of the 'quantity theory.' Whether they start from the conception of incomes, like Aftalion in the important book that he devoted to this question under the title of *Monnaie, prix et change*,[2] or whether, like

---

[1] Goschen says that exports of specie are the result of the balance of debts, or else of a difference in the value of money, or else, again, of variations in the value of money in circulation (*i.e.*, the depreciation of a currency).

[2] Sirey, Paris, 1927. This volume was to be completed by a further one in 1938 entitled *L'Or et la monnaie*.

Rueff in his *Théorie des phénomènes monétaires*,[1] they rely on the notion of 'monetary circulation,' both parties declare that the disequilibria of the balance of accounts caused by the rise of prices in the countries where the gold is discovered and the resulting exchange fluctuations determine the spread of gold and its distribution among the different countries.[2] By the term 'balance of accounts' Aftalion means the balance of external income received in the course of a year, to be distinguished from the 'balance of payments,' which in this author's terminology includes not just the annual incomes but the sum-total of a country's external debits and credits. Rueff conforms to old tradition in using 'balance of accounts' to denote all elements, whatever they may be (capital, income, and goods), which corresponds to Aftalion's 'balance of payments.' But this difference in terminology does not affect the agreement of the two writers as to the fundamental determinant of the movements of gold from country to country.

Wicksell has given a similar interpretation of the phenomenon, and explains with remarkable precision certain facts that are often not sufficiently emphasized. He observes first that the discovery of a gold-mine is accompanied by a very great rise of prices in the country where it is found. But that is only the first stage. Foreign goods soon begin to flow into the country, attracted by these high prices, "with the result that prices soon revert to normal and at the first shock possibly fall below normal." This fall in prices allows the production of gold to continue, though without this fall the cost would have become prohibitive. Profits from the mines become normal again, and the export of gold continues. It is, therefore, the gold that is exported to other countries that will henceforth affect prices in those countries, and by raising them create disequilibrium in the balance of accounts, which

---

[1] Payot, Paris, 1927.

[2] "There is at each instant one single equilibrium distribution of the world stock of gold, leading to a range of prices of such a nature that when all conditions within each country at the moment in question are taken into account (including the relations of particular prices, transport costs, individual habits in regard to the use of different forms of money, velocity of circulation, activity of trade, banking policy, discount rate . . .) *the total balances of the accounts of all the countries concerned are and remain in equilibrium.*" (Rueff, *Théorie des phénomènes monétaires*, p. 249.)

It is clear on reading this passage that it is not altogether correct to class Rueff's theory along with those of Aftalion or Wicksell. Rueff's theory is purely static; he does not take into account the dynamic hypothesis of new production of gold—a hypothesis that he will probably examine in the forthcoming volume of his work. But the world distribution of new gold is brought about, like the distribution of existing gold, by changes in the balance of accounts, and it is therefore legitimate here to associate Rueff with the other writers mentioned, although their point of view is more dynamic. In examining doctrines that present a fair number of slight individual differences it is impossible, without unduly lengthening this book, to go into all the details that a comparison of these doctrines would demand.

will in turn give rise to a new distribution of the gold. Wicksell emphasizes the fact that this rise of prices is due directly to the influx of gold, apart from any effect it may have on the rate of discount. And this is the more interesting because the author has shown elsewhere the importance he attaches to the influence of the discount rate on prices.[1]

Yet on the morrow of the First World War we watched with astonishment enormous movements of gold that seemed to contradict this simple thesis. Neither the disequilibrium of the balance of trade nor that of the balance of accounts (at least in the restricted sense given to that term by Aftalion) seemed able to account for it. The large gold payments made by England and France to the United States *during the war* were easily explained by the impossibility of exporting goods at that time to pay for the enormous amount of war material imported by those countries. They confirmed the old observation that countries with an inconvertible paper currency are gradually stripped of their stock of metal for the benefit of the foreigner. But when the war was over the flow of gold to the United States continued and even increased, even when foreign trade had been restored. Was not that a strange anomaly?

In reality the phenomenon was due to a particular circumstance not mentioned by the Classical economists because it had not shown itself in their time and because they adopted the single assumption of an international *metallic* standard. The circumstance in question was the temporary existence of *two* purchasing prices for gold, owing to the system of paper money employed by the majority of countries. Between these prices the sellers were free to choose, and they naturally chose the most advantageous. One was the official price, the other the actual market price. On the exchange market the prices of the paper pound and the paper franc in relation to the dollar convertible into gold had depreciated. But the Bank of England and the Bank of France continued to offer, for the gold brought to them, a price in paper pounds or paper francs *as low as that in force before the war* when both countries were still on the gold standard. So a dollar bought on the exchange market for paper money might cost 5s. 6d. in London and 15 francs in Paris, whereas a weight of gold equal to that contained in this same dollar was still exchangeable officially at the Bank of England for 4s. in notes, and in Paris for 4.86 francs. From this divergence between the official buying price and the free price of the gold dollar on the exchange market there was bound to result, as an inevitable consequence, that the producers of gold wishing to obtain paper pounds

---

[1] Wicksell, *Lectures on Political Economy*, English translation, Vol. II, pp. 161–163.

or francs adopted the roundabout method of *sending their gold to New York*. There they changed it into dollars, which they then sold on the exchange market in London or Paris at the price of 5s. 6d. or 15 francs —far higher than the legal buying price. Therein lies the whole secret of what was for a long time called the "cornering" of gold by the United States and the "maldistribution" of the precious metal. Cornering and maldistribution were the inevitable consequence of the absurdly prolonged refusal of the two great issuing banks to buy gold at a price corresponding to the value of the gold dollar on the exchange market. It meant the systematic exclusion of newly produced gold from their coffers. The accumulation of gold by the United States continued as long as there was this difference between the buying price of the gold dollar at the European issuing banks and that obtainable on the exchange markets.

What these events showed was this: that gold turned to those countries where it was *dearer*, not only in goods (which was the Classical doctrine) but also (and this was the new fact brought into prominence by these happenings) *in the currency of other countries*, when the rates of exchange between these currencies and between them and gold were not the same. That is the conclusion seen so clearly by Aftalion in his admirable *L'Or et la monnaie*.

Now, was this actually a *new* fact? Fundamentally it was the application to the paper-money system of phenomena often observed in bimetallic systems, when sometimes gold and sometimes silver was exported or imported, according as one could be exchanged for the other at a more favourable rate than the legal exchange rate in the country where the movements began. The influx of gold into the United States slackened after 1925 when its cause disappeared, that is to say, when first England and then France stabilized their currencies and thus did away with the difference, too long maintained, between the price of gold on the exchange market and its official purchase price.

After 1928 and 1929, and despite the stabilization of sterling, a new flow of gold began to the United States and also to France. This time a new circumstance had arisen: the exportation of capital, especially short-term capital, caused first by the enormous differences in interest rates on the great money markets, and later by *uncertainty as to the stability of the monetary standard*, this latter circumstance being predominant after the crisis of 1930. Then appeared what Aftalion calls "the attraction of sound money"—*i.e.*, the search by capital for a refuge in the securities or values of countries whose currencies seemed likely to remain more stable than elsewhere and less threatened by devaluation. No one had hitherto imagined that these influences, generally so fleeting, could ever reach the scale that they then attained, or lead to such gigantic movements of gold. Yet there was nothing in this that contradicted the Classical doctrine: events were simply showing that an "unfavourable" balance of accounts can result from circumstances far more numerous than the single movements that that doctrine took into account—i.e., movements of goods determined by price differences. According to whether or not movements of capital are included in the 'balance of accounts' (whether Rueff's or Aftalion's definition is preferred) will these movements be regarded as a simple application of the general theory or as an anomaly.[1]

In one case, moreover, the old Classical theory itself has received striking confirmation in the events of this period. This was the situation in which England found herself in relation to the United States after the return of the pound to par in 1925. The volume of means of payment for the English had greatly increased during the war, and under this influence the English price-level had risen very high. But it had been thought possible to peg the pound to the dollar *at the old rate*. The consequence followed promptly: the export of English products became more difficult, upsetting the English balance of trade and constantly driving the rate of exchange of the pound to the outgoing specie point. Hence arose an export of gold from England—though in smaller quantities than in the earlier period—or, more strictly, a tendency for gold newly extracted from the mines to go elsewhere than to England. This was a striking confirmation of the Classical doctrine. The movement did not end and gold did not begin to return to England till after the devaluation of the pound sterling.

The monetary phenomena of this period, more like those of the eighteenth century, so well described by Cantillon, than those of the nineteenth, caused surprise by the unprecedented extent of the gold movements—a surprise that was reflected in theories numerous but ephemeral. We have already mentioned the one that aroused the liveliest discussion—the theory of the 'maldistribution' of gold, debated at length at the Gold Conference at Geneva in 1928 and 1929, and in the economic reviews.[2] Aftalion has examined in detail the arguments put forward by the supporters of this theory—and particularly the influence on the general fall of prices attributed by them to this 'maldistribution'—in a most instructive book entitled *L'Or et sa*

[1] The same thing happened when the United States suddenly reduced the gold content of the dollar in 1933.

[2] See especially the articles by Strakosch in *The Economist* and the Chatham House discussions collected in a book entitled *The International Gold Problem* (Oxford, 1931).

distribution mondiale.[1] Some of the fundamental points of this theory have been briefly summarized in the preceding pages. The 'maldistribution' of gold was, in reality, the result of measures taken by the belligerent countries themselves after the First World War, and of their reluctance to restore an international monetary system after the avalanche of paper money that started during hostilities.

So nothing happened during these dramatic years to *contradict* the Classical doctrine of the distribution of gold in normal times. But, on the other hand, events have shown that other influences regarded by the Classical school as secondary or exceptional (even to the extent of leaving them unmentioned) might assume unsuspected importance as a result of the upheavals caused by the war, and set up gold movements singularly difficult to remedy. In his *Principles of Economics*, already quoted, whose superiority is as marked on this subject as on others, Pierson had already developed Ricardo's theory so as to cover other movements of gold besides those dealt with by that author. And Pierson attributed to Ricardo the particular merit of recognizing that international gold movements were due primarily to monetary and not commercial causes.[2] Aftalion's exposition of more recent experiences leads to the same conclusion.

V: COMMERCIAL POLICY: FREE TRADE, PROTECTION, AND AUTARKY

While the old Ricardian doctrine was being developed and refined into a theory both more complex and closer to the facts, the controversy among economists concerning the best commercial policy still went on, though in a far less stormy atmosphere than at the end of the nineteenth century. The triumph of an ever more restrictive protection, before and especially after the war, even in countries traditionally attached to Free Trade, like Great Britain, Holland, and Belgium, took much of the sting out of the controversies, whose influence upon practice was admittedly growing continually weaker. But this triumph did not prevent the uninterrupted progress of international trade, though from time to time the approaching end of its continued expansion was foretold by certain writers. It was predicted even before the First World War,[3] and it was predicted after it,[4] but

[1] Dalloz, Paris, 1932.
[2] See particularly pp. 536–562 of Pierson's *Principles of Economics*, Vol. I.
[3] For example, Nogaro and Oualid, in a book called *L'Évolution du Commerce* (1914), expressed the opinion that France and England "have now reached the peak of their foreign trade." (P. 416.)
[4] By Ohlin, for instance, at p. 126 of his book already quoted, though his conclusions are a little lacking in precision and may be differently interpreted.

the predictions were always belied by the facts. On the eve of the
great crisis of 1930 international trade reached a level hitherto unknown. Its decline—which was, moreover, relative, and much more
a matter of prices than of quantities—seemed only temporary. But for
the outbreak of another war it would probably have soared to new
heights through the general world expansion of production, calling
every year for more raw materials, more machinery, more tools, and
more varied foodstuffs. Nothing, it seemed, but a check to the growth
of population could seriously slow down the astounding progress of
international trade during the past hundred years. Yet nothing is less
certain.

Other circumstances intervened. To begin with, the tariff system
of a country, whether protectionist or Free Trade, seemed to have no
appreciable connexion with the more or less rapid progress of its
economy. The progress of protectionist countries like Germany and
the United States in the twenty-five years before the World War
was often more rapid than that of Free Trade countries, while, on
the other hand, the Spanish economy, strictly protectionist, made but
slow progress. In short, the amount of protection or Free Trade seems
to have played only a slight part in the development of trade and
prosperity in any country: the true motive forces are to be found
elsewhere. Charles Gide, in France, had already pointed this out,
and economists of more strictly liberal views, like Divisia, are tending
nowadays towards the same conclusion.

On the other hand, the great world movements of prices, up and
down, have obviously exercised a much more marked influence than
tariff systems on the rhythm of progress or depression of the great
economic systems. Marshall, in a famous deposition,[1] expressed the
opinion that the progress of Free Trade after 1850 had more to do
with the prosperity of England than the rise in prices that was started
at the same time by the discoveries of gold in California and Australia.
But the opposite opinion is much more likely to be the true one. The
extension of Free Trade in the middle of the nineteenth century would
have met more obstacles if the stimulus given to world economy by
the rise in prices, caused by the sudden abundance of gold, had not
made up for the temporary inconveniences inherent in any alteration
of customs duties. This was made plain when, after 1871, the fall of
prices that continued till 1895 caused a very strong protectionist
reaction against the liberal regime established in the middle of the
century, and this reaction did not end when a new rise in prices, due
to the exploitation of gold in the Transvaal, followed the preceding

[1] *Cf.* our *Histoire des Doctrines relatives au crédit et à la monnaie*, pp. 242 ff.

fall. This time the result of the rise was to mitigate the inconveniences of protection, not of Free Trade. It facilitated commercial progress, despite the hindrances that new tariff barriers tried to impose upon it.[1] Since 1930 the rapid fall in world prices has set in motion a new wave of protection. Once again it has become plain that tariffs and quotas exert only very slight influence on the extent of the crisis. In some countries they have hardly checked the fall in prices at all, and have not succeeded in preventing it. If Great Britain and the United States emerged from the crisis, it was not because of their tariff policies but because of the monetary devaluations that they both adopted. France, in spite of quotas and prohibitions, did not see her foreign trade improve till after 1936, when she resigned herself to a new devaluation, thus putting her price-level in harmony with that of her great competitors.

What was the reaction of the economists to these developments? For the Liberal ones, especially the mathematicians, Free Trade had for a long time admitted of many exceptions and much watering-down. Even Mill, following List, had admitted that the protection of an industry in its early stages might be justified: this is the 'infant industry' argument. Pareto showed that the setting-up of trade between two hitherto separate countries undoubtedly increased the total supply of wealth, though it might be concentrated in one of them alone.[2] Barone, a disciple of Pareto, after a rigorous demonstration that every protective duty gives rise to the destruction of wealth, adds that it would be erroneous to conclude "that for every country and in every age protection is harmful and Free Trade advantageous. . . . Even from the purely economic point of view it must be considered whether the destruction of wealth that is certainly one of the effects of protection may not prevent still greater destructions of wealth."[3] In short, all these writers believe, like Cournot, that freedom of trade is mainly a maxim of practical wisdom, or, like Edgeworth, who drew up a list of all the cases in which the imposition of a duty might be justified by theory, that it is one of those prudential maxims that are always good to follow—like 'honesty is the best policy.' Pareto thinks it futile to put the problem in a general form: it must be couched in the following terms: "Given all the economic and social conditions of a country at a given moment, is Free Trade or protection the better

---

[1] This is particularly true of countries like France with specific rather than *ad valorem* duties, where, in consequence, the rise in prices progressively reduces the ratio of the duty to the price of the product.

[2] See Pareto, *Manuale*, chapter ix, para. 45.

[3] Barone, *Principii*, pp. 89, 90. The same idea is to be found in Pareto, *Manuale*, chapter ix, para. 61, and note.

policy for that country at that time?"[1] List himself would not have
spoken differently.

But though the controversy about tariffs went on between economists in a different atmosphere from that of the late nineteenth
century, and though the more liberal among them were disposed to
modify their principles in many circumstances, that did not in the
least mean that the general economic arguments in favour of trade
freedom had lost for them any of their convincing force. On the contrary, they resumed and developed them after the war with a precision
that was often lacking in their predecessors. The point of view of
these economists has been perfectly defined by Robbins in his book
The Great Depression (pp. 183–184). "It is important," he says,

> that in considering this matter we should preserve a sense of propor-
> tion. . . . The existence of protective tariffs on a considerable scale
> is not in itself an obstacle to extensive business activity nor to a
> fairly rapid rate of progress. . . . No one in his senses would argue
> that the establishment of universal free trade is a *sine qua non* of
> business recovery at the present. . . . But this is not to say that there
> is anything to be said for tariffs as a positive means to prosperity.
> Nothing that has been said in recent years has served to alter in any
> substantial respect the strength of the case for the maximum inter-
> national division of labour, that is the case against protective
> tariffs; and the technical developments of modern industry have
> done much to make that case even more pertinent than in the past.
> The economies of mass production, which modern technical develop-
> ments make possible, are economies which can only be reaped to
> the full if the market is sufficiently extensive. Since tariffs necessarily
> contract markets, it follows that the existence of tariffs must prevent
> resort to the economies of mass production being as widespread as
> might otherwise be the case.

Ohlin, the most penetrating investigator of international trade,
adopts the Classical thesis, according to which trade in goods is the
only means of effecting approximately that rational distribution of
production that would be established if the factors of production
(labour, natural resources, and capital) could move about at will. "If
the factors of production," he writes at p. 39, "could move about at
will, space would no longer be of any importance. . . . Labour and
capital would be transferred from places where their marginal utility
is low to places where it is higher."[2] In this way would be brought

---

[1] Pareto, *Manuale*, chapter ix, para. 60.
[2] To be quite accurate, the hypothesis of a total transferability of the means of production that would abolish space seems to us so inconceivable that it would be better,
in our opinion, to set aside considerations of this kind. It is a relic of the ideas of
Ricardo and Mill. Space is a fact. Even if national barriers did not exist, we should
have to take account of space, and a rational world distribution of productive forces

about what Pareto called "the maximum ophelimity." But since this transferability of the means of production does not exist

> the only thing left to do is to make use of them where they are and to localize production according to the geographical distribution of the factors. . . . In this way the total volume of production is increased, and so the mobility of the products makes up to some extent for the lack of mobility of the factors of production between one country and another, or, what comes to the same thing, trade mitigates the disadvantages arising from an unfavourable distribution of the factors of production. Hence arises the profit resulting from trade between region and region (p. 42)

or between country and country, and this, he adds (going further than Pareto), is profitable *in every case* to the exchanging countries.

To sum up, trade, domestic and foreign, is the only means yet discovered by individuals and nations of sharing the advantages of which they would necessarily be deprived by the inequalities of their material or intellectual resources if they were confined to those given them by nature or history.

Another argument leading to the same conclusion has been brilliantly employed by Enrico Barone, who illustrates it by striking diagrams. It consists in showing that the immediate effect of every new protective duty is to reduce the actual revenue, in goods and services, of the country that imposes it.

So the old argument that every reduction in imports through the imposition of a customs duty tends to diminish the amount of exports has lost none of its force, though its manner of presentation in the course of discussions on reparations differs slightly from that used earlier. It can be formulated as follows. When a foreigner introduces foreign goods into France he acquires some francs. Now, these francs can be employed, either by the owner himself or by those to whom he transfers them, *only in France*, and only in the following four ways: (1) in buying French goods to be exported from France; (2) in payment of debts owed by the foreigner to France; (3) in buying capital (securities, land, houses, etc.); (4) in buying gold. So the diminution of imports through the imposition of a customs duty, by reducing the

---

would involve exchange of products because these forces would be dispersed in space, like the markets on which their products would be sold. It is simpler to say that by exchanging goods and transporting them from the places where they are made more cheaply to places where they are dearer we effect an economy which makes possible a greater amount of production for the whole world. The advantage is still more obvious when goods are exchanged which *cannot be made at all* in the places where they are in demand (copper for bananas, machinery for cotton, and so forth), and this latter case has become increasingly frequent in the international commerce of the twentieth century.

number of francs possessed by foreigners, will necessarily either injure a French exporter, or injure a French creditor who is owed money by a foreigner, or prevent foreign investments in France, or prevent an export of gold. Of these consequences the first two are by far the most frequent, and there is no doubt whatever that, considered by themselves, they weaken a country's economy. The two latter consequences are sometimes favourable and sometimes unfavourable, according to the country and the circumstances, but they are much less common and can in most cases be ignored. What we have generally to expect, therefore, if the imposition of the duty reduces imports, is either a reduction in exports or a reduction in the realization of credits, both necessarily injurious to the country's economic system, and both frequently observed in the post-war years.

To deny the applicability of these fundamental arguments would be to deny also the advantages of freedom in *internal* trade. Nor are they disputed by the immense majority of economists. If some of them sometimes support protectionist measures, it is because they regard them as temporary exceptions, to be tolerated for the time being so as to avoid certain social, political, or even military inconveniences in the country that adopts them. Haberler, in his examination of the arguments for protection, draws a distinction between two kinds. First there are the arguments that he calls undebatable—those that are not open to discussion because they disregard truths accepted by all economists (such as the 'commercial deficit' argument, a hundred times refuted and yet always reappearing in popular controversy)— and secondly those that admit the truth of these conclusions and confine themselves to showing that in certain exceptional circumstances they no longer hold good. To this latter class belongs the theory that an economic crisis causing severe unemployment may be combated or mitigated by customs duties. This thesis, often maintained since the war, is not a new one. It had been defended before that time by so convinced a Liberal as N. G. Pierson, who admitted that a sudden and heavy fall in the price of corn, for example, might justify a protective duty. "A measure that aims at preventing a too rapid fall in corn prices," he wrote, "is of advantage not only to farmers and country tradesmen but to the whole population as well."[1] What he would allow was an import duty levied at a lower rate each year until it finally disappeared, so that the advantage of a *permanent* fall in the price of corn would not be lost, but the inconvenience of a *sudden* fall would be avoided. Pierson added, however, that the inconveniences of such a duty are in other ways so great, and especially that the diffi-

[1] See Pierson, *Principles*, Vol. III, p. 197.

culty of calculating it equitably and benefiting only those who really need it is such that it is better on the whole to leave it alone (p. 200).

What Pierson accepts for agriculture Ohlin admits for the protection of industry in a period of depression and unemployment. The effect of a customs duty will be to reduce imports, but the normal repercussions of this reduction—a diminution of exports and the extension of unemployment to the export industries—will not take place in this case, for the protected industry will increase its production *without having to withdraw labour from other industries*, as it will find it among the unemployed and will simply recommence undertakings that had been held up by the crisis. Neither will there be any rise in wages or in the price of capital in the export industries. The State, on the other hand, will economize by not having to pay unemployment benefit to workers who will now be employed.[1] "All such cases as this," writes Ohlin,

> differ in one important circumstance from the case of an ordinary protective duty: the factors of production used to increase production in the protected industries do not diminish the amount of the available factors needed by other industries. The workers are drawn from the ranks of the unemployed. There is therefore no diminution of production in other industries (pp. 494–495).

No doubt, remarks Ohlin, the same result might have been obtained without a customs duty, but more slowly. The protective duty will enable a difficult obstacle to be surmounted. In the case of a *long* depression, on the other hand, the resulting movements of labour will probably reduce unemployment as effectively as a customs duty. So, to be sure of applying the duty intelligently, it would be necessary to know first whether a temporary crisis or a long depression is to be dealt with—which is not exactly an easy matter.

In his important work on international trade (*Der Internationale Handel*) Haberler, though a convinced Free Trader, maintains the same thesis as Ohlin in the case of a depression of short duration, but his argument is a different one. He agrees that a reduction of exports will necessarily correspond to the reduction of imports that follows the imposition of a customs duty. But since the protected industry is going to benefit by increased purchasing power, because of the greater activity that it owes to the protection, this purchasing power may increase the demand for the products of the export industries and make up for the loss of the purchases of foreign customers (p. 192). So by a rather different route the author reaches the same conclusion as Ohlin. He also insists that what is true of unemployment does not

[1] Ohlin, *International and Interregional Trade*, p. 493.

apply in the case of productive factors other than labour, as, for example, causing uncultivated land to lie idle.

Keynes has declared in favour of the same thesis. He admits that a customs duty, by temporarily improving the trade balance of a country, may enable it to increase its purchases of raw materials and set part of its industry going again.[1]

The theories just mentioned relate to what might be called occasional, or temporary, protection, as practised by almost all Governments. But there are also more ambitious theories, that are not content with making concessions to protection, but try to find a doctrinal basis for it and make a regular system of it. The most interesting attempt of this kind is, in our opinion, that of the Rumanian author Manoïlesco, whose *Théorie du protectionnisme et de l'échange international*, published in French in 1929, has provoked sharp contradictions but nevertheless contains original and interesting ideas. The author is first and foremost an industrialist. He wants to see his country abandon her almost exclusively agricultural economy and turn towards a more industrial one. Despite his own denial, his inspiration is much the same as that of Friedrich List, and his practical conclusions are very similar to those of the German economist. Like him, he attaches chief importance in his idea of commercial policy to productivity and nationality, and like him too he rejects a generalized protective system applying indifferently to all branches of economic activity. The basic notion in his work is that industry to-day in every country gives a bigger return than agriculture

---

[1] On this point see Haberler's book, pp. 198–200, where he discusses Keynes's position. In France it is maintained by Oulès (*Le mécanisme des échanges internationaux et la politique commerciale en temps de crise*, 1936) that the normal theory of international trade and of the equilibrium of purchases and sales between different countries, though true in periods of expansion, is not true in periods of depression or crisis, and this justifies protective duties. Just as within a country, he says, there are strong and weak businesses, and as in times of crisis the weak ones, producing at a higher price, are eliminated by the strong ones, so also there are strong and weak countries from the point of view of international commerce, and the latter tend to be eliminated in times of crisis. When general demand is active the products of the weak countries are in demand on the international market, just as in times of prosperity the products of the weak businesses find a market because the demand is very great. But in periods of crisis the strong countries, he thinks, would be able to swamp the weak ones, owing to their superior production, and bring their trade completely to an end. In this case a customs duty would be the only means by which a weak country could keep ts industry going while waiting for better times.

This argument assumes the existence of international trade machinery very different from that generally accepted, without any sufficient justification. The distinction between 'strong' and 'weak' countries does not seem to correspond to any precise economic definition. In times of crisis *all* countries find their foreign trade diminished, and the diminution is often most marked in the so-called 'strong' countries: the United States, Germany, and England, for instance, suffered far more gravely than France in the crisis of 1930.

and yields a larger income. Manoïlesco is, we believe, the first economist to emphasize with all the force it needs this important and indisputable fact which explains the continued movement of agricultural
populations towards industry. His work may in this respect be compared with a book published in the United States in 1940 by the
eminent statistician Carl Snyder under the title *Capitalism the Creator*.[1]
Based on an incomparable knowledge of statistics and history and
written in a captivating style, it is a veritable hymn of praise in
honour of the human spirit in the service of industry. With an impressive wealth of documents the author describes the marvellous
economic development of the United States during the last hundred
years, built up entirely on the basis of technical inventions put into
operation by saving. With many curves and figures he shows the
comparative yields of industry and of agriculture in the United States,
and the predominant part played by the former in this great achievement. Manoïlesco has demonstrated the same thing at a time when
this truth, still meeting with much resistance, was far from being
universally accepted. He concludes from it that protection is advantageous when duties are the only means of introducing into a country
an industry that will yield more than the country already produces,
and more, in particular, than agriculture.

The object of commercial policy being, therefore, in his view, to
raise the general level of productivity in a country, protection should
be applied only to a small number of products. "Protection," he
writes, "should cover only certain things, generally few in number
compared with all the things produced in the country." Only manufactures "whose productivity exceeds the average productivity of the
country" will be protected to the exclusion of all the rest, and so the
loss resulting from the establishment of a protective duty will be more
than compensated by the introduction into the country of more paying industries. Far from reducing international trade, industrialization
increases it. Manoïlesco emphasizes one fact whose importance
cannot be over-estimated—though it is forgotten in almost all tariff
discussions, and though Taussig has very often stated it—namely,
that "industrial countries are themselves the greatest consumers and
the greatest importers of industrial goods" (p. 258).

We are only pointing out here the fundamental conceptions in
Manoïlesco's work, without going into detail on the theoretical discussions by which he seeks to prove the falsity of the Ricardian theory
of comparative cost, and which are open to many objections. But the

[1] The sub-title is *The Economic Foundations of Modern Industrial Society* (New York,
1940).

true idea that seems to lie behind the author's theory is that a commercial policy whose sole advantage is to cause a better distribution of the existing means of production between one country and others is far less interesting and deserves less sacrifice than one that tends to *increase the productive capacity* of both the exchanging countries at once. Now, in many cases it is only industry that can achieve this result, and if protective duties are necessary to accomplish it they are justified, in the view of this author.[1]

But the reaction against Free Trade was destined to go further than protection. In quite recent years a policy has been advocated —not so much by economists as by public men—which aims not at developing international trade but at doing away with it. This is the policy of *autarky*, already outlined by the philosopher Fichte in his *Der geschlossene Handelsstaat* ("Closed Commercial State"). What it advocates is that a country should be completely independent, economically, of others. It would require from them neither consumable products, nor raw materials, nor machinery, and would therefore have no need to send them its own products. It would be sufficient unto itself, which is the meaning of the word 'autarky.' Such a system can be realized by two methods only—one that can be called restrictive, and the other expansive. On the one hand a country can restrict its needs to the level of its own resources—*e.g.*, a country without copper and aluminium can decline to create an electrical industry, a country without coal can give up metallurgy and every industry that uses steam power, such as rail transport, and a mountainous country can content itself with dairy produce and go without the corn and fruit that only the foreigner can supply, and so forth. Or, on the other hand—and this is the solution generally favoured by the autarkists—the country can seek to extend its resources to the level of its wants, in which case it will have to obtain, either by conquest or exchange, territory possessing the resources that it lacks itself. But, as man's wants are by nature unlimited, it is difficult to see where this thirst for new resources is to stop. Both solutions are fraught with such obvious inconveniences— the first for the country itself, and the second for its neighbours—

[1] A rather older but very interesting attempt to base a protectionist system on rational arguments and not merely on expediency was made in Austria by Richard Schüller. Starting from the actual theories of the Austrian school—he was a pupil of Karl Menger—and making in each case an ingenious calculation of the advantages and inconveniences of customs duties, he formulated some rules under which a protectionist policy could be justified. His book is full of originality and insight. The author was the principal commercial negotiator of the Austrian Republic after the First World War. His book *Schutzzoll und Freihandel* ("Protection and Free Trade"), which was published in 1906, is worthy of a place by itself in the literature of this subject, which is generally pretty dull and nearly always commonplace.

that there is no point in emphasizing the difficulty of practising them.

The autarkic ideal is an exaggerated form of that instinctive fear of foreign commodities that has been so well analysed by the Swedish economist Heckscher in his already classic book on Mercantilism.[1] In opposition to it he has formulated a doctrine called "exchangism" to show that it is neither exclusively Free Trade nor exclusively protectionist, but regards the extension of foreign trade and not its restriction as the fundamental object of commercial policy.

Autarky cannot be considered a mere extension of protectionism, for the latter does not deny the usefulness of trade, but simply wants to limit its too swift or sudden expansion. Autarky is a new conception, entirely opposed to the one that has guided international commercial policy from the most remote past down to the present time. What it proposes is nothing less than to reverse the line of development which for two thousand years has continued to extend trading relations between nations as between individuals. And that is a harder task than some of its advocates seem to imagine.

CHAPTER II: CONFLICTING THEORIES OF CRISES

BETWEEN the phenomena that appeared after the First World War and those that followed the Napoleonic Wars there are striking resemblances. We have already noted these in the sphere of international commerce, but they are no less impressive in the matter of crises. Hardly had the treaties of Vienna been signed than a series of industrial crises in 1815, 1818, and 1825 shook England, and, therefore, the continental countries also. A hundred years later the Treaty of Versailles had hardly been signed when the crisis of 1920 broke out in the United States, followed ten years later by the still more violent one of 1930. This latter, bringing unemployment on an unprecedented scale to the United States, to Germany, and to England, and causing the collapse of the principal currencies of the world, will always figure in history as a particularly tragic event.

Is this a mere chance resemblance? Certainly not. Every prolonged

[1] Eli F. Heckscher, *Mercantilism*, 2 vols., Stockholm, 1931. This work has been translated into English (Allen and Unwin, 1935).

z

and widespread war makes goods scarce and generally forces Governments to resort to paper money.[1] Hence comes a general rise in prices. The coming of peace brings back the ordinary volume of production and compels Governments to return to normal financial methods. The new flood of goods, and the mere ending of the creation of purchasing power (even without any withdrawal of the paper money), then cause prices to fall. The greater the previous rise the faster is this fall. When this unavoidable readjustment begins it takes the form of a crisis, but it may last for many years. If, then, the mere alternation of booms and depressions that characterizes modern industrial development provokes new crises, these are reinforced by the general tendency of prices to fall. This readjustment took place after the Napoleonic Wars, after the American War of Secession, and after the war of 1870–71. An examination of the general price-curves at each of these periods shows this so plainly that it is surprising to find so many people astonished by it when it happened after the First World War. It was particularly grave at that time because of the enormous extent to which prices had previously risen, and the severity of the crises that followed was thereby increased. The persistence of this factor must never be forgotten in interpreting these crises, for without it their extent and virulence would remain inexplicable.

But the analogy with the period after the Napoleonic Wars does not end there. The end of a great war brings not only a readjustment of prices: this readjustment extends to the whole of production. Factories doing war work are turned over to the production of consumers' goods. They have to adapt their plant and make sure of their normal markets. In primarily agricultural countries, like France in 1815, the difficulties are less, because the peasant, as soon as peace is restored, finds his land ready to receive the seed and make it grow. But even to him the dislocation of agricultural markets by the war, as well as disturbances to cultivation, present difficult problems, as we saw after 1918.

But in industrial countries it is the entire orientation of capital and labour that has to be modified. Ricardo, like Adam Smith, called attention to this in the pages already quoted. And this readaptation is made harder by the accompanying fall in prices that makes strenuous efforts necessary if cost is to be reduced. For if at the beginning of a war the necessary adaptation is made easier by the rise in prices, it is impeded after the war by their fall. After 1815 England was the

---

[1] This was not the case in France under Napoleon, however. He started the system of making conquered countries pay for the war. His horror of *assignats* made him always steer clear of paper money, but England did not escape it.

only truly industrialized country in Europe, and it was in England that the return of peace caused the most serious disturbances. Labour troubles and unemployment assumed proportions at that time which stirred the whole world. At the beginning of the twentieth century industrialization had spread to France, Germany, and the United States, and these countries experienced the difficulties from which, in 1815, England had been almost the only sufferer. But it was once again in England that unemployment lasted longest, especially after the crisis of 1920. Germany, the United States, and France did not experience it in all its gravity until after 1930. England at the beginning had her areas of unemployment, whose distress she compared to that of the French devastated regions, so that she called them her "devastated areas." The problem of unemployment, therefore, as a principal characteristic of crises, was presented with peculiar force to British economists. All their theories show the effects of it, especially those of Keynes, and the way to restore 'full employment' has the largest place in their proposals. These circumstances must be kept in mind in reading the abundant economic literature that has been evoked by these events. This abundance is itself another point of resemblance with the post-Napoleonic period.

The old controversies between Sismondi, Ricardo, and J. B. Say are still famous, and the majority of the later theories of crises have been influenced by them—not only those of Rodbertus and Marx, ascribing them to maldistribution of incomes, but also those of Tooke and the Currency School, putting the blame on excessive credit or the uncontrolled issue of bank-notes. At no time since then has this great subject ceased to occupy the economists, particularly after the crises of 1900 and 1907. But the two crises that followed the First World War in 1920 and 1929, both originating in the United States, extended so far (especially the second one), disturbed so profoundly the economic life of the great nations, had such lasting repercussions, monetary, industrial, and even political, and dislocated international trade so violently that the best-known economists in all countries have been led (as after 1815) to express their views on their causes and the remedies to be applied. These controversies recall by their extent those of the beginning of the nineteenth century. It is a significant fact that the curiosity of present-day historians and economists alike as to earlier events has been awakened and aroused by many historical works in which these events are studied in the light of the present.

These post-war theories also show signs, as is only natural, of the changes that the last hundred years have wrought in the machinery of economic life. In the matter of credit, for instance, it is no longer the bank-note that takes the first place, as in the works of Juglar or Laveleye, since for more than fifty years the bank-note has been superseded by the current account. It is, therefore, the current account, made available by the cheque, the 'written money,' that plays the chief part in modern theories of crises. In the matter of production those industries that make what are called "production goods"—such as machines, girders, rails, metal plates, steel and copper wire, etc.—have acquired increasing importance as compared with those making "consumption goods." This distinction between the two groups of undertakings, ignored by Sismondi and J. B. Say, plays a prominent part in modern theories. Particular stress is laid on the more violent fluctuations to which the first group are subject. And finally, the influence of saving on the orientation of industry is rarely mentioned by earlier writers, except Sismondi and Malthus, whereas the enormous development both of creative saving and of reserve saving during the past century has turned the attention of economists to the mechanism of saving and its influence on the birth or development of crises. So we find that theories of saving constitute a new and important part of the modern doctrines. While these doctrines emphasize certain aspects of crises that have hitherto been little studied, they none the less retain some profound resemblances to the older theories. To-day, as a century ago, they can be classified according to whether their authors ascribe decisive influence to the intervention of credit, to the uneven rhythm of industrial production, or to under-consumption.

These distinctions, however, are but secondary ones in comparison with a certain fundamental opposition that is to be observed between two classes of thinkers. There are in the first place those who, following the tradition of Ricardo and Say, continue to look on crises as fleeting and unavoidable incidents in economic progress, due to insufficient foresight, to the mistakes inseparable from all human activity, to accidents that interrupt a period of expansion, and so forth. Another and more numerous group, on the other hand, follows Sismondi in suspecting that the regular recurrence of crises indicates the influence of some factor peculiar either to the organization of credit, or to the methods of production in modern communities, or to the distribution of incomes or expenditure. The constant recurrence of booms and slumps seems to this group of writers an indication that some permanent influence, itself subject to a necessary rhythm of expansion and contraction, determines the ups and downs of economic development,[1] and they devote all their energies to discovering it. As

[1] Keynes, for instance, expresses himself thus at p. 313 of his *General Theory of*

Haberler so well puts it in the far-reaching report in which he sum-marizes and discusses all the known interpretations of the economic cycle, these economists admit that a process of expansion and con-traction cannot continue indefinitely, because it gives birth itself to forces that oppose and eventually upset it.[1] At the end of the chapter we shall see emerging from these controversies a third conception of crises, which seems to-day to be winning over those who are interested primarily in the positive study of the phenomenon. While taking into account all the influences already noticed it leaves the door open to other and new influences. Thus it envisages not one single mode of operation but several.

I: THE 'GREAT DEPRESSION' AND ITS CAUSES

Lionel Robbins is the best-known representative of the first group of economists. He has submitted 'the great depression'[2] to a pro-found analysis, in which his thought is specifically linked to the Classical tradition, which he calls the heritage of generations of subtle and disinterested thought. Since most economists use the 1930 crisis as a touchstone to test the proportion of truth contained in earlier theories, it is useful to recall its essential features as they appear to a mind of exceptional honesty and keenness.

To Robbins, then, the crisis of 1930 was the result of a combina-tion of unfavourable circumstances aggravated by a policy which, in England as much as, and perhaps even more than elsewhere, rejected some of the clearest lessons taught by past experience. One of the salient features of his book is the courage he displays in openly reject-ing some of the most popular explanations propounded in his own country under the impact of the first disasters caused by the crisis. The natural tendency in Great Britain was to cast on the economic and monetary policy of other countries responsibility for the events that brought about the resounding collapse of the pound sterling. This was ascribed first to the 'maldistribution' of gold (meaning its

---

Employment, Interest, and Money: "I suggest that the essential character of the Trade Cycle and, especially, the regularity of time-sequence and of duration which justifies us in calling it a *cycle*, is mainly due to the way in which the marginal efficiency of capital fluctuates. The Trade Cycle is best regarded, I think, as being occasioned by a cyclical change in the marginal efficiency of capital."

It is plain from this that the crisis is itself due to some more hidden factor, whose changes explain the crisis itself, and it is the movements and fluctuations of this hidden force that our authors are trying to find.

[1] G. von Haberler, *Prosperity and Depression*, p. 245 (Geneva, 1937).

[2] Robbins, *The Great Depression* (Macmillan, London, 1934).

so-called 'cornering' first by the United States and then by France), then to the 'sterilization' of gold (that is to say, the alleged refusal of the same two countries to expand their credits in proportion to their gold reserves), and finally to 'failure to observe the rules of the game' of the gold standard (without succeeding, however, in defining these 'rules of the game'). Robbins rejects all these explanations, and sees in the monetary policy of England herself one of the principal causes of the 'great depression.' And here his analysis touches on points of prime importance and interest for any theory of crises. England, he says, made her first mistake in stabilizing the pound sterling at too high a rate. Having made this mistake, she was unable to take the measures needed to determine the price-level resulting from the rate she had adopted. What were these measures? Above all, the restriction of credit. The export of gold at this point was a clear indication of the policy to be followed. But, contrary to all the 'rules of the game,' the Bank of England replaced the gold exported by new credits (p. 85). Then there was another mistake: costs of production ought by all possible means to have been reduced to the level of world prices, which had fallen below English prices, but the English preferred to maintain wages at too high a level. Thus, he concludes, the English disequilibrium was due to the choice of a false parity and a refusal to conform to the requirements of this parity (p. 97).

But this specifically English disequilibrium in turn reacted on the economies of other countries. It led other central banks in their turn to break the rules of the game. The Federal Reserve Bank of New York lowered its discount rate in 1927. Why did it do this? To come to the aid of the London market by depriving English short-term capital of the attraction of a more remunerative investment abroad. But what was the result? A speculative rise on the New York Stock Exchange which intensified the later collapse of values by which the crisis began. When it did begin it was again London that prolonged it after the fall of the pound, by leaving the world uncertain as to the rate at which the pound, now released from gold, would be stabilized afresh. Hence arose, through the truly international character of the English currency, that deplorable monetary insecurity in which the whole world was kept for too long a time (p. 106). So London, who advised everybody to observe the classical monetary rules, continued herself to break them. (Pp. 94–95.)

It remains now to explain why the crisis, once started, assumed such exceptional gravity. For it was not a 'normal' crisis when the price-index fell in three years from 93 to 63, and world trade from 68 to 26 milliard dollars, and when the number of unemployed rose to three million in Great Britain, thirteen million in the United States, and six million in Germany. It was in very truth 'the great depression.' Here again Robbins finds the principal cause in the abandonment of traditional teaching. He agrees with Ricardo, who, in a passage already quoted, casts blame upon "the restrictions and prohibitions, to which the absurd jealousies which prevail between the different states of the commercial commonwealth give rise." And Robbins himself blames also the slowness with which freedom was restored to the great markets after the war, the excessive use of customs tariffs, and the rapid multiplication of trusts and cartels.

Is this, then, a sufficient explanation? There is every probability that, when the initial mistake had been made of putting the pound back on the pre-war parity in spite of the creation of an unprecedented quantity of bank money, all the measures advocated by Robbins —which were, indeed, the logical outcome of that policy—would also have failed, as would, too, the precisely opposite measures advocated (as we shall see presently) by Hawtrey and Keynes. For the crisis of 1930 was only the second stage of the inevitable readjustment of prices which follows every great world war, and which the 1920 crisis had not sufficiently achieved, as paper money was still at that time the currency of all the belligerents except the United States. It was only the return of England to the gold standard in 1925, and the subsequent extension of that standard, that made plain the true situation. What happened then was like what was observed after the abandonment of bimetallism, when the gold extracted from the mines was not sufficient to compensate for the demonetized silver that was thrown out of employment, and world prices had to adapt themselves compulsorily to a quantity of gold that was too small to keep up the level to which universal inflation had gradually, and artificially, raised them. It was this 'deflation,' too prolonged, but inevitable in view of the return of the pound to par, that caused this great disaster. Robbins would certainly not dispute this, but his otherwise penetrating analysis does not perhaps bring out clearly enough this *superposition* of a 'normal' crisis on *a profound tendency to a fall of prices*—a superposition which in itself explains the violence of the 1930 crisis, and which rendered vain all other remedies than the harsh and abrupt adaptation that was brought about by monetary devaluations. The same subject has been dealt with by Nogaro in an important work whose views agree in many respects with those of his English colleague, but he has noted this circumstance more clearly in the following passage, which forms the conclusion of his very complete analysis of all the circumstances of the crisis: "To sum up," he writes, the actual crisis, although its immediate starting-point was the New York crash—an accidental factor—*was obviously related to a more remote antecedent, which is to be found in an essential element in the situation —viz., the movement of prices.* This movement was not merely that which ordinarily accompanies cyclic crises. The fall began well in advance of the stock exchange crisis, and affected agricultural commodities in particular. This fall was on an altogether unprecedented scale, as the preceding rise had been. The difference between wholesale prices and all other prices—prices of industrial products, retail prices, prices of services—was also on a scale hitherto unknown. It is, therefore, in this circumstance—*an entirely exceptional price movement, connected no doubt with the disturbances arising from the Great War* —that we must look for a large part of the explanation of an economic disequilibrium as serious and prolonged as that which we actually witnessed.[1]

This passage sums up perfectly the most characteristic feature of the crisis of 1930,[2] and combines the interpretations, to be dealt with presently, of Schumpeter and François Simiand.

II: 'ORGANIC' INTERPRETATIONS OF CRISES

Neither Robbins nor Nogaro has tried in connexion with the 1930 crisis to construct a theory of crises in general, or to provide an explanation of their "everlasting recurrence." They have undoubtedly rendered a signal service in concentrating their attention on all the aspects of a great and international event that marks an epoch in economic history. But the mystery of economic cycles and their evident regularity is too attractive not to have led certain thinkers once again, on the occasion of the twentieth-century crises, to search for the general mechanism of these cycles—or, if you prefer it, the hidden spring which, once discovered, could, they think, be manipulated or controlled by man's deliberate will. The most important of these attempts are associated with the names of Hawtrey, Aftalion, and Spiethoff, though many others deserve mention as well. But in such a matter an exhaustive account would distract the reader's attention too much. Each of these authors represents one important aspect of economic thought: Hawtrey by emphasizing the part played by credit, Aftalion the fluctuations of production, and Spiethoff (followed by Cassel) the role of saving. So we find in them the typical conceptions that need to be set forth in a history of economic doctrines

---

[1] B. Nogaro, *La crise économique dans le monde et en France*, p. 227 (1936).

[2] We ourself have often laid stress on this essential aspect of the great crisis: see in particular chapter i of the first volume of the *Enquête sur le Chômage* ("Enquiry into Unemployment") published by the *Institut Scientifique de Recherches*. (Sirey, 1938.)

—conceptions to which most other writers are more or less attached, though with slight variations.

I. R. G. HAWTREY

It is hard to imagine views more completely opposite to those of Robbins than those expressed by Hawtrey on the origin of the 1930 crisis and the methods by which it could have been avoided. According to Robbins restriction of credit would have made it possible to maintain the gold standard and induce the indispensable fall in costs, while for Hawtrey the same result would have been obtained by the opposite process of making credit easier. The lowering of the discount rate in 1927 by the Federal Reserve Banks is strongly criticized by Robbins, whereas Hawtrey thinks it the right method to follow,[1] and blames the United States for interrupting it. The raising of the rate in 1927 he regards as a disastrous reversal of policy, and he similarly criticizes the raising of the discount rate in London after 1929.[2] When the depression had begun an open-market policy should have been energetically followed. A half-hearted move in this direction had been made by the Federal Reserve Banks, but it was quite inadequate. The depression in the United States was precipitated just in proportion as the accumulation of gold in that country increased. In direct contradiction of Robbins's thesis Hawtrey casts the responsibility for the crisis on the insatiable demands of France and the United States for gold; demands far in excess of the production of the mines. He compares the state of the money market at that time to a tragic episode in the defence of Calcutta, in 1758, by Governor Holwell.

"In 1930 and 1931," he writes,

> producers all over the world found demand dwindling relentlessly. In desperate efforts to keep going they cut prices deeper and deeper. Their frantic competition for such demand as remained might be compared with the desperate struggles of the prisoners in the Black Hole of Calcutta to save themselves from suffocation by getting near the two small windows which were the only means of ventilation. It is said that it was only by inadvertence that Surajah Dowlah shut up 146 prisoners in a cell 18 feet by 15 feet. He merely followed precedent in committing prisoners to the guard-room. In their agony the victims sought to bribe the guards to carry an appeal for mercy to Surajah Dowlah. But he was asleep and the guards dared not awake him. He was very like a central bank.

And the writer adds:

> When, the next morning, he sent for Holwell, who had been in command of the garrison and was among the twenty-three survivors,

[1] See *The Art of Central Banking*, p. 200.   [2] *Ibid.*, pp. 213 ff.

Surajah Dowlah manifested no interest in the fate of the prisoners but wanted to find out where the East India Company's treasure was hidden.[1]

Hawtrey shows no tenderness for the central banks, which, with their eyes fixed on their gold reserves, were not interested in the gradual suffocation of the economic system. For in his eyes the fluctuations of credit—by which he means bank credit—are the sole cause of booms and depressions, and the central banks are the masters of credit. He thus joins a long line of economists going back as far as the Currency School, and where his originality lies is in combining his views with a particularly clear conception of income and its circulation, which forms as it were the skeleton of all his books. He defines income as the total of all the amounts that remunerate the various services that combine in the productive process. He does not include in it sums that come from the sale of a good previously acquired by the expenditure of earlier income. When we sell a stock-exchange security we 'disinvest' capital acquired earlier with income already expended once. The sum received is not part of income,[2] for the latter consists only of sums paid for 'new' services rendered. What Hawtrey calls "income" is what we call *net* income, as distinguished from *gross* income. Hawtrey calls it "consumers' income," where the French would say "consumable income."

Now, the price-level is a function, at each instant, of the aggregate expenditure of income by a community, and rises or falls with it. Expenditure of income includes, of course, both consumption expenditure *and saving expenditure*, the latter being only a particular way of spending income. This conception has been summed up by Hawtrey himself in his latest book[3] as follows.

By the consumers' income I mean simply the total of incomes expressed in monetary units. It is much more fundamental in monetary theory than the quantity of money. The consumers' income is the source of general demand, composed of consumption demand and of the demand for capital goods. For though it is traders, not consumers, who buy capital goods for use in production, the funds used by the traders are ultimately derived, through the investment market, from the consumers' income. And while the consumers' income is the source of demand, demand in turn is the

[1] *The Art of Central Banking* (Longmans, London, 1932), p. 220.
[2] *Cf.* chapter iii of *The Art of Central Banking*, entitled "Consumers' Income and Outlay," pp. 85, 86. Hawtrey gives the name "exterior receipts" to all sums arising from the sale of securities, properties, etc., as well as sums borrowed from banks. The whole of this chapter is essential to an understanding of Hawtrey's theory, and should be supplemented by the explanations given in his *Currency and Credit*.
[3] *A Century of Bank Rate* (Longmans, London, 1938), p. 38.

source of the consumers' income. That is to say, the money spent on the purchase of goods is the source of the incomes of those who produce and deal in the goods. So long as an unchanging stream of money continues to flow through the consumers' income to demand and back through demand to the consumers' income, activity will be maintained.

But how can income be increased? Simply and solely by *bank credit*.[1] Credit granted by one private person to another merely *displaces* income, the expenditure being made by the borrower instead of by the lender. But when banks grant credit they *create* new money and a new income. And, conversely, when they restrict or stop credit they diminish the aggregate income. Now, credit is essentially unstable.[2] An increase of credit increases consumable incomes and consequently expenditure as well. There follows a rise of prices leading to an increase in profits, which impels traders to increase production and demand new credits, which in their turn will raise prices, and so the process continues. Credit sets in motion a cumulative rise. Can this movement go on indefinitely? No, replies Hawtrey, because the banks are limited in granting credit by the extent of their reserve, which is dependent on the central gold reserve of the country. Otherwise there would be no limit to the rise of prices and the expansion of production. But, if credit ceases, a cumulative movement in the opposite direction will start. Incomes diminish, prices fall, bringing about a fresh reduction of incomes, etc., and the depression grows until the banks feel themselves in a position to resume the granting of credit.

These rises and falls of prices, therefore, result entirely from increases and reductions of bank credit, and the economic cycle is a purely monetary phenomenon.[3] Since the banks create money, they act in reality like a government which issues paper money. The process of expansion and depression under the influence of credit is identical with the process of inflation and deflation under the influence of paper money. So the conclusion follows that to deliver a country from depression, or to check too severe a depression, *credit must be facilitated* and purchasing power increased, while in the opposite case credit must be restricted. The manipulation of the discount rate—raising and lowering it—is the principal means by which the modern banking system can prevent crises, or combat them when they have begun. So

[1] And also by an increase in the rapidity of circulation of the income. But after having mentioned this influence Hawtrey does not return to it in the course of developing his theory.
[2] Cf. *The Art of Central Banking*, p. 168.
[3] *Trade and Credit*, p. 175 (1929). This is the opinion of Carl Snyder also.

it is understandable now why the views of Robbins and Hawtrey on the policy followed by England and the United States in the crisis of 1930 are in such complete disagreement.

Hawtrey's great merit is to have described with admirable clarity the creation and circulation of net income. His definitions of 'consumers' income' and 'consumers' outlay' provide a valuable plan for understanding the circulation of production incomes to consumption and *vice versa*: it ought to figure in every manual of political economy. It renders the same service to the understanding of dynamic problems as Walras's plan does to that of the interdependence of prices in a static system. It is similar and equally useful, as we shall see presently, to that constructed by Ohlin and the Stockholm school to elucidate the relations between income, saving, and investment.

On the other hand, the use that Hawtrey makes of it for the interpretation and treatment of crises (especially that of 1930) is open to grave objections, and we must call attention to the chief of these. Between inflation and deflation of paper money on the one hand and the expansion and contraction of credit on the other Hawtrey sees almost a relation of identity. We have shown elsewhere[1] how the identification of the two processes appeared in English doctrine at the beginning of the nineteenth century. From the time of Ricardo —and even from the time of John Law—the assimilation of convertible paper money created by credit with inconvertible paper is constantly reappearing. It is to be found again, implied if not expressly formulated, in all Hawtrey's works, and therein lies serious confusion. It follows that by applying to a rise in prices due to excessive issue of inconvertible paper the remedies whose aim is to prevent or correct the consequences of a *credit* crisis, he makes, in our opinion, a therapeutic error.

Bank credit is a repayable instrument. It is granted normally only for a short term. It cannot, therefore, suffice to maintain a price-level which, if it is to be lasting, assumes a certain quantity of money (metal or paper) remaining in circulation. There is no reason to think that lowering the rate of discount would have succeeded in 1930 in checking a fall in prices that was the result of the increasing volume of goods thrown on the market. To this Hawtrey would reply that credit itself creates income, for the sums lent by the banks are used as wages, for buying raw materials, and so forth, and the saving these incomes give rise to is no less genuine than that produced by other means than bank credit. We agree, but the incomes thus created are mortgaged in advance by a debt to the bank which must one day be repaid, and

[1] See our *Histoire des doctrines relatives au crédit*, etc. (Paris, 1938).

this repayment will be accomplished by a stoppage of money, and consequently of incomes. It is for this very reason that a mere lowering of the discount rate has always proved powerless to encourage *entrepreneurs* to 'start again' after a crisis.

Apart from this argument, concerned with the treatment of crises in general and that of 1930 in particular, we may follow Pigou, the shrewd successor of Alfred Marshall, in saying in opposition to Hawtrey that in a purely monetary theory account must be taken not only of the quantity of money but of its rapidity of circulation. Now, this varies, quite apart from the banks, by the action of the income-owners themselves. Moreover, if it is true that the supply of credit plays an important part in increasing or reducing purchasing power, the banks are not alone in causing these movements, for it is the merchants, the industrialists, and the State who *demand* credit, so that their state of mind exerts a powerful influence on its expansion or contraction. To concentrate attention on the *supply* of credit is to remove from the problem the often decisive influence of *demand*.[1]

Hawtrey's views, on account of the position he holds at the Treasury, have on many occasions inspired British economic policy. He, like Keynes—though the two differed from each other on many minor points—was able, and will still be able, to make the financial authorities of his country listen to him. But his views, none the less, which make everything depend on increases or decreases in purchasing power, and which may tempt statesmen by the ease with which they can be put into practice, are far from being universally accepted.

2. AFTALION AND SCHUMPETER

It is true enough that all the writers dealing with crises admit that credit plays some part in starting them. Is it not an ascertained fact that credit restrictions are generally at the bottom of the first failures that announce the coming storm? Yet most economists refuse to see in the expansion or restriction of credit the true cause of the crisis, as Hawtrey does. They seek it in the divergent and ill-synchronized movements of production, saving, or consumption, and the monetary aspect of the cycle is, in their eyes, only secondary.

It is in the rhythm of production as determined by its *technical* conditions that Aftalion finds the source of cyclic crises. For Hawtrey the fluctuations of *demand*, reflections or fluctuations of income, determine

---

[1] See Pigou on the "Monetary Theory of Crises" in the *Economic Journal*, June 1929. Pigou is himself the author of a book on crises—*Industrial Fluctuations* (London, 1927) —and especially of an important work called *Wealth and Welfare*, which laid the foundations of his reputation as an economist.

the rhythm of production.[1] Aftalion, on the contrary, regards the demand for products and services as progressing continuously, whereas the *supply* of goods proceeds by fits and starts, because of the time needed to set up the plant and machinery from which will emerge the new products and services offered for consumption. So the fall in prices comes not from an insufficiency of purchasing power but from the saturation of the wants of the public, or, in the words of the author, speaking the language of the Austrian school, from the *reduction of the final utility* of commodities that have become super-abundant.

Aftalion has provided this thesis with a copious and new documentation in which the principal industries and their behaviour before and during crises are studied with extreme care. His work, which appeared on the eve of the First World War and is based on experience of the crises of 1900 and 1907, is an example of a close combination of theoretical analysis and the most minute statistical observation. Its conclusions may be summarized as follows.

At the beginning of a period of expansion the industries making instruments of production are stimulated, because the machinery, tools, and raw materials that they provide are indispensable to all other industries. They are therefore led to make plans for extending their production. But time is needed to put these plans into operation. The construction of new factories, the increased extraction of iron ore, coal, and copper need preparation and the bringing together of many factors. Results appear only after a period of gestation which varies in different industries. Once the preparations are complete and the new manufacture is begun, a fairly long time is still needed before its effects make themselves felt on the commodity market. During this waiting period the supply of consumption goods grows but slowly. When, at length, the equipment so long in course of preparation is fully working, the sudden increase in the production of all consumable things soon meets with resistance on the part of buyers. Wants either change their direction or are sufficiently satisfied, so that demand slackens or hesitates. The new abundance of manufactured goods can then be disposed of only on condition of being offered at a lower price. That is the moment when the crisis breaks out. The fall that begins at one point extends gradually to other parts of the economic system. Faced by this hesitation on the part of the public, the makers of finished products restrict their demands for machinery, and the

[1] The reader cannot fail to notice the resemblance of this conception to the views of Sismondi, explained in an earlier chapter. This return to Sismondi on the part of the English school is one of the curiosities of the economic doctrines of 1925–35.

crisis suddenly starts—beginning in the machine-making industries. Hence there is greater distress in the industries making production goods than in those making consumption goods. The whole process is summed up by Aftalion in the following vivid simile, which we quote in full.

> If we poke the fire because a room is not warm enough we have to wait until the required temperature is reached. If the cold continues and the thermometer still records it we shall be inclined, if we have not learnt by experience, to put more coal on. We should do this even if the quantity of coal accumulated in the grate was already enough, when it had all caught fire, to throw out an unbearable heat. By letting ourselves be guided by the sensation of cold at the time, and by the present reading of the thermometer, we should fatally overheat the room. And this is the kind of mistake that the capitalist technique leads to. Since production requires a previous manufacture of fixed capital, so long as this manufacture is not accomplished the shortage of finished goods induces a belief in the possibility of preparing for new increases in production. The *entrepreneur* can only see that wants are actually unsatisfied, as shown by the high prices; he cannot know that their *virtual* satisfaction is excessive.[1]

In short, at any given moment there is over-production of certain consumption goods. It is not that *incomes are insufficient* to buy them, but that the *satisfaction they yield has diminished*: the 'final utility' of the goods supplied to the public has decreased. Once the process has started in one branch it extends to the rest. The crisis is not general but generalized, but it gradually embraces the entire economic system.

It cannot be disputed that Aftalion has noted a fact of far-reaching importance that actually characterizes the existing technique of production. It is certain that crises have nowadays a tendency to break out first, and then to grow more acute, in the machine-making industries—industries that in our day have become of prime importance. It is certain also that the forecasting of demand in these industries is subject to more mistakes than in others. The very abundance of capital that they require for their extension puts them in a particularly difficult position when the demand for their products stops, and when their productive capacity is no longer entirely employed.[2]

[1] Aftalion, *Les Crises périodiques de surproduction* (1911), Vol. II, p. 361.

[2] Almost at the same time as Aftalion a Russian economist, Bouniatian, set out the mechanism of crises in terms that often recall those used by the French economist, so that we might regard their views as the same. "Periods of prosperity and periods of depression," he says, "are signs of over-capitalization. The boom period, with its high prices and eventual over-production, the depression with its low prices and weaker economic activity, are both aspects of a single phenomenon—permanent

It is not even necessary to introduce the notion of final utility in order to express Aftalion's theory in a way that satisfies the mind. It is enough to conceive that, for one reason or another, the demand for some product does not come up to the estimated supply, either because this estimate was excessive or because *meanwhile* the desires of the public have changed. In this case some businesses find themselves deprived of their markets, their profits disappear, their workers are unemployed, and their debts remain unpaid. If the entire economy is now in a period of tension, if the banks begin to find their credit margin too much reduced, or if a saturation of markets is already apparent in some industries, then bankruptcy or stoppage of work in the businesses in question may spread quickly and widely. Difficulties that in normal circumstances would have no repercussions on other businesses, or which would have been quickly compensated by their prosperous position, will, on the hypothesis we are considering, give a shock to neighbouring industries and may start a series of

---

over-capitalization." (*Les Crises économiques*, p. 346.) But closer examination reveals that Bouniatian's conception is more akin to those which ascribe to *saving* a decisive influence in the production of crises. This "permanent over-capitalization" that he regards as one of the characteristic features of modern economic development results, in his view, from the fact that the big incomes are received primarily by large-scale undertakings. Since profits are thus concentrated in a few hands, the habit has arisen of using them almost entirely for the creation of new capital, and thus the productive forces increase incessantly while consumption is relatively stationary. At a given moment this disequilibrium becomes visible, the business undertakings no longer find for their products the markets on which they had counted, and the crisis begins. It is a phenomenon of 'decapitalization.' It reduces profits and the value of capital. The same idea could be expressed by saying that it destroys earlier saving. Thus "periodic economic crises are, to put it shortly, merely periods of compulsory decapitalization of unusual importance, arising suddenly and inevitably after a period of excessive capitalization" (p. 387).

Whereas Aftalion finds the solution of the problem in a technical circumstance—*viz.*, the time needed for the construction of plant—Bouniatian finds it in an economic circumstance—*viz.*, the concentration of profits in the hands of big businesses, and their regular employment in new industrial creations. This phenomenon of income distribution and its division between investment and consumption had been noticed already by Sismondi, and it is precisely what the theories to be mentioned in the following paragraphs are concerned with. But these theories, such as that of Keynes, to be explained later, interpret the facts differently from Bouniatian: it is the insufficiency of investments, not their excess, that they emphasize.

What Bouniatian does not explain is how consumption can remain stationary in face of increasing production, when the profits invested by *entrepreneurs* are necessarily converted by their associates in the undertaking into new incomes which will increase consumption expenditure. This stage is the chief difficulty of the problem, and Bouniatian does not solve it. We must undoubtedly make allowance here for the *delay* before the incomes created by saving can be converted into a demand for consumable products, just as at another point in the crisis there is a *delay* before the incomes set free by the fall in prices can be spent, which explains the prolongation of the fall.

repercussions that will constitute a crisis. We shall see in sec. vi the importance attached by many writers, who incorporate Aftalion's ideas in their own theories, to this background, as it were, on which there appear incidents capable of starting a general depression, like microbes causing an infectious disease.

But one point still remains obscure: how are we to account for the *simultaneous* extension of the machinery of production in a large number of industries at once?[1] Aftalion says that the development of one industry brings with it that of many others, and that thus the increase of equipment at one point of the economic field is generally accompanied by a corresponding increase at another point. This 'solidarity' of industries accounts for the circumstance in question. It appeals on the one hand to the law of substitution—"the prosperity or misfortune of one industry tends to spread to industries able to meet the same needs"—and on the other hand to the growth of incomes, "which leads to an extension of the demand for all products."[2]

It is at this very point that Schumpeter introduces his examination of the problem of crises in his brilliant *Theory of Economic Development*, the first German edition of which appeared shortly before Aftalion's book, and the two later ones after the First World War.[3]

Schumpeter belongs to the school of Walras. He came into prominence by an earlier book, where he showed himself the convinced and suggestive interpreter of the fundamental ideas of the Mathematical schools of France, Italy, and England. In his second book he supplements the 'static' views of these schools by a purely dynamic study, and, quite naturally, he takes as the centre of this dynamic system the activity of the *entrepreneur* in the modern world. According to him the social function of the *entrepreneur* is not only to introduce something new into economic development, to invent, to discover, and to diversify products, but also to spread new methods of organization and manufacture, and to adopt and popularize the inventions of others. He does not confine himself to the efficient management of the existing economic system according to the traditional rules, but at each moment, by his initiative and bold faith in the future, he 'threatens' the habits and customs and therefore the sources of profit of his more conservative competitors. He is continually renewing

[1] Lescure has called attention to this difficulty in his book *Les Crises générales et périodiques de surproduction* (5th edition, Paris, 1938).

[2] Aftalion, Vol. II, pp. 389–390.

[3] This work, translated with comments by François Perroux (Dalloz, Paris, 1935), is preceded by a study of Joseph Schumpeter's views by Perroux. We quote from the 3rd German edition of 1931. An English translation was published by the Oxford University Press in 1935.

the sources of profit—to the detriment of those already in existence—
and thus, owing to this perpetual breeding of new incomes, he feeds
the interest of the capitalist, who in a stationary economy would lose,
he believes, the reason for his existence and even come to nothing.[1]

But why is not this development *continuous*? That is what Schumpeter
considers the fundamental question raised by the phenomenon of
the cycle. Why does economic development proceed by fits and
starts? Why is not the influence of the *entrepreneurs* introduced regularly,
year by year or month by month, into the stream of economic life?
This is obviously the same question as was asked by Aftalion. Here
is Schumpeter's answer. In the modern world *entrepreneurs* do not
arise singly and sporadically but in swarms or 'troops' (*scharenweise*).
"The arrival of one or several *entrepreneurs* facilitates the arrival of
others, and they of others, who in turn cause the arrival of yet new
and ever more numerous *entrepreneurs*" (p. 339). For the single *entrepreneur* is faced at the beginning by innumerable obstacles, and if he
eventually breaks through them it is by dint of struggle and energy.

But when one or several of them have at length succeeded, then
the difficulties grow less. The first originator is followed by others
who are encouraged by his success. Their success in turn encourages
the intervention of other captains of industry until the innovation
becomes normal and enters into the current life, and its reproduction becomes a matter of imitation alone (pp. 339–340). In fact
what the observation of facts reveals is that every period of expansion
begins in one or a few branches (such as transport, electrical industries, chemistry) and is characterized by innovations introduced
in these branches. But their originators remove the obstacles not
only in the branches of production where they arose, but also, *ipso
facto*, in other branches. . . . This applies, for instance, to the opening of foreign markets. In this way the originators of new methods
extend their influence far beyond their immediate sphere of action.
The economic system is led with increasing swiftness and complete-
ness into a process of reorganization which is the very essence of the
period of expansion.

The depression appears as the inevitable consequence of this period
of expansion. If the influence of the *entrepreneurs* were continuous and
permanent, the absorption of their innovations by the economic
system would also go on continuously. But these innovations arise by
fits and starts, so that their absorption is effected in the same manner.
"This process of massive absorption is the very essence of the periodic

[1] We do not here discuss this theory, which depends on the notion that interest is
fed by profit, and that in a stationary economy when profit disappears interest must
also disappear. The idea is, in fact, that if saving becomes useless, as in a stationary
economy, the rent of saving (which is interest) must also disappear. But what about
simple advances?

depressions" (p. 342). It may be defined as "the struggle of the economic system to reach a new state of equilibrium adapted to the new circumstances created by the changes brought about by the period of expansion" (*ibid.*). The new products, in fact, do not appear until a few years after their manufacture has been put in hand. These surplus products, "*which more than compensate for the increase of purchasing power*," issue on to the market *en masse*. The interval between the start of their production and their arrival on the market in bulk determines the duration of the period of expansion. "It is, then, the massive supply of new products that causes the fall in prices and may lead to a crisis" (p. 345). Here Schumpeter's views coincide with those of Aftalion, to whom, moreover, he expressly refers in the last edition of his book.[1] But Aftalion tries to find a special explanation for the suddenness of the fall in prices, whereas Schumpeter thinks it obvious that this results automatically from the increased production, which, as he says without emphasizing it, in the sentence we have just underlined, "more than compensates for the increase of purchasing power."

Instead of reasoning as Aftalion does, in general terms of production, income, and price, Schumpeter describes the same process in terms of personality, energy, and initiative. He depicts the cycle as a function of the men who are its agents, and not of the general economic elements which determine its mode of operation. But, though his exposition gains in vividness in this way, it does not alter the fundamental notion, for the explanation of crises by the bulk appearance of *entrepreneurs* is hardly distinguishable from the bulk appearance of products suggested by Aftalion.

In conclusion, there is one remark of Schumpeter's that is worth remembering. Speaking of the post-war crises, he considers that in interpreting them phenomena connected with the war itself have been too often neglected. For him, as for Nogaro, the crisis of 1930 was largely an inevitable repercussion of the war.

3. SPIETHOFF AND CASSEL

Aftalion explains crises by the rhythm and technical conditions of the creation of capital. But does not capital itself imply a preceding condition—the formation of savings? Should not the explanation of crises be looked for beyond these technical conditions, and even in the rhythm of the formation of savings itself? This idea has attracted many economists, and lies at the root of several recent explanations

[1] See Schumpeter, *Theorie der wirtschaftlichen Entwicklung* ("Theory of Economic Development"), 3rd edition, p. 353.

of crises. It has, therefore, brought into the foreground the whole
problem of saving, its mechanism and its effects, and has given rise
to a most instructive controversy. Spiethoff in Germany, Cassel in
Sweden, Ansiaux in Belgium, and, earlier than these, the Russian
writer Tugan-Baranowski have all adopted this conception, though
with slight variations. But the author whose exposition has aroused
most interest is the German Spiethoff, who made himself the protagonist
of the notion after the crisis of 1899 which was felt more severely in
Germany than elsewhere. Of course, neither these authors nor those
mentioned earlier make any claim to having isolated a single circumstance as *the* cause of crises. They too take account of fluctuations of
credit (credit is the indispensable instrument of expansion, says
Spiethoff),[1] or of the time taken to set on foot new production industries, thus incorporating Aftalion's[2] conception in their own, or,
finally, of the influence exerted by a rise or fall in the discount rate.
But all these circumstances they regard as secondary, or, if you prefer
it, auxiliary, as compared with the one essential circumstance—first
the abundance and then the scarcity of creative saving during the
phases of depression and expansion.

They start from the fact (which is true of modern industrial
countries) that price fluctuations are particularly prominent in the
group of businesses making 'production goods.' During the first half
of the nineteenth century crises might arise from overproduction of
consumption goods, but nowadays, when machinery and building,
along with the extraction of mineral raw materials, are the principal
domain of industry, it is in this branch of production that impulses
begin. "A boom generally starts," says Spiethoff, "in the group of
firms making production goods. . . . In a capitalist age it is difficult
to imagine it starting in the group that makes consumption goods and
reaching its highest point in these industries" (p. 71). This is also
Cassel's opinion: only crises in the past, he says, could arise from
overproduction of consumable products. So on this point these
writers are already diverging from the theses of Aftalion and Schumpeter.

Now, if the firms making production goods are to extend and
develop, they need savings. We use that word, although Spiethoff,
like most German authors, prefers the word 'capital'—which we, like
Walras, reserve for the actual goods procured by saving. The distinction between saving and capital, peculiar to the French and Italian
terminology, is indispensable, if we are to get this set of ideas quite clear.

[1] Spiethoff, article on Crises in the *Handwörterbuch der Staatswissenschaften* ("Dictionary of Political Science"), p. 74.
[2] *Ibid.*, p. 77.

"Savings accumulate," says Spiethoff, "during periods of depression" (*in der Stockung staut sich das Kapital*) (p. 70). This process has been compared by a Russian author, Tugan-Baranowski, to the accumulation of steam in a steam-engine until its pressure overcomes the resistance of the piston.[1] This accumulation of savings during the depression would bring about a reduction in the rate of interest, an indispensable condition—though not (he adds) a sufficient one—of the subsequent boom. If this boom is to come, there must at the same time be new markets or new technical discoveries that *provide an opportunity* for the boldest of the *entrepreneurs* to make new profits. It is nowadays in the realm of such industries as mining, railways, electrical or siderurgical industries that these conditions are to be met with. And when once they are combined the accumulated savings are immediately attracted to businesses in this group, spreading thence into other industries, on account of the incomes created by their operation. Then the boom continues, spreading from one industry to another, increasing incomes and consumption, and stimulating alike the construction of fixed capital, electric-power stations, and means of transport—all enterprises which call for considerable capital outlay, although they provide directly consumable services.

The origin of a boom is to be found, therefore, in *accumulated savings*, and it is the inadequacy of these very savings that is destined to end it. The crisis breaks out not because the consumption of consumers' goods is reduced, but because the savings that are indispensable to the creation either of the machinery or of the fixed property and plant are not available. All such goods are different from others in that "their construction or purchase is not made out of income in the strict sense, but out of capitalized income or acquired capital" (*Erwerbskapital*, p. 75), and it is the lack of this acquired capital—or, as we should say, savings—that puts an end to the extension of the industries that make it. Their originators may see their initial forecasts completely falsified by a reduction in the saving on which they had counted, and this gives rise to a disequilibrium that provokes the crisis (p. 76). As for consumption goods, there is never any lack of the purchasing power needed to absorb them. "A limit to their market is still very far from being reached" when the crisis starts (p. 78), so it cannot be explained by any superabundance of these goods. The opposition between Spiethoff's theory and Aftalion's could not be more clearly marked.

It is obvious at once that there are two points in which the theory just described is open to criticism. To begin with, is it true that

[1] Tugan-Baranowski, *Les crises industrielles en Angleterre* (Paris, 1913), p. 273.

during a depression savings *accumulate* without being used? Profits, and therefore savings, undoubtedly diminish during this period, but none the less these savings do find employment, as Aftalion has rightly emphasized. Among other things, they are used for buying up businesses that have run into debt during the preceding period, and have been liquidated. They are used also to repay loans from the banks. Consequently the new savings are for a certain time entirely absorbed in *replacing old savings that have been destroyed*, and they do not become available for new businesses until they have facilitated this indispensable liquidation, which is generally accompanied by a fall in the rate of interest as well as in the price of services and raw materials. During this period, then, there is a combination of conditions all tending to reduce costs and adjust them to the diminished incomes, and thus making recovery easier as soon as new opportunities of expansion present themselves to the businesses, which, moreover, will need nominally less savings than in the period of maximum expansion.

The conception of a scarcity of savings in the boom period is no less open to criticism. In such a period incomes increase, and so there is a similar increase in the amount of savings. Again, savings— notwithstanding the term 'capitalized income' that Spiethoff applies to them[1]—are simply a part of income, in the same way as money used in the purchase of consumption goods. So we have to explain why these savings in a boom period are suddenly unable to absorb the increased amount of products of the firms that make machinery. Who buys this machinery if it is not the firms that make consumption goods? Why should these firms find themselves powerless to buy it, if the demand for goods for direct consumption goes on without difficulty, or even increases, as Spiethoff says it does? It must then be supposed that the consumption industries *foresee*, for some reason or other, that there is no longer any chance of increasing their existing plant because the demand for their products *is going to* diminish. Or are we to assume that the prices of consumption goods rise so fast during the boom period that they absorb an increasing proportion of income and do not leave enough to be saved? But this would imply that these goods are in great demand, which should cause those who make them to employ their profits in ordering new machinery—*i.e.*, to provide the savings which, as we are rightly told, are lacking. To these questions Spiethoff gives no answer.

Cassel and Ansiaux are more explicit. Ansiaux thinks it is the

[1] Spiethoff says that savings are 'capitalized income,' but the phrase is difficult to understand. Savings are income spent like the rest of income, but used to buy or make a special kind of goods, called capital goods.

excessive number of new business firms and the anxiety caused by growing speculation that make the savers more reluctant. The inadequacy of savings would in this case be only *apparent*; it would be an *impression*, whereas the real fact would be the excessive appeals for savings, and their surprise at meeting with no response.[1] This impression of insufficiency arises from the successive creations and extensions of firms of every kind—genuine and otherwise—that characterize the period of excitement which is the last phase of the boom. The insufficiency is relative, if you like, but it is none the less felt, and especially in the sense that it is often not the most extravagant projects that are dropped. Consequently the financing of genuine business becomes difficult, and sometimes even impossible.

Cassel has also felt the need to explain the initial abundance and then the relative scarcity of savings at the beginning and end of a period of expansion. But he does not resort to the idea of an 'accumulation' of capital during the depression, the working of which it is almost impossible to conceive.[2] He confines himself to showing[3] that the creation of savings is not equal at the beginning of a boom and at the end. This is what he writes in his book,[4] the last part of which is concerned with crises:

> As *entrepreneurs* are compelled to save by economic necessity, the savings made out of the profits of business *should* represent a larger proportion than those made out of other incomes. Consequently the formation of savings by society *should* be *relatively* greater in periods favourable to the *entrepreneur's* profits. That period is precisely the initial period of a boom. We can therefore conclude that there are *relatively* more savings at the beginning of this boom. But as soon as wages and prices begin to rise there *probably* occurs a *relative* reduction in the formation of savings in proportion to the sum total of all incomes. For the working-classes certainly consume by far the greatest part of their incomes, especially when the prices of all provisions are rising. At the same time the *entrepreneur's* income begins to fall by reason of that very rise in wages, or at all events its rate of increase becomes lower. Thus an important source of savings loses its force, and the peak of the boom period will be marked by a *relative* scarcity in the supply of savings.[5]

[1] Ansiaux, *L'Inflation du crédit et la prévention des crises* (Paris, 1934), p. 219 n.

[2] Aftalion, Bouniatian, Lescure, Haberler, and Ansiaux are unanimous on this point.

[3] Cassel, *Theoretische Sozialökonomie*, 1918, p. 531.

[4] Translated into English as *The Theory of Social Economy* (Fisher Unwin, 1923).

[5] Similar considerations, couched in almost the same terms, will be found a few pages later, pp. 534 ff. (The italics are ours.)

On the other hand, Ansiaux, like Keynes, looks at things rather differently, and his view, it may be said at once, seems infinitely nearer the truth. According to him it is in the boom period that savings are most plentiful: "No one can dispute," he says,

The author agrees with Spiethoff in thinking that in

a period of high prosperity of the modern type there is no over-production and no over-estimation of the demand of the consumer . . . but there is over-estimation of the supply of savings, that is to say of the amount of savings prepared to absorb the concrete capital that is made. What is over-estimated is the capacity of capitalists to put savings in sufficient quantity at the disposal of producers (p. 556).

The caution used by Cassel in these passages is noteworthy. The process he describes is in his view "probable," not certain. It is a plausible hypothesis, not a fact founded on experiment. The increases and decreases in savings are *relative*, whereas it is *absolute* figures that matter here. We shall see shortly that Keynes's description of the formation of savings during a crisis is exactly opposite to Cassel's.

These contradictions and uncertainties among writers who find the origin of crises in the rhythm of saving show the need for a preliminary theory of the mechanism of saving itself. What is the effect of its formation on the demand and supply of goods? Is it the same for consumption goods as for production goods? At what moment are savings most plentiful, either relatively or absolutely? Is it at the beginning or the end of a crisis? And what influence can it have on the phenomenon of unemployment? All these questions have arisen in connexion with the theory of crises, and have occupied an important place in the work of economists in the period after the First World War. It has become clear that the word 'saving' is one of those that every one thinks he understands, while it really includes very different meanings. Hence the need to clear up these meanings, and the controversies that have arisen on this subject. We must now give an account of these controversies. But first it will be as well to examine the views of the Swedish economist Knut Wicksell, whose name is constantly mentioned by economists of the first two decades of the twentieth century. By fixing his attention on the dynamic phenomena of the economic system instead of on the static phenomena which had been the chief concern of the 'theorists of equilibrium, he was led to think out methods of working which in his view made it possible to explain crises as well as general price movements. The influence of his ideas is to be seen in almost all the discussions aroused between the two World Wars by the violent fluctuations to which the world economy has been subjected, and, in particular, the discussions by economists concerning saving and investment. They deserve special examination.

"that the possibility of saving is much greater during a boom than during a depression. . . . A considerable amount of saving in the upward-moving phase is contrasted with reduced saving in the period of stagnation." (*L'Inflation du crédit*, pp. 313, 314.)

III: KNUT WICKSELL AND THE THEORY OF DIVERGENCES BETWEEN SAVING AND INVESTMENT

Great influence was exercised in the first place by Knut Wicksell over the brilliant group of Swedish economists which includes the names of Ohlin, Lindhal, and Myrdal, who are responsible for some of the most interesting theoretical investigations of 1920–40. His ideas have also met with great, though tardy, recognition among the economists of other lands. There is a striking resemblance between the problems he brought forward and those connected with the name of Keynes. But Wicksell's position as leader of a school of economists is somewhat peculiar. The Swedish economists who claim fellowship with him all begin by proclaiming their disagreement with his fundamental theses. In particular, his doctrine concerning the influence exerted on price movements by the discrepancy which appears at certain times between the bank rate of interest and what Wicksell calls the "natural rate" of interest is rejected by them all, by Ohlin as well as by Myrdal and Lindhal.[1] He himself, however, has made only a very tentative application of this idea. He formulated it in the first place to explain long-term price movements. But when it came to actually interpreting either the prolonged rise between 1895 and 1910 or the great fall that began in 1930, he reverted to the abundant gold production in the Transvaal for the first,[2] and to the intensity of the production of goods after the war for the second.[3] In other words, he eventually adopted the traditional view on this point. Ohlin felt justified in saying that Wicksell always looked upon his own contribution as a doubtful hypothesis, and was never as convinced as his pupils of its validity.[4]

So too Wicksell gave up applying his conception to the interpretation of crises, and on this point expressly adopted Spiethoff's theory,[5]

[1] Wicksell has himself given different definitions of this "natural rate." In his *Lectures on Political Economy* (Vol. II, p. 193) it is "the rate of interest at which *the demand for loan capital and the supply of savings* exactly agree, and which more or less corresponds to the expected yield on the newly created capital." In his *Geldzins und Güterpreise* (chapter viii) he defines it as "the rate which would be determined by supply and demand if money was not in use and if all loans were made in real capital."

[2] See the Preface to his *Vorlesungen* of 1906.

[3] See his study of the fall in prices after the war, in the volume of monetary studies published in 1933 by Hayek under the title *Beiträge zur Geldtheorie*.

[4] See Ohlin's Preface to the English edition of Wicksell's *Interest and Prices* (Macmillan, London, 1936), p. viii.

[5] *Lectures*, English edition, Vol. II, p. 209: "My view closely agrees with that of Professor Spiethoff."

and to some extent Aftalion's, though he never mentions the latter and seems not to have known him.[1]

It is impossible, when reading Wicksell, not to be struck by these contradictions and hesitations on the part of an intellect that yet gives proof of rare dialectical and logical vigour. His influence springs rather from the way in which he has put certain difficult problems and his criticisms of solutions already suggested, than from the originality of his own solutions. The principal question that has aroused his curiosity is how long-term price movements, whether upward or downward, are started and continue. Adopting in principle Walras's doctrine of price equilibrium, and favouring also the ideas of Böhm-Bawerk on the rate of interest, he finds great difficulty in accounting, by these theories alone, for certain price fluctuations which during the last fifty years have characterized and dominated economic development. He sees here some contradictions that had not previously been noted.

His first book, called *Geldzins und Güterpreise* (*Interest and Prices*), appeared in 1898, and is directly connected with the impassioned discussions that arose out of the prolonged fall in prices that marked the years from 1873 to 1895 and provoked so many complaints, especially from the agriculturists. Many economists who were hostile to the quantity theory, especially in Germany and France, refused at that time to attribute this fall to the stagnation or reduction of the annual production of gold. One of the arguments employed against the probability of a monetary influence was drawn from the deep fall in the discount rate observed at that time, and the simultaneous accumulation of gold in the issuing banks. How, asked the opponents of the quantity theory, could we speak in such circumstances of a scarcity of gold? Now, Wicksell declared himself an adherent of the quantity theory—the only theory, he said, which had so far accounted for the undoubted influence of money on prices. So he started to search for an interpretation by which to explain the paradox of a fall in prices accompanied by a very low discount rate when that rate seemed, on the contrary, a sign of monetary abundance that should make prices rise. That is the first problem that engaged his attention and led him

---

[1] The following passage from the *Lectures*, English edition, Vol. II, p. 211, seems to me significant: "The principal and sufficient cause of cyclical fluctuations should rather be sought in the fact that in its very nature technical or commercial advance cannot maintain the same even progress as does, in our days, the increase in needs—especially owing to the organic phenomenon of increase of population—but is sometimes precipitate, sometimes delayed. . . . There occurs the conversion of large masses of liquid into fixed capital which is an inevitable preliminary to every boom and indeed is probably the only fully characteristic sign, or at any rate one which cannot conceivably be absent." That is precisely Aftalion's thesis.

to examine all existing explanations of the way in which a rise or fall of prices is brought about.[1]

It may be said at once that the explanation of this apparent paradox is really simple enough. The fall in prices means of necessity a diminished need for specie, so that it accumulates in the banks. At the same time the demand for credit is nominally less than before for transactions of the same amount, because goods and services fetch lower prices. Wicksell, however, does not mention this explanation. What happens, according to him, is that the discount rate, though it *seems* very low, is higher than what he calls the "natural rate" of interest, which he defines sometimes as corresponding to the yield in kind of real capital and sometimes as the rate that equalizes the supply of savings and the demand for them. Hence arise losses for the *entrepreneurs* and a fall in the price of products.[2] This explanation is itself merely the application to this particular problem of a general solution to which he was led by his reflections on the wider problem of the origin of general rises and falls in prices. As we shall shortly meet with the problem again in another form, it will be enough to say that he draws a distinction here between two cases: one where the movement is due to variable relations between the production of gold and that of goods (for Wicksell has always upheld the quantity theory on this point), and the other, which is "extremely important in practice" (*Lectures*, II, p. 208), where this movement "is not due to a change in the supply of gold or to an increased demand for goods from the gold countries." It is this second case that perplexes him and leads him to think that the price movement arises from a divergence between the discount rate and the 'natural' rate of interest. Unfortunately he does not tell us what these movements are that are "extremely important in practice" and that are due neither to increased production of gold nor to that of goods. All that we know is that he was not thinking of crises. It is impossible, too, to verify his hypothesis, since the 'natural' rate is a mere figment of the brain and is not actually in existence on any market.

It is useless to dwell any longer on an explanation that is rejected even by Wicksell's followers. We mention it here—and will dwell on it no longer—only to call attention to its strangeness, and to show the direction in which Wicksell's curiosity led him when it was aroused

---

[1] This is the purpose of his first book, *Geldzins und Güterpreise* (1898), of which the English translation (Macmillan), *Interest and Prices*, with a Preface by Ohlin, appeared in 1936.

[2] The whole problem is again dealt with in his *Course*. *Cf.* pp. 205–208 of Vol. II of the English translation, *Lectures on Political Economy* (1935), and also his article in the *Economic Journal* for 1907, p. 213.

by dynamic problems very different from those solved by the Classical theories of equilibrium.

A second problem to which Wicksell rightly drew attention, and which economists had almost all neglected, is one that arises whenever there is a general fall in prices. He puts it in the following terms: "Clearly the fact is here overlooked" (when a fall in prices begins)

> that the purchasing power which on this assumption would be reduced in the case of the sellers of the former goods would be increased to a corresponding degree in the case of the buyers. If the latter have only to offer a smaller part of their income in order to satisfy their need for the goods or classes of goods in question, then they have a correspondingly greater amount left for their demand for other goods, and it is not impossible that these other goods . . . would *rise* in price and thereby perhaps compensate for the fall in price of the cheapened goods (*Lectures*, Vol. II, p. 210).

The contradiction in logic thus noted (very opportunely) by Wicksell is precisely the same as that dealt with by Keynes at the beginning of his important book on unemployment. He there poses the question why the re-employment of income liberated by the fall in the prices of certain products, which should normally take place, is not forthcoming, and why the *total* demand for products (and therefore the general price-level) and the number of workers employed do not remain always the same despite this fall. In other words, how can a general fall in prices remain and extend after it has started, and why is it not stopped at the beginning, since the aggregate purchasing power in the hands of the public has not changed?

Actually, the contradiction is solved easily enough. We have no assurance, in fact, that the income of consumers that is set free will be translated *immediately and without delay* into a new demand exerting a compensatory upward effect on the prices of other products. It is the *rapidity* of circulation of money or income that matters here. Now, we know from observation that this rapidity of circulation is very unequal. The owner of the liberated income may very well *wait* for a time before making use of it. The consumer speculates on a fall of prices just as the producer speculates on a rise. A fall in some products leads him to think that others may fall also. He is led to postpone his purchases of other commodities, and the logical compensatory rise expected by Wicksell does not take place, at least not at once. During this period of delay those business firms, or some of them, that have been hit by the fall in selling-prices will make efforts to reduce their costs, and the result will be either unemployment or a fall in wages *before* consumers have decided to transfer elsewhere their liberated purchasing power. Hence arises a diminution in the *aggregate* incomes of the working-class and the *entrepreneurs*. This diminution of incomes (and, therefore, of the aggregate demand for products), and the new fall in prices that will accompany it, will extend the circle of firms that were hit first, and the movement is thus enabled in a cumulative manner to affect more and more sections of the economic system. In short, there is a *velocity of circulation* of incomes, whose slackening diminishes the total amount of income spent in a given time. This reduction brings in its train falls in price that are added to the original fall, so as to strengthen it and prolong it until production and total demand have found a new equilibrium at a lower level of prices in general.

The solution of the problem that worried Wicksell is, therefore, simple enough, so long as we are not led astray into a purely logical discussion of its terms but consider in detail, by a microscopical examination, as it were, the reactions caused by the original fall in prices, taking due note of the *times* within which these different reactions occur. This has been very clearly shown by Ohlin and Haberler, the former in two noteworthy articles in the *Economic Journal*, and the latter in a note in his account of the theories of crises.[1] But Wicksell does not take this line: he thinks he has found another solution, which he was the first to suggest and in which Keynes in his turn found, at one time at least, a way of safety.[2] Starting from Walras's conception of saving, Wicksell declares that normally the amount of incomes exceeds that of consumption. The difference between the total incomes received and the total consumed (*i.e.*, spent on consumption goods) constitutes savings, which are invested in business enterprises or in goods intended to increase future production. These two streams, one of consumption expenditure and the other of savings expenditure, absorb together the sum total of incomes and form two continuous and parallel streams flowing side by side. So long as the amount of investment by the *entrepreneurs* coincides with the amount of saving by the savers,[3] there is no reason, says Wicksell, for any

---

[1] See Ohlin, *Some Notes on the Stockholm Theory of Savings and Investment*, in the *Economic Journal*, 1937, especially pp. 227 *ff.*, and Haberler, *Prosperity and Depression* (Geneva, 1937), p. 253 *n.* The same problem has been examined by Bouniatian in the book already mentioned (pp. 243 *ff.*). He propounds an interesting solution, but a less accurate one, in our opinion, than that given in the text (*Cf.* Bouniatian, *Les Crises économiques*, 2nd French edition, 1930).

[2] The whole of Wicksell's exposition, starting at p. 192 of his *Lectures* (Vol. II), should be carefully studied, but his concise style often makes it obscure, like all his preceding discussion of the views of Tooke and Ricardo.

[3] And assuming, of course, that no external cause comes to raise prices—such as an increase in the production of gold.

change in prices in general. On the other hand, if the sums invested by the *entrepreneurs exceed* the amount of savings (which will happen, for instance, if bank credit is more freely extended by the banks to *entrepreneurs*, especially if it is granted at a very low rate of discount), then we shall find the incomes of the *entrepreneurs*, and therefore those of their collaborators—especially the workers—increasing, and along with their incomes their consumption expenditure. We shall then see a general rise in the prices of consumable commodities, which must be attributed in the last analysis to the inequality between saving and investment which is the prelude to a general rise in the price-level. To avert this rise, therefore, it is sufficient to maintain equality between saving and investment. The method to be adopted if this is to be successful is to keep the discount rate high enough to prevent excessive investment by the *entrepreneurs*. Conversely, if the investments of the *entrepreneurs* are less than the savings that are created, then a fall in prices will take place, and this should be met by a fall in the rate of discount.[1]

This conception is obviously disconcerting to minds accustomed to the theory of the equilibrium and mutual dependence of prices, which implies, in fact, that a rise in prices may begin on the market for consumption goods as well as on the market for investment goods. Ohlin discerningly called attention to this in his introduction to the English translation of Wicksell's first book. He even admits that as a result of war-time experience Wicksell did not retain complete faith in the conception just summarized. "During his last years," he says,

> Wicksell came more and more to doubt the solidity of what had been regarded as the corner-stone of his monetary theory—the idea that if the money rate coincided with a normal rate of interest, which brought about equality between savings and investment, the commodity price-level would remain constant.

He draws the conclusion, then, from some of Wicksell's sentences, that he did admit at the end of his life, though without actually saying so, that even in a case of equilibrium between saving and investment, as generally understood, there might occur a rise or fall of prices. And so he concludes that one of the fundamental elements of Wicksell's original theory would have to be abandoned.[2]

But whatever Wicksell may have thought of his own theory, and however unacceptable it may be to his followers and those who

---

[1] The most easily accessible account of Wicksell's theory on this point is to be found in his article in the *Economic Journal* for 1907, pp. 213 *ff.*, under the title *The Influence of the Rate of Interest on Prices.*

[2] Introduction to *Interest and Prices*, p. xxi.

remain faithful to the theory of the mutual dependence of prices, this distinction between saving and investment has played a considerable part in the economic controversies of recent years, particularly in the ideas of Keynes, and it was expedient to show how it originated.

Such, then, are the salient points in the views of a writer whose function was mainly to point out the difficulties in current theories and to seek for solutions, though he himself attributed to his solutions no other value than as suggestions constantly subject to revision. Until the end of his life he never ceased to be obsessed by this problem of the great price movements, and by the desire to find methods by which price-levels could be stabilized. It is enough for us to have shown here the importance that he attached to the phenomenon of saving, to which, as we know, so many writers attribute a predominant influence in the development of crises, though they are far from agreeing about its mode of operation. To this mode of operation we must now return.

IV: THE THEORETICAL MECHANISM OF SAVING

For a long time saving was regarded as such a simple economic action that it was hardly thought necessary to make a theory of it. Adam Smith and Turgot expatiated mainly on the economic benefits that it yields, and paid little attention to the way it works. Throughout the nineteenth century authors of the most opposite views rivalled Adam Smith in singing its praises. Karl Marx considered it the essential function of the capitalist, and Keynes, who was later to criticize it so acutely, explained eloquently in his famous book on Reparations how the savings of the older countries before the First World War served to fertilize the industry of the whole world—one of the most striking pictures that his pen has drawn. Some discordant voices were heard, however—the most celebrated being that of Lord Lauderdale at the end of the eighteenth century. In a book that was widely read—it was even translated into French—and in which he often finds fault with Adam Smith's views, he protests against the too rapid liquidation of the English debt. Dupont de Nemours, in a very elaborate note on Turgot's *Réflexions*,[1] vigorously condemns all

---

[1] This note is to be found at para. 77 of Turgot's *Réflexions sur la formation et la distribution des Richesses* (see his *Œuvres*, published by Gustave Schelle, Vol. II, p. 582), and we regard it as of capital importance in the history of doctrines about saving. Dupont would like to see the term 'saving' replaced by 'productive expenditure.' He declares that we must "get rid of the simple idea of saving among the elements that go to form capital," as the word 'saving' ordinarily means merely 'putting on one side.'

saving that does not consist in 'productive expenditure.' Malthus, for his part, spoke in praise of luxury, and at the end of the nineteenth century certain less-known writers, such as Hobson, regarded excessive saving as one of the sources of the distress of the working-classes.

But many points in the theory still remain obscure, and we must call attention to them here or we shall not understand the controversies that they have given rise to. For example, economists have not managed to reach agreement as to the influence that may be exerted on the growth of saving by the rate of interest. Normally, it would seem, every rise in the rate of interest should tend to increase saving and every fall to reduce it. But experience does not seem to bear this out. Pareto thinks that saving would continue even if the rate of interest fell to zero. Another Italian author, Ricci, thinks that the amount of saving is a function of the rate of interest that follows a curve that first rises and then falls after reaching a maximum.[1] Cassel's view is that below a certain rate the reduction in saving will automatically produce a recovery in the rate and prevent its falling to zero.[2] Divisia[3] believes that the problem can only be solved inductively, and that we should stick to observed facts. But this is extremely difficult, and the answer to the question, he thinks, remains in abeyance.

The uncertainty is greater still when it comes to analysing the *mechanism* of saving. The most satisfactory description is that given by Böhm-Bawerk.[4] Saving, according to him, is merely a new direction given to the use of income. It consists in applying income not to the consumption of present goods, but to the making of instruments or the construction of factories or dwellings which will facilitate the future increase of immediately consumable goods and services. This description aims at showing how, *even if all the forces of labour in an economic system are engaged*, saving none the less provides the means for increasing the real future income of this economic system. If, *on this hypothesis*, an individual decides to save—that is, to withdraw from the consumption of his income money that was formerly applied to consumption—the process started by this saving will evidently be as follows. The former demand for consumption goods will be diminished by the amount of the savings, while on the other hand the demand for

He then develops the idea that in a society based on division of labour saving in that sense can only have the most disastrous effects by restricting the demand for products. We quote below, in dealing with Keynes, the passage in Dupont which exactly corresponds to the former's famous parable of the bananas.

[1] *Cf.* Ricci, *L'Offerta del risparmio* in *Giornale degli Economisti*, 1926 and 1927.
[2] *Cf.* Cassel, *The Nature and Necessity of Interest* (Macmillan, London, 1903).
[3] Divisia, *L'Épargne et la richesse collective* (Sirey, Paris, 1928).
[4] Böhm-Bawerk, *Positive Theorie des Kapitals*, chapter ii, sec. iv.

production goods (tools, machinery, etc.) will be increased by the same amount. The price-level of the former will tend to fall and that of the latter to rise. There follows a call for labour (which has become useless for the now reduced production of consumption goods) on the part of businesses making production goods. Saving, by diminishing consumption, will thus have served to set free labour forces that will henceforth serve to increase future production at the expense of the production of immediately consumable goods.

Nothing could be clearer than this. And it has, besides, the advantage of showing plainly that we are concerned here with community saving alone, and not with individual saving. Indeed, if we take the individual point of view only, we see at once that the savings of some may be consumed by others. The thrifty man who buys a farm, a factory, or some stocks or shares does not know whether the seller is not going to consume at once the money he receives. So these transactions do not necessarily increase the capital of the community. The best-known example is that of a State which consumes the savings of the public in war expenditure. There is no saving *for the community* unless, when account is taken of the consumption by some people of the savings of others, there remains *an actual balance* which is invested in new undertakings or in improvements of old ones. It is this actual balance, thus invested, to which the term 'savings' is applied in political economy, and to which Böhm-Bawerk's considerations apply— considerations which are very pertinent but far from exhausting the complexities of the subject.

In the mechanism here described everything turns, in fact, on the hypothesis of non-consumption, or, if preferred, reduction of consumption, by the saver. Now, this reduction is in very many cases useless. We have only to imagine a saver receiving an *addition* to his income and deciding not to consume it but to procure with it some machines that are indispensable to increase his future production. He has then no need to *reduce* his normal consumption. As a matter of fact, in the economic world of to-day, savings are *mainly* drawn from *additions* to income. It is the *increased* profits of an industry or an individual that are set aside and invested, without any diminution in the personal consumption of the saver or of society as a whole. From this follows the important consequence that the fall in the prices of consumption commodities, which was just now considered as bound up with the phenomenon of saving, *is in no way necessary*, since the demand for these commodities has not changed. *It may even have increased, if only a part of the additional income is saved*, the rest being spent in the purchase of consumable products. And that is what most frequently happens.

2A

In periods of a general rise in incomes the increase in saving is accompanied by a general increase in consumption. Even in periods when incomes in general are falling, many communities or individuals who have remained prosperous continue to save without thereby reducing their consumption. The reductions in consumption that we see, therefore, are due to the general fall in consumable incomes of the rest of the population, and not to the fact that some people save. We cannot, then, accept without serious limitations the general proposition enunciated by Keynes in his *General Theory of Employment, Interest and Money* (and asserted by many other writers as an obvious truth): "It is common ground that increased individual saving will cause a fall in the price of consumers' goods"[1] (p. 192). On the contrary, an increase in saving, or its persistence even in a period of diminishing incomes, contributes to the fall in price of consumable commodities only on the hypothesis adopted by Böhm-Bawerk, which is the least often realized in the ordinary course of events.

But still further modifications are needed in a theory constructed exclusively for cases where all economic forces are employed and nominal incomes are stationary. Even if savings are deductions from the normal consumption of the savers, even if *for them* they mean retrenchment, it does not follow that *for the community* this deduction will involve a reduction in consumption. We have only to imagine—what is, in fact, the commonest case—that the community includes some unemployed workers. In this case the new savings, by providing an income for workers who hitherto had received none, are spent on consumption. The choice of commodities consumed is altered, but the aggregate demand for consumption products, measured in purchasing power, remains unchanged. At the beginning of a boom period, when unemployment, born of the preceding crisis, is generally fairly widespread, the effect of increased saving is simply to set to work a larger number of workers and thus to provide them with incomes, and to compensate, by their demand for consumable goods, for the reduced demand of the savers. That is undoubtedly the case that Adam Smith had in mind when he said, in what seems at first sight a rather paradoxical statement, "What is annually saved, is as regularly consumed as what is annually spent."

[1] Haberler, in his *Prosperity and Depression*, often uses expressions that seem to imply adherence to this formula, either when he is quoting other writers or when he is speaking for himself. He says at p. 38, for example, that if part of one's current income is saved—*i.e.*, if all the income is not spent on consumption goods—the demand for such goods diminishes, and some factors of production are set free. See also pp. 214 and 398 of the same book. Such a formula can by its generality lead only to erroneous conclusions.

There is no need even to adopt the hypothesis of unemployment. The mere growth of population throws on the market every year a new generation of workers, whose numbers depend on the birth-rate. These new teams of workers, hitherto without any income of their own, absorb the new savings, and while creating new capital prevent the demand for consumable goods from being restricted. Let us imagine a still more familiar hypothesis, large-scale immigration, such as used to take place into the United States, or a large import of foreign labour, as in France. It is obvious that in a great many circumstances new saving does not result in any diminution of the aggregate demand for consumption products, but merely changes the nature of the things demanded.

Such are the immediate effects of an increase in saving *at the moment when it takes place*—that is to say at the time of that *change in demand* which is its first manifestation, and which must not be confused with a *reduction* in demand. But this is only the *first phase*, as has been so well stressed by Bresciani-Turroni. When saving has attained its object—*i.e.*, when savings have been transformed into more powerful or more numerous machines which serve to multiply consumption commodities—then these commodities are in more plentiful supply on the market than before. *In this new phase* a fall in prices is inevitable unless other circumstances counteract it, such as a greater abundance of gold or paper money. The deep and lasting effect of an increase in annual saving, or simply of its maintenance at the normal level it has reached at a given moment, is a fall in the prices of consumable commodities and services "as a natural consequence of their greater abundance."[1] That is the most certain result of an increase in general productivity due to saving. Whereas in the *first* phase, the creation of new savings, it is the alteration in *demand* that interests the economist, in the *second*, when saving has attained its end (the increase of production), it is the *supply*. This has been well brought out by Bresciani-Turroni in a noteworthy article in *Economica*, in which he sums up with admirable conciseness the fundamental notions that make up the modern theory of saving. Now, recent discussions on the influence of saving on crises are concerned essentially with the phenomena of the *first* phase—those that result from the new direction given to *demand*—and neglect those of the second phase which result from the increase in supply.

If we take both phases into account, we see how hard it is then to follow *in actual events* the effects of a relative increase or decrease in

[1] *Cf.* Bresciani-Turroni, *The Theory of Saving*, in *Economica*, February and May 1936, p. 69.

saving. For all the effects of the first phase are constantly being joined by those of the second, which either counterbalance or reinforce them. In our industrial communities there is a continual creation of savings. *Normally* part of the net income is saved and only the rest is consumed: it is precisely this that characterizes an economically progressive community, according to the plan set forth long ago by Walras. Can we believe that the fluctuations of savings around this normal point are sufficient to start a crisis? *Entrepreneurs* who extend their production (*e.g.*, the makers of machines) reckon that *normally* the weavers or spinners who use the machines will also extend *their* production of cotton or cloth by saving part of their profits with which to buy more machines. They may be wrong, just as the weavers or the dress-makers may be wrong in counting on the consumers of cloth and dresses to increase their purchases. Have the mistakes of the machine-makers more to do with starting crises than those of the makers of cloth or dresses? There seems no reason why it should be so. All we can say is that the more far removed the manufactured products or the extracted raw materials are, in the chain of their successive transformations, from the finished product, the more is it possible for mistakes in forecasting, if there are any, to continue before the *entrepreneurs* are enlightened by the eventual sale or non-sale of that finished product.

So a shifting of expenditure from investment to consumption, or *vice versa*, will by itself produce hardly any lasting effects. If, for a given aggregate income, the demand for consumable products is increased[1] their prices will rise, and there will be increased profits for the industrialists who make them, and they will find it advantageous to invest these profits in new manufactures. In other words, savings and investment will increase from the very fact of the increased demand for consumable products. And conversely, if it is the savings that have increased, and investments along with savings, then the new investments will result in an additional supply of consumable goods, their prices will fall, and this will stimulate purchases by consumers and again reduce that part of income that is invested. Thus an automatic correction comes into play, in whichever direction the mistake is made.

We can but agree with the conclusion reached by Bresciani-Turroni, as follows:

> The deeper we attempt to look into the saving process, the more this latter reveals to us unexpected intricacies and manifold forms. This process is by no means so simple and smooth as the conceptions

[1] Compared with what it was in the preceding period.

still prevailing not many years ago among economists would have us believe.[1]

And Divisia, for his part, asserts that "it is clear that if the growth of saving has not itself, strictly speaking, an actually contradictory character, nevertheless the analysis of its manner of working is full of pitfalls."[2] In particular, adds Bresciani-Turroni, if you wish to use a theory of saving to explain crises, a careful distinction must be made according to whether or not the increase in saving takes place at a time of 'full employment.' If there is unemployment, an extension of production may continue for a considerable time without leading to any reduction in the making of consumable commodities, for the savings provide incomes for workers hitherto without wages, and these incomes they hasten to consume. If, on the other hand, the increase in savings comes at a time when there is no unemployment—which is the case when a boom is at its height—the result will be to withdraw workers from the manufacture of consumable commodities and attract them into that of production goods. This gives rise to a reduction in the quantity of consumption commodities, followed by a rise in their prices and a nominal rise in wages, with a consequent reduction in profits *in all industries* with a tendency for production to slacken.

There we have the germ of an interesting explanation of crises. The creation of savings at the end of a boom would account in particular for what was observed in Germany in 1924 by Bresciani-Turroni, a great authority on German economy,[3] that at the moment when the 1924 crisis broke out it was consumable goods that were in short supply and whose price rose. This is in direct contradiction of the opinion of those economists who think that crises originate in a fall in the prices of consumption products, but it contradicts also the idea that they originate in a scarcity of capital. Their origin would lie rather in a shortage and dearness of labour.

Bresciani-Turroni, however, does not believe that these transfers of savings (whose effects correct themselves) are sufficient to start a crisis. His view is that crises would not occur without excessive credit. Industrialists very often start new business in production goods *with the help of credit*, which they count on being able to pay back with future savings. But if they are mistaken about the influx of future savings (and nothing is easier), the temporary expansion of production born of credit will be faced at a certain moment by an insufficiency of savings. If this mistake is widespread, a crisis may be the result. It thus has its origin in excessive credit, not excessive saving. It is

[1] *Op. cit.*, p. 181.   [2] Divisia, *L'Épargne*, pp. 225–226.
[3] *Cf.* his book *Le vicende del marco tedesco* (Milan, 1931).

obvious that the mechanism of saving becomes difficult to grasp when we try to follow it in detail.[1]

The most certain conclusion of the general theory of saving is that by the increase of productive forces it tends to increase the quantity of products and services and consequently—in the absence of any exterior causes operating in the opposite direction—to lower their prices. The *real* income of the community is increased, and the mass of products and services to be shared between its members grows unceasingly, but the price-level falls. On the whole its effects are beneficial and bring increased well-being to every one.

V: KEYNES'S THEORY OF SAVING, UNEMPLOYMENT, AND CRISES

The greatest reproach that can be levelled against Keynes's theory, as elaborated in his world-famous *General Theory of Employment, Interest and Money* in 1936, and outlined before that in his *Treatise on Money* in 1930, is that it has not taken account of all the complexities of the mechanism of saving that are revealed by careful analysis. It has been made into a simplified conception—exactly opposite to that of Adam Smith—which is summed up in the idea that saving reduces consumption, absolutely or relatively. And the whole of the demonstration is concerned with this conception.

What happens, asks Keynes, when saving reduces the demand for products? It reduces at the same time the number of employed workers. Now, if the total amount of remuneration forming the aggregate incomes of the workers is diminished, the total money income to be spent by the community is diminished, as well as the aggregate demand for products; the forecasts of the *entrepreneurs* will be falsified; production will be restricted by the disappearance of profit, the principal stimulus to production; unemployment will thereby be increased; the reduction of incomes to be shared will be intensified—leading to a new shrinking of aggregate demand, accompanied by a new reduction of profits and production. And so the process continues, until the impoverished community falls from prosperity into the depths of misery. So saving, far from being a benefit, becomes a curse, and everything should be done to discourage it and stimulate consumption. Unproductive expenditure, luxury building, public works would all be preferable to this descent into the abyss through the excessive practice of a false virtue that has yet

[1] For this mechanism I must refer the reader to my *Théorie de l'épargne* (1922), reprinted in *Essais sur quelques problèmes économiques et monétaires* (Paris, 1933).

been preached unceasingly by economists, moralists, and statesmen ever since the days of Adam Smith, the thrifty Scot who was the first to undertake its defence.[1]

Such, in broad outline, is Keynes's thesis, already elaborated more than a century earlier by Dupont de Nemours in his note on Saving appended to Turgot's *Réflexions*, paragraph 77. Here is the essential passage, whose interest needs no emphasis, despite its ungainly style.

> In countries where incomes are paid in money, if those incomes which represent the disposable portion of the harvest, are not spent by their owners, there will be a corresponding portion of the harvest which is not sold, though the cultivator will have paid its price to the owners, without having withdrawn it from his sales by which alone he had planned to be able to pay this owner every year the sum agreed upon. This unsold portion of the harvest, which the farmer would nevertheless like to dispose of, will of necessity fall very low in price. This low price will also of necessity affect other prices, which naturally find their level, as Turgot has very clearly shown (in paragraphs 30, 31, and 32 of his book). But the fall in prices will necessitate in the same way a diminution of production, as we have just seen in speaking of production which only repays its cost, and also a diminution of incomes, which are always proportional to the quantity of products to be sold, combined with the price at which they are sold, and compared with the costs of production. But the reduction of income will still be a loss to the thrifty owners, *who will find it hard to understand what they have done to ruin themselves by saving and will see nothing for it but to increase their savings, which will hasten their ruin until they reach the point where absolute destitution makes saving impossible and compels them to throw themselves, too late, into the ranks of the workers.*

This is the very thesis adopted by Keynes, who certainly had not read Dupont. He intended it to explain both the unemployment from which Great Britain had just suffered, and the continued fall of prices after 1930. It accounted for the most recent 'great depression' as well as for long-term falls in general; it provided a comprehensible and simple substitute for the much-criticized quantity theory of money, by putting the theory of prices back in the lower rank of 'subsidiary' theories (p. 32); and, finally, it set economic science free from that 'fatalism' which in all ages has made it appear as "the dismal science," and substituted for it a conception that opened up vast prospects for successful State intervention.

A scientific revolution of this kind could be attempted only by a writer gifted not only with great expository powers but also with a

---

[1] The analogy with Sismondi's doctrine of insufficiency of demand is striking, and we refer the reader to it.

fertile imagination—one, moreover, who has given brilliant proof in his earlier books of his mastery of financial and monetary problems.

The essence of the argument is contained in what Keynes himself calls the "parable" of the bananas. This occurs in an earlier work called *A Treatise on Money*, which appeared in 1930, some of whose conceptions were to be renounced in the later book, though on this point its principal ideas were retained. Imagine, says Keynes, a community living exclusively on the production and consumption of bananas, but using money for its purchases and sales. Suppose that certain members of this community, smitten by a mania for saving, decide not to buy a portion of the bananas they had hitherto consumed, and suppose, finally, that *they do not employ* the income thus 'saved' in creating new plantations that would increase their consumption in the future. Saving then "exceeds investment." What will be the result of the operation? Obviously a fall in the price of bananas, which will delight the hearts of all consumers. But there will also be a diminution of the profits of producers, which will fill them with sorrow and compel them to reduce production or dismiss their workmen. So at the following stage—the next harvest—total production will have diminished, and there will be some unemployed. If the group of savers continues every year to reduce its consumption, the impoverishment of the community will continue without limit. In this way saving will have led to disaster, under the cloak of virtue.[1]

There is nothing to be said against this reasoning—except that Keynes, by using the same word for both, is confusing 'saving' with 'hoarding.' 'Saving,' as we have said earlier, in conformity with the classical meaning of the word in the English economy—since adopted by all continental economists—is defined not as 'non-expenditure' but as expenditure of a special kind—the employment of income in the creation of new capital. Now, the saving of our banana-growers consists, it is true, in not consuming, but *without employing in new production the income thus set free*, so the result will naturally be quite different. That hoarding reduces demand, no one will dispute. But (we may note in passing) it is difficult to see any plausible motive in the action of Keynes's banana-growers. If it was not to buy more bananas sooner or later, or to increase the growing of bananas at once, what purpose could be served by their saving? Was it a mere display of asceticism?

We can see here the inconvenience of negative definitions. To define saving as 'non-consumption' is inadequate to denote the economic action we have in mind. For 'not to consume' income is

---

[1] *A Treatise on Money*, Vol. I, p. 276.

necessarily to employ it 'otherwise' than in the purchase of consumption goods, and we must therefore say what 'otherwise' we are thinking of. The sums that are 'not consumed' may be either destroyed or lost or hoarded or invested or used to pay debts. The more numerous the ways of using income the more will their effects on the general economy differ. In the traditional language of economics saving is identified with investment and distinguished from hoarding, and Keynes is here playing with words.

In his more recent book he does not return to the example of the bananas. At the same time he abandons the idea that there can be any divergence in a community between saving and investment. On this divergence he had previously built up (by a curious union with Wicksell's theories) the whole of his theory of price movements. Now he rejects it, and admits that *by definition* saving and investment are of necessity identical. But among the forms of investment he includes investment in money—*i.e.*, hoarding—so that the parable of the bananas remains incorporated in the system.

None the less, his conception of saving is no longer entirely the same. Henceforth to save is no longer to reduce consumption; it is only to reduce the *proportion* of income that is spent in consumption. When income increases, he says, there is a tendency for the recipients to increase their consumption, but *not to the extent of the whole increase of income*. There is no absolute reduction of consumption, therefore, though in more than one place Keynes returns to his old formula. But the saved income grows proportionally faster than consumption as income increases. In cases of reduced income the opposite process takes place: the *proportion* saved falls as the reduction proceeds.[1]

Even if the proportion of increased income consumed to that which is saved remains equal to what it was before the income increased, the

---

[1] "We take it as a fundamental psychological rule of any modern community that, when its real income is increased, it will not increase its consumption by an equal *absolute* amount, so that a greater absolute amount must be saved, unless a large and unusual change is occurring at the same time in other factors. . . . This means that, if employment and hence aggregate income increase, *not all* the additional employment will be required to satisfy the needs of additional consumption.

"On the other hand, a decline in income due to a decline in the level of employment, if it goes far, may even cause consumption to exceed income not only by some individuals and institutions using up the financial reserves which they have accumulated in better times, but also by the Government, which will be liable, willingly or unwillingly, to run into a budgetary deficit or will provide unemployment relief, for example, out of borrowed money. Thus, when employment falls to a low level, aggregate consumption will decline by a smaller amount than that by which real income has declined . . . which is the explanation why a new position of equilibrium can usually be reached within a modest range of fluctuation" (pp. 97–98). See also the typical passages at p. 27 and especially pp. 104 *ff.*

absolute amount saved will be greater, since the income is greater. Thus "the larger our incomes, the greater, unfortunately, is the margin between our incomes and our consumption" (p. 105). The problem of finding an investment for savings, therefore, becomes more and more difficult as income increases and the community grows richer. If, however, no solution is found—*i.e.*, if investments do not absorb savings (in other words, if hoarding takes place)—then the employment of labour will at once diminish. This means a reduction in the aggregate income of the community, an increase in unemployment, and so forth. Here again we may quote the actual words of Keynes:

> An act of individual saving means—so to speak—a decision not to have dinner to-day. But it does *not* necessitate a decision to have dinner or to buy a pair of boots a week hence or a year hence or to consume any specified thing at any specified date. Thus it depresses the business of preparing to-day's dinner without stimulating the business of making ready for some future act of consumption. It is not a substitution of future consumption-demand for present consumption-demand,—it is a net diminution of such demand. . . . If saving consisted not merely in abstaining from present consumption but in placing simultaneously a specific order for future consumption, the effect might indeed be different. . . . The absurd, though almost universal, idea that an act of individual saving is just as good for effective demand as an act of individual consumption, has been fostered by the fallacy, much more specious than the conclusion derived from it, that an increased desire to hold wealth, being much the same thing as an increased desire to hold investments, must, by increasing the demand for investments, provide a stimulus to their production; so that current investment is promoted by individual saving to the same extent as present consumption is diminished. It is of this fallacy that it is most difficult to disabuse men's minds. . . . For this overlooks the fact that there is always an alternative to the ownership of real capital-assets, namely the ownership of money and debts (pp. 210–212).

If this be admitted, the whole problem of maintaining a community in a state of full employment is, therefore, to find enough opportunities for the investment of the saved portion of income. For it is useless to try to influence saving itself, which is only a residue, the result of the public's "tendency to consumption." "Saving, in fact, is a mere residual" (p. 64). What is necessary, then, is either to increase consumption in order to reduce saving, or to find new openings for investment in order to absorb the savings.

One objection at once springs to mind. Why should an increase in consumption goods necessarily cause a fall in prices? Are there not periods of rising prices despite a great increase of products, as, for instance, when production from gold-mines is in rapid progress? But, says Keynes, the increase in incomes, and consequently in prices, that is due to the exploitation of gold-mines comes about simply because new workers are put to work in the gold-mines, and thus receive incomes and increase the general demand for products. This result might just as well be attained by a quite different method. For instance,

If the Treasury were to fill old bottles with bank-notes, bury them at suitable depths in disused coal-mines which are then filled up to the surface with town rubbish, and leave it to private enterprise on well-tried principles of *laissez-faire* to dig the notes up again . . . there need be no more unemployment and, with the help of the repercussions, the real wealth of the community, and its capital wealth also, would probably become a good deal greater than it actually is. It would, indeed, be more sensible to build houses and the like; but if there are political or practical difficulties in the way of this, the above would be better than nothing. The analogy between this expedient and the gold-mines of the real world is complete. At periods when gold is available at suitable depths experience shows that the real wealth of the world increases rapidly; and when but little of it is available, our wealth suffers stagnation or decline. Thus gold-mines are of the greatest value and importance to civilization (pp. 129–130).

If, then, the exploitation of gold-mines facilitates the raising of prices, it does so, according to Keynes, only by providing a supplementary source of labour. This is a strange thesis, not hitherto adopted by any economist, and it leads to the conclusion that any other kind of labour of equal amount, whether to provide necessaries or luxuries, would produce the same effect, so long as enough paper money is made to pay for it. The Egyptians invented the pyramid, and the Middle Ages the building of cathedrals. Only the modern age is too short-sighted to discover a way of utilizing the unemployed, providing them with incomes, and thus restoring general prosperity by the consumption of products.

In default of this unproductive expenditure new investments must be found. But the richer we become the rarer become these openings for investment. "The greater . . . the consumption for which we have provided in advance, the more difficult it is to find something further to provide for in advance" (*i.e.*, to invest in) "and the greater our dependence on present consumption as a source of demand" (p. 105).

Here we touch the weak spot in Keynes's theory—a point of far greater importance than all the other objections often raised against it in matters of detail. It can be put briefly as the fear of the disappearance of openings for productive investment, the idea that the world, having made all possible inventions, will one day find that there are no more discoveries to be made, and that when the *entrepreneurs* have exploited every conceivable opening they will be faced by a public no longer able to absorb their improved or increased products. Investment will cease when satisfaction is universal and all desires are met.

Is this a real risk? Keynes is not the first to utter these fears. So far they have always been belied by facts. Every age has unwisely boasted that it has reached the height of human knowledge and attainments. Every age, enraptured with its own achievements, has had its enthusiasts to proclaim that the human race will go no farther. And every time the following age has proved it wrong. We speak constantly of the Industrial Revolution of the late eighteenth century, but since then that Revolution has never ceased. After steam came electricity as a motive force; after the railway came the motor-car and the aeroplane to take the lead in transport. Then, after the revolution in power and transport, has come the revolution in raw materials, with plastics replacing cotton, wool, silk, and wood, and cement superseding stone. After the revolution in industry have come the changes brought about in agriculture by the use of artificial fertilizers and the extraction of nitrogen from the air. Is it likely that these changes are at an end? Are science and invention on the verge of bankruptcy? Can we really believe this? On the contrary, what frightens industry is the rapidity with which new inventions follow one upon another, causing such swift obsolescence that the profits of a business are swallowed up by the need to provide for renewal of plant in a few years. Even if invention ceased, it would be a long time before inventions already made brought benefit to entire peoples still living in sordid poverty, and entire classes, even in rich countries, who have as yet no share in the progress of hygiene and general well-being. There is a vast field open to enterprise here.

Other economists have answered the same question by a profession of faith in precisely opposite terms. Among them are Marshall, in a celebrated passage, and more recently Snyder, who sings a hymn of praise to the might of invention and saving that have brought economic greatness to the United States. Divisia, in an eloquent chapter in his book on Saving, draws the same conclusion, and quite rightly regards the building of the Pyramids[1] on the one hand and the construction of machinery on the other as marking the essential difference between

---

[1] The Pyramids have aroused the enthusiasm of many recent writers, and not the least distinguished either. See, for instance, the *Propos d'économique* of the philosopher Alain (Paris, 1934), p. 72, which is a useful reminder to economists of the need for modesty.

ancient and modern civilizations. And Hayek, in his article on Saving
in the *American Encyclopædia*, is of the same opinion.

Keynes's theory applies in principle to the general evolution of the
economic system. But as it arose in connexion with an acute crisis, with
whose circumstances the author was plainly preoccupied, it should
also provide an explanation of crises. And here he does not introduce excessive saving, as might have been expected, but the sudden
fall of profits.[1] The essential character of the cycle, which is its
regularity, is due, he says, to variations in the marginal efficiency of
capital, or, as we should say, to the sudden fall of profits (pp. 313, 315).
Hoarding does not arise till afterwards (p. 316). To remedy the
crisis, then, it would apparently suffice to lower the rate of interest
and thus supply the *entrepreneur* with new chances of profit. Unfortunately a reduction of the rate of interest, in face of what he calls
"the uncontrollable and disobedient psychology of the business
world," is generally powerless to cause "the return of confidence . . .
which is so insusceptible to control in an economy of individualistic
capitalism" (p. 317). It will be useless, then, to reduce the rate of
interest, for the pessimistic outlook of the *entrepreneurs* will make it
impossible to persuade them to make new investments.

The remedy will therefore lie in investments by the State, on the
one hand—*i.e.*, public works that will give employment to the unemployed, thus increasing the incomes to be spent and helping to increase
consumption—and, on the other hand, in measures aimed at the
direct increase of consumption. Here, after asserting that the sudden
collapse of profits is the origin of the crisis, and having declared himself not far from agreeing with the theory of over-investment, Keynes
returns to the explanation by under-consumption. He differs only
slightly from the under-consumption school, he says, and "I should
readily concede that the wisest course is to advance on both fronts at
once" (p. 325).

But if it is so difficult to contend with a crisis when once it has
started, would it not be possible to *prevent* it? Would it not be a good
preventive to raise the rate of discount, which is always identified by
Keynes with the rate of interest?[2] This also he considers inadvisable.
When pessimism gives way to optimism in the minds of *entrepreneurs*,

[1] Whence comes this fall of profits? From over-investment, says Keynes. But then,
we may reply, you believe in the theory of over-investment, and it is not the lack of
openings for investment that starts the fall. Undoubtedly, he replies (p. 320), I
accept the theory, but only in this sense, that the *entrepreneurs* have made investments
in the hope of a 6 per cent. yield, for example, and the actual yield is only 2 per cent.
Hence arise disappointment, discouragement, and crisis.

[2] This identification in the English economic system is not accepted in French
political economy, and many continental economists do not accept it either.

new investment must be encouraged. "Thus the remedy for the boom is not a higher rate of interest but a lower rate of interest!" (p. 322). He recognizes, however, that in certain circumstances the raising of the rate may be the only method to employ.[1]

But although the reduction of the rate of interest provides new openings for *entrepreneurs*, it also drives people to hoard their savings instead of investing them. What is to be done to prevent one of these effects counteracting the other? We should have to adopt a policy of a continuous fall in the rate of interest, for it is uncertainty as to the *later* direction of the rate of interest rather than its actual level that leads to hoarding. At the same time we should increase the quantity of money, which is the best way of reducing the rate of interest.[2]

Would not another solution be to reduce the cost of production by lowering wages? Keynes protests against such a suggestion, and makes a vigorous attack on Rueff and Robbins, though without naming them. The only purpose served by lowering wages, he says, is that by putting additional money into the hands of the *entrepreneurs* it makes the rate of interest fall and thereby increases the margin of possible profit. But there is a much simpler way of obtaining the same result: increasing the supply of money—and only a person who is at the same time "foolish," "unjust," and "inexperienced" would prefer the first method to the second.[3]

Here is another suggestion: could not work be redistributed by reducing the length of the working day and increasing the number of workers employed? That is what the French working-classes demanded when they asked for a forty-hour week. Keynes does not favour this solution: "I see no sufficient reason for compelling those who would prefer more income to enjoy more leisure" (p. 326).

Keynes concludes (p. 270) that the best plan would be the maintenance of a stable level of money wages. Such a policy, he says, would work best in a closed economic system, but it is still advisable in an open system, provided that equilibrium of prices with the rest of the world can be secured by means of fluctuating exchanges. This applies particularly for short periods. With regard to long periods the question arises whether it is better to keep wages stable while letting prices fall, or, conversely, to keep prices stable while letting wages rise.

---

[1] See p. 332 *n.*

[2] See pp. 167, 174, 234–236. I do not dwell on Keynes's theory of interest, which seems to me a return to ideas that were definitely abandoned by the eighteenth century and Turgot in particular. The student should read again Turgot's demonstration (*Réflexions*, para. 77), that abundance of money does not mean a reduction in the rate of interest.

[3] See pp. 268–269.

"On the whole," he says, "my preference is for the latter alternative." But as no essential point of principle is involved, he decides not to develop in detail the arguments on either side.

We will not dwell on these suggestions, which seem so simple when thus formulated. Keynes was too experienced a man to be unaware himself of the enormous difficulties concealed under this apparent simplicity. We live not in a closed system, but in an open one. Each economy is affected by what happens in other rival economies, and a system of exchange variations adopted by one country might have violent repercussions and arouse the sharpest conflicts, political as well as economic. The policy of 'exchange dumping' during the years from 1930 to 1939 provoked the liveliest international animosities and led to reprisals everywhere.

Keynes, on the other hand, speaks of the choice between a policy of wage stabilization and a policy of price stabilization as if it were easy to make, and as if States had not so far found it absolutely impossible, despite all their efforts, to keep either prices or wages stable. It is unwise to let the public think that the State has the means at its disposal to achieve such complicated ends. It was a sound observation by Mr Burgess, one of the directors of the Federal Bank of New York and closely associated with that bank's efforts at stabilization, that the price-level has never varied so much as since attempts were made to control it.[1]

In short, the practical remedy proposed by Keynes, as at an earlier date by T. R. Malthus, resolves itself into the setting-up of public works, and to calculate its effects in reducing unemployment he has constructed a complete theory—that of the 'multiplier'—which has failed to convince the British Government as well as the majority of economists.

Compared with his theory of saving Keynes's subsidiary theories are really only of secondary importance. We could go farther, and say that they are manifestly theories of circumstance, aimed at buttressing his main theme.[2] So we shall not deal with them here, but leave it to the reader to refer to them himself. The *General Theory*, like the author's earlier books, has given rise to very lively controversies. The best-known English economists, like Pigou and Hawtrey, have concentrated on defining their attitude to certain aspects of the theory,

[1] See his pamphlet *What About Money?*, published in 1940 by the National City Bank of New York.

[2] For a criticism of these monetary ideas see Marget, *The Theory of Prices* (New York, 1938, 668 pp.), and Einaudi, *Rivista di Storia Economica*, 4th year, No. 2, *Della Moneta serbatorio di valori e di altri problemi monetari*.

and Keynes has replied to them, but it cannot be said that any really new ideas have emerged from the conflict. On the other hand we must pause for a moment to mention a couple of very important articles by the Swedish economist Ohlin, who, in connexion with these discussions, summed up in the *Economic Journal*[1] some of the fundamental views of the Stockholm school on the subjects treated by Keynes and the methods of research that he advocates. These views were developed in connexion with the unemployment that began in Sweden, as elsewhere, after the 1930 crisis, and they contain several suggestions of great theoretical interest. We shall mention only the two that we consider particularly useful for analysing dynamic economic phenomena, a subject in which the Stockholm school is specially interested.

First there is the very ingenious system of notation used by Ohlin to define on the one hand the different elements in the income of a community, and on the other the different elements in its expenditure, whereby he expresses the equality of expenditure and income. I must refer the reader to the book itself, for it cannot be summarized more concisely than Ohlin has himself done. Starting from this notation he concludes that by definition the saving and the investment of a community are necessarily equal.

But then, asks Ohlin, why should Keynes be so worried about how to get savings absorbed by investment, since by definition the two are identical? The reason is, he says, that Keynes has not sufficiently realized the importance of a distinction that is fundamental in the study of dynamic problems—the distinction between forecasts and realizations. Undoubtedly, say the Swedes, if we take up a *prospective* position there is no equality between the sums that some people *wish* to invest and those that others *wish* to save. But when they both prepare to realize their intentions, their very actions result *afterwards*, through the machinery that they put into operation, in the inevitable equality of savings and investments. And he proves it. In short, Ohlin reaches the conclusion that what Proudhon would have called the "economic contradiction," so brilliantly expounded by Keynes, does not exist. Keynes put the question wrongly, and Ohlin shows how it should be put and the consequences that follow from it. The same conclusions were arrived at by a more complicated method by another eminent member of the Swedish school, Lindhal, in his *Études sur la Théorie de la monnaie et du capital*, translated into English in 1939.

The theoretical solution given by the Swedish economists, and in

[1] See the first two numbers of the *Economic Journal* for 1937, *Some Notes on the Stockholm Theory of Savings and Investment*.

particular by Ohlin,[1] is at once simple and ingenious. It takes us back
to the Classical conception of creative saving. It enriches economic
science by views that are true and ingenious, and should be regarded
as a precious acquisition. It differs in many respects from Keynes's
views. Among other points, it rejects his conception of interest and
his idea of the 'multiplier,' agreeing in this with Pigou and Hawtrey.

VI: NEW CONCEPTION OF CRISES: HABERLER, FISHER, WESLEY MITCHELL, AND DIVISIA

The contradictory views of economists as to the causes of crises and
the remedies to be adopted have not added to the prestige of political
economy among the general public. Some lay the blame on excessive
saving, some on its insufficiency. For some the crisis arises from an
unsellable surplus of consumable commodities; others think that these
same commodities are insufficient at the moment when the crisis
begins. There are some who propose to raise the discount rate when
the crisis approaches, while others would lower it. Some consider
savings to be more plentiful when the depression is drawing to an
end, others when the boom is at its height. Some demand a lowering
of wages; others think that the object should be to stabilize them. How
is it possible for statesmen responsible for taking decisions to find their
way among conceptions and suggestions as varied as the economists
whom they consult?

In addition to this there are the mistaken forecasts that well-known
specialists have permitted themselves to make. In the United States

---

[1] Ohlin's reasoning may be summarized as follows. Obviously there is no equality
at any given moment between the saving *planned* by the savers and the investments
planned by the *entrepreneurs*. But actually, after the event, this equality must of necessity
exist. Take the following example. Suppose that at a given moment, at the end of a
period of equality between investment and consumption, the public decides to reduce
its saving and increase its consumption by ten millions during the period following.
Suppose on the other hand that the *entrepreneurs* decide to invest the same amounts
as in the preceding period. There is then a margin of ten millions between the plans
of the savers and those of the *entrepreneurs*. But what will happen? Owing to the
demand created by the increase in consumption, the sales by retailers will go up by
ten millions, but at the same time their *stocks* will diminish by a certain amount—say
seven millions. The difference between the diminution in these stocks and the selling-
price of ten millions represents the retailers' profits, say three millions. These profits
that have accrued to them, and that they have in hand at the end of the period,
represent an *unforeseen* saving. Total savings have therefore diminished by seven
millions only, not ten, and the investment that was planned to be ten millions is also
diminished by the whole amount of the stocks (seven millions), and is thus reduced
to three millions. So there is a real increase in saving of three millions and a real
increase in investment of three millions only. The two are therefore in equilibrium.
(*Economic Journal*, March 1937, pp. 65–66.)

such obviously competent and undoubtedly honest men as Irving Fisher and C. E. Persons[1] have more than once announced the end of a crisis just when it was beginning to grow worse. Is it surprising that the public should feel and express scepticism about so many theories and forecasts when they are falsified by facts? To them political economy was certainly only "a poor little conjectural science," as Renan said of history. "Economics," said the philosopher Alain in 1934, "is still living in the age of the magicians whose magic book was solemnly read while things went on as best they could."[2] Would it not be better, then, to appeal to common sense or follow the inspiration of daily necessity, than to trust such doubtful theories? The same scepticism has been felt by many economists,[3] and has shown itself in a new attitude towards such a complex phenomenon as a crisis.

To begin with, are there actually general crises that recur at regular intervals? Is not this an illusion? Is there not rather in our economies a constant tendency, when a boom occurs in one part, for it to develop to a maximum? Success in one branch of industry encourages others, the banks increase their grants of credit, prices rise, and with them rises the confidence of other producers, and so on and so on. This general optimism then tends to exploit to the limit the possibilities of credit. It encourages savers to hand over their savings to the industrialists, which on the one hand increases indebtedness and on the other hand encourages less prudent or less competent *entrepreneurs* to launch out into new ventures. And at the same time the exploitation of sources of raw materials and the employment of labour are pushed to their extreme limits. In a word, the whole economic system is in *a condition of combined prosperity and fragility.* The slightest imprudence may then lead to a failure, or several failures, in one industry. Delay in the repayment of one debt may endanger one business, and by its repercussions a series of others. Some external event, such as a political crisis or the closing of a market, may have the same effect. Then credit, already extended to the utmost, becomes no longer so easily obtainable. The collapse of one bank may affect others by causing uneasiness to depositors, and the raising of the rate of discount may be enough to deprive other firms of their expected profits. To put it shortly, all the incidents inherent in normal economic life *and easily remediable in ordinary circumstances* may become fatal to the economy *in the prevailing state of tension.* In the same way an accident or strain,

---

[1] Persons is the author of a book called *Forecasting Business Cycles* (New York, 1931), and has long been in charge of the economic observation service of Harvard University.

[2] Alain, *Propos d'économique*, p. 80.

[3] An English economist, Mrs Barbara Wootton, has given utterance to this disappointment in *Lament for Economics*, published in 1938 (Allen and Unwin).

over which the human organism would easily triumph when healthy, may bring on a serious illness when it is already overworked. It is then the condition of the background or theatre of operations that must be considered as the cause.

This fragility of the economic system may be confined to a single country or may occur at the same time in several countries, but it must exist at a certain moment in every period of prosperity. This is the moment when the entire range of economic resources, including credit, has been made use of to the highest point, when many businesses have contracted debts, and when, therefore, the stoppage of payment by a single debtor puts all the rest in a difficult position, and, finally, when the quality of the new *entrepreneurs* has deteriorated and individual errors of judgment grow more numerous. The *elasticity* of the economy, if the term may be used, has diminished, and before making a new advance it has to store up a fresh supply.

What we call a crisis merely expresses in this case the impossibility of an economy to progress indefinitely to the same rhythm, from the very fact that the volume of productive forces, labour, and credit is limited. There is no 'cycle' in the strict sense, no regular periodicity, for crises can be separated by different intervals and arise from circumstances of the greatest variety. They result simply from a kind of breathlessness in the economic system, in consequence of the inevitable tendency of economic activity to quicken its pace when it is successful, so that it must needs stop to take breath. But these stoppages make little interruption in the general line of progress. Thus Carl Snyder was able to show that crises marked on a secular curve of production appear as insignificant breaks in the upward curve.

Such is the conception arrived at by some of the economists who have given the most careful study to the subject of crises. It is the one that Haberler offers us as the conclusion of his noteworthy investigation of the different theories of crises, supported by an extremely penetrating analysis. The breakdown of a particular industry, he says, may very well cause at least a temporary breakdown in total demand below the level at which it would otherwise have stood. Whether or not this will start a process of contraction depends first on the scale of the trouble and then on the general situation. If a general expansion is taking place and has not yet lost its impetus, then the trouble may be got over, if it is not too great. But if the process of expansion has already lost its impetus, the economic system will be vulnerable and may easily be precipitated into a general process of contraction.

This is the conviction also of Irving Fisher. "The old and apparently still persistent notion of the business cycle," he says, as a single, simple, self-generating cycle (analogous to that of a pendulum swinging under influence of the single force of gravity) and as actually realized historically in regularly recurring crises, is a myth. Instead of one force there are many forces. Specifically, instead of one cycle, there are many co-existing cycles, constantly aggravating or neutralizing each other, as well as co-existing with many non-cyclical forces. In other words, while a cycle, conceived as a *fact*, or historical event, is non-existent, there are always innumerable cycles, long and short, big and little, conceived as *tendencies* (as well as numerous non-cyclical tendencies), any historical event being the resultant of all the tendencies then at work. Any one cycle, however perfect and like a sine curve it may tend to be, is sure to be interfered with by other tendencies.[1]

Fisher compares a crisis to what happens when a ship capsizes which in ordinary circumstances is always near to stable equilibrium, but which, after heeling over beyond a certain angle, loses its tendency to return to equilibrium and tends instead to depart from it.

In France similar ideas have been expressed by Divisia.[2] It is apparently the view also of an American writer whose name is associated with every investigation of these 'cycles' for the last twenty-five years, and who has brought to their study not only infinite patience in detailed research but an exceptional perspicacity and flair in economic matters—Wesley Mitchell. In his view there is nothing pathological or mysterious in the process of expansion when an economy is progressing, for each step forward in one branch of activity promotes the progress of others.[3] But how are all these advances to be kept in

---

[1] Irving Fisher, in *Econometrica*, October 1933, p. 338.

[2] "Economic crises appear to be an oscillatory phenomenon of adaptation. We come across crises of over-production in the whole of industry, where production has to adapt itself to a rapid change in demand, and more generally in cases where the *entrepreneurs* make too many wrong forecasts. We also meet with crises, more or less general, on the occasion of every phenomenon of adaptation, when economic equilibria, like all equilibria, find expression in unstable reality, not in an immobility incompatible with life, but in oscillations—not necessarily sinusoidal—around the position of theoretical equilibrium. General crises may be considered to arise from a synchronization of all these movements, and each of them may have its own characteristic features according to which of the movements preponderates and comes first." (Divisia, *Cours d'Économie politique et sociale*, p. 183.)

[3] "Neither business history nor business statistics supports the view that the decisive break always comes about in the same way. The sequence in which different time series reach their highest points and turn down varies from recession to recession. Usually several stresses seem to be accumulating during a period of expansion, and the only question is which will overtax the factors of safety first. Random influences, such as harvest fluctuations, business conditions in foreign countries, the pet miscalculations of the day and the like, seem to exercise a considerable influence upon that event. And there seem to be secular changes in the character of expansions and recessions. . . . But the fundamental difficulty remains of keeping all the important processes of a business economy duly adjusted to each other in a period when all are

line with each other? There will inevitably be errors of adaptation in one branch or another, and at the point of tension reached by the different series a single error is enough to have repercussions on all the others.

Presented in this form the theory of crises has many advantages. To begin with, it avoids all recourse, as Mitchell says, to mysterious explanations. There is no *one* cause of crises, but a group of phenomena which by their juxtaposition and superposition result in a crisis. We shall not place the blame specially on under-consumption or credit expansion or saving, but shall examine how consumption, production, credit, and saving in certain conditions eventually set up *tensions* which may be transformed by an accident or an incident into ruptures.

For instance, the old and too long undecided controversy between the notions of a *general* and a *generalized* crisis disappears. No one to-day—or hardly anyone—believes in the general crisis. Every one agrees in recognizing that at a given moment a cumulative process begins, either of a rise or a fall in prices. Its starting-point may vary greatly in different crises. The real problem lies in finding in what way it spreads gradually through the national and international economy until it gives the impression of a general crisis. J. B. Say's old formula that he thought would banish the crisis bogy, "products are bought with products," still remains true as a generalization, but has no longer any but the most distant connexion with the phenomenon under discussion.

If we adopt the view described above we shall understand, too, why crises are either strengthened or mitigated by such external circumstances as the increased or reduced exploitation of gold-mines, or one of those drastic price readjustments that take place after a long war, during which goods have become scarce while monetary supplies have increased. We can understand also why there are so many circumstances that provoke a crisis or start a new boom after a depression. As it is a matter of a certain *state* of the economic system, this can be modified for the better or for the worse by any circumstance whatever that serves to increase profits or to reduce them, as the case may be. So also no one will expect the duration of these cycles to be uniform. Sometimes they are close together, sometimes far apart, precisely because they do not originate in any one definite cause so that the rhythm of their development can be determined in advance.

In conclusion, this conception opens up a vast field of work in the historical and statistical observation of crises. The economist is

expanding." (Wesley C. Mitchell, article *Business Cycles* in *Encyclopædia of the Social Sciences*, Vol. III.)

undoubtedly free to make the most varied assumptions as to the relative importance of the essential factors that cause them, but his first task is to follow the fluctuations of the different elements—price, rate of interest, production of the principal kinds of goods, saving, and so forth—which taken altogether will at a given moment start the crisis. It is on the observation of these different 'series' that the explanation of each particular crisis will depend. A study will be made on the one hand of the *order* in which the highest points of each series follow each other, and on the other hand of the *tensions* that appear between one series and another. Many interesting hypotheses have already been suggested. It has been thought, for instance, that there is a regular order of succession between these highest points, that, say, the fall in stock-exchange securities precedes the fall in the other elements. But there does not seem to be any absolute regularity there. In the matter of tensions, certain characteristic phenomena have been observed, such as the divergence between the discount rate and the interest rate, the former generally exceeding the latter on the eve of a crisis, and falling below it when the crisis has begun.

However, if there is approximate agreement as to the cumulative processes of boom and depression, it is the *critical* points that particularly attract the attention of observers and investigators. What are the incidents that start a boom or a crisis, and what is the situation of the economic system at the moment when this happens?

If we succeeded in answering this double question from observation, we should have a means of revealing the approach of the crisis and perhaps of foreseeing it. This would be the most satisfactory confirmation of the investigations that are being carried on in so many different directions. But the real difficulty lies in joining together the *whole* of the elements that play their part in starting or prolonging a crisis. This is an extremely hard task. The points of tension are so numerous, sometimes so distant from each other—even geographically—that it is difficult for a single observer to have the whole of them under his notice. It might have been thought in the United States, for instance, that the crisis of 1929 was almost overcome when a great storm was brewing in Central Europe that was to cause widespread bankruptcies in Austria and Germany and make the crisis leap over to England and the United States without anyone seeing the storm-clouds piling up.

And so, little by little, a conception has emerged that has already invalidated more than one ancient controversy. The new method, instead of *imagining* what *might be* the mechanism of crises, seeks to *observe* what they *have actually been*. Not that this observation—which began long ago—is sufficient by itself to explain them, but the perfecting of this method is the essential condition for foreseeing them and dealing with them, and already it has produced results that are far from negligible.

The two volumes of the Dutch economist Tinbergen entitled *Vérification statistique des théories des cycles économiques*, published in 1939 by the League of Nations as a supplement to Haberler's report, are typical of the kind of investigation that can be used for this purpose.[1] Making use of the statistical method of multiple correlation the author seeks to discover what influence has been exerted in the United States during a certain number of years on the other elements of the system by the factors regarded as 'causes' by the principal crisis theories. He obtains as many equations as variables calling for explanation, and is then in a position to see whether the sum total of the influences thus discovered can result in a 'cycle.' As a matter of fact, however, the positive conclusions he reaches are a little deceptive. Such a method is obviously one of the most complicated to handle. It assumes an abundance of statistical information which in many cases is still lacking. It also involves the preliminary construction of a system of 'norms' of progress for the elements of an economic system,[2] enabling us to realize at each moment the divergences from this norm of such and such an element in the system. It presupposes the assistance of regular economic laboratories like those that have now been set up in most countries, which have already done much, if not in foreseeing crises, at least in discovering important relations between the different factors in operation. Despite all obstacles it is evidently in this direction that the explanation of crises stands most chance of making progress.

VII: FRANÇOIS SIMIAND AND LONG-TERM PRICE ALTERNATIONS

In economic history there are not only relatively short 'cyclical crises,' but also long alternating periods of rising and falling prices, interrupted by shorter cyclical crises but not mingling with them. To these long periods and their alternations François Simiand has devoted his researches. He has brought to the task a measure of statistical and historical learning and a concern for scrupulous objectivity that

---

[1] See also his *Les fondements mathématiques de la Stabilisation du mouvement des affaires* (Hermann, Paris, 1938).

[2] *Cf.* the work of Dierterlen, *Les Normes économiques*, published in 1944 by the Institut Scientifique de recherches économiques (Sirey, Paris, 1944).

give a monumental quality to his works and account for the great influence he has exercised in France over a whole generation of investigators. His conclusions have a direct bearing on the theory of crises. Between the features of what Simiand calls Phase A (prolonged periods of rising prices) and Phase B (prolonged periods of falling prices) on the one hand, and the phenomena peculiar to the shorter phases of boom and depression on the other, there are striking resemblances.

According to Simiand the union of these two phases, A and B, is the essential feature of economic progress, and they are both indispensable to that progress. Their alternation is the means by which it is accomplished. Simiand almost regards this alternation as an organic rhythm in economic life and a condition necessary to its development. If it was desired to 'direct' the economic system, he says, it would be necessary to concentrate on systematically reproducing the alternation of these phases by using artificial monetary means for that purpose. No other economist had hitherto propounded a thesis like this. To them economic progress seems to result from technical causes, such as scientific discoveries and progress in means of transport, which are 'external' to the behaviour of prices, and they think that this progress can be just as well accomplished with stable prices as with those that rise or fall. Long-term price movements are in their view the effect of accidental circumstances, such as greater or less activity in the production of the precious metals or of goods. Most of them even assert (with perhaps excessive assurance) that the greatest possible stability of prices is the object to be pursued.[1]

Simiand takes up quite a different position, unlike that of almost every one else. This gives his doctrine a marked originality, besides investing his intellectual personality with a kind of austere isolation, deliberately accentuated by a literary style that often disconcerts the reader by its lack of polish.

Phase A is characterized by a general rise in incomes, profits as well as wages, and great economic activity. Now, when the fall begins and Phase B commences, a general effort is made by *entrepreneurs* and workers alike to keep their incomes at the same level, as they do not wish to lose the benefit of them. This starts the era of great technical improvements and their general extension, and thus the economic system progresses. Here are his own words:

> Being unable to increase his unit profit on reduced production, and even to maintain it with certainty at the same rate, and in any

[1] It is true that, in the opinion of an American economist more closely concerned than any other with these attempts, the means proposed for attaining this end have hardly been successful yet.

case seeing the unit amount diminishing in proportion to the fall in prices, the producer, while doing his best to defend it, both in rate and in total amount, will at least (and even more so) *defend his profit per head or per contract*, by increasing the quantities that will have to bear this reduced or limited unit profit. Such a phase seems marked by a development of economic organization, by effort and progress in technique, by the development of mechanization, intensive rather than extensive, and by a definitely faster increase in quantities— after the initial period of stoppage has passed—than the phase of monetary expansion. It may be noted in passing that this orientation of production will in such a phase require a still more rapid development of industries concerned with the means or agents of the increased and mechanized production, such as the iron and mineral industries.[1]

But what is the origin of Phases A and B? What is the motive power that sometimes raises the general price-level, and sometimes checks the rise and causes a fall to follow? After long investigations and detailed study of the curves of prices and production of the precious metals and paper money, Simiand comes to a very clear conclusion, that the origin of these movements is entirely monetary. The origin of Phase A is to be found in the increase of supplies of money, either from increased yield of gold- or silver-mines or from the manufacture of paper money, while the restriction or slackening of the production of money is the origin of Phase B. The succession of these phases between 1815 and 1914 is clearly connected with the production of the precious metals. First there is a general fall between 1815 and 1850, then between 1850 and 1873 a recovery started by the discovery of the mines of California and Australia, next a new period of falling prices from 1873 to 1895, corresponding to a period of stationary production, and finally a period of rising prices from 1895 to 1929, started originally by the enormous production of the Transvaal mines and then maintained by the universal issue of paper money during the First World War.

This explanation is valid for long-term phases, but is it equally so for the cyclical crises that occur in A and B periods alike? Simiand has not asked himself this question. His investigations are not concerned with cyclical phases. But we should hardly go wrong in thinking that for them too he would accept a monetary explanation—for instance, by substituting increase of credit for the production of the mines.

One question at once arises: does the succession of Phases A and B obey any organic necessity? Are they produced in virtue of a

[1] See pp. 462 *ff.* of Vol. II of his *Le Salaire, l'évolution sociale et la monnaie* (Alcan, Paris, 1932).

determinism like that which has been thought to determine the cyclical phases of boom and slump? In other words, is there a periodicity of phases like the alleged regular periodicity of cyclical movements? To this question Simiand gives only an evasive reply. Undoubtedly the occurrence of a B phase after an A phase seems almost inevitable. But why should a phase of rising prices or of greater creation of money be conditioned by an economic necessity? Without excluding all idea of organically necessary periodicity he yet hesitates to affirm it. Still less does he attempt to describe the mechanism by which this periodicity would be produced.[1] Moreover, he adds, this question of periodicity loses interest if it is admitted that a voluntary increase of paper money may produce the same effects as an accidental increase of the precious metals. On this point, again, our author does not go into any detail. He only admits the possibility of what he calls "a managed monetary function capable of bringing about the alternation of Phases A and B."[2]

Many objections arise here, for it seems difficult to attribute the succession of Phases A and B to any other causes than historical circumstances that are largely accidental. There seems to be no feature suggesting the operation of any mechanism connected with strictly economic development. The discovery of the Australian and Californian gold-mines in the middle of last century, like the discovery and exploitation of the Transvaal mines at the end of the century, was due, if not to pure chance, at any rate to geographical or technical discoveries independent of economic evolution. The most that can be admitted is that the general fall in prices that follows a slackening in the production of gold tends to restore its activity by reducing the costs of production of the precious metal and stimulating the search either for new deposits or for new methods of exploiting existing ones. As for the idea that the spontaneous alternation of Phases A and B can be imitated by the 'rational' manufacture of paper money, this has no support from experience, and, even assuming it to be established, it would still have to be shown that the manufacture of paper money *can* be rationalized. The typical features of booms and slumps caused

---

[1] "Is this [the increase in the precious metals] due originally to pure physical chance in some form or other? There is no doubt that the discovery of these valuable deposits, and their efficient and increasing exploitation, have shown no more regularity or dependence on general antecedents in the realm of any science than has their limitation. It appears, however, that since a fixed and regular periodicity is by no means necessary for such antecedents and consequences, the possibility of the recurrence of these alternations is likely and even probable. Or, again, there may be some other change in the quantities of the precious metals, through the progress already realized in certain sciences." (Simiand, *op. cit.*, Vol. II, p. 525.)

[2] *Ibid.*, p. 526.

by the manufacture of paper money are certainly connected in some aspects with those that follow the discovery of new metallic deposits, but they differ from them so radically in other aspects (especially in the fact that the issue of paper money is a national matter whereas the increase of metallic money is an international phenomenon) that as things are at present it is impossible to identify the two things 'rationally.'

Simiand has made a very interesting application of his theory to the world crisis of 1930.[1] In his view this was not an ordinary cyclical crises, but the starting-point of a B phase succeeding an A phase which began about 1895 and continued till about 1929, for Simiand refuses to distinguish the rise in prices due to paper money from the preceding rise due to the influx of gold from the Transvaal. So the 1930 crisis and the depression that followed were merely manifestations of the normal reversal of the trend of economic activity after a long period of rising prices. This interpretation is noteworthy, because it shows that to Simiand the 1930 crisis was not the ordinary kind of crisis but was superadded to a spontaneous long-term price movement. This view is, of course, shared by many economists. But Simiand does not regard this reversal as a result of the financial policy of the belligerents[2]—a result that appears after every long and widespread conflict —but only as the *normal* arrival of a B phase succeeding by force of circumstances a preceding A phase. Recalling the statement that— quite rightly, in our view—the 1930 crisis was a unique phenomenon, we are a little surprised that Simiand is unwilling, despite so much evidence from experience, to see in it the inevitable repercussion of war-time financial policies. Moreover, it may quite well be—and we have ourself maintained this thesis[3]—that the 1930 crisis was *both* the beginning of one of these customary reversals of price movements at the end of a period of increase in gold supplies *and* the effect of an excessive rise in prices due to the financing of the war. The 1930 crisis would in this case show the combined effects of all the circumstances making for a fall in prices, and this would explain its exceptional virulence.

Simiand's researches remain, therefore, of very great value as a description of important economic phenomena. They reveal once more the attention given by twentieth-century economists to the *dynamic* aspect of economic phenomena. On the other hand they throw no

---

[1] In a little book entitled *Les Fluctuations économiques à longue période et la crise mondiale* (Paris, 1932).

[2] *Fluctuations*, etc., p. 88.

[3] See our pamphlet *Interprétation de la chute des prix depuis 1925* (Sirey, Paris, 1936).

light at all on the mechanism or mode of operation of crises in the strict sense. In short, what Simiand's investigations have resulted in is a new verification of the quantity theory of money. The psychological reactions responsible for the fact that a new supply of the money material or a diminution in its creation affects production and prices are set by him in the clearest light. What Simiand tells us about is the human decisions that result from these increases and restrictions, and he thereby confirms a thesis that Classical economists have affirmed, though with less detail and scientific minuteness, in every age. But he has added some original views, and buttresses the whole by a wealth of arguments and harmonizing facts not previously met with.[1]

Just as this book was going to press there appeared a very important work by Professor Dupriez, of Louvain, on the same subject as that dealt with by Simiand. It is entitled *Des Mouvements économiques généraux* (Louvain, 1947, 2 vols.). In it all the economic phenomena discussed in this chapter are subjected to searching examination from the point of view of Walras's theory of interdependence, and the author associates himself in many ways with the ideas set forth in our Section VI.

All the theories examined in this chapter constitute a great effort at formulating a dynamic theory of economic phenomena. More or less regular cyclical movements, great rises and falls in prices due to paper money, movements up and down, depending sometimes on the production of the precious metals and sometimes on the extent of technical progress or the abundance of production—these things have been sifted by the authors mentioned in this chapter with a view to describing the mechanism by which these movements are brought about. The difficulty of the problem is shown by the very number of the investigations that have been undertaken, and the variety of the points of view that have been suggested for the subject by these distinguished thinkers.

The result of this enormous amount of work is by no means insignificant. Views are more and more plainly emerging which, when the dust of conflict has cleared away, will survive and remain. In this respect the work of the Swedish school, especially when made more accessible in translations to a wider public, will appear particularly useful and new. Without upsetting the notions that form the founda-

---

[1] A thorough discussion of Simiand's methods and results will be found in an article by Charles Morazé, *Essai sur la méthode de F. Simiand, Histoire d'un échec* (*Mélanges d'histoire sociale,* I and II, Paris, 1942).

tion of theories of equilibrium, and while still keeping in close contact with facts, the Swedish theories provide patiently worked-out plans, better adapted than the older ones to a variety of situations. It is on the lines traced out by these economists, and those on which certain American and continental authors are engaged, that we may hope to see established a theory more accessible to all, and more capable of supporting practical solutions. The danger to be avoided lies in the academic subtleties and controversies about ill-defined terms that have spread regrettably in some countries. They have been rightly denounced[1] by a clever English economist, D. H. Robertson.[2] The true path for political economy to follow remains always the faithful comparison of well-observed facts with theoretical constructions wide enough to take account of all these facts and not only of those that are peculiar to this country or that, as has too often happened since the First World War.

CONCLUSION

CAN a history of economic doctrines really be said to have a conclusion?

It is obviously impossible to regard the history of any science as complete so long as that science itself is not definitely constituted. This applies to all sciences alike, even to the more advanced—physics, chemistry, and mathematics, for example, all of which are continuously undergoing some modification, abandoning in the course of their progress certain conceptions that were formerly regarded as useful, but which now appear antiquated, and adopting others which, if not entirely new, are at least more comprehensive and more fruitful. And not only is this true of individual sciences, but it is equally true of the very conception of science itself. Progress in the sciences involves a modification of our ideas concerning science. The savant, as of yore, is engaged in the pursuit of truth, but the conception of scientific truth in the twentieth century is not what it was in the nineteenth century, and everything points to still further modifications

[1] At a conference of the Manchester Political Economy Society.

[2] We are sorry we have been unable to give an account of the writings of this admirable economist who has put forward many interesting ideas, especially in connexion with the theory of saving. Unfortunately circumstances have prevented a re-reading of Robertson's books, which we have been unable to procure.

of that conception in the future. It is scarcely to be expected that political economy, which is still a young science hardly out of its swaddling-clothes, will prove itself less mutable than the sciences already mentioned. All that the historian is permitted to do is to point to the distance already traversed, without pretending to be able to guess the character of the road that still remains to be covered. His object must be to appreciate the nature of the tasks that now await the economist, and for this his study of the efforts put forth in the past, to which the preceding chapters bear record, should prove of some assistance.

A simple analogy will perhaps help us to gauge the kind of impression left upon us by a study of almost two centuries of economic ideas. Imagine ourselves looking at a fan spread out in front of us. At the handle the separate radii are so closely packed together that they appear to form a single block. But as the eye travels towards the circumference the branches gradually separate from one another until they finally assume quite divergent positions. But their separation is not complete, and the more they are spread out the easier it is to detect the presence of the tissue that forms a common bond between the various sections of the fan and constitutes the basis of a new unity which is quite as powerful, if not perhaps more so, than the unity which results from their superposition at the base.

So it was with the Physiocrats, and still more with Adam Smith, whose theory of political economy was a doctrine of such beautiful simplicity that the human mind could grasp it at a single glance. But as time went on and the science progressed it was realized that the unity which characterized it at first was more apparent than real. The contradictory theories which Smith had seemed able to reconcile gave rise to new currents of thought, which tended to drift farther and farther apart as they assumed a greater degree of independence. Conflicting theories of distribution and of value began to take the field, and quarrels arose over the relative merits of the abstract and the historical method, or the claims of society and the rights of the individual.

With a view to self-defence, each of these schools took its own particular path, which it followed with varied fortune, including not a few setbacks. Each of them also surrounded itself with a network of observations and inductions, thus bringing into the common fund a wealth of new truths and useful conclusions. This has resulted in the gradual development, around each great body of economic thought, of a layer that grows ever tougher and more extensive, forming as it were a common stock of scientific knowledge, beneath which may still be seen the salient features of the main doctrines. Eventually there comes a time when what we see is no longer the sticks of the fan but the common tissue in which, at the circumference, these sticks disappear. In other words, the sum total of acquired truths is the only legacy left us by the various systems of the past, and this is the only thing that interests us to-day.

Hence one result of so much discussion and polemical warfare has been the discovery of some common ground upon which all economists, whatever their social and political aspirations, can meet. This common ground is the domain of economic science—a science that is concerned, not with the presentation of what ought to be, but with the explanation and the thorough understanding of what actually exists. The superiority of a theory is measured solely by its explanatory power. It matters little whether its author be Interventionist or Liberal, Protectionist or Free Trader, Socialist or Individualist—every one must necessarily bow before an exact observation or a scientific explanation.

But while these divergent schools tend to be lost in the unity of a more fully comprehended science, we see the emergence of other divisions, less scientific perhaps, but much more fertile so far as the progress of the science itself is concerned. It seems as if a new kind of fan arrangement were making its appearance underneath the old.

This is obviously the case with regard to method, for example, where the separation between pure and descriptive economics, or between the theoretical systematization and the mere observation of concrete phenomena, is becoming very pronounced. Both kinds of research are equally necessary, and demand different mental qualities which are very seldom found combined in the same person. Economic science, however, cannot afford to dispense either with theory or observation. The desire to seize hold of the chain of economic phenomena and to unravel its secret connexions is as strong as ever it was. On the other hand, in view of the transformation and the daily modifications which industry everywhere seems to be undergoing, it is useless to imagine that we can dispense with the task of observing and describing these. The two methods are developing and progressing together, and the violent quarrels as to their respective merits appear to be definitely laid at rest.

Accordingly what we find is a segmentation of economic science into a number of distinct sciences, each of which tends to become more or less autonomous. Such separation does not necessarily imply a conflict of opinion, but is simply the outcome of division of labour. At the outset of its career the whole of political economy was included within the compass of one or two volumes, and all those facts and theories of which an economist was supposed to have special knowledge were, according to Say and his disciples, easily grouped under the three heads of Production, Consumption, and Distribution. But since then the science has been broken up into a number of distinct branches. The term 'physics,' which was formerly employed as a name for one of the exact sciences, is just now little better than a collective name used to designate a number of special sciences, such as electricity, optics, etc., each of which might claim the lifelong devotion of the student. Similarly 'political economy' has just become a vague but useful term to denote a number of studies which often differ widely from one another. The theory of prices and the theory of distribution have undergone such modifications as entitle them to be regarded as separate studies. Social economics has carved out a domain of its own and is now leading a separate existence, the theory of population has assumed the dimensions of a special science known as demography, and the theory of taxation is now known as the science of finance. Statistics, occupying the borderland of these various sciences, has its own peculiar method of procedure. Descriptions of the commercial and industrial mechanism of banks and exchanges, the classification of the forms of industry and the study of its transformations are related to political economy much as zoology, descriptive botany, and morphology are related to the science of natural history. And although a different name must not always be taken as evidence of a different science, there is little doubt about the existence of the separate sciences already enumerated. The difficulty rather is to grasp the connexion between them and to realize the nature of that fundamental unity which binds them all together.

But there still remains a wide region over the whole of which divergences exist and conflicts continue, and where, moreover, they will probably never cease. This is the realm of *social* and *political* economics.

Despite the gradual rise of a consensus of scientific opinion among economists, the divergences concerning the object that should be pursued and the means employed to achieve that end are as pronounced as ever. Each of the chief doctrines of which we have given an exposition in the course of this work has its body of representatives. Liberals, Communists, Interventionists, State and Christian Socialists continue to preach their differing ideals and to advocate different methods of procedure. On the question of the science itself, however, they are all united. The arguments upon which they base their contentions are largely borrowed from sources other than scientific. Moral and religious beliefs, political or social convictions, individual preference or sentiment, personal experience or interest—these are among the considerations determining the orientation of each. The earlier half of the nineteenth century witnessed the science of political economy making common cause with one particular doctrine, namely, Liberalism. The alliance proved most unfortunate. The time when economic doctrines were expected to lend support to some given policy is for ever gone by. But the lesson has not been lost, and everybody realizes that nothing could be more dangerous for the development of the science than to link its teaching to the tenets of some particular school. At the same time the science might conceivably furnish valuable information to the politician by enabling him to foresee the results of such and such a measure; and it is to be hoped that such predictions, all too uncertain as yet, may, accordingly, become more precise in the future.

We cannot, then, suppose that the various currents of opinion to-day known as Liberalism, Socialism, Solidarism, Syndicalism, and Anarchism are likely to disappear in the immediate future. They may be given other names, perhaps, but they will always continue to exist in some form or other, simply because they correspond to some profound tendency in human nature or to certain permanent collective interests which alternately sway mankind.

We cannot pretend to regret this. Uniformity of belief is an illusory ideal, and from a purely practical point of view we should be sorry to see the day when there will be no conflict of opinion even about those causes or those methods which we hold most dear. Intolerance is the least effective form of propaganda, and we will end with the words of the old German writer, Jean Paul Richter, that Sainte-Beuve was so fond of quoting: "Without liberty the human spirit is like a bell standing on the ground; if it is to ring it must move freely in the air."

INDEX

In the longer paragraphs, one or more numbers standing alone, and separated by a semicolon from the preceding entry, indicate references of smaller importance, not connected with the entry preceding them.

Famine, 141; unemployment the modern form of, 421
Farmers, taxation of, 59. *See also* Agriculture
Faucher, Julius, 612
Federal Reserve Bank of New York, 706, 709, 747
Federation of Brotherhoods, 537
Federation of industries, 449
Feminism, 263, 264
Ferrara, F., his theory of value, 339 n., 340 n.
Ferrier, F., 286 n.
Festy, O., 267 n,
Fetter, F. A., 492 n.
Feudal institutions, 469 n.
Feudal society, Physiocratic criticism and, 54 n.
Feudalism, 528
Feuerbach, L. A., 612, 619 n.
Fichte, J. G., his conception of the state, 436, 437; his autarky, 700, 701
Final utility, 492-496
Fines, employees', 247
Fiscal reform and solidarity, 559. *See also* Protection
Fisher, Irving, 89 n., 100 n., 485, 492 n., 499 n., 510 n., 606, 750, 751
Fisheries, 573
Fix, Theodore, 210
Fleurant, —, 551 n.
Flower-growing, 261 n.
Fontenay, R. de, on agricultural productivity, 161 n., 171; on rent, 344 n.
Food insufficiency, Malthus's ideas on, 140, 141
Forbonnais, —, 654 n.
Foreign exchanges, sensitiveness of, 179
Foreign trade, 46 n.; colonies and navies, 280 n.
Forests, 445
Fouillée, Alfred, 557 n., 563, 585
Fourier, Charles, and population, 151 n.; 183; and Saint-Simonism, 213 n.; his own comparison with Newton, 243, 244; 'attraction of passion,' 244; his works, 245 n.; a "mere employee," 245; his work and doctrines, 255-265; his eccentricities, 255, 256; his Phalanstère, 255 n., 256-258, 261, 262, 264, 265, 274 n.; and the servant problem, 257, 258; on integral co-operation, 258; the "Phalange," 258-260; statue to his memory, 259; and education, 263; on the sex question, 263; and anti-

militarism, 264; 'Back to the Land,' 261, 262, 544; on the attractiveness of labour, 262-265; criticized by Proudhon, 304, 305; on the right to work, 308; on the co-operation of the governing classes, 472 n.; and the doctrine of solidarity, 545; on guarantism, 556; claimed as an anarchist, 611
Fourierism, Stuart Mill's opinion of, 265
Fournière, E., 467 n., 471 n.
Fourth estate, 480
Foville, — de, 170 n.
Foxwell, Professor, 241 n., 255 n., 322 n.
France, Treaty of Eden, 120, 211: Declaration of the Rights of Man, 244; the classic land of socialism, 330; unified socialism in, 473 n.
Franco-German War, doctrinal currents following, 485-487; indemnity, 663-668; crises following, 702
Frankfort, General Association at, 276
Franklin, Benjamin, 335 n., 336
Fraternity, 550; anarchists and, 625
Free competition, 184, 352, 368; Hedonists and, 108, 489; a sovereign natural law, 363; not synonymous with economic liberty, 441 n.
Free credit, 314, 325, 326
Free education, 556
Free Trade, 47-49; Walras on, 49; established in corn and Act repealed, 50; Adam Smith on, 113-118; criticized, 274 n.; and profits and rents, 178 n.; theory, triumph of, 274; Hedonists and, 511 n.; before and after 1918, 691-700
Free Trade League, French, 335 n.
Free utility and rent, French Liberals' law of, 341-346
Freedom of combination, 184; law of, 360
Freien, die, 612
French appreciation of Adam Smith, 122; Industrial Revolution, 127; economists, succession of, 133 n.; colonies, 282 n.; co-operators, 314, 561; Historical school, 391; collectivism, 467 n.; property-owners, 478; mathematical school, 499 n.; rural banks, 517; agricultural credit banks, 534; Christian socialism, 538, 539; co-operative movement, 539 n.; Radical-Socialist party, 549, 551; Constitution (1793), 552; credit societies, 562 n.; taxation of surplus value, 594; anarchism, 635; exports following 1818, 664

poor countries, 352, 353, 369, 370 *n.*;
problems after 1918, 640–643; new
theories of, 643; Ricardian theory of
644–660; why do two countries exchange products that both can produce?, 645–655; why countries import
and export, 647, 651; is it distinguished
from national trade?, 650, 655–657;
assimilated to mere barter, 657–600;
its effects on national price-levels,
677–685; high level of, 692. *See also*
Exchange
Intervention, 381, 382. *See also*
Socialism
Interventionism—*see* State Socialism
Interventionist, Sismondi as the first, 205
Intestacy, 352 *n.*
Inventions, mechanical, have not
lightened the day's toil, 377; and their
effect, 744
Investment, saving identical with, 741
Ireland: Act of Union, 120
Iron: Bastiat's theory of value, 342
'Iron law of wages,' 366, 427, 434, 435,
456 *n.*, 498, 510
Italian pasture in place of cultivation,
203
Italian School after 1918, 638
Italy, agriculture credit banks in, 534;
anarchism in, 635

JAMES, WILLIAM, 472 *n.*
Janet, Paul, 263
Jannet, Claudio, 521 *n.*, 550 *n.*
Japan, economic problems in, 637
Jaurès, J., 471 *n.*
Jenks, —, 292 *n.*
Jesus Christ, 60, 361, 471 *n.*, 514, 515,
534, 538 *n.*, 540 *n.*, 613
Jeunes Abbés, Les, 533
Jevons, Stanley, on Cantillon, 64 *n.*; on
value, 66; 92, 133; on the French economists, 133 *n.*; 163 *n.*; and the historical
school, 384; his economic theory, 384;
409, 476 *n.*; on equilibrium and prices,
485; pre-eminent in theory, 485 *n.*;
and Hedonism, 488; on final utility,
492 *n.*; his law of indifference, 495;
on Cournot, 499 *n.*; and Gossen, 499
n.; his death, 499 *n.*; ratio of exchange, 500 *n.*; on equilibrium, 506,
643; on intervention, 511; his theory
of exchange, 649
Joint-stock companies and principle, 112,
258, 414, 465, 477

Joseph II of Austria, 25
Julian, Emperor, 447
Julin, Armand, 152 *n.*
Jura Federation, 616
Juridical socialism, 563
Jurisprudence, solidarism and, 563

KARTELS, 193, 463, 465
Kantian doctrine, 618
Kautsky, K., 286 *n.*, 481 *n.*
Ketteler, Monseigneur von, 527, 531, 532
Keynes, J. M. (*afterwards* Lord Keynes),
187, 639 *n.*, 641, 660, 667, 668, 716 *n.*,
725, 729, 731, 734; his *Economic Consequences of the Peace*, 667; and payment
of reparations, 667, 674, 675; a temporary customs duty, 698; and unemployment, 703; his theory of saving,
unemployment and crises, 738–749;
his parable of the bananas, 740; his
theory of interest, 746 *n.*; his multiplier theory, 747–749
Kidd's theory, 516 *n.*
King, Gregory, 71
Kingsley, Charles, 535
Knies, K., 105 *n.*, 209, 384 *n.*, 385 *n.*,
386 *n.*, 388, 389, 392, 397, 408; on
historical study, 405
Kohler, Curt, 286 *n.*
Kraus, Professor, 121 *n.*
Kropotkin, Peter Alexeivich, 462 *n.*, 611;
anarchist doctrine and society, 612,
614 *n.*, 615, 627 *n.*; his career and
works, 615–617; on punishment,
621 *n.*; on marriage, 623; on society
and mutual aid or solidarity, 614,
626–630; and revolution, 636; on the
sovereignty of reason, 636
Kurelia, —, 607 *n.*
Kutter, Pastor, 538

LA TOUR DU PIN, MARQUIS DE, 527, 531
Labour the true source of wealth, 74;
division of, 75–78, 420 *n.*; territorial
division of, 115; a factor determining
value, 164; Saint-Simon and, 218 *n.*;
'organization' of, 238, 311; 'instrument of,' 238; attractiveness of, 262–
265; its share of total product, 346–
348 (*see also* Capital); the only source
of productive power, 353 *n.*; communion or community of, 420 *n.*;
manual, compared with directive
energy, 424; manual, Marx on, 453,
458; surplus and surplus value, 453–

Locke, J., 584
Loesewitz, J., 533
Longe, F. D., 366
Loria, Achille, and his doctrines, 471 n.;
602 n.
Lorin, Henri, 529 n.
Louis XV, 23 n.
Louis XVI, 24 n.
Louis Bonaparte, 326
Louis Philippe, 308, 352 n.
Ludlow, J. M. F., 535, 535–537
Lutfalla, —, 499 n.
Lutheran Church, 538
Luxembourg Commission, 309, 311–313
Lyons silk, 649

MABLY, ABBÉ DE, 213
Machine-making industries, do crises
tend to appear in?, 715, 736
Machinery, J. B. Say on, 127, 128;
Sismondi's and Ricardo's views on,
194–196; and rent, 574, 582; exports
and imports, 661, 662
McCulloch, S. R., 69 n., 84, 124 n.,
156 n., 164, 180 n., 181 n., 182, 189,
191, 383
Mackay, J. H., 611 n.
McKee, Samuel, 286 n.
MacVickar, J., 355
Malon, Benoît, 467 n.
Malt, tax on, 120
Malthus, T. R., 135–153, 172, 183, 331;
his career and works, 135 n.; his fears
not confirmed by history, 145; hostile
to doctrine of immaterial products,
124 n.; the Pessimist, 134, 135;
Darwin's acknowledgment to, 136;
his formula of progression, 139 n.;
the Neo-Malthusians, 148, 149; his
law of population, 135–153; on
theories of value, 156 n.; on doctrine
of rent, 157; and land cultivation, 161,
162 n.; a protectionist, 178; his theory
of population criticized, 170 n., 202 n.,
238 n., 351, 589; on public works to
reduce unemployment, 747; on misfortunes resulting from vices or habits,
333; on marriage of indigents, 364; on
identity of interests, 413; on social
extremes, 589; Malthusian theory not
approved by Henry George, 589
Man, 'economic,' 398; as a social being,
404
Mammonism, crusade against, 543

Manchester Political Economy Society,
761 n.
Manchester School and doctrine, 368,
437, 438, 469 n., 508
'Manchesterism,' 362; and Marxism,
similarity between, 448
'Manchesterthum,' 362, 439
Manchestrians, 439
Mandeville, Bernard de, 71, 72, 88 n.
Mangoldt, H. von, 574 n., 576 n., 581,
647 n.
Mankind, 'original quality' of, 517 n.;
original perfection of, 518 n.
Manoïlesco, —, his protectionist doctrine,
698–700
Mantoux, P., 83, 113 n., 119, 120 n.
Manual labour, return to, 541
Manufacturer, small, disappearance of,
200
Manufactures, List on, 282, 283
Manufacturing, large-scale, and ages of
employees, 185
Manu's law, 147
Marat, J. P., on rights of property, 212 n.
Marcet, Mrs, 134 n., 354, 355 n.
Marcus Aurelius, 545
Marget, —, 747 n.
Marginal utility, 492 n.
Marie, A. T., 309, 310 n.
Markets, Say's law of, 657
Marmande, R. de, 617
Marmontel, —, 26
Maroussem, P. du, 526 n.
Marrast, Armand, 310
Marriage, moral restraint from, 142–144;
of indigents, 364; anarchists' view of,
623
Marshall, Professor A., 393 n., 543 n.;
on Bastiat, 336; his economic chivalry,
341; on historical school, 390; and the
German economists, 393 n.; on historians' practice, 394; on chemical and
physical laws, 394–396; on provisional
nature of all laws, 394, 395; his definition of an economic law, 396; on
human motives, 398; on scientific
method and the economist, 400; on
the interpretation of history, 404; Marx
compared with, 475; on economic
equilibrium, etc., 485 n.; on consumer's rent, 497 n.; and the biological method, 513 n.; on applications of mathematics to economics,
514; on profit, 577; on composite rent,
577 n.; on a continuous series of rents,

poly price, 98 *n.*; on population, 99; on a nation's true wealth, 100; on banking, 100–102; on human conduct and personal interest, 103, 109; and the 'spontaneous order,' 104–106; his universalism or internationalism, 105 *n.*; on the investment of capital, 106, 107; on economic liberty and international trade, 109–118; on State administration, 110–112; on joint-stock companies, 112; and monopoly, 112; in agreement with work of French Physiocrats, 113; attacks mercantilism, 114; criticizes protectionism, 114–118; and prohibition of imports, 116 *n.*; political economy commenced with, 119; French and German appreciation of, 121–123; Malthus's reply to, 136; on foreign exchanges, 179; on landlords' interests, 168 *n.*; Say on, 187; Sismondi a disciple of, 188; on free competition, 196; and government, 229; his doctrine conquers Europe, 273; his disciples' constitutions, 274; List's indebtedness to, 280 *n.*; and national power, 280 *n.*; and moral forces, 282 *n.*; on ethics of utility, 361 *n.*; anæmic condition of economics following, 383; his atomic views, 384 *n.*; on man's self-interest, 396; and *laissez-faire*, 411; on the duties of the sovereign, 411; on the progress of thought since, 416; on the annual labour of a nation, 424; on *laissez-faire*, 597 *n.*; on economic effects of war, 642; on civil government, 620; influenced by the wars, 637 *n.*; on saving, 731

Smith, Prince, 380, 439
"Smithianismus," 439
Snyder, Carl, 699, 711, 751; on invention, 744
'Social' and 'national,' confusion of terms, 420 *n.*
Social being, man as a, 404
Social Catholic *syndicat*, 528, 529
Social catholicism, 449, 524–534; dismisses co-operative association, 527 *n.*; in Austria, 529 *n.*; encourages the help of the masters, 530, 531; and State intervention, 531; and corporatism, 532; and the productivity theory of capital, 533
Social Catholics usually Protectionists, 531 *n.*

Social christianity, characteristics of, 515, 516; its view of State Socialism, 516
Social classes, three, 38–42
Social Democratic Federation, 603 *n.*
'Social economics,' 21, 764
Social environment constantly changing, 403, 404
'Social function,' 341
Social legislation and solidarity, 558, 559
'Social need,' 423
'Social physics,' 126
Social protestantism, 534–540. *See also* Christian socialism
Social research, 407
Social science, school of, 525, 526
'Social' workshops, 309; Louis Blanc's, 267–271
Socialism, early use of the term, 273 *n.*; contrasted with individualism, 272, 273; Proudhon's criticism of, 299–307; discredited in the French Revolution of 1848, 308–314; Russian, 328; German National, 328; France the classic land of, 330; protection a counterfeit of, 330; 'death' of, 359; Liberal policy and, 381, 382; revival of, 381; Guild, 448, 449; unified in France, 473 *n.*; as a science, 475 *n.*; "just a movement . . . the end is nothing," 480; reconciling Liberalism with, 486, 487; 'heresy' of, 515; Christian doctrines distinct from, 516; juridical, 563; and Fabian doctrines, 603–610; its realization without conflict, 608. *See also* State Socialism
'Socialism of the chair,' 210, 419, 439. *See also* State Socialism
Socialist parties after 1870, 603
Socialists, Utopian, 513; 'the real disciples of Christ,' 538 *n.* *See also* Associated Socialists
Société d'Économie sociale, 518 *n.*
Société d'Éducation sociale, 551 *n.*
Societies, Co-operative—*See under* Co-operative
Societies, distributive, 561
Society, modern, 197, 199, 207; how built up, 301 *n.*; jurisdiction of, 414 *n.*; task of reorganizing, 561 *n.*; distinguished from government, 626, 627; various anarchist ideas on, 625, 628
Sociological evolution, 568, 569
Sociology, 392, 395, 407, 547
Solidarism, emergence of, 486; causes of its development, 545–500; bacterio-

prevent crises?, 746; stabilization of, 747

Wagner, A., 233, 396 *n.*, 397, 399 *n.* 400 *n.*, 440; on the discovery of economic laws, 406; and Rodbertus and Bismarck, 417, 418; on extreme socialism, 433 *n.*; on the functions of the State, 439 *n.*; on State socialism, 439; his principal works, 439 *n*; and rehabilitation of the State, 440; on individual effort, 443 *n.*; on State intervention, 443-445

Wakefield, Gibbon, 355 *n.*

Walker, Amasa, 575 *n.*

Walker, Francis, 367 *n.*, 575, 576, 578

Wallace, Alfred Russel, 601

Wallas, Graham, 174 *n.*

Walras, Auguste, father of Léon Walras, 499 *n.*

Walras, Léon, his free trade doctrine, 49; 92, 511 *n.*; his indebtedness to Say, 130; 170; and scarcity, 357, 492 *n.*; and the historical school, 384; on economic theory, 384; his lectures 1867-68, 416; on equilibrium and prices, 485; pre-eminent in theory, 485 *n.*; his mathematical economic work, 499 *n.*, 503, 507 *n.*, 508 *n.*, 510, 512, 514; on three interwoven markets, 505 *n.*; a Swiss, 526 *n.*; on profit, 577; on the land as State property, 586 *n.*; his scheme of land nationalization, 597-600; on the group idea, 626 *n.*; his theory of equilibrium as a basis, 638; on economic equilibrium, 643, 726; his conception of saving, 729; 736

War, caused by economic imperialism, 298; mark left by, 330; effect of paper money in, 320; 'total,' 450; state control and, 450, 451; economy, 450; and the march towards unity, 557; founders of economics strongly influenced by, 637; economic effects of, 640-642; indemnities, payment of, 663-677; leads to crises, 701, 702

War, class, 472-474, 479, 480, 482; opposition to, 485, 486

War, First World, production and exchange problems following, 487, 637-701; gradual abandonment of 'comparative-cost' doctrine after, 643-663; problem of reparations and mechanism of international transfers of capital after, 663-677; influence of inter-

national trade on national prices after, 677-685; international distribution of gold after, 685-691; question of Free Trade or Protection after, 691-700; policy of autarky following, 700, 701; crises following, 702

War, Franco-German, doctrinal currents following, 485-487; the indemnity, 663-668; crises following, 702

Wars, Napoleonic, 487, 637, 641, 645, 702

Waring, Colonel, 263 *n.*

Warville, Brissot de, 213 *n.*, 300 *n.*

Water, value of, 339; municipalization of, 445

Watteau pastorals, 25

Watt's steam-engine, 82

Wealth, circulation of, 37-62; source or origin of, 74; a nation's true, 100; of United States, 145; Saint-Simon on, 222 *n.*; its growth outstrips that of population, 352; growth of, in U.S.A. and Germany, 352; defined, 346 *n.*

Webb, Mr and Mrs Sidney, 184 *n.*, 233, 391, 448; and Fabian collectivism, 604

Weber, Max, 385 *n.*

Weill, G., 215 *n.*, 237 *n.*

Weitling, W., 330

Wellington, Duke of, 371

Wells, H. G., 604

West, Sir E., 162 *n.*, 164 *n.*

Weulersse, G., 24 *n.*, 41 *n.*, 45 *n.*

Wheat—*see* Corn

Whigs and Tories, 479

Wickett, Dr, 401 *n.*

Wicksell, Knut, defender of Malthus's thesis, 146; and the Stockholm school, 638 *n.*; on international prices, 684; on effect of gold discovery, 687, 688; and the theory of divergences between saving and investment, 724-731; on crises, 729, 730

Wieser, F. von, 492 *n.*

William II, Emperor of Germany, 53 *n.*, 446

Williams, —, 644, 656, 666

Wilson, George, 112 *n.*

Wirth, Moritz, 418 *n.*, 419 *n.*

Wollemborg, —, 534 *n.*

Wolowski, L., in the 1848 Revolution, 312

Woman, emancipation of, 263

Women and children, employment of, 185, 197, 442, 457, 529, 631

Wool and silk, 649